P9-DVT-970

International Accounting

Third Edition

Timothy Doupnik
University of South Carolina

Hector Perera
Macquarie University

McGraw-Hill Irwin

McGraw-Hill
Irwin

INTERNATIONAL ACCOUNTING, THIRD EDITION

Published by McGraw-Hill, a business unit of The McGraw-Hill Companies, Inc., 1221 Avenue of the Americas, New York, NY 10020. Copyright © 2012 by The McGraw-Hill Companies, Inc. All rights reserved. Previous editions © 2009 and 2007. No part of this publication may be reproduced or distributed in any form or by any means, or stored in a database or retrieval system, without the prior written consent of The McGraw-Hill Companies, Inc., including, but not limited to, in any network or other electronic storage or transmission, or broadcast for distance learning.

Some ancillaries, including electronic and print components, may not be available to customers outside the United States.

 This book is printed on recycled, acid-free paper containing 10% postconsumer waste.

1 2 3 4 5 6 7 8 9 0 QDB/QDB 1 0 9 8 7 6 5 4 3 2 1

ISBN 978-0-07-811095-5
MHID 0-07-811095-5

Vice President & Editor-in-Chief: *Kimberly Meriwether David*
Editorial Director: *Stewart Mattson*
Publisher: *Tim Vertovec*
Executive Editor: *Richard T. Hercher, Jr.*
Senior Administrative Assistant: *Janice Hansen*
Marketing Manager: *Dean Karampelas*
Project Manager: *Erin Melloy*
Design Coordinator: *Brenda A. Rolwes*
Cover Designer: *Studio Montage, St. Louis, Missouri*
Cover Image: *© Getty Images RF*
Buyer: *Susan K. Culbertson*
Media Project Manager: *Balaji Sundararaman*
Compositor: *Laserwords Private Limited*
Typeface: *10/12 Palatino*
Printer: *Quad/Graphics*

All credits appearing on page or at the end of the book are considered to be an extension of the copyright page.

Library of Congress Cataloging-in-Publication Data

Doupnik, Timothy S.
   International accounting/Timothy Doupnik, Hector Perera.—3rd ed.
     p. cm.
   ISBN 978-0-07-811095-5 (alk. paper)
   1. International business enterprises—Accounting. I. Perera, M. H. B. II. Title.
  HF5686.I56D68 2012
  657′.96—dc22
                                                  2011001155

www.mhhe.com

To my wife Birgit and children Stephanie and Alexander

—TSD

To my wife Sujatha and daughter Hasanka

—HBP

About the Authors

Timothy S. Doupnik *University of South Carolina*

Timothy S. Doupnik is a Professor of Accounting at the University of South Carolina, where he has been on the faculty since 1982, and primarily teaches financial and international accounting. He served as director of the School of Accounting from 2003 until 2010, when he assumed the position of Vice Provost for international affairs. He has an undergraduate degree from California State University–Fullerton, and received his master's and Ph.D. from the University of Illinois.

Professor Doupnik has published exclusively in the area of international accounting in various journals, including *The Accounting Review; Accounting, Organizations, and Society; Abacus; Journal of International Accounting Research; Journal of Accounting Literature; International Journal of Accounting;* and *Journal of International Business Studies.*

Professor Doupnik is a past president of the International Accounting Section of the American Accounting Association, and he received the section's Outstanding International Accounting Educator Award in 2008. He has taught or conducted research in the area of international accounting at universities in a number of countries around the world, including Brazil, China, Dominican Republic, Finland, Germany, and Mexico.

Hector B. Perera *Macquarie University*

Emeritus Professor Hector Perera is at Macquarie University, Australia. Prior to joining Macquarie University in January 2007, he was at Massey University, New Zealand, for 20 years. He has an undergraduate degree from University of Sri Lanka, Peradeniya, and received his Ph.D. from the University of Sydney, Australia.

Professor Perera's research has dealt mainly with international accounting issues and has been published in various journals, including *Journal of International Accounting Research; Journal of Accounting Literature; International Journal of Accounting; Advances in International Accounting; Journal of International Financial Management and Accounting; Abacus; Accounting and Business Research; Accounting, Auditing and Accountability Journal; Accounting Education; Australian Accounting Review; International Journal of Management Education;* and *Pacific Accounting Review.* In an article appearing in a 1999 issue of the *International Journal of Accounting,* he was ranked fourth in authorship of international accounting research in U.S. journals over the period 1980–1996.

Professor Perera served as chair of the International Relations Committee of the American Accounting Association's International Accounting Section in 2003 and 2004. He is currently an associate editor for the *Journal of International Accounting Research* and on the editorial boards of several other journals.

Professor Perera has been a visiting professor at a number of universities, including the University of Glasgow in Scotland; NewSouth Wales University, Wollongong University, and Northern Territory University in Australia; Turku School of Economics and Business Administration, and Åbo Akademi University in Finland; Unversiti Teknologi Mara, Malaysia; and University of Shahjah.

Preface

ORIENTATION AND UNIQUE FEATURES

International accounting can be viewed in terms of the accounting issues uniquely confronted by companies involved in international business. It also can be viewed more broadly as the study of how accounting is practiced in each and every country around the world, learning about and comparing the differences in financial reporting, taxation, and other accounting practices that exist across countries. More recently, international accounting has come to be viewed as the study of rules and regulations issued by international organizations—most notably International Financial Reporting Standards (IFRS) issued by the International Accounting Standards Board (IASB). This book is designed to be used in a course that attempts to provide an overview of the broadly defined area of international accounting, but that focuses on the accounting issues related to international business activities and foreign operations and provides substantial coverage of the IASB and IFRS.

The unique benefits of this textbook include its up-to-date coverage of relevant material; extensive numerical examples provided in most chapters; two chapters devoted to the application of International Financial Reporting Standards (IFRS); and coverage of nontraditional but important topics such as strategic accounting issues of multinational companies, international corporate governance, and corporate social reporting. This book contains several important distinguishing features:

- Numerous excerpts from recent annual reports to demonstrate differences in financial reporting practices across countries and to demonstrate financial reporting issues especially relevant for multinational corporations.

- Incorporation of research findings into the discussion on many issues.

- Extensive end-of-chapter assignments that help students develop their analytical, communication, and research skills.

- Detailed discussion on the most recent developments in the area of international harmonization/convergence of financial reporting standards.

- Two chapters on International Financial Reporting Standards that provide detailed coverage of a wide range of standards and topics. One chapter focuses on the financial reporting of assets, and the second chapter focuses on liabilities, financial instruments, and revenue recognition. (IFRS related to topics such as business combinations, foreign currency, and segment reporting are covered in other chapters.) The IFRS chapters also include numerical examples demonstrating major differences between IFRS and U.S. GAAP and their implications for financial statements.

- Separate chapters for foreign currency transactions and hedging foreign exchange risk and translation of foreign currency financial statements. The first of these chapters includes detailed examples demonstrating the accounting for foreign currency derivatives used to hedge a variety of types of foreign currency exposure.

- Separate chapters for international taxation and international transfer pricing, with detailed examples based on provisions in U.S. tax law.

- A chapter devoted to a discussion of the strategic accounting issues facing multinational corporations, with a focus on the role accounting plays in strategy formulation and implementation.
- Use of a corporate governance framework to cover external and internal auditing issues in an international context, with substantial coverage of the Sarbanes-Oxley Act of 2002.
- A new chapter on corporate social responsibility reporting, which is becoming increasingly more common among global enterprises.

CHAPTER-BY-CHAPTER CONTENT

Chapter 1 introduces the accounting issues related to international business by following the evolution of a fictional company as it grows from a domestic company to a global enterprise. This chapter provides the context into which the topics covered in the remaining chapters can be placed.

Chapters 2 and 3 focus on differences in financial reporting across countries and the international convergence of accounting standards.

- Chapter 2 presents evidence of the diversity in financial reporting that exists around the world, explores the reasons for that diversity, and describes the problems that are created by differences in accounting practice across countries. In this chapter, we also describe and compare several major models of accounting used internationally. We discuss the potential impact that culture has on the development of national accounting systems and present a simplified model of the reasons for international differences in financial reporting. The final section of this chapter uses excerpts from recent annual reports to present additional examples of some of the differences in accounting that exist across countries.
- Chapter 3 focuses on the major efforts worldwide to converge financial reporting practices with an emphasis on the activities of the International Accounting Standards Board (IASB). We explain the meaning of convergence, identify the arguments for and against convergence, and discuss the use of the IASB's International Financial Reporting Standards (IFRS), including national efforts to converge with those standards.

The almost universal recognition of IFRS as a high-quality set of global accounting standards is arguably the most important development in the world of international accounting. Chapters 4 and 5 introduce financial reporting under IFRS for a wide range of accounting issues.

- Chapter 4 summarizes the major differences between IFRS and U.S. GAAP. It provides detailed information on selected IFRS, concentrating on standards that relate to the recognition and measurement of assets—including inventories; property, plant, and equipment; intangible assets; and leased assets. Numerical examples demonstrate the application of IFRS, differences between IFRS and U.S. GAAP, and the implications for financial statements. This chapter also describes the requirements of IFRS in a variety of disclosure and presentation standards.
- Chapter 5 focuses on current liabilities, provisions, employee benefits, share-based payment, income taxes, revenue, and financial instruments, including major differences between IFRS and U.S. GAAP.

Chapter 6 describes the accounting environment in five economically significant countries—China, Germany, Japan, Mexico, and the United Kingdom—that are representative of major clusters of accounting system. The discussion related to each country's accounting system is organized into four parts: background, accounting profession, accounting regulation, and accounting principles and practices. Exhibits throughout the chapter provide detailed information on differences between each country's GAAP and IFRS, as well as reconciliations from local GAAP to U.S. GAAP.

Chapters 7, 8, and 9 deal with financial reporting issues that are of particular importance to multinational corporations. Two different surveys of business executives indicate that the most important topics that should be covered in an international accounting course are related to the accounting for foreign currency.[1] Because of its importance, this topic is covered in two separate chapters (Chapters 7 and 8). Chapter 9 covers three additional financial reporting topics of particular importance to multinational corporations—inflation accounting, business combinations and consolidated financial statements, and segment reporting. Emphasis is placed on understanding IFRS related to these topics.

- Chapter 7 begins with a description of the foreign exchange market and then demonstrates the accounting for foreign currency transactions. Much of this chapter deals with the accounting for derivatives used in foreign currency hedging activities. We first describe how foreign currency forward contracts and foreign currency options can be used to hedge foreign exchange risk. We then explain the concepts of cash flow hedges, fair value hedges, and hedge accounting. Finally, we demonstrate the accounting for forward contracts and options used as cash flow hedges and fair value hedges to hedge foreign currency assets and liabilities, foreign currency firm commitments, and forecasted foreign currency transactions.

- Chapter 8 focuses on the translation of foreign currency financial statements for the purpose of preparing consolidated financial statements. We begin by examining the conceptual issues related to translation, focusing on the concept of balance sheet exposure and the economic interpretability of the translation adjustment. Only after a thorough discussion of the concepts and issues do we then describe the manner in which these issues have been addressed by the IASB and by the U.S. FASB. We then illustrate application of the two methods prescribed by both standard-setters and compare the results. We discuss the hedging of balance sheet exposure and provide examples of disclosures related to translation.

- Chapter 9 covers three additional financial reporting issues. The section on inflation accounting begins with a conceptual discussion of asset valuation and capital maintenance through the use of a simple numerical example and then summarizes the inflation accounting methods used in different countries. The second section focuses on International Financial Reporting Standards related to business combinations and consolidations, covering issues such as the determination of control, the acquisition method, proportionate consolidation, and

---

[1] T. Conover, S. Salter, and J. Price, "International Accounting Education: A Comparison of Course Syllabi and CFO Preferences," *Issues in Accounting Education,* Fall 1994; and T. Foroughi and B. Reed, "A Survey of the Present and Desirable International Accounting Topics in Accounting Education," *International Journal of Accounting,* Fall 1987, pp. 64–82.

the equity method. The final section of this chapter focuses on International Financial Reporting Standard 8, *Operating Segments*.

Chapter 10 introduces issues related to the analysis of foreign financial statements. We explore potential problems (and possible solutions to those problems) associated with using the financial statements of foreign companies for decision-making purposes. This chapter also provides an example of how an analyst would reformat and restate financial statements from one set of GAAP to another.

Business executives rank international taxation second only to foreign currency in importance as a topic to be covered in an international accounting course.[2] International taxation and tax issues related to international transfer pricing are covered in Chapters 11 and 12.

- Chapter 11 focuses on the taxation of foreign operation income by the home-country government. Much of this chapter deals with foreign tax credits, the most important mechanism available to companies to reduce double taxation. This chapter provides a comprehensive example demonstrating the major issues involved in U.S. taxation of foreign operation income. We also discuss benefits of tax treaties, translation of foreign currency amounts for tax purposes, and tax incentives provided to attract foreign investment.

- Chapter 12 covers the topic of international transfer pricing, focusing on tax implications. We explain how discretionary transfer pricing can be used to achieve specific cost minimization objectives and how the objectives of performance evaluation and cost minimization can conflict in determining international transfer prices. We also describe government reactions to the use of discretionary transfer pricing by multinational companies, focusing on the U.S. rules governing intercompany pricing.

Chapter 13 covers strategic accounting issues of particular relevance to multinational corporations. This chapter discusses multinational capital budgeting as a vital component of strategy formulation and operational budgeting as a key ingredient in strategy implementation. Chapter 13 also deals with issues that must be addressed in designing a process for evaluating the performance of foreign operations.

Chapter 14 covers comparative international auditing and corporate governance. This chapter discusses both external and internal auditing issues as they relate to corporate governance in an international context. Chapter 14 also describes international diversity in external auditing and the international harmonization of auditing standards.

Chapter 15 introduces the current trend toward corporate social reporting (CSR) by multinational corporations (MNCs). We describe theories often used to explain CSR practices by companies and the motivations for them to engage in CSR practices. We also examine the implications of climate change for CSR. Further, we discuss some issues associated with regulation of CSR at the international level and identify international organizations that promote CSR, such as Global Reporting Initiative (GRI). Finally, we provide examples of actual CSR practices by MNCs.

---

[2] Ibid.

SUPPLEMENTARY MATERIAL

International Accounting is accompanied by supplementary items for both students and instructors. The Online Learning Center (www.mhhe.com/doupnik3e) is a book-specific website that includes the following supplementary materials.

For Students:

- Chapter Summaries
- Learning Objectives
- Links to Relevant Sites
- Online Quizzing

For Instructors:

- Access to all supplementary materials for students
- Instructor's Manual
- Solutions Manual
- PowerPoint Presentations
- Test Bank

Acknowledgments

We want to thank the many people who participated in the review process and offered their helpful comments and suggestions:

Wagdy Abdallah
Seton Hall University

Kristine Brands
Regis University

Bradley Childs
Belmont University

Teresa Conover
University of North Texas

Orapin Duangploy
University of Houston–Downtown

Gertrude Eguae-Obazee
Albright College

Emmanuel Emmenyonu
Southern Connecticut State University

Charles Fazzi
Saint Vincent College

Mark Finn
Northwestern University

Leslie B. Fletcher
Georgia Southern University

Paul Foote
California State University–Fullerton

Mohamed Gaber
State University of New York at Plattsburgh

Giorgio Gotti
University of Massachusetts–Boston

Shiv Goyal
University of Maryland University College

Robert Gruber
University of Wisconsin

Marianne James
California State University–Los Angeles

Cynthia Jeffrey
Iowa State University

Craig Keller
Missouri State University

Victoria Krivogorsky
San Diego State University

Britton McKay
Georgia Southern University

Jamshed Mistry
Suffolk University

Gregory Naples
Marquette University

Cynthia Nye
Bellevue University

Randon C. Otte
Clarion University

Obeua Persons
Rider University

Felix Pomeranz
Florida International University

Grace Pownall
Emory University

Juan Rivera
University of Notre Dame

Kurt Schulzke
Kennesaw State University

Mary Sykes
University of Houston–Downtown

We are also thankful to Gary Blumenthal, chief financial officer of The Forbes Consulting Group and instructor at Stonehill College, who revised the PowerPoint slides and Test Bank to accompany the third edition of the text.

We also pass along many thanks to all the people at McGraw-Hill/Irwin who participated in the creation of this book. In particular, Executive Editor Dick Hercher, Editorial Assistant Janice Hansen, McGraw-Hill Project Manager Erin Melloy, Laserwords Project Manager Ligo Alex, Media Project Manager Balaji Sundararaman, and Marketing Manager Dean Karampelas.

Brief Contents

Contents

Chapter **One**

Introduction to International Accounting

Learning Objectives

After reading this chapter, you should be able to

- Discuss the nature and scope of international accounting.
- Describe accounting issues confronted by companies involved in international trade (import and export transactions).
- Explain reasons for, and accounting issues associated with, foreign direct investment.
- Describe the practice of cross-listing on foreign stock exchanges.
- Explain the notion of global accounting standards.
- Examine the importance of international trade, foreign direct investment, and multinational corporations in the global economy.

WHAT IS INTERNATIONAL ACCOUNTING?

Most accounting students are familiar with financial accounting and managerial accounting, but many have only a vague idea of what international accounting is. Defined broadly, the *accounting* in international accounting encompasses the functional areas of financial accounting, managerial accounting, auditing, taxation, and accounting information systems.

The word *international* in international accounting can be defined at three different levels.[1] The first level is supranational accounting, which denotes standards, guidelines, and rules of accounting, auditing, and taxation issued by supranational organizations. Such organizations include the United Nations, the Organization for Economic Cooperation and Development, and the International Federation of Accountants.

---

[1] This framework for defining international accounting was developed by Professor Konrad Kubin in the preface to *International Accounting Bibliography 1982–1994*, distributed by the International Accounting Section of the American Accounting Association (Sarasota, FL: AAA, 1997).

At the second level, the company level, international accounting can be viewed in terms of the standards, guidelines, and practices that a company follows related to its international business activities and foreign investments. These would include standards for accounting for transactions denominated in a foreign currency and techniques for evaluating the performance of foreign operations.

At the third and broadest level, international accounting can be viewed as the study of the standards, guidelines, and rules of accounting, auditing, and taxation that exist within each country as well as comparison of those items across countries. Examples would be cross-country comparisons of (1) rules related to the financial reporting of plant, property, and equipment; (2) income and other tax rates; and (3) the requirements for becoming a member of the national accounting profession.

Clearly, international accounting encompasses an enormous amount of territory—both geographically and topically. It is not feasible or desirable to cover the entire discipline in one course, so an instructor must determine the scope of an international accounting course. This book is designed to be used in a course that attempts to provide an overview of the broadly defined area of international accounting but that also focuses on the accounting issues related to international business activities and foreign operations.

EVOLUTION OF A MULTINATIONAL CORPORATION

To gain an appreciation for the accounting issues related to international business, let us follow the evolution of Magnum Corporation, a fictional auto parts manufacturer headquartered in Detroit, Michigan.[2] Magnum was founded in the early 1950s to produce and sell rearview mirrors to automakers in the United States. For the first several decades, all of Magnum's transactions occurred in the United States. Raw materials and machinery and equipment were purchased from suppliers located across the United States, finished products were sold to U.S. automakers, loans were obtained from banks in Michigan and Illinois, and the common stock was sold on the New York Stock Exchange. At this stage, all of Magnum's business activities were carried out in U.S. dollars, its financial reporting was done in compliance with U.S. generally accepted accounting principles (GAAP), and taxes were paid to the U.S. federal government and the state of Michigan.

Sales to Foreign Customers

In the 1980s, one of Magnum's major customers, Normal Motors Inc., acquired a production facility in the United Kingdom, and Magnum was asked to supply this operation with rearview mirrors. The most feasible means of supplying Normal Motors UK (NMUK) was to manufacture the mirrors in Michigan and then ship them to the United Kingdom, thus making export sales to a foreign customer. If the sales had been invoiced in U.S. dollars, accounting for the export sales would have been no different from accounting for domestic sales. However, Normal Motors required Magnum to bill the sales to NMUK in British pounds (£), thus creating foreign currency sales for Magnum. The first shipment of mirrors to NMUK was

---

[2] The description of Magnum's evolution is developed from a U.S. perspective. However, the international accounting issues that Magnum is forced to address would be equally applicable to a company headquartered in any other country in the world.

invoiced at £100,000 with credit terms of 2/10, net 30. If Magnum were a British company, the journal entry to record this sale would have been:

Dr. Accounts receivable (+ Assets). £100,000
    Cr. Sales revenue (+ Equity) £100,000

However, Magnum is a U.S.-based company that keeps its accounting records in U.S. dollars (US$). To account for this export sale, the British pound sale and receivable must be translated into US$. Assuming that the exchange rate between the £ and US$ at the time of this transaction was £1 = US$1.60, the journal entry would have been:

Dr. Accounts receivable (£) (+ Assets) . . . . US$160,000
    Cr. Sales revenue (+ Equity) . . . . .US$160,000

This is the first time since its formation that Magnum found it necessary to account for a transaction denominated (invoiced) in a currency other than the U.S. dollar. The company added to its chart of accounts a new account indicating that the receivable was in a foreign currency, "Accounts receivable (£)," and the accountant had to determine the appropriate exchange rate to translate £ into US$.

As luck would have it, by the time NMUK paid its account to Magnum, the value of the £ had fallen to £1 = US$1.50, and the £100,000 received by Magnum was converted into US$150,000. The partial journal entry to record this would have been:

Dr. Cash (+ Asset). . . . . US$150,000
    Cr. Accounts receivable (£) (− Asset). . . . . .US$160,000

This journal entry is obviously incomplete because the debit and credit are not equal and the balance sheet will be out of balance. A question arises: How should the difference of US$10,000 between the original US$ value of the receivable and the actual number of US$ received be reflected in the accounting records? Two possible answers would be (1) to treat the difference as a reduction in sales revenue or (2) to record the difference as a separate loss resulting from a change in the foreign exchange rate. This is an accounting issue that Magnum was not required to deal with until it became involved in export sales. Specific rules for accounting for foreign currency transactions exist in the United States, and Magnum's accountants had to develop an ability to apply those rules.

Through the British-pound account receivable, Magnum became exposed to foreign exchange risk—the risk that the foreign currency will decrease in US$ value over the life of the receivable. The obvious way to avoid this risk is to require foreign customers to pay for their purchases in US$. Sometimes foreign customers will not or cannot pay in the seller's currency, and to make the sale, the seller will be obliged to accept payment in the foreign currency. Thus, foreign exchange risk will arise.

Hedges of Foreign Exchange Risk

Companies can use a variety of techniques to manage, or hedge, their exposure to foreign exchange risk. A popular way to hedge foreign exchange risk is through the purchase of a foreign currency option that gives the option owner the right, but not the obligation, to sell foreign currency at a predetermined exchange rate known as the strike price. Magnum purchased such an option for US$200 and was able to sell the £100,000 it received for a total of US$155,000 because of the option's strike price. The foreign currency option was an asset that Magnum was required to account for over its 30-day life. Options are a type of derivative financial instrument,[3] the accounting for which can be quite complicated. Foreign currency forward contracts are another example of derivative financial instruments commonly used to hedge foreign exchange risk. Magnum never had to worry about how to account for hedging instruments such as options and forward contracts until it became involved in international trade.

Foreign Direct Investment

Although the managers at Magnum at first were apprehensive about international business transactions, they soon discovered that foreign sales were a good way to grow revenues and, with careful management of foreign currency risk, would allow the company to earn adequate profit. Over time, Magnum became known throughout Europe for its quality products. The company entered into negotiations and eventually landed supplier contracts with several European automakers, filling orders through export sales from its factory in the United States. Because of the combination of increased shipping costs and its European customers' desire to move toward just-in-time inventory systems, Magnum began thinking about investing in a production facility somewhere in Europe. The ownership and control of foreign assets, such as a manufacturing plant, is known as foreign direct investment. Exhibit 1.1 summarizes some of the major reasons for foreign direct investment.

Two ways for Magnum to establish a manufacturing presence in Europe were to purchase an existing mirror manufacturer (acquisition) or to construct a brand-new plant (greenfield investment). In either case, the company needed to calculate the net present value (NPV) from the potential investment to make sure that the return on investment would be adequate. Determination of NPV involves forecasting future profits and cash flows, discounting those cash flows back to their present value, and comparing this with the amount of the investment. NPV calculations inherently involve a great deal of uncertainty.

In the early 1990s, Magnum identified a company in Portugal (Espelho Ltda.) as a potential acquisition candidate. In determining NPV, Magnum needed to forecast future cash flows and determine a fair price to pay for Espelho. Magnum had to deal with several complications in making a foreign investment decision that would not have come into play in a domestic situation.

First, to assist in determining a fair price to offer for the company, Magnum asked for Espelho's financial statements for the past five years. The financial statements had been prepared in accordance with Portuguese accounting rules, which were much different from the accounting rules Magnum's managers were familiar with. The balance sheet did not provide a clear picture of the company's

---

[3] A derivative is a financial instrument whose value is based on (or derived from) a traditional security (such as a stock or bond), an asset (such as foreign currency or a commodity like gold), or a market index (such as the S&P 500 index). In this example, the value of the British-pound option is based on the price of the British pound.

EXHIBIT 1.1
Reasons for Foreign Direct Investment

Source: Alan M. Rugman and Richard M. Hodgetts, *International Business: A Strategic Management Approach* (New York: McGraw-Hill, 1995), pp. 64–69.

Increase Sales and Profits

International sales may be a source of higher profit margins or of additional profits through additional sales. Unique products or technological advantages may provide a comparative advantage that a company wishes to exploit by expanding sales in foreign countries.

Enter Rapidly Growing or Emerging Markets

Some international markets are growing much faster than others. Foreign direct investment is a means for gaining a foothold in a rapidly growing or emerging market. The ultimate objective is to increase sales and profits.

Reduce Costs

A company sometimes can reduce the cost of providing goods and services to its customers through foreign direct investment. Significantly lower labor costs in some countries provide an opportunity to reduce the cost of production. If materials are in short supply or must be moved a long distance, it might be less expensive to locate production close to the source of supply rather than to import the materials. Transportation costs associated with making export sales to foreign customers can be reduced by locating production close to the customer.

Protect Domestic Markets

To weaken a potential international competitor and protect its domestic market, a company might enter the competitor's home market. The rationale is that a potential competitor is less likely to enter a foreign market if it is preoccupied protecting its own domestic market.

Protect Foreign Markets

Additional investment in a foreign country is sometimes motivated by a need to protect that market from local competitors. Companies generating sales through exports to a particular country sometimes find it necessary to establish a stronger presence in that country over time to protect their market.

Acquire Technological and Managerial Know-How

In addition to conducting research and development at home, another way to acquire technological and managerial know-how is to set up an operation close to leading competitors. Through geographical proximity, companies find it easier to more closely monitor and learn from industry leaders and even hire experienced employees from the competition.

assets, and many liabilities appeared to be kept off-balance-sheet. Footnote disclosure was limited, and cash flow information was not provided. This was the first time that Magnum's management became aware of the significant differences in accounting between countries. Magnum's accountants spent much time and effort restating Espelho's financial statements to a basis that Magnum felt it could use for valuing the company.

Second, in determining NPV, cash flows should be measured on an after-tax basis. To adequately incorporate tax effects into the analysis, Magnum's management had to learn a great deal about the Portuguese income tax system and the taxes and restrictions imposed on dividend payments made to foreign parent companies. These and other complications make the analysis of a foreign investment much more challenging than the analysis of a domestic investment.

Magnum determined that the purchase of Espelho Ltda. would satisfy its European production needs and also generate an adequate return on investment. Magnum acquired all of the company's outstanding common stock, and Espelho Ltda.

continued as a Portuguese corporation. The investment in a subsidiary located in a foreign country created several new accounting challenges that Magnum previously had not been required to address.

Financial Reporting for Foreign Operations

As a publicly traded company in the United States, Magnum Corporation is required to prepare consolidated financial statements in which the assets, liabilities, and income of its subsidiaries (domestic and foreign) are combined with those of the parent company. The consolidated financial statements must be presented in U.S. dollars and prepared using U.S. GAAP. Espelho Ltda., being a Portuguese corporation, keeps its accounting records in euros (€) in accordance with Portuguese GAAP.[4] To consolidate the results of its Portuguese subsidiary, two procedures must be completed.

First, for all those accounting issues in which Portuguese accounting rules differ from U.S. GAAP, amounts calculated under Portuguese GAAP must be converted to a U.S. GAAP basis. To do this, Magnum needs someone who has expertise in both U.S. and Portuguese GAAP and can reconcile the differences between them. Magnum's financial reporting system was altered to accommodate this conversion process. Magnum relied heavily on its external auditing firm (one of the so-called Big Four firms) in developing procedures to restate Espelho's financial statements to U.S. GAAP.

Second, after the account balances have been converted to a U.S. GAAP basis, they then must be translated from the foreign currency (€) into US$. Several methods exist for translating foreign currency financial statements into the parent's reporting currency. All the methods involve the use of both the current exchange rate at the balance sheet date and historical exchange rates. By translating some financial statement items at the current exchange rate and other items at historical exchange rates, the resulting translated balance sheet no longer balances, as can be seen in the following example:

Assets	€ 1,000	×	$1.35	US$1,350
Liabilities	600	×	1.35	810
Stockholders' equity.	400	×	1.00	400
	€ 1,000			US$1,210

To get the US$ financial statements back into balance, a translation adjustment of US$140 must be added to stockholders' equity. One of the major debates in translating foreign currency financial statements is whether the translation adjustment should be reported in consolidated net income as a gain or whether it should simply be added to equity with no effect on income. Each country has developed rules regarding the appropriate exchange rate to be used for the various financial statement items and the disposition of the translation adjustment. Magnum's accountants needed to learn and be able to apply the rules in force in the United States.

---

[4] Note that in 2005 Portugal adopted International Financial Reporting Standards for publicly traded companies in compliance with European Union regulations. However, as a wholly owned subsidiary, Espelho Ltda. continues to use Portuguese GAAP in keeping its books.

International Income Taxation

The existence of a foreign subsidiary raises two kinds of questions with respect to taxation:

1. What are the income taxes that Espelho Ltda. has to pay in Portugal, and how can those taxes legally be minimized?
2. What are the taxes, if any, that Magnum Corporation has to pay in the United States related to the income earned by Espelho in Portugal, and how can those taxes legally be minimized?

All else being equal, Magnum wants to minimize the total amount of taxes it pays worldwide because doing so will maximize its after-tax cash flows. To achieve this objective, Magnum must have expertise in the tax systems in each of the countries in which it operates. Just as every country has its own unique set of financial accounting rules, each country also has a unique set of tax regulations.

As a Portuguese corporation doing business in Portugal, Espelho Ltda. will have to pay income tax to the Portuguese government on its Portuguese source income. Magnum's management began to understand the Portuguese tax system in the process of determining after-tax net present value when deciding to acquire Espelho. The United States taxes corporate profits on a worldwide basis, which means that Magnum will also have to pay tax to the U.S. government on the income earned by its Portuguese subsidiary. However, because Espelho is legally incorporated in Portugal (as a subsidiary), U.S. tax generally is not owed until Espelho's income is repatriated to the parent in the United States as a dividend. (If Espelho were registered with the Portuguese government as a branch, its income would be taxed currently in the United States regardless of when the income is remitted to Magnum.) Thus, income earned by the foreign operations of U.S. companies is subject to double taxation.

Most countries, including the United States, provide companies relief from double taxation through a credit for the amount of taxes already paid to the foreign government. Tax treaties between two countries might also provide some relief from double taxation. Magnum's tax accountants must be very conversant in U.S. tax law as it pertains to foreign source income to make sure that the company is not paying more taxes to the U.S. government than is necessary.

International Transfer Pricing

Some companies with foreign operations attempt to minimize the amount of worldwide taxes they pay through the use of discretionary transfer pricing. Auto mirrors consist of three major components: mirrored glass, a plastic housing, and a steel bracket. The injection-molding machinery for producing the plastic housing is expensive, and Espelho Ltda. does not own such equipment. The plastic parts that Espelho requires are produced by Magnum in the United States and then shipped to Espelho as an intercompany sale. Prices must be established for these intercompany transfers. The transfer price generates sales revenue for Magnum and is a component of cost of goods sold for Espelho. If the transfer were being made within the United States, Magnum's management would allow the buyer and seller to negotiate a price that both would be willing to accept.

This intercompany sale is being made from one country to another. Because the income tax rate in Portugal is higher than that in the United States, Magnum requires these parts to be sold to Espelho at as high a price as possible. Transferring parts to Portugal at high prices shifts gross profit to the United States that otherwise would be earned in Portugal, thus reducing the total taxes paid to both countries. Most governments are aware that multinational companies have the ability to shift profits between countries through discretionary transfer pricing. To make sure that companies pay their fair share of local taxes, most countries have laws that regulate international transfer pricing. Magnum Corporation must be careful that, in transferring parts from the United States to Portugal, the transfer price is acceptable to tax authorities in both countries. The United States, especially, has become aggressive in enforcing its transfer pricing regulations.

Performance Evaluation of Foreign Operations

To ensure that operations in both the United States and Portugal are achieving their objectives, Magnum's top management requests that the managers of the various operating units submit periodic reports to headquarters detailing their unit's performance. Headquarters management is interested in evaluating the performance of the operating unit as well as the performance of the individuals responsible for managing those units. The process for evaluating performance that Magnum has used in the past for its U.S. operations is not directly transferable in evaluating the performance of Espelho Ltda. Several issues unique to foreign operations must be considered in designing the evaluation system. For example, Magnum has to decide whether to evaluate Espelho's performance on the basis of euros or U.S. dollars. Translation from one currency to another can affect return-on-investment ratios that are often used as performance measures. Magnum must also decide whether reported results should be adjusted to factor out those items over which Espelho's managers had no control, such as the inflated price paid for plastic parts imported from Magnum. There is no universally correct solution to the various issues that Magnum must address, and the company is likely to find it necessary to make periodic adjustments to its evaluation process for foreign operations.

International Auditing

The primary objective of Magnum's performance evaluation system is to maintain control over its decentralized operations. Another important component of the management control process is internal auditing. The internal auditor must (1) make sure that the company's policies and procedures are being followed and (2) uncover errors, inefficiencies, and, unfortunately at times, fraud. There are several issues that make the internal audit of a foreign operation more complicated than domestic audits.

Perhaps the most obvious obstacle to performing an effective internal audit is language. To be able to communicate with Espelho's managers and employees—asking the questions that need to be asked and understanding the answers—Magnum's internal auditors need to speak Portuguese. The auditors also need to be familiar with the local culture and customs, because these may affect the amount of work necessary in the audit. This familiarity can help to explain some of the behavior encountered and perhaps can be useful in planning the audit. Another important function of the internal auditor is to make sure that the company is in compliance with the Foreign Corrupt Practices Act, which prohibits a U.S. company from paying bribes to foreign government officials to obtain business. Magnum needs to make sure that internal controls are in place to provide reasonable assurance that illegal payments are not made.

External auditors encounter the same problems as internal auditors in dealing with the foreign operations of their clients. External auditors with multinational company clients must have an expertise in the various sets of financial accounting rules as well as the auditing standards in the various jurisdictions in which

EXHIBIT 1.2
The History of KPMG

Source: KPMG International, www.kpmgcampus.com/whoweare/history.shtml, accessed April 18, 2010.

KPMG was formed in 1987 through the merger of Peat Marwick International (PMI) and Klynveld Main Goerdeler (KMG). KPMG's history can be traced through the names of its principal founding members—whose initials form the name "K.P.M.G."

- **K** stands for Klynveld. Piet Klynveld founded the accounting firm Klynveld Kraayenhof & Co. in Amsterdam in 1917.
- **P** is for Peat. William Barclay Peat founded the accounting firm William Barclay Peat & Co. in London in 1870.
- **M** stands for Marwick. James Marwick founded the accounting firm Marwick, Mitchell & Co. with Roger Mitchell in New York City in 1897.
- **G** is for Goerdeler. Dr. Reinhard Goerdeler was for many years chairman of the German accounting firm Deutsche Treuhand-Gesellschaft.

In 1911, William Barclay Peat & Co. and Marwick Mitchell & Co. joined forces to form what would later be known as Peat Marwick International (PMI), a worldwide network of accounting and consulting firms.

In 1979, Klynveld joined forces with Deutsche Treuhand-Gesellschaft and the international professional services firm McLintock Main Lafrentz to form Klynveld Main Goerdeler (KMG).

In 1987, PMI and KMG and their member firms joined forces. Today, all member firms throughout the world carry the KPMG name exclusively or include it in their national firm names.

their clients operate. Magnum's external auditors, for example, must be capable of applying Portuguese auditing standards to attest that Espelho's financial statements present a true and fair view in accordance with Portuguese GAAP. In addition, they must apply U.S. auditing standards to verify that the reconciliation of Espelho's financial statements for consolidation purposes brings the financial statements in compliance with U.S. GAAP.

As firms have become more multinational, so have their external auditors. Today, the Big Four international accounting firms are among the most multinational organizations in the world. Indeed, one of the Big Four accounting firms, KPMG, is the result of a merger of four different accounting firms that originated in four different countries (see Exhibit 1.2) and currently has offices in more than 150 jurisdictions around the world.

Cross-Listing on Foreign Stock Exchanges

Magnum's investment in Portugal turned out to be extremely profitable, and over time the company established operations in other countries around the world. As each new country was added to the increasingly international company, Magnum had to address new problems associated with foreign GAAP conversion, foreign currency translation, international taxation and transfer pricing, and management control.

By the beginning of the 21st century, Magnum had become a truly global enterprise with more than 10,000 employees spread across 16 different countries. Although the United States remained its major market, the company generated less than half of its revenues in its home country. Magnum eventually decided that in addition to its stock being listed on the New York Stock Exchange (NYSE), there would be advantages to having the stock listed and traded on several foreign stock exchanges. Most stock exchanges require companies to file an annual report and specify the accounting rules that must be followed in preparing financial statements. Regulations pertaining to foreign companies can differ from those for domestic companies. For example, in the United States, the Securities and Exchange Commission requires all U.S. companies to use U.S. GAAP in preparing their financial statements. Foreign companies listed on U.S. stock exchanges may use foreign GAAP in preparing their financial statements but must provide a reconciliation of net income and stockholders' equity to U.S. GAAP. In 2007 the U.S. Securities and Exchange Commission relaxed this requirement for those companies that use International Financial Reporting Standards to prepare financial statements.

Many stock exchanges around the world now allow foreign companies to be listed on those exchanges by using standards developed by the International Accounting Standards Board (IASB). Magnum determined that by preparing a set of financial statements based on the IASB's International Financial Reporting Standards (IFRS), it could gain access to most of the stock exchanges it might possibly want to, including London's and Frankfurt's. With the help of its external auditing firm, Magnum's accountants developed a second set of financial statements prepared in accordance with IFRS and the company was able to obtain stock exchange listings in several foreign countries.

Global Accounting Standards

Through their experiences in analyzing the financial statements of potential acquisitions and in cross-listing the company's stock, Magnum's managers began to wonder whether the differences that exist in GAAP across countries were really necessary. There would be significant advantages if all countries, including the United States, were to adopt a common set of accounting rules. In that case, Magnum could use one set of accounting standards as the local GAAP in each of the countries in which it has operations and thus avoid the GAAP conversion that it currently must perform in preparing consolidated financial statements. A single set of accounting rules used worldwide also would significantly reduce the problems the company had experienced over the years in evaluating foreign investment opportunities based on financial statements prepared in compliance with a variety of local GAAP. Magnum Corporation became a strong proponent of global accounting standards.

THE GLOBAL ECONOMY

Although Magnum is a fictitious company, its evolution into a multinational corporation is not unrealistic. Most companies begin by selling their products in the domestic market. As foreign demand for the company's product arises, this demand is met initially through making export sales. Exporting is the entry point for most companies into the world of international business.

International Trade

International trade (imports and exports) constitutes a significant portion of the world economy. In 2008, companies worldwide exported more than $16.0 trillion worth of merchandise.[5] The three largest exporters were Germany, China, and the United States, in that order. The United States, Germany, and China, in that order, were the three largest importers. Although international trade has existed for thousands of years, recent growth in trade has been phenomenal. Over the

---

[5] World Trade Organization, *International Trade Statistics 2009,* Table I.8, Leading Exporters and Importers in World Merchandise Trade, 2008.

period 1996–2008, U.S. exports increased from $625 billion to $1,287 billion per year, a 106 percent increase. During the same period, Chinese exports increased sixfold to $1,428 billion in 2008. Manufactured products account for 66.5 percent of world trade, followed by fuel and mining products (22.5 percent) and agricultural products (8.5 percent).[6]

The number of companies involved in trade also has grown substantially. The number of U.S. companies making export sales rose by 233 percent from 1987 to 1999, when the number stood at 231,420.[7] Boeing is a U.S.-based company with billions of dollars of annual export sales. In 2009, 42 percent of the company's sales were outside of the United States. In addition, some of the company's key suppliers and subcontractors are located in Europe and Japan. However, not only large companies are involved in exporting. Companies with fewer than 500 workers comprise more than 90 percent of U.S. exporters.

Foreign Direct Investment

The product cycle theory suggests that, as time passes, exporters may feel the only way to retain their advantage over competition in foreign markets is to produce locally, thereby reducing transportation costs. Companies often acquire existing operations in foreign countries as a way to establish a local production capability. Alternatively, companies can establish a local presence by founding a new company specifically tailored to the company's needs. Sometimes this is done through a joint venture with a local partner.

The acquisition of existing foreign companies and the creation of new foreign subsidiaries are the two most common forms of what is known as foreign direct investment (FDI). The growth in FDI can be seen in Exhibit 1.3. The tremendous increase in the flow of FDI from 1982 to 2007 is partially attributable to the liberalization of investment laws in many countries specifically aimed at attracting FDI. Of 244 changes in national FDI laws in 2003, 220 were more favorable for foreign investors.[8]

FDI is playing a larger and more important role in the world economy. Global sales of foreign affiliates were about 1.5 times as high as global exports in 2008, compared to almost parity in 1982. Global sales of foreign affiliates comprises about 10 percent of worldwide gross domestic product.

In 2008, there were 73 cross-border acquisitions of existing companies in which the purchase price exceeded $3 billion. The largest deal was the acquisition of the U.S. firm Anheuser-Busch Cos. Inc. by InBev NV, a Belgium-based company, for a reported $52.2 billion. More than 6,000 FDI greenfield and expansion projects were announced in 2005 at an estimated cost of $716 billion.[9] The United Kingdom was the leading location of these projects, followed by the United States, and Germany.

After years of steady increases, inflows of FDI within the countries of the Organization for Economic Cooperation and Development (OECD) reached a peak of $1.2 trillion in 2000, dropping to $622 billion in 2005.[10] The most popular locations for inbound FDI in 2005 among OECD countries were, in order of importance, the

---

[6] Ibid., Table II.1, World Merchandise Exports by Product, 2008.

[7] U.S. Department of Commerce, International Trade Administration, "Small and Medium-Sized Enterprises Play an Important Role," *Export America,* September 2001, pp. 26–29.

[8] United Nations, *World Investment Report 2004,* p. xvii.

[9] Ibid., p. 6.

[10] Organization for Economic Cooperation and Development, "Trends and Recent Developments in Foreign Direct Investment," *International Investment Perspectives,* 2006, p. 13.

EXHIBIT 1.3
Growth in Foreign
Direct Investment,
1982–2008

Source: United Nations,
World Investment Report 2009,
Table I.6.

Item	Value ($ billions)			
	1982	**1990**	**2007**	**2008**
FDI inflows.	$ 58	$ 207	$1,979	$1,697
FDI outflows.	27	239	2,147	1,858
FDI inward stock.	790	1,942	15,660	14,909
FDI outward stock.	579	1,786	16,227	16,206
Sales of foreign affiliates.	2,530	6,026	31,764	30,311
Assets of foreign affiliates.	2,036	5,938	73,457	69,771
Employment by foreign affiliates (thousands).	19,864	24,476	80,396	77,386

United Kingdom, the United States, France, Luxembourg, and The Netherlands. The countries with the largest dollar amount of outbound FDI in 2005 were The Netherlands, France, the United Kingdom, Luxembourg, and Japan.

The extent of foreign corporate presence in a country can be viewed by looking at the cumulative amount of inward FDI. Over the period 1996–2005, the United States received more FDI ($1.54 trillion) than any other OECD country.[11] The United States also had the largest amount of outbound FDI ($1.41 trillion) during this period.

Multinational Corporations

A multinational corporation is a company that is headquartered in one country but has operations in other countries.[12] The United Nations estimates that there are more than 82,000 multinational companies in the world, with more than 810,000 foreign affiliates.[13] The 100 largest multinational companies account for approximately 4 percent of the world's GDP.[14]

Companies located in a relatively small number of countries conduct a large proportion of international trade and investment. These countries—collectively known as the triad—are the United States, Japan, and members of the European Union. As Exhibit 1.4 shows, 83 of the 100 largest companies in the world are located in the triad.

The largest companies are not necessarily the most multinational. Of the 500 largest companies in the United States in 2000, for example, 36 percent had no foreign operations.[15] In 2008 the United Nations measured the multinationality of companies by averaging three factors: the ratio of foreign sales to total sales, the ratio of foreign assets to total assets, and the ratio of foreign employees to total employees. Exhibit 1.5 lists the top 10 companies according to this measure.

---

[11] Ibid., p. 21.

[12] There is no universally accepted definition of a multinational corporation. The definition used here comes from Alan M. Rugman and Richard M. Hodgetts, *International Business: A Strategic Management Approach* (New York: McGraw-Hill, 1995, p. 3). Similarly, the United Nations defines *multinational corporations* as "enterprises which own or control production or service facilities outside the country in which they are based" (United Nations, *Multinational Corporations in World Development,* 1973, p. 23), and defines *transnational corporations* as "enterprises comprising parent companies and their foreign affiliates" (United Nations, *World Investment Report 2001,* p. 275).

[13] United Nations, *World Investment Report 2009,* p. 17.

[14] Ibid.

[15] T. Doupnik and L. Seese, "Geographic Area Disclosures under SFAS 131: Materiality and Fineness," *Journal of International Accounting, Auditing & Taxation,* 2001, pp. 117–38.

EXHIBIT 1.4
Home Country of Largest 100 Companies by Sales

Source: *Fortune,* "The 2009 Global 500," July 20, 2009.

United States	29	Japan	10
European Union		**Other**	
Germany	15	China	5
France	10	South Korea	4
United Kingdom	6	Russia	2
Italy	5	Brazil	1
Spain	3	Mexico	1
Netherlands	2	Norway	1
Belgium	1	Malaysia	1
Finland	1	Venezuela	1
Luxembourg	1	Switzerland	1
	44		17

Xstrata Plc was the most multinational company in the world, with more than 90 percent of its assets, sales, and employees located outside its home country of the United Kingdom. One-half the companies on this list come from the United Kingdom. The five most multinational U.S. companies in 2008, in order, were AES Corporation, Liberty Group Inc., Coca-Cola, ExxonMobil, and Procter & Gamble.

Many companies have established a worldwide presence. Nike Inc., the world's largest manufacturer of athletic footwear, apparel, and equipment, has branch offices and subsidiaries in 52 countries, sells products in more than 170 countries, and has more than 34,000 employees around the globe. Virtually all of Nike's footwear and apparel products are manufactured outside of the United States. The company generates approximately 58 percent of its sales outside the United States.[16]

Nokia, the Finnish cellular telephone manufacturer, has 10 manufacturing facilities in nine different countries around the world, including South Korea, Brazil, China, and the United States. Because these subsidiaries are outside of the euro zone, Nokia must translate the financial statements from these operations

EXHIBIT 1.5   The World's Top 10 Nonfinancial Companies in Terms of Multinationality, 2008

Source: United Nations, *World Investment Report 2009,* pp. 228–230.

Corporation	Country	Industry	MNI*
Xstrata Plc	United Kingdom	Mining and quarrying	93.2
ArcelorMittal	Luxembourg	Metals and metal products	91.4
AkzoNobel	Netherlands	Pharmaceuticals	90.3
WPP Group Plc	United Kingdom	Other business services	88.9
Vodafone Group Plc	United Kingdom	Telecommunications	88.6
Nokia	Finland	Telecommunications	88.5
Linde AG	Germany	Chemicals	88.3
Anglo American	United Kingdom	Mining and quarrying	87.5
InBev SA	Netherlands	Food, beverages, and tobacco	87.0
AstraZeneca Plc	United Kingdom	Pharmaceuticals	86.8

*Multinationality index (MNI) is calculated as the average of three ratios: foreign assets/total assets, foreign sales/total sales, and foreign employment/total employment.

[16] Nike Inc., 2009 Form 10-K, various pages.

into euros for consolidation purposes. Nokia's management states that, from time to time, it uses forward contracts and foreign currency loans to hedge the foreign exchange risk created by foreign net investments.[17]

International Capital Markets

Many multinational corporations have found it necessary, for one reason or another, to have their stock cross-listed on foreign stock exchanges. Large companies in small countries, such as Finland's Nokia, might find this necessary to obtain sufficient capital at a reasonable cost. Nokia's shares are listed on the Helsinki, Stockholm, Frankfurt, and New York stock exchanges. Other companies obtain a listing on a foreign exchange to have an "acquisition currency" for acquiring firms in that country through stock swaps. Not long after obtaining a New York Stock Exchange (NYSE) listing, Germany's Daimler-Benz acquired Chrysler in the United States in an exchange of shares.

As of January 31, 2010, there were 499 foreign companies from 47 countries cross-listed on the NYSE.[18] During 2007, 63.8 billion shares of stock in these companies were traded. The total market value of these companies' NYSE shares at the end of 2007 was $1.6 trillion. Most of these companies were required to reconcile their local GAAP financial statements to a U.S. GAAP basis.

Many U.S. companies are similarly cross-listed on non-U.S. stock exchanges. For example, more than 50 U.S. companies are listed on the London Stock Exchange, including Abbott Labs, Boeing, and Pfizer. U.S. companies such as Caterpillar, Intel, and Pepsico are listed on Euronext, a merger of the Amsterdam, Brussels, and Paris stock exchanges.

OUTLINE OF THE BOOK

The evolution of the fictitious Magnum Corporation presented earlier in this chapter highlights many of the major accounting issues that a multinational corporation must address and that form the focus for this book. The remainder of this book is organized as follows.

Chapters 2 and 3 focus on differences in financial reporting across countries and the international convergence of accounting standards. Chapter 2 provides evidence of the diversity in financial reporting that has existed internationally, explores the reasons for that diversity, and describes the various attempts to classify countries by accounting system. Chapter 3 describes and evaluates the major efforts to converge accounting internationally. The most important player in the development of global financial reporting standards is the International Accounting Standards Board (IASB). Chapter 3 describes the work of the IASB and introduces International Financial Reporting Standards (IFRS).

Chapters 4 and 5 describe and demonstrate the requirements of selected IASB standards through numerical examples. In addition to describing the guidance provided by IFRS, these chapters provide comparisons with U.S. GAAP to indicate the differences and similarities between the two sets of standards. Chapter 4 focuses on IFRS related to the recognition and measurement of assets, specifically inventories, property, plant and equipment, intangibles and goodwill, and leased assets. IFRS that deal exclusively with disclosure and presentation issues also are briefly summarized. Chapter 5 covers IFRS related to current liabilities,

---

[17] Nokia Corporation, 2009 Form 20-F, various pages.

[18] New York Stock Exchange, www.nyse.com/pdfs/Non-US_CurListofallStocks01-01-10.pdf.

provisions, employee benefits, share-based payment, income taxes, revenue, and financial instruments.

Chapter 6 describes the accounting environment in five economically significant countries—China, Germany, Japan, Mexico, and the United Kingdom—that are representative of major clusters of accounting system.

Chapters 7–9 focus on financial reporting issues that are of international significance either because they relate to international business operations or because there is considerable diversity in how they are handled worldwide. Chapters 7 and 8 deal with issues related to foreign currency translation. Chapter 7 covers the accounting for foreign currency transactions and hedging activities, and Chapter 8 demonstrates the translation of foreign currency financial statements. Chapter 9 covers several other important financial reporting issues, specifically inflation accounting, business combinations and consolidated financial statements, and segment reporting. This chapter focuses on IFRS related to these topics.

Chapter 10 introduces issues related to the analysis of foreign financial statements and explores potential problems (and potential solutions) associated with using the financial statements of foreign companies in decision making. This chapter also provides an example of how an analyst would reformat and restate financial statements from one set of GAAP to another.

International taxation and international transfer pricing are covered in Chapters 11 and 12. Chapter 11 focuses on the taxation of foreign operation income by the home country government. Much of this chapter deals with foreign tax credits, the most important mechanism available to companies to reduce double taxation. Chapter 12 covers the topic of international transfer pricing, focusing on tax implications.

Strategic accounting issues of particular relevance to multinational corporations are covered in Chapter 13. This chapter covers multinational capital budgeting as a vital component of strategy formulation and operational budgeting a key ingredient in strategy implementation. Chapter 13 also deals with issues that must be addressed in designing a process for evaluating the performance of foreign operations.

Chapter 14 covers comparative international auditing and corporate governance. This chapter discusses both external and internal auditing issues as they relate to corporate governance in an international context. Chapter 14 also describes international diversity in external auditing and the international harmonization of auditing standards. In addition to financial reports, more than 1,000 multinational companies worldwide publish a separate sustainability report, which provides environmental, social responsibility, and related disclosures. Chapter 15 introduces corporate social responsibility and sustainability reporting.

Summary

1. International accounting is an extremely broad topic. At a minimum, it focuses on the accounting issues unique to multinational corporations. At the other extreme, it includes the study of the various functional areas of accounting (financial, managerial, auditing, tax, information systems) in all countries of the world, as well as a comparison across countries. This book provides an overview of the broadly defined area of international accounting, with a focus on the accounting issues encountered by multinational companies engaged in international trade and making foreign direct investments.

2. The world economy is becoming increasingly more integrated. International trade (imports and exports) has grown substantially in recent years and is even

becoming a normal part of business for relatively small companies. The number of U.S. exporting companies more than doubled in the 1990s.

3. The tremendous growth in foreign direct investment (FDI) over the last two decades is partially attributable to the liberalization of investment laws in many countries specifically aimed at attracting FDI. The aggregate revenues generated by foreign operations outstrip the revenues generated through exporting by a two-to-one margin.

4. There are more than 82,000 multinational companies in the world, and their 810,000 foreign subsidiaries generate approximately 10 percent of global gross domestic product (GDP). A disproportionate number of multinational corporations are headquartered in the triad: the United States, Japan, and the European Union.

5. The largest companies in the world are not necessarily the most multinational. Indeed, many large U.S. companies have no foreign operations. According to the United Nations, the two most multinational companies in the world in 2008 were located in the United Kingdom and Luxembourg.

6. In addition to establishing operations overseas, many companies also cross-list their shares on stock exchanges outside of their home country. There are a number of reasons for doing this, including gaining access to a larger pool of capital.

7. The remainder of this book consists of 14 chapters. Nine chapters (Chapters 2–10) deal primarily with financial accounting and reporting issues, including the analysis of foreign financial statements. Chapters 11 and 12 focus on international taxation and transfer pricing. Chapter 13 deals with the management accounting issues relevant to multinational corporations in formulating and implementing strategy. Chapter 14, covers comparative international auditing and corporate governance. The final chapter, Chapter 15, provides an introduction to social responsibility reporting at the international level.

Questions

1. How important is international trade (imports and exports) to the world economy?

2. What accounting issues arise for a company as a result of engaging in international trade (imports and exports)?

3. Why might a company be interested in investing in an operation in a foreign country (foreign direct investment)?

4. How important is foreign direct investment to the world economy?

5. What financial reporting issues arise as a result of making a foreign direct investment?

6. What taxation issues arise as a result of making a foreign direct investment?

7. What are some of the issues that arise in evaluating and maintaining control over foreign operations?

8. Why might a company want its stock listed on a stock exchange outside of its home country?

9. Where might one find information that could be used to measure the "multi-nationality" of a company?

10. What would be the advantages of having a single set of accounting standards used worldwide?

Exercises and Problems

1. Sony Corporation reported the following in the summary of Significant Accounting Policies included in the company's 2009 annual report on Form 20-F (p. F-16):

Translation of Foreign Currencies

All asset and liability accounts of foreign subsidiaries and affiliates are translated into Japanese yen at approximate year-end current exchange rates and all income and expense accounts are translated at exchange rates that approximate those rates prevailing at the time of the transactions. The resulting translation adjustments are accumulated as a component of accumulated other comprehensive income.

Receivables and payables denominated in foreign currency are translated at appropriate year-end exchange rates and the resulting translation gains or losses are taken into income.

Required:

Explain in your own words the policies that Sony uses in reflecting in the financial statements the impact of changes in foreign exchange rates.

2. Sony Corporation reported the following in the Notes to Consolidated Financial Statements included in the company's 2009 annual report on Form 20-F (p. F-44):

Foreign Exchange Forward Contracts and Foreign Currency Option Contracts

Foreign exchange forward contracts and purchased and written foreign currency option contracts are utilized primarily to limit the exposure affected by changes in foreign currency exchange rates on cash flows generated by anticipated intercompany transactions and intercompany accounts receivable and payable denominated in foreign currencies.

Sony also enters into foreign exchange forward contracts, which effectively fix the cash flows from foreign currency denominated debt.

Required:

Explain in your own words why Sony has entered into foreign exchange forward contracts and foreign currency option contracts.

3. Cooper Grant is the president of Acme Brush of Brazil the wholly owned Brazilian subsidiary of U.S.-based Acme Brush Inc. Cooper Grant's compensation package consists of a combination of salary and bonus. His annual bonus is calculated as a predetermined percentage of the pretax annual income earned by Acme Brush of Brazil. A condensed income statement for Acme Brush of Brazil for the most recent year is as follows (amounts in thousands of Brazilian reals [BRL]):

Sales	BRL10,000
Expenses	9,500
Pretax income	BRL 500

After translating the Brazilian real income statement into U.S. dollars, the condensed income statement for Acme Brush of Brazil appears as follows (amounts in thousands of U.S. dollars [US$]):

Sales	US$3,000
Expenses	3,300
Pretax income (loss)	US$ (300)

Required:

    a. Explain how Acme Brush of Brazil's pretax income (in BRL) became a U.S.-dollar pretax loss.

    b. Discuss whether Cooper Grant should be paid a bonus or not.

4. The New York Stock Exchange (NYSE) provides a list of non-U.S. companies listed on the exchange on its Web site (www.nyse.com). (Hint: Search the internet for "NYSE List of Non-U.S. Listed Issuers.")

Required:

    a. Determine the number of foreign companies listed on the NYSE and the number of countries they represent.

    b. Determine the five countries with the largest number of foreign companies listed on the NYSE.

    c. Speculate as to why non-U.S. companies have gone to the effort to have their shares listed on the NYSE.

5. The London Stock Exchange (LSE) provides a list of companies listed on the exchange on its Web site (www.londonstockexchange.com) under "Statistics" and "List of Companies."

Required:

    a. Determine the number of foreign companies listed on the LSE and the number of countries they represent.

    b. Determine the number of companies listed on the LSE from these countries: Australia, Brazil, Canada, France, Germany, Mexico, and the United States. Speculate as to why there are more companies listed on the LSE from Australia and Canada than from France and Germany.

6. AstraZeneca PLC and Tesco PLC are two of the largest companies in the United Kingdom. The following information was provided in each company's 2009 annual report.

ASTRAZENECA
Annual Report 2009

Geographic Areas	Sales ($ million)	Total Assets ($ million)
United Kingdom	10,865	17,092
Continental Europe	13,820	6,706
The Americas	19,257	28,397
Asia, Africa, & Australasia	4,904	2,725

TESCO
Annual Report 2009

Geographical Segments	Sales (£ million)	Segment Assets (£ million)
United Kingdom	38,191	29,913
Rest of Europe	8,862	6,953
Asia	7,068	6,242
United States	206	768
Unallocated	-0-	2,115

Required:
Calculate an index of multinationality based upon the geographical distribution of Sales and Assets (employee information is not available) to determine which of these two companies is more multinational.

Case 1-1

Besserbrau AG

Besserbrau AG is a German beer producer headquartered in Ergersheim, Bavaria. The company, which was founded in 1842 by brothers Hans and Franz Besser, is publicly traded with shares listed on the Frankfurt Stock Exchange. Manufacturing in strict accordance with the almost 500-year-old German Beer Purity Law, Besserbrau uses only four ingredients in making its products: malt, hops, yeast, and water. While the other ingredients are obtained locally, Besserbrau imports hops from a company located in the Czech Republic. Czech hops are considered to be among the world's finest. Historically, Besserbrau's products were marketed exclusively in Germany. To take advantage of a potentially enormous market for its products and expand sales, Besserbrau began making sales in the People's Republic of China three years ago. The company established a wholly owned subsidiary in China (BB Pijio) to handle the distribution of Besserbrau products in that country. In the most recent year, sales to BB Pijio accounted for 20 percent of Besserbrau's sales, and BB Pijio's sales to customers in China accounted for 10 percent of the Besserbrau Group's total profits. In fact, sales of Besserbrau products in China have expanded so rapidly and the potential for continued sales growth is so great that the company recently broke ground on the construction of a brewery in Shanghai, China. To finance construction of the new facility, Besserbrau negotiated a listing of its shares on the London Stock Exchange to facilitate an initial public offering of new shares of stock.

Required:

Discuss the various international accounting issues confronted by Besserbrau AG.

Case 1-2

Vanguard International Growth Fund

The Vanguard Group is an investment firm with more than 50 different mutual funds in which the public may invest. Among these funds are 13 international funds that concentrate on investments in non-U.S. stocks and bonds. One of these is the International Growth Fund. The following information about this fund was provided in the fund's prospectus, dated December 28, 2009.

VANGUARD INTERNATIONAL GROWTH FUND
Excerpts from Prospectus
December 28, 2009

Vanguard Fund Summary

Investment Objective

The Fund seeks to provide long-term capital appreciation.

Primary Investment Strategies

The Fund invests predominantly in the stocks of companies located outside the United States and is expected to diversify its assets across developed and emerging markets in Europe, the Far East, and Latin America. In selecting stocks, the Fund's advisors evaluate foreign markets around the world and choose large-, mid-, and small-capitalization companies considered to have above-average growth potential. The Fund uses multiple investment advisors.

Market Exposure

The Fund invests mainly in common stocks of non-U.S. companies that are considered to have above-average potential for growth. The asset-weighted median market capitalization of the Fund as of August 31, 2009, was $34.7 billion.

The Fund is subject to investment style risk, which is the chance that returns from non-U.S. growth stocks and, to the extent that the Fund is invested in them, small- and mid-cap stocks, will trail returns from the overall domestic stock market. Historically, small- and mid-cap stocks have been more volatile in price than the large-cap stocks that dominate the overall market, and they often perform quite differently.

The Fund is subject to stock market risk, which is the chance that stock prices overall will decline. Stock markets tend to move in cycles, with periods of rising prices and periods of falling prices. In addition, investments in foreign stock markets can be riskier than U.S. stock investments. The prices of foreign stocks and the prices of U.S. stocks have, at times, moved in opposite directions.

The Fund is subject to country/regional risk and currency risk. *Country/regional risk* is the chance that domestic events—such as political upheaval, financial troubles, or natural disasters—will adversely affect the value of securities issued by companies in foreign countries or regions. Because the Fund may invest a large portion of its assets in securities of companies located in any one country or region, its performance may be hurt disproportionately by the poor performance of its investments in that area. Country/regional risk is especially high in emerging markets. *Currency risk* is the chance that the value of a foreign investment, measured in U.S. dollars, will decrease because of unfavorable changes in currency exchange rates.

The Fund is subject to manager risk, which is the chance that poor security selection or focus on securities in a particular sector, category, or group of companies will cause the Fund to underperform relevant benchmarks or other funds with a similar investment objective.

PLAIN TALK ABOUT
International Investing

U.S. investors who invest abroad will encounter risks not typically associated with U.S. companies, because foreign stock and bond markets operate differently from the U.S. markets. For instance, foreign companies are not subject to the same accounting, auditing, and financial-reporting standards and practices as U.S. companies, and their stocks may not be as liquid as those of similar U.S. firms. In addition, foreign stock exchanges, brokers, and companies generally have less government supervision and regulation than their counterparts in the United States. These factors, among others, could negatively affect the returns U.S. investors receive from foreign investments.

Source: Vanguard International Growth Fund Prospectus, pp. 1–11

The International Growth Fund's annual report for the year ended August 31, 2009, indicated that 94 percent of the fund's portfolio was invested in 177 non-U.S. stocks and 6 percent was in temporary cash investments. The allocation of fund net assets by region was as follows: Europe 54 percent, Pacific 24 percent, Emerging Markets 20 percent, and Canada 1 percent. The sectors and individual countries in which the fund was invested are presented in the following tables:

Sector Diversification (% of equity exposure)	
Consumer discretionary	12.5%
Consumer staples	12.5
Energy	8.7
Financials	22.7
Health care	7.2
Industrials	11.9
Information technology	8.9
Materials	9.0
Telecommunication services	4.8
Utilities	1.8

Source: Annual report, p. 14.

Country Diversification (% of equity exposure)			
Europe		**Pacific**	
United Kingdom . .	17.2%	Japan	15.4%
France	10.0	Hong Kong . . .	4.2
Switzerland	8.4	Australia	3.4
Germany	6.9	Singapore	1.3
Spain	3.5	Subtotal	24.3%
Sweden	2.8	**Emerging Markets**	
Netherlands	2.3	Brazil	6.4%
Denmark	1.8	China	5.4
Other European		Israel	2.3
Markets	1.5	Mexico	1.2
Subtotal	54.4%	South Africa . . .	1.1
		Other Emerging	
		Markets	3.7
		Subtotal	20.1%
		North America . .	
		Canada	1.2%

Source: Annual report, p. 15.

Required:

1. Explain why an individual investor might want to invest in an international growth fund.

2. Describe the risks associated with making an investment in an international growth fund. Identify the risks that would be common to domestic and international funds, and those risks that would be unique to an international fund.

3. Discuss how the fact that foreign companies are not subject to the same accounting, auditing, and financial reporting standards and practices as U.S. companies poses a risk not typically encountered when investing in the stock of U.S. companies.

4. Consider the allocation of fund assets by region. Speculate as to why the proportions of fund assets are distributed in this manner.

5. Consider the country diversification of fund assets. Identify the countries in which the fund is most heavily invested. Speculate as to why this might be the case. Are there any countries in which you would have expected the fund to be more heavily invested than it is? Are there any countries in which you would have expected the fund to be invested and it is not?

6. Consider the sector diversification of funds assets. Identify the sectors in which the fund is most heavily invested. Speculate as to why this might be the case.

References

Doupnik, T., and L. Seese. "Geographic Area Disclosures under SFAS 131: Materiality and Fineness." *Journal of International Accounting, Auditing & Taxation 2001,* pp. 117–38.

Kubin, Konrad. *Preface, International Accounting Bibliography* 1982–1994. Sarasota, FL: International Accounting Section of the American Accounting Association, 1997.

Organization for Economic Cooperation and Development. "Trends and Recent Developments in Foreign Direct Investment." *International Investment Perspectives,* 2006.

Rugman, Alan M., and Richard M. Hodgetts. *International Business: A Strategic Management Approach.* New York: McGraw-Hill, 1995.

"The 2009 Global 500." *Fortune,* July 20, 2009.

United Nations. *Multinational Corporations in World Development*, 1973.

———. *World Investment Report* 2004.

———. *World Investment Report* 2006.

U.S. Department of Commerce. "Small and Medium-Sized Enterprises Play an Important Role." *Export America,* September 2001.

World Trade Organization. *International Trade Statistics* 2009.

Chapter **Two**

Worldwide Accounting Diversity

Learning Objectives

After reading this chapter, you should be able to

- Provide evidence of the diversity that exists in accounting internationally.
- Explain the problems caused by accounting diversity.
- Describe the major environmental factors that influence national accounting systems and lead to accounting diversity.
- Describe a judgmental classification of countries by financial reporting system.
- Discuss the influence that culture is thought to have on financial reporting.
- Describe a simplified model of the reasons for international differences in financial reporting.
- Categorize accounting differences internationally and provide examples of each type of difference.

INTRODUCTION

Considerable differences exist across countries in the accounting treatment of many items. For example, companies in the United States are not allowed to report property, plant, and equipment at amounts greater than historical cost. In contrast, companies in the European Union are allowed to report their assets on the balance sheet at market values. Research and development costs must be expensed as incurred in Japan, but development costs may be capitalized as an asset in Canada and France. Chinese companies are required to use the direct method in preparing the statement of cash flows, whereas most companies in the United States and Europe use the indirect method.

Differences in accounting can result in significantly different amounts being reported on the balance sheet and income statement. In its 2009 annual report, the South Korean telecommunications firm SK Telecom Company Ltd. described 15 significant differences between South Korean and U.S. accounting rules. Under South Korean generally accepted accounting principles (GAAP), SK Telecom reported 2009 net income of 1,056 billion South Korean won (KRW). If SK Telecom had used U.S. GAAP in 2009, its net income would have been KRW 1,357 billion, approximately 28 percent larger.[1] Shareholders' equity as stated under South Korean

---

[1] The largest adjustments related to "retroactive application of equity method on business combination" and the recognition of gains on "currency and interest rate swap."

GAAP was KRW 12,345 billion but would have been KRW 14,261 billion under U.S. GAAP, a 16 percent difference. Braskem SA, a Brazilian chemical company, made 13 adjustments in 2009 to its Brazilian GAAP net income to report net income on a U.S. GAAP basis. These adjustments caused Brazilian GAAP income of 767.8 million Brazilian reais (BRL) to decrease by 70 percent, to 232.7 million reais under U.S. GAAP. Similarly, stockholders' equity of BRL 4,592.5 million on a Brazilian GAAP basis decreased to only BRL 4,379.4 million under U.S. GAAP.[2]

This chapter presents evidence of accounting diversity, explores the reasons for that diversity, and describes the problems that are created by differences in accounting practice across countries. Historically, several major models of accounting have been used internationally, with clusters of countries following them. These also are described and compared in this chapter. We describe the potential impact that culture has had on the development of national accounting systems and present a simplified model of the reasons for international differences in financial reporting.

The final section of this chapter uses excerpts from annual reports to present additional examples of some of the differences in accounting that exist across countries. It should be noted that much of the accounting diversity that existed in the past has been eliminated as countries have abandoned their local GAAP in favor of International Financial Reporting Standards (IFRS) issued by the International Accounting Standards Board (IASB). This chapter provides a historical perspective of accounting diversity that should allow readers to more fully appreciate the harmonization and convergence efforts described in the next chapter.

EVIDENCE OF ACCOUNTING DIVERSITY

Exhibits 2.1 and 2.2 present consolidated balance sheets for the British company Vodafone Group PLC and its U.S. competitor Verizon Communications Inc. A quick examination of these statements shows several differences in format and terminology between the United Kingdom and the United States. Perhaps the most obvious difference is the order in which assets are presented. Whereas Verizon presents assets in order of liquidity, beginning with cash and cash equivalents, Vodafone presents assets in reverse order of liquidity, starting with goodwill. On the other side of the balance sheet, Vodafone presents its equity accounts before liabilities. In the equity section, "Called-up share capital" is the equivalent of the common stock account on a U.S. balance sheet and "Share premium account" is the contributed capital in excess of par value. Vodafone uses a "Capital redemption reserve" to indicate an appropriation of retained earnings. Reserves are unknown in the United States. Vodafone includes "Provisions," which represent estimated liabilities related to restructurings, legal disputes, and asset retirements, in both current and noncurrent liabilities. This line item does not appear in the U.S. balance sheet.

Common for U.S. companies, Verizon includes only consolidated financial statements in its annual report. In addition to consolidated financial statements, Vodafone also includes the parent company's separate balance sheet in its annual report. This is shown in Exhibit 2.3. In the parent company balance sheet, investments in subsidiaries are not consolidated but instead are reported as

---

[2] The largest difference in stockholder's equity stems from a difference in the accounting treatment for distributions to shareholders.

EXHIBIT 2.1

VODAFONE GROUP PLC
Consolidated Balance Sheets

Consolidated Balance Sheet at 31 March

	Note	2009 £m	2008 £m
Noncurrent assets			
Goodwill	9	53,958	51,336
Other intangible assets.	9	20,980	18,995
Property, plant and equipment.	11	19,250	16,735
Investments in associated undertakings	14	34,715	22,545
Other investments	15	7,060	7,367
Deferred tax assets.	6	630	436
Postemployment benefits.	26	8	65
Trade and other receivables	17	3,069	1,067
		139,670	118,546
Current assets			
Inventory	16	412	417
Taxation recoverable		77	57
Trade and other receivables	17	7,662	6,551
Cash and cash equivalents.	18	4,878	1,699
		13,029	8,724
Total assets		152,699	127,270
Equity			
Called-up share capital.	19	4,153	4,182
Share premium account.	21	43,008	42,934
Own shares held	21	(8,036)	(7,856)
Additional paid-in capital.	21	100,239	100,151
Capital redemption reserve	21	10,101	10,054
Accumulated other recognised income and expense . .	22	20,517	10,558
Retained losses	23	(83,820)	(81,980)
Total equity shareholders' funds.		86,162	78,043
Minority interests		1,787	1,168
Written put options over minority interests		(3,172)	(2,740)
Total minority interests		(1,385)	(1,572)
Total equity		84,777	76,471
Noncurrent liabilities			
Long-term borrowings.	25	31,749	22,662
Deferred tax liabilities.	6	6,642	5,109
Postemployment benefits.	26	240	104
Provisions.	27	533	306
Trade and other payables.	28	811	645
		39,975	28,826
Current liabilities			
Short-term borrowings.	25, 35	9,624	4,532
Current taxation liabilities		4,552	5,123
Provisions.	27	373	356
Trade and other payables	28	13,398	11,962
		27,947	21,973
Total equity and liabilities		152,699	127,270

EXHIBIT 2.2

VERIZON COMMUNICATIONS, INC.
Consolidated Balance Sheets

At December 31 (Dollars in Millions, Except per Share Amounts)	2009	2008
Assets		
Current assets		
Cash and cash equivalents	$ 2,009	$ 9,782
Short-term investments	490	509
Accounts receivable, net of allowances of $976 and $941	12,573	11,703
Inventories	2,289	2,092
Prepaid expenses and other	5,247	1,989
Total current assets	22,608	26,075
Plant, property, and equipment	228,518	215,605
Less accumulated depreciation	137,052	129,059
	91,466	86,546
Investments in unconsolidated businesses	3,535	3,393
Wireless licenses	72,067	61,974
Goodwill	22,472	6,035
Other intangible assets, net	6,764	5,199
Other investments	—	4,781
Other assets	8,339	8,349
Total assets	$227,251	$202,352
Liabilities and Shareowners' Investment		
Current liabilities		
Debt maturing within one year	$ 7,205	$ 4,993
Accounts payable and accrued liabilities	15,223	13,814
Other	6,708	7,099
Total current liabilities	29,136	25,906
Long-term debt	55,051	46,959
Employee benefit obligations	32,622	32,512
Deferred income taxes	19,310	11,769
Other liabilities	6,765	6,301
Equity		
Series preferred stock ($.10 par value; none issued)	—	—
Common stock ($.10 par value; 2,967,610,119 shares issued in both periods)	297	297
Contributed capital	40,108	40,291
Reinvested earnings	17,592	19,250
Accumulated other comprehensive loss	(11,479)	(13,372)
Common stock in treasury, at cost	(5,000)	(4,839)
Deferred compensation—employee stock ownership plans and other	88	79
Noncontrolling interest	42,761	37,199
Total equity	84,367	78,905
Total liabilities and equity	$227,251	$202,352

EXHIBIT 2.3

VODAFONE GROUP PLC
Company Balance Sheets

Company Balance Sheet at 31 March

	Note	2009 £m	2008 £m
Fixed assets			
Shares in group undertakings.	3	**64,937**	64,922
Current assets			
Debtors: amounts falling due after more than one year	4	**2,352**	821
Debtors: amounts falling due within one year	4	**126,334**	126,099
		128,797	126,920
Cash at bank and in hand		**111**	—
Creditors: amounts falling due within one year	5	**(92,339)**	(98,784)
Net current assets		**36,458**	28,136
Total assets less current liabilities		**101,395**	93,058
Creditors: amounts falling due after more than one year. . .	5	**(21,970)**	(14,582)
		79,425	78,476
Capital and reserves			
Called-up share capital.	6	**4,153**	4,182
Share premium account.	8	**43,008**	42,934
Capital redemption reserve	8	**10,101**	10,054
Capital reserve.	8	**88**	88
Other reserves	8	**957**	942
Own shares held	8	**(8,053)**	(7,867)
Profit and loss account.	8	**29,171**	28,143
Equity shareholders' funds		**79,425**	78,476

"Shares in group undertakings" in the "Fixed assets" section. Liabilities are called "Creditors" and receivables are "Debtors." From the perspective of U.S. financial reporting, the UK parent company balance sheet has an unusual structure. Rather than the U.S. norm of Assets = Liabilities + Shareholders' equity, Vodafone's parent company balance sheet is presented as Assets − Liabilities = Shareholders' equity. Closer inspection shows that the balance sheet presents the left-hand side of the equation as Noncurrent assets + Working capital − Noncurrent liabilities = Shareholders' equity.

All of these superficial differences would probably cause a financial analyst little problem in analyzing the company's financial statements. More important than the format and terminology differences are the differences in recognition and measurement rules employed to value assets and liabilities and to calculate income. As was noted in the introduction to this chapter, very different amounts of net income and stockholders' equity can be reported by a company depending on the accounting rules that it uses. For example, SK Telecom's 2009 net income was 28 percent larger under U.S. GAAP than under South Korean GAAP; Braskem's 2009 net income was 70 percent smaller under U.S. GAAP than under Brazilian GAAP.

REASONS FOR ACCOUNTING DIVERSITY

Why do financial reporting practices differ across countries? Accounting scholars have hypothesized numerous influences on a country's accounting system, including factors as varied as the nature of the political system, the stage of economic development, and the state of accounting education and research. A survey of the relevant literature has identified the following five items as being commonly accepted as factors influencing a country's financial reporting practices: (1) legal system, (2) taxation, (3) providers of financing, (4) inflation, and (5) political and economic ties.[3]

Legal System

There are two major types of legal systems used around the world: common law and codified Roman law. Common law began in England and is primarily found in the English-speaking countries of the world. Common law countries rely on a limited amount of statute law, which is then interpreted by the courts. Court decisions establish precedents, thereby developing case law that supplements the statutes. A system of code law, followed in most non-English-speaking countries, originated in the Roman *jus civile* and was developed further in European universities during the Middle Ages. Code law countries tend to have relatively more statute or codified law governing a wider range of human activity.

What does a country's legal system have to do with accounting? Code law countries generally have corporation law (sometimes called a commercial code or companies act), which establishes the basic legal parameters governing business enterprises. The corporation law often stipulates which financial statements must be published in accordance with a prescribed format. Additional accounting measurement and disclosure rules are included in an accounting law debated and passed by the national legislature. In countries where accounting rules are legislated, the accounting profession tends to have little influence on the development of accounting standards. In countries with a tradition of common law, although a corporation law laying the basic framework for accounting might exist (such as in the United Kingdom), specific accounting rules are established by the profession or by an independent nongovernmental body representing a variety of constituencies. Thus, the type of legal system in a country tends to determine whether the primary source of accounting rules is the government or a nongovernmental organization.

In *code law* countries, the accounting law tends to be rather general and does not provide much detail regarding specific accounting practices and may provide no guidance at all in certain areas. Germany is a good example of this type of country. The German accounting law passed in 1985 is only 47 pages long and is silent with regard to issues such as leases, foreign currency translation, and cash flow statements.[4] When no guidance is provided in the law, German companies refer to other sources, including tax law, opinions of the German auditing profession, and standards issued by the German Accounting Standards Committee, to decide how to do their accounting. Interestingly enough, important sources of accounting practice in Germany have been textbooks and commentaries written by accounting academicians.

---

[3] Gary K. Meek and Sharokh M. Saudagaran, "A Survey of Research on Financial Reporting in a Transnational Context," *Journal of Accounting Literature,* 1990, pp. 145–82.

[4] Jermyn Paul Brooks and Dietz Mertin, *Neues Deutsches Bilanzrecht* (Düsseldorf: IDW-Verlag, 1986).

In *common law* countries, where there is likely to be a nonlegislative organization developing accounting standards, much more detailed rules are developed. The extreme case might be the Financial Accounting Standards Board (FASB) in the United States, which provides a substantial amount of implementation guidance in its accounting standards codification (ASC) and updates and has been accused of producing a "standards overload."

To illustrate this point, consider the rules related to accounting for leases established by the FASB in the United States and in German accounting law. In the United States, leases must be capitalized if any one of four very specific criteria is met. Additional guidance establishes rules for specific situations such as sales with leasebacks, sales-type leases of real estate, and changes in leases resulting from refundings of tax-exempt debt. In contrast, the German accounting law is silent with regard to leases. The only guidance in the law can be found in paragraph 285, which simply states that all liabilities must be recorded.[5]

Taxation

In some countries, published financial statements form the basis for taxation, whereas in other countries, financial statements are adjusted for tax purposes and submitted to the government separately from the reports sent to stockholders. Continuing to focus on Germany, the so-called congruency principle *(Massgeblichkeitsprinzip)* in that country stipulates that the published financial statements serve as the basis for taxable income.[6] In most cases, for an expense to be deductible for tax purposes it must also be used in the calculation of financial statement income. Well-managed German companies attempt to minimize income for tax purposes, for example, through the use of accelerated depreciation, so as to reduce their tax liability. As a result of the congruency principle, accelerated depreciation must also be taken in the calculation of accounting income.

In the United States, in contrast, conformity between the tax statement and financial statements is required only with regard to the use of the last-in, first-out (LIFO) inventory cost flow assumption. U.S. companies are allowed to use accelerated depreciation for tax purposes and straight-line depreciation in the financial statements. All else being equal, because of the influence of the congruency principle, a German company is likely to report lower income than its U.S. counterpart.

The difference between tax and accounting income gives rise to the necessity to account for deferred income taxes, a major issue in the United States in recent years. Deferred income taxes are much less of an issue in Germany; for many German companies, they do not exist at all. This is also true in other code law countries such as France and Japan.

Providers of Financing

The major providers of financing for business enterprises are family members, banks, governments, and shareholders. In those countries in which company financing is dominated by families, banks, or the state, there will be less pressure for public accountability and information disclosure. Banks and the state will often

---

[5] In compliance with European Union regulations, Germany requires publicly traded companies to use International Financial Reporting Standards (IFRS) to prepare their consolidated financial statements. German accounting law continues to be used by privately held companies and by publicly traded companies in preparing parent company financial statements.

[6] German taxable income is computed by comparing an opening and closing tax balance sheet, the *Steuerbilanz*. The tax balance sheet is based on the published balance sheet, the *Handelsbilanz*.

be represented on the board of directors and will therefore be able to obtain information necessary for decision making from inside the company. As companies become more dependent on financing from the general populace through the public offering of shares of stock, the demand for more information made available outside the company becomes greater. It simply is not feasible for the company to allow the hundreds, thousands, or hundreds of thousands of shareholders access to internal accounting records. The information needs of those financial statement users can be satisfied only through extensive disclosures in accounting reports.

There can also be a difference in financial statement orientation, with stockholders more interested in profit (emphasis on the income statement) and banks more interested in solvency and liquidity (emphasis on the balance sheet). Bankers tend to prefer companies to practice rather conservative accounting with regard to assets and liabilities.

Inflation

Countries experiencing chronic high rates of inflation found it necessary to adopt accounting rules that required the inflation adjustment of historical cost amounts. This was especially true in Latin America, which as a region has had more inflation than any other part of the world. For example, throughout the 1980s and 1990s, the average annual rate of inflation rate in Mexico was approximately 50 percent, with a high of 159 percent in 1987.[7] Double- and triple-digit inflation rates render historical costs meaningless. Throughout most of the latter half of the 20th century, this factor primarily distinguished Latin America from the rest of the world with regard to accounting.[8]

Adjusting accounting records for inflation results in a write-up of assets and therefore related expenses. Adjusting income for inflation is especially important in those countries in which accounting statements serve as the basis for taxation; otherwise, companies will be paying taxes on fictitious profits.

Political and Economic Ties

Accounting is a technology that can be relatively easily borrowed from or imposed on another country. Through political and economic links, accounting rules have been conveyed from one country to another. For example, through previous colonialism, both England and France have transferred their accounting frameworks to a variety of countries around the world. British-style accounting systems can be found in countries as far-flung as Australia and Zimbabwe. French accounting is prevalent in the former French colonies of western Africa. More recently, it is thought that economic ties with the United States have had an impact on accounting in Canada, Mexico, and Israel.

Correlation of Factors

Whether by coincidence or not, there is a high degree of correlation between legal system, tax conformity, and source of financing. As Exhibit 2.4 shows, common law countries tend to have greater numbers of domestic listed companies, relying more heavily on equity as a source of capital. Code law countries tend to link taxation to accounting statements and rely less on financing provided by shareholders.

---

[7] Joseph B. Lipscomb and Harold Hunt, "Mexican Mortgages: Structure and Default Incentives, Historical Simulation 1982–1998," *Journal of Housing Research* 10, no. 2 (1999), pp. 235–65.

[8] Mexico continued its use of inflation accounting until 2007.

EXHIBIT 2.4
Relationship
between Several
Factors Influencing
Accounting
Diversity

Sources: Number of domestic listed companies obtained from World Federation of Exchanges (2009), www. world-exchanges.org. Country populations obtained from *CIA World Fact Book* (2010).

| Country | Legal System | Domestic Listed Companies | | Tax Conformity |
		Number	Per Million of Population	
Italy	Code	296	5.1	Yes
Germany	Code	783	9.5	Yes
Japan	Code	2,335	18.4	Yes
United Kingdom	Common	2,792	45.6	No
Australia	Common	1,966	91.4	No
Canada	Common	3,700	109.6	No

PROBLEMS CAUSED BY ACCOUNTING DIVERSITY

Preparation of Consolidated Financial Statements

The diversity in accounting practice across countries causes problems that can be quite serious for some parties. One problem relates to the preparation of consolidated financial statements by companies with foreign operations. Consider General Motors Corporation, which has subsidiaries in more than 50 countries around the world. Each subsidiary incorporated in the country in which it is located is required to prepare financial statements in accordance with local regulations. These regulations usually require companies to keep books in local currency using local accounting principles. Thus, General Motors de Mexico prepares financial statements in Mexican pesos using Mexican accounting rules and General Motors Japan Ltd. prepares financial statements in Japanese yen using Japanese standards. To prepare consolidated financial statements in the United States, in addition to translating the foreign currency financial statements into U.S. dollars, the parent company must also convert the financial statements of its foreign operations into U.S. GAAP. Each foreign operation must either maintain two sets of books prepared in accordance with both local and U.S. GAAP or, as is more common, reconciliations from local GAAP to U.S. GAAP must be made at the balance sheet date. In either case, considerable effort and cost are involved; company personnel must develop an expertise in more than one country's accounting standards.

Access to Foreign Capital Markets

A second problem caused by accounting diversity relates to companies gaining access to foreign capital markets. If a company desires to obtain capital by selling stock or borrowing money in a foreign country, it might be required to present a set of financial statements prepared in accordance with the accounting standards in the country in which the capital is being obtained. Consider the case of the semiconductor manufacturer STMicroelectronics, which is based in Geneva, Switzerland. The equity market in Switzerland is so small (there are fewer than 8 million Swiss) and ST's capital needs are so great that the company has found it necessary to have its common shares listed on the Euronext-Paris and Borsa Italiana stock exchanges in Europe and on the New York Stock Exchange in the United States. To have stock traded in the United States, foreign companies must either prepare financial statements using U.S. accounting standards or provide a reconciliation of local GAAP net income and stockholders' equity to U.S. GAAP.

This can be quite costly. In preparing for a New York Stock Exchange (NYSE) listing in 1993, the German automaker Daimler-Benz estimated it spent $60 million to initially prepare U.S. GAAP financial statements; it expected to spend $15 million to $20 million each year thereafter.[9] The appendix to this chapter describes the case of Daimler-Benz in becoming the first German company to list on the NYSE. As noted in Chapter 1, the U.S. SEC eliminated the U.S. GAAP reconciliation requirement for those foreign companies using IFRS to prepare their financial statements. However, foreign companies not using IFRS continue to provide U.S. GAAP information.

Comparability of Financial Statements

A third problem relates to the lack of comparability of financial statements between companies from different countries. This can significantly affect the analysis of foreign financial statements for making investment and lending decisions. In 2003 alone, U.S. investors bought and sold nearly $3 trillion worth of foreign stocks while foreign investors traded over $6 trillion in U.S. equity securities.[10] In recent years there has been an explosion in mutual funds that invest in the stock of foreign companies. As an example, the number of international stock funds increased from 123 in 1989 to 534 by the end of 1995.[11] T. Rowe Price's New Asia Fund, for example, invests exclusively in stocks and bonds of companies located in Asian countries other than Japan. The job of deciding which foreign company to invest in is complicated by the fact that foreign companies use accounting rules different from those used in the United States and those rules differ from country to country. It is very difficult if not impossible for a potential investor to directly compare the financial position and performance of an automobile manufacturer in Germany (Volkswagen), Japan (Nissan), and the United States (Ford) because these three countries have different financial accounting and reporting standards. According to Ralph E. Walters, former chairman of the steering committee of the International Accounting Standards Committee, "either international investors have to be extremely knowledgeable about multiple reporting methods or they have to be willing to take greater risk."[12]

A lack of comparability of financial statements also can have an adverse effect on corporations when making foreign acquisition decisions. As a case in point, consider the experience of foreign investors in Eastern Europe. After the fall of the Berlin Wall in 1989, Western companies were invited to acquire newly privatized companies in Poland, Hungary, and other countries in the former communist bloc. The concept of profit and accounting for assets in those countries under communism was so different from accounting practice in the West that most Western investors found financial statements useless in helping to determine which enterprises were the most attractive acquisition targets. In many cases, the international public accounting firms were called on to convert financial statements to a Western basis before acquisition of a company could be seriously considered.

[9] Allan B. Afterman, *International Accounting, Financial Reporting, and Analysis* (New York: Warren, Gorham & Lamont, 1995), pp. C1-17, C1-22.

[10] U.S. Department of Commerce, Bureau of Economic Analysis, "U.S. International Transactions," *Survey of Current Business,* January 2005, pp. 45–76, Table 7a.

[11] James L. Cochrane, James E. Shapiro, and Jean E. Tobin, "Foreign Equities and U.S. Investors: Breaking Down the Barriers Separating Supply and Demand," NYSE Working Paper 95–04, 1995.

[12] Stephen H. Collins, "The Move to Globalization," *Journal of Accountancy,* March 1989, p. 82.

There was a very good reason why accounting in the communist countries of Eastern Europe and the Soviet Union was so much different from accounting in capitalist countries. Financial statements were not prepared for the benefit of investors and creditors to be used in making investment and lending decisions. Instead, financial statements were prepared to provide the government with information to determine whether the central economic plan was being fulfilled. Financial statements prepared for central planning purposes have limited value in making investment decisions.

Lack of High-Quality Accounting Information

A fourth problem associated with accounting diversity is the lack of high-quality accounting standards in some parts of the world. There is general agreement that the failure of many banks in the 1997 East Asian financial crisis was due to three factors: a highly leveraged corporate sector, the private sector's reliance on foreign currency debt, and a lack of accounting transparency.[13] To be sure, inadequate disclosure did not create the East Asian meltdown, but it did contribute to the depth and breadth of the crisis. As Rahman explains: "It is a known fact that the very threat of disclosure influences behavior and improves management, particularly risk management. It seems that the lack of appropriate disclosure requirements indirectly contributed to the deficient internal controls and imprudent risk management practices of the corporations and banks in the crisis-hit countries."[14] International investors and creditors were unable to adequately assess risk because financial statements did not reflect the extent of risk exposure due to the following disclosure deficiencies:

- The actual magnitude of debt was hidden by undisclosed related-party transactions and off-balance-sheet financing.
- High levels of exposure to foreign exchange risk were not evident.
- Information on the extent to which investments and loans were made in highly speculative assets (such as real estate) was not available.
- Contingent liabilities for guaranteeing loans, often foreign currency loans, were not reported.
- Appropriate disclosures regarding loan loss provisions were not made.

Because of the problems associated with worldwide accounting diversity, attempts to reduce the accounting differences across countries have been ongoing for over three decades. This process is known as *harmonization*. The ultimate goal of harmonization is to have one set of international accounting standards that are followed by all companies around the world. Harmonization is the major topic of Chapter 3.

ACCOUNTING CLUSTERS

Given the discussion regarding factors influencing accounting practice worldwide, it should not be surprising to learn that there are clusters of countries that share common accounting orientation and practices. One classification scheme identifies three major accounting models: the Fair Presentation/Full Disclosure

---

[13] M. Zubaidur Rahman, "The Role of Accounting in the East Asian Financial Crisis: Lessons Learned?" *Transnational Corporations* 7, no. 3 (December 1998), pp. 1–52.

[14] Ibid., p. 7.

EXHIBIT 2.5
Nobes's Judgmental Classification of Financial Reporting Systems

Source: Christopher W. Nobes, "A Judgemental International Classification of Financial Reporting Practices," *Journal of Business Finance and Accounting,* Spring 1983, p. 7.

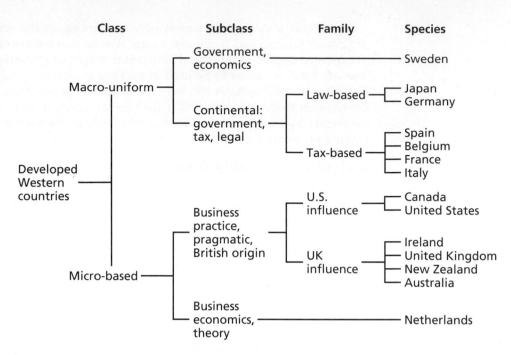

Model, the Legal Compliance Model, and the Inflation-Adjusted Model.[15] The Fair Presentation/Full Disclosure Model (also known as the Anglo-Saxon or Anglo-American model) is used to describe the approach used in the United Kingdom and United States, where accounting is oriented toward the decision needs of large numbers of investors and creditors. This model is used in most English-speaking countries and other countries heavily influenced by the United Kingdom or the United States. Most of these countries follow a common law legal system. The Legal Compliance Model originated in the code law countries of continental Europe; it is also known as the Continental European model. It is used by most of Europe, Japan, and other code law countries. Companies in this group usually are tied quite closely to banks that serve as the primary suppliers of financing. Because these are code law countries, accounting is legalistic and is designed to provide information for taxation or government-planning purposes. The Inflation-Adjusted Model is found primarily in South America. This model resembles the Continental European model in its legalistic, tax, and government-planning orientation. This model distinguishes itself, however, through the extensive use of adjustments for inflation.

A Judgmental Classification of Financial Reporting Systems

Concentrating on the Anglo-Saxon and Continental European Model countries, Nobes developed a more refined classification scheme that attempts to show how the financial reporting systems in 14 developed countries relate to one another.[16] Exhibit 2.5 presents an adaptation of Nobes's classification.

---

[15] Helen Gernon and Gary Meek, *Accounting: An International Perspective,* 5th ed. (Burr Ridge, IL: Irwin/ McGraw-Hill, 2001), pp. 10–11.

[16] Christopher W. Nobes, "A Judgemental International Classification of Financial Reporting Practices," *Journal of Business Finance and Accounting,* Spring 1983.

The terms *micro-based* and *macro-uniform* describe the Anglo-Saxon and Continental European Models, respectively. Each of these classes is divided into two subclasses that are further divided into families. Within the micro-based class of accounting system, there is a subclass heavily influenced by business economics and accounting theory. The Netherlands is the only country in this subclass. One manifestation of the influence of theory is that Dutch companies may use current replacement cost accounting to value assets in their primary financial statements. The other micro-based subclass, of British origin, is more pragmatic and is oriented toward business practice, relying less on economic theory in the development of accounting rules. The British-origin subclass is further split into two families, one dominated by the United Kingdom and one dominated by the United States. Nobes does not indicate how these two families differ.

On the macro-uniform side of the classification, a "government, economics" subclass has only one country, Sweden. Swedish accounting distinguishes itself from the other macro-uniform countries in being closely aligned with national economic policies. For example, income smoothing is allowed to promote economic stability and social accounting has developed to meet macroeconomic concerns. The "continental: government, tax, legal" subclass primarily has Continental European countries. This subclass is further divided into two families. Led by Germany, the law-based family includes Japan. The tax-based family consists of several Romance-language countries. The major difference between these families is that the accounting law is the primary determinant of accounting practice in Germany, whereas the tax law dominates in the Southern European countries.

The importance of this hierarchical model is that it shows the comparative distances between countries and could be used as a blueprint for determining where financial statement comparability is likely to be greater. For example, comparisons of financial statements between the United States and Canada (which are in the same family) are likely to be more valid than comparisons between the United States and the United Kingdom (which are not in the same family). However, the United States and the United Kingdom (which are in the same subclass) are more comparable than are the United States and the Netherlands (which are in different subclasses). Finally, comparisons between the United States and the Netherlands (which are in the same class) might be more meaningful than comparisons between the United States and any of the macro-uniform countries.

AN EMPIRICAL TEST OF THE JUDGMENTAL CLASSIFICATION

The judgmental classification in Exhibit 2.5 was empirically tested in 1990.[17] Data gathered on 100 financial reporting practices in 50 countries (including the 14 countries in Exhibit 2.5) were analyzed using the statistical procedure of hierarchical cluster analysis. The significant clusters arising from the statistical analysis are in Exhibit 2.6. Clusters are analogous to the families in Nobes's classification.

The results reported in Exhibit 2.6 clearly indicate the existence of two significantly different classes of accounting systems being used across these countries and are generally consistent with the classes, subclasses, and families of Nobes's classification. The major deviations from Nobes's classification are that

[17] Timothy S. Doupnik and Stephen B. Salter, "An Empirical Test of a Judgemental International Classification of Financial Reporting Practices," *Journal of International Business Studies,* First Quarter 1993, pp. 41–60.

EXHIBIT 2.6
Results of Hierarchical Cluster Analysis on 100 Financial Reporting Practices in 1990

Source: Timothy S. Doupnik and Stephen B. Salter, "An Empirical Test of a Judgemental International Classification of Financial Reporting Practices," *Journal of International Business Studies*, First Quarter 1993, p. 53.

Micro Class		Macro Class		
Cluster 1	**Cluster 2**	**Cluster 3**	**Cluster 5**	**Cluster 7**
Australia	Bermuda	Costa Rica	Colombia	Finland
Botswana	Canada		Denmark	Sweden
Hong Kong	Israel	**Cluster 4**	France	
Ireland	United States	Argentina	Italy	**Cluster 8**
Jamaica		Brazil	Norway	Germany
Luxembourg		Chile	Portugal	
Malaysia		Mexico	Spain	**Cluster 9**
Namibia				Japan
Netherlands			**Cluster 6**	
Netherlands Antilles			Belgium	
Nigeria			Egypt	
New Zealand			Liberia	
Philippines			Panama	
Papua New Guinea			Saudi Arabia	
South Africa			Thailand	
Singapore			United Arab Emirates	
Sri Lanka				
Taiwan				
Trinidad and Tobago				
United Kingdom				
Zambia				
Zimbabwe				

the Netherlands is located in the UK-influence cluster (Cluster 1) rather than in a subclass by itself; Japanese accounting (Cluster 9) is not as similar to German accounting (Cluster 8) as hypothesized; and Belgium (located in Cluster 6) is not in the group with France, Spain, and Italy (Cluster 5). Indeed, there appears to be more diversity among the macro countries (as evidenced by the greater number of clusters) than among the countries comprising the micro class.

The large size of the UK-influence cluster (Cluster 1) shows the influence of British colonialism on accounting development. In contrast, Cluster 2, which includes the United States, is quite small. The emergence of Cluster 4, which includes several Latin American countries, is evidence of the importance of inflation as a factor affecting accounting practice.

The two classes of accounting reflected in Exhibit 2.6 differ significantly on 66 of the 100 financial reporting practices examined. Differences exist for 41 of the 56 disclosure practices studied. In all but one case, the micro class of countries provided a higher level of disclosure than the macro class of countries. There were also significant differences for 25 of the 44 practices examined affecting income measurement. Of particular importance is the item asking whether accounting practice adhered to tax requirements. The mean level of agreement with this statement among macro countries was 72 percent, whereas it was only 45 percent among micro countries. To summarize, companies in the micro-based countries provide more extensive disclosure than do companies in the macro-uniform countries, and companies in the macro countries are more heavily influenced by taxation than are companies in the micro countries. These results are consistent with the relative importance of equity finance and the relatively weak link between accounting and taxation in the micro countries.

THE INFLUENCE OF CULTURE ON FINANCIAL REPORTING

In addition to economic and institutional determinants, national culture has long been considered a factor that affects the accounting system of a country.[18]

Hofstede's Cultural Dimensions

Using responses to an attitude survey of IBM employees worldwide, Hofstede identified four cultural dimensions that can be used to describe general similarities and differences in cultures around the world: (1) individualism, (2) power distance, (3) uncertainty avoidance, and (4) masculinity.[19] More recently, a fifth dimension, long-term orientation, was identified. *Individualism* refers to a preference for a loosely knit social fabric rather than a tightly knit social fabric (collectivism). *Power distance* refers to the extent to which hierarchy and unequal power distribution in institutions and organizations are accepted. *Uncertainty avoidance* refers to the degree to which individuals feel uncomfortable with uncertainty and ambiguity. *Masculinity* refers to an emphasis on traditional masculine values of performance and achievement rather than feminine values of relationships, caring, and nurturing. *Long-term orientation* stands for the "fostering of virtues oriented towards future rewards, in particular perseverance and thrift."[20]

Gray's Accounting Values

From a review of accounting literature and practice, Gray identified four widely recognized accounting values that can be used to define a country's accounting subculture: professionalism, uniformity, conservatism, and secrecy.[21] Gray describes these accounting values as follows:[22]

> *Professionalism versus Statutory Control*—a preference for the exercise of individual professional judgment and the maintenance of professional self-regulation as opposed to compliance with prescriptive legal requirements and statutory control.
>
> *Uniformity versus Flexibility*—a preference for the enforcement of uniform accounting practices between companies and for the consistent use of such practices over time as opposed to flexibility in accordance with the perceived circumstances of individual companies.
>
> *Conservatism versus Optimism*—a preference for a cautious approach to measurement so as to cope with the uncertainty of future events as opposed to a more optimistic, laissez-faire, risk-taking approach.
>
> *Secrecy versus Transparency*—a preference for confidentiality and the restriction of disclosure of information about the business only to those who are closely involved with its management and financing as opposed to a more transparent, open, and publicly accountable approach.

[18] One of the first to argue that accounting is determined by culture was W. J. Violet in "The Development of International Accounting Standards: An Anthropological Perspective," *International Journal of Accounting,* 1983, pp. 1–12.

[19] G. Hofstede, *Culture's Consequences: International Differences in Work-Related Values* (London: Sage, 1980).

[20] G. Hofstede, *Culture's Consequences: Comparing Values, Behaviours, Institutions, and Organizations across Nations,* 2nd ed. (Thousand Oaks, CA: Sage, 2001), p. 359.

[21] S. J. Gray, "Towards a Theory of Cultural Influence on the Development of Accounting Systems Internationally," *Abacus,* March 1988, pp. 1–15.

[22] Ibid., p. 8.

EXHIBIT 2.7
Relationships
between
Accounting Values
and Cultural
Dimensions

Source: Lee H. Radebaugh
and Sidney J. Gray, *International Accounting and
Multinational Enterprises,* 5th
ed. (New York: Wiley, 2001),
p. 49.

	Accounting Values			
Cultural Dimension	**Professionalism**	**Uniformity**	**Conservatism**	**Secrecy**
Power distance	Neg.	Pos.	n/a	Pos.
Uncertainty avoidance	Neg.	Pos.	Pos.	Pos.
Individualism	Pos.	Neg.	Neg.	Neg.
Masculinity	Pos.	n/a	Neg.	Neg.
Long-term orientation	Neg.	n/a	Pos.	Pos.

Pos. = Positive relationship hypothesized between cultural dimension and accounting value.
Neg. = Negative relationship hypothesized between cultural dimension and accounting value.
n/a = No relationship hypothesized.

Gray argues that national culture values affect accounting values, as shown in Exhibit 2.7. The accounting values of conservatism and secrecy have the greatest relevance for the information content of a set of financial statements. The relationship between culture and each of these two accounting values is explained as follows:

Conservatism can be linked perhaps most closely with the uncertainty-avoidance dimension and the short-term versus long-term orientations. A preference for more conservative measures of profits and assets is consistent with strong uncertainty avoidance following from a concern with security and a perceived need to adopt a cautious approach to cope with uncertainty of future events. A less conservative approach to measurement is also consistent with a short-term orientation where quick results are expected and hence a more optimistic approach is adopted relative to conserving resources and investing for long-term trends. There also seems to be a link, if less strong, between high levels of individualism and masculinity, on the one hand, and weak uncertainty avoidance on the other, to the extent that an emphasis on individual achievement and performance is likely to foster a less conservative approach to measurement.[23]

A preference for secrecy is consistent with strong uncertainty avoidance following from a need to restrict information disclosures so as to avoid conflict and competition and to preserve security. . . . [H]igh power-distance societies are likely to be characterized by the restriction of information to preserve power inequalities. Secrecy is also consistent with a preference for collectivism, as opposed to individualism, in that its concern is for the interests of those closely involved with the firm rather than external parties. A long-term orientation also suggests a preference for secrecy that is consistent with the need to conserve resources within the firm and ensure that funds are available for investment relative to the demands of shareholders and employees for higher payments. A significant but possibly less important link with masculinity also seems likely to the extent that in societies where there is more emphasis on achievement and material success there will be a greater tendency to publicize such achievements and material success.[24]

Gray extended Hofstede's model of cultural patterns to develop a framework that identifies the mechanism through which culture influences the development of corporate reporting systems on a national level. According to this framework (shown in Exhibit 2.8), the particular way in which a country's accounting system

[23] Lee H. Radebaugh and Sidney J. Gray, *International Accounting and Multinational Enterprises,* 5th ed. (New York: Wiley, 2001), p. 47.
[24] Ibid., p. 48.

develops is influenced by accountants' accounting values and by the country's institutional framework, both of which are influenced by cultural values. Thus, culture is viewed as affecting accounting systems indirectly in two ways: through its influence on accounting values and through its institutional consequences.

Using measures of each of the cultural values for a group of 40 countries, Hofstede classified countries into 10 different cultural areas. The Anglo cultural area, for example, is characterized by high individualism, low uncertainty avoidance, low power distance, and moderate masculinity. Given this pattern of cultural values, Gray hypothesized that Anglo countries (which include Australia, Canada, New Zealand, the United States, and the United Kingdom) would rank relatively low on the accounting values of conservatism and secrecy (or high on optimism and high on transparency). Exhibiting the opposite pattern of cultural values, the countries of the less developed Latin cultural area (which includes countries like Colombia and Mexico) are expected to rank relatively high in conservatism and secrecy. On a scale of 1 (low secrecy) to 7 (high secrecy) and a scale of 1 (low conservatism) to 5 (high conservatism), the different cultural areas were ranked as follows:

Cultural Area	Secrecy	Conservatism
Anglo	1	1
Nordic	2	2
Asian-Colonial	2	3
African	3	4
More developed Latin	3	5
Less developed Asian	4	4
Japan	5	5
Near Eastern	5	5
Germanic	6	4
Less developed Latin	7	5

These rankings show the strong positive relation expected to exist between secrecy and conservatism. Countries that require limited disclosures in financial statements (high secrecy) are expected to more strictly adhere to the notion of conservatism (high conservatism) in the measurement of assets and liabilities.

A number of studies have empirically examined the relationship between Hofstede's cultural values and national accounting systems.[25] Although the results of this research are mixed, most studies find a relationship between cultural values and disclosure consistent with Gray's hypothesis. However, these studies are unable to determine whether culture influences disclosure through its effect on accounting values or through its effect on institutional consequences. Research results on the relationship between culture and conservatism are less conclusive.

Religion and Accounting

Religion plays an important role in defining national culture in many parts of the world and can have a significant effect on business practice. Under Islam, for example, the Koran provides guidance with respect to issues such as making charitable contributions and charging interest on loans. In some Islamic countries,

[25] For a comprehensive review of this literature, see T. S. Doupnik and G. T. Tsakumis, "A Review of Empirical Tests of Gray's Framework and Suggestions for Future Research," *Journal of Accounting Literature*, 2004, pp. 1–48

EXHIBIT 2.8   Framework for the Development of Accounting Systems

Source: Adapted from S. J. Gray, "Towards a Theory of Cultural Influence on the Development of Accounting Systems Internationally," *Abacus*, March 1988, p. 7.

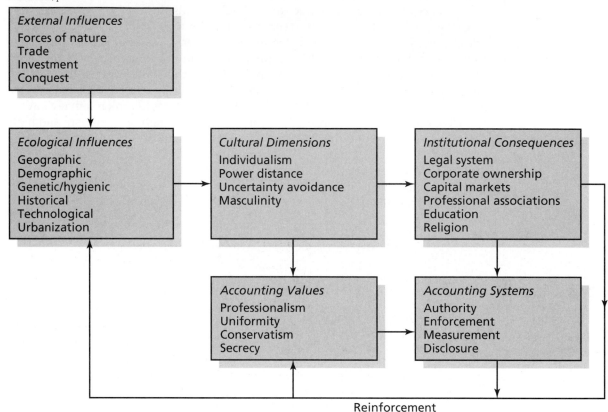

External Influences
Forces of nature
Trade
Investment
Conquest

Ecological Influences
Geographic
Demographic
Genetic/hygienic
Historical
Technological
Urbanization

Cultural Dimensions
Individualism
Power distance
Uncertainty avoidance
Masculinity

Institutional Consequences
Legal system
Corporate ownership
Capital markets
Professional associations
Education
Religion

Accounting Values
Professionalism
Uniformity
Conservatism
Secrecy

Accounting Systems
Authority
Enforcement
Measurement
Disclosure

Reinforcement

banking companies operate under Shariah, the Islamic law of human conduct derived from the Koran. Because traditional accounting rules do not cover many of the transactions carried out by Islamic financial institutions (IFIs), the Accounting and Auditing Organization for Islamic Financial Institutions (AAOIFI), a standard-setting body based in Bahrain, has been active in developing and promoting Islamic accounting standards.

Based on the AAOIFI's work, the Malaysian Accounting Standards Board (MASB) developed MASB i-1, *Presentation of Financial Statements of Islamic Financial Institutions,* in 2001. MASB i-1 states:

> The general purpose of financial statements is to provide information about the financial position, performance and cash flows of IFIs, which are useful to a wide range of users in making economic decisions. It also portrays aspects of the management's stewardship of the resources entrusted to it. All this information, along with other information in the notes to financial statements, allows users in assessing the degree of compliance of the IFIs with the prescribed Shariah requirements (para. 10).

In developing MASB i-1, the MASB consulted with the Malaysian Central Bank's National Shariah Council on issues relating to Shariah. In April 2004, the MASB announced that it would introduce four new Islamic accounting standards related to *ijarah* (leasing), *zakat* (income tax), *takaful* (insurance), and *mudarabah* (deferred payments).

A SIMPLIFIED MODEL OF THE REASONS FOR INTERNATIONAL DIFFERENCES IN FINANCIAL REPORTING

Sifting through the many reasons that have been hypothesized to affect international differences in financial reporting, Nobes developed a model with two explanatory factors: culture and the nature of the financing system.[26] Nobes argues that the major reason for international differences in financial reporting is different purposes for that reporting. A country's financing system is seen as the most relevant factor in determining the purpose of financial reporting. Specifically, whether or not a country has a strong equity financing system with large numbers of outside shareholders will determine the nature of financial reporting in a country.

Nobes divides financial reporting systems into two classes, labeled A and B. Class A accounting systems are found in countries with strong equity–outside shareholder financing. In Class A accounting systems, measurement practices are less conservative, disclosure is extensive, and accounting practice differs from tax rules. Class A corresponds to what may be called Anglo-Saxon accounting. Class B accounting systems are found in countries with weak equity–outside shareholder financing systems. Measurement is more conservative, disclosure is not as extensive, and accounting practice more closely follows tax rules. Class B corresponds to Continental European accounting.

Nobes posits that culture, including institutional structures, determines the nature of a country's financing system. Although not explicitly defined, Nobes's notion of culture appears to go beyond the rather narrow definition used in Gray's framework, which relies on Hofstede's cultural dimensions. Nobes assumes (without explaining how) that some cultures lead to strong equity-outsider financing systems and other cultures lead to weak equity-outsider financing systems. His simplified model of reasons for international accounting differences is as follows:

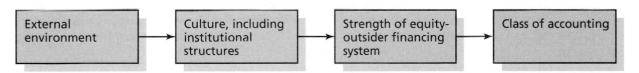

Most countries in the developed world have a self-sufficient culture. For these countries, Nobes applies his model as follows:

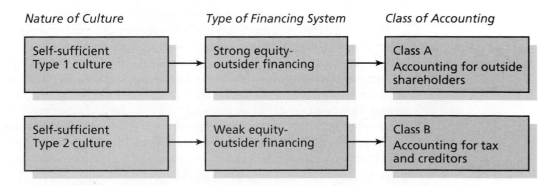

[26] Christopher W. Nobes, "Towards a General Model of the Reasons for International Differences in Financial Reporting," Abacus 34, no. 2 (1998), p. 166.

Many countries in the developing world are culturally dominated by another country often as a result of European colonialism. Nobes argues that culturally dominated countries use the accounting system of their dominating country regardless of the nature of the equity financing system. Thus, countries with a Type 1 culture as well as countries historically dominated by a Type 1 country use Class A accounting systems.

Examples of Countries with Class A Accounting

The United Kingdom is a culturally self-sufficient Type 1 country with a strong equity-outsider system. It has an outside shareholder–oriented Class A accounting system. New Zealand is culturally dominated by the United Kingdom. It also has a strong equity-outsider financing system, probably because of the influence of British culture. New Zealand also has a Class A accounting system. According to Nobes's model, this can be the result of New Zealand being culturally dominated by the United Kingdom (a Type 1 culture country), having a strong equity-outsider financing system, or both. The African nation of Malawi has a weak equity-outsider financing system, but as a former British colony (culturally dominated by the United Kingdom) it has adopted a Class A accounting system even though it has a weak equity-outsider financing system.

Nobes further suggests that as the financing system in a country evolves from weak equity to strong equity, the accounting system will also evolve in the direction of Class A accounting. He cites China as an example. Finally, Nobes argues that companies with strong equity-outsider financing will attempt to use Class A accounting even if they are located in a Class B accounting system country. He cites the German firms Deutsche Bank and Bayer and the Swiss company Nestlé as examples.

Recent Changes in Europe

The simplified model developed by Nobes appears to explain accounting developments that occurred in Europe over the past two decades. Because of the desire for companies to be competitive in attracting international equity investment, several European countries (with Class B accounting systems) developed a two-tiered financial reporting system in the late 1990s. Austria, France, Germany, Italy, and Switzerland gave stock-exchange-listed companies the option to use International Financial Reporting Standards (IFRS), a Class A accounting system, in preparing their consolidated financial statements.[27] The parent company statements, which serve as the basis for taxation, continued to be prepared using local accounting rules. Large numbers of German and Swiss companies (including Deutsche Bank, Bayer, and Nestlé), in particular, availed themselves of this opportunity to use IFRS.

This desire for companies to be competitive in the international capital market ultimately led the European Commission in 2005 to require all publicly traded companies within the European Union to use IFRS in preparing consolidated financial statements. Thus, it is no longer appropriate to think in terms of all German (or all French, all Italian, etc.) companies following the traditional Continental European model of accounting. Publicly traded companies in the EU now use a set of accounting standards based upon the Anglo-Saxon model of accounting in preparing their consolidated statements. However, in most cases, privately held companies in the EU continue to use local GAAP, as do public companies in preparing parent company financial statements.

---

[27] International Financial Reporting Standards are issued by the International Accounting Standards Board and are discussed in more detail in Chapters 3 and 4.

FURTHER EVIDENCE OF ACCOUNTING DIVERSITY

In the remainder of this chapter we provide additional evidence of some of the differences in accounting that exist across countries. We categorize accounting differences in the following manner and provide examples of each of these types of difference:

1. Differences in the financial statements included in an annual report.
2. Differences in the format used to present individual financial statements.
3. Differences in the level of detail provided in the financial statements.
4. Terminology differences.
5. Disclosures differences.
6. Recognition and measurement differences.

We illustrate these differences by considering a typical set of U.S. financial statements as a point of reference.

Financial Statements

U.S. companies are required to include a balance sheet, income statement, and statement of cash flows in a set of financial statements. In addition, schedules explaining the changes in retained earnings and accumulated other comprehensive income must be presented. Many U.S. companies provide this information in a separate statement of stockholders' equity.

Virtually all companies worldwide provide a balance sheet and an income statement in a set of financial statements. Although not universal, most countries now also require presentation of a statement of cash flows. Mexico, for example, implemented such a requirement in 2008. In addition to a balance sheet, income statement, and statement of cash flows, the Austrian firm Strabag SE includes a statement of changes in fixed assets as one of its primary financial statements. This statement provides detail on the change during the year in the historical cost of noncurrent intangible assets, tangible assets, and investment property. A statement of changes in noncurrent assets often also is found in financial statements prepared by German companies.

Format of Financial Statements

U.S. companies list assets and liabilities on the balance sheet in order of liquidity, from most liquid (cash) to least liquid (often intangible assets). The same is true in Canada, Mexico, and Japan. Companies in many countries (including most of Europe) list assets and liabilities in reverse order of liquidity. An example was presented in Exhibit 2.1 for a British company.

In the income statement format commonly used by U.S. companies, sales revenue and cost of goods sold are generally reported as separate line items, the difference being gross profit. Cost of goods sold includes manufacturing costs (materials, labor, and overhead) related to those items sold during the year. In addition to cost of goods sold, selling expense, administrative expense, research and development costs, and other operating expenses are subtracted to calculate operating income. Each of these line items includes costs related to materials (including supplies), labor, and overhead. Callaway Golf Company's income statement presented in Exhibit 2.9 illustrates the format typically used by U.S.-based companies.

EXHIBIT 2.9

CALLAWAY GOLF COMPANY
Consolidated Statements of Operations

(In Thousands, Except per Share Data)

	Year Ended December 31,		
	2009	**2008**	**2007**
Net sales	$950,799	$1,117,204	$1,124,591
Cost of sales	607,036	630,371	631,368
Gross profit	343,763	486,833	493,223
Selling expenses	260,597	287,802	281,960
General and administrative expenses	81,487	85,473	89,060
Research and development expenses	32,213	29,370	32,020
Total operating expenses	374,297	402,645	403,040
Income (loss) from operations	(30,534)	84,188	90,183
Interest and other income, net	2,685	1,863	3,455
Interest expense	(1,754)	(4,666)	(5,363)
Change in energy derivative valuation account (Note 10)	—	19,922	—
Income (loss) before income taxes	(29,603)	101,307	88,275
Income tax provision (benefit)	(14,343)	35,131	33,688
Net income (loss)	(15,260)	66,176	54,587
Dividends on convertible preferred stock	5,688	—	—
Net income (loss) allocable to common stockholders	$ (20,948)	$ 66,176	$ 54,587
Earnings (loss) per common share:			
Basic	$ (0.33)	$ 1.05	$ 0.82
Diluted	$ (0.33)	$ 1.04	$ 0.81
Weighted-average common shares outstanding			
Basic	63,176	63,055	66,371
Diluted	63,176	63,798	67,484

In contrast to the operational format income statement commonly found in the United States, many European companies present their income statement using a type of expenditure format. An example is presented in Exhibit 2.10 for Südzucker AG, a German sugar manufacturer. Rather than presenting cost of goods sold as a single line item, Südzucker presents separate line items for cost of materials, personnel expenses, and depreciation. The line item *Personnel expenses* aggregates the total amount of personnel cost incurred by the company. In contrast, Callaway Golf allocates these expenses to the various categories of operating expense (manufacturing, selling, administrative, research and development). Similarly, the line item *Depreciation* includes depreciation on manufacturing assets, as well as assets used in administration, marketing, and other departments. The second line in Südzucker's income statement, *Change in work in progress and finished goods inventories and internal costs capitalised,* adjusts for the manufacturing costs included in *Cost of materials, Personnel expenses, Depreciation,* and *Other operating expenses* that are not part of cost of goods sold in the current year. As a result of this adjustment, the amount related to the cost of goods sold subtracted in calculating operating income is the same as if cost of goods sold had been reported as a separate line item. Although much different in appearance, the format Südzucker uses to report

EXHIBIT 2.10

SÜDZUCKER AG
Consolidated Income Statement

1 March 2009 to 28 February 2010

€ million	Note	2009/10	2008/09
Income statement			
Revenues	6	**5,718.2**	**5,871.3**
Change in work in progress and finished goods inventories and internal costs capitalised	7	−256.1	−277.0
Other operating income	8	157.9	238.5
Cost of materials	9	−3,445.1	−3,449.1
Personnel expenses	10	−671.8	−662.8
Depreciation	11	−256.7	−249.7
Other operating expenses	12	−854.0	−1,125.9
Income from operations	13	**392.4**	**345.3**
Income from associated companies	14	2.0	21.6
Financial income	15	115.8	67.2
Financial expense	15	−161.8	−202.2
Earnings before income taxes		**348.4**	**231.9**
Taxes on income	16	−72.0	−48.7
Net earnings for the year	18	**276.4**	**183.2**
of which attributable to Südzucker AG shareholders		200.1	162.2
of which attributable to hybrid capital		26.2	26.2
of which attributable to minority interests		50.1	−5.2
Earnings per share (€)	18	**1.06**	**0.86**
Undiluted		−0.02	0.00
Diluted		1.04	0.86

income from operations does not affect the amount reported. The amount is the same regardless of whether the company uses the type of expenditure format or the cost of goods sold format.

The income statement prepared by Mexican companies includes a section generally not found in other countries. Exhibit 2.11 presents the income statement for Cemex S.A.B. de C.V., the world's largest supplier of building materials. After reporting *Operating income,* Cemex provides a calculation of *Comprehensive financing result* that includes interest income and expense, gains and losses on financial instruments, foreign currency gains and losses, and the *Monetary position result,* which is a measure of the purchasing power gain or loss associated with holding monetary assets and liabilities during a period of inflation.

Most companies present operating profit, pretax income, and net income as measures of performance in their income statement. Exhibit 2.12 shows the income statement for Sol Meliá SA, a Spanish hotel chain, which provides several other and different measures of performance. The first performance measure reflected in Sol Meliá's income statement is EBITDAR (earnings before interest, tax, depreciation, amortization, and rent expenses), which is then followed by EBITDA (EBITDAR minus rent expense), and then EBIT (EBITDA minus depreciation and amortization expense).

EXHIBIT 2.11

CEMEX S.A.B. DE C.V.
Consolidated Income Statements

(Millions of Mexican Pesos, Except for Earnings per Share)

	Notes	YEARS ENDED DECEMBER 31		
		2009	2008	2007
Net sales	3P	$ 197,801	225,665	228,152
Cost of sales	3Q	(139,672)	(153,965)	(151,439)
Gross profit		**58,129**	**71,700**	**76,713**
Administrative and selling expenses		(28,611)	(32,262)	(32,031)
Distribution expenses		(13,678)	(13,350)	(13,072)
Total operating expenses	3Q	(42,289)	(45,612)	(45,103)
Operating income		**15,840**	**26,088**	**31,610**
Other expenses, net	3S	(5,529)	(21,403)	(2,884)
Operating income after other expenses, net		**10,311**	**4,685**	**28,626**
Comprehensive financing result				
Financial expense	13	(13,513)	(10,199)	(8,808)
Financial income		385	513	823
Results from financial instruments	13	(2,127)	(15,172)	2,387
Foreign exchange results		(266)	(3,886)	(274)
Monetary position result	3R	415	418	6,890
Comprehensive financing result		(15,106)	(28,326)	1,018
Equity in income of associates		154	869	1,487
Income (loss) before income tax		**(4,641)**	**(22,772)**	**31,131**
Income tax	16	10,566	22,998	(4,474)
Income before discontinued operations		**5,925**	**226**	**26,657**
Discontinued operations	4B	(4,276)	2,097	288
Consolidated net income		1,649	2,323	26,945
Non-controlling interest net income		240	45	837
Controlling Interest Net Income		$ **1,409**	**2,278**	**26,108**
Basic earnings per share of continuing operations	19	$ **0.22**	**0.01**	**1.16**
Basic earnings per share of discontinued operations	19	$ **(0.16)**	**0.09**	**0.01**
Diluted earnings per share of continuing operations	19	$ **0.22**	**0.01**	**1.16**
Diluted earnings per share of discontinued operations	19	$ **(0.16)**	**0.09**	**0.01**

EXHIBIT 2.12

SOL MELIÁ SA
Consolidated Income Statements

Million Euros	12/09	12/08	Percent
Hotels	876.5	1034.0	
Leisure real estate	77.6	17.1	
Vacation club	66.5	97.4	
Other revenues	128.1	130.6	
Total revenues	**1,148.7**	**1,279.0**	**−10.2**
Raw materials	(138.0)	(155.8)	
Personnel expenses	(390.8)	(414.3)	
Other operating expenses	(338.4)	(375.0)	
Total operating expenses	**(867.2)**	**(945.1)**	**−8.2**

EBITDAR	281.5	333.9	−15.7
Rental expenses	(79.4)	(77.2)	
EBITDA	202.1	256.7	−21.3
Depreciation and amortization	(96.9)	(97.5)	
EBIT	105.2	159.2	−34.0
Net interest expense	(27.7)	(71.0)	
Exchange rate differences	1.1	(9.1)	
Other interest expense	(11.8)	(11.7)	
Total financial profit/(loss)	(38.5)	(91.8)	58.1
Profit/(loss) from equity investments	(12.8)	(6.6)	
Continuing earnings before taxes	53.9	(98.3)	−154.8
Discontinuing operations	0.0	0.0	
Profit before taxes and minorities	53.9	60.9	−11.5
Taxes	(10.4)	(6.3)	
Group net profit/(loss)	43.5	54.6	−20.4
Minorities (P)/L	(5.4)	(3.4)	
Profit/loss of the parent company	38.1	51.2	−25.6

Level of Detail

Differences exist in the level of detail provided in the individual financial statements. U.S. companies tend to provide relatively few line items on the face of the financial statements and then supplement these with additional detail in the notes. Callaway Golf's income statement presented in Exhibit 2.9 is a case in point. The level of detail provided by U.S.-based companies can be contrasted with the extremely detailed income statement provided by Thai Airways International Public Company Limited as shown in Exhibit 2.13. Instead of reporting operating expenses in only three line items as does Callaway Golf, Thai Airways presents 15 separate categories of operating expense. Even though considerable detail is provided on the face of the income statement, additional information is included in the notes to provide further detail on those line items labeled as Other. For example, Note 8.23 Other Income—Others, indicates that this line on the income statement includes gains on sales of assets, revenue from airport fees collected from passengers, and compensation revenue from the delayed delivery of aircraft.

Terminology

The examination of Vodafone PLC's balance sheet earlier in this chapter revealed a number of differences in the terminology used by Vodafone and a typical U.S. company. New Zealand–based Fletcher Building Group includes the following current assets on its balance sheet: Cash and liquid deposits, Current tax asset, Debtors, and Stocks. A "translation" of these terms into terminology commonly used in the United States would be: Cash and cash equivalents, Taxes receivable, Accounts receivable, and Inventories. Many non-English-language companies translate their annual reports into English for the convenience of English speakers. These companies typically choose between the British and the American formats and terminology in preparing convenience translations. Occasionally terms unfamiliar to both British and U.S. accounting are found in English language reports to reflect business, legal, or accounting practice unique to a specific country. For example, the Brazilian petrochemical firm, Braskem SA, includes the line

EXHIBIT 2.13

THAI AIRWAYS INTERNATIONAL PUBLIC COMPANY LIMITED
Consolidated Income Statements

For the years ended December 31, 2009 and 2008   Units: Baht

		CONSOLIDATED	
	Notes	2009	2008
Revenues			
Revenues from sale or revenues from services			
Passenger and excess baggage.		134,479,296,254	164,318,701,819
Freight.		18,525,307,811	25,840,755,700
Mail.		822,754,186	912,990,339
Other activities.		7,775,384,234	9,045,532,774
Total revenues from sale or revenues from services		**161,602,742,485**	**200,117,980,632**
Other income			
Interest income		178,067,252	493,287,861
Others.	8.23	2,093,717,478	1,994,352,142
Total other income		**2,271,784,730**	**2,487,640,003**
Total revenues.		**163,874,527,215**	**202,605,620,635**
Expenses			
Fuel and oil		47,014,753,162	89,459,872,853
Personnel.		26,191,239,889	30,534,030,465
Management benefit expenses	8.22	60,916,443	93,395,719
Flight service expenses.		17,691,615,362	19,938,599,141
Crew expenses.		5,243,530,868	6,542,134,756
Aircraft maintenance and overhaul costs		10,320,750,374	10,847,783,197
Depreciation and amortisation expenses		21,023,460,156	20,281,081,576
Lease of aircraft and spare parts.		1,531,697,470	3,650,964,476
Inventories and supplies.		8,496,583,764	8,826,777,548
Selling and advertising expenses		6,221,182,125	6,932,244,544
Insurance expenses		760,064,787	751,270,159
Damages arising from Antitrust/Competition Law	8.18.5	—	4,290,169,870
Impairment losses of assets		529,056,765	4,749,840,736
Other expenses	8.24	8,103,657,883	9,285,303,024
Losses (gains) on foreign currency exchange		(3,167,360,443)	4,471,388,154
Total expenses		**150,021,148,605**	**220,654,856,218**
Share of losses (profits) of investments by the equity method.		8,562,792	65,137,572
Profits (losses) before finance costs and income tax expenses.		**13,844,815,818**	**(18,114,373,155)**
Finance costs		5,737,562,830	5,485,264,531
Profits (losses) before income tax expenses.		**8,107,252,988**	**(23,599,637,686)**
Net tax expenses (tax income)	8.25	691,425,974	(2,285,253,584)
Net profits (losses)		**7,415,827,014**	**(21,314,384,102)**
Profits (losses) attributable to:			
Equity holders of the parent		**7,343,578,865**	**(21,379,451,415)**
Minority interests.		72,248,149	65,067,313
		7,415,827,014	**(21,314,384,102)**
Basic earnings per share.	**8.27**		
Net profits (losses) per share		**4.32**	(12.58)

EXHIBIT 2.14
Stock Market Disclosure Levels

Source: S. M. Saudagaran and G. C. Biddle, "Foreign Listing Location: A Study of MNCS and Stock Exchanges in Eight Countries," *Journal of International Business Studies,* Second Quarter 1995, p. 331.

Country	Overall Disclosure Level	Rank
United States	7.28	1
Canada	6.41	2
United Kingdom	6.02	3
Netherlands	4.75	4
France	4.17	5
Japan	3.83	6
Germany	3.81	7
Switzerland	3.17	8

item *Judicial deposits and compulsory loan* as an asset on it balance sheet. Note 11 discloses that the judicial deposits relate to *Tax contingencies* and *Labor and other claims,* but provides no further information with regard to this asset. SK Telecom includes a noncurrent asset on its balance sheet called *Guarantee deposits,* which represents the amount of cash that customers have paid as a deposit to initiate telephone service. Among its current liabilities, SK Telecom reports the line item *Withholdings,* with no further explanation as to what this might be.

Disclosure

Numerous differences exist across countries in the amount and types of information disclosed in a set of financial statements. Many of the disclosures provided by companies are required by law or other regulations. In addition, many companies around the world provide additional, voluntary disclosures often to better compete in obtaining finance in the international capital markets. The disclosures required to be made by publicly traded companies in the United States generally are considered to be the most extensive in the world. Saudagaran and Biddle developed a ranking of the level of disclosure required by stock exchanges in eight major countries (see Exhibit 2.14). Consistent with Gray's expectations with respect to secrecy the Anglo countries rank 1, 2, and 3 in the amount of disclosure provided, whereas the Germanic countries rank 7 and 8.

One must be careful in generalizing these disclosure rankings to all companies within a country. For example, the Swiss banking firm UBS AG provides extensive notes (108 pages in length) to its consolidated financial statements that are similar in scope and content to what is found in the annual reports of Anglo companies. The same can be said for other Swiss multinational corporations as well as for many multinationals in other non-Anglo countries.

There are an infinite number of differences that can exist in the disclosures provided by companies. To illustrate the wide diversity, we provide several examples of disclosures uncommon in the United States and most other countries. The Swedish appliance manufacturer AB Electrolux includes a note in its financial statements titled *Employees and Remuneration* (see Exhibit 2.15). This note reports the number of employees, their gender, and their total remuneration by geographical area. By splitting total remuneration into the amount paid to boards and senior managers and the amount paid to other employees, the statement allows interested readers to see that it is the latter group that receives the vast majority of compensation.

The Brazilian mining company Vale includes a social report in the notes to its financial statements (see Exhibit 2.16). The report is based on a model developed by the Federal Accounting Board of Brazil (CFC) and highlights the investments

EXHIBIT 2.15

AB ELECTROLUX
Excerpt from Note 27 Employees and Remuneration

Notes, all amounts in SEKm, unless otherwise stated

Average number of employees, by geographical area

	Group	
	2009	**2008**
Europe.	25,292	28,138
North America	10,384	11,398
Rest of world	14,957	15,641
Total	**50,633**	**55,177**

In 2009, the average number of employees for continuing operations was 50,633 (55,177), of whom 32,955 (35,562) were men and 17,678 (19,615) were women.

Salaries, other remuneration and employer contributions

	2009			2008		
	Salaries and remuneration	Employer contributions	Total	Salaries and remuneration	Employer contributions	Total
Parent Company	764	562	1,326	826	657	1,483
(whereof pension costs)		(159)[1]	(159)[1]		(259)[1]	(259)[1]
Subsidiaries	12,398	3,477	15,875	11,836	3,695	15,531
(whereof pension costs)		(718)	(718)		(687)	(687)
Group total	**13,162**	**4,039**	**17,201**	**12,662**	**4,352**	**17,014**
(whereof pension costs)		**(877)**	**(877)**		**(946)**	**(946)**

[1] Includes SEK 14m (20), referring to the President and his predecessors.

Salaries and remuneration by geographical area for Board members, senior managers and other employees

	2009			2008		
	Boards members and senior managers	Other employees	Total	Boards members and senior managers	Other employees	Total
Sweden						
Parent Company	48	716	764	47	779	826
Other.	8	201	209	5	230	235
Total Sweden	**56**	**917**	**973**	**52**	**1,009**	**1,061**
EU, excluding Sweden	99	5,797	5,896	88	5,765	5,853
Rest of Europe	10	768	778	10	700	710
North America	18	3,360	3,378	21	3,070	3,091
Latin America	35	1,094	1,129	38	951	989
Asia	14	326	340	12	428	440
Pacific	4	641	645	1	498	499
Africa.	2	21	23	3	16	19
Total outside Sweden.	**182**	**12,007**	**12,189**	**173**	**11,428**	**12,843**
Group total	**238**	**12,924**	**13,162**	**225**	**12,437**	**13,987**

Of the Board members in the Group, 77 were men and 12 were women, of whom 7 men and 4 women were in the Parent Company. Senior managers in the Group consisted of 186 men and 40 women, of whom 9 men and 3 women in the Parent Company. The total pension cost for Board members and senior managers in the Group amounted to 37m (48) in 2009.

EXHIBIT 2.16

VALE SA
Social Report

Consolidated

Basis for Calculations	2009	2008
Gross revenue	49,812	72,766
Operating income before financial results and equity results	13,181	27,400
Gross payroll	2,549	4,422

Labor Indicators	Amount	% of Payroll	% of Operating Income	Amount	% of Payroll	% of Operating Income
Nutrition	295	12%	2%	307	7%	1%
Compulsory payroll charges.	792	31%	6%	892	20%	3%
Transportation	159	6%	1%	152	3%	1%
Pension plan.	208	8%	2%	431	10%	2%
Health	339	13%	3%	297	7%	1%
Education.	105	4%	1%	174	4%	1%
Nursey	3	—	—	2	—	—
Employee profit sharing plan	868	34%	7%	548	12%	2%
Other.	82	3%	1%	124	3%	—
Total—Labor Indicators	**2,855**	**112%**	**22%**	**2,927**	**66%**	**11%**

Social Indicators	Amount	% of Operating Income	% of Net Operating revenue	Amount	% of Operating Income	% of Net Operating revenue
Taxes (excluding payroll charges)	**5,810**	**44%**	**12%**	**5,274**	**19%**	**7%**
Taxes paid recover	(571)	−4%	−1%	(1,955)	−7%	−3%
Citizenship investments	—	—	—	409	1%	1%
Social actions and projects.	370	3%	1%	390	1%	1%
Culture.	100	3%	1%	102	—	—
Native community.	19	—	—	19	—	—
Environmental investments	**1,397**	**11%**	**3%**	**808**	**3%**	**1%**
Total-Social indicators	**7,207**	**55%**	**14%**	**6,491**	**24%**	**9%**

Workforce indicators		
Number of employees at the end of the period . .	60,036	62,490
Number of admittances during the period	2,633	7,673

EXHIBIT 2.17

VALE SA
Statement of Added Value

Period Ended	In Millions of Reals	
	Consolidated	
	2009	**2008**
Generation of added value		
Gross revenue		
Revenue from products and services..........................	**49,812**	**72,766**
Revenue from the construction of own assets..................	13,919	17,706
Allowance for doubtful accounts	(23)	(32)
Less: Acquisition of products	(1,219)	(2,805)
Outsourced services	(6,242)	(8,244)
Materials	(20,653)	(23,958)
Fuel oil and gas..	(2,777)	(3,761)
Energy	(1,776)	(2,052)
Impairment..	—	(2,447)
Other costs..	(6,920)	(6,829)
Gross added value	**24,121**	**40,344**
Depreciation, amortization and depletion......................	(5,447)	(5,112)
Net added value	**18,674**	**35,232**
Received from third parties		
Financial revenue	866	1,221
Equity results	116	(1,325)
Total added value to be distributed	**19,656**	**35,128**
Personnel...	5,086	5,046
Taxes, rates and contribution	5,810	5,267
Taxes paid recover	(571)	(1,955)
Remuneration on third party's capital........................	3,433	4,157
Inflation and exchange rate variation, net....................	(4,519)	902
Remuneration on stockholders' equity		
Stockholders..	3,373	5,640
Reinvested	6,876	15,639
Minority interest..	168	432
Distribution of added value...............................	**19,656**	**35,128**

made by the company with respect to human resources, the environment, and social projects. In its Brazilian GAAP financial statements, Vale also presents a statement of added value (see Exhibit 2.17) that provides insight into the groups that benefit most from the company's existence. Employees and the government received the largest distributions of added value by the company in 2009. The social report indicates among other things the costs in addition to gross payroll the company incurs related to its labor force. These include costs related to food, health, education, and profit sharing. In 2009, these costs amounted to 112 percent of gross payroll, with the largest amounts going to compulsory payroll charges and profit sharing.

EXHIBIT 2.18

AKZO NOBEL NV
Note 17 Movements in Provisions

In € millions	Total	Pensions and other post-retirement benefits	Restructuring of activities	Environmental costs	Other
Balance at January 1, 2009.	2,917	1,626	165	318	**808**
Additions made during the year.	648	179	263	40	**166**
Utilization	(961)	(451)	(198)	(31)	**(281)**
Amounts reversed during the year	(64)	—	(12)	(24)	**(28)**
Unwind of discount	60	—	2	32	**26**
Acquisitions/divestments	6	1	—	—	**5**
Pension plans changing to net asset position.	77	77	—	—	**—**
Changes in exchange rates	33	7	6	17	**3**
Balance at December 31, 2009	**2,716**	**1,439**	**226**	**352**	**699**
Non-current portion of provisions	1,919	1,200	40	280	399
Current portion of provisions	797	239	186	72	300
	2,716	1,439	226	352	699

Akzo Nobel includes a noncurrent liability on its balance sheet titled *Provisions.* Provisions are accrued liabilities that by their nature involve a substantial amount of estimation. In note 17 to the financial statements, Akzo Nobel provides considerable detail about the various items for which provisions have been established and the change in each of these items during the year (see Exhibit 2.18). This information can be used to assess the quality of estimates made by the company with respect to expected future liabilities. For example, note 17 indicates that for the year 2009, Akzo Nobel had a beginning restructuring provision of €165 million and €263 million was added to the provision throughout the year. During 2009, €198 million of the estimated liability related to restructuring was paid and another €12 million was reversed as a result of overestimating the liability in a previous year. Note 17 also discloses that only €31 million of the €318 million the company expects in environmental cleanup costs was paid in 2009.

Recognition and Measurement

Perhaps the most important international differences that exist in financial reporting are those related to the recognition and measurement of assets, liabilities, revenues, and expenses. *Recognition* refers to the decision of whether an item should be reported in the financial statements. *Measurement* refers to the determination of the amount to be reported. For example, national accounting standards establish whether costs associated with acquiring the use of a resource should be recognized as an asset on the balance sheet. If so, then guidance must be provided with respect to both the initial measurement of the asset and measurement at subsequent balance sheet dates.

We close this chapter by describing the diversity that exists with respect to measuring property, plant, and equipment (PPE) subsequent to acquisition. Possible values at which these assets can be reported on the balance sheet include:

1. Historical cost (HC).
2. Historical cost adjusted for changes in the general purchasing power (GPP) of the currency.
3. Fair value (FV).

In most cases, GPP and FV accounting results in PPE being written up to an amount higher than historical cost. The counterpart to the asset write-up generally is treated as an increase in stockholders' equity, often included in a Revaluation Reserve account. The larger asset value results in a larger depreciation expense and therefore smaller net income.

U.S. GAAP requires PPE to be carried on the balance sheet at historical cost less accumulated depreciation. If an asset is impaired, that is, its carrying value exceeds the amount of cash expected to result from use of the asset, it must be written down to fair value. Upward revaluation of fixed assets is not acceptable. HC accounting also is required in Japan. Although the specific rules vary from those in the United States, write-down to a lower value is required if a permanent impairment of value has occurred.

In contrast, under IFRS, publicly traded companies in the European Union are free to choose between two different methods for valuing their assets. PPE may be carried on the balance sheet at historical cost or at revalued amounts. The basis of revaluation is the *fair value* of the asset at the date of revaluation, which in many cases will be determined through appraisals. If a company chooses to report assets at revalued amounts, it has an obligation to keep the valuations up to date, which might require annual adjustments.

Until 2008, in Mexico, PPE was reported initially at historical cost and then restated in terms of GPP at subsequent balance sheet dates. Similarly, until the early 1990s, publicly traded companies in Brazil were required to use GPP in preparing financial statements. In addition to PPE inventories and investments also were adjusted upward for inflation on each balance sheet date, and receivables were discounted to their present value. These procedures no longer are required in Brazil but still may be followed at the option of the company.

Summary

1. Considerable diversity exists across countries with respect to the form and content of individual financial statements, the rules used to measure assets and liabilities and recognize and measure revenues and expenses, and the magnitude and nature of the disclosures provided in a set of financial statements.

2. Many environmental factors are thought to contribute to the differences in financial reporting that exist across countries. Some of the more commonly mentioned factors include legal system, the influence of taxation on financial reporting, corporate financing system, inflation, political and economic ties between countries, and national culture.

3. The diversity that exists in financial reporting creates problems for multinational corporations in preparing consolidated financial statements on the basis of a single set of accounting rules. Accounting diversity also can result in increased cost for companies in tapping into foreign capital markets. The comparison of financial statements across companies located in different countries

is hampered by accounting diversity. Low-quality financial reporting contributed to the financial crisis in East Asia in the 1990s.

4. Several authors have classified countries according to similarities and differences in financial reporting. Two dominant models of accounting used in the developed world are the Anglo-Saxon model and the Continental European model.

5. Concentrating on the Anglo-Saxon and Continental model countries, Nobes developed a classification scheme that attempts to show how the financial reporting systems in 14 developed countries relate to one another. Nobes breaks down the two major classes of accounting system first into subclasses and then into families. This classification scheme shows how different families of accounting are related.

6. Culture has long been considered a determinant of accounting. Using the cultural dimensions identified by Hofstede, Gray developed a framework for the relationship between culture and accounting systems. Cultural values affect a country's accounting system in two ways: (1) through their influence on the accounting values of conservatism, secrecy, uniformity, and professionalism shared by a country's accountants and (2) through their influence on institutional factors such as the capital market and legal system.

7. In a more recent model of the reasons for international differences in financial reporting, Nobes suggests that the dominant factor is the extent to which corporate financing is obtained through the sale of equity securities to outsider shareholders. For whatever reason, some cultures lead to a strong equity-outsider financing system and other cultures lead to a weaker equity-outsider financing system. In countries with strong equity-outsider financing, measurement practices are less conservative, disclosure is extensive, and accounting practice differs from tax rules. This is consistent with what may be called Anglo-Saxon accounting. In accounting systems found in countries with weak equity–outside shareholder financing systems, measurement is more conservative, disclosure is not as extensive, and accounting practice follows tax rules. This is consistent with the Continental European accounting model.

8. Differences in financial reporting exist with regard to the financial statements provided by companies; the format, level of detail, and terminology used in presenting financial statements; the nature and amount of disclosure provided; and the principles used to recognize and measure assets, liabilities, revenues, and expenses.

Appendix to Chapter 2

The Case of Daimler-Benz

Daimler-Benz was the first German company to list on the New York Stock Exchange (NYSE), doing so in 1993. This was a major event for the NYSE and the Securities and Exchange Commission (SEC) because German companies had previously refused to make the adjustments necessary to reconcile their German law–based financial statements to U.S. generally accepted accounting principles (GAAP). After some compromise on the part of the SEC and because of Daimler's strong desire to enter the U.S. capital market (and be the first German company to do it), Daimler agreed to comply with SEC regulations.

Subsequent to its NYSE listing, Daimler-Benz filed an annual report on Form 20-F with the SEC.[1] In its 20-F filing, Daimler prepared financial statements in English, in both German deutschemarks (DM) and U.S. dollars, and, until 1996, according to German accounting principles. In the notes to the 1995 financial statements, Daimler provided a "Reconciliation to U.S. GAAP" in which adjustments were made to net income and stockholders' equity prepared in accordance with German accounting law to reconcile to U.S. GAAP. The net effect of these adjustments over the period 1993–1995 is shown in Exhibit A2.1.

The fact that in 1993 Daimler-Benz reported a profit under German GAAP but a loss under U.S. GAAP created quite a stir in the international financial community. Because German companies were well known for intentionally understating income through the creation of hidden reserves, one would have expected German GAAP income to be smaller than U.S. GAAP income (as was true in 1994). In 1993, however, Daimler incurred a net loss for the year (as can be seen from the negative amount of U.S. GAAP income). To avoid reporting this loss, the company "released" hidden reserves that had been created in earlier years, thus reporting a profit of DM 615 million under German GAAP. The difference in German GAAP and U.S. GAAP income in 1993 of some DM 2.5 billion shows just how unreliable German GAAP income can be in reflecting the actual performance of a company. In fact, the German Financial Analysts Federation (DVFA) developed a method for adjusting German GAAP earnings to a more reliable amount (known as DVFA earnings).

In 1996, Daimler-Benz decided to abandon German GAAP and implement a U.S. GAAP accounting system worldwide. The 1996 annual report was prepared using U.S. GAAP and received a clean opinion on this basis from KPMG. The rationale for this decision was outlined in the 1996 annual report and is reproduced in Exhibit A2.2. The company indicated that U.S. GAAP figures not only allowed external analysts to better evaluate the company but also served as a better basis for the internal controlling of the company. This clearly points out the differences in orientation between a typical macro-uniform accounting system that is geared toward minimizing taxes and protecting creditors, and a micro-based accounting system that has the objective of providing information that is useful for making decisions, not only by external parties but by management as well.

EXHIBIT A2.1

DAIMLER-BENZ
Excerpt from Form 20-F: Reconciliation to U.S. GAAP 1995

(all amounts in DM)

	1993	1994	1995
Net income as reported in the consolidated income statement under German GAAP.	615	895	(5,734)
Net income in accordance with U.S. GAAP.	(1,839)	1,052	(5,729)
Stockholders' equity as reported in the consolidated balance sheet under German GAAP	18,145	20,251	13,842
Stockholders' equity in accordance with U.S. GAAP.	26,281	29,435	22,860

[1] U.S. companies file their annual report with the SEC on Form 10-K; foreign companies file theirs on Form 20-F.

EXHIBIT A2.2

DAIMLER-BENZ
Excerpts from Annual Report 1996

Excerpts from *Value-Based Management, U.S. GAAP, and New Controlling Instruments*
(pages 44–45)

1996 Financial Statements Prepared Entirely in Accordance with U.S. GAAP for the First Time

Since our listing on the New York Stock Exchange we have increasingly aligned our external reporting in accordance with the information requirements of the international financial world. . . . With our 1996 annual report, we are the first German company to present an entire year's financial statements in accordance with U.S. GAAP while at the same time complying with the German Law to Facilitate Equity Borrowing. The report thus also conforms with EU guidelines and European accounting principles.

Improved External Disclosure

Instead of providing various figures concerning the economic performance of the Company that are derived using the HGB and U.S. GAAP but that in some instances differ significantly from each other because of the distinct accounting philosophies, we supply a complete set of figures in conformance with U.S. GAAP for our shareholders, the financial analysts, and the interested public. In so doing, we fulfill accounting standards of the highest reputation worldwide, and we believe our approach more clearly and accurately reflects the economic performance, financial situation, and net worth of the Company than any other accounting system available at this time. This is not least due to the fact that U.S. accounting principles focus on investor information rather than creditor protection, which is the dominant concern under German accounting principles. Discretionary valuation is greatly limited, and the allocation of income and expenses to the individual accounting period is based on strict economic considerations.

Advantages for All Shareholders

Using U.S. accounting principles makes it significantly easier to internationally active financial analysts or experienced institutional investors to accurately assess the financial situation and development of the Company. Moreover, it improves disclosure at Daimler-Benz as well as comparability on an international scale. This helps promote the worldwide acceptance of our stock.

Internal Controlling on the Basis of Balance Sheet Values in Accordance with U.S. GAAP

The U.S. GAAP not only made Daimler-Benz more transparent from an external perspective. Because the earnings figures as derived with American accounting principles accurately reflect the economic performance of the Company, we are now able to use figures from our external reporting for the internal controlling of the Company and its individual business units rather than relying on the internal operating profit used in the past. We thus make use of the same figures both internally and externally to measure the economic performance of the Company and the business units.

Excerpt from *Letter to the Stockholders and Friends of Our Company* (page 4)

1996 marks the first time we have prepared our accounts in accordance with U.S. accounting principles which gives our investors worldwide the transparency they require. This means that our success as well as our shortcomings will be reported with new clarity. The terms operating profit, return on capital employed, and cash flow have become part of the language of the entire company and part of our corporate philosophy.

Questions

1. What are the two most common methods used internationally for the order in which assets are listed on the balance sheet? Which of these two methods is most common in North America? In Europe?

2. What are the two major types of legal systems used in the world? How does the type of legal system affect accounting?

3. How does the relationship between financial reporting and taxation affect the manner in which income is measured for financial reporting purposes?

4. Who are the major providers of capital (financing) for business enterprises? What influence does the relative importance of equity financing in a country have on financial statement disclosure?

5. What are the major problems caused by worldwide accounting diversity for a multinational corporation?

6. What are the major problems caused by worldwide accounting diversity for international portfolio investment?

7. What are the hypothesized relationships between the cultural value of uncertainty avoidance and the accounting values of conservatism and secrecy?

8. How are the Anglo and less developed Latin cultural areas expected to differ with respect to the accounting values of conservatism and secrecy?

9. According to Nobes, what are the two most important factors influencing differences in accounting systems across countries?

10. What are the different ways in which financial statements differ across countries?

11. How are the various costs that comprise cost of goods sold reflected in a "type of expenditure" format income statement?

12. What information is provided in a statement of added value?

13. What are the alternative methods used internationally to present fixed assets on the balance sheet subsequent to acquisition?

Exercises and Problems

1. Refer to the income statements presented in Exhibits 2.9, 2.10, 2.11, 2.12, and 2.13 for Callaway Golf Company, Südzucker AG, Cemex S.A.B. de CV, Sol Meliá SA, and Thai Airways.

   Required:

   a. Calculate gross profit margin (gross profit/sales), operating profit margin (operating profit/sales) and net profit margin (net earnings/sales) for each of these companies. If a particular ratio cannot be calculated, explain why not.

   b. Is it valid to compare the profit margins calculated in part (a) across these companies in assessing relative profitability? Why or why not?

2. Access the financial statements from the most recent annual report of a foreign company and a domestic company with which you are familiar to complete this assignment.

   Required:

   a. Determine the accounting principles (GAAP) the foreign and domestic companies use to prepare financial statements.

   b. Determine whether the foreign and domestic companies provide a set of financial statements that includes the same components (e.g., consolidated balance sheet, consolidated income statement, consolidated cash flows statement).

   c. List five format differences in the companies' income statements.

   d. List five format differences in the companies' balance sheets.

   e. Note any terminology differences that exist between the two companies' income statements and balance sheets.

f. Assess whether the scope and content of the information provided in the notes to the financial statements is similar between the two companies.

g. Compare the overall presentation of the financial statements and notes to the financial statements between the two companies.

3. Access the financial statements from the most recent annual report of two foreign companies located in the same country to complete this assignment.

Required:

a. Determine the accounting principles (GAAP) the two foreign companies use to prepare financial statements.

b. Determine whether the two foreign companies provide a set of financial statements that includes the same components (e.g., consolidated balance sheet, consolidated income statement, consolidated cash flows statement).

c. List any format differences in the companies' income statements.

d. List any format differences in the companies' balance sheets.

e. Note any terminology differences that exist between the two companies' income statements and balance sheets.

f. Assess whether the scope and content of the information provided in the notes to the financial statements is similar between the two companies.

g. Compare the overall presentation of the financial statements and notes to the financial statements between the two companies.

4. Cultural dimension index scores developed by Hofstede for six countries are reported in the following table:

Country	Power Distance		Uncertainty Avoidance		Individualism		Masculinity		Long-Term Orientation	
	Index	Rank[a]	Index	Rank[a]	Index	Rank[a]	Index	Rank[a]	Index	Rank[b]
Belgium	65	20	94	5–6	75	8	54	22	38	18
Brazil	69	14	76	21–22	38	26–27	49	27	65	6
Korea (South)	60	27–28	85	16–17	18	43	39	41	75	5
Netherlands	38	40	53	35	80	4–5	14	51	44	11–12
Sweden	31	47–48	29	49–50	71	10–11	5	53	33	20
Thailand	64	21–23	64	30	20	39–41	34	44	56	8

[a]1 = highest rank; 53 = lowest rank.
[b]1 = highest rank; 34 = lowest rank.

Required:

Using Gray's hypothesis relating culture to the accounting value of secrecy, rate these six countries as relatively high or relatively low with respect to the level of disclosure you would expect to find in financial statements. Explain.

5. Refer to Nobes's judgmental classification of accounting systems in Exhibit 2.5 and consider the following countries: Austria, Brazil, Finland, Ivory Coast, Russia, South Africa.

Required:

Identify the family of accounting in which you would expect to find each of these countries. Explain your classification of these countries.

6. Five factors are often mentioned as affecting a country's accounting practices: (a) legal system, (b) taxation, (c) providers of financing, (d) inflation, and (e) political and economic ties.

Required:

Consider your home country. Identify which of these factors has had the strongest influence on the development of accounting in your country. Provide specific examples to support your position.

7. As noted in the chapter, diversity in accounting practice across countries generates problems for a number of different groups.

Required:

Answer the following questions and provide explanations for your answers.

a. Which is the greatest problem arising from worldwide accounting diversity?

b. Which group is most affected by worldwide accounting diversity?

c. Which group can most easily deal with the problems associated with accounting diversity?

8. Various attempts have been made to reduce the accounting diversity that exists internationally. This process is known as convergence and is discussed in more detail in Chapter 3. The ultimate form of convergence would be a world in which all countries followed a similar set of financial reporting rules and practices.

Required:

Consider each of the following factors that contribute to existing accounting diversity as described in this chapter:

- Legal system
- Taxation
- Providers of financing
- Inflation
- Political and economic ties
- Culture

Which factor do you believe represents the greatest impediment to the international convergence of accounting? Which factor do you believe creates the smallest impediment to convergence? Explain your reasoning.

Case 2-1

The Impact of Culture on Conservatism

PART I

The framework created by Professor Sidney Gray in 1988 to explain the development of a country's accounting system is presented in the chapter in Exhibit 2.8. Gray theorized that culture has an impact on a country's accounting system through its influence on accounting values. Focusing on that part of a country's accounting system comprised of financial reporting rules and practices, the model can be visualized as follows:

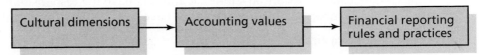

In short, cultural values shared by members of a society influence the accounting values shared by members of the accounting subculture. The shared values of the accounting subculture in turn affect the financial reporting rules and practices found within a country.

With respect to the accounting value of conservatism, Gray hypothesized that the higher a country ranks on the cultural dimensions of uncertainty avoidance and long-term orientation, and the lower it ranks in terms of individualism and masculinity, then the more likely it is to rank highly in terms of conservatism. Conservatism is a preference for a cautious approach to measurement. Conservatism is manifested in a country's accounting system through a tendency to defer recognition of assets and items that increase net income and a tendency to accelerate the recognition of liabilities and items that decrease net income. One example of conservatism in practice would be a rule that requires an unrealized contingent liability to be recognized when it is probable that an outflow of future resources will arise but does not allow the recognition of an unrealized contingent asset under any circumstances.

Required:

Discuss the implications for the global convergence of financial reporting standards raised by Gray's model.

PART II

Although Gray's model relates cultural values to the accounting value of conservatism as it is embodied in a country's financial reporting rules, it can be argued that the model is equally applicable to the manner in which a country's accountants apply those rules:

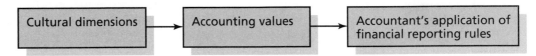

Required:

Discuss the implications this argument has for the comparability of financial statements across countries, even in an environment of substantial international accounting convergence. Identify areas in which differences in cultural dimensions across countries could lead to difference in the application of financial reporting rules.

PART III

Cancan Enterprises Inc. is a Canadian-based company with subsidiaries located in Brazil, Korea, and Sweden. (Hofstede's cultural dimension index scores for these countries are presented in Exercise 4.) Cancan Enterprises must apply Canadian GAAP worldwide in preparing consolidated financial statements. Cancan has developed a corporate accounting manual that prescribes the accounting policies based on Canadian GAAP that are to be applied by all the company's operations. Each year Cancan's internal auditors have the responsibility of ensuring that the company's accounting policies have been applied consistently companywide.

Required:

Discuss the implications that the model presented in Part II of this case has for the internal auditors of Cancan Enterprises in carrying out their responsibilities.

Case 2-2

SKD Limited

SKD Limited is a biotechnology company that prepares financial statements using internally developed accounting rules (referred to as SKD GAAP). To be able to compare SKD's financial statements with those of companies in their home country, financial analysts in Country A and Country B prepared a reconciliation of SKD's current year net income and stockholders' equity. Adjustments were based on the actual accounting policies and practices followed by biotechnology companies in Country A and Country B. The following table shows the adjustments to income and stockholders' equity made by each country analyst:

	Country A	Country B
Income under SKD GAAP.	1,050	1,050
Adjustments:		
Goodwill amortization	300	(100)
Capitalized interest.	50	50
Depreciation related to capitalized interest	(20)	(20)
Depreciation related to revalued fixed assets . .	—	(8)
Income under local GAAP	1,380	972
Stockholders' equity under SKD GAAP.	15,000	15,000
Adjustments:		
Goodwill	900	(300)
Capitalized interest.	30	30
Revaluation of fixed assets	—	56
Stockholders' equity under local GAAP	15,930	14,786

Description of Accounting Differences

Goodwill. SKD capitalizes goodwill and amortizes it over a 20-year period. Goodwill is also treated as an asset in Country A and Country B. However, goodwill is not amortized in Country A, but instead is subjected to an annual impairment test. Goodwill is amortized over a 5-year period in Country B.

Interest. SKD expenses all interest immediately. In both Country A and Country B, interest related to self-constructed assets must be capitalized as a part of the cost of the asset.

Fixed assets. SKD carries assets on the balance sheet at their historical cost, less accumulated depreciation. The same treatment is required in Country A. In Country B, companies in the biotechnology industry generally carry assets on the balance sheet at revalued amounts. Depreciation is based on the revalued amount of fixed assets.

Required:

1. With respect to the adjustments related to goodwill, answer the following:
   a. Why does the adjustment for goodwill amortization increase net income under Country A GAAP but decrease net income under Country B GAAP?
   b. Why does the goodwill adjustment increase stockholders' equity in Country A but decrease stockholders' equity in Country B?
   c. Why are the adjustments to stockholders' equity larger than the adjustments to income?

2. With respect to the adjustments made by the analyst in Country A related to interest, answer the following:
   a. Why are there two separate adjustments to income related to interest?
   b. Why does the adjustment to income for capitalized interest increase income, whereas the adjustment for depreciation related to capitalized interest decreases income?
   c. Why is the positive adjustment to stockholders' equity for capitalized interest smaller than the positive adjustment to income for capitalized interest?

3. With respect to the adjustments made by the analyst in Country B related to fixed assets, answer the following:
   a. Why does the adjustment for depreciation related to revalued fixed assets decrease income, whereas the adjustment for revaluation of fixed assets increases stockholders' equity?

References

Afterman, Allan B. *International Accounting, Financial Reporting, and Analysis.* New York: Warren, Gorham & Lamont, 1995, pp. C1-17, C1-22.

Brooks, Jermyn Paul, and Dietz Mertin. *Neues Deutsches Bilanzrecht.* Düsseldorf: IDW-Verlag, 1986.

Cochrane, James L.; James E. Shapiro; and Jean E. Tobin. "Foreign Equities and U.S. Investors: Breaking Down the Barriers Separating Supply and Demand." NYSE Working Paper, 95-04, 1995.

Collins, Stephen H. "The Move to Globalization," *Journal of Accountancy,* March 1989.

Doupnik, Timothy S., and Stephen B. Salter. "An Empirical Test of a Judgemental International Classification of Financial Reporting Practices." *Journal of International Business Studies,* First Quarter 1993, pp. 41–60.

Doupnik, Timothy S., and George T. Tsakumis. "A Review of Empirical Tests of Gray's Framework and Suggestions for Future Research." *Journal of Accounting Literature,* 2004, pp. 1–48.

Gernon, H., and Gary Meek. *Accounting: An International Perspective,* 5th ed. Burr Ridge, IL: Irwin/McGraw-Hill, 2001.

Gray, S. J. "Towards a Theory of Cultural Influence on the Development of Accounting Systems Internationally." *Abacus,* March 1988, pp. 1–15.

Hofstede, G. *Culture's Consequences: International Differences in Work-Related Values.* London: Sage, 1980.

———. *Culture's Consequences: Comparing Values, Behaviors, Institutions, and Organizations across Nations,* 2nd ed. Thousand Oaks, CA: Sage, 2001.

Malaysian Accounting Standards Board. MASB i-1, *"Presentation of Financial Statements of Islamic Financial Institutions,"* 2001.

Meek, Gary K., and Sharokh M. Saudagaran. "A Survey of Research on Financial Reporting in a Transnational Context." *Journal of Accounting Literature*, 1990, pp. 145–82.

Nobes, Christopher W. "A Judgemental International Classification of Financial Reporting Practices." *Journal of Business Finance and Accounting*, Spring 1983.

———. "Towards a General Model of the Reasons for International Differences in Financial Reporting." *Abacus* 34, no. 2 (1998), p. 166.

Radebaugh, Lee H., and Sidney J. Gray. *International Accounting and Multinational Enterprises*, 5th ed. New York: Wiley, 2002.

Rahman, Zubaidur M. "The Role of Accounting in the East Asian Financial Crisis: Lessons Learned?" *Transnational Corporations* 7, no. 3 (December 1998), pp. 1–52.

U.S. Department of Commerce. "U.S. International Transactions." *Survey of Current Business*, January 2005, pp. 45–76.

Violet, William J. 1983. "The Development of International Accounting Standards: An Anthropological Perspective." *International Journal of Accounting*, 1983, pp. 1–12.

Chapter **Three**

International Convergence of Financial Reporting

Learning Objectives

After reading this chapter, you should be able to

- Explain the meaning of convergence.
- Identify the arguments for and against international convergence of financial reporting standards.
- Discuss major harmonization efforts under the IASC.
- Explain the principles-based approach used by the IASB in setting accounting standards.
- Describe the proposed changes to the IASB's *Framework*.
- Discuss the IASB's Standards related to the first-time adoption of International Financial Reporting Standards (IFRS) and the presentation of financial statements.
- Describe the support for, and the use of, IFRS across countries.
- Examine the issues related to international convergence of financial reporting standards.
- Describe the progress made in regard to IASB/FASB convergence project.
- Explain the meaning of "Anglo-Saxon" accounting.

INTRODUCTION

In Chapter 2, we discussed worldwide diversity in accounting practices and some of the problems caused by such diversity. Sir Bryan Carsberg, former secretary-general of the International Accounting Standards Committee (IASC), explained how accounting diversity affects international capital markets:

> Imagine the case of an international business, with operations in many different countries. It is likely to be required to prepare accounts for its operations in each country, in compliance with the rules of that country. It will then have to convert those accounts to conform to the rules of the country in which the holding company is resident, for the preparation of group accounts. If the company has listings on stock exchanges outside its home country, these exchanges or their regulators

may require the accounts to be filed under some other basis. The extra cost could be enormous. Heavy costs also fall on investors in trying to compare the results of companies based in different countries and they may just be unable to make such comparisons. . . . But the biggest cost may be in limiting the effectiveness of the international capital markets. Cross border investment is likely to be inhibited.[1]

The accounting profession and standard setters have been under pressure from multinational companies, stock exchanges, securities regulators, and international lending institutions, such as the World Bank, and other international bodies such as G20, to reduce diversity and harmonize accounting standards and practices internationally. This chapter focuses on the activities of the International Accounting Standards Board (IASB), which replaced the IASC in 2001. The chapter also includes a discussion of the major harmonization efforts under the IASC. We identify the arguments for and against convergence, and discuss the adoption of International Financial Reporting Standards (IFRSs), including national efforts to converge with those standards.

CONVERGENCE AS THE BUZZ WORD IN INTERNATIONAL FINANCIAL REPORTING

The word *harmonization* appears to have had its day. It mean different things to different people. Some view harmonization as the same as standardization. However, whereas standardization implies the elimination of alternatives in accounting for economic transactions and other events, harmonization refers to the reduction of alternatives while retaining a high degree of flexibility in accounting practices. Harmonization allows different countries to have different standards as long as the standards do not conflict. For example, prior to 2005, within the European Union harmonization program, if appropriate disclosures were made, companies were permitted to use different measurement methods: German companies could use historical cost for valuing assets, while Dutch companies could use replacement costs without violating the harmonization requirements.

Harmonization is a process that takes place over time. Accounting harmonization can be considered in two ways, namely, harmonization of accounting regulations or standards (also known as formal or de jure harmonization), and harmonization of accounting practices (also known as material or de facto harmonization). Harmonization of accounting practices is the ultimate goal of international harmonization efforts. Harmonization of standards may not necessarily lead to harmonization of accounting practices adopted by companies. For example, a study in China in 2002 found that despite the Chinese government's efforts through legislation to ensure harmonization between Chinese GAAP and IASC GAAP, there was no evidence that such efforts eliminated or significantly reduced the differences that exist between earnings calculated under Chinese and IASC GAAP.[2] Other factors such as differences in the quality of audits, enforcement mechanisms, culture, legal requirements, and socioeconomic and political systems may

---

[1] Excerpt from Sir Bryan Carsberg, "Global Issues and Implementing Core International Accounting Standards: Where Lies IASC's Final Goal?" Remarks made at the 50th Anniversary Dinner, Japanese Institute of CPAs, Tokyo, October 23, 1998.

[2] S. Chen, Z. Sun, and Y. Wang, "Evidence from China on Whether Harmonized Accounting Standards Harmonize Accounting Practices," *Accounting Horizons* 16, no. 3 (2002), pp. 183–97.

lead to noncomparable accounting numbers despite similar accounting standards. An empirical study conducted in 1996 to assess the impact of the IASC's harmonization efforts, focusing on the accounting practices of major companies based in France, Germany, Japan, the United Kingdom, and the United States, concluded that the impact had been quite modest. The study considered 26 major accounting measurement issues and found that in 14 cases harmonization had increased, but in 12 cases harmonization had decreased.[3]

Convergence, like harmonization, is a process that takes place over a period of time. Unlike harmonization, however, convergence implies the adoption of one set of standards internationally. The IASB's main objective is to achieve international convergence with its standards. In other words, the efforts of the IASB are directed toward developing a high-quality set of standards for use internationally for financial reporting purposes (global standard setting). Convergence means reducing international differences in accounting standards by developing high-quality standards in partnership with national standard-setters. This process applies to all national regimes.[4]

MAJOR HARMONIZATION EFFORTS

Several international organizations were involved in harmonization efforts either regionally (such as the Association of South East Asian Nations) or worldwide (such as the United Nations). The two most important players in this effort were the European Union (regionally) and the International Accounting Standards Committee (globally). The International Organization of Securities Commissions and the International Federation of Accountants also have contributed to the harmonization efforts at the global level.

+ International Organization of Securities Commissions

Established in 1974, the International Organization of Securities Commissions (IOSCO) was initially limited to providing a *framework* in which securities regulatory agencies in the Americas could exchange information and providing advice and assistance to those agencies supervising emerging markets. In 1986, IOSCO opened its membership to regulatory agencies in other parts of the world, thus giving it the potential to become a truly international organization. Today, IOSCO is the leading organization for securities regulators around the world, with about 177 ordinary, associate, and affiliate members (including the U.S. Securities and Exchange Commission) from about 100 countries.

IOSCO aims, among other things, to ensure a better regulation of the markets on both the domestic and international levels. It provides assistance to ensure the integrity of the markets by a rigorous application of the standards and by effective enforcement.

As one of its objectives, IOSCO works to facilitate cross-border securities offerings and listings by multinational issuers. It has consistently advocated the adoption of a set of high-quality accounting standards for cross-border listings. For

---

[3] Emmanuel N. Emenyonu and Sidney J. Gray, "International Accounting Harmonization and the Major Developed Stock Market Countries: An Empirical Study," *International Journal of Accounting* 31, no. 3 (1996), pp. 269–79.

[4] G. Whittington, "The Adoption of International Accounting Standards in the European Union," *European Accounting Review,* 14, no.1 (2005), pp. 127–53.

example, a 1989 IOSCO report entitled "International Equity Offers" noted that cross-border offerings would be greatly facilitated by the development of internationally accepted accounting standards.[5] To this end, IOSCO supported the efforts of the International Accounting Standards Committee (IASC) in developing international accounting standards that foreign issuers could use in lieu of local accounting standards when entering capital markets outside of their home country. As one observer notes: "This could mean, for example, that if a French company had a simultaneous stock offering in the United States, Canada, and Japan, financial statements prepared in accordance with international standards could be used in all three nations."[6]

International Federation of Accountants

The International Federation of Accountants (IFAC) was established in October 1977 at the 11th World Congress of Accountants in Munich, with 63 founding members representing 51 countries. It is now a global organization of 158 member bodies and associates in 123 countries, representing over 2.5 million accountants employed in public practice, industry and commerce, government, and academia. Its mission is to serve the public interest and to strengthen the worldwide accountancy profession and contribute to the development of strong international economies by establishing and promoting adherence to high-quality professional standards on auditing, ethics, education, and training.

In June 1999, IFAC launched the International Forum on Accountancy Development (IFAD) in response to a criticism from the World Bank (following the Asian financial crisis) that the accounting profession was not doing enough to enhance the accounting capacity and capabilities in developing and emerging nations. IFAD's membership includes the international financial institutions (such as the World Bank, International Monetary Fund, and Asian Development Bank); other key international organizations (such as IOSCO, IASB, SEC); and the large accountancy firms.[7] The primary aim of this forum is to promote transparent financial reporting, duly audited to high standards by a strong accounting and auditing profession.

In May 2000, IFAC and the large international accounting firms established the Forum of Firms, also aimed at raising standards of financial reporting and auditing globally in order to protect the interests of cross-border investors and promote international flows of capital. The forum works alongside IFAD in achieving common objectives.

European Union

The European Union (EU) was founded in March 1957 with the signing of the Treaty of Rome by six European nations: Belgium, France, Germany, Italy, Luxembourg, and the Netherlands.[8] Between 1973 and 1995, nine other countries joined the common market (Denmark, Ireland, and the United Kingdom in 1973; Greece in 1981; Portugal and Spain in 1986; and Austria, Finland, and Sweden in January 1995), creating a 15-nation trading bloc. Another 10 new members (namely, Latvia, Estonia, Lithuania, Poland, Hungary, Czech Republic, Slovakia, Slovenia,

---

[5] This report is available from IOSCO's Web site, www.iosco.org.

[6] Stephen H. Collins, "The SEC on Full and Fair Disclosure," *Journal of Accountancy,* January 1989, p. 84.

[7] Details at www.ifad.org.

[8] The original European Economic Community (EEC) became the European Union (EU) on January 1, 1994.

and the Mediterranean islands of Cyprus and Malta) joined the EU in May 2004. Until this most recent expansion, all EU countries possessed similar traits in many respects. They all were wealthy industrial nations with similar political goals, comparable standards of living, high volumes of trade within the union, and good transportation links. The 2004 additions to EU membership are likely to change the dynamics of the group, especially considering that 8 of the 10 new entrants were members of the former Soviet bloc.

The European Commission is responsible for administering the EU. From the beginning, the EU's aim has been to create a unified business environment. Accordingly, the harmonization of company laws and taxation, the promotion of full freedom in the movement of goods and labor between member countries, and the creation of a community capital market have been high on its agenda. In July 2002, most EU members adopted a single currency, the euro, as envisaged in the Treaty of Maastricht signed in 1991.[9]

The EU attempted to harmonize financial reporting practices within the community by issuing directives that member nations had to incorporate into their laws. EU directives possess the force of law.[10] They were binding on EU members with respect to the results to be achieved, but the manner in which the desired results were achieved was left to the discretion of the individual countries.

Two directives aimed at harmonizing accounting: The Fourth Directive (issued in 1978) dealt with valuation rules, disclosure requirements, and the format of financial statements, and the Seventh Directive (issued in 1983) dealt with consolidated financial statements. The latter required companies to prepare consolidated financial statements and outlined the procedures for their preparation. It had a significant impact on European accounting, as consolidations were previously uncommon in Continental Europe.

The Fourth Directive included comprehensive accounting rules covering the content of annual financial statements, their methods of presentation, and measurement and disclosure of information for both public and private companies. It established the "true and fair view" principle, which required financial statements to provide a true and fair view of a company's assets and liabilities, and of its financial position and profit and loss for the benefit of shareholders and third parties.

The Fourth Directive provided considerable flexibility. Dozens of provisions beginning with the expression "Member states may require or permit companies to . . ." which allowed countries to choose from among acceptable alternatives. For example, under Dutch and British law, companies could write assets up to higher market values, whereas in Germany this was strictly forbidden. Both approaches were acceptable under the Fourth Directive. By allowing different options for a variety of accounting issues, the EU directives opened the door for noncomparability in financial statements. As an illustration of the effects of differing principles within the EU, the profits of one case study company were measured using the accounting principles of various member states. The results, presented in the following table, reveal the lack of comparability:[11]

[9] Several EU members—namely, Denmark, Sweden, and the United Kingdom—have not adopted the euro as their national currency.

[10] The EU has issued numerous directives covering a broad range of business issues, including directives related to accounting, auditing, taxation, e-commerce, and the prevention of money laundering.

[11] Anthony Carey, "Harmonization: Europe Moves Forward," *Accountancy*, March 1990.

Most Likely Profit—Case Study Company	
Country	**ECUs (millions)**
Spain	131
Germany	133
Belgium	135
Netherlands	140
France	149
Italy	174
United Kingdom	192

Profit measurement across EU countries differed in part because the directives failed to cover several important topics, including lease accounting, foreign currency translation, accounting changes, contingencies, income taxes, and long-term construction contracts.

Notwithstanding the flexibility afforded by the directives, their implementation into local law caused extensive change in accounting practice in several EU member countries. The following are some of the changes in German accounting practice brought about by the integration of the EU's Fourth and Seventh Directives into German law in 1985:

1. Required inclusion of notes to the financial statements.
2. Preparation of consolidated financial statements on a worldwide basis (i.e., foreign subsidiaries no longer could be excluded from consolidation).
3. Elimination of unrealized intercompany losses on consolidation.
4. Use of the equity method for investments in associated companies.
5. Disclosure of comparative figures in the balance sheet and income statement.
6. Disclosure of liabilities with a maturity of less than one year.
7. Accrual of deferred tax liabilities and pension obligations.[12]

Most of these "innovations" had been common practice in the United States for several decades.

Although the EU directives did not lead to complete comparability across member nations, they helped reduce differences in financial statements. In addition, the EU directives have served as a basic framework of accounting that has been adopted by other countries in search of an accounting model. With the economic reforms in Eastern Europe since 1989, several countries in that region found it necessary to abandon the Soviet-style accounting system previously used in favor of a Western, market-oriented system. For example, in the early 1990s, Hungary, Poland, and the Czech and Slovak Republics all passed new accounting laws primarily based on the EU directives in anticipation of securing EU membership. This is further evidence of the influence that economic ties among countries can have on accounting practice.

In 1990, the European Commission indicated that there would be no further EU directives related to accounting. Instead, the commission indicated in 1995 that it would associate the EU with efforts undertaken by the IASC toward a broader

---

[12] Timothy S. Doupnik, "Recent Innovations in German Accounting Practice Through the Integration of EC Directives," *Advances in International Accounting* 5 (1992), pp. 75–103.

international harmonization of accounting standards. In June 2000, the European Commission issued the following communication to the European Parliament:

- Before the end of 2000, the Commission will present a formal proposal requiring all listed EU companies to prepare their consolidated accounts in accordance with one single set of accounting standards, namely International Accounting Standards (IAS).
- This requirement will go into effect, at the latest, from 2005 onwards.
- Member states will be allowed to extend the application of IAS to unlisted companies and to individual accounts.[13]

+ THE INTERNATIONAL ACCOUNTING STANDARDS COMMITTEE

The International Accounting Standards Committee (IASC) was established in 1973 by an agreement of the leading professional accounting bodies in 10 countries (Australia, Canada, France, Germany, Ireland, Japan, Mexico, the Netherlands, the United Kingdom, and the United States) with the broad objective of formulating "international accounting standards." Prior to its dissolution, the IASC consisted of 156 professional accountancy bodies in 114 countries, representing more than 2 million accountants in public practice, education, government service, industry, and commerce. The IASC was funded by contributions from member bodies, multinational companies, financial institutions, accounting firms, and the sale of IASC publications.

The "Lowest-Common-Denominator" Approach

The IASC's harmonization efforts from 1973 to 2001 evolved in several different phases. In the initial phase, covering the first 15 years, the IASC's main activity was the issuance of 26 generic International Accounting Standards (IASs), many of which allowed multiple options. The IASC's approach to standard setting during this phase can be described as a lowest-common-denominator approach, as the standards reflected an effort to accommodate existing accounting practices in various countries. For example, International Accounting Standard (IAS) 11, *Construction Contracts,* as originally written in 1979, allowed companies to choose between the percentage of completion method and the completed contract method in accounting for long-term construction contracts, effectively sanctioning the two major methods used internationally. A study conducted by the IASB in 1988 found that all or most of the companies listed on the stock exchanges of the countries included in Nobes's classification presented in Chapter 2 of this book (except for Germany and Italy) were in compliance with the International Accounting Standards.[14] Given the lowest-common-denominator approach adopted by the IASC, it was obvious that IASC standards existing in 1988 introduced little if any comparability of financial statements across countries.

+The Comparability Project

Two significant activities took place from 1989 to 1993, which can be described as the IASC's second phase. The first was the 1989 publication of the *Framework for the Preparation and Presentation of Financial Statements* (hereafter referred to as

---

[13] Commission of the European Communities, "EU Financial Reporting Strategy: The Way Forward," Communication from the Commission to the Council and the European Parliament, June 13, 2000.

[14] International Accounting Standards Committee, *Survey of the Use and Application of International Accounting Standards 1988* (London: IASC, 1988).

the *Framework*), which set out the objectives of financial statements, the qualitative characteristics of financial information, definitions of the elements of financial statements, and the criteria for recognition of financial statement elements. The second activity was the Comparability of Financial Statements Project, the purpose of which was "to eliminate most of the choices of accounting treatment currently permitted under International Accounting Standards."[15] As a result of the Comparability Project, 10 revised International Accounting Standards were approved in 1993 and became effective in 1995. As an example of the changes brought about by the comparability project, IAS 11 was revised to require the use of the percentage of completion method when certain criteria are met, thereby removing the option to avoid the use of this method altogether.

+The IOSCO Agreement

The final phase in the work of the IASC began with the IOSCO agreement in 1993 and ended with the creation of the IASB in 2001. The main activity during this phase was the development of a core set of international standards that could be endorsed by IOSCO for cross-listing purposes. This period also was marked by the proposal to restructure the IASC and the proposal's final approval.

IOSCO became a member of the IASC's Consultative Group in 1987 and supported the IASC's Comparability Project. In 1993, IOSCO and the IASC agreed on a list of 30 core standards that the IASC needed to develop that could be used by companies involved in cross-border security offerings and listings. In 1995, the IASC and IOSCO agreed on a work program for the IASC to develop the set of core international standards, and IOSCO agreed to evaluate the standards for possible endorsement for cross-border purposes upon their completion.

With the publication of IAS 39, *Financial Instruments: Recognition and Measurement*, in December 1998, the IASC completed its work program to develop the set of 30 core standards. In May 2000, IOSCO's Technical Committee recommended that securities regulators permit foreign issuers to use the core IASC standards to gain access to a country's capital market as an alternative to using local standards. The Technical Committee consisted of securities regulators representing the 14 largest and most developed capital markets, including Australia, France, Germany, Japan, the United Kingdom, and the United States. IOSCO's endorsement of IASC standards was an important step in the harmonization process.[16]

U.S. Reaction to International Accounting Standards

Of the 14 countries represented on IOSCO's Technical Committee, only Canada and the United States did not allow foreign companies to use International Accounting Standards (IASs) without reconciliation to local GAAP for listing purposes.[17] In 1996, the U.S. Securities and Exchange Commission (SEC) announced three criteria IASs would have to meet to be acceptable for cross-listing purposes. Namely, IASs would have to

---

[15] International Accounting Standards Committee, *International Accounting Standards 1990* (London: IASC, 1990), p. 13.

[16] IOSCO, *Final Communique of the XXIXth Annual Conference of the International Organization of Securities Commissions,* Amman, May 17–20, 2004.

[17] The SEC allows foreign companies listed on U.S. stock exchanges to file annual reports based on IAS but only if a reconciliation from IAS to U.S. GAAP for income and stockholders' equity is included in the notes to the financial statements. Many foreign companies find this reconciliation to be very costly and view this requirement as a significant barrier to entering the U.S. capital market.

- Constitute a comprehensive, generally accepted basis of accounting.
- Be of high quality, resulting in comparability and transparency, and providing for full disclosure.
- Be rigorously interpreted and applied.

Partly in response to the third criterion, the IASC created a Standing Interpretations Committee (SIC) to provide guidance on accounting issues where there is likely to be divergent or unacceptable treatment in the absence of specific guidance in an International Accounting Standard.

The SEC began its assessment of the IASC's core set of standards in 1999 and issued a concept release in 2000 soliciting comments on whether it should modify its requirement that all financial statements be reconciled to U.S. GAAP.

The FASB conducted a comparison of IASC standards and U.S. GAAP in 1996, identifying 218 items covered by both sets of standards.[18] The following table lists the degree of similarity across these items:

	Number	Percent
Similar approach and guidance	56	26%
Similar approach but different guidance	79	36
Different approach	56	26
Alternative approaches permitted	27	12
	218	100%

Although it was widely assumed that U.S. GAAP and IASs were generally consistent, the FASB's comparison showed that differences existed for 74 percent of the accounting items covered by both sets of standards.

Compliance with International Accounting Standards

Several studies investigated the extent of compliance by those firms that claimed to follow International Accounting Standards.[19] These studies found various levels of noncompliance with IAS.[20] Former IASC Secretary-General David Cairns referred to the use of IAS with exceptions as "IAS-lite."[21] In response to the use of "IAS-lite," IAS 1 was revised in 1997 to preclude a firm from claiming to be in compliance with IAS unless it complies with all requirements (including disclosure requirements) of each standard and each applicable Interpretation. A number of firms that previously disclosed in the annual

[18] Financial Accounting Standards Board, *The IASC-U.S. Comparison Project: A Report on the Similarities and Differences between IASC Standards and U.S. GAAP,* ed. Carrie Bloomer (Norwalk, CT: FASB, 1996).

[19] See, for example, Donna L. Street, Sidney J. Gray, and Stephanie M. Bryant, "Acceptance and Observance of International Accounting Standards: An Empirical Study of Companies Claiming to Comply with IASs," *The International Journal of Accounting,* 34, no. 1 (1999), pp. 11–48; and David Cairns, *Financial Times International Accounting Standards Survey* (London: FT Finance, 1999).

[20] Apparently concerned with the lack of full compliance with IFRS, one of the SEC's major requirements to allow foreign registrants to use IFRS without reconciliation to U.S. GAAP is the existence of "an infrastructure that ensures that the standards are rigorously interpreted and applied," SEC Concept Release: International Accounting Standards (2000).

[21] David Cairns, "IAS Lite Is Alive and Well," *Accountancy,* May 2001. Cairns identifies three types of IAS lite: (1) disclosed IAS lite, where companies disclose exceptions from full IAS compliance; (2) implied IAS lite, where companies refer to the use of rather than compliance with IAS; and (3) undisclosed IAS lite, where companies claim to comply with IAS but fail to comply fully with it.

report their use of IAS "with exceptions" discontinued this disclosure subsequent to this revision to IAS 1.

In its accounting policies note to its 1998 financial statements, the French firm Thomson-CSF stated:

> In a February 1998 recommendation, the C.O.B. (the French Securities Regulator) observed that for operating periods starting as from July 1, 1998, a company could no longer state that it complied with the International Accounting Standards Committee (I.A.S.C.) reference system, if it did not apply all I.A.S.C. standards currently in force. Consequently, as from the 1998 operating period, the consolidated financial statements of Thomson-CSF, prepared in accordance with accounting principles applicable in France, as also the provisions of the 7th European Directive, no longer refer to the I.A.S.C. standards. (p. 82)

Prior to 1998, Thomson-CSF claimed to follow IAS when it apparently did not. From the excerpt above, it appears that Thomson-CSF elected not to fully comply with IAS and in 1998 no longer claimed to do so as required by the French Securities Regulator. Because the IASC itself did not have the power to enforce it, IAS 1 had to be enforced by national securities regulators and auditors.

CREATION OF THE IASB

The IASC faced problems of legitimacy with regard to constituent support, independence, and technical expertise. For example, some interested parties perceived the fact that IASC board members worked at international standard setting only part-time and were not necessarily selected because of their technical expertise as an indication of the lack of commitment on the part of the IASC to develop the highest quality standards possible. Responding to these concerns, the IASC appointed a Strategy Working Party in 1996, which issued a discussion document in December 1998 entitled "Shaping IASC for the Future." This document proposed a vastly different structure and process for the development of international accounting standards.

The final recommendations of the IASC Strategy Working Party were approved at its Venice meeting in November 1999. These recommendations, designed to deal with the issue of legitimacy, attempted to balance calls for a structure based on geographic representativeness and those based on technical competence and independence. Accordingly, it was decided that representativeness would be provided by the geographic distribution of the trustees, who would be essential to ensuring the effectiveness and independence of the board, but that board members would be selected based on their expertise.

✦On April 1, 2001, the newly created International Accounting Standards Board (IASB) took over from the IASC as the creator of international accounting standards, which were to be called International Financial Reporting Standards (IFRS). The process of restructuring the IASC into the IASB took over five years and is summarized in Exhibit 3.1. The formation of the IASB in 2001, with a change in focus from harmonization to convergence or global standard setting, marked the beginning of a new era in international financial reporting.

The Structure of the IASB

The IASB is organized under an independent foundation called the IFRS Foundation. Components of the structure are as follows (Exhibit 3.2) (the titles of some of the components are as changed in March 31, 2010):

1. International Accounting Standards Board (IASB).
2. IFRS Foundation (IFRSF).
3. Monitoring Board.
4. IFRS Interpretations Committee (IFRSIC).
5. IFRS Advisory Council (IFRSAC).
6. Working Groups (expert task forces for individual agenda projects).

+ **EXHIBIT 3.1**
**The Process of
Restructuring the
IASC into the IASB**

Date	Activity
September 1996	IASC board approves formation of a Strategy Working Party (SWP) to consider what IASC's strategy and structure should be when it completes the Core Standards work program.
December 1998	SWP publishes a discussion paper, "Shaping IASC for the Future," and invites comments.
April to October 1999	SWP holds various meetings to discuss the comments on their initial proposal and to develop final recommendations.
December 1999	SWP issues final report, *Recommendations on Shaping IASC for the Future.* IASC board passes a resolution supporting the report and appoints a nominating committee for the initial trustees.
January 2000	Nominating committee elects SEC chairman Arthur Levitt as its chair and invites nominations from public.
March 2000	IASC board approves a new constitution reflecting the SWP proposals.
May 2000	Nominating committee announces initial trustees.
May 2000	IASC member bodies approve the restructuring and the new IASC constitution.
June 2000	Trustees appoint Sir David Tweedie as the first chairman of new IASC board.
July 1, 2000	New IASC constitution takes effect.
Starting in July 2000	Trustees invite nominations for membership on the new IASC board, narrow the list to approximately 45 finalists, and conduct interviews in London, New York, and Tokyo.
January 2001	Trustees invite nominations for membership on the new advisory council.
January 2001	Members of the IASB announced.
March 2001	IASC trustees activate Part B of IASC's constitution and establish a nonprofit Delaware corporation, named the International Accounting Standards Committee Foundation, to oversee the International Accounting Standards Board.
April 2001	On April 1, 2001, the new IASB takes over from the IASC the responsibility for setting International Accounting Standards.

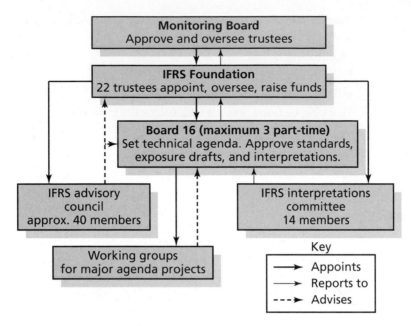

+EXHIBIT 3.2
The Structure of the IASB

Monitoring Board

The IASC Foundation Constitution was amended in February 2009 to create a Monitoring Board of public authorities. The Monitoring Board comprises the relevant leaders of the European Commission, the Japanese Financial Services Agency, the U.S. Securities and Exchange Commission, the Emerging Markets Committee of IOSCO, and the Technical Committee of IOSCO. The chairman of the Basel Committee on Banking Supervision is a nonvoting observer. The Monitoring Board oversees the IFRS Foundation Trustees, participates in the Trustee nomination process, and approves appointments to the Trustees. The specific functions of the Monitoring Board include the following:

- To enhance public accountability of the IASC Foundation.
- To participates in the Trustee nomination process and approval of appointments to the Trustees.
- To carry out oversight responsibilities in relation to the Trustees and their oversight of the IASB's activities, in particular the agenda-setting process and the IASB's efforts to improve the accuracy and effectiveness of financial reporting and to protect investors.

Trustees of the IFRS Foundation

The IFRS Foundation consists of 22 Trustees (the number of trustees was increased from 19 to 22 as a result of revisions to the IFRS Foundation in June 2005). These 22 Trustees represent different geographical areas (six from North America; six from Europe; six from the Asia/Oceania region; four from any area, subject to establishing overall geographical balance). With regard to the composition of the Trustees, the constitution requires an appropriate balance of professional backgrounds, including auditors, preparers, users, academics, and other officials serving the public interest. Two Trustees will normally be senior partners of prominent international accounting firms. The Trustees of the IFRS Foundation have responsibility, among other things, to:

- Appoint the members of the IASB and establish their contracts of service and performance criteria.
- Appoint the members of the International Financial Reporting Interpretations Committee and the IFRS Advisory Council.
- Review annually the strategy of the IASC Foundation and the IASB and its effectiveness, including consideration, but not determination, of the IASB's agenda.
- Approve annually the budget of the IFRS Foundation and determine the basis for funding.
- Review broad strategic issues affecting accounting standards, promote the IASC Foundation and its work, and promote the objective of rigorous application of International Accounting Standards and International Financial Reporting Standards—provided that the Trustees shall be excluded from involvement in technical matters relating to accounting standards.
- Establish and amend operating procedures, consultative arrangements, and due process for the IASB, the International Financial Reporting Interpretations Committee, and the Standards Advisory Council.
- Review compliance with the operating procedures, consultative arrangements, and due process procedures.
- Approve amendments to the constitution after following a due process, including consultation with the IFRS Advisory Council and publication of an Exposure Draft for public comment and subject to the voting requirements.
- Exercise all powers of the IFRS Foundation, except for those expressly reserved to the IASB, the IFRS Interpretations Committee, and the IFRS Advisory Council.
- Foster and review the development of educational program and materials that are consistent with the IFRS Foundation's objectives.

International Accounting Standards Board

The IASB has sole responsibility for establishing International Financial Reporting Standards (IFRS).

The principal responsibilities of the IASB are to:

- Develop and issue International Financial Reporting Standards and Exposure Drafts.
- Approve Interpretations developed by the International Financial Reporting Interpretations Committee (IFRIC).

The Board consists of 16 members (effective February 1, 2009), of whom at least 13 serve full-time and not more than 3 part-time.

The Board members are selected on the basis of professional competence and practical experience. They are expected to represent a geographical mix (effective February 2009), and to ensure a broad international diversity, by July 2012 there will normally be:

- Four members from the Asia/Oceania region.
- Four members from Europe.
- Four members from North America.
- One member from Africa.
- One member from South America.
- Two members appointed from any area, subject to maintaining overall geographical balance.

Due process procedures followed by the IASB include the following (the steps that are required by the IASC Foundation constitution are indicated by an asterisk*):

1. Ask the staff to identify and review the issues associated with the topic and to consider the application of the *Framework* to the issues.
2. Study national accounting requirements and practice and exchange views about the issues with national standard-setters.
3. Consult the Standards Advisory Council about the advisability of adding the topic to the IASB's agenda.*
4. Form an advisory group (generally called a "working group") to advise the IASB and its staff on the project.
5. Publish for public comment a discussion document.
6. Publish for public comment an exposure draft approved by vote of at least nine IASB members, including any dissenting opinions held by IASB members (in Exposure Drafts, dissenting opinions are referred to as "alternative views").*
7. Publish within an Exposure Draft a basis for conclusions.
8. Consider all comments received within the comment period on discussion documents and exposure drafts.*
9. Consider the desirability of holding a public hearing and the desirability of conducting field tests and, if considered desirable, holding such hearings and conducting such tests.
10. Approve a standard by the votes of at least nine IASB members and include in the published standard any dissenting opinions.*
11. Publish within a standard a basis for conclusions, explaining, among other things, the steps in the IASB's due process and how the IASB dealt with public comments on the exposure draft.

In March 2006, the Trustees of the IFRS Foundation published a new *Due Process Handbook* for the IASB. The *Handbook* describes the IASB's consultative procedures.

IFRS Advisory Council

The IFRS Advisory Council provides a forum for participation by organizations and individuals, with an interest in international financial reporting, having diverse geographical and functional backgrounds, with the objective of:

- Advising the IASB on agenda decisions and priorities in the IASB's work.
- Informing the IASB of the views of the organizations and individuals on the Council on major standard-setting projects.
- Giving other advice to the IASB or the Trustees.

The Advisory Council currently has about 40 members. The requirement is to have at least 30 members. Members are appointed by the Trustees for a renewable term of three years. They have diverse geographic and functional backgrounds.

IFRS Interpretations Committee

The IFRS Interpretations Committee (initially this committee was known as the Standing Interpretations Committee, and later changed to the International Financial Reporting Interpretations Committee) has 14 members appointed by the Trustees for terms of three years (in November 2007, the membership was increased from 12 to 14).

The Committee's Responsibilities include the following:

- To interpret the application of International Financial Reporting Standards (IFRSs) and provide timely guidance on financial reporting issues not specifically addressed in IFRSs or IASs, in the context of the IASB's framework, and undertake other tasks at the request of the Board.
- To publish Draft Interpretations for public comment and consider comments made within a reasonable period before finalizing an Interpretation.
- To report to the Board and obtain Board approval for final Interpretations.

IFRS Foundation Constitution

In January 2009, the Trustees voted to revise the constitution for changes resulting from the first phase of the review, including formation of the Monitoring Board. In January 2010, the Trustees again voted to revise the constitution for changes resulting from the second phase of the review, including name changes from IASC Foundation to IFRS Foundation, from International Financial Reporting Interpretations Committee to IFRS Interpretations Committee, and from Standards Advisory Council to IFRS Advisory Council.

Review of the IASC Foundation's Constitution

The IASC Foundation's constitution states that the trustees should undertake:

> [A] review of the entire structure of the IASC Foundation and its effectiveness, such review to include consideration of changing the geographical distribution of Trustees in response to changing global economic conditions, and publishing the proposals of that review for public comment, the review commencing three years after the coming into force of this Constitution, with the objective of implementing any agreed changes five years after the coming into force of this Constitution (6 February 2006, five years after the date of the incorporation of the IASC Foundation [Section 18 (b)]).

Consistent with Section 18 of the constitution, the IASC Foundation's Constitution Committee initiated in May 2004 a broad review of the constitution and identified 10 issues for consideration. These issues are based on the concerns expressed by important constituencies through various processes of consultation. They are as follows:

1. Whether the objectives of the IASC Foundation should expressly refer to the challenges facing small and medium-sized entities (SMEs). (*Concern:* The language of the constitution does not adequately address the position of SMEs and emerging economies.)
2. Number of trustees and their geographical and professional distribution. (*Concern:* Certain regions are overrepresented, while the Asia-Oceania region as well as emerging economies are underrepresented.)
3. The oversight role of the trustees. (*Concern:* Trustees should demonstrate more clearly how they are fulfilling the oversight function.)
4. Funding of the IASC Foundation. (*Concern:* The funding structure of the IASC Foundation needs to be examined.)
5. The composition of the IASB. (*Concern:* The geographic backgrounds of the IASB members need to be examined.)

6. The appropriateness of the IASB's existing formal liaison relationships. (*Concern:* More guidance is needed in the constitution regarding the role that liaison relationships play.)

7. Consultation arrangements of the IASB. (*Concern:* Consultative arrangements need to be improved.)

8. Voting procedures of the IASB. (*Concern:* For approval of a standard, the current "simple majority" approach should be replaced with a "super majority" approach.)

9. Resources and effectiveness of the International Financial Reporting Interpretations Committee (IFRIC). (*Concern:* given the likely increase in demand for IFRIC interpretations, the current arrangements are inadequate.)

10. The composition, role, and effectiveness of the SAC. (*Concern:* steps should be taken to make better use of the SAC.)

A recent proposal published by the Trustees of the IASC Foundation builds on governance enhancements implemented as a result of the first Constitution Review, completed in 2005 (these reviews will take place every five years). They published a report on the changes to the Foundation's constitution made as a result of the second part of their 2008–2010 constitution review. They have launched a program to enhance investors' participation in the development of IFRS. One of the proposals could see the IASB become the IFRS Board (or IFRSB) in the future.

THE IASB FRAMEWORK

+The Need for a Framework

With no conceptual framework, accounting standards would be developed unsystematically. As a result, accounting standards may be inconsistent and, according to *Gresham's law*[22] bad accounting practices will triumph over good practices. In this situation a principle or practice would be declared to be "right" because it was generally accepted, but it would not be generally accepted because it was "right." Further, it is unwise to develop standards unless there is agreement on the scope and objective of financial reporting, the type of entities that should produce financial reports, recognition, and measurement rules, and qualitative characteristics of financial information. Furthermore, by adding rigor and discipline, a conceptual framework enhances public confidence in financial reports, and preparers and auditors can use the conceptual framework as a point of reference to resolve an accounting issue in the absence of a standard that specifically deals with that issue.

The *Framework for the Preparation and Presentation of Financial Statements* was first approved by the IASC board in 1989 and was reaffirmed by the newly formed IASB in 2001. The objective of the *Framework* is to establish the concepts underlying the preparation and presentation of IFRS-based financial statements. It deals with the following:

---

[22] Gresham's Law is named after Sir Thomas Gresham (1519–1579), an English financier in Tudor times. It means, briefly, "Bad money drives out good."

1. Objective of financial statements and underlying assumptions.
2. Qualitative characteristics that affect the usefulness of financial statements.
3. Definition, recognition, and measurement of the financial statements elements.
4. Concepts of capital and capital maintenance.

Among other things, the purpose of the *Framework* is to assist the IASB in developing future standards and revising existing standards. It also is intended to assist preparers of financial statements in applying IFRS and in dealing with topics that have not yet been addressed in IFRS. The *Framework* identifies investors, creditors, employees, suppliers, customers, government agencies, and the general public as potential users of financial statements but concludes that financial statements that are designed to meet the needs of investors will also meet most of the information needs of other users. This is an important conclusion because it sets the tone for the nature of individual IFRS, that is, that their application will result in a set of financial statements that is useful for making investment decisions.

Objective of Financial Statements and Underlying Assumptions

The *Framework* establishes that the primary objective of IFRS-based financial statements is to *provide information useful for decision making.* Financial statements also show the results of management's stewardship of enterprise resources, but that is not their primary objective. To meet the objective of decision usefulness, financial statements must be prepared on an *accrual basis.* The other underlying assumption is that the enterprise for which financial statements are being prepared is a *going concern.*

Qualitative Characteristics of Financial Statements

The four characteristics that make financial statement information useful are *understandability, relevance, reliability,* and *comparability.* Information is relevant if it can be used to make predictions of the future or if it can be used to confirm expectations from the past. The *Framework* indicates that the relevance of information is affected by its nature and its materiality. An item of information is material if its misstatement or omission could influence the decision of a user of financial statements.

Information is reliable when it is neutral (i.e., free of bias) and represents faithfully what it purports to. The *Framework* specifically states that reflecting items in the financial statements based on their economic substance rather than their legal form is necessary for faithful representation. The *Framework* also states that while the exercise of prudence (conservatism) in measuring accounting elements is necessary, it does not allow the creation of hidden reserves or excessive provisions to deliberately understate income, as this would be biased and therefore would not have the quality of reliability.

+ Elements of Financial Statements: Definition, Recognition, and Measurement

Assets are defined as resources controlled by the enterprise from which future economic benefits are expected to flow to the enterprise. Note that a resource need not be owned to be an asset of an enterprise. This allows, for example, for leased resources to be treated as assets. An *asset should be recognized only when it is probable that future economic benefits will flow to the enterprise and the asset has a cost or value that can be measured reliably.* The *Framework* acknowledges that several different measurement bases may be used to measure assets including historical cost, current cost, realizable value, and present value.

+ *Liabilities* are present obligations arising from past events that are expected to be settled through an outflow of resources. Obligations need not be contractual to be treated as a liability. Similar to assets, *liabilities should be recognized when it is probable that an outflow of resources will be required to settle them and the amount can be measured reliably.* Also as with assets, several different bases exist for measuring liabilities including the amount of proceeds received in exchange for the obligation, the amount that would be required to settle the obligation currently, undiscounted settlement value in the normal course of business, and the present value of future cash outflows expected to settle the liabilities.

The *Framework* identifies income and expenses as the two elements that constitute profit. *Income,* which encompasses both revenues and gains, is defined as increases in equity, other than from transactions with owners. *Expenses,* including losses, are decreases in equity, other than through distributions to owners. *Equity* is defined as assets minus liabilities. Income should be recognized when the increase in an asset or decrease in a liability can be measured reliably. The *Framework* does not provide more specific guidance with respect to income recognition. (This topic is covered in IAS 18, *Revenue.*) Expenses are recognized when the related decrease in assets or increase in liabilities can be measured reliably. The *Framework* acknowledges the use of the matching principle in recognizing liabilities but specifically precludes use of the matching principle to recognize expenses and a related liability when it does not meet the definition of a liability. For example, it is inappropriate to recognize an expense if a present obligation arising from a past event does not exist.

Concepts of Capital Maintenance

The *Framework* describes different concepts of capital maintenance (financial capital maintenance versus physical capital maintenance) and acknowledges that each leads to a different basis for measuring assets (historical cost versus current cost). The *Framework* does not prescribe one measurement basis (and related model of accounting) over another, but indicates that it (the *Framework*) is applicable to a range of accounting models.

The IASB *Framework* is similar in content and direction to the FASB's *Conceptual Framework* embodied in *Statements of Financial Accounting Concepts 1, 2, 5,* and *6.* However, the IASB *Framework* is considerably less detailed.

Revision of the Conceptual Framework

The IASB and FASB have agreed to work together to produce a conceptual framework that will be built upon the IASB's and FASB's existing frameworks and will provide a basis for developing future accounting standards by the boards. The boards have agreed to the following phases of this project:

A. Objectives and qualitative characteristics
B. Elements and recognition
C. Measurement
D. Reporting entity
E. Presentation and disclosure
F. Purpose and status
G. Application to not-for-profit entities
H. Finalization

The two boards jointly published a discussion paper, *Preliminary Views on an Improved Conceptual Framework for Financial Reporting: The Objective of Financial Reporting and Qualitative Characteristics of Decision-useful Financial Reporting Information.*[23] As part of this project, the IASB has consulted views from interested parties with the aim of converging international and U.S. accounting standards. In response, the Institute of Chartered Accountants in Scotland pointed out that the term "fair value" is used in different ways in the two sets of standards, and suggested that the IASB develop its own higher-level guidance that could be relevant to the U.S. context. They state, "The problem is that U.S. GAAP requires fair values in much more limited circumstances than IFRS, especially for financial instruments, for some of which there are efficient markets. For other types of assets and liabilities, such as stock or a straightforward loan, applying this guidance would result in numbers that bear little resemblance to economic reality."

The preceding discussion paper sets out a draft of the first chapter of their proposed improved "conceptual framework," and includes several changes. First, it proposes a decision-useful objective and argues that information relevant to assessing stewardship will be encompassed in that objective. However, it is important to note that stewardship and decision usefulness are parallel objectives with different emphases. It can be argued that they should be defined as separate objectives. For example, there is strong support in Europe for stewardship as a core objective of financial reporting. The European Financial Reporting Advisory Group (EFRAG), the Accounting Standards Board (ASB), and a number of other European accounting standard-setters have published a brief paper discussing the rationale for including stewardship or directors' accountability to shareholders, as a separate objective of financial reporting.

Second, taking a stakeholder approach, the users of financial reports, other than capital providers, would be explicitly acknowledged in the proposed objective of financial reporting. This reflects an amendment to the current U.S. "conceptual framework," which takes a shareholder approach. Third, the IASB and the FASB have tentatively decided that an asset of an entity would be "a present economic resource to which, through an enforceable right or other means, the entity has access or can limit the access of others." Fourth, emphasis would be placed on developing principles and measurement guidance for *fair value* measurements in IFRS. In particular, the IASB plan to assess whether an "exit price" was the measurement basis intended by each standard, and when an exit price was not the measurement basis intended, whether additional guidance should be developed.

The question of whether financial reporting should be based on "decision usefulness" or it should also recognize *stewardship* as a separate objective is not new, but it has come to the fore again as a result of the publication of this discussion paper by the IASB and the FASB.

In regard to the use of "fair values" in financial statements, in November 2006, the IASB published for public comment a discussion paper on fair value measurement in financial reports. In February 2007, the FASB issued a standard,

---

[23] This "preliminary views" document deals only with financial reporting by business entities in the private sector. It does not consider issues that arise in connection with not-for-profit entities (such as charities) or entities in the public sector.

SFAS No.159, *The Fair Value Option for Financial Assets and Financial Liabilities,* which provides companies with an option to report selected financial assets and liabilities at fair value. SFAS-159 establishes a single definition of fair value together with a framework for measuring fair value for financial reports in accordance with U.S. GAAP. The standard requires companies to provide additional information that will help investors and other users of financial statements to more easily understand the effect of the company's choice to use fair value on its earnings. It also requires entities to display the fair value of those assets and liabilities for which the company has chosen to use fair value on the face of the balance sheet.[24]

IFRS require some assets, liabilities, and equity instruments to be measured at fair value. However, the current guidance on fair value measurement is inconsistent, incomplete, and scattered. The IASB has published its proposed changes to the accounting for financial liabilities. These proposed changes follow work completed on the classification and measurement of financial assets (IFRS 9, *Financial Instruments*). They involve limited changes to the accounting for liabilities, with changes to the fair value option. The proposals respond to the view that volatility in profit or loss resulting from changes in the credit risk of liabilities that an entity chooses to measure at fair value is counter-intuitive and does not provide useful information to investors.

It is clear that the revised conceptual framework will include elements of both the IASB and FASB frameworks. For example, the IASB/FASB joint project on revenue recognition has as its objective the development of a single comprehensive set of principles for revenue recognition that is based on assets and liabilities. Under the asset and liability approach revenue would be recognized based on changes in contract assets and liabilities, as opposed to the performance of obligations.

In a joint statement issued by the FASB and IASB in November 2009, the two boards affirmed June 2011 as the target date for completing the major projects in the 2006 Memorandum of Understanding (MoU), as updated in May 2008 through a Discussion Paper, "Preliminary Views on an Improved Conceptual Framework for Financial Reporting: The Reporting Entity." Accordingly, the two boards issued an Exposure Draft in March 2010, "Conceptual Framework for Financial Reporting—The Reporting Entity" (Exposure Draft ED/2010/2), with a view to bringing about significant improvement and convergence between IFRS and U.S. GAAP. Many aspects of IASB's and FASB's CFs conceptual frameworks are consistent with each other. For example, neither the IASB's *Framework for the Preparation and Presentation of Financial Statements* nor FASB Concepts Statements override authoritative standards, even though some may be inconsistent with them.

The boards focused mainly on the improvement and convergence of their existing frameworks, and they initially considered concepts applicable to business entities in the private sector. In this phase of the conceptual framework project, the boards are considering conceptual matters relating to the reporting entity. The conceptual matters considered by other phases include the

---

[24] This statement is effective as of the beginning of an entity's first fiscal year beginning after November 15, 2007.

objective of financial reporting and the qualitative characteristics of financial reporting information, the elements of financial statements, and measurement. Matters of presentation and disclosure, and the applicability of the concepts in earlier phases to other types of entities, are expected to be considered in later phases.

The IASB's *Framework* defines the reporting entity as "an entity for which there are users who rely on the financial statements as their major source of financial information about the entity." The FASB's *Statement of Financial Accounting Concepts* does not contain a definition of a reporting entity or a discussion of how to identify one. The Exposure Draft jointly issued by the IASB and FASB defines a reporting entity as "a circumscribed area of economic activities whose financial information has the potential to be useful to existing and potential equity investors, lenders, and other creditors who cannot directly obtain the information they need in making decisions about providing resources to the entity and in assessing whether the management and the governing board of that entity have made efficient and effective use of the resources provided."

This concept of reporting entity is intended to further the objective of financial reporting, which is to provide financial information about the reporting entity that is useful in making decisions about providing resources to the entity and in assessing whether the management and the governing board of that entity have made efficient and effective use of the resources provided.

INTERNATIONAL FINANCIAL REPORTING STANDARDS

As of August 2010, 41 International Accounting Standards (IAS) and 9 International Financial Reporting Standards (IFRS) had been issued (see Exhibit 3.3). Several IASs have been revised one or more times since original issuance. For example, IAS 21, *The Effects of Changes in Foreign Exchange Rates*, was originally issued in 1983 and then revised as part of the comparability project in 1993. This standard was again updated in 2003 as part of the improvements project undertaken by the IASB that resulted in revisions to 13 IASs. A minor amendment to the standard was issued in 2005, and it was amended again in 2007 as a result of the revision to IAS 1 that resulted in amendments to 23 IASs. Other IASs have been withdrawn or replaced by later standards. Of 41 IASs issued by the IASC, only 30 were still in force as of March 2008. The first IFRS was issued by the IASB in 2003, providing guidance on the important question of how a company goes about restating its financial statements when it adopts IFRS for the first time.

As Exhibit 3.3 shows, IFRS constitutes a comprehensive system of financial reporting addressing accounting concerns ranging from accounting for income taxes to the recognition and measurement of financial instruments to the preparation of consolidated financial statements. Because the IASB is a private body, it does not have the ability to enforce its standards. Instead, the IASB develops IFRS for the public good, making them available to any country or company that might choose to adopt them.

EXHIBIT 3.3 International Financial Reporting Standards (IFRS) as of August 2010

Title	Issued (Revised)	Effective Date
Framework for the Preparation and Presentation of Financial Statements[a]	1989	
IAS 1 — *Presentation of Financial Statements*[a]	1975 (1997, 2003, 2007)	Jan. 1, 2009
IAS 2 — *Inventories*[b]	1975 (1993, 2003)	Jan. 1, 2005
IAS 7 — *Cash Flow Statements*[b]	1977 (1992, 2007)	Jan. 1, 2009
IAS 8 — *Accounting Policies, Changes in Accounting Estimates and Errors*[b]	1978 (1993, 2003, 2007)	Jan. 1, 2009
IAS 10 — *Events After the Balance Sheet Date*[b]	1978 (1999, 2003, 2007)	Jan. 1, 2009
IAS 11 — *Construction Contracts*	1979 (1993, 2007)	Jan. 1, 2009
IAS 12 — *Accounting for Taxes on Income*[b]	1979 (1997, 2000, 2007)	Jan. 1, 2009
IAS 16 — *Property, Plant and Equipment*[b]	1982 (1993, 1998, 2003, 2007)	Jan. 1, 2009
IAS 17 — *Leases*[b]	1982 (1997, 2003)	Jan. 1, 2005
IAS 18 — *Revenue*[b]	1982 (1993)	Jan. 1, 1995
IAS 19 — *Employee Benefits*[b]	1983 (1997, 2000, 2007)	Jan. 1, 2009
IAS 20 — *Accounting for Government Grants and Disclosure of Government Assistance*	1983 (2007)	Jan. 1, 2009
IAS 21 — *The Effects of Changes in Foreign Exchange Rates*[c]	1983 (1993, 2003, 2007)	Jan. 1, 2009
IAS 23 — *Borrowing Costs*[b]	1984 (1993)	Jan. 1, 1995
IAS 24 — *Related Party Disclosures*[b]	1984 (2003, 2007)	Jan. 1, 2009
IAS 26 — *Accounting and Reporting by Retirement Benefit Plans*	1987	Jan. 1, 1988
IAS 27 — *Consolidated Financial Statements and Accounting for Investments in Subsidiaries*[d]	1989 (2003, 2007)	Jan. 1, 2009
IAS 28 — *Accounting for Investments in Associates*[d]	1989 (1998, 2003, 2007)	Jan. 1, 2009
IAS 29 — *Financial Reporting in Hyperinflationary Economies*[d]	1989 (2007)	Jan. 1, 2009
IAS 31 — *Financial Reporting of Interests in Joint Ventures*[d]	1990 (1998, 2003)	Jan. 1, 2005
IAS 32 — *Financial Instruments: Disclosure and Presentation*[b]	1995 (2003, 2007)	Jan. 1, 2009
IAS 33 — *Earnings per Share*[b]	1997 (2003, 2007)	Jan. 1, 2009
IAS 34 — *Interim Financial Reporting*[b]	1998 (2007)	Jan. 1, 2009
IAS 38 — *Intangible Assets*[b]	1998 (2004, 2007)	April 1, 2009
IAS 39 — *Financial Instruments: Recognition and Measurement*[b]	1998 (2000, 2003, 2004, 2007)	Jan. 1, 2009

IAS 40	Investment Property[b]	2000 (2003, 2004, 2007)	Jan. 1, 2009
IAS 41	Agriculture	2001 (2007)	Jan. 1, 2009
IFRS 1	First-time Adoption of International Financial Reporting Standards[a]	2003 (2007)	Jan. 1, 2009
IFRS 2	Share-based Payment[b]	2004	Jan. 1, 2005
IFRS 3	Business Combinations[d]	2004	March 31, 2004
IFRS 4	Insurance Contracts	2004 (2007)	Jan. 1, 2009
IFRS 5	Non-current Assets Held for Sale and Discontinued Operations[b]	2004 (2007)	Jan. 1, 2009
IFRS 6	Exploration for and Evaluation of Mineral Resources	2004	Jan. 1, 2006
IFRS 7	Financial Instruments: Disclosures	2005	Jan. 1, 2007
IFRS 8	Operating Segments[d]	2006	Jan. 1, 2009
IFRS 9	Financial Instruments	2010	Jan. 1, 2013

Standards covered in this book:

[a] Denotes standards covered in Chapter 3.
[b] Denotes standards covered in Chapter 4.
[c] Denotes standards covered in Chapters 6 and 7.
[d] Denotes standards covered in Chapter 8.

A PRINCIPLES-BASED APPROACH TO INTERNATIONAL FINANCIAL REPORTING STANDARDS

The IASB uses a principles-based approach in developing accounting standards, rather than a rules-based approach. Principles-based standards focus on establishing general principles derived from the IASB *Framework,* providing recognition, measurement, and reporting requirements for the transactions covered by the standard. By following this approach, IFRS tend to limit guidance for applying the general principles to typical transactions and encourage professional judgment in applying the general principles to transactions specific to an entity or industry.

Sir David Tweedie, IASB chairman, explained the principles-based approach taken by the IASB as follows:

> The IASB concluded that a body of detailed guidance (sometimes referred to as *bright lines*) encourages a rule-based mentality of "where does it say I can't do this?" We take the view that this is counter-productive and helps those who are intent on finding ways around standards more than it helps those seeking to apply standards in a way that gives useful information. Put simply, adding the detailed guidance may obscure, rather than highlight, the underlying principles. The emphasis tends to be on compliance with the letter of the rule rather than on the spirit of the accounting standard.
>
> We prefer an approach that requires the company and its auditors to take a step back and consider with the underlying principles. This is not a soft option. Our approach requires both companies and their auditors to exercise professional judgement in the public interest. Our approach requires a strong commitment from preparers to financial statements that provide a faithful representation of all transactions and strong commitment from auditors to resist client pressures. It will not work without those commitments. There will be more individual transactions and situations that are not explicitly addressed. We hope that a clear statement of the underlying principles will allow companies and auditors to deal with those situations without resorting to detailed rules.[25]

A report published by the Institute of Chartered Accountants in Scotland in early 2006 stated that rules-based accounting adds unnecessary complexity, encourages financial engineering, and does not necessarily lead to a true and fair view or a fair presentation. Further, it pointed out that the volume of rules would hinder the translation into different languages and cultures.

The Global Accounting Alliance supports a single set of globally accepted and principles-based accounting standards, which focus on transparency and capital market needs, and would be ideal for all stakeholders. In February 2010, the IOSCO in a report entitled "Principles for Periodic Disclosure by Listed Entities," provides securities regulators with a framework for establishing or reviewing their periodic disclosure regimes. According to the report, its principles-based format allows for a wide range of application and adaptation by securities regulators.

PRESENTATION OF FINANCIAL STATEMENTS (IAS 1)

IAS 1, *Presentation of Financial Statements,* is a single standard providing guidelines for the preparation and presentation of financial statements. In September 2007, the IASB published a revised IAS 1, effective for annual periods beginning on or after January 1, 2009. It provides guidance in the following areas:

---

[25] Excerpt from a speech delivered before the Committee on Banking, Housing and Urban Affairs of the United States Senate, Washington, DC, February 14, 2002.

- *Purpose of financial statements.* To provide information for decision making.
- *Components of financial statements.* A set of financial statements must include a balance sheet, income statement, statement of cash flows, statement of changes in equity, and notes, comprising a summary of significant accounting polices and other explanatory notes.
- *Overriding principle of fair presentation.* IAS 1 states that financial statements "shall present fairly the financial position, financial performance and cash flows of an entity. Fair presentation requires the faithful representation of the effects of transactions, other events and conditions in accordance with the definitions and recognition criteria for assets, liabilities, income and expenses set out in the *Framework.*"[26] Compliance with IFRS generally ensures fair presentation. In the *extremely rare* circumstance when management concludes that compliance with the requirement of a standard or interpretation would be so misleading that it would conflict with the objective of financial statements set out in the *Framework,* IAS 1 *requires* departing from that requirement with extensive disclosures made in the notes. If the local regulatory framework will not allow departing from a requirement, disclosures must be made to reduce the misleading aspects of compliance with that requirement.
- *Accounting policies.* Management should select and apply accounting policies to be in compliance with all IASB standards and all applicable interpretations. If guidance is lacking on a specific issue, management should refer to (a) the requirements and guidance in other IASB standards dealing with similar issues; (b) the definitions, recognition, and measurement criteria for assets, liabilities, income, and expenses set out in the IASB *Framework;* and (c) pronouncements of other standard-setting bodies and accepted industry practices to the extent, but only to the extent, that these are consistent with (a) and (b). IAS 1 does *not* indicate that this is a hierarchy. It is important to note that individual country GAAP may be used to fill in the blanks but only if consistent with other IASB standards and the IASB *Framework.*
- *Basic principles and assumptions.* IAS 1 reiterates the accrual basis and going concern assumptions and the consistency and comparative information principles found in the *Framework.* IAS 1 adds to the guidance provided in the *Framework* by indicating that immaterial items should be aggregated. It also stipulates that assets and liabilities, and income and expenses should not be offset and reported at a net amount unless specifically permitted by a standard or interpretation.
- *Structure and content of financial statements.* IAS 1 also provides guidance with respect to: (a) current/noncurrent distinction, (b) items to be presented on the face of financial statements, and (c) items to be disclosed in the notes.

IAS 1 requires companies to classify assets and liabilities as current and noncurrent on the balance sheet, except when a presentation based on liquidity provides information that is reliable and more relevant. IAS 1 also provides guidance with respect to the items, at a minimum, that should be reported on the face of the income statement or balance sheet. Exhibit 3.4 presents an illustrative income statement, and Exhibit 3.5 presents an illustrative statement of financial position demonstrating minimum compliance with IAS 1. The line items comprising profit before tax must be reflected using either a nature of expense format (common in Continental Europe) or a function of expense format (commonly found in Anglo countries). Both formats are presented in Exhibit 3.4. IAS 1 specifically precludes designating items as extraordinary on the income statement or in the notes.

---

[26] IAS 1, paragraph 13.

+ **EXHIBIT 3.4**   Illustrative IFRS Income Statement

MODEL COMPANY
Income Statement
For the year ended 31 December 20XX
(in thousands of currency units)

Nature of Expenses Format	Function of Expenses Format
Revenue	**Revenue**
Changes in inventories of finished goods and work in progress	Cost of sales
Work performed by the entity and capitalized	**Gross profit**
Raw materials and consumables used	Other income
Employee benefits expense	Distribution costs
Depreciation and amortization expense	Administrative expenses
Impairment of property, plant, and equipment	Other expenses
Other expenses	Finance costs
Finance costs	Share of profit of associates
Share of profit of associates	**Profit before tax**
Profit before tax	Income tax expense
Income tax expense	**Profit for the period from continuing operations**
Profit for the period from continuing operations	Gain (loss) from discontinued operations
Gain (loss) from discontinued operations	**Profit for the period**
Profit for the period	Attributable to:
Attributable to:	Equity holders of the parent
Equity holders of the parent	Minority interest
Minority interest	

Note: IAS 33, *Earnings per Share,* requires that basic and diluted earnings per share also be reported on the face of the income statement. Additional required disclosures must be made either on the face of the income statement or in the notes.

In Exhibit 3.5, assets are presented on one side of the balance sheet and liabilities and equity are presented on the other side. Other formats are equally acceptable so long as the current/noncurrent distinction is clear. For example, British balance sheets commonly present noncurrent assets, net current assets (working capital), and noncurrent liabilities on one side of the balance sheet and equity on the other side. In addition, assets and liabilities may be presented in order of liquidity, as is common in North America.

FIRST-TIME ADOPTION OF INTERNATIONAL FINANCIAL REPORTING STANDARDS (IFRS 1)

IFRS 1, *First-time Adoption of International Financial Reporting Standards,* issued in June 2003, was the first IFRS developed by the IASB. IFRS 1 sets out the requirements for adopting IFRS and preparing a set of IFRS financial statements for the

✝ EXHIBIT 3.5   **Illustrative IFRS Statement of Financial Position**

MODEL COMPANY
Consolidated Statement of Financial Position
As at 31 December, Year 1
(in thousands of currency units)

Assets	Equity and Liabilities
Noncurrent assets	**Equity attributable to owners of the parent**
Property, plant, and equipment	Share capital
Goodwill	Other reserves
Other intangible assets	Retained earnings
Investments in associates	
Available-for-sale financial assets	**Minority interest**
	Total equity
Current assets	
Inventories	**Noncurrent liabilities**
Trade receivables	Long-term borrowings
Other current assets	Deferred tax
Cash and cash equivalents	Long-term provisions
	Total noncurrent liabilities
Total assets	
	Current liabilities
	Trade and other payables
	Short-term borrowings
	Current portion of long-term borrowings
	Current tax payable
	Short-term provisions
	Total current liabilities
	Total liabilities
	Total equity and liabilities

Note: Additional required disclosures must be made on the face of the balance sheet or in the notes.

first time. As companies make the transition from their previous GAAP to IFRS, guidance on this issue is very important.

In general, IFRS 1 requires an entity adopting IFRS to comply with each IFRS effective at the reporting date of its first IFRS financial statements. For example, if an entity is preparing IFRS financial statements for the year ended December 31, 2005, it must comply with all IFRS in force at that date. Moreover, if the entity provides comparative financial statements for the year 2004 in its 2005 IFRS financial statements, the comparative statements also must be prepared in accordance with IFRS in force at December 31, 2005. In effect, the entity's date of transition to IFRS is January 1, 2004. IFRS 1 requires the entity to prepare an "opening IFRS balance sheet" as of that date, which becomes the starting point for accounting under IFRS.

In preparing its opening IFRS balance sheet, IFRS 1 requires an entity to do the following:

1. Recognize all assets and liabilities whose recognition is required by IFRS.
2. Derecognize items previously recognized as assets or liabilities if IFRS do not permit such recognition.
3. Reclassify items that it recognized under previous GAAP as one type of asset, liability, or component of equity, but are a different type of asset, liability, or component of equity under IFRS.
4. Apply IFRS in measuring all recognized assets and liabilities.

To understand the significance of these requirements, consider their implementation with respect to intangible assets. In preparing its opening IFRS balance sheet, an entity would need to (1) exclude previously recognized intangible assets that do not meet the recognition criteria in IAS 38, *Intangible Assets,* at the date of transition to IFRS, and (2) include intangible assets that do meet the recognition criteria in IAS 38 at that date, even if they previously had been accounted for as an expense. For example, an entity adopting IFRS must determine whether previously expensed development costs would have qualified for recognition as an intangible asset under IAS 38 at the date of transition to IFRS. If so, then an asset should be recognized in the opening IFRS balance sheet even if the related costs had been expensed previously. Furthermore, if amortization methods and useful lives for intangible assets recognized under previous GAAP differ from those that would be acceptable under IFRS, then the accumulated amortization in the opening IFRS balance sheet must be adjusted retrospectively to comply with IFRS.

In specific areas where the cost of complying with an IFRS would likely exceed the benefits to users, IFRS 1 provides exemptions from complying with IFRS. Exemptions are allowed with respect to specific aspects of accounting in the following areas: business combinations, asset revaluations, employee benefits, cumulative translation differences, and financial instruments. Recently, IFRS 1 has been further amended to assist first-time adopters.

ARGUMENTS FOR AND AGAINST INTERNATIONAL CONVERGENCE OF FINANCIAL REPORTING STANDARDS

Arguments for Convergence

Proponents of accounting convergence put forward several arguments. First, they argue that comparability of financial statements worldwide is necessary for the globalization of capital markets. Financial statement comparability would make it easier for investors to evaluate potential investments in foreign securities and thereby take advantage of the risk reduction possible through international diversification. Second, it would simplify the evaluation by multinational companies of possible foreign takeover targets. Third, convergence would reduce financial reporting costs for companies that seek to list their shares on foreign stock exchanges. Cross-listing of securities would allow companies to gain access to less expensive capital in other countries and would make it easier for foreign investors to acquire the company's stock. Fourth, national differences in corporate reporting cause loss of investor confidence, which affects the availability and cost of capital. Investors often build in a premium to the required return on their investment if there is any uncertainty or lack of comparability about the figures—such premiums can be as large as 40 percent.[27] Fifth, one set of universally accepted accounting standards would reduce the cost of preparing worldwide consolidated financial statements, and the auditing of these statements also would be simplified. Sixth, multinational companies would find it easier to transfer accounting staff to other countries. This would be true for the international auditing firms as well. Finally, convergence would help raise the quality level of accounting practices internationally, thereby increasing the credibility of financial information. In relation to this argument, some point out that as a result of convergence, developing countries would be able to adopt a ready-made set of high-quality standards with minimum cost and effort.

Arguments against Convergence

The greatest obstacle to convergence is the magnitude of the differences that exist between countries and the fact that the political cost of eliminating those differences would be enormous. One of the main obstacles is nationalism. Whether out of deep-seated tradition, indifference born of economic power, or resistance to intrusion of foreign influence, some say that national entities will not bow to any international body. Arriving at principles that satisfy all of the parties involved throughout the world seems an almost impossible task. Not only is convergence difficult to achieve, but the need for such standards is not universally accepted. A well-developed global capital market exists already. It has evolved without uniform accounting standards. Opponents of convergence argue that it is unnecessary to force all companies worldwide to follow a common set of rules. They also point out that this would lead to a situation of "standards overload" as a result of requiring some enterprises to comply with a set of standards not relevant to them. The international capital market will force those companies that can benefit from accessing the market to provide the required accounting information without convergence. Yet another argument against convergence is that because of different environmental influences, differences in accounting across countries might be appropriate and necessary. For example, countries that are at different stages of economic development or that rely on different sources of financing perhaps should have differently oriented accounting systems. Professor Frederick Choi refers to this as the dilemma of global harmonization: "The thesis of environmentally stimulated and justified differences in accounting runs directly counter to efforts at the worldwide harmonization of accounting. Hence, the dilemma." This applies equally to the idea of convergence.

INTERNATIONAL CONVERGENCE TOWARD IFRS

The IASB has earned a great deal of goodwill from many interested parties. Its new approach clearly reflects a change of role from a harmonizer to a global standard-setter. According to its chairman, the IASB's strategy is to identify the best in standards around the world and build a body of accounting standards that constitute the "highest common denominator" of financial reporting. The IASB has adopted a principles-based approach to standard setting and has obtained the support of U.S. regulators (even though U.S. standard-setters historically have taken a rules-based approach). On the other hand, the IASB's structure is similar

---

[27] David Illigworth, President of the Institute of Chartered Accountants in England and Wales, in a speech at the China Economic Summit 2004 of the 7th China Beijing International High-Tech Expo, May 21, 2004.

to that of the U.S. standard-setter recognizing that the FASB has the best institutional structure for developing accounting standards.

In 2002, the six largest public accounting firms worldwide conducted a survey of national efforts in 54 countries to promote and achieve convergence with IFRS.[28] Almost all the countries surveyed intend to converge with IFRS, indicating that the IASB is the appropriate body to develop a global accounting language. Countries indicating a plan to achieve convergence included members of the European Union, the six countries of the Western Hemisphere with the largest economies (Argentina, Brazil, Canada, Chile, Mexico, and the United States), and China, India, Malaysia, New Zealand, South Korea, and Thailand. The survey identified three different convergence strategies:

1. Replacing national GAAP with IFRS (supplemented for issues not addressed by IFRS).
2. Adopting IFRS as national GAAP on a standard-by-standard basis.
3. Eliminating differences between national GAAP and IFRS when possible and practicable.

The major concerns in achieving IFRS convergence as expressed by respondents to the 2002 survey included:

- The complicated nature of particular standards, especially those related to financial instruments and fair value accounting (51 percent of countries).
- The tax-driven nature of the national accounting regime; using IFRS as the basis for taxation is seen as a problem (47 percent of countries).
- Disagreement with certain significant IFRS, especially those related to financial statements and fair value accounting (39 percent of countries).
- Insufficient guidance on first-time application of IFRS (35 percent of countries).
- Limited capital markets, and therefore little benefit to be derived from using IFRS (30 percent of countries).
- Satisfaction with national accounting standards among investors/users (21 percent of countries).
- IFRS language translation difficulties (18 percent of countries).

The IASB has taken initiatives to facilitate and enhance its role as a global standard-setter. The issuance of IFRS 1 is one such initiative. IFRS 1 was issued in response to the concern about a lack of guidance on first-time application of IFRS. The official language of the IASB is English and IFRS are written in this language. The IASB has attempted to address the translation issue by permitting national accountancy bodies to translate IFRS into more than 30 languages including Chinese, French, German, Japanese, Portuguese, and Spanish. In addition to the problem that IFRS have not yet been translated into very many languages, research has shown that translation can be problematic as some terms in English have no direct equivalent in other languages.[29]

[28] BDO, Deloitte Touche Tohmatsu, Ernst & Young, Grant Thornton, KPMG, and PricewaterhouseCoopers. *GAAP Convergence 2002: A Survey of National Efforts to Promote and Achieve Convergence with International Financial Reporting Standards.* Available at www.ifad.net.

[29] T. S. Doupnik and M. Richter, "Interpretation of Uncertainty Expressions: A Cross-National Study," *Accounting, Organizations and Society* 28, no. 1(2003), pp. 15–35. These researchers find, for example, that German speakers do not view the English word "remote" (used in the context of the probability that a loss will occur) and its German translation "Wahrscheinlichkeit äuβerst gering" as being equivalent.

With the increasing trend in many countries including Australia and the EU member nations to adopt IFRS, a large number of companies (over 7,000 listed companies in Europe alone) now use IFRS in preparing their financial statements. The IASB's decision to hold a series of public roundtable forums to provide opportunities for those who have commented on an exposure draft to discuss their views on the proposals with members of the IASB is another important initiative.

As noted earlier, seven of the 14 board members have direct liaison responsibility with national standards setters.[30] As a result, unlike its predecessor, the IASB now is formally linked to national standard-setters in at least some countries, and the liaison board members are able to coordinate agendas and ensure that the IASB and those national bodies are working toward convergence.

IFAC supports the IASB's objective of convergence. At its July 2003 meeting, held in Quebec, Canada, IFAC approved a Compliance Program designed to provide clear benchmarks to current and potential member organizations in ensuring high-quality performance by accountants worldwide. This program requires member bodies to implement, with appropriate investigation and disciplinary regulations, both IFAC standards and IFRS. IFAC's Auditing and Assurance Standards Board (IAASB) also has issued new guidance clarifying when financial statements are in full compliance with IFRS. In its 2007 annual report, the IFAC highlights, among other things, the progress in achieving international convergence through IFRS.

As stated earlier in this chapter, the main objective of the IASB is to achieve international convergence with IFRS. However, Zeff[31] points out that some obstacles to comparability are likely to arise in areas of the business and financial culture, the accounting culture, the auditing culture, and the regulatory culture. He also warns that, in addition to the obstacles to convergence due to the problems of interpretation, language, and terminology, the impact of politics can create a "catch 22" situation. He states:

> The more rigorous the enforcement mechanism—that is, the more authority and the larger budget a country gives to its securities market regulator to fortify the effort to secure compliance with IFRS—the more lobbying pressure that will be brought on the IASB, because companies in such countries will know that they have no "escape valve," no way of side-stepping the adverse consequences, as they see them, of a proposed IASB standard or interpretation. If the auditor is strict and the regulator is strict, political lobbying of the standard setter, IASB, may become more intense. If a powerful company or group of companies do not like a draft standard, they will have an incentive to engage in politicking of the standard-setting body. Hence it becomes a Catch-22.

Regardless of the arguments against harmonization, substantial efforts to reduce differences in accounting practice have been ongoing for several decades. The question is no longer *whether* harmonization should be strived for, but going a step further, it is to ask *how to achieve convergence.*

---

[30] The IASB initially had official liaison with national standard-setters from Australia, Canada, France, Germany, Japan, New Zealand, the United Kingdom, and the United States.

[31] Zeff, S. "Political Lobbying on Proposed Standards: A Challenge to the IASB", *Accounting Horizons,* 16, no.1 (2002), pp. 43–54.

THE ADOPTION OF INTERNATIONAL FINANCIAL REPORTING STANDARDS

There are a number of different ways in which a country might adopt IFRS, including requiring (or permitting) IFRS to be used by the following:

1. *All* companies; in effect, IFRS replace national GAAP.
2. Parent companies in preparing *consolidated* financial statements; national GAAP is used in parent company-only financial statements.
3. *Stock exchange listed* companies in preparing consolidated financial statements. Nonlisted companies use national GAAP.
4. *Foreign* companies listing on domestic stock exchanges. Domestic companies use national GAAP.
5. Domestic companies that list on *foreign* stock exchanges. Other domestic companies use national GAAP.

The endorsement of IFRS for cross-listing purposes by IOSCO and the EU's decision to require domestic listed companies to use IFRS for consolidated accounts beginning in 2005 have provided a major boost to the efforts of the IASB. The results of a survey of the use of IFRS by domestic listed companies in preparing their consolidated financial statements is presented in Exhibit 3.6. Of the 130 countries included in the survey, more than 100 require or permit the use of IFRS by domestic listed companies.

IFAC supports IASB in its efforts at global standard-setting. The IFAC 2008 annual report highlights initiatives during the credit crisis and the need for convergence to global standards.

The IFAC G20 accountancy summit in July 2009 issued a renewed mandate for adoption of global standards in which they recommended that governments and regulators should step up initiatives to promote convergence to global accountancy and auditing standards. The latest IFAC Global Leadership Survey, which polled its membership of 157 accountancy organizations in 123 countries, emphasizes that investors and all consumers of financial information deserve simpler and more useful information, and that the adoption, implementation, and enforcement of international financial standards are crucial in this regard.

Recently, China, Japan, and Korea formed the Asian-Oceanian Standard Setters Group (AOSSG) as a forum for the countries in the region to exchange their ideas but also to have a joint voice in matters relating to IFRS and to bring together Asian-Oceanian standard-setters. The IASB has responded to concerns expressed by various parties. For example, it has issued amendments to IFRS 1, *First-time Adoption of IFRS,* that address the retrospective application of IFRS to particular situations and are aimed at ensuring that entities applying IFRS will not face undue cost or effort in the transition process. The IASB has also issued a revised version of IAS 24, *Related Party Disclosures,* that simplifies the disclosure requirements for government-related entities and clarifies the definition of a related party.

Many developing countries have adopted IFRS with little or no amendment as their national standards. For some of them, it may have been a less expensive option than developing their own standards. The need to attract foreign investment also may have been an influencing factor. Countries changing from

EXHIBIT 3.6   Use of IFRS in Preparing Consolidated Financial Statements

IFRS Required for All Domestic Listed Companies

Armenia	France*	Lebanon	Poland*
Australia#	Georgia	Liechtenstein	Portugal*
Austria*	Germany*	Lithuania*	Qatar
Bahamas	Greece*	Luxembourg*	Romania*
Bahrain	Guatemala	Macedonia	Singapore‡
Barbados	Guyana	Malawi	Slovak Republic*
Belgium*	Haiti	Malta*	Slovenia*
Bosnia & Herzegovina	Honduras	Mauritius	South Africa
Bulgaria*	Hong Kong†	Namibia	Spain*
Costa Rica	Hungary*	Nepal	Sweden*
Croatia	Iceland	Netherlands*	Tajikistan
Cyprus*	Ireland*	New Zealand#	Tanzania
Czech Republic*	Italy*	Nicaragua	Trinidad & Tobago
Denmark*	Jamaica	Norway	Turkey
Dominican Republic	Jordan	Oman	Ukraine
Ecuador	Kenya	Panama	United Kingdom*
Egypt	Kuwait	Papua New Guinea	Uruguay
Estonia*	Kyrgyzstan	Peru	Venezuela
Finland*	Latvia*	Philippines	Yugoslavia

IFRS Required for Some Domestic Listed Companies

China	Kazakhstan	Russian Federation	United Arab Emirates

IFRS Permitted for Domestic Listed Companies

Aruba	El Salvador	Morocco	Switzerland
Bermuda	Gibraltar	Myanmar	Uganda
Bolivia	Israel	Netherlands Antilles	Virgin Is. (British)
Botswana	Laos	Sri Lanka	Zambia
Cayman Islands	Lesotho	Suriname	Zimbabwe
Dominica	Macau	Swaziland	

IFRS Not Permitted for Domestic Listed Companies

Argentina	Colombia	Malaysia	Taiwan
Azerbaijan	Cote d'Ivoire	Mali	Thailand
Bangladesh	Fiji	Mexico	Togo
Benin	Ghana	Moldova	Tunisia
Bhutan	India	Mozambique	United States
Brazil	Indonesia	Niger	Uzbekistan
Burkina Faso	Iran	Pakistan	Vietnam
Canada	Japan	Saudi Arabia	
Chile	Korea (South)	Syria	

* Denotes EU membership. The EU has not adopted portions of IAS 39.
† Hong Kong and Philippines have adopted standards that are identical to IFRS.
‡ Singapore has adopted many IFRS word for word but has changed several IFRS when adopting them as national standards.
# Australia and New Zealand have national standards described as IFRS equivalents.

Source: Deloitte Touche Tohmatsu, "Use of IFRSs for Reporting by Domestic Listed and Unlisted Companies by Country and Region," www.iasplus.com.

centrally planned to market-based economies also have found IFRS attractive as they offer a ready-made set of standards to facilitate the development of a market system.

Although many countries do not allow domestic listed companies to use IASB standards, some of these countries nevertheless allow *foreign* companies listed on domestic stock exchanges to use IFRS in accordance with IOSCO's recommendation. Japan, for example, allows foreign companies listing on the Tokyo stock exchange to file financial statements prepared in accordance with IFRS without any reconciliation to Japanese GAAP. (The same is now true in the United States.)

In January 2005, the IASB and the Accounting Standards Board of Japan (ASBJ) announced their agreement to launch a joint project to reduce differences between IFRS and Japanese accounting standards. Convergence of Japanese GAAP and IFRS is expected by 2011. Canada, India, Brazil, and Korea also have decided that they will adopt IFRS by 2011. At the beginning of 2007, China introduced a completely new set of accounting standards that is intended to produce the same results as IFRS. A number of countries are gearing up to fully adopt IFRS in 2011.

A global leadership survey conducted by the IFAC in late 2007 revealed that, a large majority (89 percent) indicated that convergence to IFRS was "very important" or "important" for economic growth in their countries. The survey included 143 business leaders from 91 countries.[32] A majority of recent Deloitte IFRS survey respondents preferred a set date for global accounting standards.

IFRS IN THE EUROPEAN UNION

In July 2002, the European Union issued a directive (Regulation 1606/2002) requiring all listed companies of member states to prepare consolidated financial statements based on IFRS beginning January 1, 2005. The aim was to improve the quality of corporate financial reporting by increasing their comparability and transparency, and to promote the development of a single capital market in Europe.

The European Union has adopted the strategy of replacing national GAAP (supplemented for issues not addressed by IFRS) with respect to the preparation of consolidated financial statements by listed companies. Nonlisted companies continue to apply national GAAP. However, several EU countries (Denmark and Estonia) also have adopted a convergence strategy with respect to nonlisted companies, by adopting a plan to converge national GAAP with IFRS. This strategy could eventually result in no substantive differences between IFRS and a country's national GAAP. In January 2003, the European Parliament approved amendments to the EU Fourth and Seventh Directives removing all inconsistencies between the directives and IFRS.

The switch to IFRS involved significant changes to the accounting policies of listed companies. With this in mind, the U.K. Institute of Chartered Accountants in England and Wales urged British companies to provide investors and analysts with clear explanations of their preparations for adopting IFRS and changes to accounting policies ahead of publication of their 2005 accounts, as this was seen as being important in securing investor confidence.

The EU decided to adopt a version of IAS 39, *Financial Instruments: Recognition and Measurement,* with two "carve outs." The EU-approved version of IAS 39 removes specific provisions related to the use of a fair value option and of hedge

---

[32] http://accountingeducation.com/index.cfm?page=newsdetails&id=145923

accounting. This was not well received internationally, including in the United Kingdom. The concerns included that this could have adverse consequences for the cost of capital of European companies if the adopted standard prevents European companies from complying with the complete standard as issued by the IASB, as it will damage the credibility of European financial reporting. Further, it was pointed out that the adopted standard includes seriously weakened hedge accounting requirements and may give rise to artificial volatility in reported profits and difficulties in application as a result of limiting the fair value option.

Some European companies are careful to disclose the fact that they are using "IFRS as adopted by the EU," meaning that IAS 39 is not applied in its entirety. The following disclosure made by the Swedish firm AB Electrolux in Note 1 Accounting and Valuation Principles of the 2006 Annual Report is an example:

> The consolidated financial statements are prepared in accordance with International Financial Reporting Standards (IFRS) as adopted by the European Union. Electrolux's auditor, PricewaterhouseCoopers, uses similar language in its audit opinion.

So far, no research has been conducted to examine the full effect of adopting an amended version of IAS 39 in Europe. In the area of enforcement of accounting standards, there are considerable challenges in Europe. The Committee of European Securities Regulators (CESR) issued Standard No. 1, *Financial Information: Enforcement of Standards on Financial Information in Europe,* in 2003 to provide principles that could underpin the development and implementation of a common approach to the enforcement of IFRS. However, application of the standard is not mandatory and CESR will rely on the cooperation of member states in adopting the stated principles.

There is a wide variety of accounting enforcement systems used in Europe. Some countries, such as Germany, Finland, and the Netherlands, have no institutional oversight of financial reporting. Further, the enterprises that are expected to apply IFRS in Europe are heterogeneous in terms of jurisdiction, size, capital structure, ownership structure, and degree of accounting sophistication.[33] In pre-2005 Europe, there was a variety of national standards of varying degrees of completeness, sophistication, and authority, reflecting different national traditions and institutional arrangements.[34] Starting in 2005, although the European Union will have a single financial reporting standard-setter, securities regulation is subject to considerable cross-jurisdictional variation due to existing legal and cultural differences among EU jurisdictions. As a result, EU countries decided to evaluate existing enforcement strategies and introduce enforcement bodies.[35]

Recent IFRS (especially IAS 39) have increasingly required fair value measurements, with the intent of enhancing the relevance of reported numbers. A key issue for convergence is whether fair value measurements can be accepted as having sufficient reliability. One difficulty in developing fair value measures

[33] K. Schipper, "The Introduction of International Accounting Standards in Europe: Implications for International Convergence," *European Accounting Review* 14, no.1 (2005), pp. 101–26.

[34] G. Whittington, "The Adoption of International Accounting Standards in the European Union," *European Accounting Review* 14, no.1 (2005). pp. 127–53.

[35] Committee of European Securities Regulators, CESR's First Initiative towards More Robust Enforcement of Financial Information in Europe, press release CESR/03-081b, 2 April, (2003). Available at www.europefesco.org/v2/default.asp.

particularly in Europe is a lack of organized and liquid markets for many assets and obligations.

In September 2009, the EU published Commission Regulation (EC) No. 839/2009 (*Adoption of Eligible Hedged Items—Amendments to IAS 39 Financial Instruments: Recognition and Measurement*), amending Regulation (EC) No. 1226/2008, adopting certain international accounting standards in accordance with Regulation (EC) No. 1606/2002. EFRAG commented on the IASB's Exposure Draft on Fair Value Measurement, supporting most aspects of the IASB proposal to define fair value but recommending that the proposal should only apply to financial assets and financial liabilities until there has been a public consultation and debate on its use for non-financial assets and liabilities. The UK FRC also supports the view that an EU focus on principles and values in corporate reporting should be adopted and suggests that "comply or explain" should remain a fundamental cornerstone of the EU framework.

IFRS IN THE UNITED STATES

Support for a Principles-Based Approach

The U.S. Public Company Accounting Reform and Investor Protection Act of 2002 (the Sarbanes-Oxley Act) required the SEC to study the "adoption by the United States financial reporting system of a principles-based accounting system" and submit a report to specified committees of the Senate and House of Representatives.

It is interesting that support for a principles-based approach has come from many quarters including current and former U.S. regulators. It has been pointed out that as part of the commitment to convergence the FASB and SEC should change their behavior and become more like the rest of the world. For example, a former SEC chairman, expressing preference for the IASB's principles-based standards, referred to the IASB's approach as a "Ten Commandments," approach in contrast to the FASB's "cookbook" approach.[36] The SEC chairman, in a speech made in Puerto Rico in February 2002, also expressed preference for a principles-based set of accounting standards.[37] In addition, in an editorial in the June 27, 2002, edition of *Financial Times*, titled "The World after WorldCom," the U.S. regulators were urged to move to principles-based standards. The following is an extract from this editorial:

> It is time for US accounting standards to move away from prescriptive rulemaking towards the alternative used in many other countries, which focuses on "substance over form." US regulators have been suspicious of principles-based standards drafted by the International Accounting Standards Board, arguing that the US approach is superior. As the list of US accounting scandals mounts, it is hard to maintain such a position.

There also is outside pressure on the U.S. regulators to recognize IFRS. For example, on May 13, 2004, the director general of the Internal Market Directorate of the European Commission, in his testimony before the U.S. House Committee

---

[36] http://banking.senate.gov/02_02hrg/021202/index.htm.

[37] www.sec.gov/news/speech/spch539.htm.

on Financial Services, expressed a hope that the U.S. SEC would recognize IFRS as part of a program of mutual U.S.-EU recognition of each other's financial market regulations and elaborated the merits of such a recognition in detail.[38]

The Norwalk Agreement

In September 2002, at a meeting in Norwalk, Connecticut, the FASB and IASB pledged to use their best efforts to (1) make their existing financial reporting standards fully compatible as soon as is practicable and (2) to coordinate their work program to ensure that once achieved, compatibility is maintained. This has become known as the "Norwalk Agreement." Note that this agreement does not mean that the FASB will always try to move in the direction of IASB Standards to remove existing differences, but that the opposite also will occur. Significantly, the two standard-setters have agreed to work together on future issues to try to develop common solutions. In March 2003, the IASB decided to use identical style and wording in the standards issued by the FASB and IASB on joint projects.

The following are key FASB initiatives to further convergence between IFRS and U.S. GAAP:

1. *Joint projects.* Joint projects involve sharing staff resources and working on a similar time schedule. Revenue recognition, business combinations, and review of *conceptual framework* are three major topics covered by joint projects.
2. *Short-term convergence project.* The two Boards agreed to undertake a short-term project to remove a variety of differences that exist between IFRS and U.S. GAAP. The scope of the short-term convergence project is limited to those differences between the two sets of standards in which convergence is likely to be achieved in the short-term. Convergence is expected to occur by selecting either existing U.S. GAAP or IFRS requirements as the high-quality solution.
3. *Liaison IASB member.* A full-time IASB member is in residence at the FASB offices. This facilitates information exchange and cooperation between the FASB and the IASB.
4. *Monitoring of IASB projects.* The FASB monitors IASB projects according to the FASB's level of interest in the topic being addressed.
5. *The convergence research project.* The FASB staff embarked on a project to identify all the substantive differences between U.S. GAAP and IFRS and catalog differences according to the FASB's strategy for resolving them.
6. *Consideration of convergence potential in board agenda decisions.* All topics considered for addition to the FASB's agenda are assessed for the potential cooperation with the IASB.

The FASB expected that through these initiatives significant progress could be made toward convergence with IFRS in the short to medium term. Toward the end of 2004 the FASB issued three standards resulting from the short-term convergence project designed to eliminate some differences between the U.S. and IASB standards: SFAS 123 (revised 2004), *Share-based Payments*, issued in December 2004; SFAS 151, *Inventory Costs* (an amendment of ARB 43, Chapter 4), issued in November 2004; and SFAS 153, *Exchange of Non-monetary Assets* (an amendment of APB Opinion 29), issued in December 2004. SFAS 123 requires that compensation

---

[38] Full text of the testimony is available at: www.iasplus.com/index.htm.

cost relating to share-based payments transactions be recognized in financial statements. The cost is to be measured on the basis of the fair value of the equity or liability instrument issued. This standard eliminates the use of the intrinsic value method, which was allowed under Opinion 25, and it is expected to result in convergence with IFRS 2. ARB 43 states that under some circumstances, items such as idle facility expenses, excessive spoilage, double freight, and rehandling costs may be so abnormal as to require treatment as current period charges. SFAS 151 eliminates the term abnormal. The term was not defined in ARB 43. The language used in SFAS 151 is similar to that in IAS 2. SFAS 153 eliminates certain narrow differences between Opinion 29 and IAS 2. Opinion 29 provided an exception to the basic measurement principle (fair value) for exchanges of similar productive assets (commercially substantive assets). SFAS 153 eliminates that exception and brings the U.S. standard closer to IAS 16.

At a conference held in New York in April 2007, the chairmen of the IASB and FASB stressed that principles-based accounting standards would best serve users of financial statements and the public interest. More recently, the joint project on business combinations resulted in the FASB issuing a new standard on this topic in December 2007. SFAS 141 (revised), *Business Combinations,* adopts the acquisition method of accounting for business combinations that was first introduced by the IASB in IFRS 3, *Business Combinations,* in 2004. The FASB and IASB worked together to agree on solutions to a number of issues related to the application of the acquisition method. The IASB issued a revised IFRS 3 adopting these solutions in January 2008. In introducing SFAS 141 (revised 2007), the FASB states:

> This Statement, together with the IASB's IFRS 3, *Business Combinations* (as revised in 2007), completes a joint effort by the FASB and the IASB to improve financial reporting about business combinations and to promote the international convergence of accounting standards.[39]

Following the global financial crisis, the Financial Crisis Advisory Group (FCAG), a high-level group of recognized leaders with broad experience in international financial markets, was formed at the request of the IASB and FASB to consider financial reporting issues arising from the crisis. The FCAG published in July 2009 a wide-ranging review of standard-setting activities following global financial crisis. The report articulates four main principles and contains a series of recommendations to improve the functioning and effectiveness of global standard-setting. The main areas addressed in the report are:

- Effective financial reporting.
- Limitations of financial reporting.
- Convergence of accounting standards.
- Standard-setting independence and accountability.

As the co-chairmen of the FCAG stated, accounting was not a root cause of the financial crisis, but it has an important role to play in its resolution. Improved financial reporting will help restore the confidence of financial market participants and serve as a catalyst for increased financial stability and sound econimc growth. The independence and integrity of the standard-setting process, including wide

---

[39] FASB Statement of Financial Accounting Standards No. 141 (revised 2007), *Business Combinations,* p. vi.

consultation, is critical to developing high-quality, broadly accepted accounting standards responsive to the issues highlighted by the crisis.

The SEC's Policy on IFRS

In November 2007, the SEC decided to remove the requirement that foreign private issuers using IFRS reconcile their financial statements to U.S. GAAP. This reflects the recognition that IFRS is a high-quality set of accounting standards which is capable of ensuring adequate disclosure for the protection of investors and the promotion of fair, orderly, and efficient markets. This decision was supported by the experience in the European markets where there has been no market disruption or loss of investor confidence as a result of the introduction of IFRS in 2005. Substantial amounts of capital have been invested by U.S. investors in European companies which report under IFRS, thus suggesting that many U.S. investors already have concluded that IFRS is a fit-for-purpose financial reporting framework. Of the 1,100 foreign companies that file financial statements with the SEC, 180 use IFRS. Beginning in 2007, the Form 20-F filed by these companies with the SEC no longer includes a reconciliation to U.S. GAAP.

Elimination of the reconciliation requirement for foreign filers who prepare their financial reports in accordance with IFRS creates an asymmetric situation as domestic filers do not have the option of preparing their financial reports in accordance with IFRS. In July 2007, the SEC issued a concept release soliciting public comment on the idea of allowing U.S. companies to choose between the use of IFRS and U.S. GAAP. In October 2007, the AICPA recommended that the SEC should allow American public companies to report financial results using international accounting standards. Preliminary results of a survey conducted by Deloitte & Touche LLP in November 2007 show that approximately 205 of CEOs and senior finance professionals (representing approximately 300 U.S. companies) would consider adopting IFRS, if given a choice by the SEC. Even the chairmen of the FASB and Financial Accounting Foundation, which oversees the FASB, have expressed approval for a move toward the use of IFRS in the United States. They concluded that:

> Investors would be better served if all U.S. public companies used accounting standards promulgated by a single global standard setter as the basis for preparing their financial reports. This would be best accomplished by moving U.S. public companies to an improved version of International Financial Reporting Standards (IFRS).[40]

However, they state that the move to IFRS in the United States will be a complex, multiyear process that will involve making significant changes to the U.S. financial reporting system, including changes in auditing standards, licensing requirements, and how accountants are educated.

Further, for companies and financial professionals that have been using detailed rules associated with U.S. GAAP, the prospect of IFRS presents both opportunities and challenges.

The SEC is expected to consider in 2011 whether and how to incorporate IFRS into the U.S. financial system. There is widespread support for the SEC's "Roadmap for the Potential Use of Financial Statements Prepared in Accordance with

---

[40] Letter to Ms. Nancy M. Morris, Securities and Exchange Commission, signed by Robert E. Denham, Chairman, Financial Accounting Foundation, and Robert H. Herz, Chairman, Financial Accounting Standards Board, dated November 7, 2007 (www.fasb.org/FASB_FAF_Response_SEC_Release_msw.pdf).

International Financial Reporting Standards by U.S. Issuers"; for example, the UK FRC, the UK's independent regulator responsible for promoting confidence in corporate reporting and governance, emphasized that permitting U.S. domestic issuers to use IFRS will be significant to the future development and credibility of IFRS. U.S. executives want an option for early IFRS adoption, according to a KPMG IFRS institute survey, which found that nearly half of those polled say they would like the option for "early adoption" once the SEC decides to require or permit U.S. companies to use IFRS. However, the National Association of State Boards of Accountancy, supporting the joint effort by the IASB and the FASB to converge standards by 2011, has recommended that moving to convergence with, rather than adoption of, IFRS is the right path for the SEC to be following and that the SEC should withdraw its idea of a "road map" for adoption of IFRS. U.S. President Obama's administration has supported global standards in its financial reform proposal, which has been applauded by IFAC.

SOME CONCLUDING REMARKS

In the quest to achieve convergence with national accounting standards, the IASB must remain alert to the potential for it to be unduly influenced by interested parties. Commenting on the IASB's strategy to engineer convergence through a process of formal liaison with leading national standard-setters, Professor Steven Zeff warns about the political pressures that may be triggered by any board initiative to prescribe specific accounting treatments, eliminate alternative treatments, impose additional disclosure requirements, or tighten interpretations.[41] Most accounting issues are politically sensitive, because the need for standards often arises where there is controversy, and accounting can have economic consequences that affect the wealth of different groups. As a result, different groups interested in a particular accounting issue can be expected to lobby for the standard most beneficial to them, or to prevent the establishment of a proposed standard, which they believe would be less favorable than the status quo.

The issue of accounting standards convergence versus financial statement comparability also should not be overlooked. Convergence of standards does not necessarily produce comparable financial statements. Cultural and other factors could lead to different interpretations of standards and different levels of compliance across countries, leading to the production of financial statements that might not be entirely comparable.

Summary

1. Harmonization and convergence are processes of reducing differences in financial reporting practices across countries.
2. Unlike harmonization, convergence implies the adoption of one set of standards internationally. The major goal of both harmonization and convergence is comparability of financial statements.
3. Harmonization or convergence of accounting standards might not necessarily result in comparable financial statements internationally due to nation specific factors such as culture.

[41] S. Zeff, "Political Lobbying on Proposed Standards: A Challenge to the IASB," *Accounting Horizons* 16, no.1 (2002), pp. 43–54.

4. Proponents of international accounting harmonization/convergence argue that cross-country comparability of financial statements is required for the globalization of capital markets. Opponents argue that globalization is occurring without harmonization/convergence and that it might be appropriate for countries with different environments to have different standards.

5. Several organizations were involved in the harmonization efforts at global and regional levels, including IOSCO, IFAC, and the EU.

6. The IASB's main objective is to develop a set of high-quality financial reporting standards for global use.

7. To achieve a common capital market, the European Union (EU) attempted to harmonize accounting through the issuance of the Fourth and the Seventh Directives. Although the EU directives reduced differences in accounting in Europe, complete comparability was not achieved. Rather than developing additional directives, the European Commission decided to require the use of IFRS beginning in 2005.

8. The International Accounting Standards Committee (IASC) was formed in 1973 to develop international accounting standards universally acceptable in all countries. In 2001, the IASC was replaced by the International Accounting Standards Board (IASB).

9. The IASB has 16 members (13 full-time and 3 part-time). The IASB adheres to an open process in developing standards, which are principles-based (rather than rules-based). With the establishment of the IASB, there has been a shift in emphasis from harmonization to global standard setting or convergence.

10. As of August 2010, International Financial Reporting Standards (IFRS) consisted of 30 IASs, 9 IFRSs, and a number of interpretations. As a private organization, the IASB does not have the ability to require the use of its standards.

11. The International Organization of Securities Commissions (IOSCO) recommends that securities regulators permit foreign issuers to use IFRS for cross-listing. Most major stock exchanges are in compliance with this recommendation. In addition, a large and growing number of countries either require or allow domestic listed companies to use IFRS in preparing consolidated financial statements. The EU's adoption of IFRS in 2005 was a major boost to the IASB's legitimacy as a global accounting standard-setter.

12. The IASB's *Framework for the Preparation and Presentation of Financial Statements* establishes usefulness for decision making as the primary objective of financial statements prepared under IFRS. Understandability, relevance, reliability, and comparability are the primary qualitative characteristics that make financial statements useful. The *Framework* also provides workable definitions of the accounting elements. Currently, the IASB and FASB have a joint project aimed at developing a new conceptual framework acceptable to both.

13. IAS 1 is a single standard providing guidelines for the presentation of financial statements. The standard stipulates that a set of IFRS-based financial statements must include a balance sheet, an income statement, a statement of cash flows, a statement of changes in equity, and accounting polices and explanatory notes. IAS 1 establishes the overriding principle of fair presentation and permits an override of a requirement of an IASB standard in the

extremely rare situation where management concludes that compliance with a requirement of a standard would be misleading.

14. IFRS 1 provides guidance to companies that are adopting IFRS for the first time. IFRS 1 requires an entity to comply with each IFRS effective at the reporting date of its first IFRS financial statements. However, IFRS 1 provides exemptions to this rule where the cost of complying with this requirement would likely exceed the benefit to users.

15. In 2002, the FASB and IASB signed the Norwalk Agreement, in which they agreed to work toward convergence of their two sets of financial reporting standards.

16. More recently, the two boards agreed to revise their respective conceptual frameworks as a joint project.

17. In February 2007, the FASB issued SFAS 159, *The Fair Value Opinion for Financial Assets and Financial Liabilities,* which provides companies with an option to report selected financial assets and liabilities at fair values, bringing U.S. GAAP and IFRS closer together.

18. In November 2007, the SEC removed the requirement that foreign private issuers using IFRS must reconcile their financial statements to U.S. GAAP.

Appendix to Chapter 3

What Is This Thing Called Anglo-Saxon Accounting?

The term *Anglo-Saxon* or *Anglo-American* is used for a group of countries that includes the United States, the United Kingdom, Canada, Australia, and New Zealand. This group often figures in international accounting textbooks and articles, particularly with regard to international classification of accounting systems and international harmonization of accounting standards. The efforts of the IASB (and its predecessor, the IASC) are usually associated with Anglo-Saxon accounting. Some even criticize the IASB for attempting to promote Anglo-Saxon accounting throughout the world. However, many non-Anglo countries are already using IFRS. Given this, it is important to examine some of the important features of Anglo-Saxon accounting, which is the basis for IFRS.

In a broad sense, the term *Anglo-Saxon accounting* refers to the accounting systems prevalent in the English-speaking countries mentioned in the preceding paragraph. Although the accounting systems in these countries are not identical, they share some fundamental features that distinguish them from other systems of accounting:

- A focus on how businesses operate at the firm level (micro orientation), with an emphasis on the importance of professional judgment (recognition of professional rules and professional self-regulation).

- An investor orientation, with the provision of information for efficient operation of the capital market as the primary aim (recognition of the importance of being transparent).

- Less emphasis on prudence and measurement of taxable income or distributable income, and willingness to go beyond superficial legal form (substance over form).[1]

There are other recognizable commonalities that are related to the above features. For example, because of the investor orientation and emphasis on transparency in accounting reports, the principle of true and fair view or fair presentation is predominant in Anglo-Saxon financial reporting. Auditors are required to report on whether, in their opinion, the financial statements have been prepared in such a way that they adhere to this principle. In the United Kingdom, the concept of *true and fair view* has not been clearly defined in legislation. The courts have placed considerable reliance on expert witnesses in developing a meaning for this concept. The UK government's view has been that this is a highly technical matter and therefore should be dealt with by the profession. This leaves open the possibility for different interpretations. There is no single true and fair view. There are also some differences in how the concept of true and fair view is applied. For example, in the United Kingdom, it is an overriding requirement. In other words, complying with the legal requirements does not necessarily lead to a true and fair view, in which case additional information should be provided. However, in Canada and Australia, a true-and-fair-view override does not apply. Further, the U.S. equivalent to true and fair view, *present fairly*, is defined in terms of conformity with U.S. GAAP. In other words, if the financial statements have been prepared in accordance with the U.S. GAAP, then it is assumed that the information is presented fairly. In general, it is recognized that the application of the qualitative characteristics and appropriate accounting standards would normally result in financial statements that convey a true and fair view of such information, or that present it fairly.[2]

The qualitative characteristics such as understandability, relevance, reliability, and objectivity or representational faithfulness are found in the conceptual frameworks developed by all Anglo-Saxon countries and by the IASB. The use of a conceptual framework to provide guidance for developing accounting standards is another common feature among these countries. The IASB's conceptual framework is largely based on that of the U.S. FASB. This has been one of the reasons for the view that the IASB has been heavily influenced by Anglo-Saxon accounting. Another recognizable common feature among Anglo-Saxon countries is that they all have common law traditions rather than code law traditions. This means they all use common law legal systems, which tend to be flexible in terms of legislation and rely heavily on private sector and market mechanisms for regulation. Related to this, all these countries have private-sector standard-setting bodies recognizing the profession's capacity to self-regulate.[3]

Some differences can be observed among Anglo-Saxon countries with regard to the recognizable common features described in the preceding paragraph. For example, the conceptual frameworks are not always used as the basis for developing accounting standards. As a case in point, SFAS 87, *Employers' Accounting for Pensions,* in the United States specifically states that it does not follow the FASB's conceptual framework. Further, a common law legal system does not necessarily

[1] Christopher W. Nobes, "On the Myth of 'Anglo-Saxon' Financial Accounting: A Comment," *International Journal of Accounting* 38 (2003), pp. 95–104.
[2] IASC, *Framework for the Preparation and Presentation of Financial Statements* (London: IASC, 1989).
[3] Nobes (2003), op cit.

lead to flexible standards. U.S. accounting standards are increasingly becoming more detailed and rigidly prescriptive as compared to accounting standards developed in the United Kingdom. With regard to private-sector standard setting, traditionally the U.S. standard-setting system is significantly more public-sector-oriented than the UK system, because the U.S. Securities and Exchange Commission (SEC) has the ultimate responsibility for authorizing accounting standards. On the basis of these differences, some commentators have argued that Anglo-Saxon accounting is a myth.[4] However, such differences do not necessarily indicate that these countries cannot usefully be seen as members of the same group.[5]

Questions

1. How does harmonization differ from convergence?
2. What are the potential benefits that a multinational corporation could derive from the international convergence of accounting standards?
3. Were the EU directives effective in generating comparability of financial statements across companies located in member nations? Why or why not?
4. What were the three phases in the life of the IASC?
5. Why was IOSCO's endorsement of IASs so important to the IASC's efforts?
6. How does the structure of the IASB help to establish its legitimacy as a global standard-setter?
7. What is the IASB's principles-based approach to accounting standard setting?
8. Are there any major accounting issues that have not yet been covered by IFRS?
9. Do you see a major change of emphasis in the harmonization process since the establishment of the IASB? Explain.
10. What are the different ways in which IFRS might be used within a country?
11. Would the worldwide adoption of IFRS result in worldwide comparability of financial statements? Why or why not?
12. In what way is the IASB's *Framework* intended to assist firms in preparing IFRS-based financial statements?
13. As expressed in IAS 1, what is the overriding principle that should be followed in preparing IFRS-based financial statements?
14. Under what conditions should a firm claim to prepare financial statements in accordance with IFRS?
15. To what extent have IFRS been adopted by countries around the world?
16. How has the U.S. SEC policy toward IFRS changed?

Exercises and Problems

1. "The IASB has been repeatedly accused of devising accounting standards that pay insufficient attention to the concerns and practices of companies . . . . Some European banks and insurers complain about poor due process by the IASB, and Frits Bolkestein, European commissioner responsible for accounting matters, endorsed their concerns earlier this month" (*Financial Times*, March 24, 2004, p. 20).

[4] David Alexander and Simon Archer, "On the Myth of 'Anglo-Saxon' Accounting," *International Journal of Accounting* 35, no. 4 (2000), pp. 539–57.
[5] Nobes (2003), op cit.

Required:

Elaborate on the concerns raised in the preceding quote, and discuss the measures that have been taken by the IASB to alleviate those concerns.

2. Since 2005, publicly traded companies in the European Union have been required to use IFRS in preparing their consolidated financial statements.

Required:

a. Explain the EU's objective in requiring the use of IFRS.

b. Identify and describe two issues that might hamper the EU from achieving the objective underlying the use of IFRS.

3. Assume that you have been invited to advise the newly established accounting oversight body in one of the former eastern European countries that became a member of the EU in May 2004. The accounting oversight body is charged with the task of identifying the main issues to be addressed in implementing the use of IFRS.

Required:

Prepare a report outlining the key points you would include in your advice to this accounting oversight body.

4. Refer to Exhibit 3.6 in this chapter and note the countries that do not permit domestic listed companies to use IFRS.

Required:

Identify three countries from this group that are likely to have different reasons for not permitting the use of IFRS by domestic listed companies. Describe those reasons.

5. On May 19, 2004, the IASB published a single volume of its official pronouncements that will be applicable from January 1, 2005.

Required:

Access the IASB Web site (www.iasb.org), search for these pronouncements, and prepare a list of them.

6. The professional accounting bodies in many countries have taken, or are taking, steps to adopt IFRS.

Required:

Go to the Web site of a professional accounting body of your choice and outline the steps it has taken so far to facilitate adoption of IFRS.

7. The appendix to this chapter describes what is commonly referred to as Anglo-Saxon accounting.

Required:

Explain why Anglo-Saxon accounting might be of interest to Chinese accounting regulators.

8. In its 2003 annual report, Honda Motor Company Ltd. states:

Honda's manufacturing operations are principally conducted in 25 separate factories, 5 of which are located in Japan. Principal overseas manufacturing factories are located in the United States of America, Canada, The United Kingdom, France, Italy, Spain, India, Pakistan, the Philippines, Thailand, Vietnam, Brazil, and Mexico . . . . The company and its domestic subsidiaries maintain their books of account in conformity with financial accounting standards of Japan, and its foreign subsidiaries generally maintain their books of account in conformity with those of the countries of their domicile. The consolidated financial statements presented herein have been prepared in a manner and reflect the adjustments which are necessary to conform them with accounting principles generally accepted in the United States of America. (p. 59)

Required:

Discuss the possible reasons for Honda to prepare its consolidated financial statements in conformity with U.S. GAAP.

9. A list of foreign companies with shares traded on the New York Stock Exchange (NYSE) can be found on the NYSE's Web site (www.nyse.com).

   Required:
   a. Refer to Exhibit 3.6. Identify a developing country in Asia, Africa, and Latin America listed in Exhibit 3.6, and determine how many companies from each of these countries are listed on the NYSE. If the country you select first from a region does not have any NYSE-listed companies, identify another country included in Exhibit 3.6 from that region that does.
   b. Describe the manner in which IFRSs are used in each of the countries you have selected.

10. The *Financial Times*, on Tuesday, April 13, 2004, made the following comment in its editorial "Parmalat: Perennial Lessons of European Scandal: Urgent need for better enforcement and investor scepticism:"

    After the accounting scandals in the US, there was an unseemly amount of crowing in Europe. As it happens, Parmalat is a much older scandal than Enron or WorldCom. It just took longer to come out at the Italian dairy company. . . . Convergence of standards—in accounting, for instance—will help spread best practice. So will high level meetings between regulators, such as take place within the International Organisation of Securities Commission. But we are nowhere near having a world super-regulator. . . . In Italy regulation has been weak because of fragmentation and lack of clout and resources. Attempts to tackle this and to ensure regulators' independence from political interference should be urgently pursued." (p. 12)

    Required:
    Discuss the lessons referred to above concerning the objectives of the current efforts at setting global standards for accounting and financial reporting.

11. The chapter describes different phases in the harmonization efforts of the IASC.

    Required:
    Identify one such phase and prepare a brief report describing its importance in the overall scheme of international harmonization of accounting standards. You should consult relevant literature in preparing this report.

12. The IASB's main objective is to develop a set of high-quality standards for financial reporting by companies at international level.

    Required:
    Critically examine the possibility of achieving this objective.

13. Geneva Technology Company (GTC), a Swiss-based company founded in 1999, is considering the use of IFRSs in preparing its annual report for the year ended December 31, 2007. You are the manager of GTC's fixed assets accounting department.

    Required:
    Identify the steps that you will need to take in your department to comply with the requirements of IFRS 1.

14. Recently the IASB revised IFRS 1.

    Required:
    What is the main reason for this revision?

15. The SEC has lifted the requirement for foreign companies that have used IFRS as the basis for preparing their financial statements: to be eligible to list their shares in U.S. stock exchanges, they should reconcile their financial statements using U.S. GAAP.

    Required:
    Discuss the possible reasons for this relaxation of rules.

Case 3-1

Jardine Matheson Group (Part 1)

With its broad portfolio of market-leading businesses, the Jardine Matheson Group is an Asian-based conglomerate with extensive experience in the region. Its business interests include Jardine Pacific, Jardine Motors Group, Hongkong Land, Dairy Farm, Mandarin Oriental, Cycle & Carriage and Jardine Lloyd Thompson. These companies are leaders in the fields of engineering and construction, transport services, motor trading, property, retailing, restaurants, hotels and insurance broking.

The Group's strategy is to build its operations into market leaders across Asia Pacific, each with the support of Jardine Matheson's extensive knowledge of the region and its long-standing relationships. Through a balance of cash producing activities and investment in new businesses, the Group aims to produce sustained growth in shareholder value.

Incorporated in Bermuda, Jardine Matheson has its primary share listing in London, with secondary listings in Singapore and Bermuda. Jardine Matheson Limited operates from Hong Kong and provides management services to Group companies, making available senior management and providing financial, legal, human resources and treasury support services throughout the Group.[1]

Jardine Matheson uses International Financial Reporting Standards in preparing its financial statements and has done so for a number of years.

Required

Access Jardine Matheson's most recent annual report on the company's Web site (www.jardine-matheson.com). Review the company's consolidated financial statements to evaluate whether the financial statements presented comply with the presentation requirements in IAS 1, *Presentation of Financial Statements.* Document your evaluation.

---

[1] www.jardine-matheson.com/profile/intro.html.

References

Alexander, David, and Simon Archer. "On the Myth of 'Anglo-Saxon' Accounting." *International Journal of Accounting* 35, no. 4 (2000), pp. 539–57.

BDO, Deloitte Touche Tohmatsu, Ernst & Young, Grant Thornton, KPMG, PricewaterhouseCoopers. *GAAP Convergence 2002: A Survey of National Efforts to Promote and Achieve Convergence with International Financial Reporting Standards.* Available at www.ifad.net

Beresford, Dennis R. "Accounting for International Operations." *CPA Journal*, October 1988, pp. 79–80.

Cairns, David. "Compliance Must Be Enforced." *Accountancy International*, September 1998, pp. 64–65.

———. *Financial Times International Accounting Standards Survey.* London: FT Finance, 1999.

Carey, Anthony. "Harmonization: Europe Moves Forward." *Accountancy*, March 1990.

Carsberg, Sir Bryan. "Global Issues and Implementing Core International Accounting Standards: Where Lies IASC's Final Goal?" Remarks made at the 50th Anniversary Dinner, Japanese Institute of CPAs, Tokyo, October 23, 1998.

Chen, S., Z. Sun, and Y. Wang. "Evidence from China on Whether Harmonized Accounting Standards Harmonize Accounting Practices." *Accounting Horizons* 16, no. 3 (2002), pp. 183–97.

Choi, F. D. S. "A Cluster Approach to Harmonization." *Management Accounting*, August 1981, pp. 27–31.

Collins, Stephen H. "The SEC on Full and Fair Disclosure." *Journal of Accountancy*, January 1989, p. 84.

Commission of the European Communities. "EU Financial Reporting Strategy: The Way Forward." Communication from the Commission to the Council and the European Parliament, June 13, 2000.

Doupnik, Timothy S. "Recent Innovations in German Accounting Practice Through the Integration of EC Directives," *Advances in International Accounting* 5 (1992), pp. 75–103.

———, and M. Richter. "Interpretation of Uncertainty Expressions: A Cross-national Study." *Accounting, Organizations and Society* 28, no. 1 (2003), pp. 15–35.

Emenyonu, Emmanuel N., and Sidney J. Gray. "International Accounting Harmonization and the Major Developed Stock Market Countries: An Empirical Study." *International Journal of Accounting* 31, no. 3 (1996), pp. 269–79.

Ernst & Young. "Mind the GAAP: The Rise and Fall of IAS Lite." *Eye on IAS Newsletter*, June 2002, pp. 2–8.

Financial Accounting Standards Board. *The IASC-U.S. Comparison Project: A Report on the Similarities and Differences between IASC Standards and U.S. GAAP*, ed. Carrie Bloomer. Norwalk, CT: FASB, 1996.

Financial Accounting Standards Board. *The IASC-U.S. Comparison Project*, 2nd ed. Norwalk, CT: FASB, 1999.

Goeltz, Richard Karl. 1991. "International Accounting Harmonization: The Impossible (and Unnecessary?) Dream." *Accounting Horizons*, March 1991, pp. 85–86.

International Accounting Standards Committee. *Survey of the Use and Application of International Accounting Standards 1988.* London: IASC, 1988.

IOSCO. *Final Communique of the XXIXth Annual Conference of the International Organization of Securities Commissions.* Amman, May 17–20, 2004.

Nobes, Christopher W. "On the Myth of 'Anglo-Saxon' Financial Accounting: A Comment." *International Journal of Accounting* 38 (2003), pp. 95–104.

Street, Donna L., Sidney J. Gray, and Stephanie M. Bryant. "Acceptance and Observance of International Accounting Standards: An Empirical Study of Companies Claiming to Comply with IASs," *International Journal of Accounting* 34, no. 1 (1999), pp. 11–48.

"The World After WorldCom," *Financial Times,* June 27, 2002.

Zeff, S. "Political Lobbying on Proposed Standards: A Challenge to the IASB." *Accounting Horizons* 16, no. 1 (2002), pp. 43–54.

Chapter **Four**

International Financial Reporting Standards: Part I

Learning Objectives

After reading this chapter, you should be able to

- Discuss the types of differences that exist between International Financial Reporting Standards (IFRS) and U.S. generally accepted accounting standards (GAAP).
- Describe IFRS requirements related to the recognition and measurement of assets, specifically inventories; property, plant, and equipment; intangibles; and leased assets.
- Explain major differences between IFRS and U.S. GAAP on the recognition and measurement of assets.
- Describe the requirements of IFRS in a variety of disclosure and presentation standards.
- Explain major differences between IFRS and U.S. GAAP on certain disclosure and presentation issues.
- Analyze the impact that differences between IFRS and U.S. GAAP can have on the financial statements.

INTRODUCTION

As noted in Chapter 3, International Financial Reporting Standards (IFRS) have been adopted as generally accepted accounting principles (GAAP) for listed companies in many countries around the world and are accepted for cross-listing purposes by most major stock exchanges, including those in the United States.[1] Increasingly, accountants are being called on to prepare and audit, and users are finding it necessary to read and analyze, IFRS-based financial statements. With the U.S. Securities and Exchange Commission reaffirming its support for a global set of accounting standards, it is likely that IFRS will be integrated into

---

[1] The term *International Financial Reporting Standards (IFRS)* describes the body of authoritative pronouncements issued or adopted by the IASB. IFRS consist of International Accounting Standards issued by the IASC (and adopted by the IASB), International Financial Reporting Standards issued by the IASB, and interpretations developed by IFRIC or the former SIC.

the U.S. financial reporting system in the near future.[2] This chapter describes and demonstrates the requirements of selected IASB standards, particularly those relating to the recognition and measurement of assets, through numerical examples. IFRS that deal exclusively with disclosure and presentation issues also are briefly summarized.

The International Accounting Standards Committee (IASC) issued a total of 41 International Accounting Standards (IAS) during the period 1973–2001. Twelve of these standards have been superseded or withdrawn. Most of the 29 remaining standards have been revised one or more times. Since 2001, the IASB has issued nine International Financial Reporting Standards (IFRS). Exhibit 3.2 in Chapter 3 provides a list of IAS and IFRS issued by the IASB as of September 2010. In addition, more than 20 interpretations issued by the Standing Interpretations Committee (SIC) or International Financial Reporting Interpretations Committee (IFRIC) complement the standards to comprise the complete set of IFRS.

In this chapter, in addition to describing the guidance provided by IFRS, we make comparisons with U.S. GAAP to indicate the differences and similarities between the two sets of standards.[3] In this way, we can begin to appreciate the impact a choice between the two sets of standards has on financial statements.

TYPES OF DIFFERENCES BETWEEN IFRS AND U.S. GAAP

Numerous differences exist between IFRS and U.S. GAAP. The types of differences that exist can be classified as follows:

- *Definition differences.* Differences in definitions exist even though concepts are similar. Definition differences can lead to recognition or measurement differences.
- *Recognition differences.* Differences in recognition criteria and/or guidance are related to (1) whether an item is recognized or not, (2) how it is recognized (e.g., as a liability or as equity), and/or (3) when it is recognized (timing difference).
- *Measurement differences.* Differences in the *amount* recognized resulting from either (1) a difference in the method required or (2) a difference in the detailed guidance for applying a similar method.
- *Alternatives.* One set of standards allows a choice between two or more alternative methods; the other set of standards requires one specific method to be used.
- *Lack of requirements or guidance.* IFRS may not cover an issue addressed by U.S. GAAP, and vice versa.
- *Presentation differences.* Differences exist in the presentation of items in the financial statements.
- *Disclosure differences.* Differences in information presented in the notes to financial statements are related to (1) whether a disclosure is required and (2) the manner in which disclosures are required to be made.

In many cases, IFRS are more flexible than U.S. GAAP. For example, several IASB standards allow firms to choose between two alternative treatments in

---

[2] Securities and Exchange Commission, Release Nos. 33-9109; 34-61578 Commission Statement in Support of Convergence and Global Accounting Standards, February 2010.

[3] It is important to remember that both IFRS and U.S. GAAP are moving targets, constantly changing. This chapter describes IFRS and makes comparisons with U.S. GAAP as of September 2010.

accounting for a particular item. Also, IFRS generally have less bright-line guidance than U.S. GAAP; therefore, more judgment is required in applying IFRS. IFRS are said to constitute a principles-based accounting system (broad principles with limited detailed rules), whereas U.S. GAAP is a rules-based system.[4] However, for some accounting issues, IFRS are more detailed than U.S. GAAP.

Ernst & Young conducted a survey of 130 companies that provided reconciliation from IFRS to U.S. GAAP in their 2005 Form 20-F filed with the U.S. Securities and Exchange Commission.[5] Companies included in the survey were primarily located in the European Union, but it also included several companies in Switzerland, South Africa, and China. The 130 companies in the survey reported a total of 1,900 reconciling items, and 200 unique differences between IFRS and U.S. GAAP were identified. Many of the adjustments related to first-time application of IFRS. Pensions and business combinations were the two accounting issues that required adjustments by the greatest number of companies (122 companies and 100 companies, respectively). Other issues requiring adjustment by a large number of companies included provisions (74 companies), impairment of assets (62 companies), leases (49 companies), and intangibles (36 companies).

INVENTORIES

IAS 2, *Inventories,* is an example of an International Accounting Standard that provides more extensive guidance than U.S. GAAP, especially with regard to inventories of service providers and disclosures related to inventories. IAS 2 provides guidance on determining the initial cost of inventories, the cost formulas to be used in allocating the cost of inventories to expense, and the subsequent measurement of inventories on the balance sheet.

The cost of inventories includes costs of purchase, costs of conversion, and other costs:

- *Costs of purchase* include purchase price; import duties and other taxes; and transportation, handling, and other costs directly attributable to acquiring materials, services, and finished products.
- *Costs of conversion* include direct labor and a systematic allocation of variable and fixed production overhead. Fixed overhead should be applied based on a normal level of production.
- *Other costs* are included in the cost of inventories to the extent they are incurred to bring the inventories to their present location and condition. This can include the cost of designing products for specific customers. Under certain conditions, interest costs are allowed to be included in the cost of inventories for those items that require a substantial period of time to bring them to a saleable condition.

Costs that are expressly excluded from the costs of inventories are:

- Abnormal amounts of wasted materials, labor, or other production costs.
- Storage costs, unless they are necessary in the production process before a further stage of production.

---

[4] In response to several accounting scandals, including those at Enron and WorldCom, the Sarbanes-Oxley Act passed by the U.S. Congress in 2002 required the FASB to investigate the desirability of U.S. GAAP shifting to a principles-based approach.

[5] Ernst & Young, *Towards Convergence—A Survey of IFRS/US GAAP Differences* (EYGM Limited, 2007). The publication is available at www.ey.com.

- Administrative overhead that does not contribute to bringing inventories to their present location and condition.
- Selling costs.

IAS 2 does not allow as much choice with regard to cost formulas as does U.S. GAAP. First-in, first-out (FIFO) and weighted-average cost are acceptable treatments, but last-in, first-out (LIFO) is not. The standard cost method and retail method also are acceptable provided that they approximate cost as defined in IAS 2. The cost of inventories of items that are not ordinarily interchangeable and goods or services produced and segregated for specific projects must be accounted for using the specific identification method. An entity must use the same cost formula for all inventories having a similar nature and use to the entity, even if they are located in different geographical locations. For inventories with a different nature or use, different cost formulas may be justified. U.S. GAAP does not require use of a uniform inventory valuation method for inventory having a similar nature. It is common for U.S. companies to use different methods in different jurisdictions for tax reasons—for example, LIFO in the U.S. and FIFO or average cost elsewhere.

Lower of Cost or Net Realizable Value

IAS 2 requires inventory to be reported on the balance sheet at the lower of cost or net realizable value. *Net realizable value* is defined as estimated selling price in the ordinary course of business less the estimated costs of completion and the estimated costs necessary to make the sale. This rule typically is applied on an item-by-item basis. However, the standard indicates that it may be appropriate to group similar items of inventory relating to the same product line. Write-downs to net realizable value must be reversed when the selling price increases.

U.S. GAAP requires inventory to be reported at the lower of cost or market, where market is defined as replacement cost with a ceiling (net realizable value) and a floor (net realizable value less normal profit margin). The two sets of standards will provide similar results only when replacement cost is greater than net realizable value. Application of this valuation rule may be done either item by item, by groups of inventory, or on a total inventory basis. Under U.S. GAAP, write-downs to market may not be reversed if replacement costs should subsequently increase.

Example: Application of Lower of Cost or Net Realizable Value Rule

Assume that Distributor Company Inc. has the following inventory item on hand at December 31, Year 1:

Historical cost.	$1,000.00
Replacement cost.	800.00
Estimated selling price	880.00
Estimated costs to complete and sell	50.00
Net realizable value	830.00
Normal profit margin—15%	124.50
Net realizable value less normal profit margin	$ 705.50

Net realizable value is $830, which is lower than historical cost. In accordance with IFRS, inventory must be written down by $170 ($1,000 − $830). The journal entry at December 31, Year 1, is:

Inventory loss.	$170	
Inventory		$170
To record the write-down on inventory due to decline in net realizable value.		

Under U.S. GAAP, market is replacement cost of $800 (falls between $705.50 and $830), which is lower than historical cost. Inventory must be written down by $200 ($1,000 − $800).

Assume that at the end of the first quarter in Year 2, replacement cost has increased to $900, the estimated selling price has increased to $980, and the estimated cost to complete and sell remains at $50. The item now has a net realizable value of $930. This is $100 greater than carrying amount (and $70 less than historical cost). Under IFRS, $100 of the write-down that was made at December 31, Year 1, is reversed through the following journal entry:

Inventory	$100	
Recovery of inventory loss (increase in income)		$100
To record a recovery of inventory loss taken in the previous period.		

Under U.S. GAAP, the new carrying amount for the item is $800, which is less than the current replacement cost of $900. However, no adjustment is made.

In effect, under IFRS, the historical cost of $1,000 is used in applying the lower of cost or net realizable value rule over the entire period the inventory is held. In contrast, under U.S. GAAP, the inventory write-down at the end of Year 1 establishes a new cost used in subsequent periods in applying the lower of cost or market rule.

Over the period of time that inventory is held by a firm, the two sets of standards result in the same amount of expenses (cost of goods sold plus any net inventory loss). However, the amount of expense recognized in any given accounting period can differ between the two rules as can the amount at which inventory is measured on the balance sheet.

PROPERTY, PLANT, AND EQUIPMENT

IAS 16, *Property, Plant, and Equipment,* provides guidance for the following aspects of accounting for fixed assets:

1. Recognition of initial costs of property, plant, and equipment.
2. Recognition of subsequent costs.
3. Measurement at initial recognition.
4. Measurement after initial recognition.
5. Depreciation.
6. Derecognition (retirements and disposals).

Impairment of assets, including property, plant, and equipment, is covered by IAS 36, *Impairment of Assets.* Accounting for impairments is discussed later in this chapter.

Recognition of Initial and Subsequent Costs

Relying on the definition of an asset provided in the IASB's *Framework for the Preparation and Presentation of Financial Standards*, both initial costs and subsequent costs related to property, plant, and equipment should be recognized as an asset when (1) it is probable that future economic benefits will flow to the enterprise and (2) the cost can be measured reliably. Replacement of part of an asset should be capitalized if (1) and (2) are met, and the carrying amount of the replaced part should be derecognized (removed from the accounts).

Example: Replacement of Part of an Asset

Road Warriors Inc. acquired a truck with a useful life of 20 years at a cost of $150,000. At the end of the sixth year, the power train requires replacement. The remainder of the truck is perfectly roadworthy and is expected to last another 14 years. The cost of the new power train is $35,000.

The new power train will provide economic benefit to Road Warriors (it will allow the company to continue to use the truck), and the cost is measurable. The $35,000 cost of the new power train meets the asset recognition criteria and should be added to the cost of the truck. The original cost of the truck of $150,000 was not broken down by component, so the cost attributable to the original power train must be estimated. Assuming annual price increases for power trains of 5 percent, Road Warriors estimates that the cost of the original power train was $26,117 ($35,000/1.05^6). The appropriate journal entries to account for the replacement would be:

Truck	$35,000	
Cash		$35,000
Expense	$26,117	
Truck		$26,117

Measurement at Initial Recognition

Property, plant, and equipment should be initially measured at cost, which includes (1) purchase price, including import duties and taxes; (2) all costs directly attributable in bringing the asset to the location and condition necessary for it to perform as intended; and (3) an estimate of the costs of dismantling and removing the asset and restoring the site on which it is located.

An item of property, plant, and equipment acquired in exchange for a non-monetary asset or combination of monetary and nonmonetary assets should be initially measured at fair value unless the exchange transaction lacks commercial substance. Fair value is defined as the "amount for which an asset could be exchanged between knowledgeable, willing parties in an arm's length transaction."[6] If the transaction lacks commercial substance or the fair value of the asset acquired and given up cannot be determined, then the cost of the asset acquired is measured as the carrying value of the asset given up. As a result, no gain or loss is recognized.

[6] IAS 16, paragraph 6.

Example: Dismantling and Removal Costs

Caylor Corporation constructed a powder coating facility at a cost of $3,000,000: $1,000,000 for the building and $2,000,000 for machinery and equipment. Local law requires the company to dismantle and remove the plant assets at the end of their useful life. Caylor estimates that the net cost, after deducting salvage value, for removal of the equipment is $100,000, and the net cost for dismantling and removing the building will be $400,000. The useful life of the facility is 20 years, and the company uses a discount rate of 10 percent in determining present values.

The initial cost of the machinery and equipment and the building must include the estimated dismantling and removal costs discounted to present value. The present value factor for a discount rate of 10 percent for 20 periods is 0.14864 ($1/1.10^{20}$). The calculations are as follows:

Building

Construction cost	$1,000,000
Present value of dismantling and removal costs ($400,000 × 0.14864)	59,457
Total cost of the building	$1,059,457

Machinery and equipment

Construction cost	$2,000,000
Present value of dismantling and removal costs ($100,000 × 0.14864)	14,864
Total cost of the machinery and equipment	$2,014,864

The journal entry to record the initial cost of the assets would be:

Building	$1,059,457	
Machinery and equipment	2,014,864	
Cash		$3,000,000
Provision for dismantling and removal (long-term liability)		74,321

Measurement Subsequent to Initial Recognition

A substantive area of difference between IFRS and U.S. GAAP relates to the measurement of property, plant, and equipment subsequent to initial recognition. IAS 16 allows two treatments for reporting fixed assets on balance sheets subsequent to their acquisition: the cost model and the revaluation model.

Under the cost model, an item of property, plant, and equipment is carried on the balance sheet at cost less accumulated depreciation and any accumulated impairment losses. This is consistent with U.S. GAAP.

Under the revaluation model, an item of property, plant, and equipment is carried at a revalued amount, measured as fair value at the date of revaluation, less any subsequent accumulated depreciation and any accumulated impairment losses. If an enterprise chooses to follow this measurement model, revaluations must be made often enough that the carrying amount of assets does not differ materially from the assets' fair value. When revaluations are made, an entire class of property, plant, and equipment must be revalued. Revaluation increases are credited directly to the other comprehensive income component of equity as a revaluation surplus. Revaluation decreases are first recognized as a reduction in any related revaluation surplus, and, once the surplus is exhausted, additional revaluation decrease is recognized as an expense. The revaluation surplus may be transferred to retained earnings on disposal of the asset. Revalued assets may be presented either (1) at a gross amount less a separately reported accumulated depreciation (both revalued) or (2) at a net amount. Allowing firms the option to revalue fixed assets is one of the most substantial differences between IFRS and U.S. GAAP. Guidelines for applying this option are presented in more detail in the following paragraphs.

Determination of Fair Value

The basis of revaluation is the *fair value* of the asset at the date of revaluation. The definition in IAS 16 indicates that fair value is the amount at which an asset could be exchanged between knowledgeable, willing parties in an arm's-length transaction. The fair value of land and buildings is usually determined through appraisals conducted by professionally qualified valuers. The fair value of plant and equipment is also usually determined through appraisal. In the case of a specialized asset that is not normally sold, fair value may need to be estimated using, for example, a depreciated replacement cost approach. In 2009, the IASB issued an exposure draft, *Fair Value Measurement,* that is intended to provide considerably more guidance with respect to measuring the fair value of assets, including property, plant, and equipment and liabilities. If approved as a final standard, this exposure draft also will substantially converge IFRS with U.S. GAAP with respect to how fair value is measured.

Frequency of Revaluation

IAS 16 requires that revalued amounts should not differ materially from fair values at the balance sheet date. The effect of this rule is that once an enterprise has opted for the revaluation model, it has an obligation to keep the valuations up to date. Although the IASB avoids mandating annual revaluations, these will be necessary in some circumstances in order to comply with the standard. In other cases, annual changes in fair value will be insignificant and revaluation may be necessary only every several years.

Selection of Assets to Be Revalued

IAS 16 requires that all assets of the same class be revalued at the same time. Selectivity *within a class* is not permitted, but selection *of a class* is. Different classes of assets described in the standard are as follows: land; land and buildings; machinery; office equipment; furniture and fixtures; motor vehicles; ships; and aircraft.

Detailed disclosures are required for each class of property, plant, and equipment (whether revalued or not). Thus, if a company divides its assets into many classes to minimize the effect of the rule about revaluing a whole class of assets, it will incur the burden of being required to make additional disclosures for each of those classes.

Accumulated Depreciation

Two alternative treatments are described in IAS 16 for the treatment of accumulated depreciation when a class of property, plant, and equipment is revalued:

1. Restate the accumulated depreciation proportionately with the change in the gross carrying amount of the asset so that the carrying amount of the asset after revaluation equals its revalued amount. The Standard comments that this method is often used where an asset is revalued by means of an index and is the appropriate method for those companies using current cost accounting.
2. Eliminate the accumulated depreciation against the gross carrying amount of the asset, and restate the net amount to the revalued amount of the asset.

Example: Treatment of Accumulated Depreciation upon Revaluation

Assume that Kiely Company Inc. has buildings that cost $1,000,000, with accumulated depreciation of $600,000 and a carrying amount of $400,000 on December 31, Year 1. On that date, Kiely Company determines that the market value for these buildings is $750,000. Kiely Company wishes to carry buildings on the December 31, Year 1, balance sheet at a revalued amount. Under treatment 1, Kiely Company would restate both the buildings account and accumulated depreciation on buildings such that the ratio of net carrying amount to gross carrying amount is 40 percent ($400,000/$1,000,000) and the net carrying amount is $750,000. To accomplish this, the following journal entry would be made at December 31, Year 1:

Buildings	$875,000	
Accumulated depreciation—buildings		$525,000
Revaluation surplus		350,000
To revalue buildings and related accumulated depreciation		

	Original Cost		Revaluation		Total	%
Gross carrying amount	$1,000,000	+	$875,000	=	$1,875,000	100%
Accumulated depreciation	600,000	+	525,000	=	1,125,000	60
Net carrying amount	$ 400,000	+	$350,000	=	$ 750,000	40%

Under treatment 2, accumulated depreciation of $600,000 is first eliminated against the buildings account, and then the buildings account is increased by $350,000 to result in a net carrying amount of $750,000. The necessary journal entries are as follows:

Accumulated depreciation—buildings	$600,000	
Buildings		$600,000
To eliminate accumulated depreciation on buildings to be revalued.		
Buildings	$350,000	
Revaluation surplus		$350,000
To revalue buildings.		

As a result of making these two entries, the buildings account has a net carrying amount of $750,000 ($1,000,000 − 600,000 + 350,000). Under both treatments, both assets and equity are increased by a net amount of $350,000.

Treatment of Revaluation Surpluses and Deficits

On the first revaluation after initial recording, the treatment of increases and decreases in carrying amount as a result of revaluation is very straightforward:

- Increases are credited directly to a revaluation surplus in the other comprehensive income component of equity.
- Decreases are charged to the income statement as an expense.

  At subsequent revaluations, the following rules apply:

- To the extent that there is a previous revaluation surplus with respect to an asset, a decrease first should be charged against it and any excess of deficit over that previous surplus should be expensed.

- To the extent that a previous revaluation resulted in a charge to expense, a subsequent upward revaluation first should be recognized as income to the extent of the previous expense and any excess should be credited to other comprehensive income in equity.

Example: Treatment of Revaluation Surplus

Assume that Kiely Company Inc. has elected to measure property, plant, and equipment at revalued amounts. Costs and fair values for Kiely Company's three classes of property, plant, and equipment at December 31, Year 1 and Year 2, are as follows:

	Land	Buildings	Machinery
Cost.	$100,000	$500,000	$200,000
Fair value at 12/31/Y1	120,000	450,000	210,000
Fair value at 12/31/Y2	150,000	460,000	185,000

The following journal entries are made at December 31, Year 1, to adjust the carrying amount of the three classes of property, plant, and equipment to fair value:

Land	$20,000	
Revaluation surplus—land.		$20,000
Loss on revaluation—buildings (expense)	$50,000	
Buildings.		$50,000
Machinery	$10,000	
Revaluation surplus—machinery		$10,000

At December 31, Year 2, the following journal entries are made:

Land	$30,000	
Revaluation surplus—land.		$30,000
Buildings	$10,000	
Recovery of loss on revaluation—buildings (income)		$10,000
Revaluation surplus—machinery.	$10,000	
Loss on revaluation—machinery (expense)	15,000	
Machinery.		$25,000

IAS 16 indicates that the revaluation surplus in equity may be transferred to retained earnings when the surplus is realized. The surplus may be considered to be realized either through use of the asset or upon its sale or disposal. Accordingly, the revaluation surplus in equity may be transferred in one of two ways to retained earnings:

- A lump sum may be transferred at the time the asset is sold or scrapped.
- Within each period, an amount equal to the difference between depreciation on the revalued amount and depreciation on the historical cost of the asset may be transferred to retained earnings.

A third possibility apparently allowed by IAS 16 would be to do nothing with the revaluation surplus. However, this would result in a revaluation surplus being reported in equity related to assets no longer owned by the firm.

Insight into the effect the revaluation model has on financial statements can be gained by examining the U.S. GAAP reconciliations that were required of foreign companies with shares publicly traded in the United States. With shares traded on the New York Stock Exchange, until 2007 China Eastern Airlines Corporation (CEA) was required to reconcile IFRS-based income and shareholders' equity to a U.S. GAAP basis. Exhibit 4.1 presents CEA's reconciliation to U.S. GAAP, along with the note describing significant differences between IFRS and U.S. GAAP with respect to revaluation of property, plant, and equipment. In reconciling "consolidated profit/(loss) attributable to the Company's equity holders," CEA makes an adjustment for the "reversal of net revaluation surplus, net of depreciation charges." This adjustment reflects the amount of additional depreciation expense recognized under IFRS on higher revalued amounts that would not be taken under U.S. GAAP. In 2006, profit/(loss) under IFRS was increased by 53.7 million renminbi (RMB) to adjust to a U.S. GAAP basis. CEA also makes a positive adjustment in reconciling to U.S. GAAP income for the "profit/(loss) on disposals of aircraft and related assets." Revalued assets have a higher book value than assets carried at cost. As a result, when revalued assets are sold, the gain on sale is smaller than it otherwise would be. In 2006, CEA increased U.S. GAAP income by RMB 156.5 million to include the larger gain that would have been recognized if assets had been carried at cost (under U.S. GAAP) rather than revalued amounts (under IFRS).

EXHIBIT 4.1

CHINA EASTERN AIRLINES CORPORATION LIMITED
Form 20-F
2006
Revaluation of Property, Plant, and Equipment

Notes to the Consolidated Financial Statements

Excerpt from Note 40 Significant Differences between IFRS and U.S. GAAP

Differences between IFRS and U.S. GAAP which have significant effects on the consolidated profit/(loss) attributable to equity holders and consolidated net assets of the Group are summarized as follows:

	Note	2004 RMB'000	2005 RMB'000	2006 RMB'000
Consolidated profit/(loss) attributable to the Company's equity holders				
As stated under IFRS		456,371	(438,728)	(3,452,765)
Less: Minority interests	(h)	(135,680)	(28,579)	139,340
		320,691	(467,307)	(3,313,425)
U.S. GAAP adjustments:				
Net (loss)/income after tax effect attributable to CEA Northwest and CEA Yunnan	(a)	24,424	(575,326)	—
Reversal of net revaluation surplus, net of depreciation charges	(b)	57,568	73,803	53,772
Profit/(loss) on disposals of aircraft and related assets	(b)	7,099	861	156,589
Rescission of related party lease arrangements	(c)	(133,029)	—	—
Reversal of the impact of the new overhaul accounting policy adopted in 2005	(d)	227,510	(471,756)	—
Recognition of additional write-down in relation to assets held for sale	(e)	—	—	(434,561)
Reversal of gain on sale and leaseback of aircraft recognized under IFRS	(f)	—	—	(126,470)

Others	(i)	(1,518)	(3,720)	26,997
Deferred tax effect on the U.S. GAAP adjustments	(j)	(43,598)	60,122	(23,872)
As stated under U.S. GAAP		459,147	(1,383,323)	(3,660,970)
Basic and fully diluted earning/(loss) per share under U.S. GAAP		RMB 0.094	(RMB 0.284)	(RMB 0.741)
Basic and fully diluted earning/(loss) per American Depository Share ("ADS") under U.S. GAAP		RMB 9.43	(RMB 28.42)	(RMB 74.12)
Consolidated net assets				
As stated under IFRS		7,302,086	6,918,542	3,476,643
Less: Minority interests	(h)	(820,835)	(822,477)	(661,746)
		6,481,251	6,096,065	2,814,897
U.S. GAAP adjustments:				
Impact on equity before tax effect attributable to CEA Northwest and CEA Yunnan	(a)	(1,426,741)	413,841	413,841
Reversal of net revaluation surplus net of depreciation charges and profit/(loss) on disposals of aircraft and related assets	(b)	(480,010)	(405,346)	(194,985)
Reversal of impact of the new overhaul accounting policy adopted in 2005	(d)	471,756	—	—
Recognition of additional write-down in relation to assets held for sale	(e)	—	—	(434,561)
Reversal of gain on sale-and-leaseback of aircraft recognized under IFRS	(f)	—	—	(126,470)
Recognition of the funded status of postretirement benefits obligations under U.S. GAAP	(g)	—	—	(548,428)
Others	(i)	34,453	(12,140)	(12,365)
Deferred tax effect on the U.S. GAAP adjustments	(j)	(52,993)	7,129	(16,232)
As stated under U.S. GAAP		5,027,716	6,099,549	1,895,697

(b) Revaluation of property, plant, and equipment

Under IFRS, the Group's property, plant, and equipment are initially recorded at cost and are subsequently restated at revalued amounts less accumulated depreciation. The excess depreciation charge arising from the revaluation surplus was approximately RMB57,568,000, RMB73,803,000, and RMB53,772,000 for the years ended December 31, 2004, 2005, and 2006, respectively. The additional gains arising from the revaluation surplus on disposals of revalued property, plant, and equipment were approximately gains of RMB7,099,000, RMB861,000, and RMB156,589,000 for the years ended December 31, 2004, 2005, and 2006, respectively.

Under U.S. GAAP, property, plant, and equipment are stated at cost less accumulated depreciation and impairment charges, if any. Accordingly, the revaluation surplus, the related differences in depreciation charges and gains or losses on disposals on aircraft and the related assets are reversed.

In reconciling "consolidated net assets" (stockholders' equity) from IFRS to U.S. GAAP, CEA includes an adjustment for the "reversal of net revaluation surplus net of depreciation charges and profit/(loss) on disposals of aircraft and related assets." This one-line item actually combines three different adjustments:

1. The original revaluation surplus (less accumulated depreciation) included in other comprehensive income (stockholders' equity) under IFRS is reversed. This results in a smaller amount of other comprehensive income under U.S. GAAP.
2. The difference in depreciation expense under IFRS and U.S. GAAP results in an adjustment to retained earnings; U.S. GAAP retained earnings is larger.
3. The additional amount of gain on disposal of assets that would have been recognized under U.S. GAAP also results in a larger amount of U.S. GAAP retained earnings.

The first adjustment is larger in amount than the latter two. In 2006, the sum of these three adjustments caused net assets on a U.S. GAAP-basis to be RMB194 million smaller than under IFRS. This amount represents 6.9 percent of IFRS net assets.

Depreciation

Depreciation is based on estimated useful lives, taking residual value into account. The depreciation method should reflect the pattern in which the asset's future economic benefits are expected to be consumed; straight-line depreciation will not always be appropriate. IAS 16 requires estimates of useful life, residual value, and the method of depreciation to be reviewed on an annual basis. Changes in depreciation method, residual value, and useful life are treated prospectively as changes in estimates.

When an item of property, plant, and equipment is comprised of significant parts for which different depreciation methods or useful lives are appropriate, each part must be depreciated separately. This is commonly referred to as component depreciation. Components can be physical such as an aircraft engine or nonphysical such as a major inspection. Component depreciation is not commonly used under U.S. GAAP

Example: Component Depreciation

On January 1, Year 1, an entity acquires a new piece of machinery with an estimated useful life of 10 years for $120,000. The machine has an electrical motor that must be replaced every five years and is estimated to cost $10,000 to replace. In addition, by law the machine must be inspected every two years; the inspection cost is $2,000. The company has determined that the straight-line method of depreciation best reflects the pattern in which the asset's future benefits will be consumed. Assuming no residual value, depreciation of $13,800 on this machinery in Year 1 is determined in the following manner:

Component	Cost	Useful Life	Depreciation
Motor	$ 10,000	5 years	$ 2,000
Inspection	2,000	2 years	1,000
Machine	108,000	10 years	10,800
Total	$120,000		$13,800

Derecognition

Derecognition refers to the removal of an asset or liability from the balance sheet and the accounts. The carrying amount of an item of property, plant, and equipment is derecognized (1) upon disposal, or (2)when no future economic benefits are expected from its use or disposal. The gain or loss arising from the derecognition of an item of property, plant, and equipment is included in net income.

Note that an item of property, plant, and equipment should be reclassified as "noncurrent assets held for sale" when the asset's carrying amount is to be recovered by selling the asset rather than by using the asset. IFRS 5, *Noncurrent Assets Held for Sale and Discontinued Operations,* provides guidance with respect to the accounting treatment for noncurrent assets, including property, plant, and equipment, that are held for sale, as well as guidance with respect to the accounting for discontinued operations.

INVESTMENT PROPERTY

IAS 40, *Investment Property*, prescribes the accounting treatment for investment property, which is defined as land and/or buildings held to earn rentals, capital appreciation, or both. The principles related to accounting for property, plant, and equipment generally apply to investment property, including the option to use either a cost model or a fair value model in measuring investment property subsequent to acquisition. The fair value model for investment property differs from the revaluation method for property, plant, and equipment in that changes in fair value are recognized as gains or loss in current income and not as a revaluation surplus. Even if an entity chooses the cost model, it is required to disclose the fair value of investment property in the notes to financial statements. In contrast to IFRS, U.S. GAAP generally requires use of the cost model for investment property.

IMPAIRMENT OF ASSETS

IAS 36, *Impairment of Assets*, requires impairment testing and recognition of impairment losses for property, plant, and equipment; intangible assets; goodwill; and investments in subsidiaries, associates, and joint ventures. It does not apply to inventory, construction in progress, deferred tax assets, employee benefit assets, or financial assets such as accounts and notes receivable. U.S. GAAP also requires impairment testing of assets. However, several important differences exist between the two sets of standards.

Under IAS 36, an entity must assess annually whether there are any indicators that an asset is impaired. Events that might indicate an asset is impaired are:

- *External events,* such as a decline in market value, increase in market interest rate, or economic, legal, or technological changes that adversely affect the value of an asset.
- *Internal events,* such as physical damage, obsolescence, idleness of an asset, the restructuring of part of an asset, or the worse-than-expected economic performance of the asset.

If indicators of impairment are present, an entity must estimate the recoverable amount of the asset and compare that amount with the asset's carrying amount (book value).

Definition of Impairment

Under IAS 36, an asset is impaired when its carrying amount exceeds its recoverable amount.

- *Recoverable amount* is the greater of *net selling price* and *value in use.*
- *Net selling price* is the price of an asset in an active market less disposal costs.
- *Value in use* is determined as the present value of future net cash flows expected to arise from continued use of the asset over its remaining useful life and upon disposal. In calculating value in use, projections of future cash flows should be based on approved budgets and should cover a maximum of five years (unless a longer period can be justified). The discount rate used to determine present value should reflect current market assessments of the time value of money and the risks specific to the asset under review.

Under U.S. GAAP, impairment exists when an asset's carrying amount exceeds the future cash flows (undiscounted) expected to arise from its continued use and disposal. Net selling price is not involved in the test, and future cash flows are not discounted to their present value. When value in use is the recoverable amount under IAS 36, an impairment is more likely to arise under IFRS (discounted cash flows) than under U.S. GAAP (undiscounted cash flows).

Measurement of Impairment Loss

The measurement of impairment loss under IAS 36 is straightforward. It is the amount by which carrying value exceeds recoverable amount, and it is recognized in income. In the case of property, plant, and equipment carried at a revalued amount, the impairment loss is first taken against revaluation surplus and then to income.

The comparison of carrying value and undiscounted future cash flows under U.S. GAAP is done to determine whether an asset is impaired. The impairment loss is then measured as the amount by which carrying value exceeds *fair value.* Fair value may be determined by reference to quoted market prices in active markets, estimates based on the values of similar assets, or estimates based on the results of valuation techniques. It is unlikely that fair value (U.S. GAAP) and recoverable amount (IFRS) for an asset will be the same, resulting in differences in the amount of impairment loss recognized between the two sets of standards.

Example: Determination and Measurement of Impairment Loss

At December 31, Year 1, Toca Company has specialized equipment with the following characteristics:

Carrying amount	$50,000
Selling price	40,000
Costs of disposal	1,000
Expected future cash flows	55,000
Present value of expected future cash flows	46,000

In applying IAS 36, the asset's recoverable amount would be determined as follows:

Net selling price	$40,000 − 1,000 = $39,000
Value in use	$46,000
Recoverable amount (greater of the two)	$46,000

The determination and measurement of impairment loss would be:

Carrying amount	$50,000
Recoverable amount	46,000
Impairment loss	$ 4,000

The following journal entry would be made to reflect the impairment of this asset:

Impairment loss	$4,000	
Equipment		$4,000
To recognize an impairment loss on equipment.		

Under U.S. GAAP, an impairment test would be carried out as follows:

Carrying value	$50,000
Expected future cash flows (undiscounted)	55,000

Because expected future cash flows exceed the asset's carrying value, no impairment is deemed to exist. The asset would be reported on the December 31, Year 1, balance sheet at $50,000.

Reversal of Impairment Losses

At each balance sheet date, a review should be undertaken to determine if impairment losses have reversed. (Indicators of impairment reversal are provided in IAS 36.) If, subsequent to recognizing an impairment loss, the recoverable amount of an asset is determined to exceed its new carrying amount, the impairment loss should be reversed. However, the loss should be reversed only if there are changes in the estimates used to determine the original impairment loss or there is a change in the basis for determining the recoverable amount (from value in use to net selling price or vice versa). The carrying value of the asset is increased, but not to exceed what it would have been if no impairment loss had been recognized. The reversal of an impairment loss should be recognized in income immediately. U.S. GAAP does not allow the reversal of a previously recognized impairment loss.

Example: Reversal of Impairment Loss

Spring Valley Water Company purchased new water filtration equipment at the beginning of Year 1 for $1,000,000. The equipment is expected to have a useful life of 40 years with no residual value. Therefore, annual depreciation is $25,000. By the end of Year 3, Spring Valley concluded that the filtration system was not performing up to expectations. The company determined that the system had a recoverable amount based on net selling price of $740,000. The carrying amount of the asset at the end of Year 3 was $925,000 [$1,000,000 − ($25,000 × 3 years)], so the company recognized an impairment loss of $185,000 in Year 3. Annual depreciation of $20,000 [$740,000/37 years] subsequently was recognized in Years 4 and 5. The carrying amount of the equipment at the end of Year 5 was $700,000 [$740,000 − ($20,000 × 2)]. The summary journal entries to account for this asset in Years 1 through 5 are shown here:

January 1, Year 1		
Equipment	$1,000,000	
Cash		$1,000,000
December 31, Year 1, Year 2, Year 3		
Depreciation expense	$25,000	
Accumulated depreciation—equipment		$25,000
December 31, Year 3		
Impairment loss	$185,000	
Equipment		$185,000
December 31, Year 4, Year 5		
Depreciation expense	$20,000	
Accumulated depreciation—equipment		$20,000

In January, Year 6, a technician discovered that the filtration equipment had not been properly set up at the time of initial installation. Adjustments to the installation resulted in a significant boost in performance, which led the company to reevaluate whether the equipment was still impaired. New estimates of future cash flows to be generated through continued operation of the equipment resulted in a recoverable amount based on value in use of $900,000, and the company determined that it was appropriate to reverse the impairment loss recognized in Year 3. To determine the amount of impairment loss to reverse, the company calculates what the carrying amount of the equipment would have been if the impairment had never been recognized. Annual depreciation of $25,000 would have been taken for five years, resulting in a carrying amount of $875,000 [$1,000,000 − ($25,000 × 5 years)], which is less than the new recoverable amount of $900,000. With impairment, the carrying amount of the equipment at the end of Year 5 is $700,000. Therefore, early in Year 6, Spring Valley increased the carrying amount of the equipment by $175,000 to write it up to $875,000 and recorded a reversal of impairment loss of the same amount. The reversal of impairment loss results in an increase in income:

January, Year 6		
Equipment	$175,000	
Reversal of impairment loss (increase in income)		$175,000

The shares of Lihir Gold Limited, a mining company based in Papua New Guinea, are traded on the NASDAQ market in the United States. Lihir Gold uses IFRS in preparing its financial statements. The reconciliation of net income to U.S. GAAP and procedures followed by Lihir Gold in complying with IAS 36's impairment rules are summarized in Exhibit 4.2. The company explains that impairment losses on mine properties were recorded in 1999 and 2000 under IAS 36 and that these losses were partially reversed in 2004 in the amount of $205.7 million. This reversal of a previously recognized impairment loss (which increases income) is not acceptable under U.S. accounting rules, so IFRS income was reduced by $205.7 million in 2004 to reconcile to U.S. GAAP. IFRS stockholders' equity (retained earnings) was reduced by the same amount to reconcile to U.S. GAAP.

INTANGIBLE ASSETS

IAS 38, *Intangible Assets*, provides accounting rules for purchased intangible assets, intangible assets acquired in a business combination, and internally generated intangible assets. Goodwill is covered by IFRS 3, *Business Combinations*.

IAS 38 defines an intangible asset as an *identifiable*, nonmonetary asset without physical substance held for use in the production of goods or services, for rental to others, or for administrative purposes. As an asset, it is a resource *controlled* by the enterprise as a result of past events from which *future economic benefits are expected* to arise. If a potential intangible asset does not meet this definition (i.e., it is not identifiable, not controlled, or future benefits are not probable) or cannot be measured reliably, it should be expensed immediately, unless it is obtained in a business combination, in which case it should be included in goodwill.

EXHIBIT 4.2

LIHIR GOLD LIMITED
Form 20-F
2006
Impairment of Assets

Notes to the Financial Statements

Excerpt from Note 34: Reconciliation to US GAAP

The basis of preparation of these financial statements is set out in Note 1. These accounting policies vary in certain important respects from the accounting principles generally accepted in the United States (U.S. GAAP). The material differences affecting the financial statement line items between generally accepted accounting principles followed by the Company and those generally accepted in the United States are summarized below.

	Reference	2006 US $'000	2005 US $'000	2004 US $'000
Net income under IFRS		53,837	9,788	329,221
Mine properties—capitalized interest	b	559	3,661	—
Depreciation of mine properties	c	9,226	9,205	2,974
Mine properties—impairment reversal	d	—	—	(205,723)
EGS—impairment reversal	e	—	—	(90,200)
Deferred mining costs	j	—	—	(3,123)
Adjustment of deferred charges to inventory	f	25,839	—	—
Recognition of deferred waste as a charge	f	(56,349)	—	—
Deferred tax benefit adjustment for U.S. GAAP	i	3,167	(808)	108,465
Net income under U.S. GAAP		36,279	21,845	141,614

d. Impairment: Mine properties

Under IAS 36, the impairment test for determining the recoverable amount of a noncurrent asset is the higher of net selling price and its value in use. Value in use is the net present value of cash flows expected to be realized from the asset, assessed based on the current condition of the asset. Under IFRS, impairment losses may be reversed in subsequent periods.

Under SFAS 144, an impairment loss is recognized if the carrying amount of a long-lived asset (asset group) exceeds the sum of the undiscounted cash flows expected to result from the use and eventual disposition of the asset (asset group). An impairment loss is measured as the excess of the carrying amount of the long-lived asset (asset group) over its fair value. Fair value has been estimated using present value techniques. Under U.S. GAAP, impairment reversals are not permitted.

No impairments or impairment reversals occurred in 2006 or 2005. In 2004, as a result of significant changes in the critical assumptions used to determine the value in use, including increases in the life of mine and reserves and increases in the estimated long-term gold price, the directors resolved to partially reverse impairments recognized in 2000 and 1999 to the value of $205.7 million. In determining the value in use, the Company used the long-term gold price assumptions of $380 for the year ended 2004 and a pretax real discount rate of 7 percent. As a result of the reversal in 2004, all the impairments recognized in 2000 and 1999, excluding the amount that would have been depreciated of $82.7 million, have been reversed for IFRS as the impairment write-back is limited to the amount that would have been the written-down value of the assets had there been no impairment.

Purchased Intangibles

Purchased intangibles are initially measured at cost, and their useful life is assessed as finite or indefinite. The cost of intangible assets with a finite useful life is amortized on a systematic basis over the useful life. The residual value is assumed to be zero unless (1) a third party has agreed to purchase the asset at the end of its useful life or (2) there is an active market for the asset from which a residual value can be estimated.

An intangible asset is deemed to have an indefinite life when there is no foreseeable limit to the period over which it is expected to generate cash flows for the entity. If the useful life of an intangible asset is indefinite, no amortization should be taken until the life is determined to be definite. The distinction made in IAS 38 between intangibles with a finite life and those with an indefinite life and corresponding accounting treatment is consistent with U.S. GAAP.

Intangibles Acquired in a Business Combination

Under both IAS 38 and U.S. GAAP, intangibles such as patents, trademarks, and customer lists acquired in a business combination should be recognized as assets apart from goodwill at their fair value. The acquiring company should recognize these intangibles as assets even if they were not recognized as assets by the acquiree, so long as their fair value can be measured reliably. If fair value cannot be measured reliably, the intangible is not recognized as a separate asset but is included in goodwill. Similar to purchased intangibles, intangibles acquired in a business combination must be classified as having a finite or an indefinite useful life.

A special situation arises with respect to development costs that have been incurred by the acquiree prior to the business combination, often called in-process research and development. In accordance with IAS 38, in-process development costs that meet certain criteria (described in more detail in the following subsections) must be capitalized as an intangible asset unless their fair value cannot be measured reliably, in which case they are included in goodwill. In either case, the development costs are capitalized under IFRS. Recent changes in U.S. GAAP converged the treatment of in-process research and development with IFRS.

Internally Generated Intangibles

A major difference between IFRS and U.S. GAAP lies in the treatment of internally generated intangibles. To determine whether an internally generated intangible should be recognized as an asset, IAS 38 requires the expenditures giving rise to the potential intangible to be classified as either research or development expenditures. If the two cannot be distinguished, all expenditures should be classified as research expenditures. Research expenditures must be expensed as incurred. Development expenditures, in contrast, are recognized as an intangible asset when an enterprise can demonstrate all of the following:

1. The technical feasibility of completing the intangible asset so that it will be available for use or sale.
2. Its intention to complete the intangible asset and use or sell it.
3. Its ability to use or sell the intangible asset.
4. How the intangible asset will generate probable future economic benefits. Among other things, the enterprise should demonstrate the existence of a market for the output of the intangible asset or the existence of the intangible asset itself or, if it is to be used internally, the usefulness of the intangible asset.
5. The availability of adequate technical, financial, and other resources to complete the development and to use or sell the intangible asset.
6. Its ability to reliably measure the expenditure attributable to the intangible asset during its development.

Considerable management judgment is required in determining whether development costs should be capitalized as an internally generated intangible. Managers must determine the point at which research ends and development begins. IAS 38 provides the following examples of activities generally included in research:

- Activities aimed at obtaining new knowledge.
- The search for application of research findings or other knowledge.

- The search for alternatives for materials, devices, products, processes, systems, or services.
- The formulation, design, evaluation, and selection of possible alternatives for new or improved materials, devices, products, processes, systems, or services.

✦ Development activities typically include the following:

- The design, construction, and testing of preproduction prototypes and models.
- The design of tools, jigs, molds, and dies involving new technology.
- The design, construction, and operation of a pilot plant that is not of a scale economically feasible for commercial production.
- The design, construction, and testing of a chosen alternative for new or improved materials, devices, products, processes, systems, or services.

IAS 38 also provides a list of activities that are neither research nor development, including the following:

- Engineering follow-through in an early phase of commercial production.
- Quality control during commercial production, including routine testing of products.
- Troubleshooting in connection with breakdowns during commercial production.
- Routine efforts to refine, enrich, or otherwise improve upon the qualities of an existing product.
- Adaptation of an existing capability to a particular requirement or customer's need as part of a continuing commercial activity.
- Seasonal or other periodic design changes to existing products.
- Routine design of tools, jigs, molds, and dies.
- Activities, including design and construction engineering, related to the construction, relocation, rearrangement, or start-up of facilities or equipment other than facilities or equipment used solely for a particular research and development project.

Once the research and development phases of a project have been determined, management must assess whether all six criteria (listed earlier) for development cost capitalization have been met. Judgments of future circumstances often will be necessary and may be highly subjective. The ultimate decision can depend on the degree of optimism or pessimism of the persons making the judgment.

Development costs consist of (1) all costs directly attributable to development activities and (2) those costs that can be reasonably allocated to such activities, including:

- Personnel costs.
- Materials and services costs.
- Depreciation of property, plant, and equipment.
- Amortization of patents and licenses.
- Overhead costs, other than general administrative costs.

In other words, development costs are similar to costs incurred in producing inventory. Because the costs of some, but not all, development projects will be deferred as assets, it is necessary to accumulate costs for each development project as if it were a separate work in progress.

In accordance with IAS 23, *Borrowing Costs,* borrowing costs should be included as part of the cost of development activities to the extent that the costs of those activities constitute a "qualifying asset." IAS 23 is discussed in more detail later in this chapter.

Development costs capitalized as an internally generated intangible can only be treated as having a finite useful life. They must be amortized over their useful life using a method that best reflects the pattern in which the asset's economic benefits are consumed. Declining-balance, units-of-production, and straight-line methods are among the acceptable methods. Amortization begins when the intangible asset is available for sale or use.

Example: Deferred Development Costs

Szabo Company Inc. incurred costs to develop a specific product for a customer in Year 1, amounting to $300,000. Of that amount, $250,000 was incurred up to the point at which the technical feasibility of the product could be demonstrated, and other recognition criteria were met. In Year 2, Szabo Company incurred an additional $300,000 in costs in the development of the product. The product was available for sale on January 2, Year 3, with the first shipment to the customer occurring in mid-February, Year 3. Sales of the product are expected to continue for four years, at which time it is expected that a replacement product will need to be developed. The total number of units expected to be produced over the product's four-year economic life is 2,000,000. The number of units produced in Year 3 is 800,000. Residual value is zero.

In Year 1, $250,000 of development costs is expensed and $50,000 is recognized as an asset. The journal entry is as follows:

Development expense	$250,000	
Deferred development costs (intangible asset)	50,000	
Cash, payables, etc.		$300,000
To record development expense and deferred development costs.		

In Year 2, $300,000 of development costs is recognized as an asset:

Deferred development costs (asset)	$300,000	
Cash, payables, etc.		$300,000
To record deferred development costs.		

Amortization of deferred development costs begins on January 2, Year 3, when the product becomes available for sale. Szabo Company determines that the units-of-production method best reflects the pattern in which the asset's economic benefits are consumed. Amortization expense for Year 3 is calculated as follows:

Carrying amount of deferred development cost		$350,000
Units produced in Year 3	800,000	
Total number of units to be produced over economic life.	2,000,000	
% of total units produced in Year 3		40%
Amortization expense in Year 3		$140,000

The journal entry to record amortization of deferred development costs at December 31, Year 3, is as follows:

Amortization expense	$140,000	
Deferred development costs (asset).		$140,000
To record annual amortization expense.		

If Szabo Company were unable to estimate with reasonable certainty the number of units to be produced, it would be appropriate to amortize the deferred development costs on a straight-line basis over the four-year expected life. In that case, the journal entry to record amortization in Year 3 is as follows:

Amortization expense	$87,500	
Deferred development costs (asset)		$87,500
To record annual amortization expense.		

Examples of Internally Generated Intangible Assets

Items that might qualify for capitalization as internally generated intangible assets under IAS 38 include:

- Computer software costs
- Patents, copyrights
- Motion picture films
- Mortgage servicing rights
- Fishing licenses
- Franchises
- Customer or supplier relationships
- Customer loyalty
- Market share
- Marketing rights
- Import quotas

IAS 38 specifically excludes the following from being recognized as internally generated intangible assets:

- Brands
- Mastheads
- Publishing titles
- Customer lists
- Advertising costs
- Training costs
- Business relocation costs

Internally generated goodwill may *not* be recognized as an asset.

Finnish cellular telephone manufacturer Nokia Corporation is a European multinational that has used IFRS for many years. Exhibit 4.3 presents the reconciliation of net income from IFRS to U.S. GAAP provided by Nokia in its 2006 Form 20-F filed with the U.S. Securities and Exchange Commission (SEC), and the note describing the U.S. GAAP adjustment related to development costs. Adjusting for

EXHIBIT 4.3

NOKIA
Form 20-F
2006
Development Costs

Notes to the Consolidated Financial Statements

Excerpt from Note 38. Differences between International Financial Reporting Standards and U.S. Generally Accepted Accounting Principles

The Group's consolidated financial statements are prepared in accordance with International Financial Reporting Standards, which differ in certain respects from accounting principles generally accepted in the United States of America (US GAAP). The principal differences between IFRS and US GAAP are presented below together with explanations of certain adjustments that affect consolidated net income and total shareholders' equity under U.S. GAAP as of and for the years ended December 31:

	2006 EURm	2005 EURm	2004 EURm
Reconciliation of profit attributable to equity holders of the parent under IFRS to net income under US GAAP:			
Profit attributable to equity holders of the parent reported under IFRS	**4,306**	3,616	3,192
U.S. GAAP adjustments:			
Pensions	**(1)**	(3)	—
Development costs	**(55)**	10	42
Share-based compensation expense	**(8)**	(39)	39
Cash flow hedges	—	(12)	31
Amortization of identifiable intangible assets acquired	—	—	(11)
Impairment of identifiable intangible assets acquired	—	—	(47)
Amortization of goodwill	—	—	106
Other differences	**22**	(1)	(6)
Deferred tax effect of U.S. GAAP adjustments	**11**	11	(3)
Net income under U.S. GAAP	**4,275**	3,582	3,343

Development costs

Development costs are capitalized under IFRS after the product involved has reached a certain degree of technical feasibility. Capitalization ceases and depreciation begins when the product becomes available to customers. The depreciation period of these capitalized assets is between two and five years.

Under U.S. GAAP, software development costs are similarly capitalized after the product has reached a certain degree of technological feasibility. However, certain non-software-related development costs capitalized under IFRS are not capitalizable under U.S. GAAP and therefore are expensed as incurred.

The U.S. GAAP development cost adjustment reflects the reversal of capitalized non-software-related development costs under U.S. GAAP net of the reversal of associated amortization expense and impairments under IFRS. The adjustment also reflects differences in impairment methodologies under IFRS and U.S. GAAP for the determination of the recoverable amount and net realizable value of software-related development costs.

---

the capitalization of development costs under IFRS that would not be allowed under U.S. GAAP resulted in U.S. GAAP net income being €55 million less than IFRS net income in 2006. However, in 2004 and 2005, U.S. GAAP net income was €42 million and €10 million greater than IFRS income, respectively. The larger income under U.S. GAAP in these years most likely is attributable to the amount of amortization expense related to deferred development costs under IFRS exceeding the development costs expensed immediately under U.S. GAAP. Related adjustments also are made each year to reconcile stockholders' equity (retained earnings) from IFRS to U.S. GAAP. The amount of the adjustment is equal to the book value of the deferred development costs reported as an asset under IFRS; equity is smaller under U.S. GAAP.

Revaluation Model

IAS 38, *Intangible Assets,* allows the use of the revaluation model for intangible assets with finite lives, but only if the intangible has a price that is available on an active market, a condition rarely met in practice. Examples of intangible assets that may be priced on an active market include taxi licenses, fishing licenses, and production quotas. If the company chooses the revaluation method, the asset's fair value should be assessed regularly, typically annually. An increase in fair value of the asset is credited to "revaluation surplus" in equity, except to the extent it reverses a previously recorded decrease reported directly in net income. U.S. GAAP does not provide for the revaluation of intangible assets.

Impairment of Intangible Assets

Even though they are subject to amortization, finite-lived intangible assets also must be tested for impairment whenever changes in events or circumstances indicate an asset's carrying amount may not be recoverable. Goodwill and intangible assets with indefinite lives must be reviewed at least annually for impairment, regardless of the existence of impairment indicators. IAS 36, *Impairment of Assets,* allows reversals of impairment losses on intangible assets under special circumstances. However, reversal of impairment losses on goodwill is prohibited.

GOODWILL

IFRS 3, *Business Combinations,* contains the international rules related to the initial measurement of goodwill. Goodwill is recognized only in a business combination and is measured as the difference between (a) and (b):

(a) The consideration transferred by the acquiring firm plus any amount recognized as noncontrolling interest;.

(b) The fair value of net assets acquired (identifiable assets acquired less liabilities assumed).

When (a) exceeds (b), goodwill is recognized as an asset. When (a) is less than (b), a "bargain purchase" is said to have taken place and the difference between (a) and (b) (sometimes called "negative goodwill") is recognized as a gain in net income by the acquiring firm.

The amount recognized as goodwill depends on the option selected to measure any noncontrolling interest in the acquired company that might exist. Under IFRS 3, no-controlling interest may be measured at either (1) a proportionate share of the fair value of the acquired firm's net assets excluding goodwill or (2) fair value, which includes the noncontrolling interest's share of goodwill.

Example: Initial Measurement of Goodwill

George Company acquired 90 percent of the outstanding shares of Chris Company by paying $360,000 in cash. The fair value of Chris's identifiable assets is $320,000, and the liabilities assumed by George in this business combination are $40,000. George can choose between two alternatives to determine the amount to recognize as goodwill in this business combination.

Alternative 1 Noncontrolling Interest Measured at Proportionate Share of Acquired Firm's Net Assets

Fair value of Chris's identifiable net assets ($320,000 − $40,000)		$280,000
Noncontrolling interest percentage		10%
Noncontrolling interest		$ 28,000
Consideration transferred	$360,000	
Plus: Noncontrolling interest	28,000	
Subtotal.	$388,000	
Less: Fair value of Chris's identifiable net assets	280,000	
Goodwill	$108,000	

Alternative 2 Noncontrolling Interest Measured at Fair Value

Implied fair value of 100% of Chris Company ($360,000/90%)		$400,000
Noncontrolling interest percentage		10%
Noncontrolling interest		$ 40,000
Consideration transferred	$360,000	
Plus: Noncontrolling interest	40,000	
Subtotal.	$400,000	
Less: Fair value of Chris's identifiable net assets	280,000	
Goodwill	$120,000	

In Alternative 2, goodwill of $120,000 is comprised of $108,000 purchased by George plus $12,000 [$40,000 − $28,000] attributed to the no controlling interest.

Example: Gain on Bargain Purchase

Assume the same facts as in the previous example, except George acquires 90 percent of Chris for $240,000. Also, assume that no controlling interest is measured at the proportionate share of net assets (Alternative 1).

Consideration transferred	$240,000
Plus: Noncontrolling interest	28,000
Subtotal.	$268,000
Less: Fair value of Chris's identifiable net assets	280,000
Gain on bargain purchase	$ (12,000)

In this case, George would recognize a gain from a bargain purchase in net income in the year in which the acquisition takes place.

Impairment of Goodwill

As an indefinite-lived intangible asset, goodwill is not amortized. Instead, goodwill must be tested at least annually for impairment. IAS 36, *Impairment of Assets,* provides specific rules with respect to the impairment of goodwill.

Impairment testing of goodwill is performed at the level of the cash-generating unit (CGU). The CGU is the "smallest identifiable group of assets that generates cash inflows that are largely independent of the cash inflows from other assets or groups of assets." The impairment test is conducted by comparing the carrying value of the entire CGU, including goodwill attributable to that CGU, with its recoverable amount. The recoverable amount is the higher of the CGU's (1) value in use and (2) fair value less costs to sell. Under U.S. GAAP, impairment of goodwill is tested at the level of the "reporting unit," which can be different (typically larger) than a cash-generating unit.

If noncontrolling interest was originally measured at the proportionate share of net assets (alternative 1), then the carrying value of the entire CGU must be increased by the amount of goodwill attributable to the noncontrolling interest (as if alternative 2 had been applied). The impairment loss on the CGU is the amount by which the CGU's carrying amount, including goodwill, exceeds its recoverable amount. An impairment loss identified at the CGU level is first applied against goodwill. Once goodwill has been eliminated, any remaining impairment is allocated to the other assets of the CGU on a prorated basis based on their relative carrying amounts.

Example: Impairment of Goodwill

Continuing with the initial measurement of goodwill example presented earlier, at least annually, George Company must conduct an impairment test of the goodwill related to the acquisition of Chris Company. The assets of Chris Company are the smallest group of assets that generate cash inflows that are largely independent of the cash inflows from other assets or groups of assets. Therefore, Chris Company is a separate CGU. The goodwill related to the acquisition of Chris Company will be tested by comparing Chris Company's carrying amount with its recoverable amount. At the end of the year, George Company develops the following estimates for Chris Company:

Fair value	$280,000
Costs to sell	$ 30,000
Present value of future cash flows	$270,000

Alternative 1 Assuming that George Company adopted the proportionate share of acquired firm's net assets approach to measure noncontrolling interest, the impairment loss is determined as follows:

	Chris Co. Net assets	Chris Co. Goodwill	Total
Carrying amount	$280,000	$108,000	$388,000
Unrecognized noncontrolling interest in goodwill		12,000	12,000
Adjusted carrying amount	$280,000	$120,000	$400,000
Determination of recoverable amount:			
Fair value less costs to sell (1)			$250,000
Present value of future cash flows (2)			270,000
Recoverable amount [higher of (1) and (2)]			$270,000
Impairment loss (adjusted carrying amount less recoverable amount)			$130,000

In terms of allocation of impairment loss, $120,000 of the impairment loss is allocated to goodwill. The goodwill impairment is shared between the controlling and noncontrolling interest. Thus, $108,000 (90 percent) is allocated to the parent's investment in Chris Company; the remaining $12,000 (10 percent) is attributable to the noncontrolling interest (but is not recognized because the noncontrolling interest's goodwill is not recognized under this alternative). The remaining $10,000 ($130,000 − $120,000) of impairment loss is allocated to Chris Company's identifiable assets on a pro rata basis.

	Chris Co. Net assets	Chris Co. Goodwill	Total
Carrying amount	$280,000	$108,000	$388,000
Impairment loss	10,000	108,000	118,000
Carrying amount after impairment loss	$270,000	$ 0	$270,000

Alternative 2 Now assume that George Company had adopted the fair value method to measure noncontrolling interest. The impairment loss is determined in the following manner:

	Chris Co. Net assets	Chris Co. Goodwill	Total
Carrying amount	$280,000	$120,000	$400,000
Determination of recoverable amount:			
Fair value less costs to sell (1)			$250,000
Present value of future cash flows (2)			270,000
Recoverable amount [higher of (1) and (2)]			$270,000
Impairment loss (carrying amount less recoverable amount)			$130,000

Allocation of impairment loss:

	Chris Co. Net assets	Chris Co. Goodwill	Total
Carrying amount	$280,000	$120,000	$400,000
Impairment loss	10,000	120,000	130,000
Carrying amount after impairment loss	$270,000	$ 0	$270,000

Goodwill Not Allocable to Cash Generating Unit under Review

In testing goodwill for impairment, the recoverable amount is determined for the CGU to which the goodwill belongs by first applying a so-called bottom-up test. In this test, goodwill is allocated to the individual CGU under review, if possible, and impairment of that CGU is then determined by comparing (1) the carrying amount plus allocated goodwill and (2) the recoverable amount. The example presented previously demonstrated application of the bottom-up test.

If goodwill cannot be allocated on a reasonable and consistent basis to the CGU under review, then both a bottom-up test and a top-down test should be applied. Under the top-down test, goodwill is allocated to the smallest group of CGUs to which it can be allocated on a reasonable and consistent basis, and impairment of the *group* of CGUs is then determined by comparing (1) the carrying amount of the group plus allocated goodwill and (2) the recoverable amount. U.S. GAAP requires only a bottom-up test and only for that goodwill associated with those assets that are being reviewed for impairment.

Example: Application of the Bottom-Up and Top-Down Tests for Goodwill

In Year 1, La Brea Company acquired another company that operates a chain of three restaurants, paying $300,000 for goodwill. By the end of Year 4, it is clear that the restaurant located in Anaheim is not generating the profit and cash flows expected at the date of purchase. Therefore, La Brea Company is required to test for impairment.

Each restaurant is a cash-generating unit, but La Brea cannot allocate the goodwill on a reasonable and consistent basis to individual restaurants. Both a bottom-up test and a top-down test must be applied.

Bottom-Up Test A bottom-up test is applied to each restaurant by estimating the recoverable amount of the assets of each restaurant and comparing with the carrying amount of those assets excluding goodwill. An impairment loss is recognized for the amount by which a restaurant's carrying amount exceeds its recoverable amount. The loss is allocated to the impaired restaurant's assets on a pro rata basis according to the relative carrying amount of the assets. The bottom-up test checks for impairment of the assets of the individual restaurants but provides no information about the impairment of the goodwill that was purchased in the acquisition of the chain of restaurants. Assume the following carrying values and recoverable amounts for the three restaurants acquired:

Cash-Generating Unit (restaurant location)	Carrying Amount	Recoverable Amount	Impairment Loss
Anaheim	$1,000,000	$ 970,000	$30,000
Buena Park	1,000,000	1,050,000	0
Cerritos	1,000,000	1,020,000	0

An impairment loss of $30,000 is recognized, and the assets of the Anaheim restaurant are written down by that amount. The carrying amount of Anaheim's net assets is now $970,000.

Top-Down Test La Brea determines that the smallest cash-generating unit to which goodwill can be allocated is the entire chain of restaurants. Therefore, La Brea estimates the recoverable amount of the chain of restaurants and compares this with the carrying amount (after any impairment has been recognized) of the assets of all the restaurants plus goodwill. Goodwill is considered to be impaired to the extent that the carrying amount of the assets plus goodwill exceeds the restaurant chain's recoverable amount.

Cash-Generating Unit (restaurant location)	Carrying Amount
Anaheim	$ 970,000
Buena Park	1,000,000
Cerritos	1,000,000
Subtotal	2,970,000
Goodwill	300,000
Total	$3,270,000

La Brea estimates the recoverable amount of the chain of restaurants to be $3,000,000. La Brea compares this amount with the total carrying amount of $3,270,000 to determine that goodwill is impaired. A loss on the impairment of goodwill of $270,000 must be recognized.

BORROWING COSTS

Prior to its revision in 2007, IAS 23, *Borrowing Costs,* provided two methods of accounting for borrowing costs:

1. *Benchmark treatment:* Expense all borrowing costs in the period incurred.
2. *Allowed alternative treatment:* Capitalize borrowing costs to the extent they are attributable to the acquisition, construction, or production of a qualifying asset; other borrowing costs are expensed in the period incurred.

Adoption of the benchmark treatment would not have been acceptable under U.S. GAAP. As part of the FASB-IASB convergence project, IAS 23 was revised in 2007. The benchmark treatment was eliminated, and the allowed alternative treatment has become the only acceptable treatment. Borrowing costs directly attributable to the acquisition, construction, or production of a qualifying asset must be capitalized as part of the cost of that asset; all other borrowing costs must be expensed immediately.

IAS 23 (as revised in 2007) is similar to U.S. GAAP, but some definitional and implementation differences exist. IAS 23 defines *borrowing costs* as interest and other costs incurred by an enterprise in connection with the borrowing of funds. This definition is broader in scope than the definition of *interest cost* under U.S. GAAP. Borrowing costs in accordance with IAS 23 specifically include foreign exchange gains and losses on foreign currency borrowings to the extent they are regarded as an adjustment to interest costs. An asset that qualifies for borrowing cost capitalization is one that necessarily takes a substantial period to get ready for its intended use or sale. Both IAS 23 and U.S. GAAP exclude inventories that are routinely manufactured or produced in large quantities on a repetitive basis over a short period. However, IAS 23 specifically includes inventories that require a substantial period to bring them to a marketable condition.

The amount to be capitalized is the amount of interest cost that could have been avoided if the expenditure on the qualifying asset had not been made. This is determined by multiplying the weighted-average accumulated expenditures by an appropriate interest rate. The appropriate interest rate is determined similarly under both IAS 23 and U.S. GAAP, being a weighted-average interest rate on borrowings outstanding. If a specific new borrowing can be associated with a qualifying asset, the actual interest rate is used to the extent the weighted-average accumulated expenditures are less than the amount of the specific borrowing. Interest income earned on the temporary investment of a specific new borrowing is offset against the interest cost to determine the net amount of interest to be capitalized. Netting interest income against interest cost is not acceptable under U.S. GAAP. The capitalization of borrowing costs begins when expenditures for the asset are incurred and ceases when substantially all the activities necessary to prepare the asset for sale or use are completed.

Example: Capitalization of Borrowing Costs

On January 1, Year 1, Pinquill Company borrows 30,000,000 euros (€) at an annual interest rate of 8 percent to finance the construction of a new facility in Spain. The facility is expected to cost €30,000,000 and take two years to build. Pinquill temporarily invests the euros borrowed until cash is needed to pay costs. During Year 1, expenditures of €20,000,000 are incurred; the weighted-average expenditures are €12,000,000. Pinquill makes annual interest payments on the loan and will repay the loan in full on December 31, Year 2 by converting U.S. dollars into euros, The U.S. dollar/euro exchange rate was $1.42 on January 1, Year 1, and $1.40 on December 31, Year 1. The change in exchange rate is the result of the difference in interest rates on U.S. dollar and euro borrowings. The following information relates to Year 1:

Capitalizable interest cost (€12,000,000 × 8% = €960,000 × $1.40 exchange rate on 12/31/Y1)	$1,344,000
Income earned on temporary investment of borrowing (€225,000 × $1.40)	315,000
Exchange rate gain [€12,000,000 × ($1.42 − $1.40)]	240,000

The net interest cost is $1,029,000 ($1,344,000 − $315,000). After deducting the exchange rate gain, the total amount of borrowing cost to be capitalized as part of the cost of the facility is $789,000. Under U.S. GAAP, the amount of interest cost to be capitalized would be $1,344,000.

LEASES

IAS 17, *Leases*, distinguishes between finance (capitalized) leases and operating leases. IAS 17 provides guidance for classifying leases as finance or operating, and then describes the accounting procedures that should be used by lessees and lessors in accounting for each type of lease. IAS 17 also provides rules for sale-leaseback transactions. IAS 17 and U.S. GAAP are conceptually similar, but IAS 17 provides less specific guidance than U.S. GAAP.

Lease Classification

As a case in point, IAS 17 indicates that a lease should be classified and accounted for as a finance lease when it transfers substantially all the risks and rewards incidental to ownership to the lessee. The standard then provides examples of five situations that individually or in combination *normally would* lead to a lease being classified as a finance lease:

1. The lease transfers ownership of the asset to the lessee by the end of the lease term.
2. The lessee has the option to purchase the asset at a price less than fair market value.
3. The lease term is for the major part of the leased asset's economic life.
4. The present value of minimum lease payments at the inception of the lease is equal to substantially all the fair value of the leased asset.
5. The leased asset is of a specialized nature such that only the lessee can use it without major modifications.

IAS 17 provides three additional indicators of situations that individually or in combination *could* lead to a lease being classified as a finance lease:

6. The lessee bears the lessor's losses if the lessee cancels the lease.
7. The lessee absorbs the gains or losses from fluctuations in the fair value of the residual value of the asset.
8. The lessee may extend the lease for a secondary period at a rent substantially below the market rent.

In contrast, U.S. GAAP stipulates that if any one of four very specific criteria is met, a lease must be capitalized. These criteria are similar to 1 through 4 just listed; in fact, the first two are exactly the same. In the U.S. GAAP version of criterion 3, *major part* is specifically defined as 75 percent, and in criterion 4, *substantially all* is defined as 90 percent. Depending on the manner by which a financial statement preparer defines the terms *major part* and *substantially all*, application of IAS 17 and U.S. GAAP might or might not lead to similar classification of leases. In addition, there is nothing similar to criteria 5 through 8 in U.S. GAAP.

In assessing criterion 4, minimum lease payments include (1) periodic lease payments; (2) any amounts guaranteed by the lessee, such as a guaranteed residual value; and (3) the exercise price in a bargain renewal option. The discount rate to be used in determining the present value of minimum lease payments is the implicit interest rate earned by the lessor in the lease, if this is practicable to determine. If not, the lessee's incremental borrowing rate should be used. In contrast, U.S. GAAP requires the lessee's incremental borrowing rate to be used as the discount rate, unless the lessor's implicit interest rate can be determined and is less than the lessee's incremental borrowing rate.

Example: Classification of Leases

On January 1, Year 1, Creative Transportation Company (CTC) entered into a lease with Arnold Aircraft Inc. for a pre-owned airplane with the following terms:

- Lease term is seven years.
- Annual lease payments are $3,000, due on December 31.
- Fair value of the airplane at the inception of the lease is $20,000.
- The airplane has a 10-year remaining economic life.
- Estimated residual value (unguaranteed) is $5,124. CTC does not absorb any gains or losses in the fluctuations of the fair value of the residual value.
- CTC has the option to purchase the airplane at the end of the lease term for $8,000.

- Implicit annual interest rate of 5 percent (disclosed to CTC by Arnold).
- CTC's incremental annual borrowing rate is 4 percent.
- Ownership is not transferred at the end of the lease term.
- The lease may not be extended.

To determine the present value (PV) of minimum lease payments (MLP) the lessor's implicit interest rate of 5 percent is used because it is known, regardless of the lessee's incremental borrowing rate. The PV factor for an ordinary annuity of 7 payments at a 5 percent discount rate is 5.786373. The PV of MLP is calculated as $3,000 × 5.786373 = $17,359. The residual value is not included in the MLP because it is not guaranteed, and there is no renewal option to consider.

Based on the analysis presented in the following table, CTC most likely would not classify the lease as a finance lease under IFRS. However, this decision is not clear-cut. The company could decide that the lease term of seven years is the major part of the remaining economic life of the airplane and, as a result, treat this as a finance lease. Under U.S. GAAP, CTC definitely would not capitalize the lease because none of the four criteria are met.

Finance Lease Indicator	Indicator Present?
Ownership is transferred to the lessee by the end of the lease term.	No. Ownership is not transferred at the end of the lease term.
The lease contains a bargain purchase option.	No. The purchase option price of $8,000 is greater than the estimated residual value of $5,124.
The lease term is a major part of the estimated economic life of the leased property.	Maybe. The lease term is for 70% of the estimated economic life of the airplane, which might (or might not) be considered "a major part" by CTC.
The PV of MLP is substantially all of the fair value of the leased property.	Probably not. The PV of MLP is 87% of the fair value of the leased property ($17,359/$20,000). This does not appear to meet the threshold of "substantially all."
The leased assets are of such a specialized nature such that only the lessee can use them without major modifications being made.	No. There is no indication that this is the case.
The lessee bears the lessor's losses if the lessee cancels the lease.	No. There is no indication that this is the case.
The lessee absorbs the gains or losses from fluctuations in the fair value of the residual value of the asset.	No. CTC does not guarantee the residual value.
The lessee may extend the lease for a secondary period at a rent substantially below the market rent.	No. The lease may not be extended.

Finance Leases

IAS 17 requires leases classified as finance leases to be recognized by the lessee as assets and liabilities at an amount equal to the fair value of the leased property or, if lower, at the present value of the future minimum lease payments. Initial direct costs incurred by the lessee in connection with negotiating the lease are capital-ized as part of the cost of the asset under IAS 17. U.S. GAAP is silent with respect to this issue, but common practice is to defer and amortize the costs over the lease term.

Lease payments are apportioned between interest expense and a reduction in the lease obligation using an effective interest method to amortize the lease obli-gation. The leased asset is depreciated in a manner consistent with assets owned by the lessee. Normally, depreciable finance lease assets are depreciated over the shorter of useful life and lease term. If it is reasonably certain that the lessee will obtain ownership of the asset at the end of its lease term, the asset is depreciated over its expected useful life. IAS 36, *Impairment of Assets,* applies to finance lease assets the same as it does to assets owned by the entity.

A lease classified as a finance lease by the lessee should also be classified as a finance lease by the lessor. The leased asset is replaced by the "net investment" in the lease, which is equal to the present value of future minimum lease payments (including any unguaranteed residual value). Any profit on the "sale" is recog-nized at the inception of the lease, and interest is recognized over the life of the lease using an effective interest method. Under U.S. GAAP, the net investment in the lease is determined simply as the lessor's cost or carrying amount for the leased asset. Under U.S. GAAP, a lessor classifies a capital lease into either a sales-type lease (which includes the recognition of profit) or a direct-finance lease (no profit; fair value and carrying value of the leased asset are equal). IFRS does not make this distinction.

Operating Leases

Any lease not classified as a finance lease is an operating lease. With an operating lease, lease payments are recognized by the lessee as an expense and by the lessor as income. The asset remains on the books of the lessor and is accounted for in a similar fashion to any other asset owned by the lessor.

Lease payments under an operating lease are recognized as an expense on a straight-line basis over the lease term, unless another systematic basis is more representative of the time pattern of the user's benefit, in which case, that basis is used. SIC-15, *Operating Leases-Incentives,* provides guidance for situations where the lessee receives an incentive, such as a rent-free period, from the lessor to enter into the lease. In those situations, the total amount of rent to be paid over the life of the lease is allocated on a straight-line basis to the periods covered by the lease term.

Example: Operating Lease

Budget Company enters into a two-year lease for a computer with lease payments of $200 per month in the first year, and $250 per month in the second year. The total amount of lease payments will be $5,400 [($200 × 12) + ($250 × 12)]. The straight-line method accurately reflects the time pattern of the user's benefit from using the computer. On a straight-line basis, an expense in the amount of $225 ($5,400/24 months) should be recognized each month.

Sale–Leaseback Transaction

A sale–leaseback transaction involves the sale of an asset by the initial owner of the asset and the leasing of the same asset back to the initial owner. If the lease is classified as a finance lease, IAS 17 requires the initial owner to defer any gain on the sale and amortize it to income over the lease term. U.S. GAAP rules are generally similar. If the fair value of property at time of the sale–leaseback is less than its carrying amount, IAS 17 allows recognition of a loss only if the loss is due to an impairment in the value of the asset sold. U.S. GAAP requires immediate recognition of the loss regardless of its source.

If the lease in a sale–leaseback transaction is classified as an operating lease, IAS 17 requires the difference between the fair value of the asset and its carrying amount to be recognized immediately in income. Any difference between the fair value of the asset and its selling price is amortized ratably over the lease term. In contrast, U.S. GAAP requires the seller to amortize any gain over the lease term.

Example: Gain on Sale and Leaseback

Berlin Corporation sells a building to Essen Finance Company for $2,200,000. Essen Finance then leases the building back to Berlin under a 10-year agreement, which Berlin classifies as an operating lease. On the date of sale, the carrying amount of the building on Berlin's books is $1,800,000, and the building had an appraised fair value of $2,100,000.

Under IFRS, Berlin recognizes a gain on sale and leaseback of $300,000 [$2,100,000 − $1,800,000] at the date of sale for the difference between the fair value and carrying amount of the building. The company has a deferred gain of $100,000 [$2,200,000 − $2,100,000] for the difference between the fair value and selling price; this will be amortized to income at the rate of $10,000 per year over the 10-year life of the lease. Under U.S. GAAP, the entire gain of $400,000 is deferred and amortized at the rate of $40,000 per year over the lease term.

The difference in accounting treatment for gains on sale–leaseback transactions between IAS 17 and U.S. GAAP is described by Swisscom AG in Exhibit 4.4. In its 2006 reconciliation to U.S. GAAP, Swisscom made an adjustment for this accounting difference that resulted in an increase in income, as stated under U.S. GAAP, of 17 million Swiss francs. This reflects the amount of original gain on sale and leaseback that was realized in 2001 that is amortized to income in 2006 under U.S. GAAP. The gain was recognized in full in 2001 under IFRS. An adjustment also is made to stockholders' equity to reverse the difference between the full amount of gain recognized under IFRS (included in IFRS retained earnings) and the portion of the gain that has been recognized through amortization under U.S. GAAP. This adjustment reduced IFRS equity by 280 million Swiss francs in 2006 to reconcile to a U.S. GAAP basis.

Disclosure

Lessees must disclose the amount of future minimum lease payments related to operating leases and related to finance leases, separately, for each of the following periods:

1. Amount to be paid within one year (Year 1).
2. Amount to be paid after one year and not later than five years (Years 2–5) as a single amount.
3. Amount to be paid later than five years (Year 6 and beyond) as a single amount.

Also, the present value of the future minimum lease payments under finance leases must be disclosed. Entities provide more detailed information under U.S. GAAP, which requires disclosure of the amount to be paid in each of the next five years (Years 1–5) by year, as well as the amount to be paid later than five years (Year 6 and beyond) as a single amount.

EXHIBIT 4.4

SWISSCOM AG
Form 20-F
2006
Sale and Leaseback Transactions

Excerpt from Note 43. Differences between International Financial Reporting Standards and U.S. Generally Accepted Accounting Principles

The consolidated financial statements of Swisscom have been prepared in accordance with International Financial Reporting Standards (IFRS), which differ in certain significant respects from generally accepted accounting principles in the United States (U.S. GAAP). Application of U.S. GAAP would have affected the shareholders' equity as of December 31, 2006, 2005, and 2004, and net income for each of the years in the three-year period ended December 31, 2006, to the extent described below. A description of the significant differences between IFRS and U.S. GAAP as they relate to Swisscom are discussed in further detail below.

Reconciliation of net income from IFRS to U.S. GAAP

The following schedule illustrates the significant adjustments to reconcile net income in accordance with IFRS to the amounts determined in accordance with U.S. GAAP for each of the three years ended December 31.

CHF in millions	2006	2005	2004
Net income according to IFRS attributable to equity holders of Swisscom AG	**1,599**	**2,022**	**1,596**
U.S. GAAP adjustments:			
a) Capitalization of interest cost	20	14	(4)
b) Retirement benefits	(16)	(27)	(21)
c) Termination benefits	—	(31)	(10)
d) Impairment of investments	—	9	—
e) Cross-border tax leases	15	(20)	49
f) Debitel purchase accounting	—	—	(23)
g) Sale of debitel	—	254	342
g) Deferred interest	—	21	(21)
h) Revenue recognition	18	35	56
i) Outsourcing contracts	(40)	16	—
j) Site restoration	(2)	3	15
k) Goodwill and other intangible assets	—	—	106
l) Sale and leaseback transaction	17	29	24
m) Onerous contracts	(5)	6	10
o) Share buyback	(17)	—	—
p) Income taxes	—	(2)	(6)
Net income according to U.S. GAAP	**1,589**	**2,329**	**2,113**

l) Sale and leaseback transaction

In March 2001 Swisscom entered into two master agreements for the sale of real estate. At the same time, Swisscom entered into agreements to lease back part of the sold property space. The gain on the sale of the properties after transaction costs of CHF 105 million and including the reversal of environmental provisions, was CHF 807 million under IFRS.

A number of the leaseback agreements are accounted for as finance leases under IFRS and the gain on the sale of these properties of CHF 129 million is deferred and released to income over the individual lease terms. The remaining gain of CHF 678 million represents the gain on the sale of buildings which were sold outright and the gain on the sale of land and buildings which qualify as operating leases under IFRS. Under IFRS, the gain on a leaseback accounted for as an operating lease is recognized immediately. Under U.S. GAAP, in general the gain is deferred and amortized over the lease term. If the leaseback was minor, the gain was immediately recognized. In addition, certain of the agreements did not qualify as sale-and-leaseback accounting under U.S. GAAP because of continuing involvement in the form of purchase options. These transactions are accounted for under the finance method and the sales proceeds are reported as a financing obligation and the properties remain on the balance sheet and continue to be depreciated as in the past. The lease payments are split between interest and amortization of the obligation.

Exhibit 4.5 shows the disclosures made by British retailer Marks and Spencer Group plc related to operating leases.

IASB/FASB Convergence Project

In August 2010, the IASB and FASB jointly issued an exposure draft for a proposed new standard on the accounting for leases. If approved, the exposure draft would result in significant changes to the accounting requirements for both lessees and lessors. Under the proposal, lessees would recognize a "right-of-use" asset and a liability to make lease payments for all leases. Leases would no longer be classified as finance or operating; in essence, all leases would be treated as finance leases. Lease assets and liabilities would be measured based on the longest possible lease term that is more likely than not to occur, and an expected outcome approach would be used to reflect lease payments. Lessors would recognize an asset representing its right to receive lease payments and would either derecognize the leased asset or recognize a liability, depending on exposure to the risks and rewards associated with the leased asset. On sale–leasebacks, the seller would recognize the transaction either as a sale or as a borrowing, depending on whether the transaction meets conditions for recognition as a sale as stipulated in the exposure draft.

Other Recognition and Measurement Standards

The next chapter covers IASB standards pertaining to the recognition and measurement of current liabilities, provisions, employee benefits, share-based payment, income taxes, revenue, and financial instruments. IAS 21, *Foreign Currency Translation*, which provides guidance for dealing with foreign currency transactions and the translation of foreign currency financial statements, is covered in detail in Chapters 7 and 8. Standards related to financial reporting in hyperinflationary economies (IAS 29), business combinations (IFRS 3), consolidated financial statements (IAS 27), investments in associates (IAS 28), and investments in joint ventures (IAS 31) are covered in Chapter 9, Additional Financial Reporting Issues.

EXHIBIT 4.5

MARKS AND SPENCER GROUP PLC
2010
Annual Report

Excerpt from Note 27. Contingencies and Commitments

C. Commitments under operating leases

The Group leases various stores, office, warehouses, and equipment under non-cancelable operating lease agreements. The leases have varying terms, escalation clauses, and renewal rights.

	2010 £m	2009 £m
Total future minimum rentals payable under non-cancelable operating leases are as follows:		
Within one year	**228.6**	215.1
Later than one year and not later than five years	**815.2**	778.1
Later than five years	**3,005.2**	3,173.1
Total	**4,049.0**	4,166.4

The total future sublease payments to be received are £51.9m (last year £64.9m).

DISCLOSURE AND PRESENTATION STANDARDS

Several IFRS deal primarily with disclosure and presentation issues. This section summarizes some of those standards. While briefly introduced here, IFRS 8, *Operating Segments,* is discussed in greater detail in Chapter 9.

Statement of Cash Flows

IAS 7, *Statement of Cash Flows,* reiterates the requirement in IAS 1 that a company must present a statement of cash flows as an integral part of its financial statements. IAS 7 contains the following requirements:

- Cash flows must be classified as being related to operating, investing, or financing activities.
- Cash flow from operations may be presented using the direct method or the indirect method. When using the indirect method, IAS 7 does *not* specify that the reconciliation from income to cash flows must begin with any particular line item, e.g., net income. Thus, an entity could begin the reconciliation with operating income or some other measure of income. When using the direct method, there is no requirement to also present a reconciliation of income to cash from operations.
- Cash flows related to interest, dividends, and income taxes must be reported separately.
- Interest and dividends paid may be classified as operating or financing.
- Interest and dividends received may be classified as operating or investing.
- Income taxes are classified as operating unless they are specifically identified with investing or financing activities.
- Noncash investing and financing transactions are excluded from the statement of cash flows but must be disclosed elsewhere within the financial statements.
- Components of cash and cash equivalents must be disclosed and reconciled with amounts reported on the statement of financial position (balance sheet). However, the total for cash and cash equivalents in the statement of cash flows need not agree with a single line item in the balance sheet.
- IAS 7 makes an explicit distinction between bank borrowings and bank overdrafts. Overdrafts may be classified as a component (i.e., reduction) of cash and cash equivalents, if considered to be an integral part of an enterprises' cash management. Otherwise, bank overdrafts are classified as a financing activity.

Several differences exist between IFRS and U.S. GAAP in the presentation of a statement of cash flows. Under U.S. GAAP:

- Interest paid, interest received, and dividends received are all classified as operating cash flows. Dividends paid are classified as financing cash flows.
- When using the indirect method of presenting operating cash flows, the reconciliation from income to cash flows must begin with net income.
- When using the direct method of presenting operating cash flows, a reconciliation from net income to operating cash flows also must be presented.
- The cash and cash equivalents line item in the statement of cash flows must reconcile with the cash and cash equivalents line in the statement of financial position.

Example: Classification of Interest and Dividends in the Statement of Cash Flows

Star Kissed Corporation (SKC) currently reports under U.S. GAAP but is investigating the effect that the adoption of IFRS might have on its statement of cash flows. For the current year, SKC has interest received of $500, interest paid of $1,250, dividends received of $200, and dividends paid of $2,700. Under U.S. GAAP, the company classifies interest paid, interest received, and dividends received as operating activities, and dividends paid are classified as a financing activity. These items are presented in the company's U.S. GAAP statement of cash flows as follows:

Operating activities:	
Interest paid.	$(1,250)
Interest received.	500
Dividends received	200
Cash flow from operating activities	$ (550)
Investing activities:	
Nothing reported.	$ 0
Financing activities:	
Dividends paid.	(2,700)
Cash flow from financing activities.	$(2,700)
Net change in cash	$(3,250)

This classification would be acceptable under IFRS. However, the following presentation, among others, also would be acceptable under IAS 7:

Operating activities:	
Nothing reported	$ 0
Investing activities:	
Interest received	$ 500
Dividends received	200
Cash flow from investing activities	$ 700
Financing activities:	
Interest paid	$(1,250)
Dividends paid	(2,700)
Cash flow from financing activities	$(3,950)
Net change in cash	$(3,250)

Events after the Reporting Period

IAS 10, *Events after the Reporting Period,* prescribes when an entity should adjust its financial statements for events occurring after the balance sheet date (referred to in the United States as "subsequent events") and the disclosures to be made related to those events. Events after the reporting period are those events, favorable and unfavorable, that occur between the balance sheet date and the date that the financial statements are *authorized for issuance.* Under U.S. GAAP, the subsequent event period runs through the date that the financial statements are issued (or are available to be issued), which is later than the date they are authorized for issuance.

There are two types of after the reporting period events that are treated differently:

1. Adjusting events after the reporting period.
2. Nonadjusting events after the reporting period.

Adjusting Events

Those events that provide evidence of conditions that existed at the end of the reporting period are adjusting events. These events must be recognized through adjustment of the financial statements. For example, assume a company has recorded an estimated liability related to litigation on its December 31, Year 1 balance sheet of $2 million. On January 20, Year 2, before the board of directors has approved the financial statements for issuance, the judge orders the company to pay $3 million. The liability on the December 31, Year 1 balance sheet should be adjusted upward to $3 million. The judge's decision clarifies the value of the liability that existed at the balance sheet date.

Nonadjusting Events

Events that are indicative of conditions that arise after the balance sheet date but before the date the financial statements are authorized for issue are nonadjusting events. No adjustments are made to the financial statements related to these events. However, disclosures are required of:

1. The nature of the event.
2. An estimate of the financial effect, or statement that an estimate cannot be made.

For example, assume inventory carried on the December 31, Year 1 balance sheet at $3 million decreases in net realizable value to $1 million due to a change in the law on February 15, Year 2. The financial statements are approved for issuance on February 20, Year 2. The decline in market value does not relate to the condition of the inventory at the balance sheet date, so no adjustment should be made. If material, the decrease in value should be disclosed in the notes to the financial statements.

IAS 10 specifically states that financial statements should not be adjusted for cash dividends declared after the balance sheet date. The same is true for stock dividends and stock splits.

Accounting Policies, Changes in Accounting Estimates, and Errors

IAS 8, *Accounting Policies, Changes in Accounting Estimates and Errors*, provides guidance with respect to (1) the selection of accounting policies, (2) accounting for changes in accounting policies, (3) dealing with changes in accounting estimates, and (4) correction of errors.

Selection of Accounting Policies

IAS 8 establishes the following hierarchy of authoritative pronouncements to be followed in selecting accounting policies to apply to a specific transaction or event:

1. IASB Standard or Interpretation that specifically applies to the transaction or event.
2. IASB Standard or Interpretation that deals with similar and related issues.

3. Definitions, recognition criteria, and measurement concepts in the IASB *Framework.*
4. Most recent pronouncements of other standard-setting bodies that use a similar conceptual framework to develop accounting standards.

Changes in Accounting Policy

To ensure comparability of financial statements over time, an entity is required to apply its accounting policies consistently. A change in accounting policy is allowed only if the change:

1. Is required by an IFRS.
2. Results in the financial statements providing more relevant and reliable information.

If practical, the change in accounting policy should be applied retrospectively. The cumulative effect of adopting the new accounting policy is treated as an adjustment to the carrying amounts of the assets and liabilities affected and as an adjustment to the beginning balance in retained earnings. The cumulative effect is *not* included in net income.

Changes in Estimates

A change in estimate due to new developments or new information should be accounted for in the period of the change or in future periods, depending on the periods affected by the change. In other words, the change in estimate should be handled prospectively.

Correction of Errors

Material, prior-period errors should be corrected retrospectively by restating all prior reported accounts (assets, liabilities, equity) affected by the error and by recording a prior-period adjustment to the beginning balance in retained earnings. When it is impractical to determine the period-specific effects of an error on comparative information for one or more prior periods, the entity restates the opening balances in assets, liabilities, and equity for the earliest period for which retrospective restatement is practicable. This might be the current period. Whereas IFRS provides an exception if it is impractical to restate financial statements for a correction of an error, U.S. GAAP does not provide such an exception but instead requires all material errors to be corrected through restatement.

Related Party Disclosures

Transactions between related parties must be disclosed in the notes to financial statements. Parties are related if one party has the ability to control or exert significant influence over the other party. Related parties can include parent companies, subsidiaries, equity method associates, individual owners, and key management personnel. Similar rules exist in U.S. GAAP.

Earnings per Share

Basic and diluted earnings per share must be reported on the face of the income statement. IAS 33, *Earnings per Share,* provides guidance for calculating earnings per share. U.S. GAAP provides more detailed guidance with respect to the calculation of diluted earnings per share. Application of this guidance would appear to be consistent with IAS 33.

Interim Financial Reporting

IAS 34, *Interim Financial Reporting*, does not mandate which companies should prepare interim statements, how frequently, or how soon after the end of an interim period. The standard defines the minimum content to be included in interim statements by those entities required by their national jurisdiction to present them and identifies the accounting principles that should be applied. With certain exceptions, IAS 34 requires interim periods to be treated as discrete reporting periods. This differs from the position in U.S. GAAP, which treats interim periods as an integral part of the full year. As an example, IAS 34 would require annual bonuses to be recognized as expense in the interim period in which bonuses are paid. Under U.S. GAAP, on the other hand, one-fourth of the expected annual bonus is accrued each quarter.

Noncurrent Assets Held for Sale and Discontinued Operations

Noncurrent assets held for sale must be reported separately on the balance sheet at the lower of (1) carrying value or (2) fair value less costs to sell. Assets held for sale are not depreciated. Similar rules exist in U.S. GAAP.

A discontinued operation is a component of an entity that represents a major line of business or geographical area of operations that either has been disposed of or has been classified as held for sale. The after-tax profit or loss and after-tax gain or loss on disposal must be reported as a single amount on the face of the income statement. Detail of the revenues, expenses, gain or loss on disposal, and income taxes comprising this single amount must be disclosed in the notes or on the face of the income statement. If presented on the face of the income statement, it must be presented in a section identified as discontinued operations. The definition of the type of operation that can be classified as discontinued is somewhat narrower than under U.S. GAAP. In addition, U.S. GAAP requires both pre-tax and after-tax profit or loss to be reported on the income statement. Otherwise, the two sets of standards are substantially similar.

Operating Segments

As part of the short-term convergence project with the FASB, the IASB issued IFRS 8, *Operating Segments*, in 2006 to replace IAS 14, *Segment Reporting*. IFRS 8 adopted the FASB's so-called management approach. Extensive disclosures are required for each separately reportable operating segment. Operating segments are components of a business (1) that generate revenues and expenses, (2) whose operating results are regularly reviewed by the chief operating officer, and (3) for which separate financial information is available. IFRS 8 provides the following guidelines with regard to segment reporting:

- An operating segment is separately reportable if it meets any of three quantitative tests (revenue test, profit or loss test, asset test). Operating segments can be defined in terms of products and services or on the basis of geography.
- Disclosures required for each operating segment include assets, capital expenditures, liabilities, profit or loss, and the following components of profit or loss: external revenues, intercompany revenues, interest income and expense, depreciation and amortization, equity method income, income tax expense, and noncash expenses. Similar disclosures are required by U.S. GAAP except that liabilities by operating segment need not be reported.
- If the revenue reported by operating segments is less than 75 percent of total revenues, additional operating segments must be reported separately—even if

they do not meet any of the three quantitative tests—until at least 75 percent of total revenue is included in reportable segments.

- In addition to disclosures by operating segment, entitywide disclosures related to products and services, geographic areas, and major customers are required.
- If operating segments are not defined on the basis of products and services, revenue derived from each major product and service must be disclosed, even if the company has only one operating segment.
- Revenues and noncurrent assets must be disclosed for the domestic country and all foreign countries combined. These two items also must be disclosed for each foreign country in which a material amount of revenues or noncurrent assets is located. Materiality is not defined.
- The existence and amount of revenue derived from major customers must be disclosed, along with the identity of the segment generating the revenue. A major customer is defined as one from which 10 percent or more of total revenues are generated.

Summary

1. Many countries currently use IFRS, and it likely that IFRS will be integrated into the United States financial reporting system in the near future. An understanding of IFRS is important for accountants who prepare or audit financial statements.

2. Differences exist between IFRS and U.S. GAAP with respect to recognition, measurement, presentation, disclosure, and choice among alternatives. In some cases, IFRS are more flexible than U.S. GAAP. Several IFRS allow firms to choose between alternative treatments in accounting for a particular item. Also, IFRS generally have less bright-line guidance than U.S. GAAP; therefore, more judgment is required in applying individual IFRS. However, in some cases, IFRS are more detailed than U.S. GAAP.

3. Some of the more important asset recognition and measurement differences between IFRS and U.S. GAAP relate to the following issues: inventory valuation; revaluation of property, plant, and equipment; component depreciation; capitalization of development costs; measurement of impairment losses; and classification of leases.

4. IAS 2 requires inventory to be reported on the balance sheet at the lower of cost and net realizable value. Write-downs to net realizable value must be reversed when the selling price increases. Under U.S. GAAP, inventory is carried at the lower of cost or replacement cost (with a ceiling and floor), and the reversal of write-downs is not permitted. Unlike U.S. GAAP, IAS 2 does not allow the use of last-in, first-out (LIFO) in determining the cost of inventory.

5. IAS 16 allows property, plant, and equipment to be carried at cost less accumulated depreciation and impairment losses or at a revalued amount less any subsequent accumulated depreciation and impairment losses. Specific guidance is provided for those firms that choose the revaluation option. U.S. GAAP does not permit use of the revaluation model.

6. IAS 16 requires an item of property, plant, and equipment comprised of significant parts for which different useful lives or depreciation methods are appropriate to be split into component for purposes of depreciation. Component depreciation is uncommon in U.S. GAAP.

7. IAS 36 requires impairment testing of property, plant, and equipment; intangibles, including goodwill; and long-term investments. An asset is impaired when its carrying value exceeds its recoverable amount, which is the greater of net selling price and value in use. An impairment loss is the amount by which carrying value exceeds recoverable amount. If, subsequent to recognizing an impairment loss, the recoverable amount of an asset exceeds its new carrying amount, the impairment loss is reversed and the asset is written back up to the carrying amount that would have existed if the impairment had never been recognized. U.S. GAAP employs a different impairment test, and impairment losses may not be reversed.

8. IAS 38 requires development costs to be capitalized as an intangible asset when six specific criteria are met. Development costs can include personnel costs; materials and services; depreciation of property, plant, and equipment; amortization of patents and licenses; and overhead costs, other than general administrative costs. Development costs generally are not capitalized under U.S. GAAP. Intangible assets (including deferred development costs) are classified as having a finite or indefinite useful life. Finite-lived intangibles are amortized over their useful lives using a straight-line method; indefinite-lived intangibles are reviewed each year to determine if the useful life still is indefinite. If not, the intangible is reclassified as having a finite life and amortization begins.

9. Goodwill is measured as the excess of the consideration transferred in a business acquisition by the acquiring firm, plus any noncontrolling interest, over the fair value of net assets acquired. IFRS 3 allows two options in measuring noncontrolling interest, which results in two possible measures of goodwill. U.S. GAAP only allows one method for measuring noncontrolling interest.

10. Indefinite-lived intangibles and goodwill must be reviewed for impairment at least once per year. Finite-lived intangibles are tested for impairment whenever changes in circumstances indicate an asset's carrying amount may not be recoverable. IAS 36 allows the reversal of impairment losses on intangibles when certain conditions are met; however, the reversal of goodwill impairment is not allowed.

11. IAS 23 requires borrowing costs to be capitalized to the extent they are attributable to the acquisition of a qualifying asset; other borrowing costs are expensed immediately. Borrowing costs include interest and other costs, such as foreign exchange gains and losses on foreign currency borrowings, incurred in connection with a borrowing. The amount of borrowing cost to be capitalized is reduced by any interest income earned from the temporary investment of the amount borrowed. U.S. GAAP has a narrower definition of capitalizable interest costs and does not allow the netting of interest income.

12. Leases must be classified as finance leases or operating leases under both IFRS and U.S. GAAP. However, the classification guidelines differ between the two sets of standards. While there are more finance lease indicators provided in IAS 17 than in U.S. GAAP, the guidelines in IAS 17 tend to be less prescriptive and avoid the use of bright-line thresholds.

13. A sale-and-leaseback transaction generally results in a gain or loss on the sale for the seller-lessee. IFRS and U.S. GAAP differ with regard to the timing of when the gain or loss on the sale–leaseback can be recognized.

14. In addition to IAS 1, which was described in the previous chapter, several other IASB standards primarily provide guidance with respect to disclosure and presentation of information in the financial statements.

15. IAS 7 contains requirements for the presentation of the statement of cash flows. Several differences exist from U.S. GAAP, including the option to present interest and dividends paid as either operating or financing activities and interest and dividends received as either operating or investing activities.

16. IAS 10 prescribes when financial statements should be adjusted for events occurring after the end of the reporting period. The cutoff date for adjusting events is the date financial statements are authorized for issuance. Under U.S. GAAP, the cutoff date is the date financial statements are issued or are available to be issued, which is later than the date the statements are approved.

17. IAS 8 establishes a hierarchy of authoritative pronouncements to be considered in selecting accounting policies. The lowest level in the hierarchy is guidance issued by other standard-setting bodies that use a conceptual framework similar to the IASB's. This includes standards set by the FASB.

18. Once selected, an entity must use its accounting policies consistently over time. A change in accounting policy is allowed only if the change results in the financial statements providing more relevant and reliable information or the change is required by an IASB pronouncement.

19. Other disclosure and presentation standards provide guidance with respect to related party disclosures, earnings per share, noncurrent assets held for sale and discontinued operations, interim reporting, and segment reporting.

Questions

Unless otherwise indicated, questions should be answered based on IFRS.

1. What are the types of differences that exist between IFRS and U.S. GAAP?

2. How does application of the lower of cost or market rule for inventories differ between IFRS and U.S. GAAP?

3. How are the estimated costs of removing and dismantling an asset handled upon initial recognition of the asset?

4. What are the two models allowed for measuring property, plant, and equipment at dates subsequent to original acquisition?

5. Which items of property, plant, and equipment may be accounted for under the revaluation model, and how frequently must revaluation occur?

6. How is the revaluation surplus handled under the revaluation model?

7. How is depreciation determined for an item of property, plant, and equipment that is comprised of significant parts, such as an airplane?

8. In what way does the fair value model for investment property differ from the revaluation model for property, plant, and equipment?

9. How is an impairment loss on property, plant, and equipment determined and measured under IFRS? How does this differ from U.S. GAAP?

10. When a previously recognized impairment loss is subsequently reversed, what is the maximum amount at which the affected asset may be carried on the balance sheet?

11. What are the three major types of intangible asset, and how does the accounting for them differ?

12. How are internally generated intangibles handled under IFRS? How does this differ from U.S. GAAP?

13. Which intangible assets are subject to annual impairment testing?

14. How is goodwill measured in a business combination with a noncontrolling interest?

15. What is a gain on bargain purchase?

16. What is the process for determining whether goodwill allocated to a specific cash-generating unit is impaired?

17. What is the current treatment with respect to borrowing costs?

18. What are the differences in the amount of borrowing costs that can be capitalized under IFRS and U.S. GAAP?

19. How do the criteria for determining whether a lease qualifies as a finance (capitalized) lease differ between IFRS and U.S. GAAP?

20. What is the difference between IFRS and U.S. GAAP with regard to the recognition of gains and losses on sale–leaseback transactions?

21. How does the classification of interest and dividends in the statement of cash flows differ between IFRS and U.S. GAAP?

22. What is the cutoff date for the occurrence of events after the reporting period requiring adjustment to the financial statements?

23. What are the guidelines on selecting and changing accounting policies?

Exercises and Problems

Unless otherwise indicated, exercises and problems should be solved based on IFRS.

1. A company incurred the following costs related to the production of inventory in the current year:

Cost of materials	$100,000
Cost of direct labor	60,000
Allocation of variable overhead costs	30,000
Allocation of fixed overhead costs (based on normal production levels)	25,000
Storage costs (after production, prior to sale)	2,000
Selling costs	8,000

The cost of materials included abnormal waste of $10,000. What is the cost of inventory in the current year?

a. $190,000.
b. $205,000.
c. $215,000.
d. $217,000.

2. A company determined the following values for its inventory as of the end of its fiscal year:

Historical cost	$50,000
Current replacement cost.	35,000
Net realizable value	45,000
Net realizable value less a normal profit margin	40,000
Fair value	48,000

What amount should the company report for inventory on its balance sheet?

a. $35,000.
b. $40,000.
c. $45,000.
d. $48,000.

3. When an entity chooses the revaluation model as its accounting policy for measuring property, plant, and equipment, which of the following statements is correct?

a. When an asset is revalued, the entire class of property, plant, and equipment to which that asset belongs must be revalued.
b. When an asset is revalued, individual assets within a class of property, plant, and equipment to which that asset belongs may be selectively revalued.
c. Revaluations of property, plant, and equipment must be made at least every three years.
d. Increases in an asset's carrying value as a result of the first revaluation must be recognized in net income.

4. On January 1, Year 1, an entity acquires a new machine with an estimated useful life of 20 years for $100,000. The machine has an electrical motor that must be replaced every five years at an estimated cost of $20,000. Continued operation of the machine requires an inspection every four years after purchase; the inspection cost is $10,000. The company uses the straight-line method of depreciation. What is the depreciation expense for Year 1?

a. $5,000.
b. $5,500.
c. $8,000.
d. $10,000.

5. An asset is considered to be impaired when its carrying amount is greater than its

a. Net selling price.
b. Value in use.
c. Undiscounted future cash flows.
d. Recoverable amount.

6. Under IFRS, an entity that acquires an intangible asset may use the revaluation model for subsequent measurement only if

a. The useful life of the intangible asset can be reliably determined.
b. An active market exists for the intangible asset.
c. The cost of the intangible asset can be measured reliably.
d. The intangible asset has a finite life.

7. Which of the following is a criterion that must be met in order for an item to be recognized as an intangible asset?

a. The item's fair value can be measured reliably.
b. The item is part of the entity's activities aimed at gaining new scientific or technical knowledge.

    c. The item is expected to be used in the production or supply of goods or services.

    d. The item is identifiable and lacks physical substance.

8. An entity incurs the following costs in connection with the purchase of a trademark:

Purchase price of the trademark.	$80,000
Nonrefundable value added tax paid on the purchase of the trademark	4,000
Training sales department staff on the use of the trademark	2,000
Research expenditures incurred prior to the purchase of the trademark	15,000
Legal fees to register the trademark.	8,000
Salaries of personnel who negotiated purchase of the trademark during the period of negotiation	10,000

Assuming that the trademark meets the criteria for recognition as an intangible asset, at what amount should the trademark be initially measured?

    a. $84,000.
    b. $92,000.
    c. $104,000.
    d. $119,000.

9. Which of the following best describes the accounting for goodwill subsequent to initial recognition?

    a. Goodwill is amortized over its expected useful life, not to exceed 20 years.
    b. Goodwill is tested for impairment whenever impairment indicators are present.
    c. Goodwill is tested for impairment on an annual basis.
    d. Goodwill is revalued using a revaluation model.

10. An entity must adjust its financial statements for an event that occurs after the end of the reporting period if

    a. The event occurs before the financial statements have been approved for issuance and it provides evidence of conditions that existed at the end of the reporting period.
    b. The event occurs before the financial statements have been issued and it changes the value of an asset that existed at the end of the reporting period.
    c. The event occurs before the financial statements have been audited and it changes the value of a liability that existed at the end of the reporting period.
    d. The event occurs within 15 days of the end of the reporting period and it changes the level of ownership in another entity from a non-controlling to a controlling interest.

11. In selecting an accounting policy for a transaction, which of the following is the first level within the hierarchy of guidance that should be considered?

    a. The most recent pronouncements of other standard-setting bodies to the extent they do not conflict with IFRS or the IASB *Framework*.
    b. An IASB standard or interpretation that specifically relates to the transaction.

c. The definitions, recognition criteria, and measurement concepts in the IASB *Framework*.
d. An IASB standard or interpretation that deals with similar and related issues.

12. An entity can justify a change in accounting policy if

   a. The change will result in a reliable and more relevant presentation of the financial statements.
   b. The entity encounters new transactions that are substantively different from existing or previous transactions.
   c. The entity previously accounted for similar, though immaterial, transactions under an unacceptable accounting method.
   d. An alternate accounting policy gives rise to a material change in current year net income.

13. As a result of a downturn in the economy, Optiplex Corporation has excess productive capacity. On January 1, Year 3, Optiplex signed a special order contract to manufacture custom-design generators for a new customer. The customer requests that the generators be ready for pickup by June 15, Year 3, and guarantees it will take possession of the generators by July 15, Year 3. Optiplex incurred the following direct costs related to the custom-design generators:

Cost to complete the design of the generators.	$ 3,000
Purchase price for materials and parts	80,000
Transportation cost to get materials and parts to manufacturing facility.	2,000
Direct labor (10,000 labor hours at $12 per hour)	120,000
Cost to store finished product (from June 15 to June 30).	2,000

Because of the company's inexperience in manufacturing generators of this design, the cost of materials and parts included an abnormal amount of waste totaling $5,000. In addition to direct costs, Optiplex applies variable and fixed overhead to inventory using predetermined rates. The variable overhead rate is $2 per direct labor hour. The fixed overhead rate based on a normal level of production is $6 per direct labor hour. Given the decreased level of production expected in Year 3, Optiplex estimates a fixed overhead application rate of $9 per direct labor hour in Year 3.

Required:
Determine the amount at which the inventory of custom-design generators should be reported on Optiplex Corporation's June 30, Year 3 balance sheet.

14. To determine the amount at which inventory should be reported on the December 31, Year 1 balance sheet, Monroe Company compiles the following information for its inventory of Product Z on hand at that date:

• Historical cost	$20,000
• Replacement cost	14,000
• Estimated selling price.	17,000
• Estimated costs to complete and sell	2,000
• Normal profit margin as a percentage of selling price	20%

The entire inventory of Product Z that was on hand at December 31, Year 1 was completed in Year 2 at a cost of $1,800 and sold at a price of $17,150.

Required:

a. Determine the impact that Product Z has on income in Year 1 and Year 2 under (1) IFRS and (2) U.S. GAAP.

b. Summarize the difference in income, total assets, and total stockholders' equity using the two different sets of accounting rules over the two-year period.

15. Beech Corporation has three finished products (related to three different product lines) in its ending inventory at December 31, Year 1. The following table provides additional information about each product:

Product	Cost	Replacement Cost	Selling Price	Normal Profit Margin
101	$130	$140	$160	20%
202	$160	$135	$140	20%
303	$100	$ 80	$100	15%

Beech Corporation expects to incur selling costs equal to 5 percent of the selling price on each of the products.

Required:

Determine the amount at which Beech should report its inventory on the December 31, Year 1 balance sheet under (1) IFRS and (2) U.S. GAAP.

16. This is a continuation of problem 15. At December 31, Year 2, Beech Corporation still had the same three different products in its inventory. The following table provides updated information for the company's products:

Product	Cost	Replacement Cost	Selling Price	Normal Profit Margin
101	$130	$180	$190	20%
202	$160	$150	$160	20%
303	$100	$100	$130	15%

Beech Corporation still expects to incur selling costs equal to 5 percent of the selling price.

Required:

Determine the amount at which Beech should report its inventory on the December 31, Year 2 balance sheet under (1) IFRS and (2) U.S. GAAP.

17. Steffen-Zweig Company exchanges two used printing presses with a total net book value of $24,000 ($40,000 cost less accumulated depreciation of $16,000) for a new printing press with a fair value of $24,000 and $3,000 in cash. The fair value of the two used printing presses is $27,000. The transaction is deemed to lack commercial substance.

Required:

Determine the amount of gain or loss that would be recognized from this exchange of assets.

18. Stevenson Corporation acquires a one-year old building at a cost of $500,000 at the beginning of Year 2. The building has an estimated useful life of 50 years. However, based on reliable historical data, the company believes the carpeting will need to be replaced in 5 years, the roof will need to be replaced in 15 years, and the HVAC system will need to be replaced in 10 years. On the date of acquisition, the cost to replace these items would have been carpeting, $10,000; roof, $15,000; HVAC system, $30,000. Assume no residual value.

Required:

Determine the amount to be recognized as depreciation expense in Year 2 related to this building.

19. Quick Company acquired a piece of equipment in Year 1 at a cost of $100,000. The equipment has a 10-year estimated life, zero salvage value, and is depreciated on a straight-line basis. Technological innovations take place in the industry in which the company operates in Year 4. Quick gathers the following information for this piece of equipment at the end of Year 4:

Expected future undiscounted cash flows from continued use	$59,000
Present value of expected future cash flows from continued use	51,000
Net selling price in the used equipment market	50,000

At the end of Year 6, it is discovered that the technological innovations related to this equipment are not as effective as first expected. Quick estimates the following for this piece of equipment at the end of Year 6:

Expected future undiscounted cash flows from continued use	$50,000
Present value of expected future cash flows from continued use	44,000
Net selling price in the used equipment market	42,000

Required:

a. Discuss whether Quick Company must conduct an impairment test on this piece of equipment at December 31, Year 4.
b. Determine the amount at which Quick Company should carry this piece of equipment on its balance sheet at December 31, Year 4; December 31, Year 5; and December 31, Year 6. Prepare any related journal entries.

20. Godfrey Company constructed a new, highly automated chemical plant in Year 1, which began production on January 1, Year 2. The cost to construct the plant was $5,000,000: $1,500,000 for the building and $3,500,000 for machinery and equipment. The useful life of the plant (both building and machinery) is estimated to be 20 years. Local environmental laws require the machinery and equipment to be inspected by engineers after every five years of operation. The inspectors could require Godfrey to overhaul equipment at that time to be able to continue to operate the plant. Godfrey estimates that the costs of the inspection and any required overhaul to take place in five years

to be $200,000. Environmental laws also require Godfrey to dismantle and remove the plant assets at the end of their useful life. The company estimates that the net cost, after deducting any salvage value, for removal of the equipment will be $100,000, and the net cost for dismantling and removal of the building, after deducting any salvage value, will be $1,500,000. Godfrey has determined that the straight-line method of depreciation will best reflect the pattern in which the plant's future economic benefits will be received by the company. The company uses the cost model to account for its property, plant, and equipment. The company uses a discount rate of 10 percent in determining present values.

Required:
Determine the cost of the plant assets at January 1, Year 2. Determine the amount of depreciation expense that should be recognized related to the plant assets in Year 2.

21. Jefferson Company acquired equipment on January 2, Year 1 at a cost of $10 million. The equipment has a five-year life, no residual value, and is depreciated on a straight-line basis. On January 2, Year 3, Jefferson Company determines the fair value of the asset (net of any accumulated depreciation) to be $12 million.

Required:
a. Determine the impact the equipment has on Jefferson Company's income in Years 1–5 using (1) IFRS, assuming that the revaluation model is used for measurement subsequent to initial recognition, and (2) U.S. GAAP.
b. Summarize the difference in income, total assets, and total stockholders' equity using the two different sets of accounting rules over the period of Years 1–5.

22. Madison Company acquired a depreciable asset at the beginning of Year 1 at a cost of $12 million. At December 31, Year 1, Madison gathered the following information related to this asset:

Carrying amount (net of accumulated depreciation).	$10 million
Fair value of the asset (net selling price)	$7.5 million
Sum of future cash flows from use of the asset	$10 million
Present value of future cash flows from use of the asset	$8 million
Remaining useful life of the asset.	5 years

Required:
a. Determine the impact on Year 2 and Year 3 income from the depreciation and possible impairment of this equipment under (1) IFRS and (2) U.S. GAAP.
b. Determine the difference in income, total assets, and total stockholders' equity for the period of Years 1–6 under the two different sets of accounting rules.

Note: If the asset is determined to be impaired, there would be no adjustment to Year 1 depreciation expense of $2 million.

23. Iptat International Ltd. provided the following reconciliation from IFRS to U.S. GAAP in its most recent annual report (amounts in thousands of CHF):

	Net Income	Shareholders' Equity
As stated under IFRS	541,713	7,638,794
U.S. GAAP adjustments		
(a) Reversal of additional depreciation charges arising from revaluation of fixed assets	85,720	643,099
(b) Reversal of revaluation surplus of fixed assets	—	(977,240)
As stated under U.S. GAAP	627,433	7,305,653

Required:

a. Explain why U.S. GAAP adjustment (a) results in an addition to net income. Explain why U.S. GAAP adjustment (a) results in an addition to shareholders' equity that is greater than the addition to net income. What is the shareholders' equity account affected by adjustment (a)?

b. Explain why U.S. GAAP adjustment (b) results in a subtraction from shareholders' equity but does not affect net income. What is the shareholders' equity account affected by adjustment (b)?

24. In Year 1, in a project to develop Product X, Lincoln Company incurred research and development costs totaling $10 million. Lincoln is able to clearly distinguish the research phase from the development phase of the project. Research-phase costs are $6 million, and development-phase costs are $4 million. All of the IAS 38 criteria have been met for recognition of the development costs as an asset. Product X was brought to market in Year 2 and is expected to be marketable for five years. Total sales of Product X are estimated at more than $100 million.

Required:

a. Determine the impact research and development costs have on Lincoln Company's Year 1 and Year 2 income under (1) IFRS and (2) U.S. GAAP.

b. Summarize the difference in income, total assets, and total stockholders' equity related to Product X over its five-year life under the two different sets of accounting rules.

25. Xanxi Petrochemical Company provided the following reconciliation from IFRS to U.S. GAAP in its most recent annual report (amounts in thousands of RMB):

	Net Income	Shareholders' Equity
As stated under IFRS	938,655	4,057,772
U.S. GAAP adjustments		
(a) Reversal of amortization charge on deferred development costs	5,655	16,965
(b) Gain on sale and leaseback of building	(40,733)	(66,967)
As stated under U.S. GAAP	903,577	4,007,770

Required:

 a. Explain why U.S. GAAP adjustment (a) results in an addition to net income. Explain why U.S. GAAP adjustment (a) results in an addition to shareholders' equity that is greater than the addition to net income. What is the shareholders' equity account affected by adjustment (a)?

 b. Explain why U.S. GAAP adjustment (b) reduces net income. Explain why U.S. GAAP adjustment (b) reduces shareholders' equity by a larger amount than it reduces net income. What is the shareholders' equity account affected by adjustment (b)?

26. Buch Corporation purchased Machine Z at the beginning of Year 1 at a cost of $100,000. The machine is used in the production of Product X. The machine is expected to have a useful life of 10 years and no residual value. The straight-line method of depreciation is used. Adverse economic conditions develop in Year 3 that result in a significant decline in demand for Product X. At December 31, Year 3, the company develops the following estimates related to Machine Z:

Expected future cash flows	$75,000
Present value of expected future cash flows	55,000
Selling price	70,000
Costs of disposal	7,000

At the end of Year 5, Buch's management determines that there has been a substantial improvement in economic conditions resulting in a strengthening of demand for Product Z. The following estimates related to Machine Z are developed at December 31, Year 5:

Expected future cash flows	$70,000
Present value of expected future cash flows	53,000
Selling price	50,000
Costs of disposal	7,000

Required:

Determine the carrying amounts for Machine Z to be reported on the balance sheet at the end of Years 1–5, and the amounts to be reported in the income statement related to Machine Z for Years 1–5.

27. On January 1, Year 1, Holzer Company hired a general contractor to begin construction of a new office building. Holzer negotiated a $900,000, five-year, 10 percent loan on January 1, Year 1 to finance construction. Payments made to the general contractor for the building during Year 1 amount to $1,000,000. Payments were made evenly throughout the year. Construction is completed at the end of Year 1, and Holzer moves in and begins using the building on January 1, Year 2. The building is estimated to have a 40-year life and no residual value. On December 31, Year 3, Holzer Company determines that the market value for the building is $970,000.

On December 31, Year 5, the company estimates the market value for the building to be $950,000.

Required:

Use the two alternative methods allowed by IAS 16 with respect to the measurement of property, plant, and equipment subsequent to initial recognition to determine:

a. The carrying amount of the building that would be reported on the balance sheet at the end of Years 1–5.
b. The amounts to be reported in net income related to this building for Years 1–5.

In each case, assume that the building's value in use exceeds its carrying value at the end of each year and therefore impairment is not an issue.

28. Quantacc Company began operations on January 1, Year 1 and uses IFRS to prepare its financial statements. Quantacc reported net income of $100,000 in Year 5 and had stockholders' equity of $500,000 at December 31, Year 5. The company wishes to determine what its Year 5 income and December 31, Year 5 stockholders' equity would be if it had used U.S. GAAP. Relevant information follows:

    • Quantacc carries fixed assets at revalued amounts. Fixed assets were last revalued upward by $35,000 on January 1, Year 3. At that time, fixed assets had a remaining useful life of 10 years.
    • Quantacc capitalized development costs related to a new product in Year 4 in the amount of $80,000. Quantacc began selling the new product in January, Year 5 and expects the product to be marketable for a total of five years.
    • Early in January, Year 5, Quantacc realized a gain on the sale-and-leaseback of an office building in the amount of $150,000. The lease is accounted for as an operating lease, and the term of the lease is 20 years.

    Required:

    Calculate the following for Quantacc Company using U.S. GAAP (ignore income taxes):

    a. Net income for Year 5.
    b. Stockholders' equity at December 31, Year 5.

29. Stratosphere Company acquires its only building on January 1, Year 1 at a cost of $4,000,000. The building has a 20-year life, zero residual value, and is depreciated on a straight-line basis. The company adopts the revaluation model in accounting for buildings. On December 31, Year 2, the fair value of the building is $3,780,000. The company eliminates accumulated depreciation against the building account at the time of revaluation. The company's accounting policy is to reverse a portion of the revaluation surplus account related to increased depreciation expense. On January 2, Year 4, the company sells the building for $3,500,000.

    Required:

    Determine amounts to be reflected in the balance sheet related to this building for the Years 1–4 in the following table. (Use parentheses to indicate credit amounts.)

Date	Cost	Accumulated depreciation	Carrying Amount	Revaluation Surplus	Income	Retained Earnings
January 1, Year 1	$4,000,000		$4,000,000			
December 31, Year 1						
Balance						
December 31, Year 2						
Balance						
December 31, Year 3						
Balance						
January 2, Year 4						
Balance						

30. During Year 1, Reforce Company conducted research and development on a new product. By March 31, Year 2, the company had determined the new product was technologically feasible, and the company obtained a patent for the product in April, Year 2. The company developed an initial prototype by June 30, Year 2. Also, by June 30, Year 2, the company had developed a business plan including identification of a ready market for the product, and a commitment of resources to ready the product for market. After completion of the second prototype at the end of September, Year 2, the product was ready for commercial production and marketing. The company has tracked costs associated with the new product as follows:

Market research costs, Year 1	$ 25,000
Research costs, Year 1	100,000
Research costs, 1st quarter, Year 2	70,000
Legal fees to register patent, April, Year 2	25,000
Development costs for initial prototype, 2nd quarter, Year 2	500,000
Testing of initial prototype, June, Year 2	50,000
Management time to develop business plan, 2nd quarter, Year 2	15,000
Cost of revisions and second prototype, 3rd quarter, Year 2	175,000
Legal fees to defend patent, October, Year 2	50,000
Commercial production costs, 4th quarter, Year 2	400,000
Marketing campaign, 4th quarter, Year 2	80,000

Required:

Determine the amount related to this new product that will be reported as intangible assets on the company's December 31, Year 2 balance sheet.

31. Philosopher Stone Inc. incurred costs of $20,000 to develop an intranet Web site for internal use. The intranet will be used to store information related to company policies, customers, and products. Access to the intranet is password-protected and is restricted to company personnel. As the company's

auditor, you have been asked to determine whether Philosopher Stone can capitalize the Web site development costs as an intangible asset or whether the company must expense the costs in the period in which they were incurred. Your research finds that SIC 32, *Intangible Assets–Web Site Costs*, indicates that a Web site developed for internal or external use is an internally generated intangible asset that is subject to the requirements of IAS 38. Specifically, SIC 32 indicates that the recognition criteria in IAS 38 related to development costs must be satisfied. The criterion most in question is whether the company can demonstrate the usefulness of the intranet and how it will generate probable future economic benefits.

Required:

Develop a justification for why Philosopher Stone should, or should not, be allowed to account for the intranet development costs as an intangible asset.

32. Bartholomew Corporation acquired 80 precent of the outstanding shares of Samson Company in Year 1 by paying $5,500,000 in cash. The fair value of Samson's identifiable net assets is $5,000,000. Bartholomew uses the proportionate share of acquired firm's net assets approach to measure noncontrolling interest. Samson is a separate cash-generating unit. At the end of Year 1, Bartholomew compiles the following information for Samson:

Amount at which the shares of Samson could be sold	$5,000,000
Costs that would be incurred to sell the shares of Samson	$ 200,000
Present value of future cash flows from continuing to control Samson . . .	$4,750,000

Required:

At what amount should Samson's identifiable net assets and goodwill from the acquisition of Samson be reported on Bartholomew's consolidated balance sheet at the end of Year 1?

33. This exercise consists of two parts.

Part A. The following table summarizes the assets of the Rocker Division (a separate cash-generating unit) at December 31, Year 5, prior to testing goodwill for impairment. Property, Plant, and Equipment and Other Intangibles are amortized on a straight-line basis over an average useful life of 12 years and 5 years, respectively. Management has estimated the present value of future cash flows from operating the Rocker Division to be $1,560. No fair market value is available.

Required:

Complete the following table to determine the carrying amounts at 12/31/Y5 for the assets of the Rocker Division.

	Goodwill	Property, Plant, and Equipment	Other Intangibles	Total
Carrying amount, 12/31/Y4	$1,000	$1,500	$500	$3,000
Amortization expense, Year 5 . . .	0	(125)	(100)	(225)
Subtotal.	$1,000	$1,375	$400	$2,775
Impairment loss				
Carrying amount, 12/31/Y5				

Part B. Due to favorable changes in export laws, management revises its estimate of the value in use for the Rocker Division at 12/31/Y6 to be $1,930.

Required:
Complete the following table to determine the carrying amounts at 12/31/Y6 for the assets of the Rocker Division.

	Goodwill	Property, Plant, and Equipment	Other Intangibles	Total
Carrying amount, 12/31/Y5				
Amortization expense, Year 6 . . .				
Subtotal.				
Impairment loss/recovery				
Carrying amount, 12/31/Y6				

34. This exercise consists of three parts.

    Part A. On January 1, Year 1, Complete Company acquired 60 percent of the outstanding shares of Partial Company by paying $1,200,000 in cash. The fair value of Partial's identifiable assets and liabilities is $2,000,000 and $500,000, respectively.

    Required:
    Determine the possible amounts at which Complete Company should recognize goodwill from this business combination.

    Part B. Assume the same facts as in part A, except Complete Company acquires 80 percent of Partial Company for $1,100,000.

    Required:
    Determine the possible amounts at which Complete Company should recognize goodwill from this business combination.

    Part C. Assume the same facts as in part A and that Complete Company measured noncontrolling interest at the date of acquisition at the proportionate share of fair value of Partial Company's net assets. Complete Company determines that Partial Company is a separate cash-generating unit. At the end of Year 1, Complete Company develops the following estimates for Partial Company:

Fair value.	$1,900,000
Costs to sell.	$ 20,000
Present value of future cash flows	$1,860,000

    Required:
    Determine the amount of impairment loss, if any, to be recognized in the Year 2 consolidated income statement, and the amount at which Partial Company's net assets, goodwill, and noncontrolling interest would be carried on the consolidated balance sheet at the end of Year 2.

35. Thurstone Company, a U.S.-based company, borrows 1,500,000 British pounds (£) on January 1, Year 1 at an interest rate of 4 percent to finance the construction of a new office building for its employees in England. Construction is expected to take six months and cost £1,500,000. Thurstone temporarily invests the British pounds borrowed until cash is needed to pay costs. Interest earned in the first quarter of Year 1 is £5,000. During the first quarter of Year 1, expenditures of £500,000 are incurred; the weighted-average expenditures are £300,000. Thurstone will repay the borrowing plus interest on June 30, Year 1 by converting U.S. dollars into British pounds. The U.S. dollar/British pound exchange rate was $2.00 on January 1, Year 1 and $2.10 on March 31, Year 1. The change in exchange rate is the result of the difference in interest rates in the United States and Great Britain.

    Required:
    Determine the amount of borrowing costs (in U.S. dollars) that Thurstone should include in the cost of the new office building at March 31, Year 1.

36. Atlanta Tours Company entered into a five-year lease on January 1, Year 1 with Duck Boats Inc. for a customized duck boat. Duck Boats Inc. will provide a vehicle to Atlanta Tours Company with the words "Gone with the Wind" carved into the sides. Following are the terms of the lease arrangement:

    - Fair value of the wagon at the inception of the lease is $10,000.
    - There is an eight-year estimated economic life.
    - Estimated (unguaranteed) residual value is $3,500. Atlanta Tours Company does not absorb any gains or losses in the fluctuations of the fair value of the residual value.
    - Annual lease payments of $2,000 are due on January 1 of each year. The implicit interest rate in the lease is 6 percent.
    - There is an option to purchase at end of lease-term for $4,000.
    - The lease is noncancelable and may not be extended.

    Required:
    Discuss whether Atlanta Tours Company should classify this lease as an operating lease or as a finance lease under (a) IFRS and (b) U.S. GAAP.

37. This problem is comprised of three parts.

    Part A.   Fields Company sells a building to Victory Finance Company. The selling price of the building is $500,000, which approximates its fair value, and the carrying amount is $400,000. Fields then leases the building back from Victory under an operating lease for a period of three years.

    Required:
    Determine how Fields should account for the gain or loss on sale-and-leaseback.

    Part B.   Fields Company sells a building to Victory Finance Company. The selling price of the building is $500,000, which exceeds its fair value of $470,000. The carrying amount is $400,000. Fields then leases the building back from Victory under an operating lease for a period of three years.

    Required:
    Determine how Fields should account for the gain or loss on sale-and-leaseback.

Part C. Fields Company sells a building to Victory Finance Company. The selling price of the building is $500,000, which is equal to its fair value. The carrying amount of the building is $400,000. Fields then leases the building back from Victory under a finance lease for a period of 20 years.

Required:

Determine how Fields should account for the gain or loss on sale-and-lease-back.

38. Bridget's Bakery Inc. enters into a new operating lease for a 10-year term at a monthly rental of $2,500. To induce Bridget's Bakery into the lease, the lessor agreed to a free-rent period for the first three months.

Required:

Determine the amount of lease expense, if any, that Bridget's Bakery would recognize in the first month of the lease.

39. Indicate whether each of the following describes an accounting treatment that is acceptable under IFRS, U.S. GAAP, both, or neither, by checking the appropriate box.

	Acceptable under			
	IFRS	U.S. GAAP	Both	Neither
• A company takes out a loan to finance the construction of a building that will be used by the company. The interest on the loan is capitalized as part of the cost of the building.				
• Inventory is reported on the balance sheet using the last-in, first-out (LIFO) cost flow assumption.				
• The gain on a sale–leaseback transaction classified as an operating lease is deferred and amortized over the lease term.				
• A company writes a fixed asset down to its recoverable amount and recognizes an impairment loss in Year 1. In a subsequent year, the recoverable amount is determined to exceed the asset's carrying value, and the previously recognized impairment loss is reversed.				
• A company pays less than the fair value of net assets acquired in the acquisition of another company. The acquirer recognizes the difference as a gain on purchase of another company.				
• A company enters into an eight-year lease on equipment that is expected to have a useful life of 10 years. The lease is accounted for as an operating lease.				
• An intangible asset with an active market that was purchased two years ago is carried on the balance sheet at fair value.				
• In preparing interim financial statements, interim periods are treated as discrete reporting periods rather than as an integral part of the full year.				
• Development costs are capitalized when certain criteria are met.				
• Interest paid on borrowings is classified as an operating activity in the statement of cash flows.				

Case 4-1

Bessrawl Corporation

Bessrawl Corporation is a U.S.-based company that prepares its consolidated financial statements in accordance with U.S. GAAP. The company reported income in 2011 of $1,000,000 and stockholders' equity at December 31, 2011, of $8,000,000.

The CFO of Bessrawl has learned that the U.S. Securities and Exchange Commission is considering requiring U.S. companies to use IFRS in preparing consolidated financial statements. The company wishes to determine the impact that a switch to IFRS would have on its financial statements and has engaged you to prepare a reconciliation of income and stockholders' equity from U.S. GAAP to IFRS. You have identified the following five areas in which Bessrawl's accounting principles based on U.S. GAAP differ from IFRS.

1. Inventory
2. Property, plant, and equipment
3. Intangible assets
4. Research and development costs
5. Sale-and-leaseback transaction

Bessrawl provides the following information with respect to each of these accounting differences.

Inventory

At year-end 2011, inventory had a historical cost of $250,000, a replacement cost of $180,000, a net realizable value of $190,000, and a normal profit margin of 20 percent.

Property, Plant, and Equipment

The company acquired a building at the beginning of 2010 at a cost of $2,750,000. The building has an estimated useful life of 25 years, an estimated residual value of $250,000, and is being depreciated on a straight-line basis. At the beginning of 2011, the building was appraised and determined to have a fair value of $3,250,000. There is no change in estimated useful life or residual value. In a switch to IFRS, the company would use the revaluation model in IAS 16 to determine the carrying value of property, plant, and equipment subsequent to acquisition.

Intangible Assets

As part of a business combination in 2008, the company acquired a brand with a fair value of $40,000. The brand is classified as an intangible asset with an indefinite life. At year-end 2011, the brand is determined to have a selling price of $35,000 with zero cost to sell. Expected future cash flows from continued use of the brand are $42,000 and the present value of the expected future cash flows is $34,000.

Research and Development Costs

The company incurred research and development costs of $200,000 in 2011. Of this amount, 40 percent related to development activities subsequent to the point at which criteria had been met indicating that an intangible asset existed. As of the end of the 2011, development of the new product had not been completed.

Sale-and-Leaseback

In January 2009, the company realized a gain on the sale-and-leaseback of an office building in the amount of $150,000. The lease is accounted for as an operating lease, and the term of the lease is five years.

Required

Prepare a reconciliation schedule to convert 2011 income and December 31, 2011, stockholders' equity from a U.S. GAAP basis to IFRS. Ignore income taxes. Prepare a note to explain each adjustment made in the reconciliation schedule.

References

Ernst & Young. "The Evolution of IAS 39 in Europe," *Eye on IFRS Newsletter*, November 2004, pp. 1–4.

Financial Accounting Standards Board. *The IASC-U.S. Comparison Project*, 2nd ed. Norwalk, CT: FASB, 1999.

Reimers, J. L. "Additional Evidence on the Need for Disclosure Reform." *Accounting Horizons*, March 1992, pp. 36–41.

U.S. Securities and Exchange Commission. Release Nos. 33-9109; 34-61578, *Commission Statement in Support of Convergence and Global Accounting Standards*, February 2010.

Chapter **Five**

International Financial Reporting Standards: Part II

Learning Objectives

After reading this chapter, you should be able to

- Describe and apply the requirements of International Financial Reporting Standards (IFRS) related to the financial reporting of current liabilities, provisions, employee benefits, share-based payment, income taxes, revenue, and financial instruments.
- Explain and analyze the effect of major differences between IFRS and U.S. GAAP related to the financial reporting of current liabilities, provisions, employee benefits, share-based payment, income taxes, revenue, and financial instruments.

INTRODUCTION

International Financial Reporting Standards (IFRS) issued by the International Accounting Standard Board (IASB) comprise a comprehensive set of standards providing guidance for the preparation and presentation of financial statements. Chapter 4 described and demonstrated the requirements of selected IASB standards, particularly those relating to the recognition and measurement of assets. This chapter continues the study of IFRS by focusing on the recognition and measurement of current liabilities, provisions, employee benefits, share-based payment, income taxes, revenue, and financial instruments.

CURRENT LIABILITIES

IAS 1, *Presentation of Financial Statements,* requires liabilities to be classified as current or noncurrent. Current liabilities are those liabilities that a company:

1. Expects to settle in its normal operating cycle.
2. Holds primarily for the purpose of trading.
3. Expects to settle within 12 months of the balance sheet date.
4. Does not have the right to defer until 12 months after the balance sheet date.

The classification and accounting for current liabilities under IFRS is very similar to U.S. GAAP. Differences relate to the following:

- *Refinanced short-term debt:* May be reclassified as long-term debt only if refinancing is completed prior to the balance sheet date. Under U.S. GAAP, a refinancing agreement must be reached but the refinancing need not be completed by the balance sheet date.
- *Amounts payable on demand due to violation of debt covenants:* Must be classified as current unless a waiver of at least 12 months is obtained from the lender by the balance sheet date. The waiver must be obtained by the annual report issuance date under U.S. GAAP.
- *Bank overdrafts:* Are netted against cash if the overdrafts form an integral part of the entity's cash management, otherwise bank overdrafts are classified as current liabilities. Bank overdrafts are always classified as current liabilities under U.S. GAAP.

Example: Violation of Debt Covenant

On June 30, Year 1, Sprockets Inc. obtains a $100,000 loan from a bank for a manufacturing facility. The loan is due in 24 months and is subject to a number of debt covenants. In December, Year 1, Sprockets distributes too much of its cash on employee bonuses and incurs a debt covenant violation as of December 31, Year 1. As a result of the violation, the loan becomes due within 30 days. Sprockets' CFO asks the bank to waive the violation. On January 5, Year 2, the bank agrees to waive the violation, stipulating that it must be rectified within 90 days. Sprockets issues its financial statements on January 30, Year 2. In this situation, Sprockets would be required to classify the bank loan as a current liability on its December 31, Year 1 balance sheet because it did not obtain a waiver from the bank by the balance sheet date.

Now assume that Sprockets' CFO obtained a waiver from the bank on December 30, Year 1, stipulating that the debt covenant violation must be rectified within 90 days. In this case, although the waiver was obtained before the balance sheet date, Sprockets still would be required to classify the bank loan as a current liability, because the waiver is not for at least 12 months, but is for only 90 days.

PROVISIONS, CONTINGENT LIABILITIES, AND CONTINGENT ASSETS

IAS 37, *Provisions, Contingent Liabilities and Contingent Assets,* provides guidance for reporting liabilities (and assets) of uncertain timing, amount, or existence. It contains specific rules related to onerous contracts and restructuring costs. By way of examples in IAS 37, Part B, guidance also is provided with regard to issues such as environmental costs and nuclear decommissioning costs.

Contingent Liabilities and Provisions

IAS 37 distinguishes between a contingent liability, which is not recognized on the balance sheet, and a provision, which is. A *provision* is defined as a "liability of uncertain timing or amount." A provision should be recognized when

1. The entity has a *present* obligation (legal or constructive) as a result of a past event.
2. It is *probable* (more likely than not) that an outflow of resources embodying economic events will be required to settle the obligation.
3. A reliable estimate of the obligation can be made.

A *constructive obligation* exists when a company through past actions or current statements indicates that it will accept certain responsibilities and, as a result, has created a valid expectation on the part of other parties that it will discharge those responsibilities. For example, an entity has a constructive obligation to restructure when it communicates the details of the restructuring plan to those employees who will be affected by it. Another example of a constructive obligation is where a manufacturer (e.g., Sony) announces that it will honor rebates offered by a retailer that goes out of business (e.g., Circuit City) on the manufacturer's products, even though the manufacturer has no contractual obligation to do so. A constructive obligation is recognized as a provision when it meets the remaining criteria (2 and 3) just listed. U.S. GAAP does not have the concept of a constructive obligation. Thus, only legal obligations might be accrued when criteria are met.

Contingent liabilities are defined in IAS 37 as one of the following:

- *Possible* obligations that arise from past events and whose existence will be confirmed by the occurrence or nonoccurrence of a future event.
- A *present* obligation that is *not recognized* because (1) it is *not* probable that an outflow of resources will be required to settle the obligation or (2) the amount of the obligation *cannot* be measured with sufficient reliability.

Contingent liabilities are disclosed unless the possibility of an outflow of resources embodying the economic future benefits is *remote*.

The rules for recognition of a provision and disclosure of a contingent liability are generally similar to the U.S. GAAP rules related to contingent liabilities. Under U.S. GAAP, a contingent liability is neither recognized nor disclosed if the likelihood of an outflow of resources is remote; it is disclosed if such an outflow is possible but not probable; and it is recognized on the balance sheet when an outflow of resources is probable. The main difference is that U.S. GAAP requires accrual when it is probable that a loss has occurred, with no guidance as to how the word *probable* should be interpreted. Research suggests that U.S. accountants require the likelihood of occurrence to be in the range of 70 to 90 percent before recognizing a contingent liability.[1] In defining a provision, IAS 37 specifically defines *probable* as "more likely than not," which implies a threshold of just over 50 percent. Thus, in practice, the threshold for recognition of a "liability of uncertain timing or amount" is considerably lower under IFRS than U.S. GAAP.

IAS 37 establishes guidance for measuring a provision as the *best estimate* of the expenditure required to settle the present obligation at the balance sheet date. The best estimate is the probability-weighted expected value when a range of estimates exists; the midpoint within a range if all estimates are equally likely. Provisions must be discounted to present value. Provisions also must be reviewed at the end of each accounting period and adjusted to reflect the current best estimate. Under U.S. GAAP, contingent liabilities should be recognized at the low end of the range of possible amounts when a range of estimates exists. U.S. GAAP only allows discounting of a recognized contingent liability when the amount of the liability and the timing of payments are fixed or reliably determinable.

Subsequent reduction of a provision can be made only for the expenditures for which the provision was established. For example, if a provision is created for warranties, the provision can only be reduced as warranty costs are incurred.

---

[1] "The IASC-US Comparison Project: A Report on the Similarities and Differences between IASC Standards and US GAAP: 2nd Edition," published by the FASB, 1999.

A provision is reversed when it is no longer probable that an outflow of resources will occur.

With respect to disclosure of contingent liabilities, IAS 37 allows an enterprise "in extremely rare cases" to omit disclosures that "can be expected to prejudice seriously the position of the enterprise in a dispute with other parties." No such exemption exists under U.S. GAAP.

Example: Provision for Litigation Loss

Former employees of Dreams Unlimited Inc. filed a lawsuit against the company in Year 1 for alleged age discrimination. At December 31, Year 1, external legal counsel provided an opinion that it was 60 percent probable that the company would be found liable, which would result in a total payment to the former employees between $1,000,000 and $1,500,000, with all amounts in that range being equally likely.

Because it is "more likely than not" that an outflow of resources (cash) will be required as a result of the lawsuit and an amount can be reasonably estimated, Dreams Unlimited should recognize a provision. Because all amounts in the estimated range of loss are equally likely, the amount recognized would be the midpoint of the range, $1,250,000 [($1,000,000 + $1,500,000)/2]. Therefore, Dreams Unlimited would prepare the following journal entry at December 31, Year 1 to recognize a provision:

Litigation Loss	$1,250,000	
Provision for Litigation Loss		$1,250,000

Note that under U.S. GAAP, a provision probably would not be recognized because the likelihood of incurring a loss is only 60 percent. If a provision were recognized under U.S. GAAP, it would be for $1,000,000, the low end of the range.

In Year 2, Dreams Unlimited settled with the former employees, making a total payment of $1,100,000. As a result, the company would prepare the following journal entry:

Provision for Litigation Loss	$1,250,000	
Cash		$1,100,000
Reversal of Litigation Loss		150,000

The reversal of litigation loss would result in an increase in income in Year 2.

Onerous Contract

IAS 37 requires the recognition of a provision for the present obligation related to an "onerous contract," that is, a contract in which the unavoidable costs of meeting the obligation of the contract exceed the economic benefits expected to be received from it. However, recognition of a provision for expected future operating losses is not allowed. When an onerous contract exists, a provision should be recognized for the unavoidable costs of the contract, which is the lower of the cost of fulfillment and the penalty that would result from non-fulfillment under the contract. When a contract becomes onerous as a result of an entity's own action, the resulting provision should *not* be recognized until that action has actually occurred.

Example: Onerous Contract

Delicious Chocolate Company produces chocolate candies. It has a noncancelable lease on a building in Ridgeway, South Carolina, that it uses for production. The lease expires on December 31, Year 2 and is classified as an operating lease for accounting purposes. The annual lease payment is $120,000. In October, Year 1, the company closed its South Carolina facility and moved production to Mexico. The company does not believe it will be possible to sublease the building located in South Carolina.

Because there is no future economic benefit expected from the lease, it is an onerous contract. The unavoidable cost of fulfilling the lease contract for Year 2 of $120,000 should be expensed and recorded as a provision on December 31, Year 1. The journal entry would be:

Noncancelable Lease Expense	$120,000	
Provision for Future Lease Payments		$120,000

Restructuring

A restructuring is a program that is planned and controlled by management and that materially changes either

1. The scope of a business undertaken by an entity.
2. The manner in which that business is conducted.

Examples of restructurings include:

- Sale or termination of a line of business.
- Closure of business locations in a country or region.
- Change in management structure.
- Fundamental reorganization that has a material effect on the nature and focus of the entity's operations.

A difference exists between IAS 37 and U.S. GAAP with respect to when a provision should be recognized related to a restructuring plan. According to IAS 37, a restructuring provision should be recognized when an entity has a detailed formal plan for the restructuring and it has raised a valid expectation in those affected by the plan that it will carry out the restructuring, either by announcing the main features of the plan to those affected by it or by beginning to implement the plan. Also, the cost of the restructuring must be reasonably estimable and the plan must be carried out within a reasonable period of time.

U.S. GAAP does not allow recognition of a restructuring provision until a liability has been incurred. The existence of a restructuring plan and its announcement does not necessarily create a liability. Thus, the recognition of a restructuring provision and related loss may occur at a later date under U.S. GAAP than under IFRS.

Contingent Assets

A contingent asset is a probable asset that arises from past events and whose existence will be confirmed only by the occurrence or nonoccurrence of a future event. Contingent assets should not be recognized, but should be disclosed when the inflow of economic benefits is *probable.* If the realization of income from a contingency is determined to be *virtually certain,* then the related benefit is considered to meet the definition of an asset and recognition is appropriate. IAS 37 allows earlier recognition of a contingent asset (and related gain) than does U.S. GAAP, which generally requires the asset to be realized before it can be recognized.

Exhibit 5.1 provides a summary of the recognition and disclosure guidelines in IAS 37.

EXHIBIT 5.1
IAS 37 Recognition and Disclosure Guidelines

Contingent Element	Likelihood of Realization	Accounting Treatment
Uncertain liability	Probable (more likely than not)	
	—Reliably measurable	Recognize provision
	—Not reliably measurable	Disclosure
	Not probable	Disclosure
	Remote	No disclosure
Uncertain asset	Virtually certain	Recognize asset
	Probable	Disclosure
	Not probable	No disclosure

Additional Guidance

The IASB document published to accompany IAS 37 (IAS 37, Part B) provides a number of examples to demonstrate the application of the standard's recognition principles. Example 2B, for example, describes a situation involving contaminated land, which gives rise to a constructive obligation.

Example: Contaminated Land Constructive Obligation

Petrocan Company operates in the oil industry and contaminates land at a location in a foreign country. The foreign country does not have environmental legislation that will require the company to clean up the contamination. However, Petrocan has a widely published environmental policy to clean up all contamination that it causes, and the company has a record of honoring this policy.

The company applies the criteria of IAS 37 to determine whether recognition of a provision is appropriate:

1. *Present obligation as a result of a past obligating event:* The past obligating event is the contamination of the land. A present constructive obligation exists because the past conduct of the company creates a valid expectation on the part of those affected by it that the entity will clean up the contamination.

2. *An outflow of resources embodying economic benefits in settlement is probable:* Because the contamination has occurred, and the company has a policy of cleaning up all contamination, an outflow of resources to settle the constructive obligation is "more likely than not."

3. *A reliable estimate of the obligation can be made:* The company must determine whether this criterion is met. If so, a provision would be recognized for the best estimate of the costs of clean-up. If not, then disclosures would be made because there is a greater than remote likelihood of an outflow of resources to settle the obligation.

Proposed Amendments to IAS 37

The IASB intends to issue a new IFRS to replace IAS 37. The working draft in 2010 contained two major changes to the current standard:

1. The criterion of "probable outflow of resources" for recognition of a provision would be removed. As a result, a liability would be recognized for any present obligation that can be measured reliably.

2. The "best estimate" measurement rule would be replaced with the requirement that a liability should be measured at the amount that an entity would rationally pay to be relieved of the present obligation. In many cases, this will be the expected present value of the resources required to fulfill the obligation. Appendix B of the Exposure Draft to amend IAS 37 contains detailed guidance for measuring an obligation of uncertain timing or amount.

Example: Measuring the Present Value of the Resources Required to Fulfill an Obligation

Petrocan Company operates an oil well in a country with environmental laws that require the company to restore the site to its original condition once the oil well ceases operations. The company estimates the productive life of the well to be three to five years. The current three-year and five-year risk free interest rates are 4 percent and 5 percent, respectively. Petrocan identifies four outcomes that represent a reasonable estimation of the distribution of possible outcomes and develops the following schedule to estimate the expected present value of the cash outflows that will be necessary to comply with the law:

Outcome	Useful Life	Estimated Outflow	Discount Rate	Present Value of Estimated Outflow	Estimated Probability of Outcome	Present Value of Outflow × Probability of Outcome
1	3	$100,000	4%	$ 88,900	15%	$ 13,335
2	3	120,000	4%	106,680	25%	26,670
3	5	130,000	5%	101,858	35%	35,650
4	5	150,000	5%	117,529	25%	29,382
Expected present value of outflows						$105,037

As a result of this calculation, the Exposure Draft would require Petrocan to recognize a provision for site restoration of $105,037.

EMPLOYEE BENEFITS

IAS 19, *Employee Benefits,* is a single standard that covers all forms of employee compensation and benefits other than share-based compensation (e.g., stock options), which is covered in IFRS 2. IAS 19 provides guidance with respect to four types of employee benefits:

1. Short-term employee benefits (such as compensated absences and bonuses).
2. Post-employment benefits (pensions, medical benefits, and other post-employment benefits).
3. Other long-term employee benefits (such as deferred compensation and disability benefits).
4. Termination benefits (such as severance pay and early retirement benefits).

We discuss each of these types of employee benefit in turn.

Short-Term Benefits

An employer recognizes an expense and a liability at the time that the employee provides services. The amount recognized is undiscounted.

Compensated Absences

For short-term compensated absences (such as sick pay or vacation pay), an amount is accrued when services are provided only if the compensated absences accumulate over time and can be carried forward to future periods. In the case of nonaccumulating compensated absences, an expense and liability is recognized only when the absence occurs.

Profit-Sharing and Bonus Plans

An expense and a liability are accrued for profit-sharing or bonus plans only if:

- The company has a present legal or constructive obligation to make such payments as a result of past events.
- The amount can be reliably estimated.

Even if a company has no legal obligation to pay a bonus, it can have a constructive obligation to do so if it has no realistic alternative but to pay the bonus.

Post-employment Benefits

IAS 19 distinguishes between defined contribution plans and defined benefit plans. The accounting for a defined contribution plan is simple and straightforward. An employer:

1. Accrues an expense and a liability at the time the employee renders service for the amount the employer is obligated to contribute to the plan.
2. Reduces the liability when contributions are made.

The accounting for a defined post-employment benefit plan is considerably more complicated.

Defined Post-employment Benefit Plans

Under IFRS, the accounting for both defined benefit pension plans and other defined post-employment benefit plans (such as medical and life insurance benefits) is basically the same and is generally similar to the accounting under U.S. GAAP. The following discussion relates specifically to pensions, but it also is applicable to other post-employment benefits.

The two major issues in accounting for defined benefit pension plans are (1) calculation of the net pension expense (or revenue) to be recognized in current net income and (2) calculation of the net pension liability (or asset) to be reported on the balance sheet.

Income Statement Recognition and Measurement

The net pension expense (or revenue) recognized in net income is comprised of up to six components and is calculated as follows:

+ Current service cost

+ Interest cost

− Expected return on plan assets

+ / − Actuarial gains and losses (recognized in the current period)

+ Past service cost (recognized in the current period)

+ / − Curtailment or settlement gains and losses.

The first three components will exist every year for every employer who has a defined benefit plan. The last three components exist only when specific actions are taken by the employer.

Actuarial Gains and Losses

Actuarial gains and losses arise when an employer changes its actuarial assumptions used in determining the future benefit obligation or makes adjustments based on differences between past assumptions and past experience. IAS 19 allows the use of a "corridor" approach to smooth the impact that actuarial gains and losses have on net income. Under this approach, actuarial gains and losses are recognized in the current period only to the extent that they exceed 10 percent of the greater of (1) the present value (PV) of the defined pension benefit obligation at the end of the previous year or (2) the fair value (FV) of plan assets at the end of the previous year.

The amount of actuarial gain or loss recognized in the current period is the recognizable amount (the excess defined in the previous paragraph) divided by the average remaining working lives of the employees covered by the plan. The actuarial gain or loss attributable to inactive or retired employees is expensed immediately. A similar corridor approach also is used for recognition of actuarial gains and losses in U.S. GAAP, but the amount attributable to inactive or retired employees is amortized over their remaining life expectancy.

IAS 19 also permits any systematic method of amortization that results in faster recognition of actuarial gains and losses (including immediate recognition), provided the same basis is applied to both gains and losses and is applied consistently period to period. If a company chooses to recognize actuarial gains and losses in the period in which they occur, it may do so by including them either in net income or in a separate component of shareholders' equity. Bypassing income to accumulate actuarial gains and losses in equity is not acceptable under U.S. GAAP.

Past Service Cost

Past service cost arises when an employer improves the benefits to be paid employees in conjunction with a defined benefit plan. IAS 19 provides the following rules related to past service cost:

- Past service cost related to retirees and vested active employees is expensed immediately.
- Past service cost related to nonvested employees is recognized on a straight-line basis over the remaining vesting period.

In comparison, U.S. GAAP requires that the past service cost (referred to as prior service cost) related to retirees be amortized over their remaining expected life, and the past service cost related to active employees be amortized over their remaining service period. Exhibit 5.2 provides a summary of the differences in amortization rules related to past service cost and actuarial gains and losses between IFRS and U.S. GAAP.

EXHIBIT 5.2 Recognition Rules for Past Service Cost and Actuarial Gains/Losses

Employee Status	Recognition of			
	Past Service Cost		Actuarial Gains/Losses	
	IFRS	U.S. GAAP	IFRS	U.S. GAAP
Active				
Nonvested	Remaining vesting period	Remaining working life	Remaining working life	Remaining working life
Vested	Immediately	Remaining working life	Remaining working life	Remaining working life
Inactive/Retired	Immediately	Remaining expected life	Immediately	Remaining expected life

Example: Recognition of Past Service Cost

On January 1, Year 7, Eagle Company amends its defined benefit pension plan to increase the amount of benefits to be paid. The benefits vest after five years of service. At the date of the plan amendment, the increase in the present value of the defined benefit obligation attributable to vested and nonvested employees is as follows:

Employees with more than five years of service at 1/1/Y7	$10,000
Employees with less than five years of service at 1/1/Y7.......................	8,000
Total present value of additional benefits....................................	$18,000

On average, the nonvested employees have two years of service at 1/1/Y7.

Under IFRS, Eagle Company recognizes the past service cost attributable to vested employees in Year 7 and the past service cost attributable to nonvested employees is amortized on a straight-line basis over Years 7, 8, and 9 (average three years until vesting). The total amount of past service cost recognized as a component of pension expense in Year 7 is computed as follows:

Past service cost (vested employees)	$10,000
Past service cost (nonvested employees) $8,000/3 years......................	2,667
Total...	$12,667

The unrecognized past service cost of $5,333 is subtracted from the present value of the defined benefit obligation in determining the amount of asset or liability to be recognized on the balance sheet.

Under U.S. GAAP, because all of the employees affected by the plan amendment are active employees, the past service cost of $18,000 would be amortized to expense over the remaining service life of those employees. Assuming an average remaining service life of 12 years, $1,500 of past service cost would be recognized as a component of pension expense in Year 7.

Curtailments and Settlements

A pension plan curtailment arises when there is a material reduction in the number of employees covered by a plan (such as when a plant is closed as part of a restructuring) or when the future service by current employees will no longer qualify for pension benefits or will qualify only for reduced benefits. A pension plan settlement involves lump-sum cash payments to employees in exchange for their rights to received defined pension benefits. Gains and losses usually arise in conjunction with plan curtailments and settlements. IAS 19 treats these gains and losses similarly; both are recognized in income in the period in which the entity is demonstrably committed and a curtailment or settlement has been announced. U.S. GAAP treats gains and losses on plan curtailments and settlements differently, with losses generally recognized earlier than gains. A curtailment gain cannot be recognized until the related employees terminate or the plan has been adopted.

Balance Sheet Recognition and Limitation

The amount recognized on the employer's balance sheet related to a defined benefit pension plan can be either a net pension liability or a net pension asset and is calculated as follows:

+ Present value of the defined benefit obligation (PVDBO)

− Fair value of plan assets

+/− Unrecognized actuarial gains (+) and losses (−)

− Unrecognized past service cost

However, if the resulting amount is negative (net pension asset), the amount of asset to be reported on the balance sheet is limited to the lesser of two amounts

1. PVDBO plus (minus) unrecognized net actuarial gains (losses) minus unrecognized past service cost minus FV of plan assets.
2. The sum of any unrecognized actuarial losses and past service cost, and the present values of any refunds available from the plan, and any available reduction in future employer contributions to the plan.

The PVDBO is based on assumptions related to variables such as employee turnover, life expectancy, and future salary levels. The discount rate used in determining the PVDBO, current service cost, and past service cost, if applicable, is determined by reference to the yield at the end of the period on high-quality corporate bonds.

Under U.S. GAAP, the amount recognized on the balance sheet is equal to the difference between the PVDBO and the fair value of plan assets; this is known as the funded status. There is no adjustment for unrecognized actuarial gains/losses and prior service cost, and there is no limitation of the amount of pension asset to be recognized.

Example: Limitation on the Recognition of the Net Asset

The defined benefit plan of Fortsen Company Inc. has the following characteristics at December 31, Year 9:

Present value of defined benefit obligation (PVDBO)	$ 10,000
Fair value of plan assets	(10,800)
Funded status	(800)
Unrecognized actuarial losses	(50)
Unrecognized past service cost	(30)
Negative amount (possible asset)	$ (880)
Present value of available future refunds and reduction in future contributions	$ 525

The amount of pension asset that may be recognized is limited to the lesser of $880 and the following amount:

Unrecognized actuarial losses	$ 50
Unrecognized past service cost	30
Present value of available future refunds and reduction in future contributions	525
Limit	$605

Fortsen Company recognizes a prepaid pension cost (pension asset) of $605 on its 12/31/Y9 balance sheet and must disclose the fact that the limit reduces the carrying amount of the asset by $275. The asset limitation also increases the pension expense by $275. Under U.S. GAAP, Fortsen Company would recognize a pension asset in the amount of $800, equal to the difference between the PVDBO and the fair value of plan assets.

Exhibit 5.3 presents the calculation of the amounts recognized on the balance sheet and income statement by Nokia Corporation in 2009 related to its defined benefit pension plans. The company reported a net pension liability of €106 million and a net pension expense of €55 million in 2009. These amounts were larger than they would have been had the company not been limited in the amount of pension asset that it was allowed to recognize under IAS 19. Under U.S. GAAP, Nokia would have reported a net pension liability of €81 million and a net pension expense of €50 million in 2009.

Anticipation of Changes in Future Benefits

IAS 19 permits anticipation of future changes in the law in measuring the employer's pension benefit obligation. This is especially relevant in those situations where the level of pension benefits provided by the employer is linked to the level of

EXHIBIT 5.3

NOKIA CORPORATION
2009
Annual Report

Excerpt from Note 5. Pensions

The following table sets forth the changes in the benefit obligation and fair value of plan assets during the year and the funded status of the significant defined benefit pension plans showing the amounts that are recognized in the Group's consolidated statement of financial position at December 31:

EURm	2009	2008
Present value of defined benefit obligations at beginning of year	(1,205)	(2,266)
Foreign exchange	5	56
Current service cost	(55)	(79)
Interest cost	(69)	(78)
Plan participants' contributions	(12)	(10)
Past service cost	—	(2)
Actuarial gain (+)/loss (−)	(139)	105
Acquisitions	2	(2)
Curtailment	—	10

Settlements	2	1,025
Benefits paid	60	36
Present value of defined benefit obligations at end of year	**(1,411)**	**(1,205)**
Plan assets at fair value at beginning of year	1,197	2,174
Foreign exchange	(7)	(58)
Expected return on plan assets	70	71
Actuarial gain (+)/loss (−) on plan assets	56	(39)
Employer contribution	49	141
Plan participants' contributions	12	10
Benefits paid	(44)	(24)
Curtailments	—	(5)
Settlements	(2)	(1,078)
Acquisitions	(1)	5
Plan assets at fair value at end of year	**1,330**	**1,197**
Surplus (−)/deficit (+)	**(81)**	**(8)**
Unrecognized net actuarial gains (−)/losses (+)	(21)	(113)
Unrecognized past service cost	1	1
Amount not recognized as an asset in the balance sheet because of limit in IAS 19 paragraph 58(b)	(5)	—
Prepaid (−)/accrued (+) pension cost in statement of financial position	**(106)**	**(120)**

The amounts recognized in the income statement are as follows:

EURm	2009	2008	2007
Current service cost	55	79	125
Interest cost	69	78	104
Expected return on plan assets	(70)	(71)	(95)
Net actuarial (gains) losses recognized in year	(9)	—	10
Impact of paragraph 58(b) limitation	5	—	—
Past service cost gains (−)/losses (+)	—	2	—
Curtailment	—	(12)	(1)
Settlement	—	152	(12)
Total, included in personnel expenses	50	228	131

retirement benefit that will be provided by national and local governments. U.S. GAAP does *not* permit anticipation of future changes in the law.

Other Post-employment Benefits

IAS 19 does not provide separate guidance for other post-employment benefits. The procedures described earlier for pension plans are equally applicable for other forms of post-employment benefits provided to employees, such as medical benefits and life insurance. In calculating the PVDBO for post-employment medical benefit plans, assumptions also must be made regarding expected changes in the cost of medical services.

U.S. GAAP provides considerably more guidance than IAS 19 with regard to the assumptions to be used and the measurement of the employer's obligation for post-employment medical benefits. As allowed by the IASB's *Framework*, companies using IFRS could refer to the guidance provided in U.S. GAAP to identify an appropriate method for determining the amount of expense to recognize related to post-employment benefits other than pensions.

Other Long-Term Employee Benefits

Other long-term employee benefits include, for example, long-term compensated absences (e.g., sabbatical leaves), long-term disability benefits, bonuses payable 12 months or more after the end of the period, and deferred compensation paid 12 months or more after the end of the period. A liability should be recognized for other long-term employee benefits equal to the difference between:

1. The present value of the defined benefit obligation.
2. The fair value of plan assets (if any).

Termination Benefits

IAS 19 requires termination benefits to be recognized as an expense and a liability when an employer is *demonstrably committed* to either (1) terminating the employment of an employee or group of employees or (2) providing termination benefits as a result of an offer made to encourage voluntary termination. A demonstrable commitment exists when a detailed formal plan exists from which the employer cannot realistically withdraw.

In the case of an offer made to encourage voluntary termination, the amount recognized should be based on the number of employees *expected* to accept the offer, discounted to present value if the benefits will be paid more than 12 months after the balance sheet date.

U.S. GAAP distinguishes among three different types of termination benefits and provides different timing recognition criteria for each:

1. Special termination benefits should be recognized when an employee accepts the offer.
2. Contractual termination benefits should be recognized when it is probable that employees will be entitled to benefits.
3. Termination benefits offered in conjunction with a restructuring should be recognized when the plan is approved by management.

A difference also exists with respect to the amount of termination benefit to recognize related to offers to encourage voluntary termination. IAS 19 indicates that measurement should be based on the number of employees *expected to accept* the offer, discounted to present value if benefits fall due more than 12 months after the balance sheet date. Under U.S. GAAP, measurement is based on the number of employees that *actually accept* the offer, and discounting is not required.

SHARE-BASED PAYMENT

The IASB and the FASB worked closely in developing new standards related to accounting for share-based payments. Concurrent with the IASB's issuance of IFRS 2, the FASB published an exposure draft in March 2004 and subsequently issued a final standard on this topic in December 2004. Although a number of minor differences exist between the two standards, IFRS 2 and U.S. GAAP are substantially similar.

IFRS 2, *Share-based Payment*, sets out measurement principles and specific requirements for three types of share-based payment transactions:

1. *Equity-settled share-based payment transactions,* in which the entity receives goods or services as consideration for equity instruments of the entity (including stock options granted to employees).
2. *Cash-settled share-based payment transactions,* in which the entity acquires goods or services by incurring liabilities to the supplier of those goods or services for amounts that are based on the price (or value) of the entity's shares or other equity instruments of the entity (e.g., share appreciation rights).
3. *Choice-of-settlement share-based payment transactions,* in which the terms of the arrangement provide either the entity or the supplier of goods or services with a choice of whether the entity settles the transaction in cash or by issuing equity instruments.

IFRS 2 applies to share-based transactions with both employees and nonemployees and requires an entity to recognize all share-based payment transactions in its financial statements; there are no exceptions.

The standard applies a *fair value approach* in accounting for share-based payment transactions. In some situations, these transactions are recognized at the fair value of the goods or services obtained, in other cases, at the fair value of the equity instrument awarded. Fair value of shares and stock options is based on market prices, if available; otherwise a generally accepted valuation model should be used. IFRS 2, Part B, contains extensive application guidance with respect to estimating the "fair value of equity instruments granted."

Equity-Settled Share-Based Payment Transactions

Share-based payment transactions entered into by an entity that will be settled by the entity issuing equity shares are accounted for as equity transactions. Typically, a debit is made to either an asset (goods acquired) or expense (service received), and a credit is made to paid-in capital.

Share-Based Payments to Nonemployees

Entities sometimes will acquire goods or services from external suppliers using shares of the entity's stock as payment. Share-based payments to non-employees are measured at the fair value of the goods or services received. If the fair value of the goods and services received cannot be reliably determined, then the fair value of the equity instruments is used. If the fair value of the equity instruments is used, the measurement date is the date the entity obtains the goods or services. If the goods or services are received on a number of dates over a period, the fair value at each date should be used.

Under U.S. GAAP, when the transaction is accounted for using the fair value of the equity instruments, the earlier of either the date at which a commitment for performance is reached or when the performance is completed is used as the measurement date for determining the fair value of the equity instruments.

Share-Based Payments to Employees

For share-based payments to employees (including stock options), the transaction should be measured at the fair value of the equity instruments granted because the fair value of the service provided by the employees generally is not reliably measurable. The fair value of stock options must be determined at the date the options are granted (grant date).

Stock option plans typically contain vesting conditions that must be met in order for the options to become exercisable. The entity issuing stock options must estimate the number of options that are expected to vest. The product of the number of options expected to vest multiplied by the fair value of those options is the total compensation cost that will be recognized as compensation expense over the vesting period. The estimate of options expected to vest should be revised throughout the vesting period with corresponding adjustments to compensation expense. As compensation expense is recognized, it is offset by an increase in additional paid-in capital.

Compensation expense associated with stock options that vest on a single date (cliff vesting) is recognized on a straight-line basis over the service period. When stock options vest in installments (graded vesting), the compensation expense associated with each installment (or tranche) must be amortized over that installment's vesting period. U.S. GAAP allows a choice in recognizing compensation cost related to graded-vesting stock options. Entities may choose to amortize compensation cost on an accelerated basis by tranche (similar to IFRS); alternatively, compensation cost may be amortized on a straight-line basis over the vesting period.

Example: Graded-Vesting Stock Options

Glackin Corporation grants stock options with a fair value of $100,000 to select employees at the beginning of Year 1; 50 percent vest at the end of Year 1 and 50 percent vest at the end of Year 2. Under IFRS, compensation cost associated with the first tranche is fully allocated to expense in Year 1, and compensation cost associated with the second tranche is amortized to expense 50 percent in Year 1 and 50 percent in Year 2. As a result, the amount of compensation expense recognized in Year 1 is $75,000 [$50,000 + (50% × $50,000)], and the amount of compensation expense recognized in Year 2 is $25,000 [50% × $50,000]. The same pattern of compensation expense recognition would be acceptable under U.S. GAAP. Alternatively, U.S. GAAP allows the company to simply amortize the $100,000 compensation cost on a straight-line basis over the two-year vesting period, recognizing compensation expense of $50,000 in each of Year 1 and Year 2.

Modification of Stock Option Plans

Entities that grant stock options sometimes make modifications to the terms and conditions under which equity instruments were granted. For example, an entity might change the length of the vesting period or change the exercise price, which could change the fair value of the stock options. If an entity modifies the terms and conditions of a stock option, IFRS 2 requires the entity to recognize, at a minimum, the original amount of compensation cost as measured at the grant date. If the fair value of the options is reduced as a result of the modification, then there is no change in the total compensation cost to be recognized. If the modification results in an increase in the fair value of the options, then total compensation cost must be increased by the increase in fair value (the difference between the fair value at the original grant date and the fair value at the modification date). Under U.S. GAAP, when modifications are made to stock options, the fair value of the options at the date of modification determines the total amount of compensation expense to be recognized. There is no minimum amount of compensation cost to recognize as there is under IFRS.

Cash-Settled Share-Based Payment Transactions

An entity might provide employees with stock appreciation rights in which they are entitled to receive a cash payment when the entity's stock price increases above a predetermined level. Stock appreciation rights are an example of a cash-settled share-based payment transaction. This type of transaction results in the recognition of a liability (because there will be a future outflow of cash) and an expense. The liability (and expense) is measured at the fair value of the share appreciation rights using an option pricing model. Until the liability is settled it must be remeasured at each balance sheet date, with the change in fair value reflected in net income. Under U.S. GAAP, certain cash-settled share-based payment transactions are classified as equity; these transactions would be classified as a liability under IFRS.

Choice-of-Settlement Share-Based Payment Transactions

When the terms of a share-based payment transaction allow the *entity to choose* between equity settlement and cash settlement, the entity must treat the transaction as a cash-settled share-based payment transaction only if it has a present obligation to settle in cash; otherwise the entity treats the transaction as an equity-settled share-based payment transaction.

When the terms of a share-based payment transaction allow the *supplier of goods and services to choose* between equity settlement and cash settlement, the entity has issued a compound financial instrument the fair value of which must be split into separate debt and equity components. The debt component must be remeasured at fair value at each balance sheet date, with the change in fair value reflected in net income. If the supplier of goods and services chooses to receive settlement in cash, the cash payment is applied only against the debt component (reduces the liability). The equity component remains in equity. If the supplier chooses to receive settlement in equity, the debt component (liability) is transferred to equity.

Example: Choice-of-Settlement Share-Based Payment Transaction (Supplier Has Choice)

On January 1, Year 1, Leiyu Company issued 100 stock options with an exercise price of $18 each to five employees (500 options in total). The employees can choose to settle the options either (1) in shares of stock ($1 par value) or (2) in cash equal to the intrinsic value of the options on the vesting date. The options vest on December 31, Year 2 after the employees have completed two years of service. Leiyu Company expects that only four of the employees will remain with the company for the next two years and vest in the options. One employee resigns in Year 1, and the company continues to assume an overall forfeiture rate of 20 percent at December 31, Year 1. As expected, four employees vest on December 31, Year 2 and exercise their stock options. Share prices and fair values of the two settlement alternatives over the vesting period are:

Date	Share Price	Fair Value of Cash-Settlement Alternative	Fair Value of Share-Settlement Alternative
January 1, Year 1	$20	$10.00	$10.00
December 31, Year 1	$26	$11.00	$11.00
December 31, Year 2	$30	$12.00	$12.00

Because Leiyu has granted employees stock options that can be settled either in cash or in shares of stock, this is a compound financial instrument. Because this is a transaction with employees, Leiyu must determine the fair value of the compound financial instrument at the measurement date, taking into account the terms and conditions on which the rights to cash or equity instruments are granted. To determine the fair value of a compound financial instrument, the company first measures the fair value of the debt component (i.e., the cash-settlement alternative) and then measures the fair value of the equity component (i.e., the equity-settlement alternative), taking into account that the employee must forfeit the right to receive cash in order to receive the shares of stock. The fair value of the compound financial instrument is the sum of the fair values of the two components.

The stand-alone fair value of the cash-settlement alternative at the grant date (January 1, Year 1) is $5,000 (500 options × $10 per option). The stand-alone fair value of the equity-settlement alternative at the grant date also is $5,000 (500 options × $10 per option). IFRS 2 indicates that this type of share-based payment often is structured such that the fair value of the debt component and the fair value of the equity component are the same. In such cases, the fair value of the equity component is zero. Thus, the fair value of the compound financial instrument is $5,000 ($5,000 + $0).

For equity-settled share-based payment transactions, the services received and equity recognized is measured at the fair value of the equity instrument at grant date. Because the fair value of the equity component in this case is zero, there is no compensation expense recognized related to the equity component. For cash-settled share-based payment transactions, the services received and the liability incurred are initially measured at the fair value of the liability at grant date. The fair value of the liability, adjusted to reflect the number of options expected to vest, is recognized as expense over the period that the services are rendered. At each reporting date, and ultimately at settlement date, the fair value of the liability is remeasured with the change in fair value affecting the amount recognized as compensation expense. As a result, the total amount of expense recognized will be the amount paid to settle the liability.

Compensation expense for Year 1 is calculated as follows:

Fair value per option at December 31, Year 1	$ 11.00
Number of options	500
Subtotal	$ 5,500
Percentage of options expected to vest	80%
Total compensation expense	$ 4,400
Vesting period (number of years)	2
Compensation expense, Year 1	$ 2,200

The journal entry on December 31, Year 1 to recognize Year 1 compensation expense is:

Compensation Expense	$2,200	
Share-based Payment Liability		$2,200

At December 31, Year 2, the fair value of each option is equal to its intrinsic value of $12.00 ($30 share price − $18 exercise price). The fair value of the liability is $6,000 ($12.00 × 500 options). The total compensation expense is

$4,800 ($6,000 × 80%). The amount to be recognized as compensation expense in Year 2 is $2,600 ($4,800 − 2,200). The journal entry on December 31, Year 2 is:

Compensation Expense		$2,600
Share-based Payment Liability		$2,600

Accounting for the exercise of the stock options:

- *Cash-Settlement Alternative:* If the four employees choose the cash-settlement alternative upon exercise of their stock options, they will receive a total of $4,800, the intrinsic value of the 400 options that they exercise. The journal entry on December 31, Year 2 would be:

Share-based Payment Liability		$4,800
Cash		$4,800

- *Share-Settlement Alternative:* If the four employees choose the share-settlement alternative upon exercise of their stock options, they will receive a total of 400 shares of stock with a fair value of $12,000 in exchange for $7,200 (400 shares × Exercise price of $18.00 per share). The journal entry on December 31, Year 2 would be:

Cash		$7,200
Share-based Payment Liability		4,800
Common Stock ($1 par × 400)		$ 400
Additional Paid-in Capital ($29 × 400)		11,600

INCOME TAXES

IAS 12, *Income Taxes*, and U.S. GAAP take a similar approach to accounting for income taxes. Both standards adopt an asset-and-liability approach that recognizes deferred tax assets and liabilities for temporary differences and for operating loss and tax credit carry-forwards. However, differences do exist. In March 2009, the IASB issued an exposure draft (ED), *Income Tax*, which is intended to eliminate certain of the differences that currently exist between U.S. GAAP and IFRS. A final standard replacing IAS 12 had not been published when this book went to press. The accounting for income taxes is a very complex topic, and only some of the major issues are discussed here.

Tax Laws and Rates

IAS 12 requires that current and deferred taxes be measured on the basis of tax laws and rates that have been enacted or *substantively enacted* by the balance sheet date. The interpretation of substantively enacted will vary from country to country. To help make this assessment, the IASB has published guidelines that address the point in time when a tax law change is substantively enacted in many of the jurisdictions that apply IFRS. The IASB's ED on income taxes would clarify that "substantively enacted" occurs when any future steps in the enactment process cannot change the outcome. The ED notes, for example, that the point of substantive enactment in the United States is when a tax law is passed. U.S. GAAP requires measurement of income taxes using actually enacted tax laws and rates.

To minimize the double taxation of corporate dividends (tax paid by both the company and its shareholders), some countries apply a lower tax rate to profits that are distributed to shareholders than to profits that are retained by the company. Therefore, companies doing business in these countries need to know which tax rate (distributed profits versus undistributed profits) should be applied when measuring the amount of current and deferred taxes. Examples provided in IAS 12 indicate that the tax rate that applies to undistributed profits should be used to measure tax expense.

Example: Undistributed Profits

Multinational Corporation owns a subsidiary in a foreign jurisdiction where income taxes are payable at a higher rate on undistributed profits than on distributed profits. For the year ending December 31, Year 1, the foreign subsidiary's taxable income is $150,000. The foreign subsidiary also has net taxable temporary differences amounting to $50,000 for the year, thus creating the need for a deferred tax liability. The tax rate paid in the foreign country on distributed profits is 40 percent and the rate on undistributed profits is 50 percent. A tax credit arises when undistributed profits are later distributed. As of the balance sheet date, no distributions of dividends have been proposed or declared. On March 15, Year 2, Multinational's foreign subsidiary distributes dividends of $75,000 from the profit earned in Year 1.

The tax rate on undistributed profits (50 percent) is used to recognize the current and deferred tax liabilities related to earnings of the foreign subsidiary in Year 1:

Current Tax Expense	$75,000	
Taxes Payable ($150,000 × 50%)		$75,000
Deferred Tax Expense	$25,000	
Deferred Tax Liability ($50,000 × 50%)		$25,000

On March 15, Year 2, when the foreign subsidiary distributes a dividend of $75,000, a tax credit receivable from the government of $7,500 [$75,000 × (50% − 40%)] is recognized with an offsetting reduction in the current tax expense:

Tax Credit Receivable	$7,500	
Current Tax Expense		$7,500

Recognition of Deferred Tax Asset

IAS 12 requires recognition of a deferred tax asset if future realization of a tax benefit is probable, where *probable* is undefined. Under U.S. GAAP, a deferred tax asset must be recognized if its realization is more likely than not. If the word *probable* is interpreted as a probability of occurrence that is greater than the phrase *more likely than not*, then IAS 12 provides a more stringent threshold for the recognition of a deferred tax asset.

Example: Deferred Tax Asset

During the fiscal year ended December 31, Year 1, Janeiro Corporation had a net operating loss of $450,000. Because the company has experienced losses in the last several years, it cannot utilize a net operating loss carry-back. However, Janeiro has negotiated several new contracts, and management expects that it is slightly more than 50 percent likely that it will be able to utilize one-third of the net operating loss in future years. The company's effective tax rate is 40 percent.

Depending on the degree of likelihood the company assigns to the word *probable*, it either would not recognize a tax asset, or it would recognize an asset related to the amount of the net operating loss that it expects to be able to use. In the latter case, the deferred tax asset and income tax benefit would be $60,000 [$450,000 × 1/3 × 40%].

Deferred Tax Asset.	$60,000
Income Tax Benefit.	$60,000

Disclosures

IAS 12 requires extensive disclosures to be made with regard to income taxes, including disclosure of the current and deferred components of tax expense. The standard also requires an explanation of the relationship between hypothetical tax expense based on statutory tax rates and reported tax expense based on the effective tax rate using one of two approaches: (1) a numerical reconciliation between tax expense based on the statutory tax rate in the home country and tax expense based on the effective tax rate or (2) a numerical reconciliation between tax expense based on the weighted-average statutory tax rate across jurisdictions in which the company pays taxes and tax expense based on the effective tax rate.

Exhibit 5.4 demonstrates these two approaches. Tesco plc uses approach 1, showing that accounting profit multiplied by the UK statutory income tax rate of 28.2 percent would have resulted in tax expense of £833 in 2009. However, the actual tax expense is only £788 resulting in an effective tax rate of 26.7 percent. One of the reasons that the effective tax rate is different from the UK statutory tax rate is the fact that profits earned in foreign countries are taxed at different rates (differences in overseas taxation rates).

Nestlé SA uses approach 2 in reconciling its total tax expense. The reconciliation begins with the amount that would be recognized as tax expense after multiplying the profit earned in each country in which the company operates by the statutory tax rate in that country and then summing across all countries. Nestlé's effective tax rate can be measured by dividing the amount reported as taxes on continuing operations by pre-tax profit on continuing operations (not shown in Exhibit 5.4).

The expected tax expense at the weighted-average applicable tax rate results from applying the domestic statutory tax rates to profits before taxes of each entity in the country it operates. For the Group, the weighted-average applicable tax rate varies from one year to the other, depending on the relative weight of the profit of each individual entity in the Group's profit as well as the changes in the statutory tax rates.

IFRS versus U.S. GAAP

Application of IFRS can create temporary differences unknown under U.S. GAAP. For example, the revaluation of property, plant, and equipment for financial statement purposes (in accordance with IAS 16's revaluation model) with no equivalent adjustment for tax purposes will result in a temporary difference that cannot

EXHIBIT 5.4

RECONCILIATION OF ACCOUNTING PROFIT TO EFFECTIVE TAX RATE
Tesco plc
2009
Annual Report

Note 6 Taxation

Reconciliation of effective tax charge

	2009 £m	2008 £m
Profit before tax	2,954	2,803
Effective tax charge at 28.2% (2008 at 30.0%)	(833)	(841)
Effect of:		
Non-deductible expenses	(189)	(180)
Differences in overseas taxation rates	111	41
Adjustments in respect of prior years	67	215
Share of results of joint ventures and associates	3	123
Change in tax rate	25	69
Total income tax charge for the year	(788)	(673)
Effective tax rate	**26.7%**	**24.0%**

NESTLÉ
2009
Annual Report

Note 7 Taxes

Reconciliation of taxes

In millions of CHF	2009	2008
Expected tax expense at weighted average applicable tax rate	2,789	3,142
Tax effect of non-deductible or non-taxable items	(168)	(105)
Prior years' taxes	(17)	68
Transfers to unrecognized deferred tax assets	58	61
Transfers from unrecognized deferred tax assets	(44)	(14)
Changes in tax rates	(1)	(2)
Withholding taxes levied on transfers of income	340	347
Other, including taxes on capital	130	190
Taxes on continuing operations	**3,087**	**3,687**

exist under U.S. GAAP. Other differences between IFRS and U.S. GAAP can create different amounts of temporary differences. For example, because of different definitions of impairment, differences in the amount of an impairment loss can exist under the two sets of standards. With no equivalent tax adjustment, the amount of temporary difference related to the impairment loss will be different in a set of IFRS-based financial statements from the amount recognized under U.S. GAAP.

Financial Statement Presentation

Under U.S. GAAP, deferred tax assets and liabilities generally are classified as current or noncurrent based on the classification of the related asset or liability, or for tax losses and credit carry-forwards, based on the expected timing of realization. The net deferred tax amount arising from current assets and liabilities is classified as a current asset or liability; the net deferred tax amount arising from noncurrent assets and liabilities is reported as a noncurrent asset or liability. IAS 1, *Presentation of Financial Statements,* stipulates that deferred taxes may *not* be classified as a current asset or current liability, but only as noncurrent.

REVENUE RECOGNITION

IAS 18, *Revenue,* is a single standard that covers most revenues, in particular revenues from the sale of goods; the rendering of services; and interest, royalties, and dividends. There is no equivalent single standard in U.S. GAAP. U.S. rules related to revenue recognition are found in more than 200 different authoritative pronouncements, making a direct comparison between IAS 18 and U.S. GAAP difficult.

General Measurement Principle

IAS 18 requires revenue to be measured at the fair value of the consideration received or receivable.

Identification of the Transaction Generating Revenue

Revenue recognition criteria normally are applied to each transaction generating revenue. However, if a transaction consists of multiple elements, it may be appropriate to split the transaction into separate units of account and recognize revenue from each element separately. For example, if a sale of computer software is accompanied by an agreement to provide maintenance (post-contract support) for a period of time, it might be appropriate to allocate the proceeds from the sale into an amount applicable to the sale of software (revenue recognized at the time of sale) and an amount applicable to the post-contract support (revenue recognized over the period of support). Conversely, there may be situations where it is necessary to treat two or more separate transactions as one economic transaction to properly reflect their true economic substance.

Sale of Goods

Five conditions must be met in order for revenue from the sale of goods to be recognized:

1. The significant risks and rewards of ownership of the goods have been transferred to the buyer.
2. Neither continuing managerial involvement normally associated with ownership nor effective control of the goods sold is retained.
3. The amount of revenue can be measured reliably.
4. It is probable that the economic benefits associated with the sale will flow to the seller.
5. The costs incurred or to be incurred with respect to the sale of goods can be measured reliably.

Evaluating whether significant risks and rewards of ownership have been transferred to the buyer can sometimes be difficult and require the exercise of judgment. IAS 18 provides a list of examples in which significant risks and rewards might be retained by the seller. These include the following:

- The seller assumes an obligation for unsatisfactory performance not covered by normal warranty provisions.
- Receipt of revenue by the seller is contingent on the buyer generating revenue through its sale of the goods.
- Goods sold are subject to installation, installation is a significant part of the contract, and installation has not yet been completed.
- The sales contract gives the buyer the right to rescind the purchase, and the probability of return is uncertain.

Similarly, in determining whether the seller has relinquished managerial involvement or control over the goods sold, a careful evaluation is required for some types of sales.

Example: Sale of Goods with Right of Return

Qwilleran Products Inc. is a manufacturer of lighting fixtures. Qwilleran enters into an agreement with a company in Mexico, which will import and distribute Qwilleran's products locally. In December, Year 1, the first month of the agreement, Qwilleran ships $2,000,000 of lighting fixtures to the Mexican distributor to cover anticipated demand in Mexico. The distributor has the right to return products to Qwilleran if they cannot be sold in Mexico. Qwilleran has extensive experience selling its products in the United States but no experience in Mexico or other foreign countries.

Qwilleran Company must determine whether it is appropriate to recognize revenue in December, Year 1, when products are shipped to the Mexican distributor. The most important question is whether the significant risks and rewards of ownership of the goods have been transferred to the buyer. IAS 18 indicates that this might not be the case when the buyer has the right to return the purchase, and the probability of return is uncertain. Because Qwilleran has no experience selling products in Mexico, it has no basis for estimating whether the Mexican distributor will make returns. Thus, Qwilleran should conclude that it has not transferred all the significant risks of ownership to the Mexican distributor and it should defer revenue recognition until this criterion has been met.

Example: Sale of Goods with Contingent Payment

Victoria Enterprises sells small motors to Gamma Company. Gamma mounts these motors in its water pumps and sells the completed pumps to plumbing supply distributors. When Gamma receives payment from its customers, it pays Victoria for the motors. Gamma has the right to return any unused motors at the end of the year. Historically, these returns have averaged 2 percent of sales. In the month of September, Year 1, Victoria Enterprises made sales of $500,000 to Gamma Company.

IAS 18 indicates that five conditions must be met to recognize revenue from the sale of goods. In this case, it appears that conditions 2, 3, and 5 are met. It is unclear, however, whether conditions 1 and 4 are met. Because payment for the motors is only made if Gamma is able to sell its lawn mowers, it appears that a significant risk of ownership might have been retained by Victoria, and therefore condition 1 might not be met. This is reinforced by paragraph 16 of IAS 18, which indicates that an entity may retain significant risks and rewards of ownership "when the receipt of the revenue from a particular sale is contingent on the derivation of revenue by the buyer from its sale of the goods."

With respect to condition 4, from past experience, it is probable that almost all (98 percent) of "the economic benefits associated with the transaction will flow to the entity." This suggests that condition 4 is met. IAS 18, paragraph 17, indicates that when the seller retains only an insignificant risk of ownership, the transaction is a sale and revenue is recognized. The last sentence of IAS 18, paragraph 17 states: "Revenue in such cases is recognized at the time of sale provided the seller can reliably estimate future returns and recognizes a liability for returns based on previous experience and other relevant factors." As a result, it appears Victoria Enterprises would be justified in recognizing revenue for 98 percent of the sales price and would prepare the following journal entry in September, Year 1 to account for its sales to Gamma Company:

Accounts Receivable		$500,000
Sales Revenue [$500,000 × 98%]		$490,000
Deferred Revenue (liability)		10,000

Rendering of Services

When the outcome of a service transaction (1) can be estimated reliably and (2) it is probable that economic benefits of the transaction will flow to the enterprise, revenue should be recognized in proportion to some measure of the extent of services rendered (i.e., on a stage-of-completion basis). The outcome of a transaction can be estimated reliably when (1) the amount of revenue, (2) the costs incurred and the costs to be incurred, (3) and the stage of completion can all be measured reliably. The stage of completion can be estimated in a number of ways including on the basis of the percentage of total services to be performed, percentage of total costs to be incurred, and surveys of work performed. Guidelines provided in IAS 11, *Construction Contracts,* related to the application of the percentage-of-completion method on construction projects are generally applicable to the recognition of revenue for service transactions. U.S. GAAP does not allow the percentage-of-completion method to be used with service contracts.

When the outcome of a service transaction cannot be estimated reliably, revenue should be recognized only to the extent that expenses incurred are probable of recovery. If such underlying expenses are not probable of recovery, the expense should be recognized, but not the revenue.

Example: Recognition of Service Revenue

Seese & Associates, an information technology (IT) consulting firm, contracted with Drexel Manufacturing Company on January 1, Year 1 to provide services over a period of 18 months for a fixed fee of $180,000. Seese is unable to specify up-front the type and number of services that it will provide. However, based on past experience, Seese can reliably estimate the cost it will incur to fulfill its contractual obligation as $150,000. Seese incurred actual costs of $90,000 in Year 1 and received monthly payments of $10,000 from Drexel Manufacturing.

The criteria for recognizing revenue on a stage-of-completion basis are met in this situation. Drexel is making monthly payments so the criterion of probable inflow of economic benefits is met. Because this is a fixed-fee contract, the amount of revenue to be earned is known with certainty, and Seese is able to reliably estimate the stage of completion on the basis of total costs to be incurred. In Year 1, the company has incurred 60 percent [$90,000/$150,000] of the total estimated costs and therefore would recognize service revenue of $108,000 [$180,000 × 60%] with the following journal entry:

Cash [$10,000 × 12]		$120,000
Service Revenue		$108,000
Deferred Revenue		12,000

Interest, Royalties, and Dividends

If it is probable that the economic benefits of interest, royalties, and dividends will flow to the enterprise and the amounts can be measured reliably, revenue should be recognized on the following bases:

- Interest income is recognized on an effective yield basis.
- Royalties are recognized on an accrual basis in accordance with the terms of the relevant agreement.
- Dividends are recognized when the shareholders' right to receive payment is established.

Exchanges of Goods or Services

In an exchange of goods or services, if the exchanged items are similar in nature and value, no revenue (i.e., no gain or loss) is recognized. If the exchanged goods or services are dissimilar in nature, revenue is recognized at the fair value of the goods or services received, adjusted for the amount of any cash paid or received. When the fair value of the goods or services received cannot be measured reliably, revenue should be measured as the fair value of the goods or services given up, adjusted for the amount of any cash paid or received.

IAS 18, Part B

The IASB document published to accompany IAS 18 (IAS 18, Part B) provides examples illustrating the application of the standard to major types of revenue generating transactions. Most of the examples are self-explanatory, and the relationships of the examples to the underlying provisions of the standard are straightforward. The examples accompany IAS 18 but technically are not part of the standard. Issues covered in the examples include:

- *Sales transactions:* Bill-and-hold sales, goods shipped subject to conditions, lay-away sales, sale and repurchase agreements, subscription sales, installment sales, and real estate sales.
- *Service transactions:* Installation fees; servicing fees included in the price of a product; advertising commissions; insurance agency commissions; financial service fees; admission fees; initiation, entrance, and membership fees; franchise fees; and fees from the development of customized software.
- *Interest, royalties and dividends:* License fees and royalties.

We summarize the guidance provided in two of these examples next.

Bill-and-Hold Sales

The first illustrative example describes a "bill-and-hold sale" as a sale "in which delivery is delayed at the buyer's request but the buyer takes title and accepts billing." Bill-and-hold sales have been used by entities (such as Sunbeam) to shift sales to be made in future periods into the current period—a type of earnings management. To make sure that a bill-and-hold sale is truly a sale in substance, IAS 18 Part B suggests that revenue may be recognized by the seller when the buyer takes title only if four conditions are met:

1. It is probable that delivery will be made.
2. The item is on hand, identified, and ready for delivery to the buyer at the time the sale is recognized.
3. The buyer specifically acknowledges the deferred delivery instructions.
4. The usual payment terms apply.

Servicing Fees Included in the Price of the Product

The sales price of a product sometimes includes an identifiable amount for subsequent servicing. An example is after-sales support provided by a software company for a specified period of time. In such a case, IAS 18 Part B indicates a portion of the sales price should be deferred and recognized as revenue over the period during which the service is performed. The amount deferred must be sufficient to cover the expected costs of the services under the agreement and provide a reasonable profit on those services. Judgment must be applied in determining the amount to be deferred as a reasonable amount of profit is not defined in the standard.

Customer Loyalty Programs

A growing number of entities use customer loyalty programs to provide customers with incentives to buy their goods and services. In many of these programs, "points" are awarded at the time a customer makes a purchase. The question arises as to whether the entity's obligation to provide a free or discounted good or service should be recognized and measured by (1) allocating a portion of the consideration received from the sale transaction or (2) establishing a provision for the estimated future costs of providing the award.

IFRIC 13, *Customer Loyalty Programmes,* stipulates that award credits should be treated as a separately identifiable component of the sales transaction in which they are granted. The fair value of the consideration received on the sale must be allocated between the award credits and the other components of the sale. The amount allocated to the award credits is based on their fair value. If the entity supplies the award itself, it recognizes the amount allocated to award credits as revenue when award credits are redeemed and the obligation to provide a free or discounted good or service is fulfilled. The amount of revenue to be recognized is based on the number of award credits that have been redeemed, relative to the total number expected to be redeemed.

Example: Frequent-Flyer Awards Program

Redjet Airways, a regional air carrier, has a frequent-flyer program in which customers receive one point for each mile flown on Redjet flights. Frequent-flyer program members can redeem 30,000 points for a free domestic flight, which, on average, would otherwise cost $600. During Year 1, Redjet awarded 1,000,000 points to its customers on flights with total ticket sales of $600,000. Frequent-flyer points expire two years after they are awarded. By the end of Year 1, frequent-flyer program members had redeemed 300,000 points for free tickets. Redjet expects that only 10 percent of points will expire unredeemed.

Redjet must allocate the $600,000 collected in ticket sales in Year 1 between flight revenue and frequent-flyer awards (deferred revenue) based on the fair value of the points awarded. The amount to be allocated to the frequent-flyer awards is determined as follows:

Points awarded in Year 1	1,000,000
Percentage expected to be redeemed	× 90%
Points expected to be redeemed	900,000
Points needed for a free flight	÷ 30,000
Expected number of free flights	30
Average value per flight	× $600
Fair value of points awarded	$18,000

The journal entry to recognize revenue from ticket sales in Year 1 is as follows:

Cash	$600,000	
Revenue		$582,000
Deferred Revenue		18,000

During Year 1, 300,000 points were redeemed for 10 free flights, with a value of $6,000. The journal entry to recognize revenue from providing free flights under the awards program is:

Deferred Revenue	$6,000	
Revenue		$6,000

Construction Contracts

IAS 11, *Construction Contracts,* identifies two types of construction contracts: a fixed-price contract and a cost-plus contract. Revenues and expenses related to both types of contracts should be recognized using the percentage-of-completion method when the outcome of the contract can be estimated reliably. The outcome of a cost-plus contract can be estimated reliably when (1) it is probable that the economic benefits associated with the contract will flow to the entity and (2) the contract costs can be clearly identified and reliably measured. Two additional criteria must be met for a fixed-price contract to qualify for percentage-of-completion accounting treatment: (1) total contract revenues must be reliably measurable and (2) the costs to complete the contract and the stage of completion at the balance sheet date must be reliably measurable. If the outcome of a construction contract cannot be estimated reliably, a cost recovery method should be used to recognize revenue. Under this method, contract costs are expensed as incurred and revenue is recognized to the extent that contract costs incurred are likely to be recovered. If, during the construction period, the uncertainties that prevented the outcome of the contract from being estimated reliably no longer exist, then the accounting for the contract should be changed to the percentage-of-completion method.

U.S. GAAP also requires use of the percentage-of-completion when certain criteria are met. When the percentage-of-completion method is not appropriate, the completed contract method is used, which is a departure from IAS 11. Under both IAS 11 and U.S. GAAP, when the outcome of a construction contract is expected to be a loss, the loss should be recognized immediately.

IASB–FASB Revenue Recognition Project

Revenue recognition is an issue for which neither the IASB nor the FASB believes it has adequate authoritative literature that is coherent and comprehensive. In 2002, the two boards began work on a joint project to develop a single standard to deal with this important issue. The main reasons for undertaking this project are to (1) eliminate weaknesses in existing concepts and standards and (2) converge IFRS and U.S. GAAP.

In June 2010, the IASB and FASB published a joint Exposure Draft, *Revenue from Contracts with Customers,* which proposes a contract-based revenue recognition model to be applied across a wide range of transactions and industries. The proposed model requires an entity to apply the following five steps in the recognition of revenue:

1. *Identify the contract with a customer.* It might be appropriate to treat a single contract with a customer as two or more contracts when the single contract contains multiple elements that are priced independently. On the other hand, it might be appropriate to treat two or more separate contracts that are priced interdependently as a single contract.

2. *Identify the separate performance obligations in the contract.* Performance obligation is defined as "an enforceable promise (whether explicit or implicit) in a contract with a customer to transfer a good or service to the customer." The entity must evaluate all of the goods and/or services promised in a contract to determine whether there are separate performance obligations.

3. *Determine the transaction price.* If material, the time value of money should be considered in determining the transaction price in a deferred payment contract. When future payments for goods or services are not fixed in amount, the expected value should be used to determine the transaction price. A probability-weighted approach should be used to adjust the transaction price to reflect the customer's credit risk. In effect, the customer's credit risk affects how much but not whether revenue should be recognized.

4. *Allocate the transaction price to the separate performance obligations.* The transaction price should be allocated to the separate performance obligations in proportion to the stand-alone selling price of each element of the contract. When goods or services are not sold separately, the transaction price must be allocated to the separate performance obligations using a reasonable approach.

5. *Recognize the revenue allocated to each performance obligation when the entity satisfies each performance obligation.* An entity satisfies a performance obligation and recognizes revenue when control of a promised good or service is transferred to the customer. The general principle is that a customer obtains control of a good or service when the customer has the ability to direct the use of, and receive the benefit from, the good or service. Indicators that a customer has obtained control of a good or service include the following:
   - The customer has the unconditional obligation to pay for the good or service.
   - The customer has legal title to the good or service.
   - The customer has physical possession of the good or service.
   - The customer specifies the design or function of the good or service.

The Exposure Draft indicates that none of these indicators, by itself, determines whether the customer has control of the good or service. In addition, not all of the indicators will be relevant in some contracts. For example, legal title is not relevant in a contract for services.

For many revenue-generating transactions, transfer of control will occur at a specific point in time, often when the good or service is delivered to the customer. However, transfer of control also can occur on a continuous basis over a period of time. Use of the percentage-of-completion method to recognize revenue on a long-term contract will be acceptable only if the entity can demonstrate that control of the good or service is transferred to the customer on a continuous basis. The Exposure Draft provides an example with the following fact pattern to demonstrate when it would be appropriate to recognize revenue during the life of a construction contract.

Example: Construction Contract

A manufacturer enters into a fixed-price contract with a customer to build highly customized equipment. The customer is highly involved in the design of the equipment and may make changes to the design during the manufacturing process at an additional cost. The customer must make nonrefundable progress payments. Legal title passes to the customer upon delivery of the equipment. If the customer terminates the contract prior to completion of the equipment, the customer takes physical possession of the equipment and must pay for any work completed to date. The facts of this case suggest that the customer controls the equipment as it is being manufactured. Therefore, it would be appropriate for the manufacturer to use the percentage-of-completion method to recognize revenue on this contract.

Warranties

The Exposure Draft makes a distinction between warranties that cover latent defects in a product (do not constitute a separate performance obligation) and warranties that cover faults that arise after the product is transferred to the customer (do constitute a separate performance obligation). When the latter type of warranty is present, the transaction price must be allocated between two performance obligations—the promised product and the promised warranty service.

Onerous Performance Obligation

The Exposure Draft also stipulates that a liability and a loss should be recognized when a performance obligation in a contract become onerous—that is, when the total costs to be incurred in satisfying the obligation exceed the transaction price (revenue) allocated to it.

FINANCIAL INSTRUMENTS

Current IFRS guidance for the financial reporting of financial instruments is located in the following three standards:

IAS 32, *Financial Instruments: Presentation*

IAS 39, *Financial Instruments: Recognition and Measurement*

IFRS 7, *Financial Instruments: Disclosure*

In addition, the IASB issued IFRS 9, *Financial Instruments,* in November 2009 to begin the process of replacing IAS 39; IFRS 9 becomes effective in 2013.

It should be noted that the adoption of IAS 39 met with considerable resistance in the European Union. The European Commission ultimately decided in 2004 to endorse IAS 39, but with exceptions. The Commission modified the version of IAS 39 to be applied by publicly traded companies in the EU with respect to certain provisions on the use of a full fair value option and on hedge accounting. According to the European Commission, these "carve-outs" are temporary, in effect only until the IASB modifies IAS 39 in line with European requests.[2]

Definitions

IAS 32 defines a *financial instrument* as any contract that gives rise to both a financial asset of one entity and a financial liability or equity instrument of another entity. A *financial asset* is defined as any asset that is:

- Cash.
- A contractual right
  - to receive cash or another financial asset.
  - to exchange financial assets or financial liabilities under potentially favorable conditions.
- An equity instrument of another entity.
- A contract that will or may be settled in the entity's own equity instruments and is not classified as an equity instrument of the entity.

Examples of financial assets include cash, receivables, loans made to other entities, investments in bonds and other debt instruments, and investments in equity instruments of other entities. Investments in equity instruments that are accounted for under the equity method (associates, joint ventures), proportionate consolidation method (joint ventures), or are consolidated [subsidiaries and special-purpose entities (SPEs)] do not fall within the scope of IAS 32 and IAS 39. Only those investments in equity instruments that result in less than significant influence over the other entity (sometimes labeled as "marketable securities") are accounted for in accordance with IAS 32 and IAS 39.

A *financial liability* is defined as:

- A contractual obligation
  - to deliver cash or another financial asset.
  - to exchange financial assets or financial liabilities under potentially unfavorable conditions.
- A contract that will or may be settled in the entity's own equity instruments.

Examples of financial liabilities include payables, loans from other entities (including banks), issued bonds and other debt instruments, and obligations to deliver own shares for a fixed amount of cash. *Derivative financial instruments* also are financial assets or financial liabilities.

An *equity* instrument is defined as:

- Any contract that evidences a residual interest in the assets of an entity after deducting all of its liabilities.

---

[2] Ernst & Young, "The Evolution of *IAS 39* in Europe," *Eye on IFRS Newsletter,* November 2004, pp. 1–4.

Liability or Equity

IAS 32 requires financial instruments to be classified as financial liabilities or equity or both in accordance with the substance of the contractual arrangement and the definitions of financial liability and equity. If an equity instrument contains a contractual obligation that meets the definition of a financial liability, it should be classified as a liability even though its legal form is that of an equity instrument. For example, if an entity issues preferred shares that are redeemable by the shareholder and the entity cannot avoid the payment of cash to shareholders if they redeem their shares, the preferred shares should be accounted for as a liability. Preferred shares that are contingently redeemable based on future events outside the control of either the issuer or the shareholder also would be classified as a financial liability.

Example: Redeemable Preferred Shares

On October 29, Year 1, Griglia Company issued $1,000,000 of 5 percent preferred shares at par value. The preferred shareholders have the right to force the company to redeem the shares at par value if the Federal Reserve Bank interest rate rises above 5 percent. On December 10, Year 3, the Federal Reserve Bank interest rate reaches that level.

Because the future event that triggers redemption of the preferred shares is outside the control of both the company and the shareholders, the 5 percent preferred shares must be classified as a liability under IFRS. The journal entry to record issuance of the shares on October 29, Year 1 is:

Cash	$1,000,000	
Redeemable Preferred Shares Liability		$1,000,000

Under U.S. GAAP, the preferred shares initially would be classified as equity. On December 10, Year 3, when the event triggering redemption occurs, the preferred shares would be reclassified as a liability.

Compound Financial Instruments

If a financial instrument contains both a liability element and equity element, it is a *compound financial instrument* and should be split into two components that are reported separately. This is referred to as "split accounting." For example, a bond that is convertible into shares of common stock at the option of the bondholder is a compound financial instrument. From the perspective of the issuer, the bond is comprised of two components:

1. A contractual obligation to make cash payments of interest and principal as long as the bond is not converted. This meets the definition of a financial liability.

2. A call option that grants the bondholder the right to convert the bond into a fixed number of common shares. This meets the definition of an equity instrument.

Under split accounting, the initial carrying amounts of the liability and equity components are determined using what can be called the with-and-without method. The fair value of the financial instrument with the conversion feature is determined (i.e., the selling price of the instrument). Then the fair value of the financial instrument without the conversion feature is determined. This becomes the carrying amount of the financial liability component. The difference between the fair value of the instrument as a whole and the amount separately determined for the liability component is allocated to the equity component. Note that a compound financial instrument is a financial asset for the holder of the instrument.

Example: Convertible Bonds

Sharma Corporation issued $2 million of 4 percent convertible bonds at par value. The bonds have a five-year life with interest payable annually. Each bond has a face value of $1,000 and is convertible at any time up to maturity into 250 shares of common stock. At the date of issue, the interest rate for similar debt without a conversion feature is 6 percent.

The fair value of the convertible bonds is their selling price of $2 million. The fair value of the liability is calculated using the prevailing interest rate for nonconvertible bonds:

Present value of $2,000,000, n = 5, i = 6%	$2,000,000 × 0.7473 = $1,494,516
Present value of ordinary annuity of $80,000, n = 5, i = 6%.	$80,000 × 4.2124 = 336,989
Fair value of liability	$1,831,505

The present value of the bond at 6 percent is $1,831,505; this is the fair value of the liability component of the compound financial instrument. The remaining $168,495 from the proceeds of the bond issuance is allocated to the equity component.

Cash	$2,000,000
Bonds Payable	$1,831,505
Additional Paid-in Capital	168,495

Classification of Financial Assets and Financial Liabilities

IAS 39 establishes categories into which all financial assets and liabilities must be classified. The classification of a financial asset or financial liability determines how the item will be measured. A financial asset must be classified into one of the following four categories:

- *Financial assets at fair value through profit or loss (FVPL):* This includes financial assets that an entity either (1) holds for trading purposes or (2) has elected to classify into this category under the so-called fair value option (discussed in more detail later).

- *Held-to-maturity investments:* This category includes financial assets with fixed or determinable payments and fixed maturity that the entity has the intention and ability to hold to maturity. If an entity sells or reclassifies more than an insignificant amount of held-to-maturity investments prior to maturity, the entity normally will be disqualified from using this classification during the following two-year period. The entity's intentions are said to be "tainted" in this case.

- *Loans and receivables:* This includes financial assets with fixed or determinable payments that do not have a price that is quoted in an active market.

- *Available-for-sale financial assets:* This category includes all financial assets that (1) are not classified in one of the other categories or (2) the entity has elected to classify as available-for-sale. Financial assets held for trading purposes may not be classified as available-for-sale.

A financial liability must be classified as one of the following:

- *Financial liabilities at fair value through profit or loss (FVPL):* This includes financial liabilities that are held for trading or that the entity has opted to classify into this category under the "fair value option." An example of a liability held for trading is a debt instrument that the issuer intends to repurchase in the short-term to make a gain from short-term changes in interest rates.
- *Financial liabilities measured at amortized cost:* This is the default category for most financial liabilities, including accounts payables, notes payable, bonds payable, and deposits from customers.

Fair Value Option

According to IAS 39, the option to designate financial assets or financial liabilities as FVPL may be applied only if one of the following conditions is met:

1. It eliminates or significantly reduces a measurement or recognition inconsistency (sometimes referred to as "an accounting mismatch") that would otherwise arise from measuring assets or liabilities or recognizing the gains and losses on them on different bases.
2. A group of financial assets, financial liabilities, or both that is managed and its performance is evaluated on a fair value basis, in accordance with a documented risk management or investment strategy, and information about the group of instruments is provided internally on that basis to the entity's key management personnel.

Example: Fair Value Option

St. John's Inc. issued $1,000 in 5 percent bonds at par value on January 1, Year 1. The cash proceeds were used to invest in $1,000 of corporate bonds (at a fixed rate of 6 percent). The bond investment is classified as FVPL. By year-end, interest rates have increased. As a result, the fair value of the investment in bonds is $900 and the fair value of the bonds payable is $900.

The bonds payable and investment in bonds are linked. As interest rates change, the economic loss on the asset will be offset by a gain on the liability, and vice versa. However, for accounting purposes, without a fair value option, there would be a mismatch because the bonds payable are carried at amortized cost and are not revalued, whereas the bond investment is classified as FVPL and, therefore, is carried at fair value with gains/losses recognized in net income. The company would prepare the following journal entries in Year 1:

January 1		
Cash	$1,000	
Bonds Payable		$1,000
Investment in Bonds (FVPL)	$1,000	
Cash		$1,000

December 31

Interest Expense [$1,000 × 5%] $50

    Cash. $50

Cash $60

    Interest Income [$1,000 × 6%] $60

Loss on Investment in Bonds [$1,000 − $900]. $100

    Investment in Bonds (FVPL). $100

The company's Year 1 income statement would report the following:

Interest income (expense), net	$ 10
Gain (loss) on financial instruments, net.	(100)
Total	$ (90)

Under IAS 39, St. John's may use the fair value option to designate the bonds payable as FVPL to remove the accounting mismatch. If the fair value option is used, both the asset and liability will be measured at fair value with gains/losses on both recognized in income. The company would prepare the following additional journal entry on December 31:

Bonds Payable $100

    Gain on Bonds Payable $100

As a result, the company's Year 1 income statement would reflect the following:

Interest income (expense), net	$ 10
Gain (loss) on financial instruments, net.	0
Total	$ (10)

A net increase in income of $10 more accurately reflects the economic substance of holding these two financial instruments at the same time.

Transfers between Categories of Financial Assets and Financial Liabilities

To reduce the ability to "manage earnings," IAS 39 severely restricts the ability to reclassify financial assets and liabilities. Financial instruments may not be reclassified into or out of the FVPL category. Reclassification between the available-for-sale and held-to-maturity categories is possible, but as noted above, reclassification of more than an insignificant amount of held-to-maturity investments results in a two-year ban on its use.

Measurement of Financial Instruments

Initial Measurement

Financial assets and financial liabilities are initially recognized on the balance sheet at their fair value, which normally will be equal to the amount paid or received. Except for FVPL assets and liabilities, transaction costs are capitalized as part of the fair value of a financial asset or as a reduction in the fair value of a liability. Transaction costs associated with FVPL assets and liabilities are expensed as incurred.

Subsequent Measurement

Subsequent to initial recognition, financial assets and liabilities are measured using one of three values: (1) cost, (2) amortized cost, or (3) fair value. The only financial asset measured at cost is an unquoted investment in equity instruments that cannot be reliably measured at fair value. This type of asset affects income only when dividends are received (dividend income is recognized) or the asset is sold (gain or loss is realized and recognized). Unrealized gains and losses are not recognized.

Three types of financial assets and liabilities are measured at amortized cost: held-to-maturity investments, loans and receivables, and liabilities measured at amortized cost. Amortized cost is the cost of an asset or liability adjusted to achieve a constant effective interest rate over the life of the asset or liability. The effective interest rate is the internal rate of return of the cash flows of the asset or liability. Equity investments cannot be measured at amortized cost because there are no fixed cash flows; therefore, there is no constant effective interest rate.

Three categories of financial asset and liability normally are measured at fair value: (1) FVPL financial assets, (2) FVPL financial liabilities, and (3) available-for-sale financial assets. The carrying amount of these items is adjusted to fair value at each balance sheet date. The unrealized gains and loss (changes in fair value) on FVPL assets and liabilities are recognized in net income. The unrealized gains and losses on available-for-sale financial assets are deferred as a separate component of equity until they are realized (or impairment occurs).

IFRS 9 (effective January 1, 2013)

IFRS 9, *Financial Instruments,* issued in November 2009, simplifies the classification of financial assets into two categories:

1. *Financial assets measured at amortized cost:* Financial assets that are held with the objective to collect contractual cash flows that are solely in the form of principal and interest.
2. *Financial assets measured at fair value:* All other financial assets.

Example: Financial Liabilities Measured at Amortized Cost (Bonds Payable)

On January 1, Year 1, Keane Corp. issued $1,000,000 of 5 percent bonds at face value. The bonds pay interest annually and mature on December 31, Year 2. The company incurred bank and legal fees of $70,000 in conjunction with issuing the bonds.

Under IFRS, the debt issuance costs reduce the fair value of the liability. The fair value of the bonds payable at the date of issuance is $930,000 [$1,000,000 − $70,000]. The entry to initially recognize the liability is:

January 1, Year 1		
Cash.	$930,000	
Bonds Payable.		$930,000

Subsequent to initial recognition, the bonds payable are measured at amortized cost. The difference between the fair value of the bonds at the date of issuance and their face value is amortized to expense over the life of the bonds using the effective interest rate method. The effective interest rate is 8.98 percent, calculated as the internal rate of return of the following stream of payments:

January 1, Year 1: Proceeds from debt issuance $930,000
December 31, Year 1: Interest payment [$1,000,000 × 5%] ($50,000)
December 31, Year 2: Interest and principal payment ($1,050,000)

The following journal entries are made over the life of the bonds:

December 31, Year 1
Interest Expense [$930,000 × 8.98%] $83,496
   Cash. $50,000
   Bonds Payable 33,496
December 31, Year 2
Interest Expense [$963,496 × 8.98%] $86,504
   Cash. $50,000
   Bonds Payable 36,504

Bonds Payable $1,000,000
   Cash. $1,000,000

Under U.S. GAAP, debt issuance costs are deferred as an asset and amortized on a straight-line basis over the life of the debt. Total expense in Year 1 and in Year 2 would be determined as follows:

Interest expense [$1,000,000 × 5%]	$50,000
Amortization of debt issuance costs [$70,000/2]	35,000
Total	$85,000

Available-for-Sale Financial Asset Denominated in a Foreign Currency

Financial assets classified as available for sale are measured at fair value on each balance sheet date, with changes in fair value recognized as part of other comprehensive income. When an entity holds an available-for-sale financial asset that is denominated in a foreign currency, the asset's fair value in foreign currency must be translated into fair value in the entity's reporting currency. The change in fair value in the entity's reporting currency is comprised of two components, which must be accounted for separately. The two components are (1) the change in fair value in the foreign currency and (2) a foreign exchange gain or loss from changes in the exchange rate over time. IAS 39 indicates that these components are determined by treating the financial asset as if it were carried at amortized cost in the foreign currency. The foreign exchange gain or loss resulting from changes in the translated value of the amortized cost of the asset is recognized in net income, and the remaining change in fair value on the available-for-sale financial asset is recognized in other comprehensive income.

Example: Foreign Currency Financial Asset Classified as Available-for-Sale

On October 29, Year 1, Jacob Industries Inc., a U.S.-based company, purchased a Swiss treasury bond for 10,000 Swiss francs (CHF) when the exchange rate was $1.80 per Swiss franc. The bond investment has a cost of $18,000 [CHF 10,000 × $1.80] and is classified as available for sale. On December 31, Year 1, the bond has a fair value of 10,200 Swiss francs, and the exchange rate is $1.92 per Swiss franc. The bond investment now has a fair value of $19,584 [CHF 10,200 × $1.92]. Jacob must determine how to account for the $1,584 [$19,584 − $18,000] increase in the U.S. dollar fair value of this financial asset.

A foreign exchange gain or loss is recognized for the change in exchange rate applied to the amortized cost of the bond: CHF 10,000 × ($1.92 − $1.80) = $1,200 foreign exchange gain. The change in fair value in the foreign currency is then translated using the current exchange rate: (CHF 10,200 − CHF 10,000) × $1.92 = $384 fair value gain. The journal entry recorded at December 31, Year 1 is:

Investment in Bonds.		$1,584
Foreign Exchange Gain	$1,200	
Other Comprehensive Income.	384	

Impairment

IAS 39 requires an entity, at each balance sheet date, to assess whether there is any objective evidence that a financial asset is impaired. For available-for-sale equity investments, a significant or prolonged decline in the fair value below the original cost is objective evidence of impairment. FVPL financial assets are not subject to impairment testing because they already are measured at fair value with unrealized gains and losses recognized in net income.

When an investment in a loan is determined to be impaired, the creditor writes down its financial asset for the difference between (1) the investment in the loan (principal and interest) and (2) the expected future cash flows discounted at the loan's historical effective interest rate. If the loan is secured, the expected future cash flows can be estimated as the fair value of the collateral securing the loan. The investment in loan can be written down either directly or through an allowance account. The write-down is recognized as an impairment loss in net income. If in a subsequent period, the impairment loss decreases, the financial asset (investment in loan) is written back up to what its carrying amount would have been if the impairment had not been recognized. The reversal of impairment loss is recognized as a gain in net income. (Note that the counterparty debtor is not allowed to reduce the carrying amount of its financial liability due to its inability to pay unless its contractual obligation has been legally reduced by the creditor.)

Derecognition

Derecognition refers to the process of removing an asset or liability from the balance sheet. Under IAS 39, derecognition of a *financial asset* is appropriate if either of the following criteria is met:

1. The contractual rights to the cash flows of the financial asset have expired.
2. The financial asset has been transferred and the transfer qualifies for derecognition based on an evaluation of the extent to which risks and reward of ownership have been transferred.

Application of the second criterion is often complex. IAS 39, Appendix A, Application Guidance, provides a flowchart to be followed in evaluating whether a financial asset may be derecognized.

IAS 39 also provides specific guidance with respect to a so-called pass-through arrangement, which is a contractual arrangement in which an entity continues to collect cash flows from a financial asset it holds, but immediately transfers those payments to other parties. This arrangement can qualify for derecogniton of the financial asset when certain conditions listed in IAS 39 are met. If a financial asset meets the criteria for derecognition, its carrying amount is removed from the balance sheet and any difference between that amount and consideration received, if any, is recognized as a gain or loss in net income. Application of IAS 39's derecognition requirements to receivables is described in more detail later.

Derecognition of a *financial liability* is appropriate only when the obligation is extinguished—that is, when the obligation is paid, canceled, or expired. The difference between the carrying amount of the debt and the amount paid to extinguish it is recognized as a gain or loss in net income. Costs incurred in the extinguishment of debt are included as part of the gain or loss. A so-called troubled debt restructuring, in which a debtor is relieved of its obligation to the creditor due to financial hardship is treated as a debt extinguishment.

A substantial modification of the terms of existing debt should be treated as an extinguishment of old debt and the issuance of new debt. A less-than-substantial modification of the terms of existing debt is not treated as an extinguishment, but instead the modification is handled prospectively. An example would be the renegotiation of the interest rate on existing debt. Costs associated with a less-than-substantial debt modification that is not treated as an extinguishment are subtracted from the carrying amount of the debt and are amortized over the remaining term of the debt.

Under U.S. GAAP, debt modification costs are expensed as incurred. Debt extinguishment costs also are expensed as incurred, except when new debt is issued for old debt, in which case the costs are deferred and amortized over the term of the new debt.

Example: Debt Extinguishment/Modification

Champaign Company issued $10 million in 12 percent bonds several years ago at a discount. The bonds currently have a carrying amount of $9.8 million. The bond agreement allows for early extinguishment by Champaign beginning in the current year. Champaign's investment bank has arranged for the company to issue $10 million of new 10 percent bonds at face value to a group of European investors. The proceeds will be used to extinguish the 12 percent bonds. The investment banking, legal, and accounting costs to execute the transaction total $400,000.

This is a *debt extinguishment*. The costs associated with issuing the new debt are reflected in the calculation of the gain or loss on extinguishment of the old debt as follows:

Carrying amount of old debt	$ 9,800,000
Fair value of new debt	(10,000,000)
Subtotal	(200,000)
New debt issuance costs	(400,000)
Loss on extinguishment of old debt	$ (600,000)

The debt extinguishment is recognized as follows:

Bonds Payable—12% (old debt)	$9,800,000	
Loss on Extinguishment of 12% Bonds	600,000	
Bonds Payable—10% (new debt)		$10,000,000
Cash		400,000

Now assume the investment bank has negotiated a reduction in the interest rate with the 12 percent bondholder, who agrees to lower the interest rate to 10 percent based on current market conditions. Fees for the reduction in interest rate total $250,000. This is a *less than substantial debt modification*. The costs incurred adjust the carrying amount of the debt and are amortized prospectively to interest expense over the remaining life of the bonds.

Bonds Payable—12% (now 10%)		$250,000
Cash		$250,000

Derivatives

Derivatives are financial instruments such as options, forwards, futures, and swaps whose value changes in response to the change in a specified interest rate, financial instrument price, commodity price, foreign exchange rate, index, credit rating, or other variable. IFRS 39 requires derivatives to be measured at fair value. Whether the change in fair value over time is recognized in net income or deferred in stockholders' equity (i.e., other comprehensive income) depends on whether the derivative is designated as a hedge or not, and if so, what kind of a hedge. If a derivative is not designated as a hedge, the change in fair value must be recognized in net income when the fair value change occurs.

Hedge accounting results in the change in fair value on the derivative being recognized in net income in the same accounting period as gains and losses on the underlying hedged item are recognized in net income. Hedge accounting is optional and is only permitted when certain conditions are met. Similar to U.S. GAAP, IAS 39 identifies three types of hedging relationships: (1) fair value hedge, (2) cash flow hedge, and (3) hedge of a net investment in a foreign operation. We discuss fair value hedges and cash flow hedges in the context of foreign currency risks in Chapter 7 and hedges of a net investment in a foreign operation in Chapter 8.

Receivables

The accounting for receivables is governed by IAS 39, which identifies "loans and receivables" as one of four categories of financial assets. Receivables are measured initially at fair value. Subsequently, they are measured at amortized cost using an effective interest method.

Impairment of Receivables

If there is objective evidence that receivables are impaired, a loss should be recognized. Individually significant receivables should be tested for impairment individually. Individually insignificant receivables are assessed for impairment as a portfolio group. A bad debt loss and provision (allowance) for uncollectible receivables is estimated. IAS 39 states that the loss should be measured as the difference between the carrying amount of the portfolio of receivables and the present value of future cash flows expected to be received. Implementation guidance in IAS 39 suggests that the aging method of estimating the provision for uncollectible receivables is not appropriate.

Sale of Receivables

When an entity sells receivables to a third party, there is a question as to whether the sale is truly a sale of an asset or simply a borrowing secured by the accounts receivable. In the former case, it is appropriate to recognize a sale and derecognize the receivables—that is, remove them from the accounting records. In the latter case, the receivables are not derecognized and the transaction is accounted for as a borrowing. The general principle in IAS 39 is that a financial asset may be derecognized when the significant risks and rewards associated with ownership of the asset have been transferred to another entity. In some cases, the seller of receivables retains significant risks, for example, by guaranteeing the collectability of the receivables through right of recourse, and derecognition of the receivables is not appropriate. Instead, the cash received from the sale of receivables is treated as a loan payable.

A so-called pass-through arrangement exists when an entity retains the right to collect cash flows from a receivable but is obligated to transfer those cash flows to a third party. In this type of arrangement, derecognition is appropriate only if each of the following criteria is met:

1. The entity has no obligation to pay cash to the buyer of the receivables unless it collects equivalent amounts from the receivables.
2. The entity is prohibited by the terms of the transfer contract from selling or pledging the receivables.
3. The entity has an obligation to remit any cash flows it collects on the receivables to the eventual recipient without material delay. In addition, the entity is not entitled to reinvest such cash flows. An exception exists for investments in cash equivalents during the short settlement period from the collection date to the date of remittance to the eventual recipients, as long as interest earned on such investments also is passed to the eventual recipients.

The following excerpt from Fiat Group's notes to the 2009 consolidated financial statements demonstrates the impact of IAS 39's derecognition requirements with respect to receivables:

> At 31 December 2009, Current receivables include receivables sold and financed through both securitization and factoring transactions of €6,588 million (€6,190 million at 31 December 2008) which do not meet IAS 39 derecognition requirements. These receivables are recognized as such in the Group financial statements even though they have been legally sold; a corresponding financial liability is recorded in the consolidated statement of financial position as Asset-backed financing (see Note 27).

Example: Derecognition of Receivables

Edwards Inc. has receivables from unrelated parties with a face value of $1,000. Edwards transfers these receivables to Main Street Bank for $900, without recourse. The discount reflects the fact that the bank has assumed the credit risk. Edwards will continue to collect the receivables, depositing them in a non-interest-bearing bank account with the cash flows remitted to the bank at the end of each month. Edwards is not allowed to sell or pledge the receivables to anyone else and is under no obligation to repurchase the receivables from Main Street Bank.

This is a pass-through arrangement, and Edwards appears to meet the three criteria required for derecognition: (1) the company is under no obligation to pay any more than it collects, (2) it may not pledge or resell the receivables, and (3) it has agreed to remit the money collected in a timely manner. There is no interest earned on the short-term bank deposits, so there is no question whether Edwards passes on the interest to Main Street Bank. The receivables may be derecognized, as follows:

Cash	$900
Expense	100
Accounts Receivable	$1,000

Now assume that Edwards collects the receivables and deposits collections in its interest-bearing bank account. At the end of each month, Edwards remits to Main Street Bank only the amount collected on the receivables; interest earned on the short-term deposits is retained by Edwards. Because Edwards retains the interest on short-term bank deposits, the third pass-through criterion has not been met. Edwards would not be allowed to derecognize the accounts receivable. Instead, the cash received from Main Street Bank would be treated as a secured borrowing.

Cash	$900
Expense	100
Notes Payable	$1,000

Summary

1. IAS 1 requires liabilities to be classified as current or noncurrent. The classification and accounting for current liabilities under IFRS is very similar to U.S. GAAP. Differences relate to refinancing short-term debt, amounts payable on demand due to debt covenant violations, and bank overdrafts.

2. IAS 37 defines a provision as a liability of uncertain timing or amount. A provision is recognized when there is a present obligation that can be reliably estimated and for which it is probable (more likely than not) that an outflow of resources will be made. U.S. GAAP has similar requirements but does not provide guidance for the degree of likelihood needed to meet the threshold of being probable.

3. A provision should be recognized for an onerous contract, which is a contract in which the unavoidable costs of fulfilling the contract exceed the benefit expected to be received. A provision should be recognized for a restructuring when an entity has created a constructive obligation—that is, when it has raised a valid expectation in those affected by the plan that it will carry out the restructuring. U.S. GAAP does not allow recognition of a restructuring until a liability has been incurred.

4. IFRS and U.S. GAAP differ in the accounting for defined post-retirement benefit plans with respect to the periods of time over which past service cost and actuarial gains and losses are recognized, and measurement of the amount of benefit liability or asset reported on the balance sheet.

5. Under IAS 19, the amount reported on the balance sheet related to a defined post-employment benefit plan is equal to the present value of the defined benefit obligation (PVDBO) minus the fair value of plan assets minus unrecognized past service cost plus (minus) unrecognized actuarial gains (losses). Under U.S. GAAP, the amount recognized is PVDBO minus the fair value of plan assets.

6. IFRS 2 distinguishes between three types of share-based payments. Equity-settled share-based payments are treated as equity transactions; cash-settled and choice-of-settlement share-based payment transactions result in the recognition of a liability. The standard applies a fair value approach to all three types of share-based payment.

7. In a stock option plan that vests in installments, compensation cost associated with each installment is amortized over that installment's vesting period under IFRS. This approach also is acceptable under U.S. GAAP, but a simpler straight-line method also may be used.

8. Similar to U.S. GAAP, IAS 12 uses an asset-and-liability approach that requires recognition of deferred tax assets and liabilities for temporary differences and for operating loss and tax credit carry-forwards. A deferred tax asset is recognized only if it is probable that a tax benefit will be realized.

9. IFRS contain two standards specifically related to revenue recognition: IAS 18 and IAS 11. U.S. GAAP, on the other hand, has many more separate pieces of authoritative guidance that are now codified in FASB Accounting Standards Codification Topic 605. The IASB and FASB jointly issued an Exposure Draft in 2010 with the intent to converge their rules with regard to revenue recognition.

10. IAS 18 provides general principles for the recognition and measurement of revenue generated from the sale of goods; rendering of services; and interest, royalties, and dividends. The general measurement principle is that revenue should be measured at the fair value of the consideration received or receivable.

11. Five conditions must be met before revenue may be recognized from the sale of goods, including the criterion that the significant risks and rewards of ownership of the goods have been transferred to the buyer.

12. IAS 18 allows use of the stage of completion method for recognition of service revenue when several criteria are met. This method of revenue recognition is not used for service transactions under U.S. GAAP.

13. Entities that use customer loyalty programs to provide customers with incentives to purchase their goods and services must treat the award credits as a separate component of the sale transaction and recognize a portion of the sales price as deferred revenue.

14. The accounting for financial instruments is covered by IAS 32, IAS 39, IFRS 7, and IFRS 9 (which goes into effect in 2013). Financial instruments are contracts that give rise to both a financial asset for one party and either a financial liability or equity for another party.

15. IAS 32 requires financial instruments to be classified as financial liabilities or equity or both in accordance with the substance of the contractual arrangement. If an equity instrument contains a contractual obligation that meets the definition of a financial liability, it should be classified as such. Preferred shares that are redeemable at the option of the shareholders are an example of a financial liability.

16. Compound financial instruments, such as convertible bonds, must be split into a liability element and an equity element. This so-called split accounting is not followed under U.S. GAAP.

17. IAS 39 establishes four categories of financial assets and two categories of financial liabilities; both categories include the classification "at fair value through profit or loss" (FVPL). Financial assets and liabilities that otherwise would be classified in a different category may be classified as FVPL under certain conditions, such as to eliminate an accounting mismatch.

18. Financial assets and financial liabilities are initially measured at their fair value. Subsequent to initial recognition they are measured at one of three possible values: (a) cost (unquoted equity investments), (b) amortized cost (loans and receivables, held-to-maturity investments, and liabilities measured at amortized cost), or (c) fair value (FVPL financial assets, FVPL financial liabilities, and available-for-sale financial assets).

19. Under IFRS, costs associated with the issuance or modification of debt are subtracted in determining the carrying amount of the related liability. These costs are then allocated over the life of the debt as part of interest expense. Under U.S. GAAP, debt issuance costs are treated as an asset that is amortized over the life of the debt, and debt modification costs are expensed immediately.

20. According to IAS 39, the sale of receivables can be recognized as such and the receivables may be derecognized only if the significant risks and rewards from owning the receivables are transferred to the buyer. If this is not the case, the sale of receivables is treated as a borrowing with the accounts receivable acting as collateral.

Questions

Answer questions based on IFRS unless indicated otherwise.

1. What is a provision, and when must a provision be recognized?
2. What is a contingent liability? What is the financial reporting treatment for contingent liabilities?
3. What is a constructive obligation?
4. What is an onerous contract? How are onerous contracts accounted for?
5. How does a company measure the net pension benefit liability (asset) to report on the balance sheet under IFRS and U.S. GAAP?
6. In accounting for post-employment benefits, when are past service costs and actuarial gains and losses recognized in income?
7. At what point in time should a company recognize the liability and expense associated with termination benefits? What is the basis for measuring the amount of termination benefits to recognize?
8. What is the basis for determining compensation cost in an equity-settled share-based payment transaction with nonemployees? With employees?
9. What is the difference in measuring compensation expense associated with stock options that vest on a single date (cliff vesting) and in installments (graded vesting)?
10. How does an entity account for a choice-of-settlement share-based payment transaction?
11. Which income tax rates should be used in accounting for income taxes?
12. What are the rules related to the recognition of a deferred tax asset?
13. What approaches are available for disclosing the relationship between tax expense and accounting profit?
14. How are deferred taxes classified on the balance sheet?
15. What are the criteria that must be met in order to recognize revenue from the sale of goods?
16. What approaches are used to recognize revenue from the rendering of services? Under what conditions is each of these approaches used?
17. How is an exchange of goods that are similar in nature and value accounted for?
18. Under what conditions may revenue be recognized on a "bill-and-hold" sale?
19. What is a customer loyalty program, and how is such a program accounted for?

20. What are the five steps to follow in revenue recognition as proposed in the IASB/FASB exposure draft on revenue from contracts with customers?

21. What are the four classes of financial assets?

22. Under what conditions should preferred shares be recognized as a liability on the balance sheet?

23. How are convertible bonds measured initially on the balance sheet?

24. How can use of the "fair value option" solve the problem of an accounting mismatch?

25. What happens if a significant amount of held-to-maturity investments is reclassified as available-for-sale?

26. How are costs associated with the issuance of bonds payable accounted for?

27. What is the accounting treatment for debt extinguishment costs? Debt modification costs?

28. In a sale of receivables described as a pass through arrangement, under what conditions can receivables be derecognized?

Exercises and Problems

Solve exercises and problems based on IFRS unless indicated otherwise.

1. Halifax Corporation has a December 31 fiscal year end. As of December 31, Year 1, the company has a debt covenant violation that results in a 10-year note payable to Nova Scotia Bank becoming due on March 1, Year 2. Halifax will be required to classify the 10-year note payable as a current liability unless it obtains a waiver from the bank

   a. Prior to issuance of its Year 1 financial statements, that gives the company until January 1, Year 3 to rectify the debt covenant violation.

   b. Prior to December 31, Year 1, that gives the company until January 1, Year 3 to rectify the debt covenant violation.

   c. Prior to issuance of its Year 1 financial statements, that gives the company until June 30, Year 2 to rectify the debt covenant violation.

   d. Prior to December 31, Year 1, that gives the company until June 30, Year 2 to rectify the debt covenant violation.

2. Bull Arm Company has the following items at December 31, Year 1:
   - $200,000, 5 percent note payable, due March 15, Year 2. The company has reached an agreement with the bank to refinance the note for two years, but the refinancing has not yet been completed.
   - $1,000,000, 4 percent bonds payable, due December 31, Year 5. The company has violated an agreement with the bondholders to maintain a minimum balance in retained earnings, which causes the bonds to come due on January 31, Year 2.
   - $50,000 overdraft on a bank account. Overdrafts are a normal part of the company's cash management plan.

   Required:
   Related to these items, what amount should Bull Arm Company report as current liabilities on its December 31, Year 1 balance sheet?

   a. $50,000.

   b. $250,000.

   c. $1,050,000.

   d. $1,200,000.

3. Melbourne Inc. became involved in a tax dispute with the national tax authority. Melbourne's legal counsel indicates that there is a 70 percent likelihood that the company will lose this dispute and estimates that the amount the company will have to pay is between $500,000 and $700,000, with all amounts in that range being equally likely. What amount, if any, should Melbourne recognize as a provision related to this tax dispute?

a. $0.

b. $500,000.

c. $600,000.

d. $700,000.

4. Which of the following is not a criterion that must be met before an entity recognizes a provision related to a restructuring program?

a. The entity has a detailed formal plan for the restructuring.

b. The entity has begun implementation of the restructuring.

c. The restructuring plan indicates that the restructuring will be carried out in a reasonable period of time.

d. The cost of the restructuring is reasonably estimable.

5. Past service cost related to nonvested employees should be recognized as expense

a. In the period the cost is incurred.

b. Over the nonvested employees' remaining vesting period.

c. Over the nonvested employees' estimated remaining working life.

d. Over the nonvested employees' estimated life expectancy.

6. When stock options are granted to employees, what is the basis for determining the amount of compensation cost that will be recognized as expense?

a. The fair value of the service provided by the employees receiving the options at the grant date.

b. The fair value of the stock options at the exercise date.

c. The fair value of the stock options at the grant date.

d. There is no recognition of expense related to stock options.

7. Which of the following types of share-based payment (SBP) transactions always results in the recognition of a liability?

a. Equity-settled SBP transaction with employees.

b. Equity-settled SBP transaction with nonemployees.

c. Cash-settled SBP transaction with employees.

d. Choice-of-settlement SBP transaction in which the entity chooses the form of settlement.

8. Sandoval Company operates in a country in which distributed profits are taxed at 25 percent and undistributed profits are taxed at 30 percent. In Year 1, Sandoval generated pre-tax profit of $100,000 and paid $20,000 in dividends from its Year 1 earnings. In Year 2, Sandoval generated pre-tax profit of $120,000, and paid dividends of $40,000 from its Year 1 earnings. What amounts should Sandoval recognize as current tax expense in Years 1 and 2, respectively?

a. $29,000 and $34,000.

b. $30,000 and $34,000.

c. $25,000 and $30,000.

d. $30,000 and $36,000.

9. Which of the following is not a criterion that must be met to recognize revenue from the sale of goods?

a. The amount of revenue can be measured reliably.

b. The significant risks and rewards of ownership of the goods have been transferred to the buyer.

c. The costs incurred or to be incurred with respect to the sale of the goods can be measured reliably.

d. It is certain that the economic benefits associated with the sale will flow to the seller.

10. Manometer Company sells accounts receivable of $10,000 to Eck Bank for $9,000 in cash. The sale does not qualify for derecognition of a financial asset. As a result, Manometer's balance sheet will be different in which of the following ways?

a. $1,000 more in assets than under derecognition.

b. $9,000 more in assets than under derecognition.

c. $9,000 more in liabilities than under derecognition.

d. $10,000 less in equity than under derecognition.

11. Sinto Bem Company issues a two-year note paying 5 percent interest on January 1, Year 1. The note sells for its par value of $1,000,000, and the company incurs issuance costs of $22,000. Which of the following amounts best approximates the amount of interest expense Sinto Bem will recognize in Year 1 related to this note?

a. $48,900.

b. $50,000.

c. $58,680.

d. $60,670.

12. Costs incurred to accomplish a less than substantial debt modification, such as an interest rate adjustment, are treated in which of the following ways?

a. Expensed immediately.

b. Increase the carrying amount of the debt that has been modified.

c. Decrease the carrying amount of the debt that has been modified.

d. Decrease the gain on the debt modification.

13. On December 31, Year 1, Airways Corp. issued $1 million in bonds at 5 percent annual interest, due December 31, Year 6 at a discount of $100,000. Airways incurred bank fees of $100,000, legal fees of $50,000, and salaries of $25,000 for its employees in conjunction with issuing the bonds. What is the original carrying amount for these bonds?

a. $725,000.

b. $750,000.

c. $850,000.

d. $900,000.

14. In Year 1, Better Sleep Company began to receive complaints from physicians that patients were experiencing unexpected side effects from the company's sleep apnea drug. The company took the drug off the market near the end of Year 1. During Year 2, the company was sued by 1,000 customers who had had a severe allergic reaction to the company's drug and required hospitalization. At the end of Year 2, the company's attorneys estimated a 60 percent chance the company would need to make payments in the range of $1,000 to $5,000 to settle each claim, with all amounts in that range being equally likely. At the end of Year 3, while none of the cases had been resolved, the company's attorneys now estimated an 80 percent probability the company would be required to make payments in the range of $2,000 to $7,000 to settle each claim. In Year 4, 400 claims were settled at a total cost of $1.2 million. Based on this experience, the company believes 30 percent of the remaining cases will be settled for $3,000 each, 50 percent will be settled for $5,000, and 20 percent will be settled for $10,000.

Required:
Prepare journal entries for Years 1–4 related to this litigation.

15. On June 1, Year 1, Charley Horse Company entered into a contract with Good Feed Company to purchase 1,000 bales of organic hay on January 30, Year 2 at a price of $30 per bale. The hay will be grown especially for Charley Horse and is needed to feed the company's herd of buffalos. On December 1, Year 1, Charley Horse sells its herd of buffalos. As a result, the company no longer has a need for the organic hay that will be delivered on January 30, Year 2, and the company does not believe it will be able to sell the hay to a third party. Charley Horse is able to cancel the contract with Good Feed for a cancellation fee of $20,000.

Required:
Determine what accounting entries, if any, Charley Horse Company should make on December 31, Year 1 related to the contract to purchase 1,000 bales of hay on January 30, Year 2.

16. The board of directors of Chestnut Inc. approved a restructuring plan on November 1, Year 1. On December 1, Year 1, Chestnut publicly announced its plan to close a manufacturing division in New Jersey and move it to China, and the company's New Jersey employees were notified that their jobs would be eliminated. Also on December 1, Year 1, to ensure an orderly transition, management promised a termination bonus of $10,000 to any employee who remains with the company until his or her position is terminated in the fourth quarter of Year 2. Chestnut estimates it will pay termination bonuses to 120 employees for a total of $1,200,000. The present value of the estimated termination bonus is $1,000,000.

Required:
Determine the provision that should be recognized for Chestnut's restructuring plan. Identify the dates on which journal entries should be made and the amounts to be recorded.

17. The Kissel Trucking Company Inc. has a defined benefit pension plan for its employees. At December 31, Year 1, the following information is available regarding Kissel's plan:

Fair value of plan assets	$30,000,000
Present value of defined benefit obligation	38,000,000
Interest costs	1,200,000
Net unrecognized actuarial gains	300,000
Recognized actuarial gains	150,000
Unrecognized past service costs	375,000

Required:

Determine the amount that Kissel will report on the balance sheet as of December 31, Year 1 for this pension plan under (a) IFRS and (b) U.S. GAAP.

18. On January 1, Year 1, the Hoverman Corporation made amendments to its defined benefit pension plan, resulting in $150,000 of past service costs. The plan has 100 active employees, of which 60 are vested and the remaining 40 will be vested in three years. There currently are no retirees under the plan. Hoverman has determined the following information regarding the past service costs:

Unrecognized past service costs applicable to:	
Vested employees	$ 90,000
Unvested employees	60,000
Total unrecognized past service costs	$150,000

The aggregate number of future service years of employees expected to receive benefits is 500 years.

Required:

Determine the amount of past service costs to be amortized in Year 1 and subsequent years under (a) IFRS and (b) U.S. GAAP.

19. The Northeastern Company has a defined benefit pension plan. The company's actuary has determined that a loss has occurred at the beginning of Year 1 caused by demographic changes related to the composition of its workforce and revisions to life expectancy calculations. Northeastern uses the corridor approach to amortize unrecognized gains and losses. The following information relates to the actuarial loss:

Actuarial loss related to active employees	$315,000
Actuarial loss related to inactive/retired employees	85,000
Total actuarial loss	$400,000
Average remaining service lives of active employees	20 years
Average life expectancy of inactive/retired employees	15 years

Required:

Assume that the total loss of $400,000 is outside the corridor range. Calculate the amortization of the actuarial loss under (a) IFRS and (b) U.S. GAAP.

20. White River Company has a defined benefit pension plan in which the fair value (FV) of plan assets exceeds the present value of defined benefit obligations (PVDBO). The following information is available at December 31, Year 1 (amounts in millions):

PVDBO.	$3,200
FV of plan assets	3,700
Unrecognized actuarial gains	90
Unrecognized past service cost.	50

Because the FV of plan assets exceeds the PVDBO, White River will be able to reduce future contributions to the plan for several years. The present value of reductions in future contributions is $100 million.

Required:
Determine the amount at which White River Company will report a defined pension benefit asset on its December 31, Year 1 balance sheet under (a) IFRS and (b) U.S. GAAP.

21. On January 2, Year 1, Argy Company's board of directors granted 12,000 stock options to a select group of senior employees. The requisite service period is three years, with one-third of the options vesting at the end of each calendar year (graded vesting). An option-pricing model was used to calculate a fair value of $5 for each option on the grant date. The company assumes all 12,000 options will vest (i.e., there will be no forfeitures).

Required:
Determine the amount to be recognized as compensation expense in Year 1, Year 2, and Year 3 under (a) IFRS and (b) U.S. GAAP. Prepare the necessary journal entries.

22. SC Masterpiece Inc. granted 1,000 stock options to certain sales employees on January 1, Year 1. The options vest at the end of three years (cliff vesting) but are conditional upon selling 20,000 cases of barbecue sauce over the three-year service period. The grant-date fair value of each option is $30. No forfeitures are expected to occur. The company is expensing the cost of the options on a straight-line basis over the three-year period at $10,000 per year (1,000 options × $30 ÷ 3 = $10,000).

On January 1, Year 2, the company's management believes the original sales target of 20,000 units will not be met because only 5,000 cases were sold in Year 1. Management modifies the sales target for the options to vest to 15,000 units, which it believes is reasonably achievable. The fair value of each option at January 1, Year 2 is $28.

Required:
Determine the amount to be recognized as compensation expense in Year 1, Year 2, and Year 3 under (a) IFRS and (b) U.S. GAAP. Prepare the necessary journal entries.

23. Updike and Patterson Investments Inc. (UPI) holds equity investments with a cost basis of $250,000. UPI accounts for these investments as available-for-sale securities. As such, the investments are carried on the balance sheet at fair value, with unrealized gains and losses reported in other comprehensive income.

At the end of Year 1, the fair value of these investments has declined to $220,000. Consequently, UPI reports an unrealized loss for financial reporting purposes of $30,000 in other comprehensive income, which creates a temporary tax difference. As of December 31, Year 1, UPI management determines that it is more likely than not that the company will be able to deduct capital losses on these investments for tax purposes if they are realized.

As of December 31, Year 2, UPI management evaluates its assessment of tax position and determines that it is more likely than not that the company will *not* be able to take a deduction for any capital loss on these investments. UPI's tax rate is 40 percent.

Required:
Prepare journal entries to account for income taxes in Year 1 and Year 2.

24. Gotti Manufacturing Inc., a U.S.-based company, operates in three countries in addition to the United States. The following table reports the company's pretax income and the applicable tax rate in these countries for the year ended December 31, Year 1. Gotti does not have any temporary tax differences, but it does have two permanent differences: (1) nontaxable municipal bond interest of $20,000 in the United States and (2) nondeductible expenses of $5,000 in the United States.

Country	Pre-tax Income	Applicable Tax Rate
United States.	$1,450,000	35%
Country One	400,000	40%
Country Two	500,000	20%
Country Three	600,000	25%
Total	$2,950,000	
Permanent differences.	15,000	
Book income	$2,965,000	

Required:
Prepare the numerical reconciliation between tax expense and accounting profit that would appear in Gotti's income tax note in the Year 1 financial statements. Show two different ways in which this reconciliation may be presented.

25. Mishima Technologies Company introduced Product X to the market on December 1. The new product carries a one-year warranty. In its first month on the market, Mishima sold 1,000 units of the new product for a total of $1,000,000. Customers have an unconditional right of return for 90 days if they are not completely satisfied with the product. During the month of December, customers returned 200 units of the new product that they had purchased for $200,000.

Required:
Determine when it would be appropriate for Mishima Technologies Company to recognize revenue from the December sales of the new product.

26. Ultima Company offers its customers discounts to purchase goods and take title before they actually need the goods. The company offers to hold the goods for the customers until they request delivery. This relieves the customers from making room in their warehouses for merchandise not yet needed. The goods are on hand and ready for delivery to the buyer at the time the sale is made. Ultima Company pays the cost of storage and insurance prior to shipment. Customers are billed at the time of sale and are given the normal credit period (90 days) to pay.

    Required:
    Determine whether Ultima Company should recognize revenue from the sale of goods at the time title passes to the customer or whether it should defer revenue recognition until the goods are delivered to the customer.

27. The Miller-Porter Company sells powder coating equipment at a sales price of $50,000 per unit. The sales price includes delivery, installation, and initial testing of the equipment, as well as a monthly service call for one year in which a technician checks to make sure that the equipment is working properly and makes adjustments as needed. After the first year, customers are given the opportunity to enter into an extended service agreement; Miller-Porter prices these extended service agreements to earn an expected gross profit of 50 percent. Given the wages paid to technicians and the time required to make a service call, the company estimates that the cost of providing each monthly service call is $200.

    Required:
    Develop a revenue recognition policy consistent with IAS 18 for The Miller-Porter Company for its sales of power coating equipment.

28. Cypress Company enters into a fixed-fee contract to provide architectural services to the Gervais Group for $240,000. The Gervais Group, which will make monthly payments of $40,000, is a new client for Cypress Company. Cypress has agreed to provide Gervais with plans and drawings for a new manufacturing facility that will qualify for a LEED (Leadership in Energy and Environmental Design) green building certification. Cypress has no experience in designing green buildings, but it has guaranteed Gervais that the plans and drawings will be completed in six months.

    Required:
    Evaluate whether it would be appropriate for Cypress Company to account for its contract with Gervais Group on a stage-of-completion basis.

29. Phil's Sandwich Company sells sandwiches at several locations in the northeastern part of the country. Phil's customers receive a card on their first visit that allows them to receive one free sandwich for every eight sandwiches purchased in a three-month period. Customers must redeem their cards in the month after the three-month period is completed. Each time a customer purchases a sandwich, his or her card is stamped. Past experience shows that only 50 percent of customers accumulate enough stamps within a three-month period to qualify for a free sandwich, and only 80 percent of those customers actually redeem their card to receive a free sandwich. In the first quarter of the current year, Phil's sold 12,000 sandwiches at an average price of $7.00. Phil's only accepts payment in cash.

    Required:
    Prepare the summary journal entry Phil's Sandwich Company should make to recognize revenue from the sale of sandwiches for the first quarter of the current year.

30. Saffron Enterprises Inc., a U.S.-based company, purchases a 4 percent bond denominated in euros for $1,500 on January 1, Year 1 when the exchange rate is $1.50 per euro. (In other words, the purchase price was 1,000 euros.) The bond was purchased at par value. At December 31, Year 1, the fair value of the bond in the marketplace is 1,050 euros and the exchange rate is $1.40 per euro. Saffron classifies its investment in bonds as available for sale.

    Required:
    Prepare the journal entries that Saffron Enterprises should record in Year 1 related to its investment in euro-denominated bonds.

31. On January 1, Year 1, Spectrum Fabricators Inc. issues $20 million of convertible bonds at par value. The bonds have a stated annual interest rate of 6 percent, pay interest annually, and come due December 31, Year 5. The bonds are convertible at any time after issuance at the rate of 10 shares of common stock for each $1,000 of the face value of the convertible bonds. Issuance costs total $100,000. The current market interest rate for nonconvertible bonds is 8 percent.

    Required:
    Prepare the journal entries to record the issuance of the convertible bonds (round to the nearest dollar). Determine the amount of expense related to the convertible bonds that the company should recognize each year (round to the nearest dollar). [Note: You will need to calculate the effective interest rate on the bonds to determine interest expense. One way to do this is to solve for the internal rate of return (IRR) of the cash flows using Excel.]

32. The Bockster Company issues $20 million of preferred shares on January 1, Year 1 at par value. The preferred shares have a 5 percent fixed annual cash dividend.

    Part A. The preferred shareholders have the option to redeem the preferred shares for cash equal to par value any time after January 1, Year 2.

    Required:
    Discuss how Bockster should account for these redeemable preferred shares.

    Part B. The preferred shareholders do not have the option to redeem the preferred shares, but instead have the option to convert the preferred shares into a fixed number of shares of common stock any time after January 1, Year 2.

    Required:
    Discuss how Bockster should account for these convertible preferred shares.

33. On January 1, Year 1, Tempe extinguishes $10 million of 10 percent bonds payable due December 31, Year 2 that were originally issued at a discount by calling them at par value. The current carrying amount of the bonds payable is $9,950,000. To finance the debt extinguishment, management issues new debt at par with a new lender in the amount of $10 million. The new debt matures on December 31, Year 2 and has a 9 percent annual interest rate. Management incurs $100,000 in legal costs to negotiate the issuance of the new long-term bonds payable.

    Required:
    Prepare the journal entries to record the extinguishment of the debt and interest expense for Year 1.

34. Five years ago, Macro Arco Corporation (MAC) borrowed $12 million from Friendly Neighbor Bank (FNB) to finance the purchase of a new factory to be able to meet an expected increase in demand for its products. The expected increase in demand never materialized, and due to a downturn in the economy,

MAC is no longer able to make its monthly payments to FNB. After a lengthy negotiation process, which cost MAC $50,000 in legal fees, MAC will transfer the factory to the bank, along with a cash payment of $1.5 million. This will discharge MAC from the debt. The carrying amount and fair value of the factory is $8 million, and the current balance due to the bank is $10 million.

Required:
Prepare the journal entries to be recorded by MAC and FNB related to this troubled debt restructuring.

35. On November 1, Year 1, Farley Corporation sells receivables due in six months with a carrying amount of $100,000 to Town Square Bank for a cash payment of $95,000, subject to full recourse. Under the right of recourse, Farley Corporation is obligated to compensate Town Square Bank for the failure of any debtor to pay when due. In addition to the recourse, Town Square Bank is entitled to sell the receivables back to Farley Corp in the event of unfavorable changes in interest rates or credit rating of the underlying debtors.

Required:
Determine the appropriate accounting by Farley Corporation for the sale of receivables. Prepare any necessary journal entries for Year 1.

36. On December 1, Year 1, Traylor Company sells $100,000 of short-term trade receivables to Main Street Bank for $98,000 in cash by guaranteeing to buy back the first $15,000 of defaulted receivables. Traylor's historic rate of noncollection on receivables is 5 percent. Traylor notifies the customers affected that they should make payment on their accounts directly to Main Street Bank.

Required:
Determine whether the sale of receivables by Traylor Company qualifies for derecognition.

37. The Campolino Company has a defined benefit post-retirement health care plan for its employees. At the beginning of Year 1, Campolino amended the plan to provide additional benefits to all employees.

The following facts apply to the plan for the year ended December 31, Year 1:

Present value of defined benefit obligation (PVDBO) on January 1, Year 1	$650,000
Plan assets at fair value on January 1, Year 1	420,000
Unamortized past service costs (PSC) on January 1, Year 1	56,000
Plan assets at fair value on December 31, Year 1	449,000
Actual return on plan assets	21,000
Service cost	46,000
Employer contributions	48,000
Benefit payments	40,000
Average remaining vesting period	5 years
Expected return on plan assets	8 percent
Discount rate	5 percent

Other information:

- There are no retirees and none of the active employees is vested.
- There are no unamortized actuarial gains or losses at the beginning of the year.
- Benefits and employer contributions were paid on December 31, Year 1.

Required:

Use the following template to determine the post-retirement benefit expense for the year ended December 31, Year 1 and the post-retirement benefit liability at December 31, Year 1 to be reported by Campolino Company under IFRS. Prepare the necessary journal entry to reflect these amounts.

(Amounts in parentheses represent credits.)

	Campolino Company General Ledger			Benefit Fund General ledger		Off Balance Sheet	
	Benefit Expense	Cash	Benefit Asset (Liability)	PVDBO	Plan Assets	PSC	Actuarial (Gain) Loss
Balance at January 1, Year 1			$(174,000)	$(650,000)	$420,000	$56,000	
Balance at December 31, Year 1							

38. This problem consists of two parts.

Part A. On January 1, Year 1, Stone Company issued 100 stock options with an exercise price of $38 each to 10 employees (1,000 options in total). The employees can choose to settle the options either (a) in shares of stock ($1 par value) or (b) in cash equal to the intrinsic value of the options on the vesting date. The options vest on December 31, Year 3 after the employees have completed three years of service. Stone Company expects that only seven employees will remain with the company for three years and vest in the options. Two employees resign in Year 1, and the company continues to assume an overall forfeiture rate of 30 percent at December 31, Year 1. In Year 2, one more employee resigns. As expected, seven employees vest on December 31, Year 3 and exercise their stock options.

The following represents the share price and fair value at the relevant dates:

Date	Share Price	Fair Value of Cash Alternative	Fair Value of Stock Alternative
January 1, Year 1	$43	$6.00	$6.00
December 31, Year 1, Year 2	$45	$8.00	$8.00
December 31, Year 3	$47	$9.00	$9.00

Required:

Determine the fair value of the stock options at the grant date and the amount to be recognized as compensation expense in Year 1, Year 2, and Year 3. Prepare journal entries assuming that the vested employees choose (a) the cash alternative and (b) the stock alternative.

Part B. Now assume that if the employees choose to settle the stock options in shares of stock that the employees receive a 10 percent discount on the exercise price (i.e., the exercise price would be $34.20). As a result, the fair value of the share alternative on the grant date is $8.80.

Required:

Determine the fair value of the stock options at the grant date and the amount to be recognized as compensation expense in Year 1.

39. Indicate whether each of the following describes an accounting treatment that is acceptable under IFRS, U.S. GAAP, both, or neither by checking the appropriate box.

	Acceptable under			
	IFRS	**U.S. GAAP**	**Both**	**Neither**
• Bank overdrafts are netted against cash rather than being recognized as a liability when overdrafts are a normal part of cash management.				
• Uncertain legal obligations, but not constructive obligations, contingent upon a future event are recognized as liabilities when certain criteria are met.				
• A defined benefit pension liability is measured as the excess of the present value of the defined benefit obligation (PVDBO) and the fair value of plan assets.				
• Actuarial gains and losses in a defined benefit pension plan related to nonvested employees are amortized over the remaining vesting period.				
• The compensation cost associated with graded-vesting stock options is amortized to expense on a straight-line basis over the vesting period.				
• The minimum amount recognized as compensation expense on a stock option plan is the compensation cost as measured at the grant date, even if a subsequent modification to the plan decreases the total compensation cost.				
• Deferred taxes are classified as current or noncurrent based on the classification of the related asset or liability.				
• The stage of completion method is used to recognize revenue from service transactions when specified criteria are met.				
• Nonredeemable preferred shares are classified as a liability on the balance sheet.				
• Costs associated with the issuance of debt are amortized on a straight-line basis over the life of the debt.				

Case 5-1

S. A. Harrington Company

S. A. Harrington Company is a U.S.-based company that prepares its consolidated financial statements in accordance with U.S. GAAP. The company reported income in 2011 of $5,000,000 and stockholders' equity at December 31, 2011, of $40,000,000.

The CFO of S. A. Harrington has learned that the U.S. Securities and Exchange Commission is considering requiring U.S. companies to use IFRS in preparing consolidated financial statements. The company wishes to determine the impact that a switch to IFRS would have on its financial statements and has engaged you to prepare a reconciliation of income and stockholders' equity from U.S. GAAP to IFRS. You have identified the following five areas in which S. A. Harrington's accounting principles based on U.S. GAAP differ from IFRS.

1. Restructuring
2. Pension plan
3. Stock options
4. Revenue recognition
5. Bonds payable

The CFO provides the following information with respect to each of these accounting differences.

Restructuring Provision

The company publicly announced a restructuring plan in 2011 that created a valid expectation on the part of the employees to be terminated that the company will carry out the restructuring. The company estimated that the restructuring would cost $300,000. No legal obligation to restructure exists as of December 31, 2011.

Pension Plan

In 2009, the company amended its pension plan, creating a past service cost of $60,000. Half of the past service cost was attributable to already vested employees who had an average remaining service life of 15 years, and half of the past service cost was attributable to nonvested employees who, on average, had two more years until vesting. The company has no retired employees.

Stock Options

Stock options were granted to key officers on January 1, 2011. The grant date fair value per option was $10, and a total of 9,000 options were granted. The options vest in equal installments over three years: one-third vest in 2010, one-third in 2011, and one-third in 2012. The company uses a straight-line method to recognize compensation expense related to stock options.

Revenue Recognition

The company entered into a contract in 2011 to provide engineering services to a long-term customer over a 12-month period. The fixed price is $250,000, and the company estimates with a high degree of reliability that the project is 30 percent complete at the end of 2011.

Bonds Payable

On January 1, 2010, the company issued $10,000,000 of 5 percent bonds at par value that mature in five years on December 31, 2014. Costs incurred in issuing the bonds were $500,000. Interest is paid on the bonds annually.

Required

Prepare a reconciliation schedule to reconcile 2011 net income and December 31, 2011 stockholders' equity from a U.S. GAAP basis to IFRS. Ignore income taxes. Prepare a note to explain each adjustment made in the reconciliation schedule.

Chapter Six

Comparative Accounting

Learning Objectives

After reading this chapter, you should be able to

- Describe some aspects of the environment in which accounting operates in five countries, China, Germany, Japan, Mexico, and the United Kingdom.
- Explain the nature of the accounting profession in the selected countries.
- Discuss the mechanisms in place for regulating accounting and financial reporting in the selected countries.
- Examine some of the accounting principles and practices used by companies in these countries.
- Identify the areas where national accounting practices in these countries differ from International Financial Reporting Standards (IFRS).

INTRODUCTION

This chapter describes the accounting environments in five countries: China, Germany, Japan, Mexico, and the United Kingdom. We selected these countries because they are economically important and they represent a cross section of the different accounting systems used around the world. Further, their accounting systems reflect their unique historical and cultural backgrounds. Exhibit 6.1 provides comparative demographic and economic data for these countries. Germany, Japan, and the United Kingdom are among the wealthiest nations in the world, whereas China and Mexico are developing economies. China, with a population of over 1.4 billion, has been one of the fastest-growing economies in recent years. As a result of recent economic reforms, Chinese accounting is experiencing a period of rapid evolution. Germany is one of the economic powerhouses in Europe, and its accounting system is undergoing change from the Continental European approach to accounting. Japan became a major economic power within a short period after World War II, focusing on high-tech industries. Its unique system of business interrelationships has had a profound impact on accounting. Mexico is representative of Latin American countries. As a member of the North American Free Trade Agreement (NAFTA), Mexico has been under external pressure to change its accounting system. The United Kingdom represents the Anglo-Saxon model of accounting. Recently, accounting in the United Kingdom has been strongly affected by the country's membership in the European Union.

EXHIBIT 6.1 Country Profiles

Source: http://news.bbc.co.uk/2/hi/country_profiles/default.stm

	China	Germany	Japan	Mexico	United Kingdom
Area	9.6 million sq. km (3.7 million sq. miles)	357,027 sq. km (137,849 sq. miles)	377,864 sq. km (145,894 sq. miles)	1.96 million sq. km (758,449 sq. miles)	242,514 sq. km (93,638 sq. miles)
Population	1.34 billion (UN 2009)	82.2 million (UN 2009)	127.2 million (UN 2009)	109.6 million (UN 2009)	61.6 million (UN 2009)
Capital City	Beijing	Berlin	Tokyo	Mexico City	London
Life Expectancy	71 years (men) 75 years (women) (UN)	77 years (men) 82 years (women)	79 years (men) 86 (women)	74 years (men) 79 years (women)	77 years (men) 82 years (women)
Currency	Renminbi (Yuan) (1 = 10 jiao = 100 fen)	Euro (1 = 100 cents)	Yen	Peso (1 = 100 centavos)	Pound Sterling (1 = 100 pence)
GNI Per Capita	US$2,940 (World Bank, 2008)	US$42,440 (World Bank, 2008)	US$38,210 (World Bank 2008)	US$9,980 (World Bank 2008)	US$45,390 (World Bank)

The discussion related to each country's accounting system is organized into four parts: (1) background, (2) accounting profession, (3) accounting regulation, and (4) accounting principles and practices. We discuss the countries in alphabetical order.

PEOPLE'S REPUBLIC OF CHINA (PRC)

Background

The ultimate legislative authority in China rests with the National People's Congress, the highest organ of state power. It is elected for a term of five years and has the power to amend the constitution; make laws; select the president, vice president, and other leading officials of the state; approve the national economic plan, the state budget, and the final state accounts; and decide on questions of war and peace. The State Council is the highest organ of the state administration. It is composed of the premier, the vice premiers, the state councillors, heads of ministries and commissions, the auditor general, and the secretary-general.

With the formation of the People's Republic of China (PRC) in 1949, the government adopted a policy of establishing a single public ownership economy with centralized management of businesses and control of all economic resources. By 1956, all private companies had been transformed into state or collective ownership. However, these state-owned enterprises (SOEs) eventually proved to be economic failures. For example, during 1995–1997, more than half of them were in the red, and the losses in 1995 alone were close to 100 billion renminbi (US$12 billion).[1] Restructuring the loss-making SOEs was a major part of the subsequent economic reforms, which aimed at transforming the centrally planned economy into a socialist market economy, that is, a market economy based on socialist principles. Under the reform agenda, private enterprises, cooperatives, and joint ventures coexist and compete with state-run entities. The radical economic changes implemented over the last decade have made China one of the fastest-growing and largest economies, with annual economic growth rates among the highest in the world. In terms of gross domestic product (GDP), China ranks fourth behind the United States, the European Union (combined), and Japan.

To carry out its reform program, China needed capital and advanced technology. This led to an open-door policy of attracting foreign direct investment (FDI), which emphasized the importance of developing a capital market. With nearly 500,000 FDI enterprises, China is now the world's number one recipient of foreign direct investment. Today there are about half a million foreign investment entities in China, with parent entities in more than 170 countries. Foreign direct investment started to move into China in 1979, when the Equity Joint Venture Law was issued. In 2004, China received $60.6 billion worth of FDI, accounting for more than one-third of total FDI inflows in developing countries and about 15 percent of FDI inflows worldwide. The FDI inflows into China are mainly through large-scale transnational corporations, in high-tech areas and capital intensive projects, such as petroleum, automobile, and large-scale integrated circuits, and tertiary sector including securities, banking, telecommunications, transportation, and tourism.[2]

---

[1] C. J. Lee, "Financial Restructuring of State Owned Enterprises in China: the Case of Shanghai Sunve Pharmaceutical Corporation," *Accounting, Organizations and Society* 26 (2001), p. 673.

[2] T. Xiaowen, *Managing International Business in China* (Cambridge: Cambridge University Press, 2007), p.7.

Chinese companies were encouraged to raise funds on international capital markets as well as on the domestic one by issuing shares and bonds. The government took steps to develop its domestic capital market. The history of the capital market in China is short, and the market itself is relatively small. Shanghai's municipal government approved the first securities regulation in China in 1984. Share dealings did not become popular until the beginning of the next decade, when the Shanghai Stock Exchange (SHSE) was reactivated in December 1990 and a second stock exchange, the Shenzhen Stock Exchange (SZSE), was established in April 1991.[3] The capital market in China is controlled by the government. In July 1992, the Chinese Security Regulatory Commission (CSRC) was set up as China's equivalent of the U.S. Securities and Exchange Commission to monitor and regulate the stock market. This provided an encouragement for investors to engage in capital market activities. The number of companies listed on the two stock exchanges increased from 50 in 1992 to 1,831 at the end of April 2010. By the end of April 2010, according to the World Federation of Exchange, the Shanghai stock exchange had emerged as the sixth largest exchange in the world, with a market capitalization of US$2,704,778 million (market capitalization of Shenzhen stock exchange is US$868,374 million; NYSE Euronext US$11,839,793 million; Tokyo stock exchange US$3,306,082 million; NASDAQ OMX US$3,239,492 million; London stock exchange US$2,796,444 million; and Hong Kong stock exchange US42,305,143 million). The capital market in China has now become one of the largest such markets in Asia, second only to that in Tokyo. It was originally designed to offer opportunities for state-owned enterprises to raise capital, and even today nearly 90 percent of the companies listed on the two stock exchanges are still state-owned. Chinese companies also trade on exchanges outside China (about 100 companies), including the New York Stock Exchange (NYSE) (about 20 companies).

Recently, the government announced its plans to allow foreign companies to list in China, which reflects the government's desire to open up the country's financial sector and transform Shanghai into an international financial center. Further, the Minister of Finance and the CSRC have jointly issued an announcement that CPA firms in mainland China will be allowed to audit companies listed on the Hong Kong Stock Exchange. By the end of 2009, there were 54 accounting firms in China licensed to audit listed company financial statements.

Long-term investment in China's highly speculative stock market is still an exception to the rule. The turnover rates of China's two stock exchanges in 2000, for example, were more than 450 percent per annum.[4] Stock holdings typically range from days to a few months. Investors basically strive for short-term stock price gains, which are not necessarily based on fundamental company data. The validity and reliability of financial disclosure are therefore of limited importance to investors.

Companies in China issue four categories of shares:

1. "A" shares, which can be owned only by Chinese citizens, and are traded on the two stock exchanges.
2. "B" shares (introduced in 1992), which can be owned by foreigners.

---

[3] I. Haw, D. Qi, and W. Wu, "The Nature of Information in Accruals and Cash Flows in an Emerging Capital Market: The Case of China," *International Journal of Accounting* 36 (2001), pp. 391–406.

[4] China Securities Regulatory Commission, *China Securities and Futures Statistical Yearbook* (Beijing: CSRC, 2002), p. 27.

3. "C" shares, which are nontradable and held mainly by the government and other SOEs.
4. "H" shares, which can be owned only by foreigners and are traded in Hong Kong.

The market capitalization of A shares on the two stock exchanges accounts for more than 90 percent of the total market capitalization. B shares are for foreign individuals, institutional investors, and Chinese nationals able to trade in foreign currency. At the end of 1999, only about 5 percent of B shareholders were institutional investors.[5] As of late 2001, only 112 out of China's 1,160 listed firms issued B shares; approximately 50 were listed in Hong Kong, and another 20 were listed in New York.[6] Companies listed on the local capital market have a distinctive capital structure in which a large portion is made up of C shares, which cannot be traded publicly.

The categories of shares issued by Chinese companies are very different from those in the United States or Europe and they have different influences on the firm. Further, the dynamics in the Chinese boardrooms are quite different from those of Western companies. For example, chairs are full-time executives and they wield significant power. Senior managers are most likely to be former government bureaucrats and so they may have a different mind-set than top executives in U.S. firms.

With the introduction of the Qualified Foreign Institutional Investor (QFII) scheme in 2002, which was designed to allow "qualified" foreign institutional investors to purchase a limited amount of securities using Chinese currency including the A shares of any Chinese companies listed on the share market, foreign companies can now purchase the shares of Chinese companies listed on the stock market. For example, in October 2003, Kodak succeeded in purchasing 20 percent of the shares of Lucky Films, a local company listed on the Shanghai Stock Exchange. By September 2006, 40 foreign financial institutions had been granted QFII status, including, Morgan Stanley, Goldman Sachs, HSBC, Deutsche Bank, JP Morgan, Chase Bank, and Merrill Lynch International.

Accounting Profession

Accounting has a long history and a close association with the development of Chinese culture. Its roots can be found in the teachings of the philosopher and educator Confucius, which highlight the imperative to keep history and view accounting records as part of that history. The word *accounting* is noted as far back as the Hsiu Dynasty, around 2200 BC, when the stewardship function of accounting was emphasized. Later, in the Xia Dynasty (2000–1500 BC), the concept of measuring wealth and accomplishment was mentioned. In China, through thousands of years under a feudal social structure, people respected court and scholarly officials and looked down upon merchants. Accounting for business was viewed as being a nonskilled profession. More recently, the master–apprentice system was used to train accountants up until the 1900s. The first professional accounting legislation was enacted by the Northern Warloads government in 1918. Also, in the early 1900s, university study in accounting became an accepted way to understand and advance the principles and practice of accounting. The first local professional

[5] China Securities Regulatory Commission, *China Securities and Futures Statistical Yearbook* (Beijing: CSRC, 2000).

[6] CSRC, *Yearbook*, 2002.

body, the Chinese Chartered Accountants' Society of Shanghai, was established in 1925. By 1947, there were 2,619 certified accountants in China. Since 1949, Chinese scholars returning home after completing their accounting studies abroad, mainly in the Soviet Union, pioneered the development of a body of new knowledge in China, which resulted in existing practices.[7] After the revolution, accountants became totally subject to bureaucracy.

However, until the 1980s, those who carried out accounting work were not held in high regard in Chinese society compared with their Western counterparts. This was partly due to the traditional Chinese culture of "respecting the peasants and despising the merchants."[8] Consequently, accounting education has never been well developed in China and was particularly disrupted during the Cultural Revolution (beginning in the mid-1960s). Graham explains some aspects of the accounting environment in China as follows:

> Accounting became focused on reporting compliance with State economic plans, using a specified structure of accounts and following a sources and uses of funds concept. But it is commonly agreed the period of the Cultural Revolution (1966–1976) marks a dark period for the profession, as accounting was overly simplified with the objective of making accounting accessible and understandable to the "masses." University professors were ousted and occasionally brutalized, and accounting theory all but abandoned. . . . The consequence of this simplification on top of an already crude Soviet-based system was the loss of a generation or so of true accounting thought, and the absence of any need to reflect the nature of modern transactions or business concepts in the accounting system.[9]

The economic reform and the open-door policy introduced in the 1980s brought about a large number of Sino–foreign joint ventures in China. This resulted in the reemergence of a private auditing profession, supported by the Accounting Law issued in 1985 and the CPA Regulations in 1986. The CPA Regulations, promulgated by the State Council, prescribed the scope of practice for certified public accountants (CPAs) and some working and ethical rules. These developments led to the formation of the Chinese Institute of Certified Public Accountants (CICPA) in 1988, the first professional accounting body in China since the establishment of the PRC in 1949.

Unlike in the United States, accounting and auditing in China took different paths in their development processes. For many years, auditing firms mainly audited domestic companies, whereas accounting firms focused on companies using foreign investments. Accounting firms were sponsored by the Ministry of Finance (MoF), and auditing firms were under the State Administration of Audit (SAA), a department within the State Council responsible for government audits. In 1991, the SAA, in competition with the CICPA, issued its "Tentative Rules on Certified Public Auditors" to regulate auditors employed in audit firms. In 1992, the Chinese Association of Certified Practicing Auditors (CACPA) was formed under the auspices of the SAA.[10]

---

[7] L. E. Graham and C. Li, "Cultural and Economic Influences on Current Accounting Standards in the People's Republic of China," *International Journal of Accounting* 32, no. 3 (1997), pp. 247–78.

[8] Y. Chen, P. Jubb, and A. Tran, "Problems of Accounting Reform in the People's Republic of China," *International Journal of Accounting* 32, no. 2 (1997), pp. 139–53.

[9] L. E. Graham, "Setting a Research Agenda for Auditing Issues in the People's Republic of China," *International Journal of Accounting* 31, no. 1 (1996), p. 22.

[10] J. Z. Xiao, Y. Zhang, and Z. Xie, "The Making of Independent Auditing Standards in China," *Accounting Horizons* 14, no. 1 (2000), pp. 69–89.

The competition between accountants and auditors with their own rules issued by different government departments was confusing, particularly to international accounting firms. Consequently, steps were taken to merge the CICPA and CACPA. In 1993, the CPA Regulations were upgraded to become the CPA Law.[11] As a result, the MoF was given the authority to regulate both the accounting and the auditing firms. The CICPA became a member of the IASC (and IFAC) in 1997. The merger between the CICPA and the CACPA was completed in 1998.

By way of comparison, there are some clear differences between the evolution of the accounting profession in China and in other countries such as the United Kingdom. For example, in the United Kingdom, auditors enjoyed a good legislative and judicial environment during the early stages of development, whereas a market-oriented legal and judicial infrastructure is still emerging in China. Further, UK auditors were able to establish and maintain high quality because they had the support of their professional accounting bodies, which emphasized professional education, training, and examinations. By contrast, these support mechanisms are still lacking in China.[12] Finally, unlike in the United Kingdom, accounting and auditing firms in China have been treated separately. This is evident from the coexistence of the CICPA and the CACPA, with their admission requirements governed by the respective sponsoring agencies (i.e., the MoF and the SAA). By the end of 1997, there were 62,460 practicing CPAs and 6,900 accounting and auditing firms in China.[13]

The economic reform program, with its open-door policy, has stimulated the growth of accounting and related activities in China in many ways. Prior to reforms, the accounting system was no more than a way to provide information to the government. The economic reforms rapidly changed, among other things, the ownership structure of organizations.[14] The joint stock company was recognized by the state as the desired organizational structure to reform the SOEs. This created new demands for financial information from investors and other interested parties. The establishment of the two stock exchanges aiming to develop capital market activities led to major changes in China's accounting system. For example, companies that issue B shares are now required to restate their earnings according to International Financial Reporting Standards, and to provide two annual reports—one prepared by an international auditing firm, and one certified by a local accounting firm.

Many aspects of the reform program rely on accounting and auditing services to assist the market to work in an orderly manner. Various government regulations on the implementation of economic reform measures require the involvement of independent auditors. The laws on Sino–foreign joint ventures require the audit of annual statements and income tax returns and the verification of capital contributions by registered Chinese CPAs. These additional demands for accounting services created new opportunities for international accounting firms to enter the Chinese market. In the past, because only certified public accountants (CPAs) licensed by the Chinese authorities would be allowed to establish partnerships or

---

[11] In China, laws have a higher legal status than regulations, as laws are stipulated by the National Peoples' Congress, whereas regulations are promulgated by the State Council (ibid.).

[12] Xiao, Zhang, and Xie, "The Making. . . ."

[13] Y. Tang, "Bumpy Road Leading to Internationalization: A Review of Accounting Development in China," *Accounting Horizons* 14, no. 1 (2000), pp. 93–102.

[14] Z. Xiao and A. Pan, "Developing Accounting Standards on the Basis of a Conceptual Framework by the Chinese Government," *International Journal of Accounting* 32, no. 3 (1997), pp. 279–99.

limited liability accounting firms in China, to be able to operate in China, foreign accounting firms needed to affiliate with local firms.

Recently, Beijing has officially announced its plan to allow foreign companies to list in China. This reflects the government's ambitions to open up the country's financial sector and transform Shanghai into an international financial center. Further, in the process of globalization, it is necessary for investors and accountants over the world to both celebrate common ground achieved and understand the differences deeply rooted.

By providing services to foreign investors, the international accounting firms have assisted in the implementation of the open-door policy. They also have assisted in the development of the Chinese capital market by, for example, undertaking financial audits of Chinese companies that offer shares to overseas investors and that wish to obtain a foreign stock exchange listing. In addition, the international firms have been involved in training Chinese auditors and setting auditing standards. More than 200 of the world's top 500 companies have invested in China. All of the leading international accounting firms, following their clients, have moved into China by opening representative offices.

The Practice of "Hooking Up"

The practice of "hooking up" refers to an affiliate relationship between an accounting/auditing firm and its sponsoring organization, normally a government body.[15] The hooking-up relationship is rooted in the circumstances in which these professional accounting firms were originally established. At the beginning of the reform process the Chinese government required all newly established professional accounting firms to affiliate themselves with a government agency or a government-run institute. Although the government later encouraged these firms to become independent, it was difficult for them to do so because of the historical connections. As a result, most domestic professional accounting firms continued to have some government connection and truly independent private accounting firms are rarely seen in China. Further, some of the clients of these organizations are themselves directly or indirectly related to the "hooked" organization because of complex ownership and control arrangements.

Guanxi

Guanxi refers to connections or tight, close-knit networks. It can be considered an important feature of Chinese business culture. With *guanxi*, it is possible to accomplish almost anything, but, without it, life is likely to be a series of long lines and tightly closed doors, and a maze of administrative and bureaucratic hassles.[16] Although it is common practice in China, it is likely to create an ethical dilemma for foreign investors because if they do not practice *guanxi* they are unlikely to succeed in China, but if they do practice *guanxi* they may be doing something ethically wrong.

The prevalence of *guanxi* may be contributing to the large-scale corruption in China. Under its influence, *guanxi*-related considerations often prevail over ethics related considerations in accounting and auditing practice. Accountants and

---

[15] X. Dai, A.H. Lav and, J. Yang, "Hooking-up: A Unique Feature of China's Public Accounting Firms," *Managerial Finance* 26, no. 5 (2000), pp. 21–30.

[16] S. D. Seligman, "*Guanxi:* Grease for the Wheels of China," *China Business Review* 26, no.5 (1999), pp.34–38.

financial managers often have to use guanxi to do business with business partners or government officials in a way that is in violation of their professional ethics.[17]

This shows the importance of understanding the environment in which accounting is practiced in a country. In China, civil litigation is very rare and thus the CSRC is the prime discipliner of firms and their managements. Further, the relatively young Chinese auditing profession provides insufficient support for accounting standards, because auditors lack both professional training and independence.[18] Until recently, accounting education in China has been based on "Uniform Accounting Systems" and it lacked a conceptual underpinning and an international outlook. Furthermore, as a result of the absence of sophisticated users and providers of accounting information, Chinese auditors have enjoyed an almost litigation free environment.

China is said to have a set of collectivism-oriented societal values and a relatively low degree of professionalism.[19] Independence, belief in individual decisions, and respect for individual endeavour are not emphasized. People do not take responsibility for something that has not been approved by systems and rules. Collectivism thus supports devising uniform accounting systems and making accounting policy at the national level. This mentality is widely reflected in accounting and auditing practices in China.

Accounting professionalization in China over the past 60 years from the formation of Peoples' Republic of China in 1949, particularly in recent years, has been dramatic. The public practice of accountants was suspended immediately after the communist government came into power in 1949. The accounting system in the country was reformed following the Soviet Union model. As stated earlier, accountants became totally subject to bureaucracy. China revived the public practice of accountants in 1980. Since then, there has been rapid growth in the professionalization of accounting. For example, the CICPA was established in 1988. In 1991, the first national CPA qualification examination was held. The Law on Certified Public Accountants was enacted in 1993, raising the legal status of certified public accountants. However, there are many issues associated with the process of professionalization, and a lack of autonomy might be regarded as the most critical hurdle in terms of professionalization in China. The CICPA is under the direct control of the Ministry of Finance, which has the authority to appoint the leadership. In response to numerous accounting scandals, the CICPA has set up the accounting ethics code with "independence, integrity, and objectivity" at the core. However, the spirit of "professional autonomy" is not necessarily encouraged by the existing institutional structure.

In October 2007, the ICAEW and CICPA set up a joint project to facilitate and promote cooperation between the accounting professions in both countries. As a result, preparers and users of financial statements in China benefited from the ICAEW certificate in IFRS. Developed by experts and focused on an understanding of all International Standards, the Chinese edition of learning materials aims to help China to strengthen its commitment in applying rigorous accounting and

---

[17] M. Islamand and M. Gowing, "Some Empirical Evidence of Chinese Accounting System and Business Management Practices from an Ethical Perspective," *Journal of Business Ethics* 42, no.4 (2003), p. 358.

[18] B. Xiang, "Institutional Factors Influencing China's Accounting Reforms and Standards," *Accounting Horizons* 12, no. 2 (1998).

[19] L. M. Chow, G. K. Chua, and, S. J. Gray, "Accounting Reforms in China: Cultural Constraints on Implementation and Development," *Accounting and Business Research* 26, no.1 (1995).

auditing standards. This is likely to speed up the process of international convergence of accounting standards.

China's Ministry of Finance has issued Draft Interpretation 3 for Chinese new accounting standards, which are consistent with IFRS, to ensure their appropriate application. According to the *Chinese Certified Public Accountant*, the official journal of the CICPA, China had more than 7,200 accounting firms by the end of 2008. This number is 36 times more than in 1988, the year the CICPA came into being. By December 2008, China had registered more than 83,000 CPAs (population 1.34 billion). The Minister of Finance (MoF) and the China Securities Regulatory Commission (CSRC) have jointly issued an announcement that CPA firms in Mainland China will be allowed to audit H-share companies (i.e., those listed on the Hong Kong Stock Exchange) after January 2010. MoF also provided guidance at the end of 2009 on further improving accounting practice and financial reporting quality for 2010, including additional guidance on first-time adoption, appropriate use of professional judgment, elimination of the difference in A-share and H-share listed firms, and adoption of "other comprehensive income."

Accounting Regulation

The government continues to act as the accounting regulator in order to retain political control. It issues IFRS-based accounting standards mainly to meet external pressures but retains a UAS-based approach in parallel as a means of detailed regulatory control. The UAS has the benefit of familiarity, both for the regulator and for those subject to regulation. Direct government involvement in accounting regulation in China is a political tradition that originated in the era of central planning.

In Anglo-American countries, for example, setting authoritative accounting standards is the responsibility of accounting societies or independent bodies created for that purpose, whereas in China, it is the responsibility of the Ministry of Finance, rather than the Accounting Society of China (ASC) or the CICPA or any independent body.

In recent years, accounting regulation in China has been influenced mainly by China's desire to harmonize domestic accounting practices (the various uniform accounting systems used in different industries produced inconsistent practices across industries), harmonize Chinese accounting with IFRS, and meet the requirements of economic reforms. As new forms of business (such as Sino–foreign joint ventures and joint-stock companies) emerged, they created a need for international accounting harmonization. This prompted the Ministry of Finance to issue pronouncements to achieve it. These pronouncements include the following:

1. The *Accounting Systems for Sino–Foreign Joint Ventures* (1985).
2. *Accounting Systems for Companies Experimenting with a Shareholding System and the Accounting Standard for Business Enterprises* (ASBE) (1992) (the ASBE is similar to conceptual framework).
3. *The Accounting Regulations for Selected Joint Stock Limited Companies,* issued in 1991, and revised in 1998.
4. *Accounting Law* (1999).
5. *The Regulations on Financial Reporting of Enterprises* (2000).
6. *The Accounting Systems for Business Enterprises* (2001).

As these laws and regulations draw heavily on regulations and practices in Western countries, the current accounting concepts and practices in China mirror, to an extent, those in the mature market economies. Following are examples: the Accounting Law 1999 stressed the importance of "true and complete" accounting information; the Regulations on Financial Reporting of Enterprises 2000 redefined the elements of financial statements in line with the conceptual framework of the IASC and stipulated responsibilities and liabilities for parties involved in accounting, auditing, and reporting.

However, the Chinese government has retained a uniform accounting system in the Enterprise Accounting System issued in 2000 to accommodate the special circumstances of a transforming government, strong state ownership, a weak accounting profession, a weak equity market, and inertial effect of accounting tradition and cultural factors.

The movement toward private ownership has required a revision of China's accounting and disclosure standards. Several major Chinese financial scandals in the early 1990s highlighted the problems associated with the accounting system, which was modeled on the system that existed in the former Soviet Union. One of the most notorious was the Great Wall fund-raising scandal, which implicated the Zhongchen accounting firm.

> In this case, the Great Wall Electrical Engineering Science and Technology Co. illegally raised one billion Yuan in a few months between 1992 and 1993 by issuing very high coupon securities to over 100,000 private investors in 17 large cities in China. The money raised was partly embezzled and partly used to establish over 20 subsidiaries and more than 100 branches all over the country. A branch of the Zhongchen accounting firm played a key role in the fraud: its three CPAs provided an unfounded certificate confirming 0.3 billion Yuan capital after just one day's work with only 25 pages of working papers. . . . Five CPAs from the accounting firm were disqualified and the whole firm was dismantled. The president of the client company received the death penalty, a deputy minister was jailed for bribery, and the president of the People's Bank of China was terminated.[20]

The MoF establishes accounting standards and regulations, while the CSRC issues disclosure requirements for listed companies. The MoF began setting accounting standards in 1988, the same year in which the CICPA was established. The MoF adopted a policy of following international accounting practice in setting Chinese standards. To this end, in 1992, it developed the *Basic Standard of Accounting for Business Enterprises* (similar to a conceptual framework). In 1993, it appointed an international accounting firm (with technical assistance funds from the World Bank) as consultants to the MoF's standard-setting program and established two advisory committees, one consisting of international accounting experts and the other consisting of Chinese accounting experts.[21] The promulgation of a conceptual framework by the MoF in 1992 was a landmark event in the recent accounting reforms in China. It was a clear signal that Anglo-American accounting principles were to replace the rigid Soviet accounting model practiced in China since 1949.

However, extensive false reporting and earnings management by companies have discredited accounting information and hampered the development of the capital market. As a result, the Accounting Law amendment in 1999 stressed the importance of 'true and complete' accounting information. In 2000, the State Council issued an Enterprise Financial Reporting Regulation, redefining the elements

---

[20] Xiao, Zhang, and Xie, "The Making. . . ."
[21] Y. Tang, "Bumpy Road. . . ."

of financial statements in line with the conceptual framework of the IASC and stipulating responsibilities and liabilities for parties involved in accounting, auditing and reporting.[22]

The CPA Law requires auditors to audit Chinese enterprises' financial statements; verify the enterprises' capital contribution; engage in the audit work of the enterprises' merger, demerger, and liquidation; and provide professional services specified by the law and regulations.[23] Accountants who intentionally provide false certificates may be sentenced to up to five years of fixed-term imprisonment or criminal detention and a fine. The law requires a CPA to refuse to issue any relevant report where (1) the client suggests, overtly or covertly, that a false or misleading report or statement be issued; (2) the client intentionally fails to provide relevant accounting material and documents; and (3) the report to be issued by a certified public accountant cannot correctly represent all material information due to the client's unreasonable behavior.

The China Accounting Standards Committee (CASC)—comprising government experts, academics, and members of accounting firms—was established within the MoF in 1998. China has not adopted IFRS, but it has stated that it will develop its own standards based on IFRS. However, different types of companies are required to comply with different sets of standards; for example, companies with B shares must follow IFRS, companies with A shares must follow Chinese GAAP, and companies with H shares must follow either Hong Kong GAAP or IFRS.

In June 2002, the CICPA issued new guidelines on professional ethics as a supplement to the *General Standard on Professional Ethics.* The guidelines stress the importance of a CPA's independence and also contain extensive discussion on change in a professional appointment, service fees charged to clients, practice promotion, and confidentiality.[24]

The CSRC requires companies listed on the two stock exchanges to post their annual reports on the exchanges' respective Web sites.[25] The CSRC and the two stock exchanges have also adopted new corporate governance rules that require listed companies to disclose detailed related-party transaction information relating to intangible assets.[26] However, both internal and external corporate governance mechanisms are weak in China. For example, externally the market for corporate control and managerial labor market are seriously underdeveloped, while internally it was not until 2002 that independent directors and audit committees appeared in listed companies.[27] The CSRC has recently moved to require more outside directors on the boards of companies as companies with a high proportion of nonexecutive directors on the board are less likely to engage in fraud.

In November 2003 (effective January 2004), the CSRC and the MoF issued a joint document requiring companies to rotate their auditors every five years and to take a two-year break before auditing the same client again. China is following

---

[22] B. Xiang, "Institutional Factors Influencing China's Accounting Reforms and Standards," *Accounting Horizons* 12, no. 2 (1998).

[23] K. Z. Lin, and K. H. Chan, "Auditing Standards in China: A Comparative Analysis with Relevant International Standards and Guidelines," *International Journal of Accounting* 35, no. 4 (2000), pp. 559–77.

[24] For more details, see IAS PLUS, July 2002, at www.iasplus.com.

[25] Shanghai Stock Exchange Web site (www.sse.com.cn) and the Shenzhen Stock Exchange Web site (www.cninfo.com.cn).

[26] See IAS PLUS, January 2001, at www.iasplus.com.

[27] G. Chen, M. Firth, D. N Gao, and O. M. Rui, "Ownership Structure, Corporate Governance and Fraud: Evidence from China," *Journal of Corporate Finance* 12 (2006), pp. 424–48.

the international trend toward tighter regulation of auditing practices, which has gained momentum following the collapse of Arthur Andersen in the aftermath of the Enron scandal. The CSRC seems to follow the recommendations of the Sarbanes-Oxley Act in the United States.

The pressure is on for China to harmonize its accounting standards and practices with international standards. As a result, international harmonization has been recognized as a priority for the development of the profession. China's desire to join the World Trade Organization (WTO) was a major incentive for the push toward international harmonization. WTO membership, granted in 2002, was conditional upon, among other things, the adoption of internationally acceptable accounting and financial reporting practices, and the opening up of the accounting and auditing markets.

The problem of corruption and the involvement of accountants in corruption became so alarming that in 2004, the Chinese government launched a nationwide "auditing storm" campaign to check on accounting misconduct in government agencies, institutions, and enterprises. According to the report that was submitted to the National Congress, serious fraud and embezzlement of public funds were found in many government agencies and government-funded projects and often implicated accounting malpractice.

Accounting Principles and Practices

In the prereform period the aim of the accounting system in China was to help the government plan its economic activities and manage the various government funds, and it was therefore called the "fund accounting system." All accounting bodies and personnel were closely linked with the government at the central or the local level, and there were no independent accountants and independent accounting institutions. Furthermore, China's accounting system was completely closed to the outside world. The reliance on UASs is reinforced because many Chinese accountants and auditors lacked professional education and training.[28] Further, it was also supported by the Chinese culture.

With the economic reform and opening up, Chinese enterprises began to operate independently, foreign companies moved in, and a stock market emerged. All these developments required fundamental changes in the accounting system. The reform of the system gained momentum in the 1990s, following the establishment of the two stock exchanges. However, although the capital market has played an important role in accounting standard setting in China, its continued structural weaknesses and significant imperfections have seriously restricted the supply of, and demand for, decision-useful accounting information and IAS-type accounting standards.

State ownership is present in more than 90 percent of listed companies,[29] and the government remains an important influence on corporate governance by way of personnel control and resource allocation. Consequently the government is regarded as the main user of accounting information.

China is an economy in transition, and its market-based systems are still at an early stage of development. Traditionally in China, there has been a close link between taxation and accounting, and the calculation of taxable income has been a major purpose of accounting. Further, under China's communist ideological

---

[28] Xiang, "International Factors. . . ."

[29] Q. Sun, W. Tong, and J. Tong, "How Does Government Ownership Affect Firm Performance? Evidence from China's Privatization Experience," *Journal of Business Finance and Accounting* 29, no.1/2 (2002).

influences, accounting conservatism has long been criticized as a tool used to manipulate accounting numbers and maximize the profits of capitalists in exploiting workers. Accounting conservatism is the principle that stipulates that, in a situation where there are acceptable accounting alternatives, the one that produces lower current amounts for net income and net assets ought to be chosen. This accounting convention has virtually been prohibited in China since 1949.[30] A lack of conservatism in Chinese accounting standards and practices continues to be a major difference between Chinese GAAP and IFRS.

The financial statements published by Chinese companies typically include a balance sheet, an income statement, a cash flow statement, notes to financial statements, and other supporting schedules. One of the major problems associated with accounting practices adopted by enterprises in China is the lack of coherent interpretation of the relevant requirements. Regulations are subject to different interpretations and applications on the part of government agencies in different locations. As a result, the formal harmonization of accounting and auditing standards that has occurred within China has not brought about a harmonization of accounting practices. China, being a transitional economy, is only beginning to develop the infrastructure required to support credible financial reporting. As China intensifies its integration into the global economy and fulfills its obligations agreed on in the WTO accession treaty, for example, to open up its market to foreign auditors,[31] market forces in the accounting and auditing sector undoubtedly will become more active, which should strengthen the effectiveness of private safeguard mechanisms.

The conceptual framework, first issued in 1992, has since been superseded by 16 Chinese Accounting Standards (see Exhibit 6.2) and other regulations, such as the Accounting System for Business Enterprises (ASBE) issued in 2001. The ASBE aims, among other things, to enhance comparability of financial information, separate accounting and taxation treatments, and ensure harmonization with internationally accepted accounting practices.

The ASBE defines fundamental principles (going concern, accounting period, substance over form, consistency, timeliness, understandability, accrual basis, matching, impairment recognition, prudence, materiality, and measurement currency vs. presentation currency) and financial statement elements (assets, liabilities, owners' equity, revenues, expenses, and profits), which are similar to those found in IFRS. It also specifies the contents of financial reports (which financial statements are to be presented annually, semiannually, quarterly, and monthly) minimum notes to the financial statements, and how soon after the end of the accounting period reports should be published.

The ASBE also includes

1. Classifications within the asset, liability, and equity elements, as well as recognition and measurement principles for a wide variety of assets and liabilities.
2. Revenue recognition principles for goods, services, royalties, and interest.
3. Expense recognition principles for bad debts, cost of goods sold, depreciation, major overheads, and impairment of assets.

---

[30] Lin and Chan, "Auditing Standards in China."

[31] Foreign firms that have obtained CPA licenses are permitted to affiliate with Chinese firms and enter into contractual agreements to provide accounting, auditing and bookkeeping services. (World Trade Organization, *Report of the Working Party on the Accession to China, Addendum, Schedule of Specific Commitment on Services,* October 1, 2001, available at www.wto.org/english/thewto_e/completeacc_e.htm.)

4. Accounting principles for nonmonetary transactions, assets contributed by investors, accounting for income taxes, foreign currency transactions, changes in accounting policies, changes in estimates, corrections of errors, post–balance sheet events, contingencies, and related-party transactions.

5. Principles for consolidated financial statements and accounting for investments in joint ventures.

In addition, it requires that expenses be classified as operating, administrative, or financing expenses and that profit be classified between operating profit, investment income, subsidy income, and several other nonoperating income categories. Finally, its requirement to include management discussion of financial condition is similar to requirements in the United States. Further, with economic reforms, a new auditing system has emerged under which the purpose of auditing has changed from ascertaining a company's tax liabilities to ascertaining the truthfulness and fairness of a company's financial statements. Currently most

EXHIBIT 6.2
Chinese Accounting Standards as at January 1, 2002

	Accounting Standard	Effective Date	Applicability
1	Disclosure of Related Party Relationships and Transactions	January 1, 1997	Listed enterprises
2	Cash Flow Statements (minor revision in 2001)	January 1, 2001	All enterprises
3	Events Occurring After the Balance Sheet Date	January 1, 1998	Listed enterprises
4	Debt Restructuring (revised significantly in 2001)	January 1, 2002	All enterprises
5	Revenue	January 1, 1999	Listed enterprises
6	Investments (minor revision in 2001)	January 1, 2001	Joint stock limited enterprises (prior to January 1, 2001, listed enterprises only)
7	Construction Contracts	January 1, 1999	Listed enterprises
8	Changes in Accounting Policies and Estimates and Corrections of Accounting Errors (minor revision in 2001)	January 1, 2001	All enterprises (prior to January 1, 2001 listed enterprises only)
9	Non-monetary Transactions (revised significantly in 2001)	January 1, 2001	All enterprises
10	Contingencies	July 1, 2000	All enterprises
11	Intangible Assets	January 1, 2001	Joint stock limited enterprises
12	Borrowing Costs	January 1, 2001	All enterprises
13	Leases	January 1, 2001	All enterprises
14	Interim Financial Reporting	January 1, 2002	Listed enterprises
15	Inventories	January 1, 2002	Joint stock limited enterprises
16	Fixed Assets	January 1, 2002	Joint stock limited enterprises

companies in China are subject to the annual audit carried out by certified public accounting firms registered in China.

Nearly half a million enterprises in China, including all listed companies, now follow one unified ASBE. The MoF required all 170,000 SOEs to adopt the ASBE in 2005. The ASBE and Chinese Accounting Standards together form the structure of financial reporting in modern China. Since 1978 China has introduced measures to reform its accounting system, which is now converging with standard accounting practices in mature market economies. Nevertheless, significant differences remain with respect to those practices and the accounting institutional environment between China and mature market economies, for example, and fair value is not recognized for accounting purposes.

Chinese accounting practices differ in some respects from those required under IFRS. In some areas covered by IFRS, there are no specific rules in China. In other areas, transactions are treated differently under the two sets of rules. For example, there are no specific rules in the areas of business combinations, including provisions in the context of acquisitions (IAS 22); impairment of assets, particularly as (except for investments) diminutions in value are not allowed (IAS 36); the definitions of operating and finance leases (IAS 17); employee benefits obligations (IAS 19); and accounting for an issuer's financial instruments (IAS 32). Further, there are no specific rules requiring disclosures of discontinuing operations (IAS 35), segment liabilities (IAS 14), or diluted earnings per share (IAS 33). The methods of treating certain transactions are different from those required under IFRS. In China, proposed dividends are accrued before being approved (IAS 10); preoperating expenses are deferred and amortized (IAS 38); a wider definition of extraordinary items is used (IAS 8); and in segment reporting, the line of business basis is always treated as primary (IAS 14). Each of these practices is inconsistent with IFRSs. Exhibit 6.3 presents some of the differences between IFRS and Chinese GAAP.

Several Chinese companies provide financial statements prepared in accordance with both Chinese (PRC) GAAP and IFRS. Exhibit 6.4 provides an excerpt from Sinopec Shanghai Petrochemical Company Ltd.'s 2009 annual report, in which the company (1) describes major differences between PRC GAAP and IFRS and (2) quantifies the effects of these differences on net income and stockholders' equity.

The unique features in the Chinese environment include the following:

- Civil litigation is very rare and thus the CSRC is the prime discipliner of firms and their managements.
- In the ownership structure of listed firms, blockholders are usually the state and quasi-state institutions such as SOEs. (These are very different from those in Anglo-American countries and they have different influences on the firm.)
- The dynamics in Chinese boardrooms are likely to be different from those of their counterparts in Anglo-American countries. For example, chairs are full-time executives and they wield significant power; and senior management typically started their careers as government bureaucrats.
- Auditing profession in China is relatively new and it has faced a steep learning curve.
- State ownership still has an important influence on the organization and development of accounting standards.
- Wholly foreign-owned large multinational corporations competing against weaker and smaller domestic firms are becoming a major concern.

- Chinese regulators view harmonization between Chinese GAAP and IFRS as a two-way process that should permit differences and local innovation.
- The capital market in China is controlled by government. It is characterized by weak equity outsiders, strong market speculation, weak form efficiency, extensive earnings management and deceptive reporting, and large-scale market manipulation.

In recent years, Chinese regulators have taken significant steps to reform Chinese accounting standards in line with IFRS. However, due to the unique features

EXHIBIT 6.3 **Differences between Chinese GAAP and IFRS**

Issue	IFRS	Chinese GAAP
Profit or loss on disposal of fixed assets	IAS 16: Included in operating profit or loss.	Presented as a nonoperating gain or loss.
Requirement to provide segment information	IAS 14: Listed companies only.	Listed companies and other enterprises applying the system.
Measurement of property, plant, and equipment	IAS 16: May use either fair value or historical cost.	Generally required to use historical cost.
Borrowing costs related to self-use assets that take a substantial time to complete	IAS 23: May either capitalize as part of the asset's cost or charge to expenses.	Must capitalize as part of the asset's cost.
Impairment of assets that do not generate cash flows individually	IAS 36: An asset is impaired when its book value exceeds its recoverable amount, which is the greater of net realizable value and the net present value of future net cash flows expected to arise from continued use of the asset.	Specific guidance is not provided.
Research and development costs	IAS 38: Expense all research costs. Capitalize development costs if certain criteria are met.	Expense all research and development costs (except patent registration and legal costs, which are capitalized).
Preoperating expenses	IAS 38: Charged to expenses when incurred.	Deferred until the entity begins operations, then charged to expenses.
Land use rights	IAS 38: Accounted for as an operating lease. Cost of land use rights is treated as prepaid lease payments.	Accounted for as a purchased intangible asset until the construction or development commences, then accounted for as fixed assets under construction or property development costs until the construction or development is complete; on completion, total costs are transferred to property held for use.
Amortization of intangible assets	IAS 38: Amortize over the estimated useful life, which is presumed to be 20 years or less.	Amortized over the shorter of the estimated useful life and the contractual or legal life; if no contractual or legal life, amortize over the estimated useful life, but not more than 10 years.
Revaluation of intangible assets	IAS 38: Permitted only if the intangible asset trades in an active market.	Prohibited.

EXHIBIT 6.4

SINOPEC SHANGHAI PETROCHEMICAL COMPANY LTD.
Excerpts from Annual Report
2009

1. FINANCIAL DATA AND INDICATORS PREPARED IN ACCORDANCE WITH CHINA ACCOUNTING STANDARDS FOR BUSINESS ENTERPRISES ("ASBE")

(1) Principal financial data

Items	For the years ended 31 December			
	2009 *RMB millions*	2008 *RMB millions*	Change %	2007 *RMB millions*
Operating income	1,345,052	1,444,291	(6.9)	1,200,997
Operating profit/(loss)	80,202	(28,766)	—	78,083
Profit before taxation	80,076	22,025	263.6	82,817
Net profit attributable to equity shareholders of the Company	61,290	28,445	115.5	55,896
Net profit attributable to equity shareholders of the Company before extraordinary gain and loss	61,258	29,307	109.0	56,438
Net cash flow from operating activities	158,796	74,268	113.8	123,629

Items	At 31 December			
	2009 *RMB millions*	2008 *RMB millions*	Change %	2007 *RMB millions*
Total assets	866,475	763,297	13.5	740,358
Shareholders' equity attributable to equity shareholders of the Company	377,182	329,300	14.5	308,509

(2) Principal financial indicators

Items	For the years ended 31 December			
	2009 *RMB*	2008 *RMB*	Change %	2007 *RMB*
Basic earnings per share	0.707	0.328	115.5	0.645
Diluted earnings per share	0.702	0.288	143.8	0.645
Basic earnings per share (before extraordinary gain and loss)	0.707	0.338	109.0	0.651
Fully diluted return on net assets (%)	16.25	8.64	7.61	18.12
Weighted average return on net assets (%)	17.25	8.86	8.39	19.37
Fully diluted return (before extraordinary gain and loss) on net assets (%)	16.24	8.90	7.34	18.29
Weighted average return (before extraordinary gain and loss) on net assets (%)	17.24	9.13	8.11	19.56
Net cash flow from operating activities per share	1.832	0.857	113.8	1.426

Items	At 31 December			
	2009 *RMB*	2008 *RMB*	Change %	2007 *RMB*
Net assets attributable to equity shareholders of the Company per share	4.350	3.798	14.5	3.558

(3) Extraordinary items and corresponding amounts

Items	For the year ended 31 December 2009 (Income)/expense RMB millions
Gain on disposal of non-current assets.	(211)
Donations	174
Gain on holding and disposal of various investments	(322)
Net (profit)/loss of subsidiaries generated from a business combination involving entities under common control before acquisition date	(62)
Other non-operating income and expenses, net.	190
Subtotal.	(231)
Tax effect.	42
Total.	**(189)**
Attributable to:	
Equity shareholders of the Company.	(32)
Minority interests	(157)

(4) Significant changes of items in the financial statements

The table below sets forth reasons for those changes where the fluctuation was more than 30% during the reporting period, or such changes which constituted 5% or more of total assets at the balance sheet date or more than 10% of profit before taxation:

Items	At 31 December		Increase/(decrease)		Reasons for change
	2009 RMB millions	2008 RMB millions	Amount RMB millions	Percentage (%)	
Bills receivable	2,110	3,660	(1,550)	(42.3)	Mainly due to enhanced collection of cash in respond to the changes in market condition
Accounts receivable	26,592	12,990	13,602	104.7	Mainly due to the increase in scale of operations and crude oil price compared with the end of last year
Other receivables	4,454	20,525	(16,071)	(78.3)	Please refer to Note 9 to the financial statements prepared in accordance with ASBE
Prepayments	3,614	7,610	(3,996)	(52.5)	Mainly due to the decrease in prepayments in connection with construction facilities and purchase deposits
Inventories.	141,611	95,979	45,632	47.5	Mainly due to the increase in scale of operations and crude oil price compared with the end of last year
Other current assets.	856	287	569	198.3	Mainly due to the increase in the available-for-sale financial assets
Intangible assets	22,862	16,348	6,514	39.8	Please refer to Note 15 to the financial statements prepared in accordance with ASBE
Fixed assets	465,182	411,939	53,243	12.9	Please refer to Note 13 to the financial statements prepared in accordance with ASBE
Other non-current assets . . .	1,792	1,013	779	76.9	Mainly due to the increase in the available-for-sale financial assets
Short term loans	34,900	74,415	(39,515)	(53.1)	Mainly due to the Company's adjustment of its debt structure and increase in financing from issuance of bonds
Accounts payable.	97,749	56,464	41,285	73.1	Mainly due to the increase in scale of operations and crude oil price which resulted in increase in accounts payable

Continued

EXHIBIT 6.4   (*Continued*)

Items	At 31 December 2009 RMB millions	2008 RMB millions	Increase/(decrease) Amount RMB millions	Percentage (%)	Reasons for change
Employee benefits payable	4,526	1,827	2,699	147.7	Mainly due to the accrual of staff annuity and housing subsidies
Taxes payable	16,489	6,816	9,673	141.9	Please refer to Note 25 to the financial statements prepared in accordance with ASBE
Short-term debentures payable	31,000	15,000	16,000	106.7	Please refer to Note 29 to the financial statements prepared in accordance with ASBE
Non-current liabilities due	6,641	19,511	(12,870)	(66.0)	Please refer to Note 27 to the financial statements prepared within one year in accordance with ASBE
Long-term loans.	52,065	64,937	(12,872)	(19.8)	Please refer to Note 28 to the financial statements prepared in accordance with ASBE
Debentures payable	93,763	62,207	31,556	50.7	Please refer to Note 29 to the financial statements prepared in accordance with ASBE
Other non-current liabilities . . .	2,192	1,403	789	56.2	Mainly due to the increase in deferred income
Operating income	1,345,052	1,444,291	(99,239)	(6.9)	Please refer to MD&A
Operating costs	1,035,815	1,321,030	(285,215)	(21.6)	Please refer to MD&A
Sales taxes and surcharges	132,884	57,214	75,670	132.3	Please refer to Note 35 to the financial statements prepared in accordance with ASBE
Impairment losses	7,453	16,869	(9,416)	(55.8)	Please refer to Note 38 to the financial statements prepared in accordance with ASBE
Loss/(gain) from changes	365	(4,198)	4,563	Not applicable	Please refer to Note 39 to the financial statements prepared in fair value in accordance with ASBE
Investment income.	3,589	1,452	2,137	147.2	Please refer to Note 40 to the financial statements prepared in accordance with ASBE
Non-operating income.	1,275	51,911	(50,636)	(97.5)	Please refer to Note 41 to the financial statements prepared in accordance with ASBE
Income tax expense/ (benefit).	16,076	(2,846)	18,922	Not applicable	Please refer to Note 43 to the financial statements prepared in accordance with ASBE
Minority interests.	2,710	(3,574)	6,284	Not applicable	Mainly due to the increase in net profit from controlling subsidiaries

2. FINANCIAL INFORMATION EXTRACTED FROM THE FINANCIAL STATEMENTS PREPARED IN ACCORDANCE WITH INTERNATIONAL FINANCIAL REPORTING STANDARDS ("IFRS")

Items	Unit: RMB millions For the years ended 31 December				
	2009	2008	2007	2006	2005
Turnover, other operating revenues and other income	1,345,052	1,495,148	1,205,860	1,061,588	824,005
Operating profit.	84,431	26,336	85,496	81,250	71,517
Profit before taxation.	80,568	22,116	82,847	79,073	68,090
Profit attributable to equity shareholders of the Company.	61,760	28,525	55,914	53,773	43,743
Basic earnings per share (RMB).	0.712	0.329	0.645	0.620	0.505
Diluted earnings per share (RMB).	0.708	0.289	0.645	0.620	0.505
Return on capital employed (%).	11.13	5.15	11.66	12.58	12.50
Return on net assets (%)	16.44	8.70	18.16	20.30	19.31
Net cash generated from operating activities per share (RMB).	1.754	0.767	1.368	1.060	0.903

Items	Unit: RMB millions At 31 December				
	2009	2008	2007	2006	2005
Non-current assets.	676,562	613,774	556,610	471,413	400,160
Net current liabilities	112,139	121,258	88,772	76,364	32,285
Non-current liabilities.	165,570	143,974	134,616	107,815	110,195
Non-controlling interests	23,192	20,653	25,325	22,323	31,174
Total equity attributable to equity shareholders of the Company.	375,661	327,889	307,897	264,911	226,506
Net assets per share (RMB).	4.333	3.782	3.551	3.055	2.612
Adjusted net assets per share (RMB).	4.254	3.690	3.471	2.982	2.552
Debt/equity ratio*(%).	27.96	27.94	28.10	27.53	31.34

* Debt/equity ratio = long-term loans/(total equity attributable to equity shareholders of the Company + long-term loans) × 100%

3. MAJOR DIFFERENCES BETWEEN THE AUDITED FINANCIAL STATEMENTS PREPARED UNDER ASBE AND IFRS

(1) Analysis of the effects of major differences between the net profit under ASBE and profit for the year under IFRS

	For the years ended 31 December	
	2009 RMB millions	2008 RMB millions
Net profit under ASBE	**64,000**	**24,871**
Adjustments:		
Revaluation of land use rights	30	30
Government grants	462	61
Tax effects of the above adjustments.	(8)	(6)
Profit for the year under IFRS	**64,484**	**24,956**

(2) Analysis of the effects of major differences between the shareholders' equity under ASBE and total equity under IFRS

	At 31 December	
	2009 RMB millions	2008 RMB millions
Shareholders' equity under ASBE	**400,585**	**350,166**
Adjustments:		
Revaluation of land use rights	(982)	(1,012)
Government grants	(1,042)	(912)
Tax effects of the above adjustments.	292	300
Total equity under IFRS	**398,853**	**348,542**

in the Chinese cultural, economic, and political contexts, Chinese regulators seem to view harmonization between Chinese GAAP and IFRS as a two-way process that should permit differences and local innovation.

The Chinese government, has been active in developing accounting standards in harmony with international accounting standards due to self motivation and external pressure, However, it has retained a uniform accounting system in the Enterprise Accounting System issued in 2000 to accommodate the special circumstances of a transforming government, strong state ownership, a weak accounting profession, a weak equity market, and inertial effect of accounting tradition and cultural factors.[32]

At the end of 2009, the Ministry of Finance provided guidance on how to further improve financial reporting quality, which included first-time adoption of IFRS, appropriate use of professional judgment, elimination of the difference between A-share and H-share listed firms, and adoption of "other comprehensive income".

GERMANY

Background

After the Second World War, Germany was divided into American, French, British, and Soviet zones of occupation. In 1949, the Federal Republic of Germany was created out of the western zones, and the communist-led German Democratic Republic was established in the Soviet zone. After reunification in October 1990, Germany became a federal republic composed of 16 *Länder* (states): 10 from the former West, 5 from the former East, and Berlin, the capital city. The constitution provides for a president, elected by a federal convention for a five-year term; the *Bundestag* (Lower House) of 667 members elected by direct universal suffrage for a four-year term of office; and the *Bundesrat* (Upper House), composed of 69 members appointed by the governments of the *Länder* in proportion to their populations, without a fixed term of office.

Unlike in the United States, traditionally the primary source of finance for German companies is bank loans, rather than equity raised through the capital market. In Germany, banks not only provide loans to companies but also control major proportions of their equity capital, either directly or as trustees for their customers. This determines to a large extent the purpose for financial reporting by companies. Since reunification, German accounting has been greatly affected by the increasing internationalization of the German economy and the growing integration of the world's capital markets. In recent years, an increasing number of German companies, such as DaimlerChrysler and Deutsche Telekom, have been raising capital on international markets, particularly the New York Stock Exchange.

The most common legal forms of business enterprise are the *Aktiengesellschaft* (AG), which is a publicly traded stock corporation, and the *Gesellschaft mit beschränkter Haftung* (GMBH), which is a limited liability company that is not publicly traded.

Historically, Germany has had a considerable influence on the accounting systems in many countries, especially Japan, Austria, Switzerland, and some Nordic countries such as Denmark and Sweden. These countries adapted the ideas and concepts developed in Germany to suit their conditions. This is reflected in the intellectual basis of accounting and auditing education and in the source of the various laws in those countries. For example, the Commercial Code in Japan was modeled on the German Commercial Code.

---

[32] J. Z. Xiao, P. Weetman, and M. Sun, "Political Influence and Coexistence of a Uniform Accounting System and Accounting Standards: Recent Developments in China," *Abacus* 40, no. 2 (2004), pp.193–218.

Accounting Profession

Auditing dominates the financial reporting related professional activities in Germany. The title for certified auditors, *Wirtschaftsprüfer* (WP) (economic or enterprise examiner), was created by the Companies Act of 1931. *The Institut der Wirtschaftsprüfer* (Institute of Auditors) is a private association of public auditors and public audit firms. It comprises approximately 10,800 public auditors and over 900 public audit firms, and represents about 85 percent of the profession. It provides for the education and continuing professional development. Stock corporations and other large companies must be audited by WPs. Stringent requirements to become a WP are found in the *Wirtschaftsprüferordnung* (Auditors Law). These generally include obtaining a university degree in business administration, economics, law, engineering, or agriculture; passing examinations covering accounting, auditing, business adminsitration, law, taxation, and general economics; and four years of practical experience, including two years in auditing. The German auditing profession is much smaller than its counterpart in the United States (about 11,000 WPs—population 82.2 million—vs. more than 250,000 CPAs—population 307.2 million).

The auditing profession is headed by the *Wirtschaftsprüferkammer* (WPK) (Chamber of Auditors), an independent organization responsible for the supervision of its members and for the representation of the profession to other parties. It is a state-supervised organization. All public accountants are mandatory members of the WPK. A second important organization is the Institute of Auditors, whose main task is to publish statements on accounting and auditing questions, which usually serve as generally accepted accounting and auditing standards.

There also is a second-tier body of certified accountants, *vereidigte Buchprüfer* (VB). The requirements to become a VB are less onerous than to become a WP. VBs are allowed to perform only voluntary audits and audits of medium-sized limited liability companies (GMBHs). A third type of professional accountant in Germany are the *Steuerberater* (tax advisers), who focus on offering tax services to their clients.

Accounting Regulation

Financial reporting in Germany is dominated by commercial law, tax law, and pronouncements issued by the profession. Traditionally, Germany has not used a system of independent institutional oversight.[33] The German Commercial Code contains most of the country's financial reporting principles, which include the general accounting and auditing rules applicable to all companies, together with a special section relating to stock corporations and limited liability companies. It also specifies sanctions for noncompliance, such as punitive measures, penalties, and fines to be imposed by the courts. Unlike in the United States, partnership accounting is regulated in Germany. The German Stock Exchange listing requirements have much less influence on financial reporting compared to those in the United States.

A stock corporation (AG) is required to prepare statutory nonconsolidated annual financial statements comprising a balance sheet, income statement, and the notes to the financial statements, along with a management report. These financial statements should (1) be prepared in accordance with the German principles of

[33] D. Ordelheide, "Germany," in *Accounting Regulation in Europe,* ed. S. McLeary (London: Macmillan, 1999), pp. 99–146.

proper accounting applicable to all commercial business and (2) provide a true and fair view of the net assets, financial position, and results of operations of the corporation. In addition, parent companies are required to prepare statutory consolidated annual financial statements and a group management report. A parent company may be exempted from this requirement if, for example, it is itself a subsidiary of another parent company. Further, the executive board of a stock corporation is required to file at the Commercial Registrar the nonconsolidated (and consolidated, if applicable) financial statements, the management report, the auditor's report and the proposed, and resolved appropriation of retained earnings and net income (including any dividend proposal or resolution). These documents are also published in the official federal gazette, the *Bundesanzeiger.*

In Germany, the predominance of the principle of prudence (conservatism) is clearly established in the law. Accordingly, profits must be recognized only when they have been realized, but losses should be recorded as soon as they appear possible. During the worldwide economic crisis of the late 1920s and early 1930s (the Great Depression), the existing accounting practices failed to protect adequately the creditors of German companies in cases of insolvency. As a consequence, the principle of prudence was incorporated in the 1937 Stock Corporation Law, which also specifically required that the compulsory audits of public corporations be performed by WPs.

In the mid-1960s, there were signs of a change in financial reporting in Germany from a creditor orientation towards a shareholder orientation. The Companies Act of 1965 can be regarded as the initiator of this change, and for the first time it required greater financial disclosures from companies, including preparation of consolidated statements and disclosure of the valuation bases used. For two decades, the Companies Act provided the primary source of accounting regulation for listed companies, supplemented by provisions in the Commercial Code and income tax law.

More recently, German accounting regulation has been heavily influenced by the EU directives. The Accounting Act of 1985 implemented the EU's Fourth, Seventh, and Eighth Directives, and transformed them into German Commercial Law. The act specifies different financial reporting requirements according to company size. Since then the Financial Statement Directives Law, which amended the Commercial Code, has been the legal basis for financial reporting in Germany.

Until 1998 the Federal Ministry of Justice coordinated the accounting rule development process, and the accounting profession played only a relatively minor role in that process. In May 1998, German law was amended to allow a private-sector body to develop accounting standards. Accordingly, the German Accounting Standards Committee (GASC) was created in May 1998. It was charged with the responsibility of developing accounting standards for consolidated financial reporting, representing German interests in international fora, and advising the Ministry of Justice on the development of accounting legislation. The GASC is a private standard-setting body that is supported and funded by 137 German companies and individual members, and managed by an executive board of up to 14 members.

The GASC has two standing committees, the German Accounting Standards Board (GASB) and the Accounting Interpretations Committee (AIC). The GASB is solely responsible for the preparation and adoption of its pronouncements, which may consist of accounting standards, comments on accounting issues addressed to national and international bodies, working papers, and other comments and publications considered appropriate by the GASB. The main objective of the AIC is to promote international convergence of interpretations of core accounting issues in close cooperation with the IASB's International Financial Reporting Interpretations Committee (IFRIC). The GASB develops its accounting standards through a due process of public consultation, which includes the following steps:

1. Publication of exposure drafts of standards with a call for comments to be submitted within 45 days.
2. Publication of comments received (unless the party submitting the comments requests otherwise), along with an analysis and discussion of material objections and proposed amendments.
3. Publication of a revised exposure draft with a call for comments to be submitted within 30 days (in those cases where the GASB determines the comments received warrant material amendments of the original exposure draft).
4. Public discussion on the draft standard, which must be announced at least 14 days in advance; minutes of the public discussion must be published within 30 days.
5. Adoption of standards at meetings open to the public.
6. Publication of adopted standards including, where applicable dissenting votes, with a brief basis for conclusion.

The GASB was given the task of adapting German accounting principles to international norms by 2004. The establishment of this committee also provided a vehicle for the German accounting profession to participate formally in the activities of international bodies such as the IASB. The GASB, modeled on the FASB, is staffed by independent experts—three from industry, two auditors, one financial analyst, and one academic.

Germany has created a new legal code for financial accounting. Accordingly, in May 2004, representatives of 15 professional and industry associations established, under the auspices of the Federal Ministry of Justice, an independent private-sector enforcement body, the Financial Reporting Enforcement Panel (FREP). The objective of this panel is to serve as the sponsoring organization for an independent body enforcing financial reporting requirements as provided for in the draft *Bilanzkontrollgesetz* (Financial Reporting Enforcement Law). The panel's charge solely is to discover infringements of financial reporting requirements by listed companies. It does not have any authority to impose sanctions.

In November 2007, the German Federal Ministry of Justice published a draft bill of the German Accounting Law Modernization Act (BilMoG).[34]

DRSC/GASB have released their annual report for the year 2009 (in both German and English), which provides a comprehensive overview of the national and the international activities of these bodies. According to the annual report, in 2009 the work of the GASB was essentially characterized by IASB projects relating to the financial crisis. Further, the Accounting Interpretation Committee (AIC) developed or amended interpretations and application advice on different topics in 2009. The issues for GASB/DRSC in 2009 were mainly the amendments of the German Accounting Standards as a consequence of the German Accounting Law Modernization Act (BilMoG).

DRSC provided comments on IASCF constitution review proposals for enhanced public accountability. It is now available for download from the DRSC/GASB Web site. In particular, the Board takes issue with the lack of explicit

---

[34] For details, see www.stadardsetter.de/drsc/docs/press_releases/071108-RefEBilMoG.pdf (only available in German).

reference to a commitment to principle-based standards and urges the Trustees of the IFRS Foundation to review the objective of bringing about convergence with national accounting standards. They argue that as more than 100 countries now follow IFRS, the IASB should focus entirely on the quality of its standards, rather than seek convergence with a few remaining countries.

Accounting Principles and Practices

The German financial reporting requirements are mainly based on the Commercial Code. The historical cost basis for valuing tangible assets is strictly adhered to. In addition, the approved standards of the GASB must be followed in preparing the consolidated accounts of listed companies. Accordingly, starting from 2005, listed companies are required to use IFRS in their consolidated financial statements, so long as these comply with EU directives.

Given the traditional role of bank credit in corporate finance the principle of creditor protection plays an important role in German accounting practices. Accordingly, the primary function of financial accounting is the conservative determination of distributable income, which represents that part of the actual income of the company that can be paid out to shareholders without impairing the position of the creditors or the long-term prospects of the firm. Consequently, the information needs of investors and presenting a *true and fair view* in the financial statements have not been the primary focus in financial reporting.

German accounting is heavily influenced by tax law. The relationship between financial accounting and taxation in Germany is explained by the "authoritative principle," which basically states that the financial statements are the basis for taxation. There also is a "reverse authoritative principle," which requires an expense to be included in accounting income to be tax deductible. These principles have the effect of minimizing differences between tax and accounting income, thereby reducing the need to account for deferred income taxes.

The reason for the link between financial reporting and taxation in Germany is historical. The duty of bookkeeping and annual accounting was codified in the German Commercial Code in 1862. Corporate income taxation was introduced 12 years later, in 1874. The easiest course of action was to link corporate income taxation to existing financial statements. In contrast, when income tax was introduced in the United Kingdom in 1799 and reformed substantially in 1803, there was no set of accounting rules to refer to. The first accounting rules appeared only in 1844. This explains the different traditions followed in Germany and the United Kingdom with regard to the link between taxation and financial reporting.[35]

For the average company, financial accounting is influenced to a great extent by the desire to minimize taxes. For example, in years with high profits, firms will attempt to report a more moderate level of income to reduce taxes by adopting the most conservative options available under the rules. (This is less the case for companies that compete for funds in international capital markets.) In some cases, what is acceptable for tax purposes is not acceptable under German accounting rules. To meet the requirement that tax deductions must be reported in financial statements, German accounting law allows companies to report "special tax items" on the balance sheet, located between accrued liabilities and stockholders' equity. For example, assume tax law allows a special depreciation rate of

---

[35] E. L. E. Eberhartinger, "The Impact of Tax Rules on Financial Reporting in Germany, France, and the UK," *International Journal of Accounting* 34, no. 1 (1999), pp. 93–119.

75 percent in the year in which an asset with a 20-year life that costs 100 euros is acquired. Depreciation of 75 euros (a debit) would be taken in calculating both taxable and accounting income, but accumulated depreciation (a credit) would be reflected on the balance sheet in the amount of only 5 euros (5 percent annual depreciation). The difference of 70 euros is reported as a special tax item on the equity side (a credit) of the balance sheet.

The conservative measurement of income in Germany is also influenced by a desire to mitigate labor unions' demands for higher wages and to report stable income over time for dividend purposes.[36] Income stability (or smoothing) is accomplished by estimating liabilities such as provisions for warranties, pensions, and "uncertain future liabilities" at relatively high amounts, with a corresponding increase in expenses. The extra amounts accrued as liabilities on the balance sheet are known as hidden or silent reserves. In later, less profitable years, adjustments can be made to these liabilities to release the hidden reserves with a corresponding amount of revenue recognized in income. German accounting rules allow firms to smooth their profits over time in this fashion.[37] The process of using accounting options available within the accounting law to generate the desired amount of reported profit is referred to as *Bilanzpolitik* (financial statement policy).

The EU's Fourth Directive requires companies to apply the true and fair view principle in preparing financial statements. Some suggest that the German understanding of true and fair view differs from how the concept is understood in Anglo-Saxon countries. Alexander and Archer state:

> According to the thinking of the Germans, and to a certain extent of most other member states, the true and fair view is not an operational concept; accounting measurement rules are simply conventions that are agreed on by due democratic process, and if they allow hidden reserves, then such reserves are fair.[38]

The German Accounting Act of 1985 increased the required note disclosures. It appears that extensive note disclosures are seen as a way of achieving the true and fair view without changing the tax-based, income-smoothing approach to financial reporting.

Globalization has had a dramatic effect on German financial reporting in recent years. Since 1998, parent companies whose shares or other issued securities are publicly traded have been allowed to prepare their consolidated financial statements in accordance with IFRS or other internationally accepted accounting standards, such as U.S. GAAP. In 2001, of the 100 blue-chip companies making up the DAX/MDAX stock market index, 39 were using IFRS and 22 used U.S. GAAP.[39] For the 2002 financial year, 53 percent of firms listed on the Frankfurt Prime Standard adopted IFRS.[40] Since January 1, 2005, all German listed companies have been required to use IFRS in preparing their consolidated financial statements. German GAAP continue to be used by non-publicly traded companies and by

---

[36] Timothy S. Doupnik, "Recent Innovations in German Accounting Practice Through the Integration of EC Directives," *Advances in International Accounting,* 1992, p. 80.

[37] M. Glaum and U. Mandler, "Global Accounting Harmonization from a German Perspective: Bridging the GAAP," *Journal of International Financial Management and Accounting* 7, no. 3 (1996), pp. 215–42.

[38] David Alexander and Simon Archer, eds., *European Accounting Guide,* 5th ed. (New York: Aspen, 2004), p. 1.15.

[39] Ibid., p. 7.09.

[40] P. Brown, and A. Tarca, "A Commentary on Issues Relating to the Enforcement of International Financial Reporting Standards in the EU," *European Accounting Review* 14, no. 1 (2005), p. 198.

publicly traded companies in preparing their parent company, that is, nonconsolidated financial statements, which serve as the basis for taxation.

The main intention of the German Accounting Law Modernization Act is to modernize the German Accounting Law in line with IFRS. Important changes include:

- Intangible assets have to be recognized.
- Deferred tax assets will have to be recognized.
- Fair value accounting of financial assets, i.e., valuation above the initially recognized costs, will become possible.

German accounting practices differ in some respects from IFRS, partly because German accounting law contains no specific rules in some areas. For example, the law provides no guidance with respect to the translation of foreign currency financial statements of foreign subsidiaries (IAS 21), or annual impairment reviews when a useful life in excess of 20 years is used for intangible assets (IAS 38). Further, there are no specific rules requiring disclosures of a primary statement of changes in equity (IAS 1); fair values of financial assets and liabilities (IAS 32); related-party transactions other than those with equity participants (IAS 24); and earnings per share (IAS 33). There are also inconsistencies between German rules and IFRS in some areas; for example, goodwill arising on consolidation can be deducted immediately against equity (IFRS 3); foreign currency payables and receivables are generally translated at the worse of transaction and closing rates so as to avoid the recognition of gains on unsettled balances (IAS 21); leases are normally classified according to tax rules and are therefore seldom recognized as finance leases (IAS 17); and inventories can be valued at replacement cost (IAS 2). Exhibit 6.5 summarizes some of the differences between IFRS and German GAAP.

Another area where German GAAP differs from IFRS is in the management report, which is, according to the German tradition, an important part of a company's financial statements. The IFRS do not include specific requirements regarding the management report. However, even companies that publish their financial statements according to IFRS[41] still have to provide a management report providing information on a company's future situation, for example, regarding research and development or exposure to financial or operating risks.[42]

In August 2010, only about 10 German companies were listed on the New York Stock Exchange (NYSE) mainly due to overregulation of the NYSE. Prior to the adoption of IFRS in the European Union in 2005, BASF AG was one of the few NYSE-listed German companies that prepared its consolidated financial statements on the basis of German GAAP; the others used either IFRS (e.g., Bayer and Schering), or U.S. GAAP (e.g., DaimlerChrysler and Siemens). We can gain some insight into the differences that exist between German GAAP and U.S. GAAP by investigating the reconciliation to U.S. GAAP prepared by BASF in its Form

---

[41] In early February 2005, it was reported that more than half of German companies, which are in the FTSEurofirst 300 index, adopt IFRSs. Due to globalization pressures, German companies are now competing in a worldwide capital market where the quality of the information provided to investors has to match up to that of international competitors.

[42] In February 2005, the Federal Ministry of Justice published German Accounting Standard 15, *Management Reporting,* and subsequently the GASB reported that it adopted GAS 15.

EXHIBIT 6.5 Differences between German GAAP and IFRS

Issue	IFRS	German GAAP
Business combinations	IFRS 3: Must use purchase method; pooling of interests prohibited.	Certain business combinations may be accounted for as pooling of interests even though an acquirer can be identified.
Goodwill on consolidation	IFRS 3: Not amortized, but tested for impairment annually (effective March 31, 2004).	Goodwill arising on consolidation can be deducted immediately against equity.
Internally generated intangible assets	IAS 38: Internally generated goodwill can be recognized as an asset under certain conditions.	Internally generated intangible assets, which are expected to provide ongoing service to the enterprise must not be recognized.
Foreign currency translation	IAS 21: Foreign currency monetary items should be reported using the closing rate.	Foreign currency monetary balances are generally translated at the worse of transaction and closing rates so as to avoid the recognition of gains on unsettled balances.
Leases	IAS 17: Distinguishes between finance leases and operating leases, and provides guidance for classifying them.	Leases are normally classified according to tax rules; therefore, leases are seldom recognized as finance leases.
Inventory valuation	IAS 2: Requires inventories to be stated at the lower of cost and net realizable value.	Inventories can be stated at the lowest of cost, net realizable value, or replacement cost.
Construction contracts	IAS 11: The stage of completion of the contract activity at the balance sheet date should be used to recognize contract revenue.	In general the completed contract method is used for the recognition of revenue on construction contracts and services.
Exclusion of subsidiaries from consolidation	IAS 27: Subsidiaries whose activities are dissimilar to those of its parent must be consolidated.	Certain subsidiaries with dissimilar activities should be excluded from consolidation.
Start-up costs	IAS 38: Start-up costs must be charged to expenses when incurred.	Start-up costs may be capitalized and amortized over four years.

20-F annual report filed with the U.S. Securities and Exchange Commission. Exhibit 6.6 presents excerpts from this reconciliation for the year ended December 31, 2003. Note that BASF has adopted accounting policies consistent with U.S. GAAP to the extent that these practices are permissible under German GAAP. Nonetheless, BASF's accountants have determined that there are 11 accounting issues in which U.S. GAAP and German GAAP are incompatible and for which an adjustment must be made. The largest adjustments relate to the accounting for goodwill and the accrual of provisions. The adjustment related to provisions reverses accruals of liabilities (and expenses) that were made under German GAAP in 2003 that would not have met the definition of a liability under U.S. GAAP in that period.

EXHIBIT 6.6

BASF GROUP
Form 20-F
2003
Excerpt from Notes to the Consolidated Financial Statements

4. Reconciliation to U.S. GAAP

BASF Aktiengesellschaft
Form 20-F
Notes to the Consolidated Financial Statements

3. Reconciliation to U.S. GAAP

The Consolidated Financial Statements comply with IFRS as far as permissible under German GAAP. The differences between German and U.S. GAAP relate to valuation methods that are required under U.S. GAAP but which are not permissible under German GAAP.

The following is a summary of the significant adjustments to net income and stockholders' equity that would be required if U.S. GAAP had been fully applied rather than German GAAP.

	Note	Year Ended December 31,			
		2004	2004	2003	2002
			(As Restated, Note 3(1)) (Million € and Million $, Except Per Share Amounts)		
Reconciliation of Net Income to U.S. GAAP					
Net income as reported in the Consolidated Financial Statements of income under German GAAP		$2,549.2	€1,883.0	€910.2	€1,504.4
Adjustments required to conform with U.S. GAAP:					
Capitalization of interest	(a)	(6.1)	(4.5)	(7.3)	(6.4)
Capitalization of software developed for internal use	(b)	(72.4)	(53.5)	(2.8)	30.5
Accounting for pensions	(c)	55.5	41.0	69.0	71.2
Accounting for provisions	(d)	(11.0)	(8.1)	157.6	12.4
Accounting for derivatives at fair value and valuation of long-term foreign currency items at year end rates	(e)	263.3	194.5	(24.8)	(143.9)
Valuation of securities at market values	(f)	9.2	6.8	(6.2)	—
Valuation adjustments relating to companies accounted for under the equity method	(g)	(218.8)	(161.6)	62.4	12.9
Inventory valuation	(h)	(4.6)	(3.4)	(26.3)	(1.1)
Reversal of goodwill amortization and write-offs due to permanent impairment	(i)	201.3	148.7	167.3	211.0
Other adjustments	(j)	40.3	29.8	1.0	(12.9)
Deferred taxes and recognition of tax effects for dividend payments.	(k)	(284.8)	(210.4)	8.9	48.5
Minority interests.	(l)	0.7	0.5	10.7	(10.4)
Net income in accordance with U.S. GAAP.		**2,521.8**	**1,862.8**	**1,319.7**	**1,716.2**

Earnings per share

The calculation of earnings per common share is based on the weighted-average number of common shares outstanding during the applicable period. The calculation of diluted earnings per common share reflects the effect of all dilutive potential common shares that were outstanding during the respective period. Shares awarded under the BASF employee participation program "plus" have been included in the computation of diluted earnings per share. Due to a resolution by the Board of Executive Directors and the Supervisory Board in 2002, settlements of stock options from the BASF stock option program (BOP) for senior management are made in cash, therefore such stock options have no dilutive effect.

The earnings per share from continuing operations based on income from ordinary activities after taxes were not impacted by any dilutive effect in 2004, 2003 and 2002, because the impact of potential common shares was anti-dilutive in each year.

	Year Ended December 31,			
	2004	2004	2003	2002
	(Million € and Million $, Except per Share Amounts)			
Net income in accordance with U.S. GAAP	$2,521.9	€1,862.8	€1,319.7	€1,716.2
Number of shares (1,000)				
Weighted average undiluted number of shares	548,714	548,714	561,887	579,118
Dilutive effect	—	—	—	—
Weighted average diluted number of shares	548,714	548,714	561,887	579,118
Basic earnings per share in accordance with U.S. GAAP	**4.59**	**3.39**	**2.35**[1]	**2.96**[1]
Dilutive effect	—	—	—	—
Diluted earnings per share in accordance with U.S. GAAP	4.59	3.39	2.35[1]	2.96[1]

		Year Ended December 31,		
		2004	2004	2003
				(As Restated, Note 3(1))
	Note	(Million € and Million $)		
Reconciliation of Stockholders' Equity to U.S. GAAP				
Stockholders' equity as reported in the Consolidated Balance Sheets under German GAAP		$21,342.7	€15,765.0	€15,878.4
Minority interests		(449.2)	(331.8)	(388.1)
Stockholders' equity excluding minority interests		20,893.5	15,433.2	15,490.3
Adjustments required to conform with U.S. GAAP:				
Capitalization of interest	(a)	639.9	472.7	493.9
Capitalization of software developed for internal use	(b)	173.7	128.3	184.1
Accounting for pensions	(c)	1,251.3	924.3	982.5
Accounting for provisions	(d)	330.9	244.4	206.8
Accounting for derivatives at fair value and valuation of long-term foreign currency items at year end rates	(e)	4.3	3.2	(138.8)
Valuation of securities at market values	(f)	259.3	191.5	89.1
Valuation adjustments relating to companies accounted for under the equity method	(g)	52.8	39.0	182.0
Inventory valuation	(h)	25.6	18.9	167.6
Reversal of goodwill amortization and write-offs due to permanent impairment	(i)	635.6	469.5	337.1
Other adjustments	(j)	79.3	58.6	43.4
Deferred taxes and recognition of tax effects of dividend payments	(k)	(1,097.7)	(810.8)	(698.7)
Minority interests	(l)	(18.5)	(13.7)	(15.3)
Stockholders' equity in accordance with U.S. GAAP		**23,230.0**	**17,159.1**	**17,324.0**

[1]As reported in (h), BASF changed its method of inventory costing from the last-in first-out (LIFO) method to the average cost method. The new method was adopted to provide a better measure of the current value of inventory and because the LIFO method is not allowed under IFRS. The balances of U.S. GAAP shareholders' equity for 2003 and 2002 have been adjusted for the effect of retroactively not applying the LIFO method. The change in inventory costing increased shareholders' equity as of January 1, 2002 by €120.9 million. The following table presents the effect of the change on previously reported net income for 2003 and 2002.

Continued

EXHIBIT 6.6 (*Continued*)

The following table presents the effect of the change in the inventory costing method:

	As Previously Reported	Change in Inventory Costing Method	Restated
	(Million €, Except per Share Data)		
2003			
Net income	1,337.7	(18.0)	1,319.7
Basic earnings per share.	2.38	(0.03)	2.35
Diluted earnings per share	2.38	(0.03)	2.35
Stockholders' equity as of December 31.	17,221.8	102.2	17,324.0
2002			
Net income	1,716.9	(0.7)	1,716.2
Basic earnings per share.	2.96	—	2.96
Diluted earnings per share	2.96	—	2.96
Stockholders' equity as of December 31.	17,919.8	120.2	18,040.0

(a) Capitalization of interest

For U.S. GAAP purposes, the Company capitalizes interest on borrowings during the active construction period of major capital projects. Capitalized interest is added to the cost of the underlying assets and is amortized over the useful lives of the assets. The capitalization of interest relating to capital projects is not permissible under German GAAP. In calculating capitalized interest, the Company has made assumptions with respect to the capitalization rate and the average amount of accumulated expenditures. The Company's subsidiaries generally use the entity-specific weighted-average borrowing rate as the capitalization rate.

(b) Capitalization of software developed for internal use

Certain costs incurred for computer software developed or obtained for the Company's internal use are to be capitalized and amortized over the expected useful life of the software. Such costs have been expensed in these financial statements because the capitalization of self-developed intangible assets is not permissible under German GAAP.

(c) Accounting for pensions

Pension benefits under Company pension schemes are partly funded in a legally independent fund "BASF Pensionskasse VVaG" ("BASF Pensionskasse"). Pension liabilities and plan assets of BASF Pensionskasse are not included in BASF Group's balance sheet. However, contributions to the BASF Pensionskasse are included in expenses for pensions and assistance.

BASF guarantees the commitments of the BASF Pensionskasse. For U.S. GAAP purposes, BASF Pensionskasse would be classified as a defined benefit plan and therefore included in the calculation of net periodic benefit cost as well as the projected benefit obligation and plan assets. The valuation of the pension obligations under the projected unit credit method and of the fund assets of BASF Pensionskasse at market values would result in a prepaid pension asset in accordance with U.S. GAAP that is not recorded in the Consolidated Financial Statements under German GAAP.

Net periodic benefit cost in accordance with U.S. GAAP would be lower than showing the Company's contribution to the BASF Pensionskasse as expense.

Information about the funded status of the BASF Pensionskasse is provided in the following table:

	2004	2003
	(Million €)	
Plan assets as of December 31, ...	4,034.1	3,781.2
Projected benefit obligation as of December 31, ...	3,871.9	3,569.3
Funded status	162.2	211.9
Unrecognized actuarial losses............................	667.0	575.0
Prepaid pension asset..................................	829.2	786.9

The accumulated pension benefit obligation (ABO) in 2004 is €3,725.2 million and in 2003 is €3,429.8 million.

The valuation of certain pension plans of foreign subsidiaries, in accordance with SFAS 87 also resulted in prepaid pension assets. After consideration of unrecognized actuarial gains and losses, €95.1 million in 2004, and €195.6 million in 2003 were included in the reconciliation to U.S. GAAP. In addition, the change in treatment of pension liabilities explained in Note 2, and the associated charge of accumulated actuarial gains and losses to shareholders' equity is eliminated for U.S. GAAP as the SFAS 87 accounting treatment is to be continued. In the case of an additional minimum liability, equity according to U.S. GAAP is reduced.

(d) Accounting for provisions

The reconciliation item contains the following deviations:

Provisions for part-time programs for employees nearing retirement age:

In these financial statements agreed upon top-up payments within the pre-retirement part-time programs are immediately accrued in their full amount, and discounted at a rate of 3.0% (see note 22). A provision is also recorded for the expected costs for agreements that are anticipated to be concluded during the term of the collective bargaining agreements, taking into consideration the ceilings on the number of employee participants provided in such collective bargaining agreements. In accordance with U.S. GAAP, provisions may only be recorded for employees who have accepted an offer, and the supplemental payments are accrued over the employee's remaining service period. This results in a (decrease)/increase in income under U.S. GAAP of €(22.3) million in 2004, €124.4 million in 2003, and €6.0 million in 2002. Stockholders' equity increased by €154.7 million in 2004 and €140.0 million in 2003.

Provisions for omitted maintenance procedures:

German GAAP requires companies to accrue provisions as of the end of the year for expected costs of omitted maintenance procedures expected to take place in the first three months of the following year. Such costs would be expensed as incurred under U.S. GAAP. The amounts included in the reconciliation of net income related to maintenance provisions were €(8.3) million in 2004, €(1.7) million in 2003, and €(6.4) million in 2002. The amounts in the reconciliation of stockholders' equity were €23.7 million in 2004, and €32.0 million in 2003.

Provisions for restructuring measures:

SFAS 146, "Accounting for Costs Associated with Exit and Disposal Activities," requires expected costs associated with the exit or disposal of business activities to be accrued only when a liability against a third party exists. This includes severance payments for employees, the cancellation of contracts, the shutdown of production facilities, and the relocation of employees.

Since the accruals for restructuring measures under German GAAP are recorded based upon management decisions, the application of SFAS 146 (decreased)/increased net income in accordance with U.S. GAAP by €(20.9) million in 2004 (€23.5 million in 2003), and stockholders' equity by €1.6 million (€23.3 million in 2003).

Provisions for environmental measures:

In the current financial statement, obligations for recultivation obligations due to oil and gas extraction are accrued. SFAS 143, "Accounting for Asset Retirement Obligations," addresses financial accounting and reporting for obligations and costs associated with the retirement of tangible long-lived assets. The expected obligations and costs associated with the demolition of plants and removal of potential damage to the environment have to be accrued as of the start of the production as additional cost for the

Continued

EXHIBIT 6.6 (*Continued*)

related plants and are depreciated over the useful life. This also includes the change of these potential liabilities due to adjustments to the conditions as of the balance sheet date.

In addition, provisions accrued in 2004 for adaptation obligations in connection with the operation of production plants are not to be taken into consideration according to SOP 96-1, and have therefore been eliminated. Income was thereby increased by €13.9 million in 2004 and €3.8 million in 2003. Equity increased by €25.8 million in 2004 and €11.4 million in 2003.

Discounting of provisions and liabilities:

Provisions and liabilities are to be shown at nominal value according to German GAAP. According to U.S. GAAP, the values may be discounted if the aggregate amount of the liability and the timing of payments are reliably determinable. This results in an income effect in 2004 of €38.6 million, which leads to an equity increase in the same amount.

(e) Accounting for derivatives at fair value and valuation of long-term foreign currency items

As required by SFAS 133, as amended, derivative contracts are to be accounted for at fair values. Where hedge accounting is not applicable, changes in the fair values of derivative contracts are to be included in net income, together with foreign exchange gains and losses of the underlying transactions.

Under German GAAP, long-term receivables and liabilities denominated in a foreign currency are converted into euros at the exchange rates of the date when the transactions took place or the lower exchange rates at the end of the year for receivables and the higher exchange rates for liabilities. U.S. GAAP requires conversion at the exchange rate at the end of the year.

Under German GAAP, unrealized gains on swaps and other forward contracts are deferred until settlement or termination while unrealized expected losses from firm commitments are recognized as of each period end. Under U.S. GAAP, these contracts are marked to market.

Under German GAAP, hedge accounting is achieved by a combined valuation of underlying hedged transactions and derivatives. Under U.S. GAAP such accounting is not permitted. SFAS 133 requires that the hedged transaction and the derivative be accounted for separately, and extensive documentation regarding the hedge relationship be provided.

(f) Valuation of securities

Under U.S. GAAP, available-for-sale securities are recorded at market values on the balance sheet date. If the effect comes from unrealized profits or temporary decreases in value, the change in valuation is immediately recognized in a separate component of stockholders' equity. Realized profits and losses are credited or charged to income, as are other than temporary impairments of value. The major part of securities and other investments are considered to be available-for-sale. Under German GAAP, such securities and other investments are valued at the lower of acquisition cost or market value at the balance sheet date.

(g) Valuation adjustments relating to companies accounted for under the equity method

For purposes of the reconciliation to U.S. GAAP, the earnings of companies accounted for using the equity method have been determined using valuation principles prescribed by U.S. GAAP. The write-down of the interests in Basell N.V., the Netherlands, and Svalöf Weibull, Sweden, affected net income under German GAAP in 2004. This also applies to the catch-up of scheduled amortization of goodwill of these companies under U.S. GAAP that was eliminated according to SFAS 142 (Goodwill and Other Intangible Assets) in the previous years.

(h) Inventory valuation

In connection with the conversion to IFRS as of January 1, 2005, the current inventory valuation methods are being changed. This specifically affects the LIFO method, which is not allowed under IFRS. This change requires prior years' amounts to be restated, according to APB 20.27. In the current year there were differences resulting from the deductions required by German GAAP.

(i) Reversal of goodwill amortization and write-offs due to permanent impairment

Goodwill is amortized over its useful life in accordance with German GAAP, however, the U.S. GAAP standard SFAS 142, "Goodwill and Other Intangible Assets," requires write-offs only based on annual impairment tests. The recoverability of goodwill is reviewed at the reporting-unit level by comparing the fair value of the reporting unit determined using discounted future cash flows, to the carrying value. There were no material impairment write-downs required in 2004 or 2003. The regular goodwill amortization included in these financial statements is reversed and added back to net income.

(j) Other adjustments

This item primarily includes the adjustment of provisions for stock compensation.

Following a resolution by the Board of Executive Directors in 2002, stock options are to be settled in cash. Under U.S. GAAP, such obligations are to be accounted for as stock appreciation rights based on the intrinsic value of the options on the balance sheet date. However, options granted in prior years, for which cash settlement was not foreseen, are to be accounted for in accordance with SFAS 123 as equity instruments based upon the fair value on the grant date.

In the present Financial Statements, all obligations resulting from stock options are accounted for based upon the fair value on the balance sheet date. A provision is accrued over the vesting period of the options. The different accounting methods led to an increase in net income in accordance with U.S. GAAP of €16.1 million in 2004, and €17.2 million in 2003, and a decrease of €10.7 million in 2002.

In the present Financial Statements, obligations resulting from stock options are shown as provisions. In accordance with U.S. GAAP, options for which cash settlement was not originally foreseen are recorded as additions to stockholders' equity.

Overall, the accounting for stock options resulted in a decrease in stockholders' equity of €9.4 million in 2004, and €14.6 million in 2003.

(k) Deferred taxes

The adjustments required to conform with U.S. GAAP would result in taxable temporary differences between the valuation of assets and liabilities in the Consolidated Financial Statements and the carrying amount for tax purposes. Resulting adjustments for deferred taxes primarily relate to the following:

| | Note | Stockholders' Equity | | Net Income | | |
		2004	2003	2004	2003	2002
		(Million €)				
Capitalization of interest	(a)	(158.4)	(171.5)	8.9	11.0	7.3
Capitalization of software developed for internal use	(b)	(47.7)	(69.7)	21.0	1.0	(10.4)
Accounting for pensions	(c)	(351.1)	(360.6)	(14.3)	(27.7)	(22.2)
Accounting for provisions	(d)	(82.2)	(78.8)	13.9	(59.1)	(5.8)
Accounting for derivatives at fair value and valuation of long-term foreign currency items at year end rates	(e)	13.4	48.9	(58.9)	6.3	35.3
Valuation of securities at market values	(f)	(3.8)	0.1	(4.0)	(17.2)	62.2
Valuation adjustments relating to companies accounted for under the equity method	(g)	—	—	—	—	45.7
Inventory valuation	(h)	(7.2)	(65.4)	1.3	8.3	0.4
Reversal of goodwill amortization and write-offs due to permanent impairment	(i)	(122.0)	(97.0)	(31.2)	(45.9)	(60.7)
Other adjustments	(j)	55.7	95.3	(39.6)	8.0	(5.5)
Tax effects of dividend payments	(k)	(107.5)	—	(107.5)	124.2	2.2
		(810.8)	**(698.7)**	**(210.4)**	**8.9**	**48.5**

The change of the deferred taxes for foreign currency translation adjustments is recognized in other comprehensive income.

In 2004, following a change to the German Corporate Income Tax Act (Section 8b), deferred taxes were, for the first time, accrued for tax effects of future dividend payments from BASF Group companies, according to the financial plan.

In 2003, capitalized tax credits related to the distribution of retained earnings previously taxed at higher rates had to be written off in the German GAAP financial statements due to a legal change. In accordance with U.S. GAAP, such tax credits are recognized as a reduction of income tax expenses in the period in which the tax credits are recognized for tax purposes. The resulting burden on income therefore had to be eliminated in 2003 for U.S. GAAP purposes.

(l) Minority interests

The share of minority shareholders in the aforementioned reconciliation items to U.S. GAAP of net income and stockholders' equity are reported separately.

Consolidation of majority-owned subsidiaries: U.S. GAAP requires the consolidation of all controlled subsidiaries. Under German GAAP, the Company does not consolidate certain subsidiaries if their individual or their combined effect on financial position, results of operations and cash flows is not material. The effect of non-consolidated subsidiaries for 2004, 2003 and 2002, on total assets, total liabilities, stockholders' equity, net sales and net income was less than 2%.

Additionally, under German GAAP, the Company accounts on a prospective basis for previous unconsolidated subsidiaries that are added to the scope of consolidation. U.S. GAAP requires consolidation for all periods that a subsidiary is controlled. The effects of adding previously unconsolidated companies to the scope of consolidation on net sales, net income, assets and liabilities was immaterial.

Continued

EXHIBIT 6.6 (Continued)

Proportional consolidation: The Company accounts for its investments in 12 jointly operated companies (2003: 12, 2002: 11) using the proportional consolidation method, as permitted under German GAAP. Under U.S. GAAP, all investments in jointly operated companies must be accounted for using the equity method. The differences in accounting treatment between proportional consolidation and the equity method of accounting have no impact on reported stockholders' equity or net income. Rather, they relate solely to matters of classification and display. The United States Securities and Exchange Commission (SEC) permits the omission of such differences in classification and display in the reconciliation to U.S. GAAP appearing above.

Balance Sheet presentation: The classification of the balance sheet is as required by German GAAP. Noncurrent portions of receivables and prepaid expenses are disclosed in Notes 15 and 17. Current portions of provisions and liabilities are disclosed in Notes 22 and 23.

New U.S. GAAP accounting standards not yet adopted

The standards adopted in 2004—SFAS 151 "Inventory Costs," SFAS 152 "Accounting for Real Estate Time-Sharing Transactions," SFAS 153 "Exchange of Nonmonetary Assets," and EITF 03-1 "The Meaning of Other Than Temporary Impairment and its Application to Certain Investments"—were examined to determine their effect on the BASF Group financial statements. According to SFAS 151, certain abnormal costs for the production of inventories are to be charged against income in the period they occur, rather than being capitalized as production costs. SFAS 152 covers the accounting treatment of timesharing of property and property rights. SFAS 153 states that the exchange of nonmonetary assets are generally to be valued at fair value. EITF 03-1 provides guidance regarding the impairment of certain investments and the related disclosures. In September 2004, the Emerging Issues Task Force issued EITF Issue 4-10 "Determining Whether to Aggregate Operating Segments That Do Not Meet the Quantitative Thresholds" ("EITF 4-10"), which addresses the criteria for aggregating operating segments. We have reviewed our segment reporting and have determined that our aggregation of segments is consistent with the guidance in EITF Issue No. 4-10. These new standards have no effect on the financial statements of the BASF Group.

Reporting of comprehensive income

Comprehensive income in accordance with SFAS 130, "Reporting Comprehensive Income," includes the impact of expenses and earnings that are not included in net income under U.S. GAAP.

	Year Ended December 31,		
	2004	2003	2002
	(Million €)		
Comprehensive income			
Net income in accordance with U.S. GAAP (before other comprehensive income)	1,862.8	1,319.7	1,716.2
Change of foreign currency translation adjustments			
/*/ Gross	(291.3)	(729.3)	(908.6)
/*/ Deferred taxes	17.2	38.0	24.3
Changes in unrealized holding gains on securities			
/*/ Gross	95.6	(5.2)	(262.8)
/*/ Deferred taxes	0.3	17.2	71.8
Changes in unrealized losses from cash flow hedges			
/*/ Gross	(54.0)	0.5	(4.6)
/*/ Deferred taxes	18.7	(0.2)	1.6
Additional minimum liability for pensions			
/*/ Gross	(514.7)	(18.5)	(17.8)
/*/ Deferred taxes	197.0	—	5.4
Other comprehensive income (loss), net of tax	(531.2)	(697.5)	(1,090.7)
Comprehensive income, net of tax	**1,331.6**	**622.2**	**625.5**

	Year Ended December 31,	
	2004	**2003**
	(Million €)	
Statement of stockholders' equity		
Stockholders' equity in accordance with U.S. GAAP before accumulated other comprehensive income	18,694.7	18,328.4
Accumulated other comprehensive income:		
Translation adjustments		
/*/ Gross	(1,369.0)	(1,077.7)
/*/ Deferred taxes	69.2	52.0
Unrealized holding gains on securities		
/*/ Gross	196.2	100.6
/*/ Deferred taxes	(45.4)	(45.7)
Unrealized losses from cash flow hedges		
/*/ Gross	(58.1)	(4.1)
/*/ Deferred taxes	20.1	1.4
Additional minimum liability for pensions		
/*/ Gross	(551.0)	(36.3)
/*/ Deferred taxes	202.4	5.4
Accumulated other comprehensive income	(1,535.6)	(1,004.4)
Total stockholders' equity in accordance with U.S. GAAP including comprehensive income	**17,159.1**	**17,324.0**

	Year Ended December 31,	
	2004	**2003**
	(Million €)	
Stockholders' equity in accordance with U.S. GAAP on January 1.	17,324.0	18,040.0
Comprehensive income, net of tax.	1,331.6	622.2
Share buyback and cancellation, including own shares intended to be cancelled.	(725.7)	(499.8)
Dividend paid (excluding minority interests)	(774.1)	(788.7)
BASF stock option program	(9.4)	(14.6)
Change in scope of consolidation and other changes.	12.7	(35.1)
Total stockholders' equity in accordance with U.S. GAAP on December 31.	**17,159.1**	**17,324.0**

Exhibit 6.7 provides an excerpt from the annual report of 2008, which shows consolidated balance sheets prepared according to the German GAAP and IFRS.

EXHIBIT 6.7

BASF GROUP
Annual Report
2008
Excert from Notes to the Consolidated Financial Statements

Consolidated Balance Sheets (German GAAP) (million €)

	1999	2000	2001	2002	2003
Intangible assets	2,147	4,538	3,943	3,464	3,793
Property, plant and equipment.	12,416	13,641	14,190	13,745	13,070
Financial assets	1,507	3,590	3,360	3,249	2,600
Fixed assets	**16,070**	**21,769**	**21,493**	**20,458**	**19,463**
Inventories.	4,028	5,211	5,007	4,798	4,151
Accounts receivable, trade	4,967	6,068	5,875	5,316	4,954
Other receivables.	2,211	3,369	2,384	2,947	3,159
Deferred taxes.	1,225	1,270	1,373	1,204	1,247
Marketable securities.	518	364	383	132	147
Cash and cash equivalents.	990	506	360	231	481
Current assets	**13,939**	**16,788**	**15,382**	**14,628**	**14,139**
Total assets	**30,009**	**38,557**	**36,875**	**35,086**	**33,602**
Subscribed capital	1,590	1,555	1,494	1,460	1,425
Capital surplus.	2,675	2,746	2,914	2,948	2,983
Paid-in capital	4,265	4,301	4,408	4,408	4,408
Retained earnings	9,002	8,851	12,222	12,468	12,055
Currency translation adjustment	549	662	532	(330)	(972)
Minority interests.	329	481	360	396	388
Stockholders' equity.	**14,145**	**14,295**	**17,522**	**16,942**	**15,879**
Pensions and other long-term provisions	5,812	6,209	6,809	6,233	6,205
Tax and other short-term provisions.	2,826	3,334	3,332	2,764	2,982
Provisions	**8,638**	**9,543**	**10,141**	**8,997**	**9,187**
Financial indebtedness.	1,294	7,892	2,835	3,610	3,507
Accounts payable, trade.	2,316	2,848	2,467	2,344	2,056
Other liabilities.	3,616	3,979	3,910	3,193	2,973
Liabilities	**7,226**	**14,719**	**9,212**	**9,147**	**8,536**
Provisions and liabilities.	**15,864**	**24,262**	**19,353**	**18,144**	**17,723**
Thereof long-term liabilities	7,529	9,059	9,955	9,211	10,285
Total stockholders' equity and liabilities	**30,009**	**38,557**	**36,875**	**35,086**	**33,602**

Consolidated Balance Sheets (IFRS) (million €) . . . .

	2004	2005	2006	2007	2008
Intangible assets	3,607	3,720	8,922	9,559	9,889
Property, plant and equipment.	13,063	13,987	14,902	14,215	15,032
Investments accounted for using the equity method	1,100	244	651	834	1,146
Other financial assets.	938	813	1,190	1,952	1,947
Deferred taxes.	1,337	1,255	622	679	930
Other receivables and miscellaneous long-term assets	473	524	612	655	642
Long-term assets.	**20,518**	**20,543**	**26,899**	**27,894**	**29,586**
Inventories.	4,645	5,430	6,672	6,578	6,763
Accounts receivable, trade.	5,861	7,020	8,223	8,561	7,752
Other receivables and miscellaneous short-term assets.	2,133	1,586	2,607	2,337	3,948

Marketable securities	205	183	56	51	35
Cash and cash equivalents	2,086	908	834	767	2,776
Assets of disposal groups	—	—	—	614	—
Short-term assets	**14,930**	**15,127**	**18,392**	**18,908**	**21,274**
Total assets	**35,448**	**35,670**	**45,291**	**46,802**	**50,860**
Subscribed capital	1,383	1,317	1,279	1,224	1,176
Capital surplus	3,028	3,100	3,141	3,173	3,241
Retained earnings	11,923	11,928	13,302	14,556	13,250
Other comprehensive income	(60)	696	325	174	(96)
Minority interests	328	482	531	971	1,151
Stockholders' equity	**16,602**	**17,523**	**18,578**	**20,098**	**18,722**
Provisions for pensions and similar obligations	4,124	1,547	1,452	1,292	1,712
Other provisions	2,376	2,791	3,080	3,015	2,757
Deferred taxes	948	699	1,441	2,060	2,167
Financial indebtedness	1,845	3,682	5,788	6,954	8,290
Other liabilities	1,079	1,043	972	901	917
Long-term liabilities	**10,372**	**9,762**	**12,733**	**14,222**	**15,843**
Accounts payable, trade	2,372	2,777	4,755	3,763	2,734
Provisions	2,364	2,763	2,848	2,697	3,043
Tax liabilities	644	887	858	881	860
Financial indebtedness	1,453	259	3,695	3,148	6,224
Other liabilities	1,641	1,699	1,824	1,976	3,434
Liabilities of disposal groups	—	—	—	17	—
Short-term liabilities	**8,474**	**8,385**	**13,980**	**12,482**	**16,295**
Total stockholders' equity and liabilities	**35,448**	**35,670**	**45,291**	**46,802**	**50,860**

JAPAN

Background

Legislative authority in Japan rests with the *Kokkai*, the bicameral diet, which consists of a 480-member House of Representatives and a 247-member House of Councillors. Members of the House of Representatives serve a four-year term. The House of Councillors elects half of its members every three years for a six-year term.

In 1868, groups of feudal lords, known as samurai, and aristocrats overthrew the military government and installed an imperial government under the Meiji Empire. This ended Japan's self-isolation policy and led to rapid economic change. Prior to World War II, the Japanese economy was dominated by *zaibatsu* (family financial combines). They derived their power from both economic strength and political affiliations. Each of these conglomerates usually included a major bank as the source of finance for the group. During the postwar occupation of Japan by the allied forces, *zaibatsu* were dissolved by the Anti-Monopoly Law of 1947. However, when the allied forces left Japan in 1952, the old conglomerates started to reappear under a different name, *keiretsu*. Douthett and Jung describe the disappearance of *zaibatsu* and the reappearance of *keiretsu* as follows:

> An interesting aspect of Japanese ownership structure is the industrial groupings known as the *keiretsu*. The *keiretsu* is a successor of pre-war *zaibatsu*, which originated as family-controlled concerns such as Yasuda banking complex, Mitsubishi shipping conglomerate, and Mitsui trading company, and existed as early as the 1870s. After the *zaibatsu* were dissolved by the Anti-Monopoly Law (1947) during

the occupation of Japan by the allied forces following World War II, the pre-existing inter-firm relations gradually re-emerged as *keiretsu* through coordination by the previous *zaibatsu* banks and other large commercial banks.

After the occupation forces left Japan in April 1952, Ministry of International Trade and Industry (MITI) began to permit formation of cartels among the small businesses as an exception to the anti-Monopoly Law. . . . As a result, the old *zaibatsu* names were restored and MITI encouraged the formation of *keiretsu*. Banks continued to be the major nexus of inter-locking shareholding ties in these "financial *keiretsu*." The main banking groups of Mitsubishi, Sumitomo, Mitsui and Fuyo as well as the newer groups of Sanwa and Dai-ichi Kangyo Group (DKB) were the initial six financial *keiretsu*. These financial *keiretsu* are referred to as horizontal *keiretsu* since the member firms have common ties with a main bank, including shared stockholdings as well as normal banking relations. In contrast, a vertical *keiretsu* normally involves a very large trading company with many small, subservient companies such as Toyota Motor Corporation.[43]

A unique aspect of Japanese business is cross-corporate ownership. About 70 percent of the equity shares of listed firms in Japan are cross-owned by corporate shareholders such as financial institutions and other companies. *Keiretsu* control about a half of the top 200 firms in Japan through cross-corporate shareholdings, which amount to more than 25 percent of all the assets in Japan.[44] The manner in which business is organized in Japan reflects its cultural value of collectivism.

The ways in which businesses are financed influences financial reporting and attitudes of interested parties toward accounting information. The main sources of finance for Japanese business are through bank credit and cross-corporate ownership. Unlike in the United States, outside equity financing is relatively minor. In addition to providing credit, banks also have control over major portions of corporate equity capital. As "insiders," banks have access to their clients' financial information, so there is less pressure for public disclosure. This helps to explain the relatively low level of information disclosure in the annual reports of Japanese companies. The heavy reliance on bank credit and the long-term nature of cross-corporate equity ownership also lead to a weaker emphasis on short-term earnings in Japanese companies compared to those in the United States. Corporate earnings are regarded as the source of funds that can be distributed, at the discretion of the shareholders, and not as a measure of corporate performance.

In the 1990s, however, as their ability to raise capital from domestic sources contracted significantly, Japanese companies were compelled to look beyond the national borders to raise capital. This was due to the major recessionary pressures experienced by the Japanese economy during this period involving large-scale capital losses among Japanese banks and other financial companies, as well as the collapse of Japanese asset prices, including stock prices.[45] As the need to attract foreign investment grew, Japanese businesses and regulators found it necessary to respond to the demands of the international capital markets.

[43] E. B. Douthett and K. Jung, "Japanese Corporate Groupings (*Keiretsu*) and the Informativeness of Earnings," *Journal of International Financial Management and Accounting* 12, no. 2 (2001), pp. 135–36.

[44] L. Jiang and J. Kim, "Cross-Corporate Ownership, Information Asymmetry and the Usefulness of Accounting Performance Measures in Japan," *International Journal of Accounting* 35, no. 1 (2000), p. 96.

[45] W. R. Singleton and S. Globerman, "The Nature of Financial Disclosure in Japan," *International Journal of Accounting* 37 (2002), pp. 95–111.

Accounting Profession

The Certified Public Accountants Law of 1948 established the Japanese Institute of Certified Public Accountants (JICPA). This can be considered the beginning of the modern accounting profession in Japan. The JICPA has been heavily involved in the international harmonization process, being one of the nine founding members of the IASC. Compared to the AICPA in the United States, the influence of the JICPA on financial reporting in Japan has been minor. Its traditional role has been basically to implement the decisions made by the Ministry of Finance (MoF). It has issued recommendations on minor accounting issues, guidelines, and interpretations of accounting and auditing standards.[46]

Members of the accountancy profession in Japan practice with the title of CPA under the CPA Law of 1948. The CPA law deals with issues such as examinations, qualifications, registration, duties, and responsibilities of CPAs; audit corporations; the CPA board; JICPA; and disciplinary procedures. Because of the cultural value of collectivism, an independent auditor in Japan does not fit the role of someone to be trusted or relied on and the auditor has difficulty being accepted by clients. Japanese corporations do not typically trust outsiders, and that includes (Japanese) auditors.[47] The relatively low status of the accounting profession within Japanese society is reflected in the fact that very few CPAs hold top positions in industry and commerce. Instead, such positions are often held by people with engineering and science backgrounds. Japan has only about 15,000 CPAs (population 127.2 million), compared to about 250,000 in the United States (population 307.2 million).

The relatively small number of CPAs in Japan is caused partially by the rigorous requirements one must meet to become an accountant. The preliminary requirement includes a series of general examinations, but university graduates are exempt from this requirement. A candidate then must pass intermediate exams covering topics such as economics, bookkeeping, financial and cost accounting, the Commercial Code, and auditing theory. The pass rates for this exam are relatively low, but a candidate who does pass is considered to be a junior CPA. A three-year apprenticeship then is required, which includes one year in training and two years of practical experience. Upon completion of the apprenticeship, the CPA candidate must take a final technical exam and submit a written thesis. The final exam also has a very low pass rate. The JICPA recently reformed the certification process. Under this reform, the three levels of examinations have been reduced to one, the three-year internship has been reduced to two years, and the notion of junior CPA has been eliminated.

Accounting Regulation

Accounting and financial reporting in Japan are regulated primarily through a triangle of laws: the Commercial Code, the Securities and Exchange Law (SEL), and the Corporate Income Tax Law. The Commercial Code of Japan is administered by the Ministry of Justice. It was enacted in 1890, as mentioned earlier, borrowing heavily from the German Commercial Code. This law requires *kabushiki kaisha* (joint stock corporations) to prepare an annual report for submission to the general meeting of shareholders. The annual report must include a balance sheet, an

---

[46] Tax experts have their own separate profession, and it is much larger in terms of membership.

[47] J. Aono, "The Auditing Environment in Japan," in *International Auditing Environment*, ed. I. Shiobara (Tokyo: Zeimukeiri-Kyokai, 2001), pp. 199–211.

income statement, and a statement of proposed appropriation of earnings. These must be accompanied by a number of supplementary schedules, including schedules detailing the acquisition and disposal of fixed assets, transactions with directors and shareholders, and details of changes to share capital and reserves. Recent amendments to the code also require certain "large corporations" (as defined by the code) to include a *consolidated* balance sheet and income statement in annual reports for the business years ending in or after 2004. Prior to this, there was no legal requirement for consolidated financial statements in Japan.

Japan has six stock exchanges, the most important being the Tokyo Stock Exchange. From the early 1990s, while the total number of listings in the Japanese exchanges has increased rapidly, the number of foreign companies listed on Japanese stock exchanges has gradually fallen. From 1991 to 2003, the total number of companies listed on the Tokyo stock exchange increased from 1,532 to 2,194; during the same period the number of foreign listings fell from 127 to 32.

Stock exchanges in Japan are government regulated rather than self-regulated. The SEL for listed companies was enacted in 1948 and is administered by the MoF. In 1951 the SEL required that financial statements of stock-exchange-listed companies should be audited by CPAs. This requirement also was added to the Commercial Code in 1974. However, there were difficulties in implementing the SEL, particularly during its first two decades. CPA firms at the time were relatively small, often with fewer than 10 assistants, and therefore did not have the capacity to undertake audits of major corporations such as Mitsubishi, Toyota, and Sumitomo. Understandably, these small CPA firms were not able to ensure compliance with the SEL and independence was an issue. As a result, the 1966 revision to the CPA Law allowed many smaller audit companies to merge to form *kansa hajin,* large corporations that operate like partnerships in terms of their liability and auditing activities and often are affiliated with large international accounting firms. Modeled on the U.S. SEC regulations, the financial reporting requirements under SEL are more demanding compared to those of the Commercial Code. In addition to SEL requirements, the stock exchanges have their own listing requirements.

Some Japanese companies, including well-known companies such as Honda Motor Company, Sony Corporation, and Pioneer Corporation, have listed on foreign stock exchanges, in particular the New York Stock Exchange. Foreign companies that list their shares on the U.S. stock market must register with the U.S. Securities and Exchange Commission (SEC). Japanese companies are the fourth largest group of foreign SEC registrants. From 2007, foreign companies, including Japanese companies, that used IFRS in preparing their financial statements could file their 20-F forms with the SEC without reconciliation to U.S. GAAP. Most Japanese companies with U.S. stock listings use U.S. GAAP in preparing the consolidated financial statements included in their SEC filings.

Unlike in the United States, and as in Germany, financial reporting in Japan is strongly influenced by tax law. The corporate income tax law in Japan provides methods for calculating taxable income and requires revenues and expenses to be recognized in the books of account in accordance with the tax law. The tax law is considered to be less vague than the Commercial Code and the SEL, so it is often referred to for more detailed regulations. Depreciation, allowance for bad debts, and profit from installment sales are examples of accounting issues that are generally reported in financial statements in conformity with the tax law.

In addition to the three laws just discussed, all listed companies are required to comply with Business Accounting Principles issued by the MoF. Business

Accounting Principles consist of a set of seven general guidelines that form the equivalent of a conceptual framework in Japan:

1. *True and fair view.* Financial statements should provide a true and fair view of a company's financial situation.
2. *Orderly bookkeeping.* A company must use an orderly system in accounting for its activities.
3. *Distinction between capital and earnings.* A company should clearly distinguish earnings from capital, earnings being the amount that can be distributed to stockholders as a dividend.
4. *Clear presentation.* Financial statements must be presented in a manner that is straightforward and logical.
5. *Continuity.* A company should follow the same accounting principles from year to year, unless a specific and understandable reason to change arises.
6. *Conservatism.* A company should use cautious judgment in applying accounting principles.
7. *Consistency.* A company should prepare only one set of financial statements to be used by various users of financial statements.

In the 1990s, the Business Accounting Principles increasingly came under criticism, mainly from international investors, for lacking a requirement of transparency in corporate reporting.

The Business Accounting Principles are developed by the Business Accounting Deliberation Council (BADC), an advisory body to the MoF. Members of the BADC have a wide variety of backgrounds. They include accountants who work in industry, public accounting, government, and higher education. The BADC has been the primary standard-setting body in Japan.

Japan's economy experienced unprecedented growth from the mid-1950s to the 1980s. In the late 1980s, however, exports and stock prices began to fall, and economic growth ground to a halt. In November 1996, the Japanese government announced its strategy for financial reforms, and the prime minister commissioned the BADC to reform the financial reporting system. This triggered a series of major changes to the regulation of financial reporting in Japan. These changes have been referred to as the Big Bang.[48] One of the major objectives of the Big Bang is to ensure that Japanese accounting standards fall into line with international standards. As a result of the Big Bang, companies in Japan were required to

- Publish consolidated accounts, including those for all associates over which they have influence.
- Disclose the market value of pension liabilities and whether they have short-falls.
- Report tradable financial securities, such as derivatives and equities, at market values, not historical cost.[49]

Another outcome of the Big Bang was the creation, in 2001, of the Financial Accounting Standards Foundation (FASF) and a new private-sector standard-setting body modeled on the FASB, the Accounting Standards Board of Japan (ASBJ). The

[48] T. Ravlic, "Japan Looks to Higher Standards," *Australian CPA* 69, no. 10 (1999), pp. 48–49.

[49] N. Yamori and T. Baba, "Japanese Management Views on Overseas Exchange Listings: Survey Results," *Journal of International Financial Management and Accounting* 12, no. 3 (2001), pp. 312–14

FASF oversees the ASBJ. The ASBJ was established by a joint committee of the Financial Services Agency, the JICPA, and the *Keidanren* (Federation of Economic Organizations). Similar to the manner in which the FASB obtains its authority to establish U.S. GAAP from the U.S. SEC, the FASF and ASBJ derive standard-setting authority from the BADC. The BADC reserves the right, however, to override any ASBJ pronouncement that is considered to be inconsistent with the "true and fair view" principle. The FASF was established partly to facilitate harmonization with international accounting standards. The JICPA takes part in setting accounting standards by sending board members to the FASF and the ASBJ. Additionally, many CPAs participate in various technical committees at the ASBJ as technical staff.

In May 2002, the FASF confirmed that accounting standards issued by the ASBJ are considered to set forth standards for financial accounting and, together with other pronouncements such as Financial Accounting Standards Implementation Guidance and Report of Practical Issues, constitute a coherent set of standards that must be complied with or otherwise referred to by members of the founding organizations and other concerned parties.[50]

In terms of accounting regulation, Japanese tradition differs in several aspects from the approach taken in Anglo-American countries. The government has the strongest influence on accounting through the Commercial Code, the Securities Law, and the Tax Law and Regulations. Further, until recently the Japanese accounting profession, represented by the JICPA, had only a relatively minor influence on determining standards for accounting and financial reporting. Finally, stock exchanges are government regulated rather than self-regulated.

International influences have played a major role in shaping accounting regulation in Japan. The Commercial Code reflects a German influence on the Japanese company legislation, including financial reporting requirements. The Securities and Exchange Law clearly reflects the influence of U.S. securities and exchange regulations. Indications are that the forces of globalization are having a significant impact on accounting and financial reporting in Japan and will continue to do so in the future.[51]

In August 2007, the ASBJ and IASB jointly announced an agreement (known as the Tokyo Agreement) to accelerate the process of convergence between Japanese GAAP and IFRS, which began in March 2005. As part of the agreement, by 2008 the two boards will seek to eliminate major differences between the two sets of standards, identified in 2005, with the remaining differences being removed by June 2011. The target date of 2011 does not apply to any major new IFRS that will become effective after 2011, and both boards will work closely to ensure the acceptance of the international approach in Japan when new standards become effective.

In September 2009, at a meeting held in London, the chairs of the ASBJ and IASB reaffirmed their ongoing cooperation in achieving convergence of Japanese GAAP and IFRS and reported that good progress was being made toward convergence of IFRSs and Japanese GAAP. In February 2010, the JICPA joined the Global Accounting Alliance (GAA), the largest global accounting network. As a further step toward adopting IFRS in Japan, the regulatory changes announced by the

---

[50] FASF, "Concerning Treatment (Compliance) of Accounting Standards and other Pronouncements Issued by the Accounting Standards Board of Japan," May 2002. For details, go to www.jicpa.or.jp/n_eng/e200201.html.

[51] For information on developments in Japanese accounting activity, go to www.jicpa.or.jp/n_eng/e-jicpa.html.

Japan Financial Services Agency (FSA) in December 2009 permitted domestic use of IFRS and established an operational framework for the voluntary application of IFRS in Japan, starting from the fiscal year ending on or after March 31, 2010.

Accounting Principles and Practices

As mentioned earlier, Japanese disclosure requirements are based on the Commercial Code, the SEL, and ASBJ accounting standards. Accounting periods ending on March 31 are the most common in Japan. Corporate net income tends to be used as a measure of funds available for distribution to shareholders, and not as a measure of corporate performance. Financial reporting practices in Japan reflect some of the inherent cultural values in Japanese society, such as group consciousness. Prior to the U.S. occupation of Japan following World War II, there was no outside auditing profession. Many Japanese corporations viewed the introduction of the CPA law in 1949 as unnecessary, and the audit as a necessary inconvenience.[52]

In general, companies are not under pressure from their main providers of finance to disclose information publicly, and Japanese companies are reluctant to provide information voluntarily. Research has found that Japanese financial analysts are concerned that Japanese firms do not define segments meaningfully and consistently and are arbitrary in the allocation of common costs,[53] and that there is a general reluctance on the part of Japanese firms to disclose segment and other information, particularly to nonshareholders.[54]

Efforts are being made to bring Japanese accounting principles and practices closer to international standards. In January 2005, the IASB and the ASBJ announced that they had agreed to launch a joint project to reduce differences between IFRS and Japanese accounting standards. Specific elements of the agreement include the following:

- Identification and assessment of differences in their existing standards on the basis of their respective conceptual frameworks or basic philosophies with the aim of reducing those differences where economic substance or market environments such as legal systems are equivalent.
- Addressing the differences in their respective conceptual frameworks.
- Considering their respective due process requirements in arriving at agreement.
- Undertaking a study by the ASBJ to get an overall picture of major differences between Japanese accounting standards and IFRS with a view to identifying topics to be discussed.

Under this project, five topics will be considered by both boards for the first phase:

- Measurement of inventories (IAS 2).
- Segment reporting (IAS 14).
- Related-party disclosures (IAS 24).

[52] Aono, "The Auditing Environment. . . ."

[53] V. Mande and R. Ortman, "Are Recent Segment Disclosures of Japanese Firms Useful? Views of Japanese Financial Analysts," *International Journal of Accounting* 37 (2002), pp. 27–46.

[54] C. Ozu and S. Gray, "The Development of Segment Reporting in Japan: Achieving International Harmonization Through a Process of National Consensus," *Advances in International Accounting* 14 (2001), pp. 1–13; and J. L. McKinnon and G. L. Harrison, "Cultural Influence on Corporate and Governmental Involvement in Accounting Policy Determination in Japan," *Journal of Accounting and Public Policy,* Autumn (1985), pp. 201–23.

- Unification of accounting policies applied to foreign subsidiaries (IAS 27).
- Investment property (IAS 40).

The differences between Japanese accounting standards and IFRS can be identified in many areas. There are no specific Japanese rules in some areas covered by IFRS, such as classification of business combinations as acquisitions or poolings of interest (IAS 22), impairment of assets (IAS 36), and accounting for employee benefits other than severance indemnities (IAS 19). Further, there are no specific rules requiring disclosures of a primary statement of changes in equity (IAS 1), discontinuing operations (IAS 35), and segment liabilities (IAS 14). In some other areas, there are inconsistencies between Japanese GAAP and IFRS. For example, under Japanese GAAP, leases, except those that transfer ownership to the lessee, are treated as operating leases (IAS 17); inventories generally can be valued at cost rather than at the lower of cost or net realizable value (IAS 2); proposed dividends can be accrued in consolidated financial statements (IAS 10); and extraordinary items are defined more broadly (IAS 8). Exhibit 6.8 shows some of the differences between IFRS and Japanese GAAP.

Nineteen Japanese companies were listed on the New York Stock Exchange in June 2004. Each of these companies uses U.S. GAAP to prepare the financial statements included in the Form 20-F annual report filed with the U.S. Securities and Exchange Commission, so there are no reconciliations from Japanese GAAP to U.S. GAAP that we can look at to learn about the effect differences in the two sets of accounting standards have on financial statements. However, in its 2003 Form 20-F, Nidec Corporation (a Japanese motor manufacturer) provided the following information related to differences between Japanese and U.S. GAAP:

> There are differences between Japanese GAAP and U.S. GAAP. They primarily relate to the statement of cash flows, disclosure of segment information, the scope of consolidation, accounting for derivatives, deferred income taxes, accounting for investments in certain equity securities, accounting for lease transactions, accrued compensated absences, accounting for employee retirement and severance benefits, accounting for the impairment of long-lived assets, earnings per share and comprehensive income. Also, under Japanese GAAP, a restatement of prior years' financial statements reflecting the effect of a change in accounting policies is not required.
>
> Our results of operations for the year ended March 31, 2003, as reported in our U.S. GAAP and Japanese GAAP consolidated financial statements differ substantially mainly because of the difference in the scope of consolidation. For that year, we consolidated 18 more entities in our Japanese GAAP consolidated financial statements than in our U.S. GAAP consolidated financial statements. We were required to consolidate these additional entities in our Japanese GAAP consolidated financial statements because, with respect to each of those entities: (i) we were regarded as possessing a majority of the entity's voting shares because of the existence of a sufficient number of shareholders of the company that did not exercise their voting rights at the shareholders' general meetings; or (ii) our current or former executives or employees comprised a majority of the board of directors of the entity. These 18 entities had combined net sales of ¥86 billion in the year ended March 31, 2003. (p. 4)

Nidec Corporation, in its 2010 Form 20-F, provides a description of the accounting standards adopted in preparing financial statements (see Exhibit 6.9).

Tokyo Agreement

In August 2007, the ASBJ and the IASB jointly announced that they had agreed to accelerate convergence between Japanese GAAP and IFRS (the Tokyo agreement). Accordingly, the two boards will seek to eliminate the major differences between

EXHIBIT 6.8 Differences between Japanese GAAP and IFRS

Issue	IFRS	Japanese GAAP
Accounting policies for overseas subsidiaries	IAS 27: Consolidated financial statements should be prepared using uniform accounting policies for like transactions and other events in similar circumstances. If it is not practicable to use uniform accounting policies, that fact should be disclosed together with the proportions of the items in the consolidated financial statements to which the different accounting policies have been applied.	It is acceptable that overseas subsidiaries apply different accounting policies if they are appropriate under the requirements of the country of those subsidiaries.
Revaluation of land	IAS 16: Revaluations should be made with sufficient regularity such that the carrying amount does not differ materially from that which would be determined using fair value at the balance sheet date.	Land can be revalued, but the revaluation does not need to be kept up to date.
Preoperating costs	IAS 38: Start-up costs should be recognized as an expense when incurred.	Preoperating costs can be capitalized.
Inventory valuation	IAS 2: Inventories should be measured at the lower of cost or net realizable value.	Inventories can be valued at cost rather than at the lower of cost and net realizable value.
Construction contracts	IAS 11: The stage of completion of the contract activity at the balance sheet date should be used to recognize contract revenue.	The completed contract method can be used for the recognition of revenue on construction contracts.
Provisions	IAS 37: Provisions can be made only if an enterprise has a present obligation as a result of a past transaction.	Provisions can be made on the basis of decisions by directors before an obligation arises.
Segment reporting	IAS 14: Disclosure requirements for segments are provided in terms of primary and secondary reporting formats.	Segment reporting does not use the primary/secondary basis.
Financial statements of hyperinflationary subsidiaries	IAS 21: The financial statements of a foreign entity that reports in the currency of a hyperinflationary economy should be restated before they are translated into the reporting currency of the reporting entity.	There are no requirements concerning the translation of the financial statements of hyperinflationary subsidiaries.

the two sets of standards by 2008, and eliminate all the differences completely in or before June 2011 (except any major new IFRS now being developed that will become effective after 2011).

At a meeting held in London in September 2009 with the IASB, the ASBJ reported that good progress was being made toward IFRS and Japanese GAAP convergence. Further, the regulatory changes announced in December 2009 by the Japanese Financial Services Authority (FSA), established an operational framework for the voluntary application of IFRS in Japan, starting from the fiscal year on or after March 31, 2010.

EXHIBIT 6.9

NIDEC CORPORATION
Form F-20

NOTES TO CONSOLIDATED FINANCIAL STATEMENTS
For the fiscal year ended March 31, 2010

Accounting Changes

As of September 15, 2009, NIDEC adopted the FASB Accounting Standards Codification™ (ASC) 105, "Generally Accepted Accounting Principles" (formerly Statement of Financial Accounting Standards (SFAS) No. 168, "The FASB Accounting Standards Codification™ and the Hierarchy of Generally Accepted Accounting Principles—a replacement of FASB Statement No. 162"). ASC 105 replaces SFAS No. 162 "The Hierarchy of Generally Accepted Accounting Principles" and establishes the FASB Accounting Standards Codification™ as the single source of authoritative nongovernmental U.S. Generally Accepted Accounting Principles (other than guidance issued by the SEC). The adoption of ASC 105 had no impact on NIDEC's consolidated financial position, results of operations or liquidity.

As of April 1, 2009, NIDEC adopted ASC 820, "Fair Value Measurements and Disclosures" (formerly SFAS No. 157, "Fair Value Measurements") for certain nonfinancial assets and liabilities. FASB Staff Position (FSP) No. FAS 157-2, "Effective Date of FASB Statement No. 157" delays the effective date of ASC 820 for one year for nonfinancial assets and liabilities. The adoption of ASC 820 did not have a material impact on NIDEC's consolidated financial position, results of operations or liquidity.

As of April 1, 2009, NIDEC adopted ASC 805, "Business Combinations" (formerly SFAS No. 141 (revised 2007), "Business Combinations"). ASC 805 requires that assets acquired, liabilities assumed, contractual contingencies, and contingent consideration be measured at fair value as of the acquisition date, that acquisition-related costs be expensed as incurred, that restructuring costs generally be expensed in periods subsequent to the acquisition date, and the changes in accounting for deferred tax asset valuation allowances and acquired income tax uncertainties after the measurement period impact income tax expense. The adoption of ASC 805 did not have a material impact on NIDEC's consolidated financial position, results of operations or liquidity since NIDEC did not acquire any material businesses for the year ended March 31, 2010. Any future impact, however, will depend on the number, size and nature of any business combination transactions that we may complete.

As of April 1, 2009, NIDEC adopted ASC 810, "Consolidation" (formerly SFAS No. 160, "Noncontrolling Interests in Consolidated Financial Statements—an amendment of ARB No. 51"). ASC 810 recharacterizes minority interests in a subsidiary as non-controlling interests and requires the presentation of noncontrolling interests as equity in consolidated balance sheets, and separate identification and presentation in consolidated statements of income of net income attributable to the entity and the noncontrolling interest. ASC 810 also requires all transactions for changes in a parent's ownership interest in a subsidiary that do not result in the subsidiary ceasing to be a subsidiary to be recognized as equity transactions. Upon adoption, noncontrolling interests, which were previously referred to as minority interests and classified in the mezzanine section between liabilities and equity on the consolidated balance sheets, are now included as a separate component of total equity. Consolidated net income on the consolidated statements of income now includes the net income (loss) attributable to noncontrolling interests. In addition, payments for additional investments in subsidiaries, which were previously classified in the cash flows from investing activities on the consolidated statements of cash flows, are now included in cash flows from financing activities. Prior period amounts were reclassified to conform to the current period presentation.

As of June 15, 2009, NIDEC adopted ASC 855, "Subsequent Events" (formerly SFAS No. 165, "Subsequent Events"). ASC 855 establishes general standards of accounting for and disclosure of events that occur after the balance sheet date but before financial statements are issued or are available to be issued. The adoption of ASC 855 did not have a material impact on NIDEC's consolidated financial position, results of operations or liquidity.

As of December 15, 2009, NIDEC adopted ASC 715, "Compensation—Retirement Benefits", (formerly FSP No. FAS 132(R)-1, "Employers' Disclosures about Postretirement Benefit Plan Assets"). ASC 715 provides guidance on employers' disclosures of a defined benefit pension or other postretirement plan. Specifically, employers are required to disclose information about fair value measurements of plan assets. The adoption of ASC 715 did not have a material impact on Nidec's consolidated financial position, results of operations or liquidity.

Recent Accounting Pronouncements to be adopted in future periods

In December 2009, the FASB issued Accounting Standards Update (ASU) No. 2009-16, "Accounting for Transfers of Financial Assets". This accounting standard codified SFAS No.166, "Accounting for Transfers of Financial Assets—an amendment of FASB Statement No. 140". ASU 2009-16 requires more information about transfers of financial assets, including securitization transactions, and where companies have continuing exposure to the risks related to transferred financial assets. ASU 2009-16 also eliminates the concept of a "qualifying special-purpose entity," changes the requirements for derecognizing financial assets. ASU 2009-16 is effective as of the beginning of each reporting entity's first annual reporting period that begins after November 15, 2009, for interim periods within that first annual reporting period, and for interim and annual reporting periods thereafter. The adoption of ASU 2009-16 is not expected to have a material impact on its consolidated financial position, results of operations and liquidity.

In December 2009, the FASB issued ASU No. 2009-17, "Improvements to Financial Reporting by Enterprises Involved with Variable Interest Entities." This accounting standard codified SFAS No. 167, "Amendments to FASB Interpretation No. 46(R)". ASU 2009-17 requires an enterprise to perform an analysis to identify the primary beneficiary of all variable interest entities and also requires ongoing reassessments of whether an enterprise is the primary beneficiary of all variable interest entities. ASU 2009-17 is effective as of the beginning of each reporting entity's first annual reporting period that begins after November 15, 2009, for interim periods within that first annual reporting period, and for interim and annual reporting periods thereafter. The adoption of ASU 2009-17 is not expected to have a material impact on its consolidated financial position, results of operations and liquidity.

Accounting Changes

As of September 15, 2009, we adopted the FASB Accounting Standards Codification™ (ASC) 105, "Generally Accepted Accounting Principles" (formerly, Statement of Financial Accounting Standards (SFAS) No. 168, "The FASB Accounting Standards Codification™ and the Hierarchy of Generally Accepted Accounting Principles—a replacement of FASB Statement No. 162"). ASC 105 replaces SFAS No. 162 "The Hierarchy of Generally Accepted Accounting Principles," and establishes the FASB Accounting Standards Codification™ as the single source of authoritative nongovernmental U.S. Generally Accepted Accounting Principles (other than guidance issued by the SEC). The adoption of ASC 105 had no impact on our consolidated financial position, results of operations, or liquidity.

As of April 1, 2009, we adopted ASC 820, "Fair Value Measurements and Disclosures" (formerly, SFAS No. 157, "Fair Value Measurements") for certain nonfinancial assets and liabilities. FASB Staff Position (FSP) No. FAS 157-2, "Effective Date of FASB Statement No. 157" delays the effective date of ASC 820 for one year for nonfinancial assets and liabilities. The adoption of ASC 820 did not have a material impact on our consolidated financial position, results of operations or liquidity.

As of April 1, 2009, we adopted ASC 805, "Business Combinations" (formerly, SFAS No. 141 (revised 2007), "Business Combinations"). ASC 805 requires that assets acquired, liabilities assumed, contractual contingencies, and contingent consideration be measured at fair value as of the acquisition date, that acquisition-related costs be expensed as incurred; that restructuring costs generally be expensed in periods subsequent to the acquisition date; and that changes in accounting for deferred tax asset valuation allowances and acquired income tax uncertainties after the measurement period impact income tax expense. The adoption of ASC 805 did not have a material impact on our consolidated financial position, results of operations or liquidity since we did not acquire any material businesses for the year ended March 31, 2010. Any future impact, however, will depend on the number, size, and nature of any business combination transactions that we may complete.

MEXICO

Background

Mexico became an independent nation in 1821 after being held for three centuries as a Spanish colony. The legislative authority in Mexico rests with the president and the Congress. The chief executive of the government is the president, who is elected for a six-year term and may not be reelected. The Mexican Congress consists of a Senate, with 128 members, elected for six years, and a Chamber of Deputies, with 500 members, elected for three years.

Until about two decades ago, a substantial proportion of the Mexican business sector was government controlled, and a large number of business enterprises were government owned. From the mid-1970s until the late 1980s Mexico faced persistent balance-of-payments problems resulting from the government's efforts to defend the overvalued peso while incurring massive external debt. These and other economic problems were attributed largely to government acquisition and control of private enterprises. In recent years, there has been a major effort to privatize state-owned enterprises as part of a new economic program designed to accelerate long-term economic growth. Many of the restrictions on investment by foreigners have been removed, opening the door to external capital. This process has been further encouraged by Mexico's joining the United States and Canada under the North American Free Trade Agreement (NAFTA) in 1993. Among other things, NAFTA aims to reduce most barriers to trade in goods, liberalize the crossborder flow of services and capital, and open up new areas of opportunity in each country to conduct business in the other two countries. Mexico represents one of the largest trading partners of the United States, which accounts for three-quarters of Mexico's imports, more than 80 percent of Mexico's exports, and 60 percent of all direct foreign investment.

In December 1994, Mexico devalued the peso and plunged into a financial crisis (known as the Tequila crisis) as billions in short-term, dollar-denominated bonds held largely by foreigners came due. Unable to pay, Mexico accepted a $40 billion bailout from the U.S. Treasury and the International Monetary Fund. The bailout was accompanied by some tough conditions. For example, Mexico's Central Bank and Finance Secretariat had to shed light on all of their financial transactions and start communicating better with investors and creditors. Within seven months, Mexico managed to raise money on international financial markets once again. Currently, Mexico has a largely free-market economy.

Mexico has one stock exchange, the Bolsa Mexicana de Valores, located in Mexico City. Historically, the Mexican business sector has been predominantly family-owned. Firms prefer to raise capital through debt rather than equity, although this is gradually changing. The influx of foreign capital and the return of Mexican capital previously invested abroad in the late 1980s and early 1990s have stimulated the growth of the Mexican stock market. The stock exchange is a private institution jointly owned by 32 brokerage houses. Prior approval of the National Banking and Securities Commission (NBSC) is required for listing on the stock exchange. Mexican companies can issue three categories of shares, Series A, Series B, and Series N. Series A shares can be held only by Mexican nationals, and these shares account for at least 51 percent of voting rights; Series B shares are open to foreigners and may account for only up to 49 percent of ownership; and Series N shares, called neutral shares and created under the Foreign Investment Law in January 1994, involve a trust mechanism designed for foreign investors. They have no voting rights and limited corporate rights.

There are about 200 companies listed on the Mexican Stock Exchange, 80 percent of which are audited by the Big Four accounting firms; the remainder is audited by about 10 accounting firms that are associated with the second-tier international accounting firms.

Accounting Profession

The first professional organization of public accountants in Mexico, the *Asociacion de Contadores Publicos,* was established in 1917.[55] This organization was replaced by the Mexican Institute of Public Accountants (MIPA) in 1964. MIPA was officially recognized in 1977 as a federation of state and local associations of registered public accountants in Mexico. An independent, nongovernmental professional association, it is governed by three bodies, the General Conference of Members, the Governance Group, and the National Executive Committee (NEC). The first two bodies mainly perform sponsoring and oversight functions, whereas the NEC's major responsibilities relate to overseeing the day-to-day activities of MIPA. MIPA's primary responsibility is to establish and communicate, in the public interest, the accounting principles to be followed in preparing financial information for external users and to promote their acceptance and observance throughout the nation.[56] It is also empowered to conduct investigation in response to complaints against its members and impose sanctions; oversee professional

---

[55] For an excellent discussion of the early development of Mexican Accounting, see S. A. Zeff, *Forging Accounting Principles in Five Countries: A History and Analysis of Trends* (Champaign, IL: Stipes, 1972), pp. 91–109.

[56] Certain regulated enterprises, such as government-owned banks, may follow special accounting rules and thus depart from GAAP.

conduct of its members; and establish continuing professional education requirements. MIPA's Code of Ethics for professional accountants was recently revised toward alignment with IFAC's code. It includes, among other things, the adoption of a framework and principles-based approach, and additional guidance for implementation of the principles.

Public accounting services in Mexico mainly consist of bookkeeping, tax, and audit. The number of public accountants in Mexico is about 200,000, with the majority working in business or government. As stipulated in the law regulating the practice of professions, a professional diploma is required to practice as a public accountant in Mexico. Under the arrangement introduced in 1999, the MIPA organizes qualififying examination for those public accountants who intend to obtain the title of *Contador Publico Certificado* (CPC); i.e., Certified Public Accountant). The title CPC is considered equivalent to the CPA in the United States. Consequently, the Mexican CPCs can practice accountancy in the United States and Canada, subject to passing examinations on national legislation and standards in accordance with provisions of the Professional Mutual Recognition Agreement signed in September 2002 by the representatives of the U.S. NASBA/AICPA International Qualifications Appraisal Board, the CICA's International Qualifications Appraisal board, and Mexican Institute of Public Accountants and Mexican Committee for the International Practice of Accounting, agreeing on the principal elements for granting accounting certification and licenses, which include education, examination, and experience. NAFTA's Free Trade Commission affirmed the PMRA in October 2003. The implementation of the NAFTA PMRA is an example of converging national licensing requirements into an international framework. Mexico has made the most significant changes in the process and has improved the ability of Mexican CPAs to practice across national boundaries. In the past, a person would obtain a Public Accountant undergraduate degree from an approved Mexican university and would be able to practice as a Public Accountant without passing a uniform examination. Currently, Public Accountants must successfully complete the uniform examination and be certified as a Certified Public Accountant to give an audit opinion.

Accounting Regulation

Regulation of accounting and financial reporting in Mexico is through legislation, stock exchange listing requirements, and bulletins issued by MIPA. Mexican law requires all companies incorporated in Mexico to appoint one or more statutory auditors. Annual financial statements of listed companies must be audited by a Mexican CPA and be published in a nationally circulated medium. The statutory audit report must include, at a minimum, the auditor's opinion as to whether the accounting and reporting policies followed by the company are appropriate and adequate in the circumstances and have been consistently applied, and whether the information presented by management gives a true and adequate picture of the company's financial position and operating results.

The NBSC is the most important federal agency that oversees information disclosure by publicly owned companies in Mexico. It is a semi-independent entity within the Ministry of Finance that administers Mexico's securities law and regulates the operation of securities markets. The current Mexican Securities Law was enacted in 1975, with some amendments introduced in 1993, mainly to accommodate the foreign investment requirements under NAFTA.

Mexico's legal system is based on civil law; however, accounting standard setting takes an Anglo-American approach rather than a Continental European one.

Accounting in Mexico is oriented toward fairness, not legal compliance. MIPA follows a due process in developing standards, which includes issuance of exposure drafts of proposed standards for public comment.

MIPA is both the standard-setting and the enforcement body in Mexico. Accounting standards are recognized as authoritative by the government, in particular NBSC. Mexican accounting principles apply to all business entities, large and small. In some cases, the NBSC issues rules for listed companies. All companies incorporated under Mexican law must appoint at least one statutory auditor to report to the shareholders on the annual financial statements. Two special commissions within MIPA are responsible for the actual development of standards. The Auditing Standards and Procedures Commission develops auditing standards, and the Accounting Principles Commission (APC) develops accounting standards. APC members are volunteers, appointed by MIPA's NEC. About half the APC members are public accountants working as independent auditors, another 25 percent are public accountants working in other areas, and the balance consists of representatives of user, preparer, private sector, and public sector groups. MIPA also has developed a Code of Ethics, which, among other things, prohibits media advertising for public accountants.

Mexican accounting standards are known as bulletins. MIPA issues four kinds of bulletins. Series A bulletins deal with the basic accounting principles that define the framework of accounting principles. For example, Bulletin A-8 requires companies to apply IFRS for issues that are not covered by Mexican generally accepted accounting principles. MIPA has translated and published IFRS into Spanish. Series B bulletins deal with the accounting principles that are pervasive to all financial statements. For example, Bulletin B-1 states the objectives of financial statements, B-2 deals with revenue recognition, and so on. Bulletin B-10 deals with the recognition of the effects of inflation in the financial statements. Series C bulletins provide guidance with respect to specific balance sheet and income statement accounts, such as cash and short-term investments (Bulletin C-1), inventories (Bulletin C-4), liabilities (Bulletin C-9), and contingencies and commitments (Bulletin C-12). Series D bulletins deal with specific topics that are key to determining the net income of an enterprise, such as accounting for income taxes (Bulletin D-4) and leasing (Bulletin D-5). With few exceptions, bulletins are similar to U.S. GAAP.

The company law requires that shareholders appoint a *comisario*. As per requirement of the LGSM, a comisario is appointed at the annual general meeting of shareholders and is given responsibility to protect shareholder interests. This individual, for whom no professional title of any kind is required, attends board meetings without a voting right, is authorized to call a shareholders' meeting, and has full access to company information. At each annual general meeting, the comisario is required to deliver a report with respect to the accuracy, adequacy, and rationality of financial and other information presented by the board of directors, including an opinion on whether appropriate accounting policies were followed in preparing the financial statements.

Companies listed on the Mexican Stock Exchange must submit annual, December 31 year-end, consolidated financial statements, audited by a Mexican public accountant, to the Exchange and to the NBSC. Compliance with tax regulations requires a report prepared in accordance with Mexican GAAP and audited in accordance with Mexican generally accepted auditing standards.

The enactment of the Securities Market Law (LMV) of 2001 and of the CNBV's Circular Única provides the basis for enforcement of the accounting and auditing requirements in listed companies. The CNBV conducts reviews of financial statements of listed companies and other participants in the securities markets, which include brokerage firms and investment funds, as well as banks, aimed at determining compliance with applicable accounting and disclosure requirements. The CNBV also visits audit firms, selected on a random basis, to perform reviews of audit work and ensure compliance with applicable standards. For violations of accounting and auditing requirements, the CNBV is authorized under the Securities Exchange Law to impose administrative sanctions, including fines, suspension, and deprivation of the right to practice as advisers, directors, management, comisarios, and external auditors.

However, the enforcement mechanisms in Mexico are not very effective. For example, although the NBSC is responsible for enforcing insider-trading laws, these laws are rarely implemented.

Mexico is different from the United States and Canada in that a single national body, the Ministry of Education, has the authority by law to set the requirements for accounting professionals' public practice rights. The Mexican states do not have separate and different laws, as is the case in the United States and Canada.

Accounting Principles and Practices

Mexico has a conceptual framework for financial reporting, which is basically included in three bulletins: A-1, *Structure of the Basic Theory of Financial Accounting;* A-11, *Definition of Basic Concepts Integrating Financial Statements;* and B-1, *Objectives of Financial Statements.* The generally accepted accounting principles in Mexico consist of the following, in order of importance:

1. MIPA bulletins.
2. MIPA circulars or interpretations. These are opinions relating to specific topics on which there may or may not be a specific standard. Compliance with these is not mandatory, but highly recommended.
3. International Financial Reporting Standards.
4. Accounting principles of other countries that would be applicable in the circumstances. In practice, U.S. GAAP are the main source applied.

In recent years Mexican accounting principles have been heavily influenced by U.S. accounting practice because of Mexico's membership in NAFTA. The U.S. influence is through the presence of subsidiaries of U.S. companies and the prominence of local representatives of the Big Four international accounting firms. As a result, although there are differences in accounting between the two countries, Mexican and U.S. accounting standards are generally consistent. In those areas where Mexican accounting principles do not exist, such as earnings per share or line-of-business disclosures, it is common for companies to use the corresponding U.S. standard.

In addition to the basic balance sheet and income statement, a statement of changes in financial position also is prepared. This latter statement is very similar to the U.S. statement of cash flows in appearance but reflects sources and uses of funds, rather than cash. Notes to the financial statements and a report from the statutory auditor are attached to the financial statements. Mexican parent companies are required to prepare consolidated financial statements. In doing so, Mexican companies use both the purchase method and the pooling of interests method. Note that IFRS 3 eliminated option to use pooling of interests method. Goodwill is amortized over a period not exceeding 20 years.

Accounting in Mexico shares many features of accounting with other Latin American countries. In the 1980s and 1990s, inflation accounting information was being produced in several South American countries, generally using a general price index for adjustment purposes, mainly because of the absence of satisfactory specific asset indexes.

One of the unique features of Mexican accounting practice, and the greatest difference from U.S. accounting, is the treatment of the effects of inflation in financial statements by using general purchasing power accounting. Mexico has a history of high rates of inflation, often exceeding 20 percent per year. Bulletin B-10, *Recognition of the Effects of Inflation in Financial Information,* became compulsory for all Mexican companies in 1984. The bulletin has been amended and refined several times. This is an example of how accounting practices reflect specific needs of the local environment, in this case, the economic environment.

Bulletin B-10 required all nonmonetary assets and liabilities to be restated for changes in the purchasing power of the peso using the National Consumer Price Index (NCPI) published by the Central Bank. Prior to the Fifth Amendment to B-10 in 1996, estimated replacement costs were acceptable for restating inventory and fixed assets, but later this was only permissible for inventory. Equity accounts also had to be restated using the NCPI to reflect paid-in capital at constant purchasing power. The third important element of the Mexican inflation accounting system was the recognition in income of the gain or loss from the net monetary asset or liability position. All comparative financial statements from prior years also should be restated to constant pesos as of the date of the most recent balance sheet. Both large and small enterprises followed the same set of accounting standards.

Bulletin B-10 also introduced a novel concept called the integral result of financing, which was reported as a separate line item on the income statement. This is calculated by adding the nominal interest expense, the gain or loss due to price-level changes on the company's net monetary position, and the gains and losses due to exchange rate fluctuations on the company's monetary assets and liabilities denominated in foreign currencies.

Before 1996, current replacement cost based on appraisals or specific price indexes was also acceptable. This approach was eliminated because it was viewed as less reliable and less in line with international standards based on historical cost.

MIPA being one of the nine founding members of the IASC, has shown a keen interest in international harmonization of accounting standards. The United States has a dominant influence on accounting standards in Mexico. For example, many of the pioneers of the Mexican accounting profession grew up on "American accounting."[57] However, the standards issued by the FASB did not always meet the Mexican requirements, and as a result, the national standard setters have also looked for "principles-based" IFRS as a reference for upgrading Mexican GAAP. There are signs of convergence with IFRS in recent years. For example, in line with IAS 29, Mexico has given up on inflation accounting recently. Bulletin B-10 requires that nonmonetary items of the financial statements be restated for the effects of inflation, irrespective of the level of inflation. However, as a result of low inflation rates in Mexico in recent years, it does not seem to satisfy the conditions set out in IAS 29, *Financial Reporting in Hyperinflationary Economies,* for such statements. However, Mexican stakeholders strongly expressed the view that even

---

[57] Stephen A. Zeff, *Forging Accounting Principles in Five Countries: A History and an Analysis of Trends* (Champaign, Il: Stipes Publishing, 1972), pp. 96–97.

though price levels have been stabilized in the recent period, it is still more beneficial to the business community to maintain the practice of restating the effects of inflation in the country.

Mexican accounting rules require research and development costs to be expensed as incurred, and leases to be classified into financial and operating categories. Mexican GAAP differs from IFRSs in the following areas: The definition of an associate is based on a threshold of an investment of 10 percent of voting shares (IAS 28); preoperating and setup costs can be capitalized (IAS 38); a statement of changes in financial position is required instead of a statement of cash flows (IAS 7); and restatement of inflation is mandatory, irrespective of the inflation rate (IAS 29). Exhibit 6.10 summarizes some of the differences between IFRS and Mexican GAAP.

CEMEX SA de CV is one of more than 20 Mexican companies listed on the New York Stock Exchange. Note 25 to the consolidated financial statements included in the company's 2010 annual report provides a detailed description about the

EXHIBIT 6.10   Differences between Mexican GAAP and IFRS

Issue	IFRS	Mexican GAAP
Definition of an associate	IAS 28: An associate is an enterprise in which the investor has significant influence and which is neither a subsidiary nor a joint venture of the investor.	The definition of an associate is based on a threshold of an investment of 10 percent of voting shares.
Preoperating and setup costs	IAS 38: Charge to expenses when incurred.	Preoperating and setup costs can be capitalized.
Calculation of impairment of fixed assets	IAS 36: Impairment is calculated when the book value of an asset exceeds its recoverable amount, which is the greater of net realizable value and the net present value of future net cash flows expected to arise from continued use of the asset.	For the calculation of impairment, assets for sale are valued at net selling price and assets for continued use are valued at value in use.
Statement of cash flows	IAS 7: A statement of cash flows is required.	A statement of changes in financial position is required instead of a statement of cash flows.
Inflation accounting	IAS 29: Required for hyperinflationary countries.	Restatement for inflation is mandatory, irrespective of the inflation rate.
Inflation accounting method	IAS 29: Adjust the subsidiary financial statements for general effects of inflation, with the gain or loss on net monetary position in net income.	Companies can follow either the general price-level method or that method combined with the current cost method for restatement for inflation, and if the current cost method is followed, the results of holding nonmonetary assets (difference between indexed cost and current cost) is recorded in equity.
Negative goodwill	IFRS 3: Recognized in profit and loss immediately.	Negative goodwill is shown as a deferred credit and amortized over a period of up to five years.

differences between Mexican GAAP and U.S. GAAP (see Exhibit 6.11). In November 2008, the Mexican Securities and Exchange Commission (Comision Nacional Bancaria y de Valores, or CNBV) announced that all companies listed on the Mexican Stock Exchange will be required to use IFRS starting in 2012. Listed companies will have the option to use IFRS earlier—starting as early as 2008—subject to requirements that will be established by the CNBV.

EXHIBIT 6.11

CEMEX, S.A.B. DE C.V. AND SUBSIDIARIES
Notes to Consolidated Financial Statements
As of December 31, 2009
(Millions of Mexican pesos)

25. Differences between Mexican and United States Accounting Principles

(a) *Basis of Presentation under U.S. GAAP*

The consolidated financial statements are prepared in accordance with MFRS, which differ in certain significant respects from generally accepted accounting principles applicable in the United States ("U.S. GAAP"). The term "SFAS" as used herein refers to U.S. Statements of Financial Accounting Standards. Likewise, the term "FASB" refers to the U.S. Financial Accounting Standards Board. On July 1, 2009, the FASB instituted a major change in the way accounting standards are organized by the implementation of the FASB Accounting Standards Codification TM ("ASC") became the single official source of authoritative, nongovernmental U.S. GAAP. After that date, only one level of authoritative U.S. GAAP exists, other than guidance issued by the Securities and Exchange Commission ("SEC"). All other literature will be non-authoritative.

As detailed in note 3A, until December 31, 2007, the MFRS consolidated financial statements included the effects of inflation, whereas financial statements prepared under U.S. GAAP are presented on a historical cost basis. The reconciliation to U.S. GAAP includes: (i) a reconciling item to reflect the difference in the carrying value of machinery and equipment of foreign origin and related depreciation between the methodology set forth by MFRS B-10 until December 31, 2007 and the amounts that would be determined by using the historical cost/constant currency method. As described below, this provision of inflation accounting under MFRS did not meet the requirements of Rule 3-20 of Regulation S-X promulgated by the SEC. The reconciliation does not include the reversal of other MFRS inflation accounting adjustments as of and for the years ended December 31, 2009, 2008 and 2007, as these adjustments represent a comprehensive measure of the effects of price level changes in the applicable countries and, as such, are considered a more meaningful presentation than historical cost-based financial reporting for both Mexican and U.S. accounting purposes.

Reconciliation of net income under MFRS to U.S. GAAP

Considering the presentation of CEMEX's operations in Australia as discontinued operations under MFRS (note 4B), for purposes of the reconciliation of net income to U.S. GAAP, all reconciling items pertaining to CEMEX's operations in Australia for the current and prior periods were reclassified and presented in the single line item "U.S. GAAP adjustments from discontinued operations." For the years ended December 31, 2009, 2008 and 2007, the main differences between MFRS and U.S. GAAP, and their effect on consolidated net income and earnings per share, are presented below:

	2009	2008	2007
Income under MFRS from continuing operations	Ps 5,925	226	26,657
U.S. GAAP adjustments having the effect of increasing reported income from continuing operations:			
1. Financial instruments–Fair value measurements (note 25(h)).	—	1,305	—
2. Employees' statutory profit sharing (note 25(c))	—	195	226
3. Employee benefits (note 25(e)).	104	104	61
4. Other adjustments–Deferred charges (notes 25(c) and (k))	—	225	122
5. Other adjustments–Capitalized interest (note 25(k))	—	—	252
6. Other adjustments–Monetary position result (note 25(k))	—	—	588
7. Other adjustments–Discontinued operations financial expense (note 25(k))	373	388	272
8. Other adjustments–Depreciation and investments in associates (notes 25(k))	—	—	17
9. Impairment of long-lived assets (note 25(j))	920	—	—
10. Hedge accounting (note 25(h)).	1,763	—	—
11. Income taxes (note 25(c)).	3,420	—	—

U.S. GAAP adjustments having the effect of decreasing reported income from continuing operations:

1. Impairment of long-lived assets (note 25(j))	—	(46,077)	—
2. Income taxes (note 25(c)).	—	(7,861)	(1,184)
3. Hedge accounting (note 25(h)).	—	(7,716)	(339)
4. Financing transactions (note 25(f))	(2,706)	(2,596)	(1,847)
5. Accounting for uncertainty in income taxes (note 25(d)).	(3,473)	(1,584)	(2,188)
6. Financial instruments—Fair value measurements (note 25(h)).	(1,057)	—	—
7. Financial instruments—Mandatory convertible securities (note 25(h))	(65)	—	—
8. Inflation adjustment of machinery and equipment (note 25(g))	(224)	(272)	(291)
9. Other adjustments–Deferred charges (notes 25(c) and (k))	(6,104)	—	—
Income (loss) under U.S. GAAP from continuing operations.	**Ps (1,124)**	**(63,663)**	**22,346**
Income (loss) from discontinued operations as reported under MFRS	(4,276)	2,097	288
U.S. GAAP adjustments from discontinued operations (note 25(l))	(264)	(275)	(191)
Income (loss) under U.S. GAAP from discontinued operations.	**Ps (4,540)**	**1,822**	**97**
Non-controlling interest under MFRS	240	45	837
Non-controlling interest share of U.S. GAAP adjustment	—	—	239
Non-controlling income under U.S. GAAP	**Ps 240**	**45**	**1,076**
Controlling net income (loss) under U.S. GAAP	**Ps (5,904)**	**(61,886)**	**21,367**

Approximate basic and diluted earnings per share under U.S. GAAP for the years ended December 31, 2009, 2008 and 2007 are as follows:

	2009	2008	2007
Basic EPS under U.S. GAAP from continuing operations	Ps (0.05)	(2.73)	0.95
Basic EPS under U.S. GAAP from discontinued operations	(0.18)	0.04	0.01
	Ps (0.23)	**(2.69)**	**0.96**
Diluted EPS under U.S. GAAP from continuing operations[1]	Ps (0.05)	(2.73)	0.95
Diluted EPS under U.S. GAAP from discontinued operations[1]	(0.18)	0.04	0.01
	Ps (0.23)	**(2.69)**	**0.96**

[1] According to ASC 260-10-45-20 *Earnings per Share*, if there is a loss from continuing operations, diluted EPS would be computed as basic EPS not including potential common shares to avoid anti-dilution.

The following table presents summarized consolidated financial information of the statements of operations for the years ended December 31, 2009, 2008 and 2007 under U.S. GAAP, including all reconciling items described in this Note 25 as well as certain reclassifications required for purposes of U.S. GAAP:

	2009	2008[3]	2007[3]
Net sales	Ps 197,801	224,804	226,742
Operating income (loss)[1]	10,396	(42,233)	28,623
Operating income (loss) after other expenses, net	12,048	(41,427)	28,561
Comprehensive financing result[2]	(23,818)	(36,944)	(1,027)
Income (loss) before discontinued operations.	(1,124)	(63,663)	22,346
Discontinued operations	(4,540)	1,822	97
Non-controlling interest net income.	240	45	1,076
Controlling interest net income (loss).	**Ps (5,904)**	**(61,886)**	**21,367**

[1] Impairment losses as well as current and deferred Employee Statutory Profit Sharing under U.S. GAAP are included in the determination of operating income. Under MFRS, these items are part of other expenses, net. In addition, as mentioned in note 3S, under MFRS, for the years ended December 31, 2009, 2008 and 2007, other expenses, net, include several unusual or non-recurring transactions, such as restructuring costs (severance payments), results from sales of assets and impairment losses. In the summarized statements of operations under U.S. GAAP, expenses of Ps4,451 in 2009, Ps70,753 in 2008 and Ps2,083 in 2007, were reclassified from other expenses, net, under MFRS to operating expenses under U.S. GAAP.

Continued

EXHIBIT 6.11 (*Continued*)

[2] Deferred financing costs amortized under MFRS to "Other expenses, net" during 2009 in connection with the early extinguishment of the related debt for approximately Ps940 were reclassified to comprehensive financing result under U.S. GAAP.
[3] Until December 31, 2008, for MFRS purposes, CEMEX accounted for its investments in entities under joint control using the proportional consolidation method (note 3B), incorporating line-by-line all assets, liabilities, revenues and expenses according to CEMEX's equity ownership. CEMEX sold these jointly controlled entities in December 2008 (note 12A). Under U.S. GAAP, joint controlled investments are accounted for by the equity method; therefore, all revenues and expenses for the years ended December 31, 2008 and 2007 related to such joint controlled entities were removed line-by-line against the equity in associates for purposes of the statements of operations.

Reconciliation of stockholders' equity under MFRS to U.S. GAAP

At December 31, 2009 and 2008, the main differences between MFRS and U.S. GAAP, and their effect on consolidated stockholders' equity, with an explanation of the adjustments, are presented below:

	2009	2008
Total stockholders' equity reported under MFRS.	Ps 257,570	237,267
U.S. GAAP adjustments:		
1. Goodwill (notes 25(b) and (j)).	(27,760)	(31,502)
2. Other intangible assets (note 25(j)).	(179)	(179)
3. Income taxes (note 25(c)).	2,678	309
4. Accounting for uncertainty in income taxes (note 25(d)).	(13,265)	(10,236)
5. Employee benefits (note 25(e)).	(6,144)	(3,998)
6. Non-controlling interest—Financing transactions (note 25(f)).	(39,859)	(41,495)
7. Inflation adjustment for machinery and equipment (note 25(g)).	3,839	4,164
8. Financial Instruments—Fair value measurements (note 25(h)).	247	1,305
9. Financial instruments 2 Mandatory convertible securities (note 25(h)).	(2,036)	—
10. Other adjustments—Deferred charges (note 25(k)).	(5,769)	440
11. Other adjustments—Capitalized interest (note 25(k))	82	324
Approximate U.S. GAAP adjustments.	(88,166)	(80,868)
Total stockholders' equity under U.S. GAAP (note25(f))	Ps **169,404**	**156,399**

The following table presents summarized consolidated financial information of balance sheets as of December 31, 2009 and 2008, prepared under U.S. GAAP, including all reconciling items and reclassifications as compared to MFRS described in this Note 25:

	At December 31, 2009			At December 31, 2008		
	MFRS	**Change**	**U.S. GAAP**	**MFRS**	**Change**	**U.S. GAAP**
Current assets[1]	Ps 56,770	5,615	62,385	68,195	4,731	72,926
Investments in associates, other investments and non-current accounts receivable	32,144	2,600	34,744	35,702	2,461	38,163
Non-current assets of discontinued operations.	—	—	—	24,857	(10)	24,847
Property, machinery and equipment[2,3]	258,863	9,687	268,550	270,281	10,711	280,992
Goodwill, intangible assets and deferred charges	234,509	(41,647)	192,862	224,587	(36,443)	188,144
Total assets.	**5,82,286**	**(23,745)**	**558,541**	**623,622**	**(18,550)**	**605,072**
Current liabilities[1]	49,213	1,549	50,762	152,737	3,600	156,337
Long-term debt.	203,751	(149)	203,602	162,805	5	162,810
Other non-current liabilities.	71,752	23,162	94,914	69,369	17,228	86,597
Non-current liabilities of discontinued operations.	—	—	—	1,444	(10)	1,434
Perpetual debentures.	—	39,859	39,859	—	41,495	41,495
Total liabilities.	**324,716**	**64,421**	**389,137**	**386,355**	**62,318**	**448,673**
Controlling interest.	257,570	(92,031)	165,539	237,267	(85,973)	151,294
Non-controlling interest	—	3,865	3,865	—	5,105	5,105
Consolidated stockholders' equity.	**257,570**	**(88,166)**	**169,404**	**237,267**	**(80,868)**	**156,399**
Total liabilities and stockholders' equity.	Ps **582,286**	**(23,745)**	**558,541**	**623,622**	**(18,550)**	**605,072**

Additional reclassifications under U.S. GAAP

The summarized consolidated financial information under U.S. GAAP presented in the table above includes several reclassifications as compared to the summarized consolidated financial information under MFRS. The main reclassifications at December 31, 2009 and 2008 are as follows:

[1] In connection with deferred income taxes, at December 31, 2009 and 2008, current assets under U.S. GAAP include assets of Ps6,499 and Ps5,626, respectively, which are considered non-current items under MFRS. Likewise, current liabilities under U.S. GAAP include liabilities of Ps1,680 in 2009 and Ps3,542 in 2008 classified as non-current items under MFRS. As of December 31, 2008, current assets and current liabilities under both MFRS and U.S. GAAP include approximately Ps4,672 and Ps2,555, respectively, associated with Australia's discontinued operations.

[2] Assets classified as held for sale under MFRS (Note 9) for approximately Ps1,255 and Ps1,454, as of December 31, 2009 and 2008, respectively, were reclassified to long-term assets in the condensed financial balance sheet information under U.S. GAAP. These assets are stated at their estimated fair value. Estimated costs to sell these assets are not significant.

[3] At December 31, 2009 and 2008, extraction rights in the aggregates sector of approximately Ps6,302 (US$481) and Ps6,641 (US$483), respectively (Note 12), recognized as intangible assets under MFRS, were reclassified as part of the book value of the quarries in property, machinery and equipment under U.S. GAAP, in accordance with ASC 805-10-65-1, Whether Mineral Rights are Tangible or Intangible Assets.

(b) *Goodwill*

Goodwill recognized under MFRS (Note 12) has been adjusted under U.S. GAAP for: (i) the effect on goodwill from the U.S. GAAP adjustments as of the acquisition dates; (ii) beginning January 1, 2002, goodwill is not amortized under U.S. GAAP, while under MFRS goodwill was amortized until December 31, 2004; and (iii) until December 31, 2003, goodwill under MFRS was carried in the functional currencies of the holding companies for the reporting units, was translated into pesos and was then restated based on the Mexican inflation, while under U.S. GAAP, goodwill is carried in the functional currencies of the reporting units, is restated if applicable under MFRS by the inflation factor of the reporting unit's country, and is translated into Mexican pesos at the exchange rates prevailing at the reporting date. Goodwill generated beginning January 1, 2005 under MFRS is carried consistently with the treatment of goodwill under U.S. GAAP.

The reconciliation of goodwill under MFRS and U.S. GAAP for the years ended December 31, 2009, 2008 and 2007 is as follows:

	2009	2008	2007
Goodwill under MFRS	Ps 150,827	157,541	142,344
Cumulative U.S. GAAP adjustments	(27,760)	(31,502)	11,675
Goodwill under U.S. GAAP	**123,067**	**126,039**	**154,019**
U.S. GAAP adjustments:			
Cumulative U.S. GAAP adjustments at beginning of year	(31,502)	11,675	8,509
Foreign exchange results and inflation effects	2,813	2,721	3,166
Impairment charges (see note 25(j))	929	(45,898)	—
Cumulative U.S. GAAP adjustments at end of year	Ps **(27,760)**	**(31,502)**	**11,675**

(c) *Income Taxes and Employees' Statutory Profit Sharing*

Deferred Income Taxes

Under MFRS, CEMEX determines deferred income taxes in a manner similar to U.S. GAAP (note 16B). Nonetheless, there are specific differences as compared to the calculation under ASC 740, *Income Taxes* ("ASC 740"), resulting in adjustments in the reconciliation to U.S. GAAP. These differences mainly arise from: (i) the recognition of the accumulated initial effect of the asset and liability method under MFRS did not consider the deferred tax consequences of business combinations made before January 1, 2000; and (ii) the effects of deferred tax on the reconciling items between MFRS and U.S. GAAP. The tax effects of temporary differences that give rise to significant portions of the deferred tax assets and deferred tax liabilities under U.S. GAAP at December 31, 2009 and 2008 are presented below:

Continued

EXHIBIT 6.11   *(Continued)*

	2009	2008
Deferred tax assets:		
Tax loss and tax credits carryforwards	Ps 77,602	55,488
Accounts payable and accrued expenses	8,197	11,708
Others	3,832	5,696
Total gross deferred tax assets	**89,631**	**72,892**
Less valuation allowance	(32,079)	(27,194)
Total deferred tax assets under U.S. GAAP	**57,552**	**45,698**
Deferred tax liabilities:		
Property, machinery and equipment.	(51,175)	(53,797)
Others	(1,772)	(10,932)
Total deferred tax liability under U.S. GAAP	**(52,947)**	**(64,729)**
Net deferred tax asset (liability) under U.S. GAAP.	Ps **4,605**	**(19,031)**

Under U.S. GAAP, tax effects of intra-group transactions where the related assets remain in the consolidated balance sheet should be eliminated in consolidation until the time at which the asset is sold outside the group. Under MFRS, the tax effects recognized by each subsidiary as part of such intra-group sale of assets are not reversed. During 2008 (note 25(k)), in connection with an intra-group transfer of intangible assets, a deferred tax asset for the step-up in the tax basis of the assets recognized by the buyer under MFRS in the amount of Ps2,206 was eliminated for U.S. GAAP purposes. In 2009, CEMEX recorded a tax benefit of Ps220 resulting from the tax amortization of the transferred assets for which no deferred tax is recognized in consolidation under U.S. GAAP. In addition, a deferred charge for an amount of Ps215 was recognized by the seller and is being amortized over 10 years beginning in 2009, which is the period in which the acquiring entity will obtain the related tax benefit. The amortization expense recognized in the statement of operations for the year ended December 31, 2009 was Ps21.

Of the total income tax benefit of approximately Ps3,420 for the year ended December 31, 2009 and expenses of Ps7,861 and Ps1,184 for the years ended December 31, 2008 and 2007, respectively, included in the reconciliation of net income to U.S. GAAP, income tax benefit of approximately Ps2,421 in 2009 and income tax expenses of Ps2,657 in 2008 and Ps1,103 in 2007, are related to deferred income taxes.

Current Income Taxes

In addition to the reconciling items mentioned above related to deferred income taxes, according to MFRS D-4, current income taxes are presented in the income statement. For U.S. GAAP purposes, current income taxes generated by items recognized directly in equity are recognized in equity, considering also intra-period tax allocation. The reconciliation of net income to U.S. GAAP for the years ended December 31, 2009 and 2008, includes a tax benefit of approximately Ps3,353 and an expense of approximately Ps5,091, respectively, for the reclassification of current income taxes from net income under MFRS to equity under U.S. GAAP.

In connection with changes to the tax consolidation regime in Mexico (notes 3N and 16A) under MFRS based on Interpretation 18, CEMEX recognized a charge of approximately Ps2,245 against "Retained earnings," for the liability portion related to: a) the difference between the sum of the equity of the controlled entities for tax purposes and the equity for tax purposes of the consolidated entity; b) dividends from the controlled entities for tax purposes to CEMEX, S.A.B. de C.V.; and c) other transactions between the companies included in the tax consolidation that represented the transfer of resources within the group. Under U.S. GAAP, the tax effects of a new tax law enactment are recognized in the income statement, therefore, the charge to retained earnings mentioned above has been reclassified to income tax expense in the income statement for the year ended December 31, 2009.

Employees' Statutory Profit Sharing ("ESPS")

Until December 31, 2007, for purposes of U.S. GAAP, CEMEX record a deferred tax liability related to ESPS in Mexico using the asset and liability method at the statutory rate of 10%. As mentioned in note 3M, beginning January 1, 2008, deferred ESPS under MFRS is calculated and recognized under the asset and liability method. As a result, the reconciling item was eliminated and the liability under U.S. GAAP as of December 31, 2007 was cancelled during 2008 and is presented as an income adjustment of approximately Ps2,740 in the reconciliation of net income to U.S. GAAP in 2008.

(d) *Accounting for Uncertainty in Income Taxes*

Pursuant to ASC 740 under U.S. GAAP, CEMEX defines the confidence level that a tax position taken or expected to be taken must meet in order to be recognized in the financial statements. ASC 740-10-25-6 requires that the tax effects of a position must be recognized only if it is "more-likely-than-not" to be sustained based on its technical merits as of the reporting date. In making this assessment, CEMEX has assumed that the tax authorities will examine each position and have full knowledge of all relevant information. Each position has been considered on its own, regardless of its relation to any other broader tax settlement. The more-likely-than-not threshold represents a positive assertion by management that CEMEX is entitled to the economic benefits of a tax position. If a tax position is not considered more-likely-than-not to be sustained, no benefits of the position are to be recognized. Moreover, the more-likely-than-not threshold must continue to be met in each reporting period to support continued recognition of a benefit.

If during any period after recognition the threshold ceases to be met, the previously recorded benefit must be derecognized. Likewise, the benefit of a tax position that initially fails to meet the more-likely-than-not threshold should be recognized in a subsequent period if changing facts and circumstances enable the position to meet the threshold, the matter is effectively settled through negotiation or litigation with the tax authorities, or the statute of limitations has expired. A summary of the beginning and ending amount of unrecognized tax benefits recorded under U.S. GAAP as of December 31, 2009, 2008 and 2007, excluding interest and penalties, is as follows:

	2009	2008	2007
Balance of tax positions under U.S. GAAP at beginning of year	Ps 13,930	11,198	4,191
Additions for tax positions of prior years	2,368	2,217	3,635
Additions for tax positions of current year	5,110	2,126	3,356
Reductions for tax positions related to prior years and others[1]	(293)	(3,639)	(307)
Settlements	(200)	(123)	(30)
Expiration of the statue of limitations	(236)	(24)	—
Foreign currency translation effects	(346)	2,175	353
Balance of tax positions under U.S. GAAP at end of year	**Ps 20,333**	**13,930**	**11,198**
Balance of tax positions under MFRS at end of year	**Ps 9,024**	**5,474**	**5,560**

[1] During 2007, under MFRS, CEMEX released against current income tax a pre-acquisition income tax contingency, resulting in a tax benefit of approximately Ps307. Under U.S. GAAP, the resolution of a pre-acquisition income tax contingency is recognized reducing the related liability against goodwill. As a result, the reconciliation of net income to U.S. GAAP in 2007, includes the reclassification of the benefit of Ps307 under MFRS, which was recognized as a reduction of goodwill under U.S. GAAP.

CEMEX's policy is to recognize interest and penalties related to unrecognized tax benefits as part of the income tax in the consolidated income statements. Final balance for interest and penalties accrued under MFRS and U.S. GAAP was Ps1,108 and Ps3,064, respectively, as of December 31, 2009, and was Ps1,187 under MFRS and Ps2,967 under U.S. GAAP as of December 31, 2008. Interest and penalties expense (benefit) related to unrecognized tax benefits recorded in the consolidated income statement for the years ended December 31, 2009, 2008 and 2007 is as follows:

Years	MFRS	U.S. GAAP
2009	Ps (15)	154
2008	695	1,341
2007	415	621

All unrecognized tax benefits included as of December 31, 2009, 2008 and 2007, if recognized, would impact CEMEX's effective tax rate.

Tax examinations can involve complex issues, and the resolution of issues may span multiple years, particularly if subject to negotiation or litigation. Although CEMEX believes its estimates of the total unrecognized tax benefits are reasonable, uncertainties regarding the final determination of income tax audit settlements and any related litigation could affect the amount of total unrecognized tax benefits in future periods. It is difficult to estimate the timing and range of possible changes related to the uncertain tax positions, as finalizing audits with the income tax authorities may involve formal administrative and legal proceedings. Accordingly, it is not possible to reasonably estimate the expected changes to the total unrecognized tax benefits over the next 12 months, although any settlements or statute of limitations expirations may result in a significant increase or decrease in the total unrecognized tax benefits, including those positions related to tax examinations being currently conducted.

Continued

EXHIBIT 6.11 *(Continued)*

CEMEX files income tax returns in multiple jurisdictions and is subject to examination by income taxing authorities throughout the world. CEMEX's major tax jurisdictions and the years open for examination are as follows:

Country	Years
Mexico	2005–2009
United States	2005–2009
Spain	2005–2009
United Kingdom	2000–2009

(e) *Employee Benefits*

Severance payments

Under U.S. GAAP, post-employment benefits for former or inactive employees, including severance payments, which are not part of a restructuring event, are accrued over the employees' service lives. Beginning January 1, 2005, under MFRS, severance payments that are not part of a restructuring event are accrued over the employees' service lives according to actuarial computations, in a manner similar to U.S. GAAP. For the years ended December 31, 2009, 2008 and 2007, the reconciling item refers to the amortization of the cumulative initial effect from the accounting change under MFRS recognized as of January 1, 2005 as part of the unrecognized net transition obligation.

Pension and other postretirement benefits

In connection with employee pension and other postretirement benefits under MFRS, until December 31, 2007, CEMEX determined the costs of these benefits based on the obligations' net present value, and amortized any prior service cost, transition liability and actuarial results, following the corridor method (note 3M) over the employees' estimated active service lives, as permitted by ASC 715, *Compensation—Retirement Benefits 30 Defined Benefit Plans—Pensions,* under U.S. GAAP. For the year ended December 31, 2007, no adjustment was determined in the reconciliation of net income to U.S. GAAP. Beginning January 1, 2008, resulting from the adoption of new MFRS D-3, the prior service cost, transition liability and actuarial results accrued as of December 31, 2007, should be amortized to the income statement over a maximum period of five years, while the new actuarial results generated after the adoption of new MFRS D-3 are amortized normally over the employees' estimated active service lives following the corridor method. The reconciliation of net income to U.S. GAAP in 2009 and 2008 includes the reversal of the additional amortization expense recognized under MFRS of approximately Ps104 and Ps104, respectively.

For the reconciliation of stockholders' equity to U.S. GAAP, based on ASC 715, CEMEX recognizes the funded status (benefits' obligation less fair value of plan assets) of defined benefit pension and other postretirement plans as a net asset or liability and recognizes any changes in that funded status in the year in which the changes occur against other comprehensive income ("OCI") to the extent those changes are not included in the net periodic cost. The reconciliation of the funded status of postretirement benefits at December 31, 2009 and 2008 between MFRS and U.S. GAAP is as follows:

	Assets (non-current)	Liabilities (non-current)	Deferred income tax (non-current)	Total liabilities	Cumulative OCI, net of tax
Funded status under U.S. GAAP at December 31, 2008	Ps 148	10,904	(3,175)	7,729	(2,689)
Reversal of approximate ASC 715 adjustments	(148)	(4,113)	1,276	(2,837)	2,689
Funded status under MFRS at December 31, 2008	**Ps —**	**6,791**	**(1,899)**	**4,892**	**—**
Funded status under U.S. GAAP at December 31, 2008	Ps 33	13,632	(3,349)	10,283	(4,338)
Reversal of approximate ASC 715 adjustments	(33)	(6,174)	1,802	(4,372)	4,338
Funded status under MFRS at December 31, 2009	**Ps —**	**7,458**	**(1,547)**	**5,911**	**—**

The change during 2009 and 2008 in OCI under U.S. GAAP was a net loss of approximately Ps6,144 (Ps4,338 net of income tax) and a net loss of approximately Ps3,965 (Ps2,689 net of income tax), respectively, which includes: i) a curtailment gain of Ps39 in 2009 and a curtailment loss of Ps18 in 2008; ii) net losses of Ps5,619 in 2009 and Ps3,805 in 2008 from actuarial results and foreign currency translation effects during the year; and iii) expenses of approximately Ps483 in 2009 and Ps142 in 2008 from the amortization of the prior service cost, the transition liability and the actuarial results. For the years ended December 31, 2009, 2008 and 2007, ASC 715 adjustments had no effect on the summarized statements of operations under U.S. GAAP presented in note 25(a).

The expected long-term rate of return on plan assets is determined based on a variety of considerations, including the established asset allocation targets and expectations for those asset classes, historical returns of the plans' assets and other market considerations. The primary objective in the investment management for plan assets is to maximize the inflation-adjusted principal value of the assets in order to meet current and future benefit obligations to plan participants. We have a diversified portfolio composed of equity, alternative investments, fixed income and cash equivalent securities. We have independent investment consultants that provide advice to Investment Committees and Trustees to determine the annual investment strategy. Plan assets are managed on a total return and risk basis, and its performance is monitored on a quarterly basis. The Investment Committee recognizes that a certain level of risk (i.e., the uncertainty of future events), volatility (i.e., the potential for variability of asset values) and the possibility of loss in purchasing power (due to inflation) are present to some degree in all types of investment vehicles. Risk is controlled by maintaining a portfolio of assets that is diversified across a variety of asset classes, economic and industry sectors, investment styles and investment managers. Funds management complies with local legal regulations in terms of asset allocation and statutory funding requirements.

In connection with the pension plans assets by asset category (note 15), according to requirements of ASC 820, *Fair Value Measurements and Disclosure,* under U.S. GAAP, the breakdown of the assets fair value by hierarchy level (note 25(h)) as of December 31, 2009 is as follows:

	Quoted prices in active markets for identical assets (Level 1)	Significant observable inputs (Level 2)	Significant unobservable inputs (Level 3)	Total fair value
Fixed-income securities				
Cash	Ps 1,286	—	—	1,286
Investments in corporate bonds	3,860	1,772	—	5,632
Investments in government bonds	6,685	—	—	6,685
	11,831	1,772	—	13,603
Variable-income securities				
Investment in marketable securities	5,704	—	27	5,731
Other investments and private funds	1,882	42	423	2,347
	7,586	42	450	8,078
	Ps 19,417	1,814	450	21,681

(f) *Non-controlling Interest*

Financing Transactions

In connection with CEMEX's perpetual debentures (note 17D) for notional amounts of approximately US$3,045 (Ps39,859) in 2009 and US$3,020 (Ps41,495) in 2008, which are treated as equity instruments and included as part of non-controlling interest under MFRS, for purposes of the reconciliation of stockholders' equity to U.S. GAAP, such perpetual debentures were reclassified to long-term debt under U.S. GAAP, reducing stockholders' equity under U.S. GAAP in the amount of Ps39,859 in 2009 and Ps41,495 in 2008. Interest accrued on the perpetual debentures, including interest incurred in connection with perpetual loan facilities that were originated and settled during the year (note 13A and 17D), for approximately Ps2,704 in 2009, Ps2,596 in 2008 and Ps1,847 in 2007 recognized within "Other equity reserves" under MFRS were reclassified to interest expense in the reconciliation of net income to U.S. GAAP.

Non-controlling Interest under U.S. GAAP

Under MFRS, non-controlling interest in consolidated subsidiaries is presented as a separate component within stockholders' equity. For U.S. GAAP purposes, beginning on January 1, 2009, amendments to ASC 810, *Consolidation* ("ASC 810"), state that a non-controlling interest in a subsidiary is an ownership interest in the consolidated entity that should be reported as equity in the consolidated financial statements, and requires consolidated net income to be reported at amounts that include the amounts attributable to both the parent and the non-controlling interest. It also requires disclosure, on the face of the consolidated statement of income, of the amounts of consolidated net income attributable to the parent and to the non-controlling interest. These requirements must be applied prospectively as of the beginning of the fiscal year in which this statement is initially applied, except for the presentation and disclosure requirements, which must be applied retrospectively for all periods presented. Accordingly, we have

Continued

EXHIBIT 6.11 *(Continued)*

made retrospective adjustments to the previously reported balance sheet and income statement. As of December 31, 2008, previously reported stockholders' equity under U.S. GAAP was Ps151,294, which included a reconciling item related to the non-controlling interest representing a deduction of Ps5,105. Pursuant to ASC 810, this reconciling item was removed from the stockholders' equity reconciliation as of December 31, 2008 included in this annual report. In addition, the balance of non-controlling interest under MFRS is adjusted to reflect the share of the non-controlling shareholders in the corresponding reconciling entries to U.S. GAAP.

(g) *Inflation Adjustment of Machinery and Equipment*

According to Regulation S-X, when inflationary accounting is applicable under MFRS, fixed assets of foreign origin should be restated by applying the inflation rate of the country that holds the assets, regardless of the assets' origin countries, instead of using the methodology of MFRS until December 31, 2007 (note 3A and 3H), under which fixed assets of foreign origin were restated by applying a factor that considered the inflation of the asset's origin country and the fluctuation of the currency of the country that holds the asset against the currency of the asset's origin country. Depreciation expense is based upon the revised amounts. The amount recognized in the reconciliation of net income to U.S. GAAP in 2009 and 2008 refers to depreciation expense of the cumulative effect of the reconciling item as of December 31, 2007, the date on which inflationary accounting was suspended under MFRS. The amount recognized in the reconciliation of stockholders' equity to U.S. GAAP in 2009 and 2008 includes Ps2,553 (US$195) ((Ps1,685 (US$129) net of income tax) and Ps2,680 (US$195) ((Ps1,769 (US$129), net of income tax), respectively, related to the revaluation of fixed assets expropriated in Venezuela, which are presented net in the caption "Non-current accounts receivables and other assets." Beginning in 2008, if inflationary accounting is applicable under MFRS, fixed assets of foreign origin are restated using the factors derived from the general price indexes of the countries holding the assets, in a manner similar to that permitted under Regulation S-X.

(h) *Financial Instruments*

Indebtedness (note 13A)

Under MFRS, CEMEX has designated certain debt as hedges of certain investments in foreign subsidiaries and recognizes foreign exchange fluctuations on such debt within "Other equity reserves" in stockholders' equity (notes 3D and 17B). In the reconciliation of net income to U.S. GAAP, a portion of those foreign exchange results recognized in equity under MFRS was reclassified to the statement of operations under U.S. GAAP, resulting in income of Ps1,763 in 2009 and expenses of Ps7,716 in 2008 and Ps339 in 2007.

Derivative Financial Instruments (notes 3K, 13C and D)

Under both MFRS and U.S. GAAP, all derivative instruments, including those embedded in other contracts, are recognized in the balance sheet as assets or liabilities at their fair values, and changes in fair value are recognized in earnings, unless the derivatives qualify as hedges of future cash flows, in which case the effective portion of such changes in fair value is recorded temporarily in equity, and then recognized in earnings along with the related effects of the hedged items. Any ineffective portion of a hedge is reported in earnings as it occurs. However, as mentioned below, ASC 820, *Fair Value Measurements and Disclosure,* changed a definition of fair value beginning in 2008, and that created a difference between MFRS and U.S. GAAP. Except for the different amounts of fair value under MFRS and U.S. GAAP, all derivative instruments were accounted under MFRS consistently with the provisions of U.S. GAAP. For the years ended December 31, 2009, 2008 and 2007, CEMEX has not designated any derivative instrument as a fair value hedge under both MFRS and U.S. GAAP.

All energy supply contracts in which CEMEX has the obligation to acquire produced amounts of megawatts during predefined periods (note 20C), were negotiated for own-use in CEMEX's plants, do not include provisions for net cash settlement and do not have trading purposes. Such energy contracts contain features that may imply that the contracts represent derivative instruments or that they contain embedded derivative instruments. For both MFRS and U.S. GAAP, CEMEX considers these contracts under the "Normal Purchases and Normal Sales Exception" established in ASC 815, *Derivatives and Hedging*; consequently, such contracts are not recognized at fair value through the income statement.

For all hedging relationships, for accounting purposes, CEMEX formally documents the hedging relationship and its risk-management objective and strategy for undertaking the hedge, the hedging instrument, the hedged item, the nature of the risk being hedged, how the hedging instrument's effectiveness in offsetting the hedged risk will be assessed, and a description of the method of measuring ineffectiveness. This process includes linking all derivatives that are designated as cash-flow or foreign-currency hedges to specific assets and liabilities on the balance sheet or to specific firm commitments or forecasted transactions. CEMEX also formally assesses, both at the hedge's origination and on an ongoing basis, whether the derivatives that are used in hedging transactions are highly effective in offsetting changes in cash flows of hedged items. When it is determined that a derivative is not highly effective as a hedge or that it has ceased to be a highly effective hedge, CEMEX discontinues hedge accounting prospectively.

Fair Value Hierarchy

Under U.S. GAAP, CEMEX applies ASC 820, *Fair Value Measurements and Disclosure,* for fair value measurements of financial assets and financial liabilities recognized or disclosed at fair value. Beginning on January 1, 2009, CEMEX also recognizes and discloses the fair value of non-financial assets and non-financial liabilities under ASC 820.

Under MFRS, in addition to certain investments in trading securities which are recorded at their quoted market prices, CEMEX has recognized all its derivative financial instruments at their estimated fair value (notes 13C and D). For purposes of MFRS, fair value is the amount for which an asset could be exchanged, a liability settled, or an equity instrument granted could be exchanged between knowledgeable, willing parties in an arm's length transaction. Beginning in 2008 under U.S. GAAP, the concept of fair value was redefined by ASC 820 as an "Exit Value," which is the price that would be received to sell an asset or paid to transfer a liability in an orderly transaction between market participants at the measurement date. Basically, the difference between the fair value under MFRS, which is equivalent to a settlement amount at the balance sheet date, and the Exit Value under U.S. GAAP, is that the later considers the counterparty's credit risk in the valuation.

The concept of Exit Value works under the premise that there is a market and market participants for the specific asset or liability. When there is no market and/or market participants willing to make a market, ASC 820 establishes a fair value hierarchy that prioritizes the inputs to valuation techniques used to measure fair value. The hierarchy gives the highest priority to unadjusted quoted prices in active markets for identical assets or liabilities (Level 1 measurements) and the lowest priority to measurements involving significant unobservable inputs (Level 3 measurements). The three levels of the fair value hierarchy are as follows:

- Level 1 inputs are quoted prices (unadjusted) in active markets for identical assets or liabilities that CEMEX has the ability to access at the measurement date.
- Level 2 inputs are inputs other than quoted prices that are observable for the asset or liability, either directly or indirectly.
- Level 3 inputs are unobservable inputs for the asset or liability.

The fair values determined by CEMEX for its derivative financial instruments are Level 2. There is no direct measure for the risk of CEMEX or its counterparties in connection with the derivative instruments. Therefore, the risk factors applied for CEMEX's assets and liabilities originated by the valuation of such derivatives were extrapolated from publicly available risk discounts for other public debt instruments of CEMEX and its counterparties.

The following table presents a comparison of fair values between MFRS and U.S. GAAP at December 31, 2009 and 2008, which led to the reconciling adjustments for the years ended December 31, 2009 and 2008, representing a loss of approximately US$88 (Ps1,207 or Ps890 after deferred income tax) and a gain of approximately US$95 (Ps1,305 or Ps960 after deferred income tax), respectively.

(U.S. dollars millions)	2009			2008		
	MFRS	U.S. GAAP	Adjustment	MFRS	U.S. GAAP	Adjustment
Active derivative instruments (note 13C)						
Derivative instruments related to debt	US$—	—	—	(4)	5	9
Other derivative instruments	82	81	(1)	(36)	(14)	22
Derivative instruments related to equity instruments	(79)	(71)	8	225	243	18
	3	**10**	**7**	**185**	**234**	**49**
Inactive derivative instruments (note 13D)						
Cross currency swaps	—	—	—	(101)	(64)	37
Foreign exchange forward contracts	—	—	—	(284)	(275)	9
	—	—	—	(385)	(339)	46
Total	US$—	—	—	**(200)**	**(105)**	**95**

The fair values under both MFRS and U.S. GAAP presented in the table above at December 31, 2009 and 2008 include approximately US$195 (Ps2,553) and US$763 (Ps10,484), respectively, of deposits in margin accounts with financial institutions, of which in 2008, US$565 (Ps7,763) were related to active positions and US$198 (Ps2,721) to inactive positions (note 13B).

Fair Value of Perpetual Debentures

As of December 31, 2009 and 2008, the fair value of CEMEX's perpetual debentures (note 17D) was approximately Ps27,594 (US$2,108) and Ps17,464 (US$1,271), respectively. Based on ASC 820, *Fair Value Measurements and Disclosure,* such reported fair values represent Level 1 measurements which were determined considering quoted market prices of the perpetual debentures as they are available.

Continued

EXHIBIT 6.11 *(Continued)*

Effects of CEMEX's Financing Agreement under U.S. GAAP

As detailed in note 13A, on August 14, 2009, CEMEX entered into the Financing Agreement with its major creditors, which extended the maturity of approximately US$14,961 (Ps195,839) of syndicated and bilateral loans and private placement obligations. Under MFRS, the Financing Agreement qualified as the issuance of new debt and the extinguishment of the old facilities, as it did under US GAAP according to ASC 470-50, *Debt—Modifications and Extinguishments* ("ASC 470-50"). However, as opposed to MFRS in which the nominal amount of the new debt is used for the determination of gain and losses at inception, under U.S. GAAP, the new long-term debt should be measured at fair value at inception of the new debt in order to determine gains or losses on extinguishment. CEMEX segregated the extinguished instruments into long term facilities and revolving credit lines and determined the accounting treatment for each of these components as follows:

a) The fair value at measurement date of the long term facilities with a nominal amount of approximately US$11,368 (Ps148,807) was determined to be approximately US$11,357 (Ps148,663), which represents a Level 2 measurement under ASC 820 as there was no direct measure of the instrument or CEMEX's default risk. The fair value adjustment required under U.S. GAAP was a decrease in the liability and a corresponding gain in the reconciliation of net income to U.S. GAAP for approximately US$11 (Ps150). Issuance costs and commissions paid, which under MFRS were capitalized as deferred financing costs and are subject to amortization throughout the life of the instrument, have been expensed in the reconciliation of net income to U.S. GAAP for approximately Ps6,016 (US$442). A deferred income tax asset under U.S. GAAP for approximately Ps1,786 was recognized in connection with the commissions and issuance costs mentioned above.

b) The revolving credit lines retained their original carrying amount of approximately US$3,593 (Ps47,032) in accordance with ASC 470–50. The provisions of the Financing Agreement increased the borrowing capacity relative to these revolving credit lines and therefore, previously capitalized borrowing costs, which are not significant, will be amortized throughout the term of the Financing Agreement. New borrowing costs for approximately Ps811 (US$62) were capitalized as deferred financing costs during 2009 and will be amortized throughout the term of the Financing Agreement under both MFRS and U.S. GAAP.

Mandatorily Convertible Securities

Under MFRS, the mandatorily convertible securities issued in Mexico on December 10, 2009 (the "convertible securities") for approximately Ps4,126 (US$315) in exchange for CBs (note 13A), represent a compound instrument which has a liability component and an equity component. The liability component, which amounted to Ps2,090 at December 31, 2009, represents the net present value of interest payment on the principal amount, without assuming any early conversion, and was recognized within "Other financial obligations" (note 13A). The equity component, for approximately Ps2,036 at December 31, 2009, which represents the difference between the principal amount and the liability component was recognized within "Other equity reserves" net of commissions of Ps65 (note 17B).

According to ASC 470-20, *Debt with Conversion and Other Options,* under U.S. GAAP, the equity component was reclassified to debt in the reconciliation of stockholders' equity to U.S. GAAP and is presented within "Other non-current liabilities" together with the liability component in the condensed financial information of balance sheet under US GAAP. Likewise, deferred income tax asset for approximately Ps585 recognized against stockholders' equity under MFRS in connection with the mentioned transaction were eliminated (note 16B). The exchange of CBs for the convertible securities also qualified as the issuance of new debt and the extinguishment of the old facilities under ASC 470-50, which required CEMEX to measure the new financial obligation at fair value at inception and to recognize as part of the comprehensive financing result in the reconciliation of net income to U.S. GAAP: a) the issuance costs related to the liability component, which were capitalized as deferred financing costs under MFRS for approximately Ps67(US$5), and b) the issuance costs related to the equity component recognized within "Other equity reserves" under MFRS for approximately Ps65 (US$5). Under U.S. GAAP, a deferred income tax asset for Ps37 at December 31, 2009 was recognized in connection with the commissions and issuance costs mentioned above.

The fair value at measurement date approximates to the carrying value of approximately Ps4,126 (US$315) at December 31, 2009 determined by CEMEX for the convertible securities and it is considered a Level 2 fair value measurement given that the market price of these securities was available but the contract included a one-year trading restriction.

Fair Value Option

Beginning on January 1, 2008, ASC 825, *Financial Instruments* ("ASC 825"), provides entities with an option to measure many financial instruments and certain other items at fair value. Under ASC 825, unrealized gains and losses on items for which the fair value option has been elected are reported in earnings at each reporting period. As of and for the years ended December 31, 2009 and 2008, CEMEX has not elected to measure any financial instruments or other items at fair value.

Fair value of non-financial assets and non-financial liabilities

On January 1, 2009, CEMEX adopted ASC Topic 820, *Fair Value Measurements and Disclosures,* for fair value measurements of nonfinancial assets and non-financial liabilities that are recognized or disclosed at fair value in the financial statements on a non-recurring basis.

Description	Balance at December 31, 2009	Fair Value Hierarchy			Total impairment charge
		Level 1	Level 2	Level 3	
Long-lived assets held and used	Ps 174	—	—	174	(504)
Goodwill...	76,938	—	—	76,938	929
Long-lived assets held for sale	288	—	—	288	(253)
Asset retirement obligations	Ps 2,460	—	—	2,460	—

In accordance with the provisions of the ASC 360-10-35, *Property, Plant and Equipment—Impairment or Disposal of Long-Lived Assets,* long-lived assets held and used with a carrying amount of Ps677 (US$51) were written down to their fair value of Ps174 (US$13), resulting in an impairment charge of Ps504 (US$38), which was included in the consolidated statement of operations under U.S. GAAP.

Pursuant to ASC 350-20-35, *Intangibles–Goodwill and Other—Recognition and Measurement of an Impairment Loss* ("ASC 350-20-35"), goodwill with a carrying amount in 2008 of Ps76,388 (US$5,836) was adjusted in 2009 as a result of the finalization of the step 2 exercise in connection with the 2008 impairment test, to its estimated fair value of Ps76,938 (US$5,878), resulting in an impairment reversal of Ps929 (US$71), which was included as a benefit in the consolidated statement of operations under U.S. GAAP.

As indicated in ASC 360-10-35, long-lived assets held for sale with a carrying amount in 2008 of Ps541 (US$41) were written down in 2009 to their estimated fair value of Ps288 (US$22), resulting in an impairment charge of Ps253 (US$19), which was included in the consolidated statement of operations under U.S. GAAP.

Based on the requirements of ASC 40-20-35, *Asset Retirement and Environmental Obligations—Asset Retirement Obligations—Subsequent Measurement,* asset retirement obligations in the table above are calculated based on the present value of estimated removal and other closure costs using our internal risk-free rate of return or appropriate equivalent.

(i) *Stock Option Programs*

The balance of options outstanding at December 31, 2009 and 2008 and other general information regarding CEMEX's stock option programs is presented in note 18.

As mentioned in note 3T, CEMEX accounted for its stock option programs in 2008 and 2007 according to IFRS 2 and beginning on January 1, 2009 under new MFRS D-8, which provide basically the same accounting treatment. Effective January 1, 2006, under U.S. GAAP, CEMEX applies ASC 718, *Compensation–Stock Compensation* ("ASC 718"), which requires that all stock-based compensation be recognized as an expense in the financial statements and that such cost be measured at the fair value of the award. Similar to MFRS D-8 under MFRS, ASC 718 requires liabilities incurred under stock awards to be measured at fair value at each balance sheet date, with changes in fair value recorded in the income statement. Likewise, MFRS D-8 and ASC 718 require compensation cost related to awards qualifying as equity instruments to be determined considering the grant-date fair value of the awards, and be recorded during the awards' vesting period. As of and for the years ended December 31, 2009, 2008 and 2007, the compensation expense and the liabilities accrued in connection with CEMEX's stock option programs under MFRS are the same amounts that would be determined using ASC 718 under U.S. GAAP.

(j) *Impairment of Long-Lived Assets*

Under U.S. GAAP, CEMEX assesses goodwill and indefinite-lived intangibles for impairment annually unless events occur that require more frequent reviews. Other long-lived assets, including amortizable intangibles, are tested for impairment if impairment triggers occur. Discounted cash flow analyses considering the required use of market considerations are applied to assess the possible impairment of goodwill and indefinite life intangible assets; whereas if impairment indicators exist, undiscounted cash flow analyses are used to assess the impairment for other long-lived assets, including definite life intangible assets. If an assessment indicates impairment, the impaired asset is written down to its fair value based on the best information available. The useful lives of amortizable intangibles are evaluated periodically, and subsequent to impairment reviews, to determine whether revision is warranted. If cash flows related to an indefinite life intangible are not expected to continue for the foreseeable future, a useful life is assigned. Considerable management judgment is necessary to estimate undiscounted and discounted future cash flows. Assumptions used for these cash flows are consistent with internal forecasts and industry practices.

As mentioned in note 3J, under MFRS, in order to test the balances of its long-lived assets for impairment, including goodwill, definite and indefinite life intangible assets and property, machinery and equipment, CEMEX determines the value in use, which consists of the discounted amount of estimated future cash flows to be generated by the related asset. The impairment loss results from the excess of the carrying amount over the value in use related to the asset. Differences in the carrying values of certain long-lived assets under U.S. GAAP as well as other factors explained below led to different impairment losses or impairment testing results between MFRS and U.S. GAAP. As of December 31, 2009 and 2008, CEMEX has no indefinite-lived intangible assets other than goodwill under both MFRS and U.S. GAAP.

Continued

EXHIBIT 6.11 (*Continued*)

Based on impairment tests made during the last quarter of 2009, as mentioned in note 12B under MFRS, CEMEX did not recognize impairment losses of goodwill. In 2008, under MFRS, goodwill impairment losses were determined for the United States, Ireland and Thailand reporting units for approximately Ps18,314 (US$1,333), including an impairment loss related to CEMEX's Venezuelan investment in connection with its nationalization. Likewise, considering triggering events in the United States during the fourth quarter of 2008, CEMEX tested its intangible assets of definite life in that country and determined that the net book value of certain trademarks exceeded their related value in use and recorded impairment losses of approximately Ps1,598 (US$116) (note 12). In addition, as mentioned in Note 11, for the years ended December 31, 2009, 2008 and 2007, CEMEX recognized impairment losses during the fourth quarter in connection with the permanent closing of operating assets for an aggregate amount of approximately Ps503 (US$38), Ps1,045 (US$76) and Ps64 (US$6), respectively.

Goodwill

Under U.S. GAAP, if the carrying amount of the reporting unit exceeds its related fair value, CEMEX should apply a "second step" process by means of which the fair value of such reporting unit should be allocated to the fair value of its net assets in order to determine the reporting unit's "implied" goodwill. The resulting impairment loss under U.S. GAAP is the difference between the carrying amount of the related goodwill as of the valuation date and the implied goodwill amount. This situation, in addition to differences in the determination of the risk adjusted discount rates under MFRS as compared to U.S. GAAP, as well as differences in the reporting units' carrying amounts between MFRS and U.S. GAAP, originate, when applicable, different amounts of impairment losses.

To establish the fair value of its reporting units under U.S. GAAP, CEMEX initially calculated their fair value by discounting the projected future cash flows using country specific estimated weighted average cost of capital as the discount rates, and by including and blending the allocated fair value estimates based on CEMEX historical multiples, on a basis of 60% discounted cash flows and 40% Operating EBITDA (Operating income plus depreciation and amortization) multiples. As additional reference to the fair value as determined, CEMEX compared other market value indicators, including fair value estimates based on the Guided Transactions Approach and Industry Multiples. In addition, CEMEX's market capitalization, including a reasonable control premium, was taken into consideration as a reference to reconcile the aggregate fair value determined for the reporting units.

The results of the impairment test performed as of December 31, 2009 indicated that the estimated fair values of all reporting units under U.S. GAAP exceeded in each case their corresponding carrying amount and that the second step of the test was not required. Based on the results of goodwill impairment testing as of December 31, 2008 under U.S. GAAP, CEMEX recorded an estimated impairment loss in connection with its reporting unit in the United States of approximately Ps62,354 (US$4,538). The goodwill was written down to its implied fair value derived in the second step, which requires companies to determine the fair value of all the assets and liabilities of the reporting units at the measurement date. Due to the complexity of this process, CEMEX did not complete the measurement of the implied fair value of goodwill in 2008; accordingly, the goodwill impairment charge in the reconciliation of net income to U.S. GAAP in 2008 represented an estimate. After finalizing our 2008 impairment exercise under U.S. GAAP during 2009, our impairment losses in the United States were reduced by approximately US$71 (Ps929). This amount was recognized as income in the reconciliation of net income to U.S. GAAP in 2009. The reconciliation of net income under U.S. GAAP also includes a loss of Ps9 related to other impairment charges.

Complementarily, for 2008 and in connection with the goodwill associated to CEMEX's reporting units in Ireland and Thailand, as well as the goodwill associated with its Venezuelan investment, which was fully impaired under MFRS (note 12B), CEMEX did not perform the second step considering that the related goodwill was fully impaired in the first step test, the materiality of these reporting units and the goodwill balances. The reconciliation of net income to U.S. GAAP in 2008 includes an additional impairment loss of approximately Ps331 associated to the cancellation of cumulative differences in the goodwill carrying amounts of these reporting units between MFRS and U.S. GAAP. At December 31, 2008, goodwill under U.S. GAAP associated with CEMEX's reporting units in Thailand and Ireland, as well as its Venezuelan assets, was completely removed.

For purposes of the summarized statement of operations under U.S. GAAP for the years ended December 31, 2009 and 2008 (note 25(a)), the non-cash goodwill impairment losses, excluding the loss associated to CEMEX's Venezuelan investment, are included in the determination of operating income. The impairment loss recognized in 2008 and the adjustment in 2009 after finalizing the second step measurement under U.S. GAAP is explained as follows:

Item	2009	2008
Effect attributable to the different discount rates and required market considerations, net.	Ps —	51,711
Effect originated by the "second step" process	(929)	11,966
Effect resulting from different carrying amounts of goodwill between MFRS and U.S. GAAP	—	535
Total goodwill impairment losses under U.S. GAAP	(929)	64,212
Goodwill impairment losses under MFRS	—	18,314
Additional goodwill impairment losses under U.S. GAAP	**Ps (929)**	**45,898**

Discount rates under MFRS differ from those determined under U.S. GAAP. In determining an appropriate discount rate, MFRS requires company specific data such as the rate at which CEMEX can obtain financing. In contrast, under U.S. GAAP, the discount rate should reflect a market participant's perspective on the risk of the determined cash flow streams; therefore, CEMEX applied industry specific data.

The use of various rates could have an adverse change in the fair value of CEMEX's goodwill and cause it to be impaired. Undiscounted cash flows are significantly sensitive to the growth rates in perpetuity used. Likewise, discounted cash flows are significantly sensitive to the discount rate used. The higher the growth rate in perpetuity applied, the higher the amount obtained of undiscounted future cash flows by reporting unit. Conversely, the higher the discount rate applied, the lower the amount obtained of discounted estimated future cash flows by reporting unit.

CEMEX used the same growth rates in determining its projected future cash flows for both MFRS and U.S. GAAP (note 12B). The following table presents the discount rates by country at December 31, 2009 and 2008, used for the determination of CEMEX's discounted projected future cash flows under MFRS and U.S. GAAP:

	2009		2008	
Reporting units	**MFRS**	**U.S. GAAP**	**MFRS**	**U.S. GAAP**
United States.............................	8.5%	8.9%	9.2%	10.4%
Spain......................................	9.4%	9.9%	10.8%	12.0%
Mexico....................................	10.0%	10.5%	12.0%	12.9%
Colombia.................................	10.2%	10.7%	11.8%	12.6%
France.....................................	9.6%	10.1%	11.2%	12.1%
United Arab Emirates......................	11.4%	12.1%	13.0%	14.7%
United Kingdom	9.4%	9.9%	9.8%	11.2%
Egypt......................................	10.0%	10.6%	12.8%	12.1%
Range of discount rates in other countries.........	9.6%–14.6%	10.0%–15.1%	11.3%–15.0%	12.0%–18.0%

The main assumptions used in the impairment testing under U.S. GAAP of the reporting unit which, according to CEMEX's sensitivity analysis, presented a relative impairment risk in 2009, were as follows:

	At December 31, 2009			
Reporting unit	**Recognized impairment charges**	**Discount rate**	**Perpetual growth rate**	**Operating EBITDA multiple**
Spain..	Ps —	9.9%	2.5%	8.2

In connection with CEMEX's assumptions included in the table above, the impairment charges resulting from the sensitivity analysis under U.S. GAAP that would have resulted from an independent change of each one of the variables, regarding the reporting unit that presented a relative impairment risk in 2009, excluding effects that would arise from the second step process under U.S. GAAP, would have been as follows:

	Sensitivity analysis impact of described change in assumptions at December 31, 2009				
Reporting unit	**Recognized Impairment charges**	**Discount rate +1 Pt**	**Perpetual growth rate −1 Pt**	**EBITDA −10%**	**EBITDA Multiple −1 Pt**
Spain..............................	Ps —	2,980	1,374	1,484	1,818

During 2007, the fair value of the reporting units under U.S. GAAP exceeded in each case the corresponding carrying amounts. Therefore, no impairment charges resulted from the mandatory annual impairment testing of goodwill under U.S. GAAP.

Continued

EXHIBIT 6.11 (*Continued*)

Other Intangible Assets

A significant portion of CEMEX's definite-lived intangible assets under both MFRS and U.S. GAAP as of December 31, 2009 and 2008 are comprised by extraction permits, trademarks and customer relationships (note 12). When impairment indicators exist, for each intangible asset, CEMEX would determine its projected revenue streams over the estimated useful life of the asset. In order to obtain undiscounted and discounted cash flows attributable to each intangible asset, such revenues are adjusted for operating expenses, changes in working capital and other expenditures, as applicable, and discounted to net present value using the risk adjusted discount rates of return. Significant management judgment is necessary to determine the appropriate valuation method and estimates under the key assumptions, among which are: a) the useful life of the asset; b) the risk adjusted discount rate of return; c) royalty rates; and d) growth rates. Assumptions used for these cash flows are consistent with internal forecasts and industry practices.

The fair values of intangible assets are very sensitive to changes in the significant assumptions used in their calculation. Certain key assumptions are more subjective than others. In respect of trademarks, CEMEX considers the royalty rate, key in the determination of revenue streams, as the most subjective assumption. In respect of permits and customer relationships, the most subjective assumptions are revenue growth rates and estimated useful lives. CEMEX validates its assumptions through benchmarking with industry practices and the corroboration of third party valuation advisors.

During the fourth quarter of 2008, considering the existence of triggering events, CEMEX tested its U.S. intangible assets under both MFRS and U.S. GAAP. In connection with the trademarks that were adjusted to its value in use under MFRS, the impairment test under U.S. GAAP also presented an excess of the carrying amount over the undiscounted estimated future cash flows. Consequently, CEMEX discounted such estimated future cash flows using the discount rate determined under U.S. GAAP as described above, and arrived at an additional impairment loss of approximately Ps179.

In 2009 and 2007, there were no impairment indicators leading to impairment testing of CEMEX's definite-lived intangible assets under U.S. GAAP. In connection with the intangible assets arising from the acquisition of Rinker that were deemed to have an indefinite useful life as of December 31, 2007, CEMEX did not test these assets for impairment during 2007 considering the proximity between the fair value's valuation date and year-end. During 2008 (note 12), CEMEX assigned specific useful lives to these assets under both MFRS and U.S. GAAP.

Property, Plant and Equipment

For the years ended December 31, 2009, 2008 and 2007, there were no impairment charges under U.S. GAAP in addition to those described in Note 11 related to property, plant and equipment, which were recorded under MFRS. In the case of the assets subject to impairment in the related periods, the differences in carrying amounts between MFRS and U.S. GAAP were not significant as to require additional adjustments.

(k) *Other U.S. GAAP Adjustments*

Deferred charges

In prior years, under MFRS, CEMEX capitalized certain costs not qualifying for deferral under U.S. GAAP. Therefore, such costs were reversed through earnings under U.S. GAAP in the period incurred, resulting in income of Ps10 in 2008 and income of Ps122 in 2007. During 2009, 2008 and 2007, all amounts capitalized under MFRS also met the requirements for capitalization under U.S. GAAP. Accordingly, the adjustments in the reconciliation of net income to U.S. GAAP for the years ended December 31, 2008 and 2007 refer exclusively to amounts amortized under MFRS during the respective years and which were expensed in prior years under U.S. GAAP. During 2008, the accounting difference was fully amortized.

As mentioned in note 25(h), in connection with the extinguished long-term facilities under the Financing Agreement (note 13A) with an original carrying amount of approximately US$11,368 (Ps148,807), the issuance costs and commissions paid under MFRS, which were capitalized as deferred financing costs, have been expensed in the reconciliation of net income to U.S. GAAP in 2009 as part of the comprehensive financing result for approximately Ps6,016 (US$442).

Additionally and in connection with the exchange of CBs issued in Mexico for the convertible securities for approximately Ps4,126 (US$315) (see notes 13A, 17B and 25(h)), which, based on MFRS, these convertible securities represent a compound instrument which has a liability component and an equity component. Under U.S. GAAP, the exchange qualified as the issuance of new debt and the extinguishment of the old facilities according to ASC 470-50. Consequently, CEMEX reclassified as part of the comprehensive financing result under U.S. GAAP the issuance costs classified as deferred financing costs under MFRS for approximately Ps67 (US$5).

During 2009 and 2008, in connection with its perpetual debentures, CEMEX recognized issuance costs directly in equity under MFRS for approximately Ps120 and Ps276, respectively. As mentioned in note 25(f), CEMEX's perpetual debentures are treated as debt under U.S. GAAP. Consequently, issuance costs were reclassified from equity under MFRS to deferred financing costs under U.S. GAAP and are amortized over 3, 6 and 8 years, depending on each facility, which are the periods remaining before CEMEX has the option to repurchase the instrument. For the years ended December 31, 2009 and 2008, the reconciliation of net income to U.S. GAAP includes expenses of approximately Ps21 and Ps51, respectively, related to the amortization of these deferred financing costs.

In addition, during 2008, CEMEX recognized a current income tax expense of approximately Ps215 related to an intercompany transfer of intangible assets under MFRS. Under U.S. GAAP, income tax effects associated with intercompany transfers of assets should be eliminated from the income statement. Consequently, CEMEX reclassified the current income tax expense for the period under MFRS against a deferred charge under U.S. GAAP. The capitalized amount will be amortized beginning in 2009 over 10 years, which is the period in which the acquiring entity will obtain the related tax benefit. At December 31, 2009 and 2008, the reconciliation of stockholders' equity to U.S. GAAP includes a benefit of approximately Ps194 and Ps214, respectively, related to this item.

Capitalized Interest

Under both MFRS (note 11) and U.S. GAAP, CEMEX capitalizes interest related to debt incurred during significant construction projects. Capitalized interest is depreciated over the useful lives of the related assets. Under U.S. GAAP, only interest expense is considered an additional cost of constructed assets. Under MFRS, until December 31, 2007, pursuant to inflationary accounting, capitalized interest was comprehensively measured in order to include: (i) interest expense, plus (ii) any foreign exchange fluctuations, and less (iii) the related monetary position result. CEMEX does not capitalize foreign exchange fluctuations related to debt incurred during significant construction projects, considering the mix of currencies in its outstanding debt and that it is not possible to link a specific debt transaction with a corresponding construction project. In 2009 and 2008, the amount of interest capitalized by CEMEX incurred during significant construction projects under MFRS was the same as the amount that would be determined under U.S. GAAP (note 11). In the reconciliation of net income to U.S. GAAP, until December 31, 2007, the monetary position results related to debt incurred during significant construction projects and which were capitalized under MFRS were reversed to earnings under U.S. GAAP. Beginning in 2008 and thereafter, the reconciling adjustment to U.S. GAAP refers to the depreciation expense related to the cumulative adjustment as of December 31, 2007.

Monetary position result

Until December 31, 2007, monetary position result resulting from the U.S. GAAP adjustments during the periods presented was determined by (i) applying the annual inflation factor to the net monetary position of the U.S. GAAP adjustments at the beginning of the period, plus (ii) the monetary position effect of the adjustments during the period, determined in accordance with the average inflation factor for the period. Beginning in 2008, the determination of monetary position result on the U.S. GAAP adjustments was suspended.

Depreciation

Until December 31, 2006, a CEMEX's subsidiary in Colombia recorded depreciation expense for certain fixed assets using the sinking fund method. Under U.S. GAAP, depreciation is calculated on a straight-line basis over the estimated useful lives of the assets. Depreciation expense under MFRS was reduced in the reconciliation of net income to U.S. GAAP and in 2007, considering that these assets were almost fully depreciated and the small significance of the adjustment, CEMEX discontinued its quantification, resulting in the cancellation of the cumulative effect in the reconciliation of stockholders' equity to U.S. GAAP at December 31, 2006, which was released in the reconciliation of net income to U.S. GAAP in 2007, representing a benefit of Ps10.

Discontinued operations financial expense

According to ASC 205-20-45-6, *Reporting Discontinued Operations—Allocation of Interest to Discontinued Operations*, and in connection with the sale of the Australian operations (note 4B), interest on debt that is to be assumed by the buyer and interest on debt that is required to be repaid as a result of a disposal transaction shall be allocated to discontinued operations. The amounts of interest expense reclassified to discontinued operations related to the repaid debt with the funds received from the sale of our subsidiary in Australia for the years ended at December 31, 2009, 2008 and 2007 were Ps373, Ps388, and Ps272, respectively. This interest expense was reclassified net of its tax effect for approximately Ps109, Ps113 and Ps81 for 2009, 2008 and 2007, respectively, and is shown within income from discontinued operations. CEMEX elected not to reclassify other interest expenses which are not directly attributable to discontinued operations as permitted under ASC 205-20.

(l) *U.S. GAAP adjustments to discontinued operations*

The reconciling items in the reconciliation of net income to U.S. GAAP related to CEMEX's operations in Australia for the years ended December 31, 2009, 2008 and 2007 were as follows:

	2009	2008	2007
Interest expense[1]	Ps (373)	(388)	(272)
Income tax[2]	109	113	81
U.S. GAAP adjustments from discontinued operations	**Ps (264)**	**(275)**	**(191)**

[1] Represents the interest related to the repaid debt with the proceeds of the sale of our Australian operations, required to be allocated to discontinued operations by IASC 205-20-45-6 "Reporting Discontinued Operations".

[2] Income tax effects related to the interest mentioned in footnote 1 above.

Continued

EXHIBIT 6.11 *(Continued)*

(m) *Supplemental Cash Flow Information under U.S. GAAP*

Beginning in 2008 under MFRS (note 3A), as part of its primary financial statements, CEMEX includes statements of cash flows, which present the sources and uses of cash flows in following significantly the same requirements as those established by ASC 230, *Statement of cash flows,* under U.S. GAAP, instead of the statement of changes in financial position presented until December 31, 2007. In the years of transition, MFRS requires as a transitory rule (until 2010), the presentation of the former statement of changes in financial position for the prior periods presented.

For 2007, under MFRS, CEMEX presents the statement of changes in financial position, which identified the sources and uses of resources based on the differences between beginning and ending balance sheets in constant pesos. Monetary position results and unrealized foreign exchange results were treated as cash items in the calculation of resources provided by operations. Under ASC 230, statements of cash flows present only cash items and exclude non-cash items. ASC 230 does not provide guidance with respect to inflation-adjusted financial statements. The differences between MFRS and U.S. GAAP in the amounts reported are primarily due to: (i) the elimination of inflationary effects of monetary assets and liabilities from financing and investing activities against the corresponding monetary position result in operating activities; (ii) the elimination of foreign exchange results from financing and investing activities against the corresponding unrealized foreign exchange result included in operating activities; and (iii) the recognition in operating, financing and investing activities of the U.S. GAAP adjustments.

The following table reconciles the items from the statements of changes in financial position under MFRS for 2007 to the approximate cash flows under U.S. GAAP, considering the U.S. GAAP adjustments and excluding the effects of inflation required under MFRS. The following information is presented in millions of pesos on a historical peso basis and is not presented in pesos of constant purchasing power:

	2007
Net resources provided by operating activities under MFRS[1]	Ps **45,625**
Net income adjustments from MFRS to U.S. GAAP	(4,741)
Reversal of proportional consolidation	(218)
Depreciation and amortization	172
Non-controlling interest	2,095
Deferred income tax and tax uncertainties under ASC 740	3,061
Removal of estimated monetary position result and constant peso adjustments	(9,472)
Removal of unrealized foreign exchange fluctuations	(3,027)
Other adjustments	(64)
Total U.S. GAAP adjustments to operating activities	**(12,194)**
Net cash provided by operating activities under U.S. GAAP[1]	Ps **33,431**
Net resources provided by financing activities under MFRS	Ps 130,349
Removal of unrealized foreign exchange fluctuations	(3,311)
Removal of estimated constant peso adjustments	8,809
Other adjustments	44
Total U.S. GAAP adjustments to financing activities	**5,542**
Net cash provided by financing activities under U.S. GAAP	Ps **135,891**
Net resources used in investing activities under MFRS	Ps (185,798)
Reversal of proportional consolidation	172
Removal of estimated revaluation and constant peso adjustments	1,250
Removal of foreign currency translation and other equity effects	6,382
Other adjustments	287
Total U.S. GAAP adjustments to investing activities	**8,091**
Net cash used in investing activities under U.S. GAAP	Ps **(177,707)**
Decrease in cash and investments under MFRS	Ps (9,824)
Reversal of proportional consolidation	(2)
Removal of constant peso adjustments	1,441
Net U.S. GAAP adjustments to changes in cash and investments	**1,439**
Decrease in cash and investments under U.S. GAAP	Ps **(8,385)**

[1] Includes cash flows provided by our discontinued operations (note 4B) for the six months period ended December 31, 2007, for Ps1,234 (US$113).

Net cash flows from operating activities for the year ended December 31, 2007 reflect cash payments for interest and income taxes as follows:

	2007
Interest paid	Ps 8,268
Income taxes paid	4,594

MFRS requires interest expense to be classified as a financing activity within the statement of cash flows, unlike ASC 230 under U.S. GAAP, which requires it to be classified as an operating activity. The following table presents cash flows from operating, financing and investing activities under MFRS and U.S. GAAP pursuant to the reclassification of interest expense for the years ended December 31, 2009 and 2008:

	2009		**2008**	
	MFRS	**U.S. GAAP**	**MFRS**	**U.S. GAAP**
Cash flows from operating activities	Ps 34,751	20,144	41,272	29,488
Cash flows from financing activities	(37,146)	(22,539)	(23,689)	(11,905)
Cash flows from investing activities	5,715	5,715	(14,630)	(14,630)

Non-cash activities are comprised of the following:

Long-term debt assumed through the acquisition of businesses was Ps13,943 in 2007.

(n) *Other Disclosures under U.S. GAAP*

Sale of accounts receivable

CEMEX accounts for transfers of receivables under MFRS consistently with the rules set forth by ASC 860, *Transfers and Servicing* ("ASC 860"). Under ASC 860, transactions that meet the criteria for surrender of control are recorded as sales of receivables and their amounts are removed from the consolidated balance sheet at the time they are sold (note 6). ASC 860-50-30, *Transfers and Servicing—Servicing Assetsand Liabilities—Initial Measurement,* requires that all separately recognized servicing assets and servicing liabilities be initially measured at fair value, if practicable. ASC 860-50-35, *Transfers and Servicing–Servicing Assets and Liabilities– Subsequent Measurement,* permits, but does not require, the subsequent measurement of servicing assets and servicing liabilities at fair value. An entity should apply the requirements for recognition and initial measurement of servicing assets and servicing liabilities prospectively to all similar transactions.

As of and for the years ended December 31, 2009 and 2008, CEMEX did not determine any reconciling item resulting from the application of ASC 860 under U.S. GAAP and concluded that the effects of such adoption were immaterial. In arriving at this conclusion CEMEX considered that the receivables are short-term financial assets with an average collection period of approximately 42 days, and assumed a 1% servicing fee over its approximately US$735 and US$1,068 of receivables sold at December 31, 2009 and 2008, respectively. The result is a servicing asset of approximately US$7 in 2009 and US$11 in 2008 at the end of both periods that would be amortized every 42 days.

Asset retirement obligations and other environmental costs

ASC 410, Asset Retirement and Environmental Obligations ("ASC 410"), requires entities to record the fair value of an asset retirement obligation as a liability in the period in which a legal or a constructive obligation is incurred associated with the retirement of tangible long-lived assets that result from the acquisition, construction, development, and/or normal use of the assets. Such liability would be recorded against an asset that is depreciated over the life of the long-lived asset. Subsequent to the initial measurement, the obligation will be adjusted at the end of each period to reflect the passage of time and changes in the estimated future cash flows underlying the obligation. MFRS C-9, *Liabilities, Provisions, Contingent Assets and Liabilities and Commitments* ("MFRS C-9"), establishes generally the same requirements as ASC 410 in connection with asset retirement obligations. For the years ended December 31, 2009, 2008 and 2007, CEMEX did not identify any differences between MFRS and U.S. GAAP in connection with this topic.

In addition, environmental expenditures related to current operations are expensed or capitalized, as appropriate. Other than those contingencies disclosed in notes 14 and 21, CEMEX is not currently facing other material contingencies, which might result in the recognition of an environmental remediation liability.

Continued

EXHIBIT 6.11 (*Continued*)

Accounting for Costs Associated with Exit or Disposal Activities

CEMEX accrues the costs related to an exit or disposal activity, including severance payments, according to ASC 420, *Exit or Disposal Cost Obligations* ("ASC 420"), which basically requires, as a condition to accrue for such costs, that the entity communicate the plan to all affected employees and that the plan be terminated in the short-term; otherwise, associated costs should be expensed when incurred.

Guarantor's Accounting and Disclosure Requirements for Guarantees

Under U.S. GAAP, a guarantor is required to recognize, at origination of a guarantee, a liability for the fair value of the obligation undertaken. As of December 31, 2009 and 2008, CEMEX has not guaranteed any third parties' obligations. Nonetheless, with respect to the electricity supply long-term contract in Mexico discussed in note 20C, CEMEX may also be required to purchase the power plant upon the occurrence of specified material defaults or events, such as failure to purchase the energy and pay when due, bankruptcy or insolvency, and revocation of permits necessary to operate the facility. For the years ended December 31, 2009, 2008 and 2007, for accounting purposes under MFRS and U.S. GAAP, CEMEX has considered this agreement as a long-term energy supply agreement for own use and no liability has been created, based on the contingent characteristics of CEMEX's obligation and given that, absent a default under the agreement, CEMEX's obligations are limited to the purchase of energy from, and the supply of fuel to, the plant.

Variable Interest Entities

Under U.S. GAAP, CEMEX applies ASC 810, *Consolidation* ("ASC 810"). This topic addresses the consolidation of variable interest entities ("VIEs"), which are defined as those that have one or more of the following characteristics: (i) entities in which the equity investment at risk is not sufficient to finance their operations without requiring additional subordinated financing support provided by any parties, including the equity holders; and (ii) the equity investors lack one or more of the following attributes: a) the ability to make decisions about the entity's activities through voting or similar rights, b) the obligation to absorb the expected losses of the entity, and c) the right to receive the expected residual returns of the entity. Among others, entities that are deemed to be a business according to ASC 810-10-15, *Consolidation—Overall—Scope and Scope Exceptions,* including operating joint ventures, need not be evaluated to determine if they are VIEs under ASC 810.

Variable interests, among other factors, may be represented by operating losses, debt, contingent obligations or residual risks and may be assumed by means of loans, guarantees, management contracts, leasing, put options, derivatives, etc. A primary beneficiary is the entity that assumes the variable interests of a VIE, or the majority of them in the case of partnerships, directly or jointly with related parties, and is the entity that should consolidate the VIE. For the years ended December 31, 2009, 2008 and 2007, CEMEX has not identified any VIE that would require consolidation under U.S. GAAP other than those consolidated under MFRS.

Accounting for Planned Major Maintenance Activities

Under both MFRS and U.S. GAAP, CEMEX does not use the accrue-in-advance method of accounting for planned major maintenance activities considering that an obligation has not been incurred and therefore a liability should not be recognized.

(o) Newly Issued Accounting Pronouncements under U.S. GAAP not Effective in 2009

The FASB issued ASU 2009 16, *Transfers and Servicing (Topic 860): Accounting for Transfers of Financial Assets* (FASB Statement No. 166, Accounting for Transfers of Financial Assets—an amendment of FASB Statement No. 140) in December 2009. ASU 2009 16 removes the concept of a qualifying special purpose entity (QSPE) from ASC Topic 860, *Transfers and Servicing,* and the exception from applying ASC 810 10 to QSPEs, thereby requiring transferors of financial assets to evaluate whether to consolidate transferees that previously were considered QSPEs. Transferor imposed constraints on transferees whose sole purpose is to engage in securitization or asset backed financing activities are evaluated in the same manner under the provisions of the ASU as transferor imposed constraints on QSPEs were evaluated under the provisions of Topic 860 prior to the effective date of the ASU when determining whether a transfer of financial assets qualifies for sale accounting. The ASU also clarifies the Topic 860 sale accounting criteria pertaining to legal isolation and effective control and creates more stringent conditions for reporting a transfer of a portion of a financial asset as a sale. The ASU is effective for CEMEX beginning January 1, 2010, and may not be early adopted. CEMEX is evaluating the potential effect of this standard.

The FASB issued ASU 2009 17, *Consolidations (Topic 810): Improvements to Financial Reporting by Enterprises Involved with Variable Interest Entities* (FASB Statement No. 167, Amendments to FASB Interpretation No. 46(R)) in December 2009. ASU 2009 17, which amends the Variable Interest Entity (VIE) Subsections of ASC Subtopic 810 10, Consolidation—Overall, revises the test for determining the primary beneficiary of a VIE from a primarily quantitative risks and rewards calculation based on the VIE's expected losses and expected residual returns to a primarily qualitative analysis based on identifying the party or related party group (if any) with (a) the power to direct the activities that most significantly impact the VIE's economic performance and (b) the obligation to absorb losses of, or the right to receive benefits from, the VIE that could potentially be significant to the VIE. The ASU requires kick out rights and participating rights to be ignored in evaluating whether a variable interest holder meets the power criterion unless those rights are unilaterally exercisable by a single party or related party group. The ASU also revises the criteria for determining whether fees paid by an entity to a decision maker or another service provider are a variable interest in the entity and revises the Topic 810 scope characteristic that identifies an entity as a VIE if the equity at risk investors as a group do not have the right to control the entity through their equity interests to address the impact of kick out rights and participating rights on the analysis. Finally, the ASU adds a new requirement to reconsider whether an entity is a VIE if the holders of the equity investment at risk as a group lose the power, through the rights of those interests, to direct the activities that most significantly impact the VIE's economic performance, and requires a company to reassess on an ongoing basis whether it is deemed to be the primary beneficiary of a VIE. ASU 2009 17 is effective for CEMEX beginning January 1, 2010 and may not be early adopted. CEMEX expects that the adoption of ASU 2009 17 will not have a material impact on its consolidated financial statements.

In October 2009, the FASB issued ASU 2009 13, *Revenue Recognition (Topic 605): Multiple Deliverable Revenue Arrangements* (EITF Issue No. 08 1, Revenue Arrangements with Multiple Deliverables). ASU 2009 13 amends ASC 650 25 to eliminate the requirement that all undelivered elements have vendor specific objective evidence of selling price (VSOE) or third party evidence of selling price (TPE) before an entity can recognize the portion of an overall arrangement fee that is attributable to items that already have been delivered. In the absence of VSOE and TPE for one or more delivered or undelivered elements in a multiple element arrangement, entities will be required to estimate the selling prices of those elements. The overall arrangement fee will be allocated to each element (both delivered and undelivered items) based on their relative selling prices, regardless of whether those selling prices are evidenced by VSOE or TPE or are based on the entity's estimated selling price. Application of the "residual method" of allocating an overall arrangement fee between delivered and undelivered elements will no longer be permitted upon adoption of ASU 2009 13. Additionally, the new guidance will require entities to disclose more information about their multiple element revenue arrangements. ASU 2009 13 is effective for CEMEX prospectively for revenue arrangements entered into or materially modified beginning January 1, 2011. Early adoption is permitted. CEMEX expects that the adoption of ASU 2009 13 will not have a material impact on its consolidated financial statements

There is an element of secrecy in financial reporting, given the tradition of family-controlled business and the cultural orientation of Mexican society. Exhibit 6.12 shows that Mexican society is characterized by low individualism (collectivism), high masculinity, large power distance and strong uncertainty avoidance, compared to the United Kingdom. These cultural characteristics are likely to lead to high level of secrecy in accounting and financial reporting.[58]

EXHIBIT 6.12 Work-Related Cultural Value Orientation of Mexico

Source: G. Hofstede *Cultures and Organizations: Software of the Mind* (London: McGraw-Hill, 1991).

	Individualism vs. Collectivism	Masculinity vs. Femininity	Large vs. Small Power Distance	Strong vs. Weak Uncertainty Avoidance
United Kingdom	89	66	35	35
Germany	67	66	35	65
Japan	46	95	54	92
Mexico	30	69	81	82
Median score	38	49	60	68
Range	6–91	5–95	11–104	8–112

Scores above the median are considered high.

[58] S. J. Gray, "Towards a Theory of Cultural Influence on the Development of Accounting Systems Internationally," *Abacus,* March 1988, pp. 1–15.

UNITED KINGDOM

Background

The United Kingdom consists of four constituent regions: England, Wales, Scotland, and Northern Ireland. The legislative authority lies with Parliament, which includes the House of Commons and the House of Lords. The House of Commons has 659 directly elected members, whose term of office is a maximum of five years. The House of Lords is appointed and consists of 92 hereditary peers, over 500 life peers, certain senior judges, and 26 bishops of the Church of England.

The limited liability company is the main form of business organization in the United Kingdom, and the capital market provides the main source of funding for business. Consequently, facilitating the efficient working of the capital market is the primary purpose of accounting. There are approximately 15,000 private limited companies (PLCs), of which about 2,500 are listed on the London Stock Exchange.[59] The United Kingdom has by far the greatest number of companies listed on a regulated market in the European Union. Listed companies and other large companies file a full set of audited annual financial statements with the Registrar of Companies. The annual report of a UK-listed company typically includes, in addition to financial statements, a chairperson's statement, an operating and financial review, the report of the directors, the report of the remuneration committee, a statement on corporate governance, and shareholding information.

Accounting Profession

Accounting in the United Kingdom grew as an independent discipline, responding to business needs, and has had a significant influence on the development of accounting profession in many countries including the United States and member countries of the British Commonwealth such as Canada, Australia, and New Zealand. The establishment of the first professional accounting body, the Society of Accountants in Edinburgh, in 1853 can be regarded as the beginning of the modern accounting profession.[60] There are six professional bodies in the United Kingdom. In order of membership size, these are the Institute of Chartered Accountants in England and Wales (ICAEW), the Association of Chartered Certified Accountants (ACCA), the Chartered Institute of Management Accountants (CIMA), the Institute of Chartered Accountants in Scotland (ICAS), the Chartered Institute of Public Finance and Accountancy (CIPFA), and the Institute of Chartered Accountants in Ireland (ICAI). The ICAEW alone has more than 126,000 members. It is the largest professional accounting body in Europe. The UK accountancy bodies, enjoying Royal Charters, exercise considerable social power. They act as statutory regulators for the auditing and the insolvency sectors. The activities of the six bodies are coordinated through the Consultative Committee of Accountancy Bodies (CCAB), established in May 1974. Members of CIMA and CIPFA are not allowed to sign audit opinions.

[59] David Alexander and Simon Archer, eds., *European Accounting Guide,* 4th ed. (New York: Aspen, 2003), p. 14.04.

[60] For details about early developments of the accounting profession in the United Kingdom, see Zeff, *Forging Accounting Principles;* and L. Goldburgh, "The Development of Accounting," in *Accounting Concepts Readings,* ed. C. T. Gibson, G. G. Meredith, and R. Peterson (Melbourne: Cassell, 1971), pp. 18–22.

Professional accounting bodies in the United Kingdom do not require aspiring members to have an undergraduate degree in accounting. However, those who possess an undergraduate degree in accounting would qualify for exemptions from the full examination structure. The three Institutes of Chartered Accountants have been the main training bodies for the members of the big accounting firms in the respective regions of the United Kingdom. The membership of ACCA mainly consists of small practitioners and individuals from the corporate sector, while the main foci of CIMA and CIPFA are on management accounting and accounting in government organizations, respectively. All six professional accounting bodies set comprehensive exams for admission to their bodies. The examinations test knowledge at the basic, intermediate, and advanced levels. Those aspiring to be members of the three Institutes of Chartered Accountants are required to enter into training contracts with approved organizations (traditionally accounting firms but now extended to large companies) while completing their examinations.

The ICAEW in September 2000 introduced a new examination structure consisting of a professional stage and an advanced stage. The professional stage, which students can take prior to entering a training contract, consists of six subjects and two modules in law whose assessment is devolved to tuition providers. Students can gain exemptions from individual subjects at this stage if they have completed relevant diplomas, degrees, or examinations of other professional bodies. The advanced stage consists of a Test of Advanced Technical Competence (TATC) and an Advanced Case Study. The advanced stage adopts "a multidisciplinary approach, breaking down the old subject by subject 'tunnel vision,' integrating tax, audit, financial reporting and business topics, including business strategy, knowledge management and communication, digital economy, financial strategy, mergers and acquisition, change management, and business recovery."[61]

Over the years, there have been several attempts at consolidating the UK accountancy profession by a merger of the three chartered bodies (CIMA, CIPFA, and ICAEW). This would create an organization with more than 200,000 members and become the authoritative voice across the accountancy profession in the United Kingdom. However, this has not materialized as a result of the inability of the three bodies to reach an agreement on some aspects of the merger.

Traditionally, the UK accounting profession has favored a principles-based approach, rather than a rules-based approach, to standard setting. Peter Wyman, president of the ICAEW, explained the importance of this approach as follows:

> To remain a profession, accountancy must be about the exercise of professional integrity and judgment. If we are driven down the road of simply ticking boxes to show that rules have been complied with, we will end up with a clerical activity that is carried out without thought, and possibly without regard to the special context of the business at hand.
>
> Not only will this fail to attract people with intellect, but will also, inevitably from time to time, produce the wrong answers. No standard setter, no lawmaker is able to predict every likely situation. It is for this reason that we have constantly called for principles rather than rules in our standards. However, such an approach can only operate successfully if the principles are being applied by people with integrity and with the suitable skill, insight and application to do so effectively.[62]

---

[61] www.icaew.co.uk/students/newaca/document.asp.

[62] Peter Wyman, "The Enron Aftermath—Where Next?" speech delivered October 10, 2002, at a conference held in Brussels (available at www.icaew.co.uk).

Accounting Regulation

Regulation of accounting and financial reporting in the United Kingdom primarily is through legislation (Companies Act), professional pronouncements, and stock exchange listing requirements. The idea that determination of acceptable accounting principles and standards should be left in the hands of the profession has been part of the UK tradition. Unlike their counterparts in the United States, traditionally, UK legislators have never felt the need to have a powerful securities commission to regulate accounting and financial reporting with detailed rules. Recent developments, however, suggest a change to this attitude as the FRC has become the powerful independent regulator responsible for promoting confidence in corporate reporting and governance in the UK.

The United Kingdom joined the European Union in 1973. Since then, EU directives have had a strong impact on UK accounting regulation. EU directives are transformed into UK legislation through the Companies Act. The EU Fourth Directive was integrated into British law in 1981 through amendments to the Companies Act of 1948. These amendments were prescriptive to a degree previously unknown in the United Kingdom. Traditionally, the Companies Act would normally set out the general principles leaving the specific requirements to be developed through other channels, particularly the accounting profession. However, the 1981 amendments to the Companies Act state exactly how certain matters are to be disclosed, with no latitude, for example, in matters of format. Similarly, the Companies Act of 1989 introduced the EU Seventh and Eighth Directives.[63]

As a result of the EU Eighth Directive, in order to qualify to practice as an auditor in the United Kingdom, a candidate is required to be registered in a statutory register maintained by one of the professional bodies. The 1989 Companies Act also requires companies to state whether the financial statements have been prepared in accordance with applicable accounting standards and, if not, give reasons for the departure. This is also an important change, because, prior to the 1989 Companies Act, UK accounting standards were not referred to in company legislation.

In 2000, the British government, in partnership with the professional accountancy bodies, established the Accountancy Foundation, to be responsible for the nonstatutory independent regulation of the six professional chartered accountancy bodies comprising the CCAB. The purpose of establishing the Accountancy Foundation was to ensure that self-regulation would be conducted in the public interest.

In response to accounting scandals in the United States, such as those related to Enron and WorldCom, several steps have been taken to improve regulation of financial reporting in the United Kingdom. The Department of Trade and Industry initiated a review of the Accountancy Foundation in October 2002 by publishing a consultation document on how the UK accountancy and auditing professions are regulated. It highlighted a number of issues:

- Whether the professional organizations should continue to set their own ethical standards and monitor the work and conduct of audit firms, or whether there should be stronger independent oversight or intervention.

---

[63] In January 2003, the European Parliament approved amendments to the EU Fourth and Seventh Directives that removed all inconsistencies between the directives and IFRS. In December 2004, the EU adopted a directive on minimum transparency requirements for listed companies, completing a package of measures to establish a common financial disclosure regime across the EU for issuers of listed securities. The text of the directive is at www.europa.eu.int/comm/internal_market/securities/transparency/index_en.htm.

- Whether the Accountancy Foundation should focus on the company auditor rather than on the regulation of accountants in general.
- Whether the structure and funding of the Accountancy Foundation should be reviewed.

The second main element of the UK regulatory system is professional pronouncements. The establishment of the Accounting Standards Steering Committee in 1970 by the ICAEW was the beginning of the development of formal accounting standards in the United Kingdom. The committee was later redesignated as the Accounting Standards Committee (ASC), which was reconstituted as a joint committee of the six professional bodies in 1976. The ASC standard-setting mechanism came under heavy criticism in the 1980s for a lack of effective means of monitoring compliance and the low quality of its standards known as Statements of Standard Accounting Practice (SSAP). In response, the Dearing Report recommended significant changes to the UK standard-setting process, which included the creation of the following:[64]

1. The Accounting Standards Board (ASB), with the authority to issue standards in its own right.
2. The Financial Reporting Council (FRC), given the responsibility of overall policy control over the standard-setting process.
3. The Financial Reporting Review Panel (FRRP), to oversee compliance.

The creation of the ASB in August 1990 marked the beginning of a new era in accounting standards setting in the United Kingdom. It reduced the direct influence of the accounting profession on standard setting, because the ASB, like the U.S. FASB, is institutionally separated from the accounting institutes. The role of the FRC, also created in 1991, was to secure funding for the ASB and FRRP, which functioned under its purview. The FRC also acted as a high-level policy body that provided guidance to the ASB on priorities and work programs, advised the board in broad terms on issues of public concern, and encouraged compliance.

In January 2003, the Secretary of State for Trade and Industry announced a package of reforms to raise standards of corporate governance, strengthen the accountancy and audit professions, and provide for an independent system of regulation for those professions. Accordingly, the FRC assumed the functions of the Accountancy Foundation, and the FRC and its operating boards would have the following three specific roles:

- Set accounting and auditing standards.
- Proactively enforce and monitor those standards.
- Oversee the self-regulatory professional bodies.

With the assumption of these responsibilities, the FRC became the single, independent regulator of accounting and auditing in the United Kingdom. For example, it assumed responsibility for setting independence standards for auditors and for monitoring the audit of listed companies and other significant entities were transferred from the accounting professional bodies to the FRC. The FRC also retains its current responsibilities for the work of the ASB and the FRRP.

---

[64] Consultative Committee on Accountancy Bodies, *The Making of Accounting Standards: Report of the Review Committee (Dearing Committee)* (London: ICAEW, 1988).

The Companies Act of 2004, which amended the Companies Acts of 1985 and 1989, made the FRC a unified, independent regulator with the above three key roles. The FRC is funded equally by government, business, and the accountancy profession thereby guaranteeing its independence because no single interest group dominates. The annual report 2008/2009 of the FRC (published in May 2009) comments about its own effectiveness as "an effective, accountable and independent regulator, operating in the public interest and actively helping to shape UK, and to influence EU and global, approaches to corporate reporting and governance." The annual report also says,

> In view of the importance of the IASB for accounting in the UK, we continued to follow its work carefully, in particular its Memorandum of Understanding with the US FASB. The ASB continued to look for opportunities to promote the merits of reassessing the advantages of further convergence between IFRS and US GAAP. It assessed the accounting implications of current market conditions and the IASB projects related to the global liquidity squeeze, in particular consolidation and the issues around fair value measurements in illiquid markets. We continue to have significant concerns that the EU might adopt its own version of IFRS rather than the standards as published by the IASB. . . .We remain committed in principle to a future UK GAAP which is further converged with IFRS, but the strategy for achieving this remains under consideration. The ASB continued its efforts to ensure that UK converged standards remain in line with their IFRS equivalents, responding to circumstances arising from the current crisis as appropriate. (p. 5)

According to the annual report, the key themes of the FRC's work for 2009/2010 would be to influence (1) market participants to meet high standards of reporting and governance through a combination of measures to raise awareness of major risks, monitor corporate reporting and governance practices, and take enforcement action where appropriate; (2) legislators and international standards setters to encourage a proportionate and principles-based approach that promotes high standards of corporate reporting and governance; and (3) international regulatory authorities to encourage effective cooperation (p. 10).

The ASB, adopting a principles-based approach, develops its standards on the basis of a conceptual framework known as the "Statement of Principles for Financial Reporting." The ASB makes, amends, and withdraws accounting standards, assisted by four committees: (1) the Urgent Issues Task Force, (2) the Financial Sector and Other Special Industries Committee, (3) the Public Sector and Not-for-profit Committee, and (4) the Committee on Accounting for Smaller Entities. The standards issued by the ASB are called Financial Reporting Standards (FRS).

The ASB is one of several national standard-setters that have a formal liaison relationship with the IASB. The ASB is committed to align UK accounting standards with IFRS wherever practicable, by a phased replacement of existing UK standards with new UK standards based on IFRS.[65] According to the FRC annual report for 2008/2009, the ASB faces three major challenges. The first challenge is to continue to ensure an appropriate influence on the development of IFRS through high-quality submissions to, and communications with, the IASB, arguing the case for accounting standards based on clear principles rather than detailed rules. The second challenge is to work for the timely adoption of IFRS as developed

---

[65] In July 2003, the Department of Trade and Industry announced that all UK companies will be able to use IFRSs as an alternative to UK standards from 2005. (Department of Trade and Industry Press Release, "UK Extends Use of International Accounting Standards," July 17, 2003.)

by the IASB for adoption in the EU. As financial reporting has become increasingly political, the ASB will have to work hard with its European counterparts and EFRAG to maintain the policy of using IFRS in Europe. The final challenge is to develop an appropriate strategy for the future of UK GAAP.

The main purpose of the FRRP, which was established in 1991, is to review companies' financial statements to ensure fair presentation of information. The FRRP adopts a proactive role for the enforcement of accounting standards in which the Financial Services Authority (FSA), the UK finance watchdog, plays an active part.[66] The FRRP can ask directors to explain apparent departures from the accounting requirements. If the panel is not satisfied by the directors' explanations, it persuades them to adopt a more appropriate accounting treatment. Failing this, the panel can exercise its powers to secure the necessary revision of the original accounts through a court order.

Under the Companies Act of 2004, which came into effect in October 2004,[67] the authority of the FRRP would be extended to cover financial information, other than annual accounts, published by entities that have securities listed on a UK market and where mandatory accounting requirements may apply.

In May 2007, the FRRP issued a consultation paper aimed at improving the quality and credibility of annual financial statements. The panel seeks to ensure that the provision of financial statements by public and large companies complies with the reporting requirements of the Companies Act of 1985. The panel currently relies on users of accounts bringing such reports to its attention but this often happens some considerable time after publication. The panel proposes that registered audit firms disclose voluntarily to the panel any audit report they issue in respect of annual financial statements in which their opinion is qualified for failure to comply with the reporting requirements of the Companies Act.

Auditing standards in the United Kingdom are issued by the Auditing Practices Board (APB) an operating body of the FRC. They include Statements of Auditing Standards (SASs), Auditing Guidelines, and Statements of Investment Circular Reporting Standards (SIRs). The APB is funded by the CCAB, and its membership consists of practicing auditors and others from business, academia, law, and the public sector.

The third element of the UK regulatory system is stock exchange listing requirements. The London Stock Exchange (LSE) requires publication of a semi-annual interim report and disclosure of information about corporate governance and directors' remuneration. Unlike in Germany or Japan, taxation rules are not a major influence on financial reporting in the United Kingdom.

Accounting Principles and Practices

Accounting principles in the United Kingdom emphasize investor needs and the importance of transparency. UK financial statements typically include a profit and loss account, a balance sheet, a cash flow statement, a statement of total gains and losses, a statement of accounting policies, notes to financial statements, and the

---

[66] The FSA is an independent body that regulates the financial services industry in the United Kingdom. It aims to maintain confidence in the UK financial system, promote public understanding of the financial system, secure the right degree of protection for consumers, and help to reduce financial crime. For details see, www.fsa.gov.uk.

[67] The Companies (Audit, Investigations and Community Enterprise) Act of 2004 forms part of the government's stategy to help restore investor confidence in companies and financial markets following major corporate failures. The act amends relevant provisions of the Companies Acts of 1985 and 1989.

auditor's report. The United Kingdom has a differential financial reporting system in which small and medium-size companies are exempt from many reporting requirements.

The 1985 Companies Act requires corporate financial statements to provide a true and fair view of the firm's financial position and results of operations for the financial year. Auditors are given the corresponding duty to render an opinion on whether a true and fair view is provided. *True and fair view* is not specifically defined in law. The legal opinion is that compliance with accounting standards is necessary to meet the true and fair requirement. However, this requirement is overriding and may require more than just compliance with accounting standards. For example, the Companies Act specifically stipulates that if compliance with the act "would not be sufficient to give a true and fair view, the necessary additional information shall be given in the accounts or in a note to them" [Section 226 (2)]. Therefore, while accounting standards are a necessary component of a true and fair view, they may not in themselves be sufficient in all situations to provide a true and fair view. Professional judgment remains an essential additional component. In incorporating the Fourth and Seventh Directives, which had a more prescriptive approach, into the national law, extensive use was made of options in order to preserve the importance of professional judgment.

In an opinion published in May 2008, the FRC confirmed the continued relevance of the 'true and fair' concept to the preparation and audit of financial statements following the enactment of the Companies Act of 2006 and the introduction of international accounting standards.

Since January 1, 2005, UK-listed companies must use European Union–adopted IFRS to prepare their group financial statements.[68] They are permitted, but not required, to use IFRS for their individual accounts. Other companies and limited liability partnerships are permitted, but not required, to use IFRS both for their consolidated and individual accounts. UK standards will therefore still be available for all financial statements other than the consolidated accounts of listed groups. The Financial Reporting Review Panel in its 2010 annual report states that there has been a continuous improvement in the general quality of IFRS financial reporting.

Financial statements generally are prepared on the basis of historical cost, but companies are allowed to revalue tangible assets. In general, UK accounting standards are very similar to IFRS, as the international standards have been heavily influenced by British accounting. However, specific differences do exist between IFRS and UK GAAP. In some areas, there is a difference in requirements under the two sets of standards. For example, segment reporting in the United Kingdom does not follow the primary–secondary reporting format approach found in IAS 14. In other areas, UK rules are more flexible. For example, whereas IFRS 3 requires that goodwill should not be amortized systematically, but instead should be subject to an annual impairment test, UK GAAP allows amortization at the firm's discretion. Exhibit 6.13 provides a summary of several differences that exist between UK GAAP and IFRS.

Recently, the FRC published a discussion paper on reducing complexity in corporate reporting. The paper seeks to address growing concerns about the

[68] The EU made certain amendments to IAS-39 prior to its adoption. However, the ASB has adopted the unamended version of IAS 39 in the United Kingdom.

EXHIBIT 6.13 Differences between UK GAAP and IFRS

Issue	IFRS	UK GAAP
Goodwill	IFRS 3: Prohibits amortization. Must be tested for impairment annually.	Goodwill can be amortized at the firm's choice.
Proposed dividends	IAS 10: Should not be recognized as a liability at the balance sheet date.	Accrued as a liability.
Related party disclosures	IAS 24: Requires transactions to be disclosed by type of related party. Does not require names to be disclosed.	Names of transacting related parties should be disclosed.
Segment reporting	IAS 14: More disclosure for primary segments than for secondary segments.	Segment reporting does not use the primary/secondary basis. Reports net assets rather than assets and liabilities separately.
Cash flow statements	IAS 7: Cash flows include both cash and cash equivalents.	Cash flow statements reconcile to a narrowly defined "cash" rather than to "cash and cash equivalents."
Translation of profit and loss account of a foreign subsidiary	IAS 21: The average rate of exchange for the period should be used.	Allows the closing rate to be used.
Reporting on a hyperinflationary subsidiary	IAS 21: The financial statements of a foreign entity that reports in the currency of a hyperinflationary economy should be restated before they are translated into the reporting currency of the reporting entity.	The financial statements of a hyperinflationary subsidiary can be remeasured using a stable currency as the measurement currency.
Revaluation gains/losses on investment properties	IAS 40: Allows the choice of either fair value or depreciated cost as an accounting policy for measuring investment property. Where fair value is used, gains and losses from changes in fair value are recognized in the income statement.	Fair value should be used, but gains on revaluation are taken though the statement of total recognized gains and losses not through profit and loss (except for permanent deficits below cost, or their reversals).
Intangible assets	IAS 38: Requires capitalization of development expenditure in R&D. Requires Web site costs, when capitalized, to be treated as intangible asset.	Permits capitalization of development expenditure in R&D.

complexity of corporate reporting in terms of, for example, increasing length and detail of annual reports and the regulations that govern them. The paper recommends a commonsense approach to reducing complexity based on eight guiding principles divided into two categories.

Guiding Principles for Regulation

1. Regulations should focus on significant problems and be targeted to:
   - Provide relevant information that meets important user needs.
   - Reflect the reality of the business while minimizing unintended implementation consequences.

2. Regulators should limit constant change by intervening only when an area is high-risk and change will bring obvious benefit. Intervention should be as cost effective as possible—for example, by using management information already produced for internal purposes.

3. Regulators should understand what other national and international regulators are doing in a particular area. Wherever possible, they should be consistent with one another and work together in a joined-up way.

4. Regulations should be kept simple and user-friendly. They need to be understood easily by those who will apply them and those who will benefit from them. Regulations should emphasize:
   - A clear articulation of the desired outcome.
   - Principles and judgment where appropriate.
   - Plain language with well-defined terms.
   - Consistent terminology.
   - An easy-to-follow structure.

Guiding Principles for Communication

1. Highlight important messages, transactions, and accounting policies, and avoid distracting readers with immaterial clutter.

2. Provide a balanced explanation of the results—the good news and the bad.

3. Use plain language, only well-defined technical terms, consistent terminology, and an easy-to-follow structure.

4. Get the point across with a report that holds the reader's attention.

The discussion paper is focused on the activities of UK publicly traded companies, but its recommendations could be useful to all companies, and it would stimulate discussions around the world, regarding corporate reporting.

The United Kingdom has the second greatest number of foreign companies listed on the New York Stock Exchange (Canada has the most). Exhibit 6.14 provides a detailed description of the accounting standards adopted by Vodafone Group in preparing financial statements according to its 2010 Form 20-F. Note that there is no statement to reconcile the UK standards and U.S. GAAP as the financial statements were in compliance with IFRS.

The annual reports of listed companies have become too complex and focused on compliance, rather than providing useful information on the business to investors. In addressing this issue, the Institute of Chartered Accountants of Scotland (ICAS) has provided a document entitled "Making Corporate Reports Readable," which contains a pro forma short form report that uses the example of a fictional universal bank as the underlying business and produces "in less than 30 pages" the key information of interest to investors.

The ASB has issued a Financial Reporting Standard (FRS), *Improvements to Financial Reporting Standards 2009,* so as to maintain the existing levels of convergence between UK and IFRS in 2009. Recently, the FRC published a discussion paper on reducing complexity in corporate reporting. The paper seeks to address growing concerns about the complexity of corporate reporting in terms of, for example, increasing length and detail of annual reports and the regulations that govern them. The paper recommends a commonsense approach to reducing complexity based on eight guiding principles—four for better communication in reports and four for improving the quality and effectiveness of regulations.

EXHIBIT 6.14

VODAFONE GROUP PLC
Form 20-F
2010
Excerpts from Notes to the Consolidated Financial Statements

Notes to the consolidated financial statements

1. Basis of preparation

The consolidated financial statements are prepared in accordance with IFRS as issued by the IASB. The consolidated financial statements are also prepared in accordance with IFRS adopted by the EU, the Companies Act 2006 and Article 4 of the EU IAS Regulations. The preparation of financial statements in conformity with IFRS requires management to make estimates and assumptions that affect the reported amounts of assets and liabilities and disclosure of contingent assets and liabilities at the date of the financial statements and the reported amounts of revenue and expenses during the reporting period. For a discussion on the Group's critical accounting estimates see "Critical accounting estimates" on pages 71 and 72. Actual results could differ from those estimates. The estimates and underlying assumptions are reviewed on an ongoing basis. Revisions to accounting estimates are recognised in the period in which the estimate is revised if the revision affects only that period or in the period of the revision and future periods if the revision affects both current and future periods.

Amounts in the consolidated financial statements are stated in pounds sterling.

Vodafone Plc is registered in England (No. 1833679).

2. Significant accounting policies

Accounting convention

The consolidated financial statements are prepared on a historical cost basis except for certain financial and equity instruments that have been measured at fair value.

New accounting pronouncements adopted

IFRIC 13 – "Customer Loyalty Programmes"

The Group adopted IFRIC 13 on 1 April 2009. The interpretation addresses how companies that grant their customers loyalty award credits when buying goods and services should account for their obligations to provide free or discounted goods and services. It requires that consideration received be allocated between the award credits and the other components of the sale. The adoption of this interpretation did not result in a material impact on the Group's results or financial position.

IAS 23 (Revised) – "Borrowing Costs"

The Group adopted IAS 23 (Revised) on 1 April 2009. This standard requires the capitalisation of borrowing costs to the extent they are directly attributable to the acquisition, production or construction of a qualifying asset. The option of immediate recognition of those borrowing costs as an expense, previously used by the Group, has been removed. The adoption of this standard did not result in a material impact on the Group's results or financial position.

IAS 1 (Revised) – "Presentation of Financial Statements"

The Group adopted IAS 1 (Revised) on 1 April 2009. A separate consolidated statement of changes in equity is now included as part of the primary financial statements. The Group changed the naming of the primary financial statements and adopted certain new terminology set out in the revised standard.

IFRS 7 – "Financial Instruments: Disclosure"

The Group adopted an amendment to IFRS 7 on 1 April 2009. The standard requires enhanced disclosure regarding fair value measurements and liquidity risk. The adoption of this standard did not impact the Group's results or financial position.

New accounting pronouncements not yet adopted

IFRS 3 (Revised) "Business Combinations" was issued in January 2008 and will apply to business combinations occurring on or after 1 April 2010. The revised standard introduces a number of changes in the accounting for business combinations that will impact the amount of goodwill recognised, the reported results in the period that a business combination occurs and future reported results. This standard is likely to have a significant impact on the Group's accounting for business combinations post adoption.

An amendment to IAS 27 "Consolidated and Separate Financial Statements" was issued in January 2008 and is effective for annual periods beginning on or after 1 July 2009. The amendment requires that when a transaction occurs with non-controlling interests in Group entities that do not result in a change in control, the difference between the consideration paid or received and the recorded

Continued

EXHIBIT 6.14 *(Continued)*

non-controlling interest should be recognised in equity. In cases where control is lost, any retained interest should be remeasured to fair value with the difference between fair value and the previous carrying value being recognised immediately in the income statement. The Group has historically entered into transactions that would have been within the scope of the amendment to this standard and may do so in the future.

Phase I of IFRS 9 "Financial Instruments" was issued in November 2009 and is effective for annual periods beginning on or after 1 January 2013. The standard introduces changes to the classification and measurement of financial assets. The Group is currently assessing the impact of the standard on its results, financial position and cash flows. This standard has not yet been endorsed for use in the EU.

The Group has not adopted the following pronouncements, which have been issued by the IASB or the IFRIC. The Group does not currently believe the adoption of these pronouncements will have a material impact on the consolidated results, financial position or cash flows of the Group. These pronouncements have been endorsed for use in the EU, unless otherwise stated.

- "Amendment to IAS 39 Financial Instruments: Recognition and Measurement—Exposures Qualifying for Hedge Accounting", effective for annual periods beginning on or after 1 July 2009.
- "Embedded derivatives: Amendments to IFRIC 9 and IAS 39", effective for annual periods beginning on or after 30 June 2009.
- "Improvements to IFRSs" issued in April 2009 are effective over a range of dates, with the earliest being for annual periods beginning on or after 1 January 2010.
- IFRS 1, "Additional Exemptions for First-time Adopters", effective for periods beginning on or after 1 January 2010. This standard has not yet been endorsed for use in the EU.
- "IFRS for Small and Medium-Sized Entities", issued July 2009, effective immediately. This standard has not yet been endorsed for use in the EU.
- IFRS 2, "Group Cash-settled Share-based Payment Transactions", effective for periods beginning on or after 1 January 2010.
- "Amendment to IAS 32, "Classification of Rights Issues", effective for annual periods beginning on or after 1 February 2010.
- "Amendment to IAS 24, "Related Party Disclosures—State-controlled Entities and the Definition of a Related Party", effective for annual periods beginning on or after 1 January 2011. This amendment has not yet been endorsed for use in the EU.
- Amendment to IFRIC 14, "Prepayments on a Minimum Funding Requirement", effective for annual periods beginning on or after 1 January 2011. This interpretation has not yet been endorsed for use in the EU.
- IFRIC 17, "Distributions of Non-cash Assets to Owners", effective for annual periods beginning on or after 1 July 2009.
- IFRIC 19, "Extinguishing Financial Liabilities with Equity Instruments", effective annual periods beginning on or after 1 July 2010 with early adoption permitted. This interpretation has not yet been endorsed for use in the EU.

Basis of consolidation

The consolidated financial statements incorporate the financial statements of the Company and entities controlled, both unilaterally and jointly, by the Company.

Accounting for subsidiaries   A subsidiary is an entity controlled by the Company. Control is achieved where the Company has the power to govern the financial and operating policies of an entity so as to obtain benefits from its activities.

The results of subsidiaries acquired or disposed of during the year are included in the income statement from the effective date of acquisition or up to the effective date of disposal, as appropriate. Where necessary, adjustments are made to the financial statements of subsidiaries to bring their accounting policies into line with those used by the Group.

All intra-group transactions, balances, income and expenses are eliminated on consolidation.

Non-controlling interests in the net assets of consolidated subsidiaries are identified separately from the Group's equity therein. Non-controlling interests consist of the amount of those interests at the date of the original business combination and the non-controlling shareholder's share of changes in equity since the date of the combination. Losses applicable to the non-controlling shareholders in excess of the non-controlling shareholders' share of changes in equity are allocated against the interests of the Group except to the extent that the non-controlling shareholders have a binding obligation and are able to make an additional investment to cover the losses.

Business combinations   The acquisition of subsidiaries is accounted for using the purchase method. The cost of the acquisition is measured at the aggregate of the fair values, at the date of exchange, of assets given, liabilities incurred or assumed, and equity instruments issued by the Group in exchange for control of the acquiree, plus any costs directly attributable to the business combination. The acquiree's identifiable assets and liabilities are recognised at their fair values at the acquisition date.

Goodwill arising on acquisition is recognised as an asset and initially measured at cost, being the excess of the cost of the business combination over the Group's interest in the net fair value of the identifiable assets, liabilities and contingent liabilities recognised.

The interest of non-controlling shareholders in the acquiree is initially measured at the non-controlling shareholders' proportion of the net fair value of the assets, liabilities and contingent liabilities recognised.

Where the Group increases its interest in an entity such that control is achieved, previously held identifiable assets, liabilities and contingent liabilities of the acquired entity are revalued to their fair value at the date of acquisition, being the date at which the Group achieves control of the acquiree. The movement in fair value is taken to the asset revaluation surplus.

Acquisition of interests from non-controlling shareholders   Acquisitions of non-controlling interests in subsidiaries are accounted for as transactions between shareholders. There is no remeasurement to fair value of net assets acquired that were previously attributable to non-controlling shareholders.

Interests in joint ventures   A joint venture is a contractual arrangement whereby the Group and other parties undertake an economic activity that is subject to joint control; that is, when the strategic financial and operating policy decisions relating to the activities require the unanimous consent of the parties sharing control.

The Group reports its interests in jointly controlled entities using proportionate consolidation. The Group's share of the assets, liabilities, income, expenses and cash flows of jointly controlled entities are combined with the equivalent items in the results on a line-by-line basis.

Any goodwill arising from the acquisition of the Group's interest in a jointly controlled entity is accounted for in accordance with the Group's accounting policy for goodwill arising on the acquisition of a subsidiary.

Investments in associates   An associate is an entity over which the Group has significant influence and that is power to participate in the financial and operating policy decisions of the investee but is not control or joint control over those policies.

The results and assets and liabilities of associates are incorporated in the consolidated financial statements using the equity method of accounting. Under the equity method, investments in associates are carried in the consolidated statement of financial position at cost as adjusted for post-acquisition changes in the Group's share of the net assets of the associate, less any impairment in the value of the investment. Losses of an associate in excess of the Group's interest in that associate are not recognised. Additional losses are provided for, and a liability is recognised, only to the extent that the Group has incurred legal or constructive obligations or made payments on behalf of the associate.

Any excess of the cost of acquisition over the Group's share of the net fair value of the identifiable assets, liabilities and contingent liabilities of the associate recognised at the date of acquisition is recognised as goodwill. The goodwill is included within the carrying amount of the investment.

The licences of the Group's associate in the US, Verizon Wireless, are indefinite lived assets as they are subject to perfunctory renewal. Accordingly, they are not subject to amortisation but are tested annually for impairment, or when indicators exist that the carrying value is not recoverable.

Intangible assets   Identifiable intangible assets are recognised when the Group controls the asset, it is probable that future economic benefits attributed to the asset will flow to the Group and the cost of the asset can be reliably measured.

Goodwill

Goodwill arising on the acquisition of an entity represents the excess of the cost of acquisition over the Group's interest in the net fair value of the identifiable assets, liabilities and contingent liabilities of the entity recognised at the date of acquisition.

Goodwill is initially recognised as an asset at cost and is subsequently measured at cost less any accumulated impairment losses. Goodwill is held in the currency of the acquired entity and revalued to the closing rate at each end of reporting period date.

Goodwill is not subject to amortisation but is tested for impairment.

Negative goodwill arising on an acquisition is recognised directly in the income statement.

On disposal of a subsidiary or a jointly controlled entity, the attributable amount of goodwill is included in the determination of the profit or loss recognised in the income statement on disposal.

Goodwill arising before the date of transition to IFRS, on 1 April 2004, has been retained at the previous UK GAAP amounts, subject to being tested for impairment at that date. Goodwill written off to reserves under UK GAAP prior to 1998 has not been reinstated and is not included in determining any subsequent profit or loss on disposal.

Finite lived intangible assets

Intangible assets with finite lives are stated at acquisition or development cost, less accumulated amortisation. The amortisation period and method is reviewed at least annually. Changes in the expected useful life or the expected pattern of consumption of future economic benefits embodied in the asset is accounted for by changing the amortisation period or method, as appropriate, and are treated as changes in accounting estimates. The amortisation expense on intangible assets with finite lives is recognised in profit or loss in the expense category consistent with the function of the intangible asset.

Continued

EXHIBIT 6.14 *(Continued)*

Licence and spectrum fees

Amortisation periods for licence and spectrum fees are determined primarily by reference to the unexpired licence period, the conditions for licence renewal and whether licences are dependent on specific technologies. Amortisation is charged to the income statement on a straight-line basis over the estimated useful lives from the commencement of service of the network.

Computer software

Computer software comprises computer software purchased from third parties as well as the cost of internally developed software. Computer software licences are capitalised on the basis of the costs incurred to acquire and bring into use the specific software. Costs that are directly associated with the production of identifiable and unique software products controlled by the Group, and are probable of producing future economic benefits are recognised as intangible assets. Direct costs include software development employee costs and directly attributable overheads.

Software integral to a related item of hardware equipment is accounted for as property, plant and equipment.

Costs associated with maintaining computer software programs are recognised as an expense when they are incurred.

Internally developed software is recognised only if all of the following conditions are met:

- an asset is created that can be separately identified;
- it is probable that the asset created will generate future economic benefits; and
- the development cost of the asset can be measured reliably.

Amortisation is charged to the income statement on a straight-line basis over the estimated useful lives from the date the software is available for use.

Other intangible assets

Other intangible assets including brands and customer bases, are recorded at fair value at the date of acquisition. Amortisation is charged to the income statement on a straight-line basis over the estimated useful lives of intangible assets from the date they are available for use.

Estimated useful lives

The estimated useful lives of finite lived intangible assets are as follows:

- Licence and spectrum fees 3–25 years
- Computer software 3–5 years
- Brands 1–10 years
- Customer bases 2–7 years

Property, plant and equipment

Land and buildings held for use are stated in the statement of financial position at their cost, less any subsequent accumulated depreciation and subsequent accumulated impairment losses.

Equipment, fixtures and fittings are stated at cost less accumulated depreciation and any accumulated impairment losses.

Assets in the course of construction are carried at cost, less any recognised impairment loss. Depreciation of these assets commences when the assets are ready for their intended use.

The cost of property, plant and equipment includes directly attributable incremental costs incurred in their acquisition and installation.

Depreciation is charged so as to write off the cost of assets, other than land and properties under construction, using the straight-line method, over their estimated useful lives, as follows:

- Freehold buildings 25–50 years
- Leasehold premises the term of the lease

Equipment, fixtures and fittings:

- Network infrastructure 3–25 years
- Other 3–10 years

Depreciation is not provided on freehold land.

Assets held under finance leases are depreciated over their expected useful lives on the same basis as owned assets or, where shorter, the term of the relevant lease.

The gain or loss arising on the disposal or retirement of an item of property, plant and equipment is determined as the difference between the sale proceeds and the carrying amount of the asset and is recognised in the income statement.

Impairment of assets

Goodwill

Goodwill is not subject to amortisation but is tested for impairment annually or whenever there is an indication that the asset may be impaired.

For the purpose of impairment testing, assets are grouped at the lowest levels for which there are separately identifiable cash flows, known as cash-generating units. If the recoverable amount of the cash-generating unit is less than the carrying amount of the unit, the impairment loss is allocated first to reduce the carrying amount of any goodwill allocated to the unit and then to the other assets of the unit pro-rata on the basis of the carrying amount of each asset in the unit. Impairment losses recognised for goodwill are not reversed in a subsequent period.

Recoverable amount is the higher of fair value less costs to sell and value in use. In assessing value in use, the estimated future cash flows are discounted to their present value using a pre-tax discount rate that reflects current market assessments of the time value of money and the risks specific to the asset for which the estimates of future cash flows have not been adjusted.

The Group prepares and approves formal five year management plans for its operations, which are used in the value in use calculations. In certain developing markets the fifth year of the management plan is not indicative of the long-term future performance as operations may not have reached maturity. For these operations, the Group extends the plan data for an additional five year period.

Property, plant and equipment and finite lived intangible assets

At each end of reporting period date, the Group reviews the carrying amounts of its property, plant and equipment and finite lived intangible assets to determine whether there is any indication that those assets have suffered an impairment loss. If any such indication exists, the recoverable amount of the asset is estimated in order to determine the extent, if any, of the impairment loss. Where it is not possible to estimate the recoverable amount of an individual asset, the Group estimates the recoverable amount of the cash-generating unit to which the asset belongs.

If the recoverable amount of an asset or cash-generating unit is estimated to be less than its carrying amount, the carrying amount of the asset or cash-generating unit is reduced to its recoverable amount. An impairment loss is recognised immediately in the income statement.

Where an impairment loss subsequently reverses the carrying amount of the asset or cash-generating unit is increased to the revised estimate of its recoverable amount, not to exceed the carrying amount that would have been determined had no impairment loss been recognised for the asset or cash-generating unit in prior years. A reversal of an impairment loss is recognised immediately in the income statement.

Revenue

Revenue is recognised to the extent the Group has delivered goods or rendered services under an agreement, the amount of revenue can be measured reliably and it is probable that the economic benefits associated with the transaction will flow to the Group. Revenue is measured at the fair value of the consideration received, exclusive of sales taxes and discounts.

The Group principally obtains revenue from providing the following telecommunication services: access charges, airtime usage, messaging, interconnect fees, data services and information provision, connection fees and equipment sales. Products and services may be sold separately or in bundled packages.

Revenue for access charges, airtime usage and messaging by contract customers is recognised as revenue as services are performed, with unbilled revenue resulting from services already provided accrued at the end of each period and unearned revenue from services to be provided in future periods deferred. Revenue from the sale of prepaid credit is deferred until such time as the customer uses the airtime, or the credit expires.

Revenue from interconnect fees is recognised at the time the services are performed.

Revenue from data services and information provision is recognised when the Group has performed the related service and, depending on the nature of the service, is recognised either at the gross amount billed to the customer or the amount receivable by the Group as commission for facilitating the service.

Customer connection revenue is recognised together with the related equipment revenue to the extent that the aggregate equipment and connection revenue does not exceed the fair value of the equipment delivered to the customer. Any customer connection revenue not recognised together with related equipment revenue is deferred and recognised over the period in which services are expected to be provided to the customer.

Revenue for device sales is recognised when the device is delivered to the end customer and the sale is considered complete. For device sales made to intermediaries, revenue is recognised if the significant risks associated with the device are transferred to the intermediary and the intermediary has no general right of return. If the significant risks are not transferred, revenue recognition is deferred until sale of the device to an end customer by the intermediary or the expiry of the right of return.

In revenue arrangements including more than one deliverable, the arrangements are divided into separate units of accounting. Deliverables are considered separate units of accounting if the following two conditions are met: (1) the deliverable has value to the

Continued

EXHIBIT 6.14 (*Continued*)

customer on a stand-alone basis and (2) there is evidence of the fair value of the item. The arrangement consideration is allocated to each separate unit of accounting based on its relative fair value.

Commissions   Intermediaries are given cash incentives by the Group to connect new customers and upgrade existing customers.

For intermediaries who do not purchase products and services from the Group, such cash incentives are accounted for as an expense. Such cash incentives to other intermediaries are also accounted for as an expense if:

- the Group receives an identifiable benefit in exchange for the cash incentive that is separable from sales transactions to that intermediary; and
- the Group can reliably estimate the fair value of that benefit.

Cash incentives that do not meet these criteria are recognised as a reduction of the related device revenue.

Inventory

Inventory is stated at the lower of cost and net realisable value. Cost is determined on the basis of weighted average costs and comprises direct materials and, where applicable, direct labour costs and those overheads that have been incurred in bringing the inventories to their present location and condition.

Leasing

Leases are classified as finance leases whenever the terms of the lease transfer substantially all the risks and rewards of ownership of the asset to the lessee. All other leases are classified as operating leases.

Assets held under finance leases are recognised as assets of the Group at their fair value at the inception of the lease or, if lower, at the present value of the minimum lease payments as determined at the inception of the lease. The corresponding liability to the lessor is included in the statement of financial position as a finance lease obligation. Lease payments are apportioned between finance charges and reduction of the lease obligation so as to achieve a constant rate of interest on the remaining balance of the liability. Finance charges are recognised in the income statement.

Rentals payable under operating leases are charged to the income statement on a straight line basis over the term of the relevant lease. Benefits received and receivable as an incentive to enter into an operating lease are also spread on a straight line basis over the lease term.

Foreign currencies

The consolidated financial statements are presented in sterling, which is the parent Company's functional and presentation currency. Each entity in the Group determines its own functional currency and items included in the financial statements of each entity are measured using that functional currency.

Transactions in foreign currencies are initially recorded at the functional currency rate prevailing at the date of the transaction. Monetary assets and liabilities denominated in foreign currencies are retranslated into the respective functional currency of the entity at the rates prevailing on the end of reporting period date. Non-monetary items carried at fair value that are denominated in foreign currencies are retranslated at the rates prevailing on the initial transaction dates. Non-monetary items measured in terms of historical cost in a foreign currency are not retranslated.

Changes in the fair value of monetary securities denominated in foreign currency classified as available-for-sale are analysed between translation differences and other changes in the carrying amount of the security. Translation differences are recognised in the income statement and other changes in carrying amount are recognised in equity.

Translation differences on non-monetary financial assets, such as investments in equity securities, classified as available-for-sale are reported as part of the fair value gain or loss and are included in equity.

For the purpose of presenting consolidated financial statements, the assets and liabilities of entities with a functional currency other than sterling are expressed in sterling using exchange rates prevailing on the end of reporting period date. Income and expense items and cash flows are translated at the average exchange rates for the period and exchange differences arising are recognised directly in equity. On disposal of a foreign entity, the cumulative amount previously recognised in equity relating to that particular foreign operation is recognised in profit or loss.

Goodwill and fair value adjustments arising on the acquisition of a foreign operation are treated as assets and liabilities of the foreign operation and translated accordingly.

In respect of all foreign operations, any exchange differences that have arisen before 1 April 2004, the date of transition to IFRS, are deemed to be nil and will be excluded from the determination of any subsequent profit or loss on disposal.

The net foreign exchange gain recognised in the consolidated income statement is £35 million (2009: £131 million loss, 2008: £373 million gain).

Research expenditure

Expenditure on research activities is recognised as an expense in the period in which it is incurred.

Post employment benefits

For defined benefit retirement plans, the difference between the fair value of the plan assets and the present value of the plan liabilities is recognised as an asset or liability on the statement of financial position. Scheme liabilities are assessed using the projected unit funding method and applying the principal actuarial assumptions at the end of reporting period date. Assets are valued at market value.

Actuarial gains and losses are taken to the statement of comprehensive income as incurred. For this purpose, actuarial gains and losses comprise both the effects of changes in actuarial assumptions and experience adjustments arising because of differences between the previous actuarial assumptions and what has actually occurred.

Other movements in the net surplus or deficit are recognised in the income statement, including the current service cost, any past service cost and the effect of any curtailment or settlements. The interest cost less the expected return on assets is also charged to the income statement. The amount charged to the income statement in respect of these plans is included within operating costs or in the Group's share of the results of equity accounted operations as appropriate.

The Group's contributions to defined contribution pension plans are charged to the income statement as they fall due.

Cumulative actuarial gains and losses at 1 April 2004, the date of transition to IFRS, have been recognised in the statement of financial position.

Taxation

Income tax expense represents the sum of the current tax payable and deferred tax.

Current tax payable or recoverable is based on taxable profit for the year. Taxable profit differs from profit as reported in the income statement because some items of income or expense are taxable or deductible in different years or may never be taxable or deductible. The Group's liability for current tax is calculated using UK and foreign tax rates and laws that have been enacted or substantively enacted by the end of reporting period date.

Deferred tax is the tax expected to be payable or recoverable in the future arising from temporary differences between the carrying amounts of assets and liabilities in the financial statements and the corresponding tax bases used in the computation of taxable profit. It is accounted for using the statement of financial position liability method. Deferred tax liabilities are generally recognised for all taxable temporary differences and deferred tax assets are recognised to the extent that it is probable that taxable profits will be available against which deductible temporary differences can be utilised. Such assets and liabilities are not recognised if the temporary difference arises from the initial recognition (other than in a business combination) of assets and liabilities in a transaction that affects neither the taxable profit nor the accounting profit. Deferred tax liabilities are not recognised to the extent they arise from the initial recognition of goodwill.

Deferred tax liabilities are recognised for taxable temporary differences arising on investments in subsidiaries and associates, and interests in joint ventures, except where the Group is able to control the reversal of the temporary difference and it is probable that the temporary difference will not reverse in the foreseeable future.

The carrying amount of deferred tax assets is reviewed at each end of reporting period date and adjusted to reflect changes in probability that sufficient taxable profits will be available to allow all or part of the asset to be recovered.

Deferred tax is calculated at the tax rates that are expected to apply in the period when the liability is settled or the asset realised, based on tax rates that have been enacted or substantively enacted by the end of reporting period date.

Tax assets and liabilities are offset when there is a legally enforceable right to set off current tax assets against current tax liabilities and when they either relate to income taxes levied by the same taxation authority on either the same taxable entity or on different taxable entities which intend to settle the current tax assets and liabilities on a net basis.

Tax is charged or credited to the income statement, except when it relates to items charged or credited directly to equity, in which case the tax is also recognised directly in equity.

Financial instruments

Financial assets and financial liabilities, in respect of financial instruments, are recognised on the Group's statement of financial position when the Group becomes a party to the contractual provisions of the instrument.

Trade receivables

Trade receivables do not carry any interest and are stated at their nominal value as reduced by appropriate allowances for estimated irrecoverable amounts. Estimated irrecoverable amounts are based on the ageing of the receivable balances and historical experience. Individual trade receivables are written off when management deems them not to be collectible.

Other investments

Other investments are recognised and derecognised on a trade date where a purchase or sale of an investment is under a contract whose terms require delivery of the investment within the timeframe established by the market concerned, and are initially measured at cost, including transaction costs.

Continued

EXHIBIT 6.14 (*Continued*)

Other investments classified as held for trading and available-for-sale are stated at fair value. Where securities are held for trading purposes, gains and losses arising from changes in fair value are included in net profit or loss for the period. For available for- sale investments, gains and losses arising from changes in fair value are recognised directly in equity, until the security is disposed of or is determined to be impaired, at which time the cumulative gain or loss previously recognised in equity, determined using the weighted average cost method, is included in the net profit or loss for the period.

Other investments classified as loans and receivables are stated at amortised cost using the effective interest method, less any impairment.

Cash and cash equivalents

Cash and cash equivalents comprise cash on hand and call deposits, and other short-term highly liquid investments that are readily convertible to a known amount of cash and are subject to an insignificant risk of changes in value.

Trade payables

Trade payables are not interest bearing and are stated at their nominal value.

Financial liabilities and equity instruments

Financial liabilities and equity instruments issued by the Group are classified according to the substance of the contractual arrangements entered into and the definitions of a financial liability and an equity instrument. An equity instrument is any contract that evidences a residual interest in the assets of the Group after deducting all of its liabilities and includes no obligation to deliver cash or other financial assets. The accounting policies adopted for specific financial liabilities and equity instruments are set out below.

Capital market and bank borrowings

Interest bearing loans and overdrafts are initially measured at fair value (which is equal to cost at inception), and are subsequently measured at amortised cost, using the effective interest rate method, except where they are identified as a hedged item in a fair value hedge. Any difference between the proceeds net of transaction costs and the settlement or redemption of borrowings is recognised over the term of the borrowing.

Equity instruments

Equity instruments issued by the Group are recorded at the proceeds received, net of direct issuance costs.

Derivative financial instruments and hedge accounting

The Group's activities expose it to the financial risks of changes in foreign exchange rates and interest rates.

The use of financial derivatives is governed by the Group's policies approved by the Board of directors, which provide written principles on the use of financial derivatives consistent with the Group's risk management strategy. Changes in values of all derivatives of a financing nature are included within investment income and financing costs in the income statement. The Group does not use derivative financial instruments for speculative purposes.

Derivative financial instruments are initially measured at fair value on the contract date and are subsequently remeasured to fair value at each reporting date. The Group designates certain derivatives as either:

- hedges of the change of fair value of recognised assets and liabilities ('fair value hedges'); or
- hedges of net investments in foreign operations.

Hedge accounting is discontinued when the hedging instrument expires or is sold, terminated, or exercised, or no longer qualifies for hedge accounting, or the Company chooses to end the hedging relationship.

Fair value hedges

The Group's policy is to use derivative instruments (primarily interest rate swaps) to convert a proportion of its fixed rate debt to floating rates in order to hedge the interest rate risk arising, principally, from capital market borrowings. The Group designates these as fair value hedges of interest rate risk with changes in fair value of the hedging instrument recognised in the income statement for the period together with the changes in the fair value of the hedged item due to the hedged risk, to the extent the hedge is effective. The ineffective portion is recognised immediately in the income statement.

Net investment hedges

Exchange differences arising from the translation of the net investment in foreign operations are recognised directly in equity. Gains and losses on those hedging instruments (which include bonds, commercial paper and foreign exchange contracts) designated as hedges of the net investments in foreign operations are recognised in equity to the extent that the hedging relationship is effective. These amounts are included in exchange differences on translation of foreign operations as stated in the statement of comprehensive income. Gains and losses relating to hedge ineffectiveness are recognised immediately in the income statement for the period. Gains and losses accumulated in the translation reserve are included in the income statement when the foreign operation is disposed of.

Put option arrangements

The potential cash payments related to put options issued by the Group over the equity of subsidiary companies are accounted for as financial liabilities when such options may only be settled other than by exchange of a fixed amount of cash or another financial asset for a fixed number of shares in the subsidiary. The amount that may become payable under the option on exercise is initially recognised at fair value within borrowings with a corresponding charge directly to equity. The charge to equity is recognised separately as written put options over non-controlling interests, adjacent to non-controlling interests in the net assets of consolidated subsidiaries. The Group recognises the cost of writing such put options, determined as the excess of the fair value of the option over any consideration received, as a financing cost.

Such options are subsequently measured at amortised cost, using the effective interest rate method, in order to accrete the liability up to the amount payable under the option at the date at which it first becomes exercisable. The charge arising is recorded as a financing cost. In the event that the option expires unexercised, the liability is derecognised with a corresponding adjustment to equity.

Provisions

Provisions are recognised when the Group has a present obligation (legal or constructive) as a result of a past event, it is probable that the Group will be required to settle that obligation and a reliable estimate can be made of the amount of the obligation. Provisions are measured at the directors' best estimate of the expenditure required to settle the obligation at the end of reporting period date and are discounted to present value where the effect is material.

Share-based payments

The Group issues equity-settled share-based payments to certain employees. Equity-settled share-based payments are measured at fair value (excluding the effect of non market-based vesting conditions) at the date of grant. The fair value determined at the grant date of the equity-settled share-based payments is expensed on a straight-line basis over the vesting period, based on the Group's estimate of the shares that will eventually vest and adjusted for the effect of non market-based vesting conditions.

Fair value is measured using a binomial pricing model, being a lattice-based option valuation model, which is calibrated using a Black-Scholes framework. The expected life used in the model has been adjusted, based on management's best estimate, for the effects of non-transferability, exercise restrictions and behavioural considerations.

The Group uses historical data to estimate option exercise and employee termination within the valuation model; separate groups of employees that have similar historical exercise behaviour are considered separately for valuation purposes. The expected life of options granted is derived from the output of the option valuation model and represents the period of time that options are expected to be outstanding. Expected volatilities are based on implied volatilities as determined by a simple average of no less than three international banks, excluding the highest and lowest numbers. The risk-free rates for periods within the contractual life of the option are based on the UK gilt yield curve in effect at the time of grant.

Some share awards have an attached market condition, based on TSR, which is taken into account when calculating the fair value of the share awards. The valuation for the TSR is based on Vodafone's ranking within the same group of companies, where possible, over the past five years. The volatility of the ranking over a three year period is used to determine the probable weighted percentage number of shares that could be expected to vest and hence affect fair value.

The fair value of awards of non-vested shares is equal to the closing price of the Vodafone's shares on the date of grant, adjusted for the present value of future dividend entitlements where appropriate.

The paper is focused on the activities of UK publicly traded companies, but it has lessons for all companies. The FRC hopes their work will stimulate productive discussions not only in the UK but around the world, and provide a platform for lasting improvement in corporate reporting.

FRC's guiding principles for regulation to reduce complexity in financial reporting:

1. Regulations should focus on significant problems and be targeted to:
   - Provide relevant information that meets important user needs
   - Reflect the reality of the business while minimizing unintended implementation consequences.
2. Regulators should limit constant change by intervening only when an area is high-risk and change will bring obvious benefit. Intervention should be as cost effective as possible—for example, by using management information already produced for internal purposes.

3. Regulators should understand what other national and international regulators are doing in a particular area. Wherever possible, they should be consistent with one another and work together in a joined-up way.

4. Being clear means keeping regulations simple and user friendly. They need to be understood easily by those who will apply them and those who will benefit from them. Regulations should emphasise:

   - A clear articulation of the desired outcome
   - Principles and judgement where appropriate
   - Plain language with well defined terms
   - Consistent terminology
   - An easy-to-follow structure.

FRC's guiding principles for communication to reduce complexity in financial reporting:

1. Highlight important messages, transactions and accounting policies and avoid distracting readers with immaterial clutter.

2. Provide a balanced explanation of the results—the good news and the bad.

3. Use plain language, only well defined technical terms, consistent terminology and an easy-to-follow structure.

4. Get the point across with a report that holds the reader's attention.

Summary

1. China:
   a. In China, accounting and auditing have taken different paths in their development.
   b. There is strong government involvement in the activities of the stock market.
   c. The accounting profession in China has a lower social recognition compared to its counterparts in Anglo-Saxon countries.
   d. The recent economic reforms in China have had a major impact on that country's accounting standards and practices.
   e. China became a member of the IASC in 1997, and has expressed commitment to develop accounting standards based on IFRS.
   f. A number of steps have been taken toward convergence of the Chinese financial reporting standards with IFRS.

2. Japan:
   a. The Japanese economy is dominated by large conglomerates known as *keiretsu*.
   b. A unique feature of Japanese companies is cross-corporate ownership, mutual holding of equity interests among companies.
   c. In Japan, financial reporting has a creditor orientation, and is strongly influenced by tax law.
   d. Traditionally, accounting regulation in Japan is heavily influenced by government, and the accounting profession has only a minor role, compared to its counterpart in the United States.
   e. Recent developments indicate a willingness to bring Japanese accounting practices more in line with international best practice.
   f. Japan has committed to adopting IFRS through the Tokyo agreement with the IASB.

3. Germany:
   a. Traditionally, the primary source of finance for German companies has been bank credit, and as a result, financial reporting has a creditor orientation rather than an equity shareholder orientation.
   b. Company, commercial, and tax laws and regulations are the main sources of accounting requirements (or "principles of orderly bookkeeping").
   c. Financial reporting is strongly influenced by EU directives.
   d. The German stock exchange has much less influence on financial reporting compared to those in the United Kingdom or United States.
   e. Traditionally, the influence of the accounting profession on developing accounting standards has been minor compared to that of its counterpart in the United Kingdom or United States.
   f. The 2010 act to modernize German accounting systems reflects a willingness to change the traditional accounting practices and, at the same time, retain some accounting practices based on local context.

4. Mexico:
   a. In recent years, the economy has been transforming from a centrally controlled economy to a market economy.
   b. The Mexican stock exchange is a privately owned institution.
   c. Mexico has a conceptual framework for financial reporting.
   d. Until recently a unique feature of Mexican accounting was the treatment of the effects of inflation in financial statements.
   e. The changes to Mexican accounting standards in recent years highlight, among other things, the potential conflict between the pressures for international harmonization and the need to consider the local circumstances in a given country.
   f. In November 2008, the Mexican Securities and Exchange Commission (Comision Nacional Bancaria y de Valores, or CNBV) announced that all companies listed on the Mexican Stock Exchange will be required to use IFRS starting in 2012.

5. United Kingdom:
   a. The main purpose of accounting in the United Kingdom is to facilitate the effective functioning of the capital market.
   b. The primary sources of accounting standards are the Companies Act, professional pronouncements, and stock exchange listing requirements.
   c. Unlike in Germany or Japan, taxation rules do not have a major influence on financial reporting in the United Kingdom.
   d. The UK Accounting Standards Board uses a statement of principles as a conceptual framework for developing financial reporting standards.
   e. A principles-based approach is taken in setting standards for accounting and financial reporting.
   f. Traditionally, there has been no government agency similar to the U.S. SEC in the United Kingdom. However, recent changes to the regulatory structure have strengthened enforcement.
   g. Recently, the FRC published a discussion paper on reducing complexity in corporate reporting, which includes eight guiding principles.

Questions

1. How might the liberalization of accounting and auditing services in China result in an improved level of investor protection?

2. How have economic reforms affected the demand for accounting services in China?

3. In what way has the development of accounting and auditing in China differed from other countries?

4. What are the main pressures for accounting regulation in modern China?

5. Identify three features of the Chinese accounting profession that are different from its counterparts in Anglo-American countries.

6. How have cultural factors influenced accounting practices in Japan?

7. What was the accounting Big Bang in Japan?

8. What is the Tokyo agreement?

9. Why is the principle of prudence clearly established in the German law?

10. Why does tax law have a strong influence on German accounting?

11. What are the main external factors that have influenced financial reporting in Germany in recent years?

12. What was the main focus of the GASB's work in 2009?

13. What is the role of the National Banking and Securities Commission in the area of financial reporting by Mexican companies?

14. What is Professional Mutual Recognition Agreement (PMRA) signed by NAFTA participants in September 2002?

15. What is the significance of Bulletin A-8 of the Mexican Institute of Public Accountants?

16. What are the main external factors that have influenced financial reporting in Mexico in recent years?

17. What is an important contribution that Mexican accounting has made to international accounting?

18. What has been the impact of EU membership on accounting regulation in the United Kingdom?

19. What is the role of the UK Financial Reporting Council?

20. What are the main features of the approach taken in the United Kingdom in setting accounting standards?

21. What was the main objective of the discussion paper, entitled "Louder than Words," published by the FRC in 2009?

Exercises and Problems

1. This chapter describes accounting regulation in five countries: China, Germany, Japan, Mexico, and the United Kingdom.

   Required:
   Compare the mechanisms in place to regulate accounting and financial reporting in your own country with those of any of the five countries mentioned above, and explain the possible reasons for any noticeable differences.

2. The number of professional accountants in a country indicates the status of the accounting profession in that country.

   Required:
   Determine the number of accountants per 100,000 of population in the United Kingdom and Japan. Explain why the numbers are so different. The

membership details of professional accounting bodies in different countries are available at www.iasplus.com/links.htm#proforg.

3. Chapter 1 identified and described six major reasons for accounting diversity: legal system, taxation, providers of financing, inflation, political and economic ties, and culture.

   Required:
   a. Which factor or factors appear to have exerted the greatest influence on the development of accounting in each of the five countries covered in this chapter?
   b. Identify the distinguishing features of the accounting system in each of these countries.

4. Refer to the IASB Web site (www.iasb.org.uk).

   Required:
   a. Determine the manner in which IFRS are used in each of the five countries included in this chapter.
   b. Determine which of these countries has a resident who is a member of the IASB.

5. Refer to Exhibits 6.3, 6.5, 6.8, 6.9, and 6.13.

   Required:
   Identify
   a. An issue in respect of which the practices of several countries discussed in this chapter are at variance with IFRS.
   b. The most important financial accounting practice for each of the five countries, which is at variance with IFRS. Also explain the reason(s) for your selection.

6. Visit the New York Stock Exchange Web site (www.nyse.com).

   Required:
   Determine the number of companies listed on the NYSE from each of the five countries covered in this chapter.

7. This chapter describes the mechanisms in place to regulate accounting and financial reporting in five countries.

   Required:
   Compare and contrast these mechanisms in the United Kingdom and China.

8. The process of professionalization of accounting in China has been unique.

   Required:
   Discuss the unique features of professionalization of accounting in China.

9. This chapter describes the major changes that have been introduced recently in Germany and Japan in the area of accounting regulation.

   Required:
   Describe any similarities between those changes in Germany and Japan.

10. The Act of 2010 to modernize German accounting reflects both a willingness to change as well as retain traditional German accounting practices.

    Required:
    Do you agree with the preceding statement? Explain.

11. The financial reporting issues facing Mexico are different in some respects from those of other countries covered in this chapter.

    Required:
    Provide two main reasons to support the above statement.

12. Refer to Exhibits 6.3, 6.8, and 6.10.

    Required:
    Explain the main areas you would focus on in comparing financial statements prepared by companies in China, Japan, and Mexico with those prepared by companies using IFRS.

13. The JICPA has taken a number of positive steps toward convergence between Japanese GAAP and IFRS.

    Required:
    Explain the steps taken by the JICPA in this regard.

14. The NAFTA agreement has had a major impact on accounting and financial reporting by Mexican companies.

    Required:
    Discuss the nature of the impact referred to in the preceding statement.

Case 6-1

China Petroleum and Chemical Corporation

China Petroleum and Chemical Corporation (CPCC) is one of a growing number of Chinese companies that has cross-listed its stock on foreign stock exchanges. To provide information that might be useful for a wide audience of readers outside of China, CPCC provides a reconciliation of income and stockholders' equity from Chinese GAAP to IFRS. Further, to provide information specifically for its North American shareholders, the company also provides a reconciliation of net income and stockholders' equity from IFRS to U.S. GAAP. The following is the section of CPCC's 2003 annual report providing this information.

Differences between Financial Statements Prepared under the Chinese GAAP and IFRSs

The major differences are:

i. **Depreciation of oil and gas properties**

   Under the PRC accounting rules and regulations, oil and gas properties are depreciated on a straight-line basis. Under IFRS, oil and gas properties are depreciated on the unit of production method.

ii. **Disposal of oil and gas properties**

   Under the PRC accounting rules and regulations, gains and losses arising from the retirement or disposal of an individual item of oil and gas properties are recognized as income or expense in the income statement and are measured as the difference between the estimated net disposal proceeds and the carrying amount of the asset.

   Under IFRS, gains and losses on the retirement or disposal of an individual item of proved oil and gas properties are not recognized unless the retirement or disposal encompasses an entire property. The costs of the asset abandoned or retired are charged to accumulated depreciation with the proceeds received on disposals credited to the carrying amounts of oil and gas properties.

iii. Capitalisation of general borrowing costs

Under the PRC accounting rules and regulations, only borrowing costs on funds that are specially borrowed for construction are capitalized as part of the cost of fixed assets. Under IFRS, to the extent that funds are borrowed generally and used for the purpose of obtaining a qualifying asset, the borrowing costs should be capitalized as part of the cost of that asset.

iv. Acquisition of Sinopec National Star, Sinopec Maoming, Xi'an Petrochemical and Tahe Petrochemical

Under the PRC accounting rules and regulations, the acquisition of Sinopec National Star, Sinopec Maoming, Xi'an Petrochemical and Tahe Petrochemical (the "Acquisitions") are accounted for by the acquisition method. Under the acquisition method, the income of an acquiring enterprise includes the operations of the acquired enterprise subsequent to the acquisition. The difference between the cost of acquiring Sinopec National Star and the fair value of the net assets acquired is capitalized as an exploration and production right, which is amortised over 27 years.

Under IFRS, as the Group, Sinopec National Star, Sinopec Maoming, Xi'an Petrochemical and Tahe Petrochemical are under the common control of Sinopec Group Company, the Acquisitions are considered "combination of entities under common control" which are accounted in a manner similar to a pooling-of-interests ("as in pooling of interests accounting"). Accordingly, the assets and liabilities of Sinopec National Star, Sinopec Maoming, Xi'an Petrochemicals and Tahe Petrochemicals acquired have been accounted for at historical cost and the financial statements of the Group for periods prior to the Acquisitions have been restated to include the financial statements and results of operations of Sinopec National Star, Sinopec Maoming, Xi'an Petrochemicals and Tahe Petrochemical on a combined basis. The consideration paid by the Group are treated as an equity transaction.

v. Gains from issuance of shares by a subsidiary

Under the PRC accounting rules and regulations, the increase in the company's share of net assets of a subsidiary after the sale of additional shares by the subsidiary is credited to capital reserve. Under IFRS, such increase is recognised as income.

vi. Gain from debt restructuring

Under the PRC accounting rules and regulations, gain from debt restructuring resulting from the difference between the carrying amount of liabilities extinguished or assumed by other parties and the amount paid is credited to capital reserve. Under IFRS, the gain resulting from such difference is recognised as income.

vii. Revaluation of land use rights

Under the PRC accounting rules and regulations, land use rights are carried at revalued amounts. Under IFRS, land use rights are carried at historical cost less amortisation. Accordingly, the surplus on the revaluation of land use rights, credited to revaluation reserve, was eliminated.

viii. Unrecognised losses of subsidiaries

Under the PRC accounting rules and regulations, the results of subsidiaries are included in the Group's consolidated income statement to the extent that the subsidiaries' accumulated losses do not result in their carrying amount being reduced to zero, without the effect of minority interests. Further, losses are debited to a separate reserve in the shareholders' funds.

Under IFRS, the results of subsidiaries are included in the Group's consolidated income statement from the date that control effectively commences until the date that control effectively ceases.

ix. Pre-operating expenditures

Under the PRC accounting rules and regulations, expenditures incurred during the start-up period are aggregated in long-term deferred expenses and charged to the income statement when operations commence. Under IFRS, expenditures on start-up activities are recognized as an expense when they are incurred.

x. Impairment losses on long-lived assets

Under the PRC accounting rules and regulations and IFRS, impairment charges are recognized when the carrying value of long-lived assets exceeds the higher of their net selling price and the value in use which incorporates discounting the asset's estimated future cash flows. Due to the difference in the depreciation method of oil and gas properties discussed in (i) above, the provision for impairment losses and reversal of impairment loss under the PRC Accounting Rules and Regulations are different from the amounts recorded under IFRS.

xi. Government grants

Under the PRC accounting rules and regulations, government grants should be credited to capital reserve. Under IFRS, government grants relating to the purchase of equipment used for technology improvements are initially recorded as long term liabilities and are offset against the cost of assets to which the grants related when construction commences. Upon transfer to property, plant and equipment, the grants are recognized as an income over the useful life of the property, plant and equipment by way of reduced depreciation charge.

Effects of major differences between the PRC Accounting Rules and Regulations and IFRS on net profit are analysed as follows:

	Note	2003 RMB millions
Net profit under PRC GAAP		19,011
Adjustments:		
Depreciation of oil and gas properties	(i)	1,784
Disposal of oil and gas properties	(ii)	1,260
Capitalisation of general borrowing costs	(iii)	389
Acquisition of Sinopec Maoming, Xi'an Petrochemical and Tahe Petrochemical	(iv)	326
Acquisition of Sinopec National Star	(iv)	117
Gain from issuance of shares by subsidiary	(v)	136
Gain from debt restructuring	(vi)	82
Revaluation of land use rights	(vii)	18
Unrecognised losses of subsidiaries	(viii)	(182)
Pre-operating expenditures	(ix)	(169)
Effects of the above adjustments on taxation		(1,179)
*Net profit under IFRS**		*21,593*

Effects of major differences between the PRC Accounting Rules and Regulations and IFRS on shareholders' funds are analysed as follows:

	Note	2003 RMB millions
Shareholders' funds under the PRC GAAP		162,946
Adjustments:		
Depreciation of oil and gas properties	(i)	10,885
Disposal of oil and gas properties	(ii)	1,260
Capitalisation of general borrowing costs	(iii)	1,125
Acquisition of Sinopec Maoming, Xi'an Petrochemical and Tahe Petrochemical	(iv)	—
Acquisition of Sinopec National Star	(iv)	(2,812)
Revaluation of land use rights	(vii)	(870)
Effect on minority interests on unrecognised losses of subsidiaries	(viii)	61
Pre-operating expenditures	(ix)	(169)
Impairment losses on long-lived assets	(x)	(113)
Government grants	(xi)	(326)
Effect of the above adjustment on taxation		(4,088)
Shareholders' funds under IFRS		*167,899*

*The above figure is extracted from the financial statements prepared in accordance with IFRS which have been audited by KPMG.

Supplemental Information for North American Shareholders

The Group's accounting policies conform with IFRS which differ in certain significant respects from accounting principles generally accepted in the United States of America ("US GAAP"). Information relating to the nature and effect of such differences are set out below. The US GAAP reconciliation presented below is included as supplemental information, is not required as part of the basic financial statements and does not include differences related to classification, display or disclosures.

a. Foreign exchange gains and losses

In accordance with IFRS, foreign exchange differences on funds borrowed for construction are capitalized as property, plant and equipment to the extent that they are regarded as an adjustment to interest costs during the construction period. Under US GAAP, all foreign exchange gains and losses on foreign currency debts are included in current earnings.

b. Capitalisation of property, plant and equipment

In the years prior to those presented herein, certain adjustments arose between IFRS and US GAAP with regard to the capitalization of interest and pre-production results under IFRS that were reversed and expensed under US GAAP. For the years presented herein, there were no adjustments related to the capitalization of interest and pre-production results. Accordingly, the US GAAP adjustments represent the amortisation effect of such originating adjustments described above.

c. Revaluation of property, plant and equipment

As required by the relevant PRC regulations with respect to the Reorganisation, the property, plant and equipment of the Group were revalued at 30 September 1999. In addition, the property, plant and equipment of Sinopec National Star, Sinopec Maoming and Refining Assets were revalued at 31 December 2000, 30 June 2003 and 31 October 2003 respectively in connection with the Acquisitions. Under IFRS, such revaluations result in an increase in shareholders' funds with respect to the increase in carrying amount of certain property, plant and equipment below their cost bases.

Under US GAAP, property, plant and equipment, including land use rights, are stated at their historical cost less accumulated depreciation. However, as a result of the tax deductibility of the net revaluation surplus, a deferred tax asset related to the reversal of the revaluation surplus is created under US GAAP with a corresponding increase in shareholders' funds.

Under IFRS, effective 1 January 2002, land use rights, which were previously carried at revalued amount, are carried at cost under IFRS. The effect of this change resulted in a decrease to revaluation reserve net of minority interests of RMB 840 million as of 1 January 2002. This revaluation reserve was previously included as part of the revaluation reserve of property, plant and equipment. This change under IFRS eliminated the US GAAP difference relating to the revaluation of land use rights. However, as a result of the tax deductibility of the revalued land use rights, the reversal of the revaluation reserve resulted in a deferred tax asset.

In addition, under IFRS, on disposal of a revalued asset, the related revaluation surplus is transferred from the revaluation reserve to retained earnings. Under US GAAP, the gain and loss on disposal of an asset is determined with reference to the asset's historical carrying amount and included in current earnings.

d. Exchange of assets

During 2002, the Company and Sinopec Group Company entered into an asset swap transaction. Under IFRS, the cost of property, plant and equipment acquired in an exchange for a similar item of property, plant and equipment is measured at fair value. Under US GAAP, as the exchange of assets was between entities under common control, the assets received from Sinopec Group Company are measured at historical cost. The difference between the historical cost of the net assets transferred and the net assets received is accounted for as an equity transaction.

e. Impairment of long-lived assets

Under IFRS, impairment charges are recognized when a long-lived asset's carrying amount exceeds the higher of an asset's net selling price and value in use, which incorporates discounting the asset's estimated future cash flows.

Under US GAAP, determination of the recoverability of a long-lived asset is based on an estimate of undiscounted future cash flows resulting from the use of the asset and its eventual disposition. If the sum of the expected future cash flows is less than the carrying amount of the asset, an impairment loss is recognized. Measurement of an impairment loss for a long-lived asset is based on the fair value of the asset.

In addition, under IFRS, a subsequent increase in the recoverable amount of an asset is reversed to the consolidated income statement to the extent that an impairment loss on the same asset was previously recognized as an expense when the circumstances and events that led to the write-down or write-off cease to exist. The reversal is reduced by the amount that would have been recognized as depreciation had the write-off not occurred.

Under US GAAP, an impairment loss establishes a new cost basis for the impaired asset and the new cost basis should not be adjusted subsequently other than for further impairment losses.

The US GAAP adjustment represents the effect of reversing the recovery of previous impairment charge recorded under IFRS.

f. Capitalised interest on investment in associates

Under IFRS, investment accounted for by the equity method is not considered a qualifying asset for which interest is capitalized. Under US GAAP, an investment accounted for by the equity method while the investee has activities in progress necessary to commence its planned principal operations, provided that the investee's activities include the use of funds to acquire qualifying assets for its operations, is a qualifying asset for which interest is capitalized.

g. Goodwill amortisation

Under IFRS, goodwill and negative goodwill are amortised on a systematic basis over their useful lives.

Under US GAAP, with reference to Statement of Financial Accounting Standard No.142, "Goodwill and Other Intangible Assets" ("SFAS No. 142"), goodwill is no longer amortised beginning 1 January 2002, the date that SFAS No. 142 was adopted. Instead, goodwill is reviewed for impairment upon adoption of SFAS No. 142 and annually thereafter. In connection with SFAS No. 142's transitional goodwill impairment evaluation, the Group determined that no goodwill impairment existed as of the date of adoption. In addition, under US GAAP, negative goodwill of RMB 11 million, net of minority interests that existed at the date of adoption of SFAS No. 142 was written off as a cumulative effect of a change in accounting principle.

h. Companies included in consolidation

Under IFRS, the Group consolidates less than majority owned entities in which the Group has the power, directly or indirectly, to govern the financial and operating policies of an entity so as to obtain benefits from its activities, and proportionately consolidates jointly controlled entities in which the Group has joint control with other venturers. However, US GAAP requires that any entity of which the Group owns 20% to 50% of total outstanding voting stock not be consolidated nor proportionately consolidated, but rather be accounted for under the equity method. Accordingly, certain of the Group's subsidiaries of which the Group owns between 40.72% to 50% of the outstanding voting stock, and the Group's jointly controlled entities are not consolidated nor proportionately consolidated under US GAAP and instead accounted for under the equity method. This exclusion does not affect the profit attributable to shareholders or shareholders' funds reconciliation between IFRS and US GAAP.

Presented below is summarized financial information of such subsidiaries and jointly controlled entities.

	Year ended 31 December 2003 RMB millions
Revenue	21,735
Profit before taxation	1,329
Net Profit	1,090

	At 31 December 2003 RMB millions
Current assets	4,986
Total assets	27,607
Current liabilities	5,902
Total liabilities	9,238
Total equity	18,369

i. Related party transactions

Under IFRS, transactions of state-controlled enterprises with other state-controlled enterprises are not required to be disclosed as related party transactions. Furthermore, government departments and agencies are deemed not to be related parties to the extent that such dealings are in the normal course of business. Therefore, related party transactions as disclosed in Note 33 in the financial statements prepared under IFRS only refers to transactions with enterprises over which Sinopec Group Company is able to exercise significant influence.

Under US GAAP, there are no similar exemptions. Although the majority of the Group's activities are with PRC government authorities and affiliates and other PRC state-owned enterprises, the Group believes that it has provided meaningful disclosures of related party transactions in Note 33 to the financial statements prepared under IFRS.

The effect on profit attributable to shareholders of significant differences between IFRS and US GAAP is as follows:

	Reference in Note above	Year ended 12-31-2003	
		US$ millions	RMB millions
Profit attributable to shareholders under IFRS.		2,609	21,593
US GAAP adjustments			
Foreign exchange gains and losses.	(a)	9	76
Capitalisation of property, plant and equipment	(b)	1	12
Reversal of deficit on revaluation of property, plant and equipment	(c)	10	86
Depreciation on revalued property, plant	(c)	483	3,998
Disposal of property, plant and equipment.	(c)	159	1,316
Exchange of assets.	(d)	3	23

	Reference in Note above	Year ended 12-31-2003	
		US$ millions	RMB millions
Reversal of impairment of long-lived assets, Net of depreciation effect.	(e)	6	47
Capitalised interest on investments in associates	(f)	17	141
Goodwill amortisation for the year.	(g)	—	—
Cumulative effect of adopting SFAS No.142	(g)	—	—
Deferred tax effect of US GAAP adjustments		(207)	(1,715)
Profit attributable to shareholders under US GAAP		**3,090**	**25,577**
Basic and diluted earnings per share under US GAAP		**US$0.04**	**RMB0.30**
Basic and diluted earning per ADS under US GAAP*.		**US$3.56**	**RMB29.50**

*Basic and diluted earnings per ADS is calculated on the basis that one ADS is equivalent to 100 shares.

The effect on shareholders' funds of significant differences between IFRS and US GAAP is as follows:

	Reference in note above	At December 2003 US$ millions	At December 2003 RMB millions
Shareholders' funds under IFRS		20,286	167,899
US GAAP adjustments:			
Foreign exchange gains and losses.	(a)	(43)	(352)
Capitalisation of property, plant and equipment	(b)	(1)	(12)
Revaluation of property, plant and equipment	(c)	(1,564)	(12,943)
Deferred tax adjustments on revaluation	(c)	484	4,004
Exchange of assets.	(d)	(67)	(555)
Reversal of impairment of long-lived assets	(e)	(68)	(561)
Capitalised interest on investments in associates	(f)	39	321
Goodwill	(g)	2	17
Deferred tax effect of US GAAP adjustments		48	398
Shareholders' funds under US GAAP		***19,116***	***158,216***

Note: United States dollar equivalents

For the convenience of readers, amounts in Renminbi have been translated into United States dollars at the rate of US$1.00 = RMB 8.2767 being the noon buying rate in New York City on 31 December 2003 for cable transfers in Renminbi as certified for customs purposes by the Federal Reserve Bank of New York. No representation is made that the Renminbi amounts could have been, or could be, converted into United States dollars at that rate.

Source: China Petroleum and Chemical Corporation 2003 annual report, pp. 158–63.

Required

1. Critically comment on the results reported by CPCC under PRC GAAP, IFRS, and U.S. GAAP.
2. Identify the main areas of difference for CPCC between:
   a. PRC GAAP and IFRS.
   b. IFRS and U.S. GAAP.
3. Should UK readers of these financial statements find the information useful?
4. Should U.S. readers of these financial statements find the information useful?
5. Would you recommend that other companies adopt the multiple standards approach taken by CPCC? Explain.

References

Alexander, David, and Simon Archer, eds. *European Accounting Guide,* 5th ed. New York: Aspen, 2004, p. 1.15.

Aono, J. "The Auditing Environment in Japan." In *International Auditing Environment,* ed. I. Shiobara. Tokyo: Zeimukeiri-Kyokai, 2001, pp. 199–211.

Chen, S.; Z. Sun; and Y. Wang. "Evidence from China on Whether Harmonized Accounting Standards Harmonize Accounting Practices." *Accounting Horizons* 16, no. 3 (2002), pp. 183–97.

Chen, Y.; P. Jubb; and A. Tran. "Problems of Accounting Reform in the People's Republic of China." *International Journal of Accounting* 32, no. 2 (1997), pp. 139–53.

China Securities Regulatory Commission. *China Securities and Futures Statistical Yearbook.* Beijing: CSRC, 2000 and 2002.

Consultative Committee on Accountancy Bodies. *The Making of Accounting Standards: Report of the Review Committee (Dearing Committee).* London: ICAEW, 1988.

Doupnik, Timothy S. "Recent Innovations in German Accounting Practice Through the Integration of EC Directives." *Advances in International Accounting,* 1992, p. 80.

Douthett, E. B. Jr., and K. Jung. "Japanese Corporate Groupings (*Keiretsu*) and the Informativeness of Earnings." *Journal of International Financial Management and Accounting* 12, no. 2 (2001), pp. 133–59.

Eberhartinger, E. L. E. "The Impact of Tax Rules on Financial Reporting in Germany, France, and the UK." *International Journal of Accounting* 34, no. 1 (1999), pp. 93–119.

FASF. "Concerning Treatment (Compliance) of Accounting Standards and other Pronouncements Issued by the Accounting Standards Board of Japan," May 2002. For details, go to www.jicpa.or.jp/n_eng/e200201.html.

Glaum, M., and U. Mandler. "Global Accounting Harmonization from a German Perspective: Bridging the GAAP." *Journal of International Financial Management and Accounting* 7, no. 3 (1996), pp. 215–42.

Goldburgh, L. "The Development of Accounting." In *Accounting Concepts Readings,* ed. C. T. Gibson, G. G. Meredith, and R. Peterson. Melbourne: Cassell, 1971.

Graham, L. E. "Setting a Research Agenda for Auditing Issues in the People's Republic of China." *International Journal of Accounting* 31, no. 1 (1996), pp. 19–37.

Graham, L. E., and C. Li. "Cultural and Economic Influences on Current Accounting Standards in the People's Republic of China." *International Journal of Accounting* 32, no. 3 (1997), pp. 247–78.

Haw, I.; D. Qi; and W. Wu. "The Nature of Information in Accruals and Cash Flows in an Emerging Capital Market: The Case of China." *International Journal of Accounting* 36 (2001), pp. 391–406.

Hofstede, G. *Cultures and Organizations: Software of the Mind.* London: McGraw-Hill, 1991.

IASC. *Insight.* London: IASC, March 1999.

Jiang, L., and J. Kim. "Cross-Corporate Ownership, Information Asymmetry and the Usefulness of Accounting Performance Measures in Japan," *International Journal of Accounting* 35, no. 1 (2000), pp. 85–98.

Lee, C. J. "Financial Restructuring of State Owned Enterprises in China: The Case of Shanghai Sunve Pharmaceutical Corporation." *Accounting, Organizations and Society* (2001), pp. 673–89.

Lin, J., and F. Chen. "Applicability of the Conservatism Accounting Convention in China: Empirical Evidence." *International Journal of Accounting* 34, no. 4 (1999), pp. 517–37.

Lin, K. Z., and K. H. Chan. "Auditing Standards in China: A Comparative Analysis with Relevant International Standards and Guidelines." *International Journal of Accounting* 35, no. 4 (2000), pp. 559–77.

Mande, V., and R. Ortman. "Are Recent Segment Disclosures of Japanese Firms Useful? Views of Japanese Financial Analysts." *International Journal of Accounting* 37 (2002), pp. 27–46.

McKinnon, J. L., and G. L. Harrison. "Cultural Influence on Corporate and Governmental Involvement in Accounting Policy Determination in Japan." *Journal of Accounting and Public Policy,* Autumn 1985, pp. 201–23.

Ozu, C., and S. Gray. "The Development of Segment Reporting in Japan: Achieving International Harmonization Through a Process of National Consensus." *Advances in International Accounting* 14 (2001), pp. 1–13.

Ravlic, T. "Japan Looks to Higher Standards." *Australian CPA* 69, no. 10 (1999), pp. 48–49.

Singleton, W. R., and S. Globerman. "The Nature of Financial Disclosure in Japan." *International Journal of Accounting* 37 (2002), pp. 95–111.

Tang, Y. "Bumpy Road Leading to Internationalization: A Review of Accounting Development in China." *Accounting Horizons* 14, no. 1 (2000), pp. 93–102.

World Trade Organization. *Report of the Working Party on the Accession to China, Addendum, Schedule of Specific Commitment on Services,* October 1, 2001, available at www.wto.org/english/thewto_e/completeacc_e.htm.

Wyman, P. "The Enron Aftermath—Where Next?" speech delivered October 10, 2002, at a conference held in Brussels (available at www.icaew.co.uk/index/cfm?AUB=TB2I_37723).

Xiao, J. Z.; Y. Zhang; and Z. Xie. "The Making of Independent Auditing Standards in China." *Accounting Horizons* 14, no. 1 (2000), pp. 69–89.

Xiao, Z., and A. Pan. "Developing Accounting Standards on the Basis of a Conceptual Framework by the Chinese Government." *International Journal of Accounting* 32, no. 3 (1997), pp. 279–99.

Yamori, N., and T. Baba. "Japanese Management Views on Overseas Exchange Listings: Survey Results." *Journal of International Financial Management and Accounting* 12, no. 3 (2001), pp. 286–316.

Zeff, S. A. *Forging Accounting Principles in Five Countries: A History and Analysis of Trends.* Champaign, IL: Stipes, 1972.

Chapter **Seven**

Foreign Currency Transactions and Hedging Foreign Exchange Risk

Learning Objectives

After reading this chapter, you should be able to

- Provide an overview of the foreign exchange market.
- Explain how fluctuations in exchange rates give rise to foreign exchange risk.
- Demonstrate the accounting for foreign currency transactions.
- Describe how foreign currency forward contracts and foreign currency options can be used to hedge foreign exchange risk.
- Describe the concepts of cash flow hedges, fair value hedges, and hedge accounting.
- Demonstrate the accounting for forward contracts and options used as cash flow hedges and fair value hedges to hedge foreign currency assets and liabilities, foreign currency firm commitments, and forecasted foreign currency transactions.

INTRODUCTION

International trade (imports and exports) constitutes a significant portion of the world economy. According to the World Trade Organization, more than $16 trillion worth of merchandise was exported (and imported) in 2008.[1] Recent growth in trade has been phenomenal. From 1990 to 2001, global exports increased by 75 percent while global gross domestic product increased by only 27 percent.

The number of companies involved in trade also has grown substantially. From 1987 to 1999, the number of U.S. companies making export sales rose by 233 percent to a total of 231,420 companies.[2] Raytheon Company is a U.S.-based electronics and defense systems company with more than $5.2 billion of annual export

---

[1] World Trade Organization, *International Trade Statistics 2009*, Table I.8: Leading Exporters and Importers in World Merchandise Trade, 2008 (www.wto.org).

[2] U.S. Department of Commerce, International Trade Administration, "Small and Medium-Sized Enterprises Play an Important Role," *Export America*, September 2001, pp. 26–29.

sales. In 2009, 21 percent of Raytheon's sales were outside of the United States.[3] Even small businesses are significantly involved in exporting. Companies with fewer than 500 workers comprise 97 percent of U.S. exporters.

Collections from export sales or payments for imports are not always made in a company's domestic currency; they may be made in a foreign currency depending on the negotiated terms of the transaction. As the exchange rate for the foreign currency fluctuates, so does the domestic currency value of these export sales and import purchases. Companies often find it necessary to engage in some form of hedging activity to reduce losses arising from fluctuating exchange rates. For example, at the end of 2009, Raytheon reported having "foreign currency forward contracts with commercial banks to fix the foreign currency exchange rates on specific commitments and payments to vendors, and customer receipts."[4] At December 31, 2009, the company had outstanding foreign currency contracts to buy foreign currency totaling $985 million and to sell foreign currency in the amount of $632 million. At year-end 2009, Italian automaker Fiat SpA reported having contracts to hedge foreign exchange risks amounting to 9.2 billion euros (approximately $13 billion at the time).

This chapter covers accounting issues related to foreign currency transactions and foreign currency hedging activities. To provide background for subsequent discussion of the accounting issues, we begin with a description of foreign exchange markets. We then discuss the accounting for import and export transactions, followed by coverage of various types of hedging techniques. The discussion concentrates on forward contracts and options because these are the most popular types of hedging instruments. Understanding how to account for these items is important for any company engaged in international transactions.

FOREIGN EXCHANGE MARKETS

Each country uses its own currency as the unit of value for the purchase and sale of goods and services. The currency used in the United States is the U.S. dollar, the currency used in Japan is the Japanese yen, and so on. If a U.S. citizen travels to Japan and wishes to purchase local goods, Japanese merchants require payment to be made in Japanese yen. To make the purchase, a U.S. citizen has to purchase yen using U.S. dollars. The price at which the foreign currency can be acquired is known as the *foreign exchange rate.* A variety of factors determine the exchange rate between two currencies; unfortunately for those engaged in international business, the exchange rate fluctuates.[5] In some cases, a change in the exchange rate is quite large and unexpected.

Exchange Rate Mechanisms

Exchange rates have not always fluctuated. During the period 1945–1973, countries fixed the par value of their currency in terms of the U.S. dollar and the value of the U.S. dollar was fixed in terms of gold. Countries agreed to maintain the value of their currency within 1 percent of the par value. If the exchange rate for

---

[3] Raytheon Company, 2009 Form 10-K, p. 111.

[4] Ibid., p. 84.

[5] Several theories attempt to explain exchange rate fluctuations but with little success, at least in the short run. A discussion of exchange rate determination can be found in any international finance textbook. An understanding of the causes of exchange rate changes is not necessary for an understanding of the concepts underlying the accounting for changes in exchange rates.

a particular currency began to move outside of this 1 percent range, the country's central bank was required to intervene by buying or selling its currency in the foreign exchange market. Due to the law of supply and demand, the purchase of currency by a central bank would cause the price of the currency to stop falling and the sale of currency would cause the price to stop rising.

The integrity of the system hinged on the ability of the U.S. dollar to maintain its value in terms of gold and the ability of foreign countries to convert their U.S.-dollar holdings into gold at the fixed rate of $35 per ounce. As the United States began to incur balance-of-payment deficits in the 1960s, a glut of U.S. dollars arose worldwide and foreign countries began converting their U.S. dollars into gold. This resulted in a decline in the U.S. government's gold reserve from a high of $24.6 billion in 1949 to a low of $10.2 billion in 1971. In the latter year, the United States suspended the convertibility of the U.S. dollar into gold, signaling the beginning of the end for the fixed exchange rate system. In March 1973, most currencies were allowed to float in value.

Today, several different currency arrangements exist. The following are some of the more important ones and the countries they affect:

1. *Independent float.* The value of the currency is allowed to fluctuate freely according to market forces with little or no intervention from the central bank (Brazil, Canada, Japan, Mexico, Switzerland, United States).
2. *Pegged to another currency.* The value of the currency is fixed (pegged) in terms of a particular foreign currency, and the central bank intervenes as necessary to maintain the fixed value. For example, several countries peg their currency to the U.S. dollar (including the Bahamas and Ecuador).
3. *European Monetary System (euro).* In 1998, the countries comprising the European Monetary System adopted a common currency called the euro and established the European Central Bank.[6] Until 2002, local currencies such as the German mark and French franc continued to exist but were fixed in value in terms of the euro. On January 1, 2002, local currencies disappeared and the euro became the currency in 12 European countries. The value of the euro floats against other currencies such as the U.S. dollar.

Foreign Exchange Rates

Exchange rates between the U.S. dollar and most foreign currencies are published daily in major U.S. newspapers. Current and past exchange rates are readily obtainable from a variety of Web sites, such as OANDA.com and X-rates.com. U.S. dollar exchange rates at various dates for selected foreign currencies are presented in Exhibit 7.1. These are interbank rates, or wholesale prices, that banks charge one another when exchanging currencies. Prices charged when selling foreign currency to retail customers such as companies engaged in international business are higher, and prices offered to buy foreign currency from retail customers are lower. The difference between the buying and selling rates is the spread through which banks and other foreign exchange brokers earn a profit on foreign exchange trades.

The exchange rates in Exhibit 7.1 reflect the U.S. dollar price for one unit of foreign currency. These are known as direct quotes. The direct quote for the U.K. pound on February 16, 2010 was $1.5668; in other words, one British pound could be purchased for $1.5668. Indirect quotes indicate the number of foreign currency

---

[6] Most long-term members of the European Union (EU) are euro-zone countries. The major exception is the United Kingdom, which decided not to participate. Switzerland is another important European country not part of the euro zone because it is not a member of the EU.

units that can be purchased with one U.S. dollar. Indirect quotes are simply the inverse of direct quotes. If one British pound costs $1.5668, then $1.00 can purchase only 0.6382 (1/1.5668) British pounds; the indirect quote would be 0.6382. To avoid confusion, direct quotes are used exclusively in this chapter.

Exhibit 7.1 shows the U.S. dollar price for one unit of foreign currency at four dates: January 15, 2009, one year later on January 15, 2010, one month later on February 15, 2010, and one day later on February 16, 2010. The percentage changes from one date to the next also are presented. All of the currencies presented in Exhibit 7.1 increased in price or appreciated against the U.S. dollar from January 15, 2009 to January 15, 2010. However, the percentage change by which foreign currencies appreciated or strengthened against the dollar varied considerably, from 0.1 percent for the Bahraini dinar to 32.5 percent for the Brazilian real. Other than the Thai baht, all of the currencies in Exhibit 7.1 weakened against the dollar in the month from January 15, 2010 to February 15, 2010, with the euro experiencing the largest percentage decrease. Four of the nine currencies increased in value from February 15, 2010 to February 16, 2010 and five decreased in value. The percentage changes reported in Exhibit 7.1 demonstrate the great variability that exists in exchange rate changes in terms of both magnitude and direction; exchange rates fluctuate constantly.

Fluctuating exchange rates introduces considerable uncertainty with respect to the cash flows associated with foreign currency transactions. Assume that a U.S. importer placed an order for component parts with a Brazilian supplier on January 15, 2010, at a cost of 1,000,000 Brazilian reals (BRL) with delivery and payment to

EXHIBIT 7.1
Foreign Exchange Rates
U.S. Dollar per Foreign Currency (Direct Quotes)

Country (currency)	Jan. 15, 2009 $ per FC	Jan. 15, 2010 $ per FC	Feb. 15, 2010 $ per FC	Feb. 16, 2010 $ per FC
Bahrain (dinar)	2.6625	2.6649	2.6525	2.6652
Brazil (real)	0.4285	0.5677	0.5371	0.5393
China (yuan).	0.1465	0.1467	0.1463	0.1466
Euro	1.3213	1.4513	1.3636	1.3605
Mexico (peso).	0.07208	0.07867	0.07738	0.07733
Switzerland (franc) . . .	0.8953	0.9817	0.93	0.928
Taiwan (dollar)	0.03009	0.03149	0.03106	0.03115
Thailand (baht)	0.02892	0.03044	0.03059	0.03023
United Kingdom (pound).	1.4567	1.6297	1.5704	1.5668

Country (currency)	% Change for the Year*	% Change for the Month**	% Change for the Day†
Bahrain (dinar)	0.09	−0.47	0.48
Brazil (real)	32.49	−5.39	0.41
China (yuan).	0.14	−0.27	0.21
Euro	9.84	−6.04	−0.23
Mexico (peso).	9.14	−1.64	−0.06
Switzerland (franc)	9.65	−5.27	−0.22
Taiwan (dollar)	4.65	−1.37	0.29
Thailand (baht)	5.26	0.49	−1.18
United Kingdom (pound)	11.88	−3.64	−0.23

* From January 15, 2009, to January 15, 2010.
** From January 15, 2010, to February 15, 2010.
† From February 15, 2010, to February 16, 2010.

take place on February 15, 2010. On January 15, 2010, the U.S. dollar equivalent cost for the parts was $567,700 (BRL 1,000,000 × $0.5677). On February 15, 2010, the importer purchases BRL 1 million in the foreign exchange market at a price of $0.5371 per BRL. The actual cash outflow to pay for the imported parts is $537,100, which is $30,600 less than would have been paid on January 15, 2010, when the order was placed. The important thing to understand is that, because of fluctuating exchange rates, on January 15 the U.S. importer does not know how many U.S. dollars it will have to pay on February 15 for the imported parts.

Spot and Forward Rates

Foreign currency trades can be executed on a *spot* or *forward* basis. The *spot rate* is the price at which a foreign currency can be purchased or sold today. In contrast, the *forward rate* is the price today at which foreign currency can be purchased or sold sometime in the future. Because many international business transactions take some time to be completed, the ability to lock in a price today at which foreign currency can be purchased or sold at some future date has definite advantages.

The Wall Street Journal publishes forward rates quoted by New York banks for several major currencies (Canadian dollar, Japanese yen, Swiss franc, and British pound) on a daily basis. This is only a partial listing of possible forward contracts. A firm and its bank can tailor forward contracts in other currencies and for other time periods to meet the needs of the firm. There is no up-front cost to enter into a forward contract.

The forward rate can exceed the spot rate on a given date, in which case the foreign currency is said to be selling at a *premium* in the forward market, or the forward rate can be less than the spot rate, in which case it is selling at a *discount*. Currencies sell at a premium or a discount because of differences in interest rates between two countries. When the interest rate in the foreign country exceeds the interest rate domestically, the foreign currency sells at a discount in the forward market. Conversely, if the foreign interest rate is less than the domestic rate, the foreign currency sells at a premium.[7] Forward rates are said to be unbiased predictors of the future spot rate.

The spot rate for Swiss francs on March 15, 2010, was $0.9413, indicating that 1 franc could have been purchased on that date for $0.9413. On the same day, the one-month forward rate was $0.9415. The Swiss franc was selling at a premium in the one-month forward market. By entering into a forward contract on March 15 it was possible to guarantee that Swiss francs could be purchased one month later at a price of $0.9415 per franc, regardless of what the spot rate turned out to be on that date. Entering into the forward contract to purchase francs would have been beneficial if the spot rate in one month turned out to be greater than $0.9415. However, such a forward contract would have been detrimental if the future spot rate turned out to be less than $0.9415. In either case, the forward contract must be honored and Swiss francs must be purchased at $0.9415.

On the same day that the Swiss franc was selling at a premium in the forward market, the British pound was selling at a discount. On March 15, 2010, when the British pound spot rate was $1.5052, a U.S. importer of British goods could have locked in a rate of only $1.5049 to purchase British pounds in one month. This action would eliminate the risk to the importer that the British pound might

---

[7] This relationship is based on the theory of interest rate parity, which indicates that the difference in national interest rates should be equal to but opposite in sign to the forward rate discount or premium. This topic is covered in detail in international finance textbooks.

actually appreciate against the U.S. dollar over the next month, which would increase the U.S.-dollar cost of the British imports.[8]

Option Contracts

To provide companies more flexibility than exists with a forward contract, a market for *foreign currency options* has developed. A foreign currency option gives the holder of the option *the right but not the obligation* to trade foreign currency in the future. A *put option* is for the sale of foreign currency by the holder of the option; a *call option* is for the purchase of foreign currency by the holder of the option. The *strike price* is the exchange rate at which the option will be executed if the holder of the option decides to exercise the option. The strike price is similar to a forward rate. There are generally several strike prices to choose from at any particular time. Most foreign currency options are purchased directly from a bank in the so-called over-the-counter market but they also may be purchased on the Philadelphia Stock Exchange and the Chicago Mercantile Exchange.

Unlike forward contracts, where banks earn their profit through the spread between buying and selling rates, options must actually be purchased by paying an *option premium*. The option premium is a function of two components: intrinsic value and time value. The *intrinsic value* of an option is equal to the gain that could be realized by exercising the option immediately. For example, if the spot rate for a foreign currency is $1.00, a call option (to purchase foreign currency) with a strike price of $0.97 has an intrinsic value of $0.03, whereas a put option (to sell foreign currency) with a strike price of $1.00 or less has an intrinsic value of zero. An option with a positive intrinsic value is said to be "in the money."

The *time value* of an option relates to the fact that the spot rate can change over time and cause the option to become in the money. Even though a 90-day call option with a strike price of $1.00 has zero intrinsic value when the spot rate is $1.00, it will still have a positive time value because there is a chance that the spot rate could increase over the next 90 days and bring the option into the money.

The value of a foreign currency option can be determined by applying an adaptation of the Black-Scholes option pricing formula. This formula is discussed in detail in international finance books. In very general terms, the value of an option is a function of the difference between the current spot rate and strike price, the difference between domestic and foreign interest rates, the length of time to expiration, and the potential volatility of changes in the spot rate. In this book, we will give the premium originally paid for a foreign currency option and its subsequent fair value up to the date of expiration derived from applying the pricing formula.

FOREIGN CURRENCY TRANSACTIONS

Export sales and import purchases are international transactions. When two parties from different countries enter into a transaction, they must decide which of the two countries' currencies to use to settle the transaction. For example, if a U.S. computer manufacturer sells to a customer in Japan, the parties must decide whether the transaction will be denominated (i.e., whether payment will be made) in U.S. dollars or Japanese yen. In some cases, a third country's currency might be used to denominate the transaction.

---

[8] As it turned out, the spot rate for British pounds on April 15, 2010, was $1.5498, so entering into a forward contract on March 15 to purchase pounds at $1.5049 on April 15 would have been beneficial.

Assume that a U.S. exporter (Eximco) sells goods to a Spanish customer with payment to be made in euros. In this situation, Eximco has entered into a foreign currency transaction. It must restate the euro amount that actually will be received into U.S. dollars to account for this transaction. This is because Eximco keeps its books and prepares financial statements in U.S. dollars. Although the Spanish importer has entered into an international transaction, it does not have a foreign currency transaction (payment will be made in its home currency) and no restatement is necessary.

Assume that, as is customary in its industry, Eximco does not require immediate payment and allows its Spanish customer three months to pay for its purchases. By doing this, Eximco runs the risk that from the date the sale is made until the date of payment, the euro might decrease in value (depreciate) against the U.S. dollar and the actual number of U.S. dollars generated from the sale will be less than expected. In this situation Eximco is said to have an *exposure to foreign exchange risk*. Specifically, Eximco has a *transaction exposure*.

Transaction exposure can be summarized as follows:

- *Export sale.* A transaction exposure exists when the exporter allows the buyer to pay in a foreign currency and also allows the buyer to pay sometime after the sale has been made. The exporter is exposed to the risk that the foreign currency might decrease in value between the date of sale and the date of payment, thereby decreasing the amount of domestic currency (U.S. dollars for Eximco) into which the foreign currency can be converted.

- *Import purchase.* A transaction exposure exists when the importer is required to pay in foreign currency and is allowed to pay sometime after the purchase has been made. The importer is exposed to the risk that the foreign currency might increase in price (appreciate) between the date of purchase and the date of payment, thereby increasing the amount of domestic currency that has to be paid for the imported goods.

Accounting Issue

The major issue in accounting for foreign currency transactions is how to deal with the change in the domestic currency value of the sales revenue and account receivable resulting from the export when the foreign currency changes in value. The corollary issue is how to deal with the change in the domestic currency value of the foreign currency account payable and goods being acquired in an import purchase.

Assume that Eximco sells goods to a Spanish customer at a price of 1 million euros (€) when the spot exchange rate is $1.50 per euro. If payment were received at the date of sale, Eximco could have converted €1,000,000 into $1,500,000 and this amount clearly would be the amount at which the sales revenue would be recognized. Instead, Eximco allows the Spanish customer three months to pay for its purchase. At the end of three months, the euro has depreciated to $1.48 and Eximco is able to convert the €1,000,000 received on that date into only $1,480,000. How should Eximco account for this $20,000 decrease in value?

Accounting Alternatives

Conceptually, the two methods of accounting for changes in the value of a foreign currency transaction are the one-transaction perspective and the two-transaction perspective. The *one-transaction perspective* assumes that an export sale is not complete until the foreign currency receivable has been collected and converted into U.S. dollars. Any change in the U.S.-dollar value of the foreign currency will be accounted for as an adjustment to Accounts Receivable and to Sales. Under this perspective, Eximco would ultimately report Sales at $1,480,000 and an increase in the Cash account of the same amount. This approach can be criticized because it hides the fact that the company could have received $1,500,000 if the Spanish customer had been required to pay at the date of sale. The company incurs a $20,000 loss because of the depreciation in the euro, but that loss is buried in an adjustment to Sales. This approach is not acceptable under either International Financial Reporting Standards (IFRS) or U.S. GAAP.

Instead, both International Accounting Standard (IAS) 21, *The Effects of Changes in Foreign Exchange Rates,* and FASB ASC 830, *Foreign Currency Matters,* require companies to use a *two-transaction perspective* in accounting for foreign currency transactions. This perspective treats the export sale and the subsequent collection of cash as two separate transactions. Because management has made two decisions—(1) to make the export sale, and (2) to extend credit in foreign currency to the customer—the income effect from each of these decisions should be reported separately.

Under the two-transaction perspective, Eximco records the U.S. dollar value of the sale at the date the sale occurs. At that point the sale has been completed; there are no subsequent adjustments to the Sales account. Any difference between the number of U.S. dollars that could have been received at the date of sale and the number of U.S. dollars actually received at the date of payment due to fluctuations in the exchange rate is a result of the decision to extend foreign currency credit to the customer. This difference is treated as a Foreign Exchange Gain or Loss that is reported separately from Sales in the income statement. Using the two-transaction perspective to account for its export sale to Spain, Eximco would make the following journal entries:

Date of Sale:	Accounts Receivable (€)...................	1,500,000	
	Sales................................		1,500,000
	To record the sale and euro receivable at the spot rate of $1.50.		
Date of Payment:	Foreign Exchange Loss......................	20,000	
	Accounts Receivable (€)		20,000
	To adjust the U.S.-dollar value of the euro receivable to the new spot rate of $1.48 and record a foreign exchange loss resulting from the depreciation in the euro.		
	Cash	1,480,000	
	Accounts Receivable (€)		1,480,000
	To record the receipt of €1,000,000 and conversion into U.S. dollars at the spot rate of $1.48.		

Sales are reported in income at the amount that would have been received if the customer had not been given three months to pay the €1,000,000, that is, $1,500,000. A separate Foreign Exchange Loss of $20,000 is reported in income to indicate that because of the decision to extend foreign currency credit to the Spanish customer and because the euro decreased in value, fewer U.S. dollars are actually received.[9]

[9] Note that the foreign exchange loss results because the customer is allowed to pay in euros and is given 30 days to pay. If the transaction were denominated in U.S. dollars, no loss would result. There would also be no loss if the euros had been received at the date the sale was made.

Note that Eximco keeps its Account Receivable (€) account separate from its U.S.-dollar receivables. Companies engaged in international trade need to keep separate payable and receivable accounts in each of the currencies in which they have transactions. Each foreign currency receivable and payable should have a separate account number in the company's chart of accounts.

We can summarize the relationship between fluctuations in exchange rates and foreign exchange gains and losses as follows:

		Foreign Currency (FC)	
Transaction	**Type of Exposure**	**Appreciates**	**Depreciates**
Export sale	Asset	Gain	Loss
Import purchase	Liability	Loss	Gain

A foreign currency receivable arising from an export sale creates an *asset exposure* to foreign exchange risk. If the foreign currency appreciates, the foreign currency asset increases in terms of domestic currency value and a foreign exchange gain arises; depreciation of the foreign currency causes a foreign exchange loss. A foreign currency payable arising from an import purchase creates a *liability exposure* to foreign exchange risk. If the foreign currency appreciates, the foreign currency liability increases in domestic currency value and a foreign exchange loss results; depreciation of the currency results in a foreign exchange gain.

Balance Sheet Date before Date of Payment

The question arises as to what accounting should be done if a balance sheet date falls between the date of sale and the date of payment. For example, assume that Eximco shipped goods to its Spanish customer on December 10, Year 1, with payment to be received on March 1, Year 2. Assume that at December 10 the spot rate for euros is $1.50, but by December 31 the euro has appreciated to $1.51. Is any adjustment needed at December 31, Year 1, when the books are closed to account for the fact that the foreign currency receivable has changed in U.S. dollar value since December 10?

The general consensus worldwide is that a foreign currency receivable or foreign currency payable should be revalued at the balance sheet date to account for the change in exchange rates. Under the two-transaction perspective, this means that a foreign exchange gain or loss arises at the balance sheet date. The next question then is what should be done with these foreign exchange gains and losses that have not yet been realized in cash. Should they be included in net income?

The two approaches to accounting for unrealized foreign exchange gains and losses are the deferral approach and the accrual approach. Under the *deferral approach,* unrealized foreign exchange gains and losses are deferred on the balance sheet until cash is actually paid or received. When cash is paid or received, a *realized* foreign exchange gain or loss would be included in income. This approach is not acceptable under either IFRS or U.S. GAAP.

IAS 21 (as well as FASB ASC 830) requires companies to use the *accrual approach* to account for unrealized foreign exchange gains and losses. Under this approach, a firm reports unrealized foreign exchange gains and losses in net income in the period in which the exchange rate changes. The FASB justified this approach by saying: "This is consistent with accrual accounting; it results in reporting the effect of a rate change that will have cash flow effects when the event causing the effect takes place."[10] Thus, any change in the exchange rate from the date of sale to the balance sheet date would result in a foreign exchange gain or loss to be reported in income in that period. Any change in the exchange rate from the balance sheet date to the date of payment would result in a second foreign exchange gain or loss that would be reported in the second accounting period. The journal entries Eximco would make under the accrual approach would be as follows:

12/1/Y1	Accounts Receivable (€)............................	1,500,000	
	Sales.....................................		1,500,000
	To record the sale and euro receivable at the spot rate of $1.50.		
12/31/Y1	Accounts Receivable (€)............................	10,000	
	Foreign Exchange Gain		10,000
	To adjust the value of the euro receivable to the new spot rate of $1.51 and record a foreign exchange gain resulting from the appreciation in the euro since December 10.		
3/1/Y2	Foreign Exchange Loss.............................	30,000	
	Accounts Receivable (€)		30,000
	To adjust the value of the euro receivable to the new spot rate of $1.48 and record a foreign exchange loss resulting from the depreciation in the euro since December 31.		
	Cash	1,480,000	
	Accounts Receivable (€)		1,480,000
	To record the receipt of €1,000,000 and conversion at the spot rate of $1.48.		

The net impact on income in Year 1 includes Sales of $1,500,000 and a Foreign Exchange Gain of $10,000; in Year 2, a Foreign Exchange Loss of $30,000 is recorded. This results in a net increase in Retained Earnings of $1,480,000 that is balanced by an equal increase in Cash.[11]

One criticism of the accrual approach is that it leads to a *violation of conservatism* when an unrealized foreign exchange gain arises at the balance sheet date. In fact, this is one of only two situations in U.S. GAAP (the other relates to trading marketable securities reported at market value) where it is acceptable to recognize an unrealized gain in income. Historically, several European Union (EU) countries (such as Germany and Austria) more strictly adhered to the concept of conservatism. In those countries, if at the balance sheet date the exchange rate had changed such that an unrealized gain arises, the change in exchange rate was ignored and the foreign currency account receivable or payable continued to be carried on the balance sheet at the exchange rate that existed at the date of the transaction. In contrast, if the exchange rate had changed to cause a foreign exchange loss, the

---

[10] FASB Statement No. 52, *Foreign Currency Translation* (Stamford, CT, 1981), para. 124.

[11] Note that the journal entries recorded at March 1, Year 2, could have been combined into the following single entry:

3/1/Y2	Foreign Exchange Loss............................	30,000	
	Cash	1,480,000	
	Accounts Receivable (€)		1,510,000

account receivable would have been revalued and an unrealized loss would have been recorded and reported in income. This is a classic application of conservatism. With the introduction of the requirement to use IFRS, this practice is no longer used by EU-based companies in preparing consolidated financial statements.

All foreign currency assets and liabilities carried on a company's books must be restated at the balance sheet date. In addition to foreign currency payables and receivables arising from import and export transactions, companies also might have dividends receivable from foreign subsidiaries, loans payable to foreign lenders, lease payments receivable from foreign customers, and so on that are denominated in a foreign currency and therefore must be restated at the balance sheet date. Each of these foreign-currency-denominated assets and liabilities is exposed to foreign exchange risk; therefore, fluctuations in the exchange rate will result in foreign exchange gains and losses.

Many U.S. companies report foreign exchange gains and losses on the income statement in a line item often titled "Other Income (Expense)." Other incidental gains and losses such as gains and losses on sales of assets would be included in this line item as well. Companies must disclose the magnitude of foreign exchange gains and losses if material. For example, in the Notes to Financial Statements in its 2009 annual report, Merck & Company Inc. indicated that the income statement item "Other (Income) Expense, Net" included exchange gains of $12.4 million and $54.3 million in 2009 and 2007, respectively, and exchange losses of $147.4 million in 2008.[12]

HEDGING FOREIGN EXCHANGE RISK

In the preceding example, Eximco has an asset exposure in euros when it sells goods to the Spanish customer and it allows the customer three months to pay for its purchase. If the euro depreciates over the next three months, Eximco incurs a foreign exchange loss. For many companies, the uncertainty of not knowing exactly how much domestic currency will be received on this export sale is of great concern. To avoid this uncertainty, companies often use foreign currency derivatives to hedge against the effect of unfavorable changes in the value of foreign currencies.[13] The two most common derivatives used to hedge foreign exchange risk are foreign currency forward contracts and foreign currency options. Through a forward contract, Eximco can lock in the price at which it will sell the euros it receives in three months. An option establishes a price at which Eximco will be able, but is not required, to sell the euros it receives in three months. If Eximco enters into a forward contract or purchases an option on the date the sale is made, the derivative is being used as a *hedge of a recognized foreign-currency-denominated asset* (the euro account receivable).

Companies engaged in foreign currency activities often enter into hedging arrangements as soon as a noncancelable sales order is received or a noncancelable purchase order is placed. A noncancelable order that specifies the foreign currency price and date of delivery is a known as a *foreign currency firm commitment*. Assume that, on April 1, Eximco accepts an order to sell parts to a customer in Thailand at a price of 20 million Thai baht. The parts will be delivered and

---

[12] Merck & Company, Inc., Form 10-K 2009, Note 16 Other (Income) Expense, Net, p. 171.

[13] A derivative is a financial instrument whose value changes in response to the change in a specified interest rate, security price, commodity price, index of prices or rates, or other variable. The value of a foreign currency derivative changes in response to changes in foreign exchange rates.

payment will be received on May 15. On April 1, before the sale has been made, Eximco enters into a forward contract to sell 20 million Thai baht on May 15. In this case, Eximco is using a foreign currency derivative as a *hedge of an unrecognized foreign currency firm commitment*.

Some companies have foreign currency transactions that occur on a regular basis and can be reliably forecast. For example, Eximco regularly purchases components from a supplier in Singapore making payment in Singapore dollars. Even if Eximco has no contract to make future purchases, it has an exposure to foreign currency risk if it plans to continue making purchases from the Singapore supplier. Assume that, on October 1, Eximco forecasts that it will make a purchase from the Singapore supplier in one month. To hedge against a possible increase in the price of the Singapore dollar, Eximco acquires a call option on October 1 to purchase Singapore dollars in one month. The foreign currency option represents a *hedge of a forecasted foreign-currency-denominated transaction*.

ACCOUNTING FOR DERIVATIVES

In the development of a core set of standards for global use, the International Organization of Securities Commissions (IOSCO) required the International Accounting Standards Board (IASB) to include a standard on the recognition and measurement of financial instruments, off-balance-sheet items, and hedging activities. In 1988, the IASB embarked on a joint project with the Canadian Institute of Chartered Accountants to develop a comprehensive standard in this area. Due to the critical response to an early Exposure Draft, the project was subsequently divided into two parts and IAS 32, *Financial Instruments: Disclosure and Presentation*, was issued in 1995. Work continued on the recognition and measurement dimensions of the project with a discussion paper published in 1997. Comments on the discussion paper raised numerous issues that caused the IASB to conclude that developing a final standard in the near term was not possible. Therefore, to provide users of IFRS with some guidance in this area, an interim statement, IAS 39, *Financial Statements: Recognition and Measurement*, was issued in 1999. The IASB continues to work on an integrated standard on financial instruments.[14] IAS 39 provides the following general principles with respect to the accounting for derivatives:

1. All derivatives should be reported on the balance sheet at fair value (off-balance-sheet treatment is not acceptable).
2. "Hedge accounting" is acceptable for those derivatives used for hedging purposes provided the hedging relationship is clearly defined, measurable, and actually effective.

Hedge accounting is described in more detail later in this chapter.

IAS 39 (as well as FASB ASC 830) provides guidance for hedges of the following sources of foreign exchange risk:

1. Recognized foreign-currency-denominated assets and liabilities.
2. Unrecognized foreign currency firm commitments.
3. Forecast foreign-currency-denominated transactions.
4. Net investments in foreign operations.

---

[14] The IASB completed the first phase of its project to replace IAS 39 in November 2009 by issuing IFRS 9, *Financial Instruments*. IFRS 9 does not cover financial instruments used in hedging activities.

Different accounting applies to each of these different types of foreign currency hedge. This chapter demonstrates the accounting for the first three types of hedge. Hedges of net investments in foreign operations are covered in Chapter 8.

Fundamental Requirement of Derivatives Accounting

In accounting for derivative financial instruments, the fundamental requirement is that all derivatives must be carried on the balance sheet at their fair value. Derivatives are reported on the balance sheet as assets when they have a positive fair value and as liabilities when they have a negative fair value. The first issue in accounting for derivatives is the determination of fair value.

The fair value of derivatives can change over time, causing adjustments to be made to the carrying values of the assets and liabilities. The second issue in accounting for derivatives is the treatment of the unrealized gains and losses that arise from these adjustments.

Determining the Fair Value of Derivatives

The *fair value of a foreign currency forward contract* is determined by reference to changes in the forward rate over the life of the contract, discounted to the present value. Three pieces of information are needed to determine the fair value of a forward contract at any time:

1. The forward rate when the forward contract was entered into.
2. The current forward rate for a contract that matures on the same date as the forward contract entered into.
3. A discount rate—typically, the company's incremental borrowing rate.

Assume that Interco enters into a forward contract on November 1 to sell 1 million South African rand on May 1 at a forward rate of $0.15 per rand, or a total of $150,000. There is no cost to Interco to enter into the forward contract, and the forward contract has no value on November 1. On December 31, when Interco closes its books to prepare financial statements, the forward rate to sell South African rand on May 1 has changed to $0.147. On that date a forward contract for the delivery of 1 million South African rand could be negotiated that would result in a cash inflow on May 1 of only $147,000. This represents a favorable change in the value of Interco's forward contract of $3,000 ($150,000 − $147,000). The fair value of the forward contract on December 31 is $3,000, discounted to its present value. Assuming that the company's incremental borrowing rate is 12 percent per annum, the fair value of the forward contract must be discounted at the rate of 1 percent per month for four months (from the current date of December 31 to the settlement date of May 1). The fair value of the forward contract at December 31 is $2,883 ($3,000 × 0.96098).[15]

The manner in which the *fair value of a foreign currency option* is determined depends on whether the option is traded on an exchange or has been acquired in the over-the-counter market. The fair value of an exchange-traded foreign currency option is its current market price quoted on the exchange. For over-the-counter options, fair value can be determined by obtaining a price quote from an option dealer (such as a bank). If dealer price quotes are unavailable, the company can estimate the value of an option using the modified Black-Scholes option pricing model (briefly mentioned earlier in this chapter). Regardless of who does the calculation, principles similar to those in the Black-Scholes pricing model will be used in determining the fair value of the option.

---

[15] The present value factor for four months at 1 percent per month is calculated as $1/1.01^4$, or 0.96098.

Accounting for Changes in the Fair Value of Derivatives

Changes in the fair value of derivatives must be included in comprehensive income. *Comprehensive income* is defined as all changes in equity from non-owner sources and consists of two components: net income and other comprehensive income. *Other comprehensive income* consists of unrealized income items that accounting standards require to be deferred in stockholders' equity such as gains and losses on available-for-sale marketable securities. Other comprehensive income is accumulated and reported as a separate line in the stockholders' equity section of the balance sheet. The account title *Accumulated Other Comprehensive Income* is used in this chapter to describe this stockholders' equity line item.

Gains and losses arising from changes in the fair value of derivatives are recognized initially either (1) on the income statement as a part of net income or (2) on the balance sheet as a component of other comprehensive income. Recognition treatment partly depends on whether the derivative is used for hedging purposes or for speculation.[16] For speculative derivatives, the change in the fair value of the derivative (the unrealized gain or loss) is recognized immediately in net income. The accounting for changes in the fair value of derivatives used for hedging depends on the nature of the foreign exchange risk being hedged, and whether the derivative qualifies for hedge accounting.

HEDGE ACCOUNTING

Companies enter into hedging relationships to minimize the adverse effect that changes in exchange rates have on cash flows and net income. As such, companies would like to account for hedges in such a way that the gain or loss from the hedge is recognized in net income in the same period as the loss or gain on the risk being hedged. This approach is known as *hedge accounting*. Hedge accounting for foreign currency derivatives may be used only if three conditions are satisfied:

1. The derivative is used to hedge either a fair value exposure or cash flow exposure to foreign exchange risk.
2. The derivative is highly effective in offsetting changes in the fair value or cash flows related to the hedged item.
3. The derivative is properly documented as a hedge.

Each of these conditions is discussed in turn.

Nature of the Hedged Risk

A *fair value exposure* exists if changes in exchange rates can affect the fair value of an asset or liability reported on the balance sheet. To qualify for hedge accounting the fair value risk must have the potential to affect net income if it is not hedged. For example, there is a fair value risk associated with a foreign currency account receivable. If the foreign currency depreciates, the receivable must be written down with an offsetting loss recognized in net income. A fair value exposure also exists for foreign currency firm commitments.

---

[16] Companies can acquire derivative financial instruments as investments for speculative purposes. For example, assume the three-month forward rate for Swiss francs is $0.60, and a speculator believes the Swiss franc spot rate in three months will be $0.57. In that case, the speculator would enter into a three month forward contract to sell Swiss francs. At the future date, the speculator purchases francs at the spot rate of $0.57 and sells them at the contracted forward rate of $0.60, reaping a gain of $0.03 per franc. Of course, such an investment might just as easily generate a loss if the spot rate does not move in the expected direction.

A *cash flow exposure* exists if changes in exchange rates can affect the amount of cash flow to be realized from a transaction with changes in cash flow reflected in net income. A cash flow exposure exists for (1) recognized foreign currency assets and liabilities, (2) foreign currency firm commitments, and (3) forecasted foreign currency transactions.

Derivatives for which companies wish to use hedge accounting must be designated as either a *fair value hedge* or a *cash flow hedge*. For hedges of recognized foreign currency assets and liabilities and hedges of foreign currency firm commitments, companies must choose between the two types of designation. Hedges of forecasted foreign currency transactions can qualify only as cash flow hedges. Accounting procedures differ for the two types of hedge. In general, gains and losses on fair value hedges are recognized immediately in net income, whereas gains and losses on cash flow hedges are included in other comprehensive income.[17]

Hedge Effectiveness

For hedge accounting to be used initially, the hedge must be expected to be highly effective in generating gains and losses that offset losses and gains on the item being hedged. The hedge actually must be effective in generating offsetting gains and losses for hedge accounting to continue to be applied.

At inception, a foreign currency derivative can be considered an effective hedge if the critical terms of the hedging instrument match those of the hedged item. Critical terms include the currency type, currency amount, and settlement date. For example, a forward contract to purchase 1 million Japanese yen in 30 days would be an effective hedge of a liability of 1 million Japanese yen that is payable in 30 days. Assessing hedge effectiveness on an ongoing basis can be accomplished using a cumulative dollar offset method.

Hedge Documentation

For hedge accounting to be applied, the hedging relationship must be formally documented at the inception of the hedge, that is, on the date a foreign currency forward contract is entered into or a foreign currency option is acquired. The hedging company must prepare a document that identifies the hedged item, the hedging instrument, the nature of the risk being hedged, how the hedging instrument's effectiveness will be assessed, and the risk management objective and strategy for undertaking the hedge.

HEDGING COMBINATIONS

The specific entries required to account for a foreign currency hedging relationship are determined by a combination of the following factors:

1. The type of item being hedged:
   a. Foreign-currency-denominated asset/liability,
   b. Foreign currency firm commitment, or
   c. Forecasted foreign currency transaction.

---

[17] Many companies choose not to designate derivatives used to hedge recognized foreign currency assets and liabilities as hedges per se. In that case, the derivative is accounted for in exactly the same manner as if it had been designated as a fair value hedge; gains and losses are recognized immediately. As a result, designating a hedge of a recognized foreign currency asset/liability as a fair value hedge is of no importance.

2. The nature of the item being hedged:
   a. Existing (or future) asset, or
   b. Existing (or future) liability.
3. The type of hedging instrument being used:
   a. Forward contract, or
   b. Option.
4. The nature of the hedged risk:
   a. Fair value exposure, or
   b. Cash flow exposure.

To measure the fair value of a firm commitment, a choice must be made between using

1. Changes in the spot rate, or
2. Changes in the forward rate.

We do not have enough space in this chapter to demonstrate the accounting for over 20 different combinations of hedging relationships. However, it is important to see the differences in accounting for (1) foreign-currency-denominated assets/liabilities, (2) firm commitments, and (3) forecasted transactions. We show this by focusing on the accounting that would be done by an exporter who has an existing or future foreign currency asset. We also demonstrate the use of both forward contracts and options for different types of items being hedged, and we selectively demonstrate the accounting for fair value and cash flow hedges. The appendix to this chapter demonstrates the accounting for hedges entered into by an importer who has existing and future foreign currency liabilities.

HEDGES OF FOREIGN-CURRENCY-DENOMINATED ASSETS AND LIABILITIES

Hedges of foreign-currency-denominated assets and liabilities, such as accounts receivable and accounts payable, can qualify as either *cash flow hedges* or *fair value hedges*. To qualify as a cash flow hedge, the hedging instrument must completely offset the variability in the cash flows associated with the foreign currency receivable or payable. If the hedging instrument does not qualify as a cash flow hedge, or if the company elects not to designate the hedging instrument as a cash flow hedge, the hedge is designated as a fair value hedge. The following lists summarize the basic accounting for the two types of hedges.

Cash Flow Hedge
At each balance sheet date:

1. The hedged asset or liability is adjusted to fair value according to changes in the spot exchange rate, and a foreign exchange gain or loss is recognized in net income.
2. The derivative hedging instrument is adjusted to fair value (resulting in an asset or liability reported on the balance sheet), with the counterpart recognized as a change in accumulated other comprehensive income (AOCI).
3. An amount equal to the foreign exchange gain or loss on the hedged asset or liability is then transferred from AOCI to net income; the net effect is to offset any gain or loss on the hedged asset or liability.

4. An additional amount is removed from AOCI and recognized in net income to reflect (*a*) the current period's amortization of the original discount or premium on the forward contract (if a forward contract is the hedging instrument) or (*b*) the change in the *time value* of the option (if an option is the hedging instrument).

Fair Value Hedge

At each balance sheet date:

1. The hedged asset or liability is adjusted to fair value according to changes in the spot exchange rate, and a foreign exchange gain or loss is recognized in net income.

2. The derivative hedging instrument is adjusted to fair value (resulting in an asset or liability reported on the balance sheet), with the counterpart recognized as a gain or loss in net income.

FORWARD CONTRACT USED TO HEDGE A RECOGNIZED FOREIGN-CURRENCY-DENOMINATED ASSET

We now return to the Eximco example in which the company has a foreign currency account receivable to demonstrate the accounting for a hedge of a recognized foreign-currency-denominated asset. In the preceding example, Eximco has an asset exposure in euros when it sells goods to the Spanish customer and allows the customer three months to pay for its purchase. To hedge its exposure to a decline in the U.S. dollar value of the euro, Eximco decides to enter into a forward contract.

Assume that on December 1, Year 1, the three-month forward rate for euros is $1.485 and Eximco signs a contract with First National Bank to deliver €1,000,000 in three months in exchange for $1,485,000. No cash changes hands on December 1. Given that the spot rate on December 1 is $1.50, the euro is selling at a discount in the three-month forward market (the forward rate is less than the spot rate). Because the euro is selling at a discount of $0.015 per euro, Eximco receives $15,000 less than if payment had been received at the date the goods are delivered ($1,485,000 vs. $1,500,000). This $15,000 reduction in cash flow can be seen as an expense; it is the cost of extending foreign currency credit to the foreign customer.[18] Conceptually, this expense is similar to the transaction loss that arises on the export sale. It exists only because the transaction is denominated in a foreign currency. The major difference is that Eximco knows the exact amount of the discount expense at the date of sale, whereas, if the receivable is left unhedged, Eximco does not know the size of the transaction loss until three months pass. In fact, it is possible that the unhedged receivable could result in a transaction gain rather than a transaction loss.

Given that the future spot rate turns out to be only $1.48, selling euros at a forward rate of $1.485 is obviously better than leaving the euro receivable unhedged—Eximco will receive $5,000 more as a result of the hedge. This can be viewed as a gain resulting from the use of the forward contract. Unlike the discount expense, the exact size of this gain is not known until three months pass. (In fact, it is possible that use of the forward contract could result in an additional loss. This would occur if the spot rate on March 1, Year 2 is higher than the forward rate of $1.485.)

---

[18] This should not be confused with the cost associated with normal credit risk; that is, the risk that the customer will not pay for its purchase. That is a separate issue unrelated to the currency in which the transaction is denominated.

EXHIBIT 7.2 Hedge of a Foreign Currency Account Receivable with a Forward Contract

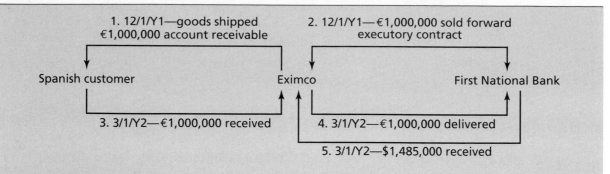

Steps on December 1, Year 1

1. Eximco ships the goods to the Spanish customer, thereby creating a €1,000,000 account receivable.

2. Eximco sells €1,000,000 three months forward to First National Bank, creating an executory contract to pay €1,000,000 and receive $1,485,000.

Steps on March 1, Year 2

3. The Spanish customer sends €1,000,000 to Eximco to settle the account receivable; Eximco now has €1,000,000 in foreign currency.

4. Eximco delivers €1,000,000 to First National Bank.

5. First National Bank pays Eximco $1,485,000.

Eximco must account for its foreign currency transaction and the related forward contract simultaneously but separately. The process can be better understood by referring to the steps involving the three parties—Eximco, the Spanish customer, and First National Bank—shown in Exhibit 7.2.

Because the settlement date, currency type, and currency amount of the forward contract match the corresponding terms of the account receivable, the hedge is expected to be highly effective. If Eximco properly designates the forward contract as a hedge of its euro account receivable position, hedge accounting may be applied. Because it completely offsets the variability in the cash flows related to the accounting receivable, the forward contract may be designated as a cash flow hedge. Alternatively, Eximco may elect to account for this forward contract as a fair value hedge.

In either case, Eximco determines the fair value of the forward contract by referring to the change in the forward rate for a contract maturing on March 1, Year 2. The relevant exchange rates, U.S.-dollar value of the euro receivable, and fair value of the forward contract are determined as follows:

| Date | Spot Rate | Account Receivable (€) | | Forward Rate to 3/1/Y2 | Forward Contract | |
		U.S.-Dollar Value	Change in U.S.-Dollar Value		Fair Value	Change in Fair Value
12/1/Y1	$1.50	$1,500,000	—	$1.485	$0	—
12/31/Y1	$1.51	$1,510,000	+$10,000	$1.496	$(10,783)*	−$10,783
3/1/Y2	$1.48	$1,480,000	−$30,000	$1.480	$5,000[†]	+$15,783

* $1,485,000 − $1,496,000 = $(11,000) × 0.9803 = $(10,783), where 0.9803 is the present value factor for two months at an annual interest rate of 12% (1% per month) calculated as $1/1.01^2$.
[†] $1,485,000 − $1,480,000 = $5,000.

Eximco pays nothing to enter into the forward contract at December 1, Year 1, and the forward contract has a fair value of zero on that date. At December 31, Year 1, the forward rate for a contract to deliver euros on March 1, Year 2 is $1.496. A forward contract could be entered into on December 31, Year 1, to sell €1,000,000 for $1,496,000 on March 1, Year 2. Because Eximco is committed to sell €1,000,000 for $1,485,000, the nominal value of the forward contract is negative $11,000. The fair value of the forward contract is the present value of this amount. Assuming that Eximco has an incremental borrowing rate of 12 percent per year (1 percent per month), and discounting for two months (from 12/31/Y1 to 3/1/Y2), the fair value of the forward contract at December 31, Year 1, is negative $10,783 (a liability). On March 1, Year 2, the forward rate to sell euros on that date is the spot rate—$1.48. At that rate, €1,000,000 could be sold for $1,480,000. Because Eximco has a contract to sell euros for $1,485,000, the fair value of the forward contract on March 1, Year 2, is $5,000. This represents an increase in fair value from December 31, Year 1, of $15,783. The original discount on the forward contract is determined by the difference in the euro spot rate and three-month forward rate on December 1, Year 1: ($1.485 − $1.50) × €1,000,000 = $15,000.

Forward Contract Designated as Cash Flow Hedge

Assume that Eximco designates the forward contract as a *cash flow hedge* of a foreign- currency-denominated asset. In this case, the original forward discount or premium is allocated to net income over the life of the forward contract using an effective interest method. The company would prepare the following journal entries to account for the foreign currency transaction and the related forward contract:

Year 1 Journal Entries—Forward Contract Designated as a Cash Flow Hedge

12/1/Y1	Accounts Receivable (€)	$1,500,000	
	Sales		$1,500,000
	To record the sale and €1,000,000 account receivable at the spot rate of $1.50 (Step 1 in Exhibit 7.2).		

There is no formal entry for the forward contract as it is an executory contract (no cash changes hands) and has a fair value of zero (Step 2 in Exhibit 7.2).

A memorandum would be prepared designating the forward contract as a hedge of the risk of changes in the cash flow to be received on the foreign currency account receivable resulting from changes in the U.S. dollar–euro exchange rate.

12/31/Y1	Accounts Receivable (€)	$10,000	
	Foreign Exchange Gain		$10,000
	To adjust the value of the euro receivable to the new spot rate of $1.51 and record a foreign exchange gain resulting from the appreciation of the euro since December 1.		
	Accumulated Other Comprehensive Income (AOCI)	$10,783	
	Forward Contract[19]		$10,783
	To record the forward contract as a liability at its fair value of $10,783 with a corresponding debit to AOCI.		

[19] "Forward Contract" is a generic account title. In practice, the balance sheet line item in which forward contract assets and liabilities are recognized will differ across companies. Chevron Corporation, for example, indicates that the fair values of forward contracts "are reported on the Consolidated Balance Sheet as "Accounts and notes receivable, net" or "Accrued liabilities," with gains and losses reported in "Other income" (2009 Form 10-K, Note 10: Financial and Derivative Instruments).

Loss on Forward Contract	$10,000	
Accumulated Other Comprehensive Income (AOCI) ...		$10,000
To record a loss on forward contract to offset the foreign exchange gain on account receivable with a corresponding credit to AOCI.		
Discount Expense.	$5,017	
Accumulated Other Comprehensive Income (AOCI).		$5,017
To allocate the forward contract discount to net income over the life of the contract using the effective interest method with a corresponding credit to AOCI.		

The first entry on 12/31/Y1 ensures that the foreign-currency-denominated asset is reported on the balance sheet at its current US$ value of $1,510,000 and that its change in US$ value is reflected as a $10,000 gain in income. The second entry recognizes the forward contract as a liability of $10,783 on the balance sheet. Because the forward contract has been designated as a cash flow hedge, the debit in the second entry is made to AOCI, which decreases stockholders' equity. The third entry achieves the objective of hedge accounting by transferring $10,000 from AOCI to a loss on forward contract. As a result of this entry, the loss on forward contract of $10,000 and the foreign exchange gain on the account receivable of $10,000 exactly offset one another, and the net impact on income is zero—this is the essence of hedge accounting. As a result of the second and third entries, the forward contract is reported on the balance sheet as a liability at its fair value of $(10,783); a loss on forward contract is recognized in the amount of $10,000 to offset the foreign exchange gain; and AOCI has a negative (debit) balance of $783. The second and third entries could be combined into one entry as follows:

Loss on Forward Contract.	10,000	
Accumulated Other Comprehensive Income (AOCI)	783	
Forward Contract.		10,783

The negative balance in AOCI of $783 can be understood as that portion of the loss on the forward contract (decrease in fair value of the forward contract) that is not recognized in net income but instead is deferred in stockholders' equity. Under cash flow hedge accounting, a loss on the hedging instrument (forward contract) is recognized only to the extent that it offsets a gain on the item being hedged (account receivable).

The last entry uses the effective interest method to allocate a portion of the $15,000 forward contract discount as an expense to net income. The company calculates the implicit interest rate associated with the forward contract by considering the fact that the forward contract will generate cash flow of $1,485,000 from a foreign currency asset with an initial value of $1,500,000. Because the discount of $15,000 accrues <u>over a three-month</u> period, the effective interest rate is calculated as $1 - \sqrt[3]{\$1,485,000/\$1,500,000} = 0.003345$. The amount of discount to be allocated to net income for the month of December Year 1 is $1,500,000 \times 0.3345\% = \$5,017$.

The impact on Year 1 net income is as follows:

Sales		$1,500,000
Foreign Exchange Gain	$10,000	
Loss on Forward Contract	(10,000)	
Net gain (loss)		0
Discount Expense.		(5,017)
Impact on net income		$1,494,983

The effect on the December 31, Year 1, balance sheet is as follows:

Assets		Liabilities and Stockholders' Equity	
Accounts receivable (€)	$1,510,000	Forward contract	$ 10,783
		Retained earnings	1,494,983
		AOCI	4,234
			$1,510,000

Year 2 Journal Entries—Forward Contract Designated as Cash Flow Hedge

3/1/Y2	Foreign Exchange Loss	$30,000	
	Accounts Receivable (€)		$30,000
	To adjust the value of the euro receivable to the new spot rate of $1.48 and record a foreign exchange loss resulting from the depreciation of the euro since December 31.		
	Forward Contract	$15,783	
	Accumulated Other Comprehensive Income (AOCI)		$15,783
	To adjust the carrying value of the forward contract to its current fair value of $5,000 with a corresponding credit to AOCI.		
	Accumulated Other Comprehensive Income (AOCI)	$30,000	
	Gain on Forward Contract		$30,000
	To record a gain on forward contract to offset the foreign exchange loss on account receivable with a corresponding debit to AOCI.		
	Discount Expense	$9,983	
	Accumulated Other Comprehensive Income (AOCI) . . .		$9,983
	To allocate the remaining forward contract discount to net income ($15,000 − $5,017 = $9,983) with a corresponding credit to AOCI.		

As a result of these entries, the balance in AOCI is zero: $4,234 − $30,000 + $15,783 + $9,983 = $0.

	Foreign Currency (€)	$1,480,000	
	Accounts Receivable (€)		$1,480,000
	To record receipt of €1,000,000 from the Spanish customer as an asset (Foreign Currency) at the spot rate of $1.48 (Step 3 in Exhibit 7.2).		
	Cash	$1,485,000	
	Foreign Currency (€).		$1,480,000
	Forward Contract		5,000

To record settlement of the forward contract, that is, record receipt of $1,485,000 in exchange for delivery of €1,000,000, and remove the forward contract from the accounts (Steps 4 and 5 in Exhibit 7.2).

The impact on Year 2 net income is:

Foreign Exchange Loss.	$(30,000)	
Gain on Forward Contract	30,000	
Net gain (loss).		0
Discount Expense.		(9,983)
Impact on net income		$(9,983)

The net effect on the balance sheet over the two years is an increase in cash of $1,485,000 with a corresponding increase in retained earnings of $1,485,000 ($1,494,983 − $9,983). The cumulative Discount Expense of $15,000 reflects the cost of extending credit to the Spanish customer.

The net benefit from having entered into the forward contract is $5,000. Eximco has a cash inflow of $1,485,000 rather than only the $1,480,000 that would have been received without a forward contract. This "gain" is reflected in net income as the difference between the net Gain on Forward Contract and the cumulative Discount Expense ($20,000 − $15,000 = $5,000) recognized over the two periods.

Effective Interest versus Straight-Line Methods

Use of the effective interest method results in allocation of the forward contract discount of $5,017 at the end of the first month and $9,983 at the end of the next two months. Straight-line allocation on a monthly basis of the $15,000 discount would result in a reasonable approximation of these amounts:

12/31/Y1	$15,000 \times \dfrac{1}{3} = \$5,000$
3/1/Y2	$15,000 \times \dfrac{2}{3} = \$10,000$

Determining the effective interest rate is complex and no conceptual insights are gained by its use. For the remainder of this chapter, we use straight-line allocation of forward contract discounts and premiums, as is allowed by the FASB. The important thing to keep in mind in this example is that, with a cash flow hedge, an expense equal to the original forward contract discount is recognized in net income over the life of the contract.

What if the forward rate on December 1, Year 1, had been $1.506 (i.e., the euro was selling at a premium in the forward market)? In that case, Eximco would receive $6,000 more through the forward sale of euros ($1,506,000) than if the euros had been received and converted into dollars at the date of sale ($1,500,000). The forward contract premium would be allocated as an increase in net income at the rate of $2,000 per month; $2,000 at 12/31/Y1 and $4,000 at 3/1/Y2.

Forward Contract Designated as Fair Value Hedge

Assume that Eximco decides not to designate the forward contract as a cash flow hedge, but instead elects to treat it as a fair value hedge. In that case, the gain or loss on the forward contract is taken directly to net income and there is no separate amortization of the original discount on the forward contract.

Year 1 Journal Entries—Forward Contract Designated as a Fair Value Hedge

12/1/Y1	Accounts Receivable (€)........................	$1,500,000	
	Sales................................		$1,500,000
	To record the sale and €1,000,000 account receivable at the spot rate of $1.50 (Step 1 in Exhibit 7.2).		

There is no formal entry for the forward contract (Step 2 in Exhibit 7.2). A memorandum would be prepared designating the forward contract as a hedge of the risk of changes in the fair value of the foreign currency account receivable resulting from changes in the U.S. dollar–euro exchange rate.

12/31/Y1	Accounts Receivable (€).............................	$10,000	
	Foreign Exchange Gain		$10,000
	To adjust the value of the euro receivable to the new spot rate of $1.51 and record a foreign exchange gain resulting from the appreciation of the euro since December 1.		
	Loss on Forward Contract	$10,783	
	Forward Contract		$10,783
	To record the forward contract as a liability at its fair value of $10,783 and record a forward contract loss for the change in the fair value of the forward contract since December 1.		

The impact on Year 1 net income is:

Sales		$1,500,000
Foreign Exchange Gain	$10,000	
Loss on Forward Contract	(10,783)	
Net gain (loss)		(783)
Impact on net income		$1,499,217

The effect on the December 31, Year 1, balance sheet is:

Assets		Liabilities and Stockholders' Equity	
Accounts receivable (€)	$1,510,000	Forward contract	$ 10,783
		Retained earnings	1,499,217
			$1,510,000

Year 2 Journal Entries—Forward Contract Designated as a Fair Value Hedge

3/1/Y2	Foreign Exchange Loss	$ 30,000	
	Accounts Receivable (€)		$ 30,000
	To adjust the value of the euro receivable to the new spot rate of $1.48 and record a foreign exchange loss resulting from the depreciation of the euro since December 31.		
	Forward Contract	$ 15,783	
	Gain on Forward Contract		$ 15,783
	To adjust the carrying value of the forward contract to its current fair value of $5,000 and record a forward contract gain for the change in the fair value since December 31.		
	Foreign Currency (€)	$1,480,000	
	Accounts Receivable (€)		$1,480,000
	To record receipt of €1,000,000 from the Spanish customer as an asset at the spot rate of $1.48 (Step 3 in Exhibit 7.2).		
	Cash	$1,485,000	
	Foreign Currency (€).		$1,480,000
	Forward Contract		5,000
	To record settlement of the forward contract, that is, record receipt of $1,485,000 in exchange for delivery of €1,000,000 and remove the forward contract from the accounts (Steps 4 and 5 in Exhibit 7.2).		

The impact on Year 2 net income is as follows:

Foreign Exchange Loss	$(30,000)
Gain on Forward Contract	15,783
Impact on Net Income	$(14,217)

The net effect on the balance sheet for the two years is an increase in cash of $1,485,000 with a corresponding increase in retained earnings of $1,485,000 ($1,499,217 − $14,217).

Under fair value hedge accounting, the original forward contract discount is not amortized systematically over the life of the contract. Instead, it is recognized in income as the difference between the Foreign Exchange Gain (Loss) on the account receivable and the Gain (Loss) on the Forward Contract, that is, $(783) in Year 1 and $(14,217) in Year 2. The net impact on net income over the two years is $(15,000), which reflects the cost of extending credit to the Spanish customer. The net Gain on Forward Contract of $5,000 ($10,783 loss in Year 1 and $15,783 gain in Year 2) reflects the net benefit—that is increase in cash inflow—from Eximco's decision to hedge the euro receivable.

The accounting for a fair value hedge of a foreign currency denominated asset or liability is the same as if the forward contract were not designated as a hedging instrument; changes in the fair value of the forward contract are immediately recognized in net income. Exhibit 7.3 provides an excerpt from the Coca-Cola Company annual report describing the accounting for forward contracts used as

EXHIBIT 7.3

COCA-COLA COMPANY
Annual Report
2009

Notes to the Consolidated Financial Statements

Excerpt from Note 4: Hedging Transactions and Derivative Financial Instruments

Cash Flow Hedging Strategy

The Company uses cash flow hedges to minimize the variability in cash flows of assets or liabilities or forecasted transactions caused by fluctuations in foreign currency exchange rates, commodity prices or interest rates. The changes in the fair values of derivatives designated as cash flow hedges are recorded in AOCI and are reclassified into the line item in the consolidated income statement in which the hedged items are recorded in the same period the hedged items affect earnings. The changes in fair values of hedges that are determined to be ineffective are immediately reclassified from AOCI into earnings. The Company did not discontinue any cash flow hedging relationships during the year ended December 31, 2009. The maximum length of time over which the Company hedges its exposure to future cash flows is typically three years.

The Company maintains a foreign currency cash flow hedging program to reduce the risk that our eventual U.S. dollar net cash inflows from sales outside the United States and U.S. dollar net cash outflows from procurement activities will be adversely affected by changes in foreign currency exchange rates. We enter into forward contracts and purchase foreign currency options (principally euros and Japanese yen) and collars to hedge certain portions of forecasted cash flows denominated in foreign currencies. When the dollar strengthens against the foreign currencies, the decline in the present value of future foreign currency cash flows is partially offset by gains in the fair value of the derivative instruments. Conversely, when the dollar weakens, the increase in the present value of future foreign currency cash flows is partially offset by losses in the fair value of the derivative instruments. The total notional value of derivatives that have been designated and qualify for the Company's foreign currency cash flow hedging program as of December 31, 2009, was approximately $3,679 million.

Economic Hedging Strategy

In addition to derivative instruments that are designated and qualify for hedge accounting, the Company also uses certain derivatives as economic hedges. Although these derivatives were not designated and/or did not qualify for hedge accounting, they are effective economic hedges. The Company primarily uses economic hedges to offset the earnings impact that fluctuations in foreign currency exchange rates have on certain monetary assets and liabilities denominated in nonfunctional currencies. The changes in fair values of these economic hedges are immediately recognized into earnings in the line item other income (loss)—net. The total notional value of derivatives related to our economic hedges of this type as of December 31, 2009, was approximately $651 million. The Company's other economic hedges are not significant to the Company's consolidated financial statements.

---

hedges of foreign-currency-denominated assets and liabilities that demonstrates this point. Coca-Cola uses the term *remeasurement* to refer to the process of adjusting the value of foreign currency "monetary assets and liabilities," that is, receivables and payables.

FOREIGN CURRENCY OPTION USED TO HEDGE A RECOGNIZED FOREIGN-CURRENCY-DENOMINATED ASSET

As an alternative to a forward contract, Eximco could hedge its exposure to foreign exchange risk arising from the euro account receivable by purchasing a foreign currency put option. A put option would give Eximco the right but not the obligation to sell €1,000,000 on March 1, Year 2, at a predetermined strike price. Assume that on December 1, Year 1, Eximco purchases an over-the-counter option from its bank with a strike price of $1.50 when the spot rate is $1.50 and pays a premium of $0.009 per euro.[20] Thus, the purchase price for the option is $9,000 (€1,000,000 × $0.009).

Because the strike price and spot rate are the same, there is no intrinsic value associated with this option. The premium is based solely on time value; that is, it is possible that the euro will depreciate and the spot rate on March 1, Year 2, will be less than $1.50, in which case the option will be in the money. If the spot rate for euros on March 1, Year 2, is less than the strike price of $1.50, Eximco will exercise its option and sell its €1,000,000 at the strike price of $1.50. If the spot rate for euros in three months is greater than the strike price of $1.50, Eximco will not exercise its option and instead will sell euros at the higher spot rate. By purchasing this option, Eximco is guaranteed a minimum cash flow from the export sale of $1,491,000 ($1,500,000 from exercising the option less the $9,000 cost of the option). There is no limit to the maximum number of U.S. dollars that could be received.

As is true for other derivative financial instruments, foreign currency options must be reported on the balance sheet at fair value. The fair value of a foreign currency option at the balance sheet date is determined by reference to the premium quoted by banks on that date for an option with a similar expiration date. Banks (and other sellers of options) determine the current premium by incorporating relevant variables at the balance sheet date into the modified Black-Scholes option pricing model. Changes in value for the euro account receivable and the foreign currency option are summarized as follows:

| Date | Spot Rate | Account Receivable (€) | | Option Premium for 3/1/Y2 | Foreign Currency Option | |
		U.S. Dollar Value	Change in U.S. Dollar Value		Fair Value	Change in Fair Value
12/1/Y1	$1.50	$1,500,000	—	$0.009	$9,000	—
12/31/Y1	$1.51	$1,510,000	+$10,000	$0.006	$6,000	−$3,000
3/1/Y2	$1.48	$1,480,000	−$30,000	$0.020	$20,000	+$14,000

The fair value of the foreign currency option can be decomposed into its intrinsic value and time value components as follows:

Date	Fair Value	Intrinsic Value	Time Value	Change in Time Value
12/1/Y1	$9,000	$0	$9,000	—
12/31/Y1	$6,000	$0	$6,000	−$3,000
3/1/Y2	$20,000	$20,000	$0	−$6,000

Because the option strike price is less than or equal to the spot rate at both December 1 and December 31, the option has no intrinsic value at those dates. The entire fair value is attributable to time value only. On March 1, the date of expiration, there is no time value remaining and the entire amount of fair value is attributable to intrinsic value.

---

[20] The price of the option (the premium) was determined by the seller of the option through the use of a variation of the Black-Scholes option pricing formula.

Option Designated as Cash Flow Hedge

Assume that Eximco designates the foreign currency option as a *cash flow hedge* of a foreign-currency-denominated asset. In this case, the change in the option's time value is recognized immediately in net income. The company prepares the following journal entries to account for the foreign currency transaction and the related foreign currency option:

Year 1 Journal Entries—Option Designated as a Cash Flow Hedge

12/1/Y1	Accounts Receivable (€)............................	$1,500,000	
	Sales.....................................		$1,500,000
	To record the sale and €1,000,000 account receivable at the spot rate of $1.50.		
	Foreign Currency Option	$ 9,000	
	Cash.......................................		$ 9,000
	To record the purchase of the foreign currency option as an asset at its fair value of $9,000.		
12/31/Y1	Accounts Receivable (€)............................	$10,000	
	Foreign Exchange Gain		$10,000
	To adjust the value of the euro receivable to the new spot rate of $1.51 and record a foreign exchange gain resulting from the appreciation of the euro since December 1.		
	Accumulated Other Comprehensive Income (AOCI)	$ 3,000	
	Foreign Currency Option		$ 3,000
	To adjust the fair value of the option from $9,000 to $6,000 with a corresponding debit to AOCI.		
	Loss on Foreign Currency Option	$10,000	
	Accumulated Other Comprehensive Income (AOCI)..		$10,000
	To record a loss on foreign currency option to offset the foreign exchange gain on the euro account receivable with a corresponding credit to AOCI.		
	Option Expense	$ 3,000	
	Accumulated Other Comprehensive Income (AOCI)..		$ 3,000
	To recognize the change in the time value of the option as a decrease in net income with a corresponding credit to AOCI.		

The impact on Year 1 net income is as follows:

Sales		$1,500,000
Foreign Exchange Gain	$10,000	
Loss on Foreign Currency Option	(10,000)	
Net gain (loss)		0
Option Expense		(3,000)
Impact on net income		$1,497,000

The effect on the December 31, Year 1, balance sheet is:

Assets		Liabilities and Stockholders' Equity	
Cash	$ (9,000)	Retained earnings	$1,497,000
Accounts receivable (€)	1,510,000	AOCI	10,000
Foreign currency option	6,000		$1,507,000
	$1,507,000		

At March 1, Year 2, the option has increased in fair value by $14,000—time value decreases by $6,000 and intrinsic value increases by $20,000. The accounting entries made in Year 2 are as follows:

Year 2 Journal Entries—Option Designated as a Cash Flow Hedge

3/1/Y2	Foreign Exchange Loss	$30,000	
	Accounts Receivable (€)		$30,000
	To adjust the value of the euro receivable to the new spot rate of $0.98 and record a foreign exchange loss resulting from the depreciation of the euro since December 31.		
	Foreign Currency Option	$14,000	
	Accumulated Other Comprehensive Income (AOCI)		$14,000
	To adjust the fair value of the option from $6,000 to $20,000 with a corresponding credit to AOCI.		
	Accumulated Other Comprehensive Income (AOCI)	$30,000	
	Gain on Foreign Currency Option		$30,000
	To record a gain on foreign currency option to offset the foreign exchange gain on account receivable with a corresponding debit to AOCI.		
	Option Expense	$6,000	
	Accumulated Other Comprehensive Income (AOCI)		$6,000
	To recognize the change in the time value of the option as a decrease in net income with a corresponding credit to AOCI.		
	Foreign Currency (€)	$1,480,000	
	Accounts Receivable (€)		$1,480,000
	To record receipt of €1,000,000 from the Spanish customer as an asset at the spot rate of $1.48.		
	Cash	$1,500,000	
	Foreign Currency (€)		$1,480,000
	Foreign Currency Option		20,000
	To record exercise of the option, that is, record receipt of $1,500,000 in exchange for delivery of €1,000,000, and remove the foreign currency option from the accounts.		

The impact on Year 2 net income is as follows:

Foreign Exchange Loss	$(30,000)	
Gain on Foreign Currency Option	30,000	
Net gain (loss)		0
Option Expense		(6,000)
Impact on net income		$(6,000)

Over the two accounting periods, Eximco would report Sales of $1,500,000 and a cumulative Option Expense of $9,000. The net effect on the balance sheet is an increase in cash of $1,491,000 ($1,500,000 − $9,000) with a corresponding increase in retained earnings of $1,491,000 ($1,497,000 − $6,000).

The net benefit from having acquired the option is $11,000. Eximco has a net cash inflow of $1,491,000 rather than only $1,480,000 if the option had not been purchased. This "gain" is reflected in net income as the net Gain on Foreign Currency Option less the cumulative Option Expense ($20,000 − $9,000 = $11,000) recognized over the two accounting periods.

Spot Rate Exceeds Strike Price

If the spot rate at March 1, Year 2, had been greater than the strike price of $1.50, Eximco would allow its option to expire unexercised. Instead it would sell its foreign currency (€) at the spot rate. The fair value of the foreign currency option on March 1, Year 2, would be zero. The journal entries for Year 1 to reflect this scenario would be the same as above. The option would be reported as an asset on the December 31, Year 1, balance sheet at $6,000 and the euro receivable would have a carrying value of $1,510,000. The entries on March 1, Year 2, assuming a spot rate on that date of $1.505 (rather than $1.48), would be as follows:

3/1/Y2	Foreign Exchange Loss	$5,000	
	Accounts Receivable (€)		$5,000
	To adjust the value of the euro receivable to the new spot rate of $1.505 and record a foreign exchange loss resulting from the depreciation of the euro since December 31.		
	Loss on Foreign Currency Option	$6,000	
	Foreign Currency Option		$6,000
	To adjust the fair value of the option from $6,000 to $0 and record a loss on foreign currency option for the change in fair value since December 31.		
	Accumulated Other Comprehensive Income (AOCI)	$5,000	
	Gain on Foreign Currency Option		$5,000
	To record a gain on foreign currency option to offset the foreign exchange loss on account receivable with a corresponding debit to AOCI.		
	Foreign Currency (€)	$1,505,000	
	Accounts Receivable (€)		$1,505,000
	To record receipt of €1,000,000 from the Spanish customer as an asset at the spot rate of $1.505.		
	Cash	$1,505,000	
	Foreign Currency (€)		$1,505,000
	To record the sale of €1,000,000 at the spot rate of $1.505.		

The preceding entries result in a credit balance in AOCI of $5,000. The following entry must be made to close AOCI and recognize a corresponding increase in net income.

AOCI	$5,000	
Adjustment to Net Income		$5,000
To close the balance in accumulated other comprehensive income as an adjustment to net income.		

As a result of the last entry, net income related to this hedged transaction is a total of $1,496,000 ($1,500,000 Sales − $9,000 Option Expense + $5,000 Adjustment to Net Income), which is exactly equal to the net increase in cash ($1,505,000 − $9,000). In practice, companies might use a variety of account titles for the adjustment to net income that results from closing AOCI.

Option Designated as Fair Value Hedge

If Eximco had decided to designate the foreign currency option as a fair value hedge, the gain or loss on the option would have been taken directly to net income and there would have been no separate recognition of the change in the time value of the option. The net gain (loss) recognized in Year 1 and Year 2 would be different from the amounts recognized under the cash flow hedge, but over the two-year period, the same amount of net income would be recognized. The accounting method (fair value hedge or cash flow hedge) has no impact on cash flows or on the net amount of income recognized.

HEDGES OF UNRECOGNIZED FOREIGN CURRENCY FIRM COMMITMENTS

In the examples thus far, Eximco does not enter into a hedge of its export sale until the sale is actually made. Assume now that on December 1, Year 1, Eximco receives and accepts an order from a Spanish customer to deliver goods on March 1, Year 2, at a price of €1,000,000. Assume further that under the terms of the sales agreement Eximco will ship the goods to the Spanish customer on March 1, Year 2, and will receive immediate payment on delivery. In other words, Eximco will not allow the Spanish customer time to pay. Although Eximco will not make the sale until March 1, Year 2, it has a firm commitment to make the sale and receive €1,000,000 in three months. This creates a euro asset exposure to foreign exchange risk as of December 1, Year 1. On that date, Eximco wants to hedge against an adverse change in the value of the euro over the next three months. This is known as a hedge of a foreign currency firm commitment. Because the results of fair value hedge accounting are intuitively more appealing, we do not cover cash flow hedge accounting for firm commitments.

Under fair value hedge accounting, (1) the gain or loss on the hedging instrument is recognized currently in net income and (2) the gain or loss (i.e., the change in fair value) on the firm commitment attributable to the hedged risk is also recognized currently in net income. This accounting treatment requires (1) measurement of the fair value of the firm commitment, (2) recognizing the change in fair value in net income, and (3) reporting the firm commitment on the balance sheet as an asset or liability. This raises the conceptual question of how the fair value of the firm commitment should be measured. Two possibilities are (1) through reference to changes in the spot exchange rate or (2) through reference to changes in the forward rate. These two approaches are demonstrated in the examples that follow.

Forward Contract Used as Fair Value Hedge of a Firm Commitment

To hedge its firm commitment exposure to a decline in the U.S.-dollar value of the euro, Eximco decides to enter into a forward contract on December 1, Year 1. Assume that on December 1, Year 1, the three-month forward rate for euros is $1.485 and Eximco signs a contract with New Manhattan Bank to deliver €1,000,000 in three months in exchange for $1,485,000. No cash changes hands on December 1, Year 1. Eximco elects to measure the fair value of the firm commitment through changes in the forward rate. As the fair value of the forward contract is also measured using changes in the forward rate, the gains and losses on the firm commitment and forward contract exactly offset. The fair value of the forward contract and firm commitment are determined as follows:

Date	Forward Rate to 3/1/Y2	Forward Contract		Firm Commitment	
		Fair Value	Change in Fair Value	Fair Value	Change in Fair Value
12/1/Y1	$1.485	$0	—	$0	—
12/31/Y1	$1.496	$(10,783)*	−$10,783	$10,783*	+$10,783
3/1/Y2	$1.48 (spot)	$5,000†	+$15,783	$(5,000)†	−$15,783

* ($1,485,000 − $1,496,000) = $(11,000) × 0.9803 = $(10,783); where 0.9803 is the present value factor for two months at an annual interest rate of 12% (1% per month) calculated as $1/1.01^2$.
† ($1,485,000 − $1,480,000) = $5,000.

Eximco pays nothing to enter into the forward contract at December 1, Year 1. Both the forward contract and the firm commitment have a fair value of zero on that date. At December 31, Year 1, the forward rate for a contract to deliver euros on March 1, Year 2, is $1.496. A forward contract could be entered into on December 31, Year 1, to sell €1,000,000 for $1,496,000 on March 1, Year 2. Because Eximco is committed to sell €1,000,000 for $1,485,000, the value of the forward contract is negative $11,000; present value is negative $10,783 (a liability). The fair value of the firm commitment is also measured through reference to changes in the forward rate. As a result, the fair value of the firm commitment is equal in amount but of opposite sign to the fair value of the forward contract. At December 31, Year 1, the firm commitment is an asset of $10,783.

On March 1, Year 2, the forward rate to sell euros on that date is the spot rate—$1.48. At that rate, €1,000,000 could be sold for $1,480,000. Because Eximco has a contract to sell euros for $1,485,000, the fair value of the forward contract on March 1, Year 2, is $5,000 (an asset). The firm commitment has a value of negative $5,000 (a liability). The journal entries to account for the forward contract fair value hedge of a foreign currency firm commitment are as follows:

Year 1 Journal Entries—Forward Contract Fair Value Hedge of Firm Commitment

12/1/Y1	There is no entry to record either the sales agreement or the forward contract as both are executory contracts. A memorandum would be prepared designating the forward contract as a hedge of the risk of changes in the fair value of the firm commitment resulting from changes in the U.S. dollar–euro forward exchange rate.		
12/31/Y1	Loss on Forward Contract	$10,783	
	Forward Contract		$10,783
	To record the forward contract as a liability at its fair value of $(10,783) and record a forward contract loss for the change in the fair value of the forward contract since December 1.		

| Firm Commitment . . . . | $10,783 | |
| Gain on Firm Commitment . . . . | | $10,783 |

To record the firm commitment as an asset at its fair value of $10,783 and record a firm commitment gain for the change in the fair value of the firm commitment since December 1.

Consistent with the objective of hedge accounting, the gain on the firm commitment offsets the loss on the forward contract and the impact on Year 1 net income is zero. The Forward Contract is reported as a liability and the Firm Commitment is reported as an asset on the 12/31/Y1 balance sheet. This achieves the objective of making sure that derivatives are recognized on the balance sheet and at the same time ensures that there is no impact on net income.

Year 2 Journal Entries—Forward Contract Fair Value Hedge of Firm Commitment

| 3/1/Y2 | Forward Contract . . . . | $15,783 | |
| | Gain on Forward Contract . . . . | | $15,783 |

To adjust the fair value of the forward contract from $(10,783) to $5,000 and record a forward contract gain for the change in fair value since December 31.

| | Loss on Firm Commitment . . . . | $15,783 | |
| | Firm Commitment . . . . | | $15,783 |

To adjust the fair value of the firm commitment from $10,783 to $(5,000) and record a firm commitment loss for the change in fair value since December 31.

| | Foreign Currency (€) . . . . | $1,480,000 | |
| | Sales . . . . | | $1,480,000 |

To record the sale and the receipt of €1,000,000 as an asset at the spot rate of $1.48.

	Cash	$1,485,000	
	Foreign Currency (€)		$1,480,000
	Forward Contract		5,000

To record settlement of the forward contract (receipt of $1,485,000 in exchange for delivery of €1,000,000), and remove the forward contract from the accounts.

| | Firm Commitment . . . . | $5,000 | |
| | Adjustment to Net Income . . . . | | $5,000 |

To close the firm commitment as an adjustment to net income.

Once again, the gain on forward contract and the loss on firm commitment offset. As a result of the last entry, the export sale increases Year 2 net income by $1,485,000 ($1,480,000 in Sales plus a $5,000 Adjustment to Net Income). This is exactly equal to the amount of cash received. In practice, companies might use a variety of account titles for the adjustment to net income that results from closing the firm commitment account.

The net Gain on Forward Contract of $5,000 ($10,783 loss in Year 1 plus $15,783 gain in Year 2) measures the net benefit to the company from hedging its firm commitment. Without the forward contract, Eximco would have sold the €1,000,000 received on March 1, Year 2, at the spot rate of $1.48, generating cash flow of $1,480,000. Through the forward contract, Eximco is able to sell the euros for $1,485,000, a net gain of $5,000.

Option Used as Fair Value Hedge of Firm Commitment

Now assume that to hedge its exposure to a decline in the U.S.-dollar value of the foreign currency firm commitment, Eximco purchases a put option to sell €1,000,000 on March 1, Year 2, at a strike price of $1.50. The premium for such an option on December 1, Year 1, is $0.009 per euro. With this option, Eximco is guaranteed a minimum cash flow from the export sale of $1,491,000 ($1,500,000 from option exercise less $9,000 cost of the option).

Eximco elects to measure the fair value of the firm commitment through reference to changes in the U.S. dollar–euro spot rate. In this case, the fair value of the firm commitment must be discounted to its present value. The fair value and changes in fair value for the firm commitment and foreign currency option are summarized as follows:

| | Option Premium for 3/1/Y2 | Foreign Currency Option | | Spot Rate | Firm Commitment | |
| | | Fair Value | Change in Fair Value | | Fair Value | Change in Fair Value |
Date						
12/1/Y1	$0.009	$9,000	—	$1.50	—	—
12/31/Y1	$0.006	$6,000	−$3,000	$1.51	$9,803*	+$9,803
3/1/Y2	$0.020	$20,000	+$14,000	$1.48	$(20,000)†	−$29,803

* $1,510,000 − $1,500,000 = $10,000 × 0.9803 = $9,803, where 0.9803 is the present value factor for two months at an annual interest rate of 12% (1% per month) calculated as $1/1.01^2$.
† $1,480,000 − $1,500,000 = $(20,000)$.

At December 1, Year 1, given the spot rate of $1.50, the firm commitment to receive €1,000,000 in three months would generate a cash flow of $1,500,000. At December 31, Year 1, the cash flow that could be generated from the firm commitment increases by $10,000 to $1,510,000. The fair value of the firm commitment at December 31, Year 1, is the present value of $10,000 discounted at 1 percent per month for two months. The fair value of the firm commitment on March 1, Year 2, is determined through reference to the change in the spot rate from December 1, Year 1, to March 1, Year 2. Because the spot rate declines by $0.02 over that period, the firm commitment to receive €1,000,000 has a fair value of negative $20,000 on March 1, Year 2. The journal entries to account for the foreign currency option and related foreign currency firm commitment are as follows:

Year 1 Journal Entries—Option Fair Value Hedge of Firm Commitment

12/1/Y1	Foreign Currency Option	$9,000	
	Cash.		$9,000
	To record the purchase of the foreign currency option as an asset.		

There is no entry to record the sales agreement as it is an executory contract. A memorandum would be prepared designating the option as a hedge of the risk of changes in the fair value of the firm commitment resulting from changes in the spot exchange rate.

12/31/Y1	Firm Commitment	$9,803	
	Gain on Firm Commitment		$9,803
	To record the firm commitment as an asset at its fair value of $9,803 and record a firm commitment gain for the change in the fair value of the firm commitment since December 1.		
	Loss on Foreign Currency Option	$3,000	
	Foreign Currency Option		$3,000
	To adjust the fair value of the option from $9,000 to $6,000 and record the change in the value of the option as a loss.		

The impact on Year 1 net income is as follows:

Gain on firm commitment	$9,803
Loss on foreign currency option	(3,000)
Impact on net income	$6,803

The effect on the December 31, Year 1, balance sheet is as follows:

Assets		**Liabilities and Stockholders' Equity**	
Cash	$(9,000)	Retained earnings	$6,803
Foreign currency option	6,000		
Firm commitment	9,803		
	$ 6,803		

Year 2 Journal Entries—Option Fair Value Hedge of Firm Commitment

3/1/Y2	Loss on Firm Commitment	$ 29,803	
	Firm Commitment		$ 29,803
	To adjust the fair value of the firm commitment from $9,803 to $(20,000) and record a firm commitment loss for the change in fair value since December 31.		
	Foreign Currency Option	$ 14,000	
	Gain on Foreign Currency Option		$ 14,000
	To adjust the fair value of the foreign currency option from $6,000 to $20,000 and record a gain on foreign currency option for the change in fair value since December 31.		
	Foreign Currency (€)	$1,480,000	
	Sales		$1,480,000
	To record the sale and the receipt of €1,000,000 as an asset at the spot rate of $1.48.		

Cash	$1,500,000	
Foreign Currency (€)		$1,480,000
Foreign Currency Option		20,000
To record exercise of the foreign currency option (receipt of $1,500,000 in exchange for delivery of €1,000,000), and remove the foreign currency option from the accounts.		
Firm Commitment	$ 20,000	
Adjustment to Net Income		$ 20,000
To close the firm commitment as an adjustment to net income.		

The impact on Year 2 net income is as follows:

Sales	$1,480,000
Loss on Firm Commitment	(29,803)
Gain on Foreign Currency Option	14,000
Adjustment to Net Income	20,000
Impact on net income	$1,484,197

The net increase in net income over the two accounting periods is $1,491,000 ($6,803 in Year 1 plus $1,484,197 in Year 2), which is exactly equal to the net cash flow realized on the export sale ($1,500,000 from exercising the option less $9,000 to purchase the option). The net gain on option of $11,000 (loss of $3,000 in Year 1 plus gain of $14,000 in Year 2) reflects the net benefit from having entered into the hedge. Without the option, Eximco would have sold the €1,000,000 received on March 1, Year 2, at the spot rate of $1.48 for $1,480,000.

HEDGE OF FORECASTED FOREIGN-CURRENCY-DENOMINATED TRANSACTION

Cash flow hedge accounting is used for foreign currency derivatives that hedge the cash flow risk associated with a forecasted foreign currency transaction. For hedge accounting to apply, the forecasted transaction must be probable (likely to occur), the hedge must be highly effective in offsetting fluctuations in the cash flow associated with the foreign currency risk and the hedging relationship must be properly documented.

The accounting for a hedge of a forecasted transaction differs from the accounting for a hedge of a foreign currency firm commitment in two ways:

1. Unlike the accounting for a firm commitment, there is no recognition of the forecasted transaction or gains and losses on the forecasted transaction.
2. The hedging instrument (forward contract or option) is reported at fair value, but because there is no gain or loss on the forecasted transaction to offset against, changes in the fair value of the hedging instrument are not reported as gains and losses in net income. Instead they are reported in other comprehensive income. On the projected date of the forecasted transaction, the cumulative change in the fair value of the hedging instrument is transferred from other comprehensive income (balance sheet) to net income (income statement).

Option Designated as a Cash Flow Hedge of a Forecasted Transaction

To demonstrate the accounting for a hedge of a forecasted foreign currency transaction, assume that Eximco has a long-term relationship with its Spanish customer and can reliably forecast that the customer will require delivery of goods costing €1,000,000 in March of Year 2. Confident that it will receive €1,000,000 on March 1, Year 2, Eximco hedges its forecasted foreign currency transaction by purchasing a €1,000,000 put option on December 1, Year 1. The facts are essentially the same as for the option hedge of a firm commitment, except that Eximco does not receive a sales order from the Spanish customer until late February, Year 2.

The option, which expires on March 1, Year 2, has a strike price of $1.50 and a premium of $0.009 per euro. The fair value of the option at relevant dates is as follows:

Date	Option Premium for 3/1/Y2	Foreign Currency Option				
		Fair Value	Change in Fair Value	Intrinsic Value	Time Value	Change in Time Value
12/1/Y1	$0.009	$9,000	—	$0	$9,000	—
12/31/Y1	$0.006	$6,000	−$3,000	$0	$6,000	−$3,000
3/1/Y2	$0.020	$20,000	−$14,000	$20,000	$0	−$6,000

Year 1 Journal Entries—Option Hedge of a Forecasted Transaction

12/1/Y1	Foreign Currency Option	$9,000	
	Cash		$9,000
	To record the purchase of the foreign currency option as an asset.		

There is no entry to record the forecasted sale. A memorandum would be prepared designating the foreign currency option as a hedge of the risk of changes in the cash flows related to the forecasted sale.

12/31/Y1	Option Expense	$3,000	
	Foreign Currency Option		$3,000
	To adjust the carrying value of the option to its fair value and recognize the change in the time value of the option as an expense.		

The impact on Year 1 net income is as follows:

Option Expense	$(3,000)
Impact on net income	$(3,000)

A Foreign Currency Option of $6,000 is reported as an asset on the December 31, Year 1, balance sheet. Cash decreases by $9,000 and retained earnings decreases by $3,000.

Year 2 Journal Entries—Option Hedge of a Forecasted Transaction

3/1/Y2	Foreign Currency Option	$14,000	
	Option Expense	6,000	
	Accumulated Other Comprehensive Income (AOCI). . .		$20,000
	To adjust the carrying value of the option to its fair value and recognize the change in the time value of the option as an expense, with a corresponding credit to AOCI.		
	Foreign Currency (€)	$1,480,000	
	Sales		$1,480,000
	To record the sale and the receipt of €1,000,000 as an asset at the spot rate of $0.98.		
	Cash	$1,500,000	
	Foreign Currency (€)		$1,480,000
	Foreign Currency Option		20,000
	To record exercise of the foreign currency option (receipt of $1,000,000 in exchange for delivery of €1,000,000), and remove the foreign currency option from the accounts.		
	Accumulated Other Comprehensive Income (AOCI)	$20,000	
	Adjustment to Net Income		$20,000
	To close AOCI as an adjustment to net income.		

The impact on Year 2 net income is as follows:

Sales	$1,480,000
Option Expense	(6,000)
Adjustment to Net Income	20,000
Impact on net income	$1,494,000

Over the two-year period, net income increases by $1,491,000($1,494,000 in Year 2 minus $3,000 in Year 1), equal to the net cash inflow realized from the export sale.

USE OF HEDGING INSTRUMENTS

There probably are as many different corporate strategies regarding hedging foreign exchange risk as there are companies exposed to that risk. Some companies simply require hedges of all foreign currency transactions. Others require the use of a forward contract hedge when the forward rate results in a greater cash inflow or smaller cash outflow than with the spot rate. Still other companies have proportional hedging policies that require hedging on some predetermined percentage (e.g., 50 percent, 60 percent, or 70 percent) of transaction exposure.

It is quite common for companies to use foreign currency derivatives to hedge the exposure to foreign exchange risk arising from forecasted foreign currency transactions. Exhibit 7.4 presents information provided by two U.S.-based companies with respect to hedging forecasted transactions. International Business Machines Corporation (IBM) uses forward contracts to hedge transactions that are

EXHIBIT 7.4
Hedges of
Forecasted
Foreign Currency
Transactions

INTERNATIONAL BUSINESS MACHINES CORPORATION
Annual Report
2006

Excerpt from Note L. Derivatives and Hedging Transactions

Anticipated Royalties and Cost Transactions

The company's operations generate significant nonfunctional currency, third-party vendor payments and intercompany payments for royalties and goods and services among the company's non-U.S. subsidiaries and with the parent company. In anticipation of these foreign currency cash flows and in view of the volatility of the currency markets, the company selectively employs foreign exchange forward contracts to manage its currency risk. These forward contracts are accounted for as cash flow hedges. The maximum length of time over which the company is hedging its exposure to the variability in future cash flows is approximately four years. At December 31, 2009, the total notional amount of forward contracts designated as cash flow hedges of forecasted royalty and cost transactions was $18.7 billion, with a weighted-average remaining maturity of 1.3 years.

THE BOEING COMPANY
Form 10-K
2006

Excerpt from Note 18—Derivative Financial Instruments

Cash Flow Hedges

Our cash flow hedges include certain interest rate swaps, cross currency swaps, foreign currency forward contracts, foreign currency option contracts, and commodity purchase contracts. Interest rate swap contracts under which we agree to pay fixed rates of interest are designated as cash flow hedges of variable-rate debt obligations. *We use foreign currency forward contracts to manage currency risk associated with certain forecasted transactions, specifically forecasted sales and purchases made in foreign currencies. Our foreign currency derivative contracts hedge forecasted transactions principally occurring within five years in the future, with certain contracts hedging transactions up to 2021.*

Derivative Instruments Not Receiving Hedge Accounting Treatment

We also hold certain derivative instruments, primarily foreign currency forward contracts, for risk management purposes but without electing any form of hedge accounting.

Author's note: Emphasis added.

anticipated to take place in no longer than four years. In contrast, Boeing Company uses both forward contracts and options to hedge future transactions principally occurring up to five years in the future, with certain contracts hedging transactions up to the year 2021.

The notes to financial statements of multinational companies also indicate the magnitude of foreign exchange risk and the importance of hedging contracts. Exhibit 7.5 presents information extracted from Abbott Laboratories' 2009 Form 10-K. At December 31, 2009, Abbott had $2.0 billion in foreign currency forward contracts related to anticipated foreign currency transactions and $7.5 billion in forward contracts used to hedge foreign-currency-denominated payables and receivables. To better appreciate the significance of these amounts, consider that Abbott had assets of $52.4 billion, sales of $30.8 billion, and net earnings of $5.7 billion in 2009.

Dell Inc. uses foreign currency options and forward contracts "to hedge our exposure on forecasted transactions and firm commitments in over 20 currencies in which we transact business. Our exposure to foreign currency movements is comprised of certain principal currencies. During fiscal 2009, these principal currencies were the Euro, British Pound, Japanese Yen, Canadian Dollar, and

EXHIBIT 7.5

ABBOT LABORATORIES
Form 10-K
2009

Notes to Consolidated Financial Statements
Note 4—Financial Instruments, Derivatives and Fair Value Measures

Certain Abbott foreign subsidiaries enter into foreign currency forward exchange contracts to manage exposures to changes in foreign exchange rates for anticipated intercompany purchases by those subsidiaries whose functional currencies are not the U.S. dollar. These contracts, totaling $2.0 billion, $129 million and $281 million at December 31, 2009, 2008, and 2007, respectively, are designated as cash flow hedges of the variability of the cash flows due to changes in foreign exchange rates and are recorded at fair value. Accumulated gains and losses as of December 31, 2009 will be included in Cost of products sold at the time the products are sold, generally through the next twelve months.

Abbott enters into foreign currency forward exchange contracts to manage currency exposures for foreign currency denominated third-party trade payables and receivables, and for intercompany loans and trade accounts payable where the receivable or payable is denominated in a currency other than the functional currency of the entity. For intercompany loans, the contracts require Abbott to sell or buy foreign currencies, primarily European currencies and Japanese yen, in exchange for primarily U.S. dollars and other European currencies. For intercompany and trade payables and receivables, the currency exposures are primarily the U.S. dollar, European currencies and Japanese yen. At December 31, 2009, 2008 and 2007, Abbott held $7.5 billion, $8.3 billion and $5.5 billion, respectively, of such foreign currency forward exchange contracts.

Australian dollar."[21] The Coca-Cola Company reports using a combination of forward contracts, options, and collars in its foreign currency hedging strategy.[22]

The Euro

The introduction of the euro as a common currency throughout much of Europe greatly reduces the need for hedging in that region of the world. For example, a Finnish company purchasing goods from a Spanish supplier no longer has an exposure to foreign exchange risk, because the two countries use a common currency. This also is true for Finnish subsidiaries of U.S. (or other non-euro-zone) parent companies. However, any transactions denominated in euros between the U.S. parent and its Finnish (or other euro-zone) subsidiary continue to be exposed to foreign exchange risk.

One advantage of the euro for U.S. (and other non-euro-zone) companies is that a euro account receivable from sales to a customer in, say, the Netherlands, will act as a *natural hedge* of a euro account payable on purchases from, say, a supplier in Italy. Assuming that similar amounts and time periods are involved, any foreign exchange loss (gain) arising from the euro payable will be offset by a foreign exchange gain (loss) on the euro receivable. There will be no need to hedge the euro account payable with a contractual hedging instrument.

FOREIGN CURRENCY BORROWING

In addition to the receivables and payables that arise from import and export activities, companies often must account for foreign currency borrowings, another type of foreign currency transaction. Companies borrow foreign currency from foreign lenders either to finance foreign operations or perhaps to take advantage

---

[21] Dell Inc., 2009 Form 10-K, p. 36.

[22] A foreign currency collar can be created by simultaneously purchasing a call option and selling a put option to fix a range of prices at which foreign currency can be purchased at a predetermined future date.

of more favorable interest rates. Accounting for a foreign currency borrowing is complicated by the fact that both the principal and interest are denominated in foreign currency and both create an exposure to foreign exchange risk.

To demonstrate the accounting for foreign currency debt, assume that on July 1, Year 1, Mapleleaf International (a company based in Canada) borrowed 1 billion Japanese yen (¥) on a one-year note at a per annum interest rate of 5 percent. Interest is payable and the note comes due on July 1, Year 2. The following exchange rates apply:

Date	Canadian Dollars (C$) per Japanese Yen (¥) Spot Rate
July 1, Year 1	C$0.00921
December 31, Year 1	0.00932
July 1, Year 2	0.00937

On July 1, Year 1, Mapleleaf borrows ¥1,000,000,000 and converts it into C$9,210,000 in the spot market. Over the life of the note, Mapleleaf must record accrued interest expense at year-end and interest payments on the anniversary date of July 1. In addition, the Japanese yen note payable must be revalued at year-end, with foreign exchange gains and losses reported in income. The journal entries to account for this foreign currency borrowing are as follows:

July 1, Year 1	Dr. Cash	9,210,000	
	Cr. Note Payable (¥)		9,210,000
	To record the yen note payable at the spot rate of C$0.00921 and the conversion of ¥1,000,000,000 into Canadian dollars.		
December 31, Year 1	Dr. Interest Expense.......................	233,000	
	Cr. Accrued Interest Payable (¥).		233,000
	To accrue interest for the period July 1–December 31, Year 2: (¥1,000,000,000 × 5% × $\frac{1}{2}$ year = ¥25,0000,000 × C$0.00932 = C$233,0000.		
	Dr. Foreign Exchange Loss	110,000	
	Cr. Note Payable (¥)		110,000
	To revalue the yen note payable at the spot rate of C$0.00932 and record a foreign exchange loss of C$110,000 (¥1,000,000,000 × [C$0.00932 – C$0.00921]).		
July 1, Year 2	Dr. Interest Expense.......................	234,250	
	Accrued Interest Payable (¥)................	233,000	
	Foreign Exchange Loss	1,250	
	Cr. Cash............................		468,500
	To record the interest payment of ¥50,000,000 acquired at the spot rate of C$0.00937 for C$468,500; interest expense for the period January 1–July 1, Year 2 (¥25,000,000 × C$0.00937); and a foreign exchange loss on the yen accrued interest payable (¥ 25,000,000 × [C$0.00937 – C$0.00932]).		

Dr. Foreign Exchange Loss	50,000	
Cr. Note Payable (¥)		50,000
To revalue the yen note payable at the spot rate of C$0.00937 and record a foreign exchange loss of C$50,000 (¥1,000,000,000 × [C$0.00937 − C$0.00932]).		
Dr. Note Payable (¥)	9,370,000	
Cr. Cash		9,370,000
To record repayment of the ¥1,000,000,000 note through purchase of yen at the spot rate of C$0.00937.		

Foreign Currency Loan

At times companies might lend foreign currency to related parties, creating the opposite situation as with a foreign currency borrowing. The accounting will involve keeping track of a note receivable and interest receivable, both of which are denominated in foreign currency. Fluctuations in the U.S.-dollar value of the principal and interest will generally give rise to foreign exchange gains and losses, which would be included in income. Under U.S. GAAP, an exception arises when the foreign currency loan is being made on a long-term basis to a foreign branch, subsidiary, or equity method affiliate. Foreign exchange gains and losses on "intercompany foreign currency transactions that are of a long-term investment nature (that is, settlement is not planned or anticipated in the foreseeable future)" are reported in other comprehensive income until the loan is repaid. Only the foreign exchange gains and losses related to the interest receivable would be recorded currently in net income.

Summary

1. There are a variety of exchange rate mechanisms in use around the world. A majority of national currencies are allowed to fluctuate in value against other currencies over time.

2. Exposure to foreign exchange risk exists when a payment to be made or received is denominated in terms of a foreign currency. Appreciation in a foreign currency will result in a foreign exchange gain on a foreign currency receivable and a foreign exchange loss on a foreign currency payable. Conversely, a decrease in the value of a foreign currency will result in a foreign exchange loss on a foreign currency receivable and a foreign exchange gain on a foreign currency payable.

3. Foreign exchange gains and losses on foreign currency balances are recorded in income in the period in which an exchange rate change occurs; this is a two-transaction perspective, accrual approach. Foreign currency balances must be revalued to their current domestic currency equivalent using current exchange rates whenever financial statements are prepared. This approach violates the conservatism principle when unrealized foreign exchange gains are recognized as income.

4. Exposure to foreign exchange risk can be eliminated through hedging. Hedging involves establishing a price today at which a foreign currency to be received in the future can be sold in the future or at which a foreign currency to be paid in the future can be purchased in the future.

5. The two most popular instruments for hedging foreign exchange risk are foreign currency forward contracts and foreign currency options. A forward contract is a binding agreement to exchange currencies at a predetermined rate. An option gives the buyer the right, but not the obligation, to exchange currencies at a predetermined rate.

6. Derivative financial instruments must be reported on the balance sheet at their fair value. Hedge accounting is appropriate if the derivative is (*a*) used to hedge an exposure to foreign exchange risk, (*b*) highly effective in offsetting changes in the fair value or cash flows related to the hedged item, and (*c*) properly documented as a hedge. Under hedge accounting, gains and losses on the hedging instrument are reported in net income in the same period as gains and loss on the item being hedged.

7. Accounting standards provide guidance for hedges of (*a*) recognized foreign-currency-denominated assets and liabilities, (*b*) unrecognized foreign currency firm commitments, and (*c*) forecasted foreign-currency-denominated transactions. Cash flow hedge accounting can be used for all three types of hedges; fair value hedge accounting can be used only for (*a*) and (*b*).

Appendix to Chapter 7

Illustration of the Accounting for Foreign Currency Transactions and Hedging Activities by an Importer

This appendix provides illustrations of the accounting for the following types of hedges used by an importing company:

1. Forward contract cash flow hedge of a recognized foreign currency liability.
2. Forward contract fair value hedge of a recognized foreign currency liability.
3. Option cash flow hedge of a recognized foreign currency liability.
4. Forward contract fair value hedge of a foreign currency firm commitment.
5. Option fair value hedge of a foreign currency firm commitment.
6. Option cash flow hedge of a forecasted foreign currency transaction.

BASIC FACTS

Telectro Company is a U.S. company that produces electronic switches for the telecommunications industry. Telectro regularly imports component parts from a supplier located in Guadalajara, Mexico, with payments made in Mexican pesos (Mex$). The following spot exchange rates, forward exchange rates, and call option premiums for Mexican pesos exist during the period August to October.

	US$ per Mexican Peso		
Date	Spot Rate	Forward Rate to October 31	Call Option Premium for October 31 (strike price $0.080)
August 1	$0.080	$0.085	$0.0052
September 30	0.086	0.088	0.0095
October 31	0.091	0.091	0.0110

1. Forward Contract Cash Flow Hedge of a Recognized Foreign Currency Liability

On August 1, Telectro imports parts from its Mexican supplier at a price of Mex$1,000,000. The parts are received on August 1, but are not paid for until October 31. In addition, on August 1, Telectro enters into a forward contract to purchase Mex$1,000,000 on October 31. The forward contract is appropriately designated as a *cash flow hedge* of the Mexican peso liability exposure. Telectro's incremental borrowing rate is 12 percent per annum (1 percent per month), and the company uses a straight-line method on a monthly basis for allocating forward discounts and premiums.

Journal Entries and Impact on the September 30 and October 31 Trial Balances

8/1	Parts Inventory	$80,000	
	Accounts Payable (Mex$)		$80,000
	To record the purchase of parts and a Mexican peso account payable at the spot rate of $0.080.		

There is no formal entry for the forward contract. A memorandum would be prepared designating the forward contract as a hedge of the risk of changes in the cash flow to be paid on the foreign currency payable resulting from changes in the U.S. dollar–Mexican peso exchange rate.

9/30	Foreign Exchange Loss	$6,000	
	Accounts Payable (Mex$)		$6,000
	To adjust the value of the peso payable to the new spot rate of $0.086 and record a foreign exchange loss resulting from the appreciation of the peso since August 1.		
	Forward Contract	$2,970	
	Accumulated Other Comprehensive Income (AOCI)		$2,970
	To record the forward contract as an asset at its fair value of $2,970 with a corresponding credit to AOCI.		
	Accumulated Other Comprehensive Income (AOCI)	$6,000	
	Gain on Forward Contract		$6,000
	To record a gain on forward contract to offset the foreign exchange loss on account payable with a corresponding debit to AOCI.		

The fair value of the forward contract is determined by reference to the change in the forward rate for a contract that settles on October 31: ($0.088 − $0.085) × Mex$1,000,000 = $3,000. The present value of $3,000 discounted for one month (from October 31 to September 30) at an interest rate of 12 percent per year (1 percent per month) is calculated as follows: $3,000 × 0.9901 = $2,970.

Premium Expense	$3,333	
Accumulated Other Comprehensive Income (AOCI)		$3,333
To allocate the forward contract premium to income over the life of the contract using a straight-line method on a monthly basis ($5,000 × $\frac{2}{3}$ = $3,333).		

The original premium on the forward contract is determined by the difference in the Mexican peso spot rate and three-month forward rate on August 1: ($0.085 − $0.080) × Mex$1,000,000 = $5,000.

Trial Balance—September 30	Debit	Credit
Parts Inventory	$80,000	
Accounts Payable (Mex$)		$86,000
Forward Contract (asset)	2,970	
AOCI		303
Foreign Exchange Loss	6,000	
Gain on Forward Contract		6,000
Premium Expense	3,333	
	$92,303	$92,303

			Debit	Credit
10/31	Foreign Exchange Loss		$5,000	
	Accounts Payable (Mex$)			$5,000
	To adjust the value of the peso payable to the new spot rate of $0.091 and record a foreign exchange loss resulting from the appreciation of the peso since September 30.			
	Forward Contract		$3,030	
	Accumulated Other Comprehensive Income (AOCI)			$3,030
	To adjust the carrying value of the forward contract to its current fair value of $6,000 with a corresponding credit to AOCI.			
	Accumulated Other Comprehensive Income (AOCI)		$5,000	
	Gain on Forward Contract			$5,000
	To record a gain on forward contract to offset the foreign exchange loss on account payable with a corresponding debit to AOCI.			

The current fair value of the forward contract is determined by reference to the difference in the spot rate on October 31 and the original forward rate: ($0.091 − $0.085) × Mex$1,000,000 = $6,000. The forward contract adjustment on October 31 is calculated as the difference in the current fair value and the carrying value at September 30: $6,000 − $2,970 = $3,030.

		Debit	Credit
Premium Expense		$1,667	
Accumulated Other Comprehensive Income (AOCI)			$1,667
To allocate the forward contract premium to income over the life of the contract using a straight-line method on a monthly basis ($5,000 × $\frac{1}{3}$ = $1,667).			
Foreign Currency (Mex$)		$91,000	
Cash			$85,000
Forward Contract			6,000

To record settlement of the forward contract; record payment of $85,000 in exchange for Mex$1,000,000, record the receipt of Mex$1,000,000 as an asset at the spot rate of $0.91, and remove the forward contract from the accounts.		
Accounts Payable (Mex$)	$91,000	
Foreign Currency (Mex$)		$91,000
To record remittance of Mex$1,000,000 to the Mexican supplier.		

Trial Balance—October 31	Debit	Credit
Cash		$85,000
Parts Inventory	$80,000	
Retained Earnings, 9/30	3,333	
Foreign Exchange Loss	5,000	
Gain on Forward Contract		5,000
Premium Expense	1,667	
	$90,000	$90,000

2. Forward Contract Fair Value Hedge of a Recognized Foreign Currency Liability

The facts are the same as in (1), with the exception that Telectro designates the forward contract as a *fair value hedge* of the Mexican peso liability exposure.

Journal Entries and Impact on the September 30 and October 31 Trial Balances

8/1	Parts Inventory	$80,000	
	Accounts Payable (Mex$)		$80,000
	To record the purchase of parts and a Mexican peso account payable at the spot rate of $0.080.		

There is no formal entry for the forward contract. A memorandum would be prepared designating the forward contract as a hedge of the risk of changes in the cash flow to be paid on the foreign currency payable resulting from changes in the U.S. dollar–Mexican peso exchange rate.

9/30	Foreign Exchange Loss	$6,000	
	Accounts Payable (Mex$)		$6,000
	To adjust the value of the peso payable to the new spot rate of $0.086 and record a foreign exchange loss resulting from the appreciation of the peso since August 1.		
	Forward Contract	$2,970	
	Gain on Forward Contract		$2,970
	To record the forward contract as an asset at its fair value of $2,970 and record a forward contract gain for the change in the fair value of the forward contract since August 1.		

Trial Balance—September 30	Debit	Credit
Parts Inventory	$80,000	
Accounts Payable (Mex$)		$86,000
Forward Contract (asset)	2,970	
Foreign Exchange Loss	6,000	
Gain on Forward Contract		2,970
	$88,970	$88,970

10/31			
	Foreign Exchange Loss	$5,000	
	Accounts Payable (Mex$)		$5,000
	To adjust the value of the peso payable to the new spot rate of $0.091 and record a foreign exchange loss resulting from the appreciation of the peso since September 30.		
	Forward Contract	$3,030	
	Gain on Forward Contract		$3,030
	To adjust the carrying value of the forward contract to its current fair value of $6,000 and record a forward contract gain for the change in fair value since September 30.		
	Foreign Currency (Mex$)	$91,000	
	Cash		$85,000
	Forward Contract		6,000
	To record settlement of the forward contract: record payment of $85,000 in exchange for Mex$1,000,000, record the receipt of Mex$1,000,000 as an asset at the spot rate of $0.91, and remove the forward contract from the accounts.		
	Accounts Payable (Mex$)	$91,000	
	Foreign Currency (Mex$)		$91,000
	To record remittance of Mex$1,000,000 to the Mexican supplier.		

Trial Balance—October 31	Debit	Credit
Cash		$85,000
Parts Inventory	$80,000	
Retained Earnings, 9/30	3,030	
Foreign Exchange Loss	5,000	
Gain on Forward Contract		3,030
	$88,030	$88,030

3. Option Cash Flow Hedge of a Recognized Foreign Currency Liability

On August 1, Telectro imports parts from its Mexican supplier at a price of Mex$1,000,000. The parts are received on August 1 but are not paid for until October 31. In addition, on August 1, Telectro purchases a three-month call option on Mex$1,000,000 with a strike price of $0.080. The option is appropriately designated as a *cash flow hedge* of the Mexican peso liability exposure.

The following schedule summarizes the changes in the components of the fair value of the Mexican peso call option with a strike price of $0.080:

Date	Spot Rate	Option Premium	Fair Value	Change in Fair Value	Intrinsic Value	Time Value	Change in TimeValue
8/1	$0.080	$0.0052	$5,200	—	$0	$5,200[a]	—
9/30	$0.086	$0.0095	$9,500	+$4,300	$ 6,000[b]	$3,500[b]	−$1,700
10/31	$0.091	$0.0110	$11,000	+$1,500	$11,000	$0[c]	−$3,500

[a] Because the strike price and spot rate are the same, the option has no intrinsic value. Fair value is attributable solely to the time value of the option.
[b] With a spot rate of $0.086 and a strike price of $0.080, the option has an intrinsic value of $6,000. The remaining $3,500 of fair value is attributable to time value.
[c] The time value of the option at maturity is zero.

Journal Entries and Impact on the September 30 and October 31 Trial Balances

8/1	Parts Inventory	$80,000	
	Accounts Payable (Mex$)		$80,000
	To record the purchase of parts and a Mexican peso account payable at the spot rate of $0.080.		
	Foreign Currency Option	$5,200	
	Cash		$5,200
	To record the purchase of a foreign currency option as an asset.		
9/30	Foreign Exchange Loss	$6,000	
	Accounts Payable (Mex$)		$6,000
	To adjust the value of the peso payable to the new spot rate of $0.086 and record a foreign exchange loss resulting from the appreciation of the peso since August 1.		
	Foreign Currency Option	$4,300	
	Accumulated Other Comprehensive Income (AOCI)		$4,300
	To adjust the fair value of the option from $5,200 to $9,500 with a corresponding credit to AOCI.		
	Accumulated Other Comprehensive Income (AOCI)	$6,000	
	Gain on Foreign Currency Option		$6,000
	To record a gain on forward currency option to offset the foreign exchange loss on account payable with a corresponding debit to AOCI.		

Option Expense	$1,700	
Accumulated Other Comprehensive Income (AOCI)		$1,700
To recognize the change in the time value of the foreign currency option as an expense with a corresponding credit to AOCI.		

Trial Balance—September 30	Debit	Credit
Parts Inventory	$80,000	
Accounts Payable (Mex$)		$86,000
Foreign Currency Option (asset)	9,500	
Cash		5,200
Foreign Exchange Loss	6,000	
Gain on Foreign Currency Option		6,000
Option Expense	1,700	
	$97,200	$97,200

10/31	Foreign Exchange Loss	$5,000	
	Accounts Payable (Mex$)		$5,000
	To adjust the value of the peso payable to the new spot rate of $0.091 and record a foreign exchange loss resulting from the appreciation of the peso since September 30.		
	Foreign Currency Option	$1,500	
	Accumulated Other Comprehensive Income (AOCI)		$1,500
	To adjust the carrying value of the foreign currency option to its current fair value of $11,000 with a corresponding credit to AOCI.		
	Accumulated Other Comprehensive Income (AOCI)	$5,000	
	Gain on Foreign Currency Option		$5,000
	To record a gain on foreign currency option to offset the foreign exchange loss on account payable with a corresponding debit to AOCI.		
	Option Expense	$3,500	
	Accumulated Other Comprehensive Income (AOCI)		$3,500
	To recognize the change in the time value of the foreign currency option as an expense with a corresponding credit to AOCI.		
	Foreign Currency (Mex$)	$91,000	
	Cash		$80,000
	Foreign Currency Option		11,000
	To record exercise of the foreign currency option: record payment of $80,000 in exchange for Mex$1,000,000, record the receipt of Mex$1,000,000 as an asset at the spot rate of $0.91, and remove the option from the accounts.		
	Accounts Payable (Mex$)	$91,000	
	Foreign Currency (Mex$)		$91,000
	To record remittance of Mex$1,000,000 to the Mexican supplier.		

Trial Balance—October 31	Debit	Credit
Cash ($5,000 credit + $80,000 credit)		$85,200
Parts Inventory	$80,000	
Retained Earnings, 9/30	1,700	
Foreign Exchange Loss	5,000	
Gain on Foreign Currency Option		5,000
Option Expense	3,500	
	$90,200	$90,200

4. Forward Contract Fair Value Hedge of a Foreign Currency Firm Commitment

On August 1, Telectro orders parts from its Mexican supplier at a price of Mex$1,000,000. The parts are received and paid for on October 31. On August 1, Telectro enters into a forward contract to purchase Mex$1,000,000 on October 31. The forward contract is designated as a *fair value hedge* of the Mexican peso firm commitment. The fair value of the firm commitment is determined through reference to changes in the forward exchange rate.

Journal Entries and Impact on the September 30 and October 31 Trial Balances

8/1	There is no formal entry for the forward contract or the purchase order. A memorandum would be prepared designating the forward contract as a fair value hedge of the foreign currency firm commitment.		
9/30	Forward Contract	$2,970	
	Gain on Forward Contract		$2,970
	To record the forward contract as an asset at its fair value of $2,970 and record a forward contract gain for the change in the fair value of the forward contract since August 1.		
	Loss on Firm Commitment	$2,970	
	Firm Commitment		$2,970
	To record the firm commitment as a liability at its fair value of $2,970 based on changes in the forward rate and record a firm commitment loss for the change in fair value since August 1.		

Trial Balance—September 30	Debit	Credit
Forward Contract (asset)	$2,970	
Firm Commitment (liability)		$2,970
Gain on Forward Contract		2,970
Loss on Firm Commitment	2,970	
	$5,940	$5,940

10/31	Forward Contract	$3,030	
	Gain on Forward Contract		$3,030

To adjust the carrying value of the forward contract to its current fair value of $6,000 and record a forward contract gain for the change in fair value since September 30.

	Loss on Firm Commitment	$3,030	
	Firm Commitment		$3,030

To adjust the value of the firm commitment to $6,000 based on changes in the forward rate and record a firm commitment loss for the change in fair value since September 30.

	Foreign Currency (pesos)	$91,000	
	Cash		$85,000
	Forward Contract		6,000

To record settlement of the forward contract; record payment of $85,000 in exchange for Mex$1,000,000, record the receipt of 1 million pesos as an asset at the spot rate of $0.91, and remove the forward contract from the accounts.

	Parts Inventory	$91,000	
	Foreign Currency (Mex$)		$91,000

To record the purchase of parts through the payment of Mex$1,000,000 to the Mexican supplier.

	Firm Commitment	$6,000	
	Adjustment to Net Income		$6,000

To close the firm commitment account as an adjustment to net income.

Note that the final entry to close the Firm Commitment as an Adjustment to Net Income will be made only in the period in which the Parts Inventory affects net income through Cost of Goods Sold. The Firm Commitment remains on the books as a liability until that time.

Trial Balance—October 31	Debit	Credit
Cash		$85,000
Parts Inventory (Cost of Goods Sold)	$91,000	
Gain on Forward Contract		3,030
Loss on Firm Commitment	3,030	
Adjustment to Net Income		6,000
	$94,030	$94,030

5. Option Fair Value Hedge of a Foreign Currency Firm Commitment

On August 1, Telectro orders parts from its Mexican supplier at a price of Mex$1,000,000. The parts are received and paid for on October 31. On August 1, Telectro purchases a three-month call option on Mex$1,000,000 with a strike price of $0.080. The option is appropriately designated as a *fair value hedge* of the

Mexican peso firm commitment. The fair value of the firm commitment is determined through reference to changes in the spot exchange rate.

Journal Entries and Impact on the September 30 and October 31 Trial Balances

8/1	Foreign Currency Option		$5,200	
	Cash			$5,200
	To record the purchase of a foreign currency option as an asset.			
9/30	Foreign Currency Option		$4,300	
	Gain on Foreign Currency Option			$4,300
	To adjust the fair value of the option from $5,200 to $9,500 and record an option gain for the change in fair value since August 1.			
	Loss on Firm Commitment		$5,940	
	Firm Commitment			$5,940
	To record the firm commitment as a liability at its fair value of $5,940 based on changes in the spot rate and record a firm commitment loss for the change in fair value since August 1.			

The fair value of the firm commitment is determined through reference to changes in the spot rate from August 1 to September 30: ($0.080 − $0.086) × Mex$1,000,000 = $(6,000). This amount must be discounted for one month at 12 percent per annum (1 percent per month): $(6,000) × 0.9901 = $(5,940).

Trial Balance—September 30	Debit	Credit
Cash		$ 5,200
Foreign Currency Option (asset)	$ 9,500	
Firm Commitment (liability)		5,940
Gain on Foreign Currency Option		4,300
Loss on Firm Commitment	5,940	
	$15,440	$15,440

10/31	Foreign Currency Option		$1,500	
	Gain on Foreign Currency Option			$1,500
	To adjust the fair value of the option from $9,500 to $11,000 and record an option gain for the change in fair value since September 30.			
	Loss on Firm Commitment		$5,060	
	Firm Commitment			$5,060
	To adjust the fair value of the firm commitment from $5,940 to $11,000 and record a firm commitment loss for the change in fair value since September 30.			

The fair value of the firm commitment is determined through reference to changes in the spot rate from August 1 to October 31: ($0.080 − $0.091) × Mex$1,000,000 = $(11,000).

	Debit	Credit
Foreign Currency (Mex$)	$91,000	
Cash		$80,000
Foreign Currency Option		11,000
To record exercise of the foreign currency option; record payment of $80,000 in exchange for Mex$1,000,000, record the receipt of Mex$1,000,000 as an asset at the spot rate of $0.91, and remove the option from the accounts.		
Parts Inventory	$91,000	
Foreign Currency (Mex$)		$91,000
To record the purchase of parts through the payment of Mex$1,000,000 to the Mexican supplier.		
Firm Commitment	$11,000	
Adjustment to Net Income		$11,000
To close the firm commitment account as an adjustment to net income.		

Note that the final entry to close the Firm Commitment as an Adjustment to Net Income will be made only in the period in which the Parts Inventory affects net income through Cost of Goods Sold. The Firm Commitment remains on the books as a liability until that point in time.

Trial Balance—October 31	**Debit**	**Credit**
Cash ($5,200 credit + $80,000 credit)		$85,200
Parts Inventory (Cost of Goods Sold)	$91,000	
Retained Earnings, 9/30	1,640	
Gain on Foreign Currency Option		1,500
Loss on Firm Commitment	5,060	
Adjustment to Net Income		11,000
	$97,700	$97,700

6. Option Cash Flow Hedge of a Forecasted Foreign Currency Transaction

Telectro anticipates that it will import component parts from its Mexican supplier in the near future. On August 1, Telectro purchases a three-month call option on Mex$1,000,000 with a strike price of $0.080. The option is appropriately designated as a *cash flow hedge* of a forecasted Mexican peso transaction. Parts costing Mex$1,000,000 are received and paid for on October 31.

Journal Entries and Impact on the September 30 and October 31 Trial Balances

8/1	Foreign Currency Option	$5,200	
	Cash		$5,200
	To record the purchase of a foreign currency option as an asset.		

9/30	Foreign Currency Option	$4,300	
	Accumulated Other Comprehensive Income (AOCI)		$4,300
	To adjust the fair value of the option from $5,200 to $9,500 with a corresponding adjustment to AOCI.		
	Option Expense	$1,700	
	Accumulated Other Comprehensive Income (AOCI)		$1,700
	To recognize the change in the time value of the foreign currency option as an expense with a corresponding credit to AOCI.		

Trial Balance—September 30	Debit	Credit
Cash		$ 5,200
Foreign Currency Option (asset)	$ 9,500	
Accumulated Other Comprehensive Income.		6,000
Option Expense	1,700	
	$11,200	$11,200

10/31	Foreign Currency Option	$1,500	
	Accumulated Other Comprehensive Income (AOCI)		$1,500
	To adjust the fair value of the option from $9,500 to $11,000 with a corresponding adjustment to AOCI.		
	Option Expense	$3,500	
	Accumulated Other Comprehensive Income (AOCI)		$3,500
	To recognize the change in the time value of the foreign currency option as an expense with a corresponding credit to AOCI.		
	Foreign Currency (Mex$)	$91,000	
	Cash		$80,000
	Foreign Currency Option		11,000
	To record exercise of the foreign currency option; record payment of $80,000 in exchange for Mex$1,000,000, record the receipt of Mex$1,000,000 as an asset at the spot rate of $0.91, and remove the option from the accounts		
	Parts Inventory	$91,000	
	Foreign Currency (Mex$)		$91,000
	To record the purchase of parts through the payment of Mex$1,000,000 to the Mexican supplier.		
	Accumulated Other Comprehensive Income (AOCI)	$11,000	
	Adjustment to Net Income		$11,000
	To close AOCI as an adjustment to net income.		

Note that the final entry to close AOCI as an Adjustment to Net Income is made at the date that the forecasted transaction was expected to occur, regardless of when the Parts Inventory affects net income.

Trial Balance—October 31	Debit	Credit
Cash ($5,200 credit + $80,000 credit)		$85,200
Parts Inventory (Cost of Goods Sold)	$91,000	
Retained Earnings, 9/30	1,700	
Loss on Foreign Currency Option	3,500	
Adjustment to Net Income		11,000
	$96,200	$96,200

Questions

1. What is the concept underlying the two-transaction perspective to accounting for foreign currency transactions?

2. A company makes an export sale denominated in a foreign currency and allows the customer one month to pay. Under the two-transaction perspective, accrual approach, how does the company account for fluctuations in the exchange rate for the foreign currency?

3. What factors create a foreign exchange gain on a foreign currency transaction? What factors create a foreign exchange loss?

4. What does the word *hedging* mean? Why do companies hedge foreign exchange risk?

5. How does a foreign currency option differ from a foreign currency forward contract?

6. How does the timing of hedges of the following differ?
   a. Foreign currency denominated assets and liabilities.
   b. Foreign currency firm commitments.
   c. Forecasted foreign currency transactions.

7. Why might a company prefer a foreign currency option rather than a forward contract in hedging a foreign currency firm commitment? Why might a company prefer a forward contract over an option in hedging a foreign currency asset or liability?

8. How are foreign currency derivatives such as forward contracts and options reported on the balance sheet?

9. How is the fair value of a foreign currency forward contract determined? How is the fair value of an option determined?

10. What is hedge accounting?

11. Under what conditions can hedge accounting be used to account for a foreign currency option used to hedge a forecasted foreign currency transaction?

12. What are the differences in accounting for a forward contract used as (*a*) a cash flow hedge and (*b*) a fair value hedge of a foreign-currency-denominated asset or liability?

13. What are the differences in accounting for a forward contract used as a fair value hedge of (*a*) a foreign-currency-denominated asset or liability and (*b*) a foreign currency firm commitment?

14. What are the differences in accounting for a forward contract used as a cash flow hedge of (*a*) a foreign-currency-denominated asset or liability and (*b*) a forecasted foreign currency transaction?

15. How are changes in the fair value of an option accounted for in a cash flow hedge? In a fair value hedge?

16. In what way is the accounting for a foreign currency borrowing more complicated than the accounting for a foreign currency account payable?

Exercises and Problems

1. Which of the following combinations correctly describes the relationship between foreign currency transactions, exchange rate changes, and foreign exchange gains and losses?

	Type of Transaction	Foreign Currency	Foreign Exchange Gain or Loss
a.	Export sale	Appreciates	Loss
b.	Import purchase	Appreciates	Gain
c.	Import purchase	Depreciates	Gain
d.	Export sale	Depreciates	Gain

2. Gracie Corporation had a Japanese yen receivable resulting from exports to Japan and a Brazilian real payable resulting from imports from Brazil. Gracie recorded foreign exchange gains related to both its yen receivable and real payable. Did the foreign currencies increase or decrease in dollar value from the date of the transaction to the settlement date?

	Yen	Real
a.	Increase	Increase
b.	Decrease	Decrease
c.	Decrease	Increase
d.	Increase	Decrease

3. On December 1, Year 1, Tackett Company (a U.S.-based company) entered into a three-month forward contract to purchase 1 million Mexican pesos on March 1, Year 2. The following U.S. dollar per peso exchange rates apply:

Date	Spot Rate	Forward Rate (to March 1, Year 2)
December 1, Year 1	$0.088	$0.084
December 31, Year 1	0.080	0.074
March 1, Year 2	0.076	

Tackett's incremental borrowing rate is 12 percent. The present value factor for two months at an annual interest rate of 12 percent (1 percent per month) is 0.9803.

Which of the following correctly describes the manner in which Tackett Company will report the forward contract on its December 31, Year 1, balance sheet?

a. As an asset in the amount of $3,921.20.

b. As an asset in the amount of $7,842.40.

c. As a liability in the amount of $13,724.20.

d. As a liability in the amount of $9,803.00.

Use the following information for Exercises 4 and 5: Reiter Corp. (a U.S.-based company) sold parts to an Israeli customer on December 1, Year 1, with payment of 100,000 Israeli shekels to be received on March 31, Year 2. The following exchange rates apply:

Date	Spot Rate	Forward Rate (to March 31, Year 2)
December 1, Year 1	$0.24	$0.23
December 31, Year 1	0.22	0.20
March 31, Year 2	0.25	

Reiter's incremental borrowing rate is 12 percent. The present value factor for three months at an annual interest rate of 12 percent (1 percent per month) is 0.9706.

4. Assuming no forward contract was entered into, how much foreign exchange gain or loss should Reiter report on its Year 1 income statement with regard to this transaction?

   a. A $5,000 gain.

   b. A $3,000 gain.

   c. A $2,000 loss.

   d. A $1,000 loss.

5. Assuming a forward contract to sell 100,000 Israeli shekels was entered into on December 1, Year 1, as a fair value hedge of a foreign currency receivable, what would be the net impact on net income in Year 1 resulting from a fluctuation in the value of the shekel?

   a. No impact on net income.

   b. A $58.80 decrease in net income.

   c. A $2,000 decrease in income.

   d. A $911.80 increase in income.

Use the following information for Exercises 6 through 8: On September 1, Year 1, Keefer Company received an order to sell a machine to a customer in Canada at a price of 100,000 Canadian dollars. The machine was shipped and payment was received on March 1, Year 2. On September 1, Year 1, Keefer Company purchased a put option giving it the right to sell 100,000 Canadian dollars on March 1, Year 2, at a price of $75,000. Keefer Company properly designates the option as a fair value hedge of the Canadian-dollar firm commitment. The option cost $1,700 and had a fair value of $2,800 on December 31, Year 1. The fair value of the firm commitment is measured through reference to changes in the spot rate. The following spot exchange rates apply:

Date	U.S. Dollar per Canadian Dollar
September 1, Year 1	$0.75
December 31, Year 1	0.73
March 1, Year 2	0.71

Keefer Company's incremental borrowing rate is 12 percent. The present value factor for two months at an annual interest rate of 12 percent (1 percent per month) is 0.9803.

6. What was the net impact on Keefer Company's Year 1 income as a result of this fair value hedge of a firm commitment?
   a. $0.
   b. An $860.60 decrease in income.
   c. A $1,100.00 increase in income.
   d. A $1,960.60 increase in income.

7. What was the net impact on Keefer Company's Year 2 income as a result of this fair value hedge of a firm commitment?
   a. $0.
   b. An $839.40 decrease in income.
   c. A $74,160.60 increase in income.
   d. A $76,200.00 increase in income.

8. What was the net increase or decrease in cash flow from having purchased the foreign currency option to hedge this exposure to foreign exchange risk?
   a. $0.
   b. A $1,000 increase in cash flow.
   c. A $1,700 decrease in cash flow.
   d. A $2,300 increase in cash flow.

   Use the following information for problems 9 and 10: On November 1, Year 1, Black Lion Company forecasts the purchase of raw materials from an Argentinian supplier on February 1, Year 2, at a price of 200,000 Argentinian pesos. On November 1, Year 1, Black Lion pays $1,200 for a three-month call option on 200,000 Argentinian pesos with a strike price of $0.35 per peso. The option is properly designated as a cash flow hedge of a forecasted foreign currency transaction. On December 31, Year 1, the option has a fair value of $900. The following spot exchange rates apply:

Date	U.S. Dollar per Argentinian Peso
November 1, Year 1	$0.35
December 31, Year 1	0.30
February 1, Year 2	0.36

9. What is the net impact on Black Lion Company's Year 1 net income as a result of this hedge of a forecasted foreign currency purchase?
   a. $0.
   b. A $200 increase in net income.
   c. A $300 decrease in net income.
   d. An $800 decrease in net income.

10. What is the net impact on Black Lion Company's Year 2 net income as a result of this hedge of a forecast foreign currency purchase? Assume that the raw materials are consumed and become a part of cost of goods sold in Year 2.
   a. A $70,000 decrease in net income.
   b. A $70,900 decease in net income.
   c. A $71,100 decrease in net income.
   d. A $72,900 decrease in net income.

11. Garden Grove Corporation made a sale to a foreign customer on September 15, Year 1, for 100,000 foreign currency units (FCU). Payment was received on October 15, Year 1. The following exchange rates apply:

Date	U.S. Dollar per FCU
September 15, Year 1	$0.40
September 30, Year 1	0.42
October 15, Year 1	0.37

Required:
Prepare all journal entries for Garden Grove Corporation in connection with this sale assuming that the company closes its books on September 30 to prepare interim financial statements.

12. On December 1, Year 1, El Primero Company purchases inventory from a foreign supplier for 40,000 coronas. Payment will be made in 90 days after El Primero has sold this merchandise. Sales are made rather quickly and El Primero pays this entire obligation on February 15, Year 2. The following exchange rates for 1 corona apply:

Date	U.S. Dollar per Corona
December 1, Year 1	$0.87
December 31, Year 1	0.82
February 15, Year 2	0.91

Required:
Prepare all journal entries for El Primero in connection with the purchase and payment.

13. On September 30, Year 1, the Lester Company negotiated a two-year loan of 1,000,000 markkas from a foreign bank at an interest rate of 2 percent per annum. Interest payments are made annually on September 30 and the principal will be repaid on September 30, Year 3. Lester Company prepares U.S.-dollar financial statements and has a December 31 year-end. Prepare all journal entries related to this foreign currency borrowing assuming the following exchange rates for 1 markka:

Date	U.S. Dollars per Markka
September 30, Year 1	$0.20
December 31, Year 1	0.21
September 30, Year 2	0.23
December 31, Year 2	0.24
September 30, Year 3	0.27

Required:
Prepare all journal entries for the Lester Company in connection with the foreign currency borrowing. What is the effective annual cost of borrowing in dollars in each of the three years Year 1, Year 2, and Year 3?

14. The Budvar Company sells parts to a foreign customer on December 1, Year 1, with payment of 20,000 crowns to be received on March 1, Year 2. Budvar enters into a forward contract on December 1, Year 1, to sell 20,000 crowns on March 1, Year 2. Relevant exchange rates for the crown on various dates are as follows:

Date	Spot Rate	Forward Rate (to March 1, Year 2)
December 1, Year 1	$1.00	$1.04
December 31, Year 1	1.05	1.10
March 1, Year 2	1.12	

Budvar's incremental borrowing rate is 12 percent. The present value factor for two months at an annual interest rate of 12 percent (1 percent per month) is 0.9803. Budvar must close its books and prepare financial statements at December 31.

Required:

a. Assuming that Budvar designates the forward contract as a cash flow hedge of a foreign currency receivable, prepare journal entries for these transactions in U.S. dollars. What is the impact on Year 1 net income? What is the impact on Year 2 net income? What is the impact on net income over the two accounting periods?

b. Assuming that Budvar designates the forward contract as a fair value hedge of a foreign currency receivable, prepare journal entries for these transactions in U.S. dollars. What is the impact on Year 1 net income? What is the impact on Year 2 net income? What is the impact on net income over the two accounting periods?

15. The same facts apply as in Exercise 14 except that Budvar Company purchases parts from a foreign supplier on December 1, Year 1, with payment of 20,000 crowns to be made on March 1, Year 2. On December 1, Year 1, Budvar enters into a forward contract to purchase 20,000 crowns on March 1, Year 2. The parts purchased on December 1, Year 1, become a part of the cost of goods sold on March 15, Year 2.

Required:

a. Assuming that Budvar designates the forward contract as a cash flow hedge of a foreign currency payable, prepare journal entries for these transactions in U.S. dollars. What is the impact on Year 1 net income? What is the impact on Year 2 net income? What is the impact on net income over the two accounting periods?

b. Assuming that Budvar designates the forward contract as a fair value hedge of a foreign currency payable, prepare journal entries for these transactions in U.S. dollars. What is the impact on Year 1 net income? What is the impact on Year 2 net income? What is the impact on net income over the two accounting periods?

16. On November 1, Year 1, Alexandria Company sold merchandise to a foreign customer for 100,000 francs with payment to be received on April 30, Year 2. At the date of sale, Alexandria Company entered into a six-month forward contract to sell 100,000 francs. The forward contract is properly designated as

a cash flow hedge of a foreign currency receivable. Relevant exchange rates for the franc are:

Date	Spot Rate	Forward Rate (to April 30, Year 2)
November 1, Year 1	$0.23	$0.22
December 31, Year 1	0.20	0.18
April 30, Year 2	0.19	

Alexandria Company's incremental borrowing rate is 12 percent. The present value factor for four months at an annual interest rate of 12 percent (1 percent per month) is 0.9610.

Required:

Prepare all journal entries, including December 31 adjusting entries, to record the sale and forward contract. What is the impact on net income in Year 1? What is the impact on net income in Year 2?

17. Artco Inc. engages in various transactions with companies in the country of Santrica. On November 30, Year 1, Artco sold artwork at a price of 400,000 ricas to a Santrican customer with payment to be received on January 31, Year 2. In addition, on November 30, Year 1, Artco purchased art supplies from a Santrican supplier at a price of 300,000 ricas; payment will be made on January 31, Year 2. The art supplies are consumed by the end of November, Year 1. To hedge its net exposure in ricas, Artco entered into a two-month forward contract on November 30, Year 1, wherein Artco will deliver 100,000 ricas to the foreign currency broker in exchange for U.S dollars at the agreed-on forward rate. Artco properly designates its forward contract as a fair value hedge of a foreign currency receivable. The following rates for the rica apply:

Date	Spot Rate	Forward Rate (to January 31, Year 2)
November 30, Year 1	$0.13	$0.12
December 31, Year 1	0.10	0.08
January 31, Year 2	0.09	

Artco Inc.'s incremental borrowing rate is 12 percent. The present value factor for one month at an annual interest rate of 12 percent (1 percent per month) is 0.9901.

Required:

Prepare all journal entries, including December 31 adjusting entries, to record these transactions and forward contract. What is the impact on net income in Year 1? What is the impact on net income in Year 2?

18. On October 1, Year 1, Butterworth Company entered into a forward contract to sell 100,000 rupees in four months (on January 31, Year 2). Relevant exchange rates for the rupee are as follows:

Date	Spot Rate	Forward Rate (to January 31, Year 2)
October 1, Year 1	$0.069	$0.065
December 31, Year 1	0.071	0.074
January 31, Year 2	0.072	

Butterworth Company's incremental borrowing rate is 12 percent. The present value factor for one month at an annual interest rate of 12 percent (1 percent per month) is 0.9901. Butterworth must close its books and prepare financial statements on December 31.

Required:
a. Prepare journal entries assuming the forward contract was entered into as a fair value hedge of a 100,000-rupee receivable arising from a sale made on October 1, Year 1. Include entries for both the sale and the forward contract.
b. Prepare journal entries assuming the forward contract was entered into as a fair value hedge of a firm commitment related to a 100,000-rupee sale that will be made on January 31, Year 2. Include entries for both the firm commitment and the forward contract. The fair value of the firm commitment is measured through reference to changes in the forward rate.

19. On August 1, Year 1, Huntington Corporation placed an order to purchase merchandise from a foreign supplier at a price of 100,000 dinars. The merchandise is received and paid for on October 31, Year 1, and is fully consumed by December 31, Year 1. On August 1, Huntington entered into a forward contract to purchase 100,000 dinars in three months at the agreed-on forward rate. The forward contract is properly designated as a fair value hedge of a foreign currency firm commitment. The fair value of the firm commitment is measured through reference to changes in the forward rate. Relevant exchange rates for the dinar are as follows:

Date	Spot Rate	Forward Rate (to October 31, Year 1)
August 1	$1.300	$1.310
September 30	1.305	1.325
October 31	1.320	

Huntington's incremental borrowing rate is 12 percent. The present value factor for one month at an annual interest rate of 12 percent (1 percent per month) is 0.9901. Huntington Corporation must close its books and prepare its third-quarter financial statements on September 30, Year 1.

Required:
Prepare journal entries for the forward contract and firm commitment. What is the impact on net income in Year 1? What is the net cash outflow on the purchase of merchandise from the foreign customer?

20. On June 1, Year 1, Tsanumis Corporation (a U.S.-based manufacturing firm) received an order to sell goods to a foreign customer at a price of 1 million euros. The goods will be shipped and payment will be received in three months on September 1, Year 1. On June 1, Tsanumis Corporation purchased an option to sell 1 million euros in three months at a strike price of $1.00. The option is properly designated as a fair value hedge of a foreign currency firm commitment. The fair value of the firm commitment is measured through reference to changes in the spot rate. Relevant exchange rates and option premiums for the euro during Year 1 are as follows:

Date	Spot Rate	Call Option Premium for September 1, Year 1 (strike price $1.00)
June 1	$1.00	$0.010
June 30	0.99	0.015
September 1	0.97	

Tsanumis Corporation's incremental borrowing rate is 12 percent. The present value factor for two months at an annual interest rate of 12 percent (1 percent per month) is 0.9803. Tsanumis Corporation must close its books and prepare its second-quarter financial statements on June 30.

Required:

Prepare journal entries for the foreign currency option and firm commitment. What is the impact on Year 1 net income? What is the net cash inflow resulting from the sale of goods to the foreign customer?

21. The Zermatt Company ordered parts from a foreign supplier on November 20 at a price of 100,000 francs when the spot rate was $0.80 per peso. Delivery and payment were scheduled for December 20. On November 20, Zermatt acquired a call option on 100,000 francs at a strike price of $0.80, paying a premium of $0.008 per franc. The option is designated as fair value hedge of a foreign currency firm commitment. The fair value of the firm commitment is measured through reference to changes in the spot rate. The parts are delivered and paid for according to schedule. Zermatt does not close its books until December 31.

Required:
a. Assuming a spot rate of $0.83 per franc on December 20, prepare all journal entries to account for the option and firm commitment.
b. Assuming a spot rate of $0.78 per franc on December 20, prepare all journal entries to account for the option and firm commitment.

22. Given its experience, Garnier Corporation expects that it will sell goods to a foreign customer at a price of 1 million lire on March 15, Year 2. To hedge this forecasted transaction, a three-month put option to sell 1 million lire is acquired on December 15, Year 1. Garnier selects a strike price of $0.15 per lire, paying a premium of $0.005 per unit, when the spot rate is $0.15. The spot rate decreases to $.14 at December 31, Year 1, causing the fair value of the option to increase to $12,000. By March 15, Year 2, when the goods are delivered and payment is received from the customer, the spot rate has fallen to $0.13, resulting in a fair value for the option of $20,000.

Required:
Prepare all journal entries for the option hedge of a forecast transaction and for the export sale assuming that December 31 is Garnier Corporation's year-end. What is the overall impact on net income over the two accounting periods? What is the net cash inflow from this export sale?

Case 7-1

Zorba Company

Zorba Company, a U.S.-based importer of specialty olive oil, placed an order with a foreign supplier for 500 cases of olive oil at a price of 100 crowns per case. The total purchase price is 50,000 crowns. Relevant exchange rates are as follows:

Date	Spot Rate	Forward Rate (to January 31, Year 2)	Call Option Premium for January 31, Year 2 (strike price $1.00)
December 1, Year 1.	$1.00	$1.08	$0.04
December 31, Year 1. . . .	1.10	1.17	0.12
January 31, Year 2.	1.15	1.15	0.15

Zorba Company has an incremental borrowing rate of 12 percent (1 percent per month) and closes the books and prepares financial statements on December 31.

Required

1. Assume the olive oil was received on December 1, Year 1, and payment was made on January 31, Year 2. There was no attempt to hedge the exposure to foreign exchange risk. Prepare journal entries to account for this import purchase.

2. Assume the olive oil was received on December 1, Year 1, and payment was made on January 31, Year 2. On December 1, Zorba Company entered into a two-month forward contract to purchase 50,000 crowns. The forward contract is properly designated as a fair value hedge of a foreign currency payable. Prepare journal entries to account for the import purchase and foreign currency forward contract.

3. The olive oil was ordered on December 1, Year 1. It was received and paid for on January 31, Year 1. On December 1, Zorba Company entered into a two-month forward contract to purchase 50,000 crowns. The forward contract is properly designated as a fair value hedge of a foreign currency firm commitment. The fair value of the firm commitment is measured through reference to changes in the forward rate. Prepare journal entries to account for the foreign currency forward contract, firm commitment, and import purchase.

4. The olive oil was received on December 1, Year 1, and payment was made on January 31, Year 2. On December 1, Zorba Company purchased a two-month call option for 50,000 crowns. The option was properly designated as a cash flow hedge of a foreign currency payable. Prepare journal entries to account for the import purchase and foreign currency option.

5. The olive oil was ordered on December 1, Year 1. It was received and paid for on December 31, Year 2. On December 1, Zorba Company purchased a two-month call option for 50,000 crowns. The option was properly designated as a fair value hedge of a foreign currency firm commitment. The fair value of the firm commitment is measured through reference to changes in the spot rate. Prepare journal entries to account for the foreign currency option, firm commitment, and import purchase.

Case 7-2

Portofino Company

Portofino Company made purchases on account from three foreign suppliers on December 15, 2009, with payment made on January 15, 2010. Information related to these purchases is as follows:

Supplier	Location	Invoice Price
Beija Flor Ltda.	São Paulo, Brazil	55,000 Brazilian reals
Quetzala SA	Guatemala City, Guatemala	255,000 Guatemalan quetzals
Mariposa SA de CV	Guadalajara, Mexico	400,000 Mexican pesos

Portofino Company's fiscal year ends December 31.

Required

1. Use historical exchange rate information available on the Internet at www.oanda.com to find interbank exchange rates between the U.S. dollar and each foreign currency for the period December 15, 2009, to January 15, 2010.
2. Determine the foreign exchange gains and losses that Portofino would have recognized in net income in 2009 and 2010, and the overall foreign exchange gain or loss for each transaction. Determine for which transaction it would have been most important for Portofino to hedge its foreign exchange risk.
3. Portofino could have acquired a one-month call option on December 15, 2009, to hedge the foreign exchange risk associated with each of the three import purchases. In each case, the option would have had an exercise price equal to the spot rate at December 15, 2009, and would have cost $200. Determine for which hedges, if any, Portofino would have recognized a net gain on the foreign currency option.

Case 7-3

Better Food Corporation

Better Food Corporation (BFC) regularly purchases nutritional supplements from a supplier in Japan with the invoice price denominated in Japanese yen. BFC has experienced several foreign exchange losses in the past year due to increases in the U.S.-dollar price of the Japanese currency. As a result, BFC's CEO, Harvey Carlisle, has asked you to investigate the possibility of using derivative financial instruments, specifically foreign currency forward contracts and foreign currency options, to hedge the company's exposure to foreign exchange risk.

Required

Draft a memo to CEO Carlisle comparing the advantages and disadvantages of using forward contracts and options to hedge foreign exchange risk. Make a recommendation for which type of hedging instrument you believe the company should employ and provide your justification for this recommendation.

References

U.S. Department of Commerce. "Small and Medium-Sized Enterprises Play an Important Role," *Export America*, September 2001.

World Trade Organization. *International Trade Statistics 2009* (www.wto.org).

Chapter Eight

Translation of Foreign Currency Financial Statements

Learning Objectives

After reading this chapter, you should be able to

- Describe the conceptual issues involved in translating foreign currency financial statements.
- Explain balance sheet exposure and how it differs from transaction exposure.
- Describe the concepts underlying the current rate and temporal methods of translation.
- Apply the current rate and temporal methods of translation and compare the results of the two methods.
- Describe the requirements of applicable International Financial Reporting Standards (IFRS) and U.S. generally accepted accounting principles (GAAP).
- Discuss hedging of balance sheet exposure.

INTRODUCTION

In today's global business environment, many companies have operations in foreign countries. In its 2009 10-K report, Ford Motor Company provided a list of subsidiaries located in some 20 different countries around the world. The German automaker Volkswagen AG reports having wholly owned subsidiaries in more than 50 countries other than Germany. Many operations located in foreign countries keep their accounting records and prepare financial statements in the local currency using local accounting principles. To prepare consolidated financial statements, parent companies must restate their foreign subsidiaries' financial statements in terms of the parent company's reporting generally accepted accounting principles (GAAP) and then translate the statements into the parent company's reporting currency. The diversity in national accounting standards and the problems associated with that diversity (such as the GAAP reconciliation for consolidation purposes) are discussed in Chapter 2.

This chapter focuses on the *translation* of foreign currency financial statements for the purpose of preparing consolidated financial statements. We begin by examining the conceptual issues related to translation and then describe the manner in which these issues have been addressed by the International Accounting

Standards Board (IASB) and by the Financial Accounting Standards Board (FASB) in the United States. We then illustrate application of the two methods prescribed by those standard-setters and compare the results from applying the two different methods. We also discuss hedging the net investment in foreign operations to avoid the adverse impact the translation of foreign currency financial statements can have on the consolidated accounts.

TWO CONCEPTUAL ISSUES

In translating foreign currency financial statements into the parent company's reporting currency, two questions must be addressed:

1. What is the appropriate exchange rate to be used in translating each financial statement item?
2. How should the translation adjustment that inherently arises from the translation process be reflected in the consolidated financial statements?

We introduce these issues and the basic concepts underlying the translation of financial statements through the following example.

Example

Parentco, a U.S.-based company, establishes a wholly owned subsidiary, Foreignco, in Foreign Country on January 1 by investing US$600 when the exchange rate between the U.S. dollar and the foreign currency (FC) is FC1 = US$1.00. The equity investment of US$600 is physically converted into FC600. In addition, Foreignco borrows FC400 from local banks on January 2. Foreignco purchases inventory that costs FC900 and maintains FC100 in cash. Foreignco's opening balance sheet appears as follows:

FOREIGNCO
Opening Balance Sheet

Cash	FC 100	Liabilities	FC 400
Inventory	900	Common stock	600
Total	FC1,000	Total	FC1,000

To prepare a consolidated balance sheet at the date of acquisition, all FC balances on Foreignco's balance sheet are translated at the exchange rate of US$1.00 per FC. There is no other exchange rate that possibly could be used on that date. A partial consolidation worksheet at the date of acquisition would appear as follows:

Consolidation Worksheet at Date of Acquisition for Parentco and Its Subsidiary Foreignco

	Parentco US$	Foreignco FC	Exchange Rate	US$	Eliminations Dr.	Eliminations Cr.	Consolidated Balance Sheet US$
Investment	600	—				(1) 600*	0
Cash	(600)	100	$1.00	100			(500)
Inventory	xx	900	$1.00	900			900
Total	xxx	1,000		1,000			400
Liabilities	xx	400	$1.00	400			400
Common stock	xx	600	$1.00	600	(1) 600		0
Total	xxx	1,000		1,000			400

* The elimination entry eliminates Parentco's Investment in Subsidiary account against Foreignco's Common Stock account.

By translating each FC balance on Foreignco's balance sheet at the same exchange rate (US$1.00), Foreignco's US$ translated balance sheet reflects an equal amount of total assets and total liabilities and equity.

Three Months Later

During the period January 1 to March 31, Foreignco engages in no transactions. However, during that period the FC appreciates in value against the US$ such that the exchange rate at March 31 is US$1.20 per FC.

In preparing the March 31 interim consolidated financial statements, Parentco now must choose between the current exchange rate of US$1.20 and the past (historical) exchange rate of US$1.00 to translate Foreignco's balance sheet into U.S. dollars. Foreignco's stockholders' equity must be translated at the historical rate of US$1.00 so that Parentco's Investment account can be eliminated against the subsidiary's common stock in the consolidation worksheet. Two approaches exist for translating the subsidiary's assets and liabilities:

1. All assets and liabilities are translated at the *current exchange rate* (the spot exchange rate on the balance sheet date).
2. Some assets and liabilities are translated at the current exchange rate, and other assets and liabilities are translated at *historical exchange rates* (the exchange rates that existed when the assets and liabilities were acquired).

All Assets and Liabilities Are Translated at the Current Exchange Rate

If the first approach is adopted, in which all assets and liabilities are translated at the current exchange rate, the consolidation worksheet on March 31 would appear as follows:

Consolidation Worksheet Three Months after Date of Acquisition for Parentco and Its Subsidiary Foreignco

	Parentco US$	Foreignco FC	Exchange Rate	US$	Change in US$ Value Since January 1	Eliminations Dr.	Cr.	Consolidated Balance Sheet US$
Investment	600	—					600	0
Cash	(600)	100	**$1.20**	120	**+20**			(480)
Inventory	xx	900	**$1.20**	1,080	**+180**			1,080
Total	xxx	1,000		1,200	+200			600
Liabilities	xx	400	**$1.20**	480	**+80**			480
Common stock	xx	600	$1.00	600	0	600		0
Subtotal	xxx	1,000		1,080	+80			480
Translation adjustment				120	**+120**			120
Total				1,200	+200			600

By translating all assets at the higher current exchange rate, assets are written up in terms of their U.S.-dollar value by US$200. Liabilities are also written up by US$80. To keep the U.S. dollar translated balance sheet in balance, a *positive* (credit) translation adjustment of US$120 must be recorded. As a result, total assets on the consolidated balance sheet are US$120 greater than on January 1, as are consolidated total liabilities and stockholders' equity.

Translating foreign currency balances at the current exchange rate is similar to revaluing foreign currency receivables and payables at the balance sheet date. The translation adjustment is analogous to the *net* foreign exchange gain or loss caused by a change in the exchange rate:

$20 gain on cash + $180 gain on inventory − $80 loss on liabilities = $120 net gain

The net foreign exchange gain (positive translation adjustment) is *unrealized*, that is, it does not result in a cash inflow of US$120 for Parentco. However, the gain can be *realized* by selling Foreignco at the book value of its net assets (FC600) and converting the proceeds into U.S. dollars at the current exchange rate (FC600 × $1.20 = US$720). In that case, Parentco would realize a gain from the sale of its investment in Foreignco that would be due solely to the appreciation in value of the foreign currency:

Proceeds from the sale	$720
Original investment	600
Realized gain	$120

The translation adjustment reflects the *change in the dollar value of the net investment* in Foreignco if the subsidiary were to be sold. In addition, a *positive* translation adjustment signals that the appreciation of the foreign currency will result in an increase in the U.S. dollar value of future foreign-currency dividends to be paid by Foreignco to its parent. For example, a dividend of FC10 distributed on March 31 can be converted into US$12, whereas the same amount of foreign-currency dividend would have been worth only US$10 at the beginning of the year.

Monetary Assets and Liabilities Are Translated at the Current Exchange Rates

Now assume that only monetary assets (cash and receivables) and monetary liabilities (most liabilities) are translated at the current exchange rate. The worksheet to translate Foreignco's financial statements into U.S. dollars on March 31 appears as follows:

Consolidation Worksheet Three Months after Date of Acquisition for Parentco and Its Subsidiary Foreignco

	Parentco US$	Foreignco FC	Foreignco Exchange Rate	Foreignco US$	Change in US$ Value Since January 1	Eliminations Dr.	Eliminations Cr.	Consolidated Balance Sheet US$
Investment	600	—					600	0
Cash	(600)	100	**$1.20**	120	**+20**			(480)
Inventory	XX	900	$1.00	900	0			900
Total	XXX	1,000		1,020	+20			420
Liabilities	XX	400	**$1.20**	480	**+80**			480
Common stock	XX	600	$1.00	600	0	600		0
Subtotal	XXX	1,000		1,080	+80			480
Translation adjustment				(60)	**−60**			(60)
Total				1,020	+20			420

Using this approach, cash is written up by US$20 and liabilities are written up by US$80. To keep the balance sheet in balance, a *negative* (debit) translation adjustment of US$60 must be recorded. As a result, both total assets and total liabilities and stockholders' equity on the consolidated balance sheet are US$20 greater than on January 1.

The translation adjustment is analogous to the *net* foreign exchange gain or loss caused by a change in the exchange rate:

$$\$20 \text{ gain on cash} - \$80 \text{ loss on liabilities} = \$60 \text{ net loss}$$

This net foreign exchange loss (negative translation adjustment) also is *unrealized.* However, the loss can be *realized* through the following process:

1. The subsidiary uses its cash (FC100) to pay its liabilities to the extent possible.
2. The parent sends enough U.S. dollars to the subsidiary to pay its remaining liabilities (FC300). At January 1, the parent would have sent US$300 to pay FC300 of liabilities (at the $1.00/FC1 exchange rate). At March 31, the parent must send US$360 to pay FC300 of liabilities (at the $1.20/FC1 exchange rate). A foreign exchange loss (negative translation adjustment) of US$60 (US$360 – US$300) arises on the net monetary liability position because the foreign currency has appreciated from January 1 to March 31.

Note that under this translation approach, the *negative* translation adjustment does not reflect the change in the U.S.-dollar value of the net investment in Foreignco. Moreover, the *negative* translation adjustment is not consistent with the change in the U.S.-dollar value of future foreign currency dividends. As the foreign currency appreciates, the U.S. dollar value of foreign currency dividends received from Foreignco increases.

Balance Sheet Exposure

As exchange rates change, assets and liabilities translated at the *current* exchange rate change in value from balance sheet to balance sheet in terms of the parent company's reporting currency (for example, U.S. dollar). These items are *exposed* to translation adjustment. Balance sheet items translated at *historical* exchange rates do not change in parent currency value from one balance sheet to the next. These items are *not* exposed to translation adjustment. Exposure to translation adjustment is referred to as balance sheet, translation, or accounting exposure. *Balance sheet exposure* can be contrasted with the *transaction exposure* discussed in Chapter 7 that arises when a company has foreign currency receivables and payables in the following way:

> Transaction exposure gives rise to foreign exchange gains and losses that are ultimately realized in cash; translation adjustments that arise from balance sheet exposure do not directly result in cash inflows or outflows.

Each item translated at the current exchange rate is exposed to translation adjustment. In effect, a separate translation adjustment exists for each of these exposed items. However, positive translation adjustments on assets when the foreign currency appreciates are offset by negative translation adjustments on liabilities. If total exposed assets are equal to total exposed liabilities throughout the year, the translation adjustments (although perhaps significant on an individual basis) net to a zero balance. The *net* translation adjustment needed to keep the consolidated balance sheet in balance is based solely on the net asset or net liability exposure.

A foreign operation will have a *net asset balance sheet exposure* when assets translated at the current exchange rate are greater in amount than liabilities translated at the current exchange rate. A *net liability balance sheet exposure* exists when liabilities translated at the current exchange rate are greater than assets translated at the current exchange rate. The relationship between exchange rate fluctuations, balance sheet exposure, and translation adjustments can be summarized as follows:

Balance Sheet Exposure	Foreign Currency (FC)	
	Appreciates	**Depreciates**
Net asset	Positive translation adjustment	Negative translation adjustment
Net liability	Negative translation adjustment	Positive translation adjustment

Exactly how the translation adjustment should be reported in the consolidated financial statements is a matter of some debate. The major question is whether the translation adjustments should be treated as a *translation gain or loss reported in income* or whether the translation adjustment should be treated as a *direct adjustment to owners' equity without affecting income*. This issue is considered in this chapter in more detail after first examining different methods of translation.

TRANSLATION METHODS

Four major methods of translating foreign currency financial statements have been used worldwide: (1) the current/noncurrent method, (2) the monetary/nonmonetary method, (3) the temporal method, and (4) the current rate (or closing rate) method.

Current/Noncurrent Method

The rules for the current/noncurrent method are as follows: current assets and current liabilities are translated at the current exchange rate; noncurrent assets, noncurrent liabilities, and stockholders' equity accounts are translated at historical exchange rates. There is no theoretical basis underlying this method. Although once the predominant method, the current/noncurrent method has been unacceptable in the United States since 1975, has never been allowed under International Financial Reporting Standards, and is seldom used in other countries.

Monetary/Nonmonetary Method

To remedy the lack of theoretical justification for the current/noncurrent method, Hepworth developed the monetary/nonmonetary method of translation in 1956.[1] Under this method, monetary assets and liabilities are translated at the current exchange rates; nonmonetary assets, nonmonetary liabilities, and stockholders' equity accounts are translated at historical exchange rates. Monetary assets are those assets whose value does not fluctuate over time—primarily cash and receivables. Nonmonetary assets are assets whose monetary value can fluctuate. They consist of marketable securities, inventory, prepaid expenses, investments, fixed assets, and intangible assets; that is, all assets other than cash and receivables.

---

[1] Samuel R. Hepworth, *Reporting Foreign Operations* (Ann Arbor: University of Michigan, Bureau of Business Research, 1956).

Monetary liabilities are those liabilities whose monetary value cannot fluctuate over time, which is true for most payables.

Under the monetary/nonmonetary method, cash, receivables, and payables carried on the foreign operation's balance sheet are exposed to foreign exchange risk. There is a net asset exposure when cash plus receivables exceed payables, and a net liability exposure when payables exceed cash plus receivables.

$$\text{Cash} + \text{Receivables} > \text{Payables} \rightarrow \text{Net asset exposure}$$
$$\text{Cash} + \text{Receivables} < \text{Payables} \rightarrow \text{Net liability exposure}$$

The previous example in which Foreignco's monetary assets and monetary liabilities were translated at the current exchange rate demonstrates the monetary/nonmonetary method. In that example, Foreignco had a net liability exposure that, when coupled with an appreciation in the foreign currency, resulted in a negative translation adjustment.

One way to understand the concept of exposure underlying the monetary/nonmonetary method is to assume that the foreign operation's cash, receivables, and payables are actually foreign currency assets and liabilities of the parent company. For example, consider the Japanese subsidiary of a New Zealand parent company. The Japanese subsidiary's yen receivables that result from sales in Japan may be thought of as Japanese yen receivables of the New Zealand parent resulting from export sales to Japan. If the New Zealand parent had yen receivables on its balance sheet, an increase in the value of the yen would result in a foreign exchange gain. There also would be a foreign exchange gain on the Japanese yen held in cash by the parent. These foreign exchange gains would be offset by a foreign exchange loss on the parent's Japanese yen payables resulting from foreign purchases. Whether a net gain or a net loss exists depends on the relative size of yen cash and receivables versus yen payables. Under the monetary/nonmonetary method, the translation adjustment measures the net foreign exchange gain or loss on the foreign operation's cash, receivables, and payables as if those items were actually carried on the books of the parent.

Temporal Method

The basic objective underlying the temporal method of translation is to produce a set of parent currency translated financial statements as if the foreign subsidiary had actually used the parent currency in conducting its operations. For example, land carried on the books of a foreign subsidiary should be translated such that it is reported on the consolidated balance sheet at the amount of parent currency that would have been spent if the parent had sent parent currency to the subsidiary to purchase the land. Assume that a piece of land costs ¥12,000,000 and is acquired at a time when one yen costs NZ$0.016. A New Zealand parent would send NZ$192,000 to its Japanese subsidiary to acquire the land—this is the land's historical cost in parent currency terms.

Consistent with the temporal method's underlying objective, assets and liabilities reported on the foreign operation's balance sheet at historical cost are translated at historical exchange rates to yield an equivalent historical cost in parent currency terms. Conversely, assets and liabilities reported on the foreign operation's balance sheet at a current (or future) value are translated at the current exchange rate to yield an equivalent current value in parent currency terms. (As is true under any translation method, equity accounts are translated at historical exchange rates.) Application of these rules maintains the underlying valuation method (historical cost or current value) used by the foreign subsidiary in accounting for its assets and liabilities.

Cash, receivables, and most liabilities are carried at current or future values under the traditional historical cost model of accounting. These balance sheet accounts are translated at the current exchange rate under the temporal method. By coincidence, the temporal method and monetary/nonmonetary method produce similar results in this situation. The two methods diverge from one another only when nonmonetary assets are carried at current value. Many national accounting standards require inventory to be carried on the balance sheet at the lower of historical cost or current market value. Although a nonmonetary asset, the temporal method requires translation of inventory at the current exchange rate when it is written down to market value. In those jurisdictions in which marketable securities are carried at current market value, such as is required by International Financial Reporting Standards (IFRS) and U.S. GAAP, marketable securities are also translated at the current exchange rate.

The temporal method generates either a net asset or a net liability balance sheet exposure depending on whether assets carried at current value are greater than or less than liabilities carried at current value. This can be generalized as follows:

$$\text{Cash} + \text{Marketable securities} + \text{Receivables} + \text{Inventory (when carried at current value)} > \text{Liabilities} \rightarrow \text{Net asset exposure}$$

$$\text{Cash} + \text{Marketable securities} + \text{Receivables} + \text{Inventory (when carried at current value)} < \text{Liabilities} \rightarrow \text{Net liability exposure}$$

Because liabilities (current plus long-term) usually are greater than assets translated at current rates, *a net liability exposure generally exists when the temporal method is used.*

Under the temporal method, income statement items are translated at exchange rates that exist when the revenue is generated or the expense is incurred. For most items, an assumption can be made that the revenue or expense is incurred evenly throughout the accounting period and an average-for-the-period exchange rate can be used for translation. Some expenses—such as cost of goods sold, depreciation of fixed assets, and amortization of intangibles—are related to assets carried at historical cost. Because these assets are translated at historical exchange rates, the expenses related to them must be translated at historical exchange rates as well.

The major difference between the translation adjustment resulting from the use of the temporal method and a foreign exchange gain or loss on a foreign currency transaction is that the translation adjustment is not necessarily realized through inflows or outflows of cash. The translation adjustment *could be realized* as a gain or loss only if (1) the foreign subsidiary collects all its receivables in yen cash and then uses its cash to pay off liabilities to the extent possible, and (2) *if there is a net asset exposure* the excess of cash over liabilities is remitted to the parent where it is converted into parent currency, or *if there is a net liability exposure* the parent sends parent currency to its foreign subsidiary which is converted into foreign currency to pay the remaining liabilities.

Current Rate Method

The fourth major method used in translating foreign currency financial statements is the current rate method. The fundamental concept underlying the current rate method is that a parent's entire investment in a foreign operation is exposed to foreign exchange risk and translation of the foreign operation's financial statements should reflect this risk. To measure the net investment's exposure to foreign exchange risk:

- All assets and liabilities of the foreign operation are translated using the *current exchange rate.*
- Equity accounts are translated at *historical exchange rates.*

The balance sheet exposure measured by the current rate method is equal to the foreign operation's net asset position (total assets minus total liabilities).

$$\text{Total assets} > \text{Total liabilities} \rightarrow \text{Net asset exposure}$$

A positive translation adjustment results when the foreign currency appreciates, and a negative translation adjustment results when the foreign currency depreciates (assuming that assets exceed liabilities). The translation adjustment arising when the current rate method is used also is unrealized. It can become a realized gain or loss if the foreign operation is sold (for its book value) and the foreign currency proceeds from the sale are converted into parent currency.

Under the current rate method, revenues and expenses are translated using the exchange rate in effect at the date of accounting recognition. In most cases an assumption can be made that the revenue or expense is incurred evenly throughout the year and an average-for-the-period exchange rate is used. However, when an income item, such as a gain or loss on the sale of an asset, occurs at a specific point in time, the exchange rate at that date should be used for translation. Alternatively, all income statement items may be translated at the current exchange rate.

The example above in which all of Foreignco's assets and liabilities were translated at the current exchange rate demonstrates the current rate method. Foreignco has a net asset exposure that, because of the appreciation in the foreign currency, resulted in a positive translation adjustment. The positive translation adjustment that arises under the current rate method becomes a realized foreign exchange gain if the foreign subsidiary is sold at its foreign currency book value and the foreign currency proceeds are converted into parent currency.

The current rate method and the temporal method are the two methods required to be used under IAS 21, *The Effects of Changes in Foreign Exchange Rates,* and FASB ASC 830, *Foreign Currency Matters.* A summary of the appropriate exchange rate for selected financial statement items under these two methods is presented in Exhibit 8.1.

Translation of Retained Earnings

Stockholders' equity items are translated at historical exchange rates under both the temporal and current rate methods. This creates somewhat of a problem in translating retained earnings, which is a composite of many previous transactions: revenues, expenses, gains, losses, and declared dividends occurring over the life of the company. At the end of the first year of operations, foreign currency (FC) retained earnings are translated as follows:

Net income in FC	[Translated per method used to translate income statement items]	=	+ Net income in PC
−Dividends in FC	× Historical exchange rate when declared	=	− Dividends in PC
Ending R/E in FC			Ending R/E in PC

EXHIBIT 8.1
Exchange Rates
Used under the
Current Rate
Method and the
Temporal Method
for Selected
Financial Statement
Items

Balance Sheet		
Assets	Exchange Rate Used under the Current Rate Method	Exchange Rate Used under the Temporal Method
Cash and receivables	Current	Current
Marketable securities	Current	Current*
Inventory at market	Current	Current
Inventory at cost	Current	Historical
Prepaid expenses	Current	Historical
Property, plant, and equipment	Current	Historical
Intangible assets	Current	Historical
Liabilities		
Current liabilities	Current	Current
Deferred income	Current	Historical
Long-term debt	Current	Current
Stockholders' Equity		
Capital stock	Historical	Historical
Additional paid-in capital	Historical	Historical
Retained earnings	Historical	Historical
Dividends	Historical	Historical

Income Statement		
	Exchange Rate Used under the Current Rate Method	Exchange Rate Used under the Temporal Method
Revenues	Average	Average
Most expenses	Average	Average
Cost of goods sold	Average	Historical
Depreciation of property, plant, and equipment	Average	Historical
Amortization of intangibles	Average	Historical

*Marketable debt securities classified as hold-to-maturity are carried at cost and therefore are translated at the historical exchange rate under the temporal method.

The ending parent currency retained earnings in Year 1 becomes the beginning parent currency retained earnings for Year 2 and the translated retained earnings in Year 2 (and subsequent years) is then determined as follows:

Beginning R/E in FC	(from last year's translation)	=	Beginning R/E in PC
+ Net income in FC	[Translated per method used to translate income statement items]		
		=	+ Net income in FC
− Dividends in FC	× Historical exchange rate when declared		
		=	− Dividends in PC
Ending R/E in PC			Ending R/E in PC

The same approach is used for translating retained earnings under both the current rate and the temporal methods. The only difference is that translation of the current period's net income is done differently under the two methods.

Complicating Aspects of the Temporal Method

Under the temporal method, it is necessary to keep a record of the exchange rates that exist when inventory, prepaid expenses, fixed assets, and intangible assets are acquired because these assets, carried at historical cost, are translated at historical exchange rates. Keeping track of the historical rates for these assets is not necessary under the current rate method. Translating these assets at historical rates makes application of the temporal method more complicated than the current rate method.

Calculation of Cost of Goods Sold (COGS)

Under the *current rate method,* cost of goods sold (COGS) in foreign currency (FC) is simply translated into the parent currency (PC) using the average-for-the-period exchange rate (ER):

$$\text{COGS in FC} \times \text{Average ER} = \text{COGS in PC}$$

Under the *temporal method,* COGS must be decomposed into beginning inventory, purchases, and ending inventory and each component of COGS must then be translated at its appropriate historical rate. For example, if beginning inventory (FIFO basis) in Year 2 was acquired evenly throughout the fourth quarter of Year 1, then the average exchange rate in the fourth quarter of Year 1 will be used to translate beginning inventory. Likewise, the fourth-quarter (4thQ) Year 2 exchange rate will be used to translate Year 2 ending inventory. If purchases were made evenly throughout Year 2, then the average Year 2 exchange rate will be used to translate purchases:

Beginning inventory in FC	× Historical ER e g., 4thQ Year 1)	=	Beginning inventory in PC
+ Purchases in FC	× Average ER, Year 2	=	+ Purchases in PC
− Ending inventory in FC	× Historical ER (e.g., 4thQ Year 2)	=	− Ending Inventory in PC
COGS in FC			COGS in PC

There is no single exchange rate that can be used to directly translate COGS in FC into COGS in PC.

Application of the Lower of Cost and Market Rule

Under the *current rate method,* the ending inventory reported on the foreign currency balance sheet is translated at the current exchange rate regardless of whether it is carried at cost or at a lower market value. Application of the *temporal method* requires the foreign currency cost and foreign currency market value of the inventory to be translated into parent currency at appropriate exchange rates, and the *lower of the parent currency cost or parent currency market value* is reported on the consolidated balance sheet. As a result of this procedure, it is possible for inventory to be carried at cost on the foreign currency balance sheet and at market value on the parent currency consolidated balance sheet, and vice versa.

Fixed Assets, Depreciation, Accumulated Depreciation

Under the *temporal method*, fixed assets acquired at different times must be translated at different (historical) exchange rates. The same is true for depreciation of fixed assets and accumulated depreciation related to fixed assets.

For example, assume that a company purchases a piece of equipment on January 1, Year 1, for FC1,000 when the exchange rate is $1.00 per FC1. Another item of equipment is purchased on January 1, Year 2, for FC4,000 when the exchange rate is $1.20 per FC1. Both pieces of equipment have a five-year useful life. Under the temporal method, the amount at which equipment would be reported on the consolidated balance sheet on December 31, Year 2, when the exchange rate is $1.50 per FC1, would be:

$$
\begin{array}{lcl}
\text{FC1,000} \times \$1.00 &=& \$1,000 \\
\underline{\text{FC4,000}} \times \$1.20 &=& \underline{\$4,800} \\
\text{FC5,000} & & \$5,800
\end{array}
$$

Depreciation expense for Year 2 under the temporal method would be calculated as follows:

$$
\begin{array}{lcl}
\text{FC}\quad 200 \times \$1.00 &=& \$\quad 200 \\
\underline{\text{FC}\quad 800} \times \$1.20 &=& \underline{\$\quad 960} \\
\text{FC1,000} & & \$1,160
\end{array}
$$

Accumulated depreciation at December 31, Year 2, under the temporal method would be calculated as follows:

$$
\begin{array}{lcl}
\text{FC}\quad 400 \times \$1.00 &=& \$\quad 400 \\
\underline{\text{FC}\quad 800} \times \$1.20 &=& \underline{\$\quad 960} \\
\text{FC1,200} & & \$1,360
\end{array}
$$

Similar procedures apply for intangible assets as well.

Under the *current rate method*, equipment would be reported on the December 31, Year 2, balance sheet at FC5,000 × $1.50 = $7,500. Depreciation expense would be translated at the average Year 2 exchange rate of $1.40: FC1,000 × $1.40 = $1,400, and accumulated depreciation would be FC1,200 × $1.50 = $1,800.

In this example, the foreign subsidiary has only two fixed assets that require translation. For subsidiaries that own hundreds and thousands of fixed assets, the temporal method, versus the current rate method, can require substantial additional work.

DISPOSITION OF TRANSLATION ADJUSTMENT

The first issue related to the translation of foreign currency financial statements is selection of the appropriate method. The second issue in financial statement translation relates to *where the resulting translation adjustment should be reported in the consolidated financial statements.* There are two prevailing schools of thought with regard to this issue:

1. *Translation gain or loss in net income.* Under this treatment, the translation adjustment is considered to be a gain or loss analogous to the gains and losses that

arise from foreign currency transactions and should be reported in income in the period in which the fluctuation in exchange rate occurs.

The first of two conceptual problems with treating translation adjustments as gains/losses in net income is the gain or loss is unrealized; that is, there is no accompanying cash inflow or outflow. The second problem is the gain or loss may not be consistent with economic reality. For example, the depreciation of a foreign currency may have a *positive* impact on the foreign operation's export sales and income, but the particular translation method used gives rise to a translation *loss*.

2. *Cumulative translation adjustment in stockholders' equity (other comprehensive income).* The alternative to reporting the translation adjustment as a gain or loss in net income is to include it in stockholders' equity as a component of other comprehensive income. In effect, this treatment defers the gain or loss in stockholders' equity until it is realized in some way. As a balance sheet account, other comprehensive income is not closed at the end of the accounting period and will fluctuate in amount over time.

The two major translation methods and the two possible treatments for the translation adjustment give rise to four possible combinations:

Combination	Translation Method	Disposition of Translation Adjustment
A	Temporal	Gain or loss in net income
B	Temporal	Deferred in stockholders' equity (other comprehensive income)
C	Current rate	Gain or loss in net income
D	Current rate	Deferred in stockholders' equity (other comprehensive income)

U.S. GAAP

Prior to 1975, there were no authoritative rules in the United States as to which translation method to use or where the translation adjustment should be reported in the consolidated financial statements. Different companies used different combinations, creating a lack of comparability across companies. In 1975, to eliminate this noncomparability, the FASB issued SFAS 8, *Accounting for the Translation of Foreign Currency Transactions and Foreign Currency Financial Statements.* SFAS 8 mandated use of the temporal method with translation gains/losses reported in income by all companies for all foreign operations (Combination A).

U.S. multinational companies were strongly opposed to SFAS 8. Specifically, they considered reporting translation gains and losses in income to be inappropriate given that the gains and losses are unrealized. Moreover, because currency fluctuations often reverse themselves in subsequent quarters, artificial volatility in quarterly earnings resulted.

After releasing two Exposure Drafts proposing new translation rules, the FASB finally issued SFAS 52, *Foreign Currency Translation,* in 1981. This resulted in a complete overhaul of U.S. GAAP with regard to foreign currency translation. SFAS 52 was approved by a narrow four-to-three vote of the FASB, indicating how contentious the issue of foreign currency translation has been. The guidance provided in SFAS 52 was incorporated into FASB ASC 830, *Foreign Currency Matters,* in 2009.

FASB ASC 830

Implicit in the *temporal method* is the assumption that foreign subsidiaries of U.S. multinational corporations have very close ties to their parent company and would actually carry out their day-to-day operations and keep their books in the U.S. dollar if they could. To reflect the integrated nature of the foreign subsidiary with its U.S. parent, the translation process should create a set of U.S.-dollar translated financial statements as if the dollar had actually been used by the foreign subsidiary. This is described as the *U.S.-dollar perspective* to translation.

Subsequently, the FASB recognized that, whereas some foreign entities are closely integrated with their parent and do in fact conduct much of their business in U.S. dollars, other foreign entities are relatively self-contained and integrated with the local economy and primarily use a foreign currency in their daily operations. For the first type of entity, the FASB determined that the U.S.-dollar perspective still applies.

For the second relatively independent type of entity, a *local-currency perspective* to translation is applicable. For this type of entity, the FASB determined that a different translation methodology is appropriate; namely, the *current rate method* should be used for translation and translation adjustments should be reported as a separate component in other comprehensive income (Combination D in the preceding table).

Functional Currency

To determine whether a specific foreign operation is (1) integrated with its parent or (2) self-contained and integrated with the local economy, the FASB developed the concept of the functional currency. The *functional currency* is the primary currency of the foreign entity's operating environment. It can be either the parent's currency (US$) or a foreign currency (generally the local currency). The functional currency orientation results in the following rule:

Functional Currency	Translation Method	Translation Adjustment
U.S. dollar	Temporal method	Gain (loss) in income
Foreign currency	Current rate method	Separate component of stockholders' equity (accumulated other comprehensive income)

When a foreign operation is sold or otherwise disposed of, the cumulative translation adjustment related to it that has been deferred in a separate component of stockholders' equity is transferred to income as a realized gain or loss.

In addition to introducing the concept of the functional currency, the FASB also introduced some new terminology. The *reporting currency* is the currency in which the entity prepares its financial statements. For U.S.-based corporations, this is the U.S. dollar. If a foreign operation's functional currency is the U.S. dollar, foreign currency balances must be *remeasured* into U.S. dollars using the temporal method with translation adjustments reported as remeasurement gains and losses in income. When a foreign currency is the functional currency, foreign currency balances are *translated* using the current rate method and a translation adjustment is reported on the balance sheet.

The functional currency is essentially a matter of fact. However, the FASB states that for many cases "management's judgment will be required to determine the functional currency in which financial results and relationships are measured with the greatest degree of relevance and reliability" (FASB ASC 830-10-55-4).

EXHIBIT 8.2
U.S. GAAP
Indicators for
Determining the
Functional Currency

	Indication That the Functional Currency Is the:	
Indicator	**Foreign Currency (FC)**	**Parent's Currency**
Cash flow	Primarily in FC and does not affect parent's cash flows	Directly impacts parent's cash flows on a current basis
Sales price	Not affected on short-term basis by changes in exchange rates	Affected on short-term basis by changes in exchange rates
Sales market	Active local sales market	Sales market mostly in parent's country or sales denominated in parent's currency
Expenses	Primarily local costs	Primarily costs for components obtained from parent's country
Financing	Primarily denominated in FC, and FC cash flows are adequate to service obligations	Primarily obtained from parent or denominated in parent currency or FC cash flows not adequate to service obligations
Intercompany transaction	Low volume of intercompany transactions; no extensive interrelationships with parent's operations	High volume of intercompany transactions and extensive interrelationships with parent's operations

U.S. GAAP provides a list of indicators to guide parent company management in its determination of a foreign entity's functional currency (see Exhibit 8.2). However, no guidance is provided as to how these indicators are to be weighted in determining the functional currency. Leaving the decision about identifying the functional currency up to management allows some leeway in this process.

Different companies approach the selection of functional currency in different ways: "For us it was intuitively obvious" versus "It was quite a process. We took the six criteria and developed a matrix. We then considered the dollar amount and the related percentages in developing a point scheme. Each of the separate criteria was given equal weight (in the analytical methods applied)."[2]

Research has shown that the weighting schemes used by U.S. multinationals for determining the functional currency might be biased toward selection of the foreign currency as the functional currency.[3] This would be rational behavior for multinationals given that, when the foreign currency is the functional currency, the translation adjustment is reported on the balance sheet and does not affect net income.

Highly Inflationary Economies

For those foreign entities located in a *highly inflationary economy*, U.S. GAAP mandates use of the *temporal method* with *translation gains/losses reported in income*. A country is defined as a highly inflationary economy if its cumulative three-year inflation exceeds 100 percent. With compounding, this equates to an average of approximately 26 percent per year for three years in a row. Countries that have met this definition in the past include Argentina, Brazil, Israel, Mexico, Turkey, and Zimbabwe. In any given year, a country may or may not be classified as highly inflationary in accordance with U.S. GAAP, depending on its most recent three-year experience with inflation.

[2] Jerry L. Arnold and William W. Holder, *Impact of Statement 52 on Decisions, Financial Reports and Attitudes* (Morristown, NJ: Financial Executives Research Foundation, 1986), p. 89.
[3] Timothy S. Doupnik and Thomas G. Evans, "Functional Currency as a Strategy to Smooth Income," *Advances in International Accounting*, 1988.

One reason for this rule is to avoid a "disappearing plant problem" that exists when the current rate method is used in a country with high inflation. Remember that under the current rate method, all assets (including fixed assets) are translated at the current exchange rate. To see the problem this creates in a highly inflationary economy, consider the following hypothetical example: The Brazilian subsidiary of a U.S. parent purchased land at the end of 1984 for 10,000,000 cruzeiros (CR$) when the exchange rate was $0.001 per CR$1. Under the *current rate method,* the land would be reported in the parent's consolidated balance sheet at $10,000.

	Historical Cost		Current Exchange Rate		Consolidated Balance Sheet
1984	CR$10,000,000	×	$0.001	=	$10,000

In 1985, Brazil experienced roughly 200 percent inflation. Accordingly, with the forces of purchasing power parity at work, the cruzeiro plummeted against the U.S. dollar to a value of $0.00025 at the end of 1985. Under the current rate method, land now would be reported in the parent's consolidated balance sheet at $2,500 and a negative translation adjustment of $7,500 would result.

	Historical Cost		Current Exchange Rate		Consolidated Balance Sheet
1985	CR$10,000,000	×	$0.00025	=	$2,500

Using the current rate method, land has lost 75 percent of its U.S.-dollar value in one year, and land is not even a depreciable asset!

High rates of inflation continued in Brazil, reaching the high point of roughly 1,800 percent in 1993. As a result of applying the current rate method, the land, which was originally reported on the 1984 consolidated balance sheet at $10,000, was carried on the 1993 balance sheet at less than $1.00.

In an Exposure Draft preceding the issuance of current authoritative guidance, the FASB proposed requiring companies with operations in highly inflationary countries to first *restate* the historical costs for inflation and then *translate* using the current rate method. For example, with 200 percent inflation in 1985, the land would have been written up to CR$40,000,000 and then translated at the current exchange rate of $0.00025. This would have produced a translated amount of $10,000, the same as in 1984.

Companies objected to making inflation adjustments, however, because of a lack of reliable inflation indexes in many countries. The FASB backed off from requiring the restate/translate approach. Instead, current U.S. GAAP requires that the temporal method be used in highly inflationary countries. In our example, land would be translated at the historical rate of $0.001 at each balance sheet date and carried at $10,000, thus avoiding the disappearing plant problem.

INTERNATIONAL FINANCIAL REPORTING STANDARDS

IAS 21, *The Effects of Changes in Foreign Exchange Rates,* contains guidance for the translation of foreign currency financial statements. To determine the appropriate translation method, IAS 21 originally required foreign subsidiaries to be classified as either (1) foreign operations that are integral to the operations of the reporting enterprise or (2) foreign entities. As part of a comprehensive improvements project, IAS 21 was revised in 2003, adopting the functional currency approach developed years earlier by the FASB. The revised standard defines *functional currency* as the currency of the primary economic environment in which a subsidiary operates. It can be either the same as the currency in which the parent presents its financial statements or it can be a different, foreign currency. IAS 21 provides a list of factors that should be considered in determining the functional currency (shown in Exhibit 8.3). Unlike U.S. GAAP, IAS 21 provides a hierarchy of primary and secondary factors to be considered in determining the functional currency of a foreign subsidiary. In addition, there are several differences in the factors to be considered under IFRS and U.S. GAAP. As a result of these differences, it is possible that a foreign subsidiary could be viewed as having one functional currency under IFRS but a different functional currency under U.S. GAAP.

IAS 21 requires the financial statements of a foreign subsidiary that has a functional currency different from the reporting currency of the parent to be translated using the current rate method, with the resulting translation adjustment reported as a separate component of stockholders' equity. Upon disposal of a foreign subsidiary, the cumulative translation adjustment related to that particular foreign subsidiary is transferred to income in the same period in which the gain or loss on disposal is recognized. The financial statements of a foreign subsidiary whose functional currency is the same as the parent's reporting currency are translated using the temporal method, with the resulting translation adjustment reported currently as a gain or loss in income. The same combinations are required under U.S. GAAP.

For foreign subsidiaries whose functional currency is the currency of a hyperinflationary economy, IAS 21 requires the parent first to restate the foreign financial statements for inflation using rules in IAS 29, *Financial Reporting in Hyperinflationary Economies,* and then translate the statements into parent company currency using the current exchange rate. All balance sheet accounts, including stockholders' equity, and all income statement accounts are translated

EXHIBIT 8.3
IAS 21 Functional Currency Indicators

Factors Considered in Determining the Functional Currency

In accordance with IAS 21, *The Effects of Changes in Foreign Exchange Rates,* the following factors should be considered first in determining an entity's functional currency:

1. The currency (*a*) that mainly influences sales prices for goods and services and (*b*) of the country whose competitive forces and regulations mainly determine the sales price of its goods and services.
2. The currency that mainly influences labor, material, and other costs of providing goods and services.

If the primary factors listed above are mixed and the functional currency is not obvious, the following secondary factors must be considered:

3. The currency in which funds from financing activities are generated.
4. The currency in which receipts from operating activities are usually retained.
5. Whether the activities of the foreign operation are an extension of the parent's or are carried out with a significant amount of autonomy.
6. Whether transactions with the parent are a large or a small proportion of the foreign entity's activities.
7. Whether cash flows generated by the foreign operation directly affect the cash flow of the parent and are available to be remitted to the parent.
8. Whether operating cash flows generated by the foreign operation are sufficient to service existing and normally expected debt or whether the foreign entity will need funds from the parent to service its debt.

at the current exchange rate. This approach is substantively different from U.S. GAAP, which requires translation of financial statements of a foreign subsidiary operating in a highly inflationary economy using the temporal method. IAS 29 provides no specific definition for hyperinflation but suggests that a cumulative three-year inflation rate approaching or exceeding 100 percent is evidence that an economy is hyperinflationary. We describe the process of adjusting financial statements for inflation under IAS 29 in Chapter 9.

THE TRANSLATION PROCESS ILLUSTRATED

To provide a basis for demonstrating the translation procedures prescribed by both IFRS and U.S. GAAP assume that Multico (a U.S.-based company) forms a wholly owned subsidiary in Italy (Italco) on December 31, Year 0. On that date, Multico invests $1,000,000 in exchange for all of the subsidiary's capital stock. Given the exchange rate of €1.00 = $1.00, the initial capital investment is €1,000,000, of which €600,000 is immediately invested in inventory and the remainder is held in cash. Thus, Italco begins operations on January 1, Year 1, with stockholders' equity (net assets) of €1,000,000 and net monetary assets of €400,000. Italco's beginning balance sheet on January 1, Year 1, is shown in Exhibit 8.4.

During Year 1, Italco purchased property and equipment, acquired a patent, and made additional purchases of inventory, primarily on account. A five-year loan was negotiated to help finance the purchase of equipment. Sales were made, primarily on account, and expenses were incurred. Income after taxes of €825,000 was generated, with dividends of €325,000 declared on December 1, Year 1. Financial statements for Year 1 (in euros) appear in Exhibit 8.5.

To properly translate the euro financial statements into U.S. dollars, we must gather exchange rates between the euro and the U.S. dollar at various times. Relevant exchange rates are as follows:

January 1, Year 1	$1.00
Rate when property and equipment were acquired and long-term debt was incurred, January 15, Year 1	0.98
Rate when patent was acquired, February 1, Year 1	0.97
Average Year 1	0.95
Rate when dividends were declared, December 1, Year 1	0.92
Average for the month of December	0.91
December 31, Year 1	0.90

As can be seen, the euro steadily declined in value against the U.S. dollar during the year.

EXHIBIT 8.4

ITALCO
Beginning Balance Sheet
January 1, Year 1

Assets	€	Liabilities and Equity	€
Cash	400,000	Capital stock	1,000,000
Inventory	600,000		1,000,000
	1,000,000		

EXHIBIT 8.5
Italco's Financial
Statements, Year 1

Income Statement
Year 1

	€
Sales	8,000,000
Cost of goods sold	6,000,000
Gross profit	2,000,000
Selling and administrative expenses	500,000
Depreciation expense	200,000
Amortization expense	20,000
Interest expense	180,000
Income before income taxes	1,100,000
Income taxes	275,000
Net income	825,000

Statement of Retained Earnings
Year 1

	€
Retained earnings, 1/1/Y1	0
Net income, Y1	825,000
Less: Dividends, 12/1/Y1	(325,000)
Retained earnings, 12/31/Y1	500,000

Balance Sheet
December 31, Year 1

Assets	€	Liabilities and Equity	€
Cash	550,000	Accounts payable	330,000
Accounts receivable	600,000	Total current liabilities . .	330,000
Inventory*	800,000	Long-term debt	2,000,000
Total current assets	1,950,000	Total liabilities	2,330,000
Property and equipment . . .	2,000,000	Capital stock	1,000,000
Less: Accumulated		Retained earnings	500,000
depreciation	(200,000)	Total	3,830,000
Patents, net	80,000		
Total assets	3,830,000		

* Inventory is carried at first-in, first-out (FIFO) cost; ending inventory was acquired evenly throughout the month of December.

TRANSLATION OF FINANCIAL STATEMENTS: CURRENT RATE METHOD

The first step in translating foreign currency financial statements is the determination of the functional currency. Assuming that the euro is the functional currency, the income statement and statement of retained earnings would be translated into U.S. dollars using the current rate method, as shown in Exhibit 8.6.

All revenues and expenses are translated at the exchange rate in effect at the date of accounting recognition. The weighted-average exchange rate for Year 1 is used because each revenue and expense in this illustration would have been recognized evenly throughout the year. However, when an income account, such as

EXHIBIT 8.6
Translation of
Income Statement
and Statement of
Retained Earnings:
Current Rate
Method

Income Statement Year 1			
	€	**Translation Rate***	**US$**
Sales	8,000,000	$0.95 (A)	7,600,000
Cost of goods sold	6,000,000	0.95 (A)	5,700,000
Gross profit	2,000,000		1,900,000
Selling and administrative expenses . .	500,000	0.95 (A)	475,000
Depreciation expense	200,000	0.95 (A)	190,000
Amortization expense	20,000	0.95 (A)	19,000
Interest expense	180,000	0.95 (A)	171,000
Income before income taxes	1,100,000		1,045,000
Income taxes	275,000	0.95 (A)	261,250
Net income	825,000		783,750

Statement of Retained Earnings Year 1			
	€	**Translation Rate***	**US$**
Retained earnings, 1/1/Y1	0		0
Net income, Year 1	825,000	From income statement	783,750
Less: Dividends, 12/1/Y1	(325,000)	0.92 (H)	(299,000)
Retained earnings, 12/31/Y1	500,000		484,750

* Indicates the exchange rate used and whether the rate is the current rate (C), the average rate (A), or a historical rate (H).

a gain or loss, occurs at a specific time, the exchange rate as of that date is applied. Depreciation and amortization expense are also translated at the average rate for the year. These expenses accrue evenly throughout the year even though the journal entry may have been delayed until year-end for convenience.

The translated amount of net income for Year 1 is transferred from the income statement to the statement of retained earnings. Dividends are translated at the exchange rate that exists on the date of declaration.

Translation of the Balance Sheet

Italco's translated balance sheet is shown in Exhibit 8.7. All assets and liabilities are translated at the current exchange rate. Capital stock is translated at the exchange rate that existed when the capital stock was originally issued. Retained earnings at December 31, Year 1, is brought down from the statement of retained earnings. Application of these procedures results in total assets of $3,447,000, and total liabilities and equities of $3,581,750. The balance sheet is brought back into balance by creating a negative translation adjustment of $134,750, which is treated as a decrease in stockholders' equity.

Note that the translation adjustment for Year 1 is a *negative* $134,750 (debit balance). The sign of the translation adjustment (positive or negative) is a function of two factors: (1) the nature of the balance sheet exposure (asset or liability) and (2) the direction of change in the exchange rate (appreciation or depreciation). In this illustration, Italco has a *net asset exposure* (total assets translated at the current

EXHIBIT 8.7
Translation of
Balance Sheet:
Current Rate
Method

Balance Sheet December 31, Year 1			
Assets	**€**	**Translation Rate***	**US$**
Cash	550,000	$0.90 (C)	495,000
Accounts receivable	600,000	0.90 (C)	540,000
Inventory	800,000	0.90 (C)	720,000
Total current assets	1,950,000		1,755,000
Property and equipment	2,000,000	0.90 (C)	1,800,000
Less: Accumulated depreciation.	(200,000)	0.90 (C)	(180,000)
Patents, net	80,000	0.90 (C)	72,000
Total assets	3,830,000		3,447,000
Liabilities and Equity			
Accounts payable	330,000	$0.90 (C)	297,000
Total current liabilities	330,000		297,000
Long-term debt	2,000,000	0.90 (C)	1,800,000
Total liabilities	2,330,000		2,097,000
Capital stock	1,000,000	1.00 (H)	1,000,000
Retained earnings	500,000	from statement of retained earnings	484,750
Cumulative translation adjustment . . .	—	to balance	(134,750)
Total equity	1,500,000		1,350,000
	3,830,000		3,447,000

exchange rate are greater than total liabilities translated at the current exchange rate), and the euro has *depreciated,* creating a *negative translation adjustment.*

The translation adjustment can be derived as a balancing figure that brings the balance sheet back into balance. The translation adjustment also can be calculated by considering the impact of exchange rate changes on the beginning balance and subsequent changes in the net asset position. The following steps are applied:

1. The net asset balance of the subsidiary at the beginning of the year is translated at the exchange rate in effect on that date.

2. Individual increases and decreases in the net asset balance during the year are translated at the rates in effect when those increases and decreases occur. Only a few events actually change net assets (e.g., net income, dividends, stock issuance, and the acquisition of treasury stock). Transactions such as the acquisition of equipment or the payment of a liability have no effect on total net assets.

3. The translated beginning net asset balance (*a*) and the translated value of the individual changes (*b*) are then combined to arrive at the relative value of the net assets being held prior to the impact of any exchange rate fluctuations.

4. The ending net asset balance is then translated at the current exchange rate to determine the reported value after all exchange rate changes have occurred.

5. The translated value of the net assets prior to any rate changes (*c*) is compared with the ending translated value (*d*). The difference is the result of exchange rate changes during the period. If (*c*) is greater than (*d*), then a negative (debit) translation adjustment arises. If (*d*) is greater than (*c*), a positive (credit) translation adjustment results.

Computation of Translation Adjustment

According to the process just described, determination of the translation adjustment to be reported for Italco in this example is calculated as follows:

	€			US$
Net asset balance, 1/1/Y1	1,000,000	×	$1.00	= 1,000,000
Change in net assets:				
Net income, Year 1	825,000	×	0.95	= 783,750
Dividends, 12/1/Y1	(325,000)	×	0.92	= (299,000)
Net asset balance, 12/31/Y1	1,500,000			1,484,750
Net asset balance, 12/31/Y1, at current exchange rate	1,500,000	×	0.90	= 1,350,000
Translation adjustment, Year 1(negative)				134,750

Since this subsidiary began operations at the beginning of the current year, $134,750 is the amount of cumulative translation adjustment reported on the consolidated balance sheet. The translation adjustment is reported as a separate component of equity only until the foreign operation is sold or liquidated. In the period in which a sale or liquidation occurs, the cumulative translation adjustment related to the particular foreign subsidiary must be removed from equity and reported as part of the gain or loss on the sale of the investment.

REMEASUREMENT OF FINANCIAL STATEMENTS: TEMPORAL METHOD

Now assume that a careful examination of the functional currency indicators leads Multico's management to conclude that Italco's functional currency is the U.S. dollar. In that case, the euro financial statements will be remeasured into U.S. dollars using the temporal method and the remeasurement gain or loss will be reported in income. To ensure that the remeasurement gain or loss is reported in income, it is easier to remeasure the balance sheet first (as shown in Exhibit 8.8).

According to the procedures outlined in Exhibit 8.1, under the temporal method, cash, receivables, and liabilities are remeasured into U.S. dollars using the current exchange rate of $0.90. Inventory, carried at first-in, first-out (FIFO) cost; property and equipment; patents; and the capital stock account are remeasured at historical rates. These procedures result in total assets of $3,604,600, and liabilities and capital stock of $3,097,000. In order for the balance sheet to balance, retained earnings must be $507,600. The accuracy of this amount is verified below.

Remeasurement of Income Statement

The remeasurement of Italco's income statement and statement of retained earnings is demonstrated in Exhibit 8.9. Revenues and expenses incurred evenly throughout the year (sales, selling and administrative expenses, interest expense, and income taxes) are remeasured at the average exchange rate. Expenses related to assets remeasured at historical exchange rates (depreciation expense and amortization expense) are themselves remeasured at relevant historical rates.

EXHIBIT 8.8
Translation of
Balance Sheet:
Temporal Method

Balance Sheet
December 31, Year 1

Assets	€	Translation Rate*	US$
Cash	550,000	$0.90 (C)	495,000
Accounts receivable	600,000	0.90 (C)	540,000
Inventory	800,000	0.91 (H)	728,000
Total current assets	1,950,000		1,763,000
Property and equipment	2,000,000	0.98 (H)	1,960,000
Less: Accumulated depreciation	(200,000)	0.98 (H)	(196,000)
Patents, net	80,000	0.97 (H)	77,600
Total assets	3,830,000		3,604,600
Liabilities and Equity			
Accounts payable	330,000	$0.90 (C)	297,000
Total current liabilities	330,000		297,000
Long-term debt	2,000,000	0.90 (C)	1,800,000
Total liabilities	2,330,000		2,097,000
Capital stock	1,000,000	1.00 (H)	1,000,000
Retained earnings	500,000	to balance	507,600
Total equity	1,500,000		1,507,600
	3,830,000		3,604,600

EXHIBIT 8.9
Translation of
Income Statement
and Statement of
Retained Earnings
Temporal Method

Income Statement
Year 1

	€	Translation Rate*	US$
Sales	8,000,000	$0.95 (A)	7,600,000
Cost of goods sold	6,000,000	calculation (H)	5,762,000
Gross profit	2,000,000		1,838,000
Selling and administrative expenses	500,000	0.95 (A)	475,000
Depreciation expense	200,000	0.98 (H)	196,000
Amortization expense	20,000	0.97 (H)	19,400
Interest expense	180,000	0.95 (A)	171,000
Income before income taxes	1,100,000		976,600
Income taxes	(275,000)	0.95 (A)	(261,250)
Remeasurement gain	—	to balance	91,250
Net income	825,000		806,600

Statement of Retained Earnings
Year 1

	€	Translation Rate*	US$
Retained earnings, 1/1/Y1	0		0
Net income, Year 1	825,000	From income statement	806,600
Less: Dividends, 12/1/Y1	(325,000)	0.92 (H)	(299,000)
Retained earnings, 12/31/Y1	500,000		507,600

Cost of goods sold is remeasured at historical exchange rates using the following procedure. Beginning inventory was acquired on January 1 and is remeasured at the exchange rate from that date ($1.00). Purchases were made evenly throughout the year and are therefore remeasured at the average rate for the year ($0.95). Ending inventory (at FIFO cost) was purchased evenly throughout the month of December and the average exchange rate for that month ($0.91) is used to remeasure that component of cost of goods sold. These procedures result in cost of goods sold of $5,762,000, calculated as follows:

	€				US$
Beginning inventory	600,000	×	$1.00	=	600,000
Plus: Purchases.	6,200,000	×	$0.95	=	5,890,000
Less: Ending inventory	(800,000)	×	$0.91	=	(728,000)
Cost of goods sold.	6,000,000				5,762,000

The ending balance in retained earnings on the balance sheet and in the statement of retained earnings must reconcile with one another. Given that dividends are remeasured into a U.S.-dollar equivalent of $299,000 and the ending balance in retained earnings on the balance sheet is $507,600, net income must be $806,600.

In order for the amount of income reported in the statement of retained earnings and in the income statement to reconcile with one another, a remeasurement gain of $91,250 is required in the calculation of income. Without this remeasurement gain, the income statement, statement of retained earnings, and balance sheet will not be consistent with one another.

The remeasurement gain can be calculated by considering the impact of exchange rate changes on the subsidiary's balance sheet exposure. Under the temporal method, Italco's balance sheet exposure is defined by its net monetary asset or net monetary liability position. Italco began Year 1 with net monetary assets (cash) of €400,000. During the year, however, expenditures of cash and the incurrence of liabilities caused monetary liabilities (Accounts payable + Long-term debt = €2,330,000) to exceed monetary assets (Cash + Accounts receivable = €1,150,000). A net monetary liability position of €1,180,000 exists at December 31, Year 1. The remeasurement gain is computed by translating the beginning net monetary asset position and subsequent changes in monetary items at appropriate exchange rates and then comparing this with the U.S.-dollar value of net monetary liabilities at year-end based on the current exchange rate.

Computation of Remeasurement Gain

	€	Translation Rate	US$
Net monetary assets, 1/1/Y1	400,000	$1.00	400,000
Increase in monetary items:			
Sales, Year 1	8,000,000	0.95	7,600,000
Decrease in monetary items:			
Purchases of inventory, Year 1	(6,200,000)	0.95	(5,890,000)
Selling and administrative expenses,			
Year 1	(500,000)	0.95	(475,000)
Payment of interest, Year 1	(180,000)	0.95	(171,000)

	€	Translation Rate	US$
Income taxes, Year 1	(275,000)	0.95	(261,250)
Purchase of property and equipment, 1/15/Y1	(2,000,000)	0.98	(1,960,000)
Acquisition of patent, 2/1/Y1	(100,000)	0.97	(97,000)
Dividends, 12/1/Y1	(325,000)	0.92	(299,000)
Net monetary liabilities, 12/31/Y	(1,180,000)		(1,153,250)
Net monetary liabilities, 12/31/Y1, at the current exchange rate	(1,180,000)	0.90	(1,062,000)
Remeasurement gain			(91,250)

If Italco had maintained its net monetary asset position (cash) of €400,000 for the entire year, a remeasurement loss of $40,000 would have resulted. (The euro amount held in cash was worth $400,000 [€400,000 × $1.00] at the beginning of the year and $360,000 [€400,0000 × $0.90] at year-end.) However, the net monetary asset position is not maintained. Indeed, a net monetary liability position arises. The *depreciation* of the foreign currency coupled with an increase in *net monetary liabilities* generates a *remeasurement gain* for the year.

COMPARISON OF THE RESULTS FROM APPLYING THE TWO DIFFERENT METHODS

The use of different translation methods can have a significant impact on Multico's consolidated financial statements. The chart below shows differences for Italco in several key items under the two different translation methods:

Item	Translation Method		Difference
	Current Rate	Temporal	
Net income	$ 783,750	$ 806,600	+ 2.9%
Total assets	$3,447,000	$3,604,600	+4.6%
Total equity	$1,350,000	$1,507,600	+11.7%
Return on equity	58.1%	53.5%	−9.4%

If the temporal method is applied, net income is 2.9 percent greater, total assets are 4.6 percent greater, and total equity is 11.7 percent greater than if the current rate method is applied. Because of the larger amount of equity under the temporal method, return on equity (net income/total equity) is only 53.5 percent as opposed to 58.1 percent using the current rate method.

It should be noted that the temporal method does not always result in larger net income (and a greater amount of equity) than the current rate method. For example, if Italco had maintained its net monetary asset position throughout the year, a remeasurement loss would have been computed under the temporal method, leading to lower income than under the current rate method. Moreover, if the euro had appreciated during Year 1, the current rate method would have resulted in higher net income.

The important point is that selection of translation method can have a significant impact on the amounts reported by a parent company in its consolidated financial statements. Different functional currencies selected by different companies in the same industry could have a significant impact on the comparability of financial statements within that industry.

In addition to differences in amounts reported in the consolidated financial statements, the results of the Italco illustration can be used to demonstrate several conceptual differences between the two translation methods.

Underlying Valuation Method

Using the temporal method, Italco's property and equipment was remeasured as follows:

Property and equipment	€2,000,000	×	$0.98 H	=	$1,960,000

By multiplying the historical cost in euros by the historical exchange rate, $1,960,000 represents the U.S.-dollar equivalent historical cost of this asset. It is the amount of U.S. dollars that the parent company would have had to pay to acquire assets having a cost of €2,000,000 when the exchange rate was $0.98 per euro.

Property and equipment was translated under the current rate method as follows:

Property and equipment	€2,000,000	×	$0.90 C	=	$1,800,000

The $1,800,000 amount is not readily interpretable. It does not represent the U.S.-dollar equivalent historical cost of the asset; that amount is $1,960,000. It also does not represent the U.S.-dollar equivalent current cost of the asset, because €2,000,000 is not the current cost of the asset in Italy. The $1,800,000 amount is simply the product of multiplying two numbers together!

Underlying Relationships

The following table reports the values for selected financial ratios calculated from the original foreign currency financial statements and from the U.S.-dollar translated statements using the two different translation methods.

		US$	
Ratio	€	Current Rate	Temporal
Current ratio (Current assets/Current liabilities)	5.91	5.91	5.94
Debt/equity ratio (Total liabilities/Total equities)	1.55	1.55	1.39
Gross profit ratio (Gross profit/Sales)	25.0%	25.0%	24.2%
Return on equity (Net income/Total equity)	55.0%	58.1%	53.5%

The temporal method distorts all of the ratios as measured in the foreign currency. The subsidiary appears to be more liquid, less highly leveraged, and less profitable than it does in euro terms.

The current rate method maintains the first three ratios, but return on equity is distorted. This distortion occurs because income was translated at the average-for-the-period exchange rate whereas total equity was translated at the current exchange rate. In fact, any ratio that combines balance sheet and income statement figures, such as turnover ratios, will be distorted because of the use of the average rate for income and the current rate for assets and liabilities.

Conceptually, when the current rate method is employed, income statement items can be translated either at exchange rates in effect when sales are made and expenses are incurred (approximated by the average rate) or at the current exchange rate at the balance sheet date. IFRS and U.S. GAAP require the average exchange rate to be used. In this illustration, if revenues and expenses had been translated at the current exchange rate, net income would have been $742,500 (€825,000 × $0.90), and the return on equity would have been 55.0 percent ($742,500/$1,350,000), exactly the amount reflected in the euro financial statements.

HEDGING BALANCE SHEET EXPOSURE

When a foreign operation is determined to have the parent's reporting currency as its functional currency, or is located in a highly inflationary economy, remeasurement gains and losses will be reported in the consolidated income statement. Management of multinational companies might wish to avoid reporting remeasurement losses in income because of the perceived negative impact this has on the company's stock price or the adverse effect on incentive compensation. Likewise, when the foreign operation has a foreign currency as its functional currency management might wish to avoid reporting negative translation adjustments in stockholders' equity because of the adverse impact on ratios such as the debt to equity ratio.

Translation adjustments and remeasurement gains/losses are a function of two factors: (1) changes in the exchange rate and (2) balance sheet exposure. While individual companies have no influence over exchange rates, there are several techniques that parent companies can use to hedge the balance sheet exposures of their foreign operations. Each of these techniques involves creating an equilibrium between foreign currency asset and foreign currency liability balances that are translated at current exchange rates.

Balance sheet exposure can be hedged through the use of a derivative financial instrument such as a forward contract or foreign currency option, or through the use of a nonderivative hedging instrument such as a foreign currency borrowing. To illustrate, assume that Italco's functional currency is the euro; this creates a *net asset balance sheet exposure.* Multico believes that the euro will lose value over the course of the next year, thereby generating a negative translation adjustment that will reduce consolidated stockholders' equity. Multico can hedge this balance sheet exposure by borrowing euros for a period of time, thus creating an offsetting euro liability exposure. As the euro depreciates, a foreign exchange gain will arise on the euro liability that offsets the negative translation adjustment arising from the translation of Italco's financial statements.

As an alternative to the euro borrowing, Multico might have acquired a euro call option to hedge its balance sheet exposure. As the euro depreciates, the fair value of the call option should increase resulting in a gain. Both IFRS and U.S. GAAP provide that the gain or loss on a hedging instrument that is designated and effective as a *hedge of the net investment in a foreign operation* should be reported in the same manner as the translation adjustment being hedged. Thus, the foreign exchange gain on the euro borrowing or the gain on the foreign currency option would be included in other comprehensive income along with the negative translation adjustment arising from the translation of Italco's financial statements. This is an exception to the general rule that foreign currency gains and losses are taken directly to net income. In the event that the gain on the hedging instrument is greater than the translation adjustment being hedged, the excess is taken to net income. Exhibit 8.10 contains disclosures made by International Business Machines Corporation (IBM) in its 2009 annual report with respect to hedging net investments in foreign operations.

The paradox of hedging a balance sheet exposure is that in the process of avoiding an unrealized translation adjustment, realized foreign exchange gains and

EXHIBIT 8.10

INTERNATIONAL BUSINESS MACHINES CORPORATION
Annual Report
2009

Excerpt from Note L. Derivatives and Hedging Transactions

Long-Term Investments in Foreign Subsidiaries (Net Investment)

A significant portion of the company's foreign currency denominated debt portfolio is designated as a hedge of net investment to reduce the volatility in stockholders' equity caused by changes in foreign currency exchange rates in the functional currency of major foreign subsidiaries with respect to the U.S. dollar. The company also uses cross-currency swaps and foreign exchange forward contracts for this risk management purpose. At December 31, 2009, the total notional amount of derivative instruments designated as net investment hedges was $1.0 billion.

losses can result. Consider Multico's foreign currency borrowing to hedge a euro exposure. At initiation of the loan, Multico will convert the borrowed euros into U.S. dollars at the spot exchange rate. When the liability matures, Multico will purchase euros at the spot rate prevailing at that date to repay the loan. The change in exchange rate over the life of the loan will generate a realized gain or loss. If the euro depreciates as expected, the result will be a realized foreign exchange gain that will offset the negative translation adjustment in other comprehensive income. Although the net effect on other comprehensive income is zero, there is a net increase in cash as a result of the hedge. If the euro unexpectedly appreciates, a realized foreign exchange loss will occur. This will be offset by a positive translation adjustment in other comprehensive income, but a net decrease in cash will arise. While a hedge of a net investment in a foreign operation eliminates the possibility of reporting a negative translation adjustment in other comprehensive income, the result can be realized gains and losses that affect cash flow.

Exhibit 8.11 presents an excerpt from the notes to the consolidated financial statements in Nokia Corporation's 2009 annual report filed on Form 20-F. Nokia prepares its financial statements in accordance with IFRS, and the excerpt describes Nokia's compliance with IAS 39 with respect to hedging of net investments. Nokia uses forward contracts, options, and foreign currency borrowings to hedge its balance sheet exposures. Hedge accounting is applied when hedges are properly documented and effective. Changes in fair value of forward contracts attributable to changes in the spot rate, changes in the intrinsic value of options, and foreign exchange gains and losses on foreign currency borrowings are deferred in stockholders' equity until the subsidiary whose balance sheet exposure is being hedged is sold or liquidated. This also is consistent with the guidance provided under U.S. GAAP.

DISCLOSURES RELATED TO TRANSLATION

Accounting standards requires an analysis of the change in the cumulative translation adjustment account to be presented in the financial statements or notes thereto. Many U.S. companies comply with this requirement by including a column titled "Accumulated Other Comprehensive Income" in their statement of stockholders' equity. Exhibit 8.12 demonstrates this method of disclosure as used by Mattel, Inc. In 2009 Mattel has three items that affect AOCI, including one labeled Currency translation adjustments. The company does not disclose the balance in currency translation adjustments at the end of each year, just the change in the account for the year. A positive translation adjustment (credit balance) was added to AOCI in 2009 ($52.210 million). Although not presented in Exhibit 8.12,

EXHIBIT 8.11

NOKIA CORPORATION
Form 20-F
2009

Excerpt from Note 1. Accounting Principles

Foreign Currency Hedging of Net Investments

The Group also applies hedge accounting for its foreign currency hedging on net investments. Qualifying hedges are those properly documented hedges of the foreign exchange rate risk of foreign currency-denominated net investments that meet the requirements set out in IAS 39. The hedge must be effective both prospectively and retrospectively.

The Group claims hedge accounting in respect of forward foreign exchange contracts, foreign currency–denominated loans, and options, or option strategies, which have zero net premium or a net premium paid, and where the terms of the bought and sold options within a collar or zero premium structure are the same.

For qualifying foreign exchange forwards the change in fair value that reflects the change in spot exchange rates is deferred in shareholders' equity. The change in fair value that reflects the change in forward exchange rates less the change in spot exchange rates is recognized in the profit and loss account within financial income and expenses. For qualifying foreign exchange options the change in intrinsic value is deferred in shareholders' equity. Changes in the time value are at all times recognized directly in the profit and loss account as financial income and expense. If a foreign currency–denominated loan is used as a hedge, all foreign exchange gains and losses arising from the transaction are recognized in shareholders' equity.

Accumulated fair value changes from qualifying hedges are released from shareholders' equity into the profit and loss account only if the legal entity in the given country is sold, liquidated, repays its share capital or is abandoned.

EXHIBIT 8.12

MATTEL, INC.
Annual Report
2009

Consolidated Statements of Stockholders' Equity (excerpt reflecting 2009 only)

	Common Stock	Additional Paid-In Capital	Treasury Stock	Retained Earnings	Accumulated Other Comprehensive (Loss) Income	Total Stockholders' Equity
			(In thousands)			
Balance, December 31, 2008	441,369	1,642,092	(1,621,264)	2,085,573	(430,635)	2,117,135
Comprehensive income:						
Net income				528,704		528,704
Change in net unrealized (loss) on derivative instruments					(19,805)	(19,805)
Defined benefit pension plans, net prior service cost, and net actuarial loss					18,696	18,696
Currency translation adjustments					52,210	52,210
Comprehensive income				528,704	51,101	579,805
Issuance of treasury stock for stock option exercises		(17,219)	48,115			30,896
Other issuance of treasury stock		(209)	209			0
Restricted stock units		(26,658)	18,566			(8,092)
Deferred compensation			(672)		(323)	(995)
Share-based compensation		49,962				49,962

Continued

EXHIBIT 8.12 *(Concluded)*

	Common Stock	Additional Paid-In Capital	Treasury Stock	Retained Earnings	Accumulated Other Comprehensive (Loss) Income	Total Stockholders' Equity
			(In thousands)			
Tax benefits from share-based payment arrangements		36,726				36,726
Dividend equivalents for restricted stock units				(3,095)		(3,095)
Dividends.				(271,353)		(271,353)
Balance, December 31, 2009	$441,369	$1,684,694	$(1,555,046)	$2,339,506	$(379,534)	$2,530,989

Mattel had a negative currency translation adjustment of $192.577 million in 2008 and a positive currency translation adjustment of $86.653 in 2007. From the signs of these translation adjustments reported in AOCI we can infer that the currencies in which Mattel's foreign subsidiaries operate, on average, appreciated against the U.S. dollar in 2007 and 2009, but depreciated against the U.S. dollar in 2008.

EXHIBIT 8.13

BASF GROUP
Annual Report
2009

Consolidated Statements of Recognized Income and Expense

Development of income and expense recognized directly in equity of shareholders of BASF SE (million €)

	Retained Earnings	Other Comprehensive Income					
	Actuarial Gains/ Losses; Asset Celling	Foreign Currency Translation Adjustment	Fair Value Changes in Available-For-Sale Securities	Cash Flow Hedges	Revaluation Due to Acquisition of Majority of Shares	Total of Other Comprehensive Income	Total Income and Expense Recognized Directly in Equity
As of January 1, 2009	(1,511)	(637)	668	(137)	10	(96)	(1,607)
Additions	(22)	—	32	206	—	238	216
Releases	—	83	—	—	(2)	81	81
Deferred taxes	108	(1)	(2)	(64)	—	(67)	41
As of December 31, 2009	(1,425)	(555)	698	5	8	156	(1,269)
As of January 1, 2008	(874)	(497)	680	(21)	12	174	(700)
Additions	(782)	(142)	—	(170)	—	(312)	(1,094)
Releases	—	—	(12)	7	(2)	(7)	(7)
Deferred taxes	145	2	—	47	—	49	194
As of December 31, 2008	(1,511)	(637)	668	(137)	10	(96)	(1,607)

IAS 21 also requires companies to provide information related to their cumulative translation adjustments. Exhibit 8.13 presents a portion of the Germany-based BASF Group's Consolidated Statement of Recognized Income and Expense, which details the "development of income and expenses recognized directly in equity." This statement shows that BASF had a cumulative translation adjustment with a negative balance of €497 million on January 1, 2008, recorded a negative translation adjustment of €142 million for the year 2008, and ended 2008 with a negative cumulative translation adjustment of €637 million. A positive translation adjustment of €83 million arose in 2009, which caused the negative balance in the cumulative translation adjustment to be only €555 million at December 31, 2009.

The cumulative translation adjustment reported in other comprehensive income relates to BASF's foreign subsidiaries that have a functional currency other than the euro. The company also has foreign subsidiaries that have the euro as functional currency for which the temporal method of translation is appropriate. Note 5 to BASF's financial statements (shown in Exhibit 8.14) states that "Income

EXHIBIT 8.14

BASF GROUP
Form 20-F
2009

---

5. Other operating income

(Million €)

	2009	2008
Reversal and adjustment of provisions	348	209
Revenue from miscellaneous revenue-generating activities.	116	178
Gains from foreign currency and hedging transactions.	171	433
Income from the translation of financial statements in foreign currencies.	34	24
Gains from disposal of property, plant and equipment and divestitures	79	70
Gains on the reversal of impairment losses on receivables	77	30
Other.	364	360
Total.	**1,189**	**1,304**

The *reversal and adjustment of provisions* primarily related to risks arising from personnel obligations, from lawsuits and damage claims as well as from various other items as part of the normal course of business and the reversal of the provisions for risks related to the pharmaceutical business divested in 2001 in the amount of €80 million. Provisions were reversed or adjusted if the circumstances on the balance sheet date are such that utilization is not expected at all or to a lesser extent.

Revenue from miscellaneous revenue-generating activities primarily represents income from rentals and logistics services.

Income from foreign currency and hedging transactions related to foreign currency transactions, the measurement of receivables and payables in foreign currencies and currency derivatives as well as other hedging transactions with market values.

Income from the translation of financial statements in foreign currencies included gains arising from the use of the temporal method.

In 2009, gains on the disposal of property, plant, and equipment and divestitures resulted primarily from the sale of parts of the polystyrene business and the sale of property, plant and equipment.

Gains on the reversal of allowances for doubtful business-related receivables resulted chiefly from receivables in the Agricultural Solutions and Performance Products segments in South America.

Other gains comprise refunds and settlements; write-ups on property, plant and equipment; gains from precious metal trading and miscellaneous sales as well as a number of other items.

from the translation of financial statements in foreign currencies" is reported in Other operating income on the income statement. Note 6 (not shown) indicates that translation losses are included in Other operating expenses.

Although there is no specific requirement to do so, many companies include a description of their translation procedures in their "summary of significant accounting policies" in the notes to the financial statements. The following excerpt from IBM's 2006 annual report illustrates this type of disclosure:

Translation of Non-U.S. Currency Amounts

Assets and liabilities of non-U.S. subsidiaries that have a local functional currency are translated to United States (U.S.) dollars at year-end exchange rates. Translation adjustments are recorded in accumulated other comprehensive income/(loss) in the Consolidated Statement of Changes in Equity. Income and expense items are translated at weighted-average rates of exchange prevailing during the year.

Inventories, plant, rental machines and other property—net, and other nonmonetary assets and liabilities of non-U.S. subsidiaries and branches that operate in U.S. dollars are translated at the approximate exchange rates prevailing when the company acquired the assets or liabilities. All other assets and liabilities denominated in a currency other than U.S. dollars are translated at year-end exchange rates with the transaction gain or loss recognized in other (income) and expense. Cost of sales and depreciation are translated at historical exchange rates. All other income and expense items are translated at the weighted-average rates of exchange prevailing during the year. These translation gains and losses are included in net income for the period in which exchange rates change.[4]

Summary

1. The two major issues related to the translation of foreign currency financial statements are (a) which method should be used, and (b) where the resulting translation adjustment should be reported in the consolidated financial statements.

2. Translation methods differ on the basis of which accounts are translated at the current exchange rate and which are translated at historical rates. Accounts translated at the current exchange rate are exposed to translation adjustment. Different translation methods give rise to different concepts of balance sheet exposure and translation adjustments of differing sign and magnitude.

3. Under the current rate method, all assets and liabilities are translated at the current exchange rate, giving rise to a net asset balance sheet exposure. Appreciation in the foreign currency will result in a positive translation adjustment. Depreciation in the foreign currency will result in a negative translation adjustment. By translating assets carried at historical cost at the current exchange rate, the current rate method maintains relationships that exist among account balances in the foreign currency financial statements but distorts the underlying valuation method used by the foreign operation.

4. Under the temporal method, assets carried at current or future value (cash, marketable securities, receivables) and liabilities are translated (remeasured) at the current exchange rate. Assets carried at historical cost and stockholders' equity are translated (remeasured) at historical exchange rates. When liabilities are greater than the sum of cash, marketable securities, and receivables, a net liability balance sheet exposure exists. Appreciation in the foreign currency will result in a negative translation adjustment (remeasurement loss). Depreciation in the

[4] IBM Corporation, 2009 Annual Report, Note A. Significant Accounting Policies, p. 76.

foreign currency will result in a positive translation adjustment (remeasurement gain). By translating (remeasuring) assets carried at historical cost at historical exchange rates, the temporal method maintains the underlying valuation method used by the foreign operation but distorts relationships that exist among account balances in the foreign currency financial statements.

5. The appropriate combination of translation method and disposition of translation adjustment is determined under both IFRS and U.S. GAAP by identifying the functional currency of a foreign operation. The financial statements of foreign operations whose functional currency is different from the parent's reporting currency are translated using the current rate method, with the translation adjustment included in stockholders' equity. The financial statements of foreign operations whose functional currency is the same as the parent's reporting currency are translated using the temporal method, with the resulting translation gain or loss reported currently in net income.

6. The only substantive difference in translation rules between IFRS and U.S. GAAP relates to foreign operations that report in the currency of a hyperinflationary economy. IAS 21 requires the parent first to restate the foreign financial statements for inflation using rules in IAS 29 and then to translate the statements into parent-company currency using the current rate method. FASB ASC 830 requires the financial statements of foreign operations that report in the currency of a highly inflationary economy to be translated using the temporal method, as if the U.S. dollar were the functional currency. A country is considered highly inflationary if its cumulative three-year inflation rate exceeds 100 percent.

7. Some companies hedge their balance sheet exposures to avoid reporting remeasurement losses in income and/or negative translation adjustments in stockholder's equity. Foreign exchange gains and losses on foreign currency borrowings or foreign currency derivatives employed to hedge translation-based exposure (under the current rate method) are treated as part of the cumulative translation adjustment in stockholders' equity. Foreign exchange gains and losses on balance sheet hedges used to hedge remeasurement-based exposure (under the temporal method) are offset against remeasurement gain and losses on the income statement.

Questions

1. What are the two major conceptual issues that must be resolved in translating foreign currency financial statements?

2. What factors create a balance sheet (or translation) exposure to foreign exchange risk? How does balance sheet exposure compare with transaction exposure?

3. What is the concept underlying the current rate method of translation? What is the concept underlying the temporal method of translation? How does balance sheet exposure differ under these two methods?

4. What are the major procedural differences in applying the current rate and temporal methods of translation?

5. How does a parent company determine the appropriate method for translating the financial statements of a foreign subsidiary?

6. What are the major differences between IFRS and U.S. GAAP in the translation of foreign currency financial statements?

7. What does the term *functional currency* mean? How is the functional currency determined under IFRS and under U.S. GAAP?

8. Which translation method does U.S. GAAP require for operations in highly inflationary countries? What is the rationale for mandating use of this method?

9. Why might a company want to hedge its balance sheet exposure? What is the paradox associated with hedging balance sheet exposure?

10. How are gains and losses on foreign currency borrowings used to hedge the net investment in a foreign subsidiary reported in the consolidated financial statements?

Exercises and Problems

1. Which of the following items is normally translated the same way under both the current rate and temporal methods of translation?
   a. Inventory
   b. Equipment
   c. Sales revenue
   d. Depreciation expense

2. In translating the financial statements of a foreign subsidiary into the parent's reporting currency under the current rate method, which of the following statements is true?
   a. Expenses are translated using a combination of current and historical exchange rates.
   b. Intangible assets are translated at the historical exchange rates in effect on the date the assets are purchased.
   c. The translation adjustment is a function of the foreign subsidiary's net assets.
   d. The translation adjustment is a function of the relative amount of monetary assets and monetary liabilities held by the foreign subsidiary.

3. A foreign subsidiary of Wampoa Ltd. has one asset (inventory) and no liabilities. The subsidiary operates with a significant degree of autonomy from Wampoa and primarily uses the local currency (the won) in carrying out its transactions. Since the date the inventory was acquired, the won has decreased in value in relation to Wampoa's reporting currency. In translating the foreign subsidiary's peso financial statements into the parent's reporting currency, which of the following is true?
   a. A translation gain must be reported in net income.
   b. A positive translation adjustment must be reported in stockholders' equity.
   c. A negative translation adjustment must be reported in stockholders' equity.
   d. A translation loss must be reported in net income.

4. Which of the following best explains how a translation loss arises when the temporal method of translation is used to translate the foreign currency financial statements of a foreign subsidiary?
   a. The foreign subsidiary has more monetary assets than monetary liabilities, and the foreign currency appreciates in value.
   b. The foreign subsidiary has more monetary liabilities than monetary assets, and the foreign currency depreciates in value.
   c. The foreign subsidiary has more monetary assets than monetary liabilities, and the foreign currency depreciates in value.

d. The foreign subsidiary has more total assets than total liabilities, and the foreign currency appreciates in value.

5. Which method of translation maintains, in the translated financial statements, the underlying valuation methods used in the foreign currency financial statements?

   a. Current rate method; income statement translated at average exchange rate for the year.

   b. Current rate method; income statement translated at exchange rate at the balance sheet date.

   c. Temporal method.

   d. Monetary/nonmonetary method.

6. In accordance with U.S. generally accepted accounting principles (GAAP), which translation combination would be appropriate for a foreign operation whose functional currency is the U.S. dollar?

	Method	Treatment of Translation Adjustment
a.	Temporal	Separate component of stockholders' equity
b.	Temporal	Gain or loss in income statement
c.	Current rate	Separate component of stockholders' equity
d.	Current rate	Gain or loss in income statement

7. The functional currency of Garland Inc.'s Japanese subsidiary is the Japanese yen. Garland borrowed Japanese yen as a partial hedge of its investment in the subsidiary. How should the transaction gain on the foreign currency borrowing be reported in Garland's consolidated financial statements?

   a. The transaction gain is reported as an adjustment to interest expense in the income statement.

   b. The transaction gain is reported as an extraordinary item in the income statement.

   c. The transaction gain is offset against the negative translation adjustment related to the Japanese subsidiary in the stockholders' equity section of the balance sheet.

   d. The transaction gain is offset against the negative translation adjustment related to the Japanese subsidiary on the income statement.

8. Selected balance sheet accounts of a foreign subsidiary of the Pacter Company have been translated into parent currency (F) as follows:

	Translated at	
	Current Rates	**Historical Rates**
Accounts receivable	F100,000	F120,000
Marketable securities, at cost	200,000	240,000
Prepaid insurance	120,000	130,000
Goodwill	250,000	300,000
	F670,000	F790,000

Required:

a. Assuming that the foreign subsidiary is determined to have the foreign currency as its functional currency in accordance with IAS 21, determine the total amount that should be included in Pacter's consolidated balance sheet for the assets listed in accordance with International Financial Reporting Standards (IFRS).

b. Assuming that the foreign subsidiary is determined to have Pacter's reporting currency as its functional currency in accordance with IAS 21, determine the total amount that should be included in Pacter's consolidated balance sheet for the assets listed in accordance with IFRS.

9. The Year 1 financial statements of the Brazilian subsidiary of Artemis Corporation (a Canadian company) revealed the following:

	Brazilian Reals (BRL)
Beginning inventory	100,000
Purchases	500,000
Ending inventory	150,000
Cost of goods sold	450,000

Canadian dollar (C$) exchange rates for 1 BRL as follows:

January 1, Year 1	C$0.45
Average, Year 1	0.42
December 31, Year 1	0.38

The beginning inventory was acquired in the last quarter of the previous year when the exchange rate was C$0.50 = BRL 1; ending inventory was acquired in the last quarter of the current year when the exchange rate was C$0.40 = BRL 1.

Required:

a. Assuming that the current rate method is the appropriate method of translation, determine the amounts at which the Brazilian subsidiary's ending inventory and cost of goods sold should be included in Artemis's Year 1 consolidated financial statements.

b. Assuming that the temporal method is the appropriate method of translation, determine the amounts at which the Brazilian subsidiary's ending inventory and cost of goods sold should be included in Artemis's Year 1 consolidated financial statements.

10. Simga Company's Turkish subsidiary reported the following amounts in Turkish lire (TL) on its December 31, Year 4, balance sheet:

Equipment	TL 100,000,000,000
Accumulated depreciation (straight-line)	32,000,000,000

Additional information related to the equipment is as follows:

Date	Amount Purchased	Useful Life	US$/TL Exchange Rate
1/1/Y1	TL 60,000,000,000	10 years	$0.0000070 = TL 1
1/1/Y3	TL 40,000,000,000	10 years	$0.0000020 = TL 1

U.S.-dollar exchange rates for the Turkish lira for Year 4 are as follows:

January 1, Year 4	$0.0000010
December 31, Year 4	0.0000006

Required:

a. Assume that Turkey is a highly inflationary economy. Determine the amounts at which the Turkish subsidiary's equipment and accumulated depreciation should be reported on Simga Company's December 31, Year 4, consolidated balance sheet in accordance with U.S. GAAP. Determine the net book value for equipment.

b. Now assume that Turkey is not a highly inflationary economy and that the Turkish subsidiary primarily uses Turkish lire in conducting its operations. Determine the amounts at which the Turkish subsidiary's equipment and accumulated depreciation should be reported on Simga Company's December 31, Year 4, consolidated balance sheet in accordance with U.S. GAAP. Determine the net book value for equipment.

11. Alliance Corporation (an Australian company) invests 1,000,000 marks in a foreign subsidiary on January 1, Year 1. The subsidiary commences operations on that date, and generates net income of 200,000 marks during its first year of operations. No dividends are sent to the parent this year. Relevant exchange rates between Alliance's reporting currency (A$) and the mark are as follows:

January 1, Year 1	A$0.15
Average, Year 1	0.17
December 31, 1997	0.21

Required:

Determine the amount of translation adjustment that Alliance will report on its December 31, Year 1, balance sheet.

12. Zesto Company (a U.S. company) establishes a subsidiary in Mexico on January 1, Year 1. The subsidiary begins the year with 1,000,000 Mexican pesos (MXN) in cash and no other assets or liabilities. It immediately uses MXN600,000 to acquire equipment. Inventory costing MXN300,000 is acquired evenly throughout the year and sold for Mex$500,000 cash. A dividend of MXN100,000 is paid to the parent on October 1, Year 1. Depreciation on the equipment for the year is MXN60,000. Currency exchange rates between the U.S. dollar and MXN for Year 1 are as follows:

January 1	U.S.$0.090
October 1	0.080
December 31	0.078
Average for the year	0.085

Required:

Determine the amount of remeasurement loss under the temporal method to be recognized in the Year 1 consolidated income statement.

13. Alexander Corporation (a U.S.-based company) acquired 100 percent of a Swiss company for 8.2 million Swiss francs on December 20, Year 1. At the date

of acquisition, the exchange rate was $0.70 per franc. The acquisition price is attributable to the following assets and liabilities denominated in Swiss francs:

Cash	1,000,000
Inventory	2,000,000
Fixed assets	7,000,000
Notes payable	(1,800,000)

Alexander Corporation prepares consolidated financial statements on December 31, Year 1. By that date, the Swiss franc appreciated to $0.75. Because of the year-end holidays, no transactions took place between the date of acquisition and the end of the year.

Required:

a. Determine the translation adjustment to be reported on Alexander's December 31, Year 1, consolidated balance sheet assuming that the Swiss franc is the Swiss subsidiary's functional currency? What is the economic relevance of this translation adjustment?

b. Determine the remeasurement gain or loss to be reported in Alexander's Year 1 consolidated income assuming that the U.S. dollar is the functional currency? What is the economic relevance of this remeasurement gain or loss?

14. Gramado Company was created as a wholly owned subsidiary of Porto Alegre Corporation on January 1, Year 1. On that date, Porto Alegre invested $42,000 in Gramado's capital stock. Given the exchange on that date of $0.84 per cruzeiro, the initial investment of $42,000 was converted into 50,000 cruzeiros (Cz). Other than the capital investment on January 1, there were no transactions involving stockholders' equity in Year 1. Gramado's cruzeiro-denominated financial statements for Year 2 are as follows:

Income Statement
Year 2

	Cz
Sales	540,000
Cost of goods sold	(310,000)
Gross profit	230,000
Operating expenses	(108,000)
Income before tax	122,000
Income taxes	(40,000)
Net income	82,000

Statement of Retained Earnings
Year 2

	Cz
Retained earnings, 1/1/Y2	154,000
Net income	82,000
Dividends (paid on 12/1/Y2)	(20,000)
Retained earnings, 12/31/Y2	216,000

Balance Sheet
December 31, Year 2

	Cz
Cash	50,000
Receivables	100,000
Inventory	72,000
Plant and equipment (net)	300,000
Less: accumulated depreciation	(70,000)
Total assets	452,000
Liabilities	186,000
Capital stock	50,000
Retained earnings, 12/31/Y2	216,000
Total liabilities and stockholders' equity	452,000

The cruzeiro is the primary currency that Gramado uses in its day-to-day operations. The cruzeiro has steadily fallen in value against the dollar since Porto Alegre made the investment in Gramado on January 1, Year 1. Relevant exchange rates for the cruzeiro for Years 1 and 2 are as follows:

January 1, Year 1	$0.84
Average for Year 1.	0.80
December 31, Year 1	0.75
Average for Year 2.	0.72
December 1, Year 2	0.71
December 31, Year 2	0.70

Required:

a. Translate Gramado Company's Year 2 financial statements into dollars.

b. Compute the translation adjustment for Year 1 and for Year 2 and reconcile these amounts to the cumulative translation adjustment reported on the translated balance sheet at December 31, Year 2.

15. Brookhurst Company (a U.S.-based company) established a subsidiary in South Africa on January 1, Year 1, by investing 300,000 South African rand (ZAR) when the exchange rate was US$0.09/ZAR 1. On that date, the foreign subsidiary borrowed ZAR 500,000 from local banks on a 10-year note to finance the acquisition of plant and equipment. The subsidiary's opening balance sheet (in ZAR) was as follows:

Balance Sheet
January 1, Year 1

Cash	300,000	Long-term debt	500,000
Plant and equipment	500,000	Capital stock	300,000
Total	800,000	Total	800,000

During Year 1, the foreign subsidiary generated sales of ZAR 1,000,000 and net income of ZAR 110,000. Dividends in the amount of ZAR 20,000 were paid to the parent on June 1 and December 1. Inventory was acquired evenly throughout the year, with ending inventory acquired on November 15, Year 1. The subsidiary's ZAR financial statements for the year ended December 31, Year 1, are as follows:

Income Statement
Year 1

	ZAR
Sales	1,000,000
Cost of goods sold	(600,000)
Gross profit	400,000
Depreciation expense.	(50,000)
Other operating expenses	(150,000)
Income before tax	200,000
Income taxes	(90,000)
Net income	110,000

Statement of Retained Earnings
Year 1

	ZAR
Retained earnings, 1/1/Y1	0
Net income	110,000
Dividends	(40,000)
Retained earnings, 12/31/Y1	70,000

Balance Sheet
December 31, Year 1

	ZAR
Cash	80,000
Receivables	150,000
Inventory	270,000
Plant and equipment (net)	450,000
Total assets	950,000
Accounts payable	80,000
Long-term debt	500,000
Common stock	300,000
Retained earnings, 12/31/Y1	70,000
Total liabilities and stockholders' equity	950,000

Relevant exchange rates for Year 1 are as follows (US$ per ZAR):

January 1, Year 1	$0.090
June 1, Year 1	0.095
Average for Year 1.	0.096
November 15, Year 1.	0.100
December 1, Year 1	0.105
December 31, Year 1	0.110

Required:

a. Translate the South African subsidiary's financial statements into U.S. dollars assuming that the South African rand is the functional currency. Compute the translation adjustment by considering the impact of exchange rate changes on the subsidiary's net assets.

b. Translate (remeasure) the South African subsidiary's financial statements into U.S. dollars assuming that the U.S. dollar is the functional currency. Compute the translation adjustment (remeasurement gain or loss) by considering the impact of exchange rate changes on the subsidiary's net monetary asset or liability position.

16. Access the most recent annual report for a U.S.-based multinational company with which you are familiar to complete the requirements of this exercise.

Required:

a. Determine whether the company's foreign operations have a predominant functional currency.

b. If possible, determine the amount of remeasurement gain or loss, if any, reported in net income in each of the three most recent years.

c. Determine the amount of translation adjustment, if any, reported in other comprehensive income in each of the three most recent years. Explain the sign (positive or negative) of the translation adjustment in each of the three most recent years.

d. Determine whether the company hedges net investments in foreign operations. If so, determine the type(s) of hedging instrument(s) used.

17. To complete the requirements of this exercise, access the most recent Form 10-K for both Exxon Mobil and Chevron.

Required:

a. Determine whether each company's foreign operations have a predominant functional currency. Discuss the implication this has for the comparability of financial statements between the two companies.

b. Determine the amount of translation adjustment, if any, reported in other comprehensive income in each of the three most recent years. Explain the sign (positive or negative) of the translation adjustment in each of the three most recent years. Compare the relative magnitude of the translation adjustments between the two companies.

c. Determine whether each company hedges the net investment in foreign operations. If so, determine the type(s) of hedging instrument(s) used.

d. Prepare a brief report comparing and contrasting the foreign currency translation and foreign currency hedging policies of these two companies.

Case 8-1

Columbia Corporation

Columbia Corporation, a U.S.-based company, acquired a 100 percent interest in Swoboda Company in Lodz, Poland, on January 1, Year 1, when the exchange rate for the Polish zloty (PLN) was $0.25. The financial statements of Swoboda as of December 31, Year 2, two years later, are as follows:

Balance Sheet
December 31, Year 2

Assets

Cash	PLN 1,000,000
Accounts receivable (net)	1,650,000
Inventory	4,250,000
Equipment.	12,500,000
Less: Accumulated depreciation	(4,250,000)
Building	36,000,000
Less: Accumulated depreciation	(15,150,000)
Land	3,000,000
Total assets	PLN 39,000,000

Liabilities and Stockholders' Equity

Accounts payable	PLN 1,250,000
Long-term debt	25,000,000
Common stock	2,500,000
Additional paid-in capital	7,500,000
Retained earnings	2,750,000
Total liabilities and stockholders' equity	PLN 39,000,000

Statement of Income and Retained Earnings
For the Year Ending December 31, Year 2

Sales	PLN 12,500,000
Cost of goods sold.	(6,000,000)
Depreciation expense—equipment	(1,250,000)
Depreciation expense—building.	(900,000)
Research and development expense.	(600,000)
Other expenses (including taxes)	(500,000)
Net income	PLN 3,250,000
Plus: Retained earnings, 1/1/Y2	250,000
Less: Dividends, Year 2.	(750,000)
Retained earnings, 12/31/Y2	PLN 2,750,000

Additional information:

- The January 1, Year 2, beginning inventory of PLN 3,000,000 was acquired on December 15, Year 1, when the exchange rate was $0.215. Purchases of inventory during Year 2 were acquired uniformly throughout the year. The December 31, Year 2, ending inventory of PLN 4,250,000 was acquired evenly throughout the fourth quarter of Year 2 when the exchange rate was $0.16.
- All fixed assets were on the books when the subsidiary was acquired except for PLN 2,500,000 of equipment which was acquired on January 3, Year 2 when the exchange rate was $0.18 and PLN 6,000,000 in buildings which was acquired on August 5, Year 2 when the exchange rate was $0.17. Equipment is depreciated on a straight-line basis over 10 years. Buildings are depreciated on a straight-line basis over 40 years. A full year's depreciation is taken in the year of acquisition.

- Dividends were declared and paid on December 15, Year 2, when the exchange rate was $0.155.
- Other exchange rates for Year 2 are:

January 1.	$0.200
Average for the year	0.175
December 31.	0.150

Required

1. Translate Swoboda's financial statements into U.S. dollars in accordance with U.S. GAAP at December 31, Year 2:
   a. Assuming the Polish zloty is the functional currency. (The December 31, Year 1, retained earnings that appeared in Swoboda's translated financial statements was $56,250. The December 31, Year 1, cumulative translation adjustment that appeared in Swoboda's translated balance sheet was negative $506,250.)
   b. Assuming the U.S. dollar is the functional currency. (The December 31, Year 1, retained earnings that appeared in Swoboda's remeasured financial statements was $882,500.)
   c. The same as (b) except Swoboda has no long-term debt. Instead, Swoboda has common stock of PLN 10,000,000 and additional paid-in capital of PLN 25,000,000. The December 31, Year 1, retained earnings that appeared in Swoboda's remeasured financial statements was negative $367,500.

2. Explain why the sign of the translation adjustments in (1a), (1b), and (1c) is positive or negative.

Case 8-2

Palmerstown Company

Palmerstown Company established a subsidiary in a foreign country on January 1, Year 1, by investing 8,000,000 pounds when the exchange rate was $1.00/pound. Palmerstown negotiated a bank loan of 4,000,000 pounds on January 5, Year 1, and purchased plant and equipment in the amount of 10,000,000 pounds January 8, Year 1. Plant and equipment is depreciated on a straight-line basis over a 10-year useful life. The first purchase of inventory in the amount of 1,000,000 pounds was made on January 10, Year 1. Additional inventory of 12,000,000 pounds was acquired at three points in time during the year at an average exchange rate of $0.86/pound. Inventory on hand at year-end was acquired when the exchange rate was $0.83/pound. The first-in, first-out (FIFO) method is used to determine cost of goods sold. Additional exchange rates for the pound during Year 1 are as follows:

January 1–31, Year 1	$1.00
Average Year 1	0.90
December 31, Year 1	0.80

The foreign subsidiary's income statement for Year 1 and balance sheet at December 31, Year 1, are as follows:

**Income Statement
For the Year Ended December 31, Year 1**

	Pounds (in thousands)
Sales	15,000
Cost of goods sold	9,000
Gross profit	6,000
Selling and administrative expenses	3,000
Depreciation expense	1,000
Income before tax	2,000
Income taxes	600
Net income	1,400
Retained earnings, 1/1/Y1	0
Retained earnings, 12/31/Y1	1,400

**Balance Sheet
At December 31, Year 1**

	Pounds (in thousands)
Cash	2,400
Inventory	4,000
Fixed assets	10,000
Less: Accumulated depreciation	(1,000)
Total assets	15,400
Current liabilities	2,000
Long-term debt	4,000
Contributed capital	8,000
Retained earnings	1,400
Total liabilities and stockholders' equity	15,400

As the controller for Palmerstown Company, you have evaluated the characteristics of the foreign subsidiary to determine that the pound is the subsidiary's functional currency.

Required

1. Use an electronic spreadsheet to translate the foreign subsidiary's financial statements into U.S. dollars at December 31, Year 1, in accordance with U.S. GAAP. Insert a row in the spreadsheet after retained earnings and before total liabilities and stockholders' equity for the cumulative translation adjustment. Calculate the translation adjustment separately to verify the amount obtained as a balancing figure in the translation worksheet.
2. Use an electronic spreadsheet to remeasure the foreign subsidiary's financial statements into U.S. dollars at December 31, Year 1, assuming that the U.S. dollar is the subsidiary's functional currency. Insert a row in the spreadsheet after depreciation expense and before income before taxes for the remeasurement gain (loss).

3. Prepare a report for the chief executive officer of Palmerstown Company summarizing the differences that will be reported in the Year 1 consolidated financial statements because the pound, rather than the U.S. dollar, is the foreign subsidiary's functional currency. In your report, discuss the relationship between the current ratio, the debt to equity ratio, and profit margin calculated from the foreign currency financial statements and from the translated U.S.-dollar financial statements. Also, include a discussion of the meaning of the translated U.S.-dollar amounts for inventory and for fixed assets.

Case 8-3

BellSouth Corporation

BellSouth Corporation invested in two wireless communications operations in Brazil in the mid-1990s that are being accounted for under the equity method. The following note is taken from BellSouth Corporation's interim report for the quarter ended March 31, 1999:

Note E—Devaluation of Brazilian Currency

We hold equity interests in two wireless communications operations in Brazil. During January 1999, the government of Brazil allowed its currency to trade freely against other currencies. As a result, the Brazilian Real experienced a devaluation against the U.S. Dollar. The devaluation resulted in the entities recording exchange losses related to their net U.S. Dollar-denominated liabilities. Our share of the foreign exchange rate losses for the first quarter was $280.

These exchange losses are subject to further upward or downward adjustment based on fluctuations in the exchange rates between the U.S. Dollar and the Brazilian Real.

In a press release announcing first quarter 1999 results, BellSouth Corporation provided the following information (as found on the company's Web site):

BellSouth Corporation (NYSE: BLS) reported a 15-percent increase in first quarter earnings per share (EPS) before special items. EPS was 46 cents before a non-cash expense of 14 cents related to Brazil's currency devaluation.

BELLSOUTH CORPORATION
Normalized Earnings Summary ($ in millions, except per share amounts) (unaudited)

	Quarter Ended		
	3/31/99	**3/31/98**	**%Change**
Reported Net Income	$615	$892	(31.1%)
Foreign currency loss [a]	280	—	
Gain on sale of ITT World Directories [b]	—	(96)	
Normalized Net Income	$895	$796	12.4%
Reported Diluted Earnings per Share	$0.32	$0.45	(28.9%)
Foreign currency loss [a]	0.14	—	
Gain on sale of ITT World Directories [b]	—	(0.05)	
Normalized Diluted Earnings per Share	$0.46	$0.40	15.0%

[a] Represents our share of foreign currency losses recorded during first quarter 1999 as a result of the devaluation of the Brazilian Real during January 1999.

[b] Represents the after-tax gain associated with additional proceeds received in first quarter 1998 on the July 1997 sale of ITT World Directories.

Required

Given the disclosure provided by BellSouth Corporation, answer the following questions:

1. Why did the company report a foreign currency loss as a result of the devaluation of the Brazilian real?

2. What does the company mean when it states: "These exchange losses are subject to further upward or downward adjustment based on fluctuations in the exchange rates between the U.S. Dollar and the Brazilian Real"?

3. What is the company's objective in reporting "Normalized Net Income"? Do you agree with the company's assessment that it had a 15 percent increase in first-quarter earnings per share?

References

Arnold, Jerry L., and William W. Holder. *Impact of Statement 52 on Decisions, Financial Reports and Attitudes.* Morristown, NJ: Financial Executives Research Foundation, 1986.

Doupnik, Timothy S., and Thomas G. Evans. "Functional Currency as a Strategy to Smooth Income." *Advances in International Accounting,* 1988.

Hepworth, Samuel R. *Reporting Foreign Operations.* Ann Arbor: University of Michigan, Bureau of Business Research, 1956.

Chapter **Nine**

Additional Financial Reporting Issues

Learning Objectives

After reading this chapter, you should be able to

- Explain the concepts underlying two methods of accounting for changing prices (inflation)—general purchasing power accounting and current cost accounting.
- Describe attempts to account for inflation in different countries, as well as the rules found in International Financial Reporting Standards (IFRS) related to this issue.
- Discuss the various issues related to the accounting for business combinations and the preparation of consolidated financial statements (group accounting).
- Present the approaches used internationally to address the issues related to group accounting, focusing on IFRS.
- Describe IFRS segment reporting requirements.

INTRODUCTION

Chapters 7 and 8 focused on accounting for foreign currency. Chapter 7 discussed foreign currency transactions and hedging activities, and Chapter 8 discussed the translation of foreign currency financial statements. These are two of the most important accounting issues for multinational corporations (MNCs).

This chapter covers three additional financial reporting topics of importance to MNCs. We describe the various alternatives available worldwide to deal with each issue, focusing on the guidance and requirements found in International Financial Reporting Standards (IFRS). The first section deals with the accounting for changing prices (inflation). Companies operating in countries experiencing high rates of inflation, including MNCs with foreign subsidiaries in such countries, must address changing prices. The second section of this chapter covers consolidations, or group accounting, and includes the accounting for business combinations. There are several approaches followed worldwide in accounting for investments in subsidiaries, joint ventures, affiliates, and the like. Whereas consolidation involves the aggregation of assets, liabilities, revenues, and expenses of all companies in a group, segment reporting does the opposite. Segment reporting, the third major topic covered in this chapter, involves the disaggregation of consolidated totals by segment for separate reporting. Geographic segment reporting is an issue that affects only those companies with foreign operations.

ACCOUNTING FOR CHANGING PRICES (INFLATION ACCOUNTING)

Conventional accounting results in a mix of attributes being reflected in the asset section of the balance sheet. Accounts receivable are reported at the net amount expected to be received in the future; short-term investments are reported at either cost or current market value; inventory is carried at the lower of cost or market value; and property, plant, and equipment is reported at cost less accumulated depreciation. Prices of most assets fluctuate, often increasing. Reporting assets on the balance sheet at their historical cost during a period of price changes can make the balance sheet information irrelevant. For example, reporting land that was purchased in 1925 at its historical cost of $1,000 is unlikely to provide financial statement readers with useful information in the 21st century.

When the prices of goods and services in an economy increase in general, we say that inflation has occurred. Economists often measure inflation by determining the current price for a "basket" of goods and services and then compare the current price with the price for the same basket of goods and services at an earlier time. For example, if a basket of goods and services costs $120 at the end of Year 1 and the same basket costs $132 at the end of Year 2, then inflation in Year 2 was 10 percent ([$132 − $120]/$120).

In this case we have measured the increase in the general price level, or the rate of inflation. The general inflation rate also reflects the decrease in the purchasing power of the currency. In our example, it takes $132 at the end of Year 2 to purchase as much as $120 could purchase at the end of Year 1. The dollar has lost 10 percent of its purchasing power during Year 2.

Not all goods and services increase in price by 10 percent when the average rate of inflation is 10 percent. The price of a new machine might increase by 15 percent, the price of component parts might increase by 12 percent, the price of janitorial services might increase by 5 percent, and the price of raw materials might actually decrease by 4 percent. These are measures of changes in specific prices. However, in our example, the changes in specific prices throughout the economy average out to an increase of 10 percent.

Impact of Inflation on Financial Statements

During a period of inflation, assets reported on the balance sheet at historical cost are understated in terms of their current value. Having understated assets results in understated expenses (especially depreciation and cost of goods sold), which in turn results in overstated net income and overstated retained earnings. Ignoring changes in the prices of assets can lead to a number of problems:

1. Understated asset values could have a negative impact on a company's ability to borrow, because the collateral is understated. Understated asset values also can invite a hostile takeover to the extent that the current market price of a company's stock does not reflect the current value of assets.

2. Overstated income results in more taxes being paid to the government than would otherwise be paid and could lead stockholders to demand a higher level of dividend than would otherwise be expected. Through the payment of taxes on inflated income and the payment of dividends out of inflated net income, both of which result in cash outflows, a company may find itself experiencing liquidity problems.

3. To the extent that companies are exposed to different rates of inflation, the understatement of assets and overstatement of income will differ across

companies; this can distort comparisons across companies. For example, a company with older fixed assets will report a higher return on assets than a company with newer assets, because income is more overstated and assets are more understated than for the comparison company. Because inflation rates tend to vary across countries, comparisons made by a parent company across its subsidiaries located in different countries can be distorted.

Purchasing Power Gains and Losses

In addition to ignoring changes in the values of nonmonetary assets, historical cost accounting also ignores the purchasing power gains and losses that arise from holding monetary assets (cash and receivables) and monetary liabilities (payables) during a period of inflation. Holding cash and receivables during inflation results in a purchasing power loss, whereas holding payables during inflation results in a purchasing power gain.

For example, when the general price level index is 120, $120 in cash can purchase one whole basket of goods and services. One year later, when the general price level index stands at 132 (10 percent inflation), the same $120 in cash can now purchase only 90.9 percent of a basket of goods and services. It now takes $132 to purchase the same amount of goods and services as at the beginning of the year. The difference between the $132 needed to maintain purchasing power and the $120 in cash actually held results in a $12 purchasing power loss. This can be computed by multiplying the amount of cash at the beginning of the year by the inflation rate of 10 percent ($120 × 10% = $12).

Borrowing money during a period of inflation results in a purchasing power gain. Assume a company expects to receive $120 in cash at the end of the current year. If it waits until the cash is received, it will be able to acquire 90.9 percent of the market basket of goods at that time when the general price level index is 132. Instead, if the company borrows $120 at the beginning of the year and repays that amount with the cash received at the end of the year, it will be able to acquire 100 percent of the basket of goods and services at the beginning of the year when the general price level index is 120. Holding a $120 liability during a period of 10 percent inflation results in a purchasing power gain of $12 ($120 × 10%). A net purchasing power gain will result when an entity maintains monetary liabilities in excess of monetary assets during inflation, and a net purchasing power loss will result when the opposite situation exists.

Methods of Accounting for Changing Prices

Two solutions have been developed to deal with the distortions caused by historical cost (HC) accounting in a period of changing prices. The first solution is to *account for changes in the general price level*. This approach makes adjustments to the historical costs of assets to update for changes in the purchasing power of the currency and therefore is referred to as general price-level-adjusted historical cost (GPLAHC) accounting or, more simply, general purchasing power (GPP) accounting. The alternative solution is to *account for specific price changes* by updating the values of assets from historical cost to the current cost to replace those assets. This is known as current replacement cost (CRC) or, simply, current cost (CC) accounting. In addition to adjusting asset values for changes in the general price level and determining expenses from GPLAHC amounts, GPP accounting also requires that purchasing power gains and losses be included in the determination of net income.

Net Income and Capital Maintenance

Application of each of the three methods of asset valuation—HC, GPP, and CC—results in a different amount of net income. Each measure of net income relates to a specific concept of capital maintenance. Much of the debate surrounding the appropriate method for asset valuation relates to determining which concept of capital maintenance is most important. The following example demonstrates the difference in net income that results from the three different accounting models.

Example

Assume that HIE Company is formed on January 1, Year 1, by investors contributing $200 in cash. The general price index (GPI) on that date is 100. HIE Company's opening balance sheet on January 1, Year 1, appears as follows:

Cash	$200	Contributed capital	$200

With the initial equity investment, one unit of inventory is purchased on January 2 at a cost of $100 and $100 remains in cash, resulting in the following financial position:

Cash	$100	Contributed capital	$200
Inventory	100		
	$200		

On January 2, Year 1, the managers of HIE Company go on vacation, returning on December 31, Year 1, at which time the inventory is sold for $150 in cash. At December 31, Year 1, the general price index is 120 (20 percent annual inflation during Year 1) and the inventory has a current replacement cost of $150. The HC income statement for Year 1 appears as follows (ignoring income taxes):

Sales	$150
Cost of sales	100
Income	$ 50

The balance sheet at December 31, Year 1, prior to any distribution of dividends is:

Cash	$250	Contributed capital	$200
		Retained earnings	50
			$250

The economic definition of income is that it is the amount that can be distributed to owners after making sure that the company is as well off at the end of the year as it was at the beginning of the year. If HIE Company were to distribute a dividend of $50 equal to Year 1 net income, the resulting balance sheet would be exactly the same as it was at the beginning of the year:

Cash	$200	Contributed capital . . .	$200

Thus, HC income is the amount that can be distributed to owners while maintaining the "nominal" amount of contributed capital at the beginning of the year. Note, however, that in terms of purchasing power, the company is not as well off at the end of the year as it was at the beginning of the year—$200 in cash at January 1, Year 1, when the GPI was 100, could purchase two baskets of goods and services. At December 31, Year 1, when the GPI has risen to 120, $200 in cash can purchase only $1\frac{2}{3}$ baskets of goods. The conventional HC model of accounting ignores the loss in purchasing power of the beginning of year amount of capital. GPP accounting explicitly takes the change in purchasing power of the currency into account.

General Purchasing Power (GPP) Accounting

Under GPP accounting, nonmonetary assets and liabilities, stockholders' equity, and all income statement items are restated from the GPI at the transaction date to the GPI at the end of the current period. Because inventory was acquired on January 1, Year 1, when the GPI was 100, and the GPI at December 31, Year 1, is 120, the cost of sales (inventory) is restated using the ratio 120/100. Fixed assets and intangible assets and the related depreciation and amortization would also be restated for changes in general purchasing power.

Because the sale occurred on December 31, Year 1, when the GPI was 120, there is no need to restate sales (or the restatement ratio can be expressed as 120/120). In addition to restating sales and cost of sales, GPP accounting also requires that a net purchasing power gain or loss be included in income. At January 1, Year 1, HIE Company has monetary assets of $100 (cash) and no monetary liabilities, yielding a net monetary asset position of $100. Because HIE Company holds this cash for the entire year, a net purchasing power loss (PPL) of $20 arises. In addition, HIE Company receives $150 in cash on December 31, Year 1, from the sale of inventory. Because this cash is received on December 31, there is no loss in purchasing power by the end of the year. The PPL is calculated as follows:

Cash, 1/1/Y1	$100 × (120/100) = $120	(amount of cash needed at 12/31/Y1 to maintain the purchasing power of $100 at 1/1/Y1)
Plus: Increase in cash, Year 1 . . .	$150 × (120/120) = $150	(amount of cash needed at 12/31/Y1 to maintain the purchasing power of $150 received on 12/31/Y1)
Subtotal.	270	
Less: Cash, 12/31/Y1	(250)	(amount of cash held, prior to distribution of dividend)
Purchasing power loss	$ 20	

Combining the restatement of the income statement items with the PPL, GPP income is calculated as follows:

	HC	Restatement Ratio	GPP
Sales	$150	× (120/120) =	$150
Cost of sales	100	× (120/100) =	120
Subtotal.	$ 50		$ 30
Purchasing power loss			20
Income			$ 10

Contributed capital must also be restated for Year 1 inflation, as follows:

	HC	Restatement Ratio	GPP
Contributed capital	$200	× (120/100) =	$240

The journal entry needed to account for GPP adjustments is as follows:

```
Dr. Inventory (Cost of Sales) . . . . . . . . . . . . . . . . . . . . . . . . . . . . . . . . . . . . . . . . .    20
    Purchasing Power Loss  . . . . . . . . . . . . . . . . . . . . . . . . . . . . . . . . . . . . . . . . .    20
        Cr. Contributed Capital . . . . . . . . . . . . . . . . . . . . . . . . . . . . . . . . . . . . .              40
```

GPP income represents the amount that can be distributed to owners while maintaining the purchasing power of capital at the beginning of the year. After paying a dividend of $10, HIE Company's balance sheet at December 31, Year 1, appears as follows:

Cash	$240	Contributed capital	$240

Note that $240 in cash at December 31, Year 1, when the GPI is 120, can purchase two baskets of goods and services, just as $200 in cash could have at January 1, Year 1, when the GPI was 100. The owners are just as well off in terms of the purchasing power of their contributed capital at the end of the year as they were at the beginning of the year.

Current Cost (CC) Accounting

Maintaining the purchasing power of equity does not necessarily ensure that the company is able to continue to operate at its existing level of capacity, because the prices of specific goods and services purchased by an individual company do not necessarily increase at the rate of average inflation. To determine the amount of income that can be distributed to owners while maintaining the company's productive capacity or physical capital, current cost (CC) accounting must be applied.

Under CC accounting, historical costs of nonmonetary assets are replaced with current replacement costs and expenses are based on these current costs. Assume that, on December 31, Year 1, the cost to replace the unit of inventory acquired at the beginning of the year is $150. In other words, this particular item has experienced a specific rate of inflation of 50 percent ([$150 − $100]/$100). The following journal entry would be made:

```
Dr. Inventory (Cost of Sales) . . . . . . . . . . . . . . . . . . . . . . . . . . . . . . . . . . . . . . . . .    50
    Cr. Holding Gain (Equity) . . . . . . . . . . . . . . . . . . . . . . . . . . . . . . . . . . . . . . . .              50
```

The CC accounting income statement would be as follows:

Sales	$150
Current cost of sales	150
Income	$ 0

There is no income to distribute as a dividend. After adding the holding gain to the beginning balance in capital, the ending balance sheet at December 31, Year 1, is as follows:

Cash	$250	Contributed capital	$200
		Holding gain	50
		Total	$250

With $250 in cash at December 31, Year 1, HIE Company can replace the inventory that was sold at its current cost of $150 and still will have $100 in cash. The company can end the year with the same physical assets as it had at the beginning of the year—$100 cash plus one unit of inventory.

Comparing the amounts of income that would be reported under GPP and CC accounting with HC income shows the potential problems that can arise if changing prices are ignored.

	HC	**GPP**	**CC**
Income	50	10	0

If HC accounting is used as the basis for taxation and dividend distribution, there is a good chance that the company will not be as well off at the end of the year in terms of either purchasing power or productive capacity at it was at the beginning of the year.

Inflation Accounting Internationally

Inflation Accounting in the United States and United Kingdom

In 1979, the Financial Accounting Standards Board (FASB) in the United States issued SFAS 33, *Financial Reporting and Changing Prices*, requiring the largest U.S. companies to provide both GPP and CC information in the notes to the financial statements. SFAS 33 was intended to be a five-year experiment to see whether financial analysts would find the supplementary information useful. In 1984, the FASB discontinued the requirement for disclosure of supplemental GPP information, citing lack of usefulness and cost to comply as reasons. Two years later, in 1986, the FASB issued SFAS 89, making optional the disclosure of CC information. Few U.S. companies continue to voluntarily provide CC information in the notes to their financial statements.

Inflation accounting was introduced in the United Kingdom in 1980 through Statement of Standard Accounting Practice (SSAP) 16. This statement required presentation of CC financial statements as either primary or supplementary statements. In either case, HC financial statements also were required to be presented. As in the United States, inflation accounting in the United Kingdom was short-lived. As a result of declining inflation rates and company complaints, SSAP 16 was rescinded in 1988.

GPP Accounting in Latin America

The countries of Latin America, from Mexico in the north to Argentina in the south, historically have experienced more inflation than any other region in the world. As a result, several countries in this region have employed or continue to use a system of inflation accounting. For years, Brazil was a leader in the use of inflation accounting. However, as a result of successful efforts in the 1990s to tame inflation, Brazil has abandoned inflation accounting.

Mexico is another country in the region that employed GPP accounting. The Mexican Institute of Public Accountants issued Bulletin B-10, *Recognition of the Inflation Effects in Financial Information,* effective in 1984. Bulletin B-10 requires all nonmonetary assets and nonmonetary liabilities to be restated using the general price level index published by the Central Bank. Initially, replacement cost accounting was allowed for inventory and property, plant, and equipment, but an amendment to Bulletin B-10 in 1997 eliminated this option. However, inventory (and the related cost of sales) may be valued at current replacement cost. In practice, this is similar to reporting inventory on a first-in, first-out (FIFO) basis and determining cost of Sales on a last-in, first-out (LIFO) basis. For imported machinery and equipment, an index comprised of the inflation rate of the country of origin coupled with the change in exchange rate between the foreign currency and the Mexican peso may be used. All other fixed assets must be restated using the general price index.

Equity must be restated with the general price index to show paid-in capital at constant purchasing power. A purchasing power gain or loss on the net monetary asset or liability position must be calculated and presented in income as a part of total financial cost, which also includes nominal interest expense and foreign exchange gains and losses. Finally, for comparative purposes, the financial statements of previous years must be restated in terms of the purchasing power of the peso at the latest balance sheet date presented. Exhibit 9.1 provides an excerpt from Industrias Peñoles's 2006 annual report that details the procedures followed by the company to comply with Bulletin B-10.

EXHIBIT 9.1

INDUSTRIAS PEÑOLES, S.A. DE C.V. AND SUBSIDIARIES
Annual Report
2006

Notes to Consolidated Financial Statements

Excerpts from Note 3 Significant Accounting Policies

b) Recognition of the Effects of Inflation on Financial Information

Grupo Peñoles restates all of its financial statements in terms of the purchasing power of the Mexican peso as of the end of the latest period, thereby comprehensively recognizing the effect of inflation. The financial statements of the prior year have been restated in terms of Mexican pesos of the latest period. The prior-year amounts presented herein differ from those originally reported in terms of Mexican pesos of the corresponding year. Consequently, all financial statement amounts are comparable, both for the current and the prior year, since all are stated in terms of Mexican pesos of the same purchasing power.

For the years ended December 31, 2006 and 2005, the annual rate of inflation, as determined based on the Mexican National Consumer Price Index (NCPI), was 4.05% and 3.33%, respectively.

The procedure for recognizing the effects of inflation in terms of Mexican pesos with year-end purchasing power is as follows:

Balance Sheet

Minerals inventories are recorded at acquisition and/or extraction cost. Metal inventories and chemical products are recognized at production cost. Such inventories are restated to reflect replacement cost, not in excess of market value.

Investments in associated companies have been valued using the equity method, which consists of the parent company's recognizing its proportional share in the stockholders' equity of the investee.

The acquisition cost of property, plant, and equipment (except for certain fixed assets that are valued at recovery value, as well as mining concessions and construction works and preoperating expenses) is restated as follows:

—The net value of property, plant, and equipment of Mexican origin is restated based on factors derived from the NCPI.

—Production machinery and equipment, computer, and transportation equipment that are identified when acquired as being of foreign origin, are controlled in the currency of the country of origin, which is restated by using the consumer price index of such country and translated to pesos at the prevailing exchange rate at the balance sheet date. Below is a list of inflation and exchange rates of the main countries as the origin of imported machinery and equipment:

			EXCHANGE RATE AT DECEMBER 31	
COUNTRY	ANNUAL RATE OF INFLATION		(NOMINAL MEXICAN PESOS)	
	2006	2005	2006	2005
United States of America (U.S. dollar)	2.9	4.4	Ps 10.88	Ps 10.71
Germany (euro)	0.7	2.4	14.51	12.66
Canada (Canadian dollar)	1.3	2.5	9.49	9.08
England (sterling pound)	3.6	2.4	21.39	18.27

The cost of mining concessions and works and preoperating expenses were restated based on factors derived from the NCPI.

The integral result of financing is restated based on the NCPI and is amortized based on the useful life of the assets that give rise to such income.

Depreciation and depletion are calculated based on the restated value (net of salvage value) of property, plant, and equipment as follows:

—Metallurgical, chemical, and industrial plants, using the straight-line method, at annual rates determined on the bases of the useful lives of the related assets.

—Mining concessions and works, preoperating expenses, facilities, and milling plants are amortized using the depletion method based on dividing the tonnage of ore milled during the year by the mine's total mineral reserves.

—Other equipment, using the straight-line method, at annual rates of 10% and 20%.

The restatement of capital contributions, capitalized reserves, retained earnings and the cumulative effect of deferred taxes is determined by applying the NCPI from the time the contributions were made, the reserves were capitalized, or the earnings were generated. This represents the amount needed to maintain the stockholders' equity investment in terms of its original purchasing power.

Statement of Income

Revenues and expenses related to monetary items are restated from the month the related transactions occurred through year-end, based on the NCPI.

Cost of sales represents replacement costs at the time inventories were sold expressed in constant year-end pesos.

Other Statements

The statement of changes in financial position identifies the sources and uses of resources representing differences between beginning and ending balances expressed in constant Mexican pesos. The result of monetary position and foreign exchange differences are not treated as a part of the resources provided by or used in operations.

The deficit from restatement of stockholders' equity shown in the statement of changes in stockholders' equity consists basically of the accumulated result of monetary position and the accumulated result from holding nonmonetary assets, which represents the difference between the replacement value of fixed assets, inventories, and the investments in associated companies compared to their value determined based on the NCPI.

k) Integral Result of Financing

Integral result of financing consists of interest income and expense, foreign-exchange gains or losses and the gains or losses from monetary position. The gains or losses from monetary position are determined by applying the NCPI to the net monetary position at the beginning of each month.

Transactions in foreign currency are recorded at the prevailing exchange rate on the day of the related transactions. Monetary assets and liabilities denominated in foreign currencies are translated to Mexican pesos at the prevailing exchange rate as of the balance sheet date. Exchange differences determined are charged or credited to the statement of income as part of the integral result of financing.

Integral result of financing generated during the construction or installation stage of major projects is capitalized.

Because the rate of inflation in Mexico was held under 5 percent for a number of years in a row, the Mexican Institute decided to abandon the requirements of Bulletin B-10 in late 2007. Mexican companies no longer are required to adjust their financial statements for inflation.

Replacement Cost Accounting in the Netherlands

No country requires companies to use current replacement cost accounting to prepare primary financial statements. However, prior to the introduction of IFRS in Europe in 2005, the Netherlands allowed companies to use replacement cost accounting in lieu of historical cost accounting in preparing financial statements. Over the years a limited number of Dutch companies, including Philips Electronics NV and Heineken NV, elected to do so. In 2003 and 2004, Heineken was the only Dutch company that continued to employ replacement cost accounting.

In 2004, Heineken carried inventories and fixed assets on the balance sheet at replacement cost, with the counterpart to the asset revaluation reflected in equity. Cost of sales (reported on Heineken's income statement as raw materials, consumables and services) and depreciation expense (included in amortization/depreciation and value adjustments) were based on current replacement costs. The schedule of changes in tangible fixed assets reported in the notes showed that €604 million (11.8 percent) of the book value of total fixed assets of €5,127 million was the result of upward revaluation to replacement cost. Of the aggregate amount of revaluation, €41 million was attributable to the year 2003 alone.

Heineken reported net profit of €537 million in 2004. This amount is based on replacement cost of sales and replacement cost depreciation expense. The company does not disclose the amount of historical cost profit that would have been recognized if replacement costs had not been used. Replacement cost profit is used in the calculation of net profit per share and is the basis for distributing dividends.

With the introduction of IFRS in the European Union in 2005, Heineken was required to implement a number of accounting and reporting changes. Two of the main changes for the company related to the valuation of tangible fixed assets and inventories. Under IFRS, Heineken now carries fixed assets at historical cost less accumulated depreciation, and inventories are carried at weighted average historical cost.

International Financial Reporting Standards

Several standards issued by the International Accounting Standards Board (IASB) deal with the issue of accounting for price changes. International Accounting Standard (IAS) 15, *Information Reflecting the Effects of Changing Prices,* issued in 1981, required supplementary disclosure of the following items reflecting the effects of changing prices:

1. The amount of adjustment to depreciation expense.
2. The amount of adjustment to cost of sales.
3. The amount of purchasing power gain or loss on monetary items.
4. The aggregate of all adjustments reflecting the effects of changing prices.
5. If current cost accounting is used, the current cost of property, plant, and equipment.

The standard applied only to enterprises "whose levels of revenues, profits, assets or employment are significant in the economic environment in which they operate" (paragraph 3) and allowed those enterprises to choose between making adjustments on a GPP or a CC basis. Because of a lack of international support for inflation accounting disclosures, the International Accounting Standards Committee (IASC) decided to make IAS 15 optional in 1989 and the IASB completely withdrew IAS 15 in 2003.

In 1989, the IASB issued IAS 29, *Financial Reporting in Hyperinflationary Economies,* which applies to the primary financial statements of any company that reports in a currency of a hyperinflationary economy. IAS 29 does not establish an absolute definition for hyperinflation, instead leaving this determination to individual companies. However, the standard does provide a list of characteristics indicative of hyperinflation:

1. The general population keeps its wealth in nonmonetary assets or in a stable foreign currency; receipts of local currency are immediately invested to maintain purchasing power.
2. The general population thinks about prices in terms of a stable foreign currency, and prices may actually be quoted in that currency.
3. Prices for credit sales and purchases include an amount to compensate for the expected loss in purchasing power during the credit period.
4. Interest rates, wages, and prices are linked to a price index.
5. The cumulative inflation rate over a three-year period is 100 percent or higher.

The procedures required by IAS 29 for the restatement of financial statements are summarized as follows:

Balance Sheet

- Monetary assets and monetary liabilities are not restated because they are already expressed in terms of the monetary unit current at the balance sheet date. Monetary items are cash, receivables, and payables.
- Nonmonetary assets and nonmonetary liabilities are restated for changes in the general purchasing power of the monetary unit. Most nonmonetary items are carried at historical cost. In these cases, the restated cost is determined by applying to the historical cost the change in general price index from the date of acquisition to the balance sheet date. Some nonmonetary items are carried at revalued amounts, for example, property, plant, and equipment revalued according to the allowed alternative treatment in IAS 16, *Property, Plant and Equipment.* These items are restated from the date of the revaluation.
- All components of owners' equity are restated by applying the change in the general price index from the beginning of the period or the date of contribution, if later, to the balance sheet date.

Income Statement

- All income statement items are restated by applying the change in the general price index from the dates when the items were originally recorded to the balance sheet date.
- The gain or loss on net monetary position (purchasing power gain or loss) is included in net income.

Comparative Information

- Information for the previous reporting period is restated in terms of the current purchasing power of the monetary unit by applying the change in general price index during the current period to each corresponding figure.

The procedures followed by the Turkish conglomerate Koç Holding AŞ in complying with IAS 29 are described in Exhibit 9.2. Application of IAS 29 was triggered by the fact that the three-year cumulative inflation in Turkey at the end of 2003 was 181.1 percent. Koç Holding reported operating profit of 832,612 billion Turkish lira (TL) in 2003. A "loss on net monetary position" of TL 34,890 million was subtracted from operating profit to determine income before taxes and minority interest. The size of this purchasing power loss was equal to 4.2 percent of operating profit and 9.1 percent of net income.

EXHIBIT 9.2

KOÇ HOLDING AŞ
Annual Report
2003

Notes to the Consolidated Financial Statements

Excerpt from Note 2—Basis of Preparation

a) Turkish Lira financial statements

The consolidated financial statements have been prepared in accordance with International Financial Reporting Standards ("IFRS") including the International Accounting Standards ("IAS") and Interpretations issued by the International Accounting Standards Board ("IASB"). Koç Holding and its Subsidiaries and Joint Ventures registered in Turkey maintain their books of account and prepare their statutory financial statements ("Statutory Financial Statements") in TL in accordance with the Turkish Commerical Code (the "TCC"), tax legislation, and the Uniform Chart of Accounts issued by the Ministry of Finance, applicable Turkish insurance laws for insurance companies and Banking law and accounting principles promulgated by the Banking Regulation and Supervising Agency for banks and for listed companies; accounting principles issued by the CMB of Turkey ("CMB Principles"). The foreign Subsidiaries and Joint Ventures maintain their books of account in accordance with the laws and regulations in force in the countries in which they are registered. These consolidated financial statements are based on the statutory records, which are maintained under the historical cost convention (except for the statutory revaluation of property, plant and equipment as discussed in Note 15), with the required adjustments and reclassifications reflected for the purpose of fair presentation in accordance with IFRS (including the restatement of the TL to match the purchasing power at the balance sheet date).

The restatement for the changes in the general purchasing power of the TL at 31 December 2003 is based on IAS 29 ("Financial Reporting in Hyperinflationary Economies"). IAS 29 requires that financial statements prepared in the currency of a hyperinflationary economy be stated in terms of the measuring unit current at the balance sheet date, and that corresponding figures for previous periods be restated in the same terms. One characteristic that necessitates the application of IAS 29 is a cumulative three-year inflation rate approaching or exceeding 100%. The restatement was calculated by means of conversion factors derived from the Turkish nationwide wholesale price index ("WPI") published by the State Institute of Statistics ("SIS"). Such indices and conversion factors used to restate the financial statements at 31 December are given below:

Dates	Index	Conversion Factors	Cumulative 3-year %
31 December 2003.	**7,382.1**	**1.000**	**181.1**
31 December 2002	6,478.8	1.139	227.3
31 December 2001	4,951.7	1.491	307.5

The main procedures for the above-mentioned restatement are as follows:

—Financial statements prepared in the currency of a hyperinflationary economy are stated in terms of the measuring unit current at the balance sheet date, and corresponding figures for previous periods are restated in the same terms.

—Monetary assets and liabilities that are carried at amounts current at the balance sheet date are not restated because they are already expressed in terms of the monetary unit current at the balance sheet date.

—Non-monetary assets and liabilities that are not carried at amounts current at the balance sheet date and components of shareholders' equity are restated by applying the relevant conversion factors.

— Comparative financial statements are restated using general inflation indices at the currency purchasing power at the latest balance sheet date.

—All items in the statements of income are restated by applying the relevant (monthly) conversion factors.

—The effect of inflation on the net monetary asset position of Koç Holding, the Subsidiaries and Joint Ventures is included in the statements of income as loss on net monetary position in the consolidated financial statements.

In March 2005, the Turkish Capital Markets Board determined that Turkish companies no longer would be required to use inflation accounting in preparing their financial statements. The reason for this change is that the cumulative three-year inflation rate as of December 31, 2004, was only 69.7 percent. "Accordingly, International Accounting Standards (IAS) 29 (*Financial Reporting in Hyperinflationary Economies*), issued by IASB, has not been applied in the consolidated financial statements for the accounting year commencing from 1 January 2005."[1]

Translation of Foreign Currency Financial Statements in Hyperinflationary Economies

If a parent company has a foreign operation located in a hyperinflationary economy, IAS 21, *The Effects of Changes in Foreign Exchange Rates,* requires application of IAS 29 to restate the foreign operation's financial statements to a GPP basis. The GPP adjusted financial statements are then translated into the parent company's reporting currency using the current exchange rate. This approach is referred to as the restate/translate method. We demonstrate this method through the following example.

Sean Regan Company formed a subsidiary in a foreign country on January 1, Year 1, through a combination of debt and equity financing. The foreign subsidiary acquired land on January 1, Year 1, which it rents to a local farmer. The foreign subsidiary's financial statements for its first year of operations, in foreign currency units (FC), are presented in Exhibit 9.3.

All revenues and expenses were realized in cash during the year. Thus, the balance in the Cash account at December 31 (FC 1,750) is equal to the beginning balance in cash (FC 1,000) plus net income for the year (FC 750).

The foreign country experienced significant inflation in Year 1, especially in the second half of the year. The general price index (GPI) during Year 1 was:

January 1, Year 1	100
Average, Year 1	125
December 31, Year 1	200

The rate of inflation in Year 1 is 100 percent [(200 − 100)/100], and the foreign country clearly meets the definition of a hyperinflationary economy.

---

[1] Koç Holding 2005 Annual Report, page 113.

EXHIBIT 9.3

SEAN REGAN COMPANY
YEAR 1 FINANCIAL STATEMENTS
Foreign Subsidiary
Income Statement
Year 1

(in FC)

Rent revenue	1,000
Interest expense	(250)
Net income	750

Foreign Subsidiary
Balance Sheets
Year 1

(in FC)	January 1	December 31
Cash	1,000	1,750
Land	9,000	9,000
Total	10,000	10,750
Note payable (5%)	5,000	5,000
Capital stock	5,000	5,000
Retained earnings	0	750
Total	10,000	10,750

As a result of the high rate of inflation in the foreign country, the FC weakened substantially during the year relative to other currencies. Relevant exchange rates between Sean Regan's parent company currency (PC) and the FC during Year 1 were:

	PC per FC
January 1, Year 1	1.00
Average, Year 1	0.80
December 31, Year 1	0.50

Assuming that Sean Regan Company prepares its consolidated financial statements in accordance with IFRS, the foreign subsidiary's FC financial statements would be (1) restated for local inflation and then (2) translated into PC using the current exchange rate as shown in Exhibit 9.4.

All financial statement items are restated to the GPI of 200 at December 31, Year 1. Rent revenue and Interest expense occurred evenly throughout the year when the average GPI was 125. Therefore, the appropriate restatement factor for these items is 200/125. Monetary assets and liabilities already are stated in terms of December 31, Year 1, purchasing power. Therefore, the restatement factor for Cash and Notes payable is 200/200. Land and capital stock are restated from the GPI of 100 that existed at the beginning of the year to the GPI of 200 at year-end; the restatement factor is 200/100.

EXHIBIT 9.4

SEAN REGAN COMPANY
Foreign Subsidiary in Hyperinflationary Economy—Application of IAS 21

	FC	Restatement Factor	Inflation-Adjusted FC	Exchange Rate	PC
Year 1					
Rent revenue	1,000	200/125	1,600	0.50	800
Interest expense	(250)	200/125	(400)	0.50	(200)
Subtotal	750		1,200		600
Purchasing power gain (loss)			3,550	0.50	1,775
Net income			4,750		2,375
December 31, Year 1					
Cash	1,750	200/200	1,750	0.50	875
Land	9,000	200/100	18,000	0.50	9,000
Total	10,750		19,750		9,875
Note payable	5,000	200/200	5,000	0.50	2,500
Capital stock	5,000	200/100	10,000	0.50	5,000
Retained earnings	750		4,750	0.50	2,375
Total	10,750		19,750		9,875

A purchasing power gain or loss must be included in the calculation of net income. The net purchasing power gain of FC 3,550 can be computed as follows:

Gain from holding note payable	FC $5,000 \times (200 - 100)/100 =$	FC 5,000
Loss from holding beginning balance in cash	$(1,000) \times (200 - 100)/100 =$	(1,000)
Loss from increase in cash during the year	$(750) \times (200 - 125)/125 =$	(450)
Net purchasing power gain (loss)		FC 3,550

Holding a note payable of FC 5,000 during a period of 100 percent inflation gives rise to a purchasing power gain of FC 5,000 on that monetary liability. Holding the beginning cash balance of FC 1,000 for the entire year generates a purchasing power loss of FC 1,000. The increase in cash of FC 750 which occurred evenly throughout the year resulted in a purchasing power loss of FC 450.

Once the FC financial statements are restated for inflation, each inflation-adjusted FC amount is translated into PC using the exchange rate at December 31, Year 1. Note that all inflation-adjusted FC amounts, including stockholders' equity accounts, are translated at the current exchange rate and therefore no translation adjustment is needed.

Now assume that Sean Regan Company wishes to comply with U.S. GAAP in preparing its consolidated financial statements. In that case, the foreign subsidiary's FC financial statements would be translated into PC using the temporal method as required by FASB ASC Topic 830, *Foreign Currency Matters*, without

EXHIBIT 9.5

SEAN REGAN COMPANY
Foreign Subsidiary in Hyperinflationary Economy—Application of U.S. GAAP

	FC	Exchange Rate	PC
Cash	1,750	0.50 C	875
Land	9,000	1.00 H	9,000
Total	10,750		9,875
Note payable	5,000	0.50 C	2,500
Capital stock	5,000	1.00 H	5,000
Retained earnings	750		2,375
Total	10,750		9,875
Revenues	1,000	0.80 A	800
Interest expense	(250)	0.80 A	(200)
Subtotal	750		600
Translation gain*			1,775
Net income			2,375

Where: C = current exchange rate; A = average-for-the-year exchange rate; H = historical exchange rate
* The increase in retained earnings is 2,375 (from the balance sheet), so Net income is 2,375. Therefore, the translation gain must be 1,775.

first adjusting for inflation. The resulting translation gain or loss is reported in net income. Application of U.S. GAAP is shown in Exhibit 9.5.

Application of the temporal method as required by U.S. GAAP in this situation results in exactly the same PC amounts as were obtained under the restate/translate approach required by IAS 21. The equivalence of results under the two approaches exists because of the exact one-to-one inverse relationship between the change in the GPI in the foreign country and the change in the PC value of the FC, as predicted by the theory of purchasing power parity. The GPI doubled and the FC lost half its purchasing power, which caused the FC to lose half its value in PC terms. To the extent that this relationship does not hold, and it rarely does, the two different methodologies for translating the foreign currency financial statements of subsidiaries located in hyperinflationary countries will generate different translated amounts. For example, if the December 31, Year 1, exchange rate had adjusted to only PC 0.60 per FC (rather than PC 0.50 per FC), then translated net income would have been PC 2,050 under U.S. GAAP and PC 2,850 under IFRS.

BUSINESS COMBINATIONS AND CONSOLIDATED FINANCIAL STATEMENTS

Business combinations are the major vehicle through which MNCs expand their international business operations. Businesses can combine their operations in a number of different ways. In many cases, the company being acquired in a business combination is legally dissolved as a separate legal entity. Either the acquired company goes out of existence and is merged into the acquiring company, or both parties to the combination are legally dissolved with a new company formed to take their place. In yet a third method of combination, one company gains control over another company by acquiring a majority of its voting shares, but the acquired company continues its separate legal existence. In this case the acquirer becomes the parent company and the acquiree becomes the subsidiary company. Here no company goes out of existence, and both the parent and the subsidiary continue to operate as separate legal entities, maintaining their own accounting records and preparing their own financial statements.

The concept of a "group" applies to this third type of business combination. IAS 27, *Consolidated and Separate Financial Statements,* defines a *group* as a parent and all its subsidiaries, and it requires parents to present consolidated financial statements. In this section, we discuss the following issues related to the accounting for business combinations and the preparation of consolidated financial statements, focusing on IFRS:

1. Determination of control.
2. Scope of consolidation.
3. Full consolidation, based on the purchase method, and the accounting for goodwill.
4. Proportionate consolidation.
5. Equity method.

The manner in which several consolidation issues are resolved in selected countries and under IFRS is summarized in Exhibit 9.6.

Determination of Control

The concept of a group is often based on *legal control,* which is usually reflected through the ownership of more than 50 percent of the shares and voting rights of another company. The ownership of shares reflecting control may be direct or indirect (through other controlled subsidiaries). Legal control also can be obtained through a contract whereby one company places itself under the legal control of another, which might not have 50 percent of the voting shares. Company legislation in Germany, for example, allows for such control contracts.

A company can effectively control another company through means other than majority ownership. Effective control also can be achieved through representation on the board of directors or because of widely distributed stock ownership. For example, if Company A owns 45 percent of the voting shares of Company B, and the other 55 percent of Company B is owned by thousands of small stockholders who do not exercise their votes, then Company A will be able to control Company B. In such cases, it might be appropriate to consolidate the investee's financial statements with those of the investor even though the latter does not own more than 50 percent of the investee's shares. For example, it is common for companies in South Korea to consolidate investees when the investor company owns more than 30 percent of the outstanding voting stock and is the largest single shareholder.

IAS 27 requires all subsidiaries to be consolidated and defines a *subsidiary* as an enterprise controlled by another enterprise, known as the parent. *Control* is defined as "the power to govern the financial and operating policies of an entity so as to obtain benefits from its activities" (paragraph 4). In essence, IAS 27 takes a substance-over-form approach to the concept of control. It recognizes that an investor owning less than 50 percent of the stock of another company nevertheless may have control when the investor has power

- Over more than half of the voting rights through agreements with other shareholders.
- To set the company's financial and operating policies because of existing statutes or agreements.
- To appoint or remove the majority of the members of the governing body (board of directors or equivalent group).
- To cast the majority of votes at meetings of the company's governing body.

EXHIBIT 9.6 Summary of Consolidation Procedures in Selected Countries

Country	Consolidated Financials Required	Reasons to Exclude Subsidiaries from Consolidation	Treatment of Goodwill	Goodwill Amortization	Pooling Method	Equity Method
European Union (IFRS)	Yes	Sold in near future and buyer being sought	Asset	Impairment test	No	Yes, 20%
United States	Yes	Bankrupt Control impaired by foreign exchange restrictions	Asset	Impairment test	No	Yes, 20%
Canada	Yes	Sold in near future Control impaired Dissimilar activities	Asset	Impairment test	No	Yes, 20%
Mexico	Yes	Bankrupt Control impaired by foreign exchange restrictions	Asset	0–40 years	No	Yes, 10%
Brazil	Yes, if subsidiaries comprise > 30% of total equity	Sold in near future Bankrupt Dissimilar activities	Asset, based on book values (not fair values)	0–20 years	No	Yes, 10%
Japan	Yes, since 1992	Sold in near future Control impaired Dissimilar activities Immaterial Information not available on time	Asset or expense	0–5 years, if asset	No	Yes, 20%
South Korea	Yes, unaudited only	Sold in near future Control impaired	Asset	5 years	No, unless regulation requires	Yes, 20%

In other words, the IASB defines control as "exclusive rights over an entity's assets and liabilities, which give access to the benefits of these assets and liabilities and the ability to increase, maintain or protect the amount of these benefits".

U.S. GAAP (Accounting Research Bulletin 51) uses *controlling financial interest* as its criterion for consolidation without specifically defining what *controlling* means. Historically, U.S. companies have relied on majority stock ownership as evidence of control. More recently, however, in the case of so-called special purpose entities, the concept of control has been expanded by FASB Interpretation 46, *Consolidation of Variable Interest Entities,* to one based on effective control.[2] A controlling financial interest in a variable interest (special purpose) entity is evidenced by one or more of the following:

- The direct or indirect ability to make decisions about the entity's activities.
- The obligation to absorb the expected losses of the entity if they occur.
- The right to receive the expected residual returns of the entity if they occur.

The level of ownership is irrelevant in determining control for this type of entity.

The IASB and FASB share the ultimate goal of adopting the improved conceptual framework for financial reporting as a replacement of their present frameworks. In March 2010, the IASB issued an Exposure Draft (ED/2010/2), entitled "Conceptual Framework for Financial Reporting—The Reporting Entity." It states, "An entity controls another entity when it has the power to direct the activities of that other entity to generate benefits for (or limit losses to) itself. If an entity that controls one or more entities prepares financial reports, it should present consolidated financial statements." It further makes a distinction between "control" and "significant influence" and states, "If one entity has significant influence, over another entity, it does not control that other entity. The entity's ability to influence the activities of another entity without actually being able to direct those activities does not constitute power over that other entity." It is clear that the IASB has taken a principles-based rather than a rules-based (or qualitative rather than quantitative) approach in defining control.

Applying the concept of legal control to identify subsidiaries may not be suitable in some countries due to their traditional business structures. For example, given Japan's extensive cross-ownership of companies, identifying legal ownership patterns of Japanese company groups (*keiretsu*) can be extremely difficult. As Radebaugh and Gray explain:

> These groups are known as keiretsu (i.e., headless combinations). Legal relationships are not the critical factor here. Relationships concerning the supply of raw materials and technology, market outlets, sources of debt finance, and interlocking directorships are also very important. Group consciousness is the key, built on a system of cooperation based on mutual trust and loyalty. Hence, Japanese consolidated accounts are not necessarily an accurate reflection of group results—both earnings and assets may be seriously understated. Many companies may report compliance with U.S. GAAP for U.S. listing purposes, but they are not strictly comparable with U.S. consolidated accounts.[3]

[2] FASB Interpretation 46, *Consolidation of Variable Interest Entities,* January 2003.
[3] Lee H. Radebaugh and Sidney J. Gray, *International Accounting and Multinational Enterprises,* 5th ed. (New York: Wiley, 2002), pp. 167–68.

Scope of Consolidation

Consolidated financial statements are the financial statements of a group presented as those of a single enterprise incorporating both the parent and its subsidiaries. The preparation of consolidated financial statements can be a highly complex task given that some MNCs have a large number of subsidiaries. For example, the Swedish home appliances group Electrolux AB has approximately 350 operating subsidiaries worldwide.

IAS 27 requires a parent to consolidate all subsidiaries, foreign and domestic, unless (1) the subsidiary was acquired with the intention to be disposed of within 12 months and (2) management is actively seeking a buyer. The only other situation in which a parent might be able to exclude a subsidiary from consolidation is when the subsidiary is dormant and its operations are insignificant to the company as a whole. This is demonstrated in Exhibit 9.7, which contains an excerpt from Volkswagen AG's annual report describing the company's basis of consolidation.

IAS 27 no longer allows a subsidiary to be excluded from consolidation when it operates under severe long-term restrictions that significantly affect its ability to send funds to its parent. It also does not allow a subsidiary to be excluded from consolidated financial statements solely because its operations are dissimilar to those of the other companies that comprise the group. A subsidiary ceases to be consolidated when the parent loses the control to govern its financial and operating policies. Loss of control by the parent can occur, for example, when a bankrupt subsidiary becomes subject to the control of a bankruptcy court, when a foreign government takes control of a foreign subsidiary, or when a contractual agreement cedes control to another party.

U.S. GAAP also requires all subsidiaries to be consolidated unless the parent has lost control as a result of bankruptcy or severe restrictions imposed by a foreign government. U.S. GAAP does not allow a subsidiary to be excluded from consolidation simply because it is being held for sale.

Full Consolidation

Full consolidation refers to the line-by-line aggregation of 100 percent of a subsidiary's assets, liabilities, revenues, and expenses even if the group owns less than 100 percent of the subsidiary's stock. The proportion of income and equity in the subsidiary that is not owned by the group is reported in the consolidated financial statements in a separate item as minority interest. As explained earlier, only those affiliates controlled by the parent are consolidated. Unconsolidated affiliates are reflected in the consolidated statements by the corresponding investment accounts. The impact that the consolidation of a subsidiary's financial statements has on the resulting consolidated financial statements depends on the method used to account for the business combination at the date of acquisition. Because the use of the pooling of interests method is prohibited under IFRS 3, the only method currently allowed to account for business combinations is the purchase method. We briefly describe this method next.

Purchase Method

Under the purchase method, when a company acquires a majority of the voting shares of another company, assets and liabilities of the acquired company (subsidiary) are revalued to fair value as of the date of acquisition. If the purchase price exceeds the revalued net assets, the excess is described as goodwill on acquisition. With this method, the acquired company contributes to group profits only after the date of acquisition.

EXHIBIT 9.7

VOLKSWAGEN AG
Annual Report
2007

Excerpts from Notes to the Consolidated Financial Statements of the Volkswagen Group for the Fiscal Year ended December 31, 2007

Basis of consolidation

In addition to Volkswagen AG, the consolidated financial statements comprise all significant companies at which Volkswagen AG is able, directly or indirectly, to govern the financial and operating policies in such a way that they can obtain benefits from the activities of these companies (subsidiaries). The subsidiaries also comprise investment funds and other special purpose entities whose net assets are attributable to the Group under the principle of substance over form. Consolidation of subsidiaries begins at the first date on which control exists, and ends when such control no longer exists.

Subsidiaries whose business is dormant or of low volume and that are insignificant for the presentation of a true and fair view of the net assets, financial position and results of operations as well as the cash flows of the Volkswagen Group are not consolidated. However, they are carried in the consolidated financial statements at the lower of cost or fair value since no active market exists for those companies and fair values cannot be reliably ascertained without undue cost or effort. The aggregate equity of these subsidiaries amounts to 0.9% (previous year: 1.2%) of Group equity. The aggregate profit after tax of these companies amounts to 0.3% (previous year: 0.4%) of the profit after tax of the Volkswagen Group.

Significant companies where Volkswagen AG is able, directly or indirectly, to significantly influence financial and operating policy decisions (associates), or directly or indirectly shares control (joint ventures), are accounted for using the equity method. Joint ventures also include companies in which the Volkswagen Group holds the majority of voting rights, but whose articles of association or partnership agreements stipulate that important decisions may only be resolved unanimously. Insignificant associates and joint ventures are generally carried at the lower of cost or fair value.

The composition of the Volkswagen Group is shown in the following table:

	2007	2006
Volkswagen AG and consolidated subsidiaries		
Germany	42	39
International	133	123
Subsidiaries carried at cost		
Germany	63	64
International	77	72
Associates and joint ventures		
Germany	24	29
International	45	51
	384	**378**

Initial Carrying Value of Acquired Net Assets When less than 100 percent of a subsidiary is acquired, two major alternatives exist for determining the initial amount at which the subsidiary's assets and liabilities are measured and carried on the consolidated balance sheet. One approach is to initially measure the acquired assets and liabilities at book value plus the parent's ownership percentage of the difference between fair value and book value at the date of acquisition. This is sometimes known as the parent company concept. For example, assume Poinsett Company acquires 80 percent of the voting stock of Sumter Company. At the date of acquisition, Sumter has land with a book value of $100,000 that is appraised to have a fair value of $150,000. Under the parent company concept, the land would be carried on Poinsett Company's consolidated balance sheet at the date of acquisition at $140,000 ($100,000 + 80% [$150,000 − $100,000]). Under this approach, the outside shareholders' interest in Sumter Company would be reported as minority interest on Poinsett Company's consolidated balance sheet in an amount equal to 20 percent of the *book value* of Sumter Company net assets.

The alternative treatment is to initially measure the acquired assets and liabilities on the parent's consolidated balance sheet at 100 percent of their fair value at the date of acquisition. Under this treatment, also known as the economic unit or entity concept, Sumter Company's land would appear on Poinsett Company's consolidated balance sheet at date of acquisition at $150,000, and the minority interest would be reported in an amount equal to 20 percent of the *fair value* of Sumter Company's net assets.

Under IAS 22, *Business Combinations,* each of these two approaches was acceptable. IFRS 3, *Business Combinations,* issued in 2004, supersedes IAS 22. With the issuance of IFRS 3, the first alternative was eliminated. The assets acquired and liabilities assumed in a business combination now must be initially measured at their acquisition-date fair value in accordance with the economic unit concept. IFRS 3 was revised in 2008 and this approach to accounting for a business combination now is refered to as the *acquisition method.*

Goodwill   Considerable variation exists in the accounting treatment of goodwill across countries. Most of the countries represented in Exhibit 9.6 require goodwill to be capitalized as an asset. However, Japan allows goodwill to be expensed immediately. In the case of Brazil, goodwill is based on the excess of purchase price over the book value, not fair value, of acquired net assets.

Most countries require the systematic amortization of goodwill to expense over a specified period of time. The maximum number of years over which goodwill can be amortized ranges from 5 to 40. Systematic amortization of goodwill is no longer required in Canada and the United States. Instead, goodwill must be subjected to an annual impairment test and written down when goodwill's implied fair value falls below its carrying value.

Under the original IAS 22, *Business Combinations* (issued in 1983), goodwill arising from application of the purchase method could be recognized as an asset or, alternatively, could be written off immediately against equity. In a revision to IAS 22 in 1993, the immediate write-off of goodwill against equity was eliminated as an acceptable alternative. IAS 22 (revised 1993) required goodwill to be recognized as an asset and amortized on a systematic basis over its useful life, which was assumed to be no longer than five years. A subsequent revision to IAS 22 in 1998 established the rebuttable presumption that the useful life of goodwill does not exceed 20 years.

IFRS 3 substantially changed the rules, prohibiting the amortization of goodwill on a systematic basis over its useful life. Instead, consistent with earlier changes in the United States and Canada, IFRS now require goodwill to be tested annually for impairment.

The term *negative goodwill* often is used to refer to the excess of the acquirer's interest in the acquiree's net assets over the acquirer's purchase price. IAS 22 adopted the view that negative goodwill could arise from expectations of future losses and expenses and, to the extent that this is the case, the negative goodwill must be deferred and recognized as income when the future losses and expenses are recognized. IFRS 3 changed this treatment, requiring negative goodwill to be recognized immediately in the income statement as a gain. This serves to substantially converge IFRS with North American practice. The difference is that negative goodwill is treated as an extraordinary gain under U.S. GAAP; classification of an item as extraordinary is not acceptable under IFRS. Current U.S. treatment of negative goodwill is reflected in the following excerpt taken from California-based Sempra Energy's 2004 Form 10-K (page 51):

Extraordinary Gain

During 2002, Sempra Commodities acquired two businesses for amounts less than the fair value of the business' net assets. In accordance with *SFAS 141*, "Business Combinations," those differences were recorded as extraordinary income.

Further Convergence of U.S. GAAP and IFRS

In 2006, there were more than 13,000 mergers and acquisitions worldwide using U.S. GAAP or IFRS. It was difficult to make comparisons when acquirers were accounting for acquisitions in different ways. Therefore, the objective of the business combinations project jointly undertaken by the IASB and FASB was to develop a single high-quality accounting standard that would ensure the accounting for business combinations is the same under both U.S. GAAP and IFRS. In January 2008, the project was completed when the IASB issued a revised version of IFRS 3, *Business Combinations,* and an amended version of IAS 27, *Consolidated and Separate Financial Statements.* The new requirements took effect on July 1, 2009, with early adoption permitted. The FASB issued its equivalent standards SFAS 141(R), *Business Combinations,* and SFAS 160, *Noncontrolling Interests in Consolidated Financial Statements,* in December 2007.

The main changes to IFRS as a result of this project include the accounting treatment of step and partial acquisitions. The requirement to measure at fair value every asset and liability at each step in an acquisition that is achieved in stages (i.e., when an acquirer has an existing holding and acquires additional shares to achieve control) has been removed. Instead, the acquirer remeasures its previously held investment in the acquiree at its fair value at the date the acquirer obtains control, with any gain or loss recognized in net income. Goodwill is measured as the difference at the acquisition date between the value of any investment in the business held before the acquisition plus the consideration transferred and the net assets acquired. For a business combination in which the acquirer achieves control without acquiring all the equity of the acquiree, the remaining (noncontrolling) equity interest is measured either at fair value or at the noncontrolling interests' proportionate share of the acquiree's net identifiable assets. Previously, only the latter was permitted.

The major changes to U.S. GAAP include requiring the use of the acquisition method for business combinations and classifying noncontrolling interests as equity. In addition, in-process research and development is required to be recognized as a separate intangible asset rather than being immediately written-off as an expense. Still there are some minor differences between U.S. GAAP and IFRS in regard to accounting for business combinations. SFAS 141(R) requires the noncontrolling interests in an acquiree to be measured at fair value, whereas IFRS allows noncontrolling equity interests to be measured either at fair value or at the noncontrolling interests' proportionate share of the acquiree's net identifiable assets. Further, in terms of the criteria for initial recognition, IFRS 3 has a "reliable measurement" threshold, whereas SFAS 141(R) has a "more likely than not" threshold for noncontractual liabilities.

Pooling of Interests Method

In the United States, until recently, the pooling of interests method was allowed when a set of restrictive criteria was satisfied. In July 2001, however, the FASB issued SFAS 141, *Business Combinations,* which requires that all business combinations be accounted for under the purchase method. Use of the pooling of interests method is no longer permitted in the United States. The pooling method also has been eliminated in Canada and is not allowed in Brazil and Mexico.

IAS 22 allowed the use of the pooling of interests method in those rare cases where it was impossible to identify an acquirer. However, with the enactment of IFRS 3 in 2004, that changed. IFRS 3 requires all business combinations to be accounted for using the purchase method; the pooling of interest method is no longer acceptable under IFRS.

Proportionate Consolidation

In some cases, two companies will jointly control another entity as a joint venture. IAS 31, *Financial Reporting of Interests in Joint Ventures,* defines *joint venture* as "a contractual arrangement whereby two or more parties undertake an activity which is subject to joint control" (paragraph 2). IAS 31 prefers proportionate consolidation for joint ventures (benchmark treatment), while equity accounting is allowed as an alternative. Proportionate consolidation is prohibited in the United States. Instead, the equity method is used to account for investments in joint ventures.

Proportionate Consolidation of a Joint Venture—Example

Assume that Alpha Company acquires 50 percent of the common shares of JV Company for cash on December 31, Year 1, at a price of $1.40 per share. (Beta Company acquires the other 50 percent of JV's shares at the same price.) The respective balance sheets for Alpha Company and JV Company at December 31, Year 1, were as follows:

ALPHA COMPANY AND JV COMPANY
Balance Sheets
December 31, Year 1

	Alpha	JV
Current assets	$ 57,200	$12,200
Fixed Assets.	100,000	8,000
Investment in JV (16,000 shares × 50% × $1.40)	11,200	
	$168,400	$20,200
Liabilities	$ 88,400	$ 4,200
Common stock ($1 par).	80,000	16,000
	$168,400	$20,200

The effect of the proportionate consolidation method is to remove the "Investment in JV" account from Alpha's balance sheet and replace it with the proportion of all the individual items that it represents. Assuming that JV's assets and liabilities are reported on its December 31, Year 1 balance sheet at fair values, the consolidated balance sheet is as follows:

ALPHA COMPANY
Consolidated Balance Sheet
December 31, Year 1

Current assets	$ 63,300[a]
Fixed assets	104,000[b]
Goodwill	3,200[d]
	$170,500
Liabilities	$ 90,500[c]
Common Stock	80,000
	$170,500

---

[a]$57,200 + (50% × $12,200) = $63,300
[b]$100,000 + (50% × $8,000) = $104,000
[c]$88,400 + (50% × $4,200) = $90,500

[d]Cost of investment	$11,200
50% of JV's net assets (50% × $16,000)	8,000
Goodwill	$ 3,200

As part of the short-term convergence project with the FASB, the IASB issued an Exposure Draft in late 2007 that would eliminate the proportionate consolidation method as an acceptable method of accounting for joint ventures. ED 9, *Joint Arrangements,* proposes using the equity method only for investments in joint ventures. However, the transitional arrangements have not yet been finalized.

Equity Method

Many investments in the stock of another company do not provide the investor with effective control of the investee but do allow the investor to exert significant influence over the investee's operating activities. An *associate* is an enterprise in which the investor has significant influence and that is neither a subsidiary nor a joint venture. Most countries require use of the equity method to account for the investment in an associate. All countries represented in Exhibit 9.6 require its use.

The key element in identifying investments in firms that are associates is determination of *significant influence.* The international norm is to assume that holding 20 percent or more of the voting shares is evidence of significant influence. This arbitrary level was first adopted in the United States and the United Kingdom in 1971 and then in the European Union's Seventh Directive in 1983. Although the use of 20 percent ownership is widely adopted as the threshold for determining significant influence, there does not seem to be any strong argument in its favor. On the contrary, Nobes points out that "the consensus about the threshold (20 percent shareholding) connected to the use of the equity method seems to have arisen by accident."[4] Countries that deviate from this norm include Brazil, Mexico, and Italy, which use a 10 percent threshold; Hungary, which uses 25 percent (10 percent for banks); and Spain, which uses 3 percent.

---

[4] Christopher W. Nobes, "An Analysis of the International Development of the Equity Method," *Abacus* 38, no. 1 (2002), p. 16.

IAS 28, *Accounting for Investments in Associates*, establishes a presumption of significant influence when the investor owns shares, directly or indirectly through subsidiaries, equivalent to 20 percent or more of the investee's voting power. Conversely, significant influence is assumed not to exist when less than 20 percent of voting shares are held, unless such influence can be clearly demonstrated.

The equity method is often known as a one-line consolidation. The procedure used in applying it to determine the carrying amount of the investment on the balance sheet is as follows: The investment is (1) initially recorded at cost; (2) increased (or decreased) for the investor's share of the associate's profit (or loss) after the date of acquisition (adjusted to eliminate the profit or loss on transactions between the investor and the associate); (3) reduced for distributions (dividends) received from the associate; (4) reduced for deprecation of the difference between fair value and book value of the investor's share of the associate's depreciable assets at the date of acquisition; and (5) adjusted for changes in the associate's equity not included in income, such as revaluation of assets and foreign exchange translation differences.

Additionally, the investor's share of the associate's profit (or loss) after the date of acquisition is treated as income (or loss). Adjustments are made to this amount to

- Eliminate the profit or loss on transactions between the investor and the associate to the extent of the investor's ownership interest in the associate.
- Depreciate the difference between fair value and book value of the investor's share of the associate's depreciable assets.

IAS 28 requires use of the equity method in accounting for investments in associates and IAS 31 allows the use of the equity method in accounting for jointly controlled entities. Exhibit 9.8 shows how the Volkswagen Group reports its share of profits and losses of investments including joint ventures, accounted for using the equity method in accordance with IFRS.

In the United States, the equity method is required for investments in both associates and joint ventures and is to be applied for these types of investment in both consolidated financial statements as well as in any parent company financial statements that are prepared. Because revaluations are not allowed under U.S. GAAP, a U.S. investor with a foreign associate that carries assets at revalued amounts cannot reflect in its investment account any revaluation of the foreign investee's assets.

EXHIBIT 9.8

VOLKSWAGEN AG
Annual Report
2007

Notes to the Consolidated Financial Statements of the Volkswagen Group for the Fiscal Year Ended December 31, 2007

5. Share of Profits and Losses of Equity-Accounted Investments

€ Million	2007	2006
Share of profits of equity-accounted investments.	820	390
of which from: Joint Ventures	(443)	(271)
of which from: Associates	(377)	(119)
Share of losses of equity-accounted investments	86	17
of which from: Joint Ventures	(86)	(5)
of which from: Associates	(0)	(12)
	734	373

When an investor exerts less than significant influence over the investee, both IFRS and U.S. GAAP require the investment to be carried on the investor's balance sheet at fair value. The fair value method is also appropriate for nonconsolidated subsidiaries.

SEGMENT REPORTING

As companies diversify internationally or in the lines of business in which they operate, the usefulness of consolidated financial statements diminishes. There are different risks and growth potential associated with different parts of the world, just as there are different risks and opportunities associated with different lines of business. The aggregation of all of a company's revenues, expenses, assets, and liabilities into consolidated totals masks these differences. United Technologies Inc., parent company of Otis (elevators), Carrier (air conditioners), and Sikorsky (helicopters), reported consolidated revenues of $53 billion and operating profit of $6.4 billion in 2009. Analysts and others might find it useful to know how much of that total was generated from each of the company's major lines of business, as there are different risks and growth prospects associated with each. In 2009, Coca-Cola Company reported consolidated revenues of $31 billion and operating income of $8.2 billion. Financial analysts and other financial statements users might want to know how much of this revenue was generated in North America, and how much was generated in Latin America, Eurasia and Africa, and other parts of the world where risks are higher.

To facilitate the analysis and evaluation of financial statements, in the 1960s several groups began to request that consolidated amounts be disaggregated and disclosed on a segment basis. Required line-of-business disclosures were introduced in the United Kingdom in 1965, and in the United States in 1969. The European Union's Fourth Directive on accounting, issued in 1978, requires both line-of-business and geographic disclosures, as does IAS 14, *Segment Reporting*, which was originally issued in 1981. Thus, segment reporting has been a part of the international accounting landscape for many years.

Notwithstanding the apparent usefulness of segment disclosures, financial analysts have consistently requested that information be disaggregated to an even greater extent than was being done in practice. Both the American Institute of Certified Public Accountants (AICPA) and the Association of Investment Management and Research (AIMR) issued reports in the 1990s recommending that segment reporting be aligned with internal reporting, with segments defined on the basis of how a company is organized and managed.

In 1992, the FASB in the United States and the Accounting Standards Board (AcSB) in Canada decided to jointly reconsider segment reporting with the objective of developing a common standard that would apply in both countries. Subsequently, the IASC began to reconsider its standard on segment reporting, IAS 14. Members of the FASB and AcSB participated in IASC meetings on segment reporting to exchange views. In 1996, all three organizations issued exposure drafts of proposed standards that were very similar. The FASB, however, made a number of changes in writing a final standard (SFAS 131), which is substantially different from what emerged from the IASC (IAS 14 revised).

In 2002, segment reporting was added to the agenda of the short-term convergence project of the IASB and the FASB. After several years of study, the IASB issued IFRS 8, *Operating Segments*, in November 2006, which substantially converges IFRS with U.S. GAAP on the issue of segment reporting.[5] With the issuance of IFRS 8, the IASB adopted the so-called management approach to segment reporting introduced by the FASB in 1996.[6]

Operating Segments—The Management Approach

The management approach to determining segments is based on the way that management disaggregates the enterprise for making operating decisions. These disaggregated components are referred to as *operating segments,* which should be evident from the enterprise's organization structure. An operating segment is a component of an enterprise if:

* It engages in business activities from which it earns revenues and incurs expenses.
* If its operating results are regularly reviewed by the chief operating decision maker to assess performance and make resource allocation decisions.
* Discrete financial information is available for it.

Even if all of an organizational unit's revenue and expense are derived from transactions with other segments it still can be an operating segment. But not all parts of a company necessarily are included in an operating segment. For example, a research and development unit that incurs expenses but does not earn revenues would not be an operating segment. After a company has identified its operating segments based on its internal reporting system, management must decide which of these segments should be reported separately. Generally, information must be reported separately for each operating segment that meets one or more quantitative thresholds.

After determining whether any segments are to be aggregated, management next must determine which of its operating segments are significant enough to justify separate disclosure. An operating segment is considered significant if it meets any one of the following tests:

1. *Revenue test.* Segment revenues, both external and intersegment, are 10 percent or more of the combined revenue, internal and external, of all reported operating segments.
2. *Profit or loss test.* Segment profit or loss is 10 percent or more of the higher (in absolute terms) of the combined reported profit of all profitable segments or the combined reported loss of all segments incurring a loss.
3. *Asset test.* Segment assets are 10 percent or more of the combined assets of all operating segments.

If the combined sales to unaffiliated customers of segments determined to be significant are less than 75 percent of total company sales made to outsiders, additional segments must be disclosed separately even though they fail to meet one of the quantitative thresholds. All segments that are neither separately reported nor combined should be included in the segment reporting disclosures as an unallocated reconciliation item or in an "all other" category.

---

[5] Only three substantive differences exist between IFRS 8 and U.S. GAAP. The first difference relates to the disclosure of segment liabilities, which is required by IFRS 8 but not U.S. GAAP. The second difference relates to the definition of long-lived assets for geographic area disclosures. IFRS 8 explicitly includes intangibles in this definition, whereas U.S. GAAP does not. When a company has a matrix form of organization, IFRS 8 allows operating segments to be based on either products and services or geographic areas. In this situation, U.S. GAAP requires operating segments to be based on products and services.

[6] IFRS 8 went into effect on January 1, 2009.

The following example demonstrates the procedures that must be followed to determine reportable operating segments.

Example: Application of Significance Tests

Diversified Printing Inc. is comprised of five business segments: Books, Cards, Magazines, Maps, and Finance. Information about each of the segments for Year 1 as reported to the chief executive officer is provided as follows:

	Books	Cards	Magazines	Maps	Finance
Revenues:					
External sales	$65.2	$13.8	$13.6	$3.1	—
Intersegment sales	13.2	2.4	—	1.6	—
Interest revenue—external	4.6	1.8	0.4	0.3	4.2
Interest revenue—intersegment	—	—	—	—	1.8
Total revenues	$83.0	$18.0	$14.0	$5.0	$6.0
Expenses:					
Operating—external	$34.1	$7.2	$14.6	$3.6	$0.6
Operating—intersegment	9.6	2.0	—	—	0.3
Interest expense	4.2	2.0	4.4	—	3.0
Income taxes	12.1	2.8	(3.0)	0.4	0.1
Total expense	$60.0	$14.0	$16.0	$4.0	$4.0
Assets:					
Tangible	$19.2	$ 2.2	$ 1.6	$1.0	$4.6
Intangible	3.8	0.8	1.4	—	—
Intersegment loans	—	—	—	—	3.4
Total assets	$23.0	$ 3.0	$ 3.0	$1.0	$8.0

Revenue Test

The combined revenue of all segments is $126.0 ($83.0 + $18.0 + $14.0 + $5.0 + $6.0). Based on the 10 percent significance level, any segment with revenues of more than $12.6 is a reportable segment. Books and Cards meet this test and should be reported separately.

Profit or Loss Test

The profit or loss (result) for each business segment is determined by subtracting segment expenses from total segment revenues. Profit or loss from each segment is determined as follows:

Segment	Total Revenues	Total Expenses	Profit	Loss
Books	$ 83.0	$60.0	$23.0	—
Cards	18.0	14.0	4.0	—
Magazines	14.0	16.0	—	$2.0
Maps	5.0	4.0	1.0	—
Finance	6.0	4.0	2.0	—
Total	$126.0	$98.0	$30.0	$2.0

The $30.0 profit from the four profitable segments is greater in absolute value than the $2.0 loss from the Magazines segment. Therefore, any segment with a profit or loss greater than $3.00 ($30.0 × 10%) is a reportable segment. Only Books and Cards qualify as reportable segments under the profit or loss test.

Asset Test

The final test is based on the segments' combined total assets of $38.0 ($23.0 + $3.0 + $3.0 + $1.0 + $8.0). According to this test, any segment with assets exceeding 10 percent of combined total assets is a separately reportable segment. Two segments, Books and Finance, meet this test as each of these segments has total assets exceeding $3.8 ($38.0 × 10%).

Only three segments meet at least one of the significance tests. Magazines and Maps do not meet any of the tests. However, if total external revenue attributable to reportable segments is less than 75 percent of the total sales made to outsiders (consolidated revenue), additional segments should be reported even if they do not meet the 10 percent threshold. To determine whether the 75 percent minimum is met, the percentage of consolidated revenues generated by reportable segments is determined as follows:

Segment	External Revenues*	Percentage of Total Consolidated Revenues
Books	$ 69.8	65.2
Cards	15.6	14.6
Magazines	14.0	Not reported
Maps	3.4	Not reported
Finance	4.2	3.9
Total consolidated revenues	$107.0	83.7

*Only external revenues are considered because intersegment revenues are eliminated in the process of preparing consolidated financial statements.

Because the Books, Cards, and Finance segments, in aggregate, comprise more than 75 percent of total consolidated revenues, the Magazines and Maps segments will be combined and reported as "All Other."

Operating Segment Disclosures

The following information must be disclosed for each separately reported operating segment:

1. *General information* about the operating segment:
   - Factors used to identify operating segments.
   - Types of products and services from which each operating segment derives its revenues.

2. *Segment profit or loss* and the following revenues and expenses included in segment profit or loss:
   - Revenues from external customers.
   - Revenues from transactions with other operating segments.
   - Interest revenue and interest expense.

- Depreciation, depletion, and amortization expense.
- Other significant noncash items included in segment profit or loss.
- Unusual items (discontinued operations and extraordinary items).
- Income tax expense or benefit.

3. *Total segment assets* and the following related items:

- Investment in equity method affiliates.
- Expenditures for additions to long-lived assets U.S. GAAP/noncurrent assets (IFRS 8).

U.S. GAAP requires disclosure of additions to long-lived assets, which are "hard assets that cannot be readily removed, which would exclude intangibles."[7] IFRS 8 requires disclosure of additions to noncurrent assets (other than financial instruments, deferred tax assets, and assets related to postretirement benefit plans), which includes both tangible fixed assets and intangibles. IFRS 8 also requires disclosure of total liabilities for each reportable segment if such an amount is regularly reported to the chief operating decision maker. U.S. GAAP does not require the disclosure of segment liabilities.

Entity-Wide Disclosures

In addition to extensive information that must be disclosed for each reportable operating segment, both IFRS and U.S. GAAP require the following types of disclosure:

1. Information about products and services.
2. Information about major customers.
3. Information about geographic areas.

Information about Products and Services

Some enterprises are not organized along product or service lines, or might have only one operating segment, yet provide a range of different products and services. To provide some comparability between enterprises, *revenues derived from transactions with external customers from each product or service* must be disclosed if a company has only one operating segment or if operating segments have not been determined based on differences in products or services.

The U.S.-based home improvement retailer Lowe's Companies, Inc., operates in only one segment. Nevertheless, the company reports "sales by product category" in its annual report. In 2009, Lowe's disclosed that it derived 10 percent of total sales from appliances and 8 percent from paint its two largest product categories.

Information about Major Customers

To assess a company's reliance on its major customers, both IFRS and U.S. GAAP require disclosures whenever 10 percent or more of a company's revenues is derived from a single customer. In this situation, the existence of all major customers must be disclosed along with the related amount of revenues and the identity of the operating segment generating the revenues. Although the identity of major

---

[7] FASB ASC 280-10-55-23.

customers need not be revealed, this information often is disclosed. For example, Walmart was identified as a major customer by 156 different U.S. companies at least once during the period 1993–2004.[8]

Information about Geographic Areas

Revenues from external customers and long-lived assets (U.S. GAAP) or non-current assets (IFRS) must be reported (1) for the *domestic country* and (2) for *all foreign countries in total* in which the enterprise derives revenues or holds assets. In addition, if revenues from external customers attributed to an *individual foreign country* are material, the specific country and amount of revenues must be disclosed separately. Similarly, a material amount of noncurrent assets located in an individual foreign country also must be disclosed separately. Even if the company has only one operating segment and therefore does not otherwise provide segment information, it must report geographic area information. In determining materiality, management should apply the concept that an item is material if its omission could change a user's decision about the enterprise as a whole.

Thus, the FASB requires U.S.-based companies to disclose the amount of revenues generated and long-lived assets held *(a)* in the United States, *(b)* in all other countries in total, and *(c)* in each material foreign country. Requiring disclosure at the individual country level is a significant change from prior rules, which required disclosures by groups of countries located in the same geographic area. Current U.S. GAAP does not preclude companies from continuing to provide information by geographic groupings of countries and for consistency purposes many companies continue to do so even if no single foreign country is determined to be material. The FASB changed the reporting requirement from geographic regions to individual countries because it believes that reporting information about individual countries has two benefits. First, it reduces the burden on preparers of financial statements because most companies are likely to have material operations in only a few countries and perhaps only in their country of domicile. Second, and more important, country-specific information is easier to interpret and therefore more useful. Individual countries within a geographic area often experience very different rates of economic growth and economic conditions. Disclosures by individual country, rather than broad geographic area, provide investors and other readers of financial statements with better information for assessing the level of risk associated with a company's foreign operations.

Disclosures about geographic areas can be an important source of information for determining the extent to which a company is diversified internationally. However, the quality of information provided is to a certain extent dependent on the company's application of the materiality threshold. To illustrate the range of detail provided by companies in complying with the geographic area disclosure requirement of U.S. GAAP, Exhibit 9.9 presents the foreign operation revenues disclosures provided in the annual report of three companies.

---

[8] Marty Gosman and Mark J., Kohlbeck, "The Effects of Wal-Mart on the Profitability and Investor Valuation of Its Suppliers." This paper has not been published in a journal. It is posted to the Web as a *working paper.* It is accessible at SSRN. Social Science Research Network www.ssrn.com. May 30, 2006. Available at SSRN: http://ssrn.com/abstract=906606.

EXHIBIT 9.9
Geographic Area
Information
for Three U.S.
Companies

INTERNATIONAL BUSINESS MACHINES CORPORATION
Annual Report
2009
Excerpt from Note W. Segment Information

Geographic Information

The following provides information for those countries that are 10 percent or more of the specific category.

Revenue*
($ in millions)

For the Year Ended December 31:	2009	2008	2007
United States	**$34,150**	$ 36,686	$36,511
Japan	**10,222**	10,403	9,632
Other countries	**51,386**	56,541	52,643
Total	**$95,758**	$103,630	$98,786

*Revenues are attributed to countries based on location of client.

Net Plant, Property and Equipment
($ in millions)

At December 31:	2009	2008	2007
United States	**$ 6,313**	$ 6,469	$ 6,592
Japan	**1,050**	1,055	890
Other countries	**5,092**	4,797	5,365
Total	**$12,455**	$12,321	$12,847

Source: IBM 2009 Annual Report, page 125.

International Business Machines Corporation (IBM) disclosed the fact that 36 percent of its 2009 revenue was generated in the United States, with an additional 11 percent generated in Japan, but there is no disclosure of the location of the remaining 53 percent of revenues attributable to "other countries." IBM explicitly states that it has used 10 percent as the threshold for determining materiality. Long-lived assets are defined as net property, plant, and equipment only.

Johnson & Johnson also discloses the amount of sales made in the United States, but provides no information with respect to any other individual country. Apparently, Johnson & Johnson has determined that no single foreign country has a material amount of the company's revenues or long-lived assets. Instead, foreign sales are reported by three broad geographic regions—Europe, Western Hemisphere excluding U.S., and Asia-Pacific and Africa. In contrast to IBM, Johnson & Johnson includes intangible assets in its measure of long-lived assets.

General Motors provides the most detailed information of the three companies, specifically reporting the amount of sales and revenue generated in seven countries other than the United States. These seven countries (four European countries, Brazil, Australia, and Korea) account for 58 percent of General Motors' sales outside North America. Similar to IBM, General Motors includes only fixed assets (including equipment held under capital lease) in its measure of long-lived assets.

JOHNSON & JOHNSON
Annual Report
2009
Excerpt from Note 8. Segments of Business and Geographic Areas

Geographic Areas

(Dollars in millions)	Sales to Customers			Long-Lived Assets		
	2009	2008	2007	2009	2008	2007
United States.	$30,889	32,309	32,444	$22,399	21,674	21,685
Europe.	15,934	16,782	15,644	17,347	14,375	15,578
Western Hemisphere excluding U.S	5,156	5,173	4,681	3,540	3,328	3,722
Asia-Pacific, Africa	9,918	9,483	8,326	1,868	1,898	1,261
Segments total.	61,897	63,747	61,095	45,154	41,275	42,246
General corporate				790	785	702
Other non-long-lived assets				48,738	42,852	38,006
Worldwide total.	$61,897	63,747	61,095	$94,682	84,912	80,954

Long-lived assets include property, plant, and equipment, net for 2009, 2008, and 2007 of $14,759, $14,365 and $14,185, respectively, and intangible assets, net for 2009, 2008, and 2007 of $31,185, $27,695 and $28,763, respectively.

Source: Johnson & Johnson, 2009 Form 10-K, p. 55.

FORD MOTOR COMPANY
Annual Report
2009
Excerpt from Note 29. Geographic Information

The following table includes information for both Automotive and Financial Services sectors (in millions):

	2009		2008		2007	
	Net Sales and Revenues	Long-lived Assets*	Net Sales and Revenues	Long-Lived Assets*	Net Sales and Revenues	Long-Lived Assets*
North America						
United States	$ 54,377	$22,489	$ 60,481	$29,158	$ 80,237	$37,174
Canada	7,974	5,000	7,964	6,369	9,332	10,280
Mexico/Other	1,336	1,393	2,224	950	2,253	1,054
Total North America	63,687	28,882	70,669	36,477	91,822	48,508
Europe						
United Kingdom.	8,448	2,388	14,406	2,259	16,634	2,899
Germany	7,843	3,468	9,146	3,845	8,239	3,849
Italy	4,529	53	5,052	31	5,537	44
France	3,102	504	3,554	502	3,580	581
Spain	2,174	1,280	3,550	1,223	5,039	1,198
Russia.	1,573	240	5,211	221	4,647	166
Belgium	1,460	1,229	2,029	1,330	1,912	1,621
Other.	8,976	344	13,286	424	14,203	842
Total Europe.	38,105	9,506	56,234	9,835	59,791	11,200
All Other	16,516	3,660	18,211	3,081	18,959	3,871
Total Company.	**$118,308**	**$42,048**	**$145,114**	**$49,393**	**$170,572**	**$63,579**

*Includes *Net investment in operating leases* and *Net property* from our consolidated balance sheet.

Source: Ford Motor Company, 2009 Annual Report, page 162.

Summary

1. Preparing financial statements using historical cost accounting in a period of inflation results in a number of problems. Assets are understated, and income generally is overstated; using historical cost income as the basis for taxation and dividend distributions can result in cash flow difficulties; and comparing the performance of foreign operations exposed to different rates of inflation can be misleading.

2. Two methods of accounting for changing prices (inflation) have been used in different countries: general purchasing power (GPP) accounting and current cost (CC) accounting. Under GPP accounting, nonmonetary assets and stockholders' equity accounts are restated for changes in the general price level. Cost of goods sold and depreciation/amortization are based on restated asset values, and the net purchasing power gain/loss on the net monetary liability/asset position is included in income. GPP income is the amount that can be paid as a dividend while maintaining the purchasing power of capital. Under CC accounting, nonmonetary assets are revalued to current cost, and cost of goods sold and depreciation/amortization are based on revalued amounts. CC income is the amount that can be paid as a dividend while maintaining physical capital.

3. Several Latin American countries have used GPP accounting in the past to overcome the limitations of historical cost accounting. Prior to the adoption of IFRS, the Netherlands allowed, but did not require, the use of CC accounting. IAS 29 requires the use of GPP accounting by firms that report in the currency of a hyperinflationary economy. IAS 21 requires the financial statements of a foreign operation located in a hyperinflationary economy to first be adjusted for inflation in accordance with IAS 29 before translation into the parent company's reporting currency.

4. Multinational corporations (MNCs) often operate as groups, and there is a need for consolidated financial statements reflecting their financial position and performance. IFRS 3 defines *group* as a parent and its subsidiaries, and requires groups to prepare consolidated financial statements. IAS 27 requires a parent to consolidate all subsidiaries, foreign and domestic, unless the subsidiary was acquired with the intention to be disposed of within 12 months and management is actively seeking a buyer.

5. The definition of *subsidiary* is based on the concept of control, which is often defined in terms of legal control through majority ownership of shares. IAS 27 also recognizes that there can be effective control without legal control, for example, through contractual agreement. Subsidiaries that are effectively controlled must be consolidated.

6. Consistent with North American practice, IFRS 3 requires the exclusive use of the purchase method in accounting for business combinations, requiring any goodwill to be recognized as an asset. Goodwill is not amortized on a systematic basis but is subjected to an annual impairment test. Negative goodwill is recognized immediately as a gain in the income statement.

7. The aggregation of all of a company's activities into consolidated totals masks the differences in risk and potential existing across different lines of business and in different parts of the world. To provide information that can be used to evaluate these risks and potentials, companies disaggregate consolidated totals and provide disclosures on a segment basis.

8. The IASB issued IFRS 8 in 2006 to converge with U.S. GAAP. Both standards require use of a so-called management approach in determining operating

segments. Three quantitative tests based on revenues, profit or loss, and assets are applied to identify which operating segments are separately reportable. Information related to products and services, revenues and expenses, assets, and capital expenditures must be disclosed for each reportable segment.

9. If operating segments are not based on geography, both standards require disclosure of revenues and noncurrent assets (or long-lived assets) for the domestic country, all foreign countries in which the company operates, and each individual country in which a material amount of revenues or assets is located. Neither standard provides a quantitative threshold for assessing materiality.

Questions

1. Why is it important that, in countries with high inflation, financial statements be adjusted for inflation?
2. What are the major differences in the calculation of income between the historical cost (HC) model and the general purchasing power (GPP) model of accounting?
3. Which balance sheet accounts give rise to purchasing power gains, and which accounts give rise to purchasing power losses?
4. What are the major differences in the calculation of income between the historical cost (HC) model and the current cost (CC) model of accounting?
5. Why is return on assets (net income/total assets) generally smaller under current cost accounting than under historical cost accounting?
6. In what ways do International Financial Reporting Standards (IFRS) address the issue of accounting for changing prices (inflation)?
7. What is a group? Compare and contrast the different concepts of a group.
8. To which specific type of business combination does the concept of a group relate?
9. Define *control*. When does control exist in accordance with IAS 27?
10. Explain why the legal concept of control may be appropriate in some countries, such as Japan.
11. What are the circumstances under which a subsidiary could, and perhaps should, be excluded from consolidation?
12. What is proportionate consolidation? Under what circumstances are companies likely to use this method?
13. In accordance with IFRS 8, how does a company determine which operating segments to report separately?
14. What are the major differences in the segment information required to be reported in accordance with IFRS and in accordance with U.S. GAAP?
15. What types of entity-wide disclosures are required by IFRS 8?
16. How does a company determine whether sales or noncurrent assets located in an individual foreign country are material?

Exercises and Problems

1. Sorocaba Company is located in a highly inflationary country and in accordance with IAS 29 prepares financial statements on a general purchasing power (inflation-adjusted) basis through reference to changes in the general price index (GPI). The company had the following transactions involving machinery and equipment in its first two years of operations:

Date	Transaction	Cost	Useful Life	GPI
January 15, Year 1	Purchase Machine X	$ 20,000	4 years	100
March 20, Year 1	Purchase Machine Y	55,000	5 years	110
October 10, Year 1	Purchase Machine Z	130,000	10 years	130
December 31, Year 1				140
April 15, Year 2	Sold Machine X			160
December 31, Year 2				180

Required:

Determine the amount that would be reported as machinery and equipment in accordance with IAS 29 on the December 31, Year 1, and December 31, Year 2, balance sheets.

2. Antalya Company borrows 1,000,000 Turkish lira (TL) on January 1, Year 1, at an annual interest rate of 60 percent by signing a two-year note payable. During Year 1, the Turkish inflation index changed from 250 at January 1 to 387.5 at December 31.

Required:

Related to this note payable, determine the following amounts for Antalya Company for Year 1:

a. Nominal interest expense.

b. Purchasing power gain on the borrowing.

c. Real interest expense (nominal interest expense less purchasing power gain). What is the real rate of interest paid by Antalya Company in Year 1 on its note payable?

3. Doner Company Inc. begins operations on January 1, Year 1. The company's unadjusted financial statements for the year ended December 31, Year 1, appear as follows:

Balance Sheets	1/1/Y1	12/31/Y1
Cash and receivables	$20,000	$35,000
Fixed assets, net	50,000	45,000
Total	$70,000	$80,000
Payables	$15,000	$15,000
Contributed capital	55,000	55,000
Retained earnings	—	10,000
Total	$70,000	$80,000
Income Statement, Year 1		
Revenues	$50,000	
Depreciation	(5,000)	
Other expenses	(35,000)	
Income	$10,000	

Revenues and expenses occur evenly throughout the year; revenues and other expenses are realized in terms of monetary assets (cash and receivables).

General price indexes for Year 1 are as follows:

1/1/Y1	100
Average Y1	120
12/31/Y1	150

Required:

a. Calculate Doner Company's Year 1 purchasing power gain or loss on net monetary items.

b. Determine Doner Company's Year 1 income on a general purchasing power basis (ignore income taxes).

4. Petrodat Company provides data processing services for companies operating in the petroleum extraction business. On January 1, Year 1, Petrodat established two foreign subsidiaries—one in Mexico and the other in Venezuela—by investing $100,000 worth of data processing equipment in each. The opening balance sheets for the two subsidiaries in local currency appear as follows:

	Mexico (pesos)	Venezuela (bolivars)
Machinery and equipment.	1,000,000	150,000,000
Total assets	1,000,000	150,000,000
Contributed capital	1,000,000	150,000,000
Total owners' equity.	1,000,000	150,000,000

The equipment is depreciated on a straight-line basis over a five-year useful life with no residual value.

The Year 1 income statement for each subsidiary appears as follows:

	Mexico (pesos)	Venezuela (bolivars)
Revenues.	400,000	60,000,000
Depreciation expense.	(200,000)	(30,000,000)
Other expenses	(150,000)	(22,500,000)
Net income	50,000	7,500,000

Revenues and other expenses occurred evenly throughout the year and were realized in cash by year-end. As a result, the balance sheets for the two companies at December 31, Year 1, appear as follows:

	Mexico (pesos)	Venezuela (bolivars)
Cash	250,000	37,500,000
Machinery and equipment.	1,000,000	150,000,000
Less: Accumulated depreciation.	(200,000)	(30,000,000)
Total assets	1,050,000	157,500,000
Contributed capital	1,000,000	150,000,000
Retained earnings	50,000	7,500,000
Total equity	1,050,000	157,500,000

For Year 1, the two subsidiaries reported the following measures of profitability:

	Mexico	Venezuela
Profit margin (net income/revenues).........................	12.5%	12.5%
Return on equity (net income/average total stockholders' equity)...	4.88%	4.88%

Values for the general price index in Mexico and Venezuela during Year 1 were as follows:

	Mexico	Venezuela
January 1.......................................	100	100
Average...	105	110
December 31.....................................	110	120

Required:
a. For each subsidiary, restate Year 1 income for changes in the general price index. Include a purchasing power gain or loss. Ignore income taxes.
b. Calculate Year 1 profit margin and return on assets for each subsidiary on an inflation-adjusted basis.
c. Comment on the impact of inflation on the comparison of profitability measures across operations located in countries with different levels of inflation.

5. Auroral Company had the following investments in shares of other companies on December 31, Year 1:

Name of Company	Country	% Voting Rights	Comments
Accurcast	Domestic	100%	Operations are dissimilar from those of the parent and other subsidiaries.
Bonello	Domestic	45	No other shareholder owns more than 0.1% of voting shares.
Cromos	Foreign	30	Cromos has incurred a net operating loss three years in a row.
Fidelis	Domestic	100	Fidelis is under jurisdiction of bankruptcy court.
Jenna	Domestic	100	Operations are immaterial to those of the parent.
Marek	Domestic	40	Management control contract provides Auroral with effective control.
Phenix	Domestic	90	Parent intends to sell one-half of its investment in the company but is not yet actively seeking a buyer.
Regulus	Foreign	50	Regulus is jointly owned with Coronal Company.
Synkron	Foreign	15	No other shareholder owns more than 10% of voting shares.
Tiksed	Foreign	70	Foreign government no longer allows dividends to be repatriated to foreign parent.
Ypsilon	Domestic	51	Remaining 49% is owned by Borealis Inc.

Required:

Determine the appropriate method for including each of these investments in Auroral Company's consolidated financial statements:

a. In accordance with IFRS.

b. In accordance with U.S. GAAP.

6. Sandestino Company contributes cash of $170,000 and Costa Grande Company contributes net assets of $170,000 to create Grand Sand Company on January 1, Year 1. Sandestino and Costa Grande each receive a 50 percent equity interest in Grand Sand. Grand Sand's financial statements for its first year of operations are as follows:

GRAND SAND COMPANY
Income Statement
Year 1

Revenues	$80,000
Expenses	50,000
Income before tax	30,000
Tax expense	10,000
Net income	$20,000

GRAND SAND COMPANY
Balance Sheet
December 31, Year 1

Cash	$ 40,000	Liabilities	$ 60,000
Inventory	60,000	Common stock	340,000
Property, plant, and equipment (net) . . .	320,000	Retained earnings	20,000
Total	$420,000	Total	$420,000

Before making any accounting entries related to its investment in Grand Sand Company, Sandestino Company's financial statements for the year ended December 31, Year 1, are as follows:

SANDESTINO COMPANY
Income Statement
Year 1

Revenues	$800,000
Expenses	450,000
Income before tax	350,000
Tax expense	100,000
Net income	$250,000

SANDESTINO COMPANY
Balance Sheet
December 31, Year 1

Cash	$ 130,000	Liabilities	$ 250,000
Inventory	200,000	Common stock	600,000
Property, plant, and equipment (net)	650,000	Retained earnings . . .	300,000
Investment in Grand Sand (at cost) . .	170,000		
Total	$1,150,000	Total	$1,150,000

Required:

a. Restate Sandestino's Year 1 financial statements to properly account for its investment in Grand Sand Company under (1) the proportionate consolidation method, and (2) the equity method.

b. Calculate and compare the following ratios for Sandestino Company under the two different methods of accounting for its investment in Grand Sand Company: (1) profit margin (net income/revenues), and (2) debt to equity (total liabilities/total stockholders' equity).

7. Horace Jones Company consists of six business segments. The consolidated income statement as well as information about each of the segments for Year 1 as reported to the chief executive officer is as follows:

HORACE JONES COMPANY	
Consolidated Income Statement	
Year 1	
Revenues.	$1,790
Cost of goods sold.	(1,060)
Depreciation and amortization.	(230)
Other operating expenses	(380)
Operating income	120
Interest expense.	(30)
Income before tax	90
Income tax.	(30)
Net income	$ 60

Summary of business segment and general corporate activity for Year 1:

	General Corporate	Segment A	B	C	D	E	F
Revenues:							
External sales revenue	—	1,030	350	20	140	130	120
Intersegment sales revenue	—	30	20	200	10	0	0
Expenses:							
Cost of goods sold.	—	600	300	130	90	60	80
Depreciation and amortization	10	80	100	10	20	5	5
Other operating expenses.	50	120	150	10	30	5	15
Interest expense	—	10	5	5	0	5	5
Income taxes	—	20	(40)	20	5	20	5
Assets:							
Current assets	10	450	150	100	80	150	70
Property, plant and equipment (net).	90	1,200	500	400	200	150	50
Purchases of property, plant and equipment	10	200	50	50	25	20	30
Intangibles.	5	100	30	20	30	10	5
Liabilities	—	750	300	250	170	140	90

Additional information:

At December 31, Year 1, consolidated total assets were $3,800 and consolidated total liabilities were $1,700. There were no significant noncash expenses other than depreciation, and no unusual items included in income. There were no investments in equity method associates or joint ventures.

Required:

The company uses International Financial Reporting Standards (IFRS) to prepare its financial statements. Prepare the note to financial statements in accordance with IFRS 8, *Operating Segments.*

8. Iskender Corporation is a Turkish conglomerate with operations located throughout Europe and the Middle East. The company recently adopted International Financial Reporting Standards and has prepared disclosures to comply with IFRS 8, *Operating Segments.* Information related to revenues:

Operating Segments	Total Revenues	Countries	Sales to External Customers
Automotive	23,093	Turkey	28,876
Food	22,875	Germany	18,765
Retail	13,987	Bulgaria	12,076
Finance	7,895	Russia	9,897
Consumer durable	7,182	Italy	7,654
Energy	6,642	Iraq	6,757
Real estate	5,400	Uzbekistan	3,049
Total	87,074		87,074

Based upon this information, Iskender prepares the following note to comply with IFRS 8:

Note 30: Segment Reporting
(amounts in millions of Turkish Lira)

Operating Segments	Automotive	Food	Retail	Other
External sales	21,678	19,781	13,987	22,397
Profit (loss)	4,076	2,007	3,467	5,563
Depreciation	222	135	142	456
Total assets	18,874	20,765	9,654	20,765
Capital expenditures	367	228	195	513
Equity method investments	398	-0-	-0-	678

Geographic Areas	Turkey	Germany	Bulgaria	Other
External sales	28,876	8,765	12,076	27,357
Property, plant, and equipment . . .	7,078	2,508	3,097	5,478

Required:

Evaluate whether Note 30 Segment Reporting is in compliance with IFRS 8 based upon the information provided.

9. Geographic segment information can be used to determine how multinational a company is and the extent to which a company is diversified internationally. Refer to the geographic segment information provided by three U.S. companies in Exhibit 9.9.

Required:

a. Develop a measure of each company's degree of multinationality.

b. Evaluate the extent to which each company is diversified internationally.

10. The following geographic segment information is provided in the 2009 annual report by two German automakers, BMW and Volkswagen:

BMW AG
Annual Report
2009

Information by region

€ million	External revenues		Noncurrent assets	
	2009	2008	2009	2008
Germany	11,436	10,739	21,136	21,916
United States	10,628	11,349	9,836	11,081
United Kingdom	4,078	4,913	1,596	1,739
Rest of Europe	12,911	15,780	3,155	3,337
Africa/Asia/Oceania	9,823	8,471	1,246	549
Rest of the Americas	1,805	1,945	590	1,169
Eliminations	—	—	(2,822)	(3,334)
Group	50,681	53,197	34,737	36,457

Source: BMW AG, 2009 Annual Report, p. 137.

VOLKSWAGEN AG
Annual Report
2009

By Region 2008

€ million	Germany	Europe and Other Regions*	North America	South America	Asia/ Oceania	Consolidation	Total
Sales revenue from external customers	27,682	55,173	12,716	9,784	8,453	—	113,808
Intangible assets, property, plant and equipment, leasing and rental assets, and investment property	17,604	18,849	7,595	1,253	388	(238)	45,451

*Excluding Germany.

Continued

(Concluded)

By Region 2009

€ million	Germany	Europe and Other Regions*	North America	South America	Asia/ Oceania	Consolidation	Total
Sales revenue from external customers.....	29,836	45,367	11,396	9,606	8,982	—	105,187
Intangible assets, property, plant and equipment, leasing and rental assets, and investment property....	18,696	19,451	7,592	1,525	591	—	47,855

*Excluding Germany.

Source: Volkswagen AG, 2009 Annual Report, p. 231.

Required:

Use the 2009 segment information provided by BMW and Volkswagen to answer the following questions:

a. Which company is more multinational?

b. Which company is more internationally diversified?

c. In which region(s) of the world did each company experience the greatest growth from 2008–2009? greatest decline?

References

American Institute of Certified Public Accountants. *Accounting Trends and Techniques,* 55th ed. New York: AICPA, 2002.

———. Accounting Research Bulletin (ARB) 51, *Consolidated Financial Statements,* 1959.

Gosman, Marty, and Mark J. Kohlbeck. "The Effects of Wal-Mart on the Profitability and Investor Valuation of Its Suppliers." May 30, 2006. Available on SSRN at http://ssrn.com/abstract=906606.

Mexican Institute of Public Accountants. Bulletin B-10, *Recognition of the Inflation Effects in Financial Information.*

Nobes, Christopher W. "An Analysis of the International Development of the Equity Method." *Abacus* 38, no. 1 (2002), pp. 16–45.

Pacter, Paul. *Reporting Disaggregated Information.* Stamford, CT: FASB, February 1993.

Radebaugh, Lee H., and Sidney J. Gray. *International Accounting and Multinational Enterprises,* 5th ed. New York: Wiley, 2002.

Chapter **Ten**

Analysis of Foreign Financial Statements

Learning Objectives

After reading this chapter, you should be able to

- Discuss reasons to analyze financial statements of foreign companies.
- Describe potential problems in analyzing foreign financial statements.
- Provide possible solutions to problems associated with analyzing foreign financial statements.
- Demonstrate an approach for restating foreign financial statements to U.S. generally accepted accounting principles (GAAP).

INTRODUCTION

There are more than 400 foreign companies listed on the New York Stock Exchange, and a similar number are listed on the London Stock Exchange. All of the major mutual fund companies—including American Century, Fidelity, and Vanguard—offer international stock funds that focus on non-U.S. firms. Many multinational companies borrow money in foreign countries and provide credit to their foreign suppliers. Investors and creditors generally find financial statements to be useful in making decisions to invest in the stock of foreign companies or extend credit to foreign borrowers.

This chapter deals with the analysis of financial statements prepared by foreign companies. The first and second sections provide an overview of financial statement analysis in general and describe several reasons for analyzing foreign financial statements. The third section describes potential problems associated with analyzing foreign financial statements and discusses possible solutions to those problems. The final section demonstrates an approach that can be used to restate a set of foreign financial statements prepared in accordance with local accounting practice to a set of generally accepted accounting principles (GAAP) more familiar to the reader.

OVERVIEW OF FINANCIAL STATEMENT ANALYSIS

Financial statement analysis is a part of *business analysis*. Business analysis is the evaluation of a company's business environment, strategies, financial position, and performance to be able to make decisions with respect to that company.

Whether to extend credit to a company or to invest in a company's equity securities are important decisions based on business analysis. Business analysis is conducted using relevant information available about a company. Financial statements are an important source of information for conducting business analysis.

Financial statement analysis consists of the following steps:

1. Accounting analysis.
2. Financial analysis.
3. Prospective analysis.

Accounting analysis begins with an evaluation of the extent to which a company's financial statements reflect economic reality. There are three common sources of distortion in financial statements:

1. Accounting standards that are inconsistent with economic reality (a rule that requires all research and development costs to be expensed immediately with no possibility of recognizing an asset is an example).
2. Estimation errors made by managers in applying accounting standards (the estimation of the cost of pension and other postretirement benefits is an example).
3. The intentional manipulation of financial statements by managers, often referred to as earnings management (the intentional overstatement of an accrued restructuring charge is an example).

Accounting analysis involves identifying distortions in financial statements and making adjustments to the financial statements where possible. The ability to make adjustments will be determined by whether a company discloses adequate information to allow an adjustment to be made. The extent to which accounting standards induce financial statement distortions will differ from country to country because of differences in national accounting rules. Differences also exist across countries with respect to the amount and type of disclosures required to be provided in financial statements.

Financial analysis involves the use of adjusted financial statement information to conduct:

1. Cash flow analysis, the analysis of how a company generates and uses cash.
2. Profitability analysis, with a focus on return on invested capital.
3. Risk analysis, including an evaluation of liquidity and solvency to assess a company's ability to meet its obligations.

Much of financial analysis is conducted through the use of ratios calculated from the financial statements. Financial ratios are compared within a company over time to determine whether the company's ability to generate cash flows, earn a return on invested capital, and so on, is improving or deteriorating. Ratios also are compared across companies operating in the same industry to evaluate companies relative to their peers. The diversity of accounting principles and practices that exists across countries hampers our ability to directly compare companies operating in the same industry but located in different countries.

Prospective analysis involves combining the results of accounting analysis and financial analysis, along with an analysis of the business environment and company strategy, to forecast future financial statement information, especially cash flows and income. Preparing forecasted future financial statements is a very important part of business analysis because decisions made today about a company are based on forecasts of the company's future prospects.

REASONS TO ANALYZE FOREIGN FINANCIAL STATEMENTS

Many users of financial statements might find it necessary to read and analyze the statements of foreign companies. Some common reasons for doing so are described in this section.

Foreign Portfolio Investment

Investors can reduce portfolio risks by diversifying internationally. Research shows that stock market returns across countries are not highly correlated.[1] For example, during the period 1997–2004, the correlation of U.S. stock returns with returns on major stock exchanges in Latin America ranged from 0.311 (Argentina) to 0.607 (Brazil). The high degree of independence across capital markets leaves substantial room for risk diversification.

Since the mid-1980s, U.S. investment firms have created a plethora of international and country-specific mutual funds. For example, Fidelity Investments offers the following targeted-country or regional stock funds: Canada, China Region, Europe, Europe Capital Appreciation, Japan, Japan Smaller Companies, Nordic, Pacific Basin, Latin America, and Southeast Asia. Fidelity's Emerging Markets Fund invests in companies located in 34 different countries, including Brazil, Turkey, and Thailand. T. Rowe Price's New Asia Fund invests in stocks of non-Japanese Asian companies, and its International Discovery Fund invests in common stocks of non-U.S. companies all over the world. The latter fund includes shares of companies from more than 36 different countries. The manager of each of these funds must decide which non-U.S. companies' stock to add to the fund's portfolio. Individual investors can invest in these funds and thereby diversify their personal portfolios internationally without incurring the costs of investing in foreign stocks directly.

International Mergers and Acquisitions

Interest in foreign financial statements also has grown with the increase in international mergers and acquisitions. Some of the largest mergers in the United States in recent years have involved foreign companies acquiring U.S. firms. The Ambev/Anheuser-Busch and BP/Amoco mergers are two examples. Over the last quarter century, Ford Motor Company acquired an equity interest in companies located in Great Britain (Jaguar, Land Rover, Aston Martin); Sweden (Volvo); and Japan (Mazda).[2] As a part of the due diligence process leading to an acquisition, financial analysts from the acquiring firm will use the financial statements of the target company as a starting point for determining how much to pay.

After the economic opening of Eastern Europe in 1989, one of the early impediments to Western investment in that region was a lack of economically meaningful financial statements for existing enterprises. Soviet-style accounting statements were prepared for national planning purposes, not for determining enterprise value. Potential buyers of privatized state-owned enterprises often found it necessary to engage one of the international public accounting firms to develop a set of financial statements based on U.S. GAAP or some other set of accounting rules that provide a more realistic picture of the company's assets and profitability.

---

[1] See, for example, Chiaku Chukwuogor, "Stock Markets Returns and Volatilities: A Global Comparison," *International Research Journal of Finance and Economics,* no. 15, 2008.

[2] In 2007, Ford sold Jaguar and Land Rover to Tata Motors of India and Aston Martin to a consortium of investors. In 2010, it reached a deal to sell Volvo to China's Zhejiang Geely Holding Group.

Other Reasons

Other reasons to evaluate foreign company financial statements include

1. Making credit decisions about foreign customers.
2. Evaluating the financial health of foreign suppliers.
3. Benchmarking against global competitors.

The next section of this chapter describes potential problems in evaluating foreign financial statements and discusses possible solutions. We focus on analyzing foreign financial statements for the purpose of making equity investment decisions.

POTENTIAL PROBLEMS IN ANALYZING FOREIGN FINANCIAL STATEMENTS

Given the information provided in earlier chapters, it should be obvious that diversity in accounting principles is one of the most significant problems in analyzing foreign financial statements. Other problems, however, may be more difficult to overcome. To appreciate the various potential problems, assume that you have taken a job with The Vanguard Group, headquartered in Valley Forge, Pennsylvania. You have been hired to assist the manager of the International Stock Fund. Your boss has decided that a certain percentage of the fund's assets should be invested in the publicly traded shares of European companies. Your job is to recommend specific companies to invest in. At least one source of information you would like to use in making your recommendations is corporate financial statements. What are the potential problems that might arise as you conduct your analysis?

Data Accessibility

Financial data for foreign companies may not be as easy to obtain as that for domestic companies. However, as international investment in equities has become more prevalent, several companies have gotten into the business of developing databases that provide financial information on foreign companies. For example, Standard & Poor's Compustat Global database provides data for 16,000 international companies in more than 80 countries. Worldscope, provided by Thomson Financial, also provides financial statement data for non-U.S. firms. In addition to providing balance sheet and income statement information, most data sources provide additional information such as financial ratios and stock prices.

There are several limitations in using commercial databases to analyze foreign companies. The first is the potential for errors when the data are entered into the database. A more serious potential problem relates to the use of a common balance sheet and income statement format for all companies in the database. Formats of financial statements differ across countries. In fact, some financial statement line items are unique to a particular country. Analysts who force all financial statements into a common format can lose information. The third, and probably greatest, limitation relates to the loss of information provided in the notes to the financial statements. None of the commercial databases provides a complete set of notes. Notes often provide important qualitative as well as quantitative information that is not available if the analyst does not have access to the actual annual report.

There are several avenues an analyst might use to obtain a copy of a foreign company's annual report. One way would be to write or call the company and request a copy. Of course, the analyst would have to know the company's address or telephone number and would have to expect some delay in receiving the report. A second way would be to use the Internet. Many companies, both domestic and foreign, maintain a Web site on which they post financial statements or through which an analyst may request an annual report. The following are Internet resources that can be helpful in obtaining financial information on foreign companies:

- Hoover's (www.hoovers.com) provides capsule information for U.S. and foreign companies, as well as links to company home pages. Access to more in-depth company profiles requires a subscription.
- The U.S. Securities and Exchange Commission (SEC; www.sec.gov) maintains a database known as Electronic Data Gathering, Analysis, and Retrieval (EDGAR), which contains the full text of reports filed electronically with the SEC, including some foreign companies listed on U.S. stock exchanges. Unfortunately, many foreign companies file annual reports with the SEC only on paper, so an electronic version is not available.
- Annual Reports.com (www.annualreports.com) allows users to search for annual reports of companies listed on stock exchanges in the United States, the United Kingdom, Canada, and Australia by name, ticker symbol, stock exchange, and industry.

Language

Even if an analyst can obtain financial statements from foreign companies, he or she must realize that those statements will be in the local language. Exhibit 10.1 presents a page from the 2009 annual report of Metso OY, a Finnish company that provides equipment and services to the paper, mining, and process industries. Although the excerpt presented in Exhibit 10.1 appears to be an accounting report, anyone who is not relatively fluent in Finnish will find it difficult to know with certainty what information is being provided. There are two possible solutions to the language problem:

1. Hire a professional translator to translate the annual report.
2. Develop a multilingual capability, possibly using a team approach in which each member of the team is fluent in a different foreign language.

The least costly solution to the language problem for the analyst would be for the foreign company to prepare a "convenience translation" of the report in a language that the analyst can read. Many large foreign companies translate their annual reports into foreign languages (especially English) for the convenience of foreign audiences of interest. Exhibit 10.2 shows the extent to which companies in a number of foreign countries provide financial statements in English.

In many cases, companies with securities registered in a foreign country are required to translate the annual report into the language of that country. Foreign companies listed on U.S. stock exchanges, for example, must file an English-language annual report with the SEC. However, quarterly reports may be filed in a foreign language. Exhibit 10.2 shows the extent to which companies in a number of non-English-speaking countries provided financial statements in English in 2004.

Few U.S.-based companies prepare convenience translations. During the 1980s, International Business Machines (IBM) prepared a translation of its annual report in French and Japanese. The French version might be explained by the fact that

EXHIBIT 10.1

METSO OY
Annual Report (in Finnish)
2009

Konsernin Tuloslaskelma

Milj. e	Liitetieto	2007	2008	2009
		31.12. päättynyt tilikausi		
Liikevaihto	32	6,250	6,400	**5,016**
Hankinnan ja valmistuksen kulut	6, 7	−4,702	−4,733	**−3,808**
Bruttokate		1,548	1,667	**1,208**
Myynnin ja hallinnon yleiskustannukset	4, 6, 7	−972	−1,043	**−938**
Liiketoiminnan muut tuotot ja kulut, netto	5, 32	1	11	**24**
Osuus osakkuusyhtiöiden tuloksista	14, 32	3	2	**0**
Liikevoitto	32	580	637	**294**
%:a liikevaihdosta		9.3%	10.0%	**5.9%**
Rahoitustuotot ja -kulut, netto	8	−33	−89	**−72**
Tulos ennen veroja		547	548	**222**
Tuloverot	9	−163	−158	**−71**
Tilikauden tulos		384	390	151
Jakautuminen:				
Emoyhtiön omistajiile		381	389	**150**
Vähemmistölle		3	1	**1**
Tilikauden tulos		384	390	151
Tulos/Osake				
Laimentamaton, euroa	12	2.69	2.75	**1.06**
Laimennettu, euroa	12	2.69	2.75	**1.06**

EXHIBIT 10.2
Extent of English-Language Annual Reports

Source: Jeanjean, T., Lesage, C., and Stolowy, H. Why do you speak English (in your annual report)?, *The International Journal of Accounting* 45 (2010), pp. 200-223.

Percentage of Companies That Provide Financial Statements in English					
Country	**%**	**Country**	**%**	**Country**	**%**
Israel	88.6	China	70.5	Indonesia	41.7
Finland	87.4	South Korea	67.6	Japan	38.3
Netherlands	87.9	Germany	59.0	Mexico	29.3
Belgium	83.3	Italy	58.1	Brazil	15.0
Switzerland	81.0	France	42.4	Chile	8.6

IBM's European headquarters were in Paris. The Japanese version probably resulted from IBM's having a large operation in Japan. IBM no longer prepares a convenience translation in either language.

Currency

Exhibit 10.3 presents the English-language version of the excerpt from Metso OY's annual report presented in Exhibit 10.1. Non-Finnish readers now can see that this is an income statement. The amounts are reported in euros. An analyst

EXHIBIT 10.3

METSO OY
Annual Report (in English)
2009

Consolidated Statements of Income

EUR million	Note	Year ended December 31,		
		2007	2008	**2009**
Net sales	**32**	6,250	6,400	**5,016**
Cost of goods sold.	**6, 7**	(4,702)	(4,733)	**(3,808)**
Gross profit		1,548	1,667	**1,208**
Selling, general and administrative expenses	**4, 6, 7**	(972)	(1,043)	**(938)**
Other operating income and expenses, net	**5, 32**	1	11	**24**
Share in profits and losses of associated companies	**14, 32**	3	2	**0**
Operating profit.	**32**	580	637	**294**
% of net sales		9.3%	10.0%	**5.9%**
Financial income and expenses, net	**8**	(33)	(89)	**(72)**
Profit before tax.		547	548	**222**
Income taxes	**9**	(163)	(158)	**(71)**
Profit		384	390	**151**
Attributable to:				
Shareholders of the company.		381	389	**150**
Minority interests		3	1	**1**
Profit		384	390	**151**
Earnings per share				
Basic, EUR	**12**	2.69	2.75	**1.06**
Diluted, EUR.	**12**	2.69	2.75	**1.06**

might like to have these amounts in, say, U.S. dollars to be able to compare with non-European companies. This requires translation from one currency to another. In translating financial statement amounts for the sake of convenience, all financial statement items, including stockholders' equity, should be translated at the current exchange rate. This avoids a translation adjustment. The analyst must be careful to translate previous years' comparative information using the exchange rate for the current year, not the current rate at the end of each year. The following example demonstrates the problem that arises when trend analysis is conducted using currency amounts translated using each year's ending exchange rate.

Assume that a European company has sales of €1,000 in Year 1 and €1,100 in Year 2, an increase of 10 percent. Assume further that the exchange rates were $1.40 per euro at the end of Year 1 and $1.50 per euro at the end of Year 2. Translation of the euro amounts using the exchange rate at the end of each year results in the following:

	Year 1	Year 2	% Change
Sales in €	€1,000	€1,100	+10%
	× $ 1.40	× $ 1.50	
Sales in $	$1,400	$1,650	+18%

Using different exchange rates to translate sales for the two years distorts the actual change in sales from Year 1 to Year 2.

Translation at the current exchange rate at the end of Year 2 maintains the percentage change in sales in terms of euros:

	Year 1	Year 2	% Change
Sales in €	€1,000	€1,100	+10%
	× $ 1.50	× $ 1.50	
Sales in $	$1,500	$1,650	+10%

In addition to translating the language, some foreign companies will also translate the currency of their financial statements in their convenience translations. This is especially true for Japanese companies that routinely translate financial statements into U.S. dollars. However, only the current-year Japanese yen amounts are translated into dollars, thus avoiding the potential problem just demonstrated. It is uncommon for European companies to translate the currency in their English-language convenience reports, perhaps because most European multinationals share a common currency, the euro.

The fact that foreign financial statements are prepared in a foreign currency is really not a problem in analyzing those statements. Much financial statement analysis is conducted using ratios. Ratios are not expressed in any currency but instead in percentage terms. For example, a company with net income of €100 and sales of €1,000 has a profit margin of 10 percent, not €10. The profit margin of a company in, say, Brazil can be compared directly with that of a company in, say, Mexico regardless of the currencies in which sales and profit are expressed. Additionally, year-to-year changes within a company also are expressed in percentage terms, thus removing the currency issue.

Terminology

Even if a foreign company has translated its financial statements into English for the convenience of English-speaking analysts, confusion can arise because of the terminology used. Differences in terminology between British and American companies are well-known and at first may cause some problems. However, it should not require much effort for an analyst in one country to become fluent in the terminology of the other country. Moreover, much of the difference in terminology that used to exist was removed in 2005 with the adoption of IFRS in the United Kingdom. IAS 1 provides standard formats for financial statements using primarily American terminology. As a result, for example, British companies now use the term *inventories* to describe this asset rather than the traditional term *stocks*. Some non-U.K. companies, however, continue to use traditional British terminology. New Zealand–based Fletcher Building Ltd., for example, continues to use the terms debtors (accounts receivable), stocks (inventories), and creditors (payables) in its balance sheet. The use of nonstandard or unusual terminology is less easy to deal with.

Several anecdotal examples of financial statement items that might lead to interpretation problems include the following:

- "Special goodwill reserve"—reported as an element of stockholders' equity in Pão de Açucar's (Brazil) balance sheet.
- "EBITDAR"—reported as a subtotal in Sol Melia's (Spain) income statement.

- "Monetary position loss"—reported as a negative item in Industrias Bachoco's (Mexico) income statement.
- "Equity method in capital adjustments"—included as a separate line item in the stockholders' equity section of SK Telecom's (South Korea) balance sheet.
- "Materials on the leach pad"—included as a separate line item in both the current asset and the noncurrent asset sections of Anglogold Ashanti Ltd.'s (South Africa) balance sheet.

Familiarity with the business environment and accounting practices in each of these countries and a careful reading of the notes to the financial statements can help alleviate problems in understanding what might appear to be odd terminology.

Format

The format of financial statements can vary across countries. Most format differences should not present much of a problem to the financial analyst. Often financial statements can be reformatted to allow for comparisons across countries. For example, whether or not interest expense is treated as an operating expense and subtracted from operating income is a trivial issue so long as it is disclosed as a separate line item. But some format differences lead to different amounts of information being provided in the financial statements. For example, the type of expense format income statement commonly found in Europe does not report the amount of cost of goods sold. An example of this format is presented in Exhibit 10.4 for the Swiss company Swatch Group Ltd. It is not possible to calculate gross profit or a gross profit margin (Gross profit/Net sales) for companies such as Swatch that use this format.

Extent of Disclosure

Amounts and types of disclosure differ across countries. An analyst's ability to reformat or adjust foreign financial statements will partially depend on whether adequate information is disclosed to allow adjustments to be made. A common adjustment made to financial statements relates to leases. Current rules under IFRS, U.S. GAAP, and other national accounting standards require leases to be capitalized when certain criteria are met. Leases not meeting the criteria for capitalization are treated as operating leases, for which certain disclosures must be made. U.S. GAAP requires the disclosure of future minimum lease payments in each of the next five years and for all years thereafter. IFRS requires disclosure of the operating lease payments to be made in the next year, for the next 2–5 years in total, and all years thereafter. Exhibit 10.5 presents typical operating lease disclosures for two companies; Southwest Airlines Co., which uses U.S. GAAP, and Turkish Airlines, which uses IFRS.

Some financial analysts believe that all leases, including operating leases, should be capitalized. To do this, the present value of future operating lease payments must be determined and both an asset and liability reflecting this amount should be reported on the balance sheet. The disclosures related to operating leases provided by Southwest Airlines are more useful than those provided by Turkish Airlines in accomplishing this adjustment. Disclosure by Southwest Airlines of the total minimum lease payments and present value of minimum lease payments related to capital leases allows an analyst to determine the implicit interest rate in capital leases. This rate can be used as the discount rate in determining the present value of the operating lease payments. Turkish Airlines does not provide similar information. Turkish Airlines also does not indicate the

EXHIBIT 10.4

SWATCH GROUP LTD.
Annual Report
2009

Consolidated Income Statement

	Notes	2009 CHF million	%	2008 CHF million	%
Gross sales		**5,421**	**105.4**	5,966	105.1
Sales reductions		**(279)**	**(5.4)**	(289)	(5.1)
Net Sales	(5, 6a)	**5,142**	**100.0**	5,677	100.0
Other operating income	(6b)	**104**	**2.0**	231	4.1
Changes in inventories		**9**	**0.2**	513	9.0
Material purchases		**(1,103)**	**(21.4)**	(1,567)	(27.6)
Personnel expense	(6c)	**(1,596)**	**(31.0)**	(1,633)	(28.8)
Other operating expenses	(6d)	**(1,433)**	**(27.9)**	(1,799)	(31.6)
Depreciation, amortization and impairment charges	(10, 11, 12, 18)	**(220)**	**(4.3)**	(220)	(3.9)
Operating profit		**903**	**17.6**	1,202	21.2
Other financial income and expense	(6f)	**59**	**1.2**	(179)	(3.2)
Interest expense	(6f)	**(18)**	**(0.4)**	(22)	(0.4)
Share of result from associates and joint ventures	(6f, 13)	**5**	**0.1**	5	0.1
Profit before taxes		**949**	**18.5**	1,006	17.7
Income taxes	(7a)	**(186)**	**(3.7)**	(168)	(2.9)
Net income		**763**	**14.8**	838	14.8
Attributable to equity holders of The Swatch Group Ltd		**759**		834	
Attributable to noncontrolling interests		**4**		4	

amount of future lease payment in each of the next five years, instead aggregating Years 2–5 into a single amount. An analyst must make an assumption with respect to the amount of lease payment in each of the next five years to be able to determine their present value. This assumption is not needed for Southwest Airlines. Neither company indicates the annual payment that will be made beyond Year 5, so an assumption must be made for both companies about the timing of payments beyond that year.

Historically, many continental European companies have used provisions (accrued liabilities) to conceal profits and create hidden reserves. In profitable years, provisions are created for items such as deferred maintenance and uncertain liabilities. The counterpart to the accrual on the balance sheet is an expense reported in income. In years in which profits are below expectations, these "cookie jar" reserves are released with an offsetting increase in income.[3] One of the most

---

[3] The term *cookie jar reserves* was made popular by former SEC chairman Arthur Levitt in describing earnings management practices by U.S. companies. See, for example, Arthur Levitt, "A Public Partnership to Battle Earnings Management," *Accounting Today*, May 24–June 6, 1999, p. 36.

EXHIBIT 10.5
Operating Lease Disclosures for Two Companies in the Airline Industry

SOUTHWEST AIRLINES
2009 Annual Report
Note 8. Leases

Total rental expense for operating leases, both aircraft and other, charged to operations in 2009, 2008, and 2007 was $596 million, $527 million, and $469 million, respectively. The majority of the Company's terminal operations space, as well as 88 aircraft, were under operating leases at December 31, 2009. Future minimum lease payments under capital leases and noncancelable operating leases with initial or remaining terms in excess of one year at December 31, 2009, were:

	Capital Leases	Operating Leases
	(In millions)	
2010	$15	$ 414
2011	12	379
2012	—	333
2013	—	254
2014	—	222
After 2014	—	1,032
Total minimum lease payments	27	$2,634
Less amount representing interest	2	
Present value of minimum lease payments	25	
Less current portion	14	
Long-term portion	$11	

TURKISH AIRLINES
2009 Annual Report
Note 23. Commitments

The Group's not accrued operational leasing debts details are as follows:

	31 December 2009	31 December 2008
Less than 1 year	312,850,973	201,619,938
Between 1–5 years	853,516,736	684,056,091
More than 5 years	422,992,569	422,009,094
Total	1,589,360,278	1,307,685,123

dramatic examples of the use of hidden reserves was carried out by Daimler-Benz in 1989 when, through the reversal of a provision for pensions, income was reported as DM 6.8 billion rather than DM 1.9 billion. Disclosures related to provisions allow analysts to assess the impact provisions have on income.

Exhibit 10.6 presents an excerpt from Südzucker AG's note related to provisions other than those related to pensions. From this note one can see that total provisions at the beginning of the 2009/2010 fiscal year were €318.2 million. During the year, €99.5 million of that amount was used, resulting in a reduction in assets with an offsetting decrease in provisions. An additional €31.4 million was released, resulting in a €31.4 million increase in pretax income. Pretax income was reduced, however, by additions to provisions in the amount of €103.3 million. Including the increase in provisions due to the change in companies consolidated, the movement in provisions during the year served to decrease pretax income by €25.7 million (€318.2 million − €292.5 million), an amount equal to 7.4 percent of reported earnings before income taxes.

EXHIBIT 10.6

SÜDZUCKER AG
Annual Report
2009/2010

Note 27. Movements in other provisions

2009/10

€ million	Personnel-related provisions	Other provisions	Total
Status as at 1 March 2009	**93.2**	**225.0**	**318.2**
Change in companies incl. in the consolidation/currency translation/other changes	0.6	1.3	1.9
Additions	13.3	90.0	103.3
Use	(20.1)	(79.4)	(99.5)
Release	(11.8)	(19.6)	(31.4)
Status as at 28 February 2010	**75.2**	**217.3**	**292.5**

Research shows that many large companies interested in attracting foreign portfolio investors or entering foreign capital markets voluntarily provide disclosures that exceed local requirements.[4] For example, although European Union rules prior to 2005 did not require presentation of a statement of cash flows, it was common for multinational firms located in the EU to provide a statement of cash flows in their annual report prior to being required to do so under IFRS.

Timeliness

The usefulness of accounting information is in part a function of its timeliness, that is, how soon after the end of the fiscal year the information is made available to the public. The time lag between the end of the year and the publication of financial statements varies considerably across countries. The variance is partly attributable to the length of time allowed by the stock market regulator in each country. U.S. companies must file their annual report with the SEC within 60 days of the end of the year. Publicly traded British companies, in contrast, are allowed six months to file their reports. Clearly, an analyst would prefer to receive financial information sooner rather than later. The usefulness of information received in June 2011 related to the period ended December 31, 2010, is questionable. The average number of days between year-end and the date auditors sign the audit report (and the annual report is ready to publish) for seven economically important countries in 1995 was as follows:[5]

Average Number of Days	Countries
31–60 days	Canada, United States
61–90 days	Japan, United Kingdom
91–120 days	France, Germany, Italy

[4] S. J. Gray, G. K. Meek, and C. B. Roberts, "International Capital Market Pressures and Voluntary Annual Report Disclosures by US and UK Multinationals," *Journal of International Financial Management and Accounting* 6, no. 1 (1995), pp. 43–68.

[5] This information was obtained from V. B. Bavishi, ed., *International Accounting and Auditing Trends, vol. 2,* 4th ed. (Princeton, NJ: CIFAR Publications, 1995).

The frequency of reporting also differs across countries. Quarterly reports are required in the United States, the United Kingdom, and Canada. European Union directives require semiannual reports. Many countries require only an annual report. In a country with only annual reports where the stock exchange authority allows a six-month time lag in publishing financial statements, there can be a 15-month period between the end of the first quarter of the fiscal year and the publication of reports related to that period. There is virtually nothing an individual analyst can do about the timeliness and frequency of reporting issues.

Differences in Accounting Principles

Differences in accounting principles for recognizing and measuring assets, liabilities, revenues, and expenses can have a significant impact on the amounts reported by companies in their financial statements. In a study conducted in France in 1990, the activities of a hypothetical company were accounted for using the accounting principles in six different countries.[6] The resulting amounts of profit are as follows:

Profit of Hypothetical Company Using Accounting Principles in Six Countries

Belgium	+460	Netherlands	+520
France	+840	United Kingdom	−160
Germany	−520	United States	−235

Profit for the hypothetical company ranged from −520 to +840 depending on which country's accounting principles were followed.

Until 2007, non-U.S. companies' listed on U.S. stock exchanges were required to reconcile net income and total stockholders' equity in terms of U.S. GAAP. Exhibit 10.7 presents the percentage difference in net income and stockholders' equity determined under local GAAP and U.S. GAAP for a group of non-U.S. biotechnology companies. Each of these companies used IFRS as its local GAAP.

EXHIBIT 10.7

Percentage Differences in Net Income and Stockholders' Equity between Local GAAP and U.S. GAAP for Selected Biotechnology Companies

Source: 2005 Form 20-F filed with the U.S. SEC obtained through the SEC's EDGAR (www.sec.gov).

Country/Company	Reconciliation from Local GAAP to U.S. GAAP	
	% Difference in Net Income	% Difference in Stockholders' Equity
United Kingdom		
Acambis	+24.8%	−5.8%
Netherlands		
Crucell	−58.1%	−4.8%
Australia		
Prana Biotechnology	−10.6%	No difference
Ireland		
Trinity Biotechnology	−51.1%	−0.6%
Switzerland		
Serono	−102.6%	−6.8%

[6] "Profits Ici Pertes Au-Dela," *L'Enterprise* No. 63, December 1990, pp. 78–79.

Across the five companies presented in Exhibit 10.7, converting to U.S. GAAP resulted in a smaller amount of net income (or larger amount of net loss) being reported by four companies, and a larger amount of net income (or smaller amount of net loss) for one company. The adjustments ranged from −102.6 percent to +24.8 percent. The effect on stockholders' equity was much smaller, ranging from −6.8 percent to no difference.

The percentages reported in Exhibit 10.7 show that differences in accounting principles can have a significant impact on the amount of income and equity reported by a company. More importantly, the *magnitude* of the change differs significantly across companies as does the *direction* of the change. There is no simple rule of thumb, such as, "Add 10 percent," that can be used to restate earnings for these companies to the common denominator of U.S. GAAP.

The important question is whether differences in accounting principles actually affect investment decisions. Choi and Levich addressed this question through interviews with 16 institutional investors in Japan, Switzerland, the United Kingdom, and the United States.[7] Their major findings are summarized as follows:

1. Nine of 16 investors indicated that accounting diversity hindered the measurement of their decision variables and ultimately affected their investment decisions. The effects of accounting diversity included limiting the geographic spread of investments and precluding certain types of companies from analysis.

2. Seven of the nine investors who found accounting diversity to be a problem attempted to cope by restating foreign financial statements to an accounting framework familiar to the analyst, such as U.S. GAAP. Two coped by adopting specific investment strategies. One invested only in government bonds. The other used a "top-down" investment approach in which investors use macroeconomic data to decide how much of the investment portfolio to allocate to a particular country. Once they decide how much to invest in a given country, the investors acquire a diversified portfolio of stocks in that country.

3. Of the seven investors who said accounting diversity did not hinder their decision making, four had developed a "multiple principles capability," in which investors use a local perspective when analyzing foreign financial statements. The idea is to use foreign GAAP statements and a well-developed knowledge of foreign accounting principles and foreign financial market conditions to make decisions. Three investors attempted to deal with the problem by using information less sensitive to accounting diversity. For example, one investor valued securities by using a discounted dividends model rather than a discounted earnings approach.

4. Countries most often mentioned as a source of concern for analysts were Japan, Switzerland, and Germany.

5. The most troublesome areas in which accounting differences existed were consolidations, valuation and depreciation of fixed assets, deferred income taxes, pensions, marketable securities, discretionary reserves, foreign currency transactions and translation, leases, goodwill, long-term construction contracts, inventory valuation, and provisions.

6. Areas in which lack of disclosure is a hindrance included segment information, method of asset valuation, information about foreign operations, frequency and completeness of interim financial statements, description of capital

[7] F. D. S. Choi and R. M. Levich, "Behavioral Effects of International Accounting Diversity," *Accounting Horizons,* June 1991, pp. 1–13.

expenditures, hidden reserves, and off-balance-sheet items. Several investors indicated overcoming the lack-of-disclosure problem by making visits to the companies being analyzed.

A significant number of investors interviewed by Choi and Levich said that they attempt to restate foreign financial statements to a familiar GAAP, focusing on restatement of earnings. One of the most sophisticated attempts to restate financial statements of companies located in different countries was carried out by Morgan Stanley Dean Witter in its so-called Apples-to-Apples project. The appendix to this chapter describes this project.

Another mechanism for dealing with accounting differences is to use a measure of earnings from which many accounting issues are removed. Sherman and Todd recommend using operating income before depreciation (OIBD) as the relevant earnings measure for evaluating company performance.[8] The logic of this approach can be seen by considering the following typical income statement:

Sales
Less: Operating expenses (cost of goods sold; general, selling, and administrative expenses)
Operating income
Less: Interest expense
Income before taxes
Less: Income tax expense
Net income

OIBD is measured by adding the depreciation included in operating expenses back to operating income. Basing analysis on OIBD removes the effect of depreciation, interest, and income taxes from the relevant measure of earnings, and any differences in the way these items are accounted for become irrelevant. Amortization of intangibles often also is added back to OIBD. The resulting measure is more commonly referred to as earnings before interest, taxes, depreciation, and amortization (EBITDA).

Additional adjustments can be made to EBITDA to further isolate the effects of accounting diversity. For example, because the determination of pension expense can vary greatly across countries, adding back the pension expense included in operating expenses to EBITDA would result in a more comparable measure of income across countries. The potential problem with this approach is that each item removed may have implications for determining the value of the firm. Removing interest expense from the earnings measure may make companies' financial statements more comparable, but it makes the earnings measure less representative of future cash flows. Carried to its logical extreme, EBITDA could be adjusted to the point where sales is the measure of performance used to analyze companies. While sales are important, they represent only one part of what determines a firm's value.

With the increased use of IFRS across countries, the problems associated with accounting diversity that once existed undoubtedly have become smaller. However, until the point is reached where all companies are using common formats, terminology, and principles in preparing their financial statements, analysts must

[8] R. Sherman and R. Todd, "International Financial Statement Analysis," in *International Accounting and Finance Handbook,* 2nd ed., ed. F. D. S. Choi (New York: John Wiley & Sons, 1997), pp. 8.1–8.61.

develop methods for coping with the potentially harmful effects of accounting diversity.

International Ratio Analysis

Even if an analyst has foreign financial statements that are prepared under a set of accounting principles with which the analyst is familiar, the use of ratio analysis can be misleading because of environmental differences across countries.

Through a comparison of financial ratios in Japan, Korea, and the United States, Choi and colleagues show that substantial differences exist that are not attributable solely to differences in accounting methods.[9] Ratios are different across these three countries also because of significant differences in economic and social environments.

Exhibit 10.8 presents the means for a number of important financial ratios for a broad cross-section of companies in Japan, Korea, and the United States in 1978. Comparing these ratios, an analyst might have concluded that Japanese and Korean firms were less liquid, less profitable, and less efficient in managing their assets than U.S. companies. Although a portion of the differences in ratios is due to accounting diversity, Choi and colleagues explain that much of the difference across the three countries can be explained by differences in economic and business environments. To demonstrate the effect that environmental differences can have on financial ratios, we discuss differences in the mean current ratio, debt ratio, and profit margin across the three countries:[10]

- *Current ratio:* The current ratio (Current assets/Current liabilities) is a measure of liquidity that is used in assessing the ability of a company to pay its short-term obligations. This ratio indicates that Japanese and Korean firms appear to have been significantly less likely to meet their short-term obligations than U.S. firms. Choi and colleagues explain that the differences in this ratio can be explained partly by the fact that Japanese and Korean companies often used short-term debt to finance fixed assets. They would borrow on a short-term basis, repay the borrowing when it came due, and then negotiate a new short-term loan at that point. By successive rollovers of short-term debt, a series of 20 three-month loans, for example, became five-year financing. Renegotiation of loans was not a problem because of close relationships between companies and banks. Companies preferred short-term loans because interest rates were lower than on long-term financing, and banks preferred short-term loans because they could adjust interest rates more frequently. Excluding short-term debt from current liabilities might have resulted in a more meaningful current ratio for these firms.

- *Debt ratio:* The debt ratio (Total liabilities/Total assets) provides a measure of financial leverage, that is, the extent to which assets are financed by liabilities. It is used to assess the risk that a firm might not be able to repay its obligations,

---

[9] F. D. S. Choi, H. Hino, S. K. Min, S. O. Nam, J. Ujiie, and A. I. Stonehill, "Analyzing Foreign Financial Statements: The Use and Misuse of International Ratio Analysis," *Journal of International Business Studies,* Spring/Summer 1983, pp. 113–31.

[10] The ratios reported in Exhibit 10.8 are for the year 1978; the discussion is based on the economic and business environment in Japan, Korea, and the United States at that time. Significant changes have occurred in these countries in the intervening years. The differences in ratios found in 1978 might or might not exist today; no recent study investigating differences in ratios across these three countries has been conducted.

EXHIBIT 10.8
Mean Financial
Ratios in Japan,
Korea, and the
United States, 1978

Source: F. D. S. Choi, H. Hino, S. K. Min, S. O. Nam, J. Ujiie, and A. I. Stonehill. "Analyzing Foreign Financial Statements: The Use and Misuse of International Ratio Analysis," *Journal of International Business Studies,* Spring/Summer 1983, p. 116.

	Current Ratio	Quick Ratio	Debt Ratio	Times Interest Earned	Inventory Turnover
Japan (*n* = 976)	1.15	0.80	0.84	1.60	5.00
Korea (*n* = 354)	1.13	0.46	0.78	1.80	6.60
United States (*n* = 902)	1.94	1.10	0.47	6.50	6.80

	Average Collection Period	Fixed Asset Turnover	Total Asset Turnover	Profit Margin	Return on Assets	Return on Equity
Japan (*n* = 976)	86	3.10	0.93	0.013	0.012	0.071
Korea (*n* = 354)	33	2.80	1.20	0.023	0.028	0.131
United States (*n* = 902)	43	3.90	1.40	0.054	0.074	0.139

both short-term and long-term, on time. As Choi and colleagues explain, high debt ratios in Japan resulted from the reliance on bank financing that was partly a function of low levels of personal savings at the end of World War II. In addition, relatively low interest rates on bank loans made debt financing attractive. In Korea, bank loans tended to be influenced by the government. Given the limited amount of financing available, the government directed funds to companies that the government wanted to promote. A high debt ratio, therefore, was a sign of government support.

- *Profit margin:* The profit margin (Net income/Net sales) is one measure of a firm's profitability. The relatively low average profit margin in Japan in 1978 can be explained in part by the fact that Japanese companies focused on sales rather than profit. To gain market share, especially in foreign markets, Japanese companies would often compete by lowering prices, thereby reducing profits. Profit margins are probably higher today, as Japanese companies have driven competitors out of the market and can therefore raise prices and, perhaps more important, as they have become more cost-efficient. Another explanation for lower profit margins for Japanese companies is that higher amounts of debt causes a higher amount of interest expense, thereby lowering net income. Korean firms also have higher levels of interest expense as a result of higher debt financing. In addition, Korean firms in 1978 tended to have newer assets purchased at higher prices than U.S. firms. As a result, depreciation expense was larger. To obtain more comparable measures of profit margin across these countries, it might have been useful to treat dividends as an expense in the United States or add back interest expense to net income in Japan and Korea.

The important point is that analysts must be careful in comparing ratios across countries. Rules of thumb that apply in one country may not apply in another country. A U.S.-based analyst blindly relying on the ratios presented in Exhibit 10.8 might have decided not to invest in or lend to Japanese or Korean companies in the 1980s. Some very respectable investment returns would have been forgone in the process. One solution to the problem is to develop a good understanding of the local business environment and learn how to identify the best companies in that environment.

RESTATING FINANCIAL STATEMENTS

As noted earlier, foreign companies listed on U.S. stock exchanges are required to provide a reconciliation of net income and stockholders' equity to U.S. GAAP in the Form 20-F annual report they file with the U.S. Securities and Exchange Commission. (An exception is made for those foreign companies using IFRS.) Foreign SEC registrants are not required to provide a complete set of financial statements on a U.S. GAAP basis. As such, the information provided is of limited usefulness in calculating financial ratios used to assess the company's financial position and profitability on a U.S. GAAP basis. The reconciliation of income and equity does allow analysts to calculate return on equity (Net income/Average stockholders' equity) on a U.S. GAAP basis. But because of a lack of detail related to the items that comprise net income and the absence of U.S. GAAP amounts for assets and liabilities, insufficient information is provided to calculate ratios such as operating profit margin (Operating profit/Net sales), total asset turnover (Net sales/Average total assets), the debt-to-equity ratio (Total liabilities/Total stockholders' equity), and the current ratio (Current assets/Current liabilities). To calculate these and other ratios, analysts must restate financial statements. In the final section of this chapter, we use information available in the annual report of the hypothetical Arcot Company to demonstrate an approach that can be used to restate financial statements to a U.S. GAAP basis.

Arcot Company began operations in Year 1. The company prepares its financial statements using the accounting rules applicable in its home country—Local GAAP, and using the currency of its home country—the crown ($\hat{C}$). Its Year 3 comparative financial statements are reproduced in Exhibits 10.9 and 10.10.

EXHIBIT 10.9

ARCOT COMPANY
Consolidated Income Statements and Statements of Retained Earnings

	Years Ended December 31		
(Millions of Crowns)	Year 3	Year 2	Year 1
Sales	9,148	8,348	7,952
Cost of goods sold	(5,163)	(4,610)	(4,415)
Gross profit	3,985	3,738	3,537
Operating expenses	(453)	(448)	(421)
Operating income	3,532	3,290	3,116
Interest expense	(156)	(128)	(186)
Other income (expense), net	132	28	(12)
Income before income taxes	3,508	3,190	2,918
Provision for income taxes	(1,052)	(957)	(875)
Net income	2,456	2,233	2,043
Retained earnings, January 1	4,276	2,043	—
Dividends	(340)	—	—
Retained earnings, December 31	6,392	4,276	2,043

EXHIBIT 10.10

ARCOT COMPANY
Consolidated Balance Sheets

(Millions of Crowns)	December 31		
	Year 3	Year 2	Year 1
Cash	1,704	1,298	1,272
Accounts receivable.	2,798	2,381	2,064
Inventories.	5,276	4,683	4,240
Total current assets	9,778	8,362	7,576
Property, plant, and equipment, net	11,807	11,104	9,524
Long-term investments	1,305	1,188	1,113
Deferred charges	436	436	345
Total assets	23,326	21,090	18,558
Accounts payable.	745	654	507
Accrued expenses	1,591	1,256	1,262
Short-term debt.	100	1,000	1,000
Dividends payable	340	—	—
Other current liabilities	204	182	115
Total current liabilities	2,980	3,092	2,884
Long-term debt	5,000	5,000	5,000
Deferred income taxes	161	98	56
Other long-term liabilities	1,007	789	612
Total liabilities	9,148	8,979	8,552
Capital.	150	150	150
Capital surplus.	8,055	7,575	7,575
Retained earnings	6,392	4,276	2,043
Revaluation reserve	200	200	200
Unrealized gains (losses)	(119)	(90)	38
Treasury stock	(500)	—	—
Total stockholders' equity	14,178	12,111	10,006
Total liabilities and stockholders' equity	23,326	21,090	18,558

Arcot identified 10 items applicable to the company in which Local GAAP and U.S. GAAP differ.[11] These differences are described in Exhibit 10.11. As a result of these differences, the company made 11 adjustments to conform net income to U.S. GAAP, including an adjustment for the deferred tax effect of the other U.S. GAAP adjustments. All income adjustments also affect stockholders' equity through retained earnings, and two differences affect stockholders' equity alone. The reconciliation of net income and stockholders' equity from Local GAAP to U.S. GAAP is presented in Exhibit 10.12.

An effective approach for restating the Local GAAP financial statements to U.S. GAAP is to construct debit/credit adjusting entries for each reconciliation item, and then post these entries to columns 2 and 3 in the restatement worksheets provided in Exhibit 10.13 (Income and Retained Earnings) and Exhibit 10.14 (Balance Sheet). An explanation of each adjustment to restate Arcot's financial statements to a U.S. GAAP basis is provided next.

[11] Although Arcot is a hypothetical company, the differences described in Exhibit 10.11 reflect actual differences between U.S. GAAP and other national accounting principles, including IFRS, as reported by various companies in Form 20-F.

EXHIBIT 10.11

ARCOT COMPANY
Differences between Local GAAP and U.S. GAAP

Note X. Differences between Local GAAP and U.S. GAAP

The accompanying consolidated financial statements included in this annual report are prepared in accordance with Local GAAP. The significant differences between Local GAAP and U.S. GAAP that affect the Company's net income and stockholders' equity are set out below.

(1) Inventory

As permitted by Local GAAP, some inventories are valued under the direct cost system, which includes material, direct labor, and other direct costs. For purposes of complying with U.S. GAAP, inventories have been valued under the full absorption cost method, which includes the indirect cost. As a result, the reconciliation reflects the difference in timing when indirect costs are recognized as expense.

(2) Revaluation of Property, Plant, and Equipment

Under Local GAAP, the Company has recorded a revaluation of certain of its fixed assets in prior years. Under U.S. GAAP, property, plant, and equipment is recorded at its historical cost and revaluations are not allowed. As a result, the reconciliation includes a reversal of such revaluation and related depreciation recognized under Local GAAP.

(3) Capitalization of Interest on Property, Plant, and Equipment

Under Local GAAP, only interest on loans obtained for the specific purpose of financing property, plant, and equipment is capitalized. For U.S. GAAP purposes, interest is capitalized during the construction period of qualifying assets, which requires capitalization of interest expense not only on loans obtained for the specific purpose of financing property, plant, and equipment. Interest is capitalized based on the average borrowing rate of the company applied to qualifying assets under construction. As a result, the reconciliation includes an adjustment for the additional amount of interest that would be capitalized under U.S. GAAP as well as an adjustment for the additional amount of depreciation on the larger cost of property, plant, and equipment.

(4) Deferred Charges

Under Local GAAP, preoperating expenses incurred in the construction or expansion of a new facility may be deferred until the facility begins commercial operations. Additionally, all costs related to the organization and start-up of a new business may be capitalized to the extent that they are considered recoverable. Deferred charges are amortized over a period of five years. Under U.S. GAAP, the rules are restrictive as to the costs that can be capitalized. The amounts recorded as deferred charges under Local GAAP do not meet the criteria for capitalization in U.S. GAAP and should be expensed as incurred. As a result, the reconciliation includes a reversal of those charges which were deferred under Local GAAP, and a reversal of the amortization of those deferred charges.

(5) Sale of Land

In connection with the sale of land in Year 3, the Company agreed to deliver the land within 24 months following the sale, free and clear of all buildings and fixtures, as well as any environmental claims. Under Local GAAP, the Company recognized a gain on the sale of land in the year of sale. Under U.S. GAAP, as a result of the Company's level of continuing involvement, the gain on the sale of land has been deferred and will be recognized in earnings during the two years over which the company will continue to utilize the property.

(6) Government Grants

Under Local GAAP, subsidized plant assets acquired in Year 1 were required to be recorded at fair value, with the related subsidy recognized as revenue. Under U.S. GAAP, the subsidy is credited against the value of the assets acquired. The reconciling difference reverses in future years as the subsidized assets depreciate.

(7) Restructuring Costs

Under Local GAAP, when a decision is taken to restructure, the necessary provisions are made for severance and other costs. U.S. GAAP requires a number of specific criteria to be met before restructuring costs can be recognized as an expense. Among these criteria is the requirement that all the significant actions arising from the restructuring plan and their completion dates must be identified by the balance sheet date. Accordingly, timing differences between Local GAAP and U.S. GAAP arise on the recognition of such costs.

(8) Derivative Financial Instruments

Both Local GAAP and U.S. GAAP require all derivative financial instruments to be recorded on the balance sheet at their fair value. Changes in the fair values of derivatives during the period are required to be included in the determination of net income unless the derivative qualifies as a hedge. The company applies hedge accounting to all qualifying instruments under Local GAAP. The company has elected not to apply hedge accounting under U.S. GAAP. Therefore, changes in the fair value of derivative financial instruments have been recorded directly in earnings for U.S. GAAP purposes.

(9) Employee Share Trust Arrangements

An employee share trust has been established in order to hedge obligations in respect of options issued under certain employee share option schemes. Under Local GAAP the Company's ordinary shares held by the employee share trust are included at historic net book value in long-term investments. Under U.S. GAAP, such shares are treated as treasury stock and included in stockholders' equity.

(10) Ordinary Dividends

Under Local GAAP, proposed dividends on ordinary shares are deducted from shareholders' equity and shown as a liability on the balance sheet at the end of the period to which they relate. Under U.S. GAAP, such dividends are only deducted from shareholders' equity at the date of declaration of the dividend. The Company has not adjusted U.S. GAAP shareholders' equity for this difference in prior years. As a result, U.S. GAAP shareholders' equity has been restated to take account of this difference.

EXHIBIT 10.12

ARCOT COMPANY
Reconciliation from Local GAAP to U.S. GAAP

The following is a summary of the material adjustments to net income and shareholders' equity, which would have been required if U.S. GAAP had been applied instead of Local GAAP (*amounts in millions of Crowns*).

Differences in Net Income		**Years Ended December 31**		
	Note	Year 3	Year 2	Year 1
Net income under Local GAAP.................		2,456	2,233	2,043
Inventory indirect costs	1	169	(41)	60
Depreciation of revaluation of property, plant, and equipment...............................	2	40	40	0
Capitalized interest.....	3	0	12	15
Depreciation of capitalized interest.....	3	(5)	(3)	0
Deferred charges...............................	4	(22)	(18)	(24)
Amortization of deferred charges..................	4	14	8	0
Gain on sale of land............................	5	(124)	0	0
Government grants	6	3	3	(27)
Restructuring costs............................	7	73	0	0
Derivative financial instruments	8	(49)	(108)	38
Deferred tax effect of U.S. GAAP adjustments		(29)	32	(19)
Net income under U.S. GAAP..................		2,526	2,158	2,086

Continued

EXHIBIT 10.12
(*Concluded*)

Differences in Stockholders' Equity

	Note	December 31 Year 3	December 31 Year 2	December 31 Year 1
Stockholders' equity under Local GAAP		14,178	12,111	10,006
Inventory indirect costs	1	188	19	60
Revaluation of property, plant, and equipment	2	(120)	(160)	(200)
Capitalized interest	3	19	24	15
Deferred charges	4	(42)	(34)	(24)
Gain on sale of land	5	(124)	0	0
Government grants	6	(21)	(24)	(27)
Restructuring costs	7	73	0	0
Employee share trust arrangement	9	(62)	(62)	0
Ordinary dividends	10	340	0	0
Deferred tax effect of U.S. GAAP adjustments		(16)	13	(19)
Stockholders' equity under U.S. GAAP		4,413	11,887	9,811

EXHIBIT 10.13

ARCOT COMPANY
Worksheet for Restatement of Income and Retained Earnings to U.S. GAAP
for the Year Ended December 31, Year 3

	(1)	(2) Debit		(3) Credit		(4)
		Reconciling Adjustments				
(*Millions of Crowns*)	**Local GAAP**	**Debit**		**Credit**		**U.S. GAAP**
Sales	9,148					9,148
Cost of goods sold	(5,163)			169	[1]	(4,994)
Gross profit	3,985					4,154
Operating expenses	(453)	22	[4]	40	[2]	(350)
		5	[3]	14	[4]	
				3	[6]	
				73	[7]	
Operating income	3,532					3,804
Interest expense	(156)					(156)
Other income (expense), net	132	124	[5]			(41)
		49	[8]			
Income before income taxes	3,508					3,607
Provision for income taxes	(1,052)	29	[11]			(1,081)
Net income	2,456					2,526
Retained earnings, January 1	4,276	34	[4]	19	[1]	4,244
		24	[6]	40	[2]	
		70	[8]	24	[3]	
				13	[11]	
Dividends	(340)			340	[10]	0
Retained earnings, December 31	6,392					6,770

EXHIBIT 10.14

ARCOT COMPANY
Worksheet for Restatement of Balance Sheet to U.S. GAAP
for the Year Ended December 31, Year 3

	(1)	(2)		(3)		(4)
		Reconciling Adjustments				
(Millions of Crowns)	**Local GAAP**	**Debit**		**Credit**		**U.S. GAAP**
Cash	1,704					1,704
Accounts receivable	2,798					2,798
Inventories	5,276	188	[1]			5,464
Total current assets	9,778					9,966
Property, plant, and equipment, net	11,807	19	[3]	120	[2]	11,685
				21	[6]	
Long-term investments	1,305			62	[9]	1,243
Deferred charges	436			42	[4]	394
Total assets	23,326					23,288
Accounts payable	745					745
Accrued expenses	1,591					1,591
Short-term debt	100					100
Dividends payable	340	340	[10]			—
Other current liabilities	204			62	[5]	266
Total current liabilities	2,980					2,702
Long-term debt	5,000					5,000
Deferred income taxes	161			16	[11]	177
Other long-term liabilities	1,007	73	[7]	62	[5]	996
Total liabilities	9,148					8,875
Capital	150					150
Capital surplus	8,055					8,055
Retained earnings	6,392					6,770
Revaluation reserve	200	200	[2]			—
Unrealized gains (losses)	(119)			119	[8]	—
Treasury stock	(500)	62	[9]			(562)
Total stockholders' equity	14,178					14,413
Total liabilities and stockholders' equity	23,326					23,288

Explanation of Reconciling Adjustments

[1] Inventory Under Local GAAP, indirect costs related to inventory are treated as operating expenses in the period they are incurred, whereas under U.S. GAAP, these costs are treated as product costs and are expensed as cost of goods sold when the inventory is sold. The reconciliation schedule in Exhibit 10.12 shows an income adjustment in Year 3 of Ĉ169 to reconcile to U.S. GAAP and an adjustment of Ĉ188 to reconcile to U.S. GAAP stockholders' equity. The adjustment to stockholders' equity is the cumulative effect on retained earnings from timing differences in the recognition of indirect costs as expense. This is the amount by which Inventory is understated on a U.S. GAAP basis at the end

of Year 3. The entry to adjust from Local GAAP to U.S. GAAP in Year 3 is as follows:

Dr. Inventories	Ĉ188		Exhibit 10.14
Cr. Cost of goods sold		Ĉ169	Exhibit 10.13
Retained earnings, 1/1/Y3 (+)		19	Exhibit 10.13

Note that the adjustment to increase the Year 3 beginning balance in retained earnings is only Ĉ19. When the reduction in cost of good sold of Ĉ169 for Year 3 is closed to retained earnings at the end of the period, the net positive adjustment to retained earnings at December 31, Year 3, will be Ĉ188, balancing the increase in inventory.

[2] Revaluation of Property, Plant, and Equipment   Exhibit 10.11 explains that, in previous years, the company revalued property, plant, and equipment, which is not acceptable under U.S. GAAP. Revaluation of property, plant, and equipment is recorded through an increase in the carrying value of assets and an offsetting increase in a revaluation reserve in stockholders' equity. Subsequent depreciation is larger as a result of the revaluation. We can see from the reconciliation schedule in Exhibit 10.12 that the revaluation must have occurred at the end of Year 1, because there is an adjustment for the revaluation in the reconciliation of stockholders' equity but not in the reconciliation of net income.

The reconciliation schedule in Exhibit 10.12 indicates an income adjustment of Ĉ40 to reverse the additional depreciation taken in Year 3 under IFRS on the revaluation amount. Note that a similar adjustment was made in Year 2. The adjustment to stockholders' equity at the end of Year 3 is Ĉ(120), which reflects the amount of the original revaluation that has not yet been depreciated. Assuming that depreciation expense is included in the "Operating expenses" line item of the income statement, the entry to adjust from Local GAAP to U.S. GAAP in Year 3 is as follows:

Dr. Revaluation reserve	Ĉ200		Exhibit 10.14
Cr. Property, plant, and equipment.		Ĉ120	Exhibit 10.14
Operating expenses (depreciation).		40	Exhibit 10.13
Retained earnings, 1/1/Y3 (+)		40	Exhibit 10.13

The debit to revaluation reserve removes the original amount recorded in this account in Year 1, and which remains on the balance sheet indefinitely. The credit to property, plant, and equipment removes the amount by which this asset was revalued Ĉ(200) less accumulated depreciation on that revaluation amount Ĉ(80). The credit to operating expenses reverses the depreciation expense taken in the current year on the revaluation amount. The adjustments to revaluation reserve, operating expenses (which is closed to retained earnings), and the beginning balance in retained earnings combine to result in a net debit (decrease) to stockholders' equity of Ĉ120.

[3] Capitalization of Interest on Property, Plant, and Equipment   Item (3) in Exhibit 10.11 indicates that Arcot only capitalizes interest to the extent that it is incurred on loans taken out for the specific purpose of financing construction of property, plant, and equipment, which is less than the amount of interest

that would be capitalized under U.S. GAAP. The reconciliation schedule in Exhibit 10.12 shows two adjustments to income as a result of the difference in accounting for capitalized interest. The first adjustment, "Capitalized interest," indicates that Ĉ15 of interest that was expensed under Local GAAP in Year 1 would have been capitalized under U.S. GAAP, and additional interest in the amount of Ĉ12 would have been capitalized in Year 2. The additional interest capitalized as part of the cost of property, plant, and equipment must be depreciated, which explains the second income adjustment to recognize "Depreciation of capitalized interest" under U.S. GAAP. In Year 3, no additional interest requires capitalization in reconciling to U.S. GAAP, so the only income adjustment is to record depreciation on the additional interest capitalized in previous years.

The adjustment to stockholders' equity at the end of Year 3 of Ĉ19 reflects the difference between the cumulative amount of interest capitalized under U.S. GAAP Ĉ27 and the accumulated depreciation on that capitalized amount Ĉ(8). Assuming that depreciation expense is included in the "Operating expenses" line item of the income statement, the entry to adjust the Year 3 financial statements from Local GAAP to a U.S. GAAP basis is:

Dr. Property, plant, and equipment, net	Ĉ19	Exhibit 10.14
Operating expenses (depreciation)	5	Exhibit 10.13
Cr. Retained earnings, 1/1/Y3 (+)	Ĉ24	Exhibit 10.13

[4] Deferred Charges   Certain costs that have been recognized as a deferred charge (asset) under Local GAAP would be expensed immediately under U.S. accounting rules. Similar to adjustment [3] described above, Exhibit 10.12 indicates that Arcot made two adjustments to income related to deferred charges. The first adjustment, "Deferred charges," reverses the deferred charges recognized under Local GAAP, instead expensing them under U.S. GAAP. This results in a decrease in U.S. GAAP income. The second adjustment, "Amortization of deferred charges," reverses the amortization expense recognized under Local GAAP on the deferred charge asset. The difference between the cumulative amount of deferred charges recognized since Year 1 Ĉ(64) and the accumulated amortization of the deferred charges Ĉ22 determines the amount of the net adjustment to stockholders' equity at the end of Year 3 Ĉ(42). The adjusting entry to restate Year 3 financial statements to U.S. GAAP is:

Dr. Operating expenses (preoperating and startup costs)	Ĉ22	Exhibit 10.13
Retained earnings, 1/1/Y3 (−)	34	Exhibit 10.13
Cr. Deferred charges	Ĉ42	Exhibit 10.14
Operating expenses (amortization of deferred charges)	14	Exhibit 10.13

The two adjustments to "Operating expenses" can be combined into one entry that increases expenses by Ĉ8. After those two adjustments are closed to retained earnings, the net decrease in retained earnings is Ĉ42, which is equal to the decrease in assets (deferred charges).

[5] Sale of Land   The gain on the sale of land recognized by Arcot in Year 3 must be deferred to Years 4 and 5 under U.S. GAAP. Assuming that the gain on sale of land is included in the "Other income (expense), net" line of the income statement,

and that the deferred gain would be included among other liabilities, the adjusting entry related to this accounting difference is:

Dr. Other income (expense), net	Ĉ124	Exhibit 10.13
Cr. Other current liabilities	Ĉ62	Exhibit 10.14
Other long-term liabilities.	62	Exhibit 10.14

The deferred gain is split into a current and long-term portion based upon the two-year period over which it will be allocated. Closing the debit (decrease) to "Other income (expense), net" to retained earnings results in a decrease in stockholders' equity of Ĉ124.

[6] Government Grants The stockholders' equity adjustments related to this item as reported in Exhibit 10.12 suggest that the company received a government grant of Ĉ30 at the beginning of Year 1 to acquire property, plant, and equipment, and that the acquired assets have a useful life of 10 years. Under Local GAAP, the assets acquired with the government grant were initially recognized at cost, and the subsidy was recognized as revenue in Year 1. Under U.S. GAAP, the assets would have been initially measured at a reduced amount after subtracting the government grant. As a result, Local GAAP revenue is higher than U.S. GAAP revenue in Year 1 by Ĉ30, and Local GAAP depreciation expense is higher in Years 1, 2, and 3 by Ĉ3. Assuming that depreciation expense is included in the "Operating expenses" line item of the income statement, the entry to adjust to a U.S. GAAP basis at the end of Year 3 is:

Dr. Retained earnings, 1/1/Y3 (−)	Ĉ24	Exhibit 10.13
Cr. Property, plant, and equipment.	Ĉ21	Exhibit 10.14
Operating expenses (depreciation).	3	Exhibit 10.13

Combining the credit (decrease) to operating expenses with the adjustment (decrease) to the beginning balance of retained earnings results in a net decrease in stockholders' equity of Ĉ21.

[7] Restructuring Costs The accounting for a restructuring results in an increase in an expense (restructuring charge) and an offsetting increase in a restructuring liability. Item 7 in Exhibit 10.11 reports that the timing of recognition of these elements differs between Local GAAP and U.S. GAAP. The income adjustment in Exhibit 10.12 for Year 3 suggests that a restructuring charge in the amount of Ĉ73 was recognized under Local GAAP that was not yet recognizable under U.S. GAAP. This amount was reversed in Year 3, along with a reversal of restructuring liability, in reconciling to U.S. GAAP. Assuming that restructuring charges are included in the line item "Operating expenses" on the income statement and restructuring liabilities are included in "Other long-term liabilities" on the balance sheet, the adjusting entry is as follows:

Dr. Other long-term liabilities.	Ĉ73	Exhibit 10.14
Cr. Operating expenses	Ĉ73	Exhibit 10.13

The reversal of the restructuring charge (operating expenses) results in an increase in retained earnings (stockholders' equity) as reflected in Exhibit 10.12.

[8] *Derivative Financial Instruments* Because the company has elected to apply hedge accounting to derivative financial instruments under Local GAAP (as described in Exhibit 10.11), changes in the fair value of derivative financial instruments are deferred on the balance sheet in an "Unrealized gains (losses)" account in stockholders' equity. The company would have elected not to use hedge accounting under U.S. GAAP, and changes in fair value therefore would have been recognized in net income. In Exhibit 10.12, the income adjustment labeled "Derivative financial instruments" serves to reclassify the amount recognized as unrealized gains (losses) in stockholders' equity under Local GAAP as a recognized gain (loss) included in net income under U.S. GAAP. The recognized gain (loss) under U.S. GAAP would be closed to retained earnings. Thus, this accounting difference has no effect on the total amount of stockholders' equity. Assuming that gains (losses) on derivative financial instruments are included in the income statement line item "Other income (expense), net," the entry to reclassify the unrealized gains and losses on derivative financial instruments is as follows:

Dr. Retained earnings, 1/1/Y3 (−)	Ĉ70	Exhibit 10.13
Other income (expense), net.	49	Exhibit 10.13
Cr. Unrealized gains (losses)	Ĉ119	Exhibit 10.14

The credit to unrealized gains (losses) removes the cumulative net unrealized loss on derivative financial instruments from the balance sheet. The debit to other income (expense), net, reclassifies the current year's unrealized loss as a recognized loss in net income. The first debit in the entry reduces the beginning balance in retained earnings for the cumulative net loss on derivatives from Years 1 and 2.

[9] *Employee Share Trust Arrangements* Item 9 in Exhibit 10.11 indicates that the company's own shares held in an employee trust are included in long-term investments under Local GAAP, but should be classified as treasury stock (contra-stockholders' equity) in accordance with U.S. GAAP. The entry to reclassify this item, which has no effect on income, is as follows:

Dr. Treasury stock	Ĉ62	Exhibit 10.14
Cr. Long-term investments	Ĉ62	Exhibit 10.14

[10] *Ordinary Dividends* Exhibit 10.11, item 10, states that a timing difference can exist in the recognition of dividends (which reduces retained earnings) and dividends payable under U.S. and Local GAAP. The reconciliation item for "Ordinary dividends" in Exhibit 10.12 indicates an increase in U.S. stockholders' equity in Year 3 of Ĉ340. Apparently, dividends proposed in Year 3 and recognized as a liability under Local GAAP had not yet been officially declared by the end of Year 3. Dividends must be reversed and dividends payable decreased by Ĉ340 to reconcile to U.S. GAAP:

Dr. Dividends payable	Ĉ340	Exhibit 10.14
Cr. Dividends	Ĉ340	Exhibit 10.13

Deferred Tax Effect of U.S. GAAP Adjustments The adjustments made to reconcile net income from Local GAAP to U.S. GAAP also affect the amounts that would be reported as provision for income taxes and deferred income taxes under U.S. GAAP. Year 3 income adjustments 1–8 reported in Exhibit 10.12 result in a net increase in U.S. GAAP before-tax income of Ĉ99. This results in an increase in provision for income taxes under U.S. GAAP of Ĉ29, which would be offset by an increase in deferred income tax liability. The tax effect of income adjustments made in Years 1 and 2 also affect the balance in deferred income tax liability at the end of Year 3. The total adjustment to deferred income taxes is determined by adding the income adjustments for the "Deferred tax effect of US GAAP adjustments" across Years 1, 2, and 3 [Ĉ(19) + Ĉ32 + Ĉ(29) = Ĉ(16)]. The entry to adjust for the tax effects of the U.S. GAAP adjustments in Year 3 is as follows:

Dr. Provision for income taxes	Ĉ29	Exhibit 10.13
Cr. Deferred income taxes (liability)	Ĉ16	Exhibit 10.14
Retained earnings, 1/1/Y3	13	Exhibit 10.13

The credit to the beginning balance in retained earnings reflects the cumulative adjustment to the provision for income taxes in Years 1 and 2 [Ĉ(19) + Ĉ32 = Ĉ(13)], which previously would have been closed to retained earnings.

Comparison of Local GAAP and U.S. GAAP Amounts

The adjusted U.S. GAAP amounts reported in Column 4 of Exhibits 10.13 and 10.14 now can be used to evaluate and compare the profitability and financial position of Arcot with other companies that use U.S. accounting principles. A comparison of the amounts reported in accordance with U.S. GAAP (Column 4) with the Local GAAP amounts (Column 1) shows that significant differences exist for some line items but that there are no differences under the two sets of accounting rules for other items.

The procedures demonstrated here for restating Arcot's financial statements could be used to transform any company's financial statements to whatever set of accounting procedures the analyst desires. For companies that do not provide a reconciliation to the analyst's target GAAP, additional steps would involve determining the major differences between the company's GAAP and the analyst's preferred GAAP and then quantifying the effect of these differences for the specific company under analysis. This requires extensive knowledge of the two sets of standards being adjusted as well as adequate disclosure provided by the company, especially with respect to the accounting principles followed. The appendix to this chapter describes a project undertaken by Morgan Stanley Dean Witter to adjust the financial statements of companies in the global airline industry to a common set of accounting principles. The analysts conducting this study did not have reconciliations to work from. They used information in the notes in combination with educated assumptions to make a number of adjustments. However, in some areas where differences in accounting principles were identified they were unable to quantify an adjustment due to insufficient disclosure of information.

Summary

1. There are many reasons one would want to analyze financial statements of foreign companies. The most important reasons relate to making investment decisions, portfolio investments by individuals and mutual fund managers, and acquisition investments by multinational companies.

2. The following are some of the problems an analyst might encounter in analyzing foreign financial statements:

   - Difficulty in finding and obtaining financial information about a foreign company.
   - An inability to read the language in which the financial statements are presented.
   - The currency used in presenting monetary amounts.
   - Terminology differences that result in uncertainty as to the information provided.
   - Differences in format that lead to confusion and missing information.
   - Lack of adequate disclosures.
   - Financial statements not being made available on a timely basis.
   - Accounting differences that hinder cross-country comparisons.
   - Differences in business environments that might make ratio comparisons meaningless even if accounting differences are eliminated.

3. Some of the potential problems can be removed by companies through their preparation of convenience translations in which language, currency, and perhaps even accounting principles have been restated for the convenience of foreign readers. Companies interested in attracting interest globally have an incentive to provide more disclosure and issue their financial statements on a more timely basis than is required by their home country.

4. A significant number of investors find that differences in accounting practices across countries hinder their financial analysis and affect their investment decisions. Some analysts cope with this problem by restating foreign financial statements to a familiar basis, such as U.S. GAAP.

5. Except for those companies using IFRS, foreign companies listed on U.S. securities markets must reconcile net income and stockholders' equity to a U.S. GAAP basis. However, there is no requirement to reconcile assets and liabilities or to provide complete financial statements in terms of U.S. GAAP. Reconciliations of net income and stockholders' equity only are of limited usefulness in analyzing a company's financial position and profitability.

6. Foreign GAAP financial statements can be restated to a preferred GAAP basis through the use of a reconciliation worksheet in which debit/credit entries summarizing the differences in GAAP are used to adjust the original reported amounts.

7. Analysts should be careful in interpreting ratios calculated for foreign companies, even if the ratios are developed from restated financial statements. Financial ratios can differ across countries as a result of differences in business and economic environments. Optimally, an analyst will develop an understanding of the accounting and business environments of the countries whose companies they wish to analyze.

Appendix to Chapter **10**

Morgan Stanley Dean Witter: *Apples to Apples*

One way to avoid the distortions to comparability caused by differences in accounting rules is to focus analysis within a country, making comparisons across companies only in that country. Using an analysis of macroeconomic variables such as expected real growth in GDP, an investor first determines how much of his or her portfolio to allocate to a specific country. The investor then makes comparisons across companies in that country to identify the best investments. International equity investing traditionally was carried out using such a "country analysis" approach.

More recently, investment advisers have moved away from country analysis to industry analysis, in which they analyze and compare the major companies within an industry worldwide. Rather than first deciding to invest 10 percent of the portfolio in Japanese stocks, the investor might decide to invest 10 percent of the portfolio in food products companies. The task then becomes one of identifying the food companies that offer the best future returns regardless of nationality. This necessitates making comparisons across companies in different countries.

In the late 1990s, analysts at Morgan Stanley Dean Witter (MSDW) embarked on a project called *Apples to Apples* to identify the types of adjustments to financial statement figures needed to make information within an industry more comparable and at the same time more useful. Rather than simply adjusting foreign companies' financial statements to a U.S. GAAP basis to improve comparability, they use a cash flow and value-driver orientation to make adjustments for all companies within an industry, including those located in the United States. Some of the global industries for which the MSDW analysts have completed this project include airlines, beverage, food products, and imaging.

MSDW analysts begin by identifying the key value drivers in a particular industry and then proceed to determine how different accounting practices affect the data related to these value drivers. The scope of the analysis is limited to those items that are relevant to stock valuation—primarily earnings and stockholders' equity. The analysts do not reconcile all accounts to a single set of rules such as IFRS or U.S. GAAP. In fact, they do not presume that U.S. GAAP provides correct data for valuing investments. Instead they make adjustments to figures reported under various GAAP to develop data that they believe more closely reflect the underlying economics. The goal is to look through the accounting rules that hinder global comparability to understand the true economics of the business. The remainder of this appendix describes the Apples to Apples process with regard to the airline industry.

GLOBAL AIRLINES

Two of the major value drivers in the airline industry are the size of a carrier's fleet of aircraft and the true cost of operations. The major accounting issues that affect the ability to value firms in this industry are capacity, capacity cost (depreciation), staff costs, taxation, and foreign currency fluctuations. The accounting problem related to each of these issues and what the MSDW analysts did to deal with them are summarized here.

Capacity

Most airlines lease a substantial portion of their fleet. Rules for capitalizing leases (reporting an asset and liability) on the balance sheet vary from country to country. MSDW believes that all leases should be capitalized and therefore made adjustments to capitalize all leases that were accounted for as operating (noncapitalized) leases. This involved removing operating lease expense (rental payments) from earnings and then adding to reported expenses depreciation on the leased asset and interest expense for the financing of the leased asset. The net effect these adjustments had on earnings ranged from +4 percent of reported earnings for KLM Royal Dutch Airlines to −59 percent of reported earnings for Japan Airlines, with the average adjustment about −10 percent. The increase in liabilities resulting from the capitalization of leases ranged from +5 percent for China Eastern to +671 percent for Delta Airlines. The change in equity was +4 percent for Southwest Airlines and −70 percent for Northwest Airlines (both are U.S. carriers). The impact on equity and pretax income was more negative for U.S. airlines than for most non-U.S. airlines, partly because U.S. airlines use more leased assets than other airlines but also because they pay higher interest rates.

Capacity Cost (Depreciation)

Depreciation is based on the historical cost of capitalized fixed assets. The analysts at MSDW believe this understates the true cost of capacity—the cost that must be incurred to maintain the revenues generated by the airline's current fleet capacity. They estimated the economic cost to sustain the current capacity by considering historical expenditures, fleet utilization, age of assets, fuel-burn rate, asset replacement policy, and the airline's market resale policy. The following steps were taken:

- Identify each airline's fleet including leased planes, and each aircraft's characteristics such as make and age.
- Estimate expenditures required to refurbish older aircraft and the amount and timing of spending on replacement aircraft.
- Estimate differences in expenses for maintenance and fuel consumption of the future fleet.
- Estimate the resulting cost outflows at present value to obtain an annual cost of capacity figure.

Reported depreciation expense was then replaced by the annual cost of capacity figure for each airline to develop a more relevant measure of earnings. For most airlines, reported depreciation undercharged for the cost of capacity. The largest adjustment resulted in a decrease in Northwest's reported income of 46 percent. Because of its aggressive depreciation policy and a relatively young fleet, China Eastern's reported income was adjusted upward by 39 percent.

Staff Costs

The major issue related to staff costs involves deferred compensation—pension and other retirement (e.g., medical) benefits promised to employees. The relevant amount for valuation is the net cash flow, on a present value basis, related to the plans. Net cash flow is the difference between cash inflows on plan assets and cash outflows to beneficiaries. In addition, an interest charge should be recognized on the underfunded portion of the benefit obligation. The extent to which benefit plans are funded and the manner in which benefit expenses are calculated varies by country. For some airlines, especially in Asia, lack of disclosures related to pension plans posed the greatest difficulty in estimating the true obligation and expense. However, the analysts were able to make assumptions and estimations to be able to develop adjustments for all airlines. The largest adjustment was a 301 percent decrease in reported income for Japan Airlines. The magnitude of this adjustment results from the fact that Japanese companies do not accrue currently an expense related to future benefit payments, which results in a large understatement of retirement benefit expense. In addition, benefits plans tend to be only partially funded so that a large interest charge must be added. Among the U.S. airlines, the cumulative adjustment for benefit obligations ranged from +23 percent (Delta) to −72 percent (Northwest) of reported equity.

Taxation

Deferred taxes are the difference between the tax expense based on accounting income and the actual taxes payable based on taxable income. For companies that use accelerated depreciation for taxes and straight-line depreciation for accounting, taxes payable are less than tax expense and a deferred tax liability will be reported on the balance sheet. Through the replacement of depreciable assets, the deferred tax liability can be deferred indefinitely. The analysts at MSDW believe the deferred tax liability reported on the balance sheet should reflect the likely amount of taxes to be paid in the future discounted to their present value. Working on the basis of certain assumptions regarding the pattern of future capital expenditures at each airline, they developed an adjustment for the present value of the deferred tax liability. This resulted in a reduction in liabilities for most companies with an offsetting increase in equity and an increase in earnings. For the U.S. airlines, the increase in income averages 15 percent and the increase in equity was greater than 20 percent in all cases. Because accounting and taxable income are closely linked in most European countries, the adjustments for the European airlines were minimal.

Foreign Currency Exposure

Airplanes and fuel are priced in U.S. dollars, so non-U.S. companies are exposed to foreign exchange risk on these items. Revenues tend to be in a variety of currencies, so net exposures to foreign exchange risk exist. The analysts attempted to determine the net exposures for the companies in the airline industry, but disclosures were inadequate to allow for a clear estimate. They believe that U.S. carriers have less risk because costs and revenues are primarily in U.S. dollars. The only adjustments that they could make were gains/losses on the local currency value of the existing fleet (used airplanes are sold for U.S. dollars) and reporting any deferred foreign exchange gains/losses in income.

Other Issues

Frequent-flyer programs represent a contingent liability for airlines. MSDW considered whether the cost of frequent-flyer programs is underreported. They concluded that giving away a seat that would otherwise not have been occupied had little if any cost, and no adjustments to reported earnings were deemed to be needed. Routes and airport slots purchased from another airline are reported as intangible assets. Routes and slots given directly to an airline are not recognized as assets but they may have value. Given the lack of disclosure by airlines about their routes and slots and the differences in regulations related to them, no direct adjustments to reported information were made.

Questions

1. Why might individual investors wish to include foreign companies in their investment portfolio?

2. Which companies might Ford Motor Company include in a benchmarking study of the automobile industry, and in which countries are those companies located?

3. What are potential problems in using commercial databases as the source of financial statement information for foreign companies?

4. How might an analyst obtain the most recent financial statements for a foreign company in which he or she is interested?

5. Why should the fact that a foreign company presents its financial statements in a foreign currency present no significant problems in analyzing those statements?

6. A foreign company prepares its financial statements in a foreign language and does not provide any convenience translations. How might this affect an analyst's decision to invest in this company?

7. How can more disclosure in the notes to the financial statements facilitate the analysis of foreign financial statements?

8. In what ways does the timeliness of the publication of financial information differ across countries?

9. What are the advantages and disadvantages in using measures such as operating income before depreciation (OIBD) or earnings before interest, taxes, depreciation and amortization (EBITDA) rather than net income in comparing profitability across foreign companies?

10. What are the different features of financial statements that a foreign company might "translate" in a convenience translation?

11. Why should analysts be careful in comparing financial ratios across companies in different countries?

12. How might differences in the extent to which countries apply the accounting concept of conservatism (some countries are more conservative than others) affect profit margins, debt-to-equity ratios, and returns on equity?

13. How might differences across countries in the extent to which debt versus equity is the major source of financing affect profit margins, debt-to-equity ratios, and return on equity?

14. A foreign company did not capitalize any interest in the current or past years, although such capitalization is required under U.S. GAAP. Why does an adjustment to reconcile this item to U.S. GAAP affect assets, expenses, and beginning retained earnings?

Exercises and Problems

1. Refer to the worksheets in Exhibits 10.13 and 10.14 in which the financial statements of Arcot Company have been restated to U.S. GAAP.

   Required:
   a. Calculate each of the ratios listed below using (1) the Local GAAP amounts in Column 1, and (2) the U.S. GAAP amounts in Column 4.
   b. Determine the percentage difference in each of these ratios using the formula: (U.S. GAAP ratio — Local GAAP ratio)/Local GAAP ratio.

c. Determine which ratios appear to be most and least affected by differences in the two sets of accounting principles.

Ratios

Current ratio (Current assets/Current liabilities)

Total asset turnover (Sales/Total assets at year-end)

Debt-to-equity ratio (Total liabilities/Total stockholders' equity)

Times interest earned ([Income before income taxes + Interest expense]/ Interest expense)

Profit margin (Net income/Sales)

Return on equity (Net income/Average total stockholders' equity)

Operating profit margin (Operating income/Sales)

Operating income as a percentage of total stockholders' equity (Operating income/Average total stockholders' equity)

2. China Petroleum & Chemical Corporation (Sinopec) provides two sets of financial statements in its annual report. One set of financial statements is prepared in accordance with Chinese (PRC) Accounting Rules and Regulations and another is prepared in accordance with IFRS. The company also provides a reconciliation of IFRS net income and net assets to U.S. GAAP. Sinopec reported the following amounts under three different sets of accounting rules in its 2006 annual report:

| | Accounting Rules | | |
RMB millions	PRC	IFRS	U.S. GAAP
Net profit attributable to equity shareholders—2006	50,664	55,408	54,862
Total equity attributable to equity shareholders—December 31, 2006	254,875	262,297	262,297
Total equity attributable to equity shareholders—December 31, 2005	215,623	222,803	222,803

Required:

a. Determine the percentage difference in net profit attributable to shareholders and average total equity attributable to equity shareholders for 2006 under the three different sets of accounting rules.

b. Calculate return on average total equity (Profit attributable to shareholders/ Average total equity) for 2006 under the three different sets of accounting rules.

c. Determine the percentage difference in return on average total equity under the three sets of rules.

d. Which of the three measures of return on average total equity is most useful in assessing Sinopec's profitability?

3. SABMiller PLC was formed when U.S.-based Miller Brewing Company merged with South African Breweries in 2002. SABMiller uses IFRS in preparing its financial statements. The following is taken from the March 31, 2010, consolidated balance sheet of SABMiller PLC:

Equity	2010 US$m	2009 US$m
Share capital	165	159
Share premium	6,312	6,198
Merger relief reserve	4,586	3,395
Other reserves*	1,322	(872)
Retained earnings	7,525	6,496
Total shareholders' equity	19,910	15,376
Minority interests in equity	689	741
Total equity	20,599	16,117

* The Statement of Changes in Shareholders' Equity indicates that "Other reserves" primarily consist of "Other comprehensive income."

Required:

Describe the content of each of the line items presented using accounting terminology commonly used in the United States.

4. The parent company balance sheet for Babcock International Group PLC at March 31, 2010, as follows:

Balance Sheet
As at 31 March 2009

	Notes	2009 £m	2008 £m
Fixed assets			
Investments in subsidiary undertakings	3	359.1	359.3
Tangible fixed assets		0.3	0.3
		359.4	359.6
Current assets			
Debtors	5	527.6	440.9
Cash and bank balances	4	48.9	53.8
		576.5	494.7
Creditors—amounts due within one year	6	104.0	62.6
Net current assets		472.5	432.1
Total assets less current liabilities		831.9	791.7
Creditors—amounts due after one year	6	355.0	380.0
Net assets		476.9	411.7
Capital and reserves			
Called-up share capital	7	137.7	137.6
Share premium account	8	148.2	148.1
Capital redemption reserve	8	30.6	30.6
Profit and loss account	8	160.4	95.4
Shareholders' funds—equity interests		476.9	411.7

Required:

Transform Babcock's March 31, 2010, balance sheet to a U.S. format.

5. China Eastern Airlines (CEA) Corporation Limited presents two sets of financial statements in its annual report; one set is prepared in accordance with Chinese (PRC) accounting regulations and one set is prepared in accordance with International Financial Reporting Standards (IFRS). The company also provides a reconciliation of consolidated profit/(loss) and consolidated net assets from PRC GAAP to IFRS. The following excerpt was taken from a recent annual report:

Significant differences between International Financial Reporting Standards ("IFRS") and PRC Accounting Regulations

(a) Under IFRS, other flight equipment is accounted for as fixed assets and depreciation charges are calculated over the expected useful lives of 20 years to residual value of 5% of cost/revalued amounts. Under PRC Accounting Regulations, such flight equipment is classified as current assets and the costs are amortized on a straight-line basis over a period of 5 years.

(b) This represents the difference on gain on disposal arising from different useful lives adopted on depreciation under IFRS and PRC Accounting Regulations.

Consolidated profit attributable to shareholders	RMB'000
As stated in accordance with PRC audited statutory accounts	132,919
Impact of IFRS and other adjustments:	
Adjustment (1).	150,794
Adjustment (2).	(13,296)
Other adjustments	271,296
As stated in accordance with IFRS	541,713

Required:

a. Determine which adjustment, (1) or (2), relates to which item, (a) or (b), described in the excerpt. Explain your answer.

b. What impact would items (a) and (b) have on the reconciliation of net assets (stockholders' equity) from PRC GAAP to IFRS?

6. China Eastern Airlines (CEA) Corporation Limited prepares a set of financial statements in accordance with IFRS (in Chinese renminbi—RMB). Until 2007, the company also provided a reconciliation of IFRS net income and net assets to U.S. GAAP. The following excerpt was taken from a recent annual report.

Required:

a. Explain the difference between (1) IFRS net income and U.S. GAAP net income and (2) IFRS net assets (owners' equity) and U.S. GAAP net assets that resulted from the accounting difference related to "revaluation of fixed assets."

b. Determine the directional impact (increase, decrease, no effect) the accounting difference described above would have on the following ratios calculated under IFRS and U.S. GAAP:

Current ratio (Current assets/Current liabilities)
Debt-to-equity ratio (Total liabilities/Total owners' equity)
Total asset turnover (Net sales/Average total assets)

Significant Differences between IFRS and U.S. GAAP

Differences between IFRS and U.S. GAAP which have significant effects on the consolidated profits/ (loss) attributable to shareholders and consolidated owners' equity of the Group are summarized as follows:

Consolidated profit/(loss) attributable to shareholders

(Amounts in thousands except per share data)

	Note	Year Ended December 31,			2003 US$ (note 2a)
		2001 RMB	2002 RMB	2003 RMB	
As stated under IFRS		541,713	83,369	(949,816)	(114,758)
U.S. GAAP adjustments:					
Reversal of difference in depreciation charges arising from revaluation of fixed assets	(a)	94,140	20,370	63,895	7,720
Reversal of revaluation deficit of fixed assets	(a)	—	171,753	—	—
Gain/(loss) on disposal of aircraft and related assets	(b)	5,791	(26,046)	(10,083)	(1,218)
Others	(c)	(11,295)	23,767	6,860	829
Deferred tax effect on U.S. GAAP adjustments.	(d)	(155,877)	(28,477)	(9,101)	(1,100)
As stated under U.S. GAAP		474,472	247,736	(892,245)	(108,527)
Basic and fully diluted earnings/(loss) per share under U.S. GAAP		RMB0.097	RMB0.051	(RMB0.185)	(US$0.022)
Basic and fully diluted earnings/(loss) per American Depository Share ("ADS") under U.S. GAAP		RMB9.75	RMB5.09	(RMB18.46)	(US$2.23)

Consolidated owners' equity

(Amounts in thousands)

	Note	December 31,		2003 US$ (note 2a)
		2002 RMB	2003 RMB	
As stated under IFRS		7,379,103	6,382,151	771,099
U.S. GAAP adjustments:				
Reversal of net revaluation surplus of fixed assets	(a)	(908,873)	(908,873)	(109,811)
Reversal of difference in depreciation charges and accumulated depreciation and loss on disposals arising from the revaluation of fixed assets	(a), (b)	637,423	691,235	83,516
Others	(c)	29,111	35,971	4,346
Deferred tax effect on U.S. GAAP adjustments	(d)	20,844	9,225	1,115
As stated under U.S. GAAP		7,157,608	6,209,709	750,264

Notes:

(a) Revaluation of fixed assets

Under IFRS, fixed assets of the Group are initially recorded at cost and are subsequently restated at revalued amounts less accumulated depreciation. Fixed assets of the Group were revalued as of June 30, 1996 as part of the restructuring of the Group for the purpose of listing. In addition, as of December 31, 2002, a revaluation of the Group's aircraft and engines was carried out and difference between the valuation and carrying amount was recognized. Under U.S. GAAP, the revaluation surplus or deficit and the related difference in depreciation are reversed since fixed assets are required to be stated at cost.

Profit margin (Net income/Net sales)
Return on equity (Net income/Average total owners' equity)

7. The following excerpts were taken from the notes to consolidated financial statements in the 2006 annual report of the Novartis Group, the Swiss pharmaceutical company:

Note 33 Significant Differences between IFRS and United States Generally Accepted Accounting Principles (U.S. GAAP)

The Group's consolidated financial statements have been prepared in accordance with IFRS, which as applied by the Group, differs in certain significant respects from U.S. GAAP.

33.9) Share-Based Compensation

There are differences in the transitional rules on adopting the expensing of share-based compensation between IFRS and U.S. GAAP, which results in a difference in the income statement charge between IFRS and U.S. GAAP. As a result of this difference, an additional expense was recognized under U.S. GAAP in 2006 of USD 5 million (2005: USD 44 million).

In addition, under IFRS, the Group accounts for all share-based compensation equity-settled transactions in equity. However, under U.S. GAAP an arrangement which is a fixed monetary amount that is settleable with a variable number of the issuer's equity shares is classified as a liability. The USD 186 million booked in the IFRS equity at December 31, 2006 (2005: USD 96 million), was reversed for U.S. GAAP purposes.

Required:

a. Determine whether the adjustments described in Note 33.9, Share-Based Compensation, caused net income for the year 2006 and stockholders' equity at December 31, 2006, to be higher under IFRS or U.S. GAAP.

b. Determine the directional impact (increase, decrease, no effect) the difference in accounting for share-based compensation in 2006 under IFRS and U.S. GAAP would have on the following ratios:

(1) Current ratio [Current assets/Current liabilities]

(2) Debt-to-equity ratio [Total liabilities/Total stockholders' equity]

(3) Total asset turnover [Net sales/Average total assets]

(4) Profit margin [Net income/Net sales]

(5) Return on equity [Net income/Average total stockholders' equity]

8. Gamma Holding NV, a Dutch textile company, provided the following information in its consolidated income statement for the year 2009 (note that "result" is equivalent to "income"):

Notes to the financial statements provided the following information related to provisions recognized in 2008 and 2009:

€ × 1,000,000	2009	2008
Group result before taxation	(45.8)	(34.1)
Income tax	(4.6)	(0.1)
Net group result from continuing operations	(50.4)	(34.2)

Notes to the financial statements provided the following information related to provisions recognized in 2008 and 2009:

€ × 1,000,000

19 Other provisions

The composition and changes were as follows:	Restructuring	Other	Total
Balance at 31-12-2007	11.5	6.4	17.9
Changes in 2008			
Additions charged to the income statement	27.0	1.7	28.7
Release credited to the income statement	(1.4)		(1.4)
Payments	(11.3)	(2.6)	(13.9)
Transfer to liabilities directly related to discontinued operations		(0.4)	(0.4)
Exchange rate differences	(0.1)		(0.1)
Balance at 31-12-2008	25.7	5.1	30.8

Changes in 2009 . . . .

Additions charged to the income statement.	12.0	1.7	13.7
Release credited to the income statement	(0.4)		(0.4)
Payments.	(26.9)	(1.4)	(28.3)
Transfer from (to) liabilities directly related to discontinued operations		(0.1)	(0.1)
Other transfers.		0.6	0.6
Balance at 31-12-2009.	**10.4**	**5.9**	**16.3**

Required:

a. Determine the percentage growth in income (loss) before tax (group result before taxation) from 2008 to 2009.

b. What impact do provisions have on income before tax?

c. What can cause the ending balance in provisions to change from one year to the next?

d. Determine what income (loss) before tax would have been in 2008 and 2009 if there had been no change in the ending balance of "other provisions." What would the percentage growth in income (loss) before tax have been in this case?

e. Is there any additional information you might like to have with respect to provisions for the time period presented earlier?

9. Gamma Holding NV, a Dutch textile company, presented the following calculation of operating profit in its 2009 consolidated income statement:

€ × 1,000,000	2009
Net turnover	658.5
Change in finished products and work in progress	(14.3)
Total operating income	644.2
Costs of raw materials and consumables	(212.9)
Contracted work and other external costs	(42.7)
Added value	388.6
Personnel costs	(236.9)
Depreciation of property, plant, and equipment	(29.4)
Impairment of property, plant, and equipment	(7.4)
Amortization of intangible assets	(4.2)
Impairment of intangible assets	(18.5)
Other operating expenses	(100.2)
Other income and expense	0.2
Total other operating expenses	(396.4)
Operating result	(7.8)

Required:

a. Determine whether finished products and work in progress inventory in total increased or decreased during the year.

b. Identify the additional information that would be needed to calculate cost of goods sold for the company in 2009.

c. Given the following assumptions with respect to the percentage of operating expenses related to manufacturing activities and nonmanufacturing activities, provide an estimate of cost of goods sold:

	% Manufacturing	% Nonmanufacturing
Costs of raw materials and consumables	90%	10%
Contracted work and other external costs	100	0
Personnel costs	50	50
Depreciation and impairment of property, plant and equipment	75	25
Amortization and impairment of intangible assets	80	20
Other operating expenses	10	90

    d. Given the estimated cost of goods sold from part (c), determine the company's gross profit margin for 2009.

10. Neopost SA is a French company operating mainly in Europe and the United States that sells and leases mailroom equipment. In accordance with IFRS, the company capitalizes development costs when certain criteria are met. The company reported the following amounts for sales and income in the consolidated income statements (in millions of euros):

Year ended 31 January	2010	2009
Sales	913.1	918.1
Income before tax	204.9	214.8
Income taxes	(57.0)	(57.9)
Net income	147.9	156.9

The following note related to intangible assets was extracted from the company's annual report (in millions of euros).

Note 6 Intangible fixed assets

	Concessions, Rights, Licenses	Development Costs	Other	Total
Gross value at 31 January 2008	**16.8**	**64.5**	**49.0**	**158.4**
Acquisitions	16.8	—	11.5	28.3
Capitalization	—	9.0	—	9.0
Disposals	—	—	(2.8)	(2.8)
Other changes	—	—	0.3	0.3
Translation difference	3.8	—	0.7	4.5
Gross value at 31 January 2009	**65.5**	**73.5**	**58.7**	**197.7**
Acquisitions	—	—	1.9	6.4
Capitalization	—	10.2	—	10.2
Disposals	(11.2)	(21.6)	(24.2)	(57.0)
Other changes	—	—	5.0	5.0
Translation difference	(1.7)	—	(1.6)	(3.3)
Gross value at 31 January 2010	**57.1**	**62.1**	**39.8**	**159.0**
Cumulative amortization	(41.1)	(35.5)	(16.6)	(93.2)
Net book value at 31 January 2010	**16.0**	**26.6**	**23.2**	**65.8**

Changes in intangible assets is mainly due to the capitalization of R&D costs and IT implementation projects (reported in column "Other").

	Concessions, Rights, Licenses	Development Costs	Other	Total
Amortization at 31 January 2008	**33.8**	**42.1**	**35.2**	**111.1**
Charges	7.2	7.1	3.1	17.4
Disposals	—	—	(0.5)	(0.5)
Other changes	—	—	0.3	0.3
Translation difference	2.9	—	0.5	3.4
Amortization at 31 January 2008	**43.9**	**49.2**	**38.6**	**131.7**
Charges	10.0	7.9	1.6	19.5
Disposals	(11.0)	(21.6)	(23.8)	(56.4)
Other changes	—	—	0.4	0.4
Translation difference	(1.8)	—	(0.2)	(2.0)
Amortization at 31 January 2010	**31.4**	**35.5**	**16.6**	**93.2**

Required:

a. Estimate the average expected useful life for development costs for the years ended January 31, 2009, and January 31, 2010.

b. Calculate income before tax and net income for the years ended January 31, 2009, and 2010 assuming that Neopost was not able to recognize development costs as an intangible asset.

c. Determine the net profit margin (Net income/Sales) for the years ended January 31, 2009, and 2010 using (1) actual reported amounts and (2) the amount calculated in part (*b*).

11. The following Statement of Added Value (in millions of Brazilian reals) was presented in the 2009 annual report of Vale S.A., a Brazilian mineral products company:

Period ended	In millions of Reais	
	Consolidated	
	2009	2008
Generation of added value		
Gross revenue		
Revenue from products and services	49,812	72,766
Revenue from the construction of own assets	13,919	17,706
Allowance for doubtful accounts	(23)	(32)
Less: Acquisition of products	(1,219)	(2,805)
Outsourced services	(6,242)	(8,244)
Materials	(20,653)	(23,958)
Fuel oil and gas	(2,777)	(3,761)
Energy	(1,776)	(2,052)
Impairment	—	(2,447)
Other costs	(6,920)	(6,829)
Gross added value	**24,121**	**40,344**
Depreciation, amortization and depletion	(5,447)	(5,112)
Net added value	**18,674**	**35,232**
Received from third parties		
Financial revenue	866	1,221
Equity results	116	(1,325)
Total added value to be distributed	**19,656**	**35,128**

(Continued)

(Concluded)

Period ended	In millions of Reais	
	Consolidated	
	2009	**2008**
Personnel	5,086	5,046
Taxes, rates and contribution	5,810	5,267
Taxes paid recover	(571)	(1,955)
Remuneration on third party's capital	3,433	4,157
Inflation and exchange rate variation, net	(4,519)	902
Remuneration on stockholders' equity		
Stockholders	3,373	5,640
Reinvested	6,876	15,639
Minority interest	168	432
Distribution of added value	19,656	35,128

Required:

a. Identify the external parties who might be interested in the information provided in Vale's Statement of Added Value.

b. In what ways does the calculation of "Total added value to be distributed" appear to differ from a calculation of net income?

c. Prepare a brief report summarizing the story being told in Vale's Statement of Added Value.

12. The consolidated income statement for Babcock International Group PLC is presented here:

Group Income Statement
For the year ended 31 March 2009

	Note	Before Acquired Intangible Amortization and Exceptional Items £m	Acquired Intangible Amortization and Exceptional Items £m	Total £m
Revenue	3	1,901.9	—	1,901.9
Operating profit	3, 4, 5, 6	147.3	(14.2)	133.1
Share of profit/loss from joint ventures		(0.2)	—	(0.2)
Finance costs	7	(32.1)	—	(32.1)
Finance income	7	5.9	—	5.9
Profit before tax		120.9	(14.2)	106.7
Income tax expense	9	(23.1)	4.0	(19.1)
Profit for the year from continuing operations		97.8	(10.2)	87.6
Discontinued operations				
Loss for the year from discontinued operations	10	—	(13.3)	(13.3)
Profit for the year	5	97.8	(23.5)	74.3

The income statement does not disclose any detail on the operating expenses that were subtracted in determining operating profit, but refers readers to several notes (Notes 3, 4, 5, and 6). The income statement also does not explain the nature or amount of "exceptional items," which are items unlikely to recur in future years.

In analyzing Babcock's financial statements, you would like to determine the company's gross profit margin for the current year and you also would like to develop an estimate of sustainable income, that is, the income generated in the current year that is likely to persist into the future.

Required:

Access Babcock International Group's 2009 annual report at www.babcock. co.uk and use the information in Notes 4 and 6 to:

a. Determine gross profit and gross profit margin (Gross Profit/Revenue) for 2009.

b. Estimate sustainable income for 2009. Sustainable income is equal to total income less items included in total income that are unlikely to recur. Indicate any assumptions made in estimating sustainable income.

13. Vale S.A., a Brazilian mineral products company, provided the following note on a voluntary basis in its 2009 annual report:

11—Cash Generation (Unaudited)

Consolidated operating cash generation measured by EBITDA (earnings before financial results, equity in subsidiaries, income taxes, depreciation, amortization and depletion, increased by dividends received was R$18,649 as of December 31, 2009, against R$35,022 as of December 31, 2008, representing a decrease of 46.8 percent.

EBITDA is not a BR GAAP measure and does not represent the expected cash flow for the reporting periods, and therefore should not be considered as an alternative measure to net income (loss), as an indicator of operating performance or as an alternative to cash flow as a liquidity source.

Vale definition of EBITDA may not be comparable with EBITDA as defined by other companies.

EBITDA—Consolidated

	2009	2008
Operating profit—EBIT	13,181	27,400
Depreciation/amortization of goodwill	5,447	5,112
Impairment	—	2,447
	18,628	34,959
Dividends received	21	63
EBITDA	18,649	35,022
Depreciation/amortization of goodwill	(5,447)	(5,112)
Dividends received	(21)	(63)
Impairment	—	(2,447)
Equity Results	116	(1,325)
Gain (loss) on disposal of assets	93	139
Financial results, net	1,952	(3,838)
Income tax and social contribution	(4,925)	(665)
Minority interests	(168)	(432)
Net income	10,249	21,279

Required:

Provide a response to each of the following questions:

a. What does EBITDA measure?

b. Why do you think Vale included Note 11, Cash Generation, in its 2009 annual report?

c. Why might a financial analyst use EBITDA in evaluating a company's performance?

d. What limitations exist in using EBITDA to evaluate a company's performance?

14. Refer to the following information provided in the chapter for Arcot Company:

- Consolidated financial statements in Exhibits 10.9 and 10.10.
- Differences between Local GAAP and U.S. GAAP in Exhibit 10.11.
- Reconciliation from Local GAAP to U.S. GAAP in Exhibit 10.12.

Use an electronic spreadsheet to complete the requirements of this problem.

Required:

a. Use the information in Exhibits 10.9 and 10.10 to create worksheets for the restatement of income and retained earnings and the balance sheet for the year ended December 31, Year 1.

b. Prepare debit/credit reconciling entries for each Year 1 reconciliation item included in the reconciliation from Local GAAP to U.S. GAAP in Exhibit 10.12.

c. Post the debit/credit reconciling entries for Year 1 to the worksheets created in (a) and determine balances for Year 1 on a U.S. GAAP basis.

d. Calculate the following ratios on a Local GAAP and a U.S. GAAP basis for Year 1 and summarize the differences.

Current ratio [Current assets/Current liabilities]

Total asset turnover [Sales/Total assets at year-end]

Debt/equity ratio [Total liabilities/Total stockholders' equity]

Times interest earned [(Income before income taxes + Interest expense)/ Interest expense]

Net profit margin [Net income/Sales]

Return on equity [Net income/Average total stockholders' equity]

Operating profit margin [Operating income/Sales]

Operating income as percent of total stockholders' equity [Operating income/ Average total stockholders' equity]

15. Refer to the following information provided in the chapter for Arcot Company:

- Consolidated financial statements in Exhibits 10.9 and 10.10.
- Differences between Local GAAP and U.S. GAAP in Exhibit 10.11.
- Reconciliation from Local GAAP to U.S. GAAP in Exhibit 10.12.

Use an electronic spreadsheet to complete the requirements of this problem.

Required:

a. Use the information in Exhibits 10.9 and 10.10 to create worksheets for the restatement of income and retained earnings and the balance sheet for the year ended December 31, Year 2.

b. Prepare debit/credit reconciling entries for each Year 2 reconciliation item included in the reconciliation from Local GAAP to U.S. GAAP in Exhibit 10.12.

c. Post the debit/credit reconciling entries for Year 2 to the worksheets created in (*a*) and determine balances for Year 2 on a U.S. GAAP basis.

d. Calculate the following ratios on a Local GAAP and a U.S. GAAP basis for Year 2 and summarize the differences:

Current ratio [Current assets/Current liabilities]
Total asset turnover [Sales/Total assets at year-end]
Debt/equity ratio [Total liabilities/Total stockholders' equity]
Times interest earned [(Income before income taxes + Interest expense)/ Interest expense]
Net profit margin [Net income/Sales]
Return on equity [Net income/Average total stockholders' equity]
Operating profit margin [Operating income/Sales]
Operating income as percent of total stockholders' equity [Operating income/Average total stockholders' equity]

Case 10-1

Swisscom AG

Swisscom AG, the principal provider of telecommunications in Switzerland, prepares consolidated financial statements in accordance with International Financial Reporting Standards (IFRS). Until 2007, Swisscom also reconciled its net income and stockholders' equity to U.S. GAAP. Swisscom's consolidated financial statements from a recent annual report are presented in their original format in Column 1 of the following worksheet. Note 27, Differences between International Financial Reporting Standards and U.S. Generally Accepted Accounting Principles, which includes Swisscom's U.S. GAAP reconciliation, also is provided.

Required

1. Use the information in Note 27 to restate Swisscom's consolidated financial statements in accordance with U.S. GAAP. Begin by constructing debit/credit entries for each reconciliation item, and then post these entries to columns 2 and 3 in the worksheets provided.

2. Calculate each of the following ratios under both IFRS and U.S. GAAP and determine the percentage differences between them using IFRS ratios as the base:

Net income/Net revenues
Operating income/Net revenues
Operating income/Total assets
Net income/Total shareholders' equity
Operating income/Total shareholders' equity

Current assets/Current liabilities

Total liabilities/Total shareholders' equity

Which of these ratios is most (least) affected by the accounting standards used?

Worksheet for the Restatement of Swisscom's Financial Statements from IFRS to U.S. GAAP

	(1) IFRS	(2) Reconciling Adjustments Debit	(3) Reconciling Adjustments Credit	(4) U.S. GAAP
Consolidated Statement of Operations				
Net revenues	**9,842**			
Capitalized cost and changes in inventories	277			
Total	10,119			
Goods and services purchased	1,666			
Personnel expenses	2,584			
Other operating expenses	2,090			
Depreciation and amortization	1,739			
Restructuring charges	1,726			
Total operating expenses	9,805			
Operating income	**314**			
Interest expense	(428)			
Financial income	25			
Income (loss) before income taxes and equity in net loss of affiliated companies	**(89)**			
Income tax expense	1			
Income (loss) before equity in net loss of affiliated companies	**(90)**			
Equity in net loss of affiliated companies	(325)			
Net income (loss)	(415)			
Consolidated Retained Earnings Statement				
Retained earnings, 1/1	**(151)**			
Net loss	(415)			
Profit distribution declared	(1,282)			
Conversion of loan payable to equity	3,200			
Retained earnings, 12/31	**1,352**			
Consolidated Balance Sheet				
Assets				
Current assets				
Cash and cash equivalents	256			
Securities available for sale	51			
Trade accounts receivable	2,052			
Inventories	169			
Other current assets	34			
Total current assets	**2,562**			

	(1) IFRS	(2) Reconciling Debit	(3) Adjustments Credit	(4) U.S. GAAP
Non-current assets				
Property, plant and equipment	11,453			
Investments	1,238			
Other non-current assets	220			
Total non-current assets	**12,911**			
Total assets	**15,473**			
Liabilities and shareholders' equity				
Current liabilities				
Short-term debt	1,178			
Trade accounts payable	889			
Accrued pension cost.	789			
Other current liabilities	**2,213**			
Total current liabilities	**5,069**			
Long-term liabilities				
Long-term debt	6,200			
Finance lease obligation	439			
Accrued pension cost.	1,488			
Accrued liabilities	709			
Other long-term liabilities.	338			
Total long-term liabilities	**9,174**			
Total liabilities	**14,243**			
Shareholders' equity				
Retained earnings	1,352			
Unrealized market value adjustment on securities available for sale	39			
Cumulative translation adjustment	(161)			
Total shareholders' equity	**1,230**			
Total liabilities and shareholders' equity	**15,473**			

27. Differences between International Financial Reporting Standards and U.S. Generally Accepted Accounting Principles

The consolidated financial statements of Swisscom have been prepared in accordance with International Financial Reporting Standards (IFRS), which differ in certain respects from generally accepted accounting principles in the United States (U.S. GAAP). Application of U.S. GAAP would have affected the balance sheet and net income (loss) to the extent described below. A description of the material differences between IFRS and U.S. GAAP as they relate to Swisscom are discussed in further detail below.

Reconciliation of net income (loss) from IFRS to U.S. GAAP

The following schedule illustrates the significant adjustments to reconcile net income (loss) in accordance with U.S. GAAP to the amounts determined under IFRS, for the current year ended December 31.

(CHF in millions)	Current Year Ended December 31
Net income (loss) according to IFRS	**(415)**
U.S. GAAP adjustments	
a) Capitalization of interest cost	8
b) Restructuring charges	205
c) Depreciation expense	(5)
d) Capitalization of software	182
e) Restructuring charges by affiliates	50
Net income according to U.S. GAAP	**25**
Reconciliation of shareholders' equity from IFRS to U.S. GAAP	

The following is a reconciliation of the significant adjustments necessary to reconcile shareholders' equity in accordance with U.S. GAAP to the amounts determined under IFRS as at December 31 of the current year.

(CHF in millions)	Current Year Ended December 31
Shareholders' equity according to IFRS	**1,230**
U.S. GAAP adjustments	
a) Capitalization of interest cost	54
b) Restructuring charges	205
c) Depreciation expense	(5)
d) Capitalization of software	475
e) Restructuring charges by affiliates	50
Shareholders' equity according to U.S. GAAP	**2,009**

a) Capitalization of interest cost

Swisscom expenses all interest costs as incurred. U.S. GAAP requires interest costs incurred during the construction of property, plant and equipment to be capitalized. Under U.S. GAAP Swisscom would have capitalized CHF 13 million and amortized CHF 5 million for the current year.

b) Restructuring charges

During the current year, Swisscom recognized under IFRS restructuring charges totaling CHF 1,726 million. The following schedule illustrates adjustments necessary to reconcile these charges to amounts determined under U.S. GAAP.

	Current Year (CHF in millions)
Restructuring charges in accordance with IFRS:	
Personnel restructuring charges	1,326
Write-down of long-lived assets.	316
Miscellaneous restructuring charges	84
Total in accordance with IFRS	1,726
Adjustments to restructuring charges to accord with U.S. GAAP	(205)
Restructuring charges in accordance with U.S. GAAP.	1,521

Reconciliation of restructuring charges	Current Year (CHF in millions)
Restructuring charges according to U.S. GAAP are comprised of the following:	
Personnel restructuring charges	1,228
Write-down of long-lived assets	209
Miscellaneous restructuring charges	84
Restructuring charges in accordance with U.S. GAAP	1,521

Note: Assume the counterpart to the personnel restructuring charge affects "other long-term liabilities."

c) Depreciation Expense

Due to the difference in carrying value of long-lived assets after write-downs described in (b), there is a difference in the amount of depreciation expense taken under IFRS and U.S. GAAP. An adjustment is made for the current year to record an additional CHF 5 million of depreciation under U.S. GAAP.

d) Capitalization of software

Swisscom has expensed software costs as incurred. For U.S. GAAP purposes external consultant costs incurred in the development of software for internal use have been capitalized. These costs are being amortized over a three year period. The capitalization of software costs accords with common practice in the U.S. telecommunications industry.

Swisscom has capitalized, as disclosed in the reconciliation of net income (loss) and shareholders' equity to U.S. GAAP, CHF 220 million and amortized CHF 37 million in the previous year and capitalized CHF 370 million and amortized CHF 188 million in the current year.

e) Restructuring charges of affiliates

During the current year, Swisscom's share of personnel and other restructuring charges recorded by affiliates amounted to CHF 50 million. These restructuring charges do not meet all the recognition criteria contained in EITF 94-3 and therefore cannot be expensed in the current year, under U.S. GAAP.

References

Bavishi, V. B., ed. *International Accounting and Auditing Trends, vol. 2*, 4th ed. Princeton, NJ: CIFAR Publications, 1995.

Choi, F. D. S.; H. Hino; S. K. Min; S. O. Nam; J. Ujiie; and A. I. Stonehill. "Analyzing Foreign Financial Statements: The Use and Misuse of International Ratio Analysis." *Journal of International Business Studies*, Spring/Summer 1983, pp. 113–31.

Choi, F. D. S., and R. M. Levich. "Behavioral Effects of International Accounting Diversity." *Accounting Horizons*, June 1991, pp. 1–13.

Chukwuogor, C. "Stock Markets Returns and Volatilities: A Global Comparison." *International Research Journal of Finance and Economics*, no. 15, 2008, pp. 7–30.

Frost, Carol A. 1998. "Characteristics and Information Value of Corporate Disclosures of Forward-Looking Information in Global Equity Markets," Dartmouth College Working Paper, as reported in Frederick D. S. Choi, Carol Ann Frost, and Gary K. Meek, *International Accounting*, 4th ed. Upper Saddle River, NJ: Prentice Hall, 2002.

Gray, S. J.; G. K. Meek; and C. B. Roberts. "International Capital Market Pressures and Voluntary Annual Report Disclosures by US and UK Multinationals," *Journal of International Financial Management and Accounting* 6, no. 1 (1995), pp. 43–68.

"Profits Ici Pertes Au-Dela." *L'Enterprise* 63 (December 1990), pp. 78–79.

Levitt, Arthur. "A Public Partnership to Battle Earnings Management," *Accounting Today,* May 24–June 6, 1999, p. 36.

Sherman, R., and R. Todd. "International Financial Statement Analysis," in *International Accounting and Finance Handbook,* 2nd ed., ed. F. D. S. Choi. New York: Wiley, 1997, pp. 8.1–8.61.

Chapter **Eleven**

International Taxation

Learning Objectives

After reading this chapter, you should be able to

- Describe differences in corporate income tax and withholding tax regimes across countries.
- Explain how overlapping tax jurisdictions cause double taxation.
- Show how foreign tax credits reduce the incidence of double taxation.
- Demonstrate how rules related to controlled foreign corporations, subpart F income, and foreign tax credit baskets affect U.S. taxation of foreign source income.
- Describe some of the benefits provided by tax treaties.
- Explain and demonstrate procedures for translating foreign currency amounts for tax purposes.
- Describe tax incentives provided by countries to attract foreign direct investment and stimulate exports.

INTRODUCTION

Taxes paid to governments are one of the most significant costs incurred by business enterprises. Taxes reduce net profits as well as cash flow. Well-managed companies attempt to minimize the taxes they pay while making sure they are in compliance with applicable tax laws. For a multinational corporation (MNC) that pays taxes in more than one country, the objective is to minimize taxes worldwide. The achievement of this objective requires expertise in the tax law of each foreign country in which the corporation operates. Knowledge of how the domestic country taxes the profits earned in foreign countries is also of great importance.

MNCs make a number of very important decisions in which taxation is an important variable. For example, tax issues are important in deciding (1) where to locate a foreign operation, (2) what legal form the operation should take, and (3) how the operation will be financed.

Investment Location Decision

The decision to make a foreign investment is based on forecasts of *after-tax* profit and cash flows. Because effective tax rates vary across countries, after-tax returns from competing investment locations could vary. The decision of whether to place an operation in either Spain or Portugal, for example, could be affected by differences in the tax systems in those two countries.

Legal Form of Operation

A foreign operation of an MNC is organized legally either as a branch of the MNC or as a subsidiary, in which case the operation is incorporated in the foreign country. Some countries tax foreign branch income differently from foreign subsidiary income. The different tax treatment for branches and subsidiaries could result in one legal form being preferable to the other because of the impact on profits and cash flows.

Method of Financing

MNCs can finance their foreign operations by making capital contributions (equity) or through loans (debt). Cash flows generated by a foreign operation can be repatriated back to the MNC either by making dividend payments (on equity financing) or interest payments (on debt financing). Countries often impose a special (withholding) tax on dividend and interest payments made to foreigners. Withholding tax rates within a country can differ by type of payment. When this is the case, the MNC may wish to use more of one type of financing than the other because of the positive impact on cash flows back to the MNC.

These examples demonstrate the importance of developing an expertise in international taxation for the management of an MNC. It is impossible (and unnecessary) for every manager of an MNC to become a true expert in international taxation. However, all managers should be familiar with the major issues in international taxation so that they know when it might be necessary to call on the experts to help make a decision.

It is not possible in this book to cover all aspects of international taxation in depth; that would require years of study and many more pages of reading than can be included here. However, there are certain issues with which international accountants and managers of MNCs should be familiar to make sure that corporate goals are being achieved. The objective of this chapter is to examine the major issues of international taxation without getting bogged down in the minutiae for which tax laws are well known. We will concentrate on taxes on income and distributions of income, ignoring other taxes such as Social Security and payroll taxes, sales and value-added taxes, and excise taxes. Although this chapter concentrates on the taxation of corporate profits, certain features of individual income taxation relevant for expatriates working overseas are described in the chapter's appendix.

TYPES OF TAXES AND TAX RATES

Corporations are subject to many different types of taxes, including property taxes, payroll taxes, and excise taxes. While it is important for managers of MNCs to be knowledgeable about these taxes, we focus on taxes on profit. The two major types of taxes imposed on profits earned by companies engaged in international business are (1) corporate income taxes and (2) withholding taxes.

Income Taxes

Most, but not all, national governments impose a direct tax on business income. Exhibit 11.1 shows that national corporate income tax rates vary substantially across countries. The corporate income tax rate in most countries is between 20 and 35 percent. Differences in corporate tax rates across countries provide MNCs with a tax-planning opportunity as they decide where to locate foreign operations. In making this decision, MNCs must be careful to consider both national and local

EXHIBIT 11.1
International Corporate Tax Rates, 2009

Sources: KPMG, Corporate and Indirect Tax Rate Survey 2009, available at www.kpmg.com (accessed on July 1, 2010).

Country	Effective Tax Rate (%)	Country	Effective Tax Rate (%)
Argentina	35	Italy	31.4
Australia	30	Japan	40.69[4]
Austria	25	Korea (South)	24.2
Belgium	33.99	Malaysia	25
Brazil	34[1]	Mexico	28
Canada	33[2]	Netherlands	25.5
Chile	17	New Zealand	30
China	25	Russia	20
Czech Republic	20	Singapore	18
Denmark	25	Spain	30
France	33.33	Sweden	26.3
Germany	29.44[3]	Switzerland	21.17[5]
Greece	25	Taiwan	25
Hong Kong	16.5	Thailand	30
Hungary	16	Turkey	20
Indonesia	28	United Kingdom	28
Ireland	12.5	United States	35[6]
Israel	26	Venezuela	34

[1] The effective tax rate on corporate profits in Brazil is the sum of a corporation income tax (25%) and a social contribution tax (9%).
[2] The Canadian effective tax rate is comprised of a federal corporate income tax rate of 19% plus a provincial corporate income tax rate, which varies by province. Ontario charges a provincial tax of 14%, which is reduced to 12% on manufacturing and processing activities.
[3] This is an approximate rate consisting of a 15% federal corporate income tax, a 0.825% solidarity tax, and an additional trade tax, which varies by locality.
[4] The effective tax rate in Japan varies by locality. The rate presented relates to a company located in Tokyo.
[5] The Swiss federal tax rate is 8.5%. Individual cantons levy an additional corporate income tax. The rate presented is for the canton of Zurich.
[6] The U.S. federal tax rate is 35%. Individual states assess different levels of local tax, ranging from 0–12%.

taxes in their analysis. In some countries, local governments impose a separate tax on business income in addition to that levied by the national government. For example, the national tax rate in Switzerland is 8.5 percent, but additional local taxes range anywhere from 6 percent to 33 percent. A company located in Zurich can expect to pay an effective tax rate of 21.17 percent to local and federal governments. Corporate income tax rates imposed by individual states in the United States vary from 0 percent (e.g., South Dakota) to as high as 12 percent (Iowa).

In a few countries, corporate income taxes can vary according to the type of activity in which a company is engaged or the nationality of the company's owners. The rate of national income tax in China is reduced from 25 percent to 15 percent for enterprises operating in certain industries. Canada imposes a lower tax rate on manufacturers, and India taxes foreign companies at a higher rate than domestic companies.

In making foreign investment decisions, MNCs often engage in a capital budgeting process in which the future cash flows to be generated by the foreign investment are forecasted, discounted to their present value, and then compared with the amount to be invested to determine a net present value. Taxes paid to the foreign government will have a negative impact on future cash flows and might affect the location decision. For example, assume that a Japanese musical instrument manufacturer is deciding whether to locate a new factory in Hungary or in Switzerland. Although the national tax rate in Hungary is much higher than in Switzerland, the effective tax rate in some parts of Switzerland would be higher than in Hungary because of the high local taxes that would have to be paid.

Of course, the amount of taxes paid to a government is not determined solely by the corporate tax rate. The manner in which taxable income is calculated also will greatly affect a company's tax liability. Just as tax rates vary from country to country, so does the way in which taxable income is calculated. Expenses that can be deducted for tax purposes can vary greatly from country to country. For example, in the United States, only the first $1 million of the chief executive officer's salary is tax deductible. Most other countries do not have a similar rule.

The United States allows companies to use the last-in, first-out (LIFO) method for inventory valuation and accelerated depreciation methods for fixed assets in determining taxable income, whereas Brazil does not. All else being equal, a company with increasing inventory prices that is replacing or expanding its fixed assets will have smaller taxable income in the United States than in Brazil. The United States has a higher corporate income tax rate than Brazil, but because taxable income is smaller, a company in the United States may actually have a smaller amount of taxes to pay.

There has been a recent and continuing international trend to reduce corporate tax rates. The United States appears to have led the way in 1986 when the corporate tax rate was reduced from 46 percent to 34 percent (it was subsequently raised to 35 percent in 1994). The United Kingdom quickly followed suit by reducing its rate from 50 percent to 35 percent, Canada from 34 percent to 29 percent, and so on. More recently, Belgium lowered its rate from 40.17 percent in 2002 to 33.99 percent in 2003, and Austria lowered its rate from 34 percent to 25 percent in 2005. Greece has gradually lowered its corporate tax rate from 40 percent in 2000 to 25 percent in 2007. This follow-the-leader effect is explained by the fact that countries compete against one another in attracting foreign investment.

One way to compete for foreign investment is to offer a so-called *tax holiday*. For example, to attract foreign investment, the prime minister of the Czech Republic announced in March 2000 that foreign enterprises that invest at least $10 million may be entitled to a 10-year exemption from income taxation and customs duties. Following the financial crisis in Asia in the late 1990s, several countries in that region adopted various measures including tax incentives to help their economies recover. In 1999, Indonesia established eight-year holidays for new projects in 22 categories of industries, including textiles, pharmaceuticals, and auto parts.

Tax Havens

There are a number of tax jurisdictions with abnormally low corporate income tax rates (or no corporate income tax at all) that companies and individuals have found useful in minimizing their worldwide income taxes. These tax jurisdictions, known as *tax havens*, include the Bahamas and the Isle of Man, which have no corporate income tax, and Liechtenstein, which has tax rates ranging from 7.5 percent to 15 percent.

A company involved in international business might find it beneficial to establish an operation in a tax haven to avoid paying taxes in one or more countries in

EXHIBIT 11.2
OECD Criteria and List of Tax Havens

Source: Organization for Economic Cooperation and Development, "The OECD's Project on Harmful Tax Practices: The 2004 Progress Report," available at www.oecd.org (accessed on March 1, 2008).

OECD criteria for tax haven status:

- No or only nominal effective tax rates
- Lack of effective exchange of information
- Lack of transparency
- Absence of substantial activities requirement

Jurisdictions meeting the OECD's criteria in June 2004 were:

Anguilla	Dominica	Niue
Antigua	Gibraltar	Panama
Aruba	Grenada	Samoa
Bahamas	Guernsey	San Marino
Bahrain	Isle of Man	Seychelles
Belize	Jersey	St. Kitts & Nevis
Bermuda	Malta	St. Lucia
British Virgin Islands	Mauritius	St. Vincent
Cayman Islands	Montserrat	Turks & Caicos
Cook Islands	Nauru	U.S. Virgin Islands
Cyprus	Netherlands Antilles	Vanuatu

which the company operates. For example, assume a Brazilian company manufactures a product for $70 per unit that it exports to a customer in Mexico at a sales price of $100 per unit. The $30 of profit earned on each unit is subject to the Brazilian corporate tax rate of 34 percent. The Brazilian manufacturer could take advantage of the fact that there is no corporate income tax in the Bahamas by establishing a sales subsidiary there that it uses as a conduit for export sales. The Brazilian parent company would then sell the product to its Bahamian sales subsidiary at a price of, say, $80 per unit, and the Bahamian sales subsidiary would turn around and sell the product to the customer in Mexico at $100 per unit. In this way, only $10 of the total profit is earned in Brazil and subject to Brazilian income tax; $20 of the $30 total profit is recorded in the Bahamas and is therefore not taxed.

The Organization for Economic Cooperation and Development (OECD) has established guidelines for tax regimes to ensure that they cannot be used to avoid taxation in other countries.[1] Because the OECD lacks enforcement power, its member countries must put pressure on tax havens in order for them to change their tax regimes. Exhibit 11.2 provides a list of criteria the OECD uses to identify tax havens and the countries meeting these criteria in 2004. Most of these countries have expressed a willingness to change their tax regimes to be removed from the OECD list and avoid any possible defensive measures by its member nations.[2]

---

[1] The OECD is a voluntary organization whose membership comprises the most developed countries in the world, located primarily in Europe and North America, but also including Japan, Korea, Australia, New Zealand, and Turkey.

[2] Organization for Economic Cooperation and Development, *The OECD's Project on Harmful Tax Practices: The 2004 Progress Report* (Paris: OECD, 2004), p. 11.

EXHIBIT 11.3
Nontreaty
Withholding
Rates in Selected
Countries

Source:
PricewaterhouseCoopers,
Worldwide Tax Summaries,
available at www.
taxsummaries.pwc.com
(accessed on July 1, 2010).

Country	Dividends	Interest	Royalties
Australia	30%	10%	30%
Austria	25	0	20
Brazil	0	15	15
Canada	25	25	25
France	25	18	33.3
Germany	20	25	15
Indonesia	20	20	20
Italy	27	0, 12.5, or 27	30
Japan	20	0, 15, or 20	20
Korea (South)	20	14 or 20	20
Malaysia	0	0 or 15	10
Mexico	0	4.9–30	5–30
New Zealand	30	15	15
Philippines	30	30	30
Singapore	0	15	10
Spain	19	19	24
Sweden	30	0	0
Switzerland	35	35	0
Taiwan	20	15 or 20	20
Thailand	10	15	15
United Kingdom	0	20	20
United States	30	30	30

Withholding Taxes

When a foreign citizen who invests in the shares of a U.S. company receives a dividend payment, theoretically he or she should file a tax return with the U.S. Internal Revenue Service and pay taxes on the dividend income. If the foreign investor does not file this tax return, the U.S. government has no recourse for collecting the tax. To avoid this possibility, the United States (like most other countries) will require the payer of the dividend (the U.S. company) to withhold some amount of taxes and remit that amount to the U.S. government. This type of tax is referred to as a *withholding tax*. The withholding tax rate on dividends in the United States is 30 percent.

To see how the withholding tax works, assume that International Business Machines Corporation (IBM), a U.S.-based company, pays a $100 dividend to a stockholder in Brazil. Under U.S. withholding tax rules, IBM would withhold $30 from the payment (which is sent to the U.S. Internal Revenue Service) and the Brazilian stockholder would be issued a check in the amount of $70.

Withholding taxes are also imposed on payments made to foreign parent companies or foreign affiliated companies. There are three types of payments typically subject to withholding tax: dividends, interest, and royalties. Withholding tax rates vary across countries, and in some countries withholding rates vary by type of payment or recipient. Exhibit 11.3 provides withholding rates generally applicable in selected countries. In many cases, the rate listed will be different for some subset of activity. For example, although the U.S. withholding rate on interest payments is generally 30 percent, interest on bank deposits and on certain registered debt instruments (bonds) is exempt (0 percent tax). In addition, many of the rates listed in Exhibit 11.3 vary with tax treaties (discussed later in this chapter).

Tax-Planning Strategy

Differences in withholding rates on different types of payments in some countries provide an opportunity to reduce taxes (increase cash flow) by altering the method of financing a foreign operation. For example, a British company planning to establish a manufacturing facility in Austria would prefer that future cash payments received from the Austrian subsidiary be in the form of interest rather than dividends because of the lower withholding tax rate (0 percent on interest versus 25 percent on dividends). This objective can be achieved by the British parent using a combination of loan and equity investment in financing the Austrian subsidiary. For example, rather than the British parent investing €10 million in equity to establish the Austrian operation, €5 million is contributed in equity and €5 million is lent to the Austrian operation by the British parent. Interest on the loan, which is a cash payment to the British parent, will be exempt from Austrian withholding tax, whereas any dividends paid on the capital contribution will be taxed at 25 percent.

Many countries have a lower rate of withholding tax on interest than on dividends. In addition, interest payments are generally tax deductible whereas dividend payments are not. Thus, there is often an incentive for companies to finance their foreign operations with as much debt and as little equity capital as possible. This is known as *thin capitalization,* and several countries have set limits as to how thinly capitalized a company may be. For example, in France, interest paid to a foreign parent will not be tax deductible for the amount of the loan that exceeds 150 percent of equity capital. In other words, the ratio of debt to equity may not exceed 150 percent for tax purposes. If equity capital is €1 million, any interest paid on loans exceeding €1.5 million will not be tax deductible. Similarly, in Mexico, subsidiaries of foreign parents run the risk of having some interest declared nondeductible when the debt-to-equity ratio exceeds 3 to 1.

Value-Added Tax

Many countries generate a significant amount of revenue through the use of a national *value-added tax (VAT).* Standard VAT rates in the European Union, for example, range from a low of 15 percent (Luxembourg and Cyprus) to a high of 25 percent (Denmark, Hungary, and Sweden).[3] Value-added taxes are used in lieu of a sales tax and are generally incorporated into the price of a product or service. This type of tax is levied on the value added at each stage in the production or distribution of a product or service. For example, if a Swedish forest products company sells lumber that it has harvested to a Swedish wholesaler at a price of €100,000, it will pay a VAT to the Swedish government of €25,000 (€100,000 × 25%). When the Swedish wholesaler, in turn, sells the lumber to its customers for €160,000, the wholesaler will pay a VAT of €15,000 (25% × €60,000 value added at the wholesale stage). The VAT concept is commonly used in countries other than the European Union, including Australia, Canada, China, Hungary, Mexico, Nigeria, Turkey, and South Africa.

---

[3] European Commission, *VAT Rates Applied in the Member States of the European Community: Situation at 1st January 2010,* available at www.eurounion.org.

Value-added taxes as well as other indirect taxes (such as sales and payroll taxes) need to be considered in determining the total rate of taxation to be paid in a country. A study conducted by the World Bank and PricewaterhouseCoopers in 2010 determined the total tax rate paid on business income in 183 countries.[4] The study was based on a case study company in its second year of operations with 60 employees and sales equal to 1,050 times per capita income. Total taxes included federal and local income taxes; VAT and other forms of sales tax; and workers compensation, Social Security, and other mandatory contributions on behalf of employees. Total tax rates ranged from 0.2 percent (Timor-Leste) to 322.0 percent (Democratic Republic of Congo). Total tax rates in selected other countries were:

Brazil	69.2%	Hong Kong	24.2%	New Zealand	32.8%
Canada	43.6%	India	64.7%	Poland	42.5%
Chile	25.3%	Italy	68.4%	Saudi Arabia	14.5%
China	63.8%	Japan	55.7%	Switzerland	29.7%
France	65.8%	Mexico	51.0%	United Kingdom	35.9%
Germany	44.9%	Namibia	9.6%	United States	46.3%

TAX JURISDICTION

One of the most important issues in international taxation is determining which country has the right to tax which income. In many cases, two countries will assert the right to tax the same income, resulting in the problem of *double taxation*. For example, consider the Brazilian investor earning dividends from an investment in IBM Corporation common stock. The United States might want to tax this dividend because it was earned in the United States, and Brazil might want to tax the dividend because it was earned by a resident of Brazil. This section discusses general concepts used internationally in determining tax jurisdiction. Subsequent sections examine mechanisms used for providing relief from double taxation.

Worldwide versus Territorial Approach

One tax jurisdiction issue is related to the taxation of income earned overseas, known as *foreign source income*. There are two approaches taken on this issue:

1. *Worldwide (nationality) approach.* Under this approach, all income of a resident of a country or a company incorporated in a country is taxed by that country regardless of where the income is earned. In other words, foreign source income is taxed by the country of residence. For example, Canada imposes a tax on dividend income earned by a Canadian company from its subsidiary in Hong Kong even though that income was earned outside of Canada. Most countries exercise tax jurisdiction on the basis of nationality and impose a tax on worldwide income.

2. *Territorial approach.* Under this approach, only the income earned within the borders of the country (domestic source income) is taxed. For example, the dividend income earned by a resident of Venezuela from investments in U.S. stocks will not be taxed in Venezuela. Few countries follow this approach, and the number is decreasing. South Africa, one of the few countries using a

[4] The World Bank and PricewaterhouseCoopers, *Paying Taxes 2010: The Global Picture*, available at www.doingbusiness.org/documents/fullreport/2010/paying-taxes-2010.pdf

territorial approach, moved to the worldwide basis of taxation beginning in 2000. The most economically important country that continues to use a territorial approach is France.

Source, Citizenship, and Residence

Regardless of the approach used in determining the scope of taxation, a second issue related to jurisdiction is the basis for taxation. Countries generally use source, citizenship, residence, or some combination of the three for determining jurisdictional authority.

Source of Income

In general, almost all countries assert the jurisdictional authority to tax income where it is earned—in effect, at its source—regardless of the residence or citizenship of the recipient. An example would be the United States taxing dividends paid by IBM Corporation to a stockholder in Canada because the dividend income was earned in the United States.

Citizenship

Under the citizenship basis of taxation, citizens are taxed by their country of citizenship regardless of where they reside or the source of the income being taxed. The United States is unusual among countries in that it taxes on the basis of citizenship. Thus, a U.S. citizen who lives and works overseas will be subject to U.S. income tax on his or her worldwide income regardless of where the citizen earns that income or resides.

Residence

Under the residence approach, residents of a country are taxed by the country in which they reside regardless of their citizenship or where the income was earned. For example, assume a citizen of Singapore resides permanently in the United States and earns dividends from an investment in the shares of a company in the United Kingdom. Taxing on the basis of residence, this individual will be subject to taxation in the United States on his or her foreign source income, even though he or she is a citizen of Singapore.

The United States is one country that taxes on the basis of residence. For tax purposes, a U.S. resident is any person who is a U.S. permanent resident as evidenced by holding a permanent resident permit issued by the Immigration and Naturalization Service (the "green card" test) or is physically present in the United States for 183 or more days in a year (physical presence test). Note that because the United States levies taxes using a worldwide approach, the worldwide income of an individual holding a U.S. permanent resident card is subject to U.S. taxation *even if he or she is not actually living in the United States.*

Companies created or organized in the United States are considered to be U.S. residents for tax purposes. The foreign *subsidiary* of a U.S. parent is not considered to be a U.S. resident, but a foreign *branch* is. Under the U.S. worldwide approach to taxation, a U.S. parent pays U.S. income tax currently on foreign branch income, but foreign subsidiary income is not taxed in the United States until dividends are paid to the U.S. parent.[5] Other countries have a similar rule.

For a U.S. MNC, establishing a foreign operation as a subsidiary (by legally incorporating in the foreign country) generally has the advantage that U.S. taxes

---

[5] An exception exists when the foreign subsidiary is located in a tax haven country and generates Subpart F income. This issue is discussed later under "Controlled Foreign Corporations."

on the subsidiary income are deferred until profits are repatriated back to the United States through the payment of dividends. The disadvantage is that if the foreign subsidiary incurs a net loss, this loss may not be taken as a tax deduction in the parent's tax return. However, the advantage of registering the foreign operation with the foreign country as a branch is that any losses are currently deductible on the U.S. tax return. The disadvantage is that any profits are taxed currently in the United States.

This provides an opportunity for strategic tax planning. U.S. MNCs often initially set up their foreign operations as branches when losses are expected in early years. The branch is then incorporated as a subsidiary when the operation becomes profitable. The disadvantage to this is that converting a branch into a subsidiary is generally considered to be the sale of the branch to the subsidiary, usually at a gain, which is taxable.

Double Taxation

The combination of a worldwide approach to taxation and the various bases for taxation can lead to overlapping tax jurisdictions that can in turn lead to double or even triple taxation. For example, a U.S. citizen residing in Germany with investment income in Austria might be expected to pay taxes on the investment income to the United States (on the basis of citizenship), Germany (on the basis of residence), and Austria (on the basis of source).

The same is true for corporate taxpayers with foreign source income. The most common overlap of jurisdictions for corporations is where the home country taxes on the basis of residence and the country where the foreign branch or subsidiary is located taxes on the basis of source. Without some relief, this could result in a tremendous tax burden for the parent company. For example, income earned by the Japanese branch of a U.S. company would be taxed at the effective Japanese corporate income tax rate of 41 percent and at the rate of 35 percent in the United States, for an aggregate tax rate of 76 percent. The U.S. parent has only 24 percent of the profit after income taxes. At that rate, there is a disincentive to establish operations overseas. Without any relief from double taxation, all investment by the U.S. company would remain at home in the United States, where income would be taxed only at the rate of 35 percent.

An important goal of most national tax systems is neutrality; that is, the tax system should remain in the background, and business, investment, and consumption decisions should be made for nontax reasons. In an international context there are three standards for neutrality, one of which is *capital-export neutrality*. A tax system meets this standard if a taxpayer's decision whether to invest at home or overseas is not affected by taxation. Double taxation from overlapping tax jurisdictions precludes a tax system from achieving capital-export neutrality; all investment will remain at home. In order to achieve capital-export neutrality, most countries have one or more mechanisms for eliminating the problem of double taxation. One mechanism is a provision in bilateral tax treaties between countries in which foreign source income is exempt. Tax treaties are discussed later in this chapter. Another major source of relief from double taxation is the *foreign tax credit*. "For U.S. citizens and residents, including domestic corporations, perhaps the most important international tax provisions are those dealing with the foreign tax credit."[6]

---

[6] Richard L. Doernberg, *International Taxation: In a Nutshell*, 4th ed. (St. Paul, MN: West, 1999), p. 13.

FOREIGN TAX CREDITS

Double taxation of income earned by foreign operations generally arises because the country where the foreign operation is located taxes the income at its source and the parent company's home country taxes worldwide income on the basis of residence. To relieve the double taxation, the question is, Which country should give up its right to tax the income? The international norm is that source should take precedence over residence in determining tax jurisdiction. In that case, it will be up to the parent company's home country to eliminate the double taxation.

This can be accomplished in several ways. One way would be to exempt foreign source income from taxation—in effect, to adopt a territorial approach to taxation. A second approach would be to allow the parent company to deduct the taxes paid to the foreign government from its taxable income. Third would be to provide the parent company with a credit for taxes paid to the foreign government.

Some countries have decided to deal with double taxation through the first option. The mechanics of applying this option are fairly straightforward; foreign source income simply is not included in the parent's tax declaration. Most countries, in contrast, have decided to use the second and third options. As a point of reference, the specific U.S. tax rules related to foreign tax credits and deductions are described here.

Credit versus Deduction

For U.S. tax purposes, U.S. companies are allowed either to (1) deduct *all* foreign taxes paid or (2) take a credit for foreign *income* taxes paid. Income taxes include withholding taxes, as discussed above, but exclude sales, excise, and other types of taxes not based on income. Unless taxes other than income taxes are substantial, it is more advantageous for a company to take the foreign tax credit rather than a tax deduction.

Example: Deduction for Foreign Taxes Paid versus Foreign Tax Credit

Assume ASD Company's foreign branch earns income before income taxes of $100,000. Income taxes paid to the foreign government are $30,000 (30 percent). Sales and other taxes paid to the foreign government are $10,000. ASD Company must include the $100,000 of foreign branch income in its U.S. tax return in calculating U.S. taxable income. The options of taking a deduction or tax credit are as follows:

ASD Company's U.S. Tax Return		
	Deduction	**Credit**
Foreign source income	$100,000	$100,000
Deduction for all foreign taxes paid	−40,000	0
U.S. taxable income	$ 60,000	$100,000
U.S. income tax before credit (35%)	$ 21,000	$ 35,000
Foreign tax credit (for income taxes paid)	0	−30,000
Net U.S. tax liability	$ 21,000	$ 5,000

Note that ASD's foreign branch earns its income in a foreign currency that must be translated into U.S. dollars for tax purposes. Foreign currency translation for tax purposes is discussed later in this chapter.

The foreign tax credit provides a dollar-for-dollar reduction in tax liability; that is, for every dollar of income tax ASD paid to the foreign government, ASD is allowed a one-dollar reduction in the amount of income taxes to be paid to the U.S. government. In this example, the foreign tax credit results in considerably less net U.S. tax liability than the deduction for foreign taxes paid. In the case of foreign branch income, the credit allowed is known as a *direct foreign tax credit* because ASD is given a credit for the taxes it paid itself to the foreign government.

In the case of foreign subsidiary income, the foreign subsidiary (as an entity legally incorporated in the foreign country) pays its own taxes to the foreign government. Remember that foreign subsidiary income will not be taxed in the United States until dividends are paid by the foreign subsidiary to the U.S. parent. At that time, ASD will include foreign source dividend income in its U.S. tax return and will be allowed an *indirect foreign tax credit* for the foreign taxes deemed to have been paid by ASD.

Calculation of Foreign Tax Credit

The rules governing the calculation of the foreign tax credit (FTC) in the United States are rather complex. In general, the FTC allowed is equal to the lower of (1) actual taxes paid to the foreign government, or (2) the amount of taxes that would have been paid if the income had been earned in the United States.

This latter amount, in many cases, can be calculated by multiplying the amount of foreign source income by the effective U.S. tax rate on worldwide taxable income. This is known as the *overall FTC limitation* because the United States will not allow a foreign tax credit greater than the amount of taxes that would have been paid in the United States. To allow an FTC greater than the amount of taxes that would have been paid in the United States would require the U.S. government to refund U.S. companies for higher taxes paid in foreign countries. More formally, the overall FTC limitation is calculated as follows:

$$\text{Overall FTC limitation} = \frac{\text{Foreign source taxable income}}{\text{Worldwide taxable income}} \times \text{U.S. taxes before FTC}$$

Example: Calculation of Foreign Tax Credit for Branches

Assume that two different U.S.-based companies have foreign branches. Alpha Company has a branch in Country A and Zeta Company has a branch in Country Z. The amount of income before tax earned by each foreign branch and the amount of income tax paid to the local government is as follows:

	Alpha Company Branch in A	Zeta Company Branch in Z
Income before taxes	$100,000	$100,000
Income tax paid	$ 25,000 (25%)	$ 37,000 (37%)

Both Alpha and Zeta will report $100,000 of foreign branch income on their U.S. tax return, and each will determine a U.S. tax liability before FTC of $35,000. For both companies, $35,000 is the amount of U.S. taxes that would have been paid if the foreign branch income had been earned in the United States. The overall FTC limitation is $35,000 for both companies.

Alpha compares the income tax of $25,000 paid to the government of Country A with the limitation of $35,000 and will be allowed an FTC of $25,000, the lesser of the two. Zeta compares actual taxes of $37,000 paid to the government of Country Z with the limitation of $35,000 and will be allowed an FTC of $35,000, the lesser of the two. The U.S. income tax return related to foreign branch income for Alpha and Zeta reflects the following:

U.S. Tax Return		
	Alpha	**Zeta**
U.S. taxable income	$100,000	$100,000
U.S. tax before FTC (35%)	$ 35,000	$ 35,000
FTC	25,000	35,000
Net U.S. tax liability	$ 10,000	$ 0

Alpha has a net U.S. tax liability after foreign tax credit on its foreign branch income of $10,000, an additional 10 percent over what has already been paid in Country A (25 percent). The United States requires Alpha to pay an effective tax rate of at least 35 percent (the U.S. rate) on all of its income, both U.S. source and foreign source.

Zeta has no U.S. tax liability after foreign tax credit on its foreign branch income. Zeta has already paid more than the U.S. tax rate in Country Z, so no additional taxes will be paid in the United States. Instead, the $2,000 difference between the $37,000 in foreign taxes paid and the foreign tax credit of $35,000 allowed in the United States becomes an *excess foreign tax credit*.

Excess Foreign Tax Credits

Excess foreign tax credits may be used to offset additional taxes paid to the United States on foreign source income in years in which foreign tax rates are lower than the U.S. tax rate. An excess FTC may be

1. Carried back 1 year. The company applies for a refund of additional taxes paid to the United States on foreign source income in the previous year.
2. Carried forward 10 years. The company reduces future U.S. tax liability in the event that additional U.S. taxes must be paid on foreign source income in any of the next 10 years.[7]

In effect, the excess FTC can be used only if, in the previous year or in the next 10 years, *the average foreign tax rate paid by the company is less than the U.S. tax rate.*

Example: Calculation of Excess Foreign Tax Credit (One Branch, Multiple Years)

Assume Zeta's foreign branch had $50,000 of pretax income in Year 1, $70,000 in Year 2, and $100,000 in Year 3. Assume the effective corporate income tax rate in Country Z in Year 1 was 34 percent. In Year 2, Country Z increased its corporate

---

[7] Prior to 2005, excess FTCs could be carried back two years and carried forward five years. The American Job Creations Act of 2004 changed these carryover periods.

income tax rate to 37 percent. The U.S. tax rate in each year is 35 percent. Zeta's U.S. income tax return would reflect the following:

	Year 1	Year 2	Year 3
Foreign source income.	$50,000	$70,000	$100,000
Foreign taxes paid	$17,000 34%	$25,900 37%	$ 37,000 37%
U.S. tax before FTC	$17,500 35%	$24,500 35%	$ 35,000 35%
FTC allowed in the United States . . .	17,000	24,500	35,000
Net U.S. tax liability	$ 500	$ 0	$ 0
Excess FTC.	$ 0	$ 1,400	$ 2,000

In Year 2, Zeta has an excess foreign tax credit of $1,400 ($25,900 foreign taxes paid less $24,500 FTC allowed in the United States). In that year, Zeta will file for a refund of $500 for the additional taxes paid on foreign source income in the previous year and will have an excess FTC to carry forward in the amount of $900. Zeta is unable to use its FTC carryforward in Year 3 because its effective foreign tax rate exceeds the U.S. tax rate. If Zeta is not able to use its excess FTC carry-forward of $900 in any of the next 10 years, the carryforward will be lost.

Example: Calculation of Foreign Tax Credit (One Company, Multiple Branches)

Let us return to the example related to two branches located in countries A and Z but now assume that both foreign branches belong to Alpha Company. In this case, Alpha has total foreign source income in Year 3 of $200,000 and the actual amount of taxes paid to foreign governments is $62,000 ([25% × $100,000 in Country A] + [37% × $100,000 in Country Z]). Alpha determines the amount of FTC allowed by the United States and its net U.S. tax liability on foreign source income as follows:

U.S. Tax Return	
	Alpha Company
U.S. taxable income	$200,000
U.S. tax before FTC (35%)	$ 70,000
FTC allowed*.	62,000
Net U.S. tax liability	$ 8,000

* Calculation of FTC allowed:

Actual tax paid   =   = $62,000

Overall FTC limitation = Foreign Source Income × U.S. Tax Rate

                        = $200,000   ×   35%   = $70,000

Lesser amount   = $62,000

In the earlier example involving Alpha and Zeta, Alpha had an additional U.S. tax liability on its foreign branch income of $10,000 and Zeta had an excess

FTC related to its foreign branch of $2,000. In this example, when both foreign branches belong to Alpha Company, the otherwise excess FTC from the branch in Country Z partially offsets the additional taxes on the branch income earned in Country A and a net U.S. tax liability of $8,000 remains.

FTC Baskets

In the United States prior to 1986, all foreign source income was combined to determine an overall FTC allowed. The Tax Reform Act of 1986 changed that by requiring foreign source income to be classified into nine separate categories (referred to as "baskets") with an FTC computed separately for each basket of foreign source income. Companies were not allowed to net FTCs across baskets. In other words, the excess FTC from one basket could not be used to reduce additional U.S. taxes owed on other baskets. The excess FTC for one basket could only be carried back and carried forward to offset additional U.S. taxes paid on that basket of income. The net effect for U.S. companies was a reduction in the total amount of FTC allowed.

The following were the different baskets of foreign source income:

1. Passive income.
2. High withholding tax interest.
3. Financial services income.
4. Shipping and aircraft income.
5. Dividends from a domestic international sales corporation (DISC).
6. Foreign trade income of a foreign sales corporation (FSC).
7. Dividends from an FSC.
8. Foreign oil and extraction income.
9. All other income.

The "all other income" basket included all foreign source income that could not be classified into one of the other baskets and included income generated from manufacturing and from sales and distribution.

Returning to the example involving Alpha Company, assume that the branch in A is a manufacturing operation and the branch in Z is involved in financial services. Country A branch income would have been placed in Basket 9 (all other income) and Country Z branch income would have been placed in Basket 3 (financial services income). Alpha Company would have an additional U.S. tax liability of $10,000 on the branch income in A and would have an excess FTC of $2,000 on the branch income in Z. Alpha would not have been allowed to use the excess FTC from Basket 3 to offset the additional tax from Basket 9. The Basket 3 excess FTC could be carried back and forward only to offset additional taxes paid on Basket 3 (financial services) income.

The American Jobs Creation Act of 2004 reduced the number of FTC baskets from nine to two: (1) a *general income* basket and (2) a *passive income* basket. This change reduces the likelihood that a company will have excess FTCs that go unused. Continuing with the Alpha Company example, since 2007, the manufacturing income earned by the branch in A and the financial services income earned by the branch in Z are included in one general income basket. Rather than a $10,000 tax liability and a $2,000 excess FTC under the previous tax regime, Alpha now has a tax liability of $8,000 on its foreign source income.

Indirect Foreign Tax Credit (FTC for Subsidiaries)

A direct FTC is allowed for foreign income taxes paid directly by a U.S. taxpayer. These include taxes paid by a U.S. company on foreign branch income and withholding taxes paid on dividends, interest, and royalties.

An *indirect FTC* is allowed for foreign income taxes paid by the foreign subsidiary of a U.S. parent. The indirect FTC may not be taken until the foreign subsidiary income is taxed in the United States.

The amount of income taxable in the United States from a foreign subsidiary is the before-tax amount of the dividend. This is referred to as the "grossed-up dividend" and is equal to the dividend plus the taxes deemed to have been paid on the income from which the dividend was paid.

To qualify for an indirect FTC, the U.S. company receiving the dividend must own a minimum of 10 percent of the voting stock of the foreign company. There is no indirect FTC allowed for dividends received from an investment where the U.S. company owns less than 10 percent of the stock of the foreign company.

Example: Calculation of Indirect FTC

The Malaysian subsidiary of MNC Company (a U.S.-based company) has $500,000 of before-tax income on which it pays an income tax of $130,000 (26 percent Malaysian corporate income tax rate). MNC Company receives a dividend of $74,000 from its Malaysian subsidiary. The U.S. corporate income tax rate is 35 percent. The grossed-up dividend is calculated as follows:

$$\text{Grossed-up dividend} = \text{Dividend received}/(1 - \text{Foreign tax rate})$$
$$\$74,000/(1 - 0.26) = \$100,000$$

In other words, the Malaysian subsidiary would have had to generate before-tax income of $100,000, on which it would pay income taxes of $26,000 (26 percent), to be able to distribute a dividend of $74,000 to its parent company. MNC Company determines the available FTC related to this dividend in the following manner:

Actual tax paid by subsidiary on income distributed as dividend	= $26,000
Overall FTC limitation = Foreign Source Income × U.S. Tax Rate	
= $100,000 × 35%	= $35,000
Lesser amount (FTC allowed)	= $26,000

The net U.S. tax liability on the dividend received from the Malaysian subsidiary is computed as follows:

U.S. Tax Return	
	MNC Company
U.S. taxable income (grossed-up dividend).	$100,000
U.S. tax before FTC (35%).	$ 35,000
FTC allowed.	26,000
Net U.S. tax liability	$ 9,000

In this example, the indirect FTC allowed is $26,000 and an additional U.S. tax liability of $9,000 will result.

Note that the *total* income earned by the foreign subsidiary and the *total* amount of income taxes paid to the foreign government are irrelevant in determining the amount of foreign source income to report in the U.S. tax return and in calculating the indirect FTC. The amount of dividend *received* is the starting point for calculating the U.S. tax liability.

Example: Calculation of Indirect FTC Including Withholding Taxes

Keppler Inc. (a U.S.-based company), receives a $1,500,000 dividend from its wholly owned subsidiary in Taiwan. The income tax rate in Taiwan is 25 percent, and the withholding rate on dividends is 20 percent. The grossed-up dividend to be reported by Keppler as foreign source income on its U.S. tax return is calculated by first grossing up the dividend for the withholding tax paid and then for the income tax paid:

> Grossed-up dividend
> $= \text{Dividend received}/(1 - \text{Withholding tax rate})/(1 - \text{Income tax rate})$
> $= \$1{,}500{,}000 \quad / \quad (1 - 0.20) \quad / \quad (1 - 0.25)$
> $= \$1{,}500{,}000 \,/\, 0.80 \,/\, 0.75 = \$2{,}500{,}000$

The grossed-up dividend can be verified as follows:

Before tax income (grossed-up dividend)	$2,500,000
Income tax (25%)	(625,000)
Income after income tax	$1,875,000
Withholding tax (20%)	(375,000)
Net dividend received by Keppler	$1,500,000

Given a 25 percent income tax and a 20 percent withholding tax on dividends, the subsidiary must generate $2,500,000 in income before tax to be able to pay its parent a net dividend (after taxes) of $1,500,000.

The foreign tax credit allowed and net U.S. tax liability related to Keppler's subsidiary in Taiwan are determined as follows:

> Actual taxes paid $= \$625{,}000 + \$375{,}000 = \$1{,}000{,}000$
> Overall FTC limitation $= \$2{,}500{,}000 \times 35\% \quad = \quad \$875{,}000$
> FTC allowed $\qquad\qquad\qquad\qquad\qquad = \quad \$875{,}000$

Grossed-up dividend	$2,500,000
US tax before FTC (35%)	$ 875,000
FTC allowed.	875,000
Net U.S. tax liability	$ 0

Keppler has an excess FTC of $125,000 ($1,000,000 − $875,000) that it can carry back 1 year or carry forward 10 years.

TAX TREATIES

Tax treaties are bilateral agreements between two countries regarding how companies and individuals from one country will be taxed when earning income in the other country. Tax treaties are designed to facilitate international trade and investment by reducing tax barriers to the international flow of goods and services.

A major problem in international trade and investment is double taxation where tax jurisdictions overlap. For example, both Australia and the United States might claim tax jurisdiction over dividends earned by an Australian citizen from investments in U.S. stocks. Treaties reduce the possibility of double taxation through the clarification of tax jurisdiction. Treaties also provide for the possibility of tax reduction through a reduction in withholding tax rates. In addition, treaties generally require the exchange of information between countries to help in enforcing their domestic tax provisions.

Model Treaties

OECD Model

Most income tax treaties signed by the major industrial countries are based on a model treaty developed by the Organization for Economic Cooperation and Development (OECD). An important article in the OECD model treaty indicates that business profits may be taxed by a treaty partner country only if they are attributable to a *permanent establishment* in that country. A permanent establishment can include an office, branch, factory, construction site, mine, well, or quarry. Facilities used for storage, display, or delivery, and the maintenance of goods solely for processing by another enterprise do not constitute permanent establishments. If there is no permanent establishment, then income that otherwise would be taxable in the country in which the income is earned if there were no treaty is not taxable in that country.

One of the most important benefits afforded by tax treaties is the reduction in withholding tax rates. The OECD model treaty recommends withholding rates of

1. 5 percent for direct investment dividends (paid by a subsidiary to its parent).
2. 15 percent for portfolio dividends (paid to individuals).
3. 10 percent for interest.
4. Zero for royalties.

Although the OECD model might be the starting point for negotiation, countries with more outbound investment than inbound investment often try to reduce the host country's right to tax, most conspicuously seeking zero withholding on interest. A very specific deviation from the model treaty is where countries that import most of their movies and TV programming seek higher withholding rates on film royalties than on other copyright royalties.

United Nations Model

The OECD model assumes that countries are economic equals. The United Nations (UN) model treaty, designed to be used between developed and developing countries, assumes an imbalance. The UN model recognizes that the host country (often a developing country) should have more taxing rights when profit repatriation essentially is a one-way street (from the developing to the developed country).

U.S. Tax Treaties

The United States also has a model treaty it uses as the basis for negotiating bilateral tax agreements. The U.S. model exempts interest and royalties from withholding tax and establishes 15 percent as the maximum withholding rate on dividends. Withholding rates from selected U.S. tax treaties are shown in Exhibit 11.4. As that exhibit shows, neither the U.S. model nor the OECD's recommendations regarding withholding rates are always followed.

EXHIBIT 11.4
Selected U.S. Tax
Treaty Withholding
Tax Rates

Source: Internal Revenue
Service, Publication 901,
"U.S. Tax Treaties,"
April 2010.

Country	Dividend Paid to Parent	Interest Paid to Parent	Royalties
Nontreaty	30%	30%	30%
Australia	5	10	0
Canada	5	0	0
China (PRC)	10	10	10
France	5	0	0
Germany	5	0	0
Hungary	5	0	0
India	15	15	10
Indonesia	10	10	10
Japan	5	10	0
Korea (South)	10	12	15
Mexico	5	15	10
New Zealand	15	10	10
Philippines	20	15	15
Russia	5	0	0
Spain	10	10	8
Thailand	10	15	8
United Kingdom	5	0	0
Venezuela	5	10	5

The United States has treaties with more than 50 countries, including all 27 members of the European Union; Australia and New Zealand; Ukraine and Russia; Egypt and Israel; Mexico and Canada; and India, Korea, Japan, and China. As of January 1, 2008, except for Venezuela, the United States did not have a tax treaty with any country in South America. This includes Brazil, which is one of the top 10 locations for U.S. foreign direct investment.

A reason there is no treaty between the United States and Brazil is that there is very little Brazilian investment in the United States. The reduction in withholding taxes that would result from a tax treaty would mostly benefit U.S. investors who are receiving interest and dividends from their Brazilian investments, but there would be little benefit for taxpayers in Brazil. The Brazilian government is not interested in entering into a treaty with the United States that would reduce the withholding taxes collected on payments made to U.S. investors without much reciprocal benefit to Brazilians.

There is also very little Polish investment in the United States. However, Poland differs from Brazil in that Poland is interested in attracting new U.S. investment. The United States/Poland tax treaty allows Poland to better compete with other countries in attracting U.S. investment.

Understanding the potential benefits to be derived from a tax treaty is very important when deciding where to locate a foreign investment. For example, of $100 of royalties paid by a subsidiary in Venezuela, $95 would be received by its U.S. parent (after paying a 5 percent withholding tax under the United States/Venezuela tax treaty). Because there is no treaty between the United States and

Brazil, for $100 of royalties paid by a subsidiary in Brazil, only $85 will land in the United States (after paying a 15 percent Brazilian withholding tax). All else being equal, a U.S.-based investor would prefer to establish a subsidiary in Venezuela rather than in Brazil to reduce the amount of withholding taxes paid.

Treaty Shopping

Treaty shopping describes a process in which a resident of Country A uses a corporation in Country B to get the benefit of Country B's tax treaty with Country C. As an example, assume that a Brazilian taxpayer has investments in U.S. shares. Because the United States has no treaty with Brazil, dividend payments made to the Brazilian investor by U.S. companies will be taxed by the U.S. government at the withholding rate of 30 percent. As demonstrated here, the Brazilian investor receives only 70 percent of the dividend:

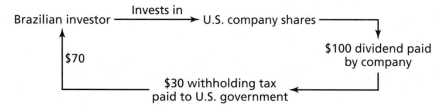

Until 1988, the Netherlands Antilles, located off the coast of South America, had a treaty with the United States that reduced the withholding rate on dividends to 10 percent. The Brazilian taxpayer could use this treaty to its advantage by establishing a wholly owned holding company in the Netherlands Antilles that in turn made investments in U.S. company shares. Dividends paid by the U.S. companies to the Netherlands Antilles (NA) stockholder would be taxed at the treaty rate of 10 percent, and income earned by the NA holding company was not taxed in the Netherlands Antilles. Dividends paid by the NA holding company to the Brazilian investor from its income, in effect, the dividend received from the U.S. companies, was not subject to NA withholding tax. In this way, the Brazilian investor was able to keep 20 percent more of the gross dividend than if the investment had been made directly from Brazil. This is demonstrated as follows:

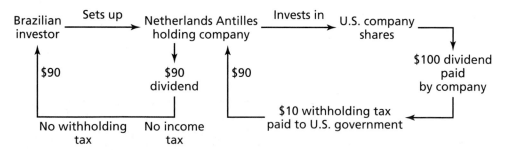

In this situation there is no incentive for Brazil to negotiate a treaty with the United States.

Since the 1980s, U.S. treaty negotiations have insisted that a "limitation of benefits" provision be included in U.S. tax treaties. A typical treaty might provide that certain treaty benefits (such as reduced withholding rates) are not available if 50 percent or more of a corporation's stock is held by third-party taxpayers (unless the stock is publicly traded). The insertion of such a limitation into the United States/Netherlands Antilles treaty would preclude the Brazilian investor from enjoying the reduced withholding rate on dividends paid by the U.S. company.

In addition to entering into new treaties, the United States has attempted to renegotiate its existing treaties with tax haven countries to include a limitation-of-benefits provision. In some cases negotiations have failed and the existing treaty has been canceled. This is true in the Netherlands Antilles case. The United States no longer has a double taxation treaty with the Netherlands Antilles.

The United States and Switzerland are leading the way in fighting treaty shopping. Switzerland has had a unilateral anti–treaty shopping provision in its domestic law since 1962. The OECD model treaty does not have a clause to combat treaty shopping.

CONTROLLED FOREIGN CORPORATIONS

To crack down on the use of tax havens by U.S. companies to avoid paying U.S. taxes, the U.S. Congress created *controlled foreign corporation (CFC)* rules in 1962.[8] A CFC is any foreign corporation in which U.S. shareholders hold more than 50 percent of the combined voting power or fair market value of the stock. Only those U.S. taxpayers (corporations, citizens, or tax residents) directly or indirectly owning 10 percent or more of the stock are considered U.S. shareholders in determining whether the 50 percent threshold is met. *All* majority-owned foreign subsidiaries of U.S.-based companies are CFCs.

As noted earlier in this chapter, the United States generally defers taxation of income earned by a foreign investment until a dividend is received by the U.S. investor. For CFCs, however, there is no deferral of U.S. taxation on so-called *Subpart F income.* Instead, Subpart F income is taxed currently similar to foreign branch income regardless of whether or not the investor receives a dividend. Subpart F of the U.S. Internal Revenue Code lists the income that will be treated in this fashion.

Subpart F Income

Subpart F income is income that is easily movable to a low-tax jurisdiction. There are four types of Subpart F income:

1. Income derived from insurance of U.S. risks.
2. Income from countries engaged in international boycotts.
3. Certain illegal payments.
4. Foreign base company income.

Foreign base company income is the most important category of Subpart F income and includes the following:

1. Passive income such as interest, dividends, royalties, rents, and capital gains from sales of assets. An example would be dividends received by a CFC from holding shares of stock in affiliated companies.

---

[8] Other countries—including Australia, Denmark, France, Italy, Sweden, the United Kingdom, and Venezuela—have similar anti–tax haven rules. For example, France uses a territorial approach to taxation and as a result does not tax profit earned by its companies outside of France. However, under French controlled foreign corporation rules, income earned by a French company outside of France may become subject to French taxation if the effective tax rate paid in the foreign country is 50 percent lower than the tax that would have been paid in France. See Ernst & Young, *Worldwide Corporate Tax Guide,* 2009, p. 293.

2. Sales income, where the CFC makes sales outside of its country of incorporation. For example, the U.S. parent manufactures a product that it sells to its CFC in Hong Kong, which in turn sells the product to customers in Japan. Sales to customers outside of Hong Kong generate Subpart F income.

3. Service income, where the CFC performs services out of its country of incorporation.

4. Air and sea transportation income.

5. Oil and gas products income.

Determination of the Amount of CFC Income Currently Taxable

The amount of CFC income currently taxable in the United States depends on the percentage of CFC income generated from Subpart F activities. Assuming that none of a CFC's income is repatriated as a dividend, the following hold true:

1. If Subpart F income is *less than 5 percent* of the CFC's total income, then none of the CFC's income will be taxed currently.

2. If Subpart F income is *between 5 percent and 70 percent* of the CFC's total income, then that percentage of the CFC's income which is Subpart F income will be taxed currently.

3. If Subpart F income is *greater than 70 percent* of the CFC's total income, then 100 percent of the CFC's income will be taxed currently.

Safe Harbor Rule

If the foreign tax rate is greater than 90 percent of the U.S. corporate income tax rate, then none of the CFC's income is considered to be Subpart F income. With the current U.S. tax rate of 35 percent, U.S. MNCs need not be concerned with the CFC rules for those foreign operations located in countries with a tax rate of 31.5 percent or higher. These countries are not considered to be tax havens for CFC purposes.

SUMMARY OF U.S. TAX TREATMENT OF FOREIGN SOURCE INCOME

Determining the appropriate U.S. tax treatment of foreign source income can be quite complicated. Factors to consider include the following:

1. Legal form of the foreign operation (branch or subsidiary).

2. Percentage level of ownership (CFC or not).

3. Foreign tax rate (tax haven or not).

4. Nature of the foreign source income (Subpart F or not) (appropriate FTC basket).

Exhibit 11.5 provides a flowchart with general guidelines for determining the amount of foreign source income to be included on the U.S. tax return, the FTC allowed, and the net U.S. tax liability on income generated by foreign operations. Use of the flowchart for determining a company's U.S. tax liability on its foreign source income is demonstrated through the following example.

Example: U.S. Taxation of Foreign Source Income

Assume that MNC Company (a U.S. taxpayer) has four subsidiaries located in four different foreign countries. The country location, MNC's percentage

EXHIBIT 11.5
Flowchart for
Determining U.S.
Taxation of Foreign
Operations

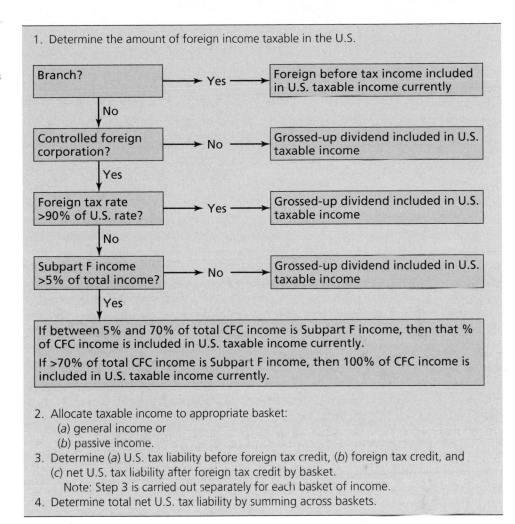

1. Determine the amount of foreign income taxable in the U.S.

Branch? → Yes → Foreign before tax income included in U.S. taxable income currently

↓ No

Controlled foreign corporation? → No → Grossed-up dividend included in U.S. taxable income

↓ Yes

Foreign tax rate >90% of U.S. rate? → Yes → Grossed-up dividend included in U.S. taxable income

↓ No

Subpart F income >5% of total income? → No → Grossed-up dividend included in U.S. taxable income

↓ Yes

If between 5% and 70% of total CFC income is Subpart F income, then that % of CFC income is included in U.S. taxable income currently.

If >70% of total CFC income is Subpart F income, then 100% of CFC income is included in U.S. taxable income currently.

2. Allocate taxable income to appropriate basket:
   (a) general income or
   (b) passive income.
3. Determine (a) U.S. tax liability before foreign tax credit, (b) foreign tax credit, and (c) net U.S. tax liability after foreign tax credit by basket.
   Note: Step 3 is carried out separately for each basket of income.
4. Determine total net U.S. tax liability by summing across baskets.

ownership, nature of activity, and income before tax for each subsidiary; the income and withholding tax rates in the host countries; and the dividend paid by each subsidiary to MNC are summarized as follows:

Foreign Entity	A	B	C	D
Country.....................	Costa Rica	Zambia	Singapore	Cayman Is.
Legal form..................	Subsidiary	Subsidiary	Subsidiary	Subsidiary
MNC's ownership	100%	51%	100%	100%
Activity	Manufacturing	Mining	Manufacturing	Investment
Before-tax income	$100,000	$100,000	$100,000	$100,000
Income tax rate	30%	35%	18%	0%
After-tax income	$70,000	$65,000	$82,000	$100,000
Gross dividend paid to MNC	$70,000	$20,000	$20,000	$0
Withholding tax rate	15%	10%	0%	0%
Net dividend received by MNC...	$59,500	$18,000	$20,000	$0

Determination of the Amount of Foreign Source Income Taxable in the United States

The amount of income from each foreign operation that will be taxable in the United States will be based on either (1) before-tax income or (2) the grossed-up dividend. Applying the flowchart in Exhibit 11.5, the first step is to determine whether the foreign operation is a branch or a subsidiary. In this example, each foreign operation is legally incorporated as a subsidiary in the country in which it resides. The next step is to determine whether the subsidiaries are controlled foreign corporations. Because MNC owns more than 50 percent of each operation, the answer to this question in each case is yes. To determine whether any of the foreign countries meets the U.S. tax law definition of a tax haven, the effective tax rate (income tax plus withholding tax) must be calculated and compared with 90 percent of the U.S. tax rate of 35 percent, or 31.5 percent. The effective tax rate is determined by adding the income tax rate plus the withholding rate applied to after-tax income:

Costa Rica	30% + 15% (1 − 30%) = 40.5%	Not a tax haven
Zambia	35% + 10% (1 − 35%) = 41.5%	Not a tax haven
Singapore	18% + 0% (1 − 18%) = 18%	Tax haven
Cayman Is	0%	Tax haven

Singapore and the Cayman Islands would be considered tax havens for purposes of the controlled foreign corporation rules. Because neither Costa Rica nor Zambia is a tax haven, only the grossed-up dividend received by MNC from those subsidiaries is subject to U.S. taxation.

The next step is to determine whether the subsidiaries in Singapore and the Cayman Islands had any Subpart F income. In general, Subpart F income is income that can be easily moved from one tax jurisdiction to another. Manufacturing income does not meet this definition, so the Singaporean subsidiary does not have any Subpart F income. Therefore, even though Singapore meets the definition of a tax haven, only the grossed-up dividend received by MNC from Subsidiary C is subject to U.S. taxation.

The Cayman subsidiary generates its income from passive investments which is specifically included in the list of Subpart F income presented earlier. Assuming that Subsidiary D generates all of its income through investments 100 percent of D's before-tax income ($100,000) will be taxable in the United States, even though D remits no dividend to its U.S. parent.

To determine the amount of income from Subsidiaries A, B, and C taxable in the United States, the net dividend received by MNC must be grossed up to a before-tax basis. The net dividend is first grossed up for withholding taxes paid, and then the before-withholding-tax dividend is grossed up for income taxes paid. The grossed-up dividend for each subsidiary is calculated as follows:

	Net Dividend		1 − Withholding Tax		Dividend before Withholding Tax		1 − Income Tax		Grossed-up Dividend
Costa Rica . . .	$59,500	/	1 − 0.15	=	$70,000	/	1 − 0.30	=	$100,000
Zambia	$18,000	/	1 − 0.10	=	$20,000	/	1 − 0.35	=	$ 30,769
Singapore . . .	$20,000	/	1 − 0.00	=	$20,000	/	1 − 0.18	=	$ 24,390

Determine Foreign Tax Credits, U.S. Tax Liability, and Excess Foreign Tax Credits, by Basket

To determine MNC's foreign tax credit, foreign taxes (both income tax and withholding tax) paid on the income taxable in the United States must be determined. For Subsidiary D, this amount is $0. For the other subsidiaries, the simplest way to determine the total amount of foreign taxes paid is to subtract the net dividend received by MNC from the grossed-up dividend—the difference between gross and net dividend is taxes deemed paid to the foreign government on the grossed-up dividend. This amount is calculated as follows:

	Costa Rica	Zambia	Singapore
Grossed-up dividend	$100,000	$30,769	$24,390
Net amount received by MNC	59,500	18,000	20,000
Taxes paid to foreign government	$ 40,500	$12,769	$ 4,390

The amount of income taxable in the United States next must be allocated to the appropriate FTC basket according to each subsidiary's activity. The income of Subsidiary D is allocated to the passive income basket, and the income of Subsidiaries A, B, and C is allocated to the general income basket. The foreign tax credit, U.S. income tax liability, and excess FTC for each basket of income can now be calculated as follows:

	Passive Income	General Income
U.S. taxable income	$100,000	$155,159
U.S. income tax before FTC (35%)	$35,000	$54,306
Less: FTC		
(a) Taxes paid to foreign government	$0	$57,659
(b) Overall FTC limitation	$35,000	$54,306
FTC allowed—lesser of (a) and (b)	0	54,306
U.S. tax liability	$35,000	$0
Excess FTC	$0	$3,353

MNC Company has a total U.S. tax liability on its foreign source passive income of $35,000 and an excess foreign tax credit on its foreign source general income of $3,353.

TRANSLATION OF FOREIGN OPERATION INCOME

In the examples presented thus far in this chapter, the income earned by foreign operations and the foreign taxes paid have been stated in terms of the parent company's domestic currency. In reality, foreign operations generate income and pay taxes in the local, foreign currency. The parent company's tax liability, however, is determined in terms of the domestic currency, for example, U.S. dollars for U.S. companies. The foreign currency income generated by a foreign operation must be translated into the parent company's currency for purposes of taxation. This section demonstrates procedures used in the United States for translating foreign currency income for U.S. tax purposes. Although we focus on U.S. tax rules, similar procedures are followed in other countries.

As is true for financial reporting, the appropriate translation procedures for determining U.S. taxable income depend on the *functional currency* of the foreign operation. The functional currency is the currency in which the foreign operation primarily conducts business and can be either a foreign currency or the U.S. dollar. For operations located in highly inflationary countries (cumulative three-year inflation exceeding 100 percent), the U.S. dollar must be used as the functional currency. Moreover, a U.S. company with a foreign branch or foreign subsidiary that primarily operates in a foreign currency can elect to use the U.S. dollar as the functional currency if it so chooses.

A foreign operation that has the U.S. dollar as its functional currency keeps its books in U.S. dollars. Any transactions that take place in a foreign currency are translated into U.S. dollars at the date of the transaction. Income of the foreign operation is directly calculated in U.S. dollars, so there is no need for translation at the end of the year.

For those foreign branches and subsidiaries that have a foreign currency as their functional currency, accounting records are kept and income is determined in the foreign currency and must be translated into U.S. dollars for U.S. tax purposes. Under U.S. tax law, foreign branch income and dividends received from foreign subsidiaries are translated into U.S. dollars differently.

Translation of Foreign Branch Income

To determine U.S. taxable income, foreign branch net income is translated into U.S. dollars using the average exchange rate for the year. Foreign branch net income is then grossed up by adding taxes paid to the foreign government translated at the exchange rate at the date of payment. When branch income is repatriated to the home office and foreign currency is actually converted into U.S. dollars, any difference in the exchange rate used to originally translate the income and the exchange rate at the date of repatriation creates a taxable foreign exchange gain or loss. The foreign tax credit is determined by translating foreign taxes at the exchange rate at the date of payment. The following example demonstrates these procedures.

Example: Translation of Foreign Branch Income

Maker Company (a U.S.-based taxpayer) establishes a branch in Mexico in January of Year 1 when the exchange rate is US$0.12 per Mexican peso (Mex$). During Year 1, the Mexican branch generates Mex$5,000,000 of pretax income. On October 15, Year 1, Mex$1,000,000 is repatriated to Maker Company and converted into U.S. dollars. The effective income tax rate in Mexico is 28 percent. Taxes were paid in Mexico on the Mexican branch income on December 31, Year 1. Relevant exchange rates for Year 1 are as follows:

	US$/Mex$
January 1	$0.125
October 15	$0.090
December 31	$0.085
Average for the year	$0.100

The amount of foreign branch income Maker Company reports on its Year 1 U.S. tax return is determined as follows:

Pretax income	Mex$6,000,000					
Taxes paid (28%).	Mex$1,400,000					
Net income × Average exchange rate	Mex$3,600,000	×	$0.100	=	$360,000	
Taxes paid × Actual exchange rate	Mex$1,400,000	×	$0.085	=	119,000	
Gain (loss) on October 15 repatriation.	Mex$1,000,000	×	($0.09 − $0.100)	=	(10,000)	
U.S. taxable income					$469,000	

The foreign tax credit (FTC) allowed by the United States is determined by comparing the actual tax paid to the Mexican government (translated into US$) and the overall FTC limitation based on the U.S. tax rate of 35 percent:

(a) Foreign taxes paid (in US$)	$119,000
(b) Overall FTC limitation ($469,000 × 35%)	164,150
FTC allowed—lesser of (a) and (b)	$119,000

The U.S. tax return would include the following:

U.S. taxable income (above).	$469,000
U.S. tax before FTC (35%).	$164,150
FTC allowed (above)	119,000
Net U.S. tax liability	$ 45,150

Translation of Foreign Subsidiary Income

Unless Subpart F income is present, the income of a foreign subsidiary is not taxable until dividends are distributed to the U.S. parent. At that time, the dividend is translated into U.S. dollars using the spot rate at the date of distribution. The dividend is grossed up by adding taxes deemed paid on the dividend translated at the spot rate at the date of tax payment. The U.S. dollar–translated amount of taxes deemed paid also is used to determine the foreign tax credit. These procedures are demonstrated using the Maker Company example presented earlier.

Example: Translation of Dividends Received from Foreign Subsidiary

Assume the same facts as in the previous example except that Maker's operation in Mexico is incorporated as a subsidiary. Relevant exchange rates are:

	US$/Mex$
October 15 (date dividends are repatriated to U.S. parent).	$0.090
December 31 (date taxes are paid to Mexican government)	$0.085

The amounts reported as Maker's U.S. taxable income, foreign tax credit, and net U.S. tax liability related to the Mexican subsidiary are calculated as follows:

Calculation of Grossed-up Dividend

Dividend received.	Mex$1,000,000	×	$0.090	=	$ 90,000
Tax deemed paid*	Mex$ 388,889	×	$0.085	=	33,056
Grossed-up dividend (U.S. taxable income). . . .					$123,056

*Taxes deemed paid can be calculated in two ways:
(Dividend/1 − Mexican tax rate) − Dividend =
(Mex$1,000,000/0.72 = Mex$1,388,889) − Mex$1,000,000 = Mex$388,889
(Dividend/Net income) × Taxes paid =
(Mex$1,000,000/Mex$3,600,000) × Mex$1,400,000 = Mex$388,889

Calculation of FTC

(a) Tax deemed paid (in US$)	$33,056
(b) Overall FTC limitation ($123,056 × 35%).	43,070
FTC allowed—lesser of (a) and (b)	$33,056

Calculation of U.S. Tax Liability

U.S. taxable income (above).	$123,056
U.S. tax before FTC (35%)	$ 43,070
FTC allowed (above).	33,056
Net U.S. tax liability.	$ 10,014

Foreign Currency Transactions

U.S. taxpayers often engage in transactions denominated in foreign currency such as export sales, import purchases, and foreign currency borrowings. In general, gains or losses arising from fluctuation in exchange rates between the date of the transaction and its settlement will be taxable only when realized—in effect, at the settlement date. For tax purposes, gains and losses on forward contracts and options used to hedge foreign currency transactions and firm commitments are integrated with the underlying item being hedged. For example, if a foreign currency receivable is hedged by a forward contract that guarantees that the foreign currency can be sold for $1,000, taxable revenue of $1,000 is reported when the receivable is collected. Any gains and losses on the foreign currency receivable and forward contract recorded for financial reporting purposes are not recognized for tax purposes.

TAX INCENTIVES

Governments often use the national tax law to encourage certain types of behavior. For example, a number of countries use tax holidays to encourage investment in specific types of assets, activities, or geographical regions. To improve the national balance of trade, an incentive to export is sometimes provided by reducing the rate of taxation on export sales. Companies doing business internationally may be able to take advantage of these incentives to reduce their global tax burden. This section provides a brief description of tax holidays and then describes the history and current status of export incentives provided by the United States.

Tax Holidays

All of the countries that comprise the Association of Southeast Asian Nations (ASEAN), as well as several other Asian countries, offer tax incentive packages to attract foreign direct investment. In Malaysia, for example, foreign corporations that qualify for "pioneer status" receive an exemption from income tax on 70 percent of annual profit for five years. Corporations that undertake a project of strategic importance involving heavy capital investment and high technology receive a 100 percent exemption for up to 10 years. The Philippines provides a 100 percent income tax holiday for three to eight years depending on the location and industry in which the foreigner invests. The country of Thailand offers a tax holiday for up to eight years for projects involving technology or human capital development, infrastructure, environmental protection, and other targeted industries. Investment projects in these industries also enjoy an exemption from import duty on machinery. Sri Lanka makes a tax holiday available to companies engaged in agriculture, electronics, machinery manufacturing, or information technology; companies involved in large-scale infrastructure development; and companies involved in small-scale projects related to power generation, tourism, recreation, warehousing, cold storage, garbage collection, or home building. It grants a five-year tax holiday for companies involved in research and development in the field of science and technology.

Countries in other parts of the world also have used tax holidays in an attempt to attract foreign direct investment. For example, several eastern European countries offered tax incentives, including tax holidays to foreign investors. Hungary, for example, offers significant tax advantages to investors. In addition to a relatively low 16 percent corporate tax rate, which itself is an investment incentive, Hungary also offers tax holidays to investors that vary with the level of investment. Companies that invest at least 3 billion Hungarian forints (HUF) and create 150 new jobs qualify for a 10-year tax holiday. Poland offers income tax exemption up to 50 percent of investment expenditure for activities carried out in any of 14 special economic zones. Lithuania and Latvia also provide tax relief for investments made in free economic zones. Croatia provides a 100 percent tax holiday for up to 10 years for investments of 8 million euros (approximately $10 million in 2010) that employ at least 75 people.

In 2002, China surpassed the United States as the largest recipient of foreign direct investment (FDI), partly as a result of tax incentives provided foreign investors for establishing production operations in China. To further enhance its competitive position in attracting FDI, China introduced legislation in 2003 that provided a two-plus-three-year tax holiday to any new company formed with at least 25 percent foreign investment. So-called foreign investment enterprises received a 100 percent exemption from taxation for the first two years in which profits are earned followed by a 50 percent exemption in the following three years. However, the Chinese government enacted new legislation in 2007 that eliminated the tax holiday for new investments beginning January 1, 2008.

Tax holidays can be of significant benefit to multinational companies as long as the income earned in the foreign country is reinvested in that country. For MNCs taxed on a worldwide basis, the benefit disappears when dividends earned in the foreign country are repatriated to the parent. At that time, the dividend is subject to home-country taxation and there is no foreign tax credit to offset the home-country liability because no income taxes were paid to the foreign government. However, some home countries grant *tax sparing* to companies that invest in developing countries. For example, Japanese companies that invest in countries with which Japan has an agreement may claim a foreign tax credit for the amount of tax that would have been paid if there were no tax holiday. This ensures that the foreign country's tax holiday provides a real incentive for investment by Japanese companies. Most of the wealthier nations provide tax sparing for investment in developing countries, but the United States does not.

U.S. Export Incentives

Prior to 1962, many U.S. companies exported through foreign base companies located in tax haven countries. By locating some of the profit earned on exports in a tax haven, companies were able to unilaterally reduce the rate of U.S. taxation on export sales. As discussed earlier in this chapter, the U.S. Congress enacted the CFC rules in 1962, which eliminated the deferral of taxation on Subpart F income and therefore the lower effective tax rate on export sales. As a result, many companies sought new legislation to create export incentives.

Domestic International Sales Corporation

In 1971, the U.S. Congress created the domestic international sales corporation (DISC) to provide companies with an incentive to export. Under the DISC provisions of the tax law, companies were able to establish export subsidiaries in the United States (DISCs) and a certain portion of the profit earned by the DISCs would be deferred from taxation until actually distributed to the parent. The U.S. parent sold goods to its DISC at a low markup, and the DISC then sold to foreign customers at higher markups, concentrating the total profit in the DISC.

The major differences from the previous use of foreign base companies in tax haven countries were that

- The DISC was located in the United States and not in a foreign country.
- The DISC was a paper company with no physical substance (the DISC did not have physical facilities or employees).
- A portion of the DISC's income was deemed to be distributed to the parent and was therefore taxed currently, even if no distribution actually took place. In the tax haven scenario, income was not taxable until actually distributed to the parent.

The DISC provisions drew immediate criticism from U.S. trading partners that were parties to the General Agreement on Tariffs and Trade (GATT), because the DISC rules violated the GATT rule against tax subsidies for exports. While not admitting any violation of GATT, the United States nevertheless withdrew the DISC and created a new export incentive in 1984—the foreign sales corporation.

Foreign Sales Corporation (FSC)

GATT did not require the taxation of export income generated from economic activity located outside of a country. Therefore, if a company funneled its exports through a foreign subsidiary that actually engaged in economic activity to earn the export income, the United States was not obligated under GATT to tax the income of the foreign subsidiary.

The U.S. Congress enacted foreign sales corporation (FSC) provisions in the Tax Reform Act of 1984. Under these provisions, a portion (generally 15 percent) of an FSC's income was tax exempt in the United States. The nonexempt portion was taxed currently regardless of whether or not dividends were paid to the parent.

To qualify as an FSC, a foreign subsidiary had to be incorporated in a foreign country (to comply with GATT) that had an exchange of information agreement or tax treaty with the United States. There was an IRS-approved list of countries in which FSCs could be established.

The European Union believed that the FSC approach violated a rule of the World Trade Organization (WTO) that prohibits export subsidies and therefore appealed to the WTO for a ruling in the late 1990s. A WTO panel ruled that the FSC did not comply with WTO rules. To comply with a settlement with the WTO, the U.S. Congress passed the FSC Repeal and Extraterritorial Income Exclusion Act (ETI) in November 2000.

The FSC Repeal and Extraterritorial Income Exclusion Act of 2000

The ETI replaced the FSC regime with an income exclusion designed to more closely model European tax systems. Under the ETI rules, U.S. taxpayers could exclude income derived from export sales from their U.S. taxable income if two tests were met. In contrast to the FSC rules, companies were not required to establish a foreign subsidiary in a qualified foreign jurisdiction to obtain ETI benefits.

The European Union (EU) argued that the ETI, like the FSC, violated international trade agreements and appealed to the WTO to disallow the new U.S. structure. The WTO sided with the EU, ruling that ETI is an unfair export subsidy, and authorized the EU to slap an unprecedented $4 billion of tariffs on U.S. goods in retaliation if the United States did not take substantive steps to repeal the ETI by January 1, 2004. The EU began imposing tariffs on U.S. products in March 2004. The tariffs began at a rate of 5 percent and were to increase by 1 percent per month, with a maximum tariff of 17 percent to be reached in March 2005. In October 2004, six months after retaliatory tariffs were implemented, the U.S. Congress passed the American Jobs Creation Act of 2004, which repealed the ETI.

American Jobs Creation Act of 2004

The American Jobs Creation Act of 2004 (AJCA) made the most sweeping changes in the taxation of overseas operations since the Tax Reform Act of 1986. In addition to reducing the number of FTC baskets from nine to two and changing the lengths of the carryover periods for excess FTCs, the AJCA also repealed the ETI for transactions occurring after December 31, 2004. However, to provide U.S. exporters with a soft landing, the repeal was phased in over a two-year period. For 2005, 80 percent of the ETI benefit was available, reducing to 60 percent in 2006. ETI benefits disappeared completely in 2007.

To replace the phasing-out ETI benefits, the AJCA introduced a phased-in deduction for domestic manufacturing. Companies engaged in domestic manufacturing activities were able to deduct 3 percent of their qualifying production activities income from taxation in 2005 and 2006, 6 percent in 2007 through 2009, and 9 percent in 2010 and beyond. When the deduction is fully phased in, the effective corporate tax rate on manufacturing income will be 31.85 percent.[9] Manufacturing firms are able to enjoy this deduction whether or not they export. Moreover, the AJCA defines *manufacturing* very broadly to include traditional manufacturing, construction, engineering, energy production, computer software development, film and videotape production, and processing of agricultural products. As a result, many companies that were unable to take advantage of the ETI rules benefit from the AJCA.

---

[9] The 9 percent deduction means that the 35 percent corporate tax rate will be applied to only 91 percent of income: 35% × 91% = 31.85%.

One additional important feature of the AJCA for multinational corporations was a provision allowing foreign source income to be repatriated to the United States at a reduced tax rate. For one year, MNCs could elect to claim a deduction equal to 85 percent of cash dividends received from controlled foreign corporations (CFCs) in excess of a base amount. This election was available either for the year prior to enactment of the AJCA (2004) or the first year after enactment (2005). To qualify for the deduction, the repatriated dividends had to be reinvested in the United States under a domestic reinvestment plan approved by senior management. Some observers estimated that more than $500 billion of foreign earnings could qualify for this "tax holiday." Many U.S. companies took advantage of the opportunity to repatriate foreign earnings at a reduced rate of taxation. Mattel Company, for example, repatriated $2.4 billion of previously unremitted foreign earnings in 2005, and Johnson & Johnson repatriated $10.8 billion. Eastman Kodak Company describes the effect the AJCA had on tax expense in 2005 as follows:

> The Jobs Creation Act was signed into law in October of 2004. The Act created a temporary incentive for U.S. multinationals to repatriate foreign subsidiary earnings by providing a 85% dividends received deduction for certain dividends from controlled foreign corporations. The deduction is subject to a number of limitations and requirements, including adoption of a specific domestic reinvestment plan for the repatriated earnings. The Company repatriated approximately $580 million in dividends subject to the 85% dividends received deduction. Accordingly, the Company recorded a corresponding tax provision of $29 million with respect to such dividends during 2005.[10]

Summary

1. Taxes are a significant cost of doing business. Taxes often are an important factor to consider in making decisions related to foreign operations. Although tax returns will be prepared by tax experts, managers of multinational corporations (MNCs) should be familiar with the major issues of international taxation.

2. Most countries have a national corporate income tax rate that varies between 20 percent and 35 percent. Countries with no or very low corporate taxation are known as tax havens. MNCs often attempt to use operations in tax haven countries to minimize their worldwide tax burden.

3. Withholding taxes are imposed on payments made to foreigners, especially in the form of dividends, interest, and royalties. Withholding rates vary across countries and often vary by type of payment within one country. Differences in withholding rates provide tax-planning opportunities for the location or nature of a foreign operation.

4. Most countries tax income on a worldwide basis. The basis for taxation can be source of income, residence of the taxpayer, and/or citizenship of the taxpayer. The existence of overlapping bases leads to double taxation.

5. Most countries provide relief from double taxation through foreign tax credits (FTCs). FTCs are the reduction in tax liability on income in one country for the taxes already paid on that income in another country. In general, the tax credit allowed by the home country is limited to the amount of taxes that would have been paid if the income had been earned in the home country.

6. The excess of taxes paid to a foreign country over the FTC allowed by the home country is an excess FTC. In the United States, an excess FTC may be

---

[10] Eastman Kodak Company, 2006 Form 10-K, p. 96.

carried back 1 year and carried forward 10 years. U.S. tax law requires companies to allocate foreign source income to two foreign tax credit baskets—general income and passive income. Excess FTCs may only be applied within the basket to which they relate.

7. In general, income earned by a foreign subsidiary is taxable in the United States only when received by the parent as a dividend. Income earned by a foreign branch is taxable in the United States currently. To crack down on U.S. companies using tax havens to avoid U.S. taxation, U.S. tax law includes controlled foreign corporation (CFC) rules. Income earned by a CFC that can be moved easily from one country to another (Subpart F income) is taxed in the United States currently, regardless of whether or not it has been distributed as a dividend.

8. Tax treaties between two countries govern the way in which individuals and companies living in or doing business in the partner country are to be taxed by that country. A significant feature of most tax treaties is a reduction in withholding tax rates. The U.S. model treaty reduces withholding taxes to zero on interest and royalties and 15 percent on dividends. However, these guidelines often are not followed.

9. Foreign branch net income is translated into U.S. dollars using the average exchange rate for the year and then grossed up by adding taxes paid to the foreign government translated at the exchange rate at the date of payment. When branch income is repatriated to the home office, any difference in the exchange rate used to originally translate the income and the exchange rate at the date of repatriation creates a taxable foreign exchange gain or loss. Dividends received from a foreign subsidiary are translated into U.S. dollars using the spot rate at the date of distribution and grossed up by adding taxes deemed paid translated at the spot rate at the date of payment.

10. Over the years, the United States has provided a variety of tax incentives to export (DISC, FSC, ETI). The Extraterritorial Income Exclusion (ETI) provisions were repealed in 2004 under pressure from the European Union and the World Trade Organization. In its place, the American Job Creation Act of 2004 allows companies engaged in domestic manufacturing activities to deduct 3 percent of their qualifying production activities income from taxation in 2005 and 2006, 6 percent in 2007 through 2009, and 9 percent in 2010 and beyond. Manufacturing firms receive this deduction whether or not they export.

Appendix to Chapter 11

U.S. Taxation of Expatriates

This chapter has concentrated on international corporate tax issues. This appendix examines several issues related to the taxation of expatriates—individuals who live and work overseas.

The United States is unusual in that it taxes its citizens on their worldwide income regardless of whether they are actually living in the United States. To make U.S. businesses more competitive by making it less expensive to use U.S. employees overseas, the U.S. Congress provides tax advantages for U.S. citizens who work abroad. These advantages are (1) a foreign earned income exclusion and (2) a foreign housing exclusion or deduction.

FOREIGN EARNED INCOME EXCLUSION

The following items of foreign earned income must be reported as income by a U.S. taxpayer:

- Wages, salaries, professional fees.
- Overseas allowance (cash payment made by employer to compensate for the "inconvenience" of living overseas).
- Housing allowance (cash payment made by employer or fair market value of housing provided by employer).
- Automobile allowance (cash allowance or fair market value).
- Cost of living allowance.
- Education allowance.
- Home leave.
- Rest and relaxation airfare.
- Tax reimbursement allowance (reimbursement for additional taxes paid to foreign government greater than what would have been paid in the home country).

If certain criteria are met, $91,400 (in 2009) of foreign earned income may be excluded from U.S. taxable income. An exclusion is allowed even if the earned income is not taxed by the foreign country (or is taxed at a lower rate than in the United States). The amount of the exclusion increases each year by the rate of inflation.

In addition, a direct foreign tax credit is allowed for foreign taxes paid on the amount of foreign earned income exceeding the amount of the exclusion. As a result, a U.S. taxpayer working in a foreign country that has a higher tax rate than the United States will pay no additional U.S. tax on his or her foreign earned income.

The real benefit of the foreign earned income exclusion arises when a U.S. taxpayer is working in a foreign country with no individual income tax or an individual tax rate less than in the United States. For example, a U.S. taxpayer working in Saudi Arabia (which has no individual income tax) would have paid no income tax at all on the first $91,400 (in 2009) of foreign earned income. Income over that amount was taxed in the United States at normal rates.

The foreign earned income exclusion is available only to U.S. taxpayers who

1. Have their *tax home* in a foreign country, and
2. Meet either (*a*) a *bona fide residence test* or (*b*) a *physical presence test*.

Tax Home

An individual's tax home is the place where he or she is permanently or indefinitely engaged to work as an employee or as a self-employed individual. An individual's tax home cannot be a foreign country if his or her abode is in the United States. *Abode* is variously defined as "home," "residence," "domicile," or "place of dwelling." It relates to where one lives rather than where one works. For your tax home to be in a foreign country, your abode must also be outside of the United States.

As an example, assume that your company transfers you to work in London for 18 months. Your home in New York is rented out and your automobile is placed in storage. In London, you purchase an automobile and you and your spouse get British driving licenses. All members of your family get a local library card and join the local golf club. You open bank accounts at the local bank. In this case, both the abode and the tax home are in London.

Bona Fide Residence Test

A bona fide residence is not necessarily the same as a domicile. A domicile is a permanent home. For example, you could have your domicile in New York and a bona fide residence in London even if you intend to return eventually to New York. Going to work in London does not necessarily mean that you have established a bona fide residence there. But if you go to London to work for an indefinite or extended period and you set up permanent quarters there for you and your family, you probably have established a bona fide residence in a foreign country, even though you intend to return to the United States eventually.

To establish a bona fide residence, you must reside in a foreign country for an uninterrupted period that includes an entire tax year. You may leave for brief trips to the United States or other foreign countries, but you must always return to the bona fide residence at the end of a trip.

The Internal Revenue Service (IRS) will determine whether you meet the bona fide residence test, given information you report in Form 2555, Foreign Earned Income.

Physical Presence Test

More objective than the bona fide residence test is the physical presence test. You meet this test if you are physically present in a foreign country or countries for 330 full days during a consecutive 12-month period. Days spent in transit to the foreign country do not count; only days in which you are in a foreign country for 24 hours count. Time spent in international waters or airspace does not count.

The minimum time requirement can be waived if you must leave a foreign country due to war, civil unrest, or similar adverse conditions. Each year, the IRS publishes a list of countries determined to have these conditions.

FOREIGN HOUSING COSTS

For those taxpayers meeting the two conditions necessary for the foreign earned income exclusion, a foreign housing exclusion is also available.

A foreign housing exclusion may be taken for the amount of housing costs paid for out of employer-provided amounts (such as salary) that exceed a base amount. The base housing amount is defined as 16 percent of the U.S. government GS-14 Step 1 pay. In 2010, that amount was $13,552 (16% × $84,697). In other words, in 2010, a U.S. taxpayer meeting the requirements for the foreign earned income exclusion could exclude foreign housing costs greater than $13,552. For example, an individual working in Hong Kong in 2010 who paid $20,000 in apartment rent could exclude $6,448 ($20,000 − $13,552) from U.S. taxable income that year. The amount taken as a foreign housing exclusion reduces the amount that may be taken as a foreign earned income exclusion. The foreign earned income exclusion is limited to the amount of foreign earned income minus the amount taken as a foreign housing exclusion.

Expenses not eligible for the foreign housing exclusion include the cost of purchasing a house or apartment, mortgage interest, property taxes, wages of housekeepers and gardeners, and any costs that are lavish and extravagant.

Questions

1. How can a country's tax system affect the manner in which an operation in that country is financed by a foreign investor?

2. Why might the effective tax rate paid on income earned within a country be different from that country's national corporate income tax rate?

3. What is a tax haven? How might a company use a tax haven to reduce income taxes?

4. What is the difference between the worldwide and territorial approaches to taxation?

5. What are the different ways in which income earned in one country becomes subject to double taxation?

6. What are the mechanisms used by countries to provide relief from double taxation?

7. Under what circumstances is it advantageous to take a deduction rather than a credit for taxes paid in a foreign country?

8. How are foreign branch income and foreign subsidiary income taxed differently by a company's home country?

9. What is the maximum amount of foreign tax credit that a company will be allowed to take with respect to the income earned by a foreign operation?

10. What are excess foreign tax credits? How are they created and how can companies use them?

11. How does the foreign tax credit basket system used in the United States affect the excess foreign tax credits generated by a U.S.-based company?

12. What is a tax treaty? What is one of most important benefits provided by most tax treaties?

13. What is treaty shopping?

14. What is a controlled foreign corporation? What is Subpart F income?

15. Under what circumstances will the income earned by a foreign subsidiary of a U.S. taxpayer be taxed as if it had been earned by a foreign branch?

16. What are the four factors that will determine the manner in which income earned by a foreign operation of a U.S. taxpayer will be taxed by the U.S. government?

17. What procedures are used to translate the foreign currency income of a foreign branch into U.S. dollars for U.S. tax purposes? What procedures are used to translate the foreign currency income of a foreign subsidiary?

18. In what way did both the domestic international sales corporation and the foreign sales corporation violate international trade agreements?

The following questions relate to the appendix to this chapter:

19. What is the benefit provided to an individual taxpayer through the foreign earned income exclusion?

20. How does an individual taxpayer qualify for the foreign earned income exclusion?

Exercises and Problems

1. In deciding whether to establish a foreign operation, which factor(s) might a multinational corporation (MNC) consider?

   a. After-tax returns from competing investment locations.

   b. The tax treatments of branches versus subsidiaries.

   c. Withholding rates on dividend and interest payments.

   d. All of the above.

2. Why might a company involved in international business find it beneficial to establish an operation in a tax haven?

   a. The OECD recommends the use of tax havens for corporate income tax avoidance.

   b. Tax havens never tax corporate income.

   c. Tax havens are jurisdictions that tend to have abnormally low corporate income tax rates.

   d. Tax havens' banking systems are less secretive.

3. Which of the following item(s) might provide an MNC with a tax-planning opportunity as it decides where to locate a foreign operation?

   a. Differences in corporate tax rates across countries.

   b. Differences in local tax rates across countries.

   c. Whether a country offers a tax holiday.

   d. All of the above.

4. Why might companies have an incentive to finance their foreign operations with as much debt as possible?

   a. Interest payments are generally tax deductible.

   b. Withholding rates are lower for dividends.

   c. Withholding rates are lower for interest.

   d. Both (a) and (c).

5. Kerry is a U.S. citizen residing in Portugal. Kerry receives some investment income from Spain. Why might Kerry be expected to pay taxes on the investment income to the United States?

   a. The United States taxes its citizens on their worldwide income.

   b. The United States taxes its citizens on the basis of residency.

   c. Portugal requires all of its residents to pay taxes to the United States.

   d. None of the above.

6. Poole Corporation is a U.S. company with a branch in China. Income earned by the Chinese branch is taxed at the Chinese corporate income tax rate of 25 percent and at the rate of 35 percent in the United States. What is this an example of?

   a. Capital-export neutrality.

   b. Double taxation.

   c. A tax treaty.

   d. Taxation on the basis of consumption.

7. What are the two most common methods of eliminating the double taxation of income earned by foreign corporations?

   a. Exempting foreign source income and deducting all foreign taxes paid.

   b. Deducting all foreign taxes paid and providing a foreign tax credit.

   c. Exempting foreign source income and providing a foreign tax credit.

   d. Deducting all foreign taxes paid and tax havens.

8. Jordan Inc., a U.S. company, is required to translate the foreign income generated by its foreign operation. To determine U.S. taxable income, what must Jordan use to translate the income of its foreign branch into U.S. dollars?

   a. The exchange rate at the end of the year.

   b. The average exchange rate for the year.

   c. The exchange rate at the beginning of the year.

   d. The previous year's ending exchange rate.

9. Bush Inc. has total income of $500,000. Bush's Polish branch has foreign source income of $200,000 and paid taxes of $38,000 to the Polish government. The U.S. corporate tax rate is 35 percent. What is Bush's overall foreign tax credit limitation?
   a. $70,000.
   b. $175,000.
   c. $150,000.
   d. $38,000.

Questions 10, 11, and 12 are based on the following information:

Information for Year 1, Year 2, and Year 3 for the Andean branch of Powell Corporation is presented in the following table. The corporate tax rate in the Andean Republic in Year 1 was 25 percent. In Year 2, the Andean Republic increased its corporate income tax rate to 29 percent. In Year 3, the Andean Republic increased its corporate tax rate to 36 percent. The U.S. corporate tax rate in each year is 35 percent.

	Year 1	Year 2	Year 3
Foreign source income.....	$75,000	$100,000	$100,000
Foreign taxes paid	18,750	29,000	36,000
U.S. tax before FTC	26,250	35,000	35,000

10. For Year 1, Year 2, and Year 3, what is the foreign tax credit allowed in the United States?
    a. $7,500, $6,000, and $0.
    b. $18,750, $29,000, and $36,000.
    c. $75,000, $100,000, and $100,000.
    d. $18,750, $29,000, and $35,000.

11. For Year 3, what is the net U.S. tax liability?
    a. $35,000.
    b. $0.
    c. $1,000.
    d. $6,000.

12. In Year 3, how much excess foreign tax credit can Powell carry back?
    a. $7,500.
    b. $6,000.
    c. $1,000.
    d. $0.

13. Bay City Rollers Inc., a U.S. company, has a branch located in São Antonio and another in the Bahian Islands. The foreign source income from the São Antonio branch is $150,000, and the foreign source income from the Bahian Island branch is $225,000. The corporate tax rates in São Antonio, the Bahian Islands, and the United States are 30 percent, 24 percent, and 35 percent, respectively.

    Required:
    Determine Bay City Rollers' (*a*) U.S. foreign tax credit and (*b*) net U.S. tax liability related to these foreign sources of income.

Problems 14 and 15 are based on the following information:

Yankee Fish n' Chips, a U.S.-based company, establishes an operation in Great Britain in January of Year 1, when the exchange rate is US$1.50 per British pound (£).

During Year 1, the British branch generates £5,000,000 of pretax income. On October 15, Year 1, £2,000,000 is repatriated to Yankee and converted into U.S. dollars. Assume the effective income tax rate in Great Britain is 30 percent. Taxes were paid in Great Britain on December 31, Year 1. Relevant exchange rates for Year 1 are provided here (US$ per £):

January 1	1.50
Average 30	1.45
October 15	1.35
December 31	1.30

Assume a U.S. tax rate of 35 percent.

14. Assume that Yankee's operation in Great Britain is registered with the British government as a branch.

    Required:
    Determine the amount of U.S. taxable income, U.S. foreign tax credit, and net U.S. tax liability related to the British branch (all in U.S. dollars).

15. Assume that Yankee's operation in Great Britain is incorporated as a subsidiary.

    Required:
    Determine the amount of U.S. taxable income, U.S. foreign tax credit, and net U.S. tax liability related to the British subsidiary (all in U.S. dollars).

16. Mama Corporation (a U.S. taxpayer) has a wholly owned sales subsidiary in the Bahamas (Bahamamama Ltd.) that purchases finished goods from its U.S. parent and sells those goods to customers throughout the Caribbean basin. In the most recent year, Bahamamama generated income of $100,000 and distributed 50 percent of that amount to Mama Corporation as a dividend. There are no income or withholding taxes in the Bahamas.

    Required:
    a. Determine the amount of income taxable in the United States assuming that Bahamamama makes 20 percent of its sales in the Bahamas and 80 percent in other countries.
    b. Determine the amount of income taxable in the United States assuming that Bahamamama makes 40 percent of its sales in the Bahamas and 60 percent in other countries.

17. Lionais Company has a foreign branch that earns income before income taxes of 500,000 currency units (CU). Income taxes paid to the foreign government are CU 150,000 (30 percent). Sales and other taxes paid to the foreign government are CU 50,000. Lionais Company must include the CU 500,000 of foreign branch income in determining its home country taxable income. In determining its taxable income, Lionais can choose between taking a deduction for all foreign taxes paid or a credit only for foreign income taxes paid. The corporate income tax rate in Lionais' home country is 40 percent.

    Required:
    Determine whether Lionais would be better off taking a deduction or credit for foreign taxes paid.

18. Avioco Limited has two branches located in Hong Kong and Australia, each of which manufactures goods primarily for export to countries in the Asia-Pacific region. The corporate income tax rate in Avioco's home country is

20 percent. The amount of income before taxes and the actual tax paid (stated in terms of Avioco's home currency) are as follows:

	Hong Kong Branch	Australia Branch
Income before taxes.	100,000	100,000
Actual tax paid.	16,500 (16.5%)	30,000 (30%)

Required:
Determine the amount of foreign tax credit Avioco will be allowed to take in determining its home country income tax liability.

19. Daisan Company is in the process of deciding where to establish a European manufacturing operation: France, Spain, or Sweden. Daisan's home country does not have a tax treaty with any of these countries. Regardless of location, the operation is expected to generate pretax income of 1 million euros annually. The operation will distribute 100 percent of its after-tax income to Daisan Company as a dividend each year.

Required:
a. Using the information on effective tax rates and withholding tax rates provided in Exhibits 11.1 and 11.3, determine the net amount of dividend that Daisan would receive annually from an investment in each of these three countries.

b. With maximizing after-tax dividends as the sole criterion, in which of the three countries should Daisan locate its European operation?

20. Pendleton Company (a U.S. taxpayer) is a highly diversified company with wholly owned subsidiaries located in South Korea and Japan. The South Korean operation manufactures electric generators that are sold in the Asian market. It generated pretax income of $200,000 in the current year. The Japanese subsidiary is a an investment company that makes passive investments in the Japanese financial markets. The Japanese subsidiary generated pretax income of $100,000 in the current year. Both companies distribute 100 percent of after-tax income to Pendleton Company as a dividend each year. Effective income tax rates and withholding rates are provided in Exhibits 11.1, 11.3, and 11.4.

Required:
a. Determine the amount of foreign tax credit allowed by the United States in the current year, and the amount of excess foreign tax credit, if any.

b. Repeat requirement (a) assuming that, rather than making passive investments in Japan, the Japanese subsidiary purchases electric generators from its South Korean sister company and distributes them in Japan.

21. Eastwood Company (a U.S.-based company) has subsidiaries in three countries: X, Y, and Z. All three subsidiaries manufacture and sell products in their host country. Corporate income tax rates in these three countries over the most recent three-year period are as follows:

Country	Year 1	Year 2	Year 3
X	50%	50%	40%
Y	25	25	25
Z	36	30	30

None of these countries imposes a withholding tax on dividends distributed to a foreign parent company. The U.S. corporate income tax rate over this period was 35 percent.

Pretax income earned by each subsidiary and the percentage of after-tax income paid to Eastwood over the most recent three-year period are as follows:

	Year 1	Year 2	Year 3
Subsidiary X			
Pretax income	$100,000	$100,000	$100,000
Dividend (% of after-tax income). . .	100%	50%	50%
Subsidiary Y			
Pretax income	$150,000	$150,000	$150,000
Dividend (% of after-tax income). . .	50%	50%	50%
Subsidiary Z			
Pretax income	$200,000	$200,000	$200,000
Dividend (% of after-tax income). . .	40%	40%	100%

Required:
a. Determine the amount of foreign source income Eastwood will include in its U.S. tax return in each of the three years.
b. Determine the amount of foreign tax credit Eastwood will be allowed to take in determining its U.S. tax liability in each of the three years.
c. Determine the amount of excess foreign tax credit, if any, Eastwood will have in each of the three years.
d. Determine Eastwood's net U.S. tax liability in each of the three years.

22. Heraklion Company (a U.S.-based company) is considering making an equity investment in an Australian manufacturing operation. The total amount of capital, in Australian dollars (A$), that Heraklion would need to invest is A$1,000,000. Heraklion has three alternatives for financing this investment:

- 100 percent equity.
- 80 percent equity and 20 percent long-term loan from Heraklion (5 percent interest rate).
- 50 percent equity and 50 percent long-term loan from Heraklion (5 percent interest rate).

Heraklion estimates that the Australian operation will generate A$200,000 of income before interest and taxes in its first year of operations. The operation will pay 100 percent of its net income to Heraklion as a dividend each year.

Required:
a. Assume there is no tax treaty between the United States and Australia. Using the information on Australian tax rates found in Exhibit 11.1 and Exhibit 11.3, determine the total amount of taxes that will be paid in Australia under each of the three financing alternatives. Which alternative results in the least amount of taxes being paid in Australia?
b. The United States/Australia tax treaty provides reduced withholding tax rates on certain payments made to a foreign parent company. Use the information on Australian tax rates found in Exhibit 11.1 and Exhibit 11.4

to determine the total amount of taxes that will be paid in Australia under each of the three financing alternatives. Which alternative results in the least amount of taxes being paid in Australia?

23. The corporate income tax rates in two countries, A and B, are 40 percent and 25 percent, respectively. Additionally, both countries impose a 30 percent withholding tax on dividends paid to foreign investors. However, a bilateral tax treaty between A and B reduces the withholding tax to 10 percent if the dividend is paid to an investor that owns more than 50 percent of the paying company's stock (parent). Both A and B use a worldwide approach to taxation but allow taxpayers to take a foreign tax credit for income taxes paid on foreign earned income. The credit is limited to the amount of tax that would have been paid in the domestic country on that income. Both countries use the same currency, so foreign currency translation is not required.

Part 1.
Albemarle Company is headquartered in Country A and has a wholly owned subsidiary in Country B. In the current year, Albemarle's foreign subsidiary generated before tax income of 100,000 and remitted 50 percent of its net income to the parent company as a dividend.

Required:
a. Determine the amount of taxes paid in Country A.
b. Determine the amount of taxes paid in Country B.

Part 2.
Bostwick Company is headquartered in Country B and has a wholly owned subsidiary in Country A. In the current year, Bostwick's foreign subsidiary generated before tax income of 100,000 and remitted 50 percent of its net income to the parent company as a dividend.

Required:
a. Determine the amount of taxes paid in Country A.
b. Determine the amount of taxes paid in Country B.

24. Intec Corporation (a U.S.-based company) has a wholly owned subsidiary located in Shanghai, China that generated income before tax of 500,000 Chinese renminbi (RMB) in the current year. The Chinese subsidiary paid Chinese income taxes at the rate of 25 percent evenly throughout the year, and paid dividends of RMB 200,000 to Intec on October 1. Assume there is no withholding tax on dividends. The following exchange rates for the current year apply:

	US$ per RMB
January 1.	$0.125
Average for the year	0.120
October 1	0.118
December 31.	0.115

Required:
Determine the following related to the income earned by Intec's Chinese subsidiary:
a. The amount of U.S. taxable income in U.S. dollars.
b. The amount of foreign tax credited allowed in the United States.
c. The amount of net U.S. tax liability.

25. Use the information provided in problem 25. Now assume that Intec Corporation's Chinese operation is organized as a branch, and repatriates after tax profits of RMB 200,000 to Intec on October 1.

Required:

Determine the following related to the income earned by Intec's Chinese branch:

a. The amount of U.S. taxable income in U.S. dollars.

b. The amount of foreign tax credited allowed in the United States.

c. The amount of net U.S. tax liability.

26. Brown Corporation has an affiliate in France (Brun SA) that sells products manufactured at Brown's factory in Columbia, South Carolina. In the current year, Brun SA earned €10 million before tax. Assume that the effective tax rate Brun SA pays in France is 30 percent. French taxes were paid at the end of the year. Cash distributions to Brown Company were made on July 1 and December 31 in the amount of €1 million each. Relevant exchange rates for the current year are as follows:

January 1.........	€1 = $1.025
July 1	€1 = $0.900
Average..........	€1 = $0.925
December 31......	€1 = $0.980

Required:

a. Assuming that Brun SA is organized as a branch, determine the amount of branch profits in U.S. dollars that Brown Corporation must include in its U.S. taxable income and the available tax credit.

b. Assuming that Brun SA is organized as a subsidiary determine the amount of foreign source income in U.S. dollars that Brown Corporation must include in its U.S. taxable income and the available tax credit.

The following exercises and problems relate to the appendix to this chapter:

27. Which of the following items is not a tax benefit provided by Congress to U.S. citizens working abroad?

a. Foreign earned income exclusion.

b. Foreign tax credit.

c. Dividend income exclusion.

d. Foreign housing exclusion.

28. The exchange rate between the U.S. dollar (US$) and Hong Kong dollar (HK$) remained constant at HK$8.00 = US$1.00 throughout 2011. Horace Gardner (a U.S. citizen) lives and works in Hong Kong. In 2008, Gardner earned income in Hong Kong of HK$960,000, and paid taxes to the local government at the rate of 15 percent. Gardner qualifies for the foreign earned income exclusion.

Required:

a. Determine the amount of foreign earned income Horace Gardner included in his calculation of U.S. taxable income for the year 2011.

b. Determine the amount of foreign tax credit Horace Gardner was allowed to take in determining his U.S. tax liability for the year 2011.

c. Assuming Horace Gardner has a marginal U.S. tax rate of 28 percent, determine the amount of U.S. income taxes he paid on his foreign earned income in the year 2011.

29. The exchange rate between the U.S. dollar (US$) and the euro (€) remained constant at €1.00 = US$1.50 throughout 2011. Elizabeth Welch (a U.S. citizen) lives and works in France. In 2011, she earned income in France of €100,000, and paid taxes to the local government at the rate of 40 percent. Welch qualifies for the foreign earned income exclusion.

Required:
a. Determine the amount of foreign earned income Elizabeth Welch included in her calculation of U.S. taxable income for the year 2011.
b. Determine the amount of foreign tax credit Elizabeth Welch was allowed to take in determining her U.S. tax liability for the year 2011.
c. Assuming Elizabeth Welch has a marginal U.S. tax rate of 28 percent, determine the amount of U.S. income taxes she paid on her foreign earned income in the year 2011.

Case 11-1

U.S. International Corporation

U.S. International Corporation (USIC), a U.S. taxpayer, has investments in Foreign Entities A–G. Relevant information for these entities for the current fiscal year appears in the following table:

Entity	Country	Percent Owned	Activity	Income before Tax ($ millions)	Income Tax Rate	Dividend Withholding Tax Rate	Net Amount Received by Parent ($ millions)
USIC	United States	—	Manufacturing	$10	35%	—	—
A	Argentina	100%	Manufacturing	$ 1	35	0%	$0.2
B	Brazil	100	Manufacturing	$ 2	34	0	$2.5*
C	Canada	100	Manufacturing	$ 3	33	5	$1.0
D	Hong Kong	100	Investment	$ 2	16.5	0	$1.5
E	Liechtenstein	100	Distribution	$ 3	10	4	$0.0
F	Japan	51	Manufacturing	$ 2	40	5	$0.5
G	New Zealand	60	Banking	$ 4	30	15	$1.0

* Some dividends were paid out of beginning-of-year retained earnings.

Additional Information
1. USIC's $10 million income before tax is derived from the production and sale of products in the United States.
2. Each entity is legally incorporated in its host country other than Entity A, which is registered with the Argentinian government as a branch.
3. Entities A, B, C, and F produce and market products in their home countries.

4. Entity D makes passive investments in stocks and bonds in the Hong Kong financial markets. Income is derived solely from dividends and interest.
5. Entity E markets goods purchased from (manufactured by) USIC. Of E's sales, 95 percent are made in Austria, Germany, and Switzerland, and 5 percent are made in Liechtenstein.
6. Entity G operates in the financial services industry in New Zealand.

Required

Determine the following:

a. The amount of U.S. taxable income for each Entity A–G.
b. The foreign tax credit allowed in the United States, first by basket and then in total.
c. The net U.S. tax liability.
d. Any excess foreign tax credits (identify by basket).

References

Doernberg, Richard L. *International Taxation: In a Nutshell*, 4th ed. St. Paul, MN: West, 1999.

Ernst & Young. *Worldwide Corporate Tax Guide,* 2009, available at www.ey.com.

European Commission. *VAT Rates Applied in the Member States of the European Community: Situation at 1st January 2010,* available at www.eurounion.org.

KPMG. "Corporate Tax Rate Survey—2009," available at www.kpmg.com.

Organization for Economic Cooperation and Development. *The OECD's Project on Harmful Tax Practices: The 2004 Progress Report.* Paris: OECD, 2004, available at www.oecd.org.

PricewaterhouseCoopers. *Worldwide Tax Summaries,* available at www.taxsummaries.pwc.com.

U.S. Internal Revenue Service. Publication 901, "U.S. Tax Treaties," available at www.irs.gov.

World Bank and PricewaterhouseCoopers. *Paying Taxes 2010: The Global Picture,* available at www.doingbusiness.org.

Chapter **Twelve**

International Transfer Pricing

Learning Objectives

After reading this chapter, you should be able to

- Describe the importance of transfer pricing in achieving goal congruence in decentralized organizations.
- Explain how the objectives of performance evaluation and cost minimization can conflict in determining international transfer prices.
- Show how discretionary transfer pricing can be used to achieve specific cost minimization objectives.
- Describe governments' reaction to the use of discretionary transfer pricing by multinational companies.
- Discuss the transfer pricing methods used in sales of tangible property.
- Explain how advance pricing agreements can be used to create certainty in transfer pricing.
- Describe worldwide efforts to enforce transfer pricing regulations.

INTRODUCTION

Transfer pricing refers to the determination of the price at which transactions between related parties will be carried out. Transfers can be from a subsidiary to its parent (upstream), from the parent to a subsidiary (downstream), or from one subsidiary to another of the same parent. Transfers between related parties are also known as *intercompany transactions*. Intercompany transactions represent a significant portion of international trade. In 2009, intercompany transactions comprised 40 percent of U.S. total goods trade: $740.5 billion (48 percent) of the $1.55 trillion in U.S. imports, and $307.2 billion (30 percent) of the $1.06 trillion in U.S. exports.[1] There is a wide range of types of intercompany transactions, each of which has a price associated with it. A list is provided in Exhibit 12.1. The basic question that must be addressed is, At what price should intercompany transfers be made? This chapter focuses on international transfers, that is, intercompany transactions that cross national borders.

---

[1] "U.S. Goods Trade: Imports and Exports by Related Parties, 2009," *U.S. Department of Commerce News,* May 12, 2010, p. 1.

EXHIBIT 12.1
Types of Intercompany Transactions and Their Associated Price

Transaction	Price
Sale of tangible property (e.g., raw materials, finished goods, equipment, buildings)	Sales price
Use of tangible property (leases) (e.g., land, buildings)	Rental or lease payment
Use of intangible property (e.g., patents, trademarks, copyrights)	Royalty, licensing fee
Intercompany services (e.g., research and development, management assistance)	Service charge, management fee
Intercompany loans	Interest rate

Two factors heavily influence the manner in which international transfer prices are determined. The first factor is the objective that headquarters management wishes to achieve through its transfer pricing practices. One possible objective relates to management control and performance evaluation. Another objective relates to the minimization of one or more types of costs. These two types of objectives often conflict.

The second factor affecting international transfer pricing is the law that exists in most countries governing the manner in which intercompany transactions crossing their borders may be priced. These laws were established to make sure that multinational corporations (MNCs) are not able to avoid paying their fair share of taxes, import duties, and so on by virtue of the fact that they operate in multiple jurisdictions. In establishing international transfer prices, MNCs often must walk a fine line between achieving corporate objectives and complying with applicable rules and regulations. In a recent survey, more respondents (39 percent) identified transfer pricing as the most important issue they face compared to all other international tax issues.[2]

We begin this chapter with a discussion of management accounting theory with respect to transfer pricing. We then describe various objectives that MNCs might wish to achieve through discretionary transfer pricing. Much of this chapter focuses on government response to MNCs' discretionary transfer pricing practices, emphasizing the transfer pricing regulations in the United States.

DECENTRALIZATION AND GOAL CONGRUENCE

Business enterprises often are organized by *division.* A division may be a profit center, responsible for revenues and operating expenses, or an investment center, responsible also for assets. In a company organized by division, top managers delegate or decentralize authority and responsibility to division managers. *Decentralization* has many advantages:

- Allowing local managers to respond quickly to a changing environment.
- Dividing large, complex problems into manageable pieces.
- Motivating local managers who otherwise will be frustrated if asked only to implement the decisions of others.[3]

[2] Ernst & Young, *2007–2008 Global Transfer Pricing Survey,* p. 9.
[3] Michael W. Maher, Clyde P. Stickney, and Roman L. Weil, *Managerial Accounting,* 8th ed. (Mason, OH: South-Western, 2004), p. 484.

However, decentralization is not without its potential disadvantages. The most important pitfall is that local managers who have been granted decision-making authority may make decisions that are in their self-interest but detrimental to the company as a whole. The corporate accounting and control system should be designed in such a way that it provides incentives for local managers to make decisions that are consistent with corporate goals. This is known as *goal congruence*. The system used for evaluating the performance of decentralized managers is an important component in achieving goal congruence.

The price at which an intercompany transfer is made determines the level of revenue generated by the seller, becomes a cost for the buyer, and therefore affects the operating profit and performance measurement of both related parties. Appropriate transfer prices can ensure that each division or subsidiary's profit accurately reflects its contribution to overall company profits, thus providing a basis for efficient allocation of resources. To achieve this, transfer prices should motivate local managers to make decisions that enhance corporate performance, while at the same time providing a basis for measuring, evaluating, and rewarding local manager performance in a way that managers perceive as fair.[4] If this does not happen (i.e., if goal congruence is not achieved), then the potential benefits of decentralization can be lost.

Even in a purely domestic context, determining a transfer pricing policy is a complex matter for multidivision organizations, which often try to achieve several objectives through such policies. For example, they may try to use transfer pricing to ensure that it is consistent with the criteria used for performance evaluation, motivate divisional managers, achieve goal congruence, and help manage cash flows. For MNCs, there are additional factors that influence international transfer pricing policy.

TRANSFER PRICING METHODS

The methods used in setting transfer prices in an international context are essentially the same as those used in a purely domestic context. The following three methods are commonly used:

1. *Cost-based transfer price.* The transfer price is based on the cost to produce a good or service. Cost can be determined as variable production cost, variable plus fixed production cost, or full cost, based on either actual or budgeted amounts (standard costs). The transfer price often includes a profit margin for the seller (a "cost-plus" price). Cost-based systems are simple to use, but there are at least two problems associated with them. The first problem relates to the issue of which measure of cost to use. The other problem is that inefficiencies in one unit may be transferred to other units, as there is no incentive for selling divisions to control costs. The use of standard, rather than actual, costs alleviates this problem.

2. *Market-based transfer price.* The transfer price charged a related party is either based on the price that would be charged to an unrelated customer or determined by reference to sales of similar products or services by other companies to unrelated parties. Market-based systems avoid the problem associated with cost-based systems of transferring the inefficiencies of one division or subsidiary to others. They help ensure divisional autonomy and provide a good basis for evaluating subsidiary performance. However, market-based pricing

---

[4] Robert G. Eccles, *The Transfer Pricing Problem: A Theory for Practice* (Lexington, MA: Lexington Books, 1985), p. 8.

systems also have problems. The efficient working of a market-based system depends on the existence of competitive markets and dependable market quotations. For certain items, such as unfinished products, there may not be any buyers outside the organization and hence no external market price.

3. *Negotiated price.* The transfer price is the result of negotiation between buyer and seller and may be unrelated to either cost or market value. A negotiated pricing system can be useful, as it allows subsidiary managers the freedom to bargain with one another, thereby preserving the autonomy of subsidiary managers. However, for this system to work efficiently, it is important that there are external markets for the items being transferred so that the negotiating parties can have objective information as the basis for negotiation. One disadvantage of negotiated pricing is that negotiation can take a long time, particularly if the process deteriorates and the parties involved become more interested in winning arguments than in considering the issues from the corporate perspective. Another disadvantage is that the price agreed on and therefore a manager's measure of performance may be more a function of a manager's ability to negotiate than of his or her ability to control costs and generate profit.

Management accounting theory suggests that different pricing methods are appropriate in different situations. Market-based transfer prices lead to optimal decisions when (1) the market for the product is perfectly competitive, (2) interdependencies between the related parties are minimal, and (3) there is no advantage or disadvantage to buying and selling the product internally rather than externally.[5] Prices based on full cost can approximate market-based prices when the determination of market price is not feasible. Prices that have been negotiated by buyer and seller rather than being mandated by upper management have the advantage of allowing the related parties to maintain their decentralized authority.

A 1990 survey of *Fortune* 500 companies in the United States found that 41 percent of respondent companies relied on cost-based methods in determining international transfer prices, 46 percent used market-based methods, and 13 percent allowed transfer prices to be determined through negotiation.[6] The most widely used approach was full production cost plus a markup. Slightly less than half of the respondents reported using more than one method to determine transfer prices.

OBJECTIVES OF INTERNATIONAL TRANSFER PRICING

Broadly speaking, there are two possible objectives to consider in determining the appropriate price at which an intercompany transfer that crosses national borders should be made: (1) performance evaluation and (2) cost minimization.

Performance Evaluation

To fairly evaluate the performance of both parties to an intercompany transaction, the transfer should be made at a price acceptable to both parties. An acceptable price could be determined by reference to outside market prices (e.g., the price that would be paid to an outside supplier for a component part), or it could be determined by allowing the two parties to the transaction to negotiate a price. Policies for establishing prices for domestic transfers generally should be based on an objective of generating reasonable measures for evaluating performance;

[5] Charles T. Horngren, Srikant M. Datar, George Foster, Madhav Ragan, and Christopher Ittner, *Cost Accounting: A Managerial Emphasis,* 13th ed. (Upper Saddle River, NJ: Prentice Hall, 2009), p. 776.

[6] Roger Y. W. Tang, "Transfer Pricing in the 1990s," *Management Accounting,* February 1992, pp. 22–26.

otherwise, dysfunctional manager behavior can occur and goal congruence does not exist. For example, forcing the manager of one operating unit to purchase parts from a related operating unit at a price that exceeds the external market price will probably result in an unhappy manager. As a result of the additional cost, the unit's profit will be less than it otherwise would be, perhaps less than budgeted, and the manager's salary increase and annual bonus may be adversely affected. In addition, as upper management makes corporate resource allocation decisions, fewer resources may be allocated to this unit because of its lower reported profitability.

Assume that Alpha Company (a manufacturer) and Beta Company (a retailer) are both subsidiaries of Parent Company, located in the United States. Alpha produces DVD players at a cost of $100 each and sells them both to Beta and to unrelated customers. Beta purchases DVD players from Alpha and from unrelated suppliers and sells them for $160 each. The total gross profit earned by both producer and retailer is $60 per DVD player.

Alpha Company can sell DVD players to unrelated customers for $127.50 per unit, and Beta Company can purchase DVD players from unrelated suppliers at $132.50. The manager of Alpha should be happy selling DVD players to Beta for $127.50 per unit or more, and the manager of Beta should be happy purchasing DVD players from Alpha for $132.50 per unit or less. A transfer price somewhere between $127.50 and $132.50 per unit would be acceptable to both managers, as well as to Parent Company. Assuming that a transfer price of $130.00 per unit is agreed on by the managers of Alpha and Beta, the impact on income for Alpha Company, Beta Company, and Parent Company (after eliminating the intercompany transaction) is as follows:

	Alpha	Beta	Parent
Sales	$130.00	$160.00	$160.00
Cost of goods sold	100.00	130.00	100.00
Gross profit	$ 30.00	$ 30.00	$ 60.00
Income tax effect	10.50 (35%)	10.50 (35%)	21.00
After-tax profit	$ 19.50	$ 19.50	$ 39.00

Now assume that Alpha Company is located in Taiwan and Beta Company is located in the United States. Because the income tax rate in Taiwan is only 25 percent, compared with a U.S. income tax rate of 35 percent, Parent Company would like as much of the $60.00 gross profit to be earned by Alpha as possible. Rather than allowing the two managers to negotiate a price based on external market values, assume that Parent Company intervenes and establishes a "discretionary" transfer price of $150.00 per unit.[7] Given this price, the impact of the intercompany transaction on income for the three companies is as follows:

	Alpha	Beta	Parent
Sales	$150.00	$160.00	$160.00
Cost of goods sold	100.00	150.00	100.00
Gross profit	$ 50.00	$ 10.00	$ 60.00
Income tax effect	12.50 (25%)	3.50 (35%)	16.00
After-tax profit	$ 37.50	$ 6.50	$ 44.00

[7] The price is "discretionary" in the sense that it is not based on market value, cost, or negotiation but has been determined at Parent's discretion to reduce income taxes.

The chief executive officer of Parent Company is pleased with this result, because consolidated income for Parent Company increases by $5.00 per unit, as will cash flow when Alpha Company and Beta Company remit their after-tax profits to Parent Company as dividends. The president of Alpha Company is also happy with this transfer price. As is true for all managers in the organization, a portion of the president's compensation is linked to profit, and this use of discretionary transfer pricing will result in a nice bonus for her at year-end. However, the president of Beta Company is less than pleased with this situation. His profit is less than if he were allowed to purchase from unrelated suppliers. He doubts he will receive a bonus for the year, and he is beginning to think about seeking employment elsewhere. Moreover, Beta Company's profit clearly is understated, which could lead top managers to make erroneous decisions with respect to Beta.

Cost Minimization

When intercompany transactions cross national borders, differences between countries might lead an MNC to attempt to achieve certain cost-minimization objectives through the use of discretionary transfer prices mandated by headquarters.

The most well-known use of discretionary transfer pricing is to minimize worldwide income taxes by recording profits in lower-tax countries. As illustrated in the preceding example, this objective can be achieved by establishing an arbitrarily high price when transferring to a higher-tax country. Conversely, this objective is also met by selling at a low price when transferring to a lower-tax country.

Conflicting Objectives

There is an inherent conflict between the performance evaluation and cost-minimization objectives of transfer pricing. To minimize costs, top managers must *dictate* a discretionary transfer price. By definition, this is not a price that has been negotiated by the two managers who are party to a transaction, nor is it necessarily based on external market prices or production costs. The benefits of decentralization can evaporate when headquarters managers assume the responsibility for determining transfer prices.

One way that companies deal with this conflict is through *dual pricing*. The official records for tax and financial reporting are based on the cost-minimizing transfer prices. When it comes time to evaluate performance, however, the actual records are adjusted to reflect prices acceptable to both parties to the transaction factoring out the effect of discretionary transfer prices. Actual transfers are invoiced so as to minimize costs, but evaluation of performance is based on simulated prices.

Other Cost-Minimization Objectives

In addition to the objective of minimizing worldwide income taxes, a number of other objectives can be achieved through the use of discretionary transfer prices for international transactions.

Avoidance of Withholding Taxes

A parent company might want to avoid receiving cash payments from its foreign subsidiaries in the form of dividends, interest, and royalties on which withholding taxes will be paid to the foreign government. Instead, cash can be transferred in the form of sales price for goods and services provided the foreign subsidiary by its parent or other affiliates. There is no withholding tax on payments for purchases of goods and services. The higher the price charged the foreign subsidiary, the more cash can be extracted from the foreign country without incurring withholding tax. For example, assume that the European subsidiary of Kerr Corporation purchases finished goods from its foreign parent at a price of €100 per unit; sells those goods in the local market at a price of €130 per unit; and remits 100 percent of its profit to the parent company, upon which it pays a 30 percent dividend withholding tax. Ignoring income taxes, the total cash flow received by Kerr Corporation from its European subsidiary is €121 per unit; €100 from the sale of finished goods and €21 (€30 − [€30 × 30%]) in the form of dividends after withholding tax. If Kerr Corporation were to raise the selling price to its European subsidiary to €120 per unit, the total cash flow it would receive would increase to €127 per unit; €120 in the form of transfer price plus €7 (€10 − [€10 × 30%]) in net dividends. Raising the transfer price even further to €130 per unit results in cash flow to Kerr Corporation of €130 per unit.

Selling goods and services to a foreign subsidiary (downstream sale) at a higher price reduces the amount of profit earned by the foreign subsidiary that will be subject to a dividend withholding tax. Sales of goods and services by the foreign subsidiary to its parent (upstream sale) at a lower price will achieve the same objective.

Minimization of Import Duties (Tariffs)
Countries generally assess tariffs on the value (based on invoice prices) of goods being imported into the country. These are known as ad valorem import duties. One way to reduce ad valorem import duties is to transfer goods to a foreign operation at lower prices.

Circumvent Profit Repatriation Restrictions
Some countries restrict the amount of profit that can be paid as a dividend to a foreign parent company. This is known as a profit repatriation restriction. A company might be restricted to paying a dividend equal to or less than a certain percentage of annual profit or a certain percentage of capital contributed to the company by its parent. When such restrictions exist, the parent can get around the restriction and remove "profit" indirectly by setting high transfer prices on goods and services provided the foreign operation by the parent and other affiliates. This strategy is consistent with the objective of avoiding withholding taxes.

Protect Cash Flows from Currency Devaluation
In many cases, some amount of the net cash flow generated by a subsidiary in a foreign country will be moved out of that country, if for no other reason than to distribute it as a dividend to stockholders of the parent company. As the foreign currency devalues, the parent currency value of any foreign currency cash decreases. For operations located in countries whose currency is prone to devaluation, the parent may want to accelerate removing cash out of that country before more devaluation occurs. One method for moving more cash out of a country is to set high transfer prices for goods and services provided the foreign operation by the parent and other related companies.

Improve Competitive Position of Foreign Operation
MNCs also are able to use international transfer pricing to maintain competitiveness in international markets and to penetrate new foreign markets. To penetrate a new market, a parent company might establish a sales subsidiary in a foreign country. To capture market share, the foreign operation must compete aggressively on

EXHIBIT 12.2
Cost Minimization
Objectives and
Transfer Prices

Objective	Transfer Pricing Rule
Minimize income taxes	
Transferring to a country with higher tax rate	High price
Transferring to a country with lower tax rate	Low price
Minimize withholding taxes	
Downstream transfer	High price
Upstream transfer	Low price
Minimize import duties	Low price
Protect foreign cash flows from currency devaluation	High price
Avoid repatriation restrictions	High price
Improve competitive position of foreign operation	Low price

price, providing its customers with significant discounts. To ensure that the new operation is profitable, while at the same expecting it to compete on price, the parent company can sell finished goods to its foreign sales subsidiary at low prices. In effect, the parent company absorbs the discount.

The parent company might want to improve the credit status of a foreign operation so that it can obtain local financing at lower interest rates. This generally involves improving the balance sheet by increasing assets and retained earnings. This objective can be achieved by setting low transfer prices for inbound goods to the foreign operation and high transfer prices for outbound goods from the foreign operation, thereby improving profit and cash flow.

Exhibit 12.2 summarizes the transfer price (high or low) needed to achieve various cost-minimization objectives. High transfer prices can be used to (1) minimize worldwide income taxes when transferring to a higher-tax country, (2) reduce withholding taxes (downstream sales), (3) circumvent repatriation restrictions, and (4) protect foreign currency cash from devaluation. However, low transfer prices are necessary to (1) minimize worldwide income taxes when transferring to a lower-tax country, (2) reduce withholding taxes (upstream sales), (3) minimize import duties, and (4) improve the competitive position of a foreign operation.

It should be noted that these different cost-minimization objectives might conflict with one another. For example, charging a higher transfer price to a foreign affiliate to reduce the amount of withholding taxes paid to the foreign government will result in a higher amount of import duties paid to the foreign government. Companies can employ linear programming techniques to determine the optimum transfer price when two or more cost-minimization objectives exist. Electronic spreadsheets also can be used to conduct sensitivity analysis, examining the impact different transfer prices would have on consolidated profit and cash flows.

Survey Results

A survey conducted in the late 1970s found the following to be the top five factors influencing the international transfer pricing policies of U.S. MNCs:[8]

1. Overall profit to the company.
2. Repatriation restrictions on profits and dividends.
3. Competitive position of subsidiaries in foreign countries.

---

[8] Roger Y. W. Tang and K. H. Chan, "Environmental Variables of International Transfer Pricing: A Japan–United States Comparison," *Abacus,* 1979, pp. 3–12.

4. Tax and tax legislation differentials between countries.
5. Performance evaluation.

For Japanese MNCs, the top five factors were the following:

1. Overall profit to the company.
2. Competitive position of subsidiaries in foreign countries.
3. Foreign currency devaluation.
4. Repatriation restrictions on profits and dividends.
5. Performance evaluation.

Differences in income tax rates between countries ranked only 14th for the Japanese MNCs surveyed.

In an updated survey of U.S. MNCs published in 1992, the top four factors remained the same.[9] Import duty rates were the fifth most important factor influencing international transfer pricing policies. Performance evaluation dropped to the 10th position.

Interaction of Transfer Pricing Method and Objectives

In a study published in 2004, Professors Chan and Lo hypothesized that MNCs would prefer either a cost-based or a market-based transfer pricing method depending on the importance of specific environmental variables that affect transfer pricing:[10]

1. Cost-based methods of determining transfer prices are preferred when the following variables are important:

   - Differences in income tax rates.
   - Minimization of import duties.
   - Foreign exchange controls and risks.
   - Restrictions on profit repatriation.
   - Risk of expropriation and nationalization.

2. Market-based methods of determining transfer prices are preferred when the following variables are important:

   - Interests of local partners.
   - Good relationship with local government.

They tested these hypotheses by conducting interviews of managers of MNCs (U.S., Japanese, and European) with operations in China, and they found support for their hypotheses related to foreign exchange controls and risk, interests of local partners, and relationship with the local government. Local partners find market-based methods to be more fair and objective and these methods also are easier to defend in disputes with the government. Cost-based methods afford more flexibility in circumventing foreign exchange controls. The other environmental variables (including differences in income tax rates and repatriation restrictions) were not important in deciding upon a transfer pricing method.

---

[9] Roger Y. W. Tang, "Transfer Pricing in the 1990s," *Management Accounting*, February 1992, pp. 22–26.

[10] K. Hung Chan and Agnes W.Y. Lo, "The Influence of Managerial Perception of Environmental Variables on the Choice of International Transfer-Pricing Methods," *International Journal of Accounting* 39 (2004), pp. 93–110.

GOVERNMENT REACTIONS

National tax authorities are aware of the potential for MNCs to use discretionary transfer pricing to avoid paying income taxes, import duties, and so on. Most countries have guidelines regarding what will be considered an acceptable transfer price for tax purposes. Across countries, these guidelines can conflict, creating the possibility of double taxation when a price accepted by one country is disallowed by another.

The Organization for Economic Cooperation and Development (OECD) developed transfer pricing guidelines in 1979 that have been supplemented or amended several times since then. The basic rule is that transfers must be made at arm's-length prices. That is, prices that would be charged between independent parties in the same circumstances. The guidelines also acknowledge the need for companies to document the arm's-length nature of their transfer prices. The idea is that OECD member countries would adopt the OECD guidelines and thereby avoid conflicts. The OECD rules are only a model and do not have the force of law in any country. However, most developed countries have transfer pricing rules generally based on OECD guidelines with some variations. The next section of this chapter discusses the specific transfer pricing rules adopted in the United States. Although the rules we discuss are specific to the United States, similar rules can be found in many other countries.

U.S. TRANSFER PRICING RULES

Understanding U.S. transfer pricing rules is important for both U.S. and non-U.S. business enterprises and tax practitioners for two reasons. First, most MNCs either are headquartered in or have significant business activities in the United States. Second, the transfer pricing reforms that took place in the United States in the 1990s have influenced changes in transfer pricing regulation in many other countries.

Section 482 of the U.S. Internal Revenue Code gives the Internal Revenue Service (IRS) the power to audit international transfer prices and adjust a company's tax liability if the price is deemed to be inappropriate. The IRS may audit and adjust transfer prices between companies controlled directly or indirectly by the same taxpayer. Thus, Section 482 applies to both upstream and downstream transfers between a U.S. parent and its foreign subsidiary, between a foreign parent and its U.S. subsidiary, or between the U.S. subsidiary and foreign subsidiary of the same parent. The IRS, of course, is primarily concerned that a proper amount of income is being recorded and taxed in the United States.

Similar to the OECD guidelines, Section 482 requires transactions between commonly controlled entities to be carried out at arm's-length prices. Arm's-length prices are defined as "the prices which would have been agreed upon between unrelated parties engaged in the same or similar transactions under the same or similar conditions in the open market." Because same or similar transactions with unrelated parties often do not exist, determination of an arm's-length price generally will involve reference to comparable transactions under comparable circumstances.

The U.S. Treasury Regulations supplementing Section 482 establish more specific guidelines for determining an arm's-length price. In general, a "best-method rule" requires taxpayers to use the transfer pricing method that under the facts and circumstances provides the most reliable measure of an arm's-length price.

There is no hierarchy in application of methods, and no method always will be considered more reliable than others. In determining which method provides the most reliable measure of an arm's-length price, the two primary factors to be considered are the degree of comparability between the intercompany transaction and any comparable uncontrolled transactions, and the quality of the data and assumptions used in the analysis. Determining the degree of comparability between an intercompany transaction and an uncontrolled transaction involves a comparison of the five factors listed in Exhibit 12.3. Each of these factors must be considered in determining the degree of comparability between an intercompany transaction and an uncontrolled transaction and the extent to which adjustments must be made to establish an arm's-length price.

Treasury Regulations establish guidelines for determining an arm's-length price for various kinds of intercompany transactions, including sales of tangible property, licensing of intangible property, intercompany loans, and intercompany services. Although we focus on regulations related to the sale of tangible property because this is the most common type of international intercompany transaction, we also describe regulations related to licensing intangible assets, intercompany loans, and intercompany services.

Sale of Tangible Property

Treasury Regulations require the use of one of five specified methods to determine the arm's-length price in a sale of tangible property (inventory and fixed assets):

1. Comparable uncontrolled price method.
2. Resale price method.
3. Cost-plus method.
4. Comparable profits method.
5. Profit split method.

If none of these methods is determined to be appropriate, companies are allowed to use an unspecified method, provided its use can be justified.

Comparable Uncontrolled Price Method

The *comparable uncontrolled price method* is generally considered to provide the most reliable measure of an arm's-length price when a comparable uncontrolled transaction exists. Assume that a U.S.-based parent company (Parentco) makes sales of tangible property to a foreign subsidiary (Subco). Under this method, the price for tax purposes is determined by reference to sales by Parentco of the same or similar product to unrelated customers, or purchases by Subco of the same or similar product from unrelated suppliers. Also, sales of the same product between two unrelated parties could be used to determine the transfer price.

To determine whether the comparable uncontrolled price method results in the most reliable measure of arm's-length price, a company must consider each of the factors listed in Exhibit 12.3. Section 1.482-3 of the Treasury Regulations indicates specific factors that may be particularly relevant in determining whether an uncontrolled transaction is comparable:

1. Quality of the product.
2. Contractual terms.
3. Level of the market.
4. Geographic market in which the transaction takes place.

EXHIBIT 12.3
Factors to Be Considered in Determining the Comparability of an Intercompany Transaction and an Uncontrolled Transaction

Source: U.S. Treasury Regulations, Sec. 1.482-1(d).

1. Functions performed by the various parties in the two transactions, including
   - Research and development.
   - Product design and engineering.
   - Manufacturing, production, and process engineering.
   - Product fabrication, extraction, and assembly.
   - Purchasing and materials management.
   - Marketing and distribution functions, including inventory management, warranty administration, and advertising activities.
   - Transportation and warehousing.
   - Managerial, legal, accounting and finance, credit and collection, training, and personnel management services.
2. Contractual terms that could affect the results of the two transactions, including
   - The form of consideration charged or paid.
   - Sales or purchase volume.
   - The scope and terms of warranties provided.
   - Rights to updates, revisions, and modifications.
   - The duration of relevant license, contract, or other agreement, and termination and negotiation rights.
   - Collateral transactions or ongoing business relationships between the buyer and seller, including arrangements for the provision of ancillary or subsidiary services.
   - Extension of credit and payment terms.
3. Risks that could affect the prices that would be charged or paid, or the profit that would be earned, in the two transactions, including
   - Market risks.
   - Risks associated with the success or failure of research and development activities.
   - Financial risks, including fluctuations in foreign currency rates of exchange and interest rates.
   - Credit and collection risk.
   - Product liability risk.
   - General business risks related to the ownership of property, plant, and equipment.
4. Economic conditions that could affect the price or profit earned in the two transactions, such as
   - The similarity of geographic markets.
   - The relative size of each market, and the extent of the overall economic development in each market.
   - The level of the market (e.g., wholesale, retail).
   - The relevant market shares for the products, properties, or services transferred or provided.
   - The location-specific costs of the factors of production and distribution.
   - The extent of competition in each market with regard to the property or services under review.
   - The economic condition of the particular industry, including whether the market is in contraction or expansion.
   - The alternatives realistically available to the buyer and seller.
5. Property or services transferred in the transactions, including any intangibles that are embedded in tangible property or services being transferred.

5. Date of the transaction.
6. Intangible property associated with the sale.
7. Foreign currency risks.
8. Alternatives realistically available to the buyer and seller.

If the uncontrolled transaction is not exactly comparable, some adjustment to the uncontrolled price is permitted in order to make the transactions more comparable. For example, assume that Sorensen Company, a U.S. manufacturer, sells the same product to both controlled and uncontrolled distributors in Mexico. The price to uncontrolled distributors is $40 per unit. Sorensen affixes its trademark to the products sold to its Mexican subsidiary but not to the products sold to the uncontrolled distributor. The trademark is considered to add approximately $10 of value to the product. The transactions are not strictly comparable because the products sold to the controlled and uncontrolled parties are different (one has a trademark and the other does not). Adjusting the uncontrolled price of $40 by $10 would result in a more comparable price and $50 would be an acceptable transfer price under the comparable uncontrolled price method. If the value of the trademark could not be reasonably determined, the comparable uncontrolled price method might not result in the most reliable arm's-length price in this scenario.

Resale Price Method

The *resale price method* determines the transfer price by subtracting an appropriate gross profit from the price at which the controlled buyer resells the tangible property. In order to use this method, a company must know *the final selling price to uncontrolled parties* and be able to determine *an appropriate gross profit for the reseller.* An appropriate gross profit is determined by reference to the gross profit margin earned in comparable uncontrolled transactions. For example, assume that Odom Company manufactures and sells automobile batteries to its Canadian affiliate, which in turn sells the batteries to local retailers at a resale price of $50 per unit. Other Canadian distributors of automobile batteries earn an average gross profit margin of 25 percent on similar sales. Applying the resale price method, Odom Company would establish an arm's-length price of $37.50 per unit for its sale of batteries to its Canadian affiliate (resale price of $50 less an appropriate gross profit of $12.50 [25 percent] to be earned by the Canadian affiliate).

In determining an appropriate gross profit, the degree of comparability between the sale made by the Canadian affiliate and sales made by uncontrolled Canadian distributors need not be as great as under the comparable uncontrolled price method. The decisive factor is the similarity of functions performed by the affiliate and uncontrolled distributors in making sales. For example, if the functions performed by the Canadian affiliate in selling batteries are similar to the functions performed by Canadian distributors of automobile parts in general, the company could use the gross profit earned by uncontrolled sellers of automobile parts in Canada in determining an acceptable transfer price. Other important factors affecting comparability might include the following:

- Inventory levels and turnover rates.
- Contractual terms (e.g., warranties, sales volume, credit terms, transport terms).
- Sales, marketing, advertising programs and services, including promotional programs, and rebates.
- Level of the market (e.g., wholesale, retail).

The resale price method is typically used when the buyer/reseller is merely a distributor of finished goods—a so-called sales subsidiary. The method is acceptable only when the buyer/reseller does not add a substantial amount of value to the product. The resale price method is not feasible in cases where the reseller adds substantial value to the goods or where the goods become part of a larger product, because there is no "final selling price to uncontrolled parties" for the goods that were transferred. Continuing with our example, if Odom Company's Canadian affiliate operates an auto assembly plant and places the batteries purchased from Odom in automobiles that are then sold for $20,000 per unit, the company cannot use the resale price method for determining an appropriate transfer price for the batteries.

Cost-Plus Method

The *cost-plus method* is most appropriate when there are no comparable uncontrolled sales and the related buyer does more than simply distribute the goods it purchases. Whereas the resale price method subtracts an appropriate gross profit from the resale price to establish the transfer price, the cost-plus method adds an appropriate gross profit to the cost of producing a product to establish an arm's-length price. This method is normally used in cases involving manufacturing, assembly, or other production of goods that are sold to related parties. Once again, the appropriate gross profit markup is determined by reference to comparable uncontrolled transactions. Physical similarity between the products transferred is not as important in determining comparability under this method as it is under the comparable uncontrolled price method. Factors to be included in determining whether an uncontrolled transaction is comparable include similarity of functions performed, risks borne, and contractual terms. Factors that may be particularly relevant in determining comparability under this method include the following:

- Complexity of the manufacturing or assembly process.
- Manufacturing, production, and process engineering.
- Procurement, purchasing, and inventory control activities.
- Testing functions.

To illustrate use of the cost-plus method, assume that Pruitt Company has a subsidiary in Taiwan that acquires materials locally to produce an electronic component. The component, which costs $4 per unit to produce, is sold only to Pruitt Company. Because the Taiwanese subsidiary does not sell this component to other, unrelated parties, the comparable uncontrolled price method is not applicable. Pruitt Company combines the electronic component imported from Taiwan with other parts to assemble electronic switches that are sold in the United States. Because Pruitt does not simply resell the electronic components in the United States, the resale price method is not available. Therefore, Pruitt must look for a comparable transaction between unrelated parties in Taiwan to determine whether the cost plus method can be used. Assume that an otherwise comparable company in Taiwan manufactures similar electronic components from its inventory of materials and sells them to unrelated buyers at an average gross profit markup on cost of 25 percent. In this case, application of the cost-plus method results in a transfer price of $5 ($4 + [$4 × 25%]) for the electronic component that Pruitt purchases from its Taiwanese subsidiary.

Now assume that Pruitt's Taiwanese subsidiary manufactures electronic components using materials provided by Pruitt on a consignment basis. To apply the cost-plus method, Pruitt would have to make a downward adjustment to the otherwise comparable gross profit markup of 25 percent, because the inventory risk assumed by the manufacturer in the comparable transaction justifies a higher gross profit markup than is appropriate for Pruitt's foreign subsidiary. If Pruitt cannot reasonably ascertain the effect of inventory procurement and handling on gross profit, the cost-plus method might not result in a reliable transfer price.

Comparable Profits Method

The *comparable profits method* is based on the assumption that similarly situated taxpayers will tend to earn similar returns over a given period.[11] Under this method, one of the two parties in a related transaction is chosen for examination. An arm's-length price is determined by referring to an objective measure of profitability earned by uncontrolled taxpayers on comparable, uncontrolled sales. Profit indicators that might be considered in applying this method include the ratio of operating income to operating assets, the ratio of gross profit to operating expenses, or the ratio of operating profit to sales. If the transfer price used results in ratios for the party being examined that are in line with those ratios for similar businesses, then the transfer price will not be challenged.

To demonstrate the comparable profits method, assume that Glassco, a U.S. manufacturer, distributes its products in a foreign country through its foreign sales subsidiary, Vidroco. Assume that Vidroco has sales of $1,000,000 and operating expenses (other than cost of goods sold) of $200,000. Over the past several years, comparable distributors in the foreign country have earned operating profits equal to 5 percent of sales. Under the comparable profits method, a transfer price that provides Vidroco an operating profit equal to 5 percent of sales would be considered arm's length. An acceptable operating profit for Vidroco is $50,000 ($1,000,000 × 5%). To achieve this amount of operating profit, cost of goods sold must be $750,000 ($1,000,000 − $200,000 − $50,000); this is the amount that Glassco would be allowed to charge as a transfer price for its sales to Vidroco. This example demonstrates use of the ratio of operating profit to sales as the profit-level indicator under the comparable profits method. The Treasury Regulations also specifically mention use of the ratio of operating profit to operating assets and the ratio of gross profit to operating expenses as acceptable profit-level indicators in applying this method.

Profit Split Method

The *profit split method* assumes that the buyer and seller are one economic unit.[12] The total profit earned by the economic unit from sales to uncontrolled parties is allocated to the members of the economic unit based on their relative contributions in earning the profit. The relative value of each party's contribution in earning the profit is based on the functions performed, risks assumed, and resources employed in the business activity that generates the profit. There are in fact two versions of the profit split method: (1) comparable profit split method and (2) residual profit split method.

Under the *comparable profit split method,* the profit split between two related parties is determined through reference to the operating profit earned by each party in a comparable uncontrolled transaction. Each of the factors listed in Exhibit 12.3 must be considered in determining the degree of comparability between the intercompany transaction and the comparable uncontrolled transaction. The degree of

---

[11] The comparable profits method is described in Treasury Regulations, Sec. 1.482-5.

[12] The profit split method is described in Treasury Regulations, Sec. 1.482-6.

similarity in the contractual terms between the controlled and comparable uncontrolled transaction is especially critical in determining whether this is the "best method." In addition, Treasury Regulations specifically state that this method "may not be used if the combined operating profit (as a percentage of the combined assets) of the uncontrolled comparables varies significantly from that earned by the controlled taxpayers."[13]

When controlled parties possess intangible assets that allow them to generate profits in excess of what is earned in otherwise comparable uncontrolled transactions, the *residual profit split method* should be used. Under this method the combined profit is allocated to each of the controlled parties following a two-step process. In the first step, profit is allocated to each party to provide a market return for its routine contributions to the relevant business activity. This step will not allocate all of the combined profit earned by the controlled parties, because it will not include a return for the intangible assets that they possess. In the second step, the residual profit attributable to intangibles is allocated to each of the controlled parties on the basis of the relative value of intangibles that each contributes to the relevant business activity. The reliability of this method hinges on the ability to measure the value of the intangibles reliably.

The transfer pricing methods allowed for tangible property transfers under U.S. regulations also are used in other countries. In a survey of 850 MNCs located in 24 different countries, Ernst & Young found the percentages of companies using various transfer pricing methods for transfers of tangible goods were:[14]

- Comparable uncontrolled price method (32 percent).
- Cost-plus method (29 percent).
- Resale price method (17 percent).
- Comparable profits method (11 percent).
- Profit-split method (4 percent).
- Other methods (6 percent).

Licenses of Intangible Property

Treasury Regulations, Section 1.482-4, list six categories of intangible property:

- Patents, inventions, formulae, processes, designs, patterns, or know-how.
- Copyrights and literary, musical, or artistic compositions.
- Trademarks, trade names, or brand names.
- Franchises, licenses, or contracts.
- Methods, programs, systems, procedures, campaigns, surveys, studies, forecasts, estimates, customer lists, or technical data.
- Other similar items. An item is considered similar if it derives its value from its intellectual content or other intangible properties rather than from physical properties.

Four methods are available for determining the arm's-length consideration for the license of intangible property:

- Comparable uncontrolled transaction method.
- Comparable profits methods.

---

[13] Treasury Regulations, Sec. 1.482-6 (c)(2).

[14] Ernst & Young, *2007–2008 Global Transfer Pricing Survey*, p. 16.

- Profit split method.
- Unspecified methods.

The comparable profits method and profit split method are the same methods as those available for establishing the transfer price on tangible property. The comparable uncontrolled transaction method is similar in concept to the comparable uncontrolled price method available for tangible property.

Comparable Uncontrolled Transaction (CUT) Method

The *comparable uncontrolled transaction (CUT)* method determines whether or not the amount a company charges a related party for the use of intangible property is an arm's-length price by referring to the amount it charges an unrelated party for the use of the intangible. Treasury Regulations indicate that if an uncontrolled transaction involves the license of the same intangible under the same (or substantially the same) circumstances as the controlled transaction, the results derived from applying the CUT method will generally be the most reliable measure of an arm's-length price.[15]

The controlled and uncontrolled transactions are substantially the same if there are only minor differences that have a definite and reasonably measurable effect on the amount charged for use of the intangible. If substantially the same uncontrolled transactions do not exist, uncontrolled transactions that involve the transfer of comparable intangibles under comparable circumstances may be used in applying the CUT method.

In evaluating the comparability of an uncontrolled transaction, the following factors are particularly relevant:[16]

- The terms of the transfer, including the exploitation rights granted in the intangible, the exclusive or nonexclusive character of any rights granted, any restrictions on use or any limitation on the geographic area in which the rights may be exploited.
- The stage of development of the intangible (including, where appropriate, necessary governmental approvals, authorizations, or licenses) in the market in which the intangible is to be used.
- Rights to receive updates, revisions or modifications of the intangible.
- The uniqueness of the property and the period for which it remains unique, including the degree and duration of protection afforded to the property under the laws of the relevant countries.
- The duration of the contract or other agreement, and any termination or renegotiation rights.
- Any economic and product liability risks to be assumed by the transferee.
- The existence and extent of any collateral transactions or ongoing business relationships between the transferee and transferor.
- The functions to be performed by the transferor and transferee, including any ancillary or subsidiary services.

Furthermore, differences in economic conditions also can affect comparability and therefore the appropriateness of the CUT method. For example, if a U.S. pharmaceutical company licenses a patented drug to an uncontrolled manufacturer in Country A and licenses the same drug under the same contractual terms to its

---

[15] In its *2007–2008 Global Transfer Pricing Survey,* Ernst & Young found the comparable uncontrolled transaction (CUT) method to be used by a majority (54 percent) of MNCs from a wide range of countries.

[16] Treasury Regulations, Sec. 1.482-4 (c)(2).

subsidiary in Country B, the two transactions are not comparable if the potential market for the drug is higher in Country B because of a higher incidence of the disease the drug is intended to combat.

Profit Split Method

Treasury Regulations provide the following example to demonstrate application of the residual profit split method to licensing intangibles. P, a U.S.-based company, manufactures and sells products for police use in the United States. P develops and obtains a patent for a bulletproof material, Nulon, for use in its protective clothing and headgear. P licenses its European subsidiary, S, to manufacture and sell Nulon in Europe. S has adapted P's products for military use and sells to European governments under brand names that S has developed and owns. S's revenues from the sale of Nulon in Year 1 are $500, and S's direct operating expenses (excluding royalties) are $300. The royalty the IRS will allow P to charge S for the license to produce Nulon is determined as follows:

1. The IRS determines that the operating assets used by S in producing Nulon are worth $200. From an examination of profit margins earned by other European companies performing similar functions, it determines that 10 percent is a fair market return on S's operating assets. Of S's operating profit of $200 (sales of $500 less direct operating expenses of $300), the IRS determines that $20 ($200 × 10%) is attributable to S's operating assets. The remaining $180 is attributable to intangibles. In the second step, the IRS determines how much of this $180 is attributable to P's intangibles and how much is attributable to S's intangibles. The amount attributable to P's intangibles is the amount the IRS will allow P to charge S for the license to produce Nulon.

2. The IRS establishes that the market values of P and S's intangibles cannot be reliably determined. Therefore, it estimates the relative values of the intangibles from Year 1 expenditures on research, development, and marketing. P's research and development expenditures relate to P's worldwide activities, so the IRS allocates these expenditures to worldwide sales. By comparing these expenditures in Year 1 with worldwide sales in Year 1, the IRS determines that the contribution to worldwide gross profit made by P's intangibles is 20 percent of sales. In contrast, S's research, development, and marketing expenditures pertain to European sales, and the IRS determines that the contribution that S's intangibles make to S's gross profit is equal to 40 percent of sales. Thus, of the portion of S's gross profit that is not attributable to a return on S's operating assets, one-third (20%/60%) is attributable to P's intangibles and two-thirds is attributable to S's intangibles (40%/60%). Under the residual profit split method, P will charge S a license fee of $60 ($180 × $\frac{1}{3}$) in Year 1.

Intercompany Loans

When one member of a controlled group makes a loan to another member of the group, Section 482 of the U.S. Internal Revenue Code requires an arm's-length rate of interest to be charged on the loan. In determining an arm's-length interest rate, all relevant factors should be considered including the principal and duration of the loan, the security involved, the credit standing of the borrower, and the interest rate prevailing for comparable loans between unrelated parties.

A safe harbor rule exists when the loan is denominated in U.S. dollars and the lender is not regularly engaged in the business of making loans to unrelated persons. Such would be the case, for example, if a U.S. manufacturing firm made a U.S.-dollar loan to its foreign subsidiary. In this situation, the stated interest rate is considered to be at arm's length if it is at a rate not less than the "applicable federal rate" and not greater than 130 percent of the applicable federal rate (AFR). The AFR is based on the average interest rate on obligations of the federal government with similar maturity dates. The AFR is recomputed each month. Assuming an AFR of 4 percent on one-year obligations, the U.S. manufacturing firm could charge an interest rate anywhere from 4 percent to 5.2 percent on a one-year U.S.-dollar loan to its foreign subsidiary without having to worry about a transfer pricing adjustment being made by the IRS.

Intercompany Services

When one member of a controlled group provides a service to another member of the group, the purchaser must pay an arm's-length price to the service provider. If the services provided are incidental to the business activities of the service provider, the arm's-length price is equal to the direct and indirect costs incurred in connection with providing the service. There is no need to include a profit component in the price in this case. However, if the service provided is an "integral part" of the business function of the service provider, the price charged must include profit equal to what would be earned on similar services provided to an unrelated party. For example, assume that engineers employed by Brandlin Company travel to the Czech Republic to provide technical assistance to the company's Czech subsidiary in setting up a production facility. Brandlin must charge the foreign subsidiary a fee for this service equal to the direct and indirect costs incurred. Direct costs include the cost of the engineers' travel to the Czech Republic and their salaries while on the assignment. Indirect costs might include a portion of Brandlin's overhead costs allocated to the engineering department. If Brandlin is in the business of providing this type of service to unrelated parties, it must also include an appropriate amount of profit in the technical assistance fee it charges its Czech subsidiary.

No fee is required to be charged to a related party if the service performed on its behalf merely duplicates an activity the related party has performed itself. For example, assume that engineers employed by Brandlin's Czech subsidiary design the layout of the production facility themselves and their plan is simply reviewed by Brandlin's U.S. engineers. In this case, the U.S. parent company need not charge the foreign subsidiary a fee for performing the review.

Arm's-Length Range

The IRS acknowledges that application of a specific transfer pricing method could result in a number of transfer prices thereby creating an "arm's-length range" of prices. A company will not be subject to IRS adjustment so long as its transfer price falls within this range. For example, assume that Harrell Company determines the comparable uncontrolled price method to be the "best method" for purchases of Product X from its wholly owned Chinese subsidiary. Four comparable uncontrolled transactions are identified with prices of $9.50, $9.75, $10.00, and $10.50. Harrell Company can purchase Product X from its Chinese subsidiary at a price anywhere from $9.50 to $10.50 without the risk of an adjustment being made by the IRS. The company may wish to choose that price within the arm's-length range (either the highest price or the lowest price) that would allow it to achieve one or more cost-minimization objectives.

Correlative Relief

Determination of an arm's-length transfer price acceptable to the IRS is very important. If the IRS adjusts a transfer price in the United States, there is no guarantee that the foreign government at the other end of the transaction will reciprocate by providing a correlative adjustment. If the foreign government does not provide correlative relief, the total tax liability for the MNC increases. For example, assume that Usco Inc. manufactures a product for $10 per unit that is sold to its affiliate in Vietnam (Vietco) for $12 per unit. The Vietnamese affiliate sells the product at $20 per unit in the local market. In that case, the worldwide income tax paid on this sale would be $2.94 per unit, calculated as follows:

	Usco	Vietco
Sales	$ 12	$ 20
Cost of sales	10	12
Taxable income	$ 2	$ 8
Tax liability	$ .70 (35%)	$2.24 (28%)

Assume further that Usco is unable to justify its transfer price of $12 through use of one of the acceptable transfer pricing methods, and the IRS adjusts the price to $15. This results in U.S. taxable income of $5 per unit. If the Vietnamese government refuses to allow Vietco to adjust its cost of sales to $15 per unit, the worldwide income tax paid on this sale would be $3.99 per unit, determined as follows:

	Usco	Vietco
Sales	$ 15	$ 20
Cost of sales	10	12
Taxable income	$ 5	$ 8
Tax liability	$1.75 (35%)	$2.24 (28%)

Article 9 of the U.S. Model Income Tax Treaty requires that, when the tax authority in one country makes an adjustment to a company's transfer price, the tax authority in the other country will provide correlative relief if it agrees with the adjustment. If the other country does not agree with the adjustment, the competent authorities of the two countries are required to attempt to reach a compromise. If no compromise can be reached, the company will find itself in the situation described earlier. In the absence of a tax treaty (such as in the case of the United States and Vietnam), there is no compulsion for the other country to provide a correlative adjustment.

When confronted with an IRS transfer pricing adjustment, a taxpayer may request assistance from the U.S. Competent Authority through its Mutual Agreement Procedure (MAP) to obtain correlative relief from the foreign government. In 2002, the IRS recommended $5.56 billion in transfer pricing adjustments. The MAP process resulted in a correlative adjustment in 38 percent of the adjustments.[17] In an additional 27 percent of cases, MAP resulted in the withdrawal of the adjustment by the IRS. The MAP process is not speedy. Over the period 1997–2002, the MAP process took an average of 679–948 days to secure a correlative adjustment.

[17] U.S. Department of the Treasury, *Current Trends in the Administration of International Transfer Pricing by the Internal Revenue Service,* September 2003, p. 13.

Penalties

In addition to possessing the power to adjust transfer prices, the IRS has the authority to impose penalties on companies that significantly underpay taxes as a result of inappropriate transfer pricing. A penalty equal to 20 percent of the underpayment in taxes may be levied for a substantial valuation misstatement. The penalty increases to 40 percent of the underpayment on a gross valuation misstatement. A substantial valuation misstatement exists when the transfer price is 200 percent or more (50 percent or less) of the price determined under Section 482 to be the correct price. A gross valuation misstatement arises when the price is 400 percent or more (25 percent or less) than the correct price.

For example, assume Tomlington Company transfers a product to a foreign affiliate for $10 and the IRS determines the correct price should have been $50. The adjustment results in an increase in U.S. tax liability of $1,000,000. Because the original transfer price was less than 25 percent of the correct price ($50 × 25% = $12.50), the IRS levies a penalty of $400,000 (40% of $1,000,000). Tomlington Company will pay the IRS a total of $1,400,000 as a result of its gross valuation misstatement.

Contemporaneous Documentation

Taxpayers must create documentation that justifies the transfer pricing method selected as the most reliable measure of arm's-length price, and they must be able to provide that documentation to the IRS within 30 days of it being requested. It has become standard practice for IRS auditors to request a taxpayer's contemporaneous documentation at the beginning of an audit involving intercompany transactions.

The documentation needed to justify the transfer pricing method chosen must include:

1. An overview of the taxpayer's business, including an analysis of economic and legal factors that affect transfer pricing.
2. A description of the taxpayer's organizational structure, including an organizational chart, covering all related parties engaged in potentially relevant transactions.
3. Any documentation specifically required by the transfer pricing regulations.
4. A description of the selected pricing method and an explanation of why that method was selected.
5. A description of alternative methods that were considered and an explanation of why they were not selected.
6. A description of the controlled transactions, including the terms of sale, and any internal data used to analyze those transactions.
7. A description of the comparable uncontrolled transactions or parties that were used with the transfer pricing method, how comparability was evaluated, and what comparability adjustments were made, if any.
8. An explanation of the economic analysis and projections relied upon in applying the selected transfer pricing method.

In 2001, the IRS commissioned a study to determine the cost incurred by companies in maintaining contemporaneous transfer pricing documentation as required. Of 567 companies surveyed, 4 percent indicated spending $0, 60 percent reported spending between $1 and $100,000, and 35 percent said they spent more than $100,000 in preparing transfer pricing documentation.[18] The survey also found that 60 percent of respondents had from 1 to 10 full-time employees handling transfer pricing issues and documentation.

A report published by PricewaterhouseCoopers in 2009 indicates that the preparation of documentation to demonstrate compliance with transfer pricing rules is an important and growing problem for MNCs. "More and more countries have established documentation rules that require companies to state clearly and with supporting evidence why their transfer pricing policies comply with the arm's-length standard. Many jurisdictions have also implemented strict penalty regimes to encourage taxpayers' compliance with these new procedures. However, some of the biggest challenges facing taxpayers in their efforts to abide by these requirements are the subtle differences in transfer pricing documentation expected across the various tax jurisdictions. These conflicting pressures need to be reviewed and managed very carefully both to meet the burden of compliance and to avoid costly penalties."[19]

Reporting Requirements

To determine whether intercompany transactions meet the arm's-length price requirement, the IRS often must request substantial information from the company whose transfer pricing is being examined. Historically, the IRS has found it extremely difficult to obtain such information when the transaction involves a transfer from a foreign parent company to its U.S. subsidiary. The information might be held by the foreign parent, which is beyond the jurisdiction of the IRS.

To reduce this problem, U.S. tax law now requires substantial reporting and record keeping of any U.S. company that (*a*) has at least one foreign shareholder with a 25 percent interest in the company and (*b*) engages in transactions with that shareholder. Accounting and other records must be physically maintained in the United States by a U.S. company meeting this definition. In addition, Form 5472 must be filed each year for each related party with whom the company had transactions during the year. Failure to keep appropriate records results in a $10,000 fine, and a fine of $10,000 is assessed for each failure to file a Form 5472. If the company does not resolve the problem within 90 days of notification by the IRS, the fine doubles and increases by $10,000 for every 30 days' delay after that. For example, a U.S. subsidiary of a foreign parent that neglects to file Form 5472 would owe the IRS $50,000 in penalties 180 days after being notified of its deficiency.

ADVANCE PRICING AGREEMENTS

To introduce some certainty into the transfer pricing issue, the United States originated and actively promotes the use of advance pricing agreements (APAs). An APA is an agreement between a company and the IRS to apply an agreed-on transfer pricing method to specified transactions. The IRS agrees not to seek any transfer pricing adjustments for transactions covered by the APA if the company uses the agreed-on method. A unilateral APA is an agreement between a taxpayer and the IRS establishing an approved transfer pricing method for U.S. tax purposes. Whenever possible, the IRS will also negotiate the terms of the APA with foreign tax authorities to create a bilateral APA, which is an agreement between the IRS and one or more foreign tax authorities that the transfer pricing method is correct.

---

[18] Ibid., p. 15.
[19] PricewaterhouseCoopers, *International Transfer Pricing 2009*, p. ii.

The APA process consists of five phases: (1) application; (2) due diligence; (3) analysis; (4) discussion and agreement; and (5) drafting, review, and execution. The request for an APA involves the company proposing a particular transfer pricing method to be used in specific transactions. Generally, one of the methods required to be followed by Treasury Regulations will be requested, but another method can be requested if none of the methods specified in the regulations is applicable or practical. In considering the request for an APA, the IRS is likely to require the following information as part of the application:

1. An explanation of the proposed methodology.
2. A description of the company and its related party's business operations.
3. An analysis of the company's competitors.
4. Data on the industry showing pricing practices and rates of return on comparable transactions between unrelated parties.

For most taxpayers, the APA application is a substantial document filling several binders.[20]

The clear advantage to negotiating an APA is the assurance that the prices determined using the agreed-on transfer pricing method will not be challenged by the IRS. Disadvantages of the APA are that it can be very time-consuming to negotiate and that it involves disclosing a great deal of information to the IRS. The IRS indicates that new unilateral agreements take an average of 25 months to negotiate and bilateral agreements take even longer (45 months).[21] Although thousands of companies engage in transactions that cross U.S. borders, by the end of 2009 only 904 APAs had been executed since the program's inception in 1991.

The first completed APA was for sales between Apple Computer Inc. and its Australian subsidiary. In 1992, Japan's largest consumer electronics firm, Matsushita (known for its Panasonic and Technics brands), announced that after two years of negotiation it had entered into an APA with both the IRS and the Japanese National Tax Administration.[22] Companies in the computer and electronics product manufacturing industry have been the greatest users of APAs.

Foreign companies with U.S. operations are as likely to request an APA as U.S. companies with foreign operations. Of a total of 61 APAs that were executed in 2009, 74 percent were between a U.S. subsidiary or branch and its foreign parent, and 26 percent involved transactions between a U.S. parent and its foreign subsidiary.[23] Through the end of 2009, almost 60 percent of all APAs were with foreign parents of U.S. companies.

In 1998, the IRS instituted an APA program for "small business taxpayers" that somewhat streamlines the process of negotiating an APA. IRS Notice 98-65 describes the special APA procedures for small businesses. In 2009, four new small-business-taxpayer APAs were completed, taking an average of 12.5 months to complete.[24]

[20] U.S. Internal Revenue Service, "Announcement and Report Concerning Advance Pricing Agreements," *Internal Revenue Bulletin: 2010–21,* April 12, 2010.

[21] Ibid., Table 2.

[22] "Big Japan Concern Reaches an Accord on Paying U.S. Tax," *New York Times,* November 11, 1992, p. A1.

[23] U.S. Internal Revenue Service, "Announcement and Report Concerning Advance Pricing Agreements," *Internal Revenue Bulletin: 2010–21,* April 12, 2010, Table 13.

[24] Ibid., Tables 10 and 11.

Most APAs cover transactions that involve a number of business functions and risks. For example, manufacturing firms typically conduct research and development, design and engineer products, manufacture products, market and distribute products, and provide after-sales services. Risks include market risks, financial risks, credit risks, product liability risks, and general business risks. The IRS indicates that in the APA evaluation process "a significant amount of time and effort is devoted to understanding how the functions and risks are allocated amongst the controlled group of companies that are party to the covered transactions."[25] To facilitate this evaluation, the company must provide a functional analysis as part of the APA application. The functional analysis identifies the economic activities performed, the assets employed, the costs incurred, and risks assumed by each of the related parties. The purpose is to determine the relative value being added by each function and therefore by each related party. The IRS uses the economic theory that higher risks demand higher returns and that different functions have different opportunity costs in making its evaluation. Each IRS APA team generally includes an economist to help with this analysis.

Sales of tangible property are the type of intercompany transaction most frequently covered by an APA, and the comparable profits method is the transfer pricing method most commonly applied.[26] This is because reliable public data on comparable business activities of uncontrolled companies may be more readily available than potential comparable uncontrolled price data, ruling out the CUP method. In addition, because the comparable profits method relies on operating profit margin rather than gross profit margin (as do the resale price and cost-plus methods), the comparable profits method is not as dependent on exact comparables being available. Companies that perform different functions may have very different gross profit margins, but earn similar levels of operating profit. The CPM also tends to be less sensitive than other methods to differences in accounting practices such as whether expenses are classified as cost of goods sold or as operating expenses.

A relatively large number of countries have developed their own APA programs. France introduced a procedure for APAs in 1999, and in 2000 the Ministry of Finance in Indonesia announced proposals to introduce APAs. Other countries in which APAs are available include, but are not limited to, Australia, Brazil, Canada, China, Germany, Japan, Korea, Mexico, Taiwan, the United Kingdom, and Venezuela. MNC respondents to a recent survey named 28 different countries in which they have some form of APA, with the United States, the United Kingdom, and Australia being the most popular places to create APAs.[27]

ENFORCEMENT OF TRANSFER PRICING REGULATIONS

The United States has made periodic attempts over the years to make sure that MNCs doing business in the United States pay their fair share of taxes. Enforcement has concentrated on foreign companies with U.S. subsidiaries, but U.S. companies with foreign operations also have been targeted. Anecdotal evidence suggests that foreign companies are using discretionary transfer pricing to waft profits out of the United States back to their home country. In one case cited in a *Newsweek* article, a foreign manufacturer was found to sell TV sets to its U.S.

[25] Ibid.

[26] Ibid., Table 19.

[27] Ernst & Young, *2007–2008 Global Transfer Pricing Survey*, p. 17.

subsidiary for $250 each, but charged an unrelated U.S. company only $150.[28] In yet two additional cases, a foreign company was found to charge its U.S. distributor $13 apiece for razor blades, and a U.S. manufacturer sold bulldozers to its foreign parent for only $551 a piece.[29] As a result, foreign companies doing business in the United States are able to pay little or no U.S. income tax. For example, according to the IRS, "Yamaha Motor U.S.A. paid only $5,272 in corporate tax to Washington over four years. Proper accounting would have shown a profit of $500 million and taxes of $127 million."[30]

In two of its biggest victories in the 1980s, the IRS was able to make the case that Toyota and Nissan had overcharged their U.S. subsidiaries for products imported into the United States. Nissan paid $1.85 billion and Toyota paid $850 million to the U.S. government as a result of adjustments made by the IRS. In both cases, however, the competent authorities in the United States and Japan agreed on the adjustments and the Japanese government paid appropriate refunds to the companies. In effect, tax revenues previously collected by the Japanese tax authority were given to the IRS. Japanese companies are not the only ones found to violate transfer pricing regulations. In a well-publicized case, Coca-Cola Japan was found by the Japanese tax authority to overpay royalties to its parent by about $360 million. In another case, the IRS proposed an adjustment to Texaco's taxable income of some $140 million.

In 1994, the IRS was armed with the ability to impose penalties (discussed earlier) for misstating taxable income through the use of non-arm's-length transfer prices. The administration hoped that the threat of additional penalties would provide an incentive for companies to comply with the regulations.

The transfer pricing saga continues. In 2004, the U.S. General Accounting Office released a report indicating that a majority of large corporations paid no U.S. income tax for the period 1996–2000.[31] During that period, from 67 percent to 73 percent of foreign-controlled corporations and from 60 to 63 percent of U.S.-controlled corporations paid no federal income tax. As a result, Congress has put renewed pressure on the IRS to enhance its enforcement of transfer pricing regulations. Discretionary transfer pricing is likely to be an issue so long as intercompany transactions exist.

Worldwide Enforcement

Over the last several years, most major countries have strengthened their transfer pricing rules, often through documentation requirements and penalties, and have stepped up enforcement. One reason for the increased challenge to taxpayers on their transfer prices is that tax authorities view transfer pricing as a "soft target."[32] Because of the difficulty in proving their transfer price is acceptable, companies might prefer to simply pay the additional tax rather than engage in a lengthy, complicated dispute. The risks associated with local tax authorities scrutinizing a company's transfer prices are:

- Increased local tax liability.
- Potential double taxation.

---

[28] "The Corporate Shell Game," *Newsweek,* April 15, 1991, pp. 48–49.

[29] "Legislators Prepare to Crack Down on Transfer Pricing," *Accounting Today,* July 13–26, 1998, pp. 10, 13.

[30] "Corporate Shell Game."

[31] U.S. General Accounting Office, *Comparison of the Reported Tax Liabilities of Foreign- and U.S.-Controlled Corporations, 1996–2000,* February 2004, p. 15.

[32] PricewaterhouseCoopers, *International Transfer Pricing 2009,* p. 1.

- Penalties and interest on overdue tax.
- Uncertainty as to the group's worldwide tax burden.
- Problems in relationships with local tax authorities.

As evidence of the extent to which tax authorities investigate MNCs' transfer pricing policies, a survey conducted by Ernst & Young in 2007 discovered that more than 50 percent of MNC respondents experienced a transfer pricing audit somewhere in the world since 2003, and 78 percent thought that an audit was likely in the next two years.[33] More than one-fourth of completed audits resulted in an adjustment being made by a tax authority and penalties were imposed in 15 percent of those cases.

Worldwide, there are certain types of transfers and certain industries that are more at risk for examination by tax authorities. For example, imports are more likely to be scrutinized than exports, partly for political reasons. Exports help the balance of trade; imports do not, and they compete with the local workforce. In addition, royalties paid for the use of intangible assets such as brand names, management service fees, research and development conducted for related parties, and interest on intercompany loans are all high on tax authorities' radar screen for examination. Intercompany services are the type of transaction most likely to be audited.[34] The industry most at risk for a transfer pricing adjustment is pharmaceuticals.[35]

There are a number of red flags that can cause a tax authority to examine a company's transfer prices. The most important of these is if the company is less profitable than the tax authority believes it should be. For example, a domestic company with a foreign parent that makes losses year after year is likely to fall under scrutiny, especially if its competitors are profitable. Price changes and royalty rate changes are another red flag. Companies that have developed a poor relationship with the tax authority are also more likely to be scrutinized. A reputation for aggressive tax planning is one way to develop a poor relationship with the local tax authority.

Summary

1. Two factors heavily influence the manner in which international transfer prices are determined: (1) corporate objectives and (2) national tax laws.

2. The objective of establishing transfer prices to enhance performance evaluation and the objective of minimizing one or more types of cost through discretionary transfer pricing often conflict.

3. Cost-minimization objectives that can be achieved through discretionary transfer pricing include minimization of worldwide income tax, minimization of import duties, circumvention of repatriation restrictions, and improving the competitive position of foreign subsidiaries.

4. National tax authorities have guidelines regarding what will be considered an acceptable transfer price for tax purposes. These guidelines often rely on the concept of an arm's-length price.

---

[33] Ernst & Young, *2007–2008 Global Transfer Pricing Survey,* December 2007, p. 1.

[34] Ibid., p. 13.

[35] Ernst & Young (2007) discovered that 56 percent of audits in the worldwide pharmaceuticals industry resulted in a transfer pricing adjustment. The industry with the second-highest incidence of transfer pricing adjustment was consumer products at 31 percent.

5. Section 482 of the U.S. tax law gives the IRS the power to audit and adjust taxpayers' international transfer prices if they are not found to be in compliance with Treasury Department regulations. The IRS also may impose a penalty of up to 40 percent of the underpayment in the case of a gross valuation misstatement.

6. Treasury Regulations require the use of one of five specified methods to determine the arm's-length price in a sale of tangible property. The best-method rule requires taxpayers to use the method that under the facts and circumstances provides the most reliable measure of an arm's-length price. The comparable uncontrolled price method is generally considered to provide the most reliable measure of an arm's-length price when a comparable uncontrolled transaction exists.

7. Application of a particular transfer pricing method can result in an arm's-length range of prices. Companies can try to achieve cost-minimization objectives by selecting prices at the extremes of the relevant range.

8. Advance pricing agreements (APAs) are agreements between a company and a national tax authority on what is an acceptable transfer pricing method. So long as the agreed-on method is used, the company's transfer prices will not be adjusted.

9. Countries have been stepping up their enforcement of transfer pricing regulations. Transfer pricing is the most important international tax issue faced by MNCs internationally. The U.S. government is especially concerned with foreign MNCs not paying their fair share of taxes in the United States.

Questions

1. What are the various types of intercompany transactions for which a transfer price must be determined?

2. What are possible cost-minimization objectives that a multinational company might wish to achieve through transfer pricing?

3. What is the performance evaluation objective of transfer pricing?

4. Why is there often a conflict between the performance evaluation and cost minimization objectives of transfer pricing?

5. How can transfer pricing be used to reduce the amount of withholding taxes paid to a government on dividends remitted to a foreign stockholder?

6. According to U.S. tax regulations, what are the five methods to determine the arm's-length price in a sale of tangible property? How does the best-method rule affect the selection of a transfer pricing method?

7. What is the arm's-length range of transfer pricing, and how does it affect the selection of a transfer pricing method?

8. Under what conditions would a company apply for a correlative adjustment from a foreign tax authority? What effect do tax treaties have on this process?

9. What is an advance pricing agreement?

10. What are the costs and benefits associated with entering into an advance pricing agreement?

Exercises and Problems

1. Which of the following objectives is not achieved through the use of lower transfer prices?
   a. Improving the competitive position of a foreign operation.
   b. Minimizing import duties.
   c. Protecting foreign currency cash flows from currency devaluation.
   d. Minimizing income taxes when transferring to a lower-tax country.

2. Which of the following methods does U.S. tax law always require to be used in pricing intercompany transfers of tangible property?
   a. Comparable uncontrolled price method.
   b. Comparable profits method.
   c. Cost-plus method.
   d. Best method.

3. Which international organization has developed transfer pricing guidelines that are used as the basis for transfer pricing laws in several countries?
   a. World Bank.
   b. Organization for Economic Cooperation and Development.
   c. United Nations.
   d. International Accounting Standards Board.

4. Which of the following types of transaction is most likely to be audited?
   a. Sales of tangible property.
   b. Licenses of intangible property.
   c. Intercompany loans.
   d. Intercompany services.

5. Which of the following is not a method commonly used for establishing transfer prices?
   a. Cost-based transfer price.
   b. Negotiated price.
   c. Market-based transfer price.
   d. Industrywide transfer price.

6. Market-based transfer prices lead to optimal decisions in which of the following situations?
   a. When interdependencies between the related parties are minimal.
   b. When there is no advantage or disadvantage to buying and selling the product internally rather than externally.
   c. When the market for the product is perfectly competitive.
   d. All of the above.

7. U.S. Treasury Regulations require the use of one of five specified methods to determine the arm's-length price in a sale of tangible property. Which of the following is not one of those methods?
   a. Cost-plus method.
   b. Market-based method.
   c. Profit split method.
   d. Resale price method.

8. Which group has negotiated the greatest number of advance pricing agreements with the U.S. Internal Revenue Service (IRS)?
   a. Foreign parent companies with branches and subsidiaries in the United States.
   b. U.S. parent companies with branches and subsidiaries in Canada and Mexico.
   c. U.S. parent companies with branches and subsidiaries in Japan.
   d. None of the above.

9. The IRS has the authority to impose penalties on companies that significantly underpay taxes as a result of inappropriate transfer pricing. Acme Company transfers a product to a foreign affiliate at $15 per unit, and the IRS determines the correct price should have been $65 per unit. The adjustment results in an increase in U.S. tax liability of $1,250,000. Due to this change in price, by what amount will Acme Company's U.S. tax liability increase?
   a. $400,000
   b. $1,250,000
   c. $1,650,000
   d. $1,750,000

Use the following information to complete Exercises 10–12:

Babcock Company manufactures fast-baking ovens in the United States at a production cost of $500 per unit and sells them to uncontrolled distributors in the United States and a wholly owned sales subsidiary in Canada. Babcock's U.S. distributors sell the ovens to restaurants at a price of $1,000, and its Canadian subsidiary sells the ovens at a price of $1,100. Other distributors of ovens to restaurants in Canada normally earn a gross profit equal to 25 percent of selling price. Babcock's main competitor in the United States sells fast-baking ovens at an average 50 percent markup on cost. Babcock's Canadian sales subsidiary incurs operating costs, other than cost of goods sold, that average $250 per oven sold. The average operating profit margin earned by Canadian distributors of fast-baking ovens is 5 percent.

10. Which of the following would be an acceptable transfer price under the resale price method?
    a. $700
    b. $750
    c. $795
    d. $825

11. Which of the following would be an acceptable transfer price under the cost-plus method?
    a. $700
    b. $750
    c. $795
    d. $825

12. Which of the following would be an acceptable transfer price under the comparable profits method?
    a. $700
    b. $750
    c. $795
    d. $825

13. Lahdekorpi OY, a Finnish corporation, owns 100 percent of Three-O Company, a subsidiary incorporated in the United States.

Required:

Given the limited information provided, determine the best transfer pricing method and the appropriate transfer price in each of the following situations:

a. Lahdekorpi manufactures tablecloths at a cost of $20 each and sells them to unrelated distributors in Canada for $30 each. Lahdekorpi sells the same tablecloths to Three-O Company, which then sells them to retail customers in the United States.

b. Three-O Company manufactures men's flannel shirts at a cost of $10 each and sells them to Lahdekorpi, which sells the shirts in Finland at a retail price of $30 each. Lahdekorpi adds no significant value to the shirts. Finnish retailers of men's clothing normally earn a gross profit of 40 percent on sales price.

c. Lahdekorpi manufacturers wooden puzzles at a cost of $2 each and sells them to Three-O Company for distribution in the United States. Other Finnish puzzle manufacturers sell their product to unrelated customers and normally earn a gross profit equal to 50 percent of the production cost.

14. Superior Brakes Corporation manufactures truck brakes at its plant in Mansfield, Ohio, at a cost of $10 per unit. Superior sells its brakes directly to U.S. truck makers at a price of $15 per unit. It also sells its brakes to a wholly owned sales subsidiary in Brazil that, in turn, sells the brakes to Brazilian truck makers at a price of $16 per unit. Transportation cost from Ohio to Brazil is $0.20 per unit. Superior's sole competitor in Brazil is Bomfreio SA, which manufactures truck brakes at a cost of $12 per unit and sells them directly to truck makers at a price of $16 per unit. There are no substantive differences between the brakes manufactured by Superior and Bomfreio.

Required:

Given the information provided, discuss the issues related to using (a) the comparable uncontrolled price method, (b) the resale price method, and (c) the cost-plus method to determine an acceptable transfer price for the sale of truck brakes from Superior Brakes Corporation to its Brazilian subsidiary.

15. Akku Company imports die-cast parts from its German subsidiary that are used in the production of children's toys. Per unit, part 169 costs the German subsidiary $1.00 to produce and $0.20 to ship to Akku Company. Akku Company uses part 169 to produce a toy airplane that it sells to U.S. toy stores for $4.50 per unit. The following tax rates apply:

German income tax	40%
U.S. income tax	35%
U.S. import duty	10% of invoice price

Required:

a. Determine the total amount of taxes and duties paid to the U.S. and German governments if part 169 is sold to Akku Company at a price of $1.50 per unit.

b. Determine the total amount of taxes and duties paid to the U.S. and German governments if part 169 is sold to Akku Company at a price of $1.80 per unit.

c. Explain why the results obtained in parts (a) and (b) differ.

16. Smith-Jones Company, a U.S.-based corporation, owns 100 percent of Joal SA, located in Guadalajara, Mexico. Joal manufactures premium leather handbags at a cost of 500 Mexican pesos each. Joal sells its handbags to Smith-Jones, which sells them under Joal's brand name in its retail stores in the United States. Joal also sells handbags to an uncontrolled wholesaler in the United States. Joal invoices all sales to U.S. customers in U.S. dollars. Because the customer is not allowed to use Joal's brand name, it affixes its own label to the handbags and sells them to retailers at a markup on cost of 30 percent. Other U.S. retailers import premium leather handbags from uncontrolled suppliers in Italy, making payment in euros, and sell them to generate gross profit margins equal to 25 percent of selling price. Imported Italian leather handbags are of similar quality to those produced by Joal. Bolsa SA also produces handbags in Mexico and sells them directly to Mexican retailers earning a gross profit equal to 60 percent of production cost. However, Bolsa's handbags are of lesser quality than Joal's due to the use of a less complex manufacturing process, and the two companies' handbags do not compete directly.

    Required:
    a. Given the facts presented, discuss the various factors that affect the reliability of (1) the comparable uncontrolled price method, (2) the resale price method, and (3) the cost-plus method.
    b. Select the method from those listed in (a) that you believe is best, and describe any adjustment that might be necessary to develop a more reliable transfer price.

17. Guari Company, based in Melbourne, Australia, has a wholly owned subsidiary in Taiwan. The Taiwanese subsidiary manufactures bicycles at a cost equal to A$20 per bicycle, which it sells to Guari at an FOB shipping point price of A$100 each. Guari pays shipping costs of A$10 per bicycle and an import duty of 10 percent on the A$100 invoice price. Guari sells the bicycles in Australia for A$200 each. The Australian tax authority discovers that Guari's Taiwanese subsidiary also sells its bicycles to uncontrolled Australian customers at a price of A$80 each. Accordingly, the Australian tax authority makes a transfer pricing adjustment to Guari's tax return, which decreases Guari's cost of goods sold by A$20 per bicycle. An offsetting adjustment (refund) is made for the import duty previously paid. The effective income tax rate in Taiwan is 25 percent, and Guari's effective income tax rate is 36 percent.

    Required:
    a. Determine the total amount of income taxes and import duty paid on each bicycle (in Australian dollars) under each of the following situations:
       (1) Before the Australian tax authority makes a transfer pricing adjustment.
       (2) After the Australian tax authority makes a transfer pricing adjustment (assume the tax authority in Taiwan provides a correlative adjustment).
       (3) After the Australian tax authority makes a transfer pricing adjustment (assume the tax authority in Taiwan does not provide a correlative adjustment).
    b. Discuss Guari Company management's decision to allow its Taiwanese subsidiary to charge a higher price to Guari than to uncontrolled customers in Australia.

c. Assess the likelihood that the Taiwanese tax authority will provide a correlative adjustment to Guari Company.

18. ABC Company has subsidiaries in Countries X, Y, and Z. Each subsidiary manufactures one product at a cost of $10 per unit that it sells to each of its sister subsidiaries. Each buyer then distributes the product in its local market at a price of $15 per unit. The following information applies:

	Country X	Country Y	Country Z
Income tax rate	20%	30%	40%
Import duty	20%	10%	0%

Import duties are levied on the invoice price and are deductible for income tax purposes.

Required:
Formulate a transfer pricing strategy for each of the six intercompany sales between the three subsidiaries, X, Y, and Z, that would minimize the amount of income taxes and import duties paid by ABC Company.

19. Denker Corporation has a wholly owned subsidiary in Sri Lanka that manufactures wooden bowls at a cost of $3 per unit. Denker imports the wooden bowls and sells them to retailers at a price of $12 per unit. The following information applies:

	United States	Sri Lanka
Income tax rate	35%	30%
Import duty	10%	—
Withholding tax rate on dividends	—	10%

Import duties are levied on the invoice price and are deductible for income tax purposes. The Sri Lankan subsidiary must repatriate 100 percent of after-tax income to Denker each year. Denker has determined an arm's-length range of reliable transfer prices to be $5.00–$6.00.

Required:
a. Determine the transfer price within the arm's-length range that would maximize Denker's after-tax cash flow from the sale of wooden bowls.
b. Now assume that the withholding tax rate on dividends is 0 percent. Determine the transfer price within the arm's-length range that would maximize Denker's after-tax cash flow from the sale of wooden bowls.

20. Ranger Company, a U.S. taxpayer, manufactures and sells medical products for animals. Ranger holds the patent on Z-meal, which it sells to horse ranchers in the United States. Ranger Company licenses its Bolivian subsidiary, Yery SA, to manufacture and sell Z-meal in South America. Through extensive product development and marketing Yery has developed a South American llama market for Z-meal, which it sells under the brand name Llameal. Yery's sales of Llameal in Year 1 were $800,000 and its operating expenses

related to these sales, excluding royalties, were $600,000. The IRS has determined the following:

Value of Yery's operating assets used in the production of Z-meal	$300,000
Fair market return on operating assets	20%
Percentage of Ranger's worldwide sales attributable to its intangibles	10%
Percentage of Yery's sales attributable to its intangibles	15%

Required:

Determine the amount that Ranger would charge as a license fee to Yery in Year 1 under the residual profit split method.

Case 12-1

Litchfield Corporation

Litchfield Corporation is a U.S.-based manufacturer of fashion accessories that produces umbrellas in its plant in Roanoke, Virginia, and sells directly to retailers in the United States. As chief financial officer, you are responsible for all of the company's finance, accounting, and tax-related issues.

Sarah Litchfield, chief executive officer and majority shareholder, has informed you of her plan to begin exporting to the United Kingdom, where she believes there is a substantial market for Litchfield umbrellas. Rather than selling directly to British umbrella retailers, she plans to establish a wholly owned UK sales subsidiary that would purchase umbrellas from its U.S. parent and then distribute them in the United Kingdom. Yesterday, you received the following memo from Sarah Litchfield.

Memorandum

SUBJECT: Export Sales Prices

It has come to my attention that the corporate income tax rate in Great Britain is only 28 percent, as compared to the 35 percent rate we pay here in the United States. Since our average production cost is $15.00 per unit and the price we expect to sell to UK retailers is $25.00 per unit, why don't we plan to sell to our UK subsidiary at $15.00 per unit. That way we make no profit here in the United States and $10.00 of profit in the United Kingdom, where we pay a lower tax rate. We have plans to invest in a factory in Scotland in the next few years anyway, so we can keep the profit we earn over there for that purpose. What do you think?

Required

Draft a memo responding to Sarah Litchfield's question by explaining U.S. income tax regulations related to the export sales described in her memo. Include a discussion of any significant risks associated with her proposal. Make a recommendation with respect to how the price for these sales might be determined.

Case 12-2

Global Electronics Company

Global Electronics Company (GEC), a U.S. taxpayer, manufactures laser guitars in its Malaysian operation (LG-Malay) at a production cost of $120 per unit. LG-Malay guitars are sold to two customers in the United States—Electronic Superstores (a GEC wholly owned subsidiary) and Walmart (an unaffiliated customer). The cost to transport the guitars to the United States is $15 per unit and is paid by LG-Malay. Other Malaysian manufacturers of laser guitars sell to customers in the United States at a markup on total cost (production plus transportation) of 40 percent. LG-Malay sells guitars to Walmart at a landed price of $180 per unit (LG-Malay pays transportation costs). Walmart pays applicable U.S. import duties of 20 percent on its purchases of laser guitars. Electronic Superstores also pays import duties on its purchases from LG-Malay. Consistent with industry practice, Walmart places a 50 percent markup on laser guitars and sells them at a retail price of $324 per unit. Electronic Superstores sells LG-Malay guitars at a retail price of $333 per unit.

LG-Malay is a Malaysian taxpayer and Electronic Superstores is a U.S. taxpayer. Assume the following tax rates apply:

U.S. ad valorem import duty	20%
U.S. corporate income tax rate	35%
Malaysian income tax rate	15%
Malaysian withholding tax rate	30%

Required

1. Determine three possible prices for the sale of laser guitars from LG-Malay to Electronic Superstores that comply with U.S. tax regulations under (*a*) the comparable uncontrolled price method, (*b*) the resale price method, and (*c*) the cost-plus method. Assume that none of the three methods is clearly the best method and that GEC would be able to justify any of the three prices for both U.S. and Malaysian tax purposes.

2. Assume that LG-Malay's profits are *not* repatriated back to GEC in the United States as a dividend. Determine which of the three possible transfer prices maximizes GEC's consolidated after-tax net income. Show your calculation of consolidated net income for all three prices. You can assume that Electronic Superstores distributes 100 percent of its income to GEC as a dividend. However, there is a 100 percent exclusion for dividends received from a domestic subsidiary, so GEC will not pay additional taxes on dividends received from Electronic Superstores. Only Electronic Superstores pays taxes on the income it earns.

3. Assume that LG-Malay's profits *are* repatriated back to GEC in the United States as a dividend and that Electronic Superstores profits are paid to GEC as a dividend. Determine which of the three possible transfer prices maximizes net after-tax cash flow to GEC. Remember that dividends repatriated back to the United States are taxable in the United States and that an indirect foreign tax credit will be allowed by the U.S. government for taxes deemed to have been

paid to the Malaysian government on the repatriated dividend. Show your calculation of net after-tax cash flow for all three prices.

4. Assume the same facts as in (3) except that a United States/Malaysia income tax treaty reduces withholding taxes on dividends to 10 percent. Determine which of the three possible transfer prices maximizes net cash flow to GEC. Don't forget to consider foreign tax credits. Show your calculation of net cash flow for all three prices.

References

"Big Japan Concern Reaches an Accord on Paying U.S. Tax." *New York Times,* November 11, 1992, p. A1.

Chan, K. Hung, and Agnes W.Y. Lo. "The Influence of Managerial Perception of Environmental Variables on the Choice of International Transfer-Pricing Methods." *International Journal of Accounting,* 39 (2004), pp. 93–110.

"The Corporate Shell Game." *Newsweek,* April 15, 1991, pp. 48–49.

Eccles, Robert G. *The Transfer Pricing Problem: A Theory for Practice.* Lexington, MA: Lexington Books, 1985.

Ernst & Young. *2007–2008 Global Transfer Pricing Survey,* December 2007, available at www.ey.com.

Horngren, Charles T.; Srikant M. Datar; George Foster; Madhav Ragan; and Christopher Ittner. *Cost Accounting: A Managerial Emphasis,* 13th ed. Upper Saddle River, NJ: Prentice Hall, 2009.

Maher, Michael W.; Clyde P. Stickney; and Roman L. Weil. *Managerial Accounting,* 8th ed. Mason, OH: South-Western, 2004.

PricewaterhouseCoopers. *International Transfer Pricing 2009,* available at www.pwc.com.

Tang, Roger Y. W. "Transfer Pricing in the 1990s." *Management Accounting,* February 1992, pp. 22–26.

———, and K. H. Chan. "Environmental Variables of International Transfer Pricing: A Japan-United States Comparison." *Abacus,* June, 1979, pp. 3–12.

U.S. Department of Commerce. "U.S. Goods Trade: Imports and Exports by Related Parties 2009." *U.S. Department of Commerce News,* May 12, 2010.

U.S. General Accounting Office. *Comparison of the Reported Tax Liabilities of Foreign- and U.S.-Controlled Corporations, 1996–2000,* February 2004, available at www.gao.gov.

U.S. Internal Revenue Service. "Announcement and Report Concerning Advance Pricing Agreements." *Internal Revenue Bulletin: 2010–21,* April 12, 2010.

Chapter **Thirteen**

Strategic Accounting Issues in Multinational Corporations

Learning Objectives

After reading this chapter, you should be able to

- Explain the role played by accounting in formulating multinational business strategy.
- Demonstrate an understanding of multinational capital budgeting.
- Describe the factors that influence strategy implementation within a multinational corporation.
- Discuss the role of accounting in implementing multinational business strategy.
- Identify issues involved in the design and implementation of an effective performance evaluation system within a multinational corporation.

INTRODUCTION

Strategies are grand plans that reflect the future direction of the organization as determined by senior management. A decision by a multinational corporation (MNC) to achieve at least 50 percent of the market share for one of its products in a particular foreign country within a specified period of time is an example of a strategic decision. *Strategic planning* refers to the determination of long-term goals and objectives of a firm, and the adoption of courses of action and the allocation of resources necessary for achieving these goals.[1] The strategic issues facing both domestic and multinational firms are similar in many respects and can be identified in two broad categories—strategy formulation and strategy implementation.

Strategy formulation is the process of deciding on the goals of the organization and the strategies for attaining those goals. This process involves both the revision of existing goals and plans and the adoption of new ones. At any point, therefore, an organization operates in accordance with a set of goals and strategies that it has adopted previously. The decisions made in formulating strategy have a long-term

[1] A. D. Chandler Jr., *Strategy and Structure* (Cambridge, MA: MIT Press, 1962), p. 13.

focus and include a capital budgeting decision, that is, decisions related to making long-term capital investments.

Strategy implementation refers to the process by which managers influence other members of the organization to behave in accordance with the organization's goals. Managerial influence is also known as *management control.* Two very important management control activities are preparing operating budgets and evaluating the performance of decentralized operations. Operating budgets are plans for the future expressed in quantitative terms that generally cover one year. Budgets provide a means for communicating management's plans throughout the organization. *Performance evaluation* is the task of ascertaining the extent to which organizational goals have been achieved. Identifying and rewarding good performance is important in achieving strategic goals. Performance is often evaluated by comparing actual results with expected results as summarized in the operating budget.

The accounting function within an organization plays an important role in strategy formulation and implementation through the activities of capital budgeting, operational budgeting, and performance evaluation. This chapter focuses on issues specifically related to carrying out these activities for foreign investments and foreign operations, including issues related to foreign currency fluctuations and the differences in culture and business environment that exist across countries.

STRATEGY FORMULATION

Information is the key to strategy formulation. Formulating a strategy involves analyzing information about both internal and external factors. Internal factors relate to the levels of skills and know-how available within the organization in such areas as technology, manufacturing, marketing, and distribution and the culture within the organization, whereas external factors relate to the competitors, customers, and suppliers, as well as to other regulatory, social, and political factors. The analysis of these factors allows managers to identify opportunities and match them with available resources to determine strategies (see Exhibit 13.1).[2] The primary objective of formulating strategy is to ensure that the organization attains its goals, which are usually aimed at increasing firm value. Accounting can help in formulating strategy by quantifying opportunities and threats, as well as strengths and weaknesses, and by developing projections of costs and benefits as financial expressions of strategy. Exhibit 13.2 provides an example of the mid-term strategy of a corporation as described in its 2009 annual report.

Accounting's primary contribution to MNC strategy formulation comes through the budgeting process. Preparing a budget is the initial step in implementing change in an organization. An important function of budgeting is to transfer information to decision makers. Budgeting forces managers to think about strategy because it formalizes the responsibilities for both short-term and long-term planning. Budgeting also identifies specific expectations that can be used as the basis for evaluating subsequent performance. We focus on capital budgeting in the remainder of this section.

[2] Robert N. Anthony and Vijay Govindarajan, *Management Control Systems,* 9th ed. (international ed.) (New York: McGraw-Hill, 1998), p. 54.

EXHIBIT 13.1
Strategy
Formulation

Source: Robert N. Anthony
and Vijay Govindarajan,
Management Control Systems,
9th ed. (international ed.)
(New York: McGraw-Hill,
1998), p. 54.

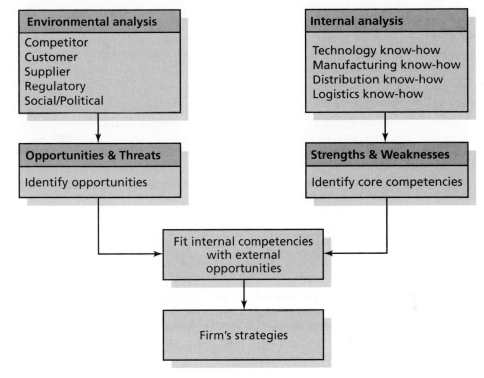

EXHIBIT 13.2

Mid-term Strategy of Sony Corporation as described by its CEO in the annual report 2009

Mid-Term Strategy

While we certainly improved our profitability dramatically in fiscal year 2009, we need to continue to transform the company to achieve our targets of a 5 percent operating profit margin and a 10 percent return on equity (ROE) in the mid-term (by the year ending March 31, 2013). To be successful, we must generate growth with consistent profitability in all of our core businesses—particularly our television and game businesses—and aggressively develop new business including network services.

Televisions

Bringing our TV business to profitability is a key short-term objective, while growing our business to a leading market position is the key mid-term objective. Although it recorded an operating loss, profitability in the TV business improved dramatically in fiscal year 2009, due to a complete overhaul of the business' cost structure and supply chain.

We have an innovative new product lineup and an aggressive sales plan with a continuously revitalized cost structure. As a result, we are targeting profitability in LCD TVs in fiscal year 2010. In addition, this autumn we will launch the Sony Internet TV. Developed in collaboration with Google, Sony Internet TV is an exciting new generation of television that not only offers new forms of enjoyment through unprecedented internet integration, but is also able to "evolve" through the download of applications. We are also developing the next generation of TV display, and over the medium term are targeting a 20 percent market share.

Game

As mentioned earlier, the PlayStation®3 platform has been gaining momentum since the launch of the slimmer, lighter and attractively priced PS3™ last year. Through continued manufacturing cost reductions on PS3™ hardware as well as an expected increase in PS3™ software sales—both disc-based and online—we are targeting profitability in the game business in fiscal year 2010.

Going forward, we will strive to make the best use of PS3™'s unique strengths to create new user experiences and generate sales. PlayStation®Move features a new motion controller that, when combined with the PlayStation®Eye camera, can very precisely track users' movements to add a new dimension to PS3™ games. Additionally, as a core aspect of Sony's Groupwide launch of 3D products, we have commenced the era of 3D gaming by enabling all existing PS3™s to be upgraded to 3D-compatibility with a free firmware download, and will release our own 3D game titles and continue to actively support the development of 3D games by third-party software developers.

Continued

EXHIBIT 13.2   *(Continued)*

Digital Imaging

Our high-margin digital imaging business, which includes cameras and camcorders, aims to maintain its leading position as the number one digital imaging brand in the world. We must continue strengthening this business through outstanding product differentiation and cost competitiveness based on key devices such as image sensors, lenses and signal processors—the pillars of our superior technology.

Great examples of this effort are our recently announced compact interchangeable lens digital cameras, which are the world's smallest and lightest*[3] of their kind, and provide the quality of a digital single lens reflex (DSLR) camera in a very compact body. At the same time, we will expand entry-segment products with increased cost competitiveness into growing markets, including developing countries. No matter the region or price point, we must constantly reinvigorate the market by offering new ways for customers to enjoy our products.

Going forward, many of Sony's digital imaging devices will be network compatible and, through our network services, will allow customers to easily upload and share their images and video with their families and friends.

3D

From black-and-white, to color, to high definition (HD), Sony has been the leader in the display of content on television. And now, with consumers and the electronics and content industries abuzz with the exciting prospects of 3D technology, we intend to take the lead in 3D.

Sony has a unique position in 3D—from the professional-use cameras that capture the images, to editing and projecting equipment, to televisions, Blu-ray Disc™ players, PS3™ and more—we are the leader in professional and consumer 3D hardware. We are also industry leaders in the production of 3D film and game content, and we also continue to work with our partners to provide the most compelling 3D content imaginable. From the lens to the living room, Sony is the only company fully immersed in every link of the 3D value chain.

Here are some examples. This June, the entire Sony Group is working in unison to bring the world of 3D to consumers' homes. In addition to launching our first Full HD 3D-integrated TVs and Blu-ray Disc players, as mentioned earlier, all existing PS3™ units (over 35 million) are already firmware upgradable to support 3D games, and will be upgradable to support 3D Blu-ray Disc playback within 2010, making PS3™ our foothold for bringing more 3D products into the living room.

In addition, we will bring 3D content into consumers' homes, starting with the 2010 FIFA World Cup™ this summer. And, together with IMAX Corporation and Discovery Communications, Inc., we are also developing the first dedicated 3D television network in the United States, and we also expect to introduce more 3D-compatible products in the near future, including VAIO and digital imaging products.

Our goal is to become the undisputed global leader in 3D. Thanks to our dedicated team at Sony, our industry-leading partners and the spirit of "make believe", we are well on the way to making this a reality.

Network Services & Mobile Products

The world of 3D is just one of many exciting new developments going on at Sony. Equally important to Sony is expanding our network service to a broader range of consumer products, bringing our products to life in the digital age.

Since we launched the PlayStation®Network (PSN) with the introduction of PS3™ in 2006, we have continuously expanded both game and non-game content being delivered through this service, and we now have online storefronts in 36 countries, delivering content to more than 47 million registered accounts as of the end of April 2010.

We have developed and launched Qriocity, a new online service platform based upon PSN. Qriocity connects many of Sony's network-enabled devices and allows consumers to enjoy high-quality entertainment across multiple devices. The first service powered by Qriocity is a video service that was launched in April 2010 in the United States, compatible with 2010 model network-enabled BRAVIA TVs and Blu-ray Disc players, as well as VAIO and other Windows-based PCs. With our network services, we are now offering a rich assortment of content, including movies, television programming, games, eBooks and more.

Our Reader digital books, as noted, have generated buzz and have strong growth prospects. Another exciting, innovative product is the Dash™ Personal Internet Viewer, which has just gone on sale in North America, and is designed to deliver personalized content from the Internet or from our network services at a glance. The continued development of innovative, networked mobile products is an important way to utilize our network services, and one of the core missions of the Networked Products & Services Group.

With these initiatives and many more, Sony has taken decisive steps to fulfill the promise of the Sony total experience—differentiating, as well as connecting, our products with stunning design and cutting-edge technology, providing unique network services and content, and embracing open platforms. We aim to establish a more intimate and rich relationship with the consumer, thus increasing the value and desirability of Sony products, as well as that of the Sony brand overall.

---

*[3] "α" NEX-5, the smallest and lightest interchangeable lens digital camera body, as of May 11, 2010.

Sony is also fully committed to putting its innovative spirit and technological expertise to use to help solve environmental challenges, from our long history with the development of superior rechargeable battery technology, to our highly successful program to take back our own products for recycling, all to provide our customers with the environmentally conscious products that they are asking for. Sony has also recently announced a new set of Green Targets, where we will strive to lower every product's power consumption by 30 percent versus 2008 levels, with a long-term goal of achieving a "Zero Environmental Footprint".

We know what we must do. We must develop the game-changing products, technologies and services that will excite our customers and deliver entirely new entertainment experiences. We must increase our speed to market with desirable and competitively priced products and services. And we must meet the aggressive financial targets we have set across all of our businesses, while maintaining integrity in everything we do, and conducting our business honestly and responsibly.

Collaboration across the Sony Group is stronger than ever, and our drive to transform this company is real and already delivering results. With Sony's ability to turn ideas into reality, and belief that anything we can imagine we can make real, I am confident that Sony will succeed and bring value to our shareholders. On behalf of the management team and all of the employees at Sony, I thank you for your continued support.

May 31, 2010

Howard Stringer
Chairman, CEO and President
Representative Corporate Executive Officer

Capital Budgeting

Multinational companies often need to commit large amounts of resources to projects with costs and benefits expected over a long period. Such projects are known as capital investments. Examples include the purchase of new equipment and the expansion into foreign territories through either greenfield investments or acquisition of existing operations. *Capital budgeting* is the process of identifying, evaluating, and selecting projects that require commitments of large sums of funds and generate benefits stretching well into the future. Sound capital investments are often a result of careful capital budgeting.[3] The evaluation of foreign investment opportunities involves a more complicated set of economic, political, and strategic considerations than those factors influencing most domestic investment decisions. Although the decision to undertake a particular foreign investment may be determined by a mix of factors, the specific project should be subjected to traditional investment analysis. We first explain the main features of traditional capital budgeting before considering the unique issues that need to be considered in foreign investment analysis.

The capital budgeting process includes three steps: (1) project identification and definition, (2) evaluation and selection, and (3) monitoring and review.[4] The first step is critical, because without a clear definition of a proposed investment project, it is difficult to estimate the associated revenues, expenses, and cash flows, which is an integral part of the second step. The second step involves identifying the cash inflows and outflows expected from a specific project and then using one or more capital budgeting techniques to determine whether the project is acceptable. The third step becomes important during implementation of the project. This refers to the possible need to alter the initial plan in response to changing circumstances.

[3] Edward J. Blocher, Kung H. Chen, Gary Cokins, and Thomas W. Lin, *Cost Management: A Strategic Emphasis* (New York: McGraw-Hill, 2005), p. 840.
[4] Ibid., p. 841.

EXHIBIT 13.3 Capital Investment Evaluation Techniques

Source: Adapted from Edward J. Blocher, Kung H. Chen, Gary Cokins, and Thomas W. Lin, *Cost Management: A Strategic Emphasis* (New York: McGraw-Hill, 2005), p. 881.

Technique	Definition	Computation Procedure	Advantages	Weaknesses
Payback period	Number of years to recover the initial investment	Number of years for the cumulative cash flow to equal the investment	• Simple to use and understand • Measures liquidity • Appraises risk	• Ignores timing and time value of money • Ignores cash flows beyond payback period
Book rate of return on investment (ROI)	Rate of average annual net income to the initial investment or average investment (book value)	Average net income ÷ Investment book value	• Data readily available • Consistent with other financial measures	• Ignores timing and time value of money • Uses accounting numbers rather than cash flows
Net present value (NPV)	Difference between the initial investment and the present value of subsequent net cash inflows discounted at a given interest rate	Present value of net cash inflows— Initial investment	• Consider time value of money • Uses realistic discount rate for reinvestment • Additive for combined projects	• Not meaningful for comparing projects requiring different amounts of investments • Favors large investments
Internal rate of return (IRR)	Discount rate that makes the initial investment equal the present value of subsequent net cash inflows	Solving the following equation for discount rate i: (Present value factor of i) Net cash inflows = Initial investment	• Considers time value of money • Easy for comparing projects requiring different amounts of investment	• Assumption on reinvestment rate of return could be unrealistic • Complex to compute if done manually

Capital Budgeting Techniques

There are four techniques often used in evaluating and making capital investment decisions: (1) payback period, (2) return on investment, (3) net present value, and (4) internal rate of return. The main features of these capital investment techniques are summarized in Exhibit 13.3.

Payback Period

The payback period of a project is the length of time required to recoup the initial investment. Calculation of payback period requires knowledge of the amount to be invested and an estimate of the after-tax cash flows to be received from the investment for each year of the project's life. For example, with an initial outlay of $600,000 and annual after-tax net cash inflows of $100,000, the payback period would be six years. If the decision rule is to accept only those projects with a payback period of five years or less, the company would reject an investment proposal with a payback period of six years. This is simple and straightforward. The length of payback period can be viewed as a measure of the investment's risk—the longer the payback period, the riskier the investment. The major limitations of this technique are its failure to consider the time value of money and an investment's total profitability. The use of payback period could lead to inappropriate investment decisions by rejecting investment proposals that provide larger cash inflows in the latter part of their useful lives. Payback period only considers the length of time required to recoup the initial investment regardless of the investment's total profitability.

Return on Investment

Calculation of return on investment (ROI) requires knowledge of the amount to be invested and an estimate of the average annual net income to be earned from an investment:

$$ROI = \frac{\text{Average annual net income}}{\text{Book value of investment}}$$

In using ROI for making capital budgeting decisions, a company must determine the minimum rate of return that makes an investment project worthwhile. Assume that a company requires ROI of at least 10 percent and has the following investment opportunities available:

Project	Required Investment	Average Annual Net Income
A.........	$800,000	$96,000
B.........	500,000	30,000
C.........	300,000	54,000

ROI for the three projects is as follows:

Project	ROI
A.............	12% ($96,000/$800,000)
B.............	6% ($30,000/$500,000)
C.............	18% ($54,000/$300,000)

Based on the company's decision rule, only projects A and C would be accepted because their ROI exceeds the 10 percent rate of return hurdle.

ROI is easy to compute using data from pro forma financial reports. Unlike payback period, it considers the entire period of an investment. However, it also ignores the time value of money. Further, it does not consider the possibility that a project may require other outlays such as working capital commitments in addition to the initial investment.

Discounted Cash Flow Techniques

Two discounted cash flow techniques are in common use in capital budgeting. They are (1) the net present value (NPV) method and (2) the internal rate of return (IRR) method. These techniques use present values of future cash flows in evaluating potential capital investments, using a discount rate. Usually the discount rate used is the firm's cost of capital or some other minimum rate of return. The Institute of Management Accountants defines cost of capital as "a composite of the cost of various sources of funds comprising a firm's capital structure."[5] A minimum

---

[5] Institute of Management Accountants, *Statement No. 4A: Cost of Capital* (Montvale, NJ: IMA, 1984), p. 1.

rate of return is often determined by referring to the strategic plan, the industry average rate of return, or other investment opportunities.

Net Present Value

The NPV of an investment is the difference between the initial investment and the sum of the present values of all future net cash inflows from the investment, calculated as follows:

$$\text{Present value of future net cash flows} - \text{Initial investment}$$
$$= \text{Net present value (NPV)}$$

The amount of NPV can be positive, negative, or zero. A positive NPV means that the investment is expected to provide a rate of return on the initial investment greater than the discount rate, whereas a negative NPV means the return provided would be less than the discount rate. If the NPV is zero, the project is expected to provide a rate of return exactly equal to the discount rate. The decision rule is to accept positive (or zero) NPV investment projects. Calculation of NPV requires knowledge of the amount of initial investment; estimation of future cash flows to be derived from the investment, including cash flows to be received upon the investment's liquidation (known as terminal value); and an appropriate discount rate based on the desired rate of return on investment.

Internal Rate of Return

A positive NPV implies that an investment's return exceeds the desired rate of return (discount rate), but it does not indicate the exact rate of return provided by the investment. This can be determined by calculating the internal rate of return (IRR). IRR is the discount rate that equates the present value of future net cash inflows to the initial investment. Essentially, a project's IRR is the discount rate at which NPV is equal to zero. The following example illustrates how IRR is determined.

IRR Illustration   Assume that a company is considering a potential investment with a four-year life, no terminal value, and the following estimated cash flows:

Total initial investment	$5,000
Net cash inflows for each of four years	$1,750

We solve the following equation to determine the present value (PV) of an annuity factor that equates the present value of the net cash inflows to the initial investment:

$$\$5,000 = \$1,750 \times \text{Present value of annuity factor (4 periods)}$$

$$\text{PV annuity factor (4 periods)} = \frac{\$5,000}{\$1,750} = 2.857$$

From a present value of annuity table, where number of periods is equal to 4, we find 2.857 to be the present value factor at a discount rate of 15 percent. Thus, the IRR for this investment project is 15 percent, which will be compared with the firm's desired rate of return in deciding whether to invest in this particular project.

Regardless of the technique used, the quality of the capital budgeting decision rests on the accuracy with which future cash flows can be estimated. Forecasting future income to be generated by a project is often the starting point for determining future cash flows.

Research shows that preference for a particular capital budgeting technique differs across countries. Shields and colleagues found that U.S. firms commonly use discounted cash flow techniques such as net present value and internal rate of return, whereas Japanese firms prefer payback period.[6] One explanation for Japanese firms' preference for payback period is that it is consistent with their corporate strategies. Many Japanese firms have adopted a strategy of creating competitive advantage through large investments in technology, and it is necessary to recoup the investment as quickly as possible to reinvest in new technologies. Another reason is that Japanese firms are increasingly competing on the basis of short product life cycles. This requires flexibility, and short payback periods increase flexibility. Japanese firms also recognize that with innovative products in the global market it is not feasible to predict cash flows in the distant future with meaningful accuracy.

Multinational Capital Budgeting

As noted earlier, application of NPV as the capital budgeting technique requires identification of the following:

1. The amount of initial capital invested.
2. Estimated future cash flows to be derived from the project over time.
3. An appropriate discount rate for determining present values.

Calculation of NPV for a foreign investment project is more complex than for a domestic project primarily because of the additional risks that affect future cash flows. The various risks facing MNCs broadly can be described as political risk, economic risk, and financial risk.

Political risk refers to the possibility that political events within a host country can adversely affect cash flows to be derived from an investment in that country. Nationalization or expropriation of assets by the host government with or without compensation to the investor is the most extreme form of political risk. Foreign exchange controls, profit repatriation restrictions, local content laws, changes in tax or labor laws, and requirements for additional local production are additional aspects of political risk. Cross-border transactions also can be affected by special rules and regulations imposed by foreign governments. For example, companies that export products to the European Union are required to comply with International Organization for Standardization (ISO) 9000 standards and certify that their products and quality control systems meet ISO 9000 minimum quality standards.

Economic risk refers to issues concerning the condition of the host country economy. Inflation and the country's balance of payments situation are aspects of economic risk. Continuous deterioration of the balance of payments situation of a country may lead to devaluation of its currency, which may aggravate the problem of inflation. Inflation affects the cost structure in an economy and the ability of the local population to afford goods and services. High inflation also increases the cost of doing business in a foreign country as managers invest time and resources in devising strategies to cope with rapidly changing prices.

Financial risk refers to the possibility of loss due to unexpected changes in currency values, interest rates, and other financial circumstances. The degree

---

[6] M. D. Shields, C. W. Chow, Y. Kato, and Y. Nakagawa, "Management Accounting Practices in the U.S. and Japan: Comparative Survey Findings and Research Implications," *Journal of International Financial Management and Accounting* 3, no. 1 (1991), pp. 61–77.

to which a firm is affected by exchange rate changes is called foreign exchange risk. As described later in this chapter, there are three types of exposure to foreign exchange risk—balance sheet exposure, transaction exposure, and economic exposure—all of which have an impact on cash flows.

The initial consideration in analyzing a potential foreign investment project is whether it should be evaluated on the basis of project cash flows (in local currency) or parent cash flows (in parent currency), taking into account the amounts, timing, and forms of transfers to the parent company. Project cash flows are especially susceptible to economic and political risk, whereas parent company cash flows can be significantly affected by political risk and foreign exchange risk. Survey results show that MNCs evaluate foreign investments from both project and parent viewpoints.[7]

Factors that vary across countries and should be considered in evaluating a potential foreign investment from a *project perspective* include the following:

1. *Taxes.* Income and other tax rates, import duties, and tax incentives directly affect cash flows.
2. *Rate of inflation.* Inflation can cause changes in a project's competitive position, cost structure, and cash flows over time.
3. *Political risk.* Host government intervention in the business environment, for example, through the imposition of local content laws or price controls, can alter expected cash flows.

Additional factors should be considered in evaluating a foreign investment from the *parent company perspective:*

1. *The form in which cash is remitted to the parent.* Different types of payments—dividends, interest, royalties—may be subject to different withholding tax rates.
2. *Expected changes in the exchange rate over the project's life.* This will directly affect the value to the parent of local cash flows.
3. *Political risk.* Foreign exchange and/or profit repatriation restrictions imposed by the host government may limit the amount of cash flow to the parent.

Incorporating these factors into the foreign investment analysis can be accomplished in two ways:

1. The factors are incorporated into estimates of expected future cash flows.
2. The discount rate used to determine the present value of expected future cash flows is adjusted (upward) to compensate for the risk associated with changes in these various factors.

It makes sense to use a common standard in choosing among competing foreign and domestic projects. Thus, making adjustments to the expected cash flows would seem to be more appropriate than making ad hoc, country-specific adjustments to the desired rate of return. While adjusting cash flows is preferable, it also is more difficult because it involves forecasting future foreign tax rates, foreign

---

[7] Vinod B. Bavishi, "Capital Budgeting Practices at Multinationals," *Management Accounting,* August 1981, pp. 32–35; and Marjorie Stanley and Stanley Block, "An Empirical Study of Management and Financial Variables Influencing Capital Budgeting Decisions for Multinational Corporations in the 1980s," *Management International Review* 3 (1983).

inflation rates, changes in exchange rates, and changes in foreign government policy. Sensitivity analysis, in which factors are varied over a relevant range of possible values, can show how sensitive the investment decision is to a particular factor. Because of the difficulty in adjusting cash flows, many companies adjust the discount rate instead. For example, a survey conducted in 1973 found that 49 percent of responding MNCs added a risk premium to their required rate of return in making foreign investment decisions.[8]

Next we illustrate how some of the complexities associated with the evaluation of potential foreign investments can be incorporated into the multinational capital budgeting process.

Illustration: Global Paper Company

Global Paper Company (GPC), a U.S.-based firm, is considering establishing a facility in Hungary to manufacture paper products locally. GPC is attracted to Hungary because of cheaper costs and substantial tax incentives offered by the local government. However, GPC is concerned about the stability of the political situation in Hungary. GPC has gathered the following information:

Initial investment. The proposed plant will be constructed in Year 0 on a turn-key basis such that GPC incurs its entire cash outflow on December 31, Year 0. The subsidiary will begin operations on January 1, Year 1. The total investment will be 50,000,000 forints (F), of which F 24,000,000 is for fixed assets to be depreciated on a straight-line basis over three years with no salvage value. The remaining F 26,000,000 is for working capital.

Financing. The project will be financed as follows:

Forint debt (10%)		F 15,000,000
Parent loan (10%)	$150,000 × F 100 =	F 15,000,000
Parent equity	$200,000 × F 100 =	F 20,000,000

The subsidiary will obtain a three-year F 15,000,000 loan from a local bank at an interest rate of 10 percent. GPC will lend the subsidiary $150,000 and make an equity investment of $200,000, for a total initial cash outlay of $350,000. The parent loan is denominated and will be repaid in U.S. dollars. Interest on the parent loan is paid at the end of each year (in U.S. dollars).

Inflation and exchange rates. Inflation in Hungary is expected to be 20 percent per year over the next three years. As a result, the forint is expected to depreciate 20 percent per year relative to the U.S. dollar. The January 1, Year 1, exchange rate is 100 forints to the dollar. Forecasted exchange rates over the next three years are as follows:

January 1, Year 1	F 100 per U.S. dollar
December 31, Year 1	F 120 per U.S. dollar
December 31, Year 2	F 144 per U.S. dollar
December 31, Year 3	F 172.8 per U.S. dollar

[8] J. C. Baker and L. J. Beardsley, "Multinational Companies' Use of Risk Evaluation and Profit Measurement for Capital Budgeting Decisions," *Journal of Business Finance,* Spring 1973, pp. 38–43.

Earnings. Expected earnings before interest and taxes (EBIT) is composed of the following:

- Sales—Year 1:
    Local: 200,000 units; sales price—F 50 per unit
    Export: 200,000 units; sales price—F 50 per unit

  Local sales in units are expected to increase 10 percent per year. Export sales in units are expected to increase by the rate of devaluation of the Hungarian forint (20 percent). The unit price (in forints) for both local and export sales is expected to increase by the rate of Hungarian inflation (20 percent).
- Variable costs (other than taxes)—40 percent of sales.
- Fixed costs (other than interest)—consists of depreciation on fixed assets only.

Taxes. The Hungarian corporate income tax rate is 25 percent, and the U.S. corporate tax rate is 35 percent. However, as an incentive to invest, the Hungarian government is offering a reduction in corporate income tax rates to 20 percent for the first three years. Hungarian withholding tax rates are 20 percent on interest and 30 percent on dividends and terminal value. Interest and dividends received in the United States from foreign sources are taxed as ordinary income and are allowed a foreign tax credit for foreign taxes paid. The repayment of the parent loan and receipt of terminal value is not taxed in the United States.

Political risk. Local political analysts have concluded that the Socialist Party might strengthen and beat the Government Party in the next election. GPC estimates this probability at 40 percent. If this occurs, it is possible that the new government will nationalize selected industries. With a change in government, GPC estimates that the probability that its Hungarian manufacturing facility would be nationalized is 60 percent. If the plant is nationalized, GPC expects that no terminal value will be recovered for the equity. However, the parent loan will still be repaid and local loans will not be repaid. If the plant is not nationalized, the company will receive its expected terminal value at the end of the third year. Given the timing of future elections, any change in government would take place at the end of the third year.

Terminal value. Cash flow forecasts are made for only three years. At the end of the third year the operation will be sold to local investors. The terminal value at the end of three years is expected to be equal to (1) the present value of an infinite stream of third-year cash flow from operations if no nationalization occurs and (2) zero if the project is nationalized.

Repatriation restrictions. Because of a shortage of foreign exchange, the Hungarian government allows only 50 percent of after-tax accounting income to be remitted as dividends to foreign parent corporations. This restriction is expected to exist for the foreseeable future. However, foreign exchange is readily available for interest and principal repayments on any foreign currency debt.

Weighted-average cost of capital. GPC's weighted-average cost of capital is 20 percent. In Hungary, similar projects would be expected to earn an after-tax return of 20 percent.

Present value factors. Present value factors at 20 percent are as follows:

Period	Factor
1	0.833
2	0.694
3	0.579

In making the decision whether to invest in Hungary, GPC's chief executive officer has requested that the accounting department conduct an analysis to determine the investment's expected NPV from both (1) a project perspective and (2) a parent company perspective.

Project Perspective

To calculate NPV from a project perspective, GPC begins by calculating cash flow from operations (CFO) in Hungarian forints over the three-year investment horizon using the following formula:

$$CFO = \text{Earnings (after tax)} + \text{Depreciation}$$

Depreciation is added back to after-tax earnings because it does not represent an annual cash outflow. Remember that sales volume and selling prices fluctuate each year. Export sales and the amount of Hungarian forint interest expense on the parent loan are a function of changes in the exchange rate.

GPC then calculates total annual cash flow (TACF) in Hungarian forints over the three-year investment horizon, where TACF is equal to CFO in Years 1 and 2. In year 3, TACF is equal to CFO plus terminal value minus repayment of local debt, if the project is not nationalized. If the project is nationalized, Year 3 TACF is equal to CFO only. TACF over the three-year life of the investment is determined as follows:

			Year 1			**Year 2**				**Year 3**
Calculation of Total Annual Cash Flow (in forints)										
Sales										
Local	200,000 u.	F50	F 10,000,000	220,000 u.	F60	F 13,200,000	242,000 u.	F72		F 17,424,000
Export	200,000 u.	F50	10,000,000	240,000 u.	F60	14,400,000	288,000 u.	F72		20,736,000
Total sales			20,000,000			27,600,000				38,160,000
Variable costs	40%		(8,000,000)	40%		(11,040,000)	40%			(15,264,000)
Depreciation			(8,000,000)			(8,000,000)				(8,000,000)
EBIT			4,000,000			8,560,000				14,896,000
Interest										
Local	F15,000,000	10%	(1,500,000)	F15,000,000	10%	(1,500,000)	F15,000,000	10%		(1,500,000)
Parent*	$15,000	120	(1,800,000)	$15,000	144	(2,160,000)	$15,000	172.8		(2,592,000)
Earnings before tax			700,000			4,900,000				10,804,000
Taxes		20%	(140,000)		20%	(980,000)		20%		(2,160,800)
Earnings after tax . .			560,000			3,920,000				8,643,200
Add: Depreciation . .			8,000,000			8,000,000				8,000,000
CFO			F 8,560,000			F 11,920,000				F 16,643,200
Terminal value[†]										83,216,000
Repayment of local debt										(15,000,000)
Total annual cash flow (without nationalization)			F 8,560,000			F 11,920,000				F 84,859,200
Total annual cash flow (with nationalization)			F 8,560,000			F 11,920,000				F 16,643,200

* Annual interest on parent loan is $15,000, which is translated into a larger amount of forints each year due to the expected decline in the value of the forint.

† Terminal value is equal to the present value of an infinite stream of Year 3 CFO calculated as: $16,643,200/0.20.

GPC next calculates the net present value of the TACF in Hungarian forints over the three-year investment horizon (1) without nationalization and (2) with nationalization, as follows:

Calculation of Net Present Value (without nationalization)		
TACF	**PV Factor**	**Present Value**
Year 1 . . . . F 8,560,000	0.833	F 7,130,480
Year 2 11,920,000	0.694	8,272,480
Year 3 84,859,200	0.579	49,133,477
		F 64,536,437
Less: Initial investment		(35,000,000)
NPV		F 29,536,437

Calculation of Net Present Value (with nationalization)		
TACF	**PV Factor**	**Present Value**
Year 1 . . . . F 8,560,000	0.833	F 7,130,480
Year 2 11,920,000	0.694	8,272,480
Year 3 16,643,200	0.579	9,636,413
		F 25,039,373
Less: Initial investment		(35,000,000)
NPV		F (9,960,627)

Finally, GPC determines the project's expected value in Hungarian forints given the probability of nationalization:

Calculation of Project Expected Value		
Net Present Value	**Probability**	**Expected NPV**
• Without nationalization . . . F29,536,437	0.76	F 22,447,692
• With nationalization . . . . F (9,960,627)	0.24*	(2,390,551)
Project expected value		F 20,057,141

* The probability of nationalization is determined by multiplying the probability of a change in government by the probability of nationalization if the government changes: 40% × 60% = 24%.

If GPC were to base the investment decision solely on the expected value from a project perspective, the positive expected value of F 20,057,141 would result in acceptance of the project.

Parent Company Perspective

To calculate NPV from a parent company perspective, GPC begins by calculating cash flows to parent (CFP) on an after-tax basis in U.S. dollars over the three-year investment horizon where

CFP = Interest on parent loan in years 1, 2, and 3 (net of withholding taxes)

+ Dividends in years 1, 2, and 3 (net of withholding taxes)

− U.S. taxes on interest and dividends in years 1, 2, and 3 (net foreign tax credit)

+ Repayment of parent loan in year 3

+ Terminal value in year 3 (net of withholding taxes)

Note that CFP is affected by Hungarian dividend repatriation restrictions (50 percent of accounting earnings), Hungarian withholding taxes (interest 20 percent, dividends 30 percent), and by changes in the exchange rate. In addition, CFP is reduced by the amount of U.S. income tax (net of foreign tax credit) that must be paid on the interest and dividends received from Hungary. Cash flows to parent in U.S. dollars are determined as follows:

Calculation of Cash Flows to Parent

			Year 1			Year 2			Year 3
Foreign exchange rates			120			144			172.8
Interest on parent loan	$150,000	10%	$15,000			$15,000			$15,000
Less: Withholding tax.		20%	(3,000)			(3,000)			(3,000)
Net interest (positive cash flow) . . .			$12,000			$12,000			$12,000
Dividend	F560,000	50%	$ 2,333	F3,920,000	50%	$13,611	F8,643,200	50%	$25,009
Less: Withholding tax.		30%	(700)		30%	(4,083)		30%	(7,503)
Net dividend (positive cash flow) . . .			$ 1,633			$9,528			$17,506

U.S. Taxes

			Year 1			Year 2			Year 3
Grossed up dividend*			$ 2,917			$17,014			$31,262
Grossed up interest			15,000			15,000			15,000
Taxable income			17,917			32,014			46,262
Tax before foreign tax credit		35%	6,271		35%	11,205		35%	16,192
Less: Foreign tax credit†			(4,283)			(10,486)			(16,192)
U.S. tax liability (negative cash flow to parent)			$ 1,988			$ 719			$ 0

Actual taxes paid in Hungary on interest and dividend:									
Interest withholding tax			3,000			3,000			3,000
Dividend withholding tax			700			4,083			7,503
Income tax (deemed paid on dividend)			583			3,403			6,252
Total			4,283			10,486			16,755

			Year 1			Year 2			Year 3
Repayment of parent loan (positive cash flow).									$150,000
Terminal value									$481,574
Less: Withholding tax								30%	(144,472)
Net terminal value (positive cash flow)									$337,102
Total cash flow to parent.			$11,646			$20,809			$516,608

* The grossed-up dividend in U.S. dollars is calculated as earnings before taxes (in forints) translated into U.S. dollars at the appropriate exchange rate multiplied by the amount that may be repatriated (50%):

$$\text{Year 1: F } 700,000/120 = \$5,833 \times 50\% = \$2,917$$
$$\text{Year 2: F } 4,900,000/144 = \$34,028 \times 50\% = \$17,014$$
$$\text{Year 3: F } 10,804,000/172.8 = \$62,524 \times 50\% = \$31,262$$

† The foreign tax credit is limited to the amount of tax before foreign tax credit.

If the project is nationalized in Year 3, terminal value will be zero, but the parent loan still will be repaid. In that case the total cash flow to parent in Year 3 is only $179,506 ($516,608 – $337,102).

GPC then calculates the net present value of cash flows to the parent over the three-year investment horizon (1) without nationalization and (2) with nationalization, as follows:

Calculation of Net Present Value (without nationalization)			
CFP		**PV Factor**	**Present Value**
Year 1	$11,646	0.833	$ 9,701
Year 2	20,809	0.694	14,441
Year 3	516,608	0.579	299,116
			$ 323,259
Less: Initial investment			(350,000)
NPV			$ (26,741)

Calculation of Net Present Value (with nationalization)			
CFP		**PV Factor**	**Present Value**
Year 1	$11,646	0.833	$ 9,701
Year 2	20,809	0.694	14,441
Year 3	179,506	0.579	103,934
			$ 128,077
Less: Initial investment			(350,000)
NPV			$(221,923)

Finally, GPC determines the expected value from a parent company perspective given the probability of nationalization:

Calculation of Parent Company Perspective Expected Value			
Net Present Value		**Probability**	**Expected NPV**
• without nationalization	$(26,741)	0.76	$ (20,323)
• with nationalization	$(221,923)	0.24	(53,262)
Expected value			$ (73,585)

If GPC bases the investment decision solely on the expected value from a parent company perspective, the negative expected value of ($73,585) would lead to rejection of the project. Evaluation of the potential Hungarian investment from both a project perspective and a parent company perspective leads to conflicting results. GPC's accountants should conduct sensitivity analyses to determine whether the results are particularly sensitive to one or more assumptions that have been made. The result may be sensitive, for example, to the assumption regarding future fluctuations in the exchange rate. Further, the company might want to consider alternative financing arrangements or attempt to obtain additional government concessions with respect to withholding and/or income taxes that could increase the likelihood of a positive NPV from a parent company perspective. Ultimately, management will need to decide whether the parent company perspective or the project perspective should dominate the decision process.

STRATEGY IMPLEMENTATION

The function of ensuring that an organization's strategies are implemented and goals are attained is known as *management control*. Management control systems are tools designed for implementing strategies and monitoring their effectiveness. Accountants play a vital role in the management control process through the development of operating budgets and in designing performance evaluation systems. Operating budgets help express a firm's long-term strategy within shorter time frames, provide a mechanism for implementing and monitoring the implementation of strategy within that time frame, and specify criteria for evaluating performance. The implementation of strategy within an organization is influenced by a variety of factors, such as organizational structure and national culture (see Exhibit 13.4). In this section, we briefly describe these other factors in relation to MNCs' management control systems.

Management Control

Management control involves planning what the organization should do to effectively implement strategy, coordinating the activities of several parts of the organization, communicating information to organizational members, evaluating information, deciding what action should be taken, and influencing organizational members to change their behavior consistent with the organization's strategy.[9]

The extent to which decision-making authority is delegated to other members of the organization is an important issue in management control. For example, in the case of MNCs, some level of delegation to subsidiary managers is generally necessary because of the need to respond to local conditions and to provide a mechanism for motivating subsidiary managers. However, the issue of delegation is particularly complex for MNCs because of the possibility that geographically dispersed subsidiary managers may work toward parochial ends, which could conflict with the interests of the organization as a whole. Therefore, with delegation of decision-making authority to subsidiary managers, the need arises for effective control systems to ensure that subsidiary managers behave in accordance

EXHIBIT 13.4 **Framework for Strategy Implementation**

Source: Robert N. Anthony and Vijay Govindarajan, *Management Control Systems,* 9th ed. (international ed.) (New York: McGraw-Hill, 1998), p. 8.

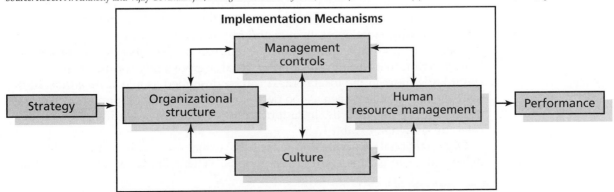

[9] Anthony and Govindarajan, *Management Control Systems,* pp. 6–7.

with organizational goals, also known as goal congruence. Determining the appropriate level of responsibility to delegate to foreign operations and designing the related control system necessary to ensure goal congruence are major issues facing MNCs in implementing strategy. Key factors that influence the design of an effective control system for an MNC include the company's organizational structure and the strategic role assigned to subsidiaries.

MNCs organize their cross-border activities in different ways depending on the main purpose of such activities. When an MNC focuses on producing products for the parent company market, its organizational structure can be described as *ethnocentric.* Firms operating on an ethnocentric principle assume that their own cultural background—including values, beliefs, language, nonverbal communication, and ways of analyzing problems—is universally applicable. In contrast, some MNCs focus on providing products to the host country with a unique product strategy. Subsidiaries in this case operate as strategic business units. The structure of such a firm can be described as *polycentric.* Polycentricism implies that the culture of the host country is important and should be adopted. Obviously, this creates the problem of adapting to multiple cultures within the overall organization. Some firms have a global networked structure, which supports both product line and geographic divisions in order to meet changing market demands. Such a structure can be described as *geocentric.* Those firms that use the principle of geocentricism believe that a synergy of ideas from different countries in which the firm operates should prevail. This, in turn, requires a common framework with enough flexibility to change when required.[10]

An MNC with a geocentric structure organizes its activities as a network of transactions in knowledge, goods, and capital among subsidiaries located in different countries. Focusing on knowledge flows, the firm can identify different roles for subsidiaries. A subsidiary that serves as the source of knowledge for other units, taking a leading role in a particular area, can be described as a *global innovator.* The Swedish company Ericsson's Italian subsidiary plays the role of a global innovator and serves as the company's global center for the development of transmission systems, while its Finnish subsidiary holds the leading global role for mobile telephones. In some cases, subsidiaries also take responsibility for creating knowledge in specific areas that other units can use. Such a subsidiary can be described as an *integrated player.* The integrator role is similar to the global innovator role. However, unlike a global innovator, which is self-sufficient in the fulfillment of its own knowledge needs, an integrated player relies on other units within the organization for some of its knowledge needs. Motorola's Chinese subsidiary is an example of an integrated player. In contrast, a unit may engage in little knowledge creation of its own and rely heavily on knowledge inflows from the parent or peer subsidiaries. Such a unit can be described as an *implementer.* Finally, a unit that has almost complete local responsibility for the creation of relevant know-how in the local context can be described as a *local innovator.* In this case, the knowledge is seen as too peculiar to be of much competitive use outside of the country in which the local innovator is located. These different subsidiary roles are shown in Exhibit 13.5.[11]

Organizational structure influences the extent to which responsibilities are delegated to individual foreign operations. Where the focus of a subsidiary's

[10] D. P. Rutenberg, *Multinational Management* (Boston: Little Brown, 1982).

[11] A. K. Gupta and V. Govindarajan, "Knowledge Flows and the Structure of Control within Multinational Corporations," *Academy of Management Review* 16, no. 4 (1991), pp. 773–75.

EXHIBIT 13.5
A Knowledge Flow-Based Framework of Generic Subsidiary Roles

Source: Adapted from A. K. Gupta and V. Govindarajan, "Knowledge Flows and the Structure of Control within Multinational Corporations," *Academy of Management Review* 16, no. 4 (1991), pp. 773–75.

Outflow of Knowledge[†] \ Inflow of Knowledge[*]	Low	High
High	Global innovator	Integrated player
Low	Local innovator	Implementer

[*] From the rest of the organization to the focal subsidiary.
[†] From the focal subsidiary to the rest of the organization.

activities is on the host country (a polycentric organizational structure), the extent of delegation to the individual foreign subsidiary would be greater than in a situation in which the focus is on the synergy of activities in different countries (a geocentric organizational structure). The extent of delegation appropriate for a particular subsidiary can also depend on the specific strategic role assigned to it. For example, a subsidiary that plays the role of a local innovator may have a higher level of responsibility compared to one that plays the role of an integrated player, because of the lower level of interdependence between a local innovator and its peer units.

Two dominant control systems are available for corporate management to control subsidiaries—bureaucratic control and cultural control.[12] A bureaucratic control system makes extensive use of rules, regulations, and procedures that clearly specify subsidiary management's role and authority and set out expected performance in terms of identified targets, such as financial targets. These targets are used as the basis for evaluating performance. In contrast, in a system of cultural control, broad organizational culture plays a crucial role.[13] A cultural control system is more implicit and informal than a bureaucratic control system. Control mechanisms such as budgeting have both bureaucratic and cultural elements. The bureaucratic element of budgeting is in setting specific targets to achieve, and the cultural element is in the role budgeting plays in changing the behavior patterns within an organization.

Another important factor that influences an MNC's decision with regard to the level of control and the extent of delegation is cultural proximity, or the extent to which the host cultural ethos permits adoption of the home (parent company) organizational culture.[14] Those countries that permit easy adoption of the parent company culture would be considered high in cultural proximity. For example, a U.S. MNC might have relatively less difficulty in transmitting its organizational culture to a subsidiary in Australia than to a subsidiary in Indonesia. In this case, the cultural proximity between the United States and Indonesia would be lower compared to that between the United States and Australia. Cultural proximity becomes crucial in the selection of control systems because the lower the cultural proximity, the higher the familiarization costs. In the preceding example, an extra

[12] B. R. Baliga and A. M. Jaeger, "Multinational Corporations: Control Systems and Delegation Issues," *Journal of International Business,* Fall 1984, pp. 25–40.

[13] *Organizational culture* can be defined as the common beliefs and expectations shared by the organization's members.

[14] Baliga and Jaeger, "Multinational Corporations."

effort would be needed to familiarize the managers of the Indonesian subsidiary with the U.S. corporate culture, incurring additional costs.[15]

The effectiveness of any MNC control system depends on the quality and cooperation of management at the foreign subsidiary level. The ability and willingness of the subsidiary management to comprehend what is involved and accept what is required are crucial to the successful implementation of any control system. Furthermore, the quality of the mechanisms and process through which information is collected, processed, and transmitted at the subsidiary level will determine the quality of performance evaluation of foreign operations.

Operational Budgeting

Accounting's primary contribution to strategy implementation is operational budgeting. Whereas long-term budgets are mainly used as a strategy formulation and long-term planning device, annual operational budgets help express a firm's long-term strategy within shorter time frames. Operational budgets provide the mechanisms to translate organizational goals into financial terms, assign responsibilities and scarce resources, and monitor actual performance. Budgeted numbers become targets for managers to achieve.

Many MNCs find it necessary to translate operational budgets of foreign subsidiaries using an appropriate exchange rate. This process is complicated by exchange rate fluctuations. The next section of this chapter discusses the issues related to performance evaluation of foreign operations.

EVALUATING THE PERFORMANCE OF FOREIGN OPERATIONS

Performance evaluation is about monitoring an organization's effectiveness in fulfilling its objectives. It is a key management control task. In addition to providing measures that can be used to evaluate management performance, corporate management also expects the performance evaluation system to help assess the profitability of current operations, identify areas that need closer attention, and allocate scarce resources efficiently. Furthermore, the performance evaluation and related reward systems are expected to motivate organizational members to behave in a manner consistent with the organization's goals. Prior studies have shown that no single criterion can be used meaningfully in evaluating the performance of all subsidiaries, as no single criterion is capable of capturing all facets of performance that are of interest to corporate management. It is common for MNCs to use a mixture of measures, financial and nonfinancial, formal and informal, and formula-based and subjective to evaluate performance. For example, when there is a lower level of perceived environmental uncertainty, firms tend to use a more formula-based type of evaluation, whereas when there is a higher level of environmental uncertainty they tend to use more subjective judgment.[16] The operating environment of a foreign subsidiary is influenced by many factors. Exhibit 13.6 shows the social, political and legal, economic, and technological factors that are likely

---

[15] Similarly, the concept of "psychic distance" (the interaction between geographic distance and culture) has been used to explain budget control of foreign subsidiaries. See Lars G. Hassel and Gary M. Cunningham, "Psychic Distance and Budget Control of Foreign Subsidiaries," *Journal of International Accounting Research* 3, no. 2 (2004), pp. 79–93.

[16] V. Govindarajan, "Appropriateness of Accounting Data in Performance Evaluation: An Empirical Examination of Environmental Uncertainty as an Intervening Variable," *Accounting, Organizations and Society* 9, no. 2 (1984), pp. 125–35.

EXHIBIT 13.6 Influences Affecting the Operating Environment of Subsidiaries in Foreign Countries

Source: H. Noerreklit and H. W. Schoenfeld, "Controlling Multinational Companies: An Attempt to Analyse Some Unresolved Issues," *International Journal of Accounting* 35, no. 3 (2000), pp. 415–30.

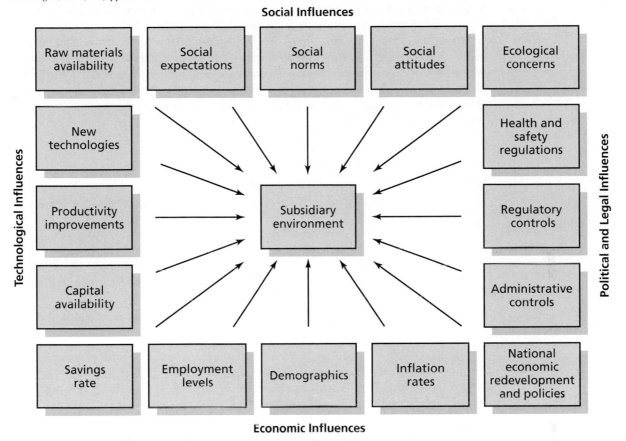

to influence a firm's operations in a national environment, creating a particular level of uncertainties and risks. Performance evaluation measures that attempt to capture these complexities are bound to contain a high degree of subjectivity.[17]

Further, companies do not seem to use any particular method of performance evaluation consistently. A study conducted by the Chartered Institute of Management Accountants (CIMA) in the United Kingdom found that, despite the consulting and academic literature on different approaches to performance measurement, most companies do not consistently use a particular technique.[18] For example, British companies adopt a contingency approach depending on the environment in which an organization operates, its structure and size, and the technological features of the organization. The CIMA study also points out that in the 1980s the focus of performance measurement was too historical. As a consequence, many organizations thought they were measuring the wrong things. In the 1990s, companies experienced difficulties in implementing measurement frameworks and

[17] For example, S. M. Robbins and R. B. Stobaugh, "The Bent Measuring Stick for Foreign Subsidiaries," *Harvard Business Review,* September–October 1973, p. 86.

[18] Chartered Institute of Management Accountants, "Latest Trends in Corporate Performance Measurement," 2002.

worried about having too many measures of performance. All these issues are still relevant in the new millennium.

Performance evaluation is a complex issue even in a purely domestic context. It becomes much more complex in an international context, particularly due to the issues that are unique to foreign operations, such as exchange rate fluctuations, varying rates of inflation in foreign countries, international transfer pricing, and cultural and environmental differences that exist across countries. It is important to ensure that the performance targets set for a foreign subsidiary are in line with overall corporate goals and strategies and at the same time appropriate for the local circumstances. In the remainder of this section, we discuss in some detail the issues relating to designing and implementing a system for evaluating the performance of a foreign subsidiary.

Designing an Effective Performance Evaluation System for a Foreign Subsidiary

Designing an effective performance evaluation system requires decisions with regard to the following:

1. The measure or measures on which performance will be evaluated.
2. The treatment of the foreign operation as a cost, profit, or investment center.
3. The issue of evaluating the foreign operating unit versus evaluating the manager of that unit.
4. The method of measuring profit for those foreign operations evaluated on the basis of profitability.

There are no universally right or wrong decisions with regard to these issues. There is no generically appropriate performance evaluation system, nor are there established guidelines that companies are required to follow. Each company will have a unique system tailored to its strategic objectives.

Performance Measures

Companies must decide whether to use financial criteria, nonfinancial criteria, or some combination of the two to measure and evaluate performance. Considering the diverse environments in which MNCs operate and the interdependencies among units in a multinational context, developing a global business strategy can be a highly complex task. A potential problem for MNCs in this regard is the tendency for headquarters to rely on simple financial control systems, often designed for home-country operations and extended to foreign subsidiaries. Subsidiary managers can be highly sensitive to these systems unless the systems are adapted to the local operating environment.[19] The danger here is that inappropriate performance standards may lead to dysfunctional behavior not in line with corporate goals.

Financial Measures

Financial measures are those measures of performance that are based on accounting information. They include sales growth, cost reduction, profit, and return on investment. Several surveys have asked MNCs which financial measures they use in evaluating the performance of foreign operations. The results of four surveys, three conducted in the United States and one conducted in the United Kingdom, are presented in Exhibit 13.7. In each survey, managers of MNCs were asked to indicate whether a particular financial measure is used in evaluating foreign subsidiary

[19] L. G. Hassel, "Headquarter Reliance on Accounting Performance Measures in a Multinational Context," *Journal of International Financial Management and Accounting* 3, no. 1 (1991), pp. 17–38.

EXHIBIT 13.7 Financial Measures Used by U.S. and UK MNCs to Evaluate Subsidiary Performance

Sources: [a] H. G. Moriscato, *Currency Translation and Performance Evaluation in Multinationals* (Ann Arbor, MI: UMI Press, 1980); [b] W. M. Abdallah and D. E. Keller, "Measuring the Multinational's Performance," *Management Accounting*, October 1985, pp. 26–30, 56; [c] A. Hosseini and Z. Rezaee, "Impact of SFAS No. 52 on Performance Measures of Multinationals," *International Journal of Accounting* 25 (1990), pp. 43–52; [d] I. S. Demirag, "Assessing Foreign Subsidiary Performance: The Currency Choice of U.K. MNCs," *Journal of International Business Studies*, Summer 1988, pp. 257–75.

	Ranking			
	United States			United Kingdom
Financial Measures	1980[a]	1984[b]	1990[c]	1988[d]
Profit	1	2	1	3
Return on investment (ROI)	2	3	3	2
Budget compared to actual profits	3	1	2	1

EXHIBIT 13.8 Comparison of Japanese and U.S. Performance Evaluation Measures

Source: J. C. Bailes and T. Assada, "Empirical Differences between Japanese and American Budget and Performance Evaluation Systems," *International Journal of Accounting* 26, no. 2 (1991), p. 137.

Percentage of Times Ranked in Top Three Budget Goals for Divisional Managers		
Measure	Japan	United States
Sales volume	86.3%	27.9%
Net profit	44.7	35.0
Production cost	40.7	12.4
Return on sales	30.7	30.5
Controllable profit	28.2	51.8
Sales growth	19.4	22.4
Return on investment	3.1	68.4

performance. In all four surveys, the top three financial measures used by both the U.S. and UK MNCs are profit, ROI, and comparison of budgeted and actual profit, although the rank order changes slightly among the four studies. Given the large percentage of companies using each measure, it is clear that MNCs use multiple financial measures in evaluating the performance of foreign operations.

By contrast, the results of a 1991 survey of U.S. and Japanese MNCs (reported in Exhibit 13.8) indicate that, compared with U.S. MNCs, Japanese MNCs are much more concerned with sales volume and production cost. In addition, Japanese MNCs are not very concerned with ROI, whereas this was the most important measure for the U.S. MNCs responding to the survey. U.S. MNCs are also more concerned with controllable profit than their Japanese counterparts. We discuss the concept of controllable profit more fully later in this chapter.

Nonfinancial Measures

Nonfinancial measures are those measures of performance that are based on information not obtained directly from financial statements. A survey of U.S. MNCs was conducted in 1983 to determine the use of various nonfinancial measures in

EXHIBIT 13.9
Importance of
Nonfinancial
Measures in
Evaluating
Performance

Source: F. D. S. Choi and
I. J. Czechowicz, "Assessing
Foreign Subsidiary Perfor-
mance: A Multinational
Comparison," *Management
International Review* 23
(1983), p. 17.

Nonfinancial Measure	Average Importance	
	Subsidiary	Manager
Increasing market share	1.8	1.5
Relationship with host country government	2.1	1.8
Quality control	2.2	1.9
Productivity improvement	2.2	2.1
Cooperation with parent company	2.4	2.0
Environmental compliance	2.4	2.3
Employee development	2.4	2.0
Employee safety	2.4	2.2
Labor turnover	2.7	2.5
Community service	2.9	2.8
Research and development in foreign subsidiary	3.1	3.2

Scale 1 = Very important to 4 = Not important

evaluating the performance of foreign operations. Respondents were asked to indicate the level of importance of each measure on a scale of 1 (very important) to 4 (not important) in evaluating (1) the foreign subsidiary and (2) the manager of the foreign subsidiary. The results are reported in Exhibit 13.9.

Survey participants indicated that market share is the most important nonfinancial measure of performance. Other important measures include relationship with host country government, quality control, and productivity improvement. Nonfinancial measures such as community service and labor turnover were deemed less important. Overall, the less quantifiable and nonfinancial measures are subjective as compared with their financial counterparts.

In general, the method of evaluation depends largely on the type of subsidiary involved. It is common to use simple and straightforward criteria for evaluating a subsidiary with specific tasks, such as a sales unit. The criteria used to evaluate such affiliates include number of new customers, market share, or a combination of similar measures.

Financial versus Nonfinancial Measures

Prior studies have found national differences with respect to the prominence given to financial and nonfinancial measures in evaluating subsidiary performance. Partial results of a study of U.S. and Japanese management accounting practices that included both types of measures are reported in Exhibit 13.10. It shows that financial measures, albeit different ones, are given primary importance in both Japan and the United States. In Japan, market share is far less important than sales as a performance measure; in the United States, market share is about as important as sales, but both sales and market share are much less important than ROI in evaluating performance. In a separate study, profit-based measures also were given primary importance by European companies.[20]

A study investigated the evaluation criteria used by MNCs from four countries (Great Britain, Canada, Germany, and Japan) with regard to their operations in the United States. Some of the results are reported in Exhibit 13.11. Although differences exist across the four countries, the MNCs ranked several criteria highly

[20] Business International Corporation, "Evaluating the Performance of International Operations" (New York: Author, 1989), p. 174.

EXHIBIT 13.10 **Comparison of Financial and Nonfinancial Measures in Japan and the United States**

Source: M. D. Shields, C. W. Chow, Y. Kato, and Y. Nakagawa, "Management Accounting Practices in the U.S. and Japan: Comparative Survey Findings and Research Implications," *Journal of International Financial Management and Accounting* 3, no. 1 (1991), p. 68.

Measure	Percentage of Time Considered Important	
	Japan	United States
Sales	69%	19%
Return on investment	7	75
Market share	12	19

EXHIBIT 13.11 **Ranking of Evaluation Criteria by MNCs with Operations in the United States**

Source: S. C. Borkowski, "International Managerial Performance Evaluation: A Five Country Comparison," *Journal of International Business Studies*, Third Quarter 1999, pp. 533–56.

Criterion	British	Canadian	German	Japanese
Profit margin	1	1,2	1	4
Sales growth	2,3,4	1,2	2	1
Cost reduction	2,3,4	3,4	5	5
Net income	12	5	4	3
Goal attainment	5	3,4	8	2
Budget adherence	2,3,4	6	9	9
Return on sales	6	13	13	7
Return on assets	7,8	10	14	13
Technical innovation	7,8	11	7	10
Return on investment	9,10	9	11	10
Product innovation	9,10	11	6	12
Market share	11	8	3	7
Company standards	13	7	10	5
Residual income	14	14	12	13

in each. Profit margin is the number one criterion for MNCs in three of the four countries (tied with sales growth in Canada) but ranks fourth in Japan. Sales growth is the number one criterion in Japan and number two in the other three countries (with some ties). Cost reduction is a top-five criterion in each country. Net income ranks in the top five in each country other than Great Britain. Market share ranks among the top five criteria only for German MNCs.

The Balanced Scorecard: Increased Importance of Nonfinancial Measures

One of the most important achievements in the design of performance evaluation systems in recent years was the introduction of the balanced scorecard in the early 1990s.[21] A balanced scorecard combines financial measures of past performance with nonfinancial measures of the drivers of future performance to

[21] For a description of this approach, see Robert S. Kaplan and David P. Norton, *The Balanced Scorecard* (Boston: Harvard University Press, 1996).

EXHIBIT 13.12
Basic Model of a Balanced Scorecard Performance System

Source: Adapted from Robert S. Kaplan and David P. Norton, "The Balanced Scorecard: Measures That Drive Performance," *Harvard Business Review*, January–February 1992, p. 72.

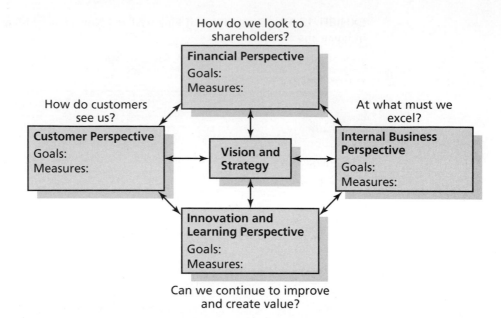

provide management with a road map for creating shareholder value. As shown in Exhibit 13.12, a balanced scorecard focuses on an integrated relationship among the key elements of a business—vision; strategy; and four perspectives, namely, financial, customer, internal business process, and learning and growth.

Financial perspective refers to the issue of how a firm should appear to its shareholders in order to succeed financially. *Customer perspective* refers to the issue of how a firm should appear to its customers in order to succeed financially. If customers are not satisfied, they will eventually find other suppliers that will meet their needs. *Internal business process perspective* refers to the business processes at which the firm must excel in order to satisfy its shareholders and customers. This allows the managers to know how well the business is running and whether its products and services conform to customer requirements. *Learning and growth perspective* refers to how the firm will sustain its ability to change and improve in order to achieve its vision. In the current environment of rapid technological change, it is becoming necessary for both managers and other employees within a firm to be in a continuous learning mode. A balanced scorecard contains performance measures related to each of the four perspectives. Nonfinancial measures are related to three of the four perspectives included in the balanced scorecard.

A 2002 survey of 167 U.S. chief financial officers conducted by PricewaterhouseCoopers found that top executives at MNCs consider nonfinancial performance measures such as product/service quality and customer satisfaction/loyalty more important than current financial results in creating long-term shareholder value (see Exhibit 13.13). According to the survey, 69 percent of MNCs have attempted to develop a balanced scorecard combining both financial and nonfinancial measures in a comprehensive system to measure performance. While nonfinancial measures are viewed as being most important for long-term shareholder value, financial results are still viewed as a key factor in making ongoing management decisions. The major advantage of profit as a measure of performance is that it embodies all the major business functions from marketing (sales revenue) to production (cost of goods sold) to financing (interest expense).

Exhibit 13.14 shows how the senior management team of Rockwater, a worldwide leader in underwater engineering and construction, transformed its vision

EXHIBIT 13.13 CFOs' Views on Factors Contributing to Long-Term Shareholder Return

Source: PricewaterhouseCoopers, "Non-financial Measures Are Highest-Rated Determinants of Total Shareholder Value, PricewaterhouseCoopers Survey Finds," Management Barometer news release, April 22, 2002.

Measure	Importance*
Product and service quality	89%
Customer satisfaction and loyalty	83
Operating efficiency	75
Current financial results	71
Innovation	62
Employee satisfaction and turnover	47

* Percentage of respondents indicating that a particular measure is important in determining long-term shareholder value.

EXHIBIT 13.14 Rockwater's Balanced Scorecard

Source: Robert S. Kaplan and David P. Norton, "Putting the Balanced Scorecard to Work," *Harvard Business Review,* September–October 1993, p. 136.

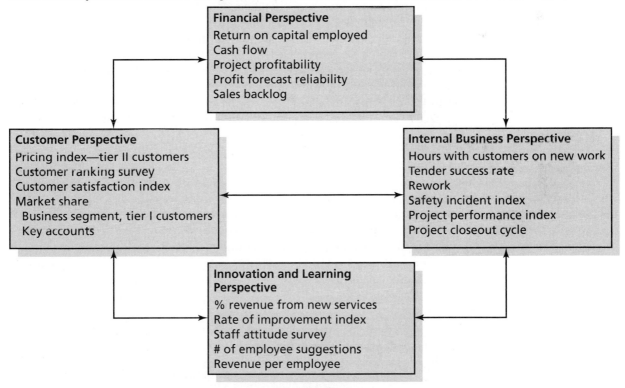

and strategy into the balanced scorecard's four sets of performance measures. Rockwater is a wholly owned subsidiary of Brown & Root/Halliburton, a global engineering and construction company. The company's vision was to be the industry leader in providing the highest standards of safety and quality to its clients.[22]

[22] Robert S. Kaplan and David P. Norton, "Putting the Balanced Scorecard to Work," *Harvard Business Review,* September–October 1993, pp. 135–40.

Responsibility Centers

A company must decide whether a foreign affiliate should be evaluated as a cost center, a profit center, or an investment center. Managers of cost centers tend to have the least amount of responsibility compared to managers of other responsibility centers within a group. They normally have no right to sell existing assets or acquire new assets. Cost centers are expected to produce as much as possible for a given amount of resources (e.g., internal service units of an organization, such as accounting, manufacturing, and research and development) or produce a given amount of output with specified quality at the lowest possible cost. Treating an operating unit as a cost center implies that responsibility is assigned only to cost control and reduction, but not to sales generation.

Evaluation as a profit center implies that profit will be used to determine whether the operating unit is achieving its objectives and that resources will be allocated according to the unit's profit. In effect, the operating unit and its management are being held responsible for generating profit. Profit center managers are given a fixed amount of assets and are ultimately responsible for both costs and revenues.

The responsibilities of an investment center manager include all the responsibilities of a profit center manager plus the responsibility for investment decisions. Return on investment is the most common investment center performance measure. If a foreign operating unit is evaluated as an investment center, the unit and its management are held responsible for generating an adequate ROI. Although identifying appropriate responsibility centers for foreign subsidiaries is a difficult task, it is also important because of the need to match the performance measure chosen to the responsibilities assigned to the responsibility center. Exhibit 13.15 summarizes major differences among the different types of responsibility centers.

Foreign Operating Unit as a Profit Center

To the extent that foreign management is not directly responsible for all of the foreign operation's activities, treating that operation as a profit center may not be useful for evaluating performance. An MNC's transfer pricing policy may not be compatible with the profit center concept. When corporate management dictates that certain transfer prices be used to achieve a specific worldwide cost-minimization objective, the local operation loses control over determination of profit. For example, it would be inappropriate to evaluate an assembly plant in a high-tax country as a profit center when it is required to purchase inputs from

EXHIBIT 13.15
Differences among Cost, Profit, and Investment Centers

Source: Adapted from Cheryl S. McWatters, Dale C. Morse, and Jerold L. Zimmerman, *Management Accounting* (New York: McGraw-Hill, 2001), p. 198.

Type of Responsibility Center	Responsibilities	Performance Measurement
Cost center	Choose output for a given cost of inputs	Output (maximize given quality constraints)
	or	or
	Choose input mix to achieve a given output	Cost (minimize given quality constraints)
Profit center	Choose inputs and outputs with a fixed level of investment	Profit (maximize)
Investment center	Choose inputs, outputs, and level of investment	Return on investment, residual income (maximize)

foreign affiliates at high prices (dictated by the parent company) in order to minimize worldwide income taxes.

Some foreign operations have strategic importance other than to generate profit. For example, a company might invest in a mining operation in a foreign country with the purpose of having a captive source of an important raw material. The original reason for making this investment was not to generate profit, and perhaps it should not be evaluated on the basis of profitability. Further, if all the output is sold (transferred) to affiliated companies, which means none is sold on the open market, then this operation may have no control over either sales volume or sales price—both are dictated by the parent or affiliated customers. For this particular type of operation, performance might be better evaluated using a measure like cost reduction or productivity, not profit. Further, if the foreign affiliate was established with the purpose to sell products produced by the parent, perhaps sales volume or market share would be a more appropriate performance measure than profit. The important point is that for some foreign operations it might not be relevant to evaluate performance on the basis of profitability. Dysfunctional behavior can occur, for example, if a parent company decides to shut down an unprofitable component-parts manufacturer when the reason it is not profitable is that the parent mandates low transfer prices. Headquarters management must decide which foreign operations should or should not be evaluated as profit centers.

In comparing the results of surveys conducted in 1978 and 1989, Business International identified a trend of companies moving away from treating individual subsidiaries as profit centers and instead treating them as cost centers. One reason for the shift is that companies have too many subsidiaries. For example, U.S.-based Cargill has 61 subsidiaries in the United Kingdom alone. Profit centers are more and more being defined at the level of strategic business unit (SBU), often product lines.[23] However, many foreign operations are legal entities in the host countries and are therefore required to maintain a complete set of accounting records and measure profit for legal and tax reasons.

Separating Managerial and Unit Performance

Intertwined with assigning levels of responsibility to foreign operating units is the question of whether the foreign operating unit and the management of that unit should be evaluated using the same performance measure. The performance of a foreign subsidiary is the result of decisions made by various parties, for example, local management, corporate management, and host governments. Local managers make most operating decisions, whereas corporate management makes transfer pricing and funds transfer decisions. Host governments may have specific rules concerning pricing and the use of foreign exchange that affect an operating unit's performance.

It is possible to have good management performance despite poor unit performance and vice versa. To properly reward and keep good managers and not inadvertently reward bad managers, the evaluation system should be able to separate subsidiary from managerial performance. The poor overall performance of the subsidiary may be largely due to the circumstances beyond the manager's control—for example, market disruption caused by terrorism—even though the manager performed well under the circumstances.

The main issue here revolves around *uncontrollable items*, that is, items that affect the performance measure over which the local manager has no control or is

[23] Business International, "Evaluating the Performance," p. 174.

not permitted to attempt to manage. The concept of *responsibility accounting* suggests that costs, revenues, assets, and liabilities should be traced to the individual manager who is responsible for them. Individual managers should not be held responsible for costs over which they have no control, nor should they be given credit for uncontrollable revenues.

Examples of Uncontrollable Items

Uncontrollable items can be classified as those that are controlled by the parent company, the host country government, and other parties. The following is a list of examples of each type:

Items Controlled by the Parent Company

- Sales revenue and cost of goods sold determined by discretionary transfer pricing.
- Allocation of corporate expenses such as the chief executive officer's salary and research and development costs to individual operating units.
- Interest expense on financing obtained from the parent (or an affiliated finance subsidiary), which sets the interest rate.

Items Controlled by the Host Government

- Restrictions on foreign exchange spending that affect the supply of imported materials and parts.
- Controls on prices that may be charged for products and services.
- Local content laws that require component parts to be sourced locally, sometimes at noncompetitive prices.

Items Controlled by Others

- Lost production due to labor strikes.
- Lost production due to power outages.
- Losses resulting from war, riots, and terrorism.
- Foreign exchange losses.

Managers normally prefer to be evaluated on the basis of controllable items because such evaluation is perceived as being fair and will make their rewards more predictable. However, costs often cannot be classified as either completely controllable or completely uncontrollable, because they are often influenced by both managerial actions and external factors.

Some companies use a measure of profit other than net profit to evaluate managers' performance. For example, using *earnings before interest and taxes* (*EBIT*) to measure performance does not hold the local manager responsible for interest and taxes. Likewise, the use of *operating profit* as the performance criterion avoids holding local management responsible for interest, taxes, and incidental gains and losses that are not a part of normal operations.

Business International asked survey participants what kinds of adjustments are made to the measures of profit and assets in measuring return on assets for evaluation purposes. Some of the results are reported in Exhibit 13.16. These results indicate, for example, that a majority of U.S.-based MNCs remove allocated corporate overhead costs from the measure of profit and intercompany receivables from the measure of total assets in calculating return on assets.

In evaluating the foreign operating unit, the decision of whether to adjust the performance measure for uncontrollable items should be based on whether the item in

EXHIBIT 13.16
Calculation of
Return on Assets
for Performance
Evaluation

Source: Rosemary Schlank,
*Evaluating the Performance of
International Operations* (New
York: Business International
Corp., 1989), p. 31.

	Percentage of MNCs	
	U.S.	European
Items Deducted from Profit		
Depreciation	68%	57%
Share of HQ administration costs	60	36
Foreign exchange gains and losses	48	50
Taxes	46	71
Interest	42	57
Share of corporate R&D	38	64
Items Included in Assets		
External receivables	80	86
Intercompany receivables	33	57
Other current assets	75	79
Fixed assets	82	71
Goodwill	44	14

question has any impact on cash flows to be received by the parent from the foreign operation. Generally, only those items controlled by the parent should be removed from the measurement of profit because all other items do affect cash flows. For example, although the local manager should not be fired over lost production due to power outages over which he or she has no control, the cost associated with lost production should be relevant in deciding whether to continue with this particular operation. In contrast, it would be dysfunctional to abandon a particular foreign operation located in a high-tax jurisdiction because of inadequate returns if the parent's discretionary transfer pricing policies contributed to the subpar ROI.

With regard to the issue of whether management and unit should be evaluated on the same basis, a 1990 survey of 109 U.S.-based MNCs found that most companies surveyed used the same performance measurement techniques in evaluating both managers and foreign operating units.[24]

Choice of Currency in Measuring Profit

It appears that most MNCs evaluate performance, at least partially, on some measure of profitability (net income, profit margin, return on investment, etc.). In using profit for performance evaluation, a major issue that companies must address is whether profit should be measured in local currency or parent company currency. If profit is to be measured in parent company currency, the company must select a *method of translation* and decide whether to include the *effects of exchange rate changes*.

Measurement of profit in the local currency is generally considered to be appropriate if the foreign subsidiary is not expected to generate parent currency for payment of dividends to stockholders. This would be true in the case where the operation provides a strategic benefit to the MNC other than an ability to generate parent currency dividends. An example would be a foreign operation that was established specifically to supply affiliated companies with raw materials.

[24] A. Hosseini and Z. Rezaee, "Impact of SFAS No. 52 on Performance Measures of Multinationals," *International Journal of Accounting* 25 (1990), p. 49.

EXHIBIT 13.17 Currency Used by U.S. and European MNCs for
Performance Evaluation

Source: Rosemary Schlank, *Evaluating the Performance of International Operations* (New York: Business International Corporation, 1989), p. 178.

Currency	U.S. (*n* = 112)	European (*n* = 14)
Local currency	17.7%	21.1%
Parent currency	40.5	21.4
Both currencies	36.7	50.0

Measurement of profit in the parent currency is considered appropriate when the foreign subsidiary is expected to generate parent currency that could be paid as dividends to stockholders. This is true for most foreign subsidiaries.

The results of the Business International study conducted in 1989 regarding this question are shown in Exhibit 13.17. It is clear that evaluating performance on the basis of profit translated into parent currency, either alone or in conjunction with local currency results, is very popular. Only about one out of every five MNCs surveyed indicated that it evaluated the performance of foreign operations from a local currency perspective only. This study also indicates that a much greater percentage of U.S. companies than European companies evaluate the performance of foreign operations on the basis of parent currency results only.

Foreign Currency Translation

If parent currency is to be used in evaluating performance, the company must translate foreign currency profit into parent currency and decide which translation method to use. For internal purposes, a company need not use the same translation methods that it is required to use for financial reporting. A U.S.-based MNC, for example, need not use SFAS 52 rules for internal performance evaluation purposes. MNCs should consider which translation method best reflects economic reality for the particular foreign operation being evaluated.

Toyota Motor Corporation's annual report for 2009, in a note to the consolidated financial statements, states its foreign currency translation policy as follows:

> All asset and liability accounts of foreign subsidiaries and affiliates are translated into Japanese yen at appropriate year-end current exchange rates and all income and expense accounts of those subsidiaries are translated at the average exchange rates for each period. The foreign currency translation adjustments are included as a component of accumulated other comprehensive income. Foreign currency receivables and payables are translated at appropriate year-end current exchange rates and the resulting transaction gains or losses are recorded in operations currently.

A corollary issue is whether the *translation adjustment* should be included in the measurement of profit. Under SFAS 52, the translation adjustment that arises when the *temporal method* is used is included as a *gain or loss in net income,* whereas the translation adjustment under the *current rate method* is *deferred on the balance sheet.* Whether to include the translation adjustment in the measure of profit used for performance evaluation purposes would seem to hinge on two issues:

1. Does the translation adjustment accurately reflect the impact on parent currency cash flows resulting from a change in the exchange rate?
2. Does the foreign operation manager have authority to hedge his or her translation exposure?

If the answer to both questions is yes, then the translation adjustment should be included in the performance evaluation measure regardless of whether this is required by financial reporting rules. If the answer to either question is no, then the translation adjustment in profit may or may not be included.

Choice of Currency in Operational Budgeting

As was shown in Exhibit 13.7, many MNCs evaluate annual performance by comparing actual operating performance to a budget. The company exerts management control by focusing on the variance between budgeted and actual profit. Budgetary control allows corporate management to trace the manager or the unit responsible for the variance between budget and actual performance. In the case of an MNC, the question arises as to whether the budget should be prepared and actual profit measured in the local currency or in the parent currency. If "actual" is compared to "budget" in *local* currency, the overall budget variance will be a function of a sales volume variance and local currency price variances. If "actual" is compared to "budget" in *parent* currency, both the budget and actual results must be translated into parent currency using appropriate exchange rates. If one exchange rate is used to translate the budget (e.g., beginning-of-year exchange rate) and another exchange rate is used to translate actual results (e.g., end-of-year exchange rate), the budget variance will be a function of sales volume and local currency price variances *and the change in exchange rates.* This can be seen as follows:

Budgeted profit in local currency	$\times$ Beginning exchange rate $=$	Budgeted profit in parent currency
vs.		vs.
Actual profit in local currency	$\times$ Ending exchange rate $=$	Actual profit in parent currency
Variance $-$ f (sales volume variance and local currency price variances)		Variance $=$ f (sales volume variance, local currency prices variances, *and exchange rate variance*)

If budget is compared to actual in parent currency, the question arises as to whether the manager of a foreign operation should be held responsible for foreign exchange risk, that is, the risk that actual results will deviate from the budget due to changes in the exchange rate. This question should be answered by determining whether foreign management has the authority to hedge, and therefore control, foreign exchange risk. If so, then it would make sense to translate the budget and actual results into parent currency and hold management responsible for the exchange rate component of the budget variance. If not, then perhaps profit measured in local currency rather than parent currency should be used for evaluation because the exchange rate variance is uncontrollable.

MNCs generally centralize their foreign exchange risk management activities and do not allow individual foreign operation managers to hedge their foreign exchange risk. Yet top management often wants to evaluate the performance of operations located in a variety of foreign countries on the basis of a common denominator—the parent currency. The question then arises as to how the local currency budget and actual results can be translated into parent currency without holding foreign management responsible for foreign exchange risk? The answer is

EXHIBIT 13.18
Combinations for Translation of Budget and Actual Results

Source: D. R. Lessard and P. Lorange, "Currency Changes and Management Control: Resolving the Centralization/Decentralization Dilemma," *Accounting Review,* July 1977, pp. 628–37.

	Rate Used to Track Actual Performance Relative to Budget		
Rate Used for Determining Budget	Actual at TOB	Projected at TOB	Actual at EOP
Actual at time of budget (TOB)	1	n/a	4
Projected at time of budget	n/a	3	5
Actual at end of period (EOP)	n/a	n/a	2

fairly obvious: Use the same exchange rate to translate both budgeted profit and actual profit.

Conceptually, there are three possible exchange rates to use in preparing the budget and in translating actual results into parent currency:[25]

1. The actual exchange rate at the time the budget is prepared.
2. A projected future exchange rate at the time the budget is prepared.
3. The actual exchange rate at the end of the budget period.

As shown in Exhibit 13.18, these three exchange rates lead to nine possible combinations, only five of which would make sense for evaluation purposes.

The five meaningful combinations of exchange rates differ as follows in the extent to which management is held responsible for fluctuations in exchange rates:

1. *Translate the budget and actual results using the spot rate that exists at the time the budget is prepared.* Under this combination, the overall budget variance is a function of sales volume and local currency price variances only. Exchange rates have no effect on evaluation. However, there is little incentive to incorporate anticipated exchange rate changes into operating decisions. This combination is equivalent to evaluating results in local currency.

2. *Translate the budget and actual results using the spot rate that exists at the end of the budget period.* The comments related to combination 1 apply equally to this combination.

3. *Translate the budget and actual results using a projected ending exchange rate (projected at the time the budget is prepared).* Under this combination, the overall budget variance also is a function of sales volume and local currency prices only. However, unlike combinations 1 and 2, the use of a projected exchange rate provides managers an incentive to incorporate expected exchange rate changes into their operating plans, but they are not held responsible for actual exchange rate changes. Because of its potential for causing local managers to consider the impact exchange rate changes will have on parent currency profit, this combination is generally favored in the literature.

4. *Translate the budget at the initial exchange rate and translate actual results using the ending exchange rate.* In this case, the overall budget variance is a function of sales volume, local currency prices, and the change in exchange rate *whether anticipated or not.* Local managers bear full responsibility for exchange rate changes. Noneconomic hedging may result if foreign managers are allowed to

---

[25] The discussion here is based on D. R. Lessard and P. Lorange, "Currency Changes and Management Control: Resolving the Centralization/Decentralization Dilemma," *Accounting Review,* July 1977, pp. 628–37.

hedge. Local managers will want to hedge their exposure even though a natural hedge may exist elsewhere in the MNC's worldwide organization.[26]

5. *Translate the budget at the projected ending exchange rate and translate actual results at the actual ending rate.* The budget variance is a function of sales volume, LC prices, and the *unanticipated* change in exchange rate. Local managers are asked to incorporate projected exchange rate changes into their operating plans. They are then held responsible for reacting to unanticipated exchange rate changes.

Illustration of the Combinations

To illustrate the five combinations of exchange rates in translating the budget and actual results, consider an example of a U.S.-based MNC with a subsidiary in Foreign Country. Budgeted amounts in foreign currency (FC) are as follows:

	Budget
Sales	FC100
Cost	90
Profit	FC 10

Assume that the foreign subsidiary's actual results in FC are exactly as budgeted and that exchange rates for the budget period are as follows:

Actual at time of budget preparation	$1.00/FC1
Projected ending	$0.90/FC1
Actual at end of period	$0.70/FC1

The following shows the translation of the budget and actual results into U.S. dollars under each of the five combinations:

	Combination									
	1		**2**		**3**		**4**		**5**	
	Budget	**Actual**	**Budget**	**Actual**	**Budget**	**Actual**	**Budget**	**Actual**	**Budget**	**Actual**
Exchange rate	$1.00	$1.00	$0.70	$0.70	$0.90	$0.90	$1.00	$0.70	$0.90	$0.70
Sales	100	100	70	70	90	90	100	70	90	70
Costs	90	90	63	63	81	81	90	63	81	63
Profit	10	10	7	7	9	9	10	7	9	7
Variance	0		0		0		3		2	

Because the foreign subsidiary exactly met its sales volume and cost targets in terms of foreign currency, any U.S.-dollar variances are due solely to the change in the exchange rate. There is no exchange rate variance in combinations 1, 2, and 3,

---

[26] A natural hedge within the MNC group exists, for example, if a subsidiary in Canada has a €1 million receivable and a subsidiary in Mexico has a €1 million payable, both due on the same date. From the group perspective, neither subsidiary should hedge its individual foreign exchange risk, because the loss (or gain) on the euro payable will be offset by a gain (or loss) on the euro receivable. If local managers are held responsible for exchange rate variances, however, there will be an incentive for both managers to hedge their specific foreign exchange exposure.

because the same exchange rate is used to translate both the budget and the actual figures. The exchange rate variance in combination 4 is $3, which is equal to the change in exchange rate from the beginning to the end of the period ($0.30) multiplied by the actual amount of FC profit (FC10). The exchange rate variance of $2 in combination 5 reflects the unanticipated change in the exchange rate ([$0.70 − $0.90] × FC10).

The 1989 Business International study referred to earlier in this chapter found that only about 14 percent of U.S. companies indicated using the same exchange rate to translate both the budget and actual results. In contrast, over one-third of the European companies included in the study indicated not holding anyone accountable for exchange rate variances.[27]

Incorporating Economic Exposure into the Budget Process

There are three types of exposure to foreign exchange risk: transaction exposure, translation (or balance sheet) exposure, and economic exposure. Transaction exposure refers to the risk that changes in exchange rates will have an adverse effect on cash flows related to foreign currency payables and receivables. Translation exposure refers to the risk that through the translation of foreign currency financial statements of its subsidiaries, a change in exchange rates will cause the parent company to report a negative translation adjustment in its consolidated financial statements. Chapters 7 and 8 covered financial accounting issues related to these two types of exposure to foreign exchange risk.

Economic exposure refers to the risk that changes in exchange rates will have a negative impact on an entity's cash flows. Transaction exposure is one aspect of economic exposure. However, the concept of economic exposure encompasses more than transaction exposure. Unlike transaction and translation exposures, economic exposure is not directly measured by the accounting system.

One example of economic exposure is the decrease in export sales that results from an *appreciation* of a company's home currency. For example, if the value of the British pound were to increase from US$1.50 to US$2.00, customers in the United States would have to pay a higher U.S.-dollar price for purchases denominated in British pounds and may therefore shift to non-British suppliers. An appreciation of the British pound creates economic exposure for British companies. The depreciation of a company's home currency also creates economic exposure through an increase in the home currency price paid for import purchases. The extent of economic exposure for a business enterprise is at least partially a function of its mix of imports and exports.

Transaction and translation exposures are often reduced through the use of financial instruments such as foreign currency forward contracts and options. Economic exposure is reduced by making operating and strategic decisions to make the company more competitive in the face of exchange rate changes. Shifting from the use of imported parts to locally produced parts and reducing the local currency price in the short term to shore up export sales are examples of actions that a company could take to reduce the economic exposure to exchange rate changes.

Economic exposure also provides opportunities to take advantage of exchange rate changes to increase local currency cash flows. For example, if the U.S. dollar were to decrease in value from $1.00 per euro to $1.25 per euro, a U.S.-based company could pursue a strategy to increase sales volume and market share in Europe without having to reduce its U.S.-dollar prices. Conversely, the company could

---

[27] Business International, "Evaluating the Performance," p. 178.

pursue a skimming strategy by increasing its U.S.-dollar price such that the euro price (and therefore European demand) after the exchange rate change remains the same as before. In either case, total U.S.-dollar sales and therefore U.S.-dollar cash flows should increase.

Designing a control system that allows the parent company to evaluate the performance of its foreign subsidiary managers on their ability to manage economic exposure and at the same time motivates them to exploit opportunities afforded by exchange rate changes is not easy. Because economic exposure deals with opportunity costs, its effects are not separately measured by the normal accounting system. Let us consider what can happen if a company does not attempt to incorporate economic exposure into the evaluation system.

Assume U.S.-based Parent Company has two subsidiaries in Foreign Country: Exporter and Importer. Exporter makes export sales to the United States but sources inputs locally, and Importer imports all of its inputs from the United States but makes no export sales. Budgets in FC and US$ (using the initial exchange rate of US$1.00 = FC1) are as follows:

	Exporter		Importer	
	FC	US$	FC	US$
Sales	100	100	100	100
Costs	90	90	90	90
Profit	10	10	10	10

During the budget period the US$ appreciates 25 percent against the FC such that the ending exchange rate is US$1.00 = FC1.25 or US$.80 = FC1. Assuming that Parent Company uses the ending exchange rate to track actual performance, actual results in FC and US$ are as follows:

	Exporter		Importer	
	FC	US$	FC	US$
Sales	118	94.4	103	82.4
Costs	101	80.8	99	79.2
Profit	17	13.6	4	3.2

Actual FC sales and FC costs are larger than budgeted for both Exporter and Importer. Because the favorable sales variance is greater than the unfavorable cost variance, Exporter's actual profit exceeds the budget in both FC and US$. Although Importer outperformed the FC sales budget, FC costs rose more rapidly and Importer's actual profit is less than budgeted in both FC and US$. Given these results, should Exporter's manager, but not Importer's manager, be rewarded? Not necessarily. Incorporating the expected effect of a currency devaluation on FC sales and FC costs paints a different picture.

Exporter

Because Exporter has only export sales, a 25 percent depreciation in the FC should allow Exporter to either (1) generate 25 percent more sales volume (if FC prices are not increased), or (2) increase FC prices by 25 percent to generate higher total FC sales revenue at the same level of sale volume. In either case, Exporter's sales should have been FC125. Actual sales are only FC118 or FC7 less than they would have been if Exporter's manager had fully exploited the opportunity to increase export sales.

Because Exporter sources all inputs locally, the depreciation in the FC should not affect costs. Exporter's manager has not effectively controlled costs; costs are FC11 (FC101 − FC90) higher than they should be.

The appreciation of the U.S. dollar should have allowed Exporter to generate the following amount of FC and US$ profit:

	FC	US$
Sales	125	100
Costs	90	72
Profit	35	28

Actual profit is only $13.60, or $14.40 less than it should have been.

Importer

Because Importer imports all inputs from the United States, a 25 percent appreciation in the U.S. dollar should cause Importer's FC costs to increase by 25 percent, from FC90 to FC101.25. Actual costs are only FC99 because Importer's manager has sourced some inputs locally rather than through imports.

Because all of Importer's sales are made locally, the appreciation in the U.S. dollar should have no effect on FC sales. Nonetheless, Importer's manager was able to outperform the FC sales budget.

The appreciation of the U.S. dollar should have caused Importer to incur the following amount of FC and US$ loss:

	FC	US$
Sales	100.00	80
Costs	101.25	81
Profit (loss)	(1.25)	(1)

Actual profit is $3.20, or $4.20 greater than it should have been.

After incorporating the effects of economic exposure into the analysis, it would appear that the manager of Importer should be rewarded and the manager of Exporter should not be.

The accounting system does not measure the amount of profit that *should have been* earned, so information provided by that system is not helpful in measuring a manager's effectiveness in coping with economic exposure. The use of translation combinations 3 and 5 outlined earlier, in which projected rates are used to prepare the budget, is a partial solution to this problem. Using projected rates to translate the budget provides an incentive for managers to take operating and strategic actions to minimize negative effects on cash flows from changes in exchange rates and take advantage of positive effects. However, this approach is limited in that projected exchange rates may not become reality. A refinement to this process would be to periodically update the projected ending exchange rate and ask local managers to update their plans as the projection changes. This has been referred to as *contingent budgeting.*[28] Clearly, this is not an easy process, but any system that forces managers of foreign operations to consider the effect that exchange rate changes have on their operating results should help in reducing the risk associated with them.

Implementing a Performance Evaluation System

The success of a performance evaluation system will be determined by its design as well as the implementation of that system. The discussion in this section is based on a recent technical briefing published by the Chartered Institute of Management Accountants (CIMA) in the United Kingdom on the latest trends in corporate performance measurement.[29] CIMA identifies six important factors that are required for a successful performance evaluation system:

1. *Integration with the overall business strategy.* It is not possible to measure performance in a meaningful way unless it is clear what an organization is trying to achieve. For example, if customer care has been identified as a critical success factor, then a fast response to complaints may be essential to achieve competitive advantage and a measure such as response time can be used to evaluate performance.

2. *Feedback and review.* The successful implementation of a performance evaluation system requires a continuous cycle of feedback on actual results in comparison with the original plan, feeding into the decision-making process. An important point to note here is that the original plan is based on certain assumptions about the nature of the business and what it takes to succeed. If performance falls short of what was expected in the original plan, then the company can take corrective action. This is an organizational learning process called single-loop learning. The term *single-loop* refers to the fact that the focus is for the organization to make decisions within the parameters of the original plan. In addition, a successful performance evaluation system should also include mechanisms to review performance measures over time. However, it may be appropriate to modify targets, change the activities being measured, or even modify the objectives. The action involved in this process is called double-loop learning. Here the focus extends to a consideration of the need to change aspects of the original plan. Single-loop learning is necessary to build core competencies, and double-loop learning is necessary to adapt to changes in the environment.

3. *Comprehensive measures.* The performance measurement system should reflect the range of factors that contribute to success. Financial performance, although the most important and widely used measure of performance, represents only one dimension of value and as such is inadequate in evaluating the strategic performance of an organization in its entirety. As explained earlier in this chapter, there is an increasing trend for MNCs to use nonfinancial measures in evaluating performance both at headquarters and subsidiary levels.

4. *Ownership and support throughout the organization.* It is important that employees throughout the organization understand and support the performance evaluation system. If they feel the system is imposed on them from above, without any consultation, they are less likely to cooperate with the system, and the system will not achieve its motivational objectives.

[28] See D. Lessard and D. Sharp, "Measuring the Performance of Operations Subject to Fluctuating Exchange Rates," *Midland Corporate Finance Journal* 2 (Fall 1984), pp. 18–30.

[29] Chartered Institute of Management Accountants, "Latest Trends."

5. *Fair and achievable measures.* Performance targets should be set at a level that is achievable and at the same time should encourage high performance. Fairness is particularly important where performance measures are used to reward managers' performance. As mentioned earlier in this chapter, performance measures should include only the elements directly controlled by managers. If this is not the case, the reward system is likely to cause frustration and demotivate managers rather than encourage better performance.

6. *A simple, clear, and understandable system.* The effectiveness of a performance evaluation system depends largely on how well the people involved understand the system and the measures used to evaluate performance. There is not much point in providing complex data about performance if these data are not readily understood by those being evaluated. If the performance evaluation system is overly complex, chances are that many will not understand it. A lack of understanding will lead to a lack of cooperation and support for the system. It is best to use simple and clear measures that can be easily understood and communicated to everyone in the organization.

CULTURE AND MANAGEMENT CONTROL

For MNCs, another factor should be added to the framework developed by CIMA for the successful implementation of a performance evaluation system: the system must be sensitive to the national cultures to which local managers belong. Indeed, cultural factors should be considered in the entire strategy implementation process. Implementing a corporate strategy that will influence human behavior in the desired manner requires cultural awareness, as a given method of implementation may not produce the desired outcome across all cultures. Noerreklit and Schoenfeld explain how differences in culturally determined value systems may lead to different managerial decisions across countries:

> Different background knowledge and culturally determined value systems exist in all MNCs, because employees grow up and are educated in different national environments and thus have non-congruent value systems. Such different values may (at a minimum) place a different emphasis on specific issues. Different emphasis and values are typically placed on specific subjects during the educational process (e.g., ethics, family relationships, work, sports, art, moral contained in children stories, songs, and proverbs). . . . Each of these influences (individually or jointly) will evoke slightly or substantially different reactions in people. This applies for day-to-day life as well as for management decisions as a special dimension of life. It suggests different actions to resolve similar problems (e.g., under-utilisation of capacity may suggest lay-offs in the US, however, in Europe, due to the existing labour law and tradition, a lay-off is too costly or unacceptable socially).[30]

Due to cultural differences, MNCs may find that changes are necessary to the manner in which strategies are implemented in different countries. For example, Japanese companies assign responsibility to the group rather than to the individual, and every group member is partially responsible for the group's performance.[31] This notion of group responsibility conflicts with the way standard costs

[30] H. Noerreklit and H. W. Schoenfeld, "Controlling Multinational Corporations: An Attempt to Analyze Some Unresolved Issues," *International Journal of Accounting* 35, no. 3 (2000), p. 418.

[31] L. Kelley, A. Whatley, and R. Worthley, "Assessing the Effects of Culture on Managerial Attitudes: A Three-Country Test," *Journal of International Business Studies,* Summer 2001, p. 22.

and budgets are used in the United States, in which responsibility is assigned to specific individuals within an organization.[32] This also calls into question the universal acceptability of one of the fundamental assumptions of the Western concept of management control—that the responsibility for specific tasks lies with the individual to whom the task is traceable. Research also has found differences between the United States and Japan in their use of budgets. U.S. managers tend to be more involved in the budgeting process, and budget variances are used as the basis for evaluating performance and determining rewards. Japanese managers, in contrast, tend to view budget variances as providing information that can be used to improve performance.[33]

Local managers' attitudes toward budgets also can be influenced by environmental factors. Researchers have discovered, for example, that managers in Central American countries view budgets as less critical than U.S. managers do.[34] Central American managers are more likely to see budgets as a source of certainty and security and as a means to protect resources amid turbulence, rather than as a performance evaluation and planning tool. The researchers argue that the differing attitudes toward budgets are due partly to the widely varying levels of environmental turbulence between the United States and Central America.

Culture also can affect management styles. Researchers have found that Mexican executives tend to use an authoritarian leadership style, do not see the need to share information with subordinates, and have little faith in participative management styles. This will have direct implications for the manner in which budgeting is applied within Mexican organizations. In particular, the idea of participative budgeting is not likely to be well received.[35]

Finally, cultural differences can influence capital budgeting decisions. For example, strong uncertainty avoidance (intolerance of uncertainty) can lead managers to require short payback periods for capital investments, because once the investment is recouped, the level of uncertainty associated with the investment is reduced significantly. This makes projects with shorter payback periods the preferred choice for some managers, even though projects with longer payback periods may produce greater longer-term benefits.

Summary

1. Accountants contribute to *strategy formulation* by providing skills to analyze customer, market, and competitor information, assess risks, develop projections as financial expressions of strategy, and prepare budgets. *Capital budgeting* is an important device used in strategy formulation.

2. *Multinational capital budgeting* is complicated by the various risks to which foreign operations are exposed. Forecasted future cash flows are likely to be influenced by factors such as local inflation, changes in exchange rates, and changes in host government policy.

[32] P. Miller and T. O'Leary, "Accounting and the Construction of the Governable Person," *Accounting, Organizations and Society* 12, no. 3 (1987), pp. 235–65.

[33] J. C. Bailes and T. Assada, "Empirical Differences between Japanese and American Budget and Performance Evaluation Systems," *International Journal of Accounting* 26, no. 2 (1991).

[34] R. Mandoza, F. Collins, and O. J. Holzmann, "Central American Budgeting Scorecard: Cross Cultural Insights," *Journal of International Accounting, Auditing and Taxation* 6 (1997), pp. 192–209.

[35] Kelley, Whatley, and Worthley, "Assessing the Effects."

3. Accountants contribute to *strategy implementation* by providing management control tools such as operational budgets and by helping to design and implement performance evaluation systems.

4. Multinational companies (MNCs) expand across national borders for various reasons, their cross-border operations can take different forms, and they adopt a variety of organizational structures. The choices made by an MNC in these areas influence the manner in which strategies are implemented.

5. Determining *the levels of control and delegation* appropriate for foreign affiliates is an important part of implementing multinational business strategy.

6. Companies must decide on *performance evaluation measures.* Although companies often use multiple measures, both financial and nonfinancial, most focus on financial measures of performance, and profit-based measures are most commonly used.

7. Companies must decide whether a foreign operation will be evaluated as *an investment center, a profit center,* or *a cost center.* Some foreign operations may have a strategic purpose other than profit creation and should therefore be evaluated differently.

8. Companies must also decide *whether the foreign operating unit and the managers of that unit should be evaluated in the same manner,* or whether they should be evaluated separately using different measures of performance. Responsibility accounting suggests that managers should not be held responsible for uncontrollable items. For foreign managers, this would consist of revenues and expenses controlled by the parent company, the host government, and others.

9. For those foreign operations evaluated on the basis of profitability, the company must decide whether profit will be measured in local or parent currency. Most companies evaluate the performance of foreign operations in parent currency, which necessitates *translation* from the local currency. These companies must decide whether the local manager will be *held responsible for the translation adjustment* that results.

10. If performance is evaluated by *comparing budgeted to actual results in parent currency,* exchange rate variances can be avoided by using the same exchange rate to translate the budget and actual results. Using a projected exchange rate to translate the budget provides an incentive for local management to factor the effects of expected exchange rate changes into the operating plans. Contingent budgeting involves periodic updating of operating budgets as exchange rates fluctuate during the period covered by the budget.

11. The success of a performance evaluation system is determined by its design as well as how it is implemented. To be successful, a performance evaluation system must be integrated with the overall strategy of the business; it must be comprehensive; it must be owned and supported throughout the organization; measures need to be fair and achievable; it needs to be simple, clear, and understandable; and there must be a system of feedback and review.

12. Management control systems also must be sensitive to the national cultures to which local managers belong. Cultural awareness is needed when implementing a system designed to influence human behavior in a particular manner, because a given method of implementation may not produce the desired outcome across all cultures.

Questions	1. What are the internal factors that influence strategy formulation within an MNC?

Questions

1. What are the internal factors that influence strategy formulation within an MNC?
2. What are the external factors that influence strategy formulation within an MNC?
3. Explain the role of accounting in strategy formulation within an MNC.
4. Compare and contrast NPV and IRR as capital budgeting techniques.
5. How does the organizational structure of an MNC influence its strategy implementation?
6. How do differences in cultural values across countries influence strategy implementation within an MNC?
7. Explain the role of accounting in implementing multinational business strategy.
8. What are the main issues that need to be considered in designing and implementing a successful performance evaluation system for a foreign subsidiary?
9. What differences can you identify between performance evaluation measures adopted by Japanese and U.S. MNCs?
10. What are the nonfinancial measures available to MNCs for evaluating foreign subsidiary performance?
11. What are the factors that influence the decision regarding the manner in which a particular subsidiary should be treated for purposes of performance evaluation (e.g., as a cost center or a profit center or an investment center)?
12. Do you think it is important to separate the evaluation of the performance of a subsidiary from that of its manager? Why?
13. What issues are associated with the calculation of profit for a foreign subsidiary?
14. What are the problems caused by inflation in evaluating the performance of a foreign subsidiary?

Exercises and Problems

1. A U.S. company is considering an investment project proposal to extend its operations in Germany. As part of the proposed project, the German operation is required to pay an annual royalty of €500,000 to the parent company.

   Required:
   Explain the cash flow implications of the payment referred to above for the parent company.

2. Refer to Exhibit 13.6.

   Required:
   Briefly explain the operating environment of a developing country of your choice using the framework that identifies the social, political, economic, and technological influences.

3. On January 1, 2009, a U.S. firm made an investment in Germany that will generate $5 million annually in depreciation, converted at current spot rate. Projected annual rates of inflation in Germany and in the United States are 5 percent and 2 percent, respectively. The real exchange rate is expected to remain constant and the German tax rate is 50 percent.

   Required:
   Calculate the expected real value (in terms of January 1, 2009 dollars) of the depreciation charge in year 2013. Assume that the tax write-off is taken at the end of the year.

4. Sedona Electronics of Arizona exports 25,000 Disc Drive Controllers (DDCs) per year to China under an agreement that covers the period 2009–2013. In China the DDCs are sold for the RMB (Chinese currency) equivalent of $50 per unit. The total costs in the United States are direct manufacturing costs and shipping costs, which amount to $35 per unit. The Market for DDCs in China is stable, and Sedona holds the major portion of the market.

In 2010, the Chinese government, adopting a policy of replacing imported DDCs with local products, invited Sedona to open an assembly plant in China. If Sedona makes the investment, it will operate the plant for five years and then sell the building and equipment to Chinese investors at net book value at the time of sale plus the current amount of any working capital. Sedona will be allowed to repatriate all net income and depreciation funds to the United States each year.

Sedona's anticipated outlay in 2010 would be $1,500,000 (buildings and equipment $750,000 and working capital $750,000). Building and Equipment will be depreciated over five years on a straight-line basis (no salvage value). At the end of the fifth year, the $750,000 of working capital may also be repatriated to the United States.

Locally assembled DDCs will be sold for the RMB equivalent of $50 each. Operating expenses per unit of DDC are as follows:

Materials purchased in China (dollar equivalent of RMB cost)	$15
Components imported from U.S. parent	$ 8
Variable costs per unit	$23

The $8 transfer price per unit for components sold by Sedona to its Chinese subsidiary consists of $4 of direct costs incurred in the U.S. and $4 of pretax profit to Sedona. There are no other operating costs in either China or the U.S.

In both China and the United States, corporate income tax rate is 40 percent. Sedona uses a 15 percent discount rate to evaluate all its investment projects.

Assume the investment is made at the end of 2010, and all operating cash flows occur at the end of 2011 through 2015. The RMB/dollar exchange rate is expected to remain constant over the five year period.

Required:

a. Do you recommend that Sedona make the investment?

b. Sedona learns that if it decides not to invest in China, a Japanese company will probably make an investment similar to that being considered by Sedona. The Japanese investment would be protected by the Chinese government against imports. How would this information affect your analysis and recommendation?

c. Assume the conditions of question (b). China reduces income tax charged to foreign firms from 40 percent to 20 percent in order to attract foreign investors. How would this information affect your analysis and recommendation?

5. Visit the Web site of Nokia Company (www.Nokia.com).

Required:

Comment on Nokia's risk management activities as reported in the company's 2009 annual report.

6. According to Exhibit 13.8, the top three budget goals for divisional managers of Japanese companies are sales volume, net profit, and production cost, in

that order, whereas those of U.S. companies are return on investment, controllable profit, and net profit, in that order.

Required:
Explain the possible reasons for differences in budget goals of Japanese and U.S. companies.

7. The concept of the balanced scorecard is becoming increasingly popular among firms internationally.

Required:
Explain the possible reasons for the popularity of the balanced scorecard.

8. It is impossible to separate the performance of a foreign subsidiary from that of its managers, and there is no need for it.

Required:
Critically comment on the preceding statement.

9. Sometimes an MNC may decide to use local currency to evaluate a foreign subsidiary.

Required:
Explain the circumstances under which it may be appropriate for an MNC to use local currency to evaluate a foreign subsidiary.

10. Developing a global business strategy for an MNC is a highly complex task.

Required:
Briefly discuss the complexities referred to in the preceding statement.

11. Globalization has made cultural values irrelevant as a factor influencing multinational business and accounting.

Required:
State whether or not you agree with the preceding statement, and develop an argument to support the position you have taken.

Case 13-1

Canyon Power Company

Late in 2009, Canyon Power Company (CPC) management was considering expansion of the company's international business activities. CPC is an Arizona-based manufacturer of specialist electric motors for use in industrial equipment. All of the company's sales were to other manufacturers in the industrial equipment industry. CPC's worldwide market was supplied from subsidiaries in Germany, Mexico, and Malaysia as well as the United States. The company was particularly successful in Asia mainly due to the high quality of its products, its technical expertise, excellent after-sale service, and of course the continued rapid economic growth in many Asian countries. This success led corporate management to consider seriously the feasibility of further expansion of its business in the Asian region.

The Malaysian subsidiary of CPC distributed and assembled electric motors. It also had limited manufacturing facilities so that it could undertake special adaptations required. With the maturing of the Asian market, particularly in the industrial sector, an expansion of capacity in that market was of strategic importance. The Malaysian subsidiary had been urging corporate management to expand its capacity since the beginning of 2009. However, an alternative scenario appeared more promising. The Indian economy, with its liberalized economic policies, was growing at annual rates much higher than those of many industrialized countries. Further, India had considerably lower labor costs and certain government incentives that were not available in Malaysia. Therefore, the company chose India for its Asian expansion project, and had a four-year investment project proposal prepared by the treasurer's staff.

The proposal was to establish a wholly owned subsidiary in India producing electric motors for the Indian domestic market as well as for export to other Asian countries. The initial equity investment would be $1.5 million, equivalent to 67.5 million Indian rupees (Rs) at the exchange rate of Rs 45 to the U.S. dollar. (Assume that the Indian rupee is freely convertible, and there are no restrictions on transfers of foreign exchange out of India.) An additional Rs 27 million would be raised by borrowing from a commercial bank in India at an interest rate of 10 percent per annum. The principal amount of the bank loan would be payable in full at the end of the fourth year. The combined capital would be sufficient to purchase plant of $1.8 million and would cover other initial expenditures including working capital. The cost of installation would be $15,000, with another $5,000 for testing. No additional working capital would be required during the four-year period. The plant was expected to have a salvage value of Rs 10 million at the end of four years. Straight-line depreciation would be applied to the original cost of the plant.

The firm's overall marginal after-tax cost of capital was about 12 percent. However, because of the higher risks associated with an Indian venture, CPC decided that a 16 percent discount rate would be applied to the project.

Present value factors at 16 percent are as follows:

Period	Factor
1	0.862
2	0.743
3	0.641
4	0.552

Sales forecasts are as follows:

	Sales (units)	
Year	(Domestic)	(Export)
1	5,000	10,000
2	6,000	12,000
3	7,000	14,000
4	8,000	16,000

The initial selling price of an electric motor was to be Rs 4,500 for Indian domestic sales and export sales in the Asian region, and the selling price in both cases was to increase at an annual rate of 10 percent. The exchange rate between the Indian rupee and the U.S. dollar was expected to vary as follows:

January 1, Year 1	Rs 45 per U.S. dollar
December 31, Year 1	Rs 45 per U.S. dollar
December 31, Year 2	Rs 43 per U.S. dollar
December 31, Year 3	Rs 40 per U.S. dollar
December 31, Year 4	Rs 38 per U.S. dollar

The cash expenditure for operating expenses, excluding interest payments, would be Rs 44 million in Year 1 and was expected to increase at a rate of 8 percent per year. The Indian subsidiary is expected to pay a royalty of Rs 20 million to the parent company at the end of each of the four years. In addition, in those years in which the subsidiary generates a profit, it will pay a dividend to CPC equal to 100 percent of net earnings. Through negotiation with the Indian government, the subsidiary will be exempt from Indian corporate income taxes and withholding taxes on payments made to the parent company. Royalties and dividends received from the Indian subsidiary are fully taxable in the United States at the U.S. corporate tax rate of 35 percent.

CPC expects to be able to sell the Indian subsidiary at the end of the fourth year for its salvage value. CPC also expects to be able to repatriate to the parent the cash balance at the end of Year 4. The cash balance will be equal to the difference between the aggregate amount of cash from operations generated by the subsidiary and the aggregate amount of dividends paid to CPC, after paying back the local bank loan. The repatriated cash balance will be taxed in the United States at 35 percent only if there is a gain after deducting the cost of the original investment.

Required

Using the information provided, you are required to

1. Calculate net present value from both a project and a parent company perspective.
2. Recommend to CPC corporate management whether or not to accept the proposal.

Case 13-2

Lion Nathan Limited

> We're in the business of satisfying thirst. We do it very well. We're also thirsty ourselves. Thirsty for continued profitable growth. Every gain delivers more for our shareholders. We're thirsty for knowledge. People and their preferences change all the time. We're open to ideas from everywhere that will make us better at beverages and brands. We're thirsty for a bigger share of the market. It's a competitive place, but we're determined to prevail through the sheer quality of our brands. We're doing all this with passion, integrity and a "can do" attitude that enables us to face reality and turn it to our advantage.[1]

[1] Lion Nathan Limited, 2001 annual report, p. 1.

Background

Lion Nathan Limited (hereafter, Lion) was formed in 1988 by the merger of two New Zealand companies: Lion Corporation, a brewer, wine and spirit manufacturer, and hotel operator, and LD Nathan & Company, a food and general merchandise retailer with consumer goods and soft drink interests. The company's strategic direction had been heavily influenced by its longtime leader, Douglas Myers, who retired from the chairmanship of the company, which he held since 1997 (Exhibit C1). Lion was the leading brewer in the duopolistic New Zealand market.

Lion quickly realized the need to transform itself from a small New Zealand–focused company into a strong Australasian business with an increasingly international outlook. In 1990 it bought 50 percent of Natbrew Holdings in Australia. The company also entered into a franchise arrangement with PepsiCo Inc. to manufacture, market, and distribute Pepsi products in Australia. In 1992 Lion Nathan acquired the remaining 50 percent of Natbrew and expanded the Pepsi franchise arrangement to NewZealand. In 1993 the company added Hahn Brewery and South Australian Breweries to the operation. The company's Australian breweries now had a 41 percent share of the Australian beer market and accounted for about 75 percent of Lion's assets (see Exhibit C2). Lion was the second largest brewer in Australasia.

Lion entered the China beer market in April 1995, when it spent NZ$21.6 million to purchase a 60 percent interest in the Taihushui brewery in Wuxi (approximately 120 kilometers west of Shanghai), with the Mashan District Government as the joint venture partner. Unlike most foreign joint-venture breweries in China, the Wuxi brewery had been turned from a loss maker to a profit center before Lion became involved. According to the 50-year agreement with Taihushui, Lion would have management control of the joint venture, and it was envisaged the local management would be retained, supplemented by Lion personnel in specialist areas such as production and marketing. In January 1996, ownership of the Taihushui brewery was increased to 80 percent.

The Taihushui purchase was funded out of Lion's operating cash flow from its existing brewing businesses in Australia and New Zealand. Lion's CEO, Myers, said the Wuxi joint venture gave Lion a significant foothold from which to build a greater presence in a high-growth area of China—the Yangtse River

EXHIBIT C1
Company Chairman

Source: Lion Nathan Limited, 2001 annual report.

Douglas Myers, Chairman since 1997, and CEO for 15 years from 1982, retired as Chairman in 2001.

Myers' formal association with the liquor industry began in 1965. It was then he became Managing Director of the family company, The Campbell & Ehrenfried Co. Ltd., continuing the Myers' already long history in brewing and liquor retailing. Six years later he founded New Zealand Wines and Spirits and by 1981 headed Lion Breweries.

Under his direction and later under his Chairmanship, Lion Nathan has grown from a small local New Zealand brewer to become one of Australasia's largest beverages companies delivering double digit compound annual growth for shareholders.

EXHIBIT C2
Lion Asset Allocation, 1989 and 1999

	New Zealand	Australia	China
1989	95%	5%	0%
1999	20%	75%	5%

Delta. Although beer consumption in China was growing rapidly, with per capita consumption increasing by 15–20 percent annually since 1990, it was still low by Western standards. Current annual per capita consumption in the Yangtse River Delta area averaged 14 liters, less than a fifth of New Zealand's or Australia's consumption. Myers said, "The time is right for the Chinese move."

Annual GDP growth in the region at the time exceeded 17 percent, and there were already more than 3,000 joint ventures in Wuxi alone. Around 70 million people lived in the delta (an area about the size of Tasmania, half the size of New Zealand's North Island). Along with its Yangtse River Delta neighbors Shanghai and Suzhou, Wuxi ranked among the five wealthiest cities in China.

Lion expanded its interests in China with the opening of a new $180 million state-of-the-art wholly owned brewery at Suzhou in March 1998. The 200-million-liter capacity at the Suzhou brewery gave the company capacity equivalent to the total New Zealand beer market, and the group had more employees in China than in New Zealand.

Introducing another twist to Lion's internationalization strategy, the Kirin Brewery Company of Japan purchased a 45 percent interest of Lion in April 1998. Although Kirin, as the dominant shareholder of Lion, affirmed that, like Lion, it saw the relationship as a long-term and enduring one, there were some concerns about their Kirin's intentions (see Exhibit C3).

In April 1999, Lion announced that it was entering into an agreement with Brauerei Beck & Company of Germany for a long-term partnership in China for the Beck's brand. The agreement would provide for Lion to brew and sell Beck's beer throughout China. Lion's managing director for China, Jim O'Mahony, said that the agreement was a clear indication of both brewers' long-term commitment to China.

In June 2000 the company shifted its domicile and primary stock exchange listing to Australia. Lion's chairman, Doug Myers, said, "The decision to relocate

EXHIBIT C3
Partnership with Kirin Breweries

Source: Lesley Springall, *The Independent*, May 30, 2001, p. 5.

Lion Seeks Foreign Fizz for Its China Operations

Lion Nathan yesterday quashed rumours that its majority shareholder, Japan's largest brewer Kirin Breweries, might take its loss-making Chinese operations off its hands. But Lion is looking for a buyer—or at least a partner—to help stem losses in China.

Lion's losses in China were reduced to $A12.9 million during the period compared to the previous half year loss of $A15.7 million.

Despite five-year prediction to the contrary, the operation has reported only bad news since Lion entered the market in 1995.

Kirin bought 46 percent of Lion in 1998 for about $1.4 billion. At the time, it said one of the reasons for its purchase was Lion's toe-hold in China which accounts for about 5 percent of Lion's overall business.

Since this "partnership agreement" lapsed last month, speculation has been rife about Kirin's long-term plans.

Lockey (Paul Lockey is Lion's Chief Financial Officer) says Kirin is not interested in Lion's Chinese operation and that it was not the key driver to the company's investment. "It is supportive of the process we're going through and has stated it has no intention to change or operate any differently as a result of the expiry of the partnership principles". Lockey denied there was a link between Friday's resignation of Lion director Mike Smith, who was instrumental in the setting-up of the Chinese operations and negotiations with Kirin, and the problems in China. After 30 years with Lion, 15 as director, Smith said it was simply time to move on. He has been a key contributor to Lion's progress from a small New Zealand brewer to a multinational of considerable clout.

the company head office is a sensible business decision which recognizes that our Australian business, which makes up 70 percent of our assets, is the main growth engine of the company." The company would remain listed on the New Zealand Stock Exchange. As a result, Lion became a New Zealand–based company that earned most of its income overseas and had an overseas-based controlling shareholder.

In August 2000, following the resignation of O'Mahony, Lion appointed James Brindley and David Carter as joint China managing directors.

Contrary to initial predictions, Lion's China operations were never profitable, for example, the reported losses for 1999, 2000, and 2001 were A$27.2 million, A$24.4 million and A$19.3 million, respectively.

In 2001, Lion's Chinese brewing operations in the Yangzte River Delta showed some improvement. While volume grew 5 percent to 83.7 million liters, revenue increased 8.6 percent with improved pricing and mix shift. In local currency, the loss of RMB 83.8 million was a 32 percent improvement on the comparable 12-month period in the prior year. In Australian dollars, the loss improved by 21 percent. Despite these improvements, the company's Chinese breweries continued to run below capacity.

In a media release on July 5, 2001, Lion announced that it had terminated all discussions with two of China's largest brewers. Commenting on this decision, Lion CEO, Gordon Cains said

> As well as successfully progressing a range of initiatives to improve the financial and operating performance of our Chinese business, we have, over the last twelve months been looking at the options available to us to participate in the consolidation of the Chinese beer market. Having patiently negotiated in good faith with a number of major brewers, we have now reached a point where we do not believe that a sensible outcome can be achieved in the foreseeable future. As a result, we have advised these two parties that we do not believe their proposals are realistic options for Lion Nathan and its shareholders. While this is disappointing, we are keen to bring an end to the uncertainty that is not helpful from an operating perspective.[2]

Opportunities were currently being investigated to address this issue.

In August 2001, following the retirement of Douglas Myers from the board and chairmanship, the board appointed GT Ricketts as the new chairman.

The Market in China

The Chinese beer market was highly fragmented, with a large number of breweries comprising regional and subregional markets. Although it has experienced some consolidation in recent years, the competitive environment was expected to remain difficult, with most brewers having real difficulty achieving adequate returns. In early 1998, there were around 860 breweries of any significant size in China. They included 40 with foreign joint-venture participation by a roll call of brewing giants: Heineken, Carlsberg, Guinness, Anheuser-Busch, Suntory, Fosters, San Miguel, Asahi.

Lion was wrestling with a number of problems in the China side of its business. Transport in the region was expensive and unreliable, with a series of canals of varying depth, width, and height clearance. To negotiate the waterways barges could be no larger than 60 tons. However, to get beer to the distribution hub in

---

[2] www.lion-nathan.co.nz.

Shanghai in sufficient volume to make the trip worthwhile required much larger vessels. Lion was spending a lot of money to recruit and train local executives with little knowledge of Western marketing and management techniques. The task was not an easy one and, at least in the initial stages, meant a heavy commitment of expatriate resources to create a corporate culture. Getting well-educated, well-trained staff was difficult, and keeping them was worse in a market full of foreign companies desperate for well-qualified locals. Many Chinese employees didn't have great loyalty to their company and would move firms for as little as an extra $20 a month.[3]

The key challenge was to adapt the Chinese *guanxi* (relationship) way of doing business to Western minds, particularly those that emphasized selling. Lion's human resources director in China, Shane Slipais, said, "Relationship building is vital to all success in China, either personal or in business. . . . Chinese spend more time on and off the job with each other than in Australia or New Zealand. . . . The secret of doing business in China is to be rigid in what you want to achieve but be flexible in the way you get there."[4] *Guanxi* worked in both formal and informal ways. Outright confrontation in the workplace was generally a no-no, and employer/employee disputes were dealt with through intermediaries.

Compliance with regulations, such as paying taxes and not polluting the environment, was far less obvious. The pecking order put multinational companies at the top of the compliance list, Chinese state-owned enterprises at the bottom and overseas-Chinese-run businesses in the middle. Corruption was endemic in any system where a form of authority, in this case the Communist Party, was above the law. It was a day-to-day reality.[5] From a Western perspective, the main problem was the need to understand different business philosophies and practices. Failure to do so could be expensive. As one commentator stated, "There is a rule of thumb about China—do your homework before you get here. Take your worst-case scenario for cost and time, multiply it by two and you have the full cost estimate."

The desire for short-term profits and/or high rates of return did not bring much success for foreign investors in China. Chinese partners emphasized long-term relationships with reasonable returns and mutual benefits. Only half of China's breweries made money, and the foreigners' track record so far had not been conspicuously better than the locals'. Both Lion's Australian archrival, Foster's, whose three loss-making breweries together notched up a deficit of $29 million in 1997, and British brewer Bass decided to quit. However, Lion appeared determined to stay back (see Exhibit C4).

Lion's Brands

In New Zealand, Lion was one major listed company that used Interbrand to value its beer brands. David Wethey stated, "Often a company would look only at brand equity when it was thinking of buying or selling the brand. But establishing the value of a brand was important right throughout its life in a company."[6]

---

[3] Nikki Mandow, "Doing Business in China: Not for the Ethnocentric," *The Independent,* January 28, 1997, p. 18.

[4] N. Gibson, "Foreigners Still Find Breaking into China a Delicate Business," *National Business Review,* August 15, 1997, p. 37.

[5] Ibid.

[6] Michele Simpson, "Love Your Brand, Get a Do-It-Yourself Valuation," *National Business Review,* July 7, 2000.

EXHIBIT C4
Lion Determination

Source: Michele Simpson, "Brewers Hit Big Trouble in China but Lion Decides to Tough It Out," *National Business Review,* April 14, 2000.

Brewers Hit Big Trouble in China but Lion Decides to Tough It Out

Brewer Lion Nathan is not going to follow competitors choosing to flee the red-ink generating Chinese market.

Despite year-upon year of huge losses since it first set up in China, Lion Nathan is ploughing on with its Asian venture as other big name brewers suddenly quit the market. British brewer Bass has decided to pull the plug on its $80 million joint venture in China, the world's second-largest market.

"There is an overcapacity in China," Lion Nathan's managing director of the Chinese operation, Jim O'Mahony said. "The industry needs consolidation and we're not overly concerned whether that process is by people exiting or folding."

Bass said talks had begun to sell its 55% share in a joint venture after it fell out with its local partner in China. Foster's last year grew tired of the much hyped potential of the 1.3 billion strong Chinese market. It sold its breweries in Tianjin and Guangzhou.

The losses for Lion's Chinese venture have risen sharply in the past three years. In 1997 it was $8.8 million, in 1998 it tripled to nearly $30 million and for the financial year ended August 31, 1999, the loss before interest and tax was $32.6 million.

… Bass has pulled out over problems with its local partner. "The gaps between our cultures have led to different views and even clashes, as the foreign party felt it didn't get what it wanted," a Bass spokeswoman said.

Lion's brands, not the beer, were worth $2.2 billion according to Lion's balance sheet (see Exhibit C5). Unlike the beer, the brand was an intangible asset and, as such, hard to pin a price tag on. However, Lion's 2001 annual report stated that its brands were revalued annually and the valuations were supported by independent valuations. Furthermore, it was claimed that the company's policy in this matter was in compliance with the applicable Australian accounting standards (see Exhibit C6).

Warwick Bryan, Lion's manager of investor relations, commented that if New Zealand's proposed accounting standard (ED 87, a photocopy of IAS 38) were to be adopted, that would mean two-thirds of the brands would have to be immediately removed from Lion's balance sheet and the remainder would have to be removed over 20 years through amortization.[7]

The Advertising Agencies Association stated that, in 1998, tangible assets represented only approximately 29 percent of the market value of Britain's FTSE 100 companies. They also stated the idea that only brands valued through a buy-and-sell process should make it to the balance sheet was "oxymoronic," because the whole point of buying a brand was to purchase something with potentially enduring, or increasing, value.[8]

Commenting on IAS 38, powerful factions felt accounting standards were heading in a different direction to commercial and economic reality. The issue was further complicated by the fact that not all companies with established brands, even within the same industry, treated the value of their brands as an asset on the balance sheet. Underlying the fuss was a fundamental debate about how well the accounting profession was serving the business and financial communities.

As one commentator stated, "In the information economy the fastest growing industries are those in which intellectual property is companies' greatest, if not only, asset. What's the value of Microsoft without Windows?"[9]

[7] Felicity Anderson, "When Is an Asset Not an Asset?" *The Independent,* December 1, 1999, p. 32.
[8] Ibid.
[9] "Barons Call Accounting Standard 'Crazy,'" *National Business Review,* June 4, 1999.

EXHIBIT C5
Financial Position

LION NATHAN LIMITED AND ITS CONTROLLED ENTITIES
Statement of Financial Position
As at 30 September 2001

	Note	Consolidated 30 Sep $m01	30 Sep $m00
Current assets			
Cash	7	10.4	5.0
Receivables	8	239.0	263.4
Inventories	9	116.0	117.6
Other	11	48.5	37.0
Total current assets		413.9	423.0
Noncurrent assets			
Receivables	8	27.9	16.3
Equity accounted investments	12	22.0	130.4
Other financial assets	10	12.0	1.3
Property, plant, and equipment	13	821.9	776.7
Deferred tax assets	14	31.3	27.4
Intangibles	15	2,136.9	1,978.7
Other	11	28.8	51.3
Total noncurrent assets		3,080.8	2,982.1
Total assets		3,494.7	3,405.1
Current liabilities			
Payables	16	280.6	264.1
Interest bearing liabilities	17	7.8	10.4
Current tax liabilities	19	2.5	7.3
Provisions	20	101.3	105.4
Total current liabilities		392.2	387.2
Noncurrent liabilities			
Interest bearing liabilities	17	1,070.2	1,291.5
Deferred tax liabilities	19	95.8	56.9
Provisions	20	12.8	3.2
Total noncurrent liabilities		1,178.8	1,351.6
Total liabilities		1,571.0	1,738.8
Net assets		1,923.7	1,666.3
Equity			
Parent entity interest			
Contributed equity	22	436.1	436.1
Reserves	23	861.0	677.1
Retained profits	24	619.0	552.7
Total parent equity		1,916.1	1,665.9
Outside equity interests in controlled entities	25	7.6	0.4
Total equity		1,923.7	1,666.3

EXHIBIT C6
Brands

Source: Lion Nathan Limited, 2001 annual report, p. 70.

Brands

Brands are stated at fair value. Revaluations are made annually and are supported by independent valuations. This policy is consistent with prior years, and complies with the revised AASB 1041 *Revaluation of Non-Current Assets*.

The fair value for beer brands owned by the Lion Nathan Group has been recognized where earnings of a brand can be separately identified, where title in them is clear, their ownership could change independently from the rest of the business, and where the brands achieve earnings in excess of those achieved by unbranded products.

Brands are considered to have no predeterminate finite economic life and are not amortized. The carrying value of each brand is subject to annual review and any permanent diminution in the aggregate value of the brands will first be charged against the Lion Nathan Group revaluation reserves.

Required

Assume Lion's new chairman decided to conduct a thorough investigation into the entire China operation, and he invited you, a U.S. consultant with accounting qualifications, to do this. Write a report identifying the main strategic issues and recommending the courses of action available to Lion in facing the current realities of this global initiative.

References

Abdallah, W. M., and D. E. Keller. "Measuring the Multinational's Performance." *Management Accounting*, October 1985, pp. 26–30, 56.

Anthony, Robert N., and Vijay Govindarajan. *Management Control Systems*, 9th ed. (international ed.). New York: McGraw-Hill, 1998.

Bailes, J. C., and T. Assada. "Empirical Differences between Japanese and American Budget and Performance Evaluation Systems." *International Journal of Accounting* 26, no. 2 (1991), pp. 131–42.

Baker, J. C., and L. J. Beardsley. "Multinational Companies' Use of Risk Evaluation and Profit Measurement for Capital Budgeting Decisions." *Journal of Business Finance,* Spring 1973, pp. 38–43.

Baliga, B. R., and A. M. Jaeger. "Multinational Corporations: Control Systems and Delegation Issues." *Journal of International Business,* Fall 1984, pp. 25–40.

Bavishi, Vinod B. "Capital Budgeting Practices at Multinationals." *Management Accounting,* August 1981.

Blocher, Edward J.; Kung H. Chen; Gary Cokins; and Thomas W. Lin. *Cost Management: A Strategic Emphasis.* New York: McGraw-Hill, 2005.

Borkowski, S. C. "International Managerial Performance Evaluation: A Five Country Comparison." *Journal of International Business Studies*, Third Quarter 1999, pp. 533–56.

Chandler, A. D., Jr. *Strategy and Structure.* Cambridge, MA: MIT Press, 1962.

Chartered Institute of Management Accountants. "Latest Trends in Corporate Performance Measurement," 2002.

Choi, F. D. S., and I. J. Czechowicz. "Assessing Foreign Subsidiary Performance: A Multinational Comparison." *Management International Review* 23 (1983), pp. 14–25.

Demirag, I. S. "Assessing Foreign Subsidiary Performance: The Currency Choice of U.K. MNCs." *Journal of International Business Studies,* Summer 1988, pp. 257–75.

Govindarajan, V. "Appropriateness of Accounting Data in Performance Evaluation: An Empirical Examination of Environmental Uncertainty as an Intervening Variable." *Accounting, Organizations and Society* 9, no. 2 (1984), pp. 125–35.

Gupta, A. K., and V. Govindarajan. "Knowledge Flows and the Structure of Control within Multinational Corporations." *Academy of Management Review* 16, no. 4 (1991), pp. 768–92.

Hassel, L. "Headquarter Reliance on Accounting Performance Measures in a Multinational Context." *Journal of International Financial Management and Accounting* 3, no. 1 (1991), pp. 17–38.

Hassel, Lars G., and Gary M. Cunningham. "Psychic Distance and Budget Control of Foreign Subsidiaries." *Journal of International Accounting Research* 3, no. 2 (2004), pp. 79–93.

Hofstede, G. *Culture's Consequences: International Differences in Work-Related Values.* Beverly Hills: Sage, 1980.

Hosseini, A., and Z. Rezaee. "Impact of SFAS No. 52 on Performance Measures of Multinationals." *International Journal of Accounting* 25 (1990), pp. 43–52.

Kaplan, Robert S., and David P. Norton. *The Balanced Scorecard.* Boston: Harvard Business School Press, 1996.

———. "The Balanced Scorecard Measures That Drive Performance." *Harvard Business Review*, January–February 1992, pp. 71–79.

———. "Putting the Balance Scorecard to Work." *Harvard Business Review*, September–October 1993, pp. 134–42.

Kelley, L.; A. Whatley; and R. Worthley. "Assessing the Effects of Culture on Managerial Attitudes: A Three-Country Test." *International Business Studies*, Summer 2001, pp. 17–31.

Lessard, D. R., and P. Lorange. "Currency Changes and Management Control: Resolving the Centralization/Decentralization Dilemma." *Accounting Review*, July 1977, pp. 628–37.

Lessard, D. R., and D. Sharp. "Measuring the Performance of Operations Subject to Fluctuating Exchange Rates." *Midland Corporate Finance Journal* 2 (Fall 1984), pp. 18–30.

Mandoza, R.; F. Collins; and O. J. Holzmann. "Central American Budgeting Scorecard: Cross Cultural Insights." *Journal of International Accounting, Auditing and Taxation* 6 (1997), pp. 192–209.

McWatters, Cheryl S.; Dale C. Morse; and Jerold L. Zimmerman. *Management Accounting*, international ed. New York: McGraw-Hill, 2001, pp. 113–14.

Miller, P., and T. O'Leary. "Accounting and the Construction of the Governable Person." *Accounting, Organizations and Society* 12, no. 3 (1987), pp. 235–65.

Morsicato, H. G. *Currency Translation and Performance Evaluation in Multinationals.* Ann Arbor, MI: UMI Research Press, 1980.

Noerreklit, H., and H. W. Schoenfeld. "Controlling Multinational Companies: An Attempt to Analyse Some Unresolved Issues." *International Journal of Accounting* 35, no. 3 (2000), pp. 415–30.

PricewaterhouseCoopers. "Non-financial Measures Are Highest-Rated Determinants of Total Shareholder Value, PricewaterhouseCoopers Survey Finds." Management Barometer, news release. New York: PWC, April 22, 2002.

Robbins, S. M., and R. B. Stobaugh. "The Bent Measuring Stick for Foreign Subsidiaries." *Harvard Business Review*, September–October 1973, pp. 80–88.

Rutenberg, D. P. *Multinational Management*. Boston: Little Brown, 1982.

Sakurai, M. "The Influence of Factory Automation on Management Practices: A Study of Japanese Companies." Working paper, January 1989.

Schlank, Rosemary. *Evaluating the Performance of International Operations*. New York: Business International Corporation, 1989.

Shields, M. D.; C. W. Chow; Y. Kato; and Y. Nakagawa. "Management Accounting Practices in the U.S. and Japan: Comparative Survey Findings and Research Implications." *Journal of International Financial Management and Accounting* 3, no. 1 (1991), pp. 61–77.

Stanley, M., and S. Block. "An Empirical Study of Management and Financial Variables Influencing Capital Budgeting Decisions for Multinational Corporations in the 1980s." *Management International Review* 3 (1983).

Chapter **Fourteen**

Comparative International Auditing and Corporate Governance

Learning Objectives

After reading this chapter, you should be able to

- Define corporate governance and discuss the circumstances that caused it to receive worldwide attention in recent years.
- Explain the link between auditing and corporate governance in an international context.
- Examine international diversity in external auditing.
- Describe the steps taken toward international harmonization of auditing standards.
- Discuss the issues concerning auditor liability and auditor independence.
- Explain the role of audit committees.
- Discuss the ethical issues involved in external auditing at the international level.
- Examine internal auditing issues in an international context.
- Describe the provisions in the Sarbanes-Oxley Act of 2002 in relation to auditing issues.

INTRODUCTION

Auditing improves the precision, quality, and reliability of information made available to users of financial statements mainly for making investment decisions regarding equities and debts in the financial markets.[1] The assurance services provided by auditing firms play an important role in ensuring the quality of financial information. Audited information helps lower the cost of debt offerings and contributes to greater investor confidence in the information provided.

[1] Auditing is "a systematic process of objectively obtaining and evaluating evidence regarding assertions about economic actions and events to ascertain the degree of correspondence between those assertions and established criteria and communicating the results to interested parties." American Accounting Association, *A Statement of Basic Auditing Concepts* (AAA Committee on Basic Auditing Concepts, 1973).

International auditing refers to the rules for auditing of financial statements to be applied internationally and the processes associated with auditing financial statements prepared by multinational corporations (MNCs). With the increasing trend toward globalization of markets and rapid growth in international transactions, the issues associated with providing reliable, high-quality information have become crucial for MNCs in their efforts to succeed in increasingly competitive global markets.

The 1997–1998 Asian financial crisis; the more recent corporate scandals, particularly in the United States, involving large companies such as Enron, World-Com, and Global Crossing; and the more recent global financial crisis (GFC) have further highlighted the importance of assurance services.

In June 2010, the UK FRC issued the new UK Corporate Governance Code. It states that the purpose of corporate governance is to facilitate effective, entrepreneurial and prudent management that can deliver the long-term success of the company. The first version of the UK Code on Corporate Governance was produced in 1992 by the Cadbury Committee. It states, "Corporate governance is the system by which companies are directed and controlled". Boards of directors are responsible for the governance of their companies. The shareholders' role in governance is to appoint the directors and the auditors and to satisfy themselves that an appropriate governance structure is in place. The responsibilities of the board include setting the company's strategic arms, providing the leadership to put them into effect, supervising the management of the business and reporting to shareholders on their stewardship. The board's actions are subject to laws, regulations and the shareholders in general meeting.

The new Code applies to accounting periods beginning on or after June 2010. The 'comply or explain' approach is the trademark of corporate governance in the UK. It is the foundation of the Code's flexibility. It is strongly supported by both companies and shareholders and has been imitated internationally.

According to the Code, the 'comply or explain' approach recognizes that an alternative to following a provision may be justified in particular circumstances if good governance can be achieved by other means. A condition of doing so is that the reasons for it should be explained clearly to shareholders (and other interested parties), who may wish to discuss the position with the company and whose voting intentions may be influenced as a result. In providing an explanation, the company should aim to illustrate how its actual practices are both consistent with the principle to which the particular provision relates and contribute to good governance.

The Sarbanes-Oxley Act, which was enacted by the U.S. Congress in 2002 following corporate debacles, was described as the most sweeping corporate legislation since the Securities Acts of 1933 and 1934. It includes detailed provisions dealing with corporate governance and various auditing issues designed to help restore investor confidence.[2] The financial regulations introduced in the United States in July 2010 following the GFC are even more sweeping. Commenting on the Asian financial crisis, the World Bank report stated that the poor system of corporate governance contributed to it by shielding the banks, financial companies, and corporations from market discipline.[3] Auditing is an integral part of corporate governance.

The international aspects of auditing, in particular harmonization of auditing standards and practices across countries, have received relatively less attention

---

[2] A summary of the Sarbanes-Oxley Act is available at www.gcwf.com/newsletter/corp/020729/sarbanes_oxley_act.htm.

[3] World Bank, *East Asia: The Road to Recovery* (Washington DC: World Bank, 1998).

during the last four decades compared to the issues concerning international harmonization of financial reporting standards. The recent debates about restoring investor confidence have brought the international issues of auditing and corporate governance to the fore.

This chapter discusses the external and internal auditing issues as they relate to corporate governance in an international context and the issues related to international harmonization of auditing. First, we explain the link between auditing and corporate governance. Then we describe international diversity in external auditing and some issues related to international harmonization of auditing standards. We also provide brief discussions on selected additional issues of international auditing, namely, auditor's liability, auditor independence, and the role of audit committees. Further, we examine issues related to internal auditing. Finally, we provide some thoughts on the future direction of international auditing and corporate governance.

INTERNATIONAL AUDITING AND CORPORATE GOVERNANCE

Corporate governance deals with the way corporations are managed and governed. As a new term, *corporate governance* suffers from a lack of definition and can mean many different things to different people.[4]

Numerous reports have been produced in recent years in many countries focusing on corporate governance.[5] In 1999, the Organization for Economic Cooperation and Development (OECD) developed a set of principles, *Principles of Corporate Governance,* to assist member and nonmember governments in their efforts to "evaluate and improve the legal, institutional and regulatory framework for corporate governance" and to "provide guidance and suggestions" for various stakeholders in corporate governance.[6] According to the OECD,

> Corporate governance . . . involves a set of relationships between a company's management, its board, its shareholders, and other stakeholders. Corporate governance also provides the structure through which the objectives of the company are set, and the means of attaining those objectives and monitoring performance are determined. Good corporate governance should provide proper incentives for the board and management to pursue objectives that are in the interests of the company and shareholders and should facilitate effective monitoring. (p. 1)

The OECD principles deal with, among other issues, the rights and fair treatment of various groups of shareholders, the role of various stakeholders, the importance of disclosure and transparency of information, and the responsibility of the board. They clarify the notion that the board of directors has the ultimate responsibility for governing (not operating on a day-to-day basis) a company. The OECD principles formed the basis of the corporate governance component of the World Bank/International Monetary Fund's Reports on the Observance of Standards and Codes (ROSC).

---

[4] The term *corporate governance* first appeared in 1962 in a book by Richard Eells of Columbia University.

[5] For major country reports on corporate governance, visit the World Bank site at www.worldbank.org/html/fpd/privatesector/cg/codes.htm.

[6] Organization for Economic Cooperation and Development, *OECD Principles of Corporate Governance,* Paris: OECD, 1999, available at www.oecd.org. The OECD member countries are Australia, Austria, Belgium, Canada, Czech Republic, Denmark, Finland, France, Germany, Greece, Hungary, Iceland, Ireland, Italy, Japan, Korea, Luxembourg, Mexico, Netherlands, New Zealand, Norway, Poland, Portugal, Slovak Republic, Spain, Sweden, Switzerland, Turkey, United Kingdom, and the United States.

In April 2004, the member governments of the OECD ratified a revised code of corporate governance that would give shareholders stronger rights in most of the member countries.[7] The revised principles emphasize, among other things, that auditors should be accountable to shareholders, not management, and that boards of directors should effectively oversee the financial reporting function, ensuring that appropriate systems of control are in place. The principles are designed to strengthen corporate governance practices in companies around the world.

The International Federation of Accountants (IFAC) has its own task force on Rebuilding Credibility in Financial Reporting.[8] In March 2003, to support this task force, IFAC introduced a new Internet resource center entitled "Viewpoints: Governance, Accountability and the Public Trust."[9]

In a report published in early 2008, based on a survey conducted in 2007, titled *Financial Reporting Supply Chain—Current Perspectives and Directions*,[10] IFAC identifies positive areas, areas of concern, and areas for further improvements. With regard to the positive, the report states that there is increased awareness that good corporate governance counts; there are new codes and standard improvements in board structure, risk management, and internal control; and more disclosure and transparency in business and financial reporting. The report identifies five areas of concern: governance in name but not in spirit; overregulation; the development of a checklist mentality; personal risk and liability for company directors and senior management; and cost-benefit concerns. IFAC makes improvements in the areas of behavioral and cultural aspects of governance; review of existing rules, since many have been introduced as a response to crises; quality of directors; the relationship of remuneration to performance; expanding the view from compliance governance to business governance.

IFAC guidance on corporate governance addresses risks and organizational accountability. The Professional Accountants in Business (PAIB) Committee of IFAC has released a new *International Good Practice Guidance* document entitled "Evaluating and Improving Governance in Organizations." The new guidance to professional accountants in business includes a framework, a series of fundamental principles, supporting guidance, and references on how they can contribute to evaluating and improving governance in organizations.

In February 2008, the FRC in the United Kingdom published *The Audit Quality Framework*. The FRC states that it will assist companies (in evaluating audit proposals), audit committees (in undertaking annual assessments of the effectiveness of external audits), all stakeholders (in evaluating the policies and actions taken by audit firms to ensure that high-quality audits are performed, whether in the United Kingdom or overseas), and regulators (when undertaking and reporting on their monitoring of the audit profession). The *Framework* identifies the following key drivers of audit quality:

1. The culture within an audit firm.
2. The skills and personal qualities of audit partners and staff.

---

[7] The 2004 *Principles of Corporate Governance* is also available from the OECD Web site.

[8] IFAC comprises more than 160 professional accounting bodies from throughout the world, representing more than 2.5 million accountants in public practice, education, the public sector, industry, and commerce.

[9] This can be accessed at www.ifac.org/credibility/viewpoints.php.

[10] The survey sought to determine the extent to which the financial reporting process, and financial reports themselves, have improved and where there is need for further action to make them more relevant. More than 340 participants from all sections of the financial reporting supply chain worldwide, including investors, preparers, company management, and directors, auditors, standard setters, and regulators, took part in the survey.

3. The effectiveness of the audit process.
4. The reliability and usefulness of audit reporting.
5. Factors outside the control of auditors affecting audit quality.

In the United States, the Sarbanes-Oxley Act's proposals for better corporate governance include the following:

- A new oversight board for the accountancy profession: the Public Company Accounting Oversight Board.
- Certification by chief executive officers (CEOs) and chief financial officers (CFOs) regarding financial statements and internal controls.
- A tightened definition of "independent" audit committee members.
- A requirement for external auditors to report directly to audit committee.
- Prohibitions on certain nonaudit services by external auditors.
- Tougher penalties for financial statement fraud.

Following the Sarbanes-Oxley Act, the New York Stock Exchange (NYSE) introduced several new listing requirements:

- Corporate boards must have a majority of independent directors.
- Listed companies must have audit, compensation, and monitoring committees composed entirely of independent directors.
- Nonmanagement directors must meet at regularly scheduled executive sessions without management.
- For a director to be deemed independent, the board must affirmatively determine that the director has no material relationship with the listed company.
- Listed companies must have an internal audit function.
- Companies must adopt and disclose governance guidelines, codes of business conduct, and charters for their audit, compensation, and nominating committees.

In December 2007, the PCAOB published a Staff Audit Practice Alert on the audit of fair value measurements in financial statements. The alert provides auditors with additional information related to auditing fair value measurements and disclosures.

The results of a survey of senior executives at U.S.-based MNCs, published in July 2004, show that a majority of the companies (over 60 percent) had made compliance with the Sarbanes-Oxley Act part of their regular corporate governance approach and had integrated it with other regulatory activities.[11]

The common issues concerning corporate governance include the quality of published information, internal controls, independent directors, auditor independence, audit committees, ethical conduct, and treatment of financial statement fraud.

The measures that have been taken around the world by governments, worldwide regulators, IFAC, accountancy organizations, and others to strengthen and improve corporate governance rules, regulations, and audit standards have had an impact on the operations of MNCs to the extent that some MNCs now include a separate section in their annual reports explaining corporate governance issues.

---

[11] Management Barometer, a quarterly survey conducted in the United States by PricewaterhouseCoopers. The report is Available at http://barometersurveys.com/production/barsurv.nsf/vwNew.

The following excerpt from the 2009 annual report of the Volkswagen Group in Germany is an example:

> Sustainable economic success can only be generated in our company if we comply with national and international rules and standards, because that is the only way to strengthen the trust of our customers and investors. Transparent and responsible corporate governance takes the highest priority in our daily work. That's why the Board of Management and the Supervisory Board of Volkswagen AG comply with the recommendations of the current German Corporate Governance Code as issued on June 18, 2009, with only a few exceptions.

Auditing issues, concerning both external and internal auditing, are directly linked to corporate governance. External auditing provides assurance to financial statement users that the information contained in those statements is of high quality. Monitoring risks and providing assurance regarding controls are two main internal auditing functions. Monitoring risks involves identifying risks, assessing their potential effect on the organization, determining the strategy to minimize them, and monitoring the possibility for new risks. As a result of recent credit market conditions, the risks to confidence in corporate reporting and governance are higher than they have been for some years. Companies may find that their precise circumstances are not expressly provided for in the standards. In fact this is one of the strengths of principles-based standards. In a multinational context, the linkages between auditing and corporate governance can be explained in terms of a set of relationships as depicted in Exhibit 14.1.

There are two main theories of corporate governance, namely, agency theory and stakeholder theory. According to agency theory, corporate governance emphasizes shareholder value, and board composition is determined by shareholder election (this view is predominant in the Anglo-American system). In contrast, the German system embraces a wider set of stakeholders with some stakeholder groups (such as employees) having a legal right to elect members of the supervisory board. However, the past decade has seen the emergence of several hybrid (or at least aligned) stakeholder–agency approaches, which recognize that if shareholders are to maximize their returns, they need to ensure they satisfy the company's various stakeholders.

EXHIBIT 14.1
International Auditing and Corporate Governance

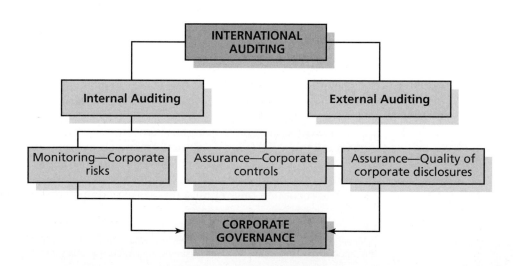

INTERNATIONAL DIVERSITY IN EXTERNAL AUDITING

External auditing is the first line of enforcement of legal and professional requirements concerning financial reporting. Given the prevalence of MNCs and the audit of nondomestic companies, issues related to international auditing are becoming increasingly important. However, there are major variations in many aspects of external auditing across different countries. These aspects include the purpose of external auditing, the audit environment, the regulation of auditing, and audit reports.

Purpose of Auditing

The external auditor's primary concern is whether the financial statements are free of material misstatement. In recent years, an increasing number of companies revealing "financial accounting irregularities" in their past financial statements and causing heavy financial losses to investors around the world has created considerable problems for the accounting profession, particularly in view of the fact that many of these companies had received clean audit reports from large international accounting firms. The investors raised doubts about the integrity of financial information disclosed by large corporations. The question often asked by investors and other interested parties is "Where was the auditor?" However, this is not new; the same question has been asked on many occasions in the past. For example, following the global financial market crisis that emerged from Asia in 1997 and 1998, the World Bank asked international accounting firms to refuse to give clean audit reports for financial statements that had not been prepared in accordance with internationally acceptable accounting standards. Later, commenting on the causes of the Asian financial crisis, an official of the U.S. Securities and Exchange Commission (SEC) pointed to the failures of (1) company accounts to show billions of dollars of debt, allowing companies to continue borrowing with no hope of repayment and (2) auditing to detect the vulnerabilities.[12]

The role of the auditor can vary in different countries. For example, in Germany the role of the statutory auditor is much wider compared to that of his or her counterparts in the United Kingdom or the United States. The UK Companies Act of 1989, which requires that audits of large and medium-sized companies must be performed by a registered auditor, specifies that the role of the auditor is to report to shareholders whether the financial statements give a true and fair view of the financial position and results of operations of the company and whether the financial reports have been properly prepared in accordance with the provisions of the act (Section 235). In Germany, Section 316 of the German Commercial Code requires that in addition to financial statements, an auditor should examine management reports of large and medium-sized corporations. The role of the statutory auditor in Germany is legally defined by the Auditors' Regulation and the German Commercial Code. German auditors take a much broader view of the concept of "client" than their counterparts in the United Kingdom or the United States. It is less problematic for German auditors to view the state and thus society as in part constituting the client.[13]

[12] L. Turner, "The 'Best of Breed' Standards: Globalising Accounting Standards Challenges the Profession to Fulfill Its Obligation to Investors," *Financial Times,* March 8, 2001.
[13] C. R. Baker, A. Mikol, and R. Quick, "Regulation of the Statutory Auditor in the European Union: A Comparative Survey of the United Kingdom, France and Germany," *European Accounting Review* 10, no. 4 (2001), pp. 763–86.

A country's corporate governance structure seems to be a major factor that determines the purpose of external auditing. In Anglo-Saxon traditions, auditors' primary reporting responsibilities are to the shareholders of companies. However, this is not the case in some other countries, which have different corporate structures. In some European countries, a two-tiered board of directors is required for a public company, in that in addition to the management board, a company is also required to have a supervisory board. In Germany, for example, limited liability companies (public companies and private companies with over 500 employees) are required to appoint a supervisory board *(Aufsichtsrat)* to oversee the management board *(Vorstand)*. The management board is composed solely of insiders and is responsible for the company's daily business activity, whereas the supervisory board has general oversight functions and is responsible for safeguarding the company's overall welfare by reviewing management board activities. The supervisory board consists of directors who are representatives of employees, creditors, and shareholder groups. The duties of the supervisory board as set out in the German Commercial Code are as follows:

> The supervisory board supervises the management of the corporation in all branches of its administration. For that purpose members of the supervisory board have the right to ask the management for information, to have access to the books of account, and to review the cash on hand. The supervisory board audits the income statement, the balance sheet and the application of profits suggested by the management *(Vorstand)*. The supervisory board is required to call a general assembly if it is deemed necessary and is in the interests of the corporation. (Article 225a, 1870 Amendment to the German Commercial Code)

The German Commercial Code establishes a duty for the supervisory board to conduct audits of the financial statements presented by the management to the shareholders' general meeting. It was envisaged that the supervisory board would perform substantive corporate governance. As accounting valuation issues became increasingly complex, supervisory boards started to use external auditors to fulfill their audit and control duties. This was the beginning of the development of the profession of external auditors in Germany. Historically, the German auditor's primary reporting responsibility is to the supervisory board and not to shareholders, as in the Anglo-Saxon traditions. The basic function of the statutory auditor in Germany is to assist the supervisory board, and the audit report is normally addressed to the supervisory board, which engages the auditor.

In China, many former state-owned enterprises are being redefined to create new economic enterprises that will be looking to list their securities on domestic and foreign stock exchanges. However, these enterprises do not conform to the Anglo-Saxon concept of an accounting entity:

> In China, the principal business of a geographical region or Province might have been historically designated as the reporting entity, and made responsible for the education and health care of its citizens as well as employment and production. The State is now "carving out" business enterprises from these former social and economic units so they can be established as independent businesses. These newly "carved-out" enterprises are just now encountering the Western concept of entity.[14]

---

[14] L. E. Graham, "Setting a Research Agenda for Auditing Issues in the People's Republic of China," *International Journal of Accounting* 31, no. 1 (1996), p. 29.

These enterprises will still have many related-party transactions with formerly related business units that are now outside the new entity. There will also be inter-company transactions involving these units. The auditor's role or responsibilities in defining the boundaries of these entities and reviewing their transactions becomes unclear.

In China, some public companies have a supervisory committee, somewhat similar to the German supervisory board. The 2009 annual report of China Eastern Airlines Corporation Ltd., for example, includes a separate report of the supervisory committee, in addition to the auditors' report; this report states,

> In 2009, the members of the Supervisory Committee, basing themselves on the powers bestowed upon them by the Company Law and the Articles of Association of the Company and their sense of responsibility toward all the shareholders, actively carried out their tasks, faithfully performed their supervisory duties, and protected the legitimate rights and interests of the Company and of all the shareholders. (p. 62)

Audit Environments

Cultural values in different countries can have an impact on the nature and quality of the audit work undertaken. For example, the perceptions of auditor's ethical conduct may be influenced by cultural norms. Similarly, the perceptions of auditor independence may vary as a result of underlying cultural and environmental differences across countries. Therefore, culture may be helpful in understanding the differences in auditor behavior patterns in different countries.[15] For example, the concept of an independent auditor is neither historically nor culturally appropriate in Japan, and legal liability suits against Japanese auditors are almost non-existent.[16] The exercise of legal rights in a court of law is not in accordance with the underlying Japanese beliefs in the maintenance of harmony in interpersonal and intergroup relationships and the avoidance of open confrontation.[17]

Chinese cultural values—including respect for seniors, the desire to avoid confrontation and look for agreeable compromises, and the concern for "saving face"—are likely to have implications in the audit judgment area. Further, history also plays a part in shaping the practice of auditing in China. As Graham explains:

> One culture shock for auditors steeped in the "risk-based audit" concepts of the 1980s, is the statutory limitation on allowances for doubtful accounts or the rule limiting the application of lower [*sic*] cost or market considerations for Chinese inventories. . . . This practice is steeped in the State enterprise system, where all products were perceived as useful for *something, someday,* thereby obviating the need for obsolescence reserves or written-downs. Foreign enterprises may now create an allowance for doubtful accounts of up to 3 percent of ending accounts receivable. Bad debt allowance accounts for Chinese enterprises are limited to between $\frac{1}{3}$ to $\frac{1}{2}$ percent of ending accounts receivable. . . . Since enterprises historically were, and most still are, State owned, State credit was always by definition "good," and bad debt provisions were/are generally unnecessary. There seems to be a "go-slow" attitude toward change that is reflected in the broadening of the Chinese principles to accommodate the expectations of business partners from more advanced nations.[18]

[15] J. Soeters and H. Schreuder, "The Interaction between National and Organizational Cultures in Accounting Firms," *Accounting, Organizations and Society* 13, no. 1 (1988), pp. 75–85.
[16] J. McKinnon, "The Accounting Profession in Japan," *Australian Accountant,* July 1983, pp. 406–10.
[17] G. G. Mueller, "Is Accounting Culturally Determined?" Paper presented at the EIASM Workshop on Accounting and Culture, Amsterdam, June 1985.
[18] Graham, "Setting a Research Agenda," p. 30.

The various environmental factors affecting auditing issues can be identified in terms of a broad concept often referred to as the accounting infrastructure, which includes producers of information; final users of information; information intermediaries; laws and regulations that govern the production, transmission, and usage of information; and legal entities that monitor and implement the laws and regulations.[19]

In less developed countries, in particular, creditors and investors play a minimal role in the accounting infrastructure and so a less developed auditing profession, compared to that in a developed country, would be expected. Further, the primary source of finance in a country may influence the degree to which the audit profession in that country has evolved. Countries in which the primary source of capital is absentee owners (stockholders) and creditors such as the United States, the United Kingdom, and Australia may have a much greater need for audit services and more sophisticated audit procedures compared to those countries in which state-controlled banks or commercial banks are the primary source of capital. In a debt-financing country such as Japan, for example, there may be a much reduced need for audited information or reliance on public financial information.

Different legal systems are also likely to influence auditing in different countries. For example, a codified Roman law system that exists in countries such as Germany and France may require more reliance on the stated legal objectives of the auditing profession. Countries with a common law system, such as the United Kingdom, Canada, or New Zealand, may allow audit characteristics to develop more freely or rely more on the auditing profession to set a general tone for the profession.[20]

The differences in the environment in which auditing operates can have implications for the transfer of auditing technology among countries. The international diversity in accounting and securities market regulations and practices, economic and political systems, patterns of business ownership, size and complexity of business firms, and stages of economic development would affect the nature of the demand for audit services and the complexity of the audit task. Therefore, audit technologies which are cost-beneficial in one national setting can be ineffective, or even dysfunctional, in a different setting.[21]

Further, audit quality is also likely to vary across different audit environments. *Audit quality* can be defined as the probability that an error or irregularity is detected and reported.[22] The detection probability is affected by the actual work done by auditors to reach their opinion. This in turn is influenced by the level of competence of the auditors (eligibility and qualifications), the requirements regarding the conduct of the audit (quality review and monitoring), and the reporting requirements. The reporting probability is affected by the auditor's independence. High independence implies a high probability of publicly reporting a detected material error or irregularity. We further discuss the issue of auditor independence later in this chapter.

[19] C. J. Lee, "Accounting Infrastructure and Economic Development," *Journal of Accounting and Public Policy,* Summer 1987, pp. 75–86.

[20] R. A. Wood, "Global Audit Characteristics across Cultures and Environments: An Empirical Examination," *Journal of International Accounting, Auditing, and Taxation* 5, no. 2 (1996), pp. 215–29.

[21] See C. W. Chow and R. N. Hwang, "The Cross-Border Transferability of Audit Technology: An Exploratory Study in the U.S.-Taiwan Context," *Advances in International Accounting* 7 (1994), pp. 217–29.

[22] L. DeAngelo, "Auditor Size and Audit Quality," *Journal of Accounting and Economics* 3 (1981), pp. 183–200.

Audit quality is also affected by the nature of the legal liability regime that exists in a country (we also discuss auditor liability later in this chapter). A strong liability regime will provide incentives for auditors to be independent and produce high-quality audits. In some Asian countries, for example, this is an unlikely scenario, because (due to cultural and other reasons) the liability regimes may not be strong and violations of professional conduct may go unpunished. This creates audit markets of uneven quality. In some countries, such as Indonesia, Malaysia, and Thailand, fraud and irregularities are required to be reported to the board of directors, not in the audit report.[23]

Regulation of Auditors and Audit Firms

The approaches taken to regulate auditing in different countries range from those that leave the task largely in the hands of the profession to those that rely heavily on the government. In Anglo-Saxon countries, mechanisms are put in place to regulate auditors within the framework of professional self-regulation. In the United States, the Public Company Accounting Oversight Board (PCAOB), composed of five independent members (not more than two of whom may be professional accountants), was established in 2002 by the SEC pursuant to the Sarbanes-Oxley Act. This act reaffirms the necessity for the auditor to be independent of management, in fact and appearance, and expands the auditor's reporting responsibility. Section 404 of the Sarbanes-Oxley Act, "Management Assessment of Internal Controls," requires public companies to include in their annual report an assessment by management of the effectiveness of the internal control structure and procedures for financial reporting. The external auditor must attest to and report on that assessment. Accordingly, the PCAOB issued an audit standard, "An Audit of Internal Control over Financial Reporting Performed in Conjunction with an Audit of Financial Statements" (PCAOB Release No.2004-003), which was approved by the SEC in June 2004.[24] The new standard requires two audit opinions: one on internal control over financial reporting and one on the financial statements.

Auditors of SEC-registered companies are required to be members of the PCAOB. This also includes non-U.S. audit firms that audit the accounts of a company or subsidiary (domestic or foreign) listed on a U.S. stock exchange. The PCAOB has the authority (1) to establish or adopt auditing standards, quality control standards, and ethical rules in relation to the conduct of audits of public companies and (2) to inspect audit firms. It also has the power to require cooperation with quality control reviews and disciplinary proceedings, and it may impose a broad range of disciplinary sanctions against auditing firms and individual members. Large firms that undertake audits of more than 100 public companies will be inspected annually. The requirement for non-U.S. audit firms to become members of PCAOB has caused some concern among the large European audit firms. Although at first the PCAOB said it should regulate both U.S. and non-U.S. accounting firms, in July 2004 announced that, for some non-U.S. audit firms that audit companies registered with the SEC (e.g., audit firms in Canada, Japan, and

---

[23] M. Favere-Marchesi, "Audit Quality in ASEAN," *International Journal of Accounting* 35, no. 1 (2000), pp. 121–49.

[24] This is effective for audits of companies with fiscal years ending on or after November 15, 2004, for accelerated filers (an accelerated filer is, generally, a U.S. company that has equity market capitalization greater than $75 million as of the last business day of its most recently completed second fiscal quarter and has filed an annual report with the SEC), or July 15, 2005, for other companies. More information can be obtained at www.sec.gov/news/press/2004-83.htm.

many European countries, including the United Kingdom), it would be willing to rely on the auditor's home-country regulators.[25]

In the United Kingdom, the word *accountant* is not defined in statute and there is no qualification requirement in order for someone to practice as an accountant. However, most accountants choose to qualify under the auspices of one of the professional bodies. The situation for *auditor* is different. The Companies Act of 1985 prescribes a statutory scheme for the regulation of auditors, under which the Department of Trade and Industries (DTI) recognizes certain accountancy bodies for the training and supervision of auditors. The Companies Act of 1985 states that every company shall appoint an auditor or auditors (except for most small companies or dormant companies). The Companies Act of 1989, which implemented the European Union's Eighth Directive, introduced stronger statutory arrangements for the regulation of auditors. It restricts qualifications for appointment as a statutory auditor to those who hold a recognized professional qualification and are subject to the requirements of a recognized supervisory body. It makes specific provision for the independence of company auditors. An officer or employee of a company being audited, for example, may not act as auditor for that company.

Under the regulatory structure for the accounting profession introduced in 1998, an independent body, the Accountancy Foundation, with a non-accountant board of trustees, was established in 2000. With the establishment of the Foundation, a strong lay and independent element was introduced into the regulatory framework. This element involved oversight arrangements concerning the regulatory activities undertaken by the principal professional accountancy bodies. The Foundation was funded by the Consultative Committee of Accountancy Bodies (CCAB).

The Foundation[26] and its related bodies[27] were responsible for the nonstatutory independent regulation of the six chartered accountancy bodies of the CCAB. This framework was developed in light of a growing recognition in the profession of the need for the regulatory arrangements to reflect the wider public interest. The regulatory functions of the Foundation included monitoring the work of accountants and auditors, handling complaints and disciplinary violations, and conducting investigations. The regulatory structure under the foundation provided an increased level of public oversight regarding statutory auditors, while essentially retaining the self-regulatory nature of the profession.[28] Accordingly, the responsibility for determining who might be recognized as a statutory auditor has been delegated primarily to four CCAB members: the Association of Chartered Corporate Accountants (ACCA), the Institute of Chartered Accountants in England and Wales (ICAEW), the Institute of Chartered Accountants in Ireland (ICAI), and the Institute of Chartered Accountants in Scotland (ICAS). Each of the four recognized professional bodies has its own examinations to assess the

---

[25] *Accountancy Magazine,* July 2004.

[26] The documents issued by the Accountancy Foundation and its related bodies are available at www.frc .org.uk.

[27] The structure of the Foundation comprises five limited companies: the Accountancy Foundation Ltd.; The Review Board Ltd. (to monitor the operation of the regulatory system to ensure that it serves the public interest); The Auditing Practices Board Ltd. (to establish and develop auditing standards): The Ethics Standards Board Ltd. (to secure the development of ethical standards for all accountants); and the Investigation and Discipline Board Ltd. (to investigate disciplinary cases of public interest).

[28] Department of Trade and Industry, *A Framework of Independent Regulation for the Accountancy Profession: A Consultation Document* (London: Department of Trade and Industry of Her Majesty's Government, 1998).

technical competence of the entry-level registered auditor (the term used in the United Kingdom for statutory auditor). In order to become a registered auditor in the United Kingdom, the professional accountant must be listed in a register maintained for that purpose by a recognized professional body.

The Auditing Practices Board (APB) was responsible for setting and developing auditing standards in the United Kingdom. The APB, as constituted under the Accountancy Foundation arrangements, continued the work of its predecessor body, which was established in 1991 under the auspices of the CCAB. Failure to abide by the professional standards issued by the APB might be grounds for disciplinary action. According to a report on audit regulation in the United Kingdom made public by the Department of Trade and Industry in July 2004, the ICAEW, ICAS, and ICAI undertook 1,030 monitoring visits during 2003. Of the firms visited, 88 percent required no action at all or, by the conclusion of the visit, had suitable plans in place to improve their audit work, and 14 firms had their registration as auditors withdrawn following a monitoring visit, compared with 11 in 2002.[29]

The Companies (Audit, Investigation and Community Enterprises) Act of 2004 provided the Financial Reporting Review Panel with statutory power to require companies, directors, and auditors to provide documents, information and explanations if it appears that accounts do not comply with relevant reporting requirements.

Under the new regime the Financial Reporting Council (FRC) is the United Kingdom's unified, independent regulator for corporate reporting and governance. Its functions, which are relevant to auditing, include the following:

- Setting, monitoring, and enforcing auditing standards, statutory oversight, and regulation of auditors.
- Operating an independent investigation and discipline scheme for public interest cases involving professional accountants.
- Overseeing the regulatory activities of the professional accountancy bodies.

The FRC is also responsible for the Combined Code of Corporate Governance and its associated guidance on internal control (the Turnbull Guidance) and audit committees (the Smith Guidance). Similar bodies have been established in Canada, Australia, Japan, France, Germany, and several other countries in the European Union.

The requirements for becoming an auditor may vary in different countries. For example, unlike in the United States, there is no uniform system of examination in the United Kingdom where four professional bodies conduct their own examinations. On the other hand, in Germany, the examinations for the prospective auditors are set by the Ministry of Economics, and self-regulation of the auditing profession takes place within the strict boundaries of the law.[30] Unlike in the United Kingdom, instead of the professional bodies, quasi-governmental agencies play a major role in the regulatory functions in Germany. The Auditors' Regulation specifies the admission requirements to become a statutory auditor and defines, among other things, the rights and duties of the auditor, the organization of the Chamber of Auditors, or *Wirtschaftsprüferkammer (WPK),* and the disciplinary measures for breaches of professional duties. The WPK is supervised by the Ministry of Justice. Statutory auditors, including audit corporations, must be

---

[29] Details are available at http://accountingeducation.com/news/news5279.html.
[30] Baker, Mikol, and Quick, "Regulation of the Statutory Auditor."

members of the WPK, a public law body created in 1961. The WPK also participates in disciplining auditors who violate standards.[31]

In China, the government is heavily involved in the regulation of the auditing
profession. China's accounting and auditing profession is sanctioned and regulated by the state. All certified public accounting (CPA) firms, both state owned
and privately owned, are under the supervision of the local Audit Bureau, which
is itself supervised by the state. The CPA firms must be approved by the state in
order to be able to audit foreign owned or joint venture companies or Chinese
companies listed on the stock exchange, as required by law. The state may also
intervene in the allocation of audit assignments among CPA firms.

Audit Reports

There are significant differences in the audit reports across different countries and
sometimes across different companies within the same country. In this section we
describe some of these differences. The appendix to this chapter provides examples of audit reports from MNCs located in Japan, Germany, the Netherlands,
United Kingdom, and China.

Audit reports on company annual reports for 2009 show a variety of applicable
audit standards and formats.

- China Southern Airline's audit report states that an audit has been conducted
in accordance with Hong Kong Standards on Auditing issued by the Hong
Kong Institute of Certified Public Accountants.

- China Eastern Airline's audit report is in both English and Chinese. It states
that the audit has been conducted in accordance with International Standards
on Auditing.

- The audit report of Bayer states that the audit has been conducted in accordance
with German Commercial Code requirements and German generally accepted
standards for the audit of financial statements promulgated by the Institute of
Public Auditors in Germany.

- The audit report of Sumitomo Metal Industries states that audit has been conducted in accordance with auditing standards generally accepted in Japan.

- Toshiba's audit report has been prepared in accordance with auditing standards generally accepted in the United States. However, the report states that
"The Company's consolidated financial statements do not disclose segment
information required by Statement of Financial Accounting Standards No.131,
Disclosures about Segments of an Enterprise and Related Information. Therefore, the
audit opinion is that financial statements present fairly, in all material respects,
except for the omission of segment information."

- The audit report of Unilever PLC has been prepared in accordance with Chapter 3
of Part 16 of the Companies Act of 2006. It also states that "Our responsibility is
to audit the consolidated financial statements in accordance with applicable law
and International Standards on Auditing (UK and Ireland). There are three sets
of opinion, namely, Opinion on financial statements, separate opinion in relation
to IFRS, and Opinion on other matter prescribed by the Companies Act 2006."

- The audit report of Unilever N.V. states that the audit has been conducted in
accordance with Dutch law.

---

[31] Ibid.

- The audit report of Kubota states that the audit has been conducted in accordance with the standards of the Public Company Accounting Oversight Board and that financial statements as of March 31, 2010, and 2009, are in conformity with U.S. GAAP. The report further states that the auditors expressed a qualified opinion in the audit report for 2009 because there was no segment information, but in the current financial statements this has been corrected.

- The audit report on Cadbury PLC's financial statements of 2008 states that the audit was conducted in accordance with International Standards on Auditing (UK and Ireland) issued by the Auditing Practices Board (UK). The audit opinion states that (*a*) the Group financial statements give a true and fair view, in accordance with IFRS as adopted by the EU, of the state of the Group's affairs as of December 31, 2008, and profit for the year then ended; (*b*) the parent company financial statements give a true and fair view, in accordance with IFRS as adopted by the EU as applied in accordance with the provisions of the Companies Act of 1985, of the state of the parent company's affairs as of December 31, 2008; (*c*) the financial statements and the part of the Directors' Remuneration Report to be audited have been properly prepared in accordance with the Companies Act of 1985 and as regards the Group financial statements, Article 4 of the IAS Regulation; and (*d*) the information given in the Directors' Report is consistent with the financial statements. The audit report also includes a separate opinion in relation to IFRS, which states that the Group, in addition to complying with its legal obligation to comply with IFRS as adopted by the EU, has also complied with the IFRS as issued by the IASB.

Some audit reports, for example, those of China Southern Airline, China Eastern Airline, Unilever PLC, and Unilever N.V., specifically mention that the auditors need to comply with ethical requirements.

As mentioned earlier, a special feature in the corporate structure in some European countries, including Germany, is the two-tiered structure with a management board and a supervisory board. The report of the supervisory board of Volkswagen AG, in the annual report 2009, states:

> During the past fiscal year, the Supervisory Board addressed the situation and the development of the Volkswagen Group regularly and in detail. In compliance with the legal requirements and the German Corporate Governance Code, we provide advice and support to the Board of Management in issues relating to the management of the Company. The Supervisory Board was consulted directly with regard to all decisions of fundamental importance to the Group. In addition, current strategic considerations were discussed with the Board of Management at regular intervals.

The Board of Management provided the Supervisory Board with regular, prompt, and comprehensive verbal and written reports on the development of business, the planning and the position of the Company, including the risk situation and risk management. These included all key aspects relating to the creation of an integrated automative group with Porsche. The Board of Management also informed us continuously about other current issues and the topic of compliance. We always received documents relevant to our decisions in good time prior to the Supervisory Board meetings. Furthermore, the Board of Management provided the Supervisory Board with detailed monthly reports on the current business position and the forecast for the year as a whole. The Board of Management explained any variations from the defined plans and targets in a comprehensive verbal or written report. The Board of Management and the Supervisory Board discussed and analyzed the reasons for the variations in detail to allow appropriate measures to be initiated. (p. 5)

INTERNATIONAL HARMONIZATION OF AUDITING STANDARDS

The audit report is the primary tool auditors use to communicate with financial statement users about the results of the audit function. The globalization of capital markets and the growth of international capital flows have heightened the significance of cross-national understanding of corporate financial reports and the associated audit reports.[32] For MNCs the ideal situation would be for both the parent company and its foreign subsidiaries to adopt one set of accounting standards, and for the auditors in both cases to use one set of auditing standards in providing their opinion on the financial statements. However, as explained in the previous sections, the audit environments and the mechanisms for audit regulation can vary significantly among different countries, and this could affect the form, content, and quality of the audit report.

International harmonization of auditing standards is important in view of the drive toward international convergence of financial reporting standards. It ensures the international capital markets that the audit process has been consistent across companies, and in particular that one set of high quality standards has been applied in auditing both the parent and its subsidiary companies. This enhances the credibility of the information in corporate financial reports. This would lead to a more efficient and effective allocation of resources in international capital markets. In addition, harmonization of auditing standards would enable audit firms to increase the efficiency and effectiveness of the audit process globally. However, efforts to harmonize auditing standards internationally have met with limited success.

The responsibility for developing international auditing standards rests mainly with IFAC through its International Auditing and Assurance Standards Board (IAASB).[33] As a condition of IFAC membership, a professional accountancy body is obliged to support the work of IFAC by informing its members of every pronouncement developed by IFAC; to work toward implementation, to the extent possible under local circumstances, of those pronouncements; and specifically to incorporate IFAC's International Standards on Auditing (ISAs) into national auditing pronouncements.[34]

The IAASB develops ISAs and International Auditing Practice Statements (IAPSs). These standards and statements outline basic principles and essential procedures for auditors, and serve as the benchmark for high-quality auditing standards and statements worldwide. The IAASB also develops quality control standards for firms and engagement teams in the practice areas of audit, assurance, and related services. Exhibit 14.2 provides a list of ISAs and International Standards on Quality Control (ISQC) issued by IFAC.[35]

---

[32] J. S. Gangolly, M. E. Hussein, G. S. Seow, and K. Tam, "Harmonization of the Auditor's Report," *International Journal of Accounting* 37 (2002), pp. 327–46.

[33] The IAASB was formerly known as the International Auditing Practices Committee (IAPC).

[34] Preface to International Standards on Auditing and Related Services.

[35] International Standards on Auditing are available at www.ifac.org.

EXHIBIT 14.2
International
Standards on
Auditing and
International
Standards on
Quality Control

ISAs and ISQC 1

The complete listing of the ISAs and ISQC 1 is set forth below, along with the Basis for Conclusions for each project. These staff-prepared documents provide background information, main comments received on the exposure drafts, and the IAASB's conclusions regarding these comments in developing the final standard.

In finalizing the 2010 *Handbook of International Quality Control, Auditing, Review, Other Assurance, and Related Services Pronouncements* (the handbook), editorial and formatting changes were made to the ISAs that had been included in the 2009 handbook. A bridging document has been prepared which provides an overview of these changes. Individual ISAs are available below via the linked version of the 2010 handbook.

ISA Number	Title
200	Overall Objectives of the Independent Auditor and the Conduct of an Audit in Accordance with International Standards on Auditing
210	Agreeing the Terms of Audit Engagements
220	Quality Control for an Audit of Financial Statements
230	Audit Documentation
240	The Auditor's Responsibilities Relating to Fraud in an Audit of Financial Statements
250	Consideration of Laws and Regulations in an Audit of Financial Statements
260	Communication with Those Charged with Governance
265	Communicating Deficiencies in Internal Control to Those Charged with Governance and Management
300	Planning an Audit of Financial Statements
315	Identifying and Assessing the Risks of Material Misstatement through Understanding the Entity and Its Environment
320	Materiality in Planning and Performing an Audit
330	The Auditor's Responses to Assessed Risks
402	Audit Considerations Relating to an Entity Using a Service Organization
450	Evaluation of Misstatements Identified during the Audit
500	Audit Evidence
501	Audit Evidence-Specific Considerations for Selected Items
505	External Confirmations
510	Initial Audit Engagements-Opening Balances
520	Analytical Procedures
530	Audit Sampling
540	Auditing Accounting Estimates, Including Fair Value Accounting Estimates, and Related Disclosures
550	Related Parties
560	Subsequent Events
570	Going Concern
580	Written Representations
600	Special Considerations-Audits of Group Financial Statements (Including the Work of Component Auditors)
610	Using the Work of Internal Auditors
620	Using the Work of an Auditor's Expert
700	Forming an Opinion and Reporting on Financial Statements

Continued

EXHIBIT 14.2
(*Concluded*)

ISA Number	Title
705	Modifications to the Opinion in the Independent Auditor's Report
706	Emphasis of Matter Paragraphs and Other Matter Paragraphs in the Independent Auditor's Report
710	Comparative Information-Corresponding Figures and Comparative Financial Statements
720	The Auditor's Responsibilities Relating to Other Information in Documents Containing Audited Financial Statements
800	Special Considerations-Audits of Financial Statements Prepared in Accordance with Special Purpose Frameworks
805	Special Considerations-Audits of Single Financial Statements and Specific Elements, Accounts or Items of a Financial Statement
810	Engagements to Report on Summary Financial Statements

International Standard on Quality Control (ISQC) 1, Quality Controls for Firms that Perform Audits and Reviews of Financial Statements, and Other Assurance and Related Services Engagements

IFAC's international regulatory and compliance regime consists of the Forum of Firms (FoF) and the Compliance Committee, with participation from outside the accounting profession. Firms that carry out transnational audit work are eligible for membership in the FoF. Membership obligations include compliance with ISAs and the IFAC Code of Ethics for Professional Accountants, and submission to periodic quality control review. The Compliance Committee monitors and encourages compliance with international standards and other measures designed to enhance the reliability of financial information and professional standards around the world.

The International Organization of Securities Commissions (IOSCO) supports IFAC's efforts in this area. IOSCO's Technical and Emerging Markets Committees participate in the discussions that take place between the IFAC and the international regulatory community regarding processes for the development of international auditing standards. In October 1992, IOSCO recommended that its members endorse ISAs and accept audits of financial statements from other countries audited in accordance with ISAs.

The issuance of ISA 13 in October 1983 by the International Auditing Practices Committee (IAPC) was an important landmark in international efforts to harmonize the audit report. The purpose of ISA 13 was to "provide guidance to auditors on the form and content of the auditor's report issued in connection with the independent audit of the financial statements of any entity" (paragraph 2). ISA 13 has been revised several times since 1983. ISA 700, *The Auditor's Report on Financial Statements,* establishes standards and provides guidance on the form and content of the auditor's report. It requires the auditor to express an opinion about whether the financial statements "give a true and fair view" or "present fairly," which in turn requires the auditor to conduct the necessary auditing procedures to support his or her expressed opinion. The requirement also helps ensure that the information satisfies the need of the international users of financial statements.

ISA 700 describes four types of audit opinion that can be expressed by the auditor: unqualified, qualified, adverse, and disclaimer of opinion. It also discusses circumstances that may result in other than an unqualified opinion, which include

EXHIBIT 14.3
ISA 700 Illustrative Audit Report

Source: ISA 700, *The Auditor's Report on Financial Statements.*

AUDITOR'S REPORT

(Appropriate Address)

We have audited the accompanying (the reference can be by page numbers) balance sheet of the ABC Company as of December 31, 20x1, and the related statements on income, and cash flows for the year then ended. These financial statements are the responsibility of the company's management. Our responsibility is to express an opinion on these financial statements based on our audit.

We conducted our audit in accordance with International Standards on Auditing (or refer to relevant national standards or practices). Those standards require that we plan and perform the audit to obtain reasonable assurance about whether the financial statements are free of material misstatement. An audit includes examining, on a test basis, evidence supporting the amounts and disclosures in the financial statements. An audit also includes assessing the accounting principles used and significant estimates made by management, as well as evaluating the overall financial statements presentation. We believe that our audit provides a reasonable basis for our opinion.

In our opinion, the financial statements give a true and fair view of (or "present fairly" in all material respects) the financial position of the company as of December 31, 20x1, and of the results of its operations and its cash flows for the year then ended in accordance with International Accounting Standards (or [title of financial reporting framework with reference to the country of origin]*) (and comply with. . . .†)

---

*In some circumstances it also may be necessary to refer to a particular jurisdiction within the country of origin to identify clearly the financial reporting framework used.
†Refer to relevant statutes or law.

---

limitation of scope, disagreement with management, and uncertainty. The appendixes to the standard include suggested expressions for the different types of opinion. For example, Exhibit 14.3 provides an illustration of an unqualified opinion that incorporates the basic requirements.

ISA 700 points out that although the auditor's opinion enhances the credibility of the financial statements, the user cannot assume that the opinion is an assurance as to the future viability of the entity or the efficiency or effectiveness with which management has conducted the affairs of the entity.

ISA 200, *Objectives and General Principles Governing an Audit of Financial Statements*, states that the objective of an audit of financial statements is to enable the auditor to express an opinion whether the financial statements are prepared, in all material respects in accordance with an identified financial reporting framework. However, this could be a problem in some cases; for example, the European Union has endorsed a modified version of IAS 39, and selecting an appropriate text for such identification may not be easy.

Auditors are expected to comply with IFAC's Code of Ethics for Professional Accountants (IFAC Handbook) and to consider the activities of internal auditing and their effect, if any, on external audit procedures (ISA 610, *Considering the Work of Internal Auditing*). In a paper published in December 2005, entitled *The Role and Domain of the Professional Accountants in Business*, IFAC's Professional Accountants in Business (PAIB) Committee states that while there is certainly high awareness of the work of accountants in audit practice and tax preparation, there is a less understood, but equally important role that professional accountants in business play in designing and maintaining mechanisms to assure effective, ethical, and responsible corporate governance and control in organizations. To provide resources for professional accountants, IFAC launched the International Center for Professional Accountants in Business in July 2007.

In June 2003, IFAC issued an IAPS providing guidance on expressing an audit opinion when the financial statements are asserted by management to have been prepared (1) solely in accordance with IFRS, (2) in accordance with IFRS and a national financial reporting framework, or (3) in accordance with a national financial reporting framework with disclosure of the extent of compliance with IFRS.[36]

In accordance with IAS 1, the IAPC specifies that financial statements should not be described as complying with IFRSs unless they comply with all the requirements of each applicable standard and each applicable interpretation of the International Financial Reporting Interpretations Committee (IFRIC). An unqualified opinion may be expressed only when the auditor is able to conclude that the financial statements give a true and fair view (or are presented fairly, in all material respects) in accordance with the identified financial reporting framework. In all other circumstances, the auditor is required to disclaim an opinion or to issue a qualified or adverse opinion depending on the circumstances. An opinion paragraph that indicates that "the financial statements give a true and fair view and are in substantial compliance with International Financial Reporting Standards" does not meet the requirements of ISA 700. Further, financial statements claimed to have complied with more than one financial reporting framework must comply with each of the indicated frameworks individually.

There have been efforts at harmonizing auditing standards at the regional level, particularly within the European Union. For example, the Fourth Directive of the European Commission requires that the auditor's report include whether the financial statements present a "true and fair view." The Eighth Directive aimed at harmonizing the educational and training prerequisites necessary to become a statutory auditor. Many EU member countries, including the United Kingdom, modified their company laws and regulations to comply with the provisions of the Eighth Directive. As a result, the UK professional bodies amended their entry requirements to include a rule that new members must have a university degree in any area. In addition, a prospective candidate for membership of one of the professional bodies would also be required to undergo a three-year training period under the supervision of a practicing member of that professional body. Recently, the representative body for the accountancy profession in Europe, the *Federation des Experts Comptables Europeens (FEE),* conducted a survey and found that fundamental requirements to be recognized as a professional accountant and auditor largely have converged across Europe.[37]

The UK Auditing Practices Board, one of the FRC's operating bodies, taking a big-bang approach, has recently issued a revised suite of auditing standards that very closely reflect the ISAs.

The IAASB has issued a series of key questions and answers in a publication titled "First-time Adoption of IFRSs, Guidance for Auditors on Reporting Issues" as well as a glossary incorporating terms used in ISAs issued as of October 31, 2004.[38] Further, in April 2005 the IFAC Education Committee issued an exposure draft on educational requirements for audit professionals proposing an International Education Standard (IES) titled "Competence Requirements for Audit Professionals."

There seems to be international cooperation in regulating auditors and audit firms. For example, the PCAOB has entered into a Statement of Protocol with

---

[36] IFAC, International Auditing and Assurance Standards Board, "Reporting by Auditors on Compliance with International Financial Reporting Standards," International Auditing Practice Statement 1014, June 1, 2003.

[37] Full survey results are available at www.fee.be.

[38] Both publications are available at www.ifac.org/store.

Australian Securities and Investment Commission (ASIC) to enhance cooperation in the supervisory oversight of auditors and public accounting firms that practice in the United States and Australia. The PCAOB is expected to enter into similar arrangements in other non-U.S. jurisdictions. In December 2007, the PCAOB issued for comment proposed guidance regarding the implementation of PCAOB Rule 4012, *Inspection of Foreign Registered Public Accounting Firms*. Accordingly, if the essential criteria as mentioned in the policy statement are met, the board may place full reliance on the inspection program of qualified non-U.S. auditor oversight entities. Rule 4012 sets out five broad principles:

1. Adequacy and integrity of the oversight system.
2. Independent operation of the oversight system.
3. Independence of the system's source of funding.
4. Transparency of the system.
5. System's historical performance.

ETHICS AND INTERNATIONAL AUDITING

Globalization of corporations and the accounting profession has raised some questions that are of fundamental importance to the accounting profession:

What does the new global profession stand for?

Can the moral standing of the accounting profession be based on a consensus of international morals and values?

Further, accounting does not operate in a static environment and is undergoing change in accordance with community and business values. What was local—including business and professional fundamentals and community values—is now global. These values are currently directed to corporate responsibility and social and environmental issues and are communicated in nonmonetary terms. These changes in community values form part of what accounting is. Further, the realm of the accounting profession's jurisdiction does not seem to remain within the boundaries of monetary symbols and financial reporting. These issues are important in judging professional credibility and integrity into the next generation.

Moral standing of the accounting profession is based on trust, which is established by the ethical conduct of its members. This is as important as an asset such as plant and equipment. At an international level, the profession has been directed to ethics education by international organizations such as IFAC. For example, IFAC membership obligations include compliance with ISAs and the IFAC Code of Ethics for Professional Accountants. The importance of consistency of ethical codes for the various professional bodies operating within individual geographical locations has also been emphasized. At the international level, the Public Interest Oversight Board (PIOB) was formed in early 2005 to oversee the work of IFAC committees, including n ethics standard-setting committee. Following the consideration and approval by the PIOB, the revised Code of Ethics for Professional Accountants was issued by the Auditing Practices Board. The revised code clarifies requirements for all professional accountants and significantly strengthens the independence requirements of auditors. Accountability over how banks are run is emphasized in the Walker Review into Corporate Governance of UK banks.

However, ethical codes may also offer opportunities for "creative accounting." Further, a focus on individual benefits has resulted in recent corporate failures. As a consequence, the accounting profession—as stewards of corporate behavior—was admonished in terms of public trust. When ethical values are falling, people often turn to government for help, as reflected during the recent global financial crisis.

The response to crises of the accounting profession in the United States has been to form committees and commissions whose recommendations end up changing little of substance. Those recommendations generally focused on rules of behavior. However, the shift from social norms to rules of behavior may not be the right path, as the focus on norms and culture are important to society.

A More Communitarian View of Professional Ethics

Professionals face their careers constrained by local laws and a set of values that appear to be universally held. Ethical standards are important in professional accounting work, and professional ethics reside in the form of a contract between a professional group and the community within which that professional group operates. Therefore, ethical issues can be local and contextual. Consequently, the notion of a universal or global set of ethical norms that is embedded in IFRS can be challenged, as the notion of an "international community" reflects the aspirations of Anglo-American culture. For example, some of the accepted methods of relationship building generally accepted in Chinese society may be considered bribery and corruption in an Anglo-American culture. Is a more communitarian view of professional ethics needed?

ADDITIONAL INTERNATIONAL AUDITING ISSUES

As a result of the renewed interest in restoring investor confidence internationally, the issues of auditor's liability, auditor independence, and the role of audit committees have figured prominently in discussion and debate. The fact that there is no international agreement on how to deal with any of these issues is of particular interest to MNCs, because they have to operate under different regulatory regimes in different countries.

Auditor's Liability

In general, auditors can be subject to three kinds of liability—civil liability, criminal liability, and professional sanctions. Civil liability arises when auditors break contractual or civil obligations or both, and criminal liability arises when they engage in criminal acts, such as intentionally providing misleading information. Professional sanctions (warnings and exclusions by professional bodies) are imposed when auditors violate the rules of the professional bodies to which they belong.[39] In terms of civil liability, the auditor may be exposed to litigation initiated by (1) the client company (the other party to the engagement contract) or (2) a third party (a party not involved in the original contract, such as a shareholder). In certain national jurisdictions, auditors are not liable to third parties. This was the case in Germany prior to 1998, but the situation changed as a consequence of a court decision in that year. Statutory auditors in Germany currently are liable to third parties in cases of negligent behavior. In the United Kingdom, under the Companies Act, the auditor reports to the members of the company but enters into

---

[39] Favere-Marchesi, "Audit Quality."

a contract with the company as a corporate entity. Accordingly, the auditor's primary duty of care is to the company and its shareholders as a group, not necessarily to individual shareholders. To be liable in negligence, the auditor must owe a "duty of care" to a third-party claimant. It is relatively difficult for individual shareholders to successfully assert claims against statutory auditors under British law.[40]

In China, the concept of legal liability extending beyond the firm to its owners does not appear to exist. This is due to the flexibility in the ownership structure of CPA firms, and the lack of a developed legal environment. A unique feature in the ownership structure of the Chinese CPA firms is that other entities, such as universities, may also have ownership interests in them. For example, Shanghai University has an ownership interest in Da Hua CPAs, one of the larger CPA firms in China.[41]

Limiting Auditor's Liability

Prompted by the collapse of Arthur Andersen, the UK government conducted a public consultation on whether it should initiate legislation to limit auditors' liability. In its response, one of the Big Four firms pointed out that the risks involved in auditing are uninsurable, unquantifiable, unmanageable, and could at any time destroy the firm or any of its competitors.[42] This should be of concern to MNCs, given that further reduction in the number of global accounting firms could seriously affect MNCs' ability to obtain the necessary professional services at reasonable prices. The remainder of this section describes some of the alternatives available for limiting auditor's liability.

Change the Ownership Structure

Audit firms, particularly in the UK tradition, are often organized as partnerships in which the principle of "joint and several liability" applies. Under this principle, each audit partner of the firm against whom a claim is made for negligence may be held liable for the whole amount of the claim. However, the joint and several liability feature is seen as a weakness of the partnership form of ownership. An effective way to limit auditor's liability would be to change the ownership structure of audit firms. Under the U.S. model of limited liability partnerships, "innocent" partners are able to protect their personal wealth from legal action. The Big Four firms are using limited liability partnerships, where permitted by law, to reduce their exposure to litigation. For example, Deloitte & Touche LLP became a limited liability partnership in August 2003.

Under UK law, limited partnerships are effective only if the limited partners are simply passive investors and take no role in the firm's professional work. Consequently, for many audit firms in the United Kingdom, the principle of joint and several liability applies to audit partners, as the firms are organized as partnerships. However, it is possible in the United Kingdom for audits to be carried out by limited liability companies.[43] It was reported recently that of the United Kingdom's top 60 accountancy firms, the majority had turned to limited liability.[44] In 1995, KPMG announced the formation of a new company, KPMG Audit PLC, to audit its top 700 clients worldwide.[45] In Germany also, statutory audits can be per-

---

[40] Baker, Mikol, and Quick, "Regulation of the Statutory Auditor," p. 769.

[41] Graham, "Setting a Research Agenda."

[42] Andrew Parker, "PwC Steps Up Litigation Fight," *Financial Times,* April 19, 2004, p. 18.

[43] Among the ASEAN countries, in Thailand and Vietnam, auditing firms may be organized as limited liability companies. Favere-Marchesi, "Audit Quality."

[44] Liz Fisher, "Firms on the Defensive," *Accountancy,* July 2004, pp. 24–26.

[45] *Accountancy Age,* October 5, 1995, p. 1.

formed by audit corporations with limited liability. However, in other countries, such as New Zealand, an audit firm cannot be incorporated.

Proportionate Liability

Another approach that has been suggested to limit auditor's liability is to apply the concept of proportionate liability, by which the claim against each auditor would be restricted to the proportion of the loss for which he or she was responsible. However, this is not a widely adopted approach. For example, in September 1998, the New Zealand Law Commission declined a proposal by the then Institute of Chartered Accountants of New Zealand (ICANZ) [now, New Zealand Institute of Chartered Accountants (NZICA)] for changing auditors' liability from "joint and several liability" to "proportionate liability." In doing so the Law Commission stated that fairness among defendants was not relevant to fairness to the injured party. German regulators seem to have taken a different view on this issue. Although German law specifies the disciplinary procedures against auditors, they are not always strictly implemented due to an overall tendency to focus on damage to the reputation of the profession rather than on the extent of the individual culpability of the auditor. Australia and Canada have recently introduced systems that recognize proportionate liability for auditors. The Companies Act of 2006 in the United Kingdom removed the longstanding bar on auditors limiting their liability to the companies they audit, which was contained in section 310 of the Companies Act of 1985. Accordingly, limits for auditor liability could be agreed upon between the company and the auditor. From an international perspective, although the current UK regime is less favourable to auditors compared to those in Australia and Germany, a reasonable degree of protection is possible.

Statutory Cap

The use of a statutory cap is yet another approach that has been suggested to limit auditor's liability. The purpose of statutory cap is to reduce the amount of money that an audit firm would have to pay if found liable for negligence. In Germany, this has been the practice for many decades. In 1931, an explicit limit on auditors' maximum exposure to legal liability damages was introduced to relieve the auditor of an overwhelming worry of unlimited liability, and to limit the premiums for liability insurance.[46] In the United Kingdom, the auditors are legally prevented from limiting their liability to their client company arising from negligence, default, breach of duty, and breach of trust.[47] As an example of the extent to which auditors may be expected to pay, damages of £65 million were awarded against the accounting firm Binder Hamlyn in 1995. The case involved a careless acknowledgement of responsibility for a set of audited accounts made to a takeover bidder by the firm's senior partner.[48]

Disclaimer

UK auditors often include disclaimers of liability in their audit opinions to protect themselves from unintended liability. In March 2003, in response to a proposal put forward by the ICAEW to promote the capping of unintended auditor liability by changing the wording in audit opinions to illustrate to whom an opinion is given, the U.S. SEC clearly stated that this would not be acceptable in the

[46] Baker, Mikol, and Quick, "Regulation of the Statutory Auditor."
[47] C. J. Napier, "Intersections of Law and Accountancy: Unlimited Auditor Liability in the United Kingdom," *Accounting, Organizations and Society* 23, no. 1 (1998), pp. 105–28.
[48] *Financial Times*, December 7, 1995, p. 1.

United States and that disclaimers of liability placed in audit opinions by UK auditors would have no validity if placed on U.S. financial reports.

Auditor Independence

One of the main principles governing auditors' professional responsibilities is independence, in particular independence from management. However, reports of independence rule violations by major international accounting firms have appeared with increasing frequency. As an example, in January 2000, the SEC made public the report by an independent consultant who reviewed possible independence rule violations by one of the Big Four firms arising from ownership of client-issued securities. The report revealed significant violations of the firm's, the profession's, and the SEC's auditor independence rules.[49] Following the corporate collapses at the beginning of this century in many countries, a series of such reports appeared and auditor independence became the subject of much debate at the international level.

IFAC Code of Ethics for Professional Accountants identifies two different categories of independence: independence in mind and independence in appearance. Independence of mind requires auditors to be in a state of mind that allows them to express opinions about the auditee without feeling that they are under pressure due to independence issues and to feel that they are allowed to act with integrity, conducting their audits objectively and with professional skepticism. Independence of mind is also referred to as "independence in fact." Independence in appearance relates to a third party's perception regarding the auditor's independence. If the third party doesn't think that the auditor appears to be independent, even though the auditor is independent in his or her mind, the third party doesn't trust the auditor due to certain circumstances or relationships that are incompatible with independence and the promise of the assurance that the auditor is supposed to provide is lost.

The NYSE Euronext Corporate Governance Guidelines require, among other things, that the board will have four committees: an Audit Committee, a Human Resources and Compensation Committee, a Nominating and Governance Committee, and an Information Technology Committee. The guidelines also require that all of the members of these committees, except for information Technology Committee, should be independent directors.

The PCAOB requires public accountancy firms to communicate to an audit client's audit committee about any relationship between the firm and the client that may reasonably be thought to bear on the firm's independence. The communication would be required both before the firm accepts a new engagement pursuant to the standards of the PCAOB and annually for continuing engagements. The remainder of this section reviews various attempts to strengthen auditors' independence.

Auditor Appointment

Having stockholders involved in the auditor appointment process is expected to strengthen the independence of auditors from management and to improve audit quality. Generally, the law, for example the UK Companies Act of 1989 (Section 384), requires that the registered (or statutory) auditor be appointed by the shareholders in an annual general meeting. However, in practice, it is the company's managers who actually select the auditor, after negotiating fees and other arrangements. The auditor often considers the managing directors of the company as the

---

[49] The full report is available at www.sec.gov/pdf/pwclaw.pdf.

client, and hence the auditor's contractual arrangement is with the management of the company, not with the individual shareholders.

Restricted or Prohibited Activities

Another issue related to auditor independence is restricted or prohibited activities, including relationships with client companies. Mandated activities such as communication between auditors could also strengthen auditor independence. On the issue of the auditor's relationship with client companies, the Sarbanes-Oxley Act has specific provisions prohibiting certain nonaudit services provided by external auditors. However, the large audit firms point out that certain consulting work in fact helps improve audit quality. For example, they argue that consulting on information systems and e-commerce puts them on the cutting edge of business, and as a result, they can (1) start to measure items, such as a company's customer service quality, that are not on balance sheets even though investors consider them to be crucial assets; (2) develop continuous financial statements that provide real-time information instead of historical snapshots; and (3) explore ways to audit other measures of value that investors use, such as Web site traffic and market share locked up by being first with a new technology.

Regulatory Oversight

In many countries, the regulation and oversight of auditors have expanded to incorporate external monitoring and oversight of auditor competence and independence. The PCAOB in the United States and the Professional Oversight Board for Accountancy (POBA) in the United Kingdom are two examples. In October 2002, IOSCO issued a document titled *Statement of Principles for Auditor Oversight*, which requires that "within a jurisdiction auditors should be subject to oversight by a body that acts and is seen to act in the public interest." In its *Statement of Principles of Corporate Governance and Financial Reporting*, IOSCO recommends the following:

- Auditors should be independent, in line with international best practice.
- Auditors should make a statement to the board concerning their independence at the time the audit report is issued.
- The audit committee should monitor the auditor's appointment, remuneration and scope of services, and any retention of the auditor to provide nonaudit services.
- The board should disclose the scope of the audit, the nature of any nonaudit services provided by the auditors, and the remuneration for these.
- The board should disclose how auditor independence has been maintained where the auditor has been approved to provide any nonaudit services.
- An independent oversight body should monitor issues of audit quality and auditor independence.

At the international level, the Public Interest Oversight Board (PIOB) was formed in early 2005 mainly to oversee the work of IFAC committees on auditing, ethics, and education standard setting.

Mandatory Rotation

Mandatory rotation of audit firms often has been advocated as a means of strengthening auditor independence, ensuring that potential conflicts of interest are avoided. A recent government inquiry into auditor independence in the

United Kingdom resulted in a recommendation for mandatory auditor rotation as a way to restore investor confidence in the market in response to investor and public concerns in the wake of corporate scandals like the one involving Enron. However, the United Kingdom's largest audit firms have overwhelmingly rejected the notion that auditors should face mandatory rotation.[50] They argue that such a change would only serve to bring down the quality of the audit and that there is no evidence that rotation will prevent corporate collapse.[51]

In revising its code of ethics for professional accountants, IFAC has specified that, for audits of listed entities, the lead engagement partner should be rotated after a predefined period, normally no more than seven years, and that a partner rotating after a predefined period should not participate in the audit engagement until a further period of time, normally two years, has elapsed.[52] This requirement may be of particular concern in countries where there may be few partners with a sufficient understanding of the particular industry involved or a particular set of accounting rules (such as U.S. GAAP or SEC regulations).

Splitting Operations

To address the independence issue, the large accounting firms have taken more drastic action, splitting into separate entities, each dealing with a specific operational area. This allows auditing and consulting arms to deal with the same customer. In 2000, Ernst & Young announced the sale of its management-consulting business to CAP Gemini Group SA for around $11 billion. One reason was to reduce SEC concerns about lack of independence. Also in 2000, PricewaterhouseCoopers decided to separate its audit and business advisory services from its other businesses (e.g., e-commerce consulting) in a decision that was "encouraged" by the SEC. In February 2000, KPMG announced the incorporation of KPMG Consulting, to be owned by KPMG LLP and its partners (80.1 percent), and Cisco Systems Inc. (19.9 percent), which in August 1999 agreed to invest $1 billion in the new company.

Stringent Admission Criteria

In the United Kingdom, the Companies Act of 1989, which implemented the EU Eighth Directive, introduced stronger statutory arrangements for the regulation of auditors. It restricts qualifications for appointment as a statutory auditor to those who hold a recognized professional qualification and are subject to the requirements of a recognized supervisory body. It makes specific provision for the independence of company auditors; for example, an officer or employee of the company being audited may not act as auditor.

A Principles-Based Approach to Auditor Independence

In a recent auditor independence standard, the Canadian Institute of Chartered Accountants (CICA) makes a shift to a more rigorous "principles-based" approach.[53] The standard reflects features of the relevant requirements included in IFAC, the U.S. Sarbanes-Oxley Act, and the SEC for public companies. Its applicability goes beyond any specific situation and mandates a proactive approach based on clearly articulated principles. The core principle of the CICA standard

---

[50] Details are available at www.accountingeducation.com.news/news3659.html.

[51] By contrast, in Singapore, the law requires the rotation of audit partners for publicly listed companies.

[52] IFAC Ethics Committee, *Revision to Paragraph 8.151 Code of Ethics for Professional Accountants* (New York: IFAC, June 2004).

[53] CICA, "Chartered Accountants Adopt New Auditor Independence Standard," news release, December 4, 2003.

is that every effort must be made to eliminate all real or perceived threats to the auditor's independence. It requires auditors to ensure that their independence is not impaired in any way. In a set of specific rules for auditors of listed entities, the standard

- Prohibits certain nonaudit services (bookkeeping, valuations, actuarial, internal audit outsourcing, information technology system design or implementation, human resource functions, corporate finance activities, legal services, and certain expert services).
- Requires rotation of audit partners (lead and concurring partners after five years with a five-year time-out period, partners who provide more than 10 hours of audit services to the client and lead partners on significant subsidiaries after seven years with a two-year time-out period).
- Prohibits members of engagement team from working for the client in a senior accounting capacity until one year has passed from the time when they were on the engagement team.
- Prohibits compensation of audit partners for cross-selling nonaudit services to their audit clients.
- Requires audit committee prior approval for any service provided by the auditor.
- Stipulates that the rules for listed entities apply only to those listed entities with market capitalization or total assets in excess of $10 million.

A Conceptual Approach to Auditor Independence

In Europe, the *Federation des Experts Comptables Europeens* describes its approach to auditor independence as a conceptual approach.[54] By focusing on the underlying aim rather than detailed prohibitions, it combines flexibility with rigor in a way that is unavailable with a rule-based approach. It is argued that this approach

- Allows for the almost infinite variations in circumstances that arise in practice.
- Can cope with the rapid changes of the modern business environment.
- Prevents the use of legalistic devices to avoid compliance.
- Requires auditors to consider actively and to be ready to demonstrate the efficiency of arrangements for safeguarding independence.

An example of this approach would be the two-tiered corporate governance structure that exists in many continental European countries, such as Germany, France, and the Netherlands, and its perceived impact on auditor independence. Under that structure, because the supervisory board monitors the activities of the management board, and the auditors report to the supervisory board, the auditors may be more independent compared to their counterparts in the United Kingdom or the United States.

The main difference between the last two approaches is that, whereas the former uses a list of specific prohibitions, the latter avoids making such a list.

Audit Committees

An audit committee is a committee of the board of directors that oversees the financial reporting process including auditing. The subject of audit committees

---

[54] Federation des Experts Comptables Europeens, *The Conceptual Approach to Protecting Auditor Independence* (Brussels: FEE, February 2001).

has drawn increased attention in recent years.[55] In a 1999 report, the U.S. Blue Ribbon Committee, which made recommendations on improving the effectiveness of audit committees, describes the role of the audit committee as first among equals in supporting responsible financial disclosure and active and participatory oversight.[56] It defines the oversight role as "ensuring that quality accounting policies, internal controls, and independent and objective outside auditors are in place to deter fraud, anticipate financial risks, and promote accurate, high quality and timely disclosure of financial and other material information to the board, to the public markets, and to shareholders."[57]

In general, the audit committee responsibilities are to

- Monitor the financial reporting process.
- Oversee the internal control systems.
- Oversee the internal audit and independent public accounting function.

The Sarbanes-Oxley Act contains specific provisions dealing with issues related to audit committees, expanding their role and responsibilities. It requires the audit committee to be responsible for the outside auditor relationship, including the responsibility for the appointment, compensation, and oversight of a company's outside auditor. It also requires that members of the audit committee be independent from company management. Further, the requirements cover audit committee's authority to engage advisors, funding for the audit committee to pay the independent auditor, and any outside advisers it engages, and procedures for handling complaints about accounting, internal control, and auditing matters (whistleblower communication).

In January 2003, responding to Section 301 of the Sarbanes-Oxley Act, the SEC proposed new rules for audit committees to prohibit the listing of companies that fail to comply with the Sarbanes-Oxley Act's and SEC's requirements.[58] The SEC's requirements relate to the independence of audit committee members, the audit committee's responsibility to select and oversee the issuer's independent accountant, procedures for handling complaints regarding the issuer's accounting practices, the authority of the audit committee to engage advisers, and funding for the independent auditor and any outside advisers engaged by the audit committee.

One of the key responsibilities of an audit committee is oversight of the external auditor. It is now widely accepted that the external auditor works for and is accountable to the audit committee and board of directors (in some cases, the supervisory board). The regulatory bodies in many countries now require listed companies to establish audit committees. For example, under the ASX Corporate Governance Guidelines, listed companies in Australia are required to set up an independent audit committee made up completely of non-executive directors. All of the audit committee members are required to be financially literate, and at least

---

[55] Each of the Big Four firms has issued audit committee guidance. See, for example, Pricewaterhouse-Coopers, *Audit Committee Effectiveness: What Works Best,* 2nd ed. (Altamonte Springs, FL: Institute of Internal Auditors Research Foundation, 2000); Blue Ribbon Committee, *Report and Recommendations of the Blue Ribbon Committee on Improving the Effectiveness of Corporate Audit Committees* (New York: New York Stock Exchange and National Association of Securities Dealers, 1999); American Institute of Certified Public Accountants, *Audit Committee Communications,* SAS No. 90 (New York: AICPA, 2000).
[56] Blue Ribbon Committee, *Report and Recommendations,* p. 7.
[57] Ibid., p. 20.
[58] Securities and Exchange Commission, *Standards Relating to Listed Company Audit Committees,* SEC Release No. 33-8173, January 8, 2003. This is available at www.SEC.gov/rules/proposed/34-47137.htm.

one must have financial expertise. Among the ASEAN countries, audit committees for publicly listed companies are required in Malaysia and Singapore.[59]

Understanding how the accountability relationship through audit committees is supposed to work effectively is very important for all parties interested in corporate reporting in an international context. One of the potential problems, at least in some countries, would be the unavailability of individuals with the desired skills to be independent directors. Another concern is that as a result of the expanded responsibilities given to audit committees, suitable individuals may now be reluctant to take on the position of audit committee member. KPMG reported that 65 percent of a sample of UK audit committee members in 2003 believed the enhanced role and responsibilities would discourage individuals from taking on such positions.[60]

INTERNAL AUDITING

Internal auditing is a segment of accounting that uses the basic techniques and methods of auditing, and functions as an appraisal activity established within an entity. The Institute of Internal Auditors (IIA)[61] defines *internal auditing* as "an independent, objective assurance and consulting activity designed to add value and improve an organization's operations."[62] The internal auditor is a person within the organization and is expected to have a vital interest in a wide range of company operations. The Sarbanes-Oxley Act specifically recognizes the importance of internal auditing in restoring credibility to the systems of business reporting, internal control, and ethical behavior. The SEC requires listed companies to have an internal audit function. The IIA is a main source of feedback to the SEC regarding implementation of the internal control provisions of the Sarbanes-Oxley Act.

The role of internal auditing is determined by management, and its scope and objectives vary depending on the size and structure of the firm and the requirements of its management. In general, the objectives of internal auditing differ from those of external auditing. As stated in ISA 610, internal auditing activities include the following:

- *Review of the accounting and internal control systems.* The establishment of adequate accounting and internal control systems is a responsibility of management that continuously demands proper attention. Internal auditing is an ordinarily assigned specific responsibility by management for reviewing these systems, monitoring their operations, and recommending improvements thereto.

- *Examination of financial and operating information.* This may include review of the means used to identify, measure, classify and report such information and specific inquiry into individual items including detailed testing of transactions, balances and procedures.

[59] Favere-Marchesi, "Audit Quality," p. 142.

[60] This research was carried out among 118 members of FTSE 350 audit committees at the recent Audit Committee Institute Round Table. (The UK Audit Committee Institute is wholly sponsored by KPMG.) Details available at http://acountingeducation.com.news/news3892.html.

[61] The Institute of Internal Auditors (IIA) was founded in the United States in 1941. For more details, see S. Ramamoorti, *Internal Auditing: History, Evolution, and Prospects* (Altamonte Springs, FL: IIA Research Foundation, 2003).

[62] The Institute of Internal Auditors, *Internal Auditing's Role in Sections 302 and 404 of the U.S. Sarbanes-Oxley Act of 2002* (Altamonte Springs, FL: IIA, May 2004).

EXHIBIT 14.4
Competing
Demands on
Internal Audit
Function

Source: A. D. Bailey,
A. A. Gramling, and
S. Ramamoorti, *Research
Opportunities in Internal
Auditing* (Altamonte
Springs, FL: IIA Research
Foundation, 2003).

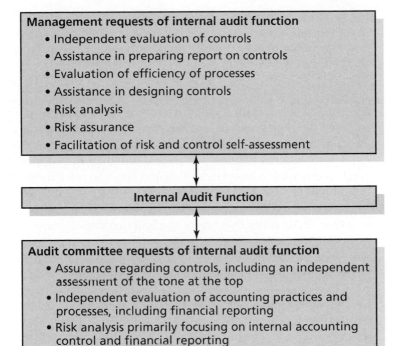

Management requests of internal audit function
- Independent evaluation of controls
- Assistance in preparing report on controls
- Evaluation of efficiency of processes
- Assistance in designing controls
- Risk analysis
- Risk assurance
- Facilitation of risk and control self-assessment

Internal Audit Function

Audit committee requests of internal audit function
- Assurance regarding controls, including an independent assessment of the tone at the top
- Independent evaluation of accounting practices and processes, including financial reporting
- Risk analysis primarily focusing on internal accounting control and financial reporting
- Fraud analysis and special investigations

- *Review of the economy, efficiency, and effectiveness of operations.* These operations include nonfinancial controls of an entity.
- *Review of compliance with laws, regulations, and other external requirements, as well as with management policies and directives and other internal requirements.*

Risk management is directly related to corporate governance and is an area in which internal auditing can make a significant contribution. Monitoring risks and providing assurance regarding controls are among the main internal audit functions (refer back to Exhibit 14.1). IFAC defines an internal control system as follows:

> An internal control system consists of all the policies and procedures (internal controls) adopted by the management of an entity to assist in achieving management's objective of ensuring, as far as practicable, the orderly and efficient conduct of its business, including adherence to management policies, the safeguarding of assets, the prevention and detection of fraud and error, the accuracy and completeness of the accounting records, and the timely preparation of reliable financial information. The internal control system extends beyond these matters which relate directly to the fairness of the accounting system.[63]

Recently, the IIA published a paper on internal auditing's role in enterprise risk management (ERM).[64] As shown in Exhibit 14.4, there are competing demands on internal audits from corporate management and audit committees. On the one hand, corporate management requests, among other things, assistance in design-

---

[63] IFAC, *Handbook of International Auditing, Assurance, and Ethics Pronouncements*, p. 122.
[64] This is available at www.theiia.org.

ing controls, self-assessment of risk and control, and preparing reports on controls. On the other hand, audit committee requests assurance regarding controls and independent evaluation of accounting practices and processes.

The PCAOB's Auditing Standard No. 5, *An Audit of Internal Control over Financial Reporting*, which is integrated with *An Audit of Financial Statements* (approved by the SEC), requires registered audit firms to use the new standard for all audits of internal control no later than for fiscal years ending on or after November 15, 2007. Adopted in May 2007, this standard implements Sections 103 and 404 of the Sarbanes-Oxley Act. The new standard reflects a principles-based approach, and allows auditors to apply professional judgment in determining the extent to which they will use the work of others. It is less prescriptive and easier to read. It directs auditors to focus on what matters most, and eliminates unnecessary procedures from the audit.

In August 2007, in a paper focused on internal control from a risk-based perspective, IFAC states that one of the best defenses against business failures and an important driver of business performance is strong internal control. In June 2008, applying the extensive expertise and experience of its members and IFAC member bodies to draw out a set of globally applicable statements of principles. These principles should (1) guide the thought processes of professional accountants in business when they tackle the relevant topic, and (2) underpin the exercise of the professional judgment that is important in their roles. They provide professional accountants in business (and those served by them) with a common frame of reference when deciding how to address issues encountered within a range of individual organizational situations.

The Demand for Internal Auditing in MNCs

In a global competitive environment, internal auditing has become an integral part of managing MNCs. The Committee of Sponsoring Organizations of the Treadway Commission (COSO) has issued its Guidance on Monitoring Internal Control Systems. The guidance is designed to help organizations better monitor the effectiveness of their internal control systems and to take timely corrective actions if needed. In China, the Ministry of Finance has provided guidance on internal control. In April 2010, five government departments jointly issued "Guidance on Internal Control." This guidance, together with the previously issued "Framework on Internal Control," is regarded as the basis for requirements on Chinese companies' internal control systems. Exhibits 14.5 and 14.6 depict a report of management on internal control over financial reporting and a report of independent registered public accounting firm on internal control over financial reporting, respectively.

There is a growing demand for risk management skills as MNCs face an increasing array of risks due to the fact that their control landscape is more extensive and complicated compared to purely domestic enterprises. The demand for internal auditing has been growing internationally during the past three decades, particularly due to regulatory and legislative requirements in many countries, for example, the U.S. Foreign Corrupt Practices Act.

U.S. Legislation against Foreign Corrupt Practices

The Foreign Corrupt Practices Act (FCPA), which became law in December 1977, requires companies to establish and maintain appropriate internal control systems so that corporate funds are not improperly used for illegal purposes. Following the FCPA internal control requirement, the SEC Act of 1934 was amended and, as a result, all the registrants of the SEC are required to install internal control systems to prevent or detect the use of firm assets for illegal activities.

EXHIBIT 14.5

COCA-COLA COMPANY AND SUBSIDIARIES
Extract from Form 10-K Report for the fiscal year ended December 31, 2008
Report of Management on Internal Control over Financial Reporting

Management of the Company is responsible for the preparation and integrity of the consolidated financial statements appearing in our annual report on Form 10-K. The financial statements were prepared in conformity with generally accepted accounting principles appropriate in the circumstances and, accordingly, include certain amounts based on our best judgments and estimates. Financial information in this annual report on Form 10-K is consistent with that in the financial statements.

Management of the Company is responsible for establishing and maintaining adequate internal control over financial reporting as such term is defined in Rule 13a-15(f) under the Securities Exchange Act of 1934 ("Exchange Act"). The Company's internal control over financial reporting is designed to provide reasonable assurance regarding the reliability of financial reporting and the preparation of the consolidated financial statements. Our internal control over financial reporting is supported by a program of internal audits and appropriate reviews by management, written policies and guidelines, careful selection and training of qualified personnel and a written Code of Business Conduct adopted by our Company's Board of Directors, applicable to all officers and employees of our Company and subsidiaries. In addition, our Company's Board of Directors adopted a written Code of Business Conduct for Non-Employee Directors which reflects the same principles and values as our Code of Business Conduct for officers and employees but focuses on matters of most relevance to non-employee Directors.

Because of its inherent limitations, internal control over financial reporting may not prevent or detect misstatements and, even when determined to be effective, can only provide reasonable assurance with respect to financial statement preparation and presentation. Also, projections of any evaluation of effectiveness to future periods are subject to the risk that controls may become inadequate because of changes in conditions, or that the degree of compliance with the policies or procedures may deteriorate.

The Audit Committee of our Company's Board of Directors, composed solely of Directors who are independent in accordance with the requirements of the New York Stock Exchange listing standards, the Exchange Act and the Company's Corporate Governance Guidelines, meets with the independent auditors, management and internal auditors periodically to discuss internal control over financial reporting and auditing and financial reporting matters. The Audit Committee reviews with the independent auditors the scope and results of the audit effort. The Audit Committee also meets periodically with the independent auditors and the chief internal auditor without management present to ensure that the independent auditors and the chief internal auditor have free access to the Audit Committee. Our Audit Committee's Report can be found in the Company's 2009 Proxy Statement.

Management assessed the effectiveness of the Company's internal control over financial reporting as of December 31, 2008. In making this assessment, management used the criteria set forth by the Committee of Sponsoring Organizations of the Treadway Commission (COSO) in *Internal Control—Integrated Framework*. Based on our assessment, management believes that the Company maintained effective internal control over financial reporting as of December 31, 2008.

The Company's independent auditors, Ernst & Young LLP, a registered public accounting firm, are appointed by the Audit Committee of the Company's Board of Directors, subject to ratification by our Company's shareowners. Ernst & Young LLP has audited and reported on the consolidated financial statements of The Coca-Cola Company and subsidiaries and the Company's internal control over financial reporting. The reports of the independent auditors are contained in this annual report.

Muhtar Kent
President and Chief Executive Officer
February 26, 2009

Harry L. Anderson
Vice President and Controller
February 26, 2009

Gary P. Fayard
Executive Vice President and Chief Financial Officer
February 26, 2009

The FCPA makes it illegal for U.S. companies to pay bribes to foreign government officials or political parties in order to secure or maintain business transactions or secure another type of improper advantage. Violation of the FCPA could result in large fines being levied against the corporation, and the executives, employees, and other individuals involved could also be fined or jailed or both. U.S. companies may be subject to liability for FCPA violations by their foreign subsidiaries or joint venture partners.

EXHIBIT 14.6

COCA-COLA COMPANY AND SUBSIDIARIES
Extract from Form 10-K Report for the fiscal year ended December 31, 2008
Report of Independent Registered Public Accounting Firm
On Internal Control over Financial Reporting

Board of Directors and Shareowners

The Coca-Cola Company

We have audited The Coca-Cola Company's internal control over financial reporting as of December 31, 2008, based on criteria established in *Internal Control—Integrated Framework* issued by the Committee of Sponsoring Organizations of the Treadway Commission (the COSO criteria). The Coca-Cola Company's management is responsible for maintaining effective internal control over financial reporting, and for its assessment of the effectiveness of internal control over financial reporting included in the accompanying Report of Management on Internal Control Over Financial Reporting. Our responsibility is to express an opinion on the Company's internal control over financial reporting based on our audit.

We conducted our audit in accordance with the standards of the Public Company Accounting Oversight Board (United States). Those standards require that we plan and perform the audit to obtain reasonable assurance about whether effective internal control over financial reporting was maintained in all material respects. Our audit included obtaining an understanding of internal control over financial reporting, assessing the risk that a material weakness exists, testing and evaluating the design and operating effectiveness of internal control based on the assessed risk, and performing such other procedures as we considered necessary in the circumstances. We believe that our audit provides a reasonable basis for our opinion.

A company's internal control over financial reporting is a process designed to provide reasonable assurance regarding the reliability of financial reporting and the preparation of financial statements for external purposes in accordance with generally accepted accounting principles. A company's internal control over financial reporting includes those policies and procedures that (1) pertain to the maintenance of records that, in reasonable detail, accurately and fairly reflect the transactions and dispositions of the assets of the company; (2) provide reasonable assurance that transactions are recorded as necessary to permit preparation of financial statements in accordance with generally accepted accounting principles, and that receipts and expenditures of the company are being made only in accordance with authorizations of management and directors of the company; and (3) provide reasonable assurance regarding prevention or timely detection of unauthorized acquisition, use, or disposition of the company's assets that could have a material effect on the financial statements.

Because of its inherent limitations, internal control over financial reporting may not prevent or detect misstatements. Also, projections of any evaluation of effectiveness to future periods are subject to the risk that controls may become inadequate because of changes in conditions, or that the degree of compliance with the policies or procedures may deteriorate.

In our opinion, The Coca-Cola Company maintained, in all material respects, effective internal control over financial reporting as of December 31, 2008, based on the COSO criteria.

We also have audited, in accordance with the standards of the Public Company Accounting Oversight Board (United States), the consolidated balance sheets of The Coca-Cola Company and subsidiaries as of December 31, 2008 and 2007, and the related consolidated statements of income, shareowners' equity, and cash flows for each of the three years in the period ended December 31, 2008, and our report dated February 26, 2009 expressed an unqualified opinion thereon.

Ernst & Young LLP
Atlanta, Georgia
February 26, 2009

The FCPA grew out of the revelations of widespread bribery of senior officials of foreign governments by American companies. In particular, the Lockheed and Watergate scandals in the mid-1970s triggered the enactment of the FCPA. The Lockheed scandal involved kickbacks and political donations paid by Lockheed, the American aircraft manufacturer, to Japanese politicians in return for aid in selling planes to All-Nippon Airlines. The scandal forced Tanaka Kakuei to resign as prime minister and as member of the ruling Liberal Democratic Party. Lockheed had paid a total of $22 million to Japanese and other government officials.

In an investigation launched by the Securities and Exchange Commission following the Watergate scandal in the 1970s, it was discovered that American companies were engaged in large-scale bribery overseas. According to the report from that investigation, by 1976 more than 450 American companies had paid bribes to foreign government officials, made contributions to political parties, or made other questionable payments. A considerable amount of "slush funds" were generated for this purpose by falsifying their accounting records. Thus, the original intention behind the enactment of the FCPA was to improve corporate accountability and transparency.

The FCPA has two main components—accounting provisions and antibribery provisions. The SEC plays the main role in enforcing the accounting provisions, which require a company to maintain books, records, and accounts fairly reflecting the transactions and dispositions of the assets. In addition, a company must devise and maintain an appropriate internal accounting controls system, execute transactions in accordance with the management's authorization, prepare financial statements in conformity with accounting principles, and record transactions to maintain accountability for assets. These requirements apply to SEC-regulated public companies— both U.S. and foreign companies—including their overseas branches.

The FCPA's accounting provisions require that a company holding a majority of a subsidiary's voting securities must cause that entity to comply with the FCPA accounting requirements. With regard to cases in which the parent holds less than a majority interest, the act requires a parent entity to "proceed in good faith to use its influence, to the extent reasonable under the circumstances" to cause compliance.

The Report of the National Commission on Fraudulent Financial Reporting in the U.S. (Treadway Commission Report, 1987), and the Report of the Committee of Sponsoring Organizations (COSO) of the Treadway Commission, 1992, also placed particular emphasis on internal controls. The 1987 Treadway Report made several recommendations designed to reduce financial statement fraud by improving control and governance. The report made it clear that the responsibility for reliable financial reporting "resides first and foremost at the corporate level, in particular at the top management level." Top management "sets the tone and establishes the financial reporting environment." The idea is that good record keeping and internal control would make it more difficult to conceal illegal activities.

The International Anti-Bribery and Fair Competition Act of 1998 expanded the scope of the FCPA for application to foreign companies (other than those regulated by the SEC) and foreign nationals, if their corrupt activity occurs within the United States. A U.S. company can be prosecuted not only when it directly authorizes an illegal payment by its foreign affiliate but also when it provides funds to that affiliate while knowing or having reason to know that the affiliate will use those funds to make a corrupt payment.

The Sarbanes-Oxley Act of 2002, Section 404(a), and the SEC's related implementing rules require the management of a public company to assess the effectiveness of the company's internal control over financial reporting, and include in the company's annual report management's conclusion about whether the company's internal control is effective, as of the end of the company's most recent fiscal year. Following these requirements, the PCAOB issued an audit standard, and in June 2004 the SEC approved the PCAOB Release No.2004-003: "An Audit of Internal Control over Financial Reporting Performed in Conjunction with an Audit of Financial Statements." Accordingly, the integrated audit results in two audit opinions: one on internal control over financial reporting and one on the financial statements.[65]

---

[65] Details are available at www.sec.gov/news/press/2004-83.htm.

Legislation in Other Jurisdictions

In December 1997, 33 countries signed the OECD Convention on Combating Bribery of Foreign Public Officials in International Business Transactions and are required to make offshore bribery a crime under domestic law.

In the United Kingdom, the Cadbury Committee, which was set up by the FRC, the London Stock Exchange, and the accounting profession to address the financial aspects of corporate governance, presented internal control frameworks in its report published in December 1992.[66] The sponsors were concerned at the perceived low level of confidence both in financial reporting and in the ability of auditors to provide the safeguards, which the users of corporate reports sought and expected. These concerns were heightened by some unexpected failures of major companies such as Polly Peck.[67] The report developed recommendations for the control and reporting functions of the board, and on the role of auditors. The main output of the committee was a Code of Best Practice for companies. It emphasized openness, integrity, and accountability, and was implemented by the London Stock Exchange. Similar proposals were made by the Criteria of Control Committee of Canada (CoCo Report) and by the OECD Convention.

In July 2007, in response to the FRC's review of impact of the Combined Code, which became effective to reporting years beginning on or after November 1, 2006, following a review by FRC, the ICAS raised the question whether the *comply or explain* approach was working. It stated that the bodies who oversee its application tion must ensure that it does not become an exercise in mindless compliance for the increasing number of companies who adhere to the principles of the code. Too often the comply or explain principle in relation to applying the code was being interpreted as *comply* meaning good and *explain* meaning bad. The ICAS suggests that the code should explicitly state that it is a good thing for a company to explain its policies and practices in support of compliance or noncompliance. It is also important that independence of directors should not be interpreted as more important than experience.

A study that examined whether the style and form of corporate governance has an effect in deterring financial fraud in China found that firms that had a high proportion of nonexecutive directors on the board were less likely to engage in fraud.[68] Both internal and external corporate governance mechanisms are weak or nonexistent in China. Externally the market for corporate control and managerial labor market are seriously underdeveloped, and internally it was not until 2002 that independent directors and audit committees appeared in listed companies. Chinese auditors have enjoyed an almost litigation-free environment because of a lack of sophisticated users and providers of accounting information.

For an MNC, an important task of monitoring risks is to develop a plan to systematically assess risk across multinational activities within the organization. In addition, the MNC needs to assess existing risk of audited area and reporting of that assessment to management or the audit committee, or both; lead the risk management activities when a void has occurred within the organization; facilitate the use of risk self-assessment techniques; evaluate risks associated with the use of

---

[66] *Report of the Committee on the Financial Aspects of Corporate Governance* (Cadbury Report) (London: Gee, December 1, 1992).

[67] For details, see David Gwilliam and Tim Russell, "Polly Peck: Where Were the Analysts?" *Accountancy,* January 1991, pp. 25–26.

[68] G. Chen, M. Firth, D. N. Gao, and O. M. Rui, "Ownership Structure, Corporate Governance and Fraud: Evidence from China," *Journal of Corporate Finance* 12 (2006), pp. 424–48.

EXHIBIT 14.7
Evaluative
Frameworks for
Internal Control

Source: Deloitte & Touche,
"Moving-forward: A Guide
to Improving Corporate
Governance through
Effective Internal Control—
A Response to Sarbanes-
Oxley," January 2003.

- *COSO—Internal Control—Integrated Framework.* Developed by the Committee of Sponsoring Organizations (COSO) of the Treadway Commission and sponsored by the AICPA, the FEI, the IIA and others, COSO is the dominant framework in the United States. The guidelines were first published in 1991, with anticipated revisions and updates forthcoming. This is believed to be the framework chosen by the vast majority of the U.S.-based public companies.
- *CoCo—The Control Model.* Developed by the Criteria of Control Committee (CoCo) of the CICA. The CoCo focuses on behavioral values rather than control structure and procedures as the fundamental basis for internal control in a company.
- *Turnbull Report—Internal Control.* Developed by the ICAEW, in conjunction with the London Stock Exchange, the guide was published in 1999. Turnbull requires companies to identify, evaluate, and manage their significant risks and to assess the effectiveness of the related internal control systems.
- *Australian Criteria of Control (ACC).* Issued in 1998 by the Institute of Internal Auditors—Australia, the ACC emphasizes the competency of management and employees to develop and operate the internal control framework. Self-committed control, which includes such attributes as attitudes, behaviors, and competency, is promoted as the most cost-effective approach to internal control.
- *The King Report.* The King Report, released by the King Committee on Corporate Governance in 1994, promotes high standards of corporate governance in South Africa. The King Report goes beyond the usual financial and regulatory aspects of corporate governance by addressing social, ethical, and environmental concerns.

new technology; and assist management in implementing a risk model across the organization covering operations in different countries. Exhibit 14.7 shows several evaluative frameworks that have been proposed for internal control.

However, in regard to internal controls, a question remains: What if the top management was involved in the illegal transaction? After all, the top management is responsible for internal control and has discretionary power to override or restructure the internal control system. Managers can commit fraud by overriding internal controls, and audits conducted in accordance with auditing standards do not always distinguish between errors and fraud.[69] Evidence suggests that, although better internal controls would prevent or discourage fraudulent conduct on the part of employees, it would be more difficult to prevent fraud at the top level:

- In 1992, General Electric (GE) allegedly misappropriated $26.5 million from the U.S. government by falsifying accounting records in conjunction with a sale of weapons to Israel. GE was accused of violating not only the FCPA but also the Money Laundering Control Act, among other laws, and was ordered to pay $69 million in fines.
- In 1995, Lockheed was prosecuted for violating the FCPA based on its alleged payment of a bribe of $1 million to a member of the Egyptian parliament in order to sell its military jets to Egypt's armed forces. The company paid a $24.8 million fine. In this case, a fine of $20,000 was also imposed on the responsible manager, and the vice president of Middle East and North Africa marketing was fined $125,000 and sentenced to 18 months in prison.
- In 1998, a large U.S. oil company, Saybolt, was prosecuted for violating the FCPA when it allegedly paid $50,000 to a Panamanian government official to obtain a lease for a site near the Panama canal, and paid a fine of $4.9 million.

[69] D. Capalan, "Internal Controls and the Detection of Management Fraud," *Journal of Accounting Research* 37, no. 1 (1999), p. 101.

- In 1996, Montedison, a major Italian company listed on the New York Stock Exchange, allegedly concealed hundreds of millions of dollars in losses by falsifying its books, and paid bribes to Italian politicians and others. The SEC filed a civil suit alleging violations of FCPA accounting standards. In response, the company reformed its internal controls and settled the case with the SEC for $300,000.

According to the results of the Management Barometer Survey 2004, referred to earlier in this chapter, 79 percent of senior executives of U.S. MNCs stated that their company needed improvements in order to comply with Section 404 of Sarbanes-Oxley Act, which requires companies to file a management assertion and auditor attestation on the effectiveness of internal controls over financial reporting. They also mentioned the areas needing remedies, which included the following:

Financial processes	55%
Computer controls	48
Internal audit effectiveness	37
Security controls	35
Audit committee oversight	26
Fraud programs	24

For effective governance, the ultimate responsibility for internal control should be vested in the board, which represents shareholders. The board is responsible for achieving corporate objectives by providing guidance for corporate strategy and monitoring management. The board is effective only if it is reasonably independent from management. Board independence usually requires a sufficient number of outsiders; an adequate time devoted by the members; and access to accurate, relevant, and timely information.

Because the board is usually not engaged in its work on a full-time basis, it needs to rely on experts for necessary information, such as the internal auditor and the external auditor. Being employees of the company, internal auditors are faced with a built-in conflict in regard to their allegiance. This makes the role of the external auditor crucial. External auditors are normally required to make an assessment of the internal control. If the external auditors are to attest to the "fair representation" or "true and fair view" of the financial position of the firm, they need to be able to form their opinion independent of the board and management. However, the issue of auditor independence is complicated by the facts that auditors are paid by the auditee company—more specifically, its management—and often the auditors provide consultancy services to the auditee company.

FUTURE DIRECTIONS

So far in this chapter we have discussed the current status with regard to various auditing issues that are important to MNCs. In this section, we provide some thoughts on the likely future developments. We identify them in terms of consumer demand for auditing, increased competition in the audit market, Big Four firms' continued high interest in the audit market, increased exposure of Big Four firms, a tendency toward a checklist approach, and the possibility that audit may not be the external auditor's exclusive domain.

Building robust corporate governance systems and processes, managing risk on a global scale, and complying with an increasingly vast web of regulatory requirements is difficult, costly, and time-consuming for MNCs.

The Sarbanes-Oxley Act has had a noticeable effect on corporate behavior, particularly in regard to disclosure of information. For example, a recent survey of 2,588 global companies found that 95 percent of U.S. companies (versus 65 percent in 2002) now report having a qualified financial expert on the audit committee.[70] However, in November 2004, a study of audit firm performance, based on interviews with 1,007 audit committee chairs and 944 CFOs, indicated that there was a significant angst among them. Top management was concerned about the costs, in terms of money and time, of implementing the extensive requirements of Sarbanes-Oxley Act. Audit committee chairs were feeling the pressure of increased accountability of the required financial reporting process.[71] Further, a survey conducted by Financial Executives International (FEI) found that the cost of complying with Sarbanes-Oxley Section 404 requirements was much more than companies expected. The Year 1 cost averaged $4.36 million, up 39 percent from the $3.14 million they expected to pay based on FEI's July 2004 cost survey.

Consumer Demand

Historically, the assurance opinion of the statutory auditor has been led by legislation rather than by consumer demand. In the future, however, there will be increasing demand to meet the needs of consumers at a global level.[72] For example, with the disclosure of corporate information on the Internet, auditors will be expected to find new ways of giving assurance on that information, which would not be limited to financial information, and on a real-time basis. A report published by the IASC in November 1999 concluded that there was a need for a generic code of conduct for Internet-based business reporting.[73] The report suggested that such a code should include conditions clearly setting out the information that is consistent with the printed annual report, which contains the audited financial statements. It also pointed out that the users of Internet-based reports are likely to be confused as to which part of the Web site relates to the audit report, signed off by an auditor. From the auditor's point of view, there is a risk involved when the financial report issued by the entity (on which the auditor provides an audit report) is materially misstated due to unauthorized tampering. This could put auditors at risk of legal action.

Attempts are being made to find solutions to some of these problems on a national basis. For example, according to recent legislation in Australia, stockholders are allowed to put questions in writing to auditors in advance of the annual general meeting. However, it appears that governments have now realized the importance of collective action at the international level in this area.

Reporting on the Internet

The AICPA and the CICA have developed a set of principles and criteria to provide assurance services in the area of electronic business. Accordingly, public accounting firms and practitioners, who have a Web Trust business license from an authorized professional accounting body, can provide assurance services to evaluate and test whether a particular Web site meets these principles and criteria. The AICPA/CICA initiative has received international recognition as a major development.[74]

---

[70] More details about rating of companies from different countries can be obtained at www.Gmiratings.com.

[71] J. D. Power and Associates, *2004 Audit Firm Performance Study Report.*

[72] J. P. Percy, "Assurance Services: Visions for the Future," *International Journal of Auditing* 3 (1999), pp. 81–87.

[73] A. Lymer, R. Debreceny, G. Gray, and A. Rahman, *Business Reporting on the Internet* (London: IASC, 1999).

[74] For example, the third version of CICA/AICPA Web Trust principles is available at www.accounting education.com/news/news497.html.

Increased Competition in the Audit Market

In the current global environment, auditor independence in the traditional sense is becoming increasingly problematic as both the audit firms and their clients grow in size and complexity. While the Sarbanes-Oxley Act has proposed more stringent independence standards, including some restrictions on the delivery of audit and nonaudit services to the same client, the Big Four international auditing firms need to ensure that they are independent both in fact and in perception. This is critical because the perception of a lack of independence will reduce the quality premium the Big Four firms are able to charge their clients and will open the audit market to more competition.

The whole area of systems, particularly technological systems, demands an assurance of their effectiveness. In addition, there is an increasing demand for assurance on the effectiveness and quality of management arrangements and corporate governance. These new demands will require new skills. This will also encourage those not trained in accountancy, but trained in investigative matters in other areas, such as the environment and technology, to develop into a competitive force. In other words, nonaccounting groups may enter the audit market, which traditionally has been the domain of the accounting profession, protected by statutory franchise.

Continued High Interest in the Audit Market

Because they have a virtual monopoly of the large-firm audit market, the Big Four have been able to use this market to build their brands.[75] The audit market will remain central to the Big Four firms' operations because it helps them to maintain their brands. This will continue to be the case in the future, as it will be more difficult for the large firms to develop a reputation for perceived quality and build brands in the nonaudit market given that they are competing against recognized competitors with their own brands, such as McKinsey and Boston Consulting Group. Thus, even though the audit market is not extremely profitable, it will be in the interest of the Big Four to protect this market from the encroachment of competitors.

Increased Exposure of the International Auditing Firms

Becoming more global also means becoming more visible. The Big Four international auditing firms audit MNCs listed in numerous jurisdictions, and as these companies grow and become more globalized, the Big Four are increasingly coming under the watchful eye of global financiers and regulatory institutions.

The Big Four accounting firms, which together audit more than 90 percent of the world's largest businesses, can expect a more intense focus on their activities than at any time since the aftermath of the scandals at Enron, WorldCom, and Parmalat. There will be renewed interest in what users can expect from an audit. The audit firms need to recognize that the nature of business has changed. It is quicker, more connected, more global, and very different to the nature of business in the last century. Questions such as these will be the subjects of discussion and debate:

Have auditors kept pace with changes in the nature of business?

Do auditors, like rating agencies, suffer from a potential conflict of interest because they are paid by those they judge?

---

[75] They audit the world's largest 100 companies, with market capitalization ranging from US\$31 billion to \$273 billion (see www.iasc.org.uk/frame/cen1_9.htm).

Particularly, with such big fees available, it is likely that politicians and regulators will be considering whether auditors face a temptation to sign off on practices that meet the rules but may present a misleading picture.

Tendency toward a Checklist Approach

The advent of litigation and the need for efficiency and effectiveness has driven the audit in some cases to be led more by process than by judgment. Given the various codes of corporate governance, regulations, and auditing standards and guidelines, there is a tendency for auditors to use a checklist approach in order to protect themselves from litigation.[76]

Auditing No Longer Only the Domain of the External Auditor

Given the increased attention on corporate governance and the resulting changes to corporate structures in recent years, no longer is auditing only the domain of the external auditor. The audit function is increasingly becoming a process that involves a partnership between the audit committee, internal auditors, and external auditors.

Different Corporate Governance Models

Currently, the UK model of splitting the roles of chairperson and chief executive is taking hold globally. As recently as 2002, more than half of incoming chief executives at North American and European companies also chaired their company's board. In 2009, that number fell to less than 17 percent in North America and 7 percent in Europe. UK good governance guidelines have long advocated splitting the job to strengthen the board's oversight role. This can be described as the *globalization of governance*. There is also growing use of the Japanese "apprenticeship" model, in which the outgoing chief executive is promoted to chairperson to oversee his or her replacement. In Japan, this happens in 75 percent of companies. This happened in more than 40 percent of North American companies in the 2005–2009 period, up from 30 percent in the prior five years.

Summary

1. Recent corporate disasters, particularly in the United States, have prompted regulatory measures that emphasize the importance of assurance services as an essential ingredient in establishing and maintaining investor confidence in markets through corporate governance.
2. Over the years, the international aspects of auditing have received relatively less attention among policymakers and researchers, compared to the international accounting standards.
3. MNCs are realizing the need to pay attention to corporate governance issues in their efforts to succeed in increasingly competitive global markets.
4. The role of the external auditor can vary in different countries. For example, the role of the statutory auditors in Germany is much broader than that of their counterparts in the United Kingdom or the United States.
5. Corporate structure is an important factor that determines the purpose of external audit. For example, some European countries have a two-tiered corporate structure, with a supervisory board and a management board. The supervisory board has general oversight function over the performance of the management board and the basic function of the statutory auditor is to assist the supervisory board. This is different from the situation that exists in Anglo-Saxon countries.

[76] Percy, "Assurance Services."

6. Audit quality is likely to vary in different audit environments, and the audit environments in different countries are determined by cultural, legal, financing, and infrastructural factors.

7. The approaches taken to regulate the audit function in different countries range from heavy reliance on the profession, for example, in the United Kingdom, to heavy reliance on the government, for example, in China.

8. The nature of the audit report varies depending largely on the legal requirements in a particular country and the listing status of the company concerned.

9. The responsibility for harmonizing auditing standards internationally rests mainly with the International Federation of Accountants (IFAC).

10. Auditors are subject to civil liability, criminal liability, and professional sanctions.

11. Different approaches have been taken in different countries to deal with the issues concerning the auditor's liability to third parties, and the principle of joint and several liability.

12. Recently many countries have turned increased attention to audit committees as an important instrument of corporate governance.

13. Currently, regulators in the United Kingdom, the United States, and some other countries have placed emphasis on public oversight bodies to monitor issues of auditor independence.

14. Large auditing firms have adopted a policy of splitting the auditing and non-auditing work into separate entities as a way of demonstrating independence.

15. Internal auditing is an integral part of multinational business management, as it helps restore/maintain credibility of the business reporting system. The demand for internal auditing has grown during the past three decades, particularly due to regulatory and legislative requirements in many countries.

Appendix to Chapter 14

Examples of 2009 Audit Reports from Multinational Corporations

The following audits were prepared in accordance with the requirements in the United States, Japan, Germany, the United Kingdom, the Netherlands and China.

INDEPENDENT AUDITORS' REPORT
China Southern Airline Co. Ltd

KPMG

Independent auditor's report to the shareholders of China Southern Airlines Company Limited
(Incorporated in the People's Republic of China with limited liability)

We have audited the consolidated financial statements of China Southern Airlines Company Limited (the "Company") and its subsidiaries (the "Group") set out on pages 46 to 138, which comprise the consolidated and company balance sheets as at 31 December 2009, and the consolidated income statement, the consolidated statement of comprehensive income, the consolidated statement of changes in equity and the consolidated cash flow statement for the year then ended, and a summary of significant accounting policies and other explanatory notes.

Directors' Responsibility for the Financial Statements

The directors of the Company are responsible for the preparation and the true and fair presentation of these financial statements in accordance with International Financial Reporting Standards issued by the International Accounting Standards Board and the disclosure requirements of the Hong Kong Companies Ordinance. This responsibility includes designing, implementing and maintaining internal control relevant to the preparation and the true and fair presentation of financial statements that are free from material misstatement, whether due to fraud or error, selecting and applying appropriate accounting policies, and making accounting estimates that are reasonable in the circumstances.

Auditor's Responsibility

Our responsibility is to express an opinion on these financial statements based on our audit. This report is made solely to you, as a body, and for no other purpose. We do not assume responsibility towards or accept liability to any other person for the contents of this report.

We conducted our audit in accordance with Hong Kong Standards on Auditing issued by the Hong Kong Institute of Certified Public Accountants. Those standards require that we comply with ethical requirements and plan and perform the audit to obtain reasonable assurance as to whether the financial statements are free from material misstatement.

An audit involves performing procedures to obtain audit evidence about the amounts and disclosures in the financial statements. The procedures selected depend on the auditor's judgement, including the assessment of the risks of material misstatement of the financial statements, whether due to fraud or error. In making those risk assessments, the auditor considers internal control relevant to the entity's preparation and true and fair presentation of the financial statements in order to design audit procedures that are appropriate in the circumstances, but not for the purpose of expressing an opinion on the effectiveness of the entity's internal control. An audit also includes evaluating the appropriateness of accounting policies used and the reasonableness of accounting estimates made by the directors, as well as evaluating the overall presentation of the financial statements.

We believe that the audit evidence we have obtained is sufficient and appropriate to provide a basis for our audit opinion.

Opinion

In our opinion, the consolidated financial statements give a true and fair view of the financial position of the Company and of the Group as at 31 December 2009 and of the Group's financial performance and cash flows for the year then ended in accordance with International Financial Reporting Standards and have been properly prepared in accordance with the disclosure requirements of the Hong Kong Companies Ordinance.

KPMG

Certified Public Accountants
8th Floor, Prince's Building
10 Chater Road
Central, Hong Kong
The People's Republic of China
12 April 2010

INDEPENDENT AUDITORS' REPORT
China Eastern Airline Corp. Ltd

To the Shareholders of China Eastern Airlines Corporation Limited
(incorporated in the People's Republic of China with limited liability)

We have audited the financial statements of China Eastern Airlines Corporation Limited (the "Company") and its subsidiaries (together, the "Group") set out on pages 66 to 164, which comprise the consolidated and Company balance sheets as at 31 December 2009, and the consolidated statement of comprehensive income, the consolidated statement of changes in equity and the consolidated cash flow statement for the year then ended, and a summary of significant accounting policies and other explanatory notes.

Directors' Responsibility for the Financial Statements

The Directors of the Company are responsible for the preparation and the true and fair presentation of these financial statements in accordance with International Financial Reporting Standards and the disclosure requirements of the Hong Kong Companies Ordinance. This responsibility include: designing, implementing and maintaining internal control relevant to the preparation and the true and fair presentation of financial statements that are free from material misstatement, whether due to fraud or error, selecting and applying appropriate accounting policies; and making accounting estimates that are reasonable in the circumstances.

Auditor's Responsibility

Our responsibility is to express an opinion on these financial statements based on our audit. We conducted our audit in accordance with International Standards on Auditing Those Standards require that we comply with ethical requirements and plan and perform the audit to obtain reasonable assurance whether the financial statements are free from material misstatement.

An audit involves performing procedures to obtain audit evidence about the amounts and disclosures in the financial statements. The procedures selected depend on the auditor's judgment, including the assessment of the risks of material misstatement of the financial statements, whether due to fraud or error. In making those risk assessments, the auditor considers internal control relevant to the entity's preparation and true and fair presentation of the financial statements in order to design audit procedures that are appropriate in the circumstances, but not for the purpose of expressing an opinion on the effectiveness of the entity's internal control. An audit also includes evaluating the appropriateness of accounting policies used and the reasonableness of accounting estimates made by the Directors, as well as evaluating the overall presentation of the financial statements.

We believe that the audit evidence we have obtained is sufficient and appropriate to provide a basis for our opinion.

Opinion

In our opinion, the financial statements give a true and fair view of the state of affairs of the Company and the Group as at 31 December 2009, and of the Group's financial performance and cash flows for the year then ended in accordance with International Financial Reporting Standards and have been properly prepared in accordance with the disclosure requirements of the Hong Kong Companies Ordinance.

Other Matters

This report, including the opinion, has been prepared for and only for you, as a body, and for no other purpose. We do not assume responsibility towards or accept liability to any other person for the contents of this report.

PricewaterhouseCoopers

Certified Public Accountants

Hong Kong, 19 April 2010

INDEPENDENT AUDITORS' REPORT
Bayer Aktiengesellschaft, Leverkusen

Auditor's Report

We have audited the consolidated financial statements prepared by Bayer Aktiengesellschaft, Leverkusen, comprising the income statement and statement of comprehensive income, statement of financial position, statement of cash flows, statement of changes in equity and the notes to the consolidated financial statements, together with the group management report for the business year from January 1, 2009 to December 31, 2009, which is combined with the management report of the company. The preparation of the consolidated financial statements and the combined management report in accordance with the IFRS, as adopted by the E.U., and the additional requirements of German commercial law pursuant to § (Article) 315a Abs. (paragraph) 1 HGB ("Handeisgesetzbuch":

German Commercial Code) are the responsibility of the parent Company's Board of Management. Our responsibility is to express an opinion on the consolidated financial statements and on the combined management report based on our audit.

We conducted our audit of the consolidated financial statements in accordance with § 317 HGB and German generally accepted standards for the audit of financial statements promulgated by the Institut der Wirtschaftsprüfer (Institute of Public Auditors in Germany) (IDW) and additionally observed the International Standards on Auditing (ISA). Those standards require that we plan and perform the audit such that misstatements materially affecting the presentation of the net assets, financial position and results of operations in the consolidated financial statements in accordance with the applicable financial reporting framework and in the combined management report are detected with reasonable assurance. Knowledge of the business activities and the economic and legal environment of the Group and expectations as to possible misstatements are taken into account in the determination of audit procedures. The effectiveness of the accounting-related internal control system and the evidence supporting the disclosures in the consolidated financial statements and the combined management report are examined primarily on a test basis within the framework of the audit. The audit includes assessing the annual financial statements of those entities included in consolidation, the determination of the entities to be included in consolidation, the accounting and consolidation principles used and significant estimates made by the Company's Board of Management, as well as evaluating the overall presentation of the consolidated financial statements and the combined management report. We believe that our audit provides a reasonable basis for our opinion.

Our audit has not led to any reservations.

In our opinion based on the findings of our audit the consolidated financial statements comply with the IFRS as adopted by the E.U., the additional requirements of German commercial law pursuant to § 315a Abs. 1 HGB and give a true and fair view of the net assets, financial position and results of operations of the Group in accordance with these requirements. The combined management report is consistent with the consolidated financial statements and as a whole provides a suitable view of the Group's position and suitably presents the opportunities and risks of future development.

Essen, February 24, 2010

PricewaterhouseCoopers
Aktiengesellschaft
Wirtschaftsprüfungsgesellschaft

Armin Slotta   Anne Böcker
Wirtschaftsprüfer   Wirtschaftsprüferin

INDEPENDENT AUDITORS' REPORT
Sumitomo Metal Industries Ltd

Independent Auditors' Report

To the Board of Directors of Sumitomo Metal Industries, Ltd.:

We have audited the accompanying consolidated balance sheets of Sumitomo Metal Industries, Ltd. ("Sumitomo Metals") and consolidated subsidiaries as of March 31, 2009 and 2008, and the related consolidated statements of income, changes in equity, and cash flows for the years then ended, all expressed in Japanese yen. These consolidated financial statements are the responsibility of Sumitomo Metals' management. Our responsibility is to express an opinion on these consolidated financial statements based on our audits.

We conducted our audits in accordance with auditing standards generally accepted in Japan. Those standards require that we plan and perform the audit to obtain reasonable assurance about whether the financial statements are free of material misstatement. An audit includes examining, on a test basis, evidence supporting the amounts and disclosures in the financial statements. An audit also includes assessing the accounting principles used and significant estimates made by management, as well as evaluating the overall financial statement presentation. We believe that our audits provide a reasonable basis for our opinion.

In our opinion, the consolidated financial statements referred to above present fairly, in all material respects, the consolidated financial position of Sumitomo Metals and consolidated subsidiaries as of

March 31, 2009 and 2008, and the consolidated results of their operations and their cash flows for the years then ended in conformity with accounting principles generally accepted in Japan.

Our audits also comprehended the translation of Japanese yen amounts into U.S. dollar amounts and, in our opinion, such translation has been made in conformity with the basis stated in Note 1. Such U.S. dollar amounts are presented solely for the convenience of readers outside Japan.

Deloitte Touche Tohaten
June 19, 2009

INDEPENDENT AUDITORS' REPORT
Toshiba Corporation
Report of Independent Auditors

The Board of Directors and Shareholders of Toshiba Corporation

We have audited the accompanying consolidated balance sheets of Toshiba Corporation and subsidiaries (the "Company") as of March 31, 2009 and 2008, and the related consolidated statements of income, shareholders' equity, and cash flows for the years then ended, all expressed in Japanese yen. These consolidated financial statements are the responsibility of the Company's management. Our responsibility is to express an opinion on these financial statements based on our audits.

We conducted our audits in accordance with auditing standards generally accepted in the United States. Those standards require that we plan and perform the audit to obtain reasonable assurance about whether the financial statements are free of material misstatement. An audit includes examining, on a test basis, evidence supporting the amounts and disclosures in the financial statements. An audit also includes assessing the accounting principles used and significant estimates made by management, as well as evaluating the overall financial statement presentation. We believe that our audits provide a reasonable basis for our opinion.

The Company's consolidated financial statements do not disclose segment information required by Statement of Financial Accounting Standards No. 131, "Disclosures about Segments of an Enterprise and Related Information." In our opinion, disclosure of segment information is required by U.S. generally accepted accounting principles.

In our opinion, except for the omission of segment information discussed in the preceding paragraph, the financial statements referred to above present fairly, in all material respects, the consolidated financial position of Toshiba Corporation and subsidiaries at March 31, 2009 and 2008, and the consolidated results of their operations and their cash flows for the years then ended in conformity with U.S. generally accepted accounting principles.

We also have reviewed the translation of the consolidated financial statements mentioned above into United States dollars on the basis described in Note 3. In our opinion, such statements have been translated on such basis.

June 24, 2009
Ernst & Young Shinnikon LLC

INDEPENDENT AUDITORS' REPORT
Unilever PLC

Auditor's report United Kingdom

Independent auditors' report to the members of Unilever PLC on the consolidated financial stetements

We have audited the consolidated financial statements of the Unilever Group for the year ended 31 December 2009 which comprise the consolidated income statement, consolidated balance sheet, consolidated cash flow statement, consolidated statement of comprehensive income, consolidated statement of changes in equity, the related notes on pages 79 to 128, and principal group companies and non-current investments on pages 131 and 132. These consolidated financial statements have been prepared under the accounting policies set out in note 1 on pages 83 to 86. The financial reporting framework that has been applied in their preparation is applicable law and international Financial Reporting Standards (IFRSs) as adopted by the European Union.

Respective responsibilities of Directors and auditors

As explained more fully in the Statement of Directors' responsibilities set out on page 76, the directors are responsible for the preparation of the group financial statements and for being satisfied that they give a true and fair view. Our responsibility is to audit the consolidated financial statements in accordance with applicable law and International Standards on Auditing (UK and Ireland). Those standards require us to comply with the Auditing Practices Board's Ethical Standards for Auditors.

This report, including the opinions, has been prepared for and only for the shareholders of Unilever PLC as a body in accordance with Chapter 3 of Part 16 of the Companies Act 2006 and for no other purpose. We do not, in giving these opinions, accept or assume responsibility for any other purpose or to any other person to whom this report is shown or into whose hands it may come save where expressly agreed by our prior consent in writing.

Scope of the audit of financial statements

An audit involves obtaining evidence about the amounts and disclosures in the financial statements sufficient to give reasonable assurance that the financial statements are free from material misstatement, whether caused by fraud or error. This includes an assessment of: whether the accounting policies are appropriate to the Group's circumstances and have been consistently applied and adequately disclosed; the reasonableness of significant accounting estimates made by the directors; and the overall presentation of the financial statements.

Opinion on financial statements

In our opinion the Group financial statements:

- give a true and fair view of the state of the Group's affairs as at 31 December 2009 and of its profit and cash flows for the year then ended;
- have been properly prepared in accordance with IFRSs as adopted by the European Union; and
- have been prepared in accordance with the requirements of the Companies Act 2006 and Article 4 of the IAS Regulation

Separate opinion in relation to IFRS as issued by the IASB

As explained in note 1 to the consolidated financial statements, the Group in addition to complying with its legal obligation to apply IFRSs as adopted by the European Union, has also applied IFRSs as issued by the International Accounting Standards Board, (IASB).

In our opinion the Group financial statements comply with IFRSs as issued by the IASB.

Opinion on other matter prescribed by the Companies Act 2006

In our opinion the information given in the Report of the Directors for the financial year for which the Group financial statements are prepared is consistent with the Group financial statements.

Matters on which we are required to report by exception

We have nothing to report in respect of the following:

Under the Companies Act 2006 we are required to report to you if, in our opinion:

- certain disclosures of directors' remuneration specified by law are not made; or
- we have not received all the information and explanations we require for our audit.

Under the Listing Rules we are required to review:

- the Directors' statement, set out on page 76, in relation to going concern; and
- the part of the Corporate Governance statement relating to the company's compliance with the nine provisions of the 2008 Combined Code specified for our review.

Other matter

We have reported separately on the parent company accounts of Unilever PLC for the year ended 31 December 2009 and on the information in the Directors' Remuneration Report that is described as having been audited.

Richard Sexton

(Senior Statutory Auditor)

For and on behalf of PricewaterhouseCoopers LLP

Chartered Accountants and Statutory Auditors

London, United Kingdom

2 March 2010

INDEPENDENT AUDITORS' REPORT
Unilever N.V.

Auditor's report Netherlands
Independent auditor's report to the shareholders of Unilever N.V.
Report on the consolidated financial statements

We have audited the consolidated financial statements which are part of the Annual Report 2009 of the Unilever Group for the year ended 31 December 2009 which comprise the consolidated income statement, consolidated balance sheet, consolidated cash flow statement, consolidated statement of comprehensive income, consolidated statement of changes in equity and the related notes on pages 79 to 128 and 131 to 132.

We have reported separately on the company accounts of Unilever N.V. for the year ended 31 December 2009.

Director's responsibility

The Directors are responsible for the preparation and fair presentation of the consolidated financial statements in accordance with International Financial Reporting Standards as adopted by the European Union and as issued by the International Accounting Standards Board and with Part 9 of Book 2 of the Netherlands Civil Code, and for the preparation of the Report of the Directors in accordance with Part 9 of Book 2 of the Netherlands Civil Code. This responsibility includes: designing, implementing and maintaining internal control relevant to the preparation and fair presentation of the consolidated financial statements that are free from material misstatement, whether due to fraud or error; selecting and applying appropriate accounting policies; and making accounting estimates that are reasonable in the circumstances.

Auditor's responsibility

Our responsibility is to express an opinion on the consolidated financial statements based on our audit. We conducted our audit in accordance with Dutch law. This law requires that we comply with ethical requirements and plan and perform the audit to obtain reasonable assurance whether the consolidated financial statements are free from material misstatement.

An audit involves performing procedures to obtain audit evidence about the amounts and disclosures in the consolidated financial statements. The procedures selected depend on the auditor's judgement, including the assessment of the risks of material misstatement of the consolidated financial statements, whether due to fraud or error. In making those risk assessments, the auditor considers internal control relevant to the entity's preparation and fair presentation of the consolidated financial statements in order to design audit procedures that are appropriate in the circumstances, but not for the purpose of expressing an opinion on the effectiveness of the entity's internal control. An audit also includes evaluating the appropriateness of accounting policies used and the reasonableness of accounting estimates made by the Directors, as well as evaluating the overall presentation of the consolidated financial statements.

We believe that the audit evidence we have obtained is sufficient and appropriate to provide a basis for our audit opinion.

Opinion

In our opinion, the consolidated financial statements give a true and fair view of the financial position of the Unilever Group as at 31 December 2009, and of its result and its cash flows for the year then ended in accordance with International Financial Reporting Standards as adopted by the European Union and as issued by the International Accounting Standards Board and with Part 9 of Book 2 of the Netherlands Civil Code.

Report on other legal and regulatory requirements

Pursuant to the legal requirement under 2:393 sub 5 part f of the Netherlands Civil Code, we report, to the extent of our competence, that the Report of the Directors is consistent with the consolidated financial statements as required by 2:391 sub 4 of the Netherlands Civil Code.

Rotterdam, The Netherlands, 2 March 2010

PricewaterhouseCoopers Accountants N.V.

R A J Swaak RA

INDEPENDENT AUDITORS' REPORT
Kubota Corporation

Report of Independent Registered Public Accounting Firm

To the Board of Directors and Shareholders of Kubota Corporation:

We have audited the accompanying consolidated balance sheets of Kubota Corporation and subsidiaries (the "Company") as of March 31, 2010 and 2009, and the related consolidated statements of income, comprehensive income (loss), changes in equity, and cash flows for each of the three years in the period ended March 31, 2010. These financial statements are the responsibility of the Company's management. Our responsibility is to express an opinion on these financial statements based on our audits.

We conducted our audits in accordance with the standards of the Public Company Accounting Oversight Board (United States). Those standards require that we plan and perform the audit to obtain reasonable assurance about whether the financial statements are free of material misstatement. An audit includes examining, on a test basis, evidence supporting the amounts and disclosures in the financial statements. An audit also includes assessing the accounting principles used and significant estimates made by management, as well as evaluating the overall financial statement presentation. We believe that our audits provide a reasonable basis for our opinion.

In our report dated June 19, 2009, we expressed a qualified opinion, because certain information required by Accounting Standards Codification ("ASC") 280, "Segment Reporting" was not presented in the consolidated financial statements for the years ended March 31, 2009 and 2008. As discussed in Note 1 to the consolidated financial statements, the Company has now presented the segment information required by ASC 280 for the years ended March 31, 2009 and 2008. Accordingly, our present opinion on the consolidated financial statements for the years ended March 31, 2009 and 2008, as expressed herein, is different from that expressed in our prior report on the previously issued consolidated financial statements for the years ended March 31, 2009 and 2008.

In our opinion, such consolidated financial statements present fairly, in all material respects, the financial position of Kubota Corporation and subsidiaries as of March 31, 2010 and 2009, and the results of their operations and their cash flows for each of the three years in the period ended March 31, 2010, in conformity with accounting principles generally accepted in the United States of America.

As discussed in Note 1 to the consolidated financial statements, the Company adopted a new accounting standard for noncontrolling interests during the year ended March 31, 2010.

We have also audited, in accordance with the standards of the Public Company Accounting Oversight Board (United States), the Company's internal control over financial reporting as of March 31, 2010, based on the criteria established in Internal Control-Integrated Framework issued by the Committee of Sponsoring Organizations of the Treadway Commission and our report dated June 18, 2010 expressed an unqualified opinion on the Company's internal control over financial reporting.

Deloitte Touche Tohmatsu LLC

June 18, 2010

INDEPENDENT AUDITORS' REPORT
Cadbury PLC

We have audited the Group and Parent Company financial statements (the "financial statements") of Cadbury plc for the year ended 31 December 2008 which comprise the Group Income Statement, the Group Statement of Recognised Income and Expense, the Group and Parent Company Balance Sheets, the Group and Parent Company Cash Flow Statement, Group Segmental reporting (a) to (d) and the related notes 1 to 40.

These financial statements have been prepared under the accounting policies set out therein. We have also audited the information in the Directors' Remuneration Report that is described as having been audited.

This report is made solely to the Company's members, as a body, in accordance with section 235 of the Companies Act 1985. Our audit work has been undertaken so that we might state to the Company's members those matters we are required to state to them in an auditors' report and for no other purpose. To the fullest extent permitted by law, we do not accept or assume responsibility to anyone other than the Company and the Company's members as a body, for our audit work, for this report, or for the opinions we have formed.

Respective responsibilities of directors and auditors

The Directors' responsibilities for preparing the Annual Report, the Directors' Remuneration Report and the financial statements in accordance with applicable law and international Financial Reporting Standards (IFRSs) as adopted by the European Union are set out in the Statement of Directors' Responsibilities.

Our responsibility is to audit the financial statements and the part of the Directors' Remuneration Report to be audited in accordance with relevant legal and regulatory requirements and International Standards on Auditing (UK and Ireland).

We report to you our opinion as to whether the financial statements give a true and fair view and whether the financial statements and the part of the Directors' Remuneration Report to be audited have been properly prepared in accordance with the Companies Act 1985 and, as regards the Group financial statements. Article 4 of the IAS Regulation. We also report to you whether in our opinion the information given in the Directors' Report is consistent with the financial statements. The information given in the Directors' Report includes that specific information presented elsewhere in the document that is cross referred from the Business Review section of the Directors' Report.

In addition we report to you if; in our opinion, the Company has not kept proper accounting records, if we have not received all the information and explanations we require for our audit, or if

information specified by law regarding Directors' remuneration and other transactions is not disclosed.

We review whether the Corporate Governance Statement reflects the Company's compliance with the nine provisions of the 2006 Combined Code specified for our review by the Listing Rules of the Financial Services Authority, and we report if it does not. We are not required to consider whether the board's statements on internal control cover all risks and controls, or form an opinion on the effectiveness of the Group's corporate governance procedures or its risk and control procedures.

We read the other information contained in the Annual Report as described in the contents section and consider whether it is consistent with the audited financial statements. We consider the implications for our report if we become aware of any apparent misstatements or material inconsistencies with the financial statements. Our responsibilities do not extend to any further information outside the Annual Report.

Basis of audit opinion

We conducted our audit in accordance with International Standards on Auditing (UK and Ireland) issued by the Auditing Practices Board. An audit includes examination, on a test basis of evidence relevant to the amounts and disclosures in the financial statements and the part of the Directors' Remuneration Report to be audited. It also includes an assessment of the significant estimates and judgements made by the Directors in the preparation of the financial statements, and of whether the accounting policies are appropriate to the Group's and Company's circumstances, consistently applied and adequately disclosed.

We planned and performed our audit so as to obtain all the information and explanations which we considered necessary in order to provide us with sufficient evidence to give reasonable assurance that the financial statements and the part of the Directors' Remuneration Report to be audited are free from material misstatement, whether caused by fraud or other irregularity or error. In forming our opinion we also evaluated the overall adequacy of the presentation of information in the financial statements and the part of the Directors' Remuneration Report to be audited.

Opinion

In our opinion:

- the Group financial statements give a true and fair view, in accordance with IFRSs as adopted by the European Union, of the state of the Group's affairs as at 31 December 2008 and of its profit for the year then ended;

- the parent company financial statements give a true and fair view, in accordance with IFRSs as adopted by the European Union as applied in accordance with the provisions of the Companies Act 1985, of the state of the parent company's affairs as at 31 December 2008;
- the financial statements and the part of the Directors' Remuneration Report to be audited have been properly prepared in accordance with the Companies Act 1985 and, as regards the Group financial statements. Article 4 of the IAS Regulation; and
- the information given in the Directors' Report is consistent with the financial statements.

Separate opinion in relation to IFRSs

As explained in Note 1(b) to the financial statements, the Group in addition to complying with its legal obligation to comply with IFRSs as adopted by the European Union, has also complied with the IFRSs as issued by the International Accounting Standards Board.

In our opinion the Group financial statements give a true and fair view, in accordance with IFRSs, of the state of the Group's affairs as at 31 December 2008 and of its profit for the year then ended.

Deloitte LLP

Chartered Accountants and Registered Auditors
London, United Kingdom
24 February 2009

Questions

1. Why should MNCs be concerned about auditing issues?
2. What are the main differences between the OECD Principles of Corporate Governance issued in 1999 and the revised version issued in 2004?
3. What are the provisions in the Sarbanes-Oxley Act 2002 and the New York Stock Exchange listing requirements that are aimed at improving corporate governance and are directly related to audit committees?
4. What determines the primary role of external auditing in a particular country?
5. What is audit quality? What determines audit quality in a given country?
6. What is the PCAOB? What is its role in audit regulation?
7. What is the PIOB? What is its role in audit regulation?
8. What was the impact of the European Union's Eighth Directive on the regulation of auditing in the United Kingdom?
9. In what ways do company audit reports vary in different countries?
10. What are the main benefits of international harmonization of auditing standards?
11. What determines whether or not to issue an unqualified audit opinion on the compliance of a set of financial statements with IFRS?
12. What are some of the strategies adopted internationally to limit the auditor's liability?
13. What are the main factors that complicate the issue of auditor independence?
14. What is the oversight role of an audit committee?
15. What are the main differences between internal auditing and external auditing within an MNC?

Exercises and Problems

1. Refer to the Report of Independent Auditors of Unilever NV and Unilever PLC, signed on 1 March 2005 (see the appendix to this chapter).

   Required:
   Identify the features in the above audit report that are unique to an MNC.

2. ISA 700 describes three types of audit opinions that can be expressed by the auditor when an unqualified opinion is not appropriate: qualified, adverse, and disclaimer of opinion.

Required:
What are the circumstances under which each of the above three
be expressed? ISA700 is accessible from the IFAC Web site (ww

3. In June 2003, IFAC issued an IAPS providing additional guid
internationally when they express an opinion on financial statements
asserted by management to be prepared in either of the following ways:

- Solely in accordance with IFRS.
- In accordance with IFRS and a national financial reporting framework.
- In accordance with a national financial reporting framework with disclosure of the extent of compliance with IFRS.

Required:
Identify the additional guidelines under each of the three categories of audit opinion.

4. In June 2004, the IFAC Ethics Committee issued its "Revision to Paragraph 8.151 Code of Ethics for Professional Accountants." Accordingly, for the audit of listed entities,

a. The lead engagement partner should be rotated after a predefined period, normally no more than seven years.

b. A partner rotating after a predefined period should not participate in the audit engagement until a further period of time, normally two years, has elapsed.

Required:
How does the revised version differ from the previous version of the paragraph mentioned in Exercise 3?

5. Internationally, legislators and professional bodies have focused on corporate governance issues in making recommendations for restoring investor confidence, and auditing is an essential part of corporate governance.

Required:
Explain the link between auditing and corporate governance.

6. Some commentators argue that the two-tiered corporate structure, with a management board and a supervisory board, prevalent in many Continental European countries, is better suited for addressing corporate governance issues, including the issue of auditor independence, compared to that with one board of directors prevalent in Anglo-Saxon countries.

Required:
Evaluate the merits of the above argument.

7. This chapter refers to a unique ownership structure of many former state-owned enterprises in China, which have been redefined to create new economic entities.

Required:
Describe the uniqueness of the ownership structure of the entities mentioned above, and explain its implications for auditing.

8. This chapter refers to the concept of accounting infrastructure, which encompasses the various environmental factors affecting the issues concerning auditing in a particular country.

Required:

Explain the environmental factors that affect the issues concerning auditing in your own country.

9. The establishment of the Public Company Accounting Oversight Board (PCAOB) in 2002 was a major step toward strengthening the auditing function in the United States.

Required:

What can the PCAOB do to strengthen the auditing function in the United States? Provide examples of two key steps it has taken so far to achieve this.

10. In Anglo-Saxon countries, mechanisms are put in place to regulate auditors within the framework of professional self-regulation, whereas in many Continental European countries, quasi-governmental agencies play a major role in this area.

Required:

a. Briefly describe the main differences between the audit regulation mechanisms in the United States and Germany.

b. Compare the audit regulation mechanisms in the United States and the United Kingdom.

11. The responsibility for harmonizing auditing standards across countries rests with IFAC.

Required:

Comment on some of the problems faced by IFAC in achieving the above goal.

12. There is no agreement internationally on how to address the issue of auditor liability.

Required:

Describe the approach taken in your own country in addressing the issue of auditor liability, and explain the rationale behind that approach.

13. The UK Corporate Governance Code takes the "comply or explain" approach.

Required:

a. Describe the main features of the comply or explain approach to corporate governance.

b. Why do think this approach seems to be popular internationally?

Case 14-1

Honda Motor Company

Following is the corporate governance report of Honda Motor Company included in its 2009 Annual Report

1. Basic Stance Regarding Corporate Governance

Based on its fundamental corporate philosophy, the Company is working to enhance corporate governance as one of its most important management issues. Our aim is to have our customers and society, as well as our shareholders and investors, place even greater trust in us and to ensure that Honda is "a company that society wants to exist."

To ensure objective control of the Company's management, outside directors and outside corporate auditors are appointed to the Board of Directors and the Board of Corporate Auditors, which are responsible for the supervision and auditing of the Company. Honda has also introduced an operating officer system, aimed at strengthening both the execution of business operations at the regional and local levels and making management decisions quickly and appropriately. The term of office of each director is limited to one year, and the amount of remuneration payable to them is determined according to a standard that reflects their performance in the Company. Our goal in doing this is to maximize the flexibility with which our directors respond to changes in the operating environment.

With respect to business execution, Honda has established a system for operating its organizational units that reflects its fundamental corporate philosophy. For example, separate headquarters have been set up for each region, business, and function, and a member of the Board of Directors or an operating officer has been assigned to each headquarters and main division. In addition, by having the Executive Council and regional operating boards deliberate important matters concerning management, the Company implements a system that enables swift and appropriate decision making.

With respect to internal control, compliance systems and risk management systems have been designed and implemented appropriately following the basic policies for the design of internal controls decided by the Board of Directors.

To enhance even further the trust and understanding of shareholders and investors, Honda's basic policy emphasizes the appropriate disclosure of Company information, such as by disclosing financial results on a quarterly basis and timely and accurately giving public notice of and disclosing its management strategies. Honda will continue raising its level of transparency in the future.

2. Company Management Organization

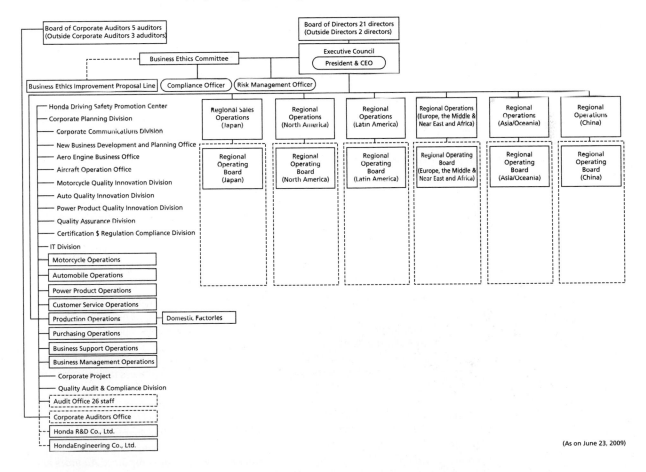

(As on June 23, 2009)

3. Internal Control System: Fundamental Position and Implementation Status

The Company is designing and implementing internal control systems in accordance with the following basic policies.

- *Systems for Ensuring that the Execution of Duties by the Directors and Employees is in Compliance with the Law and the Company's Articles of Incorporation*

  To secure compliance of Company management and employees with guidelines for conduct in conformity with applicable laws and internal rules and regulations, the Company has prepared The Honda Conduct Guidelines and implements measures to ensure that all management and employees are made aware of and follow these guidelines.

  The Company has appointed a Compliance Officer, who is a director in charge of compliance-related initiatives. Other key elements of our compliance system include the Business Ethics Committee and the Business Ethics Improvement Proposal Line.

- *Retention and Management of Information on Execution of Business by Directors*

  Minutes of the meetings of the Board of Directors and other important meetings as well as information related to the execution of business by the directors will be retained and stored appropriately following the policy for the retention and management of documents.

- *Regulations and Other Systems for Management of the Contingencies of Losses*

  Important items related to management are proposed to the Board of Directors, the Executive Council, and/or Regional Operating boards, risks are assessed, and then, decisions are made, after due consideration according to established deliberation standards.

  Regarding risks that are to be dealt with on a departmental basis, each department will work to prevent the emergence of such risk and develop policies for dealing with them. For large-scale disasters requiring Company-level crisis management, the Honda Crisis Response Rules will be applied, and the member of the Board of Directors in charge will be appointed as the Risk Management Officer, who will be responsible for designing and implementing related systems.

- *Systems for Ensuring that the Execution of Business by the Directors is Being Conducted Efficiently*

  In line with its fundamental corporate philosophy, Honda has established organizational operating systems for each region, business, and function and a member of the Board of Directors or an operating officer has been assigned to each headquarters and main division. In addition, by having the Executive Council and Regional Operating boards deliberate important matters concerning management, the Company implements a system that enables swift and appropriate decision making.

  To conduct management efficiently and effectively, business plans are prepared on an annual basis and for the medium term, and measures are taken to share these plans.

- *Systems for Ensuring that the Corporate Group, Comprising the Company and its Subsidiaries, Conducts Business Activities Appropriately*

  The Company and its subsidiaries share The Honda Conduct Guidelines and the basic policy regarding corporate governance. In addition, each subsidiary works to promote activities that are in compliance with the laws of countries where they operate and practices observed in their respective industries as they endeavor to enhance corporate governance.

  Regarding the conduct of business by subsidiaries, rules relating to monetary settlements have been established, and, regarding important management items, internal rules have been prepared that require prior approval of the Company or the submission of reports. In addition, the business management department of the Company receive reports on business plans and other matters on a periodic basis from subsidiaries and confirm the appropriateness of the conduct of activities.

  The Company's Audit Office, which is an independent unit reporting directly to the President, audits the status of conduct of business activities in each department, and works to improve the Honda Group's internal auditing systems.

  For companies accounted for under the equity method, the Company requests their understanding and cooperation with Honda's basic corporate governance policies and endeavors to improve corporate governance on a Groupwide basis.

- *Matters Relating to Assignment of Personnel to Assist the Corporate Auditors when They Request Such Assistance and Maintenance of the independence of Such Personnel from the Directors*

  The Corporate Auditors Office, which has been formed to provide staff functions for the Corporate Auditors and reports directly to them, provides such support for the Corporate Auditors.

- *Systems Providing for Reporting by Directors and Employees to the Corporate Auditors and Other Arrangements for Reporting to the Corporate Auditors*

The status of business activities of the Company's subsidiaries and other associated companies and the status of the design and operation of internal control systems, including compliance and risk management systems, are reported periodically to the Corporate Auditors. In addition, when there are matters that have a major impact on the Company, these are reported to the Corporate Auditors.

- **System for Ensuring that Other Auditing Activities of the Corporate Auditors Are Conducted Effectively**

  The Corporate Auditors and the Audit Office, which audits the conduct of business, work closely together to implement business audits in the Company, its subsidiaries, and other associated companies. In addition, the Corporate Auditors also attend the meetings of the Executive Council and other important meetings.

- **Basic Policy Regarding Exclusion of Antisocial Elements**

  Honda's basic policy is to boldly and consistently oppose antisocial elements that present a threat to social order and safety. The organizational unit in charge of responding to these elements has been specified, and it works together with the police and other related outside institutions to mount an appropriate response.

4. **Cooperation among the Internal Auditing Functions, Auditing Functions of the Corporate Auditors, and the Audits Performed by the Accounting Auditors**

- **Internal Auditing Functions**

  The Audit Office, which audits the conduct of business activities and reports directly to the President, has a staff of 26, who conduct audits of business execution in each department and endeavor to improve the Honda Group's internal auditing systems.

- **Accounting Audits**

  KPMG AZSA & Co. provided auditing services for Honda under the Company Law, Japan's Financial Instruments and Exchange Law, and the U.S. Securities Exchange Act.

  A total of 45 people from KPMG AZSA & Co. provided auditing services for Honda: three Japanese certified public accountants (Masanori Sato, Kensuke Sodegawa, and Hideaki Koyama) and 42 assistants (10 certified public accountants, 15 assistant accountants, five U.S. certified public accountants, and 12 others).

- **Cooperation among Internal Functions**

  During the fiscal year under review, the Corporate Auditors and the Accounting Auditors held meetings on six occasions. The Accounting Auditors explained and reported on the plans and results of their audits to the Corporate Auditors, and the two exchanged views.

  The Corporate Auditors and the Audit Office, which audits the conduct of business activities, maintained close contact and made adjustments regarding auditing policy and the schedule for audits. In addition, the Corporate Auditors and the Audit Office, either separately or working together, implemented audits of business activities.

5. **Personal, Capital, or Transaction Relationships or Other Matters that Might Represent a Conflict with the Reporting Company**

- **Outside Directors**

  The Company has appointed outside director Nobuo Kuroyanagi to receive advice on its corporate activities from an objective, broad-ranging and advanced viewpoint based on his extensive experience and a high level of insight in corporate management.

  The Company has appointed outside director Kensaku Hogen to receive advice on its international diplomacy from an objective, broad-ranging, and advanced viewpoint based on his extensive experience and a high level of insight in diplomacy.

  The Company has appointed Nobuo Kuroyanagi (President and Director of Mitsubishi UFJ Financial Group, Inc., and, concurrently, Chairman and Director of The Bank of Tokyo-Mitsubishi UFJ, Ltd.) as an outside director, but there are no special interest relationships between the Company and Mr. Kuroyanagi.

  There are no special interest relationships between the Company and outside director Kensaku Hogen. Please note that outside director Hogen attended all 10 meetings of the Board of Directors held during the fiscal year under review, and he made necessary and appropriate statements during the deliberation of proposals.

  The Company provides information on the Board of Directors meetings and other matters to outside directors as necessary.

- **Outside Corporate Auditors**

  The Company has appointed outside corporate auditor Koukei Higuchi to receive audit information on its corporate activities from a broad-ranging and advanced viewpoint based on his extensive experience and a high level of insight in corporate management.

The Company has appointed outside corporate auditor Fumihiko Saito to receive audit information on its corporate activities from a broad-ranging and advanced viewpoint based on his extensive experience and a high level of insight in legal affairs.

The Company has appointed outside corporate auditor Yuji Matsuda to receive audit information on its corporate activities from a broad-ranging and advanced viewpoint based on his extensive experience and a high level of insight in corporate management.

There are no special interest relationships between outside auditor Koukei Higuchi and the Company.

Outside auditor Fumihiko Saito is the representative of the Saito Law Office, but there are no special interest relationships between him and the Company.

Outside auditor Yuji Matsuda is the president and a director of the Mitsubishi UFJ Trust Investment Technology Institute Co., Ltd., but there are no special interest relationships between outside auditor Matsuda and the Company.

Outside auditor Koukei Higuchi attended 8 of the 10 meetings of the Board of Directors and 12 of the 13 meetings of the Board of Auditors held during the fiscal year under review, and he made necessary and appropriate statements during the deliberation of proposals.

Outside auditor Fumihiko Saito attended 9 of the 10 meetings of the Board of Directors and all 13 meetings of the Board of Auditors held during the fiscal year under review, and he made necessary and appropriate statements during the deliberation of proposals.

Outside auditor Yuji Matsuda attended all 10 meetings of the Board of Directors and all 13 meetings of the Board of Auditors held during the fiscal year under review, and he made necessary and appropriate statements during the deliberation of proposals.

The Company provides information on the Board of Directors meetings and other information to the outside auditors as necessary.

6. Provisions of the Articles of Incorporation

- **Items Approved by the General Meeting of Shareholders that Can Then Be Decided by the Board of Directors**

  The Articles of Incorporation provide that the Board of Directors may make decisions regarding the payment of dividends from surplus and other sources. (The Company has a policy that the final dividend for the fiscal year is determined by a decision of the Regular General Meeting of Shareholders.) This provision enables management to implement capital policy and dividend policy with greater flexibility.

- **Requirements for Special Decisions by the General Meeting of Shareholders**

  The Articles of Incorporation provide that special decisions can be made at the General Meeting of Shareholders if a quorum of shareholders are present who can exercise voting rights of one-third or more and two-thirds or more of those present vote in favor of the decision.

  This provision was included to make certain that a majority of voting shares are represented for making special decisions at the General Meeting of Shareholders.

- **Requirements for Deciding on the Election of Directors**

  The Articles of Incorporation provide that decisions on the election of candidates for director can be made if a quorum of shareholders are present who can exercise voting rights of one-third or more and a majority vote in favor of the election. Cumulative voting is not allowed in making decisions on the election of directors.

- **Number of Directors**

  The Articles of Incorporation provide for up to 30 directors.

7. Status of Measures Related to Shareholders and Others with Vested Interests

- **Measures to Invigorate Ordinary General Meetings of Shareholders and Ensure the Smooth Exercise of Voting Rights**

  To invigorate the annual Ordinary General Meeting of Shareholders, the Company holds the meeting as early as possible. The Company also presents easy-to-understand reports using videos and slides, and displays its products in the conference room.

  The Company sends convocation notices before the date required by law, and also allows shareholders to exercise their voting rights via the Internet, using personal computers or mobile phones. Convocation notices are sent in English to overseas investors.

  In these and other ways, the Company strives to make the exercise of rights as smooth as possible.

- **IR Activities**

  For analysts and institutional investors, the Company holds meetings to present its results four times a year and meetings with the president twice a year. Company representatives visit and hold information meetings as needed for major Japanese and overseas institutional investors to explain the

Honda Group's future business strategies. Representatives based in North America and Europe also hold information meetings for institutional investors as appropriate. In addition, the Company holds information meetings for investors at motor shows and other major events, where presentations on such topics as Honda Group strategies are made by the president or relevant director. Moreover, the Company conducts regular tours of facilities in Japan and overseas for shareholders and other investors.

The latest information for investors is available on the Company's Web site (http://www.honda.co.jp/investors/ in Japanese; http://world.honda.com/investors/ in English). All new information is uploaded to the site simultaneously in Japanese and English.

The Company issues a regular publication for shareholders, containing information about its businesses, products, financial status, and other matters.

- **Respecting the Perspective of Stakeholders**

Seeking to earn the unwavering trust of customers and society, the Honda Group has formulated a set of behavioral guidelines, which is observed by all individual associates (employees).

In addition to supplying products incorporating the most advanced safety and environmental technologies, the Company pursues environmental protection activities, sale driving campaigns, and social contribution activities covering all aspects of its operations, including production, logistics, and sales. These initiatives reflect the Company's effort to earn the trust and understanding of society via its corporate activities.

The Company provides information about its corporate activities via financial reports and other disclosures according to law. We also publish yearly reports on environmental protection activities, sale driving campaigns, and social contribution activities, which are posted on our Web site. In addition, we publish a corporate social responsibility (CSR) report that comprehensively explains our activities related to the environment, safety, and society.

- **Disclosure of Corporate Information**

To deliberate the accuracy and appropriateness of corporate information that is disclosed through announcements of the closing of accounts and other financial reports, the Company has formed the Disclosure Committee, which is composed of directors responsible for disclosure and other members.

8. Directors' Remuneration

The total amount of remuneration and bonuses of directors and corporate auditors is determined according to criteria that reflect their performance in the Company.

Remuneration for directors and corporate auditors is paid based on criteria approved by the Board of Directors, and it is paid within the extent of the maximum amount resolved by the Ordinary General Meeting of Shareholders.

Bonuses for directors and corporate auditors are paid based on a decision of the Ordinary General Meeting of Shareholders, taking into consideration the Company's profits during the fiscal year, past bonuses paid, and various other factors.

(Millions of yen)

Type of Remuneration	Directors		Corporate Auditors		Total	
	Number	Amount	Number	Amount	Number	Amount
Director/corporate auditor remuneration	21	724	7	123	28	848
Director/corporate auditor bonuses	21	265	5	27	26	293
Total	—	990	—	151	—	1,141

Notes:

1. The upper on directors' and corporate auditors' compensation is ¥90 million per month for services as director and, for corporate auditors, ¥18 million per month for services as auditor.

2. The figures in the table above are for services as director or corporate auditor for the fiscal year under review. The amount shown for director/corporate auditor remuneration is the amount paid during the year under review. The amount shown for director/corporate auditor bonuses is the provision to the reserve for directors'/corporate auditors' bonuses for the year under review.

3. In addition to the figures in the table above, the Company bore costs of ¥103 million related to retirement payments to 20 directors and ¥17 million related to retirement payments to 8 corporate auditors. Please note that the Company eliminated its system for retirement payments to directors and corporate auditors as of the closing of the Annual General Meeting of Shareholders [the 84th general meeting) held on June 24, 2008, and the decision was made to pay the amount of such retirement payments accrued through that shareholders' meeting as a sale and final retirement allowance payment.

Please note that the total compensation and other costs paid to the two outside directors and the three outside auditors applicable to the fiscal year under review was ¥67 million.

Companies listed on the New York Stock Exchange (NYSE) must comply with certain standards regarding corporate governance under Section 303A of the NYSE Listed Company Manual.

However, listed companies that are foreign private issuers, such as Honda, are permitted to follow home-country practice in lieu of certain provisions of Section 303A.

The following table shows the significant differences between the corporate governance practices followed by U.S. listed companies under Section 303A of the NYSE Listed Company Manual and those followed by Honda.

Corporate Governance Practices Followed by NYSE-Listed U.S. Companies	Corporate Governance Practices Followed by Honda
An NYSE-listed U.S. company must have a majority of directors meeting the independence requirements under Section 303A of the NYSE Listed Company Manual.	For Japanese companies that employ a corporate governance system based on a board of corporate auditors [the "corporate auditor system"], including Honda, Japan's Company Law has no independence requirement with respect to directors. The task of overseeing management and, together with the accounting audit firm, accounting is assigned to the corporate auditors, who are separate from the company's management and meet certain independence requirements under Japan's Company Law. In the case of Japanese companies that employ the board of corporate auditors system, including Honda, at least half of the corporate auditors must be "outside" corporate auditors who must meet additional independence requirements under Japan's Company Law. An outside corporate auditor is defined as a corporate auditor who has not served as a director, accounting councilor, executive officer, manager, or any other employee of the company or any of its subsidiaries. Currently, Honda has three outside corporate auditors which constitute 60 percent of Honda's five corporate auditors.
An NYSE-listed U.S. company must have an audit committee composed entirely of independent directors, and the audit committee must have at least three members.	Like a majority of Japanese listed companies, Honda employs the board of corporate auditors system as described above. Under this system, the board of corporate auditors is a legally separate and independent body from the board of directors. The main function of the board of corporate auditors is similar to that of independent directors, including those who are members of the audit committee, of a U.S. company: to monitor the performance of the directors, and review and express an opinion on the method of auditing by the company's accounting audit firm and on such accounting audit firm's audit reports, for the protection of the company's shareholders. Japanese companies that employ the board of corporate auditors system, including Honda, are required to have at least three corporate auditors. Currently, Honda has five corporate auditors. Each corporate auditor has a four-year term. In contrast, the term of each director of Honda is one year.

	With respect to the requirements of Rule ICA-3 under the U.S. Securities Exchange Act of 1934 relating to listed company audit committees, Honda relies on an exemption under that rule which is available to foreign private issuers with boards of corporate auditors meeting certain criteria.
An NYSE-listed U.S. company must have a nominating/corporate governance committee composed entirely of independent directors.	Honda's directors are elected at a meeting of shareholders. Its Board of Directors does not have the power to vacancies thereon. Honda's corporate auditors are also elected at a meeting of shareholders. A proposal by Honda's Board of Directors to elect a corporate auditor must be approved by a resolution of its Board of Corporate Auditors. The Board of Corporate Auditors is empowered to request that Honda's directors submit a proposal for election of a corporate auditor to a meeting of shareholders. The corporate auditors have the right to state their opinion concerning election of a corporate auditor at the meeting of shareholders.
An NYSE-listed U.S. company must have a compensation committee composed entirely of independent directors.	Maximum total amounts of compensation for Honda directors and corporate auditors are proposed to, and voted on, by a meeting of shareholders. Once the proposals for such maximum total amounts of compensation are approved at the meeting of shareholders, each of the Board of Directors and Board of Corporate Auditors determines the compensation amount for each member within the respective maximum total amounts.
An NYSE-listed U.S. company must generally obtain shareholder approval with respect to any equity compensation plan.	Currently, Honda does not adopt stock option compensation plans. When it does, Honda must obtain shareholder approval for stock options only if the stock options are issued with specifically favorable conditions or price concerning the issuance and exercise of the stock options.

Case 14-2

Daimler AG

Following is the report of the Supervisory Board included in Daimler company's 2009 Annual Report

REPORT OF THE SUPERVISORY BOARD

Dear Shareholders,

In eight meetings during the 2009 financial year, the Supervisory Board diligently fulfilled its duties and responsibilities and dealt comprehensively with the operational and strategic development of the Group. The members of the Supervisory Board representing the shareholders and the members representing the employees regularly prepared the meetings in separate preliminary discussions.

The meetings held in 2009 focused not only on numerous special topics and issues requiring the consent of the Supervisory Board, but also on the effects of the financial and economic crisis and the resulting measures to be taken by the Group. In each of its meetings, the Supervisory Board discussed the business development of the company and its most important subsidiaries. It dealt in equal measure with short-term, medium-term and long-term issues. The challenges of a more short-term nature included the decline in demand in all major sales markets that began in the second half of 2008 and worsened in the first half of 2009. The Supervisory Board therefore placed one focus of its activities on the results of the efficiency-enhancing actions that had been initiated, as well as on the cost-reducing programs and their effects on the employment situation.

The success of the measures taken by the Board of Management and followed up by the Supervisory Board was particularly apparent in the third and fourth quarters of 2009.

Other issues about which the Board of Management continually informed the Supervisory Board, in addition to the usual key figures, included:

- the Group's profitability and liquidity,
- the risk management system,
- the cost of credit risk,
- the development of raw-material prices,
- vehicles' residual values,
- the situation of suppliers,
- the development of pension obligations and pension management, and
- the effects of the insolvency of Chrysler and General Motors according to Chapter 11 of the US Bankruptcy Code.

Equal emphasis was placed on the long-term protection of competitiveness and on the measures already initiated to prepare the way for pioneering sustainable mobility. The Supervisory Board also dealt specifically with these topics in close collaboration with the Board of Management and in particular detail in a two-day strategy workshop of the Supervisory Board.

Cooperation between the Supervisory Board and the Board of Management. In all of the Supervisory Board meetings, there was an intensive and open exchange of opinions and information concerning the position of the Group, business and financial developments, fundamental issues of corporate policy and strategy, and development opportunities in particularly important growth markets. The members of the Supervisory Board prepared for decisions requiring Supervisory Board consent and decisions on investment projects on the basis of documentation provided by the Board of Management. They were also supported by the relevant committees, and discussed the projects upon which decisions were to be taken with the Board of Management. All members of the Board of Management regularly attended the meetings of the Supervisory Board. Furthermore, the Board of Management informed the Supervisory Board with the use of monthly reports about the most important performance figures and submitted the interim reports to the Supervisory Board. The Supervisory Board was kept fully informed of specific matters also between its meetings, and, as required in individual cases, following consultation with the Chairman of the Supervisory Board it was requested to pass its resolutions in writing. In addition, the Chairman of the Board of Management informed the Chairman of the Supervisory Board in regular discussions about all important developments and upcoming decisions.

Issues discussed at the meetings in 2009. In a meeting in January 2009, the Supervisory Board dealt with the possible conditions for the termination of the investigations being carried out since September 2004 by the US Securities and Exchange Commission and the US Department of Justice concerning possible violations of the US Foreign Corrupt Practices Act. In the meeting, it was emphasized that a potential termination by settlement would not have any impact on the standards or tasks of Daimler's recently established Compliance Organization. The challenge remains of securing the sustainability of these activities and of further developing them whenever required in the coming years. The Board of Management, the Audit Committee and the Supervisory Board will devote a great deal of attention to this issue also in the coming years.

At the end of February 2009, the Supervisory Board dealt with the audited 2008 financial statements of the company, the 2008 consolidated financial statements, and the management reports for Daimler AG and the Group. As preparation, the members of the Supervisory Board were provided with comprehensive documentation, some of it in draft form, including the Annual Report, the audit reports from KPMG on the year-end financial statements of Daimler AG and the consolidated financial statements according to IFRS, the management report of Daimler AG and the management report of the Daimler Group, as well as drafts of the reports of the Supervisory Board and of the Audit Committee and the annual report according to Form 20-F.

The Audit Committee and the Supervisory Board dealt in detail with these documents and discussed them in the presence of the auditors, who reported on the results of their audit. The Supervisory Board declared its agreement with the results of the audit, established in the framework of its own review that no objections were to be raised, and approved the financial statements presented by the Board of Management. The financial statements were thereby adopted. Subsequently, the Supervisory Board examined and agreed with the appropriation of earnings proposed by the Board of Management. Other items dealt with were the agenda for the Annual Meeting, including the proposal of five candidates to be elected as representatives of the shareholders, and the remuneration of the Board of Management for the year 2009. Finally, the Supervisory Board approved the external board positions and sideline business activities of the members of the Board of Management as presented in the meeting.

In an extraordinary meeting held in March, the Supervisory Board dealt with the capital increase with the preclusion of shareholders' subscription rights as proposed by the Board of Management by way of partial utilization of the Authorized/Approved Capital I that was approved by the Annual Meeting in 2008 through the issue of new shares to the investor Aabar (Abu Dhabi). The Supervisory Board was in favor of this capital increase, primarily because with a strengthened financial position, the Group would be better able to continue the substantial investment it had already started in research and development in order to approach the present opportunities and challenges in the automotive industry from a strengthened financial situation and leading position.

Two Supervisory Board meetings were held in April 2009. In the first of those two meeting, the Supervisory Board consented to the amicable termination of the Board of Management membership of Dr. Rüdiger Grube – at his own request – effective with the end of April 30, 2009, authorized the Chairman of the Supervisory Board to conclude a separation agreement, and granted its consent to the new distribution of responsibilities of the Board of Management reflecting Dr. Grube's departure.

In the second meeting held in April 2009, the Supervisory Board dealt not only with the course of business and results of the first quarter, but also with the final separation from Chrysler, i.e. with the transfer of the remaining 19.9 percent equity interest, which became possible on the basis of agreements with the US government agency Pension Benefit Guaranty Corporation (PBGC), Chrysler and Cerberus. In addition, the Board of Management explained to the Supervisory Board in this meeting the required adjustments to the operational planning and current developments in this context. This procedure was based on the decision made in the Supervisory Board meeting of December 2008 in light of the considerable uncertainty at that time regarding ongoing economic developments. In this meeting, the Supervisory Board also decided to make a solidarity contribution in relation to the measures taken to reduce labor costs and secure employment at Daimler AG, and waived 10 percent of the members' individual remuneration.

After discussing the business development and the results of the second quarter, the Supervisory Board dealt in its meeting in July with the status of the Group-wide compliance activities and the status of negotiations on the amicable termination of the investigations by the US Securities Exchange and Commission (SEC) and the US Department of Justice (DOJ). Also in this meeting, the Supervisory Board received a report by the Independent Compliance Advisor about the status of the Group's compliance activities. Fundamental questions on the financing status and management of the pension funds constituted another topic of this meeting. After that, the Supervisory Board received a report on various legal changes of particular relevance for its own activities. These changes were the corporate governance requirements of the German Accounting Law Modernization Act (BilMoG), which came into force in May 2009 and the key points of which had already been explained by the Board of Management in the meeting in December, and the German Act on the Appropriateness of Management Board Remuneration (VorstAG).

During the two-day strategy workshop in September, the Supervisory Board received detailed information on the status of the implementation of Daimler's strategic thrusts as presented by the Board of Management in previous years and of the individual divisions, taking into consideration the current economic environment. In this context, the Supervisory Board discussed the projects initiated by the divisions, the competitive positioning of the Group and its divisions, and the product strategy.

Other key points included:

- growth opportunities in developing markets,
- current strategic issues in the field of commercial vehicles and in other areas,
- the technological development of combustion engines,
- electric drive, hybrids and hydrogen drive,
- the overall technology and market strategy for safe guarding sustainable mobility and
- the latest trends in customer behavior.

In December, the Supervisory Board dealt in detail on the basis of comprehensive documentation with the operational planning for the years 2010/2011, received information on the Group's risk management and the actual risks, and decided on the financing limits for the year 2010. Other issues discussed in the December meeting included personnel matters of the Board of Management and corporate governance topics, as well as a resolution to amend the designated use of treasury shares.

Furthermore, on the basis of an independent expertise on the conformance of Board of Management remuneration with the provisions of the Act on the Appropriateness of Management Board Remuneration (VorstAG), the Supervisory Board dealt with and confirmed the preliminary decision on Board of Management remuneration in the year 2009 and the remuneration system for the year 2010, in each case based on a proposal made by the Presidential Committee.

Corporate governance. During 2009, the Supervisory Board was continually occupied with the further development of corporate governance, giving due consideration to changes in legislation and the German Corporate Governance Code as amended in June 2009.

In its meeting in February 2009, the Supervisory Board received information on the results of the efficiency review of the Audit Committee in the year 2008.

In the December meeting, pursuant to Section 161 of the German Stock Corporation Act (AktG], the Supervisory Board approved the 2009 declaration of compliance with the German Corporate Governance Code as amended on June 18, 2009, and updated the rules of procedure of the Supervisory Board and its committees in relation to the requirements of the German Accounting Law Modernization Act (BilMoG] and of the Act on the Appropriateness of Management Board Remuneration (VorstAG]; in practice, the corporate governance requirements of BilMoG and the requirements of VorstAG had been fulfilled since those two laws came into effect.

In each Supervisory Board meeting, there was a so-called executive session, in which the members of the Supervisory Board were able to discuss topics in the absence of the members of the Board of Management.

The members of the Supervisory Board of Daimler AG are obliged to disclose potential conflicts of interest to the entire Supervisory Board and not to participate in discussing or voting on topics which could lead to a conflict of interest, Dr. h.c. Bernhard Walter, Member of the Supervisory Board of Daimler AG, is also a member of the supervisory board of Henkel AG & Co. KGaA. In order to avoid a potential conflict of interest with Henkel in connection with a legal dispute (meanwhile resolved] concerning sponsoring receivables of the Brawn GP Formula 1 racing team, upon his own request, Dr. h.c. Walter did not participate in the brief discussion of this topic in the Supervisory Board and did not receive any information on it.

One member of the Supervisory Board, Mr. Arnaud Lagardere, was only able to attend fewer than half the meetings held in 2009 due to other urgent commitments.

Report on the work of the committees. The **Presidential Committee** convened four times in 2009. In addition to corporate governance issues, it also dealt with questions of remuneration, in particular resulting from the Appropriateness of Management Board Remuneration Act, and with personnel matters of the Board of Management. In February 2009, as in the previous years, the Presidential Committee once again specified compliance targets in connection with the individual target agreements of the members of the Board of Management, and evaluated the degree of goal accomplishment during the year in consultation with the Group's Compliance department and the Chairman of the Audit Committee. In November, the Presidential Committee dealt in detail with the Group's pool of potential for senior executive positions.

The **Audit Committee** met seven times in 2009. Details of these meetings are provided in a separate report of this committee (see page 154).

The **Nomination Committee** convened once in 2009; in this meeting it prepared a recommendation for the Supervisory Board's proposal on five candidates for election to the Supervisory Board of Daimler AG representing the shareholders. This took place on the basis of specifications regarding the structure, orientation and qualification profile of the members of the supervisory Board representing the shareholders with due consideration of corporate governance requirements.

As in previous years, the **Mediation Committee,** a body required by the provisions of the German Codetermination Act, had no occasion to take any action in 2009.

The Supervisory Board was continually informed about the committees' activities, and in particular about their decisions, in each case in the Supervisory Board meeting following such decisions.

Personnel changes in the Supervisory Board. After the end of the Annual Meeting held on April 8, 2009, two members representing the shareholders, William A. Owens and Dr. Mark Wössner, stepped down from the Supervisory Board of Daimler AG. As proposed by the Supervisory Board, Dr. Manfred Schneider, Dr. h.c. Bernhard Walter and Lynton R. Wilson were reelected with effect as of the end of the Annual Meeting, and Gerard Kleisterlee and Lloyd G. Trotter were elected as new representatives of the shareholders: Mr. Kleistenlee, Mr. Trotter and Dr. h.c. Walter for the period until the end of the end of the share holders' meeting that passes a resolution on the ratification of the actions of the Supervisory Board in the year 2013, and Dr. Schneider and Mr. Wilson for the period until the end of the end of the shareholders' meeting that passes a resolution on the ratification of the actions of the Supervisory Board in the year 2010. The election proposal of the Supervisory Board was based on a recommendation made by the Nomination Committee of the Supervisory Board and a resolution by the members of the Supervisory Board representing the shareholders.

Personnel changes in the Board of Management. In a Supervisory Board meeting on the occasion of the Annual Meeting in April, the Supervisory Board granted its approval for the amicable termination of the Board of Management membership of Dr. Rüdiger Grube effective at midnight on April 30, 2009. Dr. Grube left the Group at his own request and was appointed by the supervisory board of Deutsche Bahn AG as the chairman of the board of management of Deutsche Bahn AG.

In its meeting in December, the Supervisory Board approved the reappointment of Mr. Andreas Renschler as a member of the Board of Management with effect as of October 1, 2010 and until September 30, 2013 with unchanged responsibility for Daimler Trucks, and consented to the change in the Board of Management's schedule of responsibilities as proposed by the Board of Management.

In a Supervisory Board meeting in February 2010 the Supervisory Board approved the reappointments of Dr. Dieter Zetsche, Chairman of the Board of Daimler AG and Head of Mercedes-Benz Cars, and Dr. Thomas Weber, Group Research and Mercedes-Benz Cars Development, each for a term of three years effective January 1, 2011, until December 31, 2013. In addition, the Supervisory Board approved to extend the Board of Management and to appoint Dr. Wolfgang Bernhard as member of the Board of Management of Daimler AG for a term of three years with immediate effect, i.e. February 18, 2010 until February 28, 2013, with responsibility for Production and Procurement Mercedes Benz Cars and for the business unit Mercedes-Benz Vans.

Audit of the 2009 financial statements. The Daimler AG financial statements and the combined management report for the company and the Group for 2009 were duly audited by KPMG AG, Wirtschaftsprüfungsgesellschaft. Berlin, and were given an unqualified audit opinion. The same applies to the consolidated financial statements for 2009 prepared according to IFRS which were supplemented with a group management report and additional notes. The financial statements and the auditors' reports, were submitted to the Supervisory Board for its review. As preparation, the members of the Supervisory Board were provided with comprehensive documentation – some of which was in draft form — including the Annual Report, the audit report of KPMG for the company financial statements of Daimler AG and the consolidated financial statements according to IFRS and the combined management report for the Daimler AG and the Group, as well as drafts of the reports of the Supervisory Board and the Audit Committee and of the Form 20-F report. The documents were dealt with in detail by the Audit Committee and the Supervisory Board and were discussed in the presence of the auditors, who reported on the results of their audit. The Supervisory Board declared its agreement with the results of the audit, established in the framework of its own review that no objections were to be raised, and approved the Financial statements presented by the Board of Management. The financial statements are thereby adopted. Finally, the Supervisory Board approved the proposal of the Board of Management to compensate the annual deficit by partly withdrawing the capital reserve.

Appreciation. The Supervisory Board thanks all of the employees of the Daimler Group, the management and the departing members of the Board of Management and the Supervisory Board for their personal contributions and special efforts in an economic environment that presented the Group with some special challenges.

Stuttgart, March 2010
The Supervisory Board
Dr. Manfred Bischoff
Chairman

Required

1. Identify the main features of the preceding Supervisory report of Daimler company.
2. How is the preceding report different from the Board of Directors' report published by companies in the United States?

References

American Accounting Association, Committee on Basic Auditing Concepts. "A Statement of Basic Auditing Concepts," 1973.

American Institute of Certified Public Accountants. *Audit Committee Communications,* SAS No. 90, New York: AICPA, 2000.

Baker, C. R.; A. Mikol; and R. Quick. "Regulation of the Statutory Auditor in the European Union: A Comparative Survey of the United Kingdom, France and Germany." *European Accounting Review* 10, no. 4 (2001), pp. 763–86.

Blue Ribbon Committee. *Report and Recommendations of the Blue Ribbon Committee on Improving the Effectiveness of Corporate Audit Committees.* New York: New York Stock Exchange and National Association of Securities Dealers, 1999.

Canadian Institute of Chartered Accountants. "Chartered Accountants Adopt New Auditor Independence Standard." News release, December 4, 2003.

Capalan, D. "Internal Controls and the Detection of Management Fraud, *Journal of Accounting Research* 37, no. 1 (1999), pp. 101–17.

Chow, C. W., and R. N. Hwang. "The Cross-Border Transferability of Audit Technology: An Exploratory Study in the U.S.–Taiwan Context." *Advances in International Accounting* 7 (1994), pp. 217–29.

Committee of Sponsoring Organizations. *Internal Control—Integrated Framework.* COSO, 1992.

DeAngelo, L. "Auditor Size and Audit Quality." *Journal of Accounting and Economics* 3 (1981), pp. 183–200.

Deloitte & Touche. "Moving Forward: A Guide to Improving Corporate Governance through Effective Internal Control—A Response to Sarbanes-Oxley." Deloitte & Touche, January 2003.

Department of Trade and Industry. *A Framework of Independent Regulation for the Accountancy Profession: A Consultation Document.* London: DTI, 1998.

Favere-Marchesi, M. "Audit Quality in ASEAN." *International Journal of Accounting* 35, no. 1 (2000), pp. 121–49.

Federation des Experts Comptables Europeens. "The Role of Accounting and Auditing in Europe." FEE position paper, May 2002.

———. "The Conceptual Approach to Protecting Auditor Independence," February 2001.

Fisher, Liz. "Firms on the Defensive." *Accountancy,* July 2004, pp. 24–26.

Gangolly, J. S.; M. E. Hussein; G. S. Seow; and K. Tam. "Harmonization of the Auditor's Report." *International Journal of Accounting* 37 (2002), pp. 327–46.

Graham, L. E. "Setting a Research Agenda for Auditing Issues in the People's Republic of China." *International Journal of Accounting* 31, no. 1 (1996), pp. 19–37.

Gwilliam, David, and Tim Russell. "Polly Peck: Where Were the Analysts?" *Accountancy,* January 1991, pp. 25–26.

Institute of Internal Auditors. *Internal Auditing's Role in Sections 302 and 404 of the U.S. Sarbanes-Oxley Act of 2002.* Altamonte Springs, FL: IIA, May 2004.

International Federation of Accountants. "Reporting by Auditors on Compliance with International Financial Reporting Standards." International Auditing Practice Statement 1014. New York: International Auditing and Assuarance Standards Board, IFAC, June 2003.

———. "Revision to Paragraph 8.151 Code of Ethics for Professional Accountants." New York: IFAC Ethics Committee, June 2004.

Lee, C. J. "Accounting Infrastructure and Economic Development." *Journal of Accounting and Public Policy,* Summer 1987, pp. 75–86.

Lymer, A.; R. Debreceny; G. Gray; and A. Rahman. *Business Reporting on the Internet.* London: IASC, 1999.

McKinnon, J. "The Accounting Profession in Japan." *Australian Accountant,* July 1983, pp. 406–10.

Mueller, G. G. "Is Accounting Culturally Determined?" Paper presented at the EIASM Workshop on Accounting and Culture, Amsterdam, June 1985.

Napier, C. J. "Intersections of Law and Accountancy: Unlimited Auditor Liability in the United Kingdom. *Accounting, Organizations and Society* 23, no. 1 (1998), pp. 105–28.

Organization for Economic Cooperation and Development. *OECD Principles of Corporate Governance.* Paris: OECD 1999. (Available at www.oecd.org.)

Parker, Andrew. "PwC Steps Up Litigation Fight." *Financial Times,* April 19, 2004, p. 18.

Percy, J. P. "Assurance Services: Visions for the Future." *International Journal of Auditing* 3 (1999), pp. 81–87.

PricewaterhouseCoopers. *Audit Committee Effectiveness: What Works Best,* 2nd ed. Altamonte Springs, FL: The Institute of Internal Auditors Research Foundation, 2000.

Ramamoorti, S. *Internal Auditing: History, Evolution, and Prospects.* Altamonte Springs, FL: The Institute of Internal Auditors Research Foundation, 2003.

Report of the Committee on the Financial Aspects of Corporate Governance (Cadbury Report), December 1, 1992, London: Gee (a division of Professional Publishing Ltd.)

Roussey, R. S. "New Focus for the International Standards on Auditing." *Journal of International Accounting, Auditing and Taxation* 5, no. 1 (1996), pp. 133–46.

Securities and Exchange Commission. "Standards Relating to Listed Company Audit Committees." SEC Release No. 33-8173, January 8, 2003. (Available at www.SEC.gov/rules/proposed/34-47137.htm.)

Soeters, J., and H. Schreuder. "The Interaction between National and Organizational Cultures in Accounting Firms." *Accounting, Organizations and Society* 13, no. 1 (1988), pp. 75–85.

Treadway Commission. *Report of the National Commission on Fraudulent Financial Reporting.* Washington, DC: National Commission on Fraudulent Financial Reporting, 1987.

Turner, L. "The 'Best of Breed' Standards: Globalising Accounting Standards Challenges the Profession to Fulfil Its Obligation to Investors." *Financial Times,* March 8, 2001.

Wood, R. A. "Global Audit Characteristics across Cultures and Environments: An Empirical Examination." *Journal of International Accounting, Auditing, and Taxation* 5, no. 2 (1996), pp. 215–29.

Chapter Fifteen

International Corporate Social Reporting

Learning Objectives

After reading this chapter, you should be able to

- Explain the meaning of corporate social reporting (CSR).
- Identify theories used to explain the CSR practices of companies.
- Describe the current international trend of external reporting.
- Describe the steps taken at the international level to regulate CSR practices of companies.
- Discuss the factors that drive CSR practices of MNCs.
- Identify the organizations that promote CSR at the international level.
- Discuss the role played by Global Reporting Initiative (GRI).
- Explain CSR disclosures by companies at the international level with possible reasons for the current trends in this area.

INTRODUCTION

The current trend of external reporting by companies at the international level emphasizes the need to integrate economic, social, and governance (ESG) issues, reflecting sustainable development. Traditionally, external reporting has been focused on economic aspects. We discussed the issues related to economic aspects in earlier chapters of this text. We also briefly discussed the importance of governance issues in Chapter 14. The discussion in this chapter is focused mainly on the international aspects of corporate social reporting (CSR) [also known as ecological footprint reporting; environmental social governance (ESG) reporting; and triple bottom line (TBL) reporting].[1] The goal of sustainable development is to meet the needs of the present without compromising the ability of future generations to meet their own needs.[2]

In recent years, there has been a rapid increase in interest in social and environmental accounting issues among researchers, governments, professional bodies, industry groups, and corporations; there are a wide variety of reasons, not the least

[1] The discussion in the first part of this chapter is based largely on Perera, "The International and Cultural Aspects of Social Accounting", in Gray, R. and Guthrie, J. (eds), *Social Accounting, Mega Accounting, and Beyond: A Festschrift* in Honour of M.R. Mathews, Center for Social and Environmental Accounting Research, School of Management, The University of St Andrews, Scotland, pp. 215–251.

[2] World Commission on Environment and Development, *Our Common Future* (Oxford: Oxford University Press, 1987), p. 43.

of which is a growing anxiety about business ethics. Social accounting was popular in the early 1970s, but the interest in it disappeared almost completely by the end of the 1970s. In the late 1980s and early 1990s, there was a resurgence of interest in social accounting, mainly due to the renewed interest in environmental issues. In fact, there was a period in the early 1990s when social accounting was entirely swamped by environmental concerns. During this period, the national professional accounting bodies also showed an interest in environmental accounting issues. For example, in Australia both the Institute of Chartered Accountants in Australia and CPA Australia were actively involved in efforts to address environmental accounting issues. Environmental accounting largely developed out of the corporate social responsibility literature of the 1970s, which reflected widespread social concerns about the consequences of economic growth for the environment. CSR encompasses issues related to both social and environmental accounting. Following financial disasters such as Enron and WorldCom, and the more recent global financial crisis, ethical issues related to business and accounting have figured prominently in discussion and debate concerning corporate reporting and have probably added to the interest in social and environmental disclosures internationally. It has been suggested that social responsibility, financial performance, and sustainability reporting may be mutually constitutive and mutually reinforcing.[3]

Sustainable development requires new and innovative choices and ways of thinking. The developments in knowledge and technology have the potential to help address the threats to the sustainability of our social relations, environment, and economies. To support this expectation and to communicate clearly and openly about sustainability, a globally shared framework of concepts, consistent language, and metrics is required.[4]

The meaning of CSR is derived from the notion of organizational societal responsibility, which in turn is based on the notion of stewardship, defined as the accountability of management for the resources entrusted to an organization.[5] In a broad sense, accountability exists to shareholders, other stakeholders (such as employees or creditors), and to society at large. For example, it is increasingly considered morally irresponsible for companies to make profits by unnecessarily depleting natural resources or by polluting the environment. By definition, *accountability* is a proactive concept, which recognizes the responsibility associated with it. This means companies that simply react to community concerns or comply with regulations may not be truly embracing the notion of accountability.

The purpose of this chapter is to expose students to the current increasing trend toward CSR disclosures by multinational corporations (MNCs), focusing mainly on the motivation for them to do so, the regulation of CSR practices, the actual CSR practices of MNCs, and the latest efforts in this area through organizations such as Global Reporting Initiative (GRI). This chapter is structured into eight sections. The next section introduces two theories used to explain CSR practices by companies. Section three explains the drivers for CSR practices by companies. Section four examines the implications for climate change for CSR. Section five discusses regulation of CSR at international level. Section six identifies international organizations that promote CSR. Section seven describes actual CSR practices by MNCs, with some concluding remarks in the eighth and final section.

---

[3] Gray, R. "Does Sustainability Reporting Improve Corporate Behaviour: Wrong Question? Right Time?" *Accounting and Business Research* 36, Special Issue (2006), pp. 65–88.

[4] Global Research Initiative, *Sustainability Reporting Guidelines 2000–2006,* Amsterdam, GRI, 2000, p. 2.

[5] For example, the UK ASB defines stewardship in terms of accountability.

THEORIES TO EXPLAIN CSR PRACTICES

Today, stakeholders and shareholders are interested in the explanation of environmental and social impacts of company's operations and products. Sustainability reporting is now one of the greatest challenges facing the accounting profession. A number of theories have been used to explain differential social and environmental disclosures by firms, such as stakeholder theory and legitimacy theory. The stakeholder theory posits that environmental disclosures are made in response to the stakeholder demand for environmental (and social) information. Management responds to public pressure by stakeholders by voluntarily disclosing this information. A major problem with this theory, however, is that it fails to explain why firms from similar industries operating in the same geographic area provide different disclosures.

According to legitimacy theory, social reporting is a means to deal with the firm's exposure to political, economic, and social pressures. Firms behave in a way that is considered to be congruent with the society's perceived goals to legitimize their performance. Accordingly, legitimacy is "a condition or a status which exists when an entity's value system is congruent with the value system of the larger social system of which the entity is a part."[6]

The society's perceived goals are represented by various interest groups—for example, environmental public interest groups. If the members of the community are becoming more interested in the social and environmental impact of the activities of companies, it is likely that the senior management will be called upon to explain such activities. For example, researchers examined the effect of the Exxon *Valdez* oil spill on the disclosures within the annual reports of petroleum firms other than Exxon and concluded that threats to a firm's legitimacy do entice the managers to include more social responsibility information in the annual reports.[7] Similar effects can be expected as a result of the recent oil spill of the British Petroleum oil well in the Mexican Gulf.

However, in many instances, attempts at legitimacy through environmental disclosures have been greeted with increased skepticism. For example, it has been pointed out that companies in Ireland may have identified the futility of using CSR as a legitimation vehicle and have ceased to engage in its practice. This may have been caused by some unique feature in Irish culture in that there is no demand for CSR, and a more cynical, demanding, and questioning public hold a perception that CSR is doomed to fail as a legitimating vehicle.[8] This is different from the Australian context, where managers tend to consider annual report CSR to be useful to maintaining or reestablishing legitimacy.

DRIVERS OF CSR PRACTICES BY COMPANIES

There is no single motivation for managers in different countries for making social disclosures. In some countries (e.g., Australia), the level of media attention directed toward social accounting issues is a major motivating factor.[9] In some

---

[6] C. K. Lindblom, "The Implications of Organisational Legitimacy for Corporate Social Performance and Disclosure." Paper presented at the Critical Perspectives on Accounting Conference, New York, 1994.

[7] D. For example, Patten, "Intra-industry Environment Disclosures in Response to the Alaskan Oil Spill: A Note on Legitimacy Theory," *Accounting, Organizations and Society* 15, no.5 (1992), pp. 471–475.

[8] B. O'Dwyer and R. H. Gray, "Corporate Social Reporting in the Republic of Ireland: A Longitudinal Study," *Irish Accounting Review,* 5, no. 2 (1998), pp. 1–34.

[9] C. Deegan, M. Rankin, and J. Tobin, "An Examination of the Corporate Social and Environmental Disclosures of BHP from 1983 1997—A Test of Legitimacy Theory," *Accounting, Auditing & Accountability Journal* 15, no. 3 (2002), pp. 312–343.

other countries (e.g., Thailand), the social and environmental pressure groups are neither adequately proactive nor demanding in terms of information disclosure.[10]

It is now generally expected that firms not only act as good citizens, but report this good behavior to their stakeholders.[11] However, social and environmental disclosures are largely voluntary in most countries. As a result, there exists a wide diversity in such practices internationally depending on the drivers of CSR in different countries.

The relationship between the cultural context of a country and CSR practices of companies in that country may be identifiable. For example, Spanish culture and values differ from those of Anglo-Saxon countries and are closer to those of Latin-European and Latin-American countries.[12] Hofstede identified the structural elements of culture that affect behavior in organizations. He initially identified four societal cultural dimensions (namely, individualism versus collectivism, large versus small power distance, strong versus weak uncertainty avoidance, and masculinity versus femininity) and grouped countries in different cultural areas. Spain was placed in the "more developed Latin" area, characterized by large power distance, femininity, collectivism, and strong uncertainty avoidance. Gray hypothesized a relationship between accounting values (secrecy versus transparency, conservatism versus optimism, uniformity versus flexibility, and statutory control versus professionalism) and Hofstede's cultural values. Accordingly, he identified different accounting values in Anglo-Saxon countries and "more developed Latin" countries—for example, those in the "more developed Latin" countries being characterized by secrecy, conservatism, uniformity, and statutory control. Spain, being a more developed Latin country, has "secrecy" as one of the accounting values, and this applies to all areas of accounting and reporting, including CSR.

In addition to national cultural factors, CSR may also be influenced by organizational culture. CSR is often a function of the attitude of top management toward its stakeholders,[13] and culture affects moral values, which are likely to influence company managers in deciding, for example, the issues they select as being worthy of report. This was highlighted as "tone at the top" in the Treadway Commission Report in the United States.[14] Further, managers need to identify a relevant audience for implementing their legitimacy tactics, and cultural context determines, to a large extent, who is identified as a relevant audience and which legitimacy tactics will be utilized. In addition, a foreign subsidiary of a multinational company may be disclosing information to be in line with the policies of the parent company rather than in response to local demands or cultural factors.

Cultural definitions determine how the organization is understood and evaluated.[15] Organizations tend to influence these definitions or the terms on which

---

[10] N. Kuasirikun and M. Sherer, "Corporate Social Accounting Disclosure in Thailand," *Accounting, Auditing & Accountability Journal* 17, no. 4 (2004), pp. 629–660.

[11] M. J. Jones, "Accounting for Biodiversity: Operationalising Environmental Accounting," *Accounting, Auditing & Accountability Journal* 16, no. 5 (2003), pp. 762–789.

[12] G. Hofstede, *Culture's Consequences* (Thousand Oaks, CA: Sage, 1980); S. J. Gray, "Towards a Theory of Cultural Influence on the Development of Accounting Systems Internationally," *Abacus* (1988), pp. 1–15.

[13] M. Freedman, and B. Jaggi. "Global Warming, Commitment to the Kyoto Protocol, and Accounting Disclosure by the Largest Global Public Firms From Polluting Industries," *The International Journal of Accounting* 40 (2005), pp. 215–232.

[14] Treadway Commission, *Report of the National Commission on Fraudulent Financial Reporting* (Washington, DC: National Commission on Fraudulent Financial Reporting, 1987).

[15] M. C. Suchman, "Managing Legitimacy: Strategic and Institutional Approaches," *Academy of Management Review* 20, no. 3 (1995), pp. 571–610.

legitimacy is conferred by actively participating in the processes that determine them. For example, defining environmental performance is a cultural process in which various parties of interest are actively engaged. It has been pointed out that the rate of development of CSR internationally has been relatively slow and that this could be due to cultural factors, such as the economic and political conditions, the influence of the capitalist system and its social reproduction, lethargy, inertia, and the resistance to change often exhibited by the accounting profession as some of these factors are likely to influence the acceptance of CSR.[16]

Further, attitudes toward information disclosure may vary among companies in different countries. For example, research has found that Japanese companies are generally reluctant to provide information, particularly to outsiders.[17] Finally, for external audits to add value from a stakeholder perspective, they must be conducted by appropriately qualified individuals who both understand the audit process and accept the ethical, social, and environmental responsibilities of companies. However, the availability of appropriately qualified people may be a problem in many countries.

IMPLICATIONS OF CLIMATE CHANGE FOR CSR

Climate Change at a Glance

- The Intergovernmental Panel on Climate Change (IPCC) has found that concentration of carbon dioxide (CO_2) in the atmosphere has increased by 35 percent in the past 250 years, by far exceeding natural variations over the past 650,000 years, and probably the past 10 million years.
- The IPCC has concluded to a very high confidence level that the global average net effect of human activities on the atmosphere has been one of warming.
- Evidence of warming includes observations of increases in average air and ocean temperatures, widespread melting of snow and ice, and rising global mean sea level.
- Eleven years of the last 12-year period prior to 2006 (1995–2006) rank among the warmest years in the instrumental record of global surface temperature.
- New records were set for the highest temperatures reached during the summer of 2006 at locations across Europe, the United Kingdom, and the United States, including the highest European mean temperature on record for July 2006.

In 2007, the Stern Report in the United Kingdom on the Economics of Climate Change[18] stated that our actions over the coming few decades related to climate change could create risks of major disruptions to economic activity, and that costs of extreme weather alone could reach 0.5 to 1 percent of world GDP per annum by the middle of the century. It warns that the scale of economic disruption could approach those associated with the great wars and the economic depression of the first half of the 20th century.

---

[16] M. H. B. Perera and M. R. Mathews, "The Cultural Relativity of Accounting and International Patterns of Social Accounting," *Advances in International Accounting* 3 (1990), pp. 215–251.

[17] C. Ozu and S. Gray, "The Development of Segment Reporting in Japan: Achieving International Harmonization through a Process of National Consensus," *Advances in International Accounting* 14 (2001), pp. 1–13.

[18] N. Stern, *The Economics of Climate Change: The Stern Review* (Cambridge: Cabinet Office-HM Treasury, 2007).

Some Related Key Concepts

Emissions Trading

In recognition of the significant negative impacts of climate change, legislative-based emissions trading schemes have been created in certain regions (e.g., the EU Emissions Trading Scheme) and globally under the United Nations (the Kyoto Protocol), based on the concept of tradable carbon credits.

To meet its Kyoto Targets, the EU introduced the EU Emissions Trading Scheme in 2005. The scheme sets limits on emissions from more than 12,000 installations across Europe. If installations exceed the limits, they must purchase carbon credits or pay a fine. Carbon credits can be purchased from within the EU or from countries that have ratified the Kyoto Protocol and are participating in its mechanisms for international emissions trading. In the United States, Limited Emissions Trading has taken place under the Chicago Climate Exchange (CCX).

Carbon Credits

Carbon credits are reductions in greenhouse gas emissions that can be traded, have a financial value, and are created under a legal framework for emissions trading, such as the Kyoto Protocol or the EU ETS, or are generated by voluntary action outside of legal frameworks, for example, credits traded on the CCX.

Carbon Funds and Emissions Brokerages

Carbon funds are pooled funds set up to purchase carbon credits, usually on behalf of companies and other investors that will use the credits for compliance under an emissions trading scheme, or that will sell the credits at a later date. The term *emissions brokerage* is used to describe an organization that mediates between buyers and sellers of carbon credits—for example, between carbon funds and companies.

The Clean Development Mechanism

Under the Kyoto Protocol, countries are divided into two categories: developed (industrialized) countries and developing countries. In the first commitment period of the protocol, industrialized countries have targets to reduce emissions, and developing countries do not. A mechanism to promote reductions in developing countries is, however, provided in the form of the Clean Development Mechanism (CDM), which allows credits generated from emissions reduction projects in developing countries to be used in industrialized countries to assist in meeting their targets.

Carbon Neutral

The term *carbon neutral* means that emissions of carbon dioxide and/or other greenhouse gases into the atmosphere from the manufacture of a product, a company, or another activity have been offset by removing an equal amount of gas from the atmosphere. This can be achieved through the purchase of carbon credits or financing other projects to reduce or remove emissions.

Carbon Tax

A *carbon tax* is a tax on the use of fuels that cause emissions of carbon dioxide and other greenhouse gases into the atmosphere and is usually based on the quantity and type of fuel used (e.g., coal, oil, or gas). The primary purpose of a carbon tax is to create an incentive to increase the efficiency of fuel use, and thereby reduce greenhouse gas emissions from fuel and the associated contribution to climate change.

REGULATING CSR PRACTICES

Researchers have found significant shortcomings with voluntary CSR practices.[19] For example, doubts have been raised about the reliability of the disclosures. The overwhelming criticisms have been that annual report disclosures relating to the environmental performance of particular entities tend to be biased and self-laudatory with minimal disclosure of negative environmental information. Similarly, public interest groups seem to find voluntary corporate social reporting both insufficient and low in credibility, with concerns of selectivity and lack of independent verification of performance.

Due to various shortcomings of voluntary disclosures, it has been argued that some form of regulation may be necessary in order to promote more extensive and better quality reporting in the interests of the wider society.[20]

It is important to recognize in this respect that there is a difference between being accountable and being forced to be accountable; in the latter case, the spirit of the concept of accountability may not exist. In addition, regulation through legislation has some problems. First, lobbying in favor of economic interests over social and environmental interests may effectively undermine regulatory enforcement. Second, if corporate legitimizing activities are successful, then perhaps public pressure for a government to introduce disclosure legislation will be low and managers will be able to retain control of deciding what items to include in social reports. This amounts to managerial capture of the meaning of CSR. Third, for legislation to be effective, there should be a stringent enforcement mechanism. For example, in Thailand, social and environmental legislation and more severe public scrutiny do not appear to have motivated top management toward increased corporate social and environmental disclosures. Indeed, as social and environmental conditions worsened, the number of companies disclosing their social and environmental information also decreased, from 86 percent in 1993 to 77 percent in 1999.[21] This may be due to the fact that a stringent monitoring or inspection system was absent when economic downturn occurred. Social and environmental legislation in some countries is also relatively recent; for example, it was introduced in Thailand only in the 1990s. Fourth, a prime cause for the weakness of regulatory agencies may be their dependency on the expertise and the information of those very industries whose excesses they are seeking to mitigate.

Finally, it has been pointed out that the practice of corporate social disclosures in Ireland was not widespread and significantly less evident than in most other western European countries due to the absence of any form of regulation in this area.[22] On the other hand, it has been highlighted that the longer establishment/institutionalization of social legislation and more proactive social pressure groups in Germany contributed to more extensive social and ethical reporting among German companies than that made by UK companies.[23]

---

[19] R. Gray, R. Kouhy, and S. Lavers, "Corporate Social and Environmental Reporting: A Review of the Literature and a Longitudinal Study of UK Disclosures," *Accounting, Auditing & Accountability Journal* 8, no. 2 (1995), pp. 47–77.

[20] For example, S. Gallhofer and J. Haslam, "The Direction of Green Accounting Policy: Critical Reflections," *Accounting, Auditing & Accountability Journal* 1, no. 2 (1997), pp. 148–174.

[21] Kuasirikun and Sherer, "Corporate Social Accounting in Thailand."

[22] O'Dwyer, and Gray, "Corporate Social Reporting in the Republic of Ireland."

[23] C. Adams and N. Kuasirikun, "A Comparative Analysis of Corporate Reporting on Ethical Issues by UK and German Chemical and Pharmaceutical Companies," *The European Accounting Review* 9, no. 1 (2000), pp. 53–79.

Regulation of CSR in the United States

The Chicago Climate Exchange is the only cap and trade system for all six greenhouse gases (GHGs) in North America. Its emitting members make voluntary but legally binding commitments to meet annual greenhouse gas emission reduction targets. Those who reduce below the targets have surplus allowances to sell or bank; those who emit above the targets comply by purchasing CCX Carbon Financial Instrument contracts, which are a tradable commodity. Each CFI contract represents 100 metric tons of CO_2 equivalent. These contracts are comprised of exchange allowances and exchange offsets. *Exchange allowances* are issued to emitting members in accordance with their emission base line and the CCX Emission Reduction Schedule. *Exchange offsets* are generally by qualifying offset projects.

CCX has the following goals:

- To facilitate the transaction GHG allowance trading with price transparency, design excellence, and environmental integrity.
- To build the skills and institutions needed to cost effectively manage GHGs.
- To facilitate capacity-building in both public and private sectors to facilitate GHG migration.
- To strengthen the intellectual framework required for cost-effective and valid GHG reduction.
- To help inform the public debate on managing the risk of global climate change.

Membership of CCX would have the following benefits:

- Be prepared by mitigating financial, operational, and reputational risks.
- Reduce emissions using the highest compliance standards with third-party verification.
- Prove concrete action on climate change to shareholders, rating agencies, customers, and citizens.
- Establish a cost-effective, turnkey emissions management system.
- Drive policy developments based on practical, hands-on experience.
- Gain leadership recognition for taking early, credible, and binding action to address climate change.
- Establish early track record in reductions and experience with growing carbon and GHG market.

In August 2010, carbon prices dropped to a very low level of 10 cents per ton, compared to trading price during May and June 2008, when market price per ton of carbon reached $5.85 and $7.40, respectively. This was due mainly to the failure of UN Climate Summit in Copenhagen in December 2009 and the influence of campaign by "climate change skeptics."

Carbon trading is underpinned by a product called *carbon offsets*, most of which are taken on face value by the buyer. Not based on actual ton of carbon emitted, governing agencies are instead issuing certificates for a fictional commodity of emissions not emitted. It is nearly impossible to verify which of these thousands of so-called offset projects in the developing world are actually legitimate. These are some of the reasons the CCX appears to have failed.

In the United States, California and a group of nine states on the Eastern Seaboard (the Regional Greenhouse Gas Initiative) have introduced regulations on greenhouse gas emissions. Regulatory agencies such as the SEC have taken steps to introduce greater regulatory scrutiny in this area.

The discovery of toxic waste dumps across the United States eventually led to the passage of "Superfund" legislation in the 1980s, requiring corporations to become actively involved in remediation of the past problems. This was an effort to force the present users of land to clean up contaminated sites, even though they may not be responsible for the contamination. It has been pointed out that concurrent with the rise in mandated disclosures about Superfund exposures in the United States—particularly negative environmental liability disclosures—companies were also increasing the provision of other, more positive environmental information in their financial reports.[24]

International Arrangements to Regulate CSR

Internationally—for example, in Australia,[25] New Zealand,[26] the United Kingdom,[27] and the European Union[28]—environmental laws have increased dramatically. The United Kingdom, for example, has seen a steady increase in negotiated governance of releases to air, land, and water, while environmental regulation in the United States tends to be more directive-driven, wherein the EPA establishes behavioral standards and enforces compliance through punitive measures for noncompliance—a "command and control" structure.[29]

The *Kyoto Protocol* came into effect in early 2005, and more than 165 countries have now ratified the protocol, with the notable exception of the United States. The Kyoto Protocol was created under the United Nations Framework Convention on Climate Change (UNFCCC) and is a combination of country-specific greenhouse gas emissions reduction targets and emissions trading mechanisms. It is based on the recognition that the atmosphere is a shared resource and that countries have "common but differentiated responsibilities" to take action to control emissions—which is interpreted as all countries having a responsibility to take action, but that industrialized countries have a specific responsibility to take the lead.

Countries that ratify the Protocol (including the EU and Japan) are obliged to enact regulations incorporating the Protocol's provisions on disclosures related to greenhouse gases (i.e., carbon dioxide, methane, and nitrous oxides). A key aspect of this Protocol is that greenhouse gases emitted by vehicles, power plants, and certain types of industrial operations need to be brought to acceptable levels in order to control their global warming effect. The countries ratifying the Protocol are committing to reduce greenhouse gases by 5 percent from their 1990 level by the year 2011.

The *European Union Emissions Trading Scheme* (EU ETS) was launched in early 2005, and created a EU-wide market for emissions trading linked to the Kyoto Protocol. The so-called Linking Directive was introduced in the EU in 2006 to link the EU ETS to the Kyoto Protocol and allow credits generated under the protocol to be used in the EU.

---

[24] For example, D. M. Patten, "Changing Superfund Disclosure and Its Relation to the Provision of other Environmental Information," *Advances in Environmental Accounting and Management* 1, (2000), pp. 101–121.

[25] G. M. Bates, *Environmental Law in Australia* (Sydney: Butterworth, 1995).

[26] C. D. A. Milne, *Handbook of Environmental Law* (Wellington: Royal Forest and Bird Protection Society, 1992).

[27] S. Ball and S. Bell, *Environmental Law,* 2nd ed. (London: Blackstone, 1994).

[28] B. O'Dwyer, "Conceptions of Corporate Social Responsibility: The Nature of Managerial Capture," *Accounting, Auditing & Accountability Journal* 16, no. 4 (2003), pp. 523–557.

[29] J. L. Mobus, "Mandatory Environmental Disclosures in a Legitimacy Theory Context," *Accounting, Auditing & Accountability Journal* 18, no. 4 (2005), pp. 492–517.

GLOBAL REPORTING INITIATIVE (GRI)

There are several international bodies, such as the World Bank and International Federation of Accountants (IFAC), and organizations such as the Kyoto Protocol—Global Reporting Initiative (GRI) that promote CSR practices by companies. The World Bank set up one of the first carbon funds (the Prototype Carbon Fund, or PCF) to stimulate development of the emissions trading market and assist companies and governments to invest in carbon credits generated under the Kyoto Protocol. The investors in the PCF receive a pro-rata share of the carbon credits in return for their investment. Most European governments (and some non-European ones, such as Japan) also have since set up carbon funds to assist in meeting their targets under the Kyoto Protocol, and a growing number of private funds have been created to purchase carbon credits on behalf of other companies or on a speculative basis for selling later at a profit. Several of these funds have been listed on London's Alternative Investments Market (AIM), and some have been set up by large banks. The International Finance Corporation (IFC), a member of the World Bank Group, together with GRI has unveiled a Good Practice Note to help companies achieve greater business value through sustainability reporting.

The IFAC developed a Sustainability Framework, a Web-based tool (a new climate change resource) that targets professional accountants who can influence the way organizations integrate sustainability into their objectives, strategies, management, and definitions of success. Carbon disclosures, cap-and-trade, and green legislative initiatives are among the issues addressed by these new links. The International Auditing and Assurance Standards Board (IAASB) is expected to develop an assurance standard on greenhouse gas statements by firms.

In mid-2005 Australia, Canada, China, India, Japan, Korea, and the United States signed the Asia-Pacific Partnership on Clean Development and Climate aimed at deploying clean energy technology to constrain and reduce greenhouse emissions.

GRI was formed by U.S.-based nonprofits Ceres (formerly the Coalition for Environmentally Responsible Economies) and Tellus Institute, with the support of the United Nations Environment Program (UNEP) in 1997. Although the GRI is independent, with its Secretariat in Amsterdam, it remains a collaborating center of UNEP and work in cooperation with the United Nations Global Compact.

The GRI produces one of the world's most prevalent standards for sustainability reporting, which is a form of value reporting where an organization publicly communicates its economic, environmental, and social performance. As of January 2009, more than 1,500 organizations from 60 countries use the guidelines to produce their sustainability reports.

GRI Sustainability Guidelines have two parts. Part I defines report content, quality, and boundary. It provides reporting principles and reporting guidance regarding report content, ensuring the quality of reported information, and setting the report boundary. Part II provides standards for disclosure. It specifies the base content that should appear in a sustainability report. It identifies three different types of disclosure—namely, strategy and profile, management approach, and performance indicators. Strategy and profile includes disclosures that set the overall context for understanding organizational performance such as its strategy, profile, and governance. Management approach includes disclosures that cover how an organization addresses a given set of topics in order to provide context for understanding performance in a specific area. Performance indicators are those that comparable information on the economic, environmental, and social performance of the organization. Exhibit 15.1 shows the reporting framework provided by GRI. It also provides application levels for report makers to indicate that a report is GRI-based. They are required to declare the level to which they have applied the GRI reporting framework via the "application levels" system (Exhibit 15.2). Report makers have the option to request an application level check. Exhibit 15.3 provides an example of indicator protocol set specified by GRI.

EXHIBIT 15.1
GRI Reporting Framework

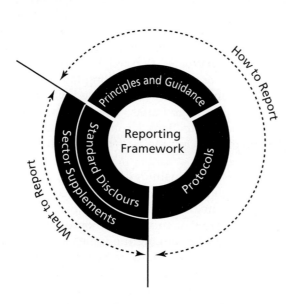

EXHIBIT 15.2   **GRI Application Level Criteria**
Reports intended to qualify for level C, C+, B, B+, A or A+ must contain each of the criteria that are presented in the column for the relevant level.

Report Application Level		C	C+	B	B+	A	A+
Standard Disclosures	G3 Profile Disclosures OUTPUT	Report on: 1.1 2.1–2.10 3.1–3.8, 3.10–3.12 4.1–4.4, 4.14–4.15		Report on all criteria listed for Level C plus: 1.2 3.9, 3.13 4.5–4.13, 4.16–4.17		Same as requirement for Level B	
	G3 Management Approach Disclosures OUTPUT	Not Required	Report Externally Assured	Management Approach Disclosures for each Indicator Category	Report Externally Assured	Management Approach disclosed for each Indicator Category	Report Externally Assured
	G3 Performance Indicators & Sector Supplement Performance Indicators OUTPUT	Report on a minimum of 10 Performance Indicators, including at least one from each of: social, economic, and environment.		Report on a minimum of 20 Performance Indicators, at least one from each of: economic, environment, human right, labor, society, product responsibility.		Respond on each Core 63 and Sector Supplement* Indicator with due regard to the materiality Principle by either: a) reporting on the indicator or b) explaining the reason for its omission.	

*Sector supplement in final version

EXHIBIT 15.3
Example of Indicator Protocol Set Specified by GRI

Source: *GRI Sustainability Guidelines 2000–2006.*

Aspects of Performance Indicators:

Environment	Material; energy; water; biodiversity; emissions, effluents, and waste; products and services; compliance; transport; overall
Economic	Economic performance; market presence; indirect economic impacts
Human Rights	Investment and procurement practices; nondiscrimination; freedom of association and collective bargaining; child labor; forced and compulsory labor; security practices; indigenous rights
Labor Practices and Decent Work	Employment; labor/management relationship; occupational health and safety; training and education; diversity and equal opportunity
Product Responsibility	Customer health and safety; product and service labeling; marketing communications; customer privacy; compliance
Society	Community; corruption; public policy; anti-competitive behavior; compliance

Reporting leads to improved sustainable development outcomes because it allows organizations to measure, track, and improve their performance on specific issues. As well as helping organizations manage their impacts, sustainability reporting promotes transparency and accountability. Performance can be monitored year on year or can be compared to other similar organizations.

The G3 are the so-called third generation of the GRI's Sustainability Reporting Guidelines. They were launched in October 2006. The G3 consist of principles and disclosure items. The principles help reporters define the report content, the quality of the report, and give guideline on how to set the report boundary. Principles include those such as materiality, stakeholder inclusiveness, comparability, and timeliness. Disclosure items include disclosures on management of issues, as well as performance indicators themselves—for example, "total water withdrawal by source."

GRI is a network-based organization that has developed the world's most widely used sustainability reporting framework. This framework has been developed through a consensus-seeking process with participants drawn globally from business, civil society, labor, and professional institutions. This framework sets out the principles and indicators for organizations to measure and report their economic, environmental, and social performance. It includes Sustainability Reporting Guidelines published in 2006, which outline core content for reporting and are relevant to all organizations regardless of size, sector, or location. The GRI board calls for governments to require companies to report on sustainability factors—or to explain why they are unable to report on sustainability factors. GRI also issued a document entitled "Biodiversity—A GRI Reporting Resource" in January 2007. Among other things, it assists reporting organizations in understanding biodiversity issues and its relationship to their activities and operations and offers insights on specific issues and challenges related to biodiversity reporting.

In an effort to create a worldwide common knowledge on sustainability reporting process, as well as to apply and use the GRI reporting framework, the GRI launched its international certified training program to be implemented by local partners, "GRI-Certified Training Program," in 2007. The first implementation waves include Brazil, India, and the United States. The first memorandum of understanding (MoU) was signed by GRI and a Brazilian association [Associacao Brasileira de Comunicacao Empresarial (ABERJE)] in July 2007, signaling the start of an international program and an important local partnership. GRI introduced the Readers' Choice Award to draw attention to the fact that sustainability reporting complements traditional reporting by offering shareholders and stakeholders' insight into sustainability as one of the most burning issues of our time. It is interesting that in a GRI survey of 2,000 companies from 60 countries that had submitted their CSR for the competition on Readers' Choice, the Brazilian companies won most of the awards. For example, the audit report for Banco Bradeco's CSR report for 2009 refers to GRI-G3 sustainability guidelines (Exhibit 15.4).

GRI sponsored the Global Conference on Sustainability and Transparency in Amsterdam in May 2008, where issues of reporting and assurance related to sustainability—namely, the risk of divergent financial reporting practices developing in different countries and the lack of an assurance framework for these types of engagement. The main outcome of the conference includes two key propositions:

- By 2015, all large and medium-size companies in Organization for Economic Cooperation and Development (OECD) countries and large emerging economics should be required to report on their ESG performance and, if they do not do so, to explain why.

- By 2020, there should be a generally accepted and applied international standard that would effectively integrate financial and ESG reporting by all organizations.

The Prince of Wales's Accounting for Sustainability Project and the GRI announced in August 2010 the formation of the International Integrated Reporting Committee (IIRC), recognizing that it may not be possible to meet 21st-century challenges with 20th-century decision-making and reporting systems. The IIRC's remit is to strive for a globally accepted framework for accounting for sustainability. The aim is to develop a framework that brings together financial, environmental, social, and governance information in a clear, concise, consistent, comparable, and integrated manner. The following views reflect the rationale behind the establishment of the IIRC:

> To make our economy sustainable we have to relearn everything we have learnt from the past. That means making more from less and ensuring that governance, strategy and sustainability are inseparable. Integrated Reporting builds on the practice of Financial Accounting, and Environmental, Social and Governance—or ESG—Reporting, and equips companies to strategically manage their operations, brand and reputation to stakeholders and be better prepared to manage any risk that may compromise the long-term sustainability of the business.—Professor Mervin King, chair of the GRI

> The case for globally consistent financial reporting standards is well understood and accepted. It is appropriate to apply the same global approach to other aspects of corporate reporting. This initiative represents an important stem on that journey.—Sir David Tweedie, chair of the IASB

> The goal of the IIRC is not to increase the reporting burden on companies and other entities. Rather, it is to help them and all their stakeholders make better resource allocation decisions. All of us have a stake in a sustainable society. While integrated

EXHIBIT 15.4   Auditor's report on Banco Bradesco's Sustainability Report 2009

To Banco Bradesco S.A.'s Management

Introduction

We have been hired with the goal of assuring Banco Bradesco S.A.'s *2009 Sustainability Report,* prepared under the responsibility of the company's management. This responsibility includes the design, implementation and maintenance of internal controls for the appropriate preparation and presentation of the *2009 Sustainability Report.* Our responsibility is to issue a report of limited assurance for the information disclosed in Banco Bradesco S.A.'s *Sustainability Report* for 2009.

Criteria for the Preparation of the *2009 Sustainability Report*

The 2009 Sustainability Report was prepared according to Global Reporting Initiative (GRI) guidelines at the A+ application level. Following these guidelines, Banco Bradesco S.A. reported on 61 core and additional indicators, as well as 16 supplementary performance indicators for the financial sector.

Applied Procedures

The limited assurance report was prepared in accordance with NPO 1 Assurance Standards and Procedures issued by the Brazilian Institute of Independent Auditors (IBRACON) and thus consisted of: (i) planning the report, taking into account the relevance and the volume of information presented by Bradesco S.A.'s Sustainability Report; (ii) understanding internal controls; (iii) verification of the evidence supporting the quantitative and qualitative data of the Sustainability Report based on tests; (iv) interviews with the managers in charge of preparing the information; and (v) comparing the financial information with the accounting records. Thus, the procedures above were deemed sufficient to allow a limited assurance level but do not meet the requirements for the issuance of a more comprehensive assurance report, as established by the NPO 1 Assurance Standards and Procedures. Our limited assurance evaluation also covered the verification of the requirements for GRI-G3 for reports with an A+ Application Level.

Scope and Limitations

The chief objective of our report was to identify and assess whether the data included in the *2009 Sustainability Report*—in terms of obtaining qualitative information, measuring, and calculating quantitative information complies with the following criteria: (i) Brazilian Accounting Standard NBCT IS—Social and Environmental Information, and (ii) the Global Reporting Initiative's sustainability guidelines (GRI-G3). The opinions, background information, descriptive information and information subject to subjective assessment are not included in the scope of the report.

Conclusion

Based on our limited review, we are not aware of any relevant changes that should be made to the information contained in Banco Bradesco S.A.'s *Sustainability Report* relating to the period ended on December 31, 2009 for this information to be properly presented, in all relevant aspects, with regard to the criteria used for the A+ Application Level.

Additional Considerations

In relation to the definition of content of the *2009 Sustainability Report,* following the GRI-G3 principals, we recommend the following changes in the reporting process:

- Adaptation of the *Report's* themes to better match those asked for by Banco Bradesco S.A.'s stakeholders.
- More transparency under the Balance principal, with the inclusion of both the positive and negative aspects of the Organization's performance.
- More objective comparison with the information contained in the previous report.

São Paulo, February 11, 2010

PricewaterhouseCoopers
Independent Auditors
CRC 2SP000160/O-5

Washington Luiz Pereira Cavalcanti
Accountant CRC ISP172940/O-6

reporting alone cannot ensure sustainability it is a powerful mechanism to help us all make better decisions about the resources we consume and the lives we lead.—Ian Ball, CEO of the IFAC

I believe we will look back on the creation of this Committee as a turning point in the development of corporate reporting.—Jane Diplock, chair of the executive committee of the IOSCO

It is clear there are several efforts made at international level to encourage companies to engage in CSR.

CSR PRACTICES BY MNCs

There is an increasing trend for *Fortune* 500 companies to provide a sustainability report and make reference to the GRI guidelines. For example, in its sustainability report for 2009, United Parcel Service Inc. (UPS) states that it has followed GRI guidelines. UPS has adopted a plan to cut the carbon emissions of its airline by an additional 20 percent by 2020, for a cumulative reduction of 42 percent since 1990. UPS plans to achieve this goal by investing in more fuel-efficient aircraft types and engines, by instituting fuel-saving operational initiatives, and by introducing bio-fuels. The report, which can be downloaded from the company's Web site, includes a section on GRI Index—Strategy and Analysis, showing how UPS responds to each of the G3 indicators. It is important that this report has been assured by the auditors (Exhibit 15.5) and by GRI (for the first time in 2009).

The GRI survey report analyzed a sample of 50 sustainability reports published in 2006 for the year 2005 by leading international companies. The selected companies were from energy, financial services, telecommunications and information technology, consumer goods and pharmaceutical, industrial, and mining industries. They were all from the *Financial Times'* top 500 list (FT500) and used the GRI guidelines.

GRI research findings indicate that there is a worldwide trend toward sustainability reporting by companies, suggesting that sustainability reporting is becoming a well-utilized tool in maintaining and building brand—often a company's most valuable asset. The findings also show that there is a strong correlation between high profitability and sustainability reporting in the world's top businesses. For example, the world's top five most valued brands (as ranked by *Interbrand*'s and *BusinessWeek*'s top 100 Global Brands)—Coca-Cola, Microsoft, IBM, General Electric, and Nokia—all produce reports of their economic, environment, and social performance based on metrics from the GRI. Exhibit 15.6 provides a list of company-provided CSR reports in 2010. Exhibit 15.7 provides an extract from IBM Corporation's CSR report in 2009.

Findings indicate that with the growing significance of climate change, many companies are taking steps to quantify, report, and reduce greenhouse gas emissions from their own operations. Many companies are also taking similar steps to disclose their energy use, which is also useful for assessing climate impacts. In many cases, reports make an explicit link between greenhouse gas emissions and energy. In some companies, senior management has clearly expressed its commitment to CSR (Exhibit 15.8).

The majority of companies reported greenhouse gas or CO_2 emissions from the company with quantities in units such as tons. Most companies that reported their

EXHIBIT 15.5 Independent Accountants' Review Report on Corporate Sustainability Report 2009

Board of Directors, Shareowners, and Stakeholders

United Parcel Service, Inc.

Atlanta, Georgia

We have reviewed the 2009 UPS Corporate Sustainability Report of United Parcel Service, Inc. (the "Company") for the year ended December 31, 2009. This report is the responsibility of the Company's management.

We conducted our review in accordance with attestation standards established by the American Institute of Certified Public Accountants. A review consists principally of applying analytical procedures, considering management assumptions, methods, and findings, and making inquiries of persons responsible for sustainability and operational matters. It is substantially less in scope than an examination, the objective of which is the expression of an opinion on the presentation. Accordingly, we do not express such an opinion. A review of the sustainability report is not intended to provide assurance on the entity's compliance with laws or regulations.

The preparation of the sustainability report requires management to interpret the criteria, make determinations as to the relevancy of information to be included, and make estimates and assumptions that affect reported information. Different entities may make different but acceptable interpretations and determinations. The sustainability report includes information regarding the Company's sustainability initiatives and targets, the estimated future impact of events that have occurred or are expected to occur, commitments, and uncertainties. Actual results in the future may differ materially from management's present assessment of this information because events and circumstances frequently do not occur as expected.

Based on our review, nothing came to our attention that caused us to believe that such sustainability report does not include, in all material respects, the required elements of the Global Reporting Initiative G3 Guidelines, for Application Level B sustainability reports; that the 2009 amounts included therein have not been accurately derived, in all material respects, from the Company's records; or that the underlying information, determinations, estimates, and assumptions of the Company do not provide a reasonable basis for the disclosures contained therein.

The comparative disclosures for periods prior to 2009 were not reviewed by us and, accordingly, we do not express any form of assurance on them.

Deloitte & Touche LLP
July 9, 2010
Detroit, Michigan

greenhouse gas emissions or CO_2 emissions also reported a target to reduce their emissions. No examples were found of companies that quantify the financial cost (or benefit) of reducing greenhouse emissions, although examples were found where companies reported financial benefits from reductions in energy use.

A handful of companies reported on the financial implications of targets. In all cases, these companies reported financial savings or positive returns on investment from their actions to achieve their targets, such as improving energy efficiency. These companies were in the oil and gas, pharmaceutical, and information technology sectors.

The items disclosed and the methods of disclosure in corporate social reports can vary in different countries. For example, the most disclosed items of social disclosures in the annual reports of the United Kingdom, the United States, and Australia are human resources and community involvement,[30] whereas the most disclosed items in Thai corporate annual reports are employee information and

[30] J. Guthrie and L. Parker, "Corporate Social Disclosure Practice: A Comparative International Analysis," *Advances in Public Interest Accounting*, 3 (1990), pp. 159–176.

EXHIBIT 15.6 List of CSR Reports in 2010

ConAgra Foods Inc. (NYSE: CAG)

This report focuses of the three planks of the company's corporate responsibility platform: "Good for You, Good for the Community, and Good for the Planet."

MTR Corporation (HKG: 66)

This report covers 2009 and reveals that sustainability is mainstreamed through the company's Promise, Policy, and Programs.

Banco Bradesco (NYSE: BBD)

This report presents the company's sustainability vision, that is, how sustainability is inserted into the company's strategy, divided into three pillars.

Fuji Xerox Australia

This report is an account of the company's impact and efficiency in delivering a sustainable business and details the company's progress against its economic, social, and environmental sustainability targets.

WestLB AG

This report includes relevant information and ratios on the current status of developments in sustainability management as well as related products and financial services.

Fluor Corporation (NYSE: FLR)

This report emphasizes the importance "alignment," which begins with the company's clients and culminates in the execution of its projects.

Thales (EPA: HO)

This report demonstrates the company's commitment to constantly improve its risk prevention policy.

NEC Corporation (TYO: 6701)

This report discloses the company's practices carried out in pursuit of CSR during the year ended March 2010.

Medtronic Inc (NYSE: MDT)

This report provides a comprehensive view of the company's commitment to global economic, social, and environmental stewardship.

Hellenic Petroleum Group (ATH: ELPE)

This report is the fifth of the company's annual sustainability reports produced since 2005.

USG Corporation (NYSE: USG)

This report reviews the company's efforts throughout the past year and describes some of the company's future objectives.

Tamro Group

This report describes the development and results of the company's corporate responsibility.

Kinross Gold Corporation (TSE: K)

This report chronicles the company's progress over the past two years in delivering on the strong commitment to corporate responsibility.

Provident Financial (LON: PFG)

This report is designed to provide all the people that matter to the company's business with an account of how the social, environmental, and economic impacts are managed.

Barilla Group

This report represents a key marker in the company's journey toward renewing its corporate culture and approach to business.

Network Rail

This report includes an introduction to how the company manages corporate responsibility and how it is committed to being a responsible business.

Johnson Matthey (LON: JMAT)

This report reviews the company's progress toward its "Sustainability 2017" vision and the work it is doing to reduce its own environmental footprint.

EXHIBIT 15.7 **Extract from IBM Corporate Responsibility Report 2009**

IBM Disaster response (since 2001)

2001 New York City, September 11; Gujarat, India, earthquake

2004 Thailand, India, Indonesia and Sri Lanka, tsunami

2005 U.S. Gulf Coast, hurricanes Katrina and Rita, Mexico, hurricanes/flooding; Pakistan, earthquake

2006 Indonesia, Mt. Merapi, volcano/earthquake; Guinsaugon, Philippines, landslides

2007 San Diego, wildfires; Peru, earthquake; Tabasco, Mexico, flooding; Indonesia, mud slides; Bangladesh, cyclone; Sri Lanka, flooding

2008 Myanmar, cyclone Nargis; Sichuan Province, China, earthquake; Bihar, India, flooding

2009 Mexico, H1n1 response; Atlanta CDC, H1n1 response; server donation; Philippines, typhoon Ketsana/Ondoy; Indonesia, earthquakes; Vietnam, flooding; Italy, earthquake; Taiwan, typhoon; Kamataka and Andhra Pradesh, India, flooding Victoria, Australia, bush fires.

2010 Haiti, earthquake; Chile, earthquake.

Disaster response

For decades IBM employees have rallied in response to natural disasters around the world, donating money, time, and technology to aid in disaster management and recovery efforts. But our approach is not only to address the acute needs in the immediate aftermath of a disaster, but also to provide critical capabilities that are systematic and repeatable, enabling faster and smarter responses in the future, even to unforeseen disasters.

Throughout 2009, IBMers responded to brushfires in Australia, typhoons in the Philippines, H1N1 outbreaks in Mexico, floods in Vietnam and India, and, of course, the devastating earthquake in Haiti. From developing emergency communications infrastructure to providing servers and software for missing persons registries, asset tracking, and logistics management, IBMers consistently contribute their expertise to assist in these efforts. For example, floods in India and the Philippines and the earthquake in China (2008), led to the deployment of Sahana, an integrated, free open-source disaster management system, designed to run rescue, relief and rehabilitation operations.

In Haiti, though the company maintains no presence in the country, IBM worked in coordination with World Vision, a leading global NGO, to develop a sophisticated vehicle tracking system. For longer-term recovery, IBM is also creating a design plan for a mobile Humanitarian Data Center that can be installed when the telecommunications and grid infrastructure are stronger. Both solutions will be reuseable in other situations going forward. To date, IBM employees around the world have donated more than $1.1 million through the employee payroll program, which allows IBMers to automatically contribute to charitable causes through their paycheck. And IBMers are continuing to volunteer as we identify opportunities in their communities through on demand community.

EXHIBIT 15.8 A Letter from Our Chairman and Chief Executive Officer

Dear Stakeholders:

In the midst of the global financial downturn, the economic, environmental and social implications of business are more important than ever. There's no question that the world is undergoing a massive resetting of priorities, values and expectations. The Coca-Cola Company brands are among the world's most recognized and valued. The strength and sustainability of our brands are directly related to our social license to operate, which we must earn daily by keeping our promises to our customers, consumers, associates, investors, communities and partners. It is an honor, and a responsibility that we take very seriously.

We are dedicated to offering quality beverages for every lifestyle, life stage and occasion, marketing those beverages responsibly, and providing information that consumers can trust. In 2008, we launched more than 160 low- and no-calorie beverages and continued to increase our number of fortified products globally. And just a few weeks ago, we announced that we will list the energy information per serving for our beverages on the front of nearly all of our packages worldwide by the end of 2011.

Productivity

We constantly challenge ourselves, and our partners, to find innovative ways to make our products and services affordable and our operations and supply chains economically beneficial to the communities we serve.

In 2008, our Company committed to drive out $500 million in operating expenses by the end of 2011, allowing us to reinvest in innovation and fuel our business growth for years to come. We are assessing everything to increase productivity, minimize waste and maximize resources—a clear example of where sustainability goals and business objectives align. By reducing packaging material use, improving water efficiency, installing more efficient lighting and using energy conservation tools, among other productivity initiatives, we intend to deliver more than half of the savings by the end of 2009. At the same time, we have invested in the world's largest bottle-to-bottle recycling facility, which is expected to generate long-term savings in the cost of materials for the Coca-Cola system and provide benefits to local communities.

Sustainable Communities

The private sector plays a pivotal role in developing sustainable communities through economic development and community involvement. At Coca-Cola, we have witnessed the effect that critical issues—like water needs—can have on a developing economy and how addressing those needs helps both the community and our business. In Kenya, for example, our system built a new water well for a remote village where women spent the majority of their day walking miles to the nearest clean water source for their families' needs. Now, instead of walking hours a day to get water, the women are able to focus their time on creating and operating a local catering and events business.

I also have seen our unique business model create opportunity in developing economies, most notably, our micro distribution program in Africa. Instead of trying to use large trucks to serve thousands of small retail outlets in areas where the roads are often in poor condition, our bottling partners distribute to carefully selected entrepreneurs who sell our products exclusively to small retailers, often by bicycle or pushcart. People who set up what are commonly called Manual Distribution Centers, or MDCs, employ others in the area, who then sell and distribute our beverages to retailers. Today, there are more than 2,600 MDCs in Africa, employing approximately 12,000 people.

Live Positively

Building a culture of sustainability and social responsibility begins at home, with the people who work for our Company and our bottling partners. We have embedded our commitment to sustainability into a framework we call LIVE POSITIVELY.

LIVE POSITIVELY is a way for us to think holistically and globally about sustainability efforts throughout the Coca-Cola system. It is a modern expression of our Company's heritage of caring about our people and our planet. LIVE POSITIVELY includes goals, metrics and principles for our work in developing beverage benefits; supporting active healthy living programs; building sustainable communities; improving environmental programs for our operations; and creating a safe, inclusive work environment for our associates.

Ultimately, LIVE POSITIVELY is about all of us making the right decisions each day—the smart decisions—to be the Company we know we can be. It is about continuing to challenge ourselves to improve and do more. We discuss LIVE POSITIVELY in more detail throughout this report.

Transparency

Commitment is meaningless without accountability. The scrutiny we face from a global audience is high, and the need for increased transparency continues to grow beyond the requests of our critics to those of our customers and partners. We value an open and honest dialogue with our stakeholders, and we are prepared to advance the conversation.

In this report, you will see global targets for water stewardship, climate protection, sustainable packaging, active healthy living and the expansion of our MDCs in Africa, as well as increased data disclosure. Though we highlight accomplishments, we also note areas where we need to improve. We provide a four-year look at performance data for the Company and the Coca-Cola system, where available. And later this year, we are publishing our Company's first full report against the Global Reporting Initiative G3 Guidelines.

We are making progress. In fact, in 2009 our Company was placed on the Dow Jones Sustainability World Index for the first time, after being on the North America Index since 2005. We joined some of our bottling partners who also are on the World list and respective geography lists.

This report was developed to share our commitments and our progress in meeting them, and it is one chapter in an ongoing story. We have accomplished many good things, but we still have work to do to continue earning your trust and keeping our promises to you and the communities we serve. We are dedicated to upholding those promises every day.

My best regards,

Muhtar Kent
Chairman and Chief Executive Officer
November 2, 2009

environmental information.[31] In terms of methods of disclosure, the United Kingdom and the United States, for example, manifest both monetary and nonmonetary disclosure, whereas Australian companies tend to be limited to nonmonetary quantification.[32] Further, the methods of social disclosure in Australia are favorable to the company concerned, even to the point of increasing positive disclosures around the time of negative events.[33]

In terms of style of reporting, Australian companies have not adopted the compliance-with-standard style of reporting to stakeholders being observed in Europe, and their policies contain little reference to reporting standards or the necessity of disclosure.[34] In some cases, The CSR report has been certified by independent auditors (Exhibit 15.9).

The extent of environmental disclosures can also vary among different countries. Research has shown that Canadian firms provide more extensive environmental disclosure than U.S. firms,[35] whereas U.S. firms are associated with greater environmental disclosures compared to Australian or U.K. firms.[36] Further, firms using the Anglo-American model tend to provide more environmental disclosure compared to firms from other countries.[37] These studies were based on data that

[31] Kuasirikun and Sherer, "Corporate Social Accounting in Thailand."

[32] Guthrie and Parker, "Corporate Social Disclosure Practice."

[33] C. Deegan and B. Gordon, "A Study of Environmental Disclosure Practices of Australian Corporations," *Accounting and Business Research* 26, no. 3 (1996), pp. 187–199.

[34] C. A. Tilt, "The Content and Disclosure of Australian Corporate Environmental Policies," *Accounting, Auditing & Accountability Journal* 14, no. 2 (2001), pp. 190–212.

[35] N. Buhr and M. Freedman, "Culture, Institutional Factors, and Differences in Environmental Disclosures between Canada and the United States," *Critical Perspectives on Accounting* 12 (2001), pp. 293–322.

[36] Guthrie and Parker, "Corporate Social Disclosure Practice."

[37] G. Gamble, K. Hsu, C. Jackson, and C. Tollerson, "Environmental Disclosures in Annual Reports: An International Perspective," *Accounting Horizons* 31 (1996), pp. 293–331.

EXHIBIT 15.9 Sony Corporation Independent Verification of CSR Report 2009

Purpose and Scope of Verification

(Updated on September 28th, 2009)

Sony has obtained third-party verification since fiscal 2001 to ensure the credibility of data reported and facilitate the ongoing improvement of its environmental management. Since fiscal 2003, Sony has sought independent verification from the Bureau Veritas (BV) Group, the external auditing organization for the Sony Group's global environmental management system. In fiscal 2008, Sony asked the BV Group to undertake independent verification of the reliability of data collection and reporting processes, as well as the accuracy and the appropriateness of conclusions drawn from such data, at production sites, non-manufacturing sites, design sites and Sony's headquarters.

CSR Report 2009

Independent Verification Report

To: Sony Corporation

Objective of verification

To verify the reliability of environmental data selected by Sony Corporation (Sony) for inclusion in the Sony CSR Report 2009 (the Report), issued under the responsibility of Sony's management. The aim of this verification is to consider the accuracy of environmental performance data detailed in the Report and to provide a verification opinion based on objective evidence.

Scope of work

The scope of the verification work covered the activities of the following Sony business entities for which environmental data is generated:

Sony Corporation Headquarters, Sony Computer Entertainment Inc., Sony Manufacturing Systems Corporation Isehara Piant, Sony Supply Chain Solutions, Inc. Main Office and Odaiba Operation Center, Sony Mobile Display Corporation Higashiura Plant, Sony Semiconductor Corporation Nagasaki Technology Center, Sony Electronics (Wdx) Co., Ptc. Ltd., Sony EMCS (Malaysia) Sdn. Bhd. PG Tec.

In total nine sites were visited as part of the verification coverage including five manufacturing sites, two logistics department sites, one design and development site and the Sony headquarters.

Verification Methodology and Standard

Bureau Veritas has conducted its verification activities as follows:

Sony Headquarters

1. The reliability of data collection and aggregation systems, process adequacy and the effectiveness of internal verification
2. The accuracy of data aggregation carried out at Headquarters (April 2006 to March 2009)
3. The validity of conclusions drawn from and reported against aggregated data

Sites

1. The relevance of the scope of data collection
2. The effectiveness of data measurement, collection and aggregation methods and of internal verification
3. The reliability of data collection and aggregation and the accuracy of final aggregated data

This verification was conducted against Bureau Veritas' standard procedures and guidelines for external verification of non-financial reporting, based on current best practice. Bureau Veritas has referred to the international Standard on Assurance Engagements (ISAE) 3000 in providing a limited assurance:

Verification and review findings

Bureau Veritas is of the opinion that:

1. The environmental data from sites and products are considered to be reliable and free from significant error. Some inconsistencies were identified in the data during the verification process which were corrected.
2. Sony's systems for the monitoring, collection and aggregation of performance data is considered to be reliable and appropriately conducted at each of the visited sites.

were disclosed before the Kyoto Protocol was signed. A number of major initiatives, such as GRI, have recently been undertaken to encourage CSR practices by companies. Some companies have clearly stated their CSR policy in their annual reports (Exhibit 15.10).

In a study conducted in 2005, based on disclosures made in the annual reports, environmental reports, and Web sites of 10 of the largest (in terms of revenues) public firms from the chemical, oil and gas, energy, and motor vehicles and casualty insurance industries, it has been pointed out that firms from countries that ratified the Kyoto Protocol have higher disclosure indexes related to pollution and greenhouse gas emissions as compared to firms in other countries.[38]

A large U.S.-based industrial and electronics group reported that it undertook nearly 500 energy conservation projects within its global operations in 2004 and 2005. This was part of the company's commitment to reduce the intensity of greenhouse gas emissions by 30 percent and improve energy efficiency by 30 percent within the next six years. The company reported the reduction in total tons of greenhouse gas emissions and converted this into removing an equivalent number of cars (in thousands of cars) from the roads. The company also reported a total annual cost saving in millions of U.S. dollars from its energy conservation projects.

A large European electricity utility reported on the involvement of the company chairman and CEO in the process of updating the company environmental policy to focus on global warming. The updated policy includes offering energy efficiency services to customers, considering global warming in investment choices, investing in research and development, and developing renewable energy. The company also reported on the involvement of the company chairman and CEO in an industry-led initiative to fight global warming.

The joint research report by KPMG and GRI published in July 2007, entitled "Reporting the Business implications of Climate Change in Sustainability Reports," shows that companies are keen to report climate change as a new business bearer than a cause of risk. The research surveyed a sample of annual sustainability reports, published by international companies in the *Financial Times'* FT Global 500 list that reported the Business Implications of Climate Change in Sustainability Reports. According to the report, companies currently tend to report extensively on new business opportunities rather than on the business risks that stem from climate change and its effects. These data contrast with recent evidence that climate change poses significant risk to the global economy, as documented in the UK government's Stern Report on the Economics of Climate Change in 2007.

Exhibit 15.11 provides a list of companies that have expressed a commitment to CSR according to 2009 Progress Report published by Business Roundtable, entitled "Enhancing our Commitment to a Sustainable Future." Business Roundtable is an association of chief executives of leading U.S. companies with more than $45 trillion in annual revenues and nearly 10 million employees. Member companies comprise nearly a third of the total value of the U.S. stock market and pay nearly half of all corporate income taxes paid to the federal government.

---

[38] Freedman and Jaggi, "Global Warming, Commitment to the Kyoto Protocol, and Accounting Disclosure by the Largest Global Public Firms From Polluting Industries."

EXHIBIT 15.10 Extracts from Toyota Annual Report 2010

Toyota CSR Policy

CSR Policy: Contribution toward Sustainable Development (adopted in 2005 and revised in 2008) explains how we adapt the Guiding Principles at Toyota with regard to social responsibilities to our stakeholders.

We, Toyota Motor Corporation and our subsidiaries, take initiative to contribute to harmonious and sustainable development of society and the earth through all business activities that we carry out in each country and region, based on our Guiding Principles.

We comply with local, national, and international laws and regulations as well as the spirit thereof and we conduct our business operations with honesty and integrity.

In order to contribute to sustainable development, we believe that management interacting with its stakeholders as described on the following page is of considerable importance, and we will endeavor to build and maintain sound relationships with our stakeholders through open and fair communication. We expect our business partners to support this initiative and act in accordance with it. (p. 20)

"To maintain stable, long-term growth in international society, companies have to earn the respect and trust of society and individuals. Rather than simply contributing to economic development through operational activities, growing in harmony with society is a must for good corporate citizens. Mindful of the foregoing, Toyota has a range of committees that are tasked with monitoring corporate activities and management in relation to social responsibilities, including the CSR Committee and the Toyota Environment Committee." (p. 25)

Extracts from Toyota Sustainability Report 2010

In FY2009, during the economic doldrums caused by the Lehman Shock, issues concerning product quality surfaced, causing great concern to certain Toyota stakeholders. In the resulting circumstances, the Sustainability Report 2010 focused on three main points: (1) proper disclosure of information pertinent to the quality issue: (2) clarifying mid- and long-term environmental actions for CO_2 reduction and other programs, despite the severe business climate: (3) showing how Toyota contributes to society, including emerging countries, through making cars.

In addition, the black-and-white portions of the report as well as its binding were done at Toyota Loops, a company that provides employment to the severely disabled.

Key Issues (Materiality)

Quality	• The quality issue: background and future prospects
	• Response to quality issues in each area
	• Promotion of TQM for improvement of working quality
	• Briefing sessions for dealers to explain safety, quality Issues
	• Internal/external quality communication
Mid- and long-term environmental actions	• Development and expansion of next-generation environment-considering vehicles
	• Fifth (next FY) Toyota Environmental Action Plan
	• Outlines of activities for CO_2 reduction in each area
Contribution to society through making cars	• Contribution to society and economy in emerging countries by making cars
	• Employment initiatives in response to economic activities and production changes
	• Contribution to social and economic growth in countries and regions by global expansion

Period Covered

The period covered in the report's data is from April 2009 to March 2010. For major ongoing initiatives, the most recent status update in 2010 has been included.

Scope of Report

Environmental Aspects: Includes Toyota Motor Corporation's (TMC) own initiatives and examples of those of its overseas consolidated subsidiaries, as well as the progress of consolidated environmental management in Japan and overseas.

Social Aspects: Includes Toyota Motor Corporation's (TMC) own initiatives and examples of those of its overseas consolidated affiliates, and so on.

Economic Aspects: Includes financial results and global expansion.

Editorial Policy (for Web site edition)

In issuing its Sustainability Report, Toyota's fundamental policy has been to place an emphasis on being comprehensive and accurate, to incorporate as much data as possible, and to have the information bear up to the evaluation by relevant experts. Toyota has been striving to make its reports easy to read by using universal design colors and fonts, and through such efforts as including special pages highlighting its activities throughout the year and examples of overseas initiatives.

In this year's report, Toyota has responded to the requests for more concise information by creating the abridged Sustainability Report 2010 Web edition, featuring the main highlights. This abridged version can serve as the starting point to learn about Toyota's sustainability activities, and can be used by our customers in general or as a material for university courses and the like. Those interested in learning more can then consult either the Sustainability Report or the Toyota Web site.

Respond to society's changing needs and enrich people's lives by making safe and reliable vehicles. Never forget to appreciate our customers and all other stakeholders. Embracing these principles, the hearts of all Toyota associates are united in an effort to make better vehicles.

EXHIBIT 15.11   List of companies expressed a commitment to CSR

ABB Inc.	CSX Corporation
Abbot	Cummins Inc.
Accenture	Deere & Company
ACE Limited	Deloitte (U.S.)
Aetna	The Dow Chemical Company
Alcoa Inc.	Duke Energy
Altec Inc.	DuPont
American Electric Power	Eastman Chemical Company
Anadarko Petroleum Corporation	Eastman Kodak Company
ArvinMeritor Inc.	Eaton Corporation
AT&T	ExxonMobil Corporation
Avery Dennison Corporation	FedEx Corporation
Bechtel Group Inc.	FPL Group Inc.
BNSF Railway Company	General Electric Company
The Boeing Company	General Motors Corporation
The Brink's Company	W.W. Grainger
Caterpillar Inc.	The Hartford Financial Services Group Inc.
Ceridian Corporation	Honeywell
Chevron	HSBC
The Chubb Corporation	Humana Inc.
Citi	IBM Corporation
The Coca-Cola Company	Ingersoll Rand Company Limited

Continued

EXHIBIT 15.11   *(Concluded)*

International Paper Company	SAP
ITT Corporation	Sara Lee Corporation
Johnson Controls	SAS Institute Inc.
KPMG LLP	Siemens Corporation
The McGraw-Hill Companies	Southern Company
McKesson Corporation	State Farm
Merck	The Travelers Companies Inc.
Motorola	Tyco International
National Gypsum Company	Union Pacific
Navistar	United Technologies Corporation
Norfolk Southern Corporation	Verizon Communications Inc.
Office Depot Inc.	Western & Southern Financial Group
Owens Corning	Weyerhaeuser Company
Pfizer Inc.	Whirlpool Corporation
Praxair Inc.	The Williams Companies Inc.
Principal Financial Group	Xerox Corporation
The Proctor & Gamble Company	

Japan stands out as a country with a high rate of reporting on climate change, with all Japanese companies including a dedicated section on climate change and most including a specific statement from the CEO or company chairman on climate change. Japan is closely followed by Europe; for example, in Sweden, the number of firms reporting on their sustainability performance has reached a record high, and the number of people using those reports to gain information about firms has also grown rapidly. In general, companies tend to focus on the benefits of climate change. Few companies reported on the risk of legal action (such as class action lawsuits related to climate change), and hardly any companies report on risks or business disruptions caused by extreme weather events (such as floods, storms and droughts, increased forest fires, or long-term physical changes such as reduced water availability). The SEC Climate Change Guidance is available on the SEC Web site. The current trend of external reporting by companies is to integrate reporting on economic, social, and governance (ESG) and financial reporting.

CONCLUDING REMARKS

While there has been increased interest in CSR in recent years, there exists a wide range of national differences of such practices due mainly to cultural reasons. The distinctive nature of the culture of a particular people implies that its programs may represent alternative solutions to common problems. This may be relevant to understanding the international diversity in CSR patterns and also in formulating strategies to promote CSR at international level.

The cultural relativity of CSR imposes serious methodological limitations to research in the area. Hypothesis testing is critical to scientific research, but hypotheses may not capture the impact of culture. Even if the hypotheses do capture some of the relevant cultural aspects, there can be limitations in the testing process. For example, hypotheses are tested using observable evidence, gathered using particular techniques that are amenable to statistical analysis. If the evidence is not observable, then the hypothesis is rejected as being unsupported. But absence of evidence does not always mean evidence of absence. Evidence may not be there to observe in some cases due to cultural reasons, such as the influence of religion. For example, according to Islam, firms are expected to conduct themselves ethically, but not advertise the fact that they are doing so. As a result, firms following the principles of Islam may not disclose information regarding some issues, including social issues. This does not necessarily mean that they are not concerned about such issues.

Generalizability is another essential feature of scientific research, and focus on it may require factors such as culture, which may not be generalizable, to be left out from the analysis. This will invariably make the findings of limited value in understanding the issues associated with CSR.

The findings show that firms from countries that have ratified the Kyoto Protocol provide greater pollution disclosures as compared to firms whose home countries have not ratified the Protocol, even though they are firms operating in Protocol countries.

Summary

1. Traditionally, companies have focused on economic aspects in external reporting. However, the current trend is to integrate economic, social, and governance aspects for this purpose.

2. Social accounting was popular in the 1970s, but in the 1990s, social accounting was swamped by environmental accounting with the title "corporate social reporting" (CSR), which is based on the notion of organizational social responsibility.

3. The organizational social responsibility exists to shareholders and other stakeholders such as employers, creditors and society at large.

4. The two theories are often used to explain CSR: stakeholder theory and legitimacy theory. Stakeholder theory posits that CSR is in response to the stakeholder demand for such information, while according to legitimacy theory, CSR is a means to deal with firms' exposure to political and social pressures.

5. It is now expected that firms not only act as good citizens, but report this good behavior to their stakeholders.

6. CSR disclosures are made on a voluntary basis in many countries.

7. National and organizational cultural values are among the main influencing factors for firms to engage in CSR practices.

8. It has been pointed out that climate change has implications for CSR by firms, and as a result, the concepts such as "emissions trading," "carbon credits," "carbon funds," "emissions brokerage," "carbon neutral," and "carbon tax" have become common usage in discussions on CSR.

9. Due to shortcomings of voluntary disclosures, there have been several attempts at the international level to regulate CSR practices by firms—for example, the Kyoto Protocol, Global Reporting Initiative (GRI), European Union Emission Trading scheme, and Asia-Pacific Partnership on Climate Change.

10. GRI research findings indicate that there is a worldwide trend toward CSR practices; in particular, firms from countries that have ratified the Kyoto Protocol provide greater pollution disclosures compared to firms from other countries.

11. International organizations such as the World Bank and IFAC, and programs such as Kyoto Protocol and GRI, are actively promoting CSR.

Questions

1. What is corporate social reporting (CSR)?
2. What are the theories often used to explain the CSR practices of firms?
3. What is the conceptual basis for CSR?
4. What motivates firms to engage in CSR practices?
5. What are the implications of climate change for CSR?
6. Identify five key terms used in assessing the impact of climate change on a firm.
7. Why is it necessary to regulate CSR practices of firms?
8. Identify five mechanisms for regulating CSR practices at the international level.
9. What are some of the problems of trying to regulate CSR practices through legislation?
10. What are the items often included in CSR reports?
11. What is the Kyoto Protocol?
12. What is the Global Reporting Initiative?

Exercises and Problems

1. The Corporate Responsibility Report 2010 of Coca-Cola Amatil Company is at http://ccamatil.com/InvestorRelations/AnnualReports/2009/2010%20Sustainability%20Report.pdf. It mentions four global pillars.

   Required:
   Discuss the strategies, programs, and targets of the company in relation to each of those global pillars, as mentioned in the report.

2. Exhibit 15.4 provides an example of an audit report of a Brazilian company for 2009, which refers to GRI-G3 sustainability guidelines.

   Required:
   Identify a 2010 audit report for a U.S. company, which refers to GRI-G3 sustainability guidelines and compare the two audit reports.

3. Exhibit 15.7 provides an extract from the CSR report of a company in the IT industry, IBM corporation.

   Required:
   Discuss the motivations for a company in another industry of your choice to prepare a CSR report, and identify the nature of the information, which is most likely to be included in such a report.

4. Exhibit 15.10 provides an example of a company, which has clearly stated its CSR policy in its annual report.

   Required:
   Identify another company, which has stated its CSR policy in its 2010 annual report, and compare the main points highlighted by the two companies.

References

Adams, C., and Kuasirikun, N. "A Comparative Analysis of Corporate Reporting on Ethical Issues by UK and German Chemical and Pharmaceutical Companies." *The European Accounting Review* 9, no.1 (2000), pp. 53–79.

Ball, S., and Bell, S. *Environmental Law*, 2nd ed. London: Blackstone, 1994.

Bates, G. M. *Environmental Law in Australia.* Sydney: Butterworth, 1995.

Bebbington, J., Gray, R. and Owen, D. "Seeing the Wood for the Trees—Taking the Pulse of Social and Environmental Accounting." *Accounting, Auditing & Accountability Journal* 12, no. 1 (1999), pp. 47–51.

Buhr, N., and Freedman, M. "Culture, Institutional Factors, and Differences in Environmental Disclosures between Canada and the United States." *Critical Perspectives on Accounting* 12 (2001), pp. 293–322.

Deegan, C., Rankin, M. and Tobin, J. "An Examination of the Corporate Social and Environmental Disclosures of BHP from 1983–1997—A Test of Legitimacy Theory." *Accounting, Auditing & Accountability Journal* 15, no. 3 (2002), pp. 312–343.

Deegan, C., and Gordon, B. "A Study of Environmental Disclosure Practices of Australian Corporations." *Accounting and Business Research* 26, no. 3 (1996), pp. 187–199.

Freedman, M., and B. Jaggi. "Global Warming, Commitment to the Kyoto Protocol, and Accounting Disclosure by the Largest Global Public Firms from Polluting Industries." *The International Journal of Accounting* 40 (2005), pp. 215–232.

Gallhofer, S., and Haslam, J. "The Direction of Green Accounting Policy: Critical Reflections." *Accounting, Auditing & Accountability Journal* 1, no. 2 (1997), pp. 148–174.

Gamble, G., Hsu, K., Jackson, C., and Tollerson, C. "Environmental Disclosures in Annual Reports: An International Perspective." *Accounting Horizons,* 31, (1996), pp. 293–331.

Gray, R. "Does Sustainability Reporting Improve Corporate Behaviour: Wrong Question? Right Time?" *Accounting and Business Research* 36, Special Issue (2006), pp. 65–88.

Gray, R., Dey, C., Owen, D., Evans, R. and Zadek, S. "Struggling with the Praxis of Social Accounting—Stakeholders, Accountability, Audits and Procedures." *Accounting, Auditing & Accountability Journal* 10, no. 3 (1997), pp. 325–364.

Gray, R., Kouhy, R. and Lavers, S. "Corporate Social and Environmental Reporting: A Review of the Literature and a Longitudinal Study of UK Disclosures." *Accounting, Auditing & Accountability Journal* 8, no. 2 (1995), pp. 47–77.

Gray, S. J. "Towards a Theory of Cultural Influence on the Development of Accounting Systems Internationally." *Abacus* (1988), pp. 1–15.

Guthrie, J., and Parker, L. "Corporate Social Disclosure Practice: A Comparative International Analysis", *Advances in Public Interest Accounting,* 3, (1990), pp. 159–176.

Hofstede, G. *Culture's Consequences.* Thousand Oaks, CA: Sage, 1980.

Jones, M. J. "Accounting for Biodiversity: Operationalising Environmental Accounting." *Accounting, Auditing & Accountability Journal* 16, no. 5 (2003), pp. 762–789.

Kuasirikun, N., and Sherer, M. "Corporate Social Accounting Disclosure in Thailand." *Accounting, Auditing & Accountability Journal* 17, no. 4 (2004), pp. 629–660.

Lindblom, C. K. "The Implications of Organisational Legitimacy for Corporate Social Performance and Disclosure." Paper presented at the Critical Perspectives on Accounting Conference, New York (1994).

Milne, C. D. A. *Handbook of Environmental Law.* Wellington: Royal Forest and Bird Protection Society, 1992.

Mobus, J. L. "Mandatory Environmental Disclosures in a Legitimacy Theory Context." *Accounting, Auditing & Accountability Journal* 18, no. 4 (2005), pp. 492–517.

O'Dwyer, B. "Conceptions of Corporate Social Responsibility: The Nature of Managerial Capture." *Accounting, Auditing & Accountability Journal* 16, no. 4 (2003), pp. 523–557.

O'Dwyer, B., and Gray, R. H. "Corporate Social Reporting in the Republic of Ireland: A Longitudinal Study." *Irish Accounting Review* 5, no. 2 (1998), pp.1–34.

Ozu, C., and S. Gray "The Development of Segment Reporting in Japan: Achieving International Harmonization through a Process of National Consensus." *Advances in International Accounting* 14 (2001), pp. 1–13.

Patten, D. M. "Changing Superfund Disclosure and Its Relation to the Provision of Other Environmental Information." *Advances in Environmental Accounting and Management* 1 (2000), pp. 101–121.

Patten, D. "Intra-industry Environment Disclosures in Response to the Alaskan Oil Spill: A Note on Legitimacy Theory." *Accounting, Organizations and Society* 15, no. 5 (1992), pp. 471–475.

Perera, H. "The International and Cultural Aspects of Social Accounting." In R. Gray and J. Guthrie, Eds., *Social Accounting, Mega Accounting and Beyond: A Festschrift in Honour of M. R. Mathews,* City, Scotland: Centre for Social and Environmental Accounting Research, School of Management, The University of St Andrews, 2007, Ch. 8.

Perera, M. H. B. and Mathews, M. R. "The Cultural Relativity of Accounting and International Patterns of Social Accounting." *Advances in International Accounting* 3 (1990), pp. 215–251.

Stern, N. *The Economics of Climate Change: The Stern Review* Cambridge: Cabinet Office-HM Treasury, 2007.

Suchman, M. C. "Managing Legitimacy: Strategic and Institutional Approaches." *Academy of Management Review* 20, no. 3 (1995), pp. 571–610.

Tilt, C. A. "The Content and Disclosure of Australian Corporate Environmental Policies." *Accounting, Auditing & Accountability Journal* 14, no. 2 (2001), pp. 190–212.

Tilt, C. A. "The Influence of External Pressure Groups on Corporate Social Disclosure: Some Empirical Evidence." *Accounting, Auditing & Accountability Journal* 7, no. 4 (1994), pp. 24–46.

Treadway Commission, *Report of the National Commission on Fraudulent Financial Reporting.* Washington, DC: National Commission of Fraudulent Financial Reporting, 1987.

Index

A

G